Arguing in Communities

Arguing in Communities: Reading and Writing Arguments in Context

Third Edition

Gary Layne Hatch

Brigham Young University

Boston Burr Ridge, IL Dubuque, IA Madison, WI New York
San Francisco St. Louis Bangkok Bogotá Caracas Kuala Lumpur
Lisbon London Madrid Mexico City Milan Montreal New Delhi
Santiago Seoul Singapore Sydney Taipei Toronto

McGraw-Hill Higher Education

*A Division of The **McGraw-Hill** Companies*

ARGUING IN COMMUNITIES:
READING AND WRITING ARGUMENTS IN CONTEXT

Published by McGraw-Hill, a business unit of The McGraw-Hill Companies, Inc., 1221 Avenue of the Americas, New York, NY, 10020.

This book is printed on acid-free paper.

4567890 BKM BKM 098

ISBN-13: 978-0-7674-1681-8

ISBN-10: 0-7674-1681-3

President of McGraw-Hill Humanities/Social Sciences: *Steve Debow*
Executive editor: *Lisa Moore*
Director of development, English: *Carla Kay Samodulski*
Senior developmental editor: *Renee Deljon*
Senior marketing manager: *David S. Patterson*
Senior media producer: *Todd Vaccaro*
Project manager: *Ruth Smith*
Production supervisor: *Susanne Riedell*
Senior designer: *Jenny El-Shamy*
Lead supplement producer: *Marc Mattson*
Photo research coordinator: *Alexandra Ambrose*
Typeface: *10/12 Galliard*
Compositor: *G&S Typesetters*

Library of Congress Cataloging-in-Publication Data

Hatch, Gary Layne.
Arguing in communities : reading and writing arguments in context / Gary Layne Hatch.—3rd ed.
p. cm.
Includes index.
ISBN 0-7674-1681-3 (acid-free paper)
1. Persuasion (Rhetoric) 2. Reasoning. 3. Communication—Social aspects. 4. Rhetoric—Research—Methodology. I. Title.
P301.5.P47H38 2003
808—dc21 2002069596

www.mhhe.com

Preface

Students are often asked to study arguments apart from any social context, and when they take courses in argumentative writing, they are often presented with an anthology of written arguments lined up like zoo animals removed from their native habitats. These anthologized arguments are usually so far removed from their social contexts that they no longer have any connection to the real world, and students aren't given the chance to see that arguments are all around them. De-contextualized arguments can be studied like zoological specimens, their elements dissected, their structures analyzed, but rarely can they be brought to life, and so students studying them do not learn that arguing and arguments are vitally important to us as social beings. *Arguing in Communities* is an attempt to take students where arguments live, so to speak, to the communities where we live and argue every day. My hope for the book is that it will help students to see argument as a positive part of life, that it will help to improve the quality of our arguments, and with luck, that it will help to improve communities in the process.

My central premise in the text is that arguing productively is an important part of living healthfully in any community and among other communities. Without effective arguing, communities have difficulty making decisions, coming to consensus, living with and negotiating difference, and simply getting things done. Negotiating difference, though, is the key, because difference is a given of human life, of every community. It's usually when arguing breaks down in the face of difference that people resort to some sort of force to accomplish their goals, whether it's through raised voices, physical violence, or legal action. The better able we are to argue effectively about our differences within our own communities and across community lines, the better chance we have at living more peaceful, productive, and satisfying lives.

HIGHLIGHTED FEATURES

I'm not certain that a class in argumentative writing can actually make communities more productive at resolving their differences, but *Arguing in Communities* is my contribution to that effort. By focusing on how arguments function in and across communities as well as on what makes arguments effective, this book offers a unique approach to teaching argumentation. Its features include the following:

- **Consistent focus on arguments within and across communities.** As I discuss above, arguments begin in and travel among communities, groups of people who have something, sometimes many things, in common, such as history, culture, language, values, beliefs, customs, viewpoints, interests, or, within the academy, common bodies of knowledge, methods of inquiry, and domains of study. Most fundamentally, the focus on communities keeps arguments "real" for students. It reinforces the fact that arguments are human responses to particular situations.
- **An emphasis on arguments as part of social processes.** I present the essential principles of argument—claims, reasons, and assumptions—after I've established that arguing can be something we do along with, as opposed to against, others, and that it helps us to sort out our differences and even helps us find good reasons for believing what we do. I emphasize that, through argument, we can generate new and better ideas, and that much social change depends on the arguments that precede or surround it.
- **An emphasis on arguments as conversations.** I present arguing not only as a part of social processes but as conversations that take place within and among communities. In my experience, and that of many colleagues, students respond well to the conversation metaphor, its familiarity diminishing the relative unfamiliarity of written communication. Students learn how to identify, record, and evaluate conversations, from conversations as immediate as those taking place on their school campuses to those as seemingly distant as the debates taking place in the U.S. Congress.
- **An emphasis on arguments in context.** Throughout the book I emphasize the importance of studying arguments in context, within, that is, the broader conversation in which a particular argument is a response. The text is therefore grounded in thorough coverage of the rhetorical situation. Between the general introduction (which begins on page xiii) and Chapter 1, over 10 pages are devoted to presenting this central concept, and it is consistently discussed thereafter.
- **Integrated readings that serve as applications of principles.** Integrated sets of readings on contemporary issues are presented within each chapter. These sets of three to four readings on timely, high-interest topics present a range of perspectives and model communities in conversation, while also illustrating the principles covered in the chapter.

- **Consistent attention to the effect of electronic technology on arguments.** From the telephone to electronic bulletin boards to instant messaging, electronic technology affects how we argue, and in this text I pay consistent attention to its influences, especially in regard to the proliferation of visual arguments in our lives. Similarly, the text consistently discusses electronic communities and arguments in electronic contexts, among them listservs, chat rooms, instant messaging, and email.
- **Acknowledgment of the logic within emotion.** I describe the ways in which ethos and pathos are integrated with logos and logical appeals, and how, as part of a social process, arguing cannot be reduced to just logic. In particular, I challenge the tendency to discredit emotion as illogical and irrational, and show that to move people to action, arguing must include appropriate emotional appeals as well as logical appeals. Students learn how to use emotional appeals effectively and ethically.
- **Presentation of several models for organizing arguments.** In teaching students how to analyze audiences and adapt arguments to audiences' different needs, I present several models for organizing arguments. In addition to the "classical" form most frequently used in academic writing, this text provides detailed instruction for organizing arguments according to the following patterns: delayed thesis, conciliatory argument, Rogerian argument, William Safire's "option three," and motivated sequence.
- **Extensive discussion of logical fallacies.** The 20 fallacies of reasoning, often called "informal fallacies," covered in Chapter 4 weaken or invalidate arguments in both student writing and public discourse. In this chapter, I present three categories of fallacies (of ethos, of pathos, and of logos), and explain how each fallacy works and how it can be revised into a more legitimate argument.
- **Thorough, up-to-date coverage of writing and research.** *Arguing in Communities* provides thorough coverage of writing arguments in general (Chapter 5), and the research process for writing and documenting research-based arguments (Chapter 6). Chapter 6 includes guidelines and models for both the Modern Language Association (MLA) and the American Psychological Association (APA) documentation styles, as well as sample papers in MLA and APA format.
- **Numerous student and everyday arguments.** *Arguing in Communities* presents nearly 20 examples of student and everyday arguments. These arguments encourage student writers by showing them that students and nonprofessional writers can and do make important contributions (sometimes published) to arguments within communities. Student and "My Turn" (from *Newsweek*) essay topics include graduated driver licensing, Hollywood and actors, and online shopping.
- **Numerous activities.** Every chapter presents activities for both individual and collaborative work. Activities and assignments are located under the headings "Practicing the Principles" and the project-oriented "Applying the Principles."

NEW TO THE THIRD EDITION

Instructors who have used the previous edition or editions of this text will recognize several new features that I developed in response to reviewers' helpful suggestions.

- **More writing guidelines and student models.** Step-by-step guidelines for analyzing arguments and the process of writing arguments, including summarizing, paraphrasing, and quoting, appear in Part One. Nearly 20 student and everyday model arguments now appear throughout the text, as do new boxes that summarize and highlight key information.
- **Streamlined organization and instruction.** The coverage of the rhetorical appeals (ethos, pathos, and logos) has been consolidated into three chapters (down from six), each of which addresses both identifying and evaluating the type of appeal. Additionally, research is covered in one chapter, and, for greater flexibility, the text no longer includes an anthology of additional readings.
- **New chapter on visual argument.** The new Chapter 12 (Arguing with Images) provides a substantial introduction to visual rhetoric. It covers topics such as the variety of visual arguments, images and persuasion, and strategies of visual argument, and presents images ranging from *Guernica* to the flag being raised over Iwo Jima, to John F. Kennedy, Jr., saluting his father's casket, to Elian Gonzalez being forcibly taken from his relatives' home.
- **Two new case studies.** An extended case study on the topic of the Columbine high school shootings and youth violence, including both verbal and visual arguments, appears in installments throughout Part One to show how arguments change as the number and types of communities participating in them increases. A briefer case study on Napster and Internet music swapping appears in Chapter 6, Writing Researched Arguments.
- **Over 75 percent new readings and visuals.** Over 75 percent of the more than 100 written arguments are new to this edition and address such current issues as cloning, youth culture, and male body image. Over 20 new visuals, including web pages, cartoons, photographs, advertisements, and a logo also appear throughout the book.

OVERVIEW OF THE BOOK'S ORGANIZATION AND CONTENTS

Aiming to enhance its ease of use, I have divided the book into two parts: Part One, The Essential Principles, and Part Two, Types of Claims. The general introduction (pages xiii–xix that precedes Part One grounds students in the book's basic concepts by defining and beginning discussions of terms such as *arguing, visual argument, technology, difference, context,* and *rhetorical situation.*

Part One presents arguing as a means of rational persuasion within and among communities, developing students' understanding of the rhetorical situation and writing processes, particularly in regard to a general method for arguing (Chapter 1). It is here, in Chapter 1, that I give students the opportunity to identify the communities in which they live and teach them how to record, analyze, and evaluate the conversations that take place in their communities so that they can make useful contributions to these conversations.

Chapters 2, 3, and 4 cover argument's classical appeals. Chapter 2 explains *ethos*, focusing on how writers use their standing in communities to establish their credibility to be persuasive. I teach students how to share personal information about themselves, identify with their readers, and adopt an appropriate voice in order to sound credible. Chapter 3 focuses on *pathos*, the use of emotion in arguing. In this chapter students learn to give their arguments immediacy and presence for their readers by using concrete examples and choosing words that evoke an emotional response. Chapter 4 covers *logos*, identifying the role of logic in arguing and teaching students how to identify and avoid logical fallacies, manipulative or deceptive language, and misleading statistical arguments. This chapter also guides students through the process of analyzing arguments—both how to identify the parts of an argument and explain how these parts work together to persuade.

The last two chapters of Part One describe how to combine all of the above aspects of arguing into an effective written or oral argument that is a response to a conversation taking place within or between communities. In particular, in Chapter 5, students learn two major argumentative strategies: adapting to the conventions and beliefs of the community and challenging the community. Students also learn to identify and use the six common forms that arguments take: classical, delayed thesis, conciliatory, motivational, Rogerian, and Option Three. In Chapter 6, students are guided through research processes so that they can effectively use sources to support their arguments, and so that they have access to the broadest range of conversations that they might want to join.

All but one chapter in the second part of the book (Chapters 7 through 11) focus on the different kinds of claims that members of communities can argue: claims about existence, causality, language, values, and actions. Throughout these chapters, students learn how to ask a set of standard questions in order to identify what is at issue in a particular debate or disagreement, what kind of claims are being made, and how someone can evaluate and respond to those claims. Part Two sustains the emphasis on rhetorical situations, community contexts, and conversations present throughout Part One.

Finally, a new chapter concludes Part Two: Chapter 12, Arguing with Images. In this chapter, I describe the variety of visual arguments we encounter, discuss images and persuasion, and identify various common strategies of visual arguments. I wrote this new chapter to help students develop their critical awareness of and ability to discuss the rhetoric of visual arguments, particularly by approaching visual and multimedia arguments as human responses (often for commercial purposes) within community contexts and conversations. Chapter 12 includes numerous images, readings, and activities.

PRINT AND ELECTRONIC SUPPLEMENTS

- **Instructor's Resource Manual.** This teachers guide begins with a discussion of the original idea for *Arguing in Communities,* the social process approach to argument and how to teach it, and different ways to organize courses around the text. (A sample 15-week syllabus is provided.) The manual's chapter-by-chapter coverage addresses each chapter's goal and suggests possible answers to questions that accompany reading selections in the text.
- ***Arguing in Communities* Website <www.mhhe.com/hatch>.** In addition to providing links for all of the URLs presented in the book, the site offers abundant links relevant to the authors and issues represented in the text, as well as a glossary of terms and links to resources for research projects.
- **Teaching Composition Faculty Listserv at <www.mhhe.com/tcomp>.** Moderated by Chris Anson at North Carolina State University and offered by McGraw-Hill as a service to the composition community, this listserv brings together senior members of the college composition community with newer members—junior faculty, adjuncts, and teaching assistants—through an online newsletter and accompanying discussion group to address issues of pedagogy, both in theory and in practice.
- **PageOut.** McGraw-Hill's own PageOut service is available to help you get your course up and running online in a matter of hours—at no cost. Additional information about the service is available online at <http://www.pageout.net>.
- **Webwrite.** This online product, available through our partner company MetaText, makes it possible for writing teachers and students to, among other things, comment on and share papers online.

For further information about these and other electronic resources, contact your local McGraw-Hill representative, visit the English pages on the McGraw-Hill Higher Education website at <www.mhhe.com/catalogs/hss/english>, or visit McGraw-Hill's Digital Solutions pages at <www.mhhe.com/catalogs/solutions>.

ACKNOWLEDGMENTS

I would like to thank the editors and staff at McGraw-Hill who have helped me extensively with both the second and first editions and this new edition of the text. They have made me feel a part of their family. In particular, I would like to thank Renee Deljon, who guided me through another revision that turned out to be much more interesting and extensive than either of us first imagined. I am also particularly indebted to the production team at McGraw-Hill for securing permissions and keeping everything on schedule.

For my first introduction to many of the ideas in this book, I thank Gregory Clark, from my undergraduate days at Brigham Young University, as well as my former graduate instructors and colleagues at Arizona State University: Frank D'Angelo, David Schwalm, Keith Muller, John Ramage, Jackie Wheeler, and Elizabeth Vander Lei.

Thanks are also again due to the reviewers of this book's previous editions. Their advice was essential: Vincent Casaregola, St. Louis University; Scott Cawelti, University of Northern Iowa; Susan M. Grant, University of Missouri, St. Louis; Steven D. Krause, Eastern Michigan University; Katherine Ploeger, California State University, Stanislaus; and Donald L. Soucy, New England Institute of Technology.

And for their abundantly thoughtful and useful suggestions, I wish to thank the reviewers whose comments shaped this new edition of the book:

Dawn Jeppesen Anderson, Ricks College
Marck L. Beggs, Henderson State University
Martha F. Bowden, Kennesaw State University
Lauren Sewell Coulter, University of Tennessee–Chattanooga
Chad Klinger, North Idaho College
Catherine Schutz, University of Central Florida
Mary L. Tobin, Rice University
Lynne Viti, Wellesley College
Mary B. Zeigler, Georgia State University

Finally, my most humble apologies and sincere thanks to AnneMarie, who endured with me the trials and rewards of writing, and to Aubrey, Carson, and Maren.

Introduction

All around us, we find arguments. In simple terms, an argument is a statement, called a claim, supported by other statements called reasons and assumptions. The claim is the statement under dispute. It is the focus of the argument, a proposition about which at least some people would disagree. But not all disagreements are arguments. Some arguments are constructive and some are destructive. In the media, arguments are often represented as shouting matches between emotional participants. You may even have experienced such arguments. When people become involved in a heated debate with others, where all they do is contradict one another, they often come away from the experience frustrated and angry and no closer to resolving the conflict that caused the disagreement in the first place. These kinds of arguments are typically destructive. In many cases, such disagreements aren't really arguments. Merely setting forth an opinion or making a claim isn't arguing. Neither is contradicting or disagreeing with someone. To argue is to justify or support with reasons what you claim to be true. Reasons are statements that lend credibility and support to the claim, which is disputed. Like reasons, assumptions are also statements that support an argument, but assumptions are often unstated or implied—assumed to be true. Assumptions are often general principles, definitions, and values that help readers make the connection between the reasons and the claim; they fill in the gaps in reasoning.

WHAT MAKES AN ARGUMENT GOOD?

Not all arguments are good arguments. Not all claims are based on good reasons. Some argue to win at any cost, even if winning involves manipulation, deception, or aggression. There are books that will tell you how to "win every argument" or "sell anything." These books teach you how to get your way through intimidation, name-calling, distortion, and deception. But people usually don't need training to argue this way. Just turn on any daytime television talk show, or listen to talk radio. Watch political debates. In these contests, the candidates rarely address the issues raised by their opponents. Instead, they just try to "get their message out" or make their opponents look foolish. Often they don't even answer the questions posed by the moderator: They're too busy responding to the last question or answering a question that was never asked. Often, public debate descends into calling names, the way children do on the playground.

But arguments don't have to be this way. Good arguments are constructive. They clarify your position as they persuade. In fact, the word *argument* itself comes from the Latin word for "silver" and literally means to make an idea clear, just as you can see your reflection clearly in polished silver. Because of its social nature, arguing well can bring people together, resolve conflict, and help us work collaboratively. When we argue, we argue *with* others. When we persuade, we are persuading *someone*. Arguing doesn't have to be combative. We don't necessarily have to argue *against* someone. And we don't always have to win by defeating someone else, by having our opinion prevail over another's. Often we argue *along with* others, to sort out our differences and to find good reasons for believing the way we do, perhaps even producing some new or better ideas in the process. Arguing well involves critical thinking, the process of analyzing and evaluating ideas in the pursuit of truth. College provides students an excellent opportunity to develop this ability to think critically. In college, you can clarify your own ideas by testing them against the ideas of others and by working together with other students to improve your skills in arguing well. These skills will help you learn how to learn, and they provide the foundation for a solid education.

According to the traditional definition, arguing is primarily a verbal activity. In other words, whether they are delivered orally or written down, arguments use words. As a verbal activity, arguments reveal themselves through language. Many of the arguments you encounter in your college experience will be verbal arguments. Speeches, lectures, newspaper and magazine articles, scholarly essays, technical reports, reviews, and books are all verbal arguments. But even verbal arguments often have a visual dimension. Although arguing is mainly a verbal activity, arguments may also rely on nonverbal elements, such as gestures and facial expressions (when we are speaking to each other) or symbolic and visual elements of print documents (such as images or document design). These visual elements contribute to the effectiveness of the verbal argument.

Whether we realize it or not, visual arguments are everywhere around us: T-shirts, bumper stickers, billboards, company logos, signs, symbols, television ads, magazine ads. This includes even the way in which we dress, how we interact with others, how we speak, and what we drive. We constantly make claims on others' beliefs—sometimes without being fully aware that we are doing so. We receive thousands of messages every day advancing some claim; often these claims are not stated. For example, look at all the messages people have on their clothes. In addition to brand names and logos, they may have images or actual verbal messages that make some kind of implied argument.

Because they don't rely as much on language, visual arguments are usually implicit and more highly compact than verbal arguments. This allows you to respond to these arguments without necessarily articulating the claims and reasons. For example, if you are on a dark street and someone threatens you with a knife, you face a situation that demands a response. You may not realize it, but you are part of an argument. You probably wouldn't take the time at that moment to try to translate that argument into language, but you could easily do so. This person's body language is saying, "Give me what I want or I will harm you with this knife." That's a simple claim supported by a reason. Implicit in this argument are also the assumptions that you don't want to be harmed, that you have something this person wants, and that this is a credible threat. Your potential attacker can communicate all of this without using a single word. In addition to being implicit, visual arguments also make an impression or argue a claim in a very short time or very small space. An ad designer might have only 15 seconds of television time, one page of a magazine, a 1-by-8-inch Internet banner, or a small space on a T-shirt, mug, or pen. The need for immediacy and the lack of space or time are reasons people might choose to make a visual argument rather than a verbal argument.

Technology has made visual arguments an increasingly important part of our lives. Television, video, and film are primarily visual media, and even traditional print media, such as newspapers and magazines and books, are using more and more visual content. Recent advances in the development of the Internet and multimedia technology bring the visual and verbal together in ways other media cannot. These media provide not only a new channel for receiving information but also a way for millions of people to publish and disseminate information.

Whether verbal or visual, you will find arguments everywhere around you. We are involved in arguing all the time: It is part of using language and symbols and part of being human. Arguments make up the fabric of the communities in which we live, the groups that we identify with because of our shared language, beliefs, values, activities, and interests. And if you are to be a successful member of these communities, particularly the college community, you need to understand how to argue well and how to respond effectively with arguments of your own.

THE ROLE OF ARGUING IN RESPONDING TO DIFFERENCE

As noted earlier, arguments are everywhere, and they are an important part of the life of a community. Why is this so? Even though members of a community have much in common—that which defines them as a group—there is also much that divides them. Although humans are genetically similar, no two people have experienced the world in exactly the same way. Each person is unique, and because of our unique physical makeup and social background, each one of us will see things in a slightly different way. Our language divides us as well. Language makes understanding and community possible. Language allows us to build common beliefs and values, but it can also create misunderstanding, confusion, and division. The problem of difference within a community is compounded by the fact that most of us belong to a number of different communities, each with its own language, rules, beliefs, and values. If individuals within the same community can misunderstand or disagree with each other, imagine the potential for disagreement that exists between those belonging to different communities.

Our diversity ensures that within any community, there will be disagreement and differences of opinion. Our differences can lead to conflict—even among individuals or communities that have much in common. Because of our differences, some conflict within a community is inevitable.

One way communities respond to conflict is by using force: punishing, silencing, or expelling members of the community who disagree or dissent. This force may be exerted by powerful members of the community, by vote of the majority, through the power of law, through military or physical strength, or through subtle pressure from peers to conform or risk ridicule and alienation. Individuals who dissent or disagree may choose either to fall in line, to accept the punishment and continue to dissent, or to withdraw from the community. Most communities acknowledge what they consider to be legitimate uses of force; however, the use of force, if taken to an extreme, can result in the kind of totalitarian intolerance that led to the Holocaust in Germany and Poland, the "killing fields" of Cambodia, and "ethnic cleansing" in Bosnia.

Another way to respond to difference is through tolerance—learning to live with and accept the difference of others. Members of a community can "agree to disagree" as long as they can accept the consequences of leaving the disagreement unresolved. For instance, people who work together may disagree about political, religious, or moral issues, but they will probably set these aside when they come to work—at least they will if they want to get any work done. Most communities tolerate a certain amount of difference; however, when taken to an extreme, accepting difference of every kind can lead to anarchy, apathy, inertia, and the dissolution of the community.

The strength of arguing in responding to difference is that arguing well seeks to bring about change, but without force. Threats of force may cause people to change, but they may do so grudgingly, resenting those who have threatened them. Arguing, on the other hand, may cause people to change their opinions and actions willingly. Ideally, arguing is a decision-making process that involves everyone concerned in a forum of free and open debate, each presenting his or her opinion in good faith, each willing to abide by the consensus or compromise that results from negotiation. Arguing in this manner resolves diverse opinions into a synthesis that is essentially agreeable to all.

Learning to argue effectively is particularly important in a democratic society, which attempts to allow the majority the right to rule and at the same time protects the rights of those who disagree with the majority opinion: to build consensus, but allow individualism. Of course, this kind of arguing is an ideal that is rarely realized, but perhaps many more conflicts could be resolved peacefully if community members understood more about arguing effectively. If we are ever to coexist and survive as humans, we must learn to live together reasonably, accepting some of our differences and negotiating others. It may be the best hope for humanity.

WHAT IS CONTEXT?

Students often study arguments removed from any social context. Students taking a course in argumentative writing are often presented with an anthology of written arguments lined up like zoo animals removed from their native habitat. Consequently, many students fail to realize that arguments are all around them. They fail to realize that arguments make up an important part of how they live, work, and study every day.

Whenever we are engaged with ideas and reasons, we are arguing. Whenever someone else makes a claim on our opinions, beliefs, and values, we are arguing. But placing arguments in context includes more than simply identifying who is engaged in arguing—the speakers and listeners or readers and writers. The context for arguing also includes the time, place, and circumstances of arguing. When you understand the complete context for an argument, you will be better able to make sense of the argument and respond effectively.

Writing that matters, including arguing, responds to the needs of actual people in real situations. When you argue, you are part of a conversation made up of the members of a community who care about the issue you are discussing. Others may respond to your argument, inviting you to reply to their response. Writing teachers often refer to the interaction between writers and readers in a particular context as a "rhetorical situation."

Rhetoric is the art of persuasion, really the art of arguing effectively for a particular audience, occasion, and purpose.[1] A *rhetorical situation* is one that calls for the use of persuasion—it's a situation in which an argument would be an appropriate response. Of course, because arguments are everywhere, rhetorical situations are all around us, too. Whenever true arguing occurs, it happens within the context of a rhetorical situation. Figure 1 identifies the primary parts of the rhetorical situation: the writer, the reader, and the issue.

[1] Some teachers may make a distinction between argument and persuasion, or they may see argument as just one type of persuasion. The distinction they make is primarily between explicit, verbal arguments and implicit, visual arguments. Or they may be limiting argument to "logic." In this more limited view, argument is "rational" and persuasion is "irrational." In this text, I will use argument and persuasion interchangeably because I am arguing that every message, whether verbal or visual, is an argument: Arguing and seeking to persuade are the same activity.

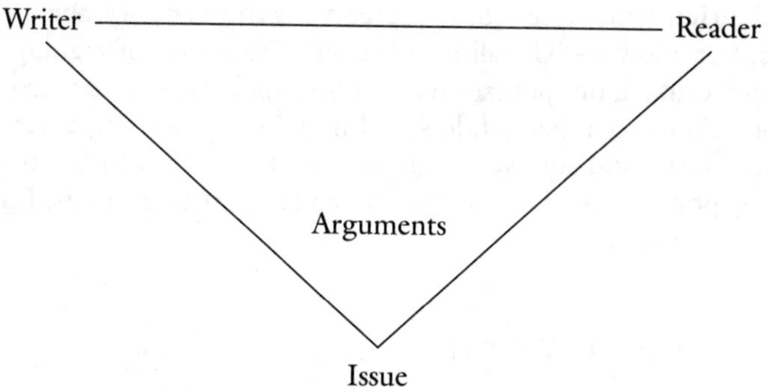

Figure 1 The Rhetorical Situation

This interaction is mediated through symbols—language, of course, but visual elements as well. If you are in the position of the "writer," then you are making an argument through language or visual elements that addresses the issue under discussion. If you are the "reader," then you are trying to understand someone else's argument. In a real conversation, the participants will take turns being "writer" (speaker) or "reader" (listener), but they will all use the tools of rhetoric—the tools of effective argumentation. Regardless of the reading or writing task, determining the rhetorical situation is key to understanding your role as a reader or writer. Understanding the rhetorical situation will help you define your purpose, audience, and subject much more clearly. And identifying your position in the rhetorical situation is essential to arguing effectively.

LOOKING AHEAD

Throughout your life, you will be called upon to write for a variety of contexts and purposes. Many of these writing situations will require you to argue effectively. Part One of this text introduces the process of arguing for a variety of rhetorical situations. Chapter 1 elaborates more fully on the topic of arguing in context and identifying rhetorical situations. In this chapter, you will learn how to define "community" and identify the communities you belong to. You will also learn to identify rhetorical situations and to describe how rhetorical situations can change. By understanding your place in a community and rhetorical situation, you will be able to respond effectively to the arguments that are all around you.

Chapter 2 explains *ethos*, how to use your standing in the community or establish your credibility as a writer in order to be persuasive. In particular, I will explain how to share personal information about yourself, identify with your readers, and adopt an appropriate voice in order to sound credible. Chapter 3 focuses on *pathos*, the use of emotion in arguing. You will learn how to give your argument immediacy and presence for your readers by using concrete examples and choosing words that evoke an emotional response.

Chapter 4 identifies the role of logic in arguing. In this chapter, you will learn how to analyze arguments—identify the parts of an argument and explain how these parts work together to persuade. In this chapter, you will also learn how to identify and avoid logical fallacies, manipulative or deceptive language, and misleading statistical arguments. Chapter 5 describes how to combine all these aspects of arguing into an effective written or oral argument. In particular, you will learn two major argumentative strategies: adapting to the conventions and beliefs of the community and challenging the community. You will learn to identify six common forms that arguments take: the classical argument, delayed thesis, conciliatory argument, motivational argument, Rogerian argument, and Option Three.

Chapter 6 focuses on how to use research as part of the process of composing an argument. You will learn how to find sources for your arguments in the library and also how to use computer databases and the Internet to find information. In this chapter, you will learn how to analyze and evaluate the sources you've found and then incorporate these sources into your argument, using proper methods of citation.

After completing Part One of this text, you should be able to write with confidence arguments for a variety of occasions, audiences, and purposes. As you put these principles into practice in your own life and become more sensitive to the needs of the communities you belong to, you should find that you can use your skills in arguing not just to get your way but rather to use your influence to strengthen the community by mediating conflict.

Brief Contents

Contents

* Indicates that the selection is new to this edition.

2 Analyzing and Evaluating Ethos 67

3 Analyzing and Evaluating Pathos 109

6 Writing Researched Arguments 327

PART TWO
Types of Claims 443

8 Arguing Claims about Causality 499

9 Arguing Claims about Language 555

Readings by Issue

Language/Public Discourse/The Media

The Environment

Education

U.S. Legal and Justice System

Communities

Civil Rights/Human Rights/Social Justice

Cultural Differences

Science/Medical Ethics

Business/Advertising/Consumer Culture

Parenting and Families

Visual Arguments

Columbine High School Massacre/Violence in the United States

Technology

Popular Culture

Health and Fitness

PART ONE

The Essential Principles

Chapter 1

Arguments in Context

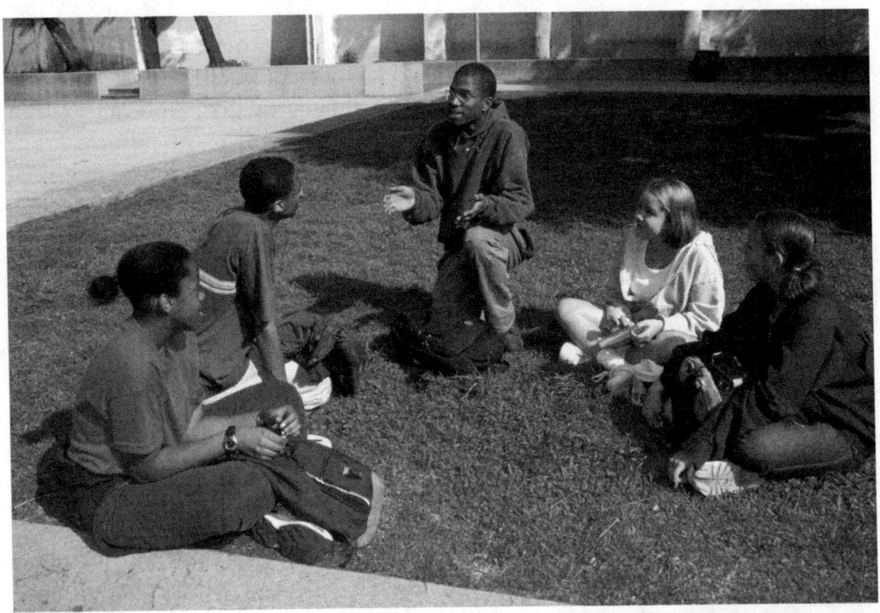

Community and Context

This book emphasizes the importance of studying arguments in context—reading an argument within the broader conversation in which a particular argument is a response. This broader conversation, along with the beliefs, values, and assumptions identified with those who participate in the conversation, forms the *context* for an argument. This context includes the *rhetorical situation,* a situation that calls for the use of rhetoric, a situation where an argument would be an appropriate response. A rhetorical situation identifies the interaction between writers and readers or speakers and listeners in relation to a particular issue, and refers to the set of elements involved in any act of communication: the writer/speaker, the audience, the purpose, the occasion, and the topic.

But just as real arguments can best be understood in context, rhetorical situations should be studied in context, too. They should be studied in relationship to other rhetorical situations and to the broader life of a community of which these situations are a part. A rhetorical situation brings members of a community together to discuss a particular issue, but the issue and the relationships among the participants in the conversation make sense only if you can identify the community or communities that these participants belong to.

DEFINING *COMMUNITY*

The word *community* comes from a Latin word that means "common" or "shared." In its broadest sense, *community* describes a group of people who have something in common. Communities may be defined by geographical location or may consist of people sharing a common history, language, or culture. Communities may be formed by those who share the same social or business interests, or political or religious views. Disciplines within a college or university, academic departments, and scholarly organizations often define themselves according to a common body of knowledge, method of inquiry, or domain of study. Communities overlap and intersect in a lot of interesting ways. Communities formed by common interests or beliefs may transcend geographical boundaries, and a geographical community may contain many smaller communities based on language or culture. People may claim membership in a lot of different communities. For example, members of your class may belong to the same fraternity or sorority you do. Or you may belong to the same campus club, live in the same housing unit, attend the same church, participate in the same social events, or come from the same area. You may recognize each other at a political rally or a sporting event. We all belong to different communities, but we also share our membership in communities with others. Identifying ourselves with different communities creates commonalities among us, but also gives us our diversity.

LANGUAGE AND COMMUNITY

Nearly all people who interact with one another in any community do so, to a certain extent, through a common language. This common language helps to define any community, as language initiates us into the world of a community and allows us to participate by giving us the power to communicate. As members of a community, we learn the common names for people, places, objects, actions, and emotions, and through the language of the community, we receive the community's common values and beliefs. The common language that binds a community is "discourse," and a community defined by this common language is a "discourse community."

A university or college is a discourse community. It is separated from the world around it not only by geographical boundaries and physical barriers but also by language. Terms from the college discourse community include, among many others, "associate professor," "credit hour," "add/drop," "general education," "syllabus," "rush week," and "quad." Some first-time college students struggle with this language, and often no one bothers to define these terms for them because experienced members of the community have forgotten that there was a time when the terms weren't familiar. The problem is compounded by the fact that the larger university is made up of many smaller discourse communities defined by separate disciplines, departments, majors, and fields of study.

UNDERSTANDING HOW COMMUNITIES ARE STRUCTURED

Every community has a structure, an organization of power, a hierarchy of positions or roles taken by individuals within the community. The structure of the community can be highly complex, as with a corporation or government body, or it can be fairly simple. There may be a formal recognized structure as well as an "unofficial" structure behind the official one, a "shadow" organization. Considerable power, for example, may lie in the hands of staff or support people who work behind the scenes. The structure of a community may also contain organizations within organizations.

For example, the university or college community that you belong to as a student is a complex organization, an organization made up of many smaller organizations, where the structures of these organizations overlap, often in confusing ways. Beginning students are often frustrated because they don't understand whom to go to for help with a problem, who has the power to make and enforce decisions, or whom they can talk to when they have questions. And even those students who know whom to talk to sometimes can't get access to these people.

Within every community is a distribution of power as well as processes for communicating, making decisions, and enforcing decisions. The structure of the community may govern conditions for the use of language: who speaks, when they speak, where they speak, how, in what manner, for how long, and, sometimes, what they are allowed to say. The community structure may determine how decisions are made, enacted, and enforced: Who makes decisions? How are they made? When and where are they made? In what manner? To what end or purpose? The communications and decision-making processes of a community may be explicit and formal, as in the case of legislative bodies, committees, and courts, or they may be implicit and essentially informal, as in the case of families and social groups.

Understanding the structure of the community—its distributions of power, its processes for communication and decision making—is an essential part of living in any community. Persuasive power can come from knowing how to say something that matters to the people that matter. For instance, you can debate an important social issue with your friends around the lunch table, but this debate probably won't have as much of an impact on the life of the community as it would if you could somehow present your views to a member of Congress, a lobbyist, or an influential member of the media. The influence a group of individuals can have on community matters may seem quite small, but understanding something about arguing and the structure of organizations may allow individuals greater access to power than they realized was possible. Sometimes a few letters to a congressional representative can influence his or her vote on an issue, particularly when the issue is not a highly publicized one. And students can wield considerable power in their local or campus communities if they understand how these communities are organized and how to argue effectively within the organization.

Rhetorical Situations within Communities

IDENTIFYING THE PARTICIPANTS

As explained earlier, a rhetorical situation is one that calls for the use of persuasion—it's a situation in which an argument would be an appropriate response. A rhetorical situation brings people together to debate or discuss an issue that is important to them. These participants are the potential audience for arguments made in response to the rhetorical situation. Although a rhetorical situation is part of the structure of a community, it is not the same as this structure. Furthermore, the participants in a rhetorical situation—the potential audience—will generally be only part of the larger community. For example, no means of communication can include everyone who lives in the United States. Even if you were to broadcast your message on all the major networks, you would reach only those who have their televisions on and are watching a major network. Likewise, if you published your argument in the *Wall Street Journal* or the *New York Times,* you would reach a large number of people but only those who read these newspapers—and took the time to read your piece—not the full community. As you try to identify the participants in a rhetorical situation, remember that you are limited to those who participate in a particular conversation, usually defined by a particular time, place, and medium.

But it isn't enough to know who is participating in a particular rhetorical situation. If you are going to address these people as an audience, you need to know something about them as well. How much do they know or care about the issue? What is their current position? What values and opinions do they share? How does your position and how do your values and opinion differ from those of other participants? Answering these questions will help you understand the relationship of your position to the positions held by other participants in the conversation. Since conversation surrounding a particular issue may involve several positions, answering these questions will also help you understand as well how the participants in a rhetorical situation relate to each other.

When you are analyzing the relationships among participants in a rhetorical situation, it helps to use yourself as a point of reference. Let's call those with whom you basically agree your "in-group." Those who hold an opinion much different from yours are your "out-group." Between your opinion and the opinion of your out-group lie people with a spectrum of opinions, including those who share your position to a certain degree but not as fully as you and your in-group do. The following diagram shows a simple relationship:

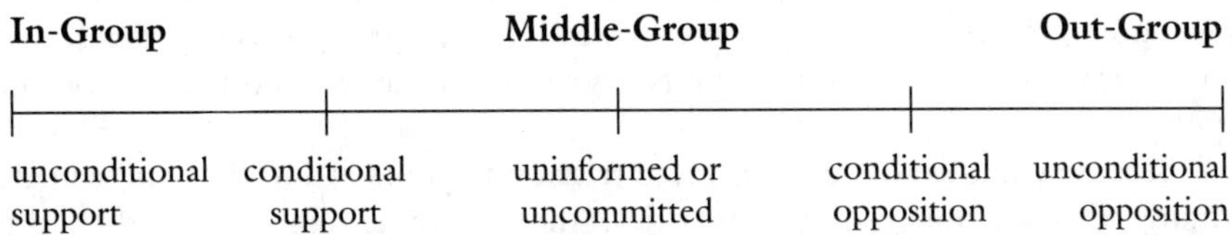

At one extreme, your out-group is characterized by "unconditional opposition." This group is completely opposed to your position, able to offer strong reasons to support its opposition, and reluctant to make any show of support or conciliation toward your view. At the other extreme, your in-group, consisting of those most closely associated with your position, offers unconditional support and is able to offer strong reasons for that support. Between these two positions lie other positions. A less extreme out-group will be characterized by conditional opposition, opposing your view but perhaps unable to offer strong reasons for its opposition or willing to concede some support for your position. Likewise, a less extreme in-group will be characterized by conditional support, unable perhaps to offer strong reasons for that support or to commit fully to your view. In the middle are those who have not made much of a commitment either way or who may not know much about the issue.

In another situation, you and your in-group might represent a middle ground between what you consider two extreme positions. Here is a diagram of that situation:

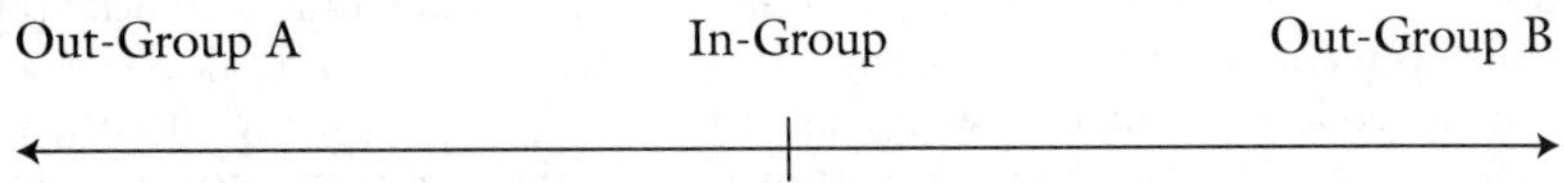

When the audience holds multiple opinions, you may come up with a more complex diagram, particularly if you try to represent the relationship of these different groups to one another as well as to you and your in-group:

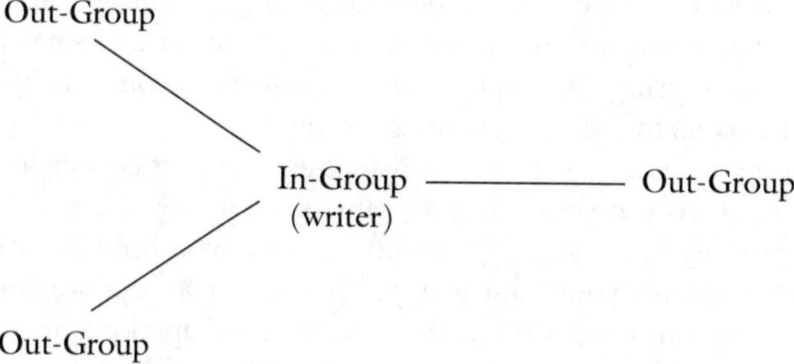

In this diagram the two out-groups on the left agree with each other more than they agree with the out-group on the right. The in-group position lies somewhere between the positions of the two groups on the left and the one on the right.

Because you define these groups in relation to yourself and the issue you are arguing, they are not absolute categories. Another writer might define them differently, as you might when writing about another issue. Your out-group on one issue might become your in-group on another. This type of grouping is not meant to be judgmental or evaluative, merely descriptive. You might sympathize with people in your out-group on a different issue. The model is merely designed to help you analyze the possible relationships among participants in a rhetorical situation.

KAIROS: IDENTIFYING THE RIGHT MOMENT

What Is Kairos? In the life of any community, there are times and places of significance. The Greeks used the term *kairos* to describe such moments. Kairos is a critical or opportune moment, the meeting of the right people at the right time and place. Kairos describes the proper time to act. The Romans described a similar idea as ***decorum,*** acting in the proper manner for the circumstances, or ***carpe diem,*** taking advantage of the moment. The Hebrew author of Ecclesiastes expressed a similar view in a passage that provides the basis for the folk song "Turn, Turn, Turn":

> To every thing there is a season, and a time to every purpose under heaven: A time to be born, and a time to die; a time to plant, and a time to pluck up that which is planted; a time to kill, and a time to heal; a time to break down, and a time to build up; a time to weep, and a time to laugh; a time to mourn, and a time to dance; a time to cast away stones, and a time to gather stones together; a time to embrace, and a time to refrain from embracing; a time to get, and a time to lose; a time to keep, and a time to cast away; a time to rend, and a time to sew; a time to keep silence, and a time to speak; a time to love, and a time to hate; a time of war, and a time of peace. (KJV 3:1–8)

These critical moments may take different forms. They may be regular meetings, such as town council meetings, court sessions, public hearings, stockholders' meetings, church meetings, committee meetings. They may be ceremonies or rituals, such as weddings, funerals, graduations, birthdays. Kairos refers to any moment that is somehow a critical junction of time, space, and action.

One kind of action that kairos can call forth is communicating. Guests at a wedding may toast the newlyweds. Graduation ceremonies and funerals have speakers. Proclaiming a new national monument, winning or losing an election, announcing a new tax plan all require a suitable speech—and so constitute rhetorical situations because they call for appropriate responses in language.

Real Times and Places Some critical moments are located in real time and real space. Such spaces include church buildings, courtrooms, boardrooms, student unions, and town halls. Getting the right people in the right place is crucial. For instance, if you met the nine members of the Supreme Court at a party in Washington and asked for their opinions on the landmark abortion rights case *Roe v. Wade,* you still wouldn't have a Supreme Court opinion because, although you have the right people, you have them in the wrong place and the wrong circumstances.

Nearly every university has a place on campus that is considered the "right place" to speak out on public issues. At Arizona State University, where I was a graduate student, people gather near the fountain in front of the student union or on the lawn west of the library. There they discuss religion and politics but also promote campus and club events. At Brigham Young University, students generally meet at a place called the "checkerboard quad," a grassy area broken up by concrete squares. The student organization occasionally sponsors a "soapbox" here, an open microphone for students to speak out on issues of local concern. Colleges also have more formal forums: classrooms, seminars, panel discussions, debates. These have a different set of rules from, say, the fountain in front of the student union.

Time is also a consideration. Some occasions for arguing are regularly scheduled in a community. City councils, courts, legislatures, stockholders' meetings, and government hearings, for example, all follow a regular schedule for conducting their business. If you want to argue a local issue in front of the city council, you need to know both the place and the time of the meeting and how to get your issue on the agenda. At other times, occasions for arguing arise in response to a crisis or moment of decision.

Virtual Times and Places Technology allows the extension of times and places. These extensions of time, space, and human experience are called *virtual.* We have come to think of virtual realities only as the extension of human experience through computers, but many kinds of virtual time, space, and experience exist. Telephones can create a virtual place where two people can narrow distances in physical space, and conference calling can bring the voices of several people together at once. You can even use the telephone to participate in a conversation about political issues. For instance, you can call the White House to register your opinion on an issue or to find out when a bill was signed or vetoed. You can call the Sierra Club for the latest environmental news, get information on AIDS from the AIDS hotline, or find out about cancer research by calling the American Cancer Society.

Television and radio create a kind of virtual space where viewers from around the planet can watch or hear events as they happen. Tape delays create virtual time and space so that we can participate in these events at our own convenience. The 2000 Summer Olympics in Sydney, Australia, were taped and broadcast during prime time in the United States, but viewers could participate in the events just as though they were broadcast live. Television, radio, and film also allow multiple viewpoints and perspectives through editing. The combination of the telephone and the Internet with radio and television even allows viewers to respond to broadcasters directly.

Perhaps the most powerful electronic medium of all is created by computers. The Internet has become an important part of how we in the United States live in communities. You may already be familiar with e-mail, electronic discussion groups, and newsgroups. Many businesses and other organizations now strive for "paperless" offices where all correspondence occurs electronically. You can fire off a quick note to the White House or to Congress through e-mail. The Internet affords people the power of a television broadcaster or of a magazine or newspaper editor. Many people have set up home pages on the World Wide Web to describe themselves, their families, their hobbies and interests, their school work, and their employment. Usually, anyone with access to the Internet can access these pages. People now buy all kinds of things electronically and can browse vast databases of information. People can participate in chat groups, MUDs, or MOOs where they can carry on virtual conversations in real time.

You don't, however, always need high-tech electronic media to create a virtual experience. The regular mail system is slower than e-mail, telephone, or fax, but it still extends our experience through time and space. And if you can't visit the president personally and don't have access to e-mail, you can still contact the White House the old-fashioned way by writing a letter. Newspapers are not as fast as the Internet, television, or radio, but they can still take readers to places and events that they wouldn't be able to witness in reality. Diaries, journals, and books give readers a virtual experience with authors who have long since died, enabling them to reconstruct the conversations these writers carried on in their own communities.

Kairos and Power To argue effectively, it is important to understand how kairos works within the structure of a community. The critical moments in the life of a community—the appropriate action for the right people at the right time and place—relate to the community's structure of power and decision making. Not everyone in a community is equal: Some have greater access to the important people and locations. Not everyone has equal access to the decision makers in the community. Although you can e-mail your congressional representative, you probably wouldn't have the same influence as someone who can visit the representative face to face or hire an expensive team of lobbyists. Lawyers have greater access to the courts than ordinary citizens. Newspapers and magazines have editors and publishers who decide which voices are heard in their publications. Television and radio stations have managers who decide what gets on the air. Even radio call-in programs, which seem rather democratic, have a producer who decides which callers get on the air. Scarcity of time, space, and money limits the number of people who can join the conversation and how much they can contribute. Those who control access to the conversation are called "gatekeepers." To make a real difference, you need to know the process by which gatekeepers will allow access to meaningful conversations. Here are some important questions to ask:

- How do individuals within a community routinely communicate with one another?
- Where do people routinely meet? Under what circumstances?
- In what ways do people communicate? Who is allowed to speak? Under what conditions?
- What occasions call for people to respond? What is considered an appropriate response to these occasions?
- How is the communication process tied to the decision-making process and the work or mission of the community?
- Who are the gatekeepers? What barriers limit access to the conversation?

Rhetorical Situations Are Cyclical

To argue effectively, you need to know the right time to make an appropriate response to a rhetorical situation. Knowing the right time requires that you understand something about how rhetorical situations change over time. Rhetorical situations are not static; they evolve. Lloyd Bitzer, an important rhetorical theorist, calls the evolution of a rhetorical situation its "life cycle."

In the earliest stages of this cycle, a need for debate exists, but the occasion and circumstances may not be clearly defined. Some people may not be aware of the issue or may not have organized themselves to respond to it. At this point, arguing can define the issue more clearly and raise awareness of the problem. As the situation evolves, it reaches a period of maturity where people are forming their opinions, arguing their positions, and beginning to make decisions. This time of maturity is kairos, the crucial moment to respond to the right people at the right place. As this critical moment begins to pass, Bitzer explains that rhetorical situations enter a period of deterioration. At this stage, many people may already have formed their opinions, made their decisions, or begun to take

■■ THE LIFE CYCLE OF A RHETORICAL SITUATION

Origin The awareness of the issue is still forming, and the implications are unclear. Many people are unfamiliar with the issue or may not have strongly held opinions. The processes for deciding the issue and the groups involved are largely undetermined.

Maturity The issues are more clearly defined, and processes for deciding the issue are in place. The moment of decision is approaching. Many different groups are engaged in the decision-making process.

Deterioration The prime moment for influencing the opinion of those who decide has passed, and a solution may be in the early stages of implementation. Positions on the issues are very well established.

Disintegration The process of change becomes practically irreversible. Decisions are made and put into action. Many groups have moved on to other issues.

action or implement plans. It grows more and more difficult for arguing to have an effect. Finally, the rhetorical situation enters a period of disintegration in which arguing can have little or no effect. Perhaps the audience that can really make a difference is no longer present or has turned to other issues. Perhaps plans are already completed or well under way.

Here is an example of the life cycle of a rhetorical situation. The state of Utah considers building a freeway that would pass through wetlands near the shores of the Great Salt Lake. Proponents of this freeway believe it is needed to handle current levels of traffic as well as anticipated growth. Many environmentalists and local residents fear that the freeway will destroy hundreds of acres of wetlands. In the early stages of this project, opponents of the freeway raise public awareness of the issue and of the importance of wetlands and also shape the process the government would follow in debating and deciding this issue. Once this process is accomplished, the rhetorical situation reaches a point of maturity, and all parties need to put forth their best arguments. In this case, the state decides to hold a series of local hearings before debating the issue in legislative committee and making a decision. Once these hearings end and the committee meets, this situation enters a period of deterioration. It becomes harder and harder to influence legislators and shape public opinion. As building proceeds on the freeway (or after the freeway is voted down), the rhetorical situation disintegrates, and a rhetorical response becomes difficult.

Responding to a Rhetorical Situation

FINDING PLACES TO ENTER THE CONVERSATION

The best arguments are those that are part of a conversation, that respond to issues facing a real community. To join the conversation in a meaningful way, you need to identify a place where you can enter the conversation. Your response may originate in a disagreement or controversy that already exists in the community, or you may wish to present a position that has not been presented. In the process of listening to others and recording and evaluating their ideas, you may have found gaps in their reasoning, areas that have not been considered. These would be natural points to enter the conversation.

You might find yourself presenting a new argument to your community, answering objections others may raise, educating those who are uninformed, and motivating those who lack interest. You could also enter a conversation by stirring things up a bit, taking a provocative position to get the debate about an issue moving along or to cause others to see an issue in a new way.

It is difficult to describe exactly how to identify a proper time and place for you to add your voice to the conversation. Usually, when you really try to get involved in the intellectual life of a community, the opportunities present themselves. Finding your place in the conversation depends a lot on the relationship you have to other members of the community, as well as your position on the particular issue in relation to others. In deciding how you should enter a conversation, you need to make some inferences about others who are participating in the conversation. These others are your potential audience.

Understanding your relationship to your audience provides you with some opportunities for joining in the conversation. For example, you can address yourself to those who basically agree with your position in order to consolidate that belief and motivate them to act on their beliefs. You can also provide good reasons for sharing the belief you hold. If you address yourself to those who are uninformed, undecided, or uncommitted, you can try to build their interest and help them form an opinion. You can explain why you feel your position is better than other positions. You can invite these others to get involved in the conversation. If you are addressing those who disagree with you, you have an opportunity to explore common ground and resolve conflict. You can also "agree to disagree" and outline exactly where that disagreement lies, clarifying your position. Perhaps you can get these others to see things a little more your way (although you are not likely to persuade them to embrace your position entirely).

As you engage in debate and discussion with others, you try to clarify your own position as well as find the best arguments for persuading others, both framing your ideas for yourself and explaining to others why you feel the way you do.

You can prepare to join the conversation by trying to anticipate how others will respond to your argument. Try placing yourself in their position. Pretend that you oppose your own views. Think of all the reasons you can to support this opposing point of view. Anticipate any objections to this opposing view (including what you consider your own best reasons). This "doubting game" may cause you to rethink your original position. You may decide that you need to modify or even reject your original claim. But you may also discover a new position that you can support with more confidence. Whether or not you change your original position, seeing your argument from the perspective of others in the community will help you find places where your argument is poorly supported or inadequately explained. Remember that diversity is a strength. You can develop your argument by seeking out positions different from your own—the more diverse, the better.

The most straightforward way to join the conversation is to adapt your argument to the needs, values, and language of the community. You are generally more persuasive if you can identify with those you are trying to persuade. Occasionally, however, you may want to challenge the community, to help others see an issue in a new way, to get a conversation going, or to take the conversation in a new direction.

THE ELEMENTS OF EFFECTIVE ARGUMENTATION

Arguing comes as naturally to humans as language. Children learn early on how to use language to get what they want from their parents, older siblings, and friends. In trying to get their way, children learn the power of trust and emotion—as well as the effectiveness of stubborn repetition. The practice of persuasion is as old as human civilization, but the Greeks were really the first, in the European cultural tradition, to try to understand how persuasion works. The Greeks gave us the word *rhetoric* to identify the arts of persuasion. The Greek philosopher Aristotle, in his *Art of Rhetoric,* defined three elements of persuasion, identified by the Greek words *ethos, pathos,* and *logos:* persuasion through the credibility of the writer, persuasion through emotion, and persuasion through logic. To argue effectively, you need to learn how to use these three elements of persuasion in connection with one another.

Ethos: Arguing from Credibility Ethos is related to the English word *ethics* and refers to the trustworthiness or credibility of a speaker or writer, based on how others perceive his or her character. Ethos is an effective persuasive strategy because whom we believe is often as important as what we believe. Some people can convey the "goodness" of their character through their speaking and writing, and others will respond positively because they trust the character that is presented. Can you think of a time when you have done something or accepted an opinion for no other reason than that you trusted the person giving the advice or offering the opinion? For example, when a trusted physician gives you advice, you may not understand all the medical reasons behind the advice, but you follow it anyway because you believe the physician knows what he or she is talking about. Similarly, a religious leader may argue for the rightness of a particular way of living, and because you trust this leader's character, you choose to accept this way of life. In another instance you trust that a firefighter teaching the proper method for administering CPR has saved many lives using the method, so you accept its effectiveness and value. These are all examples of persuasion through ethos.

Pathos: Arguing from Emotion Pathos is related to the English words *pathetic*, *sympathy*, and *empathy*. The Greek word for "emotion" or "feeling," pathos refers to the ability of language to evoke feelings in us, to put us in a particular emotional state. Whenever you act or accept an opinion based on your feelings, even without fully understanding why, you are acting on pathos. These feelings don't have to be feelings of pity, as the word *pathetic* implies. They may be any emotion: love, fear, patriotism, guilt, hate, joy. As you examine the emotional aspects of arguments, make sure that you consider the full range of emotions.

Arguments that rely heavily on pathos are common. For example, advertisers, who have to present a convincing message in a 30-second television spot, on a single magazine page, or in a narrow Web banner, often try to evoke an emotional response in consumers. Ads may make you laugh so that you'll feel good about a product or company. Clothing ads may appeal to your sense of vanity, to your need to belong, to your fear of rejection, or to your desire to succeed. Tire ads may appeal to your fear of being stranded on the road. Food ads appeal to your hunger. And many ads use the appeal of sex to sell their products.

Although the emotional appeal can be manipulative, it is also essential for moving people to action. People can be convinced logically that they ought to do something but still not follow through. When people are made to feel strongly about something, they will often act on those feelings—even when they're not sure why. Human feelings are powerful, but the key to sustained work and commitment is acting upon a decision even when the powerful emotions have waned. The emotional appeal can be a way of sustaining such emotions and, consequently, the commitment to act.

Logos: Arguing from Logic The Greek word *logos* is the basis for the English word *logic*. To the Greeks, this word could mean "word," "thought," or "law." It refers to "the expression of thought in language." Logos is a broader idea than formal logic—the highly symbolic and mathematical logic that you might study in a philosophy course. Logos refers to any attempt to appeal to the intellect, the general meaning of "logical argument." When you argue through logos, you use examples, facts, documents, direct observation, measurements, experiments, and statistics—things that can be verified, tested, or reproduced.

Everyday arguments rely heavily on ethos and pathos, but academic arguments depend on logos. Certainly, academic writers want to sound credible and trustworthy, but readers of academic arguments will usually demand some logical support for a claim, no matter how much they trust the reputation of the scholar making the argument. Historians want eyewitness accounts and historical artifacts and documents. Scientists want careful observation and experimentation. Social scientists want theoretical models that make sense and that can be tested empirically. Literary critics will ask for examples from the literary work being analyzed and interpreted. Logical arguments have to make sense to the mind, and they need to follow accepted methods of reasoning, analyzing, and interpreting.

A General Method for Arguing

You've already learned a lot about arguing. It may help to reduce everything to a general method for arguing. First, you need to find an issue. You may already have an issue that you are interested in. Perhaps you've got an idea that you would like to share with others or have heard an argument that you would like to respond to. Perhaps you have a question that you would like answered. If you don't have a clear issue in mind, all you really need to do is join in a conversation in one of the communities you belong to (or would like to join) and issues will present themselves.

Second, you need to identify and analyze the rhetorical situation. To identify the rhetorical situation, you need to determine who is involved in the conversation and what positions they hold. You need to find out what occasions bring people together to discuss this issue. Where and when do they meet? Do they meet face to face, or is their discussion mediated in some way? You also need to look at the life cycle of the particular situation. How has the situation evolved? What stage is it in now? How might the situation change?

Third, you need to analyze and evaluate the arguments others make about these issues. To analyze their arguments, you need to first identify the claims

A GENERAL METHOD FOR ARGUING

1. Find an issue.
2. Identify and analyze the rhetorical situation.
3. Analyze and evaluate the arguments others make about this issue.
4. Determine your relationship to your audience.
5. Identify the right time and place to make a response.
6. Use the means of persuasion available to you to compose an argument.

they make. Then find the reasons they give to support their claims and the assumptions that are implied in those claims and reasons. To evaluate their arguments, you need to consider how consistent the arguments are as well as how well these arguments correspond with the beliefs and values of the author and of the community. You also need to consider how well these claims, reasons, and assumptions correspond with your own beliefs and values. In Chapters Two, Three, and Four, I describe how to analyze and evaluate different kinds of arguments.

Fourth, determine your relationship to your audience. Comparing the arguments made by others to your own beliefs will not only help you evaluate these arguments, but it will also help you form your own position and determine how closely your position corresponds with your audience's position. If, for example, you and your audience share a lot of beliefs and values, your primary task as a writer will probably be to increase the audience's adherence to the position you both share and to move your audience to action. If, on the other hand, you and your audience differ quite a bit, then your goal will probably be to build common ground and understanding. In Chapter Five, I will talk more about the particular strategies you might use to address the needs of different audiences.

Fifth, you need to identify the right time and place to make a response—the kairos of the issue. If you have done a good job of analyzing the rhetorical situation, then it should be apparent whom you should talk to, where and when you should make a response, and how you should adapt your response to the life stage of this particular situation. Finally, you need to use the best means of persuasion available to you to make a response appropriate to your audience and situation. You need to build your credibility with the audience (ethos); construct a logical, consistent, reasonable argument (logos); and evoke an emotional response in your audience appropriate to the issue and occasion (pathos).

The Principles in Action: Readings

UNDERSTANDING COMMUNITIES

Academic communities are important for students and professors, but most students leave the academic community when they graduate. This book is primarily designed to help you succeed in your academic writing, but you can apply the same techniques you used in analyzing your college community to analyzing other communities you belong to and understanding how language works within these communities.

In the following essay, J. B. Priestley describes three types of communities: regional, national, and international. He argues that we have given too much emphasis to the national community and not enough to the regional or international. As you read this essay, consider the following questions:

1. What are the effects of emphasizing nationalism over regionalism or internationalism?
2. What are the "landscape and speech," "traditional customs," "food and drink," and "songs and jokes" that reflect the region you come from? How important are these to understanding your identity?
3. Is there such a thing as national culture? What is the relationship between your regional culture and a national culture?
4. What kind of communities are international in scope? What kind of membership or allegiance do you have to international communities? Is there a culture that crosses national boundaries?
5. How do popular media, such as television, movies, newspapers, and magazines, create a sense of national, international, or regional culture?
6. Priestley lived long before computer technology, but what role might new information technology have in strengthening regional and international communities?

Wrong Ism

J. B. PRIESTLEY

THERE are three isms that we ought to consider very carefully—regionalism, nationalism, internationalism. Of these three the one there is most fuss about, the one that starts men shouting and marching and shooting, the one that seems to have all the depth and thrust and fire, is of course nationalism. Nine people out of 10, I fancy, would say that of this trio it is the one that really counts, the big boss. Regionalism and internationalism, they would add, are comparatively small, shadowy, rather cranky. And I believe all this to be quite wrong. Like many another big boss, nationalism is largely bogus. It is like a bunch of flowers made of plastics. 1

The real flowers belong to regionalism. The mass of people everywhere may never have used the term. They are probably regionalists without knowing it. Because they have been brought up in a certain part of the world, they have formed perhaps quite unconsciously a deep attachment to its landscape and speech, its traditional customs, its food and drink, its songs and jokes. (There are of course always the rebels, often intellectuals and writers, but they are not the mass of people.) They are rooted in their region. Indeed, without this attachment a man can have no roots.

So much of people's lives, from earliest childhood onwards, is deeply intertwined with the common life of the region, they cannot help feeling strongly about it. A threat to it is a knife pointing at the heart. How can life ever be the same if bullying strangers come to change everything? The form and colour, the very taste and smell of dear familiar things will be different, alien, life-destroying.

It would be better to die fighting. And it is precisely this, the nourishing life of the region, for which common men have so often fought and died.

This attachment to the region exists on a level far deeper than that of any political hocus-pocus. When a man says "my country" with real feeling, he is thinking about his region, all that has made up his life, and not about that political entity, the nation. There can be some confusion here simply because some countries are so small—and ours is one of them—and so old, again like ours, that much of what is national is also regional.[1] Down the centuries, the nation, itself, so comparatively small, has been able to attach to itself the feeling really created by the region. (Even so there is something left over, as most people in Yorkshire or Devon, for example, would tell you.) This probably explains the fervent patriotism developed early in small countries. The English were announcing that they were English in the Middle Ages, before nationalism had arrived elsewhere.

If we deduct from nationalism all that it has borrowed or stolen from re- 5
gionalism, what remains is mostly rubbish. The nation, as distinct from the region, is largely the creation of power-men and political manipulators. Almost all nationalist movements are led by ambitious frustrated men determined to hold office. I am not blaming them. I would do the same if I were in their place and wanted power so badly. But nearly always they make use of the rich warm regional feeling, the emotional dynamo of the movement, while being almost untouched by it themselves. This is because they are not as a rule deeply loyal to any region themselves. Ambition and a love of power can eat like acid into the tissues of regional loyalty. It is hard, if not impossible, to retain a natural piety and yet be forever playing both ends against the middle.

Being itself a power structure, devised by men of power, the nation tends to think and act in terms of power. What would benefit the real life of the region, where men, women, and children actually live, is soon sacrificed for the power and prestige of the nation. (And the personal vanity of presidents and ministers themselves, which historians too often disregard.) Among the new nations of our time innumerable peasants and labourers must have found themselves being cut down from five square meals a week to three in order to provide unnecessary airlines, military forces that can only be used against them and nobody else, great conference halls and official yachts and the rest. The last traces of imperialism and colonialism may have to be removed from Asia and Africa, where men can no longer endure being condemned to a permanent inferiority by the colour of their skins; but even so, the modern world, the real world of our time, does not want and would be far better without more and more nations, busy creating for themselves the very paraphernalia that western Europe is now trying to abolish. You are compelled to answer more questions when trying to spend half a day in Cambodia than you are now travelling from the Hook of Holland to Syracuse.

[1] Priestley (1894–1984) was English. [Ed.]

This brings me to internationalism. I dislike this term, which I used only to complete the isms. It suggests financiers and dubious promoters living nowhere but in luxury hotels; a shallow world of entrepreneurs and impresarios. (Was it Sacha Guitry who said that impresarios were men who spoke many languages but all with a foreign accent?) The internationalism I have in mind here is best described as world civilisation. It is life considered on a global scale. Most of our communications and transport already exist on this high wide level. So do many other things from medicine to meteorology. Our astronomers and physicists (except where they have allowed themselves to be hush-hushed) work here. The UN special agencies, about which we hear far too little, have contributed more and more to this world civilisation. All the arts, when they are arts and not chunks of nationalist propaganda, naturally take their place in it. And it grows, widens, deepens, in spite of the fact that for every dollar, ruble, pound, or franc spent in explaining and praising it, a thousand are spent by the nations explaining and praising themselves.

This world civilisation and regionalism can get along together, especially if we keep ourselves sharply aware of their quite different but equally important values and rewards. A man can make his contribution to world civilisation and yet remain strongly regional in feeling: I know several men of this sort. There is of course the danger—it is with us now—of the global style flattening out the regional, taking local form, colour, flavour, away for ever, disinheriting future generations, threatening them with sensuous poverty and a huge boredom. But to understand and appreciate regionalism is to be on guard against this danger. And we must therefore make a clear distinction between regionalism and nationalism.

It is nationalism that tries to check the growth of world civilisation. And nationalism, when taken on a global scale, is more aggressive and demanding now than it has ever been before. This in the giant powers is largely disguised by the endless fuss in public about rival ideologies, now a largely unreal quarrel. What is intensely real is the glaring nationalism. Even the desire to police the world is nationalistic in origin. (Only the world can police the world.) Moreover, the nation-states of today are for the most part far narrower in their outlook, far more inclined to allow prejudice against the foreigner to impoverish their own style of living, than the old imperial states were. It should be part of world civilisation that men with particular skills, perhaps the product of the very regionalism they are rebelling against, should be able to move easily from country to country, to exercise those skills, in anything from teaching the violin to running a new type of factory to managing an old hotel. But nationalism, especially of the newer sort, would rather see everything done badly than allow a few non-nationals to get to work. And people face a barrage of passports, visas, immigration controls, labour permits; and in this respect are worse off than they were in 1900. But even so, in spite of all that nationalism can do—so long as it keeps its nuclear bombs to itself—the internationalism I have in mind, slowly creating a world civilisation, cannot be checked.

Nevertheless, we are still backing the wrong ism. Almost all our money goes 10
on the middle one, nationalism, the rotten meat between the two healthy slices of bread. We need regionalism to give us roots and that very depth of feeling which nationalism unjustly and greedily claims for itself. We need internationalism to save the world and to broaden and heighten our civilisation. While regional man enriches the lives that international man is already working to keep secure and healthy, national man, drunk with power, demands our loyalty, money and applause, and poisons the very air with his dangerous nonsense.

The essay that follows describes what it's like for newcomers to enter a community. Bill Wodraska writes about moving from the city to the country and trying to master the art of "hunkering." In this article, he describes the conflict and confusion that can arise when new members enter a community and outlines the role of language and communication in joining a community. As you read this essay, consider the following questions:

1. Have you ever had the experience of being a newcomer to a community? If so, what was your experience?
2. Have you ever had the experience of being a long-standing member of a community? What was it like when someone new tried to join?
3. To what extent does language distinguish new members of a community from long-standing members? How does one go about learning the language of a community?
4. What kinds of conflict can arise when newcomers try to join a community? How do communities typically resolve these conflicts? How should communities resolve these conflicts?

The Gentle Art of Hunkering

BILL WODRASKA

ALL OF US who move to the country are trying to make successful new lives 1
for ourselves. But I conjecture that some of us will fail because we don't *hunker* . . . and never learn how.

On one level, hunkering is the squatting-on-the-haunches posture assumed by many countryfolk outdoors, especially when there's something serious to discuss or ponder. But the art of hunkering goes far beyond physical posture to encompass tact, sensitivity, and all the other aspects of effective communication between human beings. And I believe that mastering this skill just might be the key to successful living in a rural area.

Say you need to know when to plant strawberries, how deep to sink a fence posthole, or the answer to any one of a thousand other day-to-day questions. No amount of reading—even in MOTHER[1]—is going to provide you with *all* the information you need. Occasionally, you'll require on-the-spot aid and advice . . . and what better source is there than your neighbor who most likely met up with and solved the same problem 40 years ago?

OK, you're willing to ask for assistance. That's half the battle, but only half . . . because that man up the road is not an automated teaching device but a human being. And if he thinks you're nothing but an imported city slicker or stuck-up "foreigner" (who should have stayed where you came from), he won't lift a finger for you.

So my first suggestion is to rid yourself of any notion that you're "bringing 5
yourself down to the level of the local people." True, you may be better educated, more widely traveled and perhaps even wealthier than your new neighbors. *But you're the one going to them for help and advice, not the other way around.* Their experience has made them experts at the kind of life you're seeking. You aren't lowering yourself in this interaction . . . you're just *moving over* toward the other fellow's position. I hope that point seems obvious to you. It took a devil of a long time for *me* to learn it!

With that basic ground rule established, let's say you're approaching Ed Hopkins—the owner of the next farm over—with a specific problem: You need to know who owns the fence between your field and his. Although you might view your visit as a fairly straightforward errand, Ed sees the transaction in a somewhat different light. You need only some basic information, but he wants to know who you are, where you come from, what you're doing over there on the old McAllister place, and the identity of those other people living with you. That's the conversational small change he'll spend talking down at the store with his cronies . . . and that's part of the price you have to pay for what you want to know. It's no use bemoaning the infringement on your precious privacy. The "nosiness" of rural neighbors is inevitable. If you want perfect isolation, you might be able to get it in a warrenlike Manhattan apartment house, but you won't in the country.

So you find your neighbor in his driveway, fiddling with his hay baler . . . and, willy-nilly, you start getting your message across even before you open your mouth. The speed with which you walk up to him, the expression on your face, whether you're smiling or not, your posture, and the way you hold your arms all speak volumes about your intentions toward him. You can appear hostile and threatening—by closing the distance between Ed and yourself too rapidly—or you can be diffident and respectful in your advance. Bear down on your neighbor with a tense, clenched manner and you've created an atmosphere that makes it easy for him to dislike you. But draw near in a relaxed, easygoing, candid fashion . . . and you're in business.

[1] *Mother Earth News,* which calls itself "the original country magazine." [Ed.]

You need to move in slowly and know when to stop (Ed's body language will tell you) to avoid his recoiling away from you. Also, take care not to be too aggressive when you look at your neighbor. Good communication calls for a frank, nonfurtive meeting of the eyes, but it's possible to have too much of a good thing. If you don't shift your gaze just before or just after Ed does, he'll regard your stare—at least on some subconscious level—either as insolence or as a downright threat.

If you think my description sounds a bit overdone, please recall one fact: Although the city person may have dozens of contacts with strangers every day, the country dweller may go for weeks without seeing anyone but family and longtime friends. What is a casual meeting for you may be an event for him or her.

Now, what do you say when you do open the conversation, and how do you 10
say it? Chances are—rural communication systems being what they are—Ed already knows your name and something about you . . . but it won't hurt to introduce yourself with a smile and a "Good morning, Mr. Hopkins." (If you don't know his name, "sir" will do nicely.) Then you'll want to observe the universal rapport-breeding ritual of brief chitchat about the weather and the crops.

These preliminaries serve not only to break the ice but also to give you an idea of Ed's reactions to you and your approach. If he's sullen, cold, and defensive, you'll have to work on building a warmer climate before popping your question. On the other hand, if he's friendly and receptive, much of the work is done.

What judgment Ed will make of you will depend, at least in part, on *how* you talk during this meeting and those to come. Your voice needs to be low, slow, modulated, and friendly . . . not brisk or clipped. Also, although your natural tendency may be to ask your question and get out of there, this just can't be done in rural intercourse. If you're like me, you may have to continually force yourself to take your time about coming to the point, to slow your speech, and even to allow occasional silences. It seems to me—though I have no real evidence for my belief—that countryfolk are less upset than city dwellers by lapses in conversation, and they feel less need to fill the pauses with idle chatter.

Now what can be said about the point itself; that is, the phrasing of your question or request? Probably best is an indirect form that gives Ed an out and leaves him the option of helping you or not, rather than putting him into a situation he has to wiggle away from. Master such phrasing as "Say, I've been wondering how . . ." instead of "Do you know how . . ." and "Do you know anyone who might . . ." instead of "Will you . . ." When you use these graceful and considerate forms, Ed can back out easily—turn you down—without feeling like an ogre. In addition, he has the option of referring you to someone else better able to handle the problem if he's unwilling, or unable, to help you himself.

Moreover, your query or request ought to be just as specific and well thought out as you can make it. After all, your accent may be strange, your appearance distracting, and your question somewhat out of the ordinary. You want to avoid confusing Mr. Hopkins. There's nothing quite so pitiful as two people talking at each other when neither has anything but the haziest idea of what the other is driving at.

15 And don't be surprised if your neighbor prefers to transact business outside in good weather . . . probably hunkered down in the yard. After some practice the position is comfortable, and the conversation is less strained outdoors than it would be sitting stiffly in the parlor. When you find yourself quite automatically lowering yourself to your haunches and looking for something to do with your hands (twisting a piece of grass or baling twine, poking at the gravel, or maybe drawing designs in the dust with a stick), you're on your way to productive rural communication.

Finally, when you have the information you need, don't break off the contact abruptly as you might with a clerk or TV repairman. The code of rural neighborliness requires more than perfunctory conversation before taking leave. (And who knows but that you'll find out something you hadn't thought to ask?) This brings up the necessity for having contact with your neighbors at times when you *don't* need anything from them, just to be neighborly. You'll probably have to take the initiative for the first visits on yourself.

Eventually—if you're going about all this in the right way and the folks nearby come to like you as a person—you'll find yourself being tested in a friendly, nonmalevolent way. You may be invited to swallow a raw clam (as I was by French-speaking clam diggers in New Brunswick) or to try your hand at some demanding chore like tobacco stripping. The point here is not whether you "pass" or "fail" the test but whether you play the game with grace and goodwill. You may bungle the "job," but if you're willing to laugh at your own ineptness and not take your own dignity too seriously, you'll prove the stuff you're made of and come through the *initiation* in good style.

Finally, consider this summation of the art of hunkering written many years ago by Horace Kephart, a man who made a new life for himself among the people of the southern Appalachians:

> Tact . . . implies the will and the insight to put yourself truly in the other man's place. Imagine yourself born, bred, circumstanced like him. It implies, also, the courtesy of doing as you would be done by if you were in that fellow's shoes. No arrogance, no condescension, but man to man on a footing of equal manliness.

The following essay tries to understand how electronic communities differ from physical communities. In "Finding One's Own in Cyberspace," Amy Bruckman answers concerns that critics of the Internet raise about the treatment of women online. Bruckman argues that all users, including women, need to find (or start) an online community that fits their interests. Bruckman was the founder of the MediaMOO, a MUD, or virtual space, designed for researchers of media, one of the few MUDs dedicated to scholarly research and education. She also created MOOSE CROSSING, a MUD designed to help children learn reading, writing, and programming skills. This essay originally appeared in

MIT's *Technology Review* (January 1996), but it is available online through Bruckman's Web page at <http://www.cc.gatech.edu/~asb>.

As you read this essay, consider the following questions:

1. How does the author define *community*?
2. What kind of metaphors or analogies does she provide for the Internet? Is it a "highway," a "home," a "place" or "space," a "network," an "organism"? How does the metaphor you use to describe the Internet affect how you view it?
3. What are the advantages and disadvantages of participating in an online community?
4. What restrictions are placed on who can join or participate in an online community? Who decides? What role does the technology itself play in deciding who can participate?
5. Based on your experience or research, is there a race or gender gap in online communities?

Finding One's Own in Cyberspace

AMY BRUCKMAN

THE WEEK the last Internet porn scandal broke, my phone didn't stop ringing: "Are women comfortable on the Net?" "Should women use gender-neutral names on the Net?" "Are women harassed on the Net?" Reporters called from all over the country with basically the same question. I told them all: Your question is ill-formed. "The Net" is not one thing. It's like asking: "Are women comfortable in bars?" That's a silly question. Which woman? Which bar? 1

The summer I was 18, I was the computer counselor at a summer camp. After the campers were asleep, the counselors were allowed out, and would go bar hopping. First everyone would go to Maria's, an Italian restaurant with red-and-white-checked tablecloths. Maria welcomed everyone from behind the bar, greeting regular customers by name. She always brought us free garlic bread. Next we'd go to the Sandpiper, a disco with good dance music. The Sandpiper seemed excitingly adult—it was a little scary at first, but then I loved it. Next, we went to the Sportsman, a leather motorcycle bar that I found absolutely terrifying. Huge, bearded men bulging out of their leather vests and pants leered at me. I hid in the corner and tried not to make eye contact with anyone, hoping my friends would get tired soon and give me a ride back to camp.

Each of these bars was a community, and some were more comfortable for me than others. The Net is made up of hundreds of thousands of separate communities, each with its own special character. Not only is the Net a diverse place, but "women" are diverse as well—there were leather-clad women who loved the

Sportsman, and plenty of women revel in the fiery rhetoric of Usenet's *alt.flame*. When people complain about being harassed on the Net, they've usually stumbled into the wrong online community. The question is not whether "women" are comfortable on "the Net," but rather, what types of communities are possible? How can we create a range of communities so that everyone—men and women—can find a place that is comfortable for them?

If you're looking for a restaurant or bar, you can often tell without even going in: Is the sign flashing neon or engraved wood? Are there lots of cars parked out front? What sort of cars? (You can see all the Harleys in front of the Sportsman from a block away.) Look in the window: How are people dressed? We are accustomed to diversity in restaurants. People know that not all restaurants will please them, and employ a variety of techniques to choose the right one.

It's a lot harder to find a good virtual community than it is to find a good 5
bar. The visual cues that let you spot the difference between Maria's and the Sportsman from across the street are largely missing. Instead, you have to "lurk"—enter the community and quietly explore for a while, getting the feel of whether it's the kind of place you're looking for. Although published guides exist, they're not always very useful—most contain encyclopedic lists with little commentary or critical evaluation, and by the time they're published they're already out of date. Magazines like *NetGuide* and *Wired* are more current and more selective, and therefore more useful, but their editorial bias may not fit with your personal tastes.

Commonly available network-searching tools are also useful. The World Wide Web is filled with searching programs, indexes, and even indexes of indexes ("meta-indexes"). Although browsing with these tools can be a pleasant diversion, it is not very efficient, and searches for particular pieces of information often end in frustration. If you keep an open mind, however, you may come across something good.

SHAPING AN ONLINE SOCIETY

But what happens if, after exploring and asking around, you still can't find an online environment that suits you? Don't give up, start your own! This doesn't have to be a difficult task. Anyone can create a new newsgroup in Usenet's "alt" hierarchy or open a new chat room on America Online. Users of Unix systems can easily start a mailing list. If you have a good idea but not enough technical skill or the right type of Net access, there are people around eager to help. The more interesting question is: How do you help a community to become what you hope for? Here, I can offer some hard-won advice.

In my research at the MIT Media Lab (working with Professor Mitchel Resnick), I design virtual communities. In October of 1992, I founded a professional community for media researchers on the Internet called MediaMOO. Over the past three years, as MediaMOO has grown to 1,000 members from 33 countries, I have grappled with many of the issues that face anyone attempting to establish a virtual community. MediaMOO is a "multi-user dungeon" or MUD—a virtual world on the Internet with rooms, objects, and people from all around the world. Messages typed in by a user instantly appear on the screens of all other users who are currently in the same virtual "room." This real-time interaction distinguishes MUDs from Usenet newsgroups, where users can browse through messages created many hours or days before. The MUD's virtual world is built in text descriptions. MOO stands for MUD object-oriented, a kind of MUD software (created by Pavel Curtis of the Xerox Palo Alto Research Center and Stephen White, now at InContext Systems) that allows each user to write programs to define spaces and objects.

The first MUDs, developed in the late 1970s, were multiplayer fantasy games of the dungeons-and-dragons variety. In 1989, a graduate student at Carnegie Mellon University named James Aspnes decided to see what would happen if you took away the monsters and the magic swords but instead let people extend the virtual world. People's main activity went from trying to conquer the virtual world to trying to build it, collaboratively.

10 Most MUDs are populated by undergraduates who should be doing their homework. I thought it would be interesting instead to bring together a group of people with a shared intellectual interest: the study of media. Ideally, MediaMOO should be like an endless reception for a conference on media studies. But given the origin of MUDs as violent games, giving one an intellectual and professional atmosphere was a tall order. How do you guide the evolution of who uses the space and what they do there?

A founder/designer can't control what the community ultimately becomes—much of this is up to the users—but can help shape it. The personality of the community's founder can have a great influence on what sort of place it becomes. Part of what made Maria's so comfortable for me was Maria herself. She radiated a warmth that made me feel at home.

Similarly, one of the most female-friendly electronic communities I've visited is New York City's ECHO (East Coast Hang Out) bulletin board, run by Stacy Horn. Smart, stylish, and deliberately outrageous, Horn is role model and patron saint for the ECHO-ites. Her outspoken but sensitive personality infuses the community, and sends a message to women that it's all right to speak up. She added a conference to ECHO called "WIT" (women in telecommunications), which one user describes as "a warm, supportive, women-only, private conference where women's thoughts, experiences, wisdom, joys, and despairs are shared." But Horn also added a conference called "BITCH," which the ECHO-ite calls "WIT in black leather jackets. All-women, riotous and raunchy."

Horn's high-energy, very New York brand of intelligence establishes the kind of place ECHO is and influences how everyone there behaves. When ECHO was first established, Horn and a small group of her close friends were the most active people on the system. "That set the emotional tone, the traditional style of posting, the unwritten rules about what it's OK to say," says

Marisa Bowe, an ECHO administrator for many years. "Even though Stacy is too busy these days to post very much, the tone established in the early days continues," says Bowe, who is now editor of an online magazine called *Word*.

Beyond the sheer force of a founder's personality, a community establishes a particular character with a variety of choices on how to operate. One example is to set a policy on whether to allow participants to remain anonymous. Initially, I decided that members of MediaMOO should be allowed to choose: They could identify themselves with their real names and e-mail addresses, or remain anonymous. Others questioned whether there was a role for anonymity in a professional community.

As time went on, I realized they were right. People on MediaMOO are sup- 15
posed to be networking, hoping someone will look up who they really are and where they work. Members who are not willing to share their personal and professional identities are less likely to engage in serious discussion about their work and consequently about media in general. Furthermore, comments from an anonymous entity are less valuable because they are unsituated—"I believe X" is less meaningful to a listener than "I am a librarian with eight years of experience who lives in a small town in Georgia, and I believe X." In theory, anonymous participants could describe their professional experiences and place their comments in that context; in practice it tends not to happen that way. After six months, I proposed that we change the policy to require that all new members be identified. Despite the protests of a few vocal opponents, most people thought that this was a good idea, and the change was made.

Each community needs to have its own policy on anonymity. There's room for diversity here too: Some communities can be all-anonymous, some all-identified, and some can leave that decision up to each individual. An aside: Right now on the Net no one is either really anonymous or really identified. It is easy to fake an identity; it is also possible to use either technical or legal tools to peer behind someone else's veil of anonymity. This ambiguous state of affairs is not necessarily unfortunate: it's nice to know that a fake identity that provides a modicum of privacy is easy to construct, but that in extreme cases such people can be tracked down.

FINDING BIRDS OF A FEATHER

Another important design decision is admissions policy. Most places on the Net have a strong pluralistic flavor, and the idea that some people might be excluded from a community ruffles a lot of feathers. But exclusively is a fact of life. MIT wouldn't be MIT if everyone who wanted to come was admitted. Imagine if companies had to give jobs to everyone who applied! Virtual communities, social clubs, universities, and corporations are all groups of people brought together for a purpose. Achieving that purpose often requires that there be some way to determine who can join the community.

A key decision I made for MediaMOO was to allow entry only to people doing some sort of "media research." I try to be loose on the definition of "media"—writing teachers, computer network administrators, and librarians are all working with forms of media—but strict on the definition of "research." At first, this policy made me uncomfortable. I would nervously tell people, "It's mostly a self-selection process. We hardly reject anyone at all!" Over time, I've become more comfortable with this restriction, and have enforced the requirements more stringently. I now believe my initial unease was naive.

Even if an online community decides to admit all comers, it does not have to let all contributors say anything they want. The existence of a moderator to filter postings often makes for more focused and civil discussion. Consider Usenet's two principal newsgroups dealing with feminism—*alt.feminism* and *soc.feminism.* In *alt.feminism,* anyone can post whatever they want. Messages in this group are filled with the angry words of angry people; more insults than ideas are exchanged. (Titles of messages found there on a randomly selected day included "Women & the workplace (it doesn't work)" and "What is a feminazi?") The topic may nominally be feminism, but the discussion itself is not feminist in nature.

The huge volume of postings (more than 200 per day, on average) shows 20
that many people enjoy writing such tirades. But if I wanted to discuss some aspect of feminism, *alt.feminism* would be the last place I'd go. Its sister group, *soc.feminism,* is moderated—volunteers read messages submitted to the group and post only those that pass muster. Moderators adhere to *soc.feminism's* lengthy charter, which explains the criteria for acceptable postings—forbidding ad hominem attacks, for instance.

Moderation of a newsgroup, like restricting admission to a MUD, grants certain individuals within a community power over others. If only one group could exist, I'd have to choose the uncensored *alt.feminism* to the moderated *soc.feminism.* Similarly, if MediaMOO were the only virtual community or MIT the only university, I'd argue that they should be open to all. However, there are thousands of universities and the Net contains hundreds of thousands of virtual communities, with varying criteria for acceptable conduct. That leaves room for diversity: some communities can be moderated, others unmoderated. Some can be open to all, some can restrict admissions.

The way a community is publicized—or not publicized—also influences its character. Selective advertising can help a community achieve a desired ambiance. In starting up MediaMOO, for example, we posted the original announcement to mailing lists for different aspects of media studies—not to the general-purpose groups for discussing MUDs on Usenet. MediaMOO is now rarely if ever deliberately advertised. The group has opted not to be listed in the public, published list of MUDs on the Internet. Members are asked to mention MediaMOO to other groups only if the majority of members of that group would probably be eligible to join MediaMOO.

New members are attracted by word of mouth among media researchers. To bring in an influx of new members, MediaMOO typically "advertises" by organizing an online discussion or symposium on some aspect of media studies. Announcing a discussion group on such topics as the techniques for studying behavior in a virtual community or strategies for using computers to teach writing attracts the right sort of people to the community and sets a tone for the kinds of discussion that take place there. That's much more effective than a more general announcement of MediaMOO and its purpose.

In an ideal world, virtual communities would acquire new members entirely by self-selection: people would enter an electronic neighborhood only if it focused on something they cared about. In most cases, this process works well. For example, one Usenet group that I sometimes read—*sci.aquaria*—attracts people who are really interested in discussing tropical fishkeeping. But self-selection is not always sufficient. For example, the challenge of making MediaMOO's culture different from prevailing MUD culture made self-selection inadequate. Lots of undergraduates with no particular focus to their interests want to join MediaMOO. To preserve MediaMOO's character as a place for serious scholarly discussions, I usually reject these applications. Besides, almost all of the hundreds of other MUDs out there place no restrictions on who can join. MediaMOO is one of the few that is different.

Emotionally and politically charged subject matter, such as feminism, makes 25
it essential for members of a community to have a shared understanding of the community's purpose. People who are interested in freshwater and saltwater tanks can coexist peacefully in parallel conversations on *sci.aquaria*. However, on *alt.feminism,* people who want to explore the implications of feminist theory and those who want to question its basic premises don't get along quite so well. Self-selection alone is not adequate for bringing together a group to discuss a hot topic. People with radically differing views may wander in innocently, or barge in deliberately—disrupting the conversation through ignorance or malice.

Such gate crashing tends to occur more frequently as the community grows in size. For example, some participants in the Usenet group *alt.tasteless* decided to post a series of grotesque messages to the thriving group *rec.pets.cats,* including recipes for how to cook cat. A small, low-profile group may be randomly harassed, but that's less likely to happen.

In the offline world, membership in many social organizations is open only to those who are willing and able to pay the dues. While it may rankle an American pluralistic sensibility, the use of wealth as a social filter has the advantages of simplicity and objectivity: No one's personal judgment plays a role in deciding who is to be admitted. And imposing a small financial hurdle to online participation may do more good than harm. Token fees discourage the random and pointless postings that dilute the value of many newsgroups. One of the first community networks, Community Memory in Berkeley, California, found that charging a mere 25 cents to post a message significantly raised the level of discourse, eliminating many trivial or rude messages.

Still, as the fee for participation rises above a token level, this method has obvious moral problems for a society committed to equal opportunity. In instituting any kind of exclusionary policy, the founder of a virtual community should first test the key assumption that alternative, nonexclusionary communities really do exist. If they do not, then less restrictive admissions policies may be warranted.

BUILDING ON DIVERSITY

Anonymity policy, admission requirements, and advertising strategy all contribute to a virtual community's character. Without such methods of distinguishing one online hangout from another, all would tend to sink to the least common denominator of discourse—the equivalent of every restaurant in a town degenerating into a dive. We need better techniques to help members of communities develop shared expectations about the nature of the community, and to communicate those expectations to potential new members. This will make it easier for people to find their own right communities.

Just as the surest way to find a good restaurant is to exchange tips with 30
friends, word of mouth is usually the best way to find out about virtual communities that might suit your tastes and interests. The best published guides for restaurants compile comments and ratings from a large group of patrons, rather than relying on the judgment of any one expert. Approaches like this are being explored on the Net. Yezdi Lashkari, cofounder of Agents Inc., designed a system called "Webhound" that recommends items of interest on the World Wide Web. To use Webhound, you enter into the system a list of web sites you like. It matches you with people of similar interests, and then recommends other sites that they like. Not only do these ratings come from an aggregate of many opinions, but they also are matched to your personal preferences.

Webhound recommends just World Wide Web pages, but the same basic approach could help people find a variety of communities, products, and services that are likely to match their tastes. For example, Webhound grew out of the Helpful Online Music Recommendation Service (HOMR), which recommends musical artists. A subscriber to this service—recently renamed Firefly—first rates a few dozen musical groups on a scale from "the best" to "pass the earplugs"; Firefly searches its database for people who have similar tastes, and uses their list of favorites to recommend other artists that might appeal to you. The same technique could recommend Usenet newsgroups, mailing lists, or other information sources. Tell it that you like to read the Usenet group *rec.arts.startrek.info,* and it might recommend *alt.tv.babylon-5*—people who like one tend to like the other. While no such tool yet exists for Usenet, the concept would be straightforward to implement.

Written statements of purpose and codes of conduct can help communities stay focused and appropriate. MediaMOO's stated purpose, for example, helps set its character as an arena for scholarly discussion. But explicit rules and mission statements can go only so far. Elegant restaurants don't put signs on the door saying "no feet on tables" and fast food restaurants don't post signs saying "feet on tables allowed." Subtle cues within the environment indicate how one is expected to behave. Similarly, we should design regions in cyberspace so that people implicitly sense what is expected and what is appropriate. In this respect, designers of virtual communities can learn a great deal from architects.

Vitruvius, a Roman architect from the first century B.C., established the basic principles of architecture as commodity (appropriate function), firmness (structural stability), and delight. These principles translate into the online world, as William Mitchell, dean of MIT's School of Architecture and Planning, points out in his book *City of Bits: Space, Place, and the Infobahn:*

> Architects of the twenty-first century will still shape, arrange, and connect spaces (both real and virtual) to satisfy human needs. They will still care about the qualities of visual and ambient environments. They will still seek commodity, firmness, and delight. But commodity will be as much a matter of software functions and interface design as it is of floor plans and construction materials. Firmness will entail not only the physical integrity of structural systems, but also the logical integrity of computer systems. And delight? Delight will have unimagined new dimensions.

Marcos Novak of the University of Texas at Austin is exploring some of those "unimagined dimensions" with his notion of a "liquid architecture" for cyberspace, free from the constraints of physical space and building materials. But work of this kind on the merging of architecture and software design is regrettably rare; if virtual communities are buildings, then right now we are living in the equivalent of thatched huts. If the structure keeps out the rain—that is, if the software works at all—people are happy.

35 More important than the use of any of these particular techniques, however, is applying an architect's design sensibility to this new medium. Many of the traditional tools and techniques of architects, such as lighting and texture, will translate into the design of virtual environments. Depending on choice of background color and texture, type styles, and special fade-in effects, for instance, a Web page can feel playful or gloomy, futuristic or old-fashioned, serious or fun, grown-up or child-centered. The language of the welcoming screen, too, conveys a sense of the community's purpose and character. An opening screen thick with the jargon of specialists in, say, genetic engineering, might alert dilettantes that the community is for serious biologists.

As the Net expands, its ranks will fill with novices—some of whom, inevitably, will wander into less desirable parts of cybertown. It is important for such explorers to appreciate the Net's diversity—to realize, for example, that the newsgroup *alt.feminism* does not constitute the Internet's sole contribution to feminist debate. Alternatives exist.

I'm glad there are places on the Net where I'm not comfortable. The world would be a boring place if it invariably suited any one person's taste. The great promise of the Net is diversity. That's something we need to cultivate and cherish. Unfortunately, there aren't yet enough good alternatives—too much of the Net is like the Sportsman and too little of it is like Maria's. Furthermore, not enough people are aware that communities can have such different characters.

People who accidentally find themselves in the Sportsman, *alt.feminism*, or *alt.flame*, and don't find the black leather or fiery insults to their liking, should neither complain about it nor waste their time there—they should search for a more suitable community. If you've stumbled into the wrong town, get back on the bus. But if you've been a longtime resident and find the community changing for the worse—that's different. Don't shy away from taking political action within that community to protect your investment of time: speak up, propose solutions, and build a coalition of others who feel the same way you do.

With the explosion of interest in networking, people are moving from being recipients of information to creators, from passive subscribers to active participants and leaders. Newcomers to the Net who are put off by harassment, pornography, and just plain bad manners should stop whining about the places they find unsuitable and turn their energies in a more constructive direction: help make people aware of the variety of alternatives that exist, and work to build communities that suit their interests and values.

ANALYZING EVERYDAY ARGUMENTS

By now, I hope you realize that arguments are all around. Even what we wear and how we dress can be an argument. Why do people choose to wear the clothes they do? Often, it is because they are trying to say something about themselves or identify with a certain group. Maybe they're trying to show off their sense of fashion or demonstrate that they can afford to buy the very best (meaning the most expensive). Maybe they "dress down" to resist what is fashionable or to convey a more relaxed attitude. A lot of people still believe that "the clothes make the man" (or woman). Sometimes we communicate something about ourselves even by something as small as a logo—the small symbol that identifies the brand of our clothing. Take the Nike "swoosh" as an example. Studies indicate that among young people, this small mark (which looks like a fat check mark) is the most recognized logo in the world. Why do people recognize the swoosh? Why do people wear it on their shoes, hats, jackets, socks, bags, shorts, and T-shirts? What would make one athlete even tattoo the swoosh on his chest? What values and beliefs are associated with this little mark? Obviously, Nike is trying to sell shoes and clothing, but the swoosh seems to be selling much more. The following readings try to explain the appeal of the swoosh. In "The Swooshification of the World," *Sports Illustrated* writer Rick Reilly takes a satiric perspective on the pervasiveness of the swoosh. In the second selection, advertising professors Robert Goldman and Stephen Papson try to explain the persuasive power of Nike's icon.

As you read these selections, consider the following questions:

1. What articles of clothing or accessories that have the Nike swoosh do you or other members of the class own?
2. How do you characterize people who wear the swoosh? Which celebrities wear it? What sports teams have Nike logos on their uniforms? (Take a close look at the Denver Broncos uniforms, redesigned by Nike.)
3. What other logos do you as a class recognize? What values or beliefs are associated with these logos?
4. How does a logo or brand gain prominence? What role does advertising play? To what degree do people participate in advertising when they wear certain brands or logos?
5. How important is it to you and your classmates to buy certain brands or display certain logos?

The Swooshification of the World

RICK REILLY

I MUST GET more Swoosh in my life. More, more, more. It's not enough 1
to have the Swoosh on every jersey and scoreboard and dugout rook. It's not enough that the Swoosh is on basketballs, footballs, soccer balls, and volleyballs. It's not enough that the Swoosh is slapped all over more than 40 universities, eight NFL teams, six NHL teams (two more next season), and five Major League Soccer teams.

I want the eye black under baseball and football players' eyes to take the form of a Swoosh. I want hockey sticks, nine-irons, and yardage markers to be made in the shape of a Swoosh. I want to know who's in the on-deck Swoosh. I want to watch the Swoosh channel. I want Swoosh condoms (Just Do It).

It's not enough that the Swoosh is on Michael Jordan's beret and Mary Pierce's headband and Gabrielle Reece's beach volleyball top. It's not enough that the center on the Hawaii basketball team had his sideburns shaped into Swooshes. I want a Swoosh tatoo. I want a Swoosh lasered onto my retinas. I want to name my son Swoosh. (If it's a girl, Swooshie.)

I want these things because the Swoosh is the most ubiquitous symbol in sports history. The swoosh is so huge that the name of the company that goes with the Swoosh doesn't even appear anymore. In the ads, on the shoes, even on the company letterhead, all you get is the Swoosh, and you just *know*. Try that with Keds, pal.

Happiness is a warm Swoosh. Do you see the way it *swooshes* upward, a 5
snappy little check mark, letting you know that everything in your life is A-OK?

It's airy, windswept, uplifting. It's the delighted little final stroke your pen makes when endorsing the biggest check of your life.

But there is not enough of it in our lives yet. From here on in, instead of H-O-R-S-E, I want kids to play S-W-O-O-S-H. I want skis to go *swoosh*! I want to get the autograph of Sheryl Swoosh.

Woe to you who underestimate the Swoosh. Tiger Woods, the coolest athlete on Planet Swoosh, has the Swoosh on the front of his hat and the side of his hat and the back of his hat and on his turtleneck and on his shirt and on his sweater and on his vest and on his pants and on his socks and on his shoes. But when Woods arrived in Thailand two weeks ago, he found that his luggage had been misplaced, and he had to play a pro-am without his usual complement of Swooshes. He lasted just 13 holes before heat and exhaustion got to him. Don't you see? The Swoosh is the source of all his powers!

I wasn't always like this. I used to rage against the Swoosh. "Why?" I yelped at strangers. "Why must the Swoosh run the world?" Why, I asked, after almost 30 years, did the Denver Broncos let the Swoosh people redesign the team's uniforms and logo so that they were suddenly uglier than the jerseys of a meat-market softball team. I cried out against the subliminal Swooshing all over the new Denver uniform. "Don't you see it?" I railed, pointing to the Broncos' new logo. "The horse's nostril! It's a Swoosh!"

In protest I determined to go an entire day without getting Swooshed. I made it 14 minutes, just past my Eggo, when my wife came down in her Swoosh sports bra. Something snapped in me that morning. I gave in. You cannot fight the Swoosh.

10 I want my kids to attend the University of California at Swoosh. I want to get up in the morning and eat a big bowlful of chocolate Swooshios as part of a nutritionally balanced breakfast. I want to meet Carolyn Davidson. She's the graphic designer who, after graduating from Portland State in 1972, came up with the Swoosh for Phil Knight, Zeus of Swoosh, for $35. Thirty-five dollars! When she handed it to Knight, she remembers, he said, "I don't love it, but maybe it'll grow on me." Twenty-five years and a zillion dollars later, you think it's all right now, Phil? (Davidson, who in 1983 was given some Nike stock by Knight, who recently retired, says her second most famous work is the wallpaper she designed for a motel in Yakima, Washington.) Carolyn Davidson, stand up and take your place in world history!

Some experts believe the Swoosh is better known than McDonald's golden arches. Nine national soccer teams, including Brazil's, wear the Swoosh. The Tour de France leader wears the Swoosh. When the United States played Russia in hockey's recent World Cup, both teams were wearing the Swoosh.

The Swoosh is like Jell-O: There's alway's room for the Swoosh. I want Swoosh on the periodic table of elements right next to boron. I want Swoosh to be the 27th letter of the alphabet. I want to order raw eel at a Swooshi bar.

Do not fight it, brothers and sisters. Trust in the Swoosh. The Swoosh is good and powerful. If our government leaders would only get it, the Swoosh could bail us out of this deficit thing like *that*. Of course, we would have to make a few small concessions.

Al, does the presidential seal look different to you?

Suddenly the Swoosh Is Everywhere

ROBERT GOLDMAN and STEPHEN PAPSON

The credo in today's arenas: no *swoosh*, no swagger.[1]

WE LIVE IN a cultural economy of signs and Nike's swoosh is currently the most recognizable brand icon in that economy.[2] Nike's swoosh is a commercial symbol that has come to stand for athletic excellence, a spirit of determination, hip authenticity, and playful self-awareness. While the logo carries the weight of currency, Nike's "Just do it" slogan has become part of the language of everyday life. Indeed, the Nike swoosh is so firmly lodged in the public consciousness that Nike no longer necessarily includes its name in its ads or on billboards. The shoe vanished from Nike TV ads some time ago. Then in the mid-1990s the Nike name has also quietly disappeared, leaving only the swoosh logo to mark the ads. Nike signs its ads with only its icon, so confident is it that the swoosh can be interpreted minus any accompanying text. Nike's 1997 annual report makes just this point: the "company has come to be known by a symbol—the swoosh." 1

The swoosh achieved visual omnipresence. And yet this, precisely, has been Nike's Achilles' heel. The visual embedding of the swoosh onto all environments—the clothing products we use, the social spaces we occupy, and the media we watch—gave rise to overswooshification (when every surface has a swoosh across it like the Air Max running shoes with seven swoosh exposures on each shoe). Overexposure, for Nike, overswooshification, presents the peril of sign inflation—the more common the swoosh becomes the less value it has. Nike sought to combat this in December 1997 by moving away from its swoosh signature to signing its commercials as Nike, in a small, tight cursive font.

Nike and its advertising agency, Wieden & Kennedy, currently stand out as leaders in what may be described as a cultural economy of images. The Nike swoosh sign has rapidly gained an identification level that rivals the Coca-Cola icon, while its brand value is currently unparalleled. The preeminence of the Nike logo has translated into record corporate earnings fiscal quarter after fiscal quarter, making Nike a blue chip stock. Instantly recognized throughout the world, the Nike swoosh sometimes seems to be everywhere—on shirts and caps and pants. The icon is no longer confined to shoes as sponsorship deals have plastered the swoosh across jerseys and sporting arenas of all manner, from basketball to football to volleyball to track to soccer to tennis to hockey. Nike's growth strategy is based on penetrating new markets in apparel while making acquisitions in sporting goods. The value of the swoosh now runs so deep that visitors to remote, rural, and impoverished regions of the Third World report finding peasants sewing crude swoosh imitations on to shirts and caps, not for the world market but for local consumption. Even in the hinterlands of places like Jamaica and Guatemala, the swoosh symbol carries recognition and status. As the Nike symbol has grown ascendant in the marketplace of images, Nike has become the sign some people love to love and the sign others love to hate.

It is now a commonplace to observe that Nike advertising is no longer about selling shoes but about keeping the swoosh highly visible and highly valued. This does not surprise us because we view advertising as a cultural space in which competitors try to maximize the value of their visual logo in an always-fluctuating economy of signs. We view advertising as a vehicle for articulating a brand's sign value. This means that an ad campaign gives visibility and meaning to a brand image, and that it joins together meanings of the product with meanings evoked by the imagery. Virtually every ad these days is an investment in this kind of brand identity. In Nike's case this involved joining images of Michael Jordan with the meaning of Nike shoes—Michael Jordan joined to Nike shoes lends value to the meaning of the swoosh. Since he provided the initial source of value in this exchange, it is no surprise that Michael Jordan himself has long since been transformed into a global iconic presence in the media, so much so that in 1996 Nike introduced a "Brand Jordan" line of shoes and apparel.

5 Consumer ads usually invite viewers into fantasies of individualism, although the promise of individualism is likely premised on conformity of consumption preferences. Since the 1960s advertising has grown reliant on formulas for branding goods with the imagery of individual identity and well-being. But as the number of consumer products has steadily increased, so has advertising clutter. Ads became predictable and boring, and what is worse, too many of them looked the same. Hence, though every advertiser seeks to differentiate its product name and symbol from competitors, when it uses the same formulas and clichés everyone else uses, it thwarts its own purpose. Every once in a while, someone will break away from the pack, but competitors usually respond by imitating the innovative look or style until it is no longer distinctive. By the early 1980s, widespread consumer discontent with the recipes of advertising had developed. By the late 1980s, a few leading-edge advertising agencies recognized that media-literate baby boomers and post–baby boomers had grown alienated from slick ads built around appeals to consuming individualism and status through commodities.

Nike and its advertising agency, Wieden & Kennedy, have built their reputation on advertising that is both distinctive and avoids claims of packaged individualism. Their ads have garnered public admiration because they seem to speak in a voice of honesty and authenticity. Paradoxically, their aura of authenticity has been a product of their willingness to address alienated spectators about feeling alienated from media-contrived images. Wieden & Kennedy has cobbled together a style that sometimes ventures into the waters of political provocation; a style situated at the intersection between public and private discourses where themes of authenticity and personal morality converge with the cynical and nihilistic sensibility that colors contemporary public exchanges. Ranging from moral indictment to showers of praise, Nike ad campaigns have sometimes provoked intense public interest. Within the realm of popular culture, Nike ads constantly surprise and excite, because they are unafraid of being controversial. This willingness to take chances in its ads has translated into Nike's dominance in the sign economy.

Looking at Nike's advertising from the late 1980s through the mid-1990s, we find Nike ads come in two basic flavors. One flavor is of an irreverent, winking attitude toward everything that smacks of commodity culture. Nike adopts a self-reflexive posture about the formulas of consumer-goods advertising as well as a self-aware attitude about its own position as a wealthy and powerful corporation in an industry based on influencing desires and tastes. These ads speak to savvy and jaded viewers about the glossy, staged exultations of one brand or another that daily assault us. In these ads, Nike hails viewers wary of the continuous incursion of commodified discourses into all life spheres. In the second flavor, however, Nike constructs itself as the vehicle of an ethos that integrates themes of personal transcendence, achievement, and authenticity. We call this Nike's motivational ethos. By mixing these two flavors of advertising, Nike has created an advertising discourse that is able to present itself as a legitimate public discourse. Nike advertising has ventured beyond the typical advertising agenda of merely building up its own sign to construct what appears to be a personal philosophy of daily life.

Nike's advertising has invested the swoosh with a sensibility that resists the profane and cheesy tendencies that consumers associate with commercial culture. Nike advertising does more than simply sell shoes as commodities, it gives voice to important cultural contradictions that define our era. In this regard, we see Nike advertising as representative of a newly unfolding stage of commodity culture mixed with cultural politics. This is evident where Nike has pursued a calculated approach to provoking public debate and controversy, something that previous rounds of consumer advertising sought to avoid at all costs. In this vein, Nike's method of advertising as storytelling interests us because of the way it draws on the rhetorical legacy of middle-class morality to raise questions that are not immediately resolvable through recourse to commodities. We believe that Nike's advertising is popular because of the way it speaks to, and embraces, the contradictions of both middle-class morality and the language of commodities.

LOGOMANIA

"Brand consciousness" of Nike's "global power brand" now extends "anywhere there is the faint possibility of a growing middle class."[3] To get a sense of how people value and rank their brand preferences, survey researchers routinely ask them to make lists. One recent study by Teenage Research Unlimited asked 200 teenagers for their top 20 brands, regardless of product category. The results cast light on how important logos or signs are to the athletic footwear industry. Out of the top 20, the survey reveals that five are in the athletic footwear industry—Nike, Reebok, Adidas, Fila, and Converse. Of all the brands to choose from, including Coke, Nike led the list with a whopping 38 percent of teens ranking it number one. Guess jeans came in a distant second at 17 percent.[4]

In 1993, Nike spent roughly $250 million on advertising, marketing, and 10
promoting the Nike brand; by 1997 that total had grown to $978 million. The visibility and power of Nike's swoosh sign has been largely a function of Nike being the current leader in a competitive advertising system geared to producing and maintaining the highest sign values. We call it sign value to pinpoint the primary product of consumer-goods advertising today. In this following section we will briefly discuss what we mean by sign values, noting how they are constructed and circulated, and how the competition between brands for recognition and dominance has led to what we call sign wars.[5]

The swoosh logo was born of business necessity. By 1971 Phil Knight's fledgling shoe distribution company, named Blue Ribbon Sports, had grown to the point where its product line consisted of a haphazard combination of Japanese Knockoffs of German running shoes (Adidas) and a few shoes of BRS's own design. But it had also outgrown its relationship as exclusive distributor of Onitsuka Tiger, its Japanese shoe supplier, and Knight engineered "a partnership with Nissho-Iwai, a large Japanese sogo sosha (trading company). Nissho agreed to contract independent manufacturing sources (Nihon-Koyo and Nippon Rubber) for the BRS line of shoes."[6] In 1971, Knight decided he needed a logo and a change of name as he moved to market his own brand of shoes. Knight asked a Portland State University arts student named Carolyn Davidson to design a "stripe, or logo, for the side of the shoe. Because Adidas used stripes as its logo, all athletic shoe logos, no matter what shape, were called stripes."[7] Davidson's fee for the task was $35. Knight asked her to try to make it suggest movement and speed, make it visible from a distance, while also functionally contributing to the shoe support system. At the time, the stripes on other athletic shoes served a structural or functional purpose: the "distinctive three stripes" on Adidas shoes held the upper and lower soles together while the Puma stripe supported the ball of the foot. By contrast, despite Knight's desire for something comparable to the Adidas stripe, the swoosh was from the outset strictly a symbolic and aesthetic accouterment.[8] Knight and his associates did not particularly like the design, but halfheartedly accepted it because they had nothing better. Knight reportedly said "I don't love it. But I think it will grow on me."[9] Nike insiders would come to call it the swoosh, so the story goes, after a customer placed an order for the shoe with the "swooshie fiber" on the side. Shortly thereafter, the story of the Nike name change bears a striking similarity to the birth of the swoosh logo. Knight had been toying with the name Dimension Six, but nobody else liked that name. The pressure for a new name was spurred by a printer's deadline to put a name—any name—on the side of the shoe boxes that were being made. When an employee named Jeff Johnson came up with the name Nike, after the winged Greek goddess of victory, it too was met with a lack of either recognition or enthusiasm. "I guess we'll go with the Nike thing for now," said Knight. "I really don't like any of them [the names], but I guess that's the best of the bunch."[10]

The point here is that initially, the swoosh logo was an empty vessel—a visual marker that lacked any intrinsic meaning. At first, people described it as a fat check mark. The swoosh has acquired meaning and value through repeated association with other culturally meaningful symbols. By placing the swoosh in the same frame with Michael Jordan, Nike was able to draw upon the value and meaning of Michael Jordan as a star basketball player. The meaning of "Air" Jordan was transferred to the meaning of "Air" Nike. Only through a process of abstracting and "emptying out" the meanings of other cultural images did the Nike logo become invested with the value and meaning it possesses today. Today, that fat check mark is not only instantly identifiable, it has also come to inspire devotion. Today, the Nike swoosh is so rich in meaning that it is now capable of extending value to other objects and persons. In 1991 Nike was inducted into the American Marketing Association's Hall of Fame because its ads "have had a dramatic impact on our lifestyle, becoming enshrined as American icons."[11]

These days, concerns about selecting the right logo may seem ho-hum since every company that wants to compete in this arena must be able to compete at the level of logo recognition. Companies like Nike, Reebok, Adidas, Fila, Starter, and Champion all acknowledge that branded sales are essential to their growth, and each competes to try to convince viewers that they want to wear the company name or symbol. David Chandler, vice president of Reebok International's apparel marketing, observes that consumers are "looking for brands that mesh with their personalities."[12] So the name of the game is to invest one's logo with recognizability and cultural desirability. To a certain extent, consumers (wearers) become advertisements themselves for the brand logo they have chosen to display.

Think about it. Everyone knows the name of Nike's icon is the swoosh, but do you know what Reebok calls its icon? They call it the vector. Though historically Nike's chief competitor, Reebok's advertising has not established a similarly viable or coherent sign or logo. However, it is instructive to note that Reebok advertising circa 1995 shifted to emulate the Nike concentration on the logo. Indeed, Reebok advertising has become notable for its attention to what might be called sign-work. Reebook's commercials from the 1996 Summer Olympics each ended by turning the vector on its side so that it could double as the symbol for the Olympic torch. We could not invent a better example of a company trying to leverage the value of one meaning system (the Olympics) to add value to its brand symbol.

As the stakes of logo identification and sign value escalate so too does the 15
amount of energy that goes into both promoting these signs and protecting the value of those logos. There is certainly nothing in the following headline that would make us blink twice: "Athletic wear companies are pumping billions into the world's sports tank, fueling a proliferation of logos in places such as high school gyms and Olympic victory stands; draped in logos and letters."[13] And yet

it speaks to a fundamental penetration of more and more social spaces by the discourse of signs and logos. At the same time that companies are investing to cover our consciousness in logos that seem genuine, we have also begun to hear a new phrase bandied about—the logo police. They were at the 1996 Summer Olympics to make sure everyone followed the logo rules, and "logo cops prowl the sidelines in the NFL, protecting a $3 billion licensing business by making sure everyone is wearing the right cap. A player caught wearing the wrong logo faces a $5,000 fine, $100,000 if he does it in the Super Bowl."[14] We've heard anecdotal stories of Nike going to great lengths to protect the value of its logo, such as squads of enforcers who tour Asian factories to guard against counterfeiters.

THE GREAT AMERICAN PHILOSOPHY: "JUST DO IT"

> It's the only company that has successfully managed to sell a way of life with its products.[15]

We believe that Nike's overall image—its commodity sign—is less about a particular commodity than the corporation itself. Nike has constructed itself as an icon that embraces a larger image system that possesses both a philosophy and a personality.

Since signs and icons do not exist in a vacuum, but in relation to one another, it is important to contrast Nike's sign representations with those of competitors such as Reebok and Converse and Fila and Asics and Adidas and British Knights and L.A. Gear and New Balance. Perhaps Nike's greatest advertising accomplishment has been its ability to attach the aura of a philosophy to its name via its sign and slogan. One aspect of the Nike philosophy emerges from how its ads communicate a philosophic identity embedded in the codes of its photographic style and tone. Yet, no serious deconstruction skills are required to recognize Nike's basic philosophy in its most frequently stated maxim: "Just do it." Nike says its slogan "is cemented in consumers' minds as a rallying cry to get off the couch and play sports." More than just a slogan, "Just do it" receives almost daily mass media interpretation and affirmation. For example, the July 13, 1995, *USA Today* carried what seemed to be a press release: "Sponsor finds epitome of do it attitude." As Nike entered yet another sport, IndyCar racing, it sponsored race car driver Scott Pruett, in the Molson Indy in Toronto. Pruett, the story tells us, "was chosen for the 'Just do it' attitude he showed in recovering from a 1990 crash that left him with a broken back, knees, and ankles. Ten months later, he won an International Race of Champions event at Daytona Beach, Florida." Pruett is quoted [as saying] that "the values instilled in me when I was young—determination and perseverance—were the strengths I relied on during my recovery and return." A corresponding Nike campaign will "showcase people who have triumphed against disabilities through athletics."[16]

Why does "Just do it" resonate with so many people? It speaks to the restraint and inhibition in everyday life that keep people from the experience of transcendence. Nike provides a language of self-empowerment—no matter who you are, no matter what your physical, economic or social limitations. Transcedence is not just possible, it is waiting to be called forth. Take control of your life and don't submit to the mundane forces that can so easily weigh us down in daily life. No more rationalizations and justifications, it's time to act. The phrase is wonderfully ambiguous. It hails all of us about any action that we have avoided, put off, or rationalized. The Nike philosophy challenges us to confront, and hopefully, to overcome barriers. Specific images encapsulate and honor this, such as the culminating scene in a spirited Nike ad called "A Time of Hope" in which a wheelchair marathoner exultantly rips opens his shirt as he crosses the finish line to reveal the superman insignia tattooed on his chest.[17]

Such moral lessons are hardly new to our culture: grit, determination, and effort are frequently cast as enabling us to conquer all obstacles in our way. Nothing touches the heart of traditional American ideologies of individual achievement more than sports conceptualized as a level playing field for competition, because when the playing field is level, the individual may prevail. Contemporary advertising is replete with what we call motivation ads. Frequently these motivational stories rely on athletic metaphors. Texaco draws on the equivalence between the performance of Olympic athletes and the performance of its gasoline. Champion's solemn inspirational lyrics state that "it takes a little more to never say never." This genre of ads proclaim if you have "what is deep inside" and are willing to go the extra mile of hard work, you can become the best. If this ideological appeal is so pervasive, why then does Nike's construction of it seem to stand out above the rest? We suspect the answer lies in the domain of aesthetic style and expression: it's not just what they say, but how they say it.

NOTES

1. Nike and the swoosh are trademarks of the Nike Corporation.
2. B.G. Brooks, "*Swoosh,* the Mark of Success in '90s," *Rocky Mountain News,* October 13, 1995, p. 12B.
3. Donald Katz, *Just Do It: The Nike Spirit in the Corporate World* (New York: Random House, 1994), p. 198.
4. Laurie McDonald, "Selling High Tech; Marketing Footwear," *Footwear News,* May 20, 1996, p. 1.
5. Robert Goldman and Stephen Papson, *Sign Wars* (New York: Guilford, 1996).
6. Michael Donaghu and Richard Barff, "*Nike* Just Did It: International Subcontracting and Flexibility in Athletic Footwear Production," *Regional Studies* 24 (December 1990), p. 541.
7. J.B. Strasser and Laurie Becklund, *Swoosh: The Unauthorized Story of Nike and the Men Who Played There* (New York: Harcourt Brace Jovanovich, 1991), p. 125.
8. Miguel Korzeniewicz, "Commodity Chains and Marketing Strategies: Nike and the Global Athletic Footwear Industry," in *Commodity Chains and Global Capitalism,* ed. Gary Gereffi and Miguel Korzeniewicz (Westport, CT: Greenwood Press, 1994), p. 254. Davidson could not find a way to reconcile support and movement as Knight had instructed. "Support was static, she explained, movement was

the opposite" (Strasser and Becklund, *Swoosh,* p. 126). Instead, she recommended the shoe support be included in the shoe itself and the mark and the stripe be used to convey movement.

9. Strasser and Becklund, *Swoosh,* p. 126.

10. Ibid., p. 129.

11. Katz, *Just Do It,* p. 151.

12. Quoted in Brenda Lloyd, "Activewear Firms Banking on Increased Brand Interest; Super Show," *Daily News Record,* February 13, 1996, p. 4.

13. Bob Baum, "Athletic Wear Companies Are Pumping Billions into the World's Sports Tank, Fueling a Proliferation of Logos in Places such as High School Gyms and Olympic Victory Stands," *Chicago Tribune,* May 12, 1996, p. 10C.

14. Ibid.

15. Joachim Schroder, purchasing director for Germany's Karstadt department stores, cited in Linda Himelstein, "The *Swoosh* Heard Round the World," *Business Week,* May 12, 1997, pp. 76 ff.

16. Beth Tuschak, "Pruett Lures *Nike* on Board at Toronto: Sponsor Finds Epitome of "Do It" Attitude," *USA Today,* July 13, 1995, p. 10C.

17. One of the first "Just do it" ads in 1988 also featured a wheelchair athlete, Craig Blanchette. Like Levi's and the Bank of America, Nike's usage of a wheelchair athlete points to his/her signifying role in the cosmology of the emerging global capitalist system. The wheelchair person now signifies an inclusivity of spirit in a new stage of capitalism that ostensibly has removed all barriers of entry into markets and competitions.

CONSIDERING COLUMBINE: THE RHETORICAL SITUATIONS

The worst school shooting in U.S. history occurred on April 20, 1999, at Columbine High School in Littleton, Colorado. On that day, Eric Harris and Dylan Klebold killed 12 of their classmates and one teacher and wounded 23 others before taking their own lives. There had been other school shootings before Columbine, but this event captured the attention of the nation like no other. It's difficult to determine exactly why the Columbine shooting had such an impact on the national consciousness. Certainly, some of this impact came from the scale of the violence—even though the events of that day could have been much worse. For instance, had the propane bomb placed in the kitchen of the high school cafeteria gone off, hundreds could have been killed. Many were also struck by the fact that such a violent act could occur in an otherwise peaceful, middle-class neighborhood.

But some of the impact of the Columbine shooting has to do with the rhetorical moment in which it occurred. The debate about gun violence in the United States has been going on for decades, but it had reached a stage of maturity—a moment of kairos—in Colorado in 1999. In the spring of 1999, Colorado had become the focus of the national debate over gun violence. Over the course of several weeks, the state legislature had been debating a concealed weapons law that would give Colorado some of the most liberal gun laws in the

United States. Republican senators Doug Dean and Ken Chlouber had cosponsored SB 84, which would require county sheriffs to give a concealed weapons permit to nearly anyone over age 21 who had completed the required training and who was not a convicted felon. A second bill, HB 1305, would have allowed the state to overrule local laws preventing juveniles from buying firearms other than handguns. (The state law prohibited juveniles from buying handguns, but allowed them to buy any other kind of legal firearm.) A third bill, SB 205, would have protected handgun manufacturers from lawsuits. These bills had strong support from Colorado Governor Bill Owens.

The debate over these bills was an important local issue, but it became a national issue when the National Rifle Association decided to hold its national convention in Denver, beginning April 30, 1999. The NRA had been pushing for more relaxed concealed weapons laws in several states, and when the state of Missouri rejected a referendum to relax its laws, the NRA was eager for a political victory in Colorado. Supporters of the bills moved to get them passed by the time of the NRA convention, and the convention brought the state legislature under the scrutiny of the national press. Clearly, the rhetorical situation regarding the Colorado gun debate had reached a point of maturity.

But the debate changed considerably with the shooting at Columbine High School, just a week before the NRA was to hold its annual convention in Denver. The shootings set off a series of rhetorical events that spanned the next year. It changed the nature of the gun violence debate as both supporters and opponents of gun control had to account for the shootings. The community and the nation also found several ways to remember those who died and who were wounded. At some points, these memorial events and the political debates overlap.

The following readings outline the evolution of the rhetorical situations surrounding the Columbine shootings. The first selection, "Columbine Timeline," describes events from April 20, 1999, to April 16, 2000. This timeline, compiled by *Denver Post* librarians Regina Avila, Judi Acre, and Jan Torpy, not only provides information about this tragic event, but it also chronicles various rhetorical moments—some verbal and some visual—that respond to the shootings. The second selection, "Tragedy Focuses Attention on Gun Bills," written the day following the event, describes the immediate impact that the shootings had on the life cycle of the Colorado gun debate. (All three gun bills were shelved within a few days after the shooting, but Columbine quickly became the focus of a renewed national debate over gun control.) The third selection, "It's Time to Find Out What's Wrong with our Hateful Society," is an attempt by *Denver Post* columnist Chuck Green to respond to the Columbine tragedy. Written just the day after the shooting, Green's essay is addressing a rhetorical situation in its infancy—the origin of the life cycle. The implications of this situation are still unclear, and Green is trying to set the tone for the debate.

As you read these selections, consider the following questions:

1. Which stages of the life cycle of a rhetorical situation are apparent in the events described in the timeline? What is the kairos of these events (the right people at the right place and time)?

2. How well do these essays and the rhetorical events described in the timeline respond to needs of the rhetorical situations? What kinds of responses or debates were considered inappropriate or untimely?
3. In what ways do the attempts to respond to the Columbine shooting become part of the debate on gun violence, both the local debate about Colorado's gun laws and the larger debate?
4. Why did the Columbine shooting have such a profound effect on the national consciousness and the national debate about gun violence?
5. What memories do you have of the Columbine shooting? If you were in high school at the time, what effect did the shooting have on your school? What were some of the rhetorical events in your own community that resulted from Columbine (i.e., memorials, protests, debates, discussions)?

The *Denver Post* maintains an archive of articles, editorials, and letters related to the Columbine tragedy. These are found at <http://www.denverpost.com/news/shotmain.htm>. (If this link is not active, then check the *Denver Post* website and search for "Columbine.") You may want to consult this archive to enhance your reading and discussion of the rhetorical events brought about by the shooting.

What Are You Wearing to the Prom?

Newsweek, May 1, 1999, p. 23.

Columbine Timeline

DENVER POST LIBRARIANS REGINA AVILA, JUDI ACRE, and JAN TORPY

1 APRIL 20, 1999: Seniors Eric Harris and Dylan Klebold storm Columbine High School shooting four guns and carrying dozens of pipe bombs. They kill 12 classmates, one teacher, and then themselves. They also wound 23 others in the worst school shooting in U.S. history.

APRIL 21: Jefferson County schools Superintendent Jane Hammond closes all district schools. Clement Park, just north of the Columbine, becomes the unofficial gathering place for mourners. Gov. Bill Owens declares a state of emergency. The Legislature abandons three gun-related bills, the Colorado Avalanche cancels the first of two playoff games, and the NRA announces it will drastically scale back its Denver convention next week.

APRIL 22: Authorities find a powerful 20-pound propane-tank bomb Harris and Klebold had planted in the school's kitchen. Officials later say if it had gone off, hundreds of people would have been killed.

APRIL 25: 70,000 mourners crowd a movie theater parking lot near Columbine for a communitywide memorial service attended by Vice President Al Gore and his wife, Tipper; Gov. Owens and his wife; evangelist Billy Graham's son; and Christian performing artists Amy Grant and Michael W. Smith.

5 APRIL 26: Officials learn three guns used in the massacre at Columbine High School were bought last year by Dylan Klebold's girlfriend shortly after her 18th birthday.

APRIL 29: The last of the funerals for those killed is held.

APRIL 30: Brian Rohrbough, whose son, Daniel, was murdered, takes down crosses erected at Clement Park for Harris and Klebold, saying it's inappropriate to honor the killers alongside the victims.

MAY 1: An estimated 12,000 placard-waving people rally at the state Capitol against gun violence and protest the National Rifle Association's annual meeting four blocks away.

MAY 2: A remembrance service for Columbine students, staff, and parents is held at Red Rocks Amphitheatre.

10 MAY 3: Mark E. Manes, 22, surrenders to Jefferson County authorities to face a felony charge of selling a handgun to a minor. He admits selling a TEC-DC9 semiautomatic handgun to Harris and Klebold for $500 in January, but denies any knowledge of their plans for the massacre. Columbine students head back to school for the first time since the massacre, finishing out the school year at nearby Chatfield High.

MAY 20: President Bill and first lady Hillary Rodham Clinton meet with Columbine victims and families. Later in the day, they commemorate the one-month anniversary of the rampage before a crowd of 2,200 at Dakota Ridge High School. In Conyers, Ga., a 15-year-old student carries two guns into his suburban Atlanta high school and opens fire on his schoolmates. Six were wounded, none killed.

MAY 22: Columbine seniors graduate. There is a moment of silence for the seniors that had been killed on April 20.

MAY 26: The SHOUTS center—Students Helping Others Unite Together Socially—opens in the Ascot Theater on West Bowles Avenue. An owner of a video arcade at Denver International Airport removes five violent games in response to the Columbine massacre.

MAY 27: The family of victim Isaiah Shoels files a $250 million wrongful-death lawsuit against the parents of the two killers.

MAY 28: Jefferson County District Court Judge Henry Nieto seals the au- 15
topsy reports of the 13 Columbine High victims and the two killers.

JUNE 1: Students return to Columbine to retrieve their belongings.

JUNE 2: Victim families receive letters of remorse from Klebold's parents.

JUNE 3: Work begins to repair Columbine High for the start of classes in August.

JUNE 4: Robyn Anderson admits on "Good Morning America" she bought three of the four guns used by Harris and Klebold, but denies knowledge of their deadly plan.

JUNE 15: Parents of slain Columbine students announce their desire to 20
keep the school library closed forever. The library was the scene of most of the carnage; Harris and Klebold killed 10 students and themselves there.

JUNE 16: Authorities say the surveillance videotape recorded in Columbine High's cafeteria on April 20, enhanced by the FBI, doesn't substantiate the theory of a third gunman.

JUNE 17: Prosecutors file charges against Philip Joseph Duran, 22, who worked with the gunmen at a Blackjack Pizza store and introduced them to friend Mark Manes, who sold them the TEC-DC9. Duran is charged with unlawfully providing a handgun to minors and possessing a dangerous or illegal weapon.

JUNE 22: Rashad Williams, 15, a San Francisco high school track star, gives Columbine shooting victim Lance Kirklin $18,000 he raised during a running event.

JULY 2: The Healing Fund announces it will distribute $50,000 each to the families of the 12 students and one teacher who were slaying victims, and $150,000 to the families of five severely injured students. Twenty-five others injured in the attack will receive $10,000. Another $1.1 million will go for outreach and other direct services for Columbine students and faculty, including $150,000 already given to establish a youth center and $50,000 given to the Colorado Office of Victim Assistance. Ballistics tests confirm that "friendly fire" from police officers did not harm anyone at Columbine, authorities say.

JULY 20: Columbine students and families return to school to decorate tiles 25
that will be affixed to hallway walls.

AUG. 11: Jefferson County law enforcement officers are "strongly encouraged" to establish a presence in schools as the new academic year starts, according to a letter sent from John Kiekbusch, a division chief with the Jefferson County Sheriff's Office.

AUG. 16: Columbine students return to school. Freshly painted swastikas are found outside the school and in the bathrooms.

AUG. 18: Mark Manes agrees to plead guilty. It is the first criminal conviction stemming from the Columbine massacre.

AUG. 20: Partially paralyzed student Richard Castaldo heads home from Craig Hospital. He is the last of the wounded students to leave the hospital.

AUG. 30: Gov. Owens sharply criticizes a recommendation from mental- 30
health experts that the state seek $5.5 million in federal funds to pay for counseling for anyone in Colorado affected by the shootings.

AUG. 31: The Healing Fund accepts its last donations, topping off the largest account established for the victims at $4.4 million.

SEPT. 1: Jefferson County school officials tighten security and send reassuring memos to parents after five high schools receive another in a series of anonymous letters threatening violence.

SEPT. 10: Before the Columbine Rebels girls' softball team's first game of the season, the new Dave Sanders Memorial Softball Field is dedicated.

SEPT. 14: - Standing alongside the Rev. Al Sharpton in New York, the Shoels family accuses the Healing Fund of misappropriating funds and calls on the public to stop donating to the United Way.

SEPT. 15: Larry Gene Ashbrook, 47, enters a church service for teenagers 35
at Wedgwood Baptist Church in Fort Worth, Texas, and opens fire before turning the gun on himself. Ashbrook kills seven people, wounded seven more, and then takes his own life.

SEPT. 22: An Internet magazine, Salon.com, publishes purported excerpts from Eric Harris' diary in which the Columbine High School killer calls for the extermination of mankind.

SEPT. 24: Howard Cornell, 60, the chief of security for Jefferson County schools, abruptly retires after splitting with other district officials over how best to safeguard students. Sheriff's spokesman Steve Davis says it looks unlikely that Cassie Bernall was ever asked by her killers whether she believed in God before they shot her. Patrick Ireland is named homecoming king.

SEPT. 26: Relatives and friends of slain students Daniel Rohrbough and Kyle Velasquez chop down 2 of the 15 trees recently planted by members of the West Bowles Community Church. The families contend that the two killers shouldn't be remembered alongside those they killed.

SEPT: 29: Gov. Owens announces the creation of a 14-member Columbine Review Commission to study law enforcement's response to the tragedy and make recommendations aimed at preventing similar massacres.

OCT. 1: Celine Dion opens the new Pepsi Center with a concert, providing 40 front-row seats and back-stage passes to Columbine victims and their families. She dedicates $500,000 from the concert to helping the victims.

OCT. 4: The families of slain students Kelly Fleming and Daniel Rohrbough file a federal lawsuit claiming the school district violated their rights when it removed their commemorative art tiles painted with religious themes from Columbine.

OCT. 12: CBS News airs a portion of the surveillance videotape from the Columbine cafeteria. The sheriff's department had released the tape to other law enforcement agencies for training purposes. An Albuquerque TV crew copied it at a law enforcement training seminar and then fed it to CBS for nationwide viewing.

OCT. 15: Columbine teacher Patricia Nielson, who made the frantic 911 call from the school library on April 20, takes a leave of absence.

OCT. 17: The families of 20 Columbine students—including the Klebolds—file notices of intent to sue either the sheriff's department or school district over the massacre.

OCT. 19: A 17-year-old Columbine student is arrested on suspicion 45
of threatening to "finish the job" started by his former classmates, Harris and Klebold.

OCT. 22: Carla Hochhalter, 48, the mother of partially paralyzed student Anne Marie Hochhalter, walks into an Englewood pawnshop, asks to look at a handgun and then shoots herself. Her suicide reopens wounds for the entire community and causes a flood of calls to counseling hotlines.

OCT. 25: For the first time since the shootings, Eric Harris' parents, Wayne and Kathy Harris, meet with investigators. The Harrises agree to the interview only if some questions—such as whether Wayne found one of Eric's pipe bombs and detonated it in a field with him—are off-limits.

NOV. 2: Arthur Leon Thomas, 19, allegedly sent a threat over the Internet to Brenda Parker of Broomfield, who is a former girlfriend of Eric Harris.

NOV. 12: Mark Manes is sentenced to six years in prison for selling the semiautomatic handgun to Harris and Klebold.

NOV. 19: Garlin Newton completes his 700-mile Oklahoma-City-to- 50
Columbine walk, carrying a cross in hopes of reviving prayer in schools. His arrival, though, is met by jeers from both students and motorists.

DEC. 4: The Columbine Rebels win the school's first statewide varsity football title. The season was dedicated to Matt Kechter, a junior-varsity lineman and one of the 12 students killed in April.

DEC. 13: *Time* magazine's cover story, "The Columbine Tapes," discloses details of three hours of suicide tapes left behind by Harris and Klebold. The tapes cause a furor not only because of the chilling words of the two killers, but because the sheriff's office allowed a reporter to see the tapes before they were shown to victims' families.

DEC. 15: Columbine junior Erin Walton receives an Internet message from Michael Ian Campbell, 18, of Florida. Campbell, using the screen name Soup81, threatens to "finish what begun" at Columbine and warns Walton to stay home from school the next day.

DEC. 16: Because of the threat, school officials end the semester two days early, canceling finals.

DEC. 17: FBI agents arrest Campbell at his Cape Coral, Fla., home and 55
seize his computer.

DEC. 22: Campbell appears in federal court in Florida and apologizes for the threat. He is ordered to undergo counseling at his own expense and appear in U.S. District Court in Denver on Jan. 11.

JAN. 5, 2000: Tom Mauser, father of victim Daniel Mauser, becomes a full-time lobbyist for the Colorado-based bipartisan gun-control group, Sane Alternatives to the Firearms Epidemic (SAFE). Mauser has taken a leave of absence from his job at the Colorado Department of Transportation to become director of political affairs for SAFE Colorado.

JAN. 7: Pueblo authorities confiscate a computer they believe a 15-year-old boy used to send a threatening message to a Littleton resident. The chat message appeared on New Year's Eve on the computer of a 20-year-old Colorado State University student who was home for the holidays.

JAN. 10: Arthur Leon Thomas, 19, of Houston, who was indicted on three counts of transmitting threats, appears in court in Denver. Thomas mailed a threat to Columbine High School and a threat to Jefferson County Sheriff John Stone on Sept. 30, according to the indictment. On Nov. 2, according to the indictment, he sent a threat over the Internet to Brenda Parker of Broomfield, who is a former girlfriend of Eric Harris.

JAN. 12: A temporary restraining order is issued barring Jefferson County 60
Sheriff John Stone from further releasing a videotape made by Eric Harris regarding the April 20 rampage at Columbine High School.

JAN. 20: The Jefferson County school board votes 4–1 to support a plan to tear down the existing library at Columbine, build an atrium in its place and build a new library elsewhere at the school. Duran pleads not guilty to charges against him.

JAN. 21: Benefactor and local businesswoman Sharon Magness announces a pledge of $250,000 to build a new library at Columbine High School.

JAN. 26: Robyn Anderson releases a statement about how she bought guns for Harris and Klebold, and how she wished there had been laws requiring background checks at the time of the purchase.

JAN. 27: Tom Mauser attends the president's State of the Union speech. Denver Mayor Wellington Webb unveils the latest version of the "Wall of Death" posterboard list, now bearing 3,094 names. The names belong to victims of gun violence in the nation's 100 largest cities since the April 20 massacre.

JAN. 31: The family of Isaiah Shoels settles in a suburb of Houston. 65

FEB. 9: Campbell pleads guilty to one felony count of communicating a threat across state lines. He rejects his attorney's defense of "Internet intoxication," calling it ridiculous.

FEB. 11: The Gov. Owens-endorsed HB 1272, by Rep. Dorothy Gotlieb, R-Denver, fails in the House. The bill would allow local police to enforce a federal law banning licensed gun dealers from selling guns to anyone between 18 and 20.

FEB. 14: Columbine students Stephanie Hart and Nick Kunselman are found shot to death inside a Subway Sandwich Shop in Littleton. Authorities reveal the number of bombs planted by Harris and Klebold are more than previously thought. Dave Sanders is posthumously honored with the Arthur Ashe Award for Courage at the annual ESPY awards in Las Vegas.

MARCH 3: Bill Tuthill, assistant county attorney for Jefferson County, announces the sheriff's office will not make public videotapes, diaries, or lists made by Harris and Klebold until litigation over the materials concludes.

MARCH 7: John and Janet Elway meet with some of the families of the students injured or slain in the Columbine massacre. Gov. Bill Owens signs legislation to reauthorize the state's background check on gun purchases, or InstaCheck Program.

MARCH 11: Stonemasons and volunteers rebuild a staircase outside the library at Columbine.

MARCH 12: Dawn Anna, mother of victim Lauren Townsend, receives the Sportswomen of Colorado's award for courage and inspiration.

MARCH 27: Jefferson County Undersheriff John Dunaway tells a special gubernatorial review commission that the Columbine report won't be released until late May.

MARCH 30: Lawyers for the victims of the Columbine massacre ask President Clinton to establish a multimillion-dollar disaster fund to help survivors and the families of the 13 who were slain. Bruce Springsteen donates 50 seats at his concert as a fundraiser for HOPE, the organization trying to raise money for a new library at Columbine.

APRIL 5: The SHOUTS teen center that opened in response to the Columbine shootings says it is likely to close after June 30 because funds for the center will be exhausted.

APRIL 7: The White House announces it will be unable to provide disaster relief for the families of those killed and injured at Columbine High School. Gov. Bill Owens announces he will not join President Clinton at an April 12 rally for stronger gun control.

APRIL 10: The families of slain students Kelly Fleming and Daniel Rohrbough demand release of the Jefferson County sheriff department's investigative report on the shooting and other related materials.

Tragedy Focuses Attention on Gun Bills

MIKE SORAGHAN

1 IT DIDN'T take long for House Speaker Russ George to start getting messages Tuesday blaming the Legislature's gun debate for the shooting at Columbine High School in Littleton.

"I'm getting e-mails right now that say, 'See what happens?'" George, R-Rifle, said in an interview, as students still were fleeing the gruesome scene.

The tragedy occurred against the backdrop of a fierce Statehouse debate over guns.

Even as the shooters still were inside the school, legislators realized that the gun debate had hit home in an unimaginable way. Both chambers of the Legislature decided not to meet today out of respect for the victims and their families. Many legislators noted that the gun proposals being debated under Colorado's golden dome wouldn't apply to Tuesday's scenario—students carrying guns into schools.

5 But one of the sponsors of a bill to allow more adults to carry concealed weapons said his bill might have helped the situation.

"I would feel safer knowing that there was a teacher at my kid's school who was a concealed weapons permit holder who could intervene in a situation like this," said House Majority Leader Doug Dean, R-Colorado Springs.

But anti-gun leaders said the shooting showed the need for gun control.

"The more guns you put in circulation, the more people get shot," said Sen. Pat Pascoe, D-Denver. "It's common sense."

Gov. Bill Owens, who has generally supported this year's gun legislation, said it wasn't appropriate to talk about legislation in the press of tragedy. But he did note that the shooters were not obeying gun laws.

10 "These killers broke every gun law in the books when they walked in today," Owens said.

Owens has demanded, very specifically, that concealed handguns not be allowed in schools. State law already bans other kinds of guns in schools.

In the past few weeks, Colorado has become a focal point in the national debate over guns. The National Rifle Association has been pushing for more states to allow concealed carry of handguns. After Missouri voters rejected a concealed-carry referendum, Colorado became the most likely place to pass such a law this year.

In addition, Denver will host the NRA's national convention at the end of this month. Critics say legislators are pushing to get some gun laws passed in time for the convention.

Owens has been invited to speak at the convention May 1, but had not committed to the engagement.

Dean and Sen. Ken Chlouber, R-Leadville, co-sponsored SB 84, which 15
would require sheriffs to issue concealed weapons permits to just about anyone 21 or older who has undergone training and isn't a felon.

Another bill, HB 1305, would wipe out most local gun laws. According to a local government lobbying group, the bill would wipe out any local laws that ban juveniles from buying or possessing guns other than handguns. State law prohibits juveniles from buying or possessing handguns.

A third bill, SB 205, would block lawsuits against gun manufacturers.

As details from the shooting scene kept trickling out, it started becoming clear that some people linked the school incident to the legislative push on guns. The Rev. Lucia Guzman, director of the Colorado Council of Churches, said, "If the NRA doesn't cancel its convention in Denver at this tragic time, it's a slap in the face to Denver."

She said she saw Owens on TV and he said this is not the time to talk about the gun legislation.

"Then when is the time to talk about the gun legislation?" Guzman asked. 20

The NRA said it wasn't time for politics.

"It would be inappropriate for anyone to comment on it (the incident at the school) until we know what happened," spokesman Bill Powers said.

But another, more militant, gun group echoed the sentiments of Dean, saying the shooting showed that the concealed carry bill should not bar handguns from schools and other places. The current draft of the legislation says concealed handguns could not be carried into schools or onto school grounds unless they are locked in a car.

"It just goes to show that gun control does not work," said Damien Veatch, chairman of Rocky Mountain Gun Owners. "When a criminal shoots at innocents, it is clear he has no concern for the law. We'd rather that teachers could protect themselves and their classrooms, if they so choose."

Sen. Norma Anderson, a Republican whose district includes Columbine, 25
found her phone message list filled with anti-gun sentiments after the shooting. But she wasn't talking about them.

"I'm not thinking about the impact here, I'm thinking about the impact on the families," Anderson said.

Rep. Ken Gordon of Denver, who leads the Democratic minority in the House and has ardently fought the gun bills, also declined to tie the shootings to the gun bills.

"I just hope to God it's not the Legislature that's causing this," Gordon said.

It's Time to Find Out What's Wrong with Our Hateful Society

CHUCK GREEN

SOMETHING is terribly wrong in America. But that's not the worst part. 1

The worst part is that we don't know what the problem is, and we don't seem to care enough to find out.

We can land people on the moon, and we can peer inside the human cell, but we can't raise our own children with decent values.

While the planet still is populated with starving children, and while religious wars still keep the morticians busy in places as civilized as Ireland, and while gangs terrorize the inner-city streets of America, we have a problem.

The problem is that the most privileged among us—among the most priv- 5
ileged of the privileged in the history of human existence—still hate.

In suburban Colorado—and in Fargo, North Dakota, and in Tallahassee, Florida—hate thrives.

It goes unnoticed, at worst, or is tolerated, at best, throughout America. Those are pretty narrow parameters—and they are unacceptable.

As the visions of bloody murder flicker across the screens of our TV sets this morning, we must stop and ask ourselves if this is the best the human condition can deliver.

Jefferson County, Colorado.

We have indoor plumbing. We have full employment. We have public edu- 10
cation. We have big-screen TVs and leather-interior luxury cars and super highways and bicycle paths and Internet connections and day-care centers and public defenders for indigent defendants and wilderness areas for hikers and luxury boxes for corporate guests during Monday-night football and first-class tickets to Europe.

Yet we can't stop killing each other.

And we don't seem to care enough to find out why.

Well, there is no better place to start, and there is no better time to begin, than here and now.

This week, in Colorado.

Gov. Bill Owens ought to make a passionate plea for a national pathology of 15
violence in America. And President Bill Clinton ought to provide it.

It's time we cared enough to find out what is wrong with the most advanced, the most civilized, the most privileged, the most tolerant, the most educated, the most compassionate society ever to populate the Earth.

What is wrong with us?

There isn't an easy answer. It probably lies somewhere deep inside the human spirit, beyond the known boundaries of politics and civilized history.

For some reason, apparently, people like to kill. And we like to watch people get killed, in our living rooms on TV and in our movie theaters at the mall.

We like Mafia movies as much as we like "Star Wars." We are equally entertained by neighborhood gang killings and intergalactic battles.

There is something about the human pathology that seems determined to hate, to become predatory and to kill. Our international enemies or our schoolmates—no matter.

But what is even worse than that is that we don't seem to care. We don't seem to be determined to find out what the problem is.

And if we don't find out, if we don't devote the resources, who will?

Now is the time; here is the place.

Practicing the Principles: Activities

REFLECTING ON THE NATURE OF ARGUING

Freewrite for five minutes about a time when you had a quarrel or disagreement—the playground variety of argument. How did you feel at the time? How productive was the activity? What was the outcome? What could you have done to make your experience more productive? Share your experience with your classmates. How did your experience compare with theirs?

FINDING ARGUMENTS ALL AROUND

Bring to class anything you can find that you think might be making a claim: print ads, campaign literature, junk mail, T-shirts, bumper stickers, coffee mugs, personal ads, product packaging, letters to the editor, music lyrics or videos, Web pages, whatever. The more outrageous, the better. Sort through these as a class and try to identify the arguments these objects are making (the claims, reasons, and assumptions—remember that in everyday arguments, claims are often implied rather than stated). How do these objects establish credibility, appeal to your emotions, or rely on logic? After you have attempted to reconstruct these arguments, write briefly about how your knowledge of the context for the artifact helps you in reconstructing these arguments. Pay particular attention to instances where you may disagree about what claim the object is making.

THE SPECTRUM OF VIEWPOINTS

Deborah Tannen, in her recent book *The Argument Culture,* argues that in American public debate, we focus too often on opposition: winners and losers, right and wrong, for and against, pro and con. For Tannen, complex social issues can rarely be reduced to only two positions. Make a list of some current political or social issues, and then a further list of the positions people generally take for or against each issue. In most cases, do these positions tend to fall into two groups: for and against? For instance, we often talk of people being pro-life or pro-choice, for gun control or against gun control, in favor of capital punishment or against capital punishment, pro-war or anti-war. As a class, brainstorm about what possible other positions one could take on some of these issues. Then select one of these issues and represent the variety of views on a spectrum.

COMPARING COMMUNITIES

Generate a list of the communities you belong to and share it with other members of the class. Use the following list to remind you of all the ways that community can be defined: geographical location; common values and beliefs; common characteristics; shared economic, political, and professional interests; shared social and recreational interests; a common history, culture, and language; family; race; gender; or common educational background. You might consider interviewing another student and describing for other class members the communities of the person you interviewed. Take some time as a class to discuss the similarities and differences among the communities you belong to. (Remember that communities often overlap one another.) Note, in particular, the similarities and differences in language. Generate a list of terms and phrases that are used in one of these communities that would be unfamiliar to or misunderstood by a newcomer. Explain these terms to a classmate. To finish this activity, freewrite about how language creates and maintains boundaries between communities.

MAPPING THE ORGANIZATION OF YOUR COLLEGE

One way of understanding the organization of your college is to compare your experience of the college community with how the community represents itself. Begin with the buildings and grounds. Bring in a map of your campus or else sketch one from memory. What does the organization of the campus say about the kinds of activities that are important? What is located near the center of the map? What kinds of buildings are near the edges? How does one building differ from another? What does each building say about the kinds of activities that occur there? Now consider your classroom. Discuss how one classroom differs from another, not just physically but in how the class is organized. Are the classes large or small? Do students interact much with the instructor or with each other? What effect does the physical makeup of the room have on the organization of the class? Are chairs bolted to the floor, facing forward? Can students move around or rearrange their desks or chairs? Are some parts of the class closer to the instructor? What does the organization of your campus—its buildings, offices, classrooms, public spaces—say about how, when, and where people discuss and decide issues?

READING THE ORGANIZATION OF YOUR COLLEGE

Do some research to understand how your college community presents itself to its students and to others. Bring to your class your course catalogs and bulletins, orientation pamphlets, advisement sheets, Web pages, or any other document that attempts to introduce the college to students in an official way. If you can, get a copy of your college's mission statement. As a class, you can then compare your experience of the college organization with how the organization is described in official documents. Compare your experience of the college community with your classmates' experiences.

OBSERVING KAIROS

Visit some of the places on your campus or in your local community where people go to speak out on issues. Observe the kairos of these conversations: When do they happen? What is special about the place? Who is typically involved? What rules or conventions (either formal or implicit) govern the conversations? In what are considered appropriate responses? If you have access to the Internet, try visiting a chat room, discussion forum, or MUD. What is the kairos of these virtual conversations?

IDENTIFYING THE LIFE CYCLE OF A RHETORICAL SITUATION

Lloyd Bitzer outlines four stages in the life of a rhetorical situation: origin, maturity, deterioration, and disintegration. As a class, brainstorm about some issues that face your college community. Select two or three of these and try to describe the life cycle of these issues in specific terms. What stage is the issue in now? In what direction is the discussion and decision-making process turning? When do you think the issue will enter a new stage?

As an alternative to analyzing a rhetorical situation at your college, you may want to research the life cycle of the ballot dispute in Florida during the 2000 presidential election. Begin as a class by creating a timeline for the dispute from election night through inauguration day (January 20, 2001). Then record and analyze the different rhetorical events that led to the Florida electors being awarded to George W. Bush. What were some of the crucial rhetorical moments? How appropriate were the responses to these moments? How might different responses have changed the outcome?

"JUST DO IT": THE PERSUASIVE POWER OF A LOGO

In this chapter, I talked about the persuasive power of the Nike swoosh, one of the most easily recognized logos in the world. A logo or brand name becomes powerful as a persuasive tool when people begin immediately to associate certain values and beliefs with the logo or name. Since Nike sells athletic shoes and clothing, it wants to associate with its logo anything that is good about sports: commitment, endurance, sacrifice, desire, competition, strength, skill. To understand how Nike has done this, you need to look at a lot of ads. As a class, look at recent issues of magazines to find Nike ads. You can also find television ads on www.industry.adcritic.com. What values and beliefs do these ads convey? How do they convey these values and beliefs?

As an extension of this activity, examine some other logo or brand in the same way you analyzed Nike. Brainstorm for a few moments about some logos or brands (IBM, Microsoft, Chevrolet, Texaco, Nabisco, Budweiser). Then gather some ads that promote these brands. What values and beliefs do these ads convey?

Now consider the world of higher education. Many colleges and universities also have logos or symbols. Can a college name also be a brand name? How does a college try to associate itself with certain values and beliefs?

VIRTUAL DISCUSSIONS

The Internet offers many opportunities to engage in discussion and debate. These discussions take a variety of formats. Some are fairly structured. *Wired Online* sponsors a forum called "Brain Tennis: Debate as a Spectator Sport." *Wired* invites two experts to debate a topic over the course of two weeks. (These topics usually focus on society and technology.) While the experts debate each other, visitors to the site can debate each other in an online forum. You can find "Brain Tennis" at <hotwired.lycos.com/braintennis>. Some forums focus directly on political issues. Try <www.votervoices.com> for a list of forums divided by issue as well as by region and state. You can find a similar site at <www.youdebate.com>. "The Debate Couch" describes itself as "a friendly place for civilized and intelligent conversation." This forum is open to all participants and any issue, but "juvenile trash-talking, personal attacks, and obscene language" are not allowed. The Internet has hundreds of forums for debating and discussing issues. To find these, try a keyword search on "chats and forums."

Applying the Principles: Analytical Projects

THE USE OF PRODUCT LOGOS IN ADVERTISING

Find some print advertisements that use product logos. As a class, analyze the persuasive strategies these ads use and identify the values and beliefs each ad is associating with the logo. Look for these logos elsewhere and try to discover how consistently the logo is associated with a certain set of values. You can easily find ads by looking through current magazines, especially sports magazines. You can also find television commercials to analyze at <industry.adcritic.com>. Just do a keyword search on the brand name (for example, "Nike").

THE USE OF NATIVE AMERICAN NAMES AND IMAGES AS LOGOS

Over the past decade, a heated debate has continued about whether sports teams using Native American names and logos are offensive. Teams such as the Atlanta Braves, the Washington Redskins, the Cleveland Indians, and the Florida State Seminoles have come under attack from various groups. In the 1970s, Stanford University changed its mascot from the "Indians" to the "Cardinal" (with a "pine tree" logo). The controversy has surfaced recently at San Diego State University. San Diego State University's sports teams are known as the Aztecs, a nickname dating to the 1920s. The mascot is specifically named "Monty Montezuma." The campus is located on Montezuma Mesa, and one of the main streets leading to campus is Montezuma Drive. In fall 2000, the Native American Student Alliance at SDSU demanded that the name and image be dropped because it demeans and offends Native Americans. Despite strong support for the mascot from current students and alumni, and others in San Diego, the student council recommended that the university president remove the mascot. The council's recommendation led to a passionate discussion in the community.

SDSU is currently in the process of redesigning its logo; the controversial logo has been discontinued. The following letters to the editor of the *San Diego Union-Tribune* all respond to the question, "Is the SDSU Aztec logo offensive?" As a class, read and analyze these letters and discuss this issue. To enrich your discussion, you may want to research the broader question of whether Native American team names and logos are offensive.

SDSU Aztec Warrior

Is the SDSU Aztec Logo Offensive?

SAN DIEGO UNION-TRIBUNE

LETTERS TO THE EDITOR, OCTOBER 4, 2000

It's pathetically unfortunate that, because of a minuscule band of offensive, left-leaning, self-servicing panderers (the San Diego State Student Council), our endeared university may be about to become the laughing stock of all rational-thinking people by dropping its nickname.

What do these names have in common: Adirondack, Delaware, Massachusetts, Potomac, Illinois, Miami, Alabama, Waco, Wichita, Mohave, Shasta, Yuma, Laguna, Santa Ana, Santee and Santa Clara? They're names of Indian tribes used to identify states, cities and places in this country. Are these next on the Student Council's agenda! When a poll was taken on the Aztec nickname not long ago, 91 percent of the students wanted to keep it. The Student Council is turning a deaf ear to the desires of the very students they are supposed to be representing.

ANDREA BALTAZAR
San Diego

If the Aztec logo or Monty Montezuma's antics on the field are offensive, then get rid of them. Have a recognized Aztec scholar help design a new logo that is historically accurate. But before the university drops the Aztec name, it should explain how its use is offensive. Most reasonable, open-minded people will respond to a logical, non-emotional argument.

DAVID P. KILEY
San Diego

For those who are indignant at the local Indian criticism of Monty, think about that dark, forlorn-looking statue of Montezuma that sits at the entrance to SDSU—about which no real understanding of its meaning is broadcast, discussed or ever spoken of. It's ignored as if it were not there. Neither that statue nor that shameful image of a mascot belongs on the SDSU campus.

What we should be asking ourselves is what is the true meaning of having any mascot in an athletic event on this or any other campus, especially when it pertains to Indians or any other politically deprived and decimated group who are ignored in order not to bring up a horrendous past for which we are responsible?

If we truly wish to honor Native-Americans, let's show it by admitting our previous sins by trying to understand and to show respect for their existence, rather than stooping so low as to steal their own heroes as ours and flaunting them in the most undignified manner.

JAMES AJEMIAN
San Diego

As a note of practicality, someone should be considering the expense to change the signage, stationery and everything else with the Aztec logo. Once this cost is determined, it should be passed on to the hypersensitive student leadership (or their parents) in the form of a onetime tuition increase.

What's more important: the quality and price of education or the misperceived indignity cast upon the decendents of our ancient and proud Aztec forebears?

GEORGE LONGWORTH and
MELISSA DRESCHER
San Diego

(*Editor's note: The letter above was cosigned by five other SDSU alumni.*)

I have a simple solution to where the money can come from to pay for the expensive switching of the mascot at SDSU: We can get the U.S. government to pay for it with the wealth they stole from the indigenous people when they first invaded and raped our land.

SIMON JARA
San Diego

It appears that there is a small group of young American Indians at SDSU who are actually more embarrassed by their heritage than proud of it, and therefore want to keep it out of public view.

What school ever chooses a name and mascot to be an object of derision? Rather, it chooses one that represents strength, honor and valor; one they feel they can be proud of and relate to.

ANNE L. SKALAK
San Diego

I graduated from San Diego State University in 1999. I chose SDSU because I have many friends and family members who have also graduated from the university. I am also of Mexican descent, so I consider myself an Aztec both by blood and educational lines. I am honored to consider myself a part of this heritage. The mascot issue is a ridiculous waste of time.

GERARDO DERARDO
San Diego

The 10th-grade World History class at San Diego High School believes there are enough real problems in the world that require attention. Pseudo controversy by some people who have too much time on their hands does not deserve consideration.

The Indians protesting the Aztec name are not even Aztecs. The name itself does anything but dishonor the long and proud traditions of SDSU and the memory of the mighty Aztec Empire. The name honors the strength, greatness and cultural contributions of the Aztecs.

Where will this all stop? If Monty Montezuma is removed we will be offended. We may not be college students yet, but we can recognize racism when we see it and it is not in the Aztec mascot. It is found in those who are raising this protest.

(*Editor's note: The letter above was signed by 23 members of the 10th-grade World History class at San Diego High School.*)

SAN DIEGO UNION-TRIBUNE
LETTERS TO THE EDITOR, OCTOBER 8, 2000

LOGO DROP NONSENSICAL

My wife and I have been season ticket holders to Aztecs football games since they started playing at the Mission Valley stadium. I believe that was around 1969, when Dennis Shaw was leaving his mark on college football record books. We have seen all the great quarterbacks: Brian Sipe, Jesse Freitas, Todd Santos, et al. Aztecs football was fun to watch in those days: winning and setting college records for passing and receiving. We had a tailgate party of over 30 people. It was a great way to spend a Saturday night.

Times have changed. The football program is not nearly as strong as it used to be. The team is not winning anymore. Support for the Aztecs is down. Now we are down to about 10 or 12 loyal Aztecs fans in our tailgate party. I think we are there for the friendship more than anything else.

We are all appalled by what is happening at SDSU. Drop the Aztecs logo? You must be kidding! Didn't we recently read about all of the men's and women's sports programs being dropped by the athletic department? The reason? Lack of funds!

Just how much money would be spent in removing the Aztecs logo? Must be in the millions.

Who's going to pay for this? Should they drop another sport?

It doesn't make any sense. The Aztecs name is offensive to Native Americans? Why? They should be proud. Proud of the fact that a major university has recognized them and has chosen their name to represent them. Proud that their heritage is displayed and connected with all university functions.

Are they upset because "a non-Native American is portraying Monty Montezuma this year"?—as the Native American Student Alliance stated in a letter to Viewpoints (U-T, Oct. 1).

Wouldn't it be a whole lot cheaper just to change the person portraying Monty? Or better yet, just drop him. They haven't changed his opening act for years.

BILL MILLER
La Mesa

Keeping the Faith

As a registered Chippewa American Indian, I am proud to have graduated from an institution that honors itself by calling itself "Aztecs."

In my 40 years of attending Aztecs athletic events, I can honestly say that I never heard one disparaging remark against the Aztecs. I have always been proud to call myself an Aztec rather than a Horned Frog, a Gator or even a Duck.

As for Aztecs football, the problem is one of recruiting. There's no reason we can't get quality athletes to come to San Diego. Remember Moses Moreno and 16 other San Diego kids who went to Colorado State and won a Western Athletic Conference title and made a Holiday Bowl appearance?

There are thousands of good athletes in Southern California—so let's get our share. We need to work harder to compete to get the best to come here. There's no reason why the Trojans, Bruins and, yes, the Aztecs, can't be the best. Build through recruiting and they will come.

JERRY WALDRON
SDSU, Class of 1971

Aztec Heritage Runs Deep

The Aztec people, as their nation came into being, had many cultures contributing to it. The Tarastecs were expert weavers, the Toltecs were master builders and skilled at pottery work, while the Zapotec honored priesthood and higher education. The Olmeca people developed a unique art and enjoyed ball-games and good sportsmanship. The Mayan culture contributed a calendar, corn agriculture and writing with mathematics and astronomy. The Aztec nation was derived from all of these and other precultures.

The first five dormitories built on the Aztec campus were named for these cultures. The men's residence halls found on the West side of the campus took the names of Toltec, Tarastec and Zapotec, those cultures found west of the Aztec nation. Likewise, the original women's dormitories, Maya and Olmeca, found on the east side of the Aztec campus, took the names of the cultures found east of the Aztec nation. Thus, symbolically, the residence halls contribute individually and collectively to the Aztec campus.

I find no comparison with the nomadic American Indians and the Aztec people, who established a truly great civilization of permanency in a spirit of co-operation amongst so many cultures. What are the fractions of pure Indian blood in the 20 students who object about another culture, the Aztec culture, which is not their own? There is no way they are the true spokesmen for the Aztec heritage. It is ironic that they want their Indian culture built up while tearing down San Diego State's Aztec culture. Don't they know that an Indian does not stand taller by knocking down an Aztec?

JIM MALIK
Emeritus Professor of Chemistry, SDSU

SAN DIEGO UNION-TRIBUNE

LETTERS TO THE EDITOR, OCTOBER 22, 2000

SDSU Alumni Want Aztec Mascot Kept

One of the greatest traditions of San Diego is under attack. If the citizens of San Diego County don't stand up and stop this attack, we will lose what few traditions we have. I am talking about the Aztec tradition of San Diego State University.

Few things in society have ever received as much support as the retention of Monty Montezuma and the Aztec tradition. If a poll were conducted and asked what color the sky is, it is doubtful that there would be as much consensus as there is on the Aztec mascot.

The SDSU Alumni Association sent out 12,000 e-mails asking whether the Aztec name should be kept. Of the 4,000 responses received, 98 percent supported keeping the Aztec tradition as part of San Diego. Due to that overwhelming support by the alumni, the Alumni Association resolved that the Aztec name, logo and human mascot should be kept.

With all this support, why is there still the possibility of Monty Montezuma becoming extinct? Because a few students at San Diego State have called the Aztec tradition "racist" and "culturally degrading." That small group of students could not be further from the truth. Ash Hayes, former president of the Alumni Association, said, "The Aztec tradition is based on honor, vigor, glory and heritage." That is truly what the Aztec tradition of SDSU is all about.

We must fight to keep that tradition of honor, vigor, glory and heritage alive.

BILL HORN
County Supervisor 5th District

Numerous comparisons have been made between SDSU and other schools with Indian mascots. But SDSU is the only school to name a specific leader as the mascot. Although I am somewhat ambivalent about the use of Aztecs as a nickname, I do feel regret over the flippant treatment of the noted leader Montezuma.

It is the statue of Montezuma that is objectionable. Carved in 1937 by the famous artist Donal Hord, it has been widely praised for its artistic quality. The artist originally named it "The Aztec," but the statue later assumed the label of Montezuma. This was unfortunate because the facial features, particularly the nose and ears, have been exaggerated, possibly as a concession to the statue's role as a mascot. It is doubtful that it bears any likeness to the subject. I could understand why some native Aztecs might take offense.

Although the statue is a fine work of art in its own way, it has outlived its usefulness as "Montezuma." Perhaps this would be a good time to retire it, change it back to "The Aztec," or rename it "The San Diego State Aztec."

MARC B. LOGAN
San Diego

Chapter 2
Analyzing and Evaluating Ethos

Ethos: Arguing from Credibility

Ethos is a persuasive strategy based on the credibility of the writer—the writer's perceived character. An argument grounded in ethos succeeds when the audience trusts what the writer says. Think about people you trust. Why do you trust them? You might trust them because they have authority. For example, some people have credibility because of the position they hold in the community. Religious leaders, teachers, police officers, and other public officials have authority because of the position they hold. The uniform, the badge, the sign of office are all persuasive in some contexts. Their authority can make them more credible.

SOURCES OF CREDIBILITY

- Position or role in the community.
- Character, prior behavior, decent and fair actions.
- Knowledge, education, training, expertise.

For instance, the president of the United States has certain authority because of his position—he can put ideas into action—and the office he holds conveys a certain degree of credibility on whoever holds the position.

Others gain our trust, not because of the position they hold, but rather because of the qualities of character they demonstrate. Generally, we trust people who are knowledgeable and experienced, who are decent, fair, reliable, and honorable, and who demonstrate goodwill with others. We tend to trust people who are more like us, who identify with our values and beliefs. And we trust people in our communities who demonstrate good qualities over a long period. You might also trust someone because of his or her knowledge of an issue. Because we can't know everything about every issue we need to decide, we often value the opinion of experts (as long as they show other good qualities). For instance, most people want to find a good doctor or dentist, one who is not only knowledgeable and skilled, but also honest and caring.

Of course, ethos can also work against a writer. People who demonstrate a consistent pattern of misbehavior may have a hard time earning the trust of others, even when they have good intentions or even if they hold an important position. For instance, a political leader whose behavior doesn't fit with the values associated with his or her office may lose credibility with voters. If someone has authority because of his or her position and exercises that authority in ways that are decent and fair, then they gain even greater credibility in their community.

Long-standing or high-ranking members of a community can usually rely on their position in the community to establish credibility. For example, within the Catholic community, the Pope has credibility because of his position, and his credibility is enhanced by his well-known acts of service and devotion, his theological writings, and his years of experience in church leadership. When the Pope speaks or writes on religious issues, he can rely heavily on his position and reputation. Supreme Court justices also have considerable credibility by virtue of their position, education, and experience. Even though other members of the legal community may know as much or more about particular legal issues, a Supreme Court justice has considerable influence by virtue of having been appointed to the court. But you don't have to be a religious leader or judge to have credibility. Your position and reputation would give you some influence in certain communities.

Even those with great influence in their communities still have to rely to some extent on the arts of rhetoric to build trust with their audience. When participating in a rhetorical situation, they would need to assume a role that is consistent with their position in the community and appropriate to the situation. They would need to decide how to present themselves, what information about themselves to share with their audience, how to use their authority, and how to identify their values with the values of the community.

Those who are relatively unknown in the community must rely even more than others on the arts of rhetoric to establish credibility. For instance, because of their traditional role in the academic community, students typically have very little credibility. Even though a student may be quite knowledgeable and experienced, the educational system defines the teacher as the expert and the student as the beginner. As a result, even when students know what they are talking about, they must still use ethos effectively to persuade others. This is particularly true when the teacher or other students don't know very much about you or judge you based on first impressions or stereotypes, believing, for example, that women don't do well in math and sciences, that men are generally not creative, or that athletes are not as well prepared as other students. It usually isn't enough to know what you are talking about; you also have to *sound* like you know what you are talking about.

Consider the traditional research paper, for example. Teachers expect students to include their own reflections and conclusions, but teachers also expect students to rely heavily on the opinions of experts and authorities. Students quote, paraphrase, and summarize other writers, merging their voices with voices of authority to create credibility and show what they have learned about their topic. If a research paper came in with very few references, the teacher would probably be suspicious, perhaps wondering whether the student was guilty of plagiarism.

Teachers have different expectations for their fellow teachers and scholars. In an essay by an established scholar, a lot may be left unsaid because there is a body of common knowledge and assumptions about the topic that one has mastered as an expert. Established scholars rely much more upon their own authoritative voices and less upon the voices of others. Saying something that everyone else knows can label one as a beginner. For instance, if there are three primary scientific theories to explain a certain event, and experts are all familiar with them, then an authoritative writer may refer to them in an article without citing the works in which the theories were originally explained. Students, however, would be expected to cite all such works. Experts can also make generalizations about their field that students can't. When a student opens an essay with a sweeping, panoramic introduction, beginning with "Throughout the ages . . . ," for example, or "In today's society . . . ," teachers may fault the student for overgeneralization and lack of support. But a famous historian can make sweeping claims about the course of history without a lot of specific detail and without always quoting the opinions of other historians. Ethos makes a difference.

Creating Ethos

Ethos is present in every act of communication—written, spoken, or visual. Whether favorable or otherwise, we are always giving others an impression of ourselves. The key in arguing is to be in control of one's ethos as much as possible. We can control ethos by presenting ourselves in the best possible way, establishing a relationship with our audience that is appropriate to the situation.

SHARING PERSONAL INFORMATION

Trust can come from what we know about a speaker or writer: his or her position or role in the community, prior behavior, and knowledge or expertise. According to Aristotle, we tend to believe those who hold positions of trust, those who observe the ethical principles of the community and develop a reputation for fairness and goodwill, and those who have a lot of experience and education. People trust doctors, religious leaders, and firefighters in part because of the position they hold in the community, because of their reputation, and because of their training and experience. People who are not well known in a community may need to share more information about themselves to establish credibility than would long-standing members of the community.

When analyzing the credibility of written arguments, the first step is to consider a writer's background. If you don't know much about the writer, then consider the background information he or she reveals. Look for stories the writer tells or examples the writer gives from his or her own life. Look for information about the author provided by an editor. You might even do some research to find out even more about the author. Then consider the following questions:

What is the writer's standing in the community?
What position does he or she hold?
What kind of authority and influence come with this position?
What is the writer's reputation?
What is the writer's education, experience, or expertise?

TECHNIQUES FOR CREATING ETHOS

- Sharing personal information.
- Adopting an authoritative voice.
- Identifying with the reader.
- Selecting an appropriate point of view.

What about the author's life is particularly appropriate for the issue under discussion?

ADOPTING AN AUTHORITATIVE VOICE

Writers can also establish credibility through the way in which they present themselves. For instance, it is important for a job applicant to make a good impression through a résumé and in an interview. Even if an applicant has experience, education, and expertise, if these qualities do not come through on the résumé or during the interview, then he or she may not be hired.

Writers can sound credible by adopting an authoritative voice. We trust doctors, scientists, and other experts because they sound like experts. They speak the language of science and education, languages that our American society recognizes as authoritative. Experts also know how to support their claims with well-documented, appropriate evidence. Studies, expert opinion, and statistics are not just an important part of a logical argument; citing them can also establish credibility.

It is also possible to assume an authoritative voice through a technique called "voice merging." Voice merging occurs when a writer quotes, paraphrases, or alludes to an authoritative voice or to a voice that represents the values of the community, transferring some of that authority to the writer. A political speaker, for example, might quote Thomas Jefferson, James Madison, George Washington, or some other political hero to lend authority to the argument. A religious leader might quote the Bible or some other sacred text. Some writers quote or allude to the works of literary figures considered great or important by the community: William Shakespeare, Charles Dickens, George Bernard Shaw, Virginia Woolf, W. E. B. Dubois, Toni Morrison, or others. Citing such authorities is more than decoration; it also lends authority to the writer.

Some people have mastered the art of sounding credible even though they have very little idea of what they are talking about. Think of the "infomercials" you might have seen on late-night television. In most cases, it is easier to sound credible if you really *do* know what you are talking about, but there are people who can manipulate others by sounding credible when they really are not—con artists, for example, and people who falsify credentials in order to get into a prestigious school or obtain an important job. Like other forms of communication, persuasion through ethos can be abused.

IDENTIFYING WITH THE READER

When analyzing written arguments, consider how writers convey or create credibility by identifying with the values of the community. When politicians show themselves with their families, playing football with a group of marines, hiking in the Grand Canyon, or visiting a school or homeless shelter, they are trying to show that they identify themselves with the values of the community. A writer does the same thing by using recognizable examples, sharing personal information, or appealing to reasons that support community values.

Choosing the right words is another way to identify with the reader. We trust those who "speak our language." One who speaks the language of the community seems to belong. For example, Martin Luther King, Jr., when addressing the African-American community, spoke the language of that community, drawing upon his experience and training as a folk preacher. But when he addressed liberal white audiences, a main source of support for his campaign for civil rights, he adapted his language, drawing upon his university training. In both instances, he strengthened his credibility by speaking the language of the community he was addressing.

SELECTING AN APPROPRIATE POINT OF VIEW

Point of view refers to the relationship the writer tries to establish with his or her readers. A first-person point of view (using "I" or "we") can create an intimate, personal, and friendly relationship between writer and readers, but "I" also draws attention to the writer as an individual. Doing so can be useful when a writer has particular expertise or relevant personal experience or when he or she can speak as a representative member of the community. Using "I" may not be as effective, however, on formal occasions or when the personal experience of the writer may appear irrelevant, limited, or biased. Some teachers believe that the first-person point of view is never appropriate in academic writing, but in recent years, more and more academic authors are using "I" when sharing relevant personal information. Using "we" emphasizes what a writer shares with readers, but "we" can also alienate people who feel that they share very little with the writer. Readers might also reject a writer who seems to be overly intimate in order to draw them in, like avoiding a stranger who insists on giving them a hug.

A second-person point of view (using "you") immediately gains a reader's attention, as when someone calls your name out in a crowd or looks directly into your eyes. The second-person point of view is often used in giving instructions or warnings, and it lends itself very well to giving commands. Used too much, it can make a writer appear dictatorial, preachy, or condescending. Using "you" can also create a distance between the writer and reader or put readers on the defensive, particularly when they have some doubts about the writer's claims or motives.

A third-person point of view (using "he," "she," "it," "they," or "one") gives a sense of objectivity and formality. The third-person point of view creates a distance between the writer, the reader, and the issue, and it can give the impression that the writer is a detached and unbiased observer. For this reason, scientists and scholars often use the third-person point of view. However, the third-person point of view can make a writer appear apathetic and impassive.

The Principles in Action: Readings

ETHOS AND PERSONAL EXPERIENCE

Ethos is present in any act of communication, but some arguments rely more heavily on ethos than others. This is particularly true when writers share a lot of personal experience to build credibility with their readers. In the first essay, author Leslie Marmon Silko considers the human cost of increasingly strict control of the southern borders of the United States. Silko is a Native American and is well known as a creative writer. Here, she gives a personal account of her encounter with the Border Patrol in New Mexico. In the second selection, Carolyn Edy, a single mother living in New Hampshire, writes about her decision to keep her baby and become a single mother—against the advice of her family and the dire predictions of experts. In the final selection, Chang-Lin Tien, former chancellor of the University of California at Berkeley, argues against the decision of California voters to abolish affirmative action in higher education in 1996.

As you read each of these essays, consider the following questions:

1. What kind of status or position does each author have in the communities he or she belongs to? In what ways does the author demonstrate this?
2. What kind of authority comes with this status or position? How important is this status or position in establishing credibility?
3. How does each author create ethos? How well does this created ethos conform to the author's status?
4. How does each author reveal information about himself or herself? What is the effect on each author's ethos of writing from a first-person point of view and revealing personal information?
5. How does each author try to adopt an authoritative voice? To what extent does the author merge his or her voice with the voices or others?
6. How does each author try to identify with his or her readers?
7. How does each author try to convey knowledge, experience, honesty, fairness, reliability, and goodwill?

The Border Patrol State

LESLIE MARMON SILKO

1 I USED TO travel the highways of New Mexico and Arizona with a wonderful sensation of absolute freedom as I cruised down the open road and across the vast desert plateaus. On the Laguna Pueblo reservation, where I was raised, the people were patriotic despite the way the U.S. government had treated Native Americans. As proud citizens, we grew up believing the freedom to travel was our inalienable right, a right that some Native Americans had been denied in the early 20th century. Our cousin, old Bill Pratt, used to ride his horse 300 miles overland from Laguna, New Mexico, to Prescott, Arizona, every summer to work as a fire lookout.

In school in the 1950s, we were taught that our right to travel from state to state without special papers or threat of detainment was a right that citizens under communist and totalitarian governments did not possess. That wide open highway told us we were U.S. citizens; we were free . . .

Not so long ago, my companion Gus and I were driving south from Albuquerque, returning to Tucson after a book promotion for the paperback edition of my novel *Almanac of the Dead*. I had settled back and gone to sleep while Gus drove, but I was awakened when I felt the car slowing to a stop. It was nearly midnight on New Mexico State Road 26, a dark, lonely stretch of two-lane highway between Hatch and Deming. When I sat up, I saw the headlights and emergency flashers of six vehicles—Border Patrol cars and a van were blocking both lanes of the highway. Gus stopped the car and rolled down the window to ask what was wrong. But the closest Border Patrolman and his companion did not reply; instead, the first agent ordered us to "step out of the car." Gus asked why, but his question seemed to set them off. Two more Border Patrol agents immediately approached our car, and one of them snapped, "Are you looking for trouble?" as if he would relish it.

I will never forget that night beside the highway. There was an awful feeling of menace and violence straining to break loose. It was clear that the uniformed men would be only too happy to drag us out of the car if we did not speedily comply with their request (asking a question is tantamount to resistance, it seems). So we stepped out of the car and they motioned for us to stand on the shoulder of the road. The night was very dark, and no other traffic had come down the road since we had been stopped. All I could think about was a book I had read—*Nunca Mas*—the official report of a human rights commission that investigated and certified more than 12,000 "disappearances" during Argentina's "dirty war" in the late 1970s.

5 The weird anger of these Border Patrolmen made me think about descriptions in the report of Argentine police and military officers who became addicted

to interrogation, torture and the murder that followed. When the military and police ran out of political suspects to torture and kill, they resorted to the random abduction of citizens off the streets. I thought how easy it would be for the Border Patrol to shoot us and leave our bodies and car beside the highway, like so many bodies found in these parts and ascribed to "drug runners."

Two other Border Patrolmen stood by the white van. The one who had asked if we were looking for trouble ordered his partner to "get the dog," and from the back of the van another patrolman brought a small female German shepherd on a leash. The dog apparently did not heel well enough to suit him, and the handler jerked the leash. They opened the doors of our car and pulled the dog's head into it, but I saw immediately from the expression in her eyes that the dog hated them, and that she would not serve them. When she showed no interest in the inside of the car, they brought her around back to the trunk, near where we were standing. They half-dragged her up into the trunk, but still she did not indicate any stowed-away human beings or illegal drugs.

The mood got uglier; the officers seemed outraged that the dog could not find any contraband, and they dragged her over to us and commanded her to sniff our legs and feet. To my relief, the strange violence the Border Patrol agents had focused on us now seemed shifted to the dog. I no longer felt so strongly that we would be murdered. We exchanged looks—the dog and I. She was afraid of what they might do, just as I was. The dog's handler jerked the leash sharply as she sniffed us, as if to make her perform better, but the dog refused to accuse us: She had an innate dignity that did not permit her to serve the murderous impulses of those men. I can't forget the expression in the dog's eyes; it was as if she were embarrassed to be associated with them. I had a small amount of medicinal marijuana in my purse that night, but she refused to expose me. I am not partial to dogs, but I will always remember the small German shepherd that night.

Unfortunately, what happened to me is an everyday occurrence here now. Since the 1980s, on top of greatly expanding border checkpoints, the Immigration and Naturalization Service and the Border Patrol have implemented policies that interfere with the rights of U.S. citizens to travel freely within our borders. I.N.S. agents now patrol all interstate highways and roads that lead to or from the U.S.-Mexico border in Texas, New Mexico, Arizona and California. Now, when you drive east from Tucson on Interstate 10 toward El Paso, you encounter an I.N.S. check station outside Las Cruces, New Mexico. When you drive north from Las Cruces up Interstate 25, two miles north of the town of Truth or Consequences, the highway is blocked with orange emergency barriers, and all traffic is diverted into a two-lane Border Patrol checkpoint—ninety-five miles north of the U.S.-Mexico border.

I was detained once at Truth or Consequences, despite my and my companion's Arizona driver's licenses. Two men, both Chicanos, were detained at the same time, despite the fact that they too presented ID and spoke English without the thick Texas accents of the Border Patrol agents. While we were stopped, we watched as other vehicles—whose occupants were white—were waved through the checkpoint. White people traveling with brown people, however, can expect to be stopped on suspicion they work with the sanctuary movement, which shelters refugees. White people who appear to be clergy, those who wear ethnic clothing or jewelry and women with very long hair or very short hair (they could be nuns) are also frequently detained; white men with beards or men with long hair are likely to be detained, too, because Border Patrol agents have "profiles" of "those sorts" of white people who may help political refugees. (Most of the political refugees from Guatemala and El Salvador are Native American or mestizo because the indigenous people of the Americas have continued to resist efforts by invaders to displace them from their ancestral lands.) Alleged increases in illegal immigration by people of Asian ancestry means that the Border Patrol now routinely detains anyone who appears to be Asian or part Asian, as well.

Once your car is diverted from the Interstate Highway into the checkpoint 10
area, you are under the control of the Border Patrol, which in practical terms exercises a power that no highway patrol or city patrolman possesses: They are willing to detain anyone, for no apparent reason. Other law-enforcement officers need a shred of probable cause in order to detain someone. On the books, so does the Border Patrol; but on the road, it's another matter. They'll order you to stop your car and step out; then they'll ask you to open the trunk. If you ask why or request a search warrant, you'll be told that they'll have to have a dog sniff the car before they can request a search warrant, and the dog might not get there for two or three hours. The search warrant might require an hour or two past that. They make it clear that if you force them to obtain a search warrant for the car, they will make you submit to a strip search as well.

Traveling in the open, though, the sense of violation can be even worse. Never mind high-profile cases like that of former Border Patrol agent Michael Elmer, acquitted of murder by claiming self-defense, despite admitting that as an officer he shot an "illegal" immigrant in the back and then hid the body, which remained undiscovered until another Border Patrolman reported the event. (Last month, Elmer was convicted of reckless endangerment in a separate incident, for shooting at least 10 rounds from his M-16 too close to a group of immigrants as they were crossing illegally into Nogales in March 1992.) Or that in El Paso a high school football coach driving a vanload of players in full uniform was pulled over on the freeway and a Border Patrol agent put a cocked revolver to his head. (The football coach was Mexican-American, as were most of the players in his van; the incident eventually caused a federal judge to issue a restraining order against the Border Patrol.) We've a mountain of personal experiences like that which never make the newspapers. A history professor at U.C.L.A. told me she had been traveling by train from Los Angeles to Albuquerque twice a month doing research. On each of her trips, she had noticed that the Border Patrol agents were at the station in Albuquerque scrutinizing the passengers. Since she is six feet tall and of Irish and German ancestry, she was not particularly concerned. Then one day when she stepped off the train in Albuquerque, two Border Patrolmen accosted her, wanting to know what she was doing, and why she was traveling between Los Angeles and Albuquerque twice a month. She presented identification and an explanation deemed "suitable" by the agents, and was allowed to go about her business.

Just the other day, I mentioned to a friend that I was writing this article and he told me about his 73-year-old father, who is half Chinese and had set out alone by car from Tucson to Albuquerque the week before. His father had become confused by road construction and missed a turnoff from Interstate 10 to Interstate 25; when he turned around and circled back, he missed the turnoff a second time. But when he looped back for yet another try, Border Patrol agents stopped him and forced him to open his trunk. After they satisfied themselves that he was not smuggling Chinese immigrants, they sent him on his way. He was so rattled by the event that he had to be driven home by his daughter.

This is the police state that has developed in the southwestern United States since the 1980s. No person, no citizen, is free to travel without the scrutiny of the Border Patrol. In the city of South Tucson, where 80 percent of the respondents were Chicano or Mexicano, a joint research project by the University of Wisconsin and the University of Arizona recently concluded that one out of every five people there had been detained, mistreated verbally or nonverbally, or questioned by I.N.S. agents in the past two years.

Manifest Destiny may lack its old grandeur of theft and blood—"lock the door" is what it means now, with racism a trump card to be played again and again, shamelessly, by both major political parties. "Immigration," like "street crime" and "welfare fraud," is a political euphemism that refers to people of color. Politicians and media people talk about "illegal aliens" to dehumanize and demonize undocumented immigrants, who are for the most part people of color. Even in the days of Spanish and Mexican rule, no attempts were made to interfere with the flow of people and goods from south to north and north to south. It is the U.S. government that has continually attempted to sever contact between the tribal people north of the border and those to the south.[1]

Now that the "Iron Curtain" is gone, it is ironic that the U.S. government 15
and its Border Patrol are constructing a steel wall 10 feet high to span sections of the border with Mexico. While politicians and multinational corporations extol the virtues of NAFTA and "free trade" (in goods, not flesh), the ominous curtain is already up in a six-mile section at the border crossing at Mexicali; two miles are being erected but are not yet finished at Naco; and at Nogales, 60 miles south of Tucson, the steel wall has been all rubber-stamped and awaits construction likely to begin in March. Like the pathetic multimillion-dollar

[1] The Treaty of Guadalupe Hidalgo, signed in 1848, recognizes the right of the Tohano O'Odom (Papago) people to move freely across the U.S.-Mexico border without documents. A treaty with Canada guarantees similar rights to those of the Iroquois nation in traversing the U.S.-Canada border.

"antidrug" border surveillance balloons that were continually deflated by high winds and made only a couple of meager interceptions before they blew away, the fence along the border is a theatrical prop, a bit of pork for contractors. Border entrepreneurs have already used blowtorches to cut passageways through the fence to collect "tolls," and are doing a brisk business. Back in Washington, the I.N.S. announces a $300 million computer contract to modernize its record-keeping and Congress passes a crime bill that shunts $255 million to the I.N.S. for 1995, $181 million earmarked for border patrol, which is to include 700 new partners for the men who stopped Gus and me in our travels, and the history professor, and my friend's father, and as many as they could from South Tucson.

It is no use; borders haven't worked, and they won't work, not now, as the indigenous people of the Americas reassert their kinship and solidarity with one another. A mass migration is already under way; its roots are not simply economic. The Uto-Aztecan languages are spoken as far north as Taos Pueblo near the Colorado border, all the way south to Mexico City. Before the arrival of the Europeans, the indigenous communities throughout this region not only conducted commerce, the people shared cosmologies, and oral narratives about the Maize Mothers, the Twin Brothers and their Grandmother, Spider Woman, as well as Quetzalcoatl the benevolent snake. The great human migration within the Americas cannot be stopped; human beings are natural forces of the Earth, just as rivers and winds are natural forces.

Deep down the issue is simple: The so-called "Indian Wars" from the days of Sitting Bull and Red Cloud have never really ended in the Americas. The Indian people of southern Mexico, of Guatemala and those left in El Salvador, too, are still fighting for their lives and for their land against the "cavalry" patrols sent out by the governments of those lands. The Americas are Indian country, and the "Indian problem" is not about to go away.

One evening at sundown, we were stopped in traffic at a railroad crossing in downtown Tucson while a freight train passed us, slowly gaining speed as it headed north to Phoenix. In the twilight I saw the most amazing sight: Dozens of human beings, mostly young men, were riding the train; everywhere, on flat cars, inside open boxcars, perched on top of boxcars, hanging off ladders on tank cars and between boxcars. I couldn't count fast enough, but I saw 50 or 60 people headed north. They were dark young men, Indian and mestizo; they were smiling and a few of them waved at us in our cars. I was reminded of the ancient story of Aztlán, told by the Aztecs but known in other Uto-Aztecan communities as well. Aztlán is the beautiful land to the north, the origin place of the Aztec people. I don't remember how or why the people left Aztlán to journey farther south, but the old story says that one day, they will return.

Single Motherhood Is a Joy, Not a Disaster

CAROLYN EDY

JUST AFTER Christmas '97, I went to Video Thunder with my mom and 1
my grandmother. We were three single mothers in search of a way to spend a cold New Hampshire evening. My mother was divorced, my grandmother was recently widowed, and I was three weeks shy of becoming an unwed mother.

My grandmother held up a video box and hollered across the store to me: "Oh, this is it! The perfect movie for you." In her hand was the movie *Bastard Out of Carolina*. I laughed and told her I'd already seen it. I'd rented it after I'd discovered I was pregnant.

I was 25 and had just received a master's degree from the University of North Carolina. A week after listening to graduation speeches telling me how far I could go, I sat on the edge of a twin bed, listening to the object of my affection give me his canned "It's not you—it's me" speech. Two weeks after that I sat at Planned Parenthood, where I'd gone for a $10 pregnancy test, waiting for my name to be called. A hip 22-year-old told me I was "definitely pregnant" and offered me cheerful sympathy, a tissue, a bag of congratulatory paraphernalia, and several abortion pamphlets.

I had always known I would never have an abortion or give up my child. Now I was sure that my life was over. Media portrayals of single mothers confirmed this—unless, like Murphy Brown, I was over-35 and already a success. But I felt so strongly I had to keep my child that it didn't take long to change my perspective. I began to rejoice and become hopeful—and I saw that these emotions were considered inappropriate.

While waddling around a national magazine as its first pregnant intern, I re- 5
ceived a press release from the Census Bureau stating that families headed by single mothers were among the country's poorest. That same month I listened to a man on C-SPAN radio predicting doom for the children of single mothers—in the form of dropouts, drugs, and divorce.

A pregnant co-worker spoke excitedly with me about our pregnancies, until I told her I was planning to deliver the baby in New Hampshire. She asked if my husband had been transferred. I told her I wasn't married, that I was going to live near my family. The conversation ended, and my pregnancy was never mentioned again.

Premarital sex is a given these days, and half of U.S. pregnancies are unintended. Yet living among the young and privileged—in four years of prep school, four years of college, and one year in Manhattan—I knew of no peers who were pregnant. I learned of friends' abortions only after they learned I was having a baby.

The shock value of my pregnancy was blaming those who believe in a woman's right to choose. The pro-choice, feminist movement often forgets that it is advocating a *choice*. Many who view abortion as an uncomplicated operation see my decision as incomprehensible. And whether they support a woman's right to have an abortion or oppose it, many would agree that I am depriving my daughter and one loving, infertile couple of a happy family.

To those who said I needed to think of my child, I responded with questions of my own. How could I be sure my child would be well cared for by someone else? And as for depriving her of an in-house father, I asked: How many children are abandoned by their fathers later in life? How many have to deal with divorce? When people said I needed to think of my own life, I replied that I couldn't live with myself if I did not keep this baby.

10 Most of my family viewed my optimism as pure naiveté. "She has no idea what she's in for" was a favorite line during my pregnancy—and continued into my daughter's first few months. This when I was already up every hour feeding, diapering and rocking a newborn.

But so far this prediction has come true: I really had no idea what I was in for. As much as I knew I would love my child, I love her more. I had hoped I would enjoy being a mother, and in fact I thrive in my new role.

After a yearlong silence, my daughter's father asked to be a part of her life. He resented me for not giving him a choice in whether she was born or whether I kept her. But I did allow him to choose whether he became involved, and that has greatly changed the way he views her. Now he feels as I do—proud that there is no other baby like her.

It's hard now to remember the panic I felt two summers ago. I have become so accustomed to my life with my daughter that I never know quite what to say to people who shake their heads and say, "It must be so hard." The truth sounds saccharine. I am hopelessly in love with my child.

Whenever I do complain that single motherhood is hard, I've got my mom and grandmother to tell me I have it easy—I don't have a husband to take care of as well.

A View from Berkeley

CHANG-LIN TIEN

1 WHEN the debate over affirmative action in higher education started to simmer, the stance I took as the chancellor of the University of California at Berkeley seemed to surprise many people.

To be sure, my view—that we *should* consider race, ethnicity, and gender along with many other factors in admissions—has put me at odds with some constituencies, including the majority of the Regents of the University of California. Last July, these officials voted to end affirmative action admission policies.

And with California voters to decide later this year whether to end all state affirmative action programs, silence might seem a more prudent course for the head of a major public university. We already have enough battles to fight, my staff sometimes reminds me: declining public funding, for example.

A few students and friends have hinted that it might make more sense for me, as an Asian-American, to oppose affirmative action.

5 Asian-Americans, who are not considered underrepresented minorities under affirmative action, have divergent views. Some are disturbed by the "model minority" stereotype; they say it pits them against other minorities and hides the discrimination they still face. Others—including the two Asian-American Regents who voted to end affirmative action—believe the only fair approach is to base admissions on academic qualifications. That also opens the door to more Asians.

So why do I strongly support affirmative action? My belief has been shaped by my role in higher education. And by my experience as a Chinese immigrant. I know firsthand that America can be a land of opportunity. When I came here, I was a penniless 21-year-old with a limited grasp of the language and culture. Yet I was permitted to accomplish a great deal. My research in heat transfer contributed to better nuclear reactor safety and space shuttle design. My former students are professors and researchers at some of America's best schools and business concerns.

But as I struggled to finish my education here, I also encountered the ugly realities of racial discrimination. This, too, is part of America's legacy and it is inextricably connected to the need for affirmative action.

When I first arrived in this country in 1956 as a graduate student, for example, I lived in Louisville, Kentucky. One day I got on a bus and saw that all the black people were in the back, the white people in the front. I didn't know where I belonged, so for a long time I stood near the driver. Finally, he told me to sit down in the front, and I did. I didn't take another bus ride for a whole year. I would walk an hour to avoid that.

I served as a teaching fellow at Louisville for a professor who refused to pronounce my name. He addressed me as "Chinaman." One day he directed me to adjust some valves in a large laboratory apparatus. Climbing a ladder, I lost my balance and instinctively grabbed a nearby steam pipe. It was scorchingly hot and produced a jolt of pain that nearly caused me to faint. Yet I did not scream. Instead, I stuffed my throbbing hand into my coat pocket and waited until the class ended. Then I ran to the hospital emergency room, where I was treated for a burn that had singed all the skin off my palm.

Outwardly, my response fit the stereotype of the model-minority Asian: I 10
said nothing and went about my business. But my silence had nothing to do with stoicism. I simply did not want to endure the humiliation of having the professor scold me in front of the class.

Of course, four decades later, there have been major civil rights advances in America. But serious racial divisions remain. That's why colleges and universities created affirmative admissions programs. The idea was to open the doors to promising minority students who lacked educational and social opportunities.

As Berkeley's chancellor, I have seen the promise of affirmative action come true. No racial or ethnic group constitutes a majority among our 21,000 undergraduates. And Berkeley students enter with higher grades and test scores than their predecessors. They graduate at the highest rate in our history.

I think that affirmative action should be a temporary measure, but the time has not yet come to eliminate it. Educational opportunities for inner-city minority students, for example, still contrast dramatically with those of affluent students in the suburbs, where many white families live.

And as a public institution, the university needs to look at broader societal needs, including greater leadership training of California's African-American and Hispanic population.

I try to explain this when, as occasionally happens, Asian-American or white 15
friends complain to me that their child, a straight-A student, didn't get into Berkeley because we give spaces to others. I also say that we use admission criteria other than test scores, grades, and ethnicity, including a genius for computers, musical talent, geographical diversity.

Besides, a straight-A average wouldn't guarantee admission to Berkeley even if there were no affirmative action. For a freshman class with 3,500 places, we get about 25,000 applicants. This year, 10,784 of them had a 4.0 high school record.

What's more, helping minority students may not be the most compelling reason for preserving affirmative action.

Every time I walk across campus, I am impressed by the vibrant spirit of this diverse community. In teeming Sproul Plaza, the dozens of student groups who set up tables represent every kind of social, political, ethnic, and religious interest. In the dorms, students from barrios, suburbs, farm towns, and the inner city come together.

When there are diverse students, staff, and faculty (among whom there are still too few minorities) everybody stands to gain.

Of course, interactions between students of different backgrounds can bring 20
misunderstanding. Some white students tell me they feel squeezed out by black and Latino students they believe are less deserving, as well as by over-achieving Asian-American students. Some African-American and Latino students confide they sometimes feel their professors and white classmates consider them academically inferior, a view that's slow to change even when they excel.

Still, the overall message I get time and again from students and recent graduates is that they have valued the chance to challenge stereotypes.

So I was stunned by the Regents' decision to end affirmative action admissions policies, which goes into effect by 1998. I even debated whether to resign.

In Chinese, however, the character for "crisis" is actually two characters: one stands for danger and the other for opportunity. And I took the Chinese approach. Noting that the Regents had reaffirmed their commitment to diversity when they discarded affirmative action, I decided to stay to try to make a difference.

Recently, I joined the superintendents of the major urban school districts of the San Francisco Bay area to announce a campaign: The Berkeley Pledge.

Under this program, Berkeley is deepening its support for disadvantaged 25
youth trying to qualify for admission. One way will be to provide educational expertise for teachers; another will be to create incentives for pupils at selected school "pipelines" that begin in kindergarten. We also are stepping up our recruitment of exceptional minority students.

America has come a long way since the days of Jim Crow segregation. It would be a tragedy if our nation's colleges and universities slipped backward now, denying access to talented but disadvantaged youth and eroding the diversity that helps to prepare leaders.

ETHOS IN VISUAL ARGUMENTS: CORPORATE IMAGE MAKING

Just as writers have to establish credibility to persuade people effectively, so do companies. Corporations have ethos, just like people do. They have a standing in the community. We often even talk about "corporate citizenship." All companies hope to establish and maintain a positive image. That's why most large companies have a public relations department. A lot of corporate ethos is established through customer service—how the company treats its clients—but many companies also have ad campaigns that are designed to build a positive image of the company in the mind of the public. In these ads, the company is selling its name and its image, not just its products. Because ads have limited space for their message, many rely on visual elements as well as text. Some of these visual elements are designed to persuade: pictures, logos, appealing typeface and layout, famous people, beautiful people. These visual arguments work much the same way as other arguments do. A company may reveal information about itself visually by showing employees doing good deeds or by representing employees as common folk who are just like everyone else. A company may build credibility by associating itself with a famous person or an important cause or movement, representing an image, person, or logo we normally associate with another organization. Or a company may portray scenes in its ads that are associated with values we share as members of a community: public health, environmental quality, care of children or the elderly, integrity, expertise, and so on. In many ways, companies present an image that challenges the view the public might hold of them.

As you read print ads, pay particular attention to the visual elements of the ad and consider these questions:

1. What company or organization is sponsoring the ad? What kind of work does this company do? What kind of products does it sell?
2. What do you know about each company? What, in your opinion, is the public image of the company? How did the ad affect your opinion about the company?
3. What information does the company reveal about itself in its ad? How does it portray its employees, customers, or corporate leaders?
4. What other people, organizations, causes, or movements does the company associate itself with? What values does the company transfer to itself through this association?
5. How does the company convey trust and credibility through other visual elements such as graphic design, layout, or typeface?
6. What message does the company seek to send in its ad?

CONSIDERING COLUMBINE: RESPONDING TO THE TRAGEDY

High school students do not normally find themselves in a position to speak out in national forums about controversial issues such as gun violence and control. But experiencing an event as momentous as the Columbine shootings conveys tremendous credibility on ordinary people.

The following readings are included to show how experience and status can provide people access to a much broader audience than they might otherwise have. The first selection is a speech given by Darrell Scott before a subcommittee of the House Judiciary Committee. Darrell Scott is the father of Rachel Scott, a victim of the Columbine shootings. In this speech, Scott used the credibility given to him as the father of one of the victims to appeal for the right to pray in public schools. In the second selection, Devon Adams writes about her experience as a survivor of the shooting and as a friend of both Rachel Scott and Dylan Klebold, one of the shooters, along with Eric Harris. Her experience provides her with the opportunity to write for *Newsweek,* an uncommon forum for a high school sophomore. She uses the power of her experience to argue that

Eric Harris and Dylan Klebold deserve to be remembered along with the others who died that day. She also argues for "safe alternatives to the firearms epidemic." The third selection is the speech that Charlton Heston gave at the annual NRA meeting held in Denver, Colorado, May 1, 1999—less than two weeks after the shooting. In this speech, NRA President Heston responds directly to criticisms directed at the NRA and the convention. Although the NRA scaled back its activities in Denver in response to the Columbine shootings, many believed the organization should have canceled its meetings. Many also thought the broad freedom to buy and possess guns supported by the NRA contributed to the shootings. As president of the NRA, Charlton Heston has credibility with members of his organization and with those sympathetic to its cause. Moreover, as a famous actor, Heston has ethos with many other people and groups. It's difficult for some to think of Charlton Heston without picturing him in one of his many film roles, such as Moses in Cecil B. DeMille's production of *The Ten Commandments* or as Judah Ben-Hur in the Biblical film epic *Ben Hur.* (Heston doesn't refer to his celebrity in his speech, but it is so well known—especially among his supporters—that he doesn't really need to.) The last selection contrasts with those that precede it because it presents excerpts from a panel discussion, and so is an example of a group, not just an individual, with credibility. It's important to note that each member of the panel is considered credible (and was asked to participate) for different reasons related to position or experience: Wayne LaPierre is the executive director of the NRA, Jack Valenti is president of the Motion Picture Association of America, Hillary Rosen is president of the Recording Industry Association of America, Doug Lowenstein is president of the Interactive Digital Software Association, Marshall Herskovitz is a TV and movie producer and director, and Jonah Green is a New York high-school student.

As you read each of these essays, consider the following questions:

1. What kind of status does each author have in the communities to which he or she belongs?
2. How does each author create ethos? How well does this created ethos conform to the author's status?
3. What is the effect on each author's ethos of writing from a first-person point of view and revealing personal information?
4. In what ways does each author try to identify himself or herself with readers?
5. How does each author try to convey knowledge, experience, honesty, fairness, reliability, and goodwill?
6. What is each author's experience of the Columbine shootings? In your opinion, do some of these experiences have more weight than others?

Speech to Congress after the Columbine Massacre

DARRELL SCOTT

WE ALL CONTAIN the seeds of kindness or the seeds of violence. The death 1
of my wonderful daughter, Rachel Joy Scott, and the deaths of that heroic teacher, and the other 11 children who died must not be in vain. Their blood cries out for answers. The first recorded act of violence was when Cain slew his brother Abel out in the field. The villain was not the club he used. Neither was it the NCA, the National Club Association. The true killer was Cain, and the reason for the murder could only be found in Cain's heart.

In the days that followed the Columbine tragedy, I was amazed at how quickly fingers began to be pointed at groups such as the NRA. I am not a member of the NRA. I am not a hunter. I do not even own a gun. I am not here to represent or defend the NRA because I don't believe that they are responsible for my daughter's death. Therefore I do not believe that they need to be defended. If I believed they had anything to do with Rachel's murder I would be their strongest opponent. I am here today to declare that Columbine was not just a tragedy—it was a spiritual event that should be forcing us to look at where the real blame lies! Much of the blame lies here in this room. Much of the blame lies behind the pointing fingers of the accusers themselves.

I wrote a poem just four nights ago that expresses my feelings best. This was written way before I knew I would be speaking here today.

> Your laws ignore our deepest needs
> Your words are empty air
> You've stripped away our heritage
> You've outlawed simple prayer.
> Now gunshots fill our classrooms
> And precious children die
> You seek for answers everywhere
> And ask the question "Why"
> You regulate restrictive laws
> Through legislative creed
> And yet you fail to understand,
> That God is what we need!

Men and women are three-part beings. We all consist of body, soul, and 5
spirit. When we refuse to acknowledge a third part of our makeup, we create a void that allows evil, prejudice, and hatred to rush in and wreak havoc. Spiritual influences were present within our educational systems for most of our nation's history. Many of our major colleges began as theological seminaries. This is a historical fact. What has happened to us as a nation?

We have refused to honor God, and in doing so, we open the doors to hatred and violence. And when something as terrible as Columbine's tragedy occurs politicians immediately look for a scapegoat such as the NRA. They immediately seek to pass more restrictive laws that continue to erode away our personal and private liberties.

We do not need more restrictive laws. Eric and Dylan would not have been stopped by metal detectors. No amount of gun laws can stop someone who spends months planning this type of massacre. The real villain lies within our own hearts. Political posturing and restrictive legislation are not the answers. The young people of our nation hold the key. There is a spiritual awakening taking place that will not be squelched! We do not need more religion. We do not need more gaudy television evangelists spewing out verbal religious garbage. We do not need more million-dollar church buildings built while people with basic needs are being ignored. We do need a change of heart and a humble acknowledgment that this nation was founded on the principle of simple trust in God!

As my son Craig lay under that table in the school library and saw his two friends murdered before his very eyes, he did not hesitate to pray in school. I defy any law or politician to deny him that right! I challenge every young person in America, and around the world, to realize that on April 20, 1999, at Columbine High School, prayer was brought back to our schools.

Do not let the many prayers offered by those students be in vain. Dare to move into the new millennium with a sacred disregard for legislation that violates your God-given right to communicate with him. To those of you who would point your finger at the NRA—I give to you a sincere challenge. Dare to examine your own heart before casting the first stone! My daughter's death will not be in vain! The young people of this country will not allow that to happen!

Mourn for the Killers, Too

DEVON ADAMS

THIS YEAR, I went back to school early. My junior year at Columbine High School officially begins this week. But last Friday, I was back in the building to show incoming freshmen around. The idea was basically to have fun—and we did. The serious part of the program was to let the freshmen know that there are people they can turn to when they have questions, or if they're in some kind of trouble. We finished last year at another school, but I've been inside Columbine several times since April, when Eric Harris and Dylan Klebold killed a teacher, 12 kids, and themselves. The library, where the worst bloodshed occurred, has been sealed off by a wall of lockers and replaced by a temporary library. By now, I've walked past the lockers so many times that I almost forget 1 what's behind them. It looks so normal, and I think that's healthy. If the new kids see us treating the area as normal, then they won't be spooked by it.

Columbine has been the biggest part of my life since I was an incoming freshman. I'm glad I have two more years here—in a way, I never want to leave. And I never want to forget the people who died, including Eric and Dylan. I think we should mourn all of them. Dylan was my friend, and I still don't understand why he did it. At first, I blamed myself: I could have been a better friend. But then I began to see that all of society was to blame. Eric and Dylan were constantly ridiculed by many kids. And it was too easy for them to obtain guns.

Not long after the shooting, I joined a new, bipartisan organization called SAFE Colorado; the acronym stands for Sane Alternatives to the Firearms Epidemic. Our goal is to obtain reasonable gun legislation. We need to find compromises. Some people say background checks on gun purchasers should be completed within 24 hours. Others say five days. I think there's a happy medium: three days. Finding out if someone is dangerous takes more than 24 hours but less than five days.

Littleton is not the Wild West. It's more like a typical American suburb. I know that some of my friends' parents have handguns in the house, though I have never seen them because they are locked up. I don't want to outlaw all guns. I can even see someone having a handgun in the home for protection. But we need restrictions on automatic guns with a dozen or more bullets in their clips. The only purpose for that kind of gun is to kill lots of people quickly. I also think guns should be licensed, just like cars. And the minimum age for gun purchasers should be raised from 18 to 21—the drinking age. If you're not responsible enough to drink alcohol, you're not responsible enough to buy a gun.

5 Last July, a group of us from SAFE went to Washington, D.C., to lobby for gun legislation, including an end to unregulated sales at gun shows. We talked to the president and the vice president, but half of Colorado's congressional delegation turned a deaf ear to us. My lobbying experience has left me disappointed in politicians. They just don't get it—that 13 young people die every day in this country from gun violence. And they don't seem to care that 70 to 80 percent of Americans support reasonable gun legislation.

I'm also saddened by a lot of the news coverage of Columbine. Some reporters respected our grief, but many were insulting. As one TV reporter primped for the camera, he was heard to say: "Do I look devastated enough?" And even people who hated Dylan and Eric were appalled by the magazine cover that called them "The Monsters Next Door." They were our friends, too. They were just kids. But someone had to make monsters out of them.

After the shootings, it was reported that Eric and Dylan wanted to kill nonwhite students and athletes, but many of their victims didn't fall into either category. One of them was a dear friend of mine, Rachel Scott. She was no athlete, she was a theater person. Rachel was beautiful, inside and out. She was a hard worker with a great sense of humor. After I got out of the school on the day of the shooting, I watched the news coverage on TV, trying to find out who had been shot. I saw videotape of students running past a body on the ground. All you could see clearly was the victim's hair, but that was enough. I had helped to cut Rachel's hair, so I knew she was the one lying there. The sad thing is that Rachel would have been a perfect friend for Eric and Dylan, if only they had known her well, because she would have accepted them. I still can't believe they meant to kill her.

And now the shooting in Los Angeles. It was horrible enough that, at the age of 17, I had to run for my life from my own high school. It is even more hideous when guns are turned against preschoolers. This must stop, and it must stop now.

Address to Denver, Colorado, May 1 NRA Meeting

CHARLTON HESTON

THANK YOU. Thank you very much. Good morning. I am very happy to 1
welcome you to this abbreviated annual gathering of the National Rifle Association. Thank you all for coming and thank you for supporting your organization. I also want to applaud your courage in coming here today. Of course, you have a right to be here. As you know, we've canceled the festivities and the fellowship we normally enjoy at our annual gatherings. This decision has perplexed a few and inconvenienced thousands. As your president, I apologize for that. But it is fitting and proper that we should do this. Because NRA members are, above all, Americans. That means that whatever our differences, we are respectful of one another, and we stand united, especially in adversity.

I have a message from the mayor, Mr. Wellington Webb, the mayor of Denver. He sent me this. It says, "Don't come here. We don't want you here."

I say to the mayor, well, my reply to the mayor is, "I volunteered for the war they wanted me to attend when I was 18 years old. Since then, I have run small errands for my country, from Nigeria to Vietnam." I know many of you here in this room could say the same thing. But the mayor said, "Don't come."

I'm sorry for that. I'm sorry for the newspaper ads saying the same thing, "Don't come here." This is our country. As Americans, we are free to travel wherever we want, in our broad land.

They say we'll create a media distraction. But we were preceded here by 5
hundreds of intrusive news crews. They say we'll create political distraction. But it's not been the NRA pressing for political advantage, calling press conferences to promote vast new packages of legislation. Still they say, "Don't come here."

I guess what saddens me the most is how that suggests complicity. It implies that you and I and 80 million honest gun owners are somehow to blame. That we don't care as much as they do. Or that we don't deserve to be as shocked and horrified as every other soul in America mourning for the people of Littleton.

Don't come here. That's offensive. It's also absurd. Because we live here. There are thousands of NRA members in Denver and tens upon tens of thousands in the state of Colorado. NRA members labor in Denver's factories, they populate Denver's faculties, run Denver corporations, play on Colorado's sports teams, work in media and across the front range, parent and teach and coach Denver's children, attend Denver's churches, and proudly represent Denver in uniform on the world's oceans and in the skies over Kosovo at this very moment. NRA members are in City Hall, Fort Carson, NORAD, the Air Force Academy, and the Olympic training center. And yes, NRA members are surely among the police and fire and SWAT team heroes who risked their lives to rescue the students at Columbine.

Don't come here? We're already here! This community is our home. Every community in America is our home. We are a 128-year-old fixture of mainstream America. The Second Amendment ethic of lawful, responsible firearm ownership spans the broadest cross section of American life imaginable. So, we have the same rights as all other citizens to be here. To help shoulder the grief, to share our sorrow, and to offer our respectful, reassured voice to the national discourse that has erupted around this tragedy.

One more thing: Our words and our behavior will be scrutinized more than ever this morning. Those who are hostile towards us will lie in wait to seize on a sound bite out of context, ever searching for an embarrassing moment to ridicule us. So, let us be mindful. The eyes of the nation are on us today . . .

I see our country teetering on the edge of an abyss. At its bottom brews the 10
simmering bile of deep, dark hatred. Hatred that is dividing our country. Politically. Racially. Geographically. In every way, whether it's political vendettas, sports brawls, corporate takeovers, high school gangs and cliques.

The American competitive ethic has changed from "let's beat the other guy" to "let's destroy the other guy."

Too many, too many are too willing to stigmatize and demonize others for political advantage, for money, or for ratings. The vilification is savage.

This week, Representative John Conyers slandered 3 million Americans when he called the NRA "merchants of death" on national television, as our first lady nodded in agreement. A hideous editorial cartoon by Mike Peters ran nationally. It showed children's dead bodies sprawled out to spell NRA.

The countless requests we've received in the last week or so for media appearances are in fact summons to public floggings, where those who hate firearms will predictably don the white hat and give us the black one. This harvest of hatred is then sold as news, as entertainment, as government policy. Such hateful, divisive forces are leading us to one awful end: America's own form of Balkanization. A weakened country of rabid factions each less free, united only by hatred of one another.

15 In the past 10 days we've seen these brutal blows attempting to fracture America into two such camps. One camp would be the majority, people who believe our founders guaranteed our security with the right to defend ourselves, our families, and our country.

The other camp would be a large minority of people who believe that we will buy security if we will just surrender these freedoms. This debate would be accurately described as those who believe in the Second Amendment versus those who don't.

But instead it is spun as those who believe in murder versus those who don't. The struggle between the reckless and the prudent. Between the dim-witteds and the progressives. Between inferior citizens who don't know and elitists who know what's good for society.

But we're not the rustic reckless radicals they wish for.

No, the NRA spans the broadest range of American demography imaginable. We defy stereotype, except for love of country. Look in your mirror, your shopping mall, your church, or grocery store. That's us. Millions of ordinary people and extraordinary people. War heroes, sports idols, several U.S. presidents, and yes, movie stars.

20 But the screeching hyperbole leveled at gun owners has made these two camps so wary of each other, so hostile, and confrontational and disrespectful. On both sides.

It is forgotten that we are first, Americans. I am asking all of us on both sides to take one step back from the edge. Then another step. And another. However many it takes to get back to that place where we are all Americans. Different, imperfect, diverse, but one nation, indivisible.

This cycle of tragedy-driven hatred must stop. Because so much more connects us than that which divides us. And because tragedy has been and will always be with us. Somewhere right now evil people are planning evil things. All of us will do everything meaningful, everything we can do to prevent it. But each horrible act can't become an axe for opportunists to cleave the very bill of rights that binds us.

America must stop this predictable pattern of reaction; when an isolated terrible event occurs, our phones ring demanding that the NRA explain the inexplicable. Why us? Because their story needs a villain. They want us to play the heavy in their drama of packaged grief. To provide riveting programming to run between commercials for cars and cat food.

The dirty secret of this day and age is that political gain and media ratings all too often bloom on fresh graves.

25 I remember a better day when no one dared politicize or profiteer on drama. We kept a respectful distance then, as the NRA has tried to do now. Simply being silent is so often the right thing to do. But today carnage comes with a catchy title, splashy graphics, regular promos, and a reactionary passage of legislation. Reporters perch like vultures on the balconies of hotels for a hundred miles

around. Cameras jockey for shocking angles, as news anchors race to drench their microphones with the tears of victims.

Injury, shock, grief, and despair shouldn't be brought to you by sponsors. That's pornography. It trivializes the tragedy it abuses. It abuses vulnerable people, and maybe worst of all, it makes the unspeakable seem commonplace.

We are often cast as the villain. That is not our role in American society, and we will not be forced to play it.

Our mission is to remain, as our [NRA] vice president said, a steady beacon of strength and support for the Second Amendment, even if it has no other friend on this planet. We cannot—we must not—let tragedy lay waste to the most rare and hard-won human right in history. A nation cannot gain safety by giving up freedom. This truth is older than our country.

"Those who would give up essential liberty to purchase a little temporary safety, deserve neither liberty nor safety." Ben Franklin said that.

Now, if you like your freedoms of speech, and of religion, freedom from 30
search and seizure, freedom of the press, and of privacy and to assemble, and to redress grievances, then you better give them the eternal bodyguard called the Second Amendment.

The individual right to bear arms is freedom's insurance policy. Not just for your children, but for infinite generations to come. That is its singular sacred beauty, and why we preserve it so fiercely. No, it's not a right without rational restrictions. And it's not for everyone. Only the law-abiding majority of society deserves the Second Amendment.

Abuse it once, and lose it forever. That's the law.

But, curiously, the NRA is far more eager to prosecute gun abusers than are those who oppose gun ownership altogether. As if the tool could be more evil than the evil doers. I don't understand that.

The NRA also spends more and works harder than anybody in America to promote safe, responsible use of firearms. From 38,000 certified instructors, training millions of police, hunters, women, and youth, to 500 law enforcement agencies promoting our Eddie Eagle gun safety program Wayne told you about, distributed to 11 million kids, 11 million and counting.

But our essential reason for being is this: as long as there is a Second Amend- 35
ment, evil can never conquer us. Tyranny in any form can never find footing within a society of law-abiding, armed, ethical people. The majesty of the Second Amendment that our founders so divinely created and crafted to your birthright guarantees that no government despot, no renegade faction of armed forces, no roving gangs of criminals, no breakdown of law and order, no massive anarchy, no force of evil or crime, or oppression from within or from without, can ever rob you of the liberties that define your Americanism.

So, when they ask you, "Well, indeed, you would bear arms against government tyranny?" The answer is: "No. That could never happen precisely because we have the Second Amendment."

Let me be absolutely clear. The Founding Fathers guaranteed this freedom because they knew no tyranny could ever arise among a people endowed with the right to keep and bear arms. That's why you and your descendants need never fear fascism, refugee camps, brainwashing, ethnic cleansing, or especially submission to the wanton will of criminals. The Second Amendment: there could be no more precious inheritance.

Now, that's what the NRA preserves. Now, if you disagree, that's your right. I respect that. But we will not relinquish it or be silenced about it, or be told, "Do not come here. You are unwelcome in your own land."

Let us go from this place, from this huge room, renewed in spirit and dedicated against hatred. We have work to do, hearts to heal, evil to defeat, and a country to unite. We may have differences, and we will again suffer tragedy almost beyond description. But when the sun sets on Denver tonight, and forever more, let it always set on We, the People. Secure in our land of the free and home of the brave. I for one plan to do my part, thank you.

Moving Beyond the Blame Game

A MONTH AFTER the Littleton Tragedy, the conversation continues—in schools, in homes, and at this week's White House conference on youth violence. The theories of why Eric Harris and Dylan Klebold went on their rampage have given way to a broader discussion of the deeper sources of the problem and where to go from here. Obviously, there are no quick fixes; everything from more values education to better supervision of antidepressant medication has been introduced into the debate. But Americans have singled out a few issues for special attention. According to the new *Newsweek* Poll, about half of all Americans want to see the movie industry, the TV industry, computer-game makers, Internet services, and gun manufacturers and the NRA make major policy changes to help reduce teen violence. Slightly fewer want the music industry to change fundamentally. Younger Americans are less concerned about media violence than their elders are. On guns, there's a racial gap, with 72 percent of nonwhites and 41 percent of whites seeking major changes. 1

To further the conversation, *Newsweek* assembled a panel last week to explore the complexities. One after another, the people who actually make heavily violent movies, records, and games declined to participate, just as they did when the White House called. This could be a sign that they are feeling the heat—or perhaps just avoiding it. Those who did take part in the *Newsweek* forum include Wayne LaPierre, executive director of the NRA; Jack Valenti, president of the Motion Picture Association of America; Hillary Rosen, president of the Recording

Industry Association of America; Doug Lowenstein, president of the Interactive Digital Software Association; Marshall Herskovitz, TV and movie producer and director; and Jonah Green, a 15-year-old New York high-school student. *Newsweek's* Jonathan Alter moderated the discussion. Excerpts:

Alter: **Youth shall be served, so I want to start with Jonah. You seem to think that there's a lot of scapegoating going on.**

Green: Well, I have to say that America is very confused and scared. There's no one simple answer to teen violence. It's understandable because we're seeking answers, but right now people are focusing too much on putting the blame somewhere. We should be focusing on solutions.

OK, Wayne, wouldn't making guns less easily accessible be at least a partial solution? 5

LaPierre: You can't talk about easy access to guns by people we all don't want to have guns without talking about the shameful secret that really hasn't been reported. Which is the complete collapse of enforcement of the existing firearm laws on the books by the Department of Justice the last six years. The proof is in the statistics. Six thousand kids illegally brought guns to school the last two years. We've only had 13 [federal] prosecutions. And only 11 prosecutions for illegally transferring guns to juveniles.

Do you think that if an 11-year-old brings his father's gun to school, the child should be prosecuted?

LaPierre: Yes, I do. They did not prosecute Kip Kinkel out in Oregon after he was blowing up cats, threatening people. He walks into school with a gun. They do nothing to him except send him home. And he comes back to the school two days later with a gun and shoots those kids. I mean, the fact is we're either serious about this situation or we're not.

How about Clinton's gun-limit proposal? Why does anyone need to buy more than one gun a month?

LaPierre: That's just a sound bite. 10

Doug, some of your industry's games are a long way from Pac-Man, right?

Lowenstein: Oh, absolutely. There are some very violent videogames, although they represent only a small fraction of the market. There's a critical parental role here: It costs over $1,000 to own a computer. A hundred dollars plus to own a videogame machine. There's a very conscious choice involved in bringing this kind of entertainment into your home. And the parent needs the tools to make an informed choice.

You don't think it desensitizes kids to violence to play games over and over?

Green: Personally, I think some kids use videogames, especially the violent ones, just as some violent movies, as a vent. You know, they like to live vicariously and vent their anger through that. And Doug was right that we can't really map out everything a kid has and how they use it and what makes them able to kill somebody.

Hillary, MTV is doing a stop-the-violence campaign, but then 15
they air—and you supported—something like Eminem's song about stuffing a woman into the trunk of a car. Don't you see a contradiction here?

Rosen: Young people are so much smarter than anybody—the media or politicians or most adults, in fact—may give them credit for being. They understand the difference between fantasy and reality, and that's why giving them concrete steps to take when they face personal conflict or when they face a gang conflict or school bullying, or those sorts of things, are much more productive means for giving them tools to be nonviolent in their lives than taking away their culture.

Do you think that a music-rating system just makes it forbidden fruit and makes kids want to play or see it more?

Rosen: We've done surveys that show it doesn't encourage young people to buy artists. People buy music that they connect with, that they like, that has a good beat, that sounds good. The label is there for parents and for retailers.

Green: I actually think artists like Eminem are very sarcastic. It is more playful than hard core. I find rap being a little more human than it used to be. Gangsta rap isn't as big anymore, and now sampling is.

Rosen: It's true. 20

Green: Edgar Allan Poe talked about death—he was dark, but he was a celebrated poet. It's about having an edge, a hook. That can be violence.

You don't have any problem with Marilyn Manson naming himself after a serial killer?

Green: I think it's in bad taste. It was just stupid and controversial.

Hillary, how about you?

Rosen: Well, I agree with Jonah that it's bad taste, but that's the point. 25
Marilyn Manson is an act. It's an act that's sort of designed to create a persona of empowering the geek. Unfortunately, Charles Manson was a real person. People don't have to make up horrible tragedies in this world.

Green: Entertainment and the media were never really for getting across good, moral messages like "I love my school and my mother." People rarely feel they need to express bland feelings like that.

Rosen: But it is on some level, because Britney Spears sells more records than Marilyn Manson. You know there's been a resurgence of young pop music. B* Witched and the Dixie Chicks and Britney Spears and 'N Sync. I mean, these artists are selling a hell of a lot more records than Marilyn Manson.

Do you think that kids have kind of gotten that message and are less interested in gratuitously violent lyrics than they used to be? Because they've seen so much death, either in their own neighborhoods or on TV?

Rosen: Well, there's no question that what used to be known as gangsta rap is definitely played out. Rap is much more light-hearted. It's about getting money and getting women. The music has evolved.

Why is that?

Rosen: Well, this might be controversial, but I'm actually one of those people who believes that young people are a lot more positive about the world today than most of the media is giving them credit for in the last couple of weeks. Surveys have shown that young people are more optimistic about their future, they're more positive, they're more connected to their parents than they have been in generations. And these all speak to really good, positive things.

Marshall, what do you think are some of Hollywood's responsibilities in this area?

Herskovitz: I think we now have virtual reality available to people that is nihilistic, anarchic, and violent. And it is possible for a person to so completely live in that virtual reality that they come to confuse it for the real world around them.

But you know from firsthand experience that violence sells.

Herskovitz: "Legends of the Fall" was a very violent movie. I think violence has a potentially strong part in any artistic venture. It's not something I would ever want to talk about legislatively. I would like to talk about it in terms of individual responsibility, yes.

So where should the thoughtful consumer of all of this draw the line between gratuitous violence and necessary violence for dramatic purposes?

Herskovitz: Oh, I think that's the point. The thoughtful consumers feel it in their gut. I think the problem in this culture is that thoughtful consumers are not particularly influencing their children.

But isn't it a little too easy to just say it's all the parent's responsibility?

Valenti: Well, I don't think the movie industry can stand *in loco parentis.* Over 30 years ago I put in place a movie-rating system, voluntary, which gives advanced cautionary warnings to parents so that parents can make their own judgments about what movies they want their children to see.

I think what a lot of parents wonder is, why is it that NC-17 is not applied to gratuitously violent movies? 40

Valenti: Well, it's because the definition of "gratuitous" is shrouded in subjectivity. There is no way to write down rules. I think Marshall can tell you that creative people can shoot a violent scene a hundred different ways. Sex and language are different, because there are few ways that you can couple on the screen that—there's only a few. And language is language. It's there or it isn't. But violence is far more difficult to pin down. It's like picking up mercury with a fork.

A movie director told me recently that he went to see "The Matrix," and there was a 5-year-old at the film with his mother. Isn't that a form of child abuse?

Valenti: If a parent says he wants his 5-year-old to be with him, who is to tell this parent he can't do it? Who is to tell him?

But if it was NC-17, that 5-year-old wouldn't be allowed to go, right?

Valenti: Well, that's right. 45

So why allow them in when it's R?

Valenti: Because the way our system is defined, we think there's a dividing line.

When parents aren't doing their job properly, where does the responsibility of everybody else begin?

LaPierre: I was talking with John Douglas, the FBI's criminal profiler. And he said, "Wayne, never underestimate the fact that there are some people that are just evil." And that includes young people. We go searching for solutions, and yet some people are just plain bad apples. You look around the country—the cities that are making progress across the board are really combining prevention and working with young people when you get the first warning signs. And making sure they find mentors. Making sure they're put into programs. And they're combining that with very, very tough enforcement of things like the gun laws.

Herskovitz: I have a fear that modern society, and in particular television, may 50
be beyond the ability of parents to really control. I think movies are different, because the kid has to go out of the house and go there. TV is a particular problem because it's in the house.

But Marshall, maybe that's because the values that are being propagated by the media, broadly speaking, are so much more powerful that parents can't compete as easily as they used to.

Herskovitz: I don't believe that. I accept a lot of responsibility for the picture the media create of the world. But I don't think there's a conflict between that and the responsibility of parents to simply sit down and talk with their children. Most violent crime is committed by males. Young men are not being educated in the values of masculinity by their fathers.

So why then let all of these boys see scenes of gratuitous violence that don't convey human values to them?

Valenti: There are only three places where a child learns what Marshall was talking about, values. You learn them in the church. You learn them in school. And you learn them at home. And if you don't have these moral shields built in you by the time you're 10 or 12 years old, forget it.

I'm not sure that people in Hollywood are thinking, "Is what we do part of the solution on this values question, or does it just contribute to the problem?"

Herskovitz: The answer is the people who aren't contributing to the problem are thinking about it a lot, and the people who are contributing to the problem are not thinking about it.

Valenti: Well, how does *Newsweek* then condone its putting on the cover of your magazine Monica Lewinsky? What kind of a value system does that convey?

Well, that's a separate discussion.

Valenti: Oh, I don't think it is.

Well, let me say this. We very explicitly did not put Dylan Klebold and Eric Harris on our cover the first week. We're wrong in these judgments sometimes, but we do at least try to think about the consequences of what we put out there, instead of just saying it's up to the parents. That seems to me a cop-out.

Lowenstein: What you're looking for is an elimination of any problematic content.

No, I'm not. I'm looking for a sense of shame and a sense of responsibility. I'm wondering where it is in all of the industries that we have represented here today.

Hersovitz: Most people, especially in electronic journalism, don't think at all about this, and their role is incredibly destructive, just like most people in the movie and television business don't think at all about this. And their role is destructive. I think there's a great need for shame. Most people I know and speak to are very ashamed, but unfortunately they're not the people who make violent movies.

Practicing the Principles: Activities

RECALLING MOMENTS OF TRUST

Freewrite for a few minutes about a time when you did something because you trusted someone. For example, have you ever joined an organization because someone suggested it to you? Have you ever taken a particular class because someone you respected recommended it to you? What was the person you trusted like? What position did he or she hold in your community? What qualities did he or she possess that inspired trust? These are the qualities that a writer needs to convey. As a class, select some examples of essays, articles, or ads that you find particularly persuasive. What kind of qualities does the author convey? What techniques does the author use?

FINDING CREATED ETHOS IN LETTERS TO THE EDITOR

One of the best ways to analyze how writers try to establish credibility is by looking at short arguments by people who are not well known in their community or who lack official status. Short arguments are especially useful for this type of analysis because a writer must establish credibility rather quickly. And people who lack status must rely heavily on constructing credibility in developing their arguments. Letters to the editor of a newspaper provide especially good examples for analysis. The writers of such letters have a range of abilities, knowledge, and experience and show a surprising variety of approaches to establishing ethos.

As a class, collect letters to the editor from a campus or local newspaper. Or if you have access to papers from your hometown, you might select letters that focus on an important issue facing your home community. Gather letters from several local sources if you can (campus papers, local weeklies and dailies). For this assignment, stay away from large regional or national papers such as the *Washington Post, Los Angeles Times,* or *New York Times.* Collect letters from several editions of the paper so that you can track the evolution of an issue over time. This also allows you to follow a conversation, as writers respond and react to each other. You may also want to review the letters to the editor of the *San Diego Union-Tribune* regarding "Monty Montezuma," the San Diego State University mascot (found in Chapter 1). Bring the letters you have found to class for discussion and then write a brief analysis of the letters or make an oral report on the issue, using the letters as examples.

As you read letters to the editor, consider the following questions:

1. What status does each writer have in the community? What information does each writer share to reveal this status?

2. How does each writer try to create an authoritative voice? What other people does the writer quote or refer to? What kind of authority do these other sources lend to the writer? Do some letters sound more "expert" than others?
3. How does each writer try to establish a relationship with readers? What is the point of view? How does the writer try to identify with readers? Do some sound more like "representative members of the community" than others?
4. Which writers sound more like they know what they are talking about? Which are you more ready to believe and why?

As a variation of this assignment, select some issues that are covered by local writers in a local or campus paper. Check articles, editorials, and letters to the editor. Then look for information about these same issues in a regional or national newspaper. Collect these articles as a class and then compare how these authors establish credibility. Is there a difference between the ethos for a writer for a local paper and a national paper? To what extent does the publication itself convey some authority on the writer?

ETHOS IN EVERYDAY OBJECTS

Return to the pile of artifacts that you assembled for the activity at the end of Chapter 1: the print ads, campaign literature, junk mail, T-shirts, bumper stickers, coffee mugs, product packaging, letters to the editor, music lyrics or videos, and so on. You may also want to review the discussion of the Nike logo and corporate images in Chapter 1. As you examine these artifacts, try to identify examples of ethos. For instance, many of these objects are decorated with corporate images. What values are associated with these images? How does a company try to inspire trust in its message and its product, even on a coffee cup or T-shirt? Many consumer products also associate themselves with famous people. What standing do these figures have in the community? What kind of trust do they inspire? Why do some companies market their products by inviting you to identify yourself with a well-known person? How is that trust transferred to the product itself? How do consumers feel about these people? How do they feel about the products because these products are associate with these people? To what extent do feelings of trust depend on your knowledge of the community that the artifacts you've collected belong to?

ETHOS ONLINE

Websites provide a wonderful opportunity for both ordinary people and official organizations to provide information about themselves. How do these websites allow organizations to build their image? How do the visual elements of the website convey trust and credibility? For example, consider the websites for these well-known companies:

Philip Morris, <www.philipmorrisusa.com>
Phillips 66, <www.phillips66.com>
Ford, <www.ford.com>
Texaco, <www.texaco.com>
American Airlines, <www.aa.com>
DuPont, <www.dupont.com>
Pfizer, <www.pfizer.com>

If you have the expertise, construct a website for a hypothetical organization in such a way that you convey a sense of trust, responsibility, knowledge, and expertise. Keep in mind the effect you wish to have on your audience with each element of the website.

Applying the Principles: Analytical Project

As you read the following essays, apply what you've learned in this chapter to identify each author's main idea. Analyze and evaluate how each author uses ethos to be persuasive. The first essay, "The Big Bash," was written by Sylvia Cary, a licensed therapist in Southern California, for *Men's Fitness.* The second essay, "Reflections from a Life Behind Bars," is by James Gilligan, a clinical psychiatrist and the former director of mental health for the prison system in Massachusetts. This essay was first published in *The Chronicle of Higher Education,* a periodical for college teachers and administrators.

The Big Bash

SYLVIA CARY

IN A P.C. WORLD, why are men the butt of everybody's jokes? 1

Two guys go into a store to buy a brain. The male brain costs $100 and the female brain costs $25. When they ask the store clerk why the female brain costs so much less, he tells them, "Because the female brain has been used."

—JOKE TOLD BY ACTRESS SHARON STONE DURING A MARCH 1998 TV TRIBUTE TO BETTY FORD

Think that's funny? The audience certainly did. But can you imagine if the joke had been reversed—as it might have been, say, 50 years ago? We've come a long way—so long that the pendulum is swinging in the other direction, and now it's aimed directly at you.

5 Thirty years after the women's movement began, there's really only one politically correct target group left: guys. Particularly rich white guys, but guys in general will do. Examples of male-bashing are all around us—in books and movies that denigrate men as ridiculously immature and entirely ruled by their little heads, in sitcoms that make husbands the butt of every family joke, in TV commercials that disparage male pride (if they're lost, it's because he's too stubborn to ask for directions) or portray them as unable to care for themselves (the only reason the macho guy recovers from his really tough headache is because she cajoles him into taking a pill). Meanwhile, the phrase "testosterone poisoning" has come to symbolize everything supposedly wrong with behaving like a typical male.

Now, it's not that there isn't any truth to these portrayals, or that the jokes weren't kind of funny the first time we heard them. But I have to admit, if I were a guy, I would be pretty steamed by now.

What's strange about all this is that men aren't upset, says Warren Farrell, PhD, the San Diego-based author of *Why Men Are the Way They Are and The Myth of Male Power.* Most have just come to accept male-bashing as a part of life. "The war between the sexes is continuing, but now only one side is showing up," he says. Many men even see a little bashing as their due, adds Gordon Bruning, PhD, an admitting psychologist at the Betty Ford Center in Rancho Mirage, California. "Men still have guilt from years of discrimination against women, so it's like the men are saying to themselves, OK, ladies, we'll let you get a few licks in."

Of course, a lot of media male-bashing happens just because it's easy—who else are you going to make jokes about in the '90s? Make fun of women, minorities, religious or ethnic groups anywhere outside the Howard Stern show and you'll get hisses, not laughs.

But it's also true that some women really are angry at men, Farrell says. This is in part, he argues, because in the decades since World War II, women have had to abandon their "primary fantasy" that men will provide them with lifelong economic security. (Although feminists have argued with this idea, there's no question that the "knight in shining armor" myth still has a strong hold on our culture—just look at movies like *Pretty Woman,* or even *As Good as It Gets.*) Instead, many women have found themselves divorced, often facing the double burden of child care and financial responsibilities that used to be divided among couples.

10 At the same time, women who fought hard for their independence are reluctant to admit they still like the idea of a rescuer in the wings, comments Stephen Johnson, PhD, founder and director of The Men's Center of Los Angeles. It may be easier to believe that men are useless than to admit a need for them, particularly when that need is not easily fulfilled. "I have a hunch that at the heart of it, women are lonely and longing for good relationships with men,

but they're afraid such relationships are few and far between," Johnson says. "On top of that is their anger: 'If I can't have the kind of man that I want, I'm going to throw stones at the image.'"

If you're unaware of that anger, maybe it's because what you hear is just the tip of the iceberg, says Irving Zaroff, a licensed attorney, businessman, and marriage and family counselor. "When I was studying to become a counselor, I interned at a counseling center with about 30 women," he recalls. "The only other male there was the director. When I'd go into staff meetings, I had a feeling that certain issues were being skirted." After a while, Zaroff learned that it wasn't his imagination. One female staff member told him that in the past there had been lots of male-bashing at these meetings, but that his presence had curbed it. He was left to wonder what had been said behind closed doors.

What if someone close to you—even someone you care about—says something you consider a form of male-bashing? It could be a joke about men in general, or maybe something that hits closer to home—a statement that says you're being a guy, and that there's something wrong with that.

The first thing to consider is whether or not it comes out of truth. Maybe you are being a jerk. Maybe you should have been more considerate, put the toilet seat down, done a little less talking and a little more listening. After all, you may not be wrong all the time, but you certainly aren't right all the time, either.

But if you hear a woman putting down you in particular or guys in general just for being men, don't just accept it—speak up. Tell her it bothers you, and try to find out where all that hostility is coming from.

In most cases, simply talking about it will dissipate her anger, anyway— 15
especially since the main complaint many women have about the men in their lives is that they won't communicate. Deep down, most women really want to be educated about what men think and feel, Zaroff says. They're hungry for it. Otherwise, a woman may assume that the man doesn't feel much at all.

"When you don't do anything about male-bashing, you encourage it," says Zaroff. "When the bashing hits closer to home and comes from somebody I deeply care about, then my tendency is to be pretty direct. I try to describe how I feel when they make a crack I don't like."

According to Farrell, when responding to a male-bashing joke or comment, it's important to keep things light. "Always maintain a tone of respect in your voice, and make it clear that you're not taking it too seriously," he says. "Usually the point is so powerful that you don't need to say it with a negative tone."

Most people will get the point quickly if you simply reverse the roles involved, Farrell adds. "If they say some version of 'All men are stupid,' then say, 'How would you feel if somebody said all women are stupid?' Or, to put it in racial terms, 'How would you feel if someone made a similar remark about blacks? Would you still consider it to be just a joke?' What's helpful about this is that it allows people to see things in a way they haven't before."

Trading information and insights about male-bashing can really help, so start educating yourself and your female friends about the issue. It would be nice if there were an influential men's organization to help you do this—but the nascent men's movement never really got off the ground after it was depicted in the media as a bunch of hairy idiots drumming in the woods. (Talk about a bashing!) Recovery from that period is still going on, Johnson says. But individual men and women actually talking to one another will make for a good start.

Reflections from a Life Behind Bars: Build Colleges, Not Prisons

JAMES GILLIGAN

1 NEITHER words nor pictures, no matter how vivid, can do more than give a faint suggestion of the horror, brutalization, and degradation of the prisons of this country. I speak from extensive personal knowledge of this subject, for I have spent 25 years of my professional life behind bars—not as an inmate, but as a prison psychiatrist.

I am a physician, and I see violence (whether it is legal or illegal, homicidal or suicidal, intentional or careless) as a public-health problem—indeed, the most important and dangerous threat to public health in our time. Because it affects mostly the young, violence kills more people under the age of 65 in this country than do cancer and heart disease, the two illnesses that are often (and mistakenly) thought to be the most significant causes of death.

So I cannot emphasize too strongly how seriously I take the problem of violence. Far from being tolerant or permissive toward it, I am far more strongly opposed to violence in all its forms and in all its legal statuses, and far less tolerant and permissive toward it than are those who believe that our salvation lies in building more and more punitive (i.e., violent) prisons.

There is a widespread misimpression that punishment deters violence—in other words, that punishment is one means of preventing violence. However, the overwhelming weight of empirical evidence suggests that exactly the opposite is true—namely, that punishment, far from inhibiting or preventing violence, is the most potent stimulus or cause of violence that we have yet discovered. Several different lines of evidence, from several different populations and stages of the life cycle, converge in supporting that conclusion.

5 For example, child-rearing is such an inherently and inescapably complicated subject that there are relatively few findings from the past several decades of research on it that are so clear, so unmistakable, and so consistently replicated that they are virtually universally agreed on. But among those few is this: The more severely punished children are, the more violent they become, both as chil-

dren and as adults. This is especially true of violent punishments. For example, children who are subjected to corporal discipline are significantly more likely to subject other people to physical punishments (i.e., inflict violence on them), both while they are still children and after they have reached adulthood. That is hardly surprising, of course, for corporal discipline is simply another name for physical violence; it would be called assault and battery if committed against an adult.

In fact, even with respect to nonviolent behavior, such as bed-wetting or excessive dependency or passivity ("laziness"), punishment has a counterproductive effect; that is, the more severely children are punished for a given behavior, the more strongly they persist in repeating it. To put it the other way around: If we want to produce as violent a generation of children and adults as possible, the most effective thing we can do is to punish our children and adults as severely as possible.

While the research just referred to can be found in the literature on child development and child abuse, there is no reason to think that the psychology of adults differs in this respect from that of children, and every reason to think that it is the same. In fact, I have been able to confirm those findings on children from my own clinical experience of over 25 years with violent adult criminals and the violent mentally ill. The degree of violent child abuse to which this population had been subjected was so extreme that the only way to summarize it is to say that the most violent people in our society—those who murder others—are disproportionately the survivors of attempted murder themselves, or of the completed murders of their closest relatives, siblings, or parents.

Thus, if punishment could prevent violence, these men would never have become violent in the first place, for they were already punished, even before they became violent, as severely as it is possible to punish a person without actually killing him. Many were beaten nearly to death as children, so when they became adults, they did beat someone else to death.

Fortunately, we not only know what stimulates violence (punishment, humiliation), we also know what prevents violence, both in society in general and in the criminal-justice and prison systems in particular. Unfortunately, we Americans have been dismantling the conditions that do prevent violence as rapidly as we could over the past 25 years, with the entirely predictable result that the levels of violent crimes, such as murder, have repeatedly reached the highest recorded levels in our history. For example, for the last quarter of a century our murder rates have been twice as high as they were 40 years ago, and five to ten times as high as they currently are in any other democracy and developed economy on earth.

What are the conditions that prevent violence? Among general social condi- 10
tions, there are several, but space permits mentioning only the most powerful one: a relatively classless society, with an equitable social and economic system in which there are minimal discrepancies in wealth, income, and standard of

living between the poorest and the wealthiest fractions of the population (people are vulnerable to feelings of shame and inferiority if they are poor, or economically inferior, while other people are rich, or economically superior).

Around the world, the nations with the most equitable economic systems, such as Sweden and Japan, are significantly more likely to have the lowest murder rates. And those with the greatest economic discrepancies between the rich and the poor (of which the United States is the world leader among developed democracies) have the highest murder rates (a statistic in which the United States is also the world leader). Even within the United States, the most equitable or "classless" states have the lowest murder rates, and those with the most inequitable degrees of class stratification have the highest. Yet the last Congress dismantled one of the few programs we had that tended to equalize income in this country—the earned-income tax credit.

Among the conditions in the prison system that prevent violent behavior (both during imprisonment and after release to the community), the most powerful is education. In Massachusetts, for example, when I headed the prison mental-health service, we did a study to see what programs within the prison had been most effective in preventing recidivism among prison inmates after they had been released from prison and returned to the community. While several programs had worked, the most successful of all, and the only one that had been 100 percent effective in preventing recidivism, was the program that allowed inmates to receive a college degree while in prison. Several hundred prisoners in Massachusetts had completed at least a bachelor's degree while in prison over a 25-year period, and not one of them had been returned to prison for a new crime.

Immediately after I announced this finding in a public lecture at Harvard, and it made its way into the newspapers, our new governor, William Weld, who had not previously been aware that prison inmates could take college courses, gave a press conference on television in which he declared that Massachusetts should rescind that "privilege," or else the poor would start committing crimes in order to be sent to prison so they could get a free college education! And lest one think that that was merely the rather bizarre response of one particularly cynical demagogue, it is worth noting that the U.S. Congress responded the same way. The last Congress declared that inmates throughout the federal prison system would no longer be eligible to receive Pell grants.

It is too late now to even begin to attempt to "reform" prisons. The only thing that can be done with them is to tear them all down, for their architecture alone renders them unfit for human beings. Or even animals: No humane society permits animals in zoos to be housed in conditions as intolerable as those in which we cage humans. The reason for the difference, of course, is clear: Zoos are not intended for punishment; prisons are. That is why it would benefit every man, woman, and child in this country, and it would hurt no one, to demolish the prisons and replace them with much smaller, locked, secure residential schools and colleges in which the residents could acquire as much education as their intelligence and curiosity would permit.

Such institutions would of course be most effective in their only rational purpose, which would be to prevent crime and violence, if they were designed to be as humane and homelike as possible, and as near the prisoners' own homes as possible, so that their families could visit as freely as possible (including frequent conjugal visits), and so they could visit their families as freely as possible. (For conjugal and home visits have repeatedly been shown, in this country and around the world, to be associated with lowered rates of violence, both during incarceration and after release into the community—which is probably why both have been effectively abolished in this country.)

Since there is no reason to isolate anyone from the community against his will unless he poses a danger of physically harming others, these residential schools would need to be limited to those who have been, or have threatened or attempted to be, violent. (Very few, if any, nonviolent "criminals" need to be removed from the community at all. Nor should those who have committed only nonviolent crimes ever have to be housed with those who have been seriously violent; and there are many reasons why they should not be.)

Thus one of the most constructive responses I can think of . . . would be the designing of an "anti-prison"—not prison reform, but prison replacement; not prison construction, but prison deconstruction. If we replaced prisons with a boarding-school "home away from home" for many people who are literally homeless in the so-called community, and provided them with the tools they need in order to acquire knowledge and skill, self-esteem and self-respect, and the esteem and respect of others, these new facilities could actually reduce the rates of crime and violence in our society, instead of feeding them, as our current prisons do.

Of course, before we could do that, we would need to overcome our own irrational need to inflict revenge (i.e., punishment) on those who are weaker than we. Nothing corrodes the soul of the vengeful person as thoroughly as his own vengeful impulses. Thus the main reason we need to abolish [prisons] is not only, or even primarily, for the sake of those who get imprisoned in them, but in order to heal our own souls—and indeed, our whole society, which is sick with an epidemic of violence, both legal and illegal.

Chapter 3

Analyzing and Evaluating Pathos

Pathos: Arguing through Emotion

When arguments are presented in an academic setting, the focus is usually placed on logic. If emotion is mentioned, it is usually described as an illegitimate argumentative strategy, something that detracts from thinking rationally. In some cases, the appeal to emotions is even presented as a logical fallacy or an inherently manipulative approach. But examining arguments in context shows that emotion is an important part of how arguments work in real communities. A logical argument can be convincing, but it won't usually be compelling. People can change their minds because of a logical argument, but pathos is usually more likely to cause them to change their behavior. Like other means of persuasion, pathos can be used to manipulate, deceive, and take advantage of others. But used properly, pathos can inspire and motivate others to act on their convictions.

Although the Greek word *pathos* is the root for the English words *pathetic*, *empathy*, and *sympathy*, pathos concerns a much wider range of emotions than pity. In his *Art of Rhetoric*, Aristotle writes that pathos can stir feelings of "anger and mildness; friendship and enmity; fear and boldness; shame and shamelessness; gratitude; pity and indignation; envy and emulation." A skillful writer can use fear, anger, humor, or compassion to put audience members in a particular emotional state such that they would receive a message that they might otherwise reject or act upon beliefs they already hold. As you analyze an author's appeal to emotion or when you find yourself responding emotionally to an argument, consider whether the emotions you are feeling are consistent with the issue and appropriate for the magnitude of the problem.

Emotional arguments can be found through an essay, but the direct emotional appeal is often stated at the beginning or the end. An emotional appeal placed near the beginning can catch readers' interest and predispose them to read the argument with a favorable attitude. An emotional appeal at the end of an essay can move readers to action.

In most academic writing, the appeal to emotions is considered less convincing than ethos or logos, particularly when the appeal is exaggerated or manipulative. The academic community usually expects that any appeal to emotions will be used to reinforce a logical argument.

Creating Pathos

CONCRETE EXAMPLES

One way that writers evoke an emotional response in their readers is through descriptive language. Instead of telling readers how they should feel, writers try to re-create an experience in such a way that readers actually do feel the associated emotion. Mark Twain once gave the following advice to fiction writers: "Don't say, 'The woman screamed.' Bring her on and let her scream!" Concrete examples and detailed descriptions give an argument presence. They make the argument real and immediate for readers. Journalists recognize that running a photograph along with a news story makes the story more immediate. Showing a picture of a young child who has been kidnaped will create a much greater emotional response than merely reporting the child's kidnaping. Providing personal information about the child (showing her toys and family, interviewing classmates) heightens the emotional response. A news story may contain

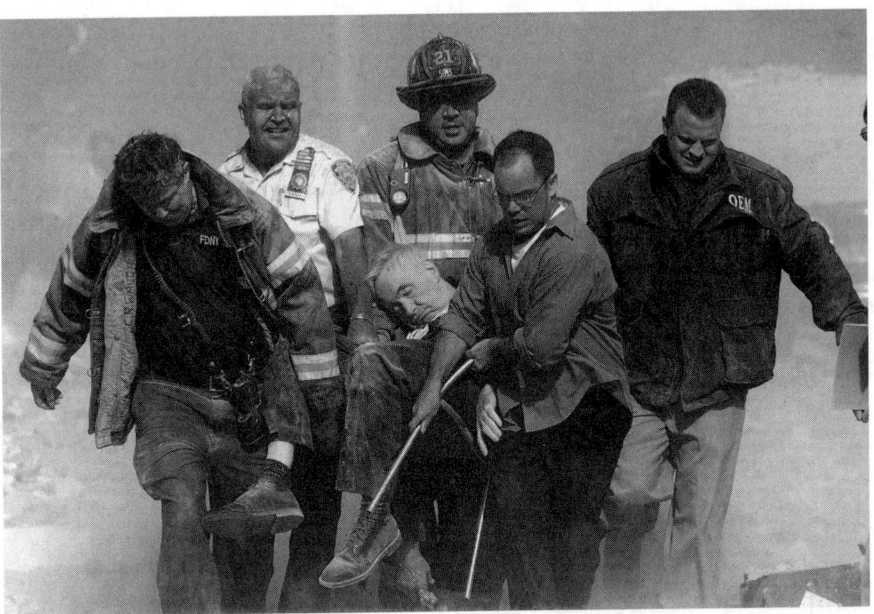

AP Photo/Charles H. Porter IV

statistics on how many families are without adequate food, shelter, or clothing, but no one responds. But if a reporter describes the plight of one particular family, then readers are likely to provide help.

The emotional response created by the second kind of story makes the difference between action and inaction. For example, on September 11, 2001, the nation watched in horror as a terrorist attack destroyed the twin towers of the World Trade Center in New York City, killing almost 3,000 people, including over 300 firefighters. The horror and emotion of the event were captured in Charles Porter's photo of firefighters carrying the limp body of Father Mychal Judge, chaplain of the New York City Fire Department, from the scene of the devastation. This picture, and others like it, touched an emotional chord in the American people, causing a public outpouring of grief and sympathy.

WORD CHOICE

Word choice is also important in creating an emotional response. Some words carry more emotional weight than others. Writers need to pay particular attention to the connotations of words, their suggested or implied meanings, in addition to their denotative or dictionary meanings. For instance, the words *cheap* and *inexpensive* both have similar denotative meanings. They both refer to something that can be bought at a lower price than expected. However, *cheap* can carry a negative connotation of "lower quality" as well as "lower price." To say that a person is "cheap" means that he or she is careful with money but with the negative connotation of "miserly" or "stingy." More positive words with roughly the same denotation are "frugal" or "thrifty."

Some words carry such powerful emotional overtones that they color other terms that are associated with them. Richard Weaver, a political philosopher, literary critic, and rhetorical theorist, called such terms "ultimate terms." These are highly emotional terms around which other terms cluster. Ultimate terms with a positive connotation, Weaver calls "god terms." Those with a negative connotation are called "devil terms." For instance, in the 1950s and 1960s, *communism* was a devil term for many Americans. Anything or anyone associated with communism—even obliquely—was painted by anti-communists with the same broad brush. In the 1950s, at the height of the anti-communist crusade by Republican Senator Joseph McCarthy of Wisconsin, even the slightest association of a person with communism or left-wing politics could ruin that person's life. For more obvious reasons, the word *Nazi* is another example of a devil term. A god term provides positive associations. The following words would be god terms for many Americans: *democracy, liberty, family, prosperity.* When you analyze emotional language in an argument, check to see if these emotional words form a pattern or cluster of related terms that may be related to an ultimate term, either a god or a devil term.

Writers must also pay close attention to figurative language, such as metaphor, simile, hyperbole, understatement, personification, and irony. A metaphor is an implied comparison that is not meant to be taken literally. For instance, if you call someone a "snake," you are using a metaphor. You don't mean that the person is literally a snake, but *snake* suggests similarities between the person and the characteristics traditionally associated with snakes (such as sneakiness, quickness, or deception). A simile is a similar kind of comparison using *like* or *as:* "slippery as a snake," for example. Well-chosen metaphors and similes give presence to an argument through concrete images that are vivid and memorable. Hyperbole is an extreme exaggeration or overstatement used for emphasis. If you plan a party and call it the "party of the century," then you are using hyperbole. Understatement is the opposite of hyperbole. To say that a devastating earthquake "did a bit of damage" would be an understatement and would actually draw attention to the extensive damage. Personification is assigning human characteristics to nonhuman objects. If you argue that a certain river should not be dammed because it is the "lifeblood" of a wilderness area, you are personifying the river and the wilderness in order to emphasize the importance of the river. Finally, irony is an incongruity or difference between what is said and what is meant or between what is expected and what actually happens. For instance, a writer might use irony to criticize an idea by seeming to praise it or to attack an idea by pretending to defend it. One of the most famous uses of irony is "A Modest Proposal" by Jonathan Swift, the 17th-century author of *Gulliver's Travels.* In this essay Swift suggests that the Irish economy could be improved if the children of the Irish were raised like cattle to provide food for the English.

In seeming to promote this idea, he is really attacking the exploitation of the Irish by the English landowners.

Figures draw attention to themselves because they deviate from the expected. For instance, an environmental activist might refer to the clear-cutting of forests as a "rape of the earth." *Rape* is a highly emotional term with seriously negative connotations. It suggests violence and domination. Readers would have difficulty responding positively to a word such as *rape.* At the same time, the word *rape* is used metaphorically, and the comparison of clear-cutting with the act of rape is obviously meant to shock. The comparison also suggests personification because rape is an attack by one person on another. Presenting the earth as a woman in this way may gain the unconscious sympathy of readers who feel for other victims of sexual violence. On the other side, supporters of clear-cutting might refer to this act as "harvesting," using a word that carries much more benign connotations. *Harvesting* suggests farming and gaining the benefits of one's own labors. It may also evoke the nostalgia and respect that many Americans have for the traditional farmer

The Principles in Action: Readings

UNDERSTANDING PATHOS

It is often easier to recognize pathos when it is not working well. When a writer is effective in evoking an emotional response in his or her readers, then readers are probably so caught up in the emotion that they don't notice how the writer is working. Still, because persuasion through emotions can be so powerful, it is important to learn how to recognize when a writer is trying to make you feel something. It is particularly important to recognize when a writer is trying to play on your emotions as a reader, trying to create an emotional response in the audience that isn't warranted by the situation.

As you read the following article by Gretchen Letterman, consider these questions:

1. Identify words that seem to carry emotional weight. How do you respond to these words? How do you think the writer wants you to respond?
2. Identify instances where the writer provides concrete examples or detailed descriptions. What kind of emotional response do these examples evoke?
3. Find instances of figurative language: metaphor, simile, hyperbole, understatement, personification, or irony. In what way do these figures deviate from the meaning you would normally expect? What kind of emotional weight do these figures carry? What do these figures emphasize? How do they focus your attention?
4. To what extent has "tobacco industry" become an ultimate term?

Tobacco's Tiniest Victims

GRETCHEN LETTERMAN

FEW SIGHTS make such an unforgettable impression on the mind and heart 1
as the neonatal intensive care unit at All Children's Hospital in St. Petersburg, Fla. Babies more tiny than seems imaginable are fighting, with the help of tubes and machines and hovering nurses, to get big enough and strong enough to go home to their families.

Depending on their sizes and conditions, some stay in this post-natal womb longer than others. Their Isolettes are adorned with sweet touches (a hand-lettered sign proclaiming "Robin's Nest," a cuddly teddy bear keeping watch from atop a monitor) in the hope that babies burdened with life-threatening complications will soak up the same love they would if they were snugly nestled in their own cribs at home.

Many newborns have to take such a detour before they can leave the hospital in their parents' arms because they are born too small, organs too immature to function properly.

There are many reasons for this cruel reality, but one that is completely preventable is highlighted by the recent work of two doctors from the University of Massachusetts.

Doctors Joseph DiFranza and Robert Lew analyzed 40 years of research to 5
determine that 53,000 babies a year are born with low birthweight and 22,000 need intensive care at birth because their mothers smoked while they were pregnant. Their analysis also found that pregnant women's smoking caused 1,900 babies to die each year from Sudden Infant Death Syndrome and that an additional 3,700 infants die within one month of birth due to complications from the smoke their mothers inhaled during pregnancy. The doctors also attribute 115,000 miscarriages annually to smoking.

It's not news that a woman's smoking can harm her fetus, but this is the first time the numbers have been calculated, and they are astonishing. Smoking women, addicted to a legal substance, are poisoning their children, some with fatal conclusion, by the thousands every year.

The sins of tobacco are being reported with increasing frequency. Just two weeks ago a thorough review of research damned secondhand smoke more soundly than ever before. The hearts of nonsmokers are more vulnerable to damage from passive smoking than are the hearts of smokers to the firsthand drag, researchers concluded, because their bodies haven't built up defenses to tobacco's toxins. That's especially bad news for children.

Yet the tobacco industry keeps winning, even in the face of unprecedented legal attack such as lawsuits by Florida, Mississippi, and other states against tobacco companies to recoup the cost of state-financed medical care for sick smokers.

A bill that would have banned smoking in Florida restaurants is likely dead because, preposterously, lawmakers didn't want to take the time needed to debate it—"at least an hour and a half," according to Rep. Ben Graber, who chairs the health-care committee that would have had to spare the precious moments.

Children are still being hooked, despite efforts in schools to keep them smoke-free, by kid-appealing advertisements and promotional products. Despite all we know about what smoke in a woman's lungs can do to a fetus she carries, pregnant women continue to light up.

For some, stopping the smoking habit is as easy as making up their minds to do so, especially when the health or pleas of a loved one are influencing factors. For the majority of smokers, however, quitting is either an undesired goal or a seemingly impossible one. That's the power of addiction.

Anyone who spends a minute in a neonatal intensive care unit gazing at a premature baby, the translucent skin stretched tight over miniature ribs, shouldn't have any trouble feeling heartache for the little life struggling to survive, especially for the 22,000 babies a year whose struggle could have been avoided if their mothers hadn't smoked.

Who knows, the experience might even have an effect on tobacco industry executives and their lobbyists.

An Analysis of Letterman's Essay In this essay, Gretchen Letterman denounces what she calls the "sins of the tobacco industry." She focuses on the harmful effects that smoking during pregnancy can have on an unborn baby. Letterman's main emotional appeals are found at the beginning and end of her essay, common positions for emotional appeals.

Letterman begins her essay by describing a concrete example, a particular scene of suffering babies born prematurely. Letterman doesn't indicate exactly why these particular babies are premature but allows her readers to make the connection between their suffering and the suffering of babies whose mothers smoked. The scene is All Children's Hospital in St. Petersburg, Florida (where Gretchen Letterman lives). She describes seeing "babies more tiny than seems imaginable" hooked up to "tubes and machines." Hospitals are an uncomfortable place for most people anyway. If you are nervous about getting a shot or giving blood, then imagine having all kinds of strange tubes running in and out of your body. Then imagine this being done to a newborn. This is the powerful image that Letterman is trying to convey. In her second paragraph, Letterman elaborates on this disturbing image by describing the "sweet touches" that "adorn" their special care cribs: "a hand-lettered sign proclaiming 'Robin's Nest'" and "a cuddly teddy bear keeping watch from atop a monitor." In the next-to-last paragraph, Letterman focuses on one particular detail to capture the suffering of these infants: "the translucent skin stretched tight over miniature ribs." This detail calls to my mind the pictures of starving, diseased, and malnourished children so familiar from advertisements for children's aid programs.

It also reminds me somewhat of pictures of Holocaust survivors. Whether Letterman intended these associations doesn't really matter. The image of a suffering child speaks to something instinctual in most human beings. By describing these details, Letterman changes these infants from statistics to real people.

Letterman also uses words that carry a lot of emotional weight: the "cuddly teddy bear," "cruel reality," "poisoning their children," "sins of tobacco," "tobacco's toxins." She uses words with a negative connotation when referring to the suffering of the children and the actions of the tobacco industry and legislators. She uses words with positive connotations to describe those who care for these infants.

Letterman's argument does not rely solely on emotion. She establishes her credibility as a writer by sharing her first-hand experience in a post-natal ward. She speaks with the authoritative voice of science by citing the "40 years of research" analyzed by Joseph DiFranza and Robert Lew. She also refers to "a thorough review of research" that showed the harm of secondhand smoke. Letterman gives the impression that she is knowledgeable by reviewing the legislative history of antismoking legislation. And she demonstrates her goodwill by identifying with an important value in the community: the protection of innocent children.

PATHOS IN ADVERTISEMENTS

Like letters to the editor, advertisements provide excellent examples for analysis because those who compose these arguments frequently use emotional appeals. People who write letters to the editor are usually trying to get readers to change their minds about something or to do something, and their letters often result from powerful emotions in the writers, who are upset enough or feel strongly enough about something that they need to express their feelings in public. It is difficult, however, to convey such strong emotion in such a short space, usually fewer than 500 words.

Advertisers face a similar problem. The typical television ad runs 30 to 60 seconds—not much time to make a pitch for a product. Some ads are as short as 15 seconds. Most print ads must create an emotional response in a page or less, trying to catch the attention of readers as they thumb through a magazine or newspaper. Further, the nature of an advertisement does not allow for a detailed elaboration of a logical argument. So most ads try to create an immediate emotional response. According to one old advertising adage, "Don't sell the steak; sell the sizzle." In other words, if you get people excited about your product, they will want to buy what you are selling.

The following three ads all try to create an immediate emotional response. The first ad is for Dakin toys, soft, furry, stuffed animals. The creators of this ad use visual images to contrast Dakin toys with other toys. Featured in the center of the ad is a cute stuffed puppy, an image that calls to mind the dogs I had as pets when I was younger, as well as the stuffed animals I owned. This picture speaks "soft and cuddly." The phrase underneath the dog's foot contains an interesting double meaning: "Gifts you can feel good about." They are gifts that literally feel good because they are soft and cuddly, but parents can also rest assured that Dakin stuffed animals are not going to lead to violence. After reading this phrase, the reader's eye is led to the Dakin logo, a cuddly teddy bear.

The contrasting image in this ad is the collection of combat toys: the squirt gun in the shape of a real gun, the tank, the fighter plane, and the action figure. Most disturbing of all to me is the commando knife with dried blood along the blade. This knife is placed just above the dog, and the point of the knife leads your eye over and then down to the puppy. The large typeface at the top of the ad emphasizes the link between combat toys and violence in adults: "Is it any wonder the prisons are full?"

The elements of the ad are enough to send a message and associate an emotional image with that message: If you don't want your kids to be violent, then buy the kind of toys that Dakin sells. The ad does have a logical argument, however. The ad copy, which doesn't receive as much emphasis as the emotional imagery, cites studies linking violent toys to increased violence. The ad copy also contains an ethical appeal, an attempt to establish Dakin's credibility as a company that distances itself from toy makers that care only about profits and to appeal to the community value of teaching a child "how to love" rather than "how to maim."

The next two ads also seek to make an immediate emotional connection to the reader. As you view these ads, consider the following questions:

1. What emotions are the creators of each ad trying to evoke in viewers?
2. How do visual features of the ad reinforce this emotion?
3. How does the copy relate to the emotional response? Does the ad copy also present a logical argument?
4. What do these ads want you to do based on the emotions you feel? In what ways are the ads motivational?
5. How effective are these ads? Do you immediately feel something? How legitimate is this attempt to persuade through emotion?

Dakin Toy Advertisement

Is it any wonder the prisons are full?
In the mid 1950's, researchers at the University of Pennsylvania began conducting what has become a landmark study.
Its purpose: to determine the effect violent toys have on our children.
What they found was rather disturbing. The researchers stated that violent toys cause children to become more violent. That they actually may, in fact, teach children to become violent.
At Dakin, we've always tried to produce toys that teach children some other things.
Toys that, rather than teach a child how to maim, would teach a child how to love.
That, rather than teach a child how to hurt, would teach a child how to care for something.
Toys that, rather than being designed to be played with in only one way, would challenge the child's imagination to use them in a variety of ways. From playing house. To playing veterinarian. To playing Mr. Big Shot Hollywood movie director.
Naturally, researchers and child psychologists have had something to say about toys like the Dakin stuffed animal you see on the left: That they can play a very important role in helping children develop into secure, well-adjusted individuals.
You see, as parents ourselves, we at Dakin don't design toys solely on the basis of whether or not they'll make money.
We design them on the basis of whether we'd want our children playing with them.
DAKIN
Gifts you can feel good about.

American Red Cross Advertisement[1]

When you give blood
you give another birthday,
another anniversary,
another day at the beach,
another night under the stars,
another talk with a friend,
another laugh,
another hug,
another chance.

American Red Cross

Please give blood.

Ad Council

Courtesy of the American Red Cross.

[1] In the original ad, the cross and the words "American Red Cross" are in red. [ED.]

Humane Farming Association Advertisement

Q: Why can't this veal calf walk?

A: He has only two feet.

Actually, less than two feet. Twenty two inches to be exact. His entire life is spent chained in a wooden box measuring only 22 inches wide and 56 inches long. The box is so small that the calf can't walk or even turn around.

Most people think animal abuse is illegal. It isn't. In veal factories, it's business as usual. "Milk-fed" veal is obtained by making a calf anemic. The calf is *not* fed mother's milk. He's fed an antibiotic laced formula that causes severe diarrhea. He must lie in his own excrement – choking on the ammonia gases. He's chained in a darkened building with hundreds of other baby calves suffering the same fate. They are immobilized, sick, and anemic.

Toxic Veal

The reckless use of oxytetracycline, mold inhibiting chemicals, chloramphenicol, neomycin, penicillin, and other drugs is not just bad for calves. It is toxic to you.

But doesn't the USDA prevent tainted veal from being sold? Absolutely not. The USDA itself admits that most veal is never checked for toxic residue.

Antibiotics in veal and other factory farm products create virulent strains of bacteria that wreak havoc on human health. *Salmonella* poisoning is reaching epidemic proportions.

Veal factories maximize profits for agribusiness drug companies because they are a breeding ground for disease. To keep calves alive under such torturous conditions, they are *continually* given drugs which are passed on to consumers.

It doesn't have to be this way. And with your help, it won't be. Please, don't buy veal!

Campaign Against Factory Farming

YES! Factory farms must be stopped from misusing drugs, abusing farm animals, and destroying America's family farms. Enclosed is my tax-deductible contribution of:

☐ $20 ☐ $50 ☐ $100 ☐ $500 ☐ Other________

Name________________________

Address________________________

City/State/Zip________________________

A free Consumer Alert pack is available upon request.

THE HUMANE FARMING ASSOCIATION

1550 California Street • Suite 4 • San Francisco, CA 94109

CONSIDERING COLUMBINE: REMEMBERING THE VICTIMS

The tragedy at Columbine High School was not the first school shooting. And it wasn't the first mass murder, either. But it was the most extensive attack on a group of students, and it touched the community of Littleton, Colorado, and the nation deeply. The event itself warrants disbelief, horror, and grief. But the emotional impact of the shootings was intensified by the continual coverage of the event—the photographs, video footage, stories, and discussion. The Internet also played an important part in this communal grieving as several websites appeared memorializing those who were injured and killed that day. Many people sought to honor and remember those who suffered, but some also sought to use Columbine as an emotional symbol to argue about other issues as well: educational reform, handgun control and safety, high school culture, the effect of violent movies and video games. Following are some stories and images that attempt to capture the grief, pain, sadness, and recovery associated with the Columbine tragedy. In "The Making of a Martyr," *Newsweek* writer Kenneth Woodward describes how Cassie Bernall has been memorialized as an unofficial Christian martyr because she reportedly gave her life rather than deny her faith. "Voices of Columbine" represents a special section of the *Denver Post* online remembering the Columbine victims a year after the event. The image on the page is taken from the Columbine memorial reunion. The next two selections come from "Voices of Columbine." In the first of these, *Denver Post* writer Janet Bingham tells the story of how Holocaust survivor Gerda Weissmann Klein sought to comfort Columbine survivor Melissa Pillow. In the second of these, Bingham tells the story of Crystal Woodman, a Columbine library survivor, and her correspondence with Donika Sokoli, a survivor of the conflict in Kosovo. In "A Note for Rachel Scott," *Time* magazine author Roger Rosenblatt gives his own personal response to the death of Rachel Scott. Following Rosenblatt's essay are selections from the Fox News photoessay "High School Shooting in Littleton." The complete photoessay is available online at www.foxnews.com/photoessay/schoolshooting2. The final image in this section is from a Columbine memorial site, representative of several that are found on the Internet. (A list of these memorial sites is available at denverpost.com or www.columbinememorial.org.

As you read these stories and analyze these images, consider the following questions:

1. What is the central message of each story or image? What is the purpose of each story or image? Are there any that appear to have more than one message or purpose?
2. What emotions is each story or image trying to convey? What techniques does each author use? How effective are these techniques?
3. Would you characterize these stories or images as excessive in their use of

emotion or restrained? What are the advantages and disadvantages of restraint when dealing with a highly emotional issue?

4. What memories and emotions do you associate with the shootings at Columbine High School or the aftermath of this tragedy?

The Making of a Martyr

KENNETH L. WOODWARD

EVANGELICAL Christians have been urging teens for years to just say no to drugs and sex. During the Columbine High School massacre in Littleton, Colo., 17-year-old Cassie Bernall said yes when asked if she believed in God—and instantly became an evangelical saint. The day she walked into the Columbine killing field she was just one of 12 ordinary students who would be cut down by Eric Harris and Dylan Klebold. But because of her last words, she is now being hailed in evangelical circles as an authentic martyr for the faith—a crown of Christian witness that eluded even Martin Luther King Jr., who died a victim of racial, not religious, hatred. 1

Turning martyrs into saints is something that Catholics, not Protestants, are known for. But in the world of evangelical Web sites, where pious adolescents meet like Christians in the catacombs, Cassie is the subject of countless prayers, personal testimonials and songs like "You Went Home at Lunchtime." As the budding hagiography has it, Cassie's death was part of God's plan to bring forth witnesses out of the Columbine killings who would then win others to Christ. That certainly was the message of Franklin Graham (Billy's son and successor), who used the public memorial service in Littleton last April to call the mourners—including Jews—to conversion. That's the message on Cassie T-shirts. And that's the message that will continue in a series of teen rallies in 28 states this summer planned by Revival Generation, a new evangelistic organization created in response to the Littleton shootings.

Cassie's family isn't speaking to the media about the the outpouring of interest in their daughter. But the title of a book by her mother, Misty, to be published by religious imprint Plough suggests that they too are interested in transforming her death from tragedy to triumph: "She Said Yes: The Unlikely Martyrdom of Cassie Bernall" will be out in September. For the religious, this should not be entirely surprising. Christians have long found consolation in believing that their brethren, even their children, have died defending the faith. Throughout Christian history, martyrdom has been seen as God's greatest gift of grace, and that belief has made the stories of the martyrs Christian classics.

To die a victim of simple adolescent outrage isn't martyrdom in any religious sense. But Cassie's case appears to fit the classic Christian mold. The male student who killed her was part of a group which had ardently embraced atheism.

That made them resident aliens in a neighborhood thick with evangelical churches and evening youth groups like Warriors for Christ. The killers hated Jews, athletes and blacks as well. But of the dozen students they killed, four were members of a Bible-study society that meets daily for prayer. Inside the school, some evangelical kids were known to be concerned about their "unsaved" classmates, and many of the believers were easily distinguishable by the Bibles they carried to school. In short, evangelical kids formed one of the high-school cliques that the killers were out to punish.

Still, there would be no Christian martyrs at Columbine if Eric Harris and 5
Dylan Klebold hadn't asked for proclamations of belief—and in this, Cassie wasn't alone. Here, in a late 20th-century American high-school library, two deeply troubled adolescent killers replayed the role of early Christianity's Roman persecutors: they demanded a confession of faith. Rachel Scott, 17, another victim who died outside the school, did as well, according to her pastor. So, reportedly, did two survivors: Kacey Ruegsegger, 17, who was shot in the face and shoulder, and Valerie Schnurr, who was shot in the leg. In the early Christian church, the survivors would have been hailed as confessors—believers who were prepared to suffer martyrdom but were spared.

To some critics, casting Cassie as a martyr is an opportunistic reach for conversions. Lutheran pastor Don Maxhousen thinks it is "escapist theology" to claim that "she's happy, she's with God now" and wonders who will be there to help her parents over holidays when there's no Cassie there to share Thanksgiving or celebrate Christmas. "As a Lutheran, I would be helping a family focus on getting through a long and dark period in their life." Others would prefer to see attention focused on different agendas, like banning the sale of guns, posting the Ten Commandments or permitting organized prayer in public schools. "People desperately want a national conversation on this, and that is what I am going to do in the campaign," says Gary Bauer, a conservative Christian candidate for the Republican presidential nomination.

Still, how long—and how well—Cassie and her fellow Christian victims will be remembered is hard to guess. T-shirts have a much shorter hang time than stained-glass windows. Moreover, Americans generally prefer secular saints like Abraham Lincoln and Dr. King, who died for social causes. "We've never had a teenage Christian martyr, especially in this country," says Josh Weideman, 17, who'll be running this summer's rallies. It'd be nice to think that she will be the last.

Columbine Memorial

Gerda Weissmann Klein and Melissa Pillow: Holocaust Survivor Comforts Columbine Student

JANET BINGHAM

IT WAS A simple act of kindness: the gift of a raspberry. 1

More than 50 years ago it sustained the courage of a young teenage girl in a Nazi slave labor camp.

Today, in the retelling, it sustains the courage of another teenager, 16-year-old Melissa Pillow, a survivor of the April 20 shootings at Columbine.

Holocaust survivor Gerda Weissmann Klein told the story recently to Columbine students. She was 15 in 1939 when the Nazis invaded her Polish homeland and took her brother away. She was eventually sent off to a series of slave labor camps for three years and never saw any of her family again.

One day, in a camp called Grunberg, her friend Ilse found a raspberry in the 5
gutter on the way to the factory in which they worked. She carried the treasure

all day in her pocket and presented it on a fresh leaf to Gerda that night. Ilse did not live to taste another raspberry. But the gesture lives in Gerda's memory as an example of how, under terrible circumstances, kindness and caring can exist.

Hearing that story, Melissa said she was filled "with this feeling of hope that love can overcome evil, that love can overcome hate." In January, Klein spoke with Melissa and other juniors in a world history class, to faculty later and to hundreds of parents and community members the same night.

Melissa, one of many students who sent letters of gratitude to Klein, wrote to her: "Please know that you have changed one life for the better." "I can never minimize their pain," Klein said in an interview from her home in Scottsdale, Arizona.

"I was their age. I know exactly how it was. It is a balm on my wounds to think that my own pain has helped someone else. And they have helped me—by their response to my feelings. They have done an incredible good.

"Then you somehow feel it wasn't totally in vain.

"Today when you say Columbine you think of a day of horror and loss and 10
destruction. I hope it can be turned around, that today each of those young people will do something good, something kind, and that they will become the leaders for hope and reconciliation." In sharing her story, Klein said that whenever the going was difficult she envisioned an evening at home, she and her brother doing their homework, her father reading the evening paper, her mother working on her needlepoint or knitting or embroidery. Once she might have called it a "boring" evening at home, she said, but in retrospect it became precious.

Melissa said she too had realized the importance of her family while sitting trapped in the school on April 20 with about 30 other students and a teacher. They spent four hours in a room some 40 feet from the library where most of the fatal shootings took place.

"I realized I would not allow myself to die. I was going to see my sister play basketball in high school. I was going to see her graduate. I was going to see her fulfill her life. The hope of seeing my family again got me through those four long hours." The experience "made me appreciate what I have. . . . Now I try to live so that if I die within the next five minutes I won't have regrets." She recognizes now that "it is the little things you remember and miss the most, the simplicity of life." A little thing like a raspberry.

Melissa says that if, like Ilse who presented the gift of the raspberry, "I can just love, maybe I can make changes, even if only in one person's life."

Crystal Woodman: Columbine Library Survivor

JANET BINGHAM

1 FROM HER dining room table, Crystal Woodman picks up a letter, hand-delivered from Kosovo, the word "love" written in yellow highlighter across it.

It is from the dark-haired girl she met in the village of Meja. "I am very thankful that I was able to meet with you, and to share your and my pain together," writes 18-year-old Donika Sokoli.

Crystal, 17, had told Donika how she heard the shots that murdered her classmates as she huddled with two friends under a table in the Columbine library. It amazes her still that Donika knew about the Columbine tragedy, from faraway Kosovo, and felt a bond with her.

"When she heard I was in the library, her face turned solemn. She looked like she would cry. She said, 'I am so sorry.' After everything she had gone through."

5 Donika shared her own story. Serb soldiers had rousted her family from their house, taken away her father, torched her home. She saw flames, heard gunshots, saw blood spilled. She has never seen her father again.

In her letter to Crystal, Donika writes, "I thought my life was over. There's so many years I thought I would never find a true friend. You have come into my life like an angel."

Crystal, now a senior, had read the newspaper headlines and seen the TV images of devastation in Kosovo, but it meant little to her before she went there in December, invited by the Christian relief organization Samaritan's Purse to help distribute hundreds of thousands of Christmas boxes.

Also invited were two teens who had seen seven of their friends killed in a shooting during a youth-group meeting at a Fort Worth, Texas, church. The three Americans felt a special connection with each other and with the young survivors of violence a world away.

They spent only three days in Kosovo, but Crystal thinks about it every day. There was the little girl who never smiled. She had lost both parents.

10 Then there was the little boy who clowned for her camera wearing the Groucho Marx nose and eyeglasses he'd received for Christmas.

Others smiled. "But there was so much pain deep inside that when they smiled, it didn't get to their eyes."

Most of the children spoke no English. But words weren't needed. The American teens blew bubbles, put on a puppet show, sang, and played with Slinkies and a Hacky Sack.

And they handed out the Christmas boxes that had been filled with gifts by American children. The first box distributed had been packed by Craig Scott, whose sister, Rachel, was killed at Columbine.

Crystal had packed a box with a doll, a stuffed animal, a red fleece blanket, a toothbrush, socks, gloves, jewelry, a chalk board, a notebook, a bracelet. It was the notebook that most delighted Verona, the little girl who opened it.

Crystal's father, who came with her, had packed a box that included a flannel shirt and flashlight. It went to Arzim, age 14, the oldest male left alive in his village after a massacre of the adult men.

Arzim and 11 other orphaned children now live with two adults in a one-room shelter with no electricity.

"When we gave him the flashlight," Crystal says, "it was like we gave him the world.

"I can't come close to understanding what they went through. What we went through at Columbine was devastating and hard, but it's something we experienced for one day. For these kids, the violence and suffering went on for day after day, month after month.

"We had families to go home to. We had the nurturing and comfort and love of our parents and our family. To know that so many of these kids don't have parents, don't have houses, don't even have the bare necessities.

"We have to step out of our own comfort bubbles. We give so little of what we have to others in the world. It doesn't touch our hearts. In America we are very selfish. What if we loved everyone in the world the way we love ourselves?

"Violence happens in suburban Littleton and we're devastated. But suffering goes on all over the world.

"I realize I can't take anything for granted. As teenagers, we think we're invincible. Now I realize I might not be here the next hour, the next day. I realize I must do what I can while I am able.

"We need to tell these children they're not forgotten. We still love them.

"I think about Kosovo all the time. The relationship with Donika, it was so incredible. It put a lot of things into perspective. It was an experience that changed my life."

Before she left Kosovo, Crystal said a special goodbye to Donika's mother. "I was in the bus. Her mother reached up and pinched my cheeks. She was crying. I was crying. It wasn't about words. There was a connection there like no other connection. Christ was bonding us together, planting seeds in our lives."

A Note for Rachel Scott

ROGER ROSENBLATT

YOUR friends were shown on television, writing goodbye messages on the 1
white casket provided for you. I hope you will not mind if a stranger writes a message of his own. Of course, this is a literary device (as a young writer, you will recognize it as such), a way of doing an essay on the thought your death evokes. But this is also for you alone, Rachel, dead at 17, yet ineradicable because of the photograph of your bright and witty face, now sadly familiar to the country, and because of the loving and admiring testimonies of your family.

Your dad said in an interview last week that while there were many legal and legislative questions to be answered in the aftermath of the Columbine High School murders, these did not touch "the deep issues of the heart." He was referring specifically to the forgiveness that he, your mother, and stepfather were dredging up for Dylan and Eric; and he may also have been thinking about the two boys' deep issues of the heart, realized out of a terrible darkness, and about the nightmares of your schoolmates who survived—all deep issues, reachable with great pain and difficulty.

But the deep issue I want to touch upon has to do with me and my colleagues—journalists who, for all our recurrent, usually unattractive display of know-it-all confidence, occasionally come upon a story such as yours and recognize our helplessness before it. Most honest journalists will admit that they never really understand the events they attempt to organize and clarify, and that more often than not it makes a "better story," one that comes closer to the truth, to swim around in the mystery of things.

I, who have lived more then three times your years, have rarely understood the occurrences and the people in the world that I have pretended to give order to. Yet I write sentences that end in periods. An odd word, sentence, don't you think? It means an authoritative decision, a judgment (one is sentenced in a courtroom), as well as a definite part of the language. Yet anybody who writes one knows that in reality sentences roll on and come to no conclusions; typically, they are questions disguised as answers, even cries for help.

So, Rachel, when I write, "This is what I want to tell you," please read, 5
"This is what I want to ask": Where do we, who ply our trade in this magazine and elsewhere, find the knowledge of the unknowable? How do we learn to trust the unknowable as news—those deep issues of the heart?

The problem belongs both to us and to those we hope to serve. Journalists are pretty good at unearthing the undeep issues. Give us a presidential scandal, even a war, and we can do a fair job of explaining the explicable. But give us the killings at Columbine, and in an effort to cover the possibilities we will miss what people are thinking in their secret chambers—thinking, feeling—about their

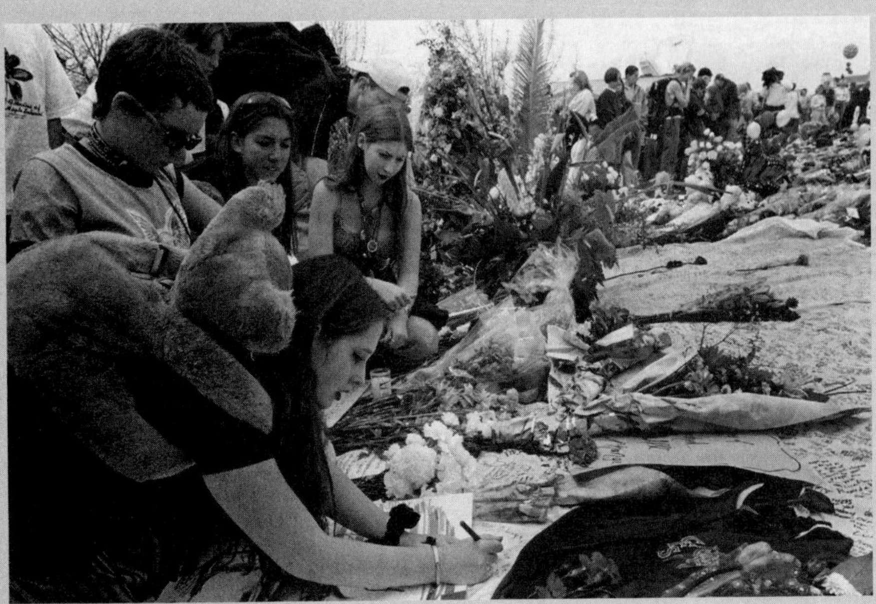

own loves and hatreds, about the necessity of attentiveness to others, about their own children: about *you,* Rachel.

I have never believed that life is revealed in its cataclysmic moments, its "wake-up calls," but rather in repose, when people go about the quieter business of being who they are. Journalists tend to turn to where the noise is. One of the things your death bequeaths is a reminder to where the noise is not. One can tell far more interesting things about a crowd at a picnic [than] a mob in the streets, or about someone like you when you were writing poems and performing in school plays, or just dreaming without a sound, [than] when murder made you a "national symbol."

Your other bequest may be more useful still—to journalists and everyone else. No life ends on a period, no matter how long it is lived. But your abbreviated life makes one especially aware of how much there is to the unknowable and untidy. In their private hours, your parents will imagine you as a wife, a mother, an actress in the movies or at the village playhouse. For myself, I see you married—as my own daughter was married a year ago—in a church ceremony the antipode of the one you were the center of last week.

The deeper unknowable, though, is who you were before the guns locked you into a sentence. The only question that ever ought to matter to my colleagues and our customers is the one we do not ask except in retrospect, after the guns or the scandal: Who are we all in silence—at a table in the cafeteria, at a table in the library? What can journalists tell others about the mind we all share, the innocent mind and the murderous? That is the real news of your death. That is the news I want to remember next week, when Kosovo is over or not over, and Congress debates gun control, and Al Hirt's trumpet is no longer heard.

I would like to have remembered it before Tuesday, April 20, when the news 10
of the day supposedly brought you to light. Rachel, you were always in the light.

Practicing the Principles: Activities

RECALLING MOMENTS OF EMOTION

Freewrite for five minutes on a time when you did something because you felt strongly that you should or because you felt a powerful emotion. How would you describe the emotion you felt? What caused you to feel the way you did? Would you have acted the same way without the emotion? What role does emotion play in how you regularly make decisions? Revise your freewrite by relating the episode where you felt this intense emotion. Use descriptive language to re-create this experience for your classmates so that they have a sense of what it was like to experience what you experienced. Then share your story with other members of your class.

ILLUSTRATING AN EMOTION

As a class, brainstorm a list of emotions, such as pity, fear, anger, hate, love, compassion, and joy. Then select one or two of these emotions and freewrite for five minutes about that emotion. Revise your freewrite to identify a story that illustrates that emotion. Draw upon your own experience or upon your reading or knowledge of others' experience. Try to use descriptive language to re-create this experience for your classmates.

IDENTIFYING ULTIMATE TERMS

As a class, brainstorm a list of ultimate terms, both god terms and devil terms. Then select one of these terms and create a "bubble map" (or "semantic web") of terms that cluster around this term. To create a bubble map, write the term on the board or on a piece of paper. Draw a circle around it. Then write related terms in a cluster around this term. Draw a circle around each of these and then draw a line from the original term to these clusters. Then select one of the circled cluster terms and repeat this process for each of these terms. Eventually, your map should look something like this:

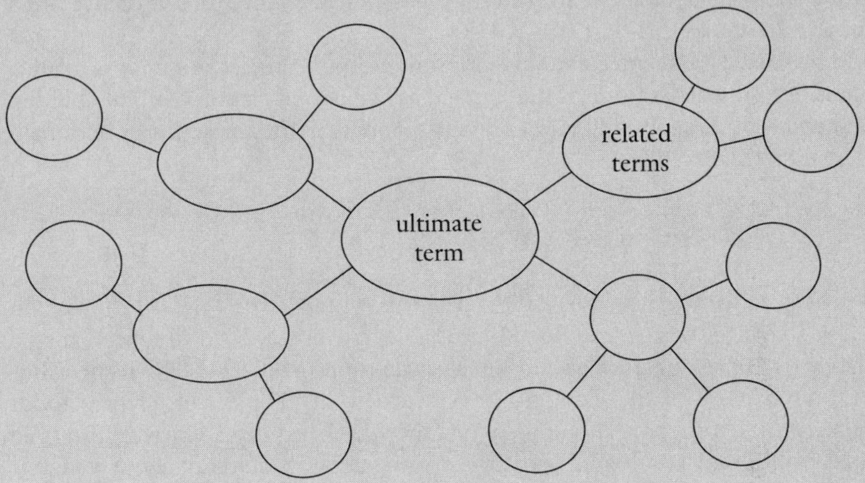

related terms

ultimate term

FINDING EMOTION IN THE MEDIA

As a class, either review a couple of weeks of newspapers or videotape an evening's worth of television commercials. Look for examples of emotional arguments. In the newspaper, you might look at news photos, editorials, letters to the editor, or advertisements. On television, you will find that most television commercials use emotional arguments in some way, particularly humor. Try writing a script for a television commercial or newspaper ad that makes a brief emotional argument in order to sell a product or image.

ENCOMIUM AND INVECTIVE

In classical times, an *encomium* was a speech of praise and an *invective* was a speech of blame delivered at formal ceremonies, such as funerals, dramatic performances, or sporting events. You can still find these kinds of speeches in our own time: speeches given at graduations, funerals, or awards ceremonies; toasts at weddings; or acceptance speeches at political conventions. The memorials in honor of the victims of the Columbine tragedy are examples of encomia. In traditional style, an encomium is associated with some kind of ceremony (such as a memorial service) and remembers the past while looking toward the future. An encomium usually celebrates the values of the community as they are exemplified in the person being praised. An invective usually denigrates the negative qualities of an individual in order to reinforce the positive values of the communities. Occasionally, encomium and invective are combined in one as the person being praised is compared to the person being blamed. Because they involve praise and blame and relate to community values, encomium and invective often involve emotional arguments.

For this activity, pick a famous person, event, or object to praise or blame. Consider the background of the person, his or her education, natural abilities, and accomplishments. Tell stories about that person that make his or her qualities real for the reader.

WRITING YOUR OWN OBITUARY

This activity can be a tiny bit morbid, but only if you take it seriously. In Mark Twain's *Huckleberry Finn,* Huck is able to overhear his own funeral and all the nice things people say about him after he supposedly died. The scene is humorous because of the incongruity between what people typically say about Huck and what they say about him when they think he's dead. Try writing a brief speech that someone would give at *your* funeral or an obituary about you that would be printed in the newspaper. Consider writing two versions, one with exaggerated praise and highly emotional language, and one where you show more restraint. Which version is more effective as a serious obituary or funeral speech?

Applying the Principles: Analytical Projects

PERSONAL EXPERIENCE AND EMOTION

As you read the following essays, apply what you've learned in this chapter to identify each author's main idea. Analyze and evaluate how each author uses pathos to be persuasive. The first essay, "Me, My Clone, and I," was written by Jonathan Colvin, a technical writer who lives in Vancouver, British Columbia. This essay was originally published in *The Humanist,* a publication of the American Humanist Association, an organization dedicated to "critical inquiry and social concern." The second essay, "In Search of Brotherhood," was written by Ron Stodghill, II, a writer for *Time* magazine. This essay was originally published in *Essence,* a magazine written primarily for African-American readers.

Me, My Clone, and I (or In Defense of Human Cloning)

JONATHAN COLVIN

1 CLONE. To many people the word has sinister overtones; it's a disturbing amalgam of flesh and technology. A recent poll revealed that 88 percent of Canadians believe that human cloning should be illegal, and most governments are moving to concur.

Interested in this near-unanimous sentiment, I carried out my own impromptu survey of friends and strangers. Most said they agreed with the prohibition of human cloning. But when I asked them to explain exactly why they thought it should be illegal, the poll became much more revealing.

Many mumbled about the dangers of "cloning Hitler" or creating a subclass of slaves. Others brought up the specter of basketball teams full of identical seven-foot-tall players. A smaller, more thoughtful percentage believed it would be unnatural or the ultimate in narcissism. In general, however, public attitudes toward human cloning seem to be based on a diet of science-fiction B-movies and paperbacks.

But should human cloning be feared as the next Frankenstein's monster of genetic engineering?

5 While undoubtedly fascinating, few people would perceive identical twins to be the least bit sinister. And yet identical twins are in fact natural clones, formed from the same egg and sharing the same genotype. If natural clones are not to be feared, why should we fear the deliberate ones?

Many of the attitudes concerning human cloning are reminiscent of the arguments against in vitro fertilization in the 1960s, when accusations of "playing God" and interfering with nature were common. Today, however, "test tube" babies are celebrated for their own individuality and as people in their own right. Exactly, say opponents of cloning. Babies born in vitro are unique individuals; clones are photocopies of people who already exist. What will happen to individuality if we can stamp out copies of ourselves like so many cookies on a tray?

Interestingly, many of those who make this argument also tend to emphasize nurture over nature and deny that our genes determine ourselves—whether it be IQ, athletic ability, or our favorite ice cream flavor. But these arguments contradict each other. For if nurture triumphs over nature, then a clone will be an individual as unique as any other, determined for the most part by the environment in which she or he was reared.

Perhaps the most weighty argument against cloning is that, by eliminating the mixing of genes that occurs during conventional reproduction, human biodiversity will be diminished and human evolution will cease. It is the serendipitous mixing of genes that produces the Einsteins and Mozarts of the world; take away this process and surely the potential for new genius will cease. However, the fact is that human biological evolution for all intents and purposes has become insignificant compared to cultural evolution.

At this point, it is appropriate that I reveal the source of my interest in this subject. For the truth is, I wish to clone myself. Before my gate is stormed by villagers wielding branding irons, let me explain why.

I am 32 years old and have cystic fibrosis, an inherited genetic disease that 10
prohibits those who suffer from it from conceiving children and usually kills by the mid-30s. My dream is to clone myself, repair my clone's genetic defect, and give him the opportunity to fulfill the potential that has been denied to me by a cruel quirk of nature.

Perhaps my clone will climb Mount Everest, singlehandedly sail around the world, or simply marry and raise a family without the fear that his children will be prematurely fatherless and his wife a widow. The clone will not be me, but perhaps he will be who I could have been.

My body, my self. Surely also my DNA, my self.

With the coming genetic revolution, we will be directing our own evolution rather than relying on a natural (and sometimes disastrous) lottery to do it for us. And surely cloning will remain an esoteric and unusual method of reproduction, with most people choosing to do it the old-fashioned (and far more pleasurable) way. But should government be able to tell me what I can or cannot do with what is, after all, an intrinsic part of what and who I am?

Criminalizing an activity may be easier than answering the thorny philosophical questions raised by it. But before government rushes to outlaw my dream, it should at least seriously consider whether the opposition to human cloning is based on real dangers.

In Search of Brotherhood

RON STODGHILL II

I AM NOT REALLY SURE when our boundaries went up. Men tend to build 1
walls quietly, without warning. All I know is that when I looked up, me and my buddy weren't talking anymore. Somehow we had become like strangers. This rift—a simple misunderstanding magnified by male ego—didn't happen overnight. Men aren't like some women I know; we don't announce that we are cutting each other off. Instead we just slowly starve the relationship of anything substantive until it fades away. Me and my buddy had let our friendship evaporate to a point where we hadn't spoken in almost two years. Then one morning my mother called me at work and shared something she'd heard about him. "You know his wife is sick with cancer," she said.

I had to close my office door. I don't cry often, but the news broke me down. I thought of his wedding day four years ago and a picture I snapped of him beaming at me as he wrapped his bride in his arms. I remember telling my wife that I'd never seen him so happy, so sure about something. As it hit me that he now faced the possibility of losing his love, a deep sense of shame came over me. I wondered how he was coping and who was helping him through this crisis. I thought how devastated I'd be if my own wife were suffering. And I wondered whether he and I could ever be tight again.

We had always been like family, sharing an unusual history that dated back to the turn of the century when our great-grandparents were pals growing up in a small town not far from Nashville. Both our families migrated north to Detroit for better-paying jobs, and remained close through the generations. When I was born 36 years ago, he was among my first playmates. As we grew older, we became what we called true boys—real aces, spending most of our time together running the streets, hanging at bars and clubs, watching games, and chasing women. Our friendship came so easily that we took it for granted, and when it began to unravel, neither of us had a clue how to mend it.

WHAT REAL MEN ARE—AND AREN'T

Like so many brothers, I have always been clumsy talking openly to other men about matters beyond box scores, babes, or general BS on the job. Not that I believe male kinship is for "soft" or "weak" or "gay" types. It's just that expressing my most personal thoughts to another man, no matter how close we are, feels awkward at times, unnatural. Growing up, I learned from the males in my life that real men are tough, independent, dispassionate. Women, while they may possess these attributes, are also allowed to be tender, vulnerable, and compassionate. But I am learning that men, too, must grant ourselves more freedom in defining how we communicate. If we don't, we risk losing what's most important to us—our women, families, friends, and even ourselves.

5 A few years ago my father and I went to the Million Man March. It was a rare opportunity for us to spend an entire day together, amid the throngs of other black fathers and sons and friends. For hours we stood on the Mall in the crisp October air while the world marveled at our historic moment. There were many things I could have shared with my father that day—mistakes I'd made in my life, triumphs big and small, times he'd made me proud and times he'd disappointed me. Instead we both stood there, soaking in the event and retreating into our own thoughts. Around us I noticed a profound silence. My memory of that day will always be somewhat bittersweet because it revealed that beneath a dramatic facade of togetherness, black men—myself included—mostly chose to stand apart.

Most of us brothers understand the nature of intimacy. Through the women in our lives, we have witnessed the bounty of wisdom, counsel, and encouragement that comes channeling through their tight female networks. A few years ago, when word spread that my wife, Robyn, was pregnant with our first child, the phone rang constantly for months with female relatives and friends eager to talk about everything from breast-feeding to keeping the marital flame burning with an infant in the house. It became clear that sisters are able to benefit from a deep reservoir of insight offered to them by other wise and generous sisters.

TRANSCENDING THE MYTHOLOGY OF OUR MASCULINITY

My impending role as new father brought up a host of issues, too. I was trying to navigate Robyn's mild mood swings and a much-altered sex life brought on by her hormonal and physical changes. And I was grappling with how a new baby would affect our finances. With a needy newborn, would we ever get out of the house, or should we plan on life becoming a blur of working and changing diapers? But the fathers I knew seemed caught off guard by my questions, offering little more than a pat on the back and a vow to share a congratulatory cigar once the baby was born. I realized that discussing our experiences might have required us to reveal shortcomings or failures and compromise that fragile thing we call our masculinity.

It's tough to transcend the powerful mythology of masculinity, to imagine our heroes as anything less than solitary dudes who depended only on God and their own wits and brawn to triumph. We just can't picture Nelson Mandela, during his 27-year imprisonment, turning to a cell mate and confiding: "Man, I've got this weird feeling. I hope Winnie ain't cheatin' on me." Or Martin Luther King, Jr., after the March on Washington, mumbling to Ralph Abernathy, "I was so nervous speaking in front of all those people." Or even Michael Jordan, during his brief venture into pro baseball, lamenting over a beer, "It hurts when fans tell me I suck at this. Am I really that bad?"

Though we may rarely admit it, men are plagued with many of the same doubts, fears, and insecurities as women. And to survive our humiliating legacy—the enslavement of our families, the rape and exploitation of our women, the auctioning off of our children, and our groping for dignity in the shadowy freedoms that form our reality today—black men have withdrawn, adopting a vow of silence. But we can't expect to become better husbands, fathers, friends, and everything else we say we want to become without talking to one another. Our definition of manhood must include having the confidence and trust in our brothers to share our most intimate feelings. Brick by brick we must deconstruct the fortress that has kept our pain, insecurities, and even our dreams locked away for fear of scorn or ridicule. We must unburden ourselves and our sons from a warped and limited notion of masculinity, from thinking that intimacy is the exclusive terrain of women and that showing any emotion beyond anger makes us sissies. Like women, we have our own rich bank of wisdom and insight, but the vaults have been closed much too long.

BRIDGING TIME, BRIDGING DISTANCE

The day after my mother called, my wife and I drove over to visit my buddy 10
and his family. It was a sweet reunion, warm and easy. We all embraced and apologized for letting so much time slip between us. His wife looked frail, but her spirits were up. For the first time they saw our 2-year-old boy and marveled at

the blessing. Their little girl, 2½, instantly took to our son, and the two darted off together.

With yet another generation of our families starting a new relationship, my friend and I stepped outside, hoping to rebuild our old one. As he sat beside me on the patio, I could see the anguish in his face. Knowing that a pat on the back simply wasn't enough to touch all he was going through, I put my hand on his. We both knew there was no longer a place for bravado, false pride or ego in our friendship. Yet for a moment we just sat there, not really knowing how to begin. "So how are you survivin', my brother?" I asked finally.

He looked at me directly. "Damn, man," he said, his jaw tightening. "This s--- is real. It's been hard."

He stood up and paced for a moment, then sat back down. And then we began to talk, about our lives, ourselves, in a way we had never done before. He spoke about the sudden trip to the hospital, the grim diagnosis, the countless tests and surgery, and his own pain at watching his wife suffer while his daughter tried to figure out why. I told him how glad I was to be back in touch with him, and that I would be there for him, to talk, to laugh, to help bear this load. When I told him that, he seemed suddenly energized. He sat back in his chair, gazed up at the sky and began telling me some of the lessons he'd been learning about faith and courage and pushing forward even when things look bleak. As he shared these things with me, I listened closely and learned something from my boy about what it really takes to be a man.

PATHOS IN ADVERTISING

The following advertisement uses emotion to persuade readers. As you read and discuss this advertisement as a class, make sure you pay attention to the visual as well as the verbal arguments.

American Civil Liberties Union Advertisement

THE MAN ON THE LEFT
IS 75 TIMES MORE LIKELY TO BE STOPPED BY THE POLICE WHILE DRIVING THAN
THE MAN ON THE RIGHT.

It happens every day on America's highways. Police stop drivers based on their skin color rather than for the way they are driving. For example, in Florida 80% of those stopped and searched were black and Hispanic, while they constituted only 5% of all drivers. These humiliating and illegal searches are violations of the Constitution and must be fought. Help us defend your rights. Support the ACLU.

american civil liberties union
125 Broad Street, 18th Floor, NY, NY 10004 www.aclu.org

Chapter 4
Analyzing and Evaluating Logos

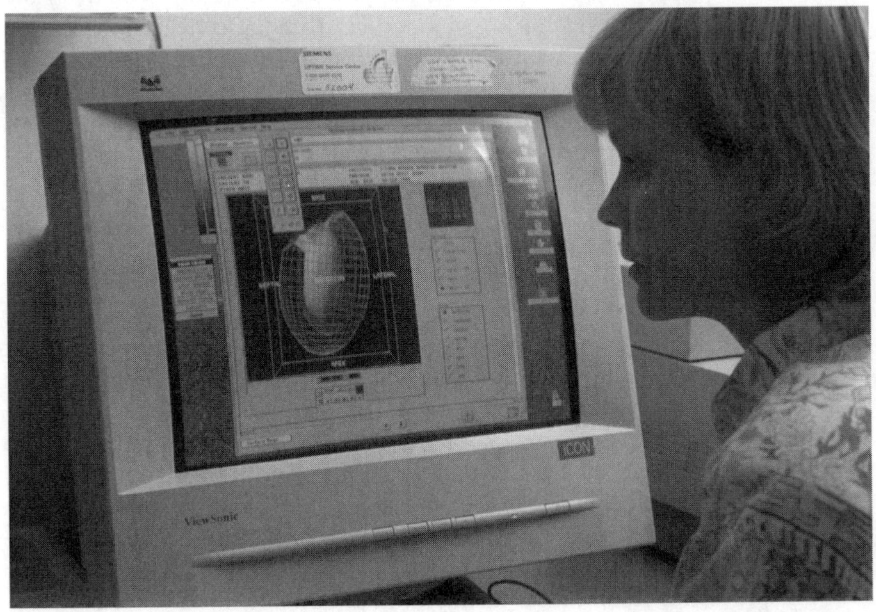

Logos: Arguing through Reasoning

The Greek word *logos* has several different meanings. It can mean word, thought, reason, or order. Our English word *logic* derives from *logos,* but logos has a broader meaning than logic. Logos refers to arguing through reasoning—the presentation of rational thought through language. Logos appeals to the rational, to our ability to think; ethos and pathos typically work on our non-rational faculties, our abilities to trust and feel. Although ethos and pathos can be more compelling, logos provides the backbone of arguing, particularly in academic communities. In *The Art of Rhetoric,* Aristotle considers logos the primary persuasive appeal. Logos provides an overall framework of which ethos and pathos are a part. Arguments from ethos and pathos can be rationalized. In other words, they can be explained in terms of claims and reasons, but arguments from logos require claims and reasons for their basic structure. And although ethos and pathos are important to move people to action, it is logos that leads to conviction, to belief that lasts after the emotion passes. Logos protects us against illegitimate or manipulative uses of language and allows us to reflect on what we feel and what we believe. Although logos may not inspire people as much as ethos and pathos, logos will often prevent people from acting foolishly or rashly.

The power of reflection and contemplation associated with logos is what makes this appeal so important in academic communities. Academic authors typically value certainty, and they will usually approach conclusions tentatively until a preponderance of evidence convinces them that the conclusion is true or useful. This is why academic authors want to test one another's arguments and have their arguments tested by others. This is why scientists usually try to replicate the experiments of other scientists, why social scientists compare their data with the data of other social scientists, or why art critics will check an author's interpretation or evaluation of a work against their own. At its worst, academic argument can become as contentious and rancorous as any other argument. But at its best, academic argument leads to critical thinking, the ability to judge for ourselves the rightness of a claim based on the available evidence. Logos provides the key to this critical judgment.

When we supply reasons to support our opinions, we discover—perhaps for the first time—why we hold the opinions we do. We may also discover that some cherished opinions have no rational basis. In this way, logical argument and critical thinking not only create new knowledge for the community, but they also lead to self-knowledge, to a better understanding of who we are and what we believe. Critical thinking is part of the process of gaining an education. Through informed and responsible arguing, we recognize truths that would otherwise have gone unnoticed.

The process of testing ideas through logical argument is a particularly important part of a college education. According to the philosopher Richard Rorty, a college serves two functions: providing students with "cultural literacy" and with "critical literacy." Cultural literacy is an awareness of the common knowledge of the community, what members of the community are expected to know. A degree in law or medicine, for example, certifies that the student who receives the degree has adequately learned the body of knowledge that scholars in the legal or medical communities value. But a university serves the additional function of teaching critical literacy. Critical literacy is the ability to question or explore what is believed to be true, to challenge or dispute the claims and opinions of others in an attempt to clarify and understand. Ideally, a college is a place where members of the community or members of different communities come together to ask questions, debate, and discuss ideas in a responsible fashion. This process of questioning and responding is critical thinking. It takes place primarily through language, through reading, writing, and speaking. Critical thinking can create tension, but it also represents the ideal for education.

FIVE KINDS OF CLAIMS

Claims about existence—What is the nature of reality?

Claims about causality—What are the causes or effects of an event?

Claims about language—How should words be defined or interpreted?

Claims about values—What do we value? What is the value of a particular object?

Claims about actions—What should we do? How should we act? What will solve a particular problem?

Creating Logos

A logical argument consists of three parts: claims, reasons, and assumptions

CLAIMS

The claim is the statement under dispute. It is the focus of the argument, a statement that is controversial, a proposition about which at least some people disagree. For many people, the first three statements that follow would be claims or "opinions" because they are under dispute; the fourth statement would be a "fact," a statement that is commonly accepted as true.

> The wealthy should pay a greater percentage of their income in taxes than the poor.
>
> The U.S. government is hiding the remains of an alien spacecraft.
>
> The U.S. government should guarantee basic health care.
>
> Paris is the capital of France.

Of course, what is a fact for some people may be an opinion for others; what some accept as true, others may dispute.

The level of disagreement depends on the people involved. Some people dispute the existence of a supreme being, while others take this existence for granted. Some accept a religious text such as the Bible or the Koran as authoritative, as a reliable index of truth; others dispute such a claim. Some take as a given that capital punishment is always wrong, while others hold the opposite view.

If a group of people all agree on a particular belief, then its status as a claim might not be noticed. Such a belief becomes part of the "common sense" or "self-evident truths" shared by that community. In fact, our opinions and biases often go unnoticed until someone calls them into question by raising an alternative opinion.

To question or discuss a claim, you first have to identify it. To do so, begin by asking "What is the topic or issue?" Then ask "What positions can people take on this issue?" Here is an example:

What is the issue? Secondhand smoke.

What positions can people take on this issue? Secondhand smoke causes cancer.

In academic writing, the claim of an argument is often the thesis, and this thesis usually comes near the beginning of the essay, following some kind of introduction. But this need not always be the pattern. The claim may come at the end of an argument and, in some cases, even in the middle. A claim may not be explicitly stated anywhere in the argument itself, and sometimes it may begin as a question. When the purpose of arguing is to discover for yourself what you believe, the claim you state may be only an initial attempt to take a position. Note that claims are *not* examples, background information, evidence, or data.

Some claims are absolute. They are either always true, or they are true for all cases:

All humans are mortal.

Copenhagen is the capital of Denmark.

No one has ever visited Mars.

Some claims are modified. They either may be true, or they are true only in some cases. Modified claims refer to what is generally the case or what is probable or possible rather than to what must always, absolutely be:

Most mass murderers are men.

It might snow tomorrow.

Eating broccoli may prevent cancer in some patients.

To identify an absolute claim look for words such as *every, all, each, everyone, anyone, always, must, never, none, no one*. To identify a modified claim, look for words such as *some, many, most, sometimes, someone, may, might, could, possibly, probably*. The philosopher Stephen Toulmin uses the term *qualifier* to describe words or phrases such as these, that modify the scope of a claim.

The different types of claims will be described in detail in later chapters, but here I will introduce each of them briefly.

Arguing about Existence Some claims relate to our experience of reality. One type of claim about reality is the claim about existence. A claim about existence responds to abstract questions such as these: What is really there? What is happening? What happened in the past? What will happen in the future? Here are some examples of claims about existence:

There is a hole in the ozone.

There is a 10th planet in the solar system.

Three million people live in Phoenix, Arizona.

The accused was at the scene of the crime between 11:00 and 11:30 P.M.

The Cleveland Indians will win the World Series.

Other claims about existence involve measuring or describing our experience of reality, responding to questions such as these: How large? How long? How much? How far? How many? How fast? Here are some examples:

That horse is brown with white spots.

The recent earthquake was the largest in over a decade.

It is 65 miles to the next gas station.

Claims that describe or characterize experience may require elaborate models and maps. For instance, no one has experienced a black hole directly. The claim that black holes exist relies upon mathematical models about the structure of the universe. And when the earth is viewed from space, no national boundaries are visible; these boundaries can only be shown on a map.

Arguing about Causality Our experience of the world may lead us to make claims about causes and effects, responding to abstract questions such as these: What will happen if we do that? What brought this about? Why are we doing this? What will this lead to? What caused that? What will that do? What is the purpose or motive? Can it be changed? Here are some sample claims about causality:

Smoking causes lung disease.

Violence on television contributes to the high rate of violent crime in America.

He is saying that only because he wants your money. (Motivation is a type of cause.)

Raising interest rates further will put the economy into recession.

The economic differences between the North and the South made the Civil War inevitable.

Like existence, claims about causes and effects can refer to past and future experience as well as to present experience.

Arguing about Language Language is made up of symbols, representations of our experience, our thinking about experience, or our thinking about symbols themselves. The word *tree* is not a concrete tree that we experience outside. It is a symbol that refers to our experience of trees, our concept of "a tree." Other symbols could be used to refer to the same concept. Danes use the symbol "træ." Germans use the symbol "baum." One could just as easily represent the concept of tree through some sort of picture or visual image.

Since all arguing takes place through symbols—usually written and spoken language—all arguing is to some extent "about symbols." But claims about symbols express arguments about the nature of symbols themselves, about what they mean or represent. Some claims relate to the definitions of terms:

> Anyone who tells ethnic jokes is racist.
>
> Most great artists are insane.
>
> You have to be able to read a job application to be considered literate.

Acceptance of these claims depends upon how one defines "racist," "insane," and "literate." Some claims about symbols may relate to the interpretation of a text, particularly an authoritative text such as the Constitution, the Bible, the Koran, or the rules for major-league baseball.

> The First Amendment does not protect pornographic or obscene speech.
>
> The Bible does not forbid homosexual relations.
>
> The Koran requires death for those who blaspheme.
>
> The rules of baseball indicate that a ball going under a fence should be considered a double.

Some claims about symbols relate to how we use symbols and answer questions such as these: How should we read or understand symbols? Are there symbols that cannot be used? Who should be allowed to use language? Under what circumstances and in what manner should one use particular symbols?

Arguing about Values A value is something that an individual or community holds to be of worth or esteem. Our values are related to our desires. To say that we desire to be free means that we value "freedom." If we desire to have the esteem and regard of others, we hold "fame" or "success" as a value. Sometimes, values are stated explicitly in an argument, but often they are implied or understood. Whenever an argument contains claims about what is "good" or "bad," or about what we "should" or "ought" to do, then it is an argument about values. The claim may not actually use the words *good/bad* or *should/should not,* but the force of these words will be there. Value claims always pass judgment or "evaluate":

> That painting is beautiful.
>
> The proposed landfill will be an eyesore.
>
> Plagiarism is wrong.
>
> Euthanasia is ethical.
>
> This diamond is priceless.
>
> What a great film!
>
> I didn't care for the plot.

Values come into conflict with each other when we have to choose between two things we desire (or dislike) or when we disagree with one another about what we desire. In such cases, we may have to choose between the better of two good things or the lesser of two evils. Some claims about values refer to the order or hierarchy of values, to what desires we should prefer above others:

Mexican food is better than Italian food.

It is best to find a parking space close to the store.

He is the "most-preferred man" on campus.

Camping in the mountains is more fun than camping in the desert.

A woman's right to privacy takes precedence over any government interest in the life of the fetus during the first trimester of pregnancy.

A fetus's right to life is more important than any right of the mother.

Arguing about Actions Claims about actions are closely related to claims about values; they usually imply an evaluation of an action and recommend some different action. Any judgment about good/bad, right/wrong, beautiful/ugly, or moral/immoral usually implies a "should" or "ought," and "should" and "ought" refer to actions. We first observe how others act; then we argue about how they should or ought to act. Or we recognize a state of inaction—no one is doing anything—and recommend some type of action. Claims about actions typically propose a change in the way things are now.

Action implies some degree of choice on the part of the performer or performers of the action. To explain how action implies choice, the philosopher Kenneth Burke distinguishes between action and motion. A lot of things move but don't act. Gold balls and baseballs move, for example, but humans act by swinging clubs and bats. Action, then, implies movement with a purpose and a direction. Humans choose to act, but they may "move" without choosing. If I trip and fall down a flight of stairs, I am definitely moving, but unless I tripped myself intentionally, I'm not acting. Actions always require some agent, some person or group of people performing the action. The agent may be stated in the claim or may be implied:

The federal government should impose national standards for education.

Students ought to graduate from college in four years.

Students should be taught foreign languages in elementary school.

This river needs to be cleaned up.

Let's eat out.

Practice your piano lesson!

The last three claims in this example show instances where the agent, the one performing the action, is implied or understood. (For the action of cleaning up the river, the agent is an unspecified "someone.")

REASONS

Just because people have a disagreement about something does not mean that they are arguing, at least not in the way that I am describing arguing in this book. And merely setting forth an opinion or making a claim is not arguing or reasoning either. Logical argument is rational persuasion. It is based on reasons. So to be a logical argument, a claim must be supported by one or more reasons. Stephen Toulmin calls reasons "data," the Latin root for which literally means "that which is given." Reasons, or data, are the evidence given for a claim. If you believe the reason or reasons, then you also believe the claim.

Identifying the Reasons Like claims, reasons are statements. After you have identified the claim, you should then look for the reason or reasons given to support that claim. A word such as *because* may be used to show that a "reason" is about to follow. Here is an example: You should wear a heavy coat today because it will probably snow. In this example, the claim is "you should wear a heavy coat today" (a claim about actions). The word *because* indicates that the reason for the claim is that "it will probably snow." (The reason, in this case, is a statement about existence, a statement about what will happen in the future.) Note that sometimes the reason precedes the claim, particularly when the claim is signaled by a word such as *so* or *therefore:*

> It will probably snow (reason), so you should wear a heavy coat today (claim).
>
> It will probably snow (reason); therefore, you should wear a heavy coat (claim).

Once you have identified the claim, the reason is often close by, particularly in academic writing, where reasons often follow the claim as part of a thesis statement. In some cases, however, the reason may be implied rather than stated. In such a case, you need to ask a further question: What do I need to believe in order to accept the claim the author is making?

Chains of Reasons In a simple argument, the claim is the only statement under dispute because the reason is something that others accept as true. In a more complex argument, however, the statement offered as a reason may itself require support before others will accept its truth. In a complex argument, the statements offered as reasons may actually be "claims" requiring further reasons. In the example I have been using, what if the person being addressed is not convinced that "it will probably snow"? The reason is then under dispute and needs to be justified. So the statement functioning as the reason itself becomes a claim:

> You should wear a heavy coat today because it will probably snow. I watched the weather report this morning, and the meteorologist reported a 90 percent chance of snow today and tomorrow.

The simple argument now becomes a complex argument with a chain of claims and reasons. If you accept the statement about existence (the meteorologist reported a 90 percent chance of snow), then you will accept the statement that it will probably snow. Of course, it is possible that these additional supporting statements may also be disputed. You might not accept the authority of the meteorologist, for example, or believe that she really predicted snow. If supporting statements are disputable, then they in turn need to be justified or explained through further reasons, extending the chain.

Non Sequiturs Some of the reasons in a chain of reasons may be implied rather than stated. If so, you will need to reconstruct these links in the chain based on what you can infer from the argument. Sometimes so much of the chain is left unstated that it is difficult to make the connections. A reason or chain of reasons that cannot be connected to the claim in some logical way is called a *non sequitur.* This Latin phrase means "does not follow" and refers to an argument in which the claim does not clearly follow from the reasons. Here are some examples:

> You should buy our product because we are showing you a picture of a beach.
>
> Our pizza is the best because we give away free soft drinks.

Some arguments appear to be non sequiturs but make sense with a little more background information. Consider the following instance:

> You should wear your coat today because I'm going shopping.

Without having more information about this argument, it is difficult to make any connection between the claim and the reason. With a little more information about context, however, this non sequitur makes more sense:

> You should wear your coat today because I'm going shopping. I won't be able to pick you up after school, so you will have to walk home.

Actually, we make statements all the time, particularly among those we know quite well, that others may take to be non sequiturs because they don't understand the context or background implied in the statement. When my wife calls me at work and says, "Pick up something to eat on the way home because I couldn't get a baby-sitter," I can fill in the context enough to know that the reason she gives is not a non sequitur. Here is the reconstructed chain of reasons:

> (You should) Pick up something (for us) to eat on the way home. (claim)
>
> We don't have anything for the two of us to eat for dinner. (implied reason)
>
> We were planning on going out for dinner. (implied reason)
>
> Now we are eating at home. (implied reason)
>
> I couldn't get a baby-sitter. (stated reason)

ASSUMPTIONS

In discussing reasons, I suggested that arguments usually don't make much sense without some information in addition to the claim and the reason. Even if you accept the reason, there may be gaps you have to fill in before accepting the claim. The statements that fill in these gaps are called assumptions. They are sometimes stated, but more often they are implied, even in academic writing. Found in the movement from reasons to claims, assumptions fill in the gaps in a chain of reasons. In his system for describing the structure of arguments, Stephen Toulmin refers to assumptions as "warrants."

Identifying Assumptions To identify an assumption, first identify the claim and reason, then ask the following question: If the reason is true, what else must be true for the claim to be true? An assumption can usually be identified from the actual language of the claim and reason. Here is an example:

Claim: Richard Nixon was a good president.

Reason: He was skilled at foreign policy.

Assumption: Any president who is skilled at foreign policy is a good president.

To identify the assumption in this case, look for the term that is common to both the claim and the reason (Richard Nixon) and replace it with a more general term (any president). Here is another example:

Claim: You should visit Paris.

Reason: Paris has the world's best art museums.

Assumption: You should visit a place that has the best art museums.

In this argument, "Paris" is the common element between the claim and the reason. Replace it with a more general term, "place," and combine the remaining elements of the claim and reason.

Let's go back to the example I used in discussing reasons:

You should wear a heavy coat today because it will probably snow.

The assumption here is that, in general, one should wear a coat when it snows: Snow justifies the wearing of a coat. A related assumption is that what is true of the general is true of the particular. In other words, if you should generally wear a coat on a snowy day, then you should wear a coat on this particular snowy day. This second assumption may seem like a statement of the obvious, and it is obvious in an argument this simple. Most arguments are not laid out this simply, however, and in more complex arguments, it can be challenging to identify all the assumptions.

Assumptions can often be the most crucial part of an argument. Identifying assumptions may lead to qualification of the claim, reservations about the claim, or possible objections to it. When you find yourself agreeing with the reason or reasons but still having difficulty accepting the claim, take a implied assumptions. Consider the following dialogue:

Student Y: What a dumb movie. There was no action ir
Student X: I really liked it. It made me think.
Student Y: But nothing happened!
Student X: You just don't appreciate a good movie.

This appears to be an argument: Both students are making claims and putting forth reasons. But their arguing is not very productive because they have not examined the assumptions implied in each of their arguments. Take the first argument: The movie was dumb because it had no action. First, identify the claim: The movie was dumb (a statement about value). Then, identify the reason: It had no action (a statement about existence). Obviously, the two students disagree about the claim; yet they agree about the reason, that the movie had no action. So why do they disagree? Because they have different assumptions about what makes a movie a good movie (an issue of value). In the first student's argument, the implied assumption is that a good movie must have action. The second student's argument implies that a movie must make a viewer think. Once these assumptions have been recognized, the argument might be recast as follows:

Student Y: What a dumb movie. There was no action in it.
Student X: That's true, but does a movie need action to be a good movie? I think that a good movie is one that makes you think.
Student Y: This movie does make you think. I just prefer an action movie.
Student X: Perhaps we should find a movie that does both.

Student X's final statement is probably overly optimistic, but at least the discussion now focuses on the crucial point of disagreement between the two: What makes a movie good? Before they resolve this point, they will never agree on a good movie.

Assumptions in a Chain of Reasoning As the previous example shows, an assumption, like a reason, can be disputed and become a "claim" in a new chain of reasoning. Identifying assumptions takes an argument in a new direction. In the example, the focus of the argument shifts from whether a particular movie is good to the larger question of what a good movie should have or do. As with any chain of reasons, the chain can continue until the two sides agree to disagree or until they together identify some common ground that can help resolve the issue. Perhaps our two student moviegoers could appeal to an authority they both accept, such as a movie critic. Or perhaps they could agree on a higher value than "action" or "thought" that determines the value of a movie.

Identifying assumptions in a chain of reasoning can be particularly difficult when some elements of the chain are implied rather than stated. In such a case, you must first identify or reconstruct the claims and reasons before identifying the assumptions. I recently saw the following statement on a bumper sticker:

Abortion stops a heart from beating.

lthough only a single statement, this is an argument. But it only makes sense as an argument if we know something about the context. Only one part of the argument is stated; the others are implied or understood. But what element is stated here? Claim, reason, or assumption? The people who produced this bumper sticker took for granted that their audience would know what an abortion is and be aware of the controversy over legalized abortions. So the statement on this bumper sticker is probably not intended as a claim: Anyone who knows what an abortion is understands that, if a fetus has developed a heart, then an abortion will stop that heart from beating. (Those who disagree that abortion *always* stops a heart from beating might see this as a claim, however. They could point out that abortions may take place at any point during a pregnancy, even before the fetus's heart is formed. There are, they would argue, some abortions that do not stop a heart from beating.)

In fact, this statement is probably intended as a reason for a claim that is understood, the claim that abortion is wrong or that it should be made illegal. Interpreted this way, the argument can be reconstructed as follows:

Claim: Abortion is wrong.

Reason: Abortion stops a heart from beating.

Assumption: Any act that stops a heart from beating is wrong.

As an argument, the statement on the bumper sticker is a bit deceptive because it *appears* to be a claim rather than a reason. And taken as a claim, the statement is much less controversial and more factual than the actual claim "Abortion is wrong." Reconstructing this argument is crucial for understanding and responding to it.

To reconstruct the argument on the bumper sticker, I had to conjecture about the people who made the bumper sticker and their intended audience. In order to do this, I relied upon my interpretation of contemporary American culture and politics. Someone else might reconstruct the argument differently, and the two of us might even disagree about how the argument should be reconstructed. The point is that reconstructing arguments and identifying assumptions can never be an exact process. Arguing in everyday life is not, like quantitative logic or mathematics, governed by strict rules. Understanding an argument requires some understanding of its context and its history, some understanding of the community in which the argument occurs. You have to understand the definitions of key terms used in the argument, and you have to understand, as much as possible, what people accept as true and what they still disagree about.

Consider the argument implied by the bumper sticker. The assumption is "Any act that stops a heart from beating is wrong." This statement is so broad that it is nearly impossible to defend, without qualification, against all objections. Consider the exceptions, all the "things" that could stop a heart from beating but are not necessarily "wrong." Old age stops a heart from beating, but is it wrong? Again, relying on my knowledge of the context, I can suggest that the creators of this bumper sticker probably mean that any unnatural and intentional act that stops a heart from beating is wrong. But my restatement of the assumption is only a conjecture. To be sure, I would need more information about the conversation and context for this argument.

Common Types of Assumptions An assumption will make sense only within the context of a particular argument. However, you frequently will encounter some general types of assumptions. Authors use these general strategies to make the connections between reasons and claims. The general patterns are often identified by the acronym GASCAP[1]:

G—Generalization

A—Analogy

S—Sign

C—Causality

A—Authority

P—Principles

When a generalization forms the basis of an argument, the assumption is that "whatever is true of a representative sample will be true of the whole group." Many arguments are based on generalizations: consumer research, opinion polls, Nielsen television ratings, quality control checks in industry, scientific experiments, teacher evaluations, taste testing. When an argument is based on an analogy, the assumption is that "situations that are similar in some ways will be similar in others." Many arguments are based on comparisons or precedents. For example, legal arguments often compare the case under consideration with previous similar cases. And politicians may make decisions on what to do in a particular community based on what was done in a similar community. Scientists also make arguments about scientific principles based on what they observed in similar experiments or conditions.

An argument based in signs is usually an argument about existence. In such an argument, the assumption is that "certain signs indicate an unobserved object or event." Historians and archeologists argue from signs when they try to re-create the past based on evidence left behind. Geologists try to understand the history of the earth by examining the signs found in rock formations or fossils. A police detective could try to identify a criminal based on signs found at the crime scene.

If an argument is based on causality, then the assumption will be that "if X occurs, then Y will follow." Many arguments about actions are based on assumptions about causality. You push on the brake because you assume it will stop the car. You watch a weather forecast to determine what to wear to school because you assume that the forecast gives a reasonable prediction of the weather. You wear your raincoat because you assume that it will keep the water

[1]Richard Fulkerson provides a detailed discussion of GASCAP in Chapter 3 of his *Teaching the Argument in Writing* (Urbana: NCTE, 1996). Many of the examples of arguments used here come from Fulkerson's chapter.

■■ ASSUMPTIONS BASED ON GASCAP

G—Generalization: Whatever is true of a representative sample will be true of the whole group.

A—Analogy: Situations that are similar in some ways will be similar in others.

S—Sign: Certain signs indicate an unobserved object or event.

C—Causality: If X occurs, then Y will follow.

A—Authority: Whatever a trusted expert says about a subject is probably right.

P—Principles: What is generally true will be true in a particular case.

out. Politicians pass laws because they assume that people will obey them or that the laws can be enforced.

In an argument based on authority, the assumption is that what a trusted export says about a subject is probably right. Arguments based on authority are closely related to ethos—the assumption relies on how much you trust the expert's opinion. As mentioned in Chapter 2, we make decisions every day based on assumptions about authority. If we refused to accept any authority, we would have a hard time getting anything done. For example, you ask a reasonable-looking person for directions because you trust that the person knows how to get to where you are going. If that person seems hesitant or unsure, you will probably ask another reasonable-looking person. But the reason you stop in the first place is that you are willing to accept an opinion given on authority.

An argument from principles is based on the assumption that "what is generally true will be true in a particular case." Most arguments about what is right or wrong, or good or bad, are based on assumptions about principles. Laws, rules, accepted patterns of behavior, scientific truths—these are all examples of principles that help us draw conclusions.

Evaluating Logos

As noted earlier, what often passes for arguing is really just quarreling, bickering, and contending with words. Logical argument, on the other hand, should be rational and reasonable and should attempt to clarify, not just refute. To understand and respond to a logical argument, you must be able to identify its parts so that you can isolate points of agreement and disagreement. To find the parts of an argument, ask the following questions:

1. What is the issue?
2. What claim is being made about the issue?
3. What kind of claim is it?
4. What reasons are given to support the claim?
5. What assumptions are implied by these reasons?
6. What additional reasons or chains of reasons and assumptions support the statements made in the reasons and assumptions?
7. Where do I agree or disagree with this argument?

Once you have identified the parts of the argument, ask the following questions to evaluate the quality of the logical argument:

1. Is the claim an idea? Does it state an assertion in a complete sentence?
2. Does it answer a question that is at issue for the community?
3. Is it framed in precise language? If it is your own claim, does it say exactly what you mean?
4. Is it justified by reasons and assumptions that are acceptable to the community being addressed?
5. Is it justified by reasons and assumptions that are acceptable to you? If not, then what would be required to convince you?

If you answer "no" to any of these questions, then you have found a place where you can respond to the claim. If it is your own claim, then you have found where your argument needs to be revised. If you can answer "yes" to these questions, then you are ready to evaluate the reasons that are used to justify or explain the claim. Here are some questions to ask when evaluating a reason:

1. Is the reason an idea? Does it state an assertion in a complete sentence?
2. Does it answer the question "What makes the claim true?"
3. Is it framed in precise language? If it is your own claim, does it say exactly what you mean?
4. Can you identify the assumptions that allow you to make the logical connection between the claim and reason?
5. Will the community accept the reason, or does it need to be supported with additional reasons?
6. Do you accept the reason? If not, then what would be required to convince you?

Again, if your answer to any of these questions is "no," you have discovered a place where you can respond to those who are using this reason to support their claim. If the reason is your own, then you have discovered a place where you can revise and improve your argument. If you can answer "yes" to the above questions, then you need to evaluate each of the assumptions you identified in response to Question 4:

1. Is the assumption an idea? Does it state an assertion in a complete sentence?
2. Does it answer the question, "If the reason is true, then what else must be true for the claim to be true?"
3. If stated, is it framed in precise language? If implied, can it be reconstructed in precise terms?
4. Is the assumption one of the six GASCAP strategies (generalization, analogy, sign, causality, authority, principle)?
5. Will the community accept the assumption, or does it need to be supported with additional reasons?
6. Do you accept the assumption? If not, then what would be required to convince you?

Fallacies

An important part of evaluating logos is looking for fallacies: arguments that sound persuasive but contain errors in reasoning or manipulative strategies. Because they sound persuasive, fallacies can be very dangerous, particularly when people don't take time to think. Fallacies are easy arguments to make (because they stem from lazy thinking) and they seem to be true. Many of them resemble legitimate arguments. Most fallacies are related to logos, but there are fallacies of ethos and pathos as well.

FALLACIES OF ETHOS

Ethical fallacies work in two ways. In the first case, a person misuses ethos by misrepresenting his or her authority. In this case, an author might try to win the trust of an audience by presenting himself or herself as knowledgeable, trustworthy, or interested, when in reality he or she is just trying to take advantage of the audience's trust. In the second case, an author might attack an individual who really is credible in order to destroy that individual's authority.

Ad Hominem This Latin phrase means "to the person," and this term refers to a personal attack that has nothing to do with the argument. Of course, questioning a person's character or credibility is not necessarily fallacious. It becomes so when the attack on a person's character is used as a distraction from the real issue. For instance, it would not be fallacious to attack a scientist's experimental results if you had reason to believe that he or she had falsified data. An attack would be fallacious, however, if you based your criticism on the fact that he or she had a string of outstanding parking tickets. Some politicians use personal attacks as part of their campaign strategy. This is called "negative campaigning" or "mudslinging." A politician may rake up an opponent's past behavior, even things the opponent did when he or she was quite young, looking for anything that might damage the opponent's public image. Sometimes, politicians will even point to the irresponsible behavior of an opponent's relatives (siblings, children, in-laws, cousins) as a way of attacking the candidate's current credibility.

Guilt by Association This fallacy is an attack on an individual's credibility based upon that individual's membership in a particular group. This fallacy usually works in this way. You generalize from the behavior of some members of the group to the group as a whole, stereotyping all members of the group, and then you identify the individual you are attacking with that group. Racial stereotyping is one type of guilt by association. For instance, a neighbor said he didn't like the fact that an Asian family had moved into our neighborhood because he had worked with some Chinese people and found them untrustworthy. He assumed that because he didn't trust some Chinese people, he couldn't trust anyone Chinese. He also assumed that anyone with Asian features must be Chinese. (This particular family was Laotian.)

Poisoning the Well A writer who "poisons the well" presents an argument in such a biased or emotional way that it is difficult for an opponent to respond without looking dishonest or immoral. This strategy is also meant as a distraction from the real issue and may involve personal attacks. Here's an example: "Of course, this liar will tell you that he didn't steal my stuff. You can't believe a thief. Go ahead and ask him; he'll deny it." How is the accused supposed to respond? The very act of asserting innocence in this case can be construed as a sign of guilt. The emotional and manipulative nature of the language in this case is a distraction from the real issue: Who is guilty of stealing?

False Authority This fallacy occurs when an author tries to establish credibility without any real authority or when an audience is more willing to listen to a person who is popular rather than one who is knowledgeable. Con men use the

■■ FALLACIES OF ETHOS

Ad hominem—Attacking the person rather than the issue.

Guilt by association—Attacking the individual's membership in a group.

Poisoning the well—Presenting an opponent's argument in a biased and emotional way.

False authority—Attempting to establish credibility without real authority; authority based on popularity rather than expertise.

fallacy of false authority to trick people out of their money. Advertisements may also use false authorities, often by using celebrities to endorse various products. A basketball player may be an expert on athletic shoes, but is an athlete any more qualified to endorse deodorant? (I suppose they sweat a lot.) Does playing a doctor on a daytime soap opera qualify someone to endorse a particular medical product or service? Just because someone is an expert in one area, doesn't make them an expert in another. Having a Ph.D. in chemistry doesn't make you an expert on educational issues.

FALLACIES OF PATHOS

Emotions play an important role in persuasion, particularly in moving people to act on their convictions. But emotions can be easily manipulated as well. Fallacies of pathos occur when an author uses emotions to obscure an issue, divert attention away from the real issue, lead others into errors in reasoning, or exaggerate the significance of an issue. Teachers occasionally hear fallacious appeals to emotion from their students. I once had a student who missed a lot of class and skipped some major assignments. He turned in a final essay, but it showed signs of being thrown together at the last minute. When I told him he wouldn't be passing the class, he complained about how angry his parents would be if he lost his scholarship. His implied argument was "You should give me a passing grade because my parents will be angry with me." The assumption here is that performance in college courses should be measured by how parents will react to the final grades (an assumption of principle related to a causal argument). This assumption was unacceptable to me, but the student was hoping that the vividness of his emotional appeal would distract me from the flimsiness of the argument.

Ad Populum This Latin phrase means "to the people." The term refers to a fallacious argument that appeals to popular prejudices. One of these is the *bandwagon appeal,* an appeal to popularity—if everyone else is doing it, it must be right. Here are a couple of examples: "It is all right for me to cheat on my taxes because everyone else does"; "It's all right for me to break the speed limit because I'm just keeping up with the flow of traffic. Besides, other people go faster than I do." The assumption in these arguments is that "just because something is popular or common practice, it must be right." Another ad populum fallacy is the *appeal to traditional wisdom.* This fallacy is an appeal to what has been done in the past: "That's just the way we've always done it." A related fallacy is the *appeal to provincialism,* the belief that the familiar is automatically superior to the unfamiliar: "That's just how it's done around here."

Threats/Rewards The appeal to force is another name for a threat. A threat diverts attention from the real issue to the negative consequences of not accepting the argument. Extortion, blackmail, intimidation, hate speech, racial slurs,

FALLACIES OF PATHOS

Ad populum—Appealing to popular prejudices, including the bandwagon appeal, the appeal to traditional wisdom, and the appeal to provincialism.

Appeal to force/reward—Using threats or bribes to persuade.

Red herring—Attempting to draw attention aware from the issue by raising irrelevant, usually emotional, issues.

and sexual harassment are all examples of threats. The appeal to reward is just the opposite of a threat, diverting attention from the issue to what will be gained by accepting the point of view. Buying votes, trading favors, and bribery are all examples of the appeal to reward.

Red Herring The name of this fallacy probably comes from a trick once used by escaping prisoners: dragging a fish across their path of escape to throw dogs off the scent. A red herring is any attempt to draw attention away from the issue by raising irrelevant issues. This diversion often involves obscuring the issue with more emotional issues. Here is an example: "I don't think the president's economic plan is a good idea. I mean, what is he going to do about the violence in our inner cities?"

FALLACIES OF LOGOS

Logical fallacies are arguments that look rational, fair, and valid, but aren't. If you take a logic class, you will learn a lot about formal fallacies—arguments that don't follow the proper form of a logical syllogism. Following are common informal fallacies: errors in reasoning related claims, reasons, and assumptions.

Begging the Question This term describes an argument in which the reason is really no more than a restatement of the conclusion. For example, "You should exercise because it is good for you" is just another way of saying "You should exercise because you should exercise." A writer also begs the question when he or she offers a conclusion without adequate support or uses reasons or assumptions that are just a controversial as the conclusion. Consider the familiar argument "Abortion is wrong because it is murder." This argument doesn't really advance the conversation about abortion because it offers as a reason one of the primary points of contention in the abortion issue: a fetus is really an individual life that can be "murdered."

Complex Question A complex or "loaded" question is really two questions phrased as one. A famous example is "Have you stopped beating your wife?" The two questions phrased here as one are "Have you ever beaten your wife?" and "If so, have you stopped?" As the question is phrased, answering either "yes" or "no" will get a husband in trouble: "Yes (I used to beat her, but I stopped)"; "No (I still beat her)."

Equivocation Equivocation is using one term for two different definitions. When using this fallacy, an author will often have one definition in mind while allowing the audience to think that he or she means something else. When President Clinton was asked about his relationship with Monica Lewinsky, he insisted that he did not have "sexual relations" with "that woman." Many Americans accused him of equivocating in this case with the commonplace definition of "sexual relations."

Hasty Generalization/Sweeping Generalization A hasty generalization is another name for "jumping to conclusions." It is a conclusion formed on scant evidence. Here is an example:

> The country is probably going into a recession because they laid off five people at my office.

The assumption in this argument is that a few people being laid off at one office is a sure sign of a coming recession. But the economy is so large and complex that five people being laid off at one office would have no effect. This conclusion requires more evidence. A sweeping generalization is similar to a hasty generalization. It involves applying a statement that is true for one particular situation to another situation without considering how the two situations might be different. Here is an example:

> My accounting degree really prepared me well for law school. Everyone who wants to go to law school should major in accounting.

The assumption in this argument is that what is true for the writer is true for everyone. The argument ignores important differences among students. Some people feel well prepared for law school after studying English, political science, or philosophy.

False Analogy An analogy is a powerful persuasive tool because it presents an argument in interesting and memorable terms. As mentioned earlier, analogies also provide the assumptions for many kinds of arguments. An analogy becomes fallacious, however, when the differences between the things compared are greater than the similarities. When the United States got involved in wars against communists in Korea and Vietnam, government leaders justified their actions by referring to the "domino theory." According to this theory, if communists were allowed to take over one country, neighboring countries would also fall to communism like a line of dominoes, risking world domination by communist nations. This analogy is a powerful and memorable image, but it ignores the fact that international politics is much more complex than a game of dominoes. The domino theory was also based on the assumption that Asian nations were like European nations in their politics and that one Asian nation (Korea) was pretty much like another (Vietnam). These assumptions proved to be false as well.

Post Hoc The full Latin name for this fallacy is *post hoc, ergo propter hoc,* "after this, therefore because of this." This fallacy refers to an error in reasoning based on the assumption that just because one event follows another, the first caused the second. A lot of superstitions originate in this fallacy. A person walks under a ladder, and a bucket of paint falls on his head, so he tells people that walking under a ladder brings bad luck. The problem is that walking under the ladder did not cause the bucket to fall (unless he bumped the ladder); further, to jump to the conclusion that there is a connection between ladders and bad luck is a hasty generalization. Buckets don't fall every time someone walks under a ladder.

Slippery Slope This fallacy is another fallacy of causality. It occurs when you argue that one event will inevitably lead through a series of events resulting in disaster. It's found in the familiar warning given to kids: "If you steal a candy bar, then you will steal toys, then bikes, then cars, and then you'll find yourself on death row." It is true that most hard criminals started with petty crimes, but it isn't true that every kid who steals a candy bar will turn into a murderer. This argument is just designed to scare them; logically, it doesn't work. The slippery slope fallacy is a favorite of political extremists who argue that voting for one candidate (or the other) will drive the country to ruin. It is true that voting has consequences, but a lot of other decisions would have to be made before an individual could ruin the government. You'll hear extremists argue that one particular bill, this one Supreme Court nominee, just a slight increase in taxes will all bring the country to unavoidable disaster. Of course, fatal decisions can be made, but as with any causal argument, the writer should be prepared to explain exactly how the causal chain works.

Oversimplification. This fallacy occurs when a writer makes an argument that reduces a complex issue to a simple argument. An oversimplification may have some truth, but because it leaves out important information, it distorts the truth. Here is an example:

> Jogging is good for you. Everybody ought to jog every day.

It may be true *all other things being equal* that jogging is good for humans, but some people may have conditions that make jogging harmful or inappropriate. One kind of oversimplification is an *oversimplified cause.* This fallacy occurs when a writer tries to reduce a complex event or phenomenon to one simple cause. When former Vice President Dan Quayle blamed the television show "Murphy Brown" for the breakdown of the American family, he reduced a complex social phenomenon to a ridiculously simple cause. The same fallacy occurred when people blamed talk radio programs for the bombing of the federal building in Oklahoma City in 1995 or the movie *The Matrix* for the shootings at Columbine High School in 1999. Although these may have been contributing causes, it would be fallacious to identify these as the sole causes. Because causality typically involves complex relationships, the oversimplified cause is quite common.

Stacking the Deck Gamblers "stack the deck" in their favor by arranging the cards so that they will win. Writers "stack the deck" by ignoring any evidence or arguments that don't support their position. For example, a drug company would stack the deck by realizing only the positive results of experiments on a new drug, suppressing any negative results. I once experienced "stacking the deck" when buying a used car. The person trying to sell me the car talked about how wonderful the car was. After I bought the car, another person tried to sell me an extended warranty by pointing out all the things that could break down. In both cases, these sales representatives were stacking the deck by ignoring either the bad or good qualities of the car. Whenever you're hearing only one side of a story, you should wonder what's being left out.

Appeal to Ignorance The burden of supporting an argument falls on the person making it. A writer who makes an appeal to ignorance refuses to accept this burden of proof and tries to use the lack of evidence *as* evidence to support a claim. Here is an example:

> Bigfoot, the Loch Ness monster, and extraterrestrials must really exist because no one has ever proved that they don't.

In fact, those who make the claim "Bigfoot exists" are the ones who need to support the claim. It would be a mistake, however, to assume that "Bigfoot does not exist" just because you don't accept the argument that he does. "Bigfoot does not exist" is also a claim that carries with it a burden of proof.

Non Sequitur This Latin phrase means "it does not follow" and refers to a conclusion that has no apparent connection to the reasons. Non sequiturs are often used in advertising. For example, a car may be pictured with a beautiful woman inside, the implied argument being "You should buy this car because a beautiful woman is sitting in it." But there is no clear connection between the conclusion and the reason. The woman is just there to get your attention. It is not possible to identify an assumption or chain of reasons that would link the reason and the conclusion in a sensible way.

False Dilemma The false dilemma, or "either/or" fallacy, involves trying to force readers to accept a conclusion by presenting only two options, one of which is clearly more desirable than the other. Rarely are there only two possibilities. I have to admit, however, that my wife and I often use this strategy with our kids: "Do you want to finish your dinner or go straight to bed?" "Hard sell"

■■ FALLACIES OF LOGOS

Begging the question—Restating or assuming a conclusion.

Complex question—Phrasing two questions as one.

Equivocation—Using one term for two different definitions.

Hasty generalization—Drawing a conclusion on scant evidence.

Sweeping generalization—Applying a principle true in one instance to all instances.

False analogy—Comparing two objects or events that are more dissimilar than similar.

Post hoc—Assuming that just because one event follows another, the first caused the second.

Slippery slope—Arguing that one event will inevitably lead through a series of events resulting in disaster.

Oversimplification—Reducing a complex issue to a simple reason or cause.

Stacking the deck—Ignoring evidence that is not favorable.

Appeal to ignorance—Using the lack of evidence to the contrary as a reason.

Non sequitur—Providing a reason that cannot be reasonably connected to the conclusion by an assumption or chain of reasons.

False dilemma—Forcing a reader to accept a conclusion by presenting only two extreme options.

Strawperson—Weakening or distorting another's argument to make it easier to refute.

salespersons and negotiators often use the false dilemma to try to close a deal: "Do you want to pay cash or credit for that?" (eliminating the option that you may not want to buy at all); "If you don't act now, you will never get another chance!"; "Would you rather buy whole life insurance or risk leaving your family without any income?"

Strawperson Imagine how much easier it would be to knock over a scarecrow than a real person. The strawperson is an oversimplified and distorted version of another's viewpoint that is easy to refute. A writer usually resorts to setting up a strawperson when his or her own arguments are not particularly strong. In such a case, the writer has to weaken the other point of view to the point that it can be easily challenged. The strawperson works best when the other person is unable to respond or to give a proper account of his or her own viewpoint.

Quantitative Arguments

Our society places a great deal of trust in statistics, which are really just another way of describing our experience. Statistics help us count and quantify certain aspects of the world we live in and allow us to say something about the collective experience of a community. But just because they are subject to mathematical principles, statistics are still not absolute truth. Some experiences cannot be counted and measured, and the quality of an argument based on statistics depends on how the information was gathered and interpreted. Statistics can be deceiving. For instance, there are problems with averaging. The ***average***, or ***mean***, for a group is calculated by adding together the data relating to each member of the group and then dividing that total by the number of members. If you want to calculate the average weight of a football team's defensive line, for example, you take the weight of each player added together and divide that total weight by the number of players on the defensive line. When there are great differences among the numbers being totaled, averages can be deceiving. Let's say that the average weight of the defensive line is 300 pounds (a total of 1,200 pounds divided by four players). Sounds like a nightmare for the opposing quarterback. But suppose the weight is distributed as follows:

Left end	450 pounds
Left tackle	450 pounds
Right tackle	150 pounds
Right end	150 pounds

Now it sounds like a quarterback's dream. The opposing team can play to the right side of the defensive line and run right over those 150-pounders or play to the left side and run right past those 450-pounders.

As this example suggests, it is always important to know how the numbers being averaged are distributed among the members of the group. Take average income, as another example. If it is reported that the average yearly income for a household of four is $35,000, you should not assume that most households of four actually make that much. There are individuals in the United States who make millions of dollars annually, and these pull the "average" income above the average household's income. To evaluate the figure, it might help to know the ***median***, the level at which half the incomes are higher and half are lower, or the ***mode***, the income that shows up most frequently.

Averages can also be deceiving when there are only a few numbers being averaged. If two students take a class and one gets an A while the other fails, then the average grade for that class is C. But that average doesn't really say much about the performance of the class: Too few numbers are being averaged.

Percentages can be deceiving as well. A percentage is calculated by dividing a part of a group by the total number of members in the group (for example, 50 ÷ 200 = .25). A percentage is always expressed as a part of 100, so .25 is

25/100, or 25 percent. When dealing with percentages, it is always important to know the "raw" numbers from which they are calculated. A percentage is particularly deceiving when it is calculated from only a few numbers. Suppose that you ask three of your classmates what kind of music they prefer, and two of them tell you country music, while the third mentions jazz. Based on this you could say that almost 70 percent of the students you surveyed at your school prefer country music, but the number would be deceiving because you only surveyed three students.

Even raw numbers can be deceiving. It doesn't mean much to take second place, for instance, if there are only two competitors in the contest. Raw numbers have to be put in some context. If your school reports that 300 students flunked out last year, is that good or bad? It depends. How many have flunked out in previous years? Maybe 300 represents a real improvement. How many students attend your school? If the total student body is 50,000, 300 dropouts might not be too bad. For a school with 1,500 students, however, a dropout rate of 300 looks much worse.

Sometimes statistics are intentionally used to mislead or deceive. When an ad claims that a "new, improved" toothpaste is "twice as good" (or "200 percent better"), what does that mean? Twice as good as it was before? Twice as good as other brands? Twice as good in one or two ways? What information has been omitted from an ad like this? As noted earlier, admitting only information that proves your case while ignoring other statistical information is an example of "stacking the deck."

When evaluating statistics, it may help to ask questions such as these:

What is really being counted or measured?

How have the statistics been gathered?

What can one really conclude from these statistics?

Is any information missing?

Is the experience these statistics quantify reliable? Is it an experience that can be quantified?

The Principles in Action: Readings

PLAYING THE NUMBERS

The following essays each discuss the prominence of statistical arguments in our contemporary culture and the ways in which statistical arguments can be misunderstood, manipulated, and distorted. Stephen Budiansky, the author of "The Numbers Racket," is a scientist and a correspondent for *The Atlantic*. He has written several books, including works on cryptography and on animal intelligence. In this selection, Budiansky explains how polls and statistics are routinely used in political discourse to deceive and manipulate. The author of the second selection, William Lutz, is an English professor and the well-known author of *Doublespeak,* from which this excerpt is taken. Lutz is an expert on how language can be used to deceive, and he edits the *Quarterly Review of Doublespeak,* a "watchdog" newsletter published by the National Council of Teachers of English. The final two selections come from Bill Bryson, a popular humorist and travel writer. These two short essays both come from *I'm a Stranger Here Myself,* a collection of essays on American culture he wrote for an English newspaper when he returned to live in the United States after living in England more than 20 years. As you read these essays, consider the following questions:

1. According to each author, what is the importance of statistical arguments in American society?
2. According to each author, what are legitimate and illegitimate uses of statistical arguments?
3. What are some of the particular ways described in these essays that numbers can be misunderstood or misrepresented?
4. How convincing are the examples these authors provide? What other examples can you think of?

The Numbers Racket: How Polls and Statistics Lie

STEPHEN BUDIANSKY

STATISTICS are an American obsession. In an election year, they become a positive mania. The poll data pour in daily on everything a person could conceivably have an opinion about—and some things it's hard to imagine anyone having an opinion about. One recent survey reports that by a narrow, 42-to-40 margin, American women believe the first lady should be active in "all" as opposed to "just some" aspects of presidential business. 1

It's not just polls. Numbers of every description have become the currency of American life. Politicians and advocacy groups burnish their positions with them, sports commentators dissect them, advertisers bombard us with them, corporations make multimillion-dollar decisions based on them. The Census Bureau used to count just people; now, it tabulates everything from coffee consumption to the number of coin-operated video games. School-reform advocates once pressed their case with anecdotes of ill-trained teachers and out-of-date textbooks; now, they cite scores on the 50 million or more standardized tests that are administered to elementary and high-school students each year. A campaign against drugs that swept the country in the 1930s featured lurid tales of marijuana-crazed children killing their parents; today's war on drugs features lurid numbers of drug profits.

"Numbers suggest understanding," says Peter Reuter, an economist at the RAND Corporation. "People believe that you can't have a policy debate if you don't have numbers."

But that faith in numbers means that all too rarely is the truth behind the numbers questioned—and all too easily are they manipulated. Whatever your position, a statistic is available to back it up. Crime? It's going down. Except, that is, if you're a law-enforcement official pleading for a higher budget. Then crime is going up. The crisis in education? School superintendents can prove it's not their fault. A new study shows that students' test scores are above the national average. Everywhere. The explosive issues of abortion and gun control? A majority of Americans, polls clearly show, are against both. A majority are also for them. Take your pick.

THE NUMBER THAT WOULD NOT DIE

Numbers concocted to support a position may be complete guesses—but 5
once in the public record, they take on a life of their own that belies their shadowy origins. Take the figure of $140 billion for the size of the U.S. illegal-drug-trafficking industry. In its various incarnations, this figure has been cited in countless newspaper articles, in congressional testimony, in speeches by attorneys general and most prominently this year by Representative Charles Rangel (D-N.Y.), chairman of the House Select Committee on Narcotics Abuse and Control, in his push for an expanded war on drugs. Not only is it a large number, it's also a seemingly precise number—140, not 100 or 150—that implies some real knowledge of the scope of the problem. But where does it come from? The figure seems to have originated in 1978, when the National Narcotics Intelligence Consumers Committee, the government unit once charged with keeping track of such things, put the drug trade at $50 billion. It jumped mysteriously to $80 billion in 1980. After some internal wrangling—and much external criticism—NNICC quietly dropped the estimate a few years ago. But then the cause was taken up by Rangel's committee. John Cusack, the panel's former staff director, recalls that when he noticed that the NNICC estimate had risen to $90 billion by 1982, "adding $10 billion a year seemed to make sense"—and that's what the committee has done ever since. The figure "is not scientifically accurate," admits Cusack, now a drug consultant to the Attorney General of the Bahamas. "It's an educated guess."

THE VANISHING DEFICIT

If there were any doubt about the power that statistics have come to command, consider last October's stock-market crash[1]—triggered in large measure by the release of government trade figures showing a deficit $1.5 billion greater

[1]This article was originally published in the summer of 1988. [Ed.]

than Wall Street expected. Never mind that trade figures are notoriously unreliable because of the difficulty of tracking our own exports and the flow of capital. It was a number, it came from the government—and that was enough to base billions of dollars in financial decisions upon. That market-crashing trade figure has since been revised downward—by $1.3 billion.

The abuse of numbers is almost a matter of course in the burgeoning business of polling. Even many of the major polling firms routinely do work for interest groups that are interested in one thing only: getting a poll that supports their position. The essence of such "tactical polling"—as the member of one Washington advocacy group unabashedly termed it—is to phrase questions or sequences of questions in a way that leads respondents to the "right" response.

Studies have shown how easy that can be to do. A 1978 CBS–*New York Times* poll, for example, asked: "Do you agree or disagree that the federal government ought to help people get medical care at low cost?" When 81 percent agreed, the results were reported as evidence of support for an expanded federal government. But critics pointed out that it was absurd to draw that conclusion without having presented an alternative. To prove the point, the North American Newspaper Alliance conducted another poll that asked the same question, substituting the words "private enterprise" for "federal government"—and found that 71 percent agreed with *that* proposition.

So it's not surprising that groups with an ax to grind manage to get the results they pay for (see "How to Skew a Poll"—on page 167). "It is genuinely becoming 'pollster wars' out there," says Democratic pollster Alan Secrest. "Too many people are playing fast and loose with polling data. It is unconscionable, but understandable with so much at stake." Adds Mervin Field, head of the respected Field Research Corporation: "There's a real danger. Legislation is being tailored and the public manipulated with these polls."

This year's political primaries have shown the power of numbers as never before. 10
Thomas Patterson, professor of political science at Syracuse University, warns that coverage of the candidates is being dictated to a dangerous degree by poll results—and some extremely shoddy poll results at that. "There is a poll craziness out there. If you are high in the polls, you almost automatically have some good things said about you in the press." Adds Everett Ladd, director of the Roper Center for Public Opinion Research at the University of Connecticut: "The numbers contribute to a misplaced concreteness."

The trouble is that in the frenzied media competition over polling, little distinction is made between good polls and bad polls, and many news organizations aren't willing to spend the money on the extra effort needed to eliminate biases in their polls—using an adequate sample group, taking the trouble to reach everyone in that sample group even if it means calling back repeatedly, and phrasing questions properly. "Any damn fool with 10 phones and a typewriter thinks he can conduct a poll," says Warren Mitofsky, director of elections and surveys for CBS News.

How to Skew a Poll: Loaded Questions and Other Tricks

Even polls taken at the same time can produce dramatically different results depending on how the question is phrased. Some examples:

CONTRA AID

Aid the rebels in Nicaragua "to prevent Communist influence from spreading"?

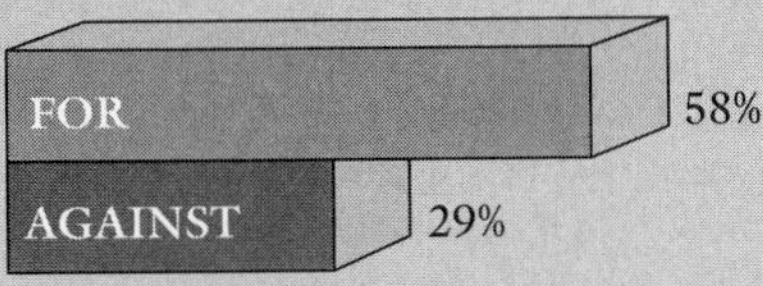

(Yankelovich-Clancy-Shulman poll for *Time*)

Assist "the people trying to overthrow the government of Nicaragua"?

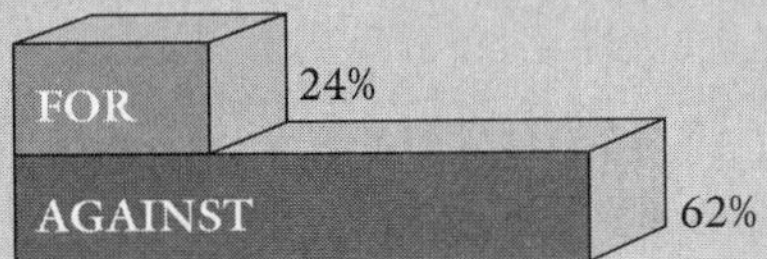

(CBS-*New York Times* poll)

ABORTION

Constitutional amendment "prohibiting abortion"?

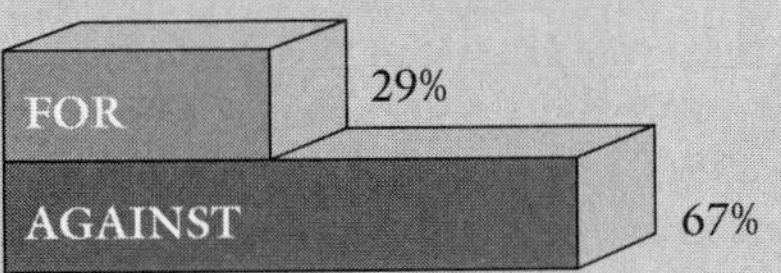

Constitutional amendment "protecting the life of the unborn"?

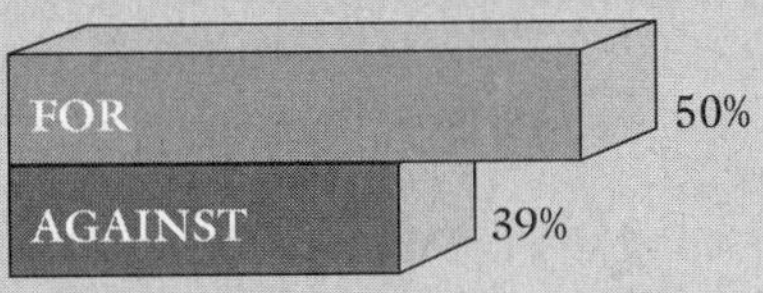

(*New York Times* poll)

GUN CONTROL

Waiting period and background check before guns can be sold?

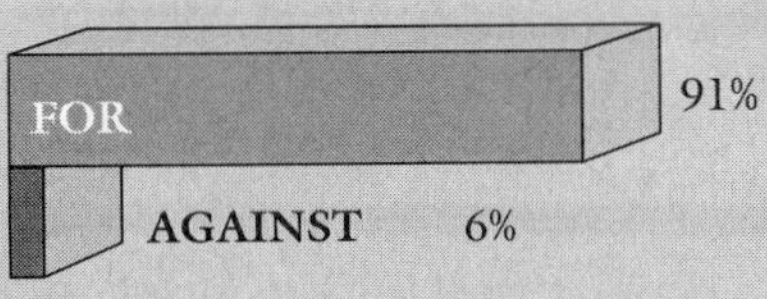

(Gallup Poll)

"National gun-registration program costing about 20% of all dollars now spent on crime control?"

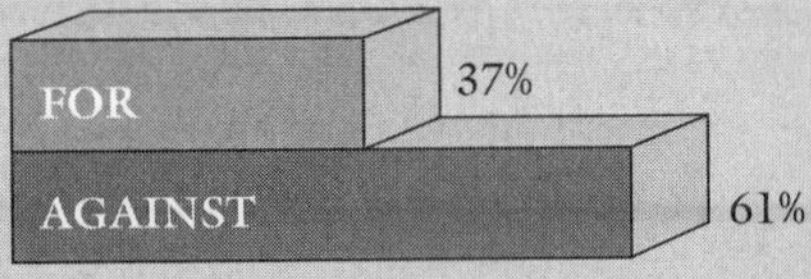

(Write-in poll for National Rifle Association)

WELFARE

"Are we spending too much, too little, or about the right amount on welfare?"

"Are we spending too much, too little, or about the right amount on assistance to the poor?"

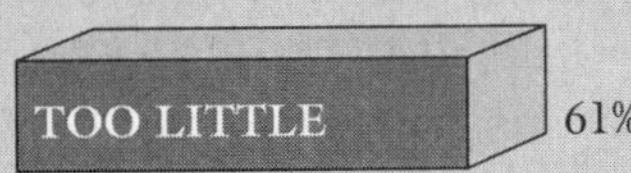

(Survey of the National Opinion Research Center of the University of Chicago)

What does it mean when a poll says "margin of error of plus or minus 3 percent?" Not as much as most people think. That standard warning label refers only to the most obvious possible source of error—the statistical chance that a perfect, randomly selected sample doesn't reflect the country as a whole. In practice, political polls are off by an average of 5.7 percent, according to polling consultant Irving Crespi of Princeton, New Jersey; one third are off by more than 6.4 percent.

Loaded questions, such as those above, are one way results can be tilted. Some other major sources of error:

The Skewed Sample

Women answer the phone 70 percent of the time. A poll that doesn't take that into account by making extra calls to get enough men is likely to be slanted. But biases can slip in by much less obvious ways. A test poll conducted in the 1984 presidential election found that if the poll were halted after interviewing only those subjects who could be reached on the first try, Reagan showed a 3-percentage point lead over Mondale. But when interviewers made a determined effort to reach everyone on their lists of randomly selected subjects—calling some as many as 30 times before finally reaching them—Reagan showed a 13 percent lead, much closer to the actual election result. As it turned out, people who were planning to vote Republican were simply less likely to be at home.

The Ignorance Factor

Not many people want to appear unpatriotic, uninformed, or socially unacceptable. So when the pollster calls, they say they intend to vote when they don't, offer what they believe are less controversial opinions, or express a view—any view—to cover up their ignorance of an issue. One study found that almost a third of respondents offered opinions when asked about the nonexistent "Public Affairs Act."

The "Pseudo Poll"

The least reliable polls are not even polls at all—experts call them "pseudo polls" because they don't even make an attempt at surveying a random sample. AT&T has been marketing call-in polls using its area-code 900 numbers. TV stations ask viewers to call one number to register a "Yes" vote, another for "No." The results are then tallied and aired. The trouble is that only those who feel strongly enough to spend the 50 cents AT&T charges for each call are likely to phone in—hardly a representative sample.

OFF BY A MILE

Even a casual glance at the contradictory poll results of this political year demonstrates that the uncertainties far surpass the standard 3-percent-plus-or-minus warning. For example, an NBC news poll a month before the New Hampshire primary had Michael Dukakis trailing Richard Gephardt 18 points to 19. A *Los Angeles Times* poll conducted the same day showed Dukakis leading 37 to 8. The actual result: Dukakis 36, Gephardt 20. In fact, the usual plus-or-minus warning only refers to the smallest source of possible error—the probability that a randomly chosen sample group differs from the population as a whole. It

Statistical Myths

All Children Are Above Average

Test scores are up. Children are scoring above the national norm in reading and math. The education crisis is over.

Dr. John Cannell of Beaver, West Virginia, smelled a rat. A family physician, he was troubled by the low self-esteem of his teenage patients. Many had apparently been assigned to grade levels beyond their academic abilities. So how could West Virginia be above the national average?

Simple: *All* states are above average. One reason is that the sample group of students that was used to establish the "average" had been required to take all of the tests—but when schools later administered the tests, they could pick only those tests that best matched their curricula. "The testing industry wants to sell lots of tests, and the school superintendents desperately need high and improving scores," says Cannell. "Nobody is disappointed."

3 Million Americans Are Homeless

While homeless advocates fiercely defend this number, it has a strange history. In 1980, homeless advocate Mitch Snyder conducted interviews with local agencies, and listed estimates of the number of homeless in 14 cities. The numbers ranged from a few hundredths of a percent in some cities to 1 percent in a few cases. While he made no national estimate at that time, by 1982 Snyder was claiming that his 1980 survey had found that "1 percent of the population, or 2.2 million people, lacked shelter." He went on to say that the number "could" reach 3 million in 1983. That number was picked up and widely quoted.

More-scientific surveys have found the number to be 8 to 10 times too large. Part of the discrepancy is also due to advocates' having included in their definition of the "homeless" people who live in substandard housing. But Snyder subsequently told a congressional hearing: "These numbers are in fact meaningless. We have tried to satisfy your gnawing curiosity for a number because we are Americans with Western little minds that have to quantify everything in sight, whether we can or not."

doesn't account for the fact that people may refuse to answer, may lie, or may be influenced by leading questions.

The media fascination with polls is part and parcel of the wider fascination with statistics of all kinds. Numbers seem concrete; numbers seem objective. "It is a safe kind of journalism. You can't generally be accused of ideological or political bias," says Michael Jay Robinson, a consultant to the Gallup-Times Mirror survey.

The case of all test scores being above average (see "Statistical Myths" above) is a classic example—both of the political impact of unsubstantiated numbers and of the many ways available to manipulate statistics. For several years, virtually every state's department of education and even most urban school districts had reported in glowing terms that their students had scored above the national average on standardized reading, writing, and math tests. Obviously, if the average really had been an average, some states would have had to be below it. It turned out that the "average" was calculated using a skewed sample group that included students with learning disabilities. It also was seven years out of date, and thus failed to reflect an overall rise in the average that had taken place.

Such fiddling with the sample group is in fact one of the most common ways to tease a desired result out of an otherwise valid statistic. That's how partisans on both sides of the 65-mile-per-hour-speed-limit debate were able to use the same data to prove their case. Depending on which states you include in the sample, you can prove that the higher speed limit has caused more traffic fatalities—or fewer fatalities.

A variation on that theme is regularly practiced by environmental activists who discover a cancer "hot spot," or political reporters who discover a "key" county that always picks the winner in presidential elections. But pure chance alone will dictate that some areas will have a much higher cancer rate than the average (just as some will have a much lower rate). And while picking the right presidential candidate in 10 straight elections might seem remarkable, someone who voted by tossing a coin would have 1 chance in 1,024 of duplicating that feat. With more than 3,000 counties in the country, those odds don't seem so long.

Why are we so impressed by numbers? "Human judgment and intuition are fallible," says Stanford University psychology Prof. Amos Tversky. Some of the errors people make in interpreting statistics in fact fall into definable patterns. One rule is that losses loom larger than gains. People are more willing to support public-health programs when told of the numbers of lives that would be lost without it—as opposed to lives saved by it. Psychologists have also found that people rarely question the context of numbers—as in accepting the statement that a detergent is "35 percent better" without asking, "35 percent better than what?"

But most important, numbers have taken on the role of the compelling anecdote—the story that people take to repeating without ever asking where it came from. Numbers that begin their lives as total guesses often persist for years, being quoted and requoted—usually for a lack of any more-reliable data. (The 3 million homeless people in the United States is one such famous statistic that would not die; see "Statistical Myths.")

FOOLING THE PROS

Number blindness even besets people who should be experts. That mainstay of economic statistics, the gross national product, is the basis of countless economic projections. Yet it is a number fraught with uncertainties. At times recently, it has even showed economic growth dramatically slowing when it was really accelerating. Frank de Leeuw, chief statistician for the Bureau of Economic Analysis that puts together the figure, admits that the GNP estimates err, on average, by almost 2 percentage points. One reason: The data that go into the figure are still heavily tilted toward industries that were dominant in the 1930s and 1940s; it is a poor measure of the newly ascendant service industries.

20 Those who make multimillion-dollar decisions every day have been no less susceptible to the allure of numbers. When General Foods decided to launch a new instant-drink mix called Great Shakes, it test-marketed it in several cities with what appeared to be a resounding success. Customers, the numbers showed, seemed to be enthusiastically purchasing all of the various flavors. General Foods immediately launched it nationally—to a resounding thud. The company finally pieced together what had happened: Customers were trying one flavor after another, hoping that the next one surely would taste better than the last. When they had run through them all, they stopped buying any of them. "There's an overreliance on numbers," says Bruce Meyers, marketing-research director of the BBD&O advertising agency. "Any research should be an aid to judgment, not a replacement for it." But here's one number that shows what American business thinks of that advice: The survey-research industry now earns more than $2 billion a year—and is growing at a rate of about 15 percent a year.

From Doublespeak

WILLIAM LUTZ

BEWARE OF THE POLLS

1 STATISTICAL doublespeak is a particularly effective form of doublespeak, since statistics are not likely to be closely scrutinized. Moreover, we tend to think that numbers are more concrete, more "real" than mere words. Quantify something and you give it a precision, a reality it did not have before.

We live in an age where people love numbers. Computer printouts are "reality." You identify yourself with your Social Security number; your American Express, MasterCard, or Visa number; your driver's license number; your telephone number (with area code first); your ZIP code. Three out of four doctors recommend something, we are told; a recent poll reveals 52.3 percent are opposed; Nielsen gives the new television program a 9.2; the movie grossed $122 million.

Baseball produces not just athletic contests but an infinity of statistics, which all true fans love to quote endlessly. Crowds at football and basketball games chant, "We're number one!" while the Dow Jones index measures daily our economic health and well-being. Millions of people legally (and illegally) play the daily number. Millions of pocket calculators are sold every year. The list could go on to include the body count of Vietnam and the numbers of nuclear warheads and intercontinental ballistic missiles cited as the measure of national security.

The computer scientist, the mathematician, the statistician, and the accountant all deal with "reality," while the poet, the writer, the wordsmith deal with, well, just words. You may find, however, that the world of numbers is not as accurate as you think it is, especially the world of the public opinion poll.

5 If you believe in public opinion polls, I've got a bridge you might like to buy. Depending upon which poll you believed just before the New Hampshire primary in February 1988, you would have known that Robert Dole would beat George Bush 35 percent to 27 (Gallup); or Dole would win 32 percent to Bush's 28 percent (*Boston Globe*); or that Dole and Bush were even at 32 percent each (ABC–*Washington Post*); or Bush would win 32 percent to Dole's 30 (WBZ-TV); or Bush would win 34 percent to Dole's 30 percent (CBS–*New York Times*). Of course, George Bush won the actual vote 38 percent to 29 percent.

Things weren't much better on the Democratic side, either. While most primary polls were correct in identifying Michael Dukakis as the winner, the margin of victory varied from 47 percent to 38 percent. Dukakis won with 36 percent of the vote. For second place, though, the polls really missed the call. Two had Paul Simon ahead of Richard Gephardt for second place, while a third had the two tied, and the others had Simon behind by a thin margin. In the actual vote, Simon finished third, with 17 percent of the vote, while Gephardt finished second with 20 percent. No one predicted Gephardt's 20 percent of the vote, *not even the surveys of voters leaving the polling places after they had voted*. This last point should not be overlooked, for it reminds us that no poll is worth anything unless people tell the pollster the truth. Since no pollster can ever know whether or not people are telling the truth, how can we ever be sure of any poll?

Things didn't improve during the presidential campaign either. In August 1988, before the Republican National Convention, seven polls gave seven different answers to the question of who was ahead. The CBS–*New York Times* poll had Dukakis leading Bush 50 percent to 33 percent, while a poll taken by KRC Communications/Research had Dukakis ahead only 45 percent to 44 percent. When the ABC News poll came out with Bush ahead 49 percent to 46 percent, many people in the polling business discounted the results. ABC promptly took another poll three days later which showed Dukakis ahead 55 percent to 40 percent. That was more like it, said the other professional poll takers.

Even as presented, such polls are deceptive. Any poll has a margin of error inherent in it, but pollsters don't discuss that margin very much. They like their polls to have an air of precision and certainty about them. The KRC polls just mentioned had a margin of error of plus or minus 4 percent. This means that, in the first poll KRC took, Dukakis really had anywhere from 49 to 41 percent, while Bush had anywhere from 48 to 40 percent. In other words, Dukakis could have been ahead 49 to 40 percent, or Bush could have been ahead 48 to 41 percent. The poll didn't tell you anything.

Polls have become important commodities to be sold. Television news programs and newspapers use polls to show that they have the inside information, thus boosting their ratings and their circulation. Also, the more dramatic or unexpected the results of a poll, the better the chances the poll will be featured prominently on the evening news program. In addition to all this hype and use of polls as news, politicians, corporations, special-interest groups, and others have vested interests in the results of particular polls. Such people and groups have been known to design and conduct polls that will produce the results they want. In other words, polls can be and are a source of a lot of doublespeak.

10 How do you read a poll? Actually, it's not all that hard, but the problem is that most poll results don't give you enough information to tell whether the poll is worth anything. In order to evaluate the results of a poll, you need to know the wording of the question or questions asked by the poll taker, when the poll was taken, how many people responded, how the poll was conducted, who was polled, how many people were polled, and how they were selected. That's a lot of information, and rarely does a poll ever give you more than just the results.

In 1967, two members of Congress asked their constituents the following question: "Do you approve of the recent decision to extend bombing raids in North Vietnam aimed at the strategic supply depots around Hanoi and Haiphong?" Sixty-five percent said yes. When asked, "Do you believe the U.S. should bomb Hanoi and Haiphong?" however, only 14 percent said yes. In 1973, when Congress was considering articles of impeachment against President Nixon, a Gallup poll asked the question, "Do you think President Nixon should be impeached and compelled to leave the Presidency, or not?" Only 30 percent said yes to this question. They were then asked, "Do you think the President should be tried and removed from office if found guilty?" To this, 57 percent said yes.

The most popular form of polling these days is the telephone poll, where a few hundred people are called on the telephone and asked a couple of questions. The results are then broadcast the next day. The two ABC polls mentioned earlier were based on telephoning 384 and 382 people, respectively. Just remember that the U.S. population is over 245 million.

According to Dennis Haack, president of Statistical Consultants, a statistical research company in Lexington, Kentucky,

> Most national surveys are not very accurate measures of public opinion. Opinion polls are no more accurate than indicated by their inability to predict Reagan's landslide in 1980 or Truman's win in 1948. The polls were wrong then and they have been wrong many other times when they tried to measure public opinion. The difference is that with elections we find out for sure if the polls were wrong; but for nonelection opinion polls there is no day of reckoning. We never know for sure how well surveys measure opinion when elections are not involved. I don't have much confidence in nonelection opinion surveys.

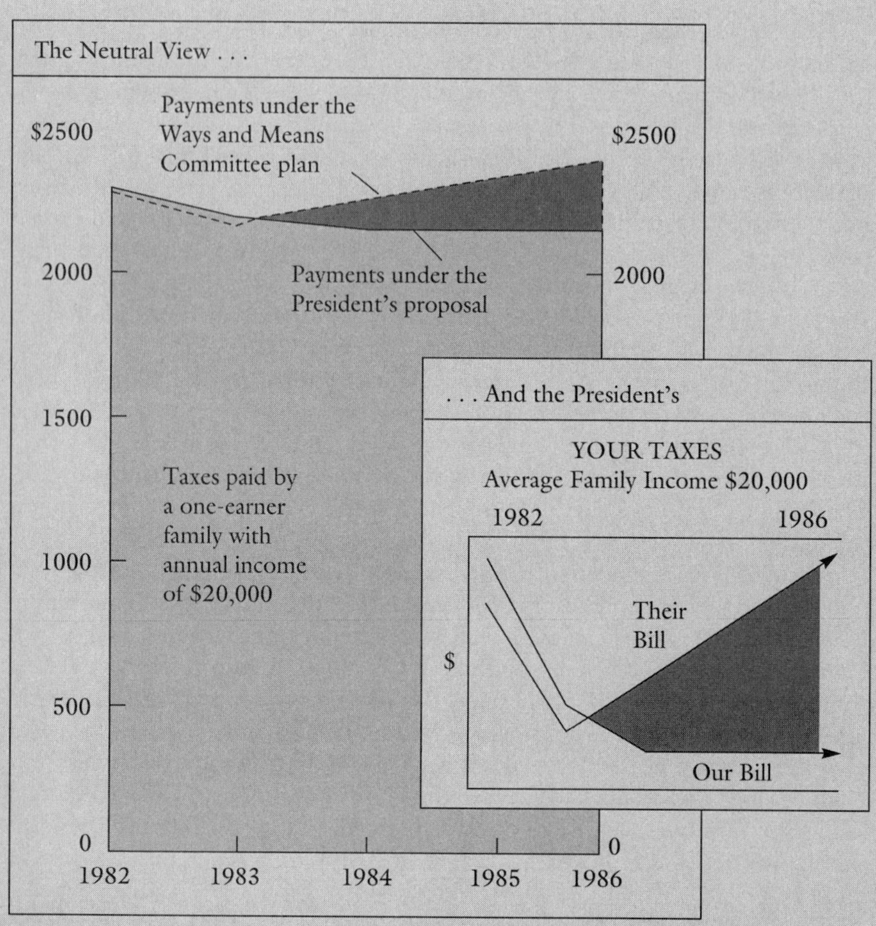

Figure 1 President Reagan's misleading and biased chart, compared with a neutral presentation regarding the same tax proposals.

THE DOUBLESPEAK OF GRAPHS

Just as polls seem to present concrete, specific evidence, so do graphs and charts present information visually in a way that appears unambiguous and dramatically clear. But, just as polls leave a lot of necessary information out, so can graphs and charts, resulting in doublespeak. You have to ask a lot of questions if you really want to understand a graph or chart.

15 In 1981 President Reagan went on television to argue that citizens would be paying a lot more in taxes under a Democratic bill than under his bill. To prove his point, he used a chart that appeared to show a dramatic and very big difference between the results of each bill (see Figure 1). But the president's

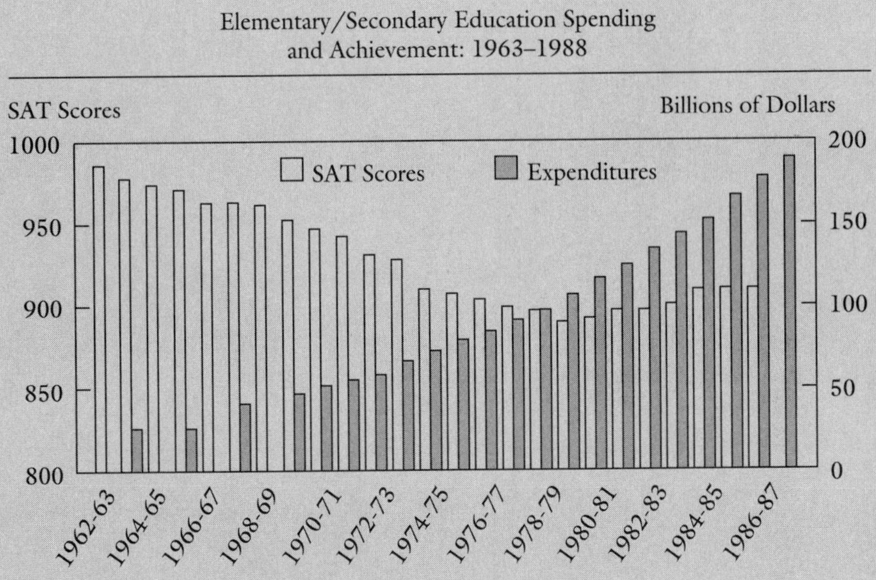

Elementary/Secondary Education Spending
and Achievement: 1963–1988

SAT Scores — Billions of Dollars

1000 950 900 850 800 — 200 150 100 50 0

SAT Scores — Expenditures

1962-63 1964-65 1966-67 1968-69 1970-71 1972-73 1974-75 1976-77 1978-79 1980-81 1982-83 1984-85 1986-87

Figure 2 Misleading graph from the Department of Education, showing school spending relative to SAT scores.

chart was doublespeak, because it was deliberately designed to be misleading. Pointing to his chart, President Reagan said, "This red space between the two lines is the tax money that will remain in your pockets if our bill passes, and it's the amount that will leave your pockets if their bill is passed. On the one hand, you see a genuine and lasting commitment to the future of working Americans. On the other, just another empty promise." That was a pretty dramatic statement, considering that the maximum difference between the two bills, after five years, would have been $217.

The president's chart showed a deceptively dramatic difference because his chart had no figures on the dollar scale and no numbers for years except 1982 and 1986. The difference in tax payments was exaggerated in the president's chart by "squashing" or tightening the time scale as much as possible, while stretching the dollar scale, starting with an oddly unrounded $2,150 and winding up at $2,400. Thus, the chart had no perspective. Using the proper method for constructing a chart would have meant starting at $0 and going up to the first round number after the highest point in the chart, as done in the "neutral view" in Figure 1. Using that method, the $217 seems rather small in a total tax bill of $2,385.

What happened to the numbers on the president's chart? "The chart we sent over to the White House had all the numbers on it," said Marlin Fitzwater, then a press officer in the Treasury Department. Senior White House spokesperson

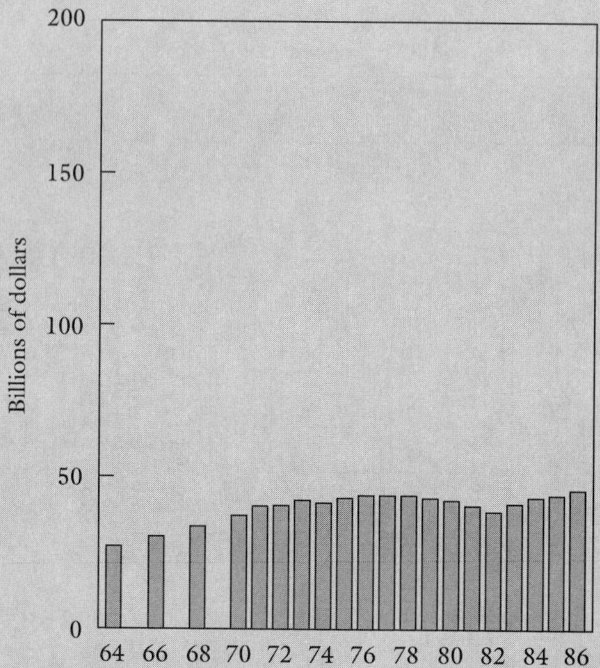

Figure 3 Elementary/secondary education spending in constant dollars (billions).

David Gergen said, "We took them off. We were trying to get a point across, not the absolute numbers." So much for honesty.

In 1988 the Department of Education issued a graph that seemed to prove that there was a direct connection between the rise in elementary and secondary school spending and the decline in scores on the Scholastic Aptitude Test (see Figure 2 on page 175). The Reagan administration had been arguing that spending more money doesn't improve education and may even make it worse. But the chart was doublespeak. First, it used current dollars rather than constant dollars, adjusted for inflation. Because each year it takes more money to buy the same things, charts are supposed to adjust for that increase so the measure of dollars remains constant over the years illustrated in the chart. If the Department of Education had figured in inflation over the years on the chart, it would have shown that the amount of constant dollars spent on education had increased modestly from 1970 to 1986, as Figure 3 shows.

Second, scores on the Scholastic Aptitude Test go from 400 to 1,600, yet the graph used by the Education Department (Figure 2) used a score range of only 800 to 1,000. By limiting the range of scores on its graph, the department showed what appeared to be a severe decline in scores. A properly prepared graph, shown in Figure 4, shows a much more gradual decline.

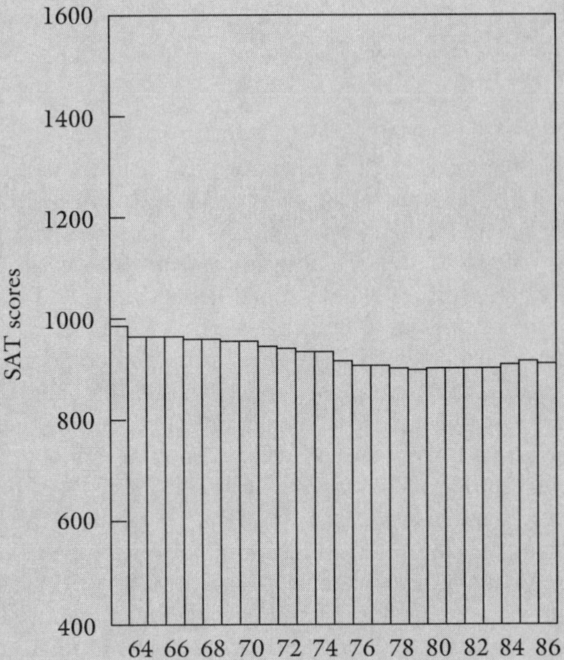

Figure 4 SAT scores, 1963–1986.

20 The Department of Education's presentation is a good example of diagrammatic doublespeak. Without all the information you need in order to understand the chart, you can be easily misled, which of course was the purpose of the chart. You should always be skeptical whenever you see a graph or chart being used to present information, because these things are nothing more than the visual presentation of statistical information. And as for statistics, remember what Benjamin Disraeli is supposed to have said: "There are three kinds of lies—lies, damn lies, and statistics."

The Risk Factor

BILL BRYSON

1 NOW HERE is something that seems awfully unfair to me. Because I am an American it appears that I am twice as likely as an English person to suffer an untimely and accidental death. I know this because I have just been reading something called *The Book of Risks: Fascinating Facts about the Chances We Take Every Day* by a statistical wonk named Larry Laudan.

It is full of interesting and useful charts, graphs, and factual analyses, mostly to do with coming irremediably a cropper in the United States. Thus, I know that if I happen to take up farm work this year I am three times more likely to lose a limb, and twice as likely to be fatally poisoned, than if I just sit here quietly. I now know that my chances of being murdered sometime in the next 12 months are 1 in 11,000; of choking to death 1 in 150,000; of being killed by a dam failure 1 in 10 million; and of being fatally conked on the head by something falling from the sky about 1 in 250 million. Even if I stay indoors, away from the windows, it appears that there is a 1 in 450,000 chance that something will kill me before the day is out. I find that rather alarming.

However, nothing is more galling than the discovery that just by being an American, by standing to attention for "The Star-Spangled Banner" and having a baseball cap as a central component of my wardrobe, I am twice as likely to die in a mangled heap as, say, Prince Philip or Posh Spice. This is not a just way to decide mortality, if you ask me.

Mr. Laudan does not explain why Americans are twice as dangerous to themselves as Britons (too upset, I daresay), but I have been thinking about it a good deal, as you can imagine, and the answer—very obvious when you reflect for even a moment—is that America is an outstandingly dangerous place.

5 Consider this: Every year in New Hampshire a dozen or more people are killed crashing their cars into moose. Now correct me if I am wrong, but this is a fate unlikely to await anyone in the United Kingdom. Nor, we may safely assume, is anyone there likely to be eaten by a grizzly bear or mountain lion, butted senseless by bison, seized about the ankle by a seriously perturbed rattlesnake, or subjected to an abrupt and startling termination from tornadoes, earthquakes, hurricanes, rock slides, avalanches, flash floods, or paralyzing blizzards—all occurrences that knock off scores, if not hundreds, of my fellow citizens each year.

Finally, and above all, there is the matter of guns. There are 200 million guns in the United States and we do rather like to pop them off. Each year, 40,000 Americans die from gun-shot wounds, the great majority of them by accident. Just to put that in perspective for you, that's a rate of 6.8 gunshot deaths per 100,000 people in America, compared with a decidedly unambitious 0.4 per 100,000 in the United Kingdom.

America is, in short, a pretty risky place. And yet, oddly, we get alarmed by all the wrong things. Eavesdrop on almost any conversation at Lou's Cafe here in Hanover and the talk will all be of cholesterol and sodium levels, mammograms and resting heart rates. Show most Americans an egg yolk and they will recoil in terror, but the most palpable and avoidable risks scarcely faze them.

Forty percent of the people in this country still don't use a seat belt, which I find simply amazing because it costs nothing to buckle up and clearly has the potential to save you from exiting through the windshield like Superman. (Vermont, which is one of the few states to keep careful track of these things, reported that in the first 10 months of 1998, 81 people were killed on the state's roads—and 76 percent of those people were not wearing seat belts.) Even more remarkably, since a spate of recent newspaper reports about young children being killed by airbags in minor crashes, people have been rushing to get their airbags disconnected. Never mind that in every instance the children were killed because they were sitting in the front seat, where they should not have been in the first place, and in nearly all cases weren't wearing seat belts. Airbags save thousands of lives, yet many people are having them disabled on the bizarre assumption that they present a danger.

Much the same sort of statistical illogic applies to guns. Forty percent of Americans keep guns in their homes, typically in a drawer beside the bed. The odds that one of those guns will ever be used to shoot a criminal are comfortably under one in a million. The odds that it will be used to shoot a member of the household—generally a child fooling around—are at least 20 times that figure. Yet over 100 million people resolutely ignore this fact, even sometimes threaten to pop you one themselves if you make too much noise about it.

10 Nothing, however, better captures the manifest irrationality of people toward risks as one of the liveliest issues of recent years: passive smoking. Four years ago, the Environmental Protection Agency released a report concluding that people who are over 35 and don't smoke but are regularly exposed to the smoke of others stand a 1 in 30,000 risk of contracting lung cancer in a given year. The response was immediate and electrifying. All over the country smoking was banned at work and in restaurants, shopping malls, and other public places.

What was overlooked in all this was how microscopically small the risk from passive smoking actually is. A rate of 1 in 30,000 sounds reasonably severe, but it doesn't actually amount to much. Eating one pork chop a week is statistically more likely to give you cancer than sitting routinely in a roomful of smokers. So, too, is consuming a carrot every seven days, a glass of orange juice twice a month, or a head of lettuce every two years. You are five times more likely to contract lung cancer from your pet parakeet than you are from secondary smoke.

Now I am all for banning smoking on the grounds that it is dirty and offensive, unhealthy for the user, and leaves unsightly burns in the carpet. All I am saying is that it seems a trifle odd to ban it on grounds of public safety when you are happy to let any old fool own a gun or drive around unbuckled.

But then logic seldom comes into these things. I remember some years ago watching my brother buy a lottery ticket (odds of winning: about 1 in 12 million), then get in his car and fail to buckle up (odds of having a serious accident in any year: 1 in 40). When I pointed out the inconsistency of this, he looked at me for a moment and said: "And what are the odds, do you suppose, that I will drop you four miles short of home?"

Since then, I have kept these thoughts pretty much to myself. Much less risky, you see.

The Numbers Game

BILL BRYSON

THE U.S. CONGRESS, which never ceases to be amazing, recently voted to 1
give the Pentagon $11 billion more than it had asked for. Do you have any idea how much $11 billion is? Of course you don't. Nobody does. It is not possible to conceive of a sum that large.

No matter where you turn with regard to America and its economy you are going to bump into figures that are so large as to be beyond meaningful comprehension. Consider just a few figures culled at random from this week's papers. California has an economy worth $850 billion. The annual gross domestic product of the United States is $6.8 trillion. The federal budget is $1.6 trillion, the federal deficit nearly $200 billion.

It's easy to lose sight of just how enormous these figures really are. America's cumulative debt at last count, according to *Time* magazine, was "a hair" under $4.7 trillion. The actual figure was $4.692 trillion, so that statement is hard to argue with, yet it represents a difference of $8 billion—a pretty large hair in anybody's book.

I worked long enough on the business desk of a national newspaper in England to know that even the most experienced financial journalists often get confused when dealing with terms like *billion* and *trillion,* and for two very good reasons. First, they have usually had quite a lot to drink at lunch, and, second, such numbers really are confusing.

And that is the whole problem. Big numbers are simply beyond what we are 5
capable of grasping. On Sixth Avenue in New York there is an electronic billboard, erected and paid for by some anonymous source, that announces itself as "The National Debt Clock." When I was last there, it listed the national debt at $4,533,603,804,000—that's $4.5 trillion—and the figure was growing by $10,000 every second, or so fast that the last three digits on the electronic meter were a blur. But what does $4.5 trillion actually mean?

Well, let's just try to grasp the concept of $1 trillion. Imagine that you were in a vault filled with dollar bills and that you were told you could keep each one you initialed. Say, too, for the sake of argument that you could initial one dollar bill per second and that you worked straight through without ever stopping. How long do you think it would take to count a trillion dollars? Go on, humor me and take a guess. Twelve weeks? Two years? Five?

If you initialed one dollar per second, you would make $1,000 every seventeen minutes. After 12 days of nonstop effort you would acquire your first $1 million. Thus, it would take you 120 days to accumulate $10 million and 1,200 days—something over three years—to reach $100 million. After 31.7 years you would become a billionaire, and after almost a thousand years you would be as wealthy as Bill Gates. But not until after 31,709.8 years would you count your trillionth dollar (and even then you would be less than one-fourth of the way through the pile of money representing America's national debt).

That is what $1 trillion is.

What is interesting is that it is becoming increasingly evident that most of these inconceivably vast sums that get bandied about by economists and policy makers are almost certainly miles out anyway. Take gross domestic product, the bedrock of modern economic policy. GDP was a concept that was originated in the 1930s by the economist Simon Kuznets. It is very good at measuring physical things—tons of steel, board feet of lumber, potatoes, tires, and so on. That was all very well in a traditional industrial economy. But now the greater part of output for nearly all developed nations is in services and ideas—things like computer software, telecommunications, financial services—which produce wealth but don't necessarily, or even generally, result in a product that you can load on a pallet and ship out to the marketplace.

Because such activities are so difficult to measure and quantify, no one really 10
knows what they amount to. Many economists now believe that America may have been underestimating its rate of GDP growth by as much as two to three percentage points a year for several years. That may not seem a great deal, but if it is correct then the American economy—which obviously is already staggeringly enormous—may be one-third larger than anyone had thought. In other words, there may be hundreds of billions of dollars floating around in the economy that no one suspected were there. Incredible.

Here's another even more arresting thought. None of this really matters because GDP is in any case a perfectly useless measurement. All that it is, literally, is a crude measure of national income—"the dollar value of finished goods and services," as the textbooks put it—over a given period.

Any kind of economic activity adds to the gross domestic product. It doesn't matter whether it's a good activity or a bad one. It has been estimated, for instance, that the O. J. Simpson trial added $200 million to America's GDP through lawyers' fees, court costs, hotel bills for the press, and so on, but I don't think many people would argue that the whole costly spectacle made America a noticeably greater, nobler place.

In fact, bad activities often generate more GDP than good activities. I was recently in Pennsylvania at the site of a zinc factory whose airborne wastes were formerly so laden with pollutants that they denuded an entire mountainside. From the factory fence to the top of the mountain there was not a single scrap of growing vegetation to be seen. From a GDP perspective, however, this was wonderful. First, there was the gain to the economy from all the zinc the factory had manufactured and sold over the years. Then there was the gain from the tens of millions of dollars the government must spend to clean up the site and restore the mountain. Finally, there will be a continuing gain from medical treatments for workers and townspeople made chronically ill by living amid all those contaminants.

In terms of conventional economic measurement, all of this is gain, not loss. So too is overfishing of lakes and seas. So too is deforestation. In short, the more recklessly we use up natural resources, the more the GDP grows.

15 As the economist Herman Daly once put it: “The current national accounting system treats the earth as a business in liquidation.” Or as three other leading economists dryly observed in an article in the *Atlantic Monthly* last year: “By the curious standard of the GDP, the nation’s economic hero is a terminal cancer patient who is going through a costly divorce.”

So why do we persist with this preposterous gauge of economic performance? Because it’s the best thing that economists have come up with yet. Now you know why they call it the dismal science.

CONSIDERING COLUMBINE: LOOKING FOR ANSWERS

In the wake of the tragedy at Columbine High School, students, teachers, families, and members of the community all sought answers: Why here? Why us? What does the future hold? As the tremendous emotional impact of the shootings eventually passed, experts began to look for answers within a broader national context and tried to place the Columbine shootings within the conversation about other cultural movements. Each of the following authors is looking for causes and explanations for the shootings. The first two are part of a set of articles on Columbine published in the *National Review,* May 17, 1999, a few weeks after the shootings. Barbara Lerner, author of “The Killer Narcissists,” is a psychologist and writer living in Chicago. As a psychologist, Lerner tries to understand how Eric Harris and Dylan Klebold could have committed this act after having just completed individual counseling, including anger-management training. In the second selection, “Levittown to Littleton,” Christopher Caldwell, a senior writer for *The Weekly Standard,* examines how the suburban environment itself may have contributed to the tragedy. In the final selection, “Cultivating Killers,” Judith Reisman examines the relationship between social violence and violence in popular computer games, music, and media. Reisman is the president of the Institute for Media Education, a nonprofit organization concerned about the prevalence of sex and violence in the media. As you read these essays, consider the following questions:

1. What claim does each author make about the causes of the Columbine shootings?
2. What reasons are given to support the claim?
3. What assumptions are implied by these reasons? Are any of these assumptions found on the GASCAP list?
4. Do any of these authors commit logical fallacies (particularly the post hoc or oversimplified cause)?
5. How does these authors use statistical arguments?
6. To what extent do you agree or disagree with these authors' claims? Are there other causes that these authors haven't considered?

The Killer Narcissists: The Missing Explanation

BARBARA LERNER

THE QUESTIONS won't go away. The recent shooting spree—the eighth in two years—forces us to face them again. Why all these wanton killings by schoolboys, this senseless spiral of schoolhouse slaughter? Who are these kids? Why are they doing it? What can we do? In the '90s, most parents look to psychology for answers, but psychology doesn't have one set—it has two: pre-'60s answers and post-'60s answers. And they conflict. 1

Every sensate American knows the post-'60s answers. You hear them from all the talking heads. Not just establishment experts, but mainstream teachers, preachers, politicians, and journalists. All subscribe to the conventional wisdom of the '90s: Kids who kill are in great distress, they've been neglected, rejected, and abused, their self-esteem is low, they are crying out for help. They need more love and understanding, more communication and parental attention, more early intervention, professional counseling, and anger-management training. And the reason we have more of these kids today is that we have more absent parents, more media violence, more guns.

Will the Colorado killers fit this profile? Were they the abused offspring of harsh, uncaring parents and a cold, indifferent community, desperately unhappy beings with nowhere to turn for help? It doesn't look like it. Eric Harris and Dylan Klebold both came from intact middle-class families variously described by neighbors as "solid," "sensitive," and "utterly normal," and both had already been through the therapeutic mill. Each boy had gotten individual counseling; each got anger-management training as well. Both finished their therapy in

February, two months before the crime, and both got glowing reports from their counselors.

Maybe, when all the facts are known, Harris and Klebold will turn out to be a lot more like Kip Kinkel, the 15-year-old Oregon shooter who vanished from the news as soon as his life story began to emerge because it didn't fit the profile at all. Kinkel was a problem for the conventional wisdom because he had it all, everything '90s experts recommend. His parents were popular teachers, one of them was always there for him when he came home from school, and both did their best to make him happy, spending time with him, taking him on family vacations, helping him get whatever he wanted, even when the things he wanted unnerved them. They made few demands, rejected firm discipline as too harsh, and sought professional help, early and often. They were in counseling, along with Kip, when, in May 1998, he shot them both dead, killed two of his many school friends, and wounded 22 others.

Looking at cases like this, psychologists in the 1950s and earlier had a set of 5
answers you don't hear much anymore. Here's an updated sample: We have more wanton schoolboy killers today because we have more narcissists, and the step from being a narcissist to being a wanton killer is a short one, especially in adolescence. A narcissist is a person who never progressed beyond the self-love of infancy, one who learned superficial social skills—narcissists are often charming—but never learned to love another and, through love, to view others as separate persons with an equal value. To the narcissist, other people have no intrinsic worth; their value is purely instrumental. They are useful when they satisfy his desires and enhance his self-esteem, disposable as bottle caps when they don't.

Only the narcissist matters, and because his sense of self-importance is so grossly inflated, his feelings are easily hurt. When [he does] get hurt—when others thwart him or fail to give him the excessive, unearned respect he demands—he reacts with rage and seeks revenge, the more dramatic the better. Take guns away from kids like these, and many won't settle for knives and baseball bats: They'll turn to deadlier weapons—to explosives, as that overgrown schoolboy, Ted Kaczynski did, or to environmental poisons, as the young subway saboteurs of Japan did. Kip was on his way—police found five bombs at his house. And the Colorado killers upped the ante: They made more than 30 bombs and used shrapnel as well as bullets to blow away their victims.

Will more counseling and anger-management classes help? At best, they are palliatives, in cases like these. They can put a patch over the hole at the core of these kids, the moral void, but they cannot fill the hole. No brand of psychology can, and earlier brands—Freud's especially—had the humility to recognize that. He saw the hole for what it is, a moral hole that only moral training can fill. Not just calm, rational, smiley-face, didactic lessons, but the kind of intense, gut-level experiences children have when their parents draw a sharp moral line and demonstrate a willingness to go all out to defend it.

Through experiences like these, normal children learn that the parental love they could take for granted as infants and toddlers can no longer be taken for granted. That love is no longer unconditional; it can be withdrawn. And to avoid that frightening outcome, the child learns to see his parents as more than human piñatas, full of goodies he has only to bang away at to get. He learns to see them as moral beings with standards and values that are more important than his own immature wishes, and he begins to internalize those standards and values, making them his own, and developing a conscience.

Many '90s experts don't understand this process. They focus only on self-esteem, not on esteem for others, and they obsess about the methods parents use to teach their kids, ignoring the content, the moral lessons they are trying to teach, insisting that any physical punishment, however infrequently and judiciously applied, is child abuse. These experts have no real solutions to offer, when the problem is overindulgence rather than abuse, as it now so often is. They are part of the problem. And the sooner we recognize that, the better.

Levittown to Littleton: How the Suburbs Have Changed

CHRISTOPHER CALDWELL

THE DAY after the shootings at Columbine High, many newspapers ran a 2×2 inset map of the school neighborhood in Littleton, Colorado. There was a grid of high-speed roads a mile to a block. There were residential cul-de-sacs squiggling into empty quadrants. And looming up in the corner like a 747 hangar was the monolithic high-school building. 1

Such brand-new landscapes, almost wholly unfamiliar to northeasterners, make up virtually all of the middle-class neighborhoods in any western metropolis—Phoenix, Albuquerque, Houston. What was odd was that the Littleton map generally ran amid columns of copy seeking out the root causes of the shooting, and seeking them most everywhere: guns, television, affluence, big schools, divorce, Hollywood, the Internet, Goth music. Looking for simple explanations for a tragedy like Littleton is probably a fool's errand. But if one is going to engage in the exercise, the suburban layout described in the little map belongs on the list.

In the weeks following the massacre, many Americans have begun to think so too. News articles and television specials have cast towns like Littleton as un-"nurturing" at best, an adolescent hell on earth at worst. People are once again deeply troubled by "suburbia." Fifty-five percent of Americans live in suburbs now—but only 25 percent of that number mention the suburbs as the place they'd most like to live.

Well, yeah, yeah, one might say. People have been beating up on suburbs since Bill Levitt developed his first neighborhood on Long Island in 1947. So what else is new?

As it turns out, *everything* is new. 5

The argument over the sterility of suburban developments like the various Levittowns was thrashed out decades ago, and largely settled in favor of suburbia. Witnesses for the prosecution began appearing in the 1950s: Allen Ginsberg's poetry, the Pete Seeger folk song (written by Malvina Reynolds) called "Little Boxes" (". . . made of ticky-tacky / And they all look the same"), novels of corporate anomie like Sloan Wilson's *Man in the Gray Flannel Suit*. For the campus protestors of the 1960s, the suburbs were synonymous with conformity, repression, and racism. For the radicals' largely conservative opponents, they meant family, patriotism, and decency. In retrospect, we can view this as an early sign of the Left's conversion to elite snobbery: What really bothered the Left about Levittowns was that they were so *working class*. Happily, and unsurprisingly, conservatives won this battle.

But the Littleton problem is not the Levittown problem. And conservatives' victory in earlier battles has made them too quick to dismiss the complaints that have spawned dozens of panicky books in the past two years and have come to a boil in the wake of the shootings. Al Gore's attacks on suburban "sprawl" may retain much of the earlier anti-suburban liberal snobbery. The "livability agenda" that he plugs may lack intellectual seriousness. But Gore's very lack of seriousness should alert us that there's a real problem here. The vice president is a sufficiently unoriginal man that he would not be flailing about for a solution if he hadn't already found deep discontent in suburban focus groups.

The problem with Levittown was its physical monotony, a problem that diminishes over time, as trees grow and suburbanites modify their homes. What's more, since Tocqueville we've been told that a tendency to uniformity comes with the democratic territory. The problem in affluent "McMansion" suburbs like Littleton is that children grow up in almost hermetic seclusion—a newer and more soul-destroying condition, with dismal implications for democracy. Large lots, dead-end streets, and draconian zoning laws mean that there are vast distances to travel to reach any kind of public space. For parents, this means dependence on cars. For children unlucky enough to inhabit a dead-end that has no children on it, this means: No friends for you. Until adolescence, not even a child who is an ambitious walker can escape, since other neighborhoods are separated from his not by streets but by highways. (Town planners may christen them "avenues" or "boulevards," and real-estate agents may sell them as such, but they're highways.) No child in Levittown faced this problem.

This seclusion, in turn, creates an abject dependence on parents for automobile travel, and with it, a breakdown in any socialization of children that could be called normal. In the largely suburban eastern town where I grew up, a 5-year-old could walk about the neighborhood, and a 10-year-old could walk all over town. Twelve-year-olds could ride their bikes most places, and 14-year-olds could ride them to other towns. When you were 16, you could take the car if you really needed it. Entry into adult mobility was gradual and supervised. By contrast, a 15-year-old Littleton resident lives in a state of dependence considerably greater than that of my 5-year-old neighbors—or of 5-year-olds in any Levittown, for that matter. When a child of the western suburbs reaches driving age, his parents face a choice: either maintain the kid in his infantile seclusion until you send him off to college (where he can go nuts) or buy him a car and unleash him as a demigod of the highways.

There are, no doubt, cultural and historic factors at work along with ques- 10
tions of suburban landscape. For one, anonymity—which the locals describe as "privacy"—is a cherished cultural value in the western United States. (So is rootlessness: How many kids in Littleton High have parents from Littleton? How many were born in Littleton themselves?) For another, western suburbs were always doomed to be more sterile than their eastern counterparts, since the East was already too heavily settled for automobile-based suburbs to gain absolute dominion over the landscape: Drive out of a planned development in Massachusetts or New Jersey and you can easily wind up on a village green.

The upshot is that Levittown has as much in common with the Olde Village Greene as it does with Littleton—and is a much better place to live for that reason. The ghastly solitude of much of the American upper-middle class was well evoked by Edward Luttwak in his recent book *Turbo-Capitalism:* "There is a lot of lonely space not only between but inside the ideal dwellings of the American dream, the veritable mansions of the richest suburbs, which could house parents, grown children and their children in familial communion if only all were poor enough, but which mostly house only one ever-so-busy male and as busy a female, with surviving parents in their own retirement abodes, distant children pursuing their budding careers, and few friends, whose degree of loyal commitment might rate them as mere acquaintances in other climes."

Littleton is perhaps best described as Levittown plus affluence plus limitless buildable land—and the result is something qualitatively different, even unprecedented. If in Levittown the issue is conformity, in Littleton it's identity. In Levittown, you get kids banding together lamenting that their life is less heroic than that of their parents: It's *Rebel Without a Cause*. In Littleton, you get kids building the wildest fantasies in their interminable solitude, with the help of their computers, their televisions, and their stereos: It's a high-tech version of *The Wild Boy of Aveyron*. (As the architecture professor William Morrish told the *New York Times:* "They're basically an unseen population until they pierce their noses.")

Critics of the Fifties complained that Levittown's sameness could lead to conformity—although there was never much proof that it did. Today's critics warn that the loneliness of Littleton produces something very like the opposite of conformity. We can only hope that the evidence they're right doesn't continue to mount.

Cultivating Killers

JUDITH A. REISMAN

> Michael Carneal had never fired a pistol before stealing the gun he used that day. But in the ensuing melee, he fired eight shots, hit eight people, and killed three of them. When Michael Carneal was shooting, he fired one shot at each kid. . . . He simply fired one shot at everything that popped up on his screen.
>
> —COLONEL DAVE GROSSMAN, EXPERT ON VIOLENCE IN SOCIETY

COMMENTING after the April 20 shooting spree and suicide by students 1
Eric Harris and Dylan Klebold at their Littleton, Colorado, high school, Hillary Clinton told an audience of public school teachers in New York, "We can no longer shut our eyes to the impact the media is having on all our children. . . . We're awash in it." And syndicated columnist Peggy Noonan added her opinion in the April 22 *Wall Street Journal:* "The kids who did this are responsible. They did it. They killed. But they came from a place and time, and were yielded forth by a culture."

Culture, indeed, seems to be a key factor in the violence and murder that permeate our society today, and are touching greater numbers of our youth across the nation.

There are still many unknowns in the Colorado tragedy, but one thing is certain: The Columbine tragedy has ratcheted up the anxiety and debate over America's at-risk youth. While the last few years have witnessed horrible acts of murder by kids at schools, the determined and premeditated destruction and murder wrought by Harris and Klebold leave us particularly stunned. What inspired these kids from an affluent suburb of Denver to such vicious carnage—accomplished with a sense of triumph and glee?

For at least two decades, experts have warned that television, movies, music, and other entertainment media are desensitizing young people to violence and death. Murder, rape, and physical assault are common fare in movies and in weekly episodes of award-winning television dramas, and some popular music genres have taken to glorifying sex, violence, murder, and even suicide. Adolescents have been immersed, in many cases without the clear understanding of their parents and other adults, in a culture of sex, death, and violence. Unless the media and entertainment industry are factored into the dialogue over this cultural crisis, there will be no remedy—and Columbine and the other school killings will be merely an introduction to more violent and sensational acts of terror and murder.

Until recent times, three institutions have been responsible for socializing 5
America's children: the home, the church, and the school. By far the most influential of these three elements has been the home—and more specifically the parents.

The values modeled by mom and dad, and instilled by them into the characters of their children, have traditionally charted the moral course of those kids. Good parenting by and large produced good kids, and bad parenting bad kids. But something has changed in the last couple of decades: An outside force has militated against the positive influence provided by parents, church, and (not so long ago) school.

While every generation has certainly had its share of both "good" and "bad" parents, one can state with some certainty that young people have not murdered their schoolmates based on the quality of the parenting they received. Moreover, there is no evidence that "bad" parents have taught or modeled mass murder to their children. So if kids like Eric Harris and Dylan Klebold did not learn to murder from their parents, what influence was present that pushed them to this madness? Clearly the mass media, with its unnatural fixation on violence and murder, must assume much of the blame.

Guns, of course, have been a constant in our nation since its founding, and the Second Amendment has ever guaranteed that the right of firearms ownership holds a place close to the hearts of free and independent Americans.

Guns have also held center stage in Hollywood fare since the very beginning of the movie industry. Shoot-'em-up cowboy films have been popular since the days of silent movies, as well as cops-and-robbers pictures. But there is a distinct difference between movies through the mid-1960s and the majority which have been made since then. Previously, the viewer always knew the difference between the good guys and the bad guys, and graphic scenes of violence (often with perverted overtones) were never permitted as they are with a vengeance today.

Today's movies are often little more than thinly veiled excuses for displays of sex, violence, and murder, depicted as graphically as possible. And such disturbing images are assaulting young children through video rental outlets, on cable and direct-dish television, as well as in popular music, computer games, and Internet sites. The end result is a polluting of the hearts, minds, and spirits of America's children—often without the knowledge of well-meaning parents.

During Hollywood's "Golden Age," from the early 1930s through the mid- 10
1960s, filmmakers followed the Motion Picture Code (MPC), a guide approved by America's religious leadership, which prohibited movie content which was explicitly sexual, violent, profane, or blasphemous. This was a voluntary code enforced by public pressure and moral suasion. But there were also state and local laws which protected society.

No such restrictions guide today's moviemakers and other entertainment producers, and what has resulted is a veritable sewer line of filth flowing from Hollywood and its subsidiaries into the heart of our nation's culture. Without even trying one can name a handful of popular films of recent years which have been marketed on their content of graphic sex and violence: *Natural Born Killers, The Basketball Diaries, Pulp Fiction, Face-off, The Matrix, Blade, The Terminator, Payback, Alien, Halloween* (and its umpteen sequels). In 1975, Earl Warren Jr. noted with obvious disapproval that for many years obscenity laws had included "bloodshed" and gratuitous "crime" as well as sexual matters.

In 1957, the U.S. Supreme Court, led by his father Earl Warren Sr., overturned those laws with its revolutionary decision in *Roth v. United States.* The younger Warren was greatly relieved by this decision, remarking that illegal obscenity was "at last narrowed to matters of a sexual nature."

Until *Roth,* American common law held that any part of a public display which disordered susceptible persons could be illegal. The law allowed that while "normal" people might view obscene materials, including "bloodshed" and "crime," and remain unaffected, society had an obligation to protect juveniles and other vulnerable persons from such harmful stimuli.

That crime and violence were thus controlled said a good deal about America's moral views. Addressing the impact of the law on society, Dr. Wanda Franz, president of National Right to Life, noted that the law teaches the public what is "moral," or at least "O.K." Since 1957, first "bloodshed and crime," and then "sex and violence," became acceptable fare for entertainment and media. Trusting our justice system, parents everywhere have been lulled into a false sense of security about the harmless nature of today's entertainment for their children.

The sexual revolution, begun by Alfred Kinsey in the late 1940s, paved the way for a legal revolution—a revolution which cited Kinsey's fraudulent science as proof that there was really no division between moral and immoral, right and wrong, normal and abnormal. Science became our new god, and the Judeo-Christian foundations of our culture were gradually replaced by the tenets of secular humanism. By 1962 public school prayer was banned, in 1963 Bible reading, and gradually "Thou shalt not kill" was replaced in our school classrooms with "lifeboat ethics."

As common law's biblically based "right and wrong" standard was legally 15
wrested from American life, a new relative standard had to be crafted as a replacement. The attack on our culture was key to this change, and increasingly explicit sexual and violent content in movies, television, video games, and other media forms have been used to push our nation into that new, "values-free," social and legal standard.

Over the decades since the *Roth* decision, films, television, and operant conditioning "video games" have become increasingly sexual and violent—and the market has focused its attention on children. With today's anything-goes media mindset, respected companies are making big money on sex, satanism, and death. For example, Seagram's, known in the past mainly as an alcoholic beverage giant, now makes millions of dollars promoting satanic rock guru and suicide peddler Marilyn Manson, whose "music" has been linked to the Littleton massacre and other carnage by adolescents. Witness the following example of Marilyn Manson's message of hate and rebellion, which morally rudderless teens all over America are eating up and emulating in their dress, their attitudes, and, unfortunately, their actions:

- "I am so all american, I'd sell you suicide I am totalitarian, I've got abortions in my eyes . . . "
- "Let's just kill everyone and let your god sort them out . . . "

- "I'm gonna f*** you 'til somebody better comes along . . . "
- "The living are dead and I hope to join them too . . . "
- "Got no religion. . . . I wanna die young and sell my soul . . . "

On March 8, 1999, the U.S. Supreme Court ruled that distributors Time Warner Inc. and director Oliver Stone could be used by the family of a shooting victim in a crime allegedly inspired by the film *Natural Born Killers. Entertainment News* quoted media lawyers who swore to defend the right of "artists and directors to express their creative ideas without fear of liability."

Science magazine quoted University of California neuroscientist Robert Malenka as he spoke at the National Academy of Sciences: "Because of the advances we've made over the last decade . . . [it is] now clear that environmental influences, from learning to medications . . . modify thought and behavior by modifying brain structure and functioning."

So how did Oliver Stone's "creative ideas" modify thought and behavior by "modifying brain structure and functioning" of those teenagers who repeatedly viewed *Natural Born Killers?* In the movie, Stone depicts the murder victims as more depraved than the young killer-lovers. Using background screams of horror, pain, sex, joy, and profanity, Stone cynically intercuts color and black/white footage to subtly encourage his audience to identify with the killer anti-heroes. Viewers find themselves rooting for the couple as they murder her incestuous father, set her mother afire, and gaily shoot passersby. Finally, Stone has the couple drive off, their toddlers in tow, to live happily ever after, with no price to pay—legally, psychologically, or emotionally—for their heinous crimes.

20 Stone, of course, is unoriginal. His film is nothing more than standard indoctrination fare. War violence experts Dave Grossman and James Gibson note that part of the conditioning some soldiers get in training them to kill their enemies includes exposure to films heavy with sadosexual content.

A $130 million lawsuit filed on April 12, 1999, in Paducah, Kentucky, lists among the defendants Time Warner and Polygram Filmed Entertainment, Inc., computer game makers, and Internet sex sites. On December 1, 1997, Michael Carneal, a 14-year-old student at Paducah's Heath High School, shot and killed three girls in a group of praying classmates gathered in the school lobby. The lawsuit contends that the "video game industry," "sex porn sites" and *Basketball Diaries,* a 1995 Polygram film, inspired Carneal's brutal murders.

In *Basketball Diaries,* a teenager, played by Leonardo DiCaprio, shoots his Catholic school teacher and classmates as they sit defenseless before him. A preview for the movie *Coldblooded* was included with the *Basketball Diaries* video. In the preview, television teen idol Jason Priestly modeled murder for millions of impressionable and vulnerable youth. Priestly's paternal mentor opens the short preview by saying:

"Ever killed a guy before?"

"No," replies our hero.

25 "You lead a pretty boring life, don't you," remarks his mentor. "You've never fired a gun before?"

"Never."

But after practicing on a "pop up" firing range, Priestly asks:

"When do we do our first job?"

"Hang on tiger," replies his mentor. "Be patient, something always comes up."

30 Next, the preview cuts to a close-up of an obese man on the floor, on his knees, hands spread out before him, eyes closed, begging for his life, followed by the loud report of a gun and the unmistakable impression that the man has been killed.

Priestly's character is thrilled to kill scores of unarmed men and women in the quick film cuts, saying, "I've never been good at anything before. It's exciting!"

Sex and violence are interwoven throughout the movie. Scenes depict Priestly's character freely shooting unarmed people, and are intercut with scenes of partial nudity and simulated physical intimacy with a willing, young girl. This portrayal of sex, crime, and violence, especially to hormonally challenged youngsters, is a powerful influence, and neurological experts argue that such stimuli, after enough consumption, do alter a young person's brain patterns. Is it all that surprising that a vulnerable adolescent like Michael Carneal, who consumed countless hours of these kinds of images, shot to death defenseless Jessica James, Kayce Steger, and Nicole Hadley, and wounded five other praying students?

Media elites insist that only the mentally disturbed would act out the toxic images which have been poured into the nation's environment 24 hours a day over the past years. This was the group, "mentally disturbed," that the obscenity laws, pre-1957, sought to protect. In 1989 the Institute of Medicine (IoM) claimed that 12 to 22 percent of American youth have a "diagnosable mental illness." So, the IoM would argue, on that evidence, between 10 million and 18 million of roughly 80 million American youths are demonstrably vulnerable to modified brain structure and function, some of whom will be inspired to act out the sexual brutality and murder modeled by mass media entertainment.

Corporations are regularly held accountable for dumping their toxic waste into our physical environment. Tobacco companies are now being held liable for the deaths of adult smokers who voluntarily used their products. But filmmakers and movie distributors like Oliver Stone and Warner have yet to be held responsible for the deadly effects their products inspire—particularly on the young. Producers of visual media which incite sex, violence, and crime must be held accountable for influencing our mental and cultural environment.

35 Since the Supreme Court's *Roth* decision, violent and pornographic images have improperly come under the First Amendment, which was designed by the Founding Fathers to protect thought, debate, and dialogue. In the April 26 *New York Times,* Denise Caruso noted that hundreds of scientific studies since 1972 establish the "direct correlation between exposure to media violence—now including video games—and increasing aggression."

The media have long applied desensitization, conditioning, and vicarious learning techniques to unsuspecting audiences, functionally restructuring and remolding the national mind. The '90s were declared by the U.S. Congress "The Decade of the Brain," and what we have learned since 1900 about our executive organ must again inform laws protecting the vulnerable.

Dr. Gary Lynch, a neuroscientist at the University of California–Irvine, observes that an "event which lasts half a second within five to ten minutes has produced a structural change that is in some ways as profound as the structural changes one sees in [brain] damage." This rudimentary observation addresses the brain's processing of visual stimuli. Lynch's research is critical for any evaluation of today's toxic media. Michael Carneal typifies the profile of one molded by demonic music, violent video games, violent films, pornography, and racist ideology. America's heartless killers clearly hearken to German Nazi youth, and it is useful to recall some aspects of German National Socialist indoctrination.

Nazi youth were taught that brutalizing, even killing, was their right as supermen and that their parents' religious beliefs were irrelevant. Hitler's understanding of how to sway the masses is textbook, and can inform us about the power of the imagery forced upon us by moviemakers like Oliver Stone. Hitler's own words (as recorded in *Propaganda: The Art of Persuasion in World War II,* by Anthony Rhodes) predict other tragedies similar to those in Littleton and Paducah: "Propaganda must be addressed to the emotions and not to the intelligence, and it must concentrate on a few simple themes . . . with lurid photographs of the . . . sexual and physical."

Certainly current movies, television programs, music videos, and video games fit Hitler's brainwashing technique. Over a century ago scientists understood that certain images stir "emotions" from the right hemisphere of the brain, triggering visceral, red-alert responses and inevitably subverting the left-hemisphere "intelligence" tasks of reason, debate, and dialogue. If images reach the right hemisphere and compromise left hemisphere reasoning, cognition—"free speech"—is subverted by visual experience. Richard Restak, author of *The Brain* (1984) observes: "Inhibition rather than excitation is the hallmark of the healthy brain. . . . If all the neurons in the brain were excitatory we would be unable to do something as simple as reaching out for a glass of water."

The prefrontal cortex, our rational "command center," controls our psyche, 40
and neurochemical research provides evidence of the increasingly noxious effect of common media imagery on psyche and conduct. *Science* magazine noted, "Maintaining normal brain function . . . requires a delicate balancing act: too much neuronal activity can be as bad as too little."

And educational psychologist Jane Haley, in *Endangered Minds: Why Our Children Don't Think* (1990), reiterated that the human brain "is plastic," and noted that "large areas of uncommitted brain tissue can be molded . . . to the demands of a particular environment."

Dr. Lynch writes that "in a matter of seconds, taking an incredibly modest signal, a word . . . which is in your head as an electrical signal for no more than a few seconds, can . . . leave a trace that will last for years."

What "trace" have the myriad violent and cynical films, television programs, pornographic magazines, obscene Internet sites, and occult video games left on our own future youth? David Gottlieb reported in *Scientific American* that one of the most important functions of the nervous system is to inhibit human excitation. He noted that inhibitory transmitters are so "widespread in the brain and spinal cord that they must fulfill a significant function." UCLA psychologist Dr. Margaret Kemeny cites ways in which the brain is impacted by exposure to violent, sexual, altruistic, or religious media: "Although it seems intangible, anytime we feel anything, anytime we think anything, anytime we imagine anything, there is activity in the brain that is taking place in the body at that time. That activity can then lead to a cascade of changes in the body."

Viewing obscene, violent, or sexual images does structurally alter a child's brain, mind, and memories, with brain tissue "molded" by excitatory media.

For roughly four decades, our nation's children have been guinea pigs for 45
"entertainment" brain experiments. The deadly and grievous results are seen all around us, and were witnessed in Littleton, Paducah, and elsewhere.

Former President Theodore Roosevelt once observed: "To educate a man in mind and not in morals is to educate a menace to society." Stripping legal protections from the vulnerable few has made all of America vulnerable.

Practicing the Principles: Activities

FALLACIES IN LETTERS TO THE EDITOR

In one of the explorations for an earlier chapter, I invited you to collect letters to the editor in order to analyze ethos in arguments about a local issue. You may have noticed that letters to the editor also provide a lot of examples of logical fallacies. They are often written quickly, without a lot of thought, so writers often make errors in reasoning. Return to the letters you collected earlier, or begin a new collection, looking for common fallacies.

In addition to collecting letters to the editor, you might try examining other media sources for logical fallacies: commercials, advertisements, radio call-in shows, daytime talk shows on television, or political speeches.

EAVESDROPPING

Try "eavesdropping" on some conversations around campus to collect some fallacies in their natural habitat. Hang out at the student union, listen in on your roommates' conversations, or ride the city bus to and from school. Try to find some places on campus where students will be informally debating and discussing community issues. Bring your examples to class to share with other students.

CURING THE FALLACY

Jackie Wheeler, one of my former colleagues at Arizona State University, taught me a game called "Cure the Fallacy." She believed that most logical fallacies are perversions of perfectly acceptable persuasive strategies. Therefore, most can be "cured." For instance, a hasty or sweeping generalization might be changed into a legitimate generalization by gathering additional evidence or by limiting the scope of the generalization. A fallacious appeal to emotion might be changed into a genuine appeal to pathos if you revise the emotional description to fit the situation. An oversimplified cause might by cured by identifying more likely causes.

Examine the list of fallacies that I provide in this chapter or—even better—the list of fallacies that you have gathered on your own, and working in small groups, see how many of these you can "cure."

THE NUMBERS DON'T LIE

In this chapter, I provide some questions to answer when evaluating statistical arguments, but I'm no expert on statistics. Consider inviting a statistician to your class to talk about the dangers of using numerical and statistical arguments. If you encounter questionable statistical arguments or graphs in your reading, then bring these to class for discussion.

If you have access to spreadsheet or graphing software in a computer classroom, you can easily examine how graphs and statistics can be manipulated. Generate a graph and then change the type of graph, the scale, and the labeling to find out how elastic graphs can be and how easily graphs can be used to demonstrate nearly anything.

Applying the Principles: Analytical Projects

PRACTICE WITH FALLACIES

The first set of logical fallacies come from Zachary Seech's *Logic in Everyday Life*. The second set comes from *Logical Self-Defense,* by Ralph Johnson and J. Anthony Blair. These examples provide you with additional opportunities to practice identifying and explaining fallacies. Do each of the following:

1. Identify the argument: claims, reasons, and assumptions. If the parts of the argument are not explicit, then try to infer them from the example.
2. Explain why (or why not) the example is a fallacy.
3. If the example is a fallacy, then identify the kind of fallacy it is and describe how it works.
4. Think of a way to "cure" the fallacy. How could you revise each example to make it a legitimate argument?

Exercises from Logic in Everyday Life

ZACHARY SEECH

1. I heard that the nation's educational community is opposing the new tax bill. George, you're a teacher. Just why do you think the bill is a bad one?
2. Despite constant criticism of the Electoral College system, it's clear that this is the best method for selecting a national leader. After all, it has been accepted as a fair and good method for a couple of centuries now.
3. What will *you* do? Will you give every penny you can afford for helping the pathetically starving people in Africa? Or will you clutch desperately to each dollar you earn, using all of your abundance of wealth for personal comfort and convenience?
4. I see nothing wrong with doing my civic duty and casting my my vote in a local election even if I am uninformed on the issues. Why, I'll bet that half of the people who vote have done essentially no research prior to election day.
5. Just disregard Ralph Nader's latest list of reasons to require stricter safety standards on new cars. He has been critical of the United States auto industry for years. Why should we expect anything different now?
6. You can't prove he was to blame for her misfortune, so it must actually have been someone else who was responsible.
7. *Bank officer:* You say, Dr. Selch, that you will repay this unsecured loan. How does my bank know that you are honest and trustworthy so we can take your word for that?
   Dr. Selch: You can ask my department chairperson, Dr. Velnoy.
   Bank officer: But how do we know we can rely on the word of Dr. Velnoy?
   Dr. Selch: Oh, don't worry about that. I can vouch for him without reservation!
8. A high-school teacher comments:

   My students don't seem to be doing as well on the tests I've been giving lately. Students are apparently not as smart as they used to be.

9. Altruism, the view that people do not always act out of self-interest, is clearly false. There is no proof that, when you consider ultimate motivations, any motive other than pure self-interest is at work.
10. *Of course* women are more emotional than men. Everybody knows that!
11. Even the ancient Egyptians believed in a form of life after death. So there must be some truth in that idea.
12. In the movie *The Bishop's Wife,* the bishop (played by David Niven) asks the angel (played by Cary Grant) who he is. The angel replies, "I'm an angel." The bishop's challenge, "How do I know that?" meets with the following reply: "Surely you, of all people, know you can believe an angel."
13. A mother to her daughter over breakfast:

    "You wouldn't have to deal with this problem of coming up with enough money to repair the car if you hadn't taken the car last night. I *told* you to stay home and leave the car in the garage. You got just what you deserved for not listening to me."

14. From *National Geographic,* December 1985 ("How We Found *Titanic,*" by Robert D. Ballard):

    It was from [the crow's nest of the *Titanic*] that lookout Fred Fleet, who survived, first sighted the iceberg one-fourth of a mile dead ahead. Instinctively he gave three rings on the bell above the crow's nest . . . Fleet warned the bridge [by telephone], "Iceberg right ahead!"

    Ironically, Fleet's words doomed *Titanic.* In response to the warning her officer-in-charge tried to reverse engines and turn hard to starboard. The reversal actually turned the ship slowly to port, and she suffered the fatal gash in her starboard side. Had she rammed the berg head-on, she would likely have flooded only two or three compartments and remained afloat.

15. From a letter to the editor of the *New York Times,* February 25, 1986:

    There is not an iota of evidence to suggest that Moslems in North Africa have been involved, directly or indirectly, in any terrorist activity.

16. Yes, I cheated on the test, but so did a lot of other people. To be fair, you should punish all of the offenders equally.
17. The only life in the universe may be right here on this planet. On the other hand, there *may be* life elsewhere in the universe. Who knows which of these claims is true? Certainly one or the other is true.
18. We know that Pope John XXIII was moved by compassion, since all popes have been moved by compassion.
19. Don't look to your physician for sympathy on medical costs, George. Dr. Diaz will undoubtedly be unsympathetic. The medical community has strongly opposed virtually all significant cost-containment efforts and shown no practical concern to limit the costs of health care to the public.

20. The Atlanta Braves are going to win the National League pennant this year. It's true! I heard Ted Turner, the owner of the team, say so himself.
21. I don't see how you can think you have a moral obligation to feed the starving masses overseas. No one else seems to feel that way.
22. How can you doubt that good and right will eventually triumph? This has been a basic assumption of Western thought for ages.
23. From *The San Diego Union*, April 21, 1985:

    With two outs in the bottom of the 10th, first base was open with Alan Wiggins, off to a 2-for-22 start, in the on-deck circle. [Los Angeles Dodgers manager Tommy] Lasorda could have walked [San Diego Padres player Kurt] Bevacqua.

    Instead he had reliever Ken Howell pitch to Bevacqua. [Bevacqua batted in the winning run.]

    "I didn't want to walk him," said Lasorda. When asked why, the Dodger manager tersely replied, "because I didn't want to."

Exercises from Logical Self-Defense

RALPH JOHNSON and J. ANTHONY BLAIR

1. The excerpt below is from "In Defense of Culture: The Unravelling Tie that Binds," by Robert Solomon. Solomon is arguing that American cultural identity is threatened and that neither television nor contemporary music is capable of forging the cultural ties needed to bind Americans together. He writes:

    Consider the case of contemporary music: The Beatles are only a name to most 12-year-olds. Beethoven, by contrast, continues to provide the musical themes we can assume (even if wrongly) that all of us have heard, time and time again. This isn't snobbery; it's continuity.

2. The argument below is adapted from a Canadian magazine article entitled "The Case against Abortion":

    In 1988, more than 152,000 women had their children killed before they could be born. These numbers are on the increase every year. By the end of 1995, we will have reached the 200,000 level. The percentages are similar in western Europe. They are greater in the Soviet Union. No one would be against abortion when the woman's life is at stake, but that situation is now exceedingly rare. The present mass feticide takes place almost always for convenience. Medical professionals tell us that 95 percent of abortions now performed kill the healthy offspring of healthy women. How has this quiet medical slaughter become part of modern societies everywhere?

3. The debate about the aggressive behavior of men brought this letter to a newspaper:

   I don't want to hear any more of this talk about how barbaric and brutal men are. I work in the emergency room of Parkview Hospital. Allow me to tell you what I have seen lately. The other night, they brought in a man who had been beaten silly by his wife while he was sleeping. In another case, a man came in complaining of a headache that had lasted for several days. X-rays revealed a bullet in his head; later he found a note from his wife explaining that she had shot him while he was asleep and that he should go to the hospital. A young baby boy was brought in with bruises all over his body; his mother had beaten him. That's the kind of thing that makes me think this talk of men being the aggressive ones is overblown.

4. The following was sent to the *San Francisco Examiner* (July 19, 1992) by a doctor in San Jose:

   Your article about Kate Michelman was well done and, I think, unbiased. However, I must take issue with the so-called "logic" of the abortion rights movement. Nature includes human gestation, and human gestation involves the development and growth of the human, always a person, no matter how small or how immature. The end, the adult, is in the beginning the zygote. The zygote is a person, no matter how many persons deny the fact. Some people even deny their own existence. Some people even deny that 2 plus 2 equals 4.

5. In a debate about apartheid, one arguer declared: "Apartheid is a crime against humanity. It is on the same level as genocide and slavery." One response to this was:

   As unjust and debasing as apartheid is, it is not on the same level as genocide. European Jewry, Armenians, and members of the Baha'i religion would hardly agree with the arguer's view. What she is saying is that Soweto is equal to Auschwitz. Where are the gas chambers and the ovens in Soweto? Although apartheid may also have been labeled a crime against humanity, in no way are genocide and apartheid on the "same level." Anyone who equates Soweto to Auschwitz demonstrates an abysmal lack of understanding of what Auschwitz was. Are the gas chambers running twenty-four hours a day in Soweto?

6. In "Three Days of the Con Job" (*GQ*, March 1992), Joe Queenan relates his experiences at the First International Men's Conference held in Austin,

Texas, and refers to a comment by Robert Bly warning that the movement was still in its infancy. Queenan writes:

> Of course it's easy for Robert Bly to say "Hold the publicity!" now that Bill Moyers has anointed him the Saint Thomas Aquinas of the late twentieth century on a widely viewed PBS special, now that Bly has had a number-one book on the *New York Times* best-sellers list, now that Bly has banked a few big ones by preaching an esoteric philosophy whose highly debatable central tenet is that the industrial revolution ruined everything for men, that things were a whole lot better back in the Middle Ages, when Dad stayed home. (Yes, Bob, it's true that Dad stayed home, but the Visigoths didn't.)

7. This is an excerpt from a review of *You Just Don't Understand: Women and Men in Conversation* by Deborah Tannen. (The review, by Mary Beard, appeared in the *London Review of Books,* August 1991, p. 18.)

> Judging the matter as it stands, I find it hard to interpret the man's actions as anything other than rudeness verging on exploitation. First he gets his sex, then he gets his breakfast cooked and paper provided. [That is how Tannen recounted the incident in question.] For her it is a matter of language again. In fact, she congratulates the woman concerned, who apparently realized that different genderlects were at stake here: "She realized that unlike her, he did not feel the need for talk to reinforce their intimacy." Any women who actually believed this ridiculous interpretation would no doubt also believe that washing-up and nappy-changing are somehow at odds with men's sense of their own language. She would probably accept, too, the inevitability of male abuse—just "getting attention" again, she would say.

8. In 1991, there was a heated dispute that originated when a chemistry professor published a paper in the *Canadian Journal of Physics* (Vol. 68, 1990), a respectable peer-refered scientific journal, on the subject of what causes the problems of teenagers and young adults. The professor's argument, in brief outline, went something like this:

> There is a significant correlation between teenagers and young adults who have problems and the lack of full-time parent in their homes when they are growing up. Most women who work outside the home do so to protect themselves against the possibility that their husbands will leave them, not because the feminist movement is correct. Most women are equipped by nature to be nurturers, whereas most men are not. Without the socioeconomic pressure to work, most women would choose to remain in their natural roles. The growth of feminism is merely a symptom of unstable families and therefore of an unstable society. Feminism could not sustain an economically stable society.

9. Farley Mowat (author of *Never Cry Wolf*) was asked on his 70th birthday what he thought about the prospects of the human species. He replied in the following vein:

   Humans today are acting like yeast in a brewer's vat, multiplying mindlessly, all the while greedily consuming the limited subsistence of our world. If we continue to act like the yeasts, we will perish as they do, having exhausted our resources and poisoned ourselves in the lethal brew of our own wastes.

10. A study done by Jane Maulden, a researcher at the University of California at Berkeley, and reported on in the August 1990 issue of the journal *Demographics,* discussed the effects of a marital breakup on the health of the children.

    Maulden studied 6,000 children's health histories. In families in which divorce had occurred, the children averaged 0.13 more illnesses per year after the divorce than before. Such children ran a 35 percent risk of developing health problems over a three-year period, as compared with a 26 percent risk among all children.

    Nearly one-third of the illnesses reported were accounted for by ear infections and pneumonia. Others included allergies, asthma, chronic skin conditions, chronic lung problems, and urinary infections.

    Maulden said that "children are likely to experience very significant stress because their living standards change dramatically. . . . They probably also lose many of the resources that contribute to good health: a safe, comfortable environment relatively free of environmental hazards and the risks of infection; good food; and constant adult supervision."

11. The plan in the United States to commemorate Elvis Presley with a postage stamp provoked the following letter:

    It's ridiculous to honor Elvis with a postage stamp. In the 1960s, drugs hit the American scene like a tidal wave. Rock 'n' roll entertainers, Elvis among them, encouraged drug use by example and promoted it in their music. Today, we see the social wreckage that resulted. Lives were destroyed and are still being destroyed. The human and economic costs have been enormous. That money could have been put to much better use—for example, to help the poor. It's a crying shame to whitewash the past with this stupid stamp.

12. The abortion debate is the occasion for innumerable arguments. The following argument is adapted from a letter written by someone who took issue with the claim of columnist Clair Hoy that the fetus is an innocent human being:

    Hoy misunderstands innocence. Innocence is not absence of guilt; it's freedom from guilt. Freedom from guilt implies the ability to choose to do wrong. A fetus is no more innocent than I am innocent of speeding on the highway on my bicycle. I'm incapable of going that fast. But a fetus is incapable of any freedom of action whatsoever. So a fetus cannot be innocent.

13. A newspaper editorial once made the claim that abortion should be a matter entirely between the woman concerned and her doctor and that this needn't violate the consciences of those women and medical practitioners who are opposed to abortion. That opinion drew the following response:

    Your concept of conscience is indeed narrow.

    One who is opposed to smoking, for instance, is not content to leave the matter between the child and the tobacconist. Indeed he or she seeks to have glamorous advertising of the product banned and tries to make smoking as difficult as possible (e.g., banning it in schools, in food establishments, and so on) to create a deterrent to immature as well as casual smokers.

    Similarly, one who is opposed to abortion cannot possibly leave this matter between an often immature or panic-stricken woman and a doctor often too busy and too materialistic to oppose her wishes.

14. An excerpt from an advertisement for numerology contained the following claim. (It's not relevant, but Dionne Warwick has since dropped the final *e* from her surname.)

    We have found that numerology is a very useful tool in producing good luck. For example, each letter in the alphabet has an assigned number. Singer Dionne Warwick took the advice of her numerologist and added an *e* to the end of her name. Her numerologist told her that this would bring about the correct, fortunate combination.

    She immediately skyrocketed to fame. She has told the story about her numerologist on the Johnny Carson show twice.

15. This writer objects to the organized killing of pigeons.

    We would like to praise those who protested the pigeon slaughter. We are appalled to think that anyone could be so insensitive and inhumane. To starve and then slaughter these poor creatures is unthinkable. Of those who say that "these protesters have no right to interfere with our freedoms," we ask, How can cruelty to animals be considered a cherished freedom? And how about the remark made by the man who said that he shoots skeets but prefers live birds because they are more unpredictable. Whatever happened to live and let live? Murder for sport is still murder.

16. In an article in the *Windsor Star*, a local columnist argued against pornography. Distinguishing between "erotica," which she defined as sexual expression between people who have enough power to be there by choice, and "pornography," she wrote:

It may be that what the country needs, besides more employment, is more erotica. What we don't need, and should not tolerate, is pornography. Pornography makes half the human race feel like malleable objects at best and like helpless or debased subjects at worst. Surely if pornography insults or injures half the population and may possibly incite or negatively influence the other half, then it has no place in our shops and homes.

17. In a letter to *Mother Jones* (April 1992), Robert Simonds, president of the Citizens for Excellence in Education (CEE), responded to an earlier article suggesting that the Christian Right is a very dangerous movement.

    Children are being brutalized by left-wing groups presently in control of our schools. How? Through atheistic and immoral programs such as Planned Parenthood; by forcing boys to hold bananas in class while girls practice putting condoms on the bananas; and by teaching children that homosexuality is as normal and fulfilling as heterosexuality. CEE wants parents—Christian or otherwise—to be elected to school boards. CEE has never "endorsed" a candidate. We educate and encourage parents to run for office.

18. In March 1993, Dr. David Gunn, a doctor who ran an abortion clinic in Pensacola, Florida, was murdered. A man named Michael Griffin was charged with the crime. In a nationally syndicated article titled "Why Weep for an Abortionist When the Score Is 30 Million to 1?" Joseph Sobran argued:

    The man who shot (Gunn) was not even a member of an anti-abortion organization. . . . Nevertheless, Peter Jennings and his colleagues made the most of it, leading off the evening news and filling the front pages with the murder of the poor "doctor." The moral was supplied by Kate Michelman of the National Abortion Rights Action League, who decried "anti-choice terrorism." Terrorism? Why not just call it murder? The killer's intent was to kill, not to terrify.

19. In the debate over fighting in professional hockey games, one argument often heard runs as follows:

    If you don't allow fighting, you're going to spoil the game. Hockey isn't a namby-pamby game like cricket or shuffleboard. Hockey players are skating fast and hitting hard. Somebody's always bound to run into another fellow too hard or with his stick up or whatever, and the other guy's got to defend himself because he has to go back and play the guy that hit him next week. Plus, if you get a reputation for being soft around the league, you're done for. You have to be able to stand up for yourself, and that means fighting. If you cut out the fighting, then players will retaliate in other ways, like with the stick work, which can get really dangerous and cause bad injuries. Fights aren't dangerous—nobody ever gets hurt. That's the way hockey has always been, and that's the way it's got to stay or else you change the game, and for the worse.

20. From an article titled "Men, Inexpressiveness and Power" in *Language, Gender and Society* (1983) comes the following:

    Sexism is not significantly challenged simply by changing men's capacity to feel or express themselves. Gender relationships in this society are constructed in terms of social power, and to forget that fact . . . is to assume that men can somehow unproblematically experience "men's liberation"—as if there existed for men some directly analogous experience to the politics created by feminist and gay struggles. Men are not oppressed *as men* and hence are not in a position to be liberated *as men*.

AMERICAN OVERCONSUMPTION

Each of the following essays focuses on one of the defining problems of American culture: obesity. It's an odd paradox in our culture that we are obsessed with both gaining weight and losing weight. These authors examine some of the causes and effects of obesity in American culture. As you read the following essays, discuss and apply as a class the principles you have learned from this chapter. The first selection, "Let Them Eat Fat," is by Greg Critser and appeared in *Harper's* magazine, March 2000. The second selection, "The Fat of the Land," comes from Bill Bryson's *I'm a Stranger Here Myself,* a collection of short essays about American culture written after his return from living in England. The final selection, "Fat Like Me," is by Leslie Lambert, senior editor for *Ladies' Home Journal.* To obtain the personal experience and expertise for this article, she went undercover as an obese woman for a week to evaluate how a person's weight affects the way he or she is viewed by others.

Let Them Eat Fat

GREG CRITSER

NOT LONG AGO, a group of doctors, nurses, and medical technicians wheeled a young man into the intensive care unit of Los Angeles County-USC Medical Center, hooked him to a ganglia of life-support systems—pulse and respiration monitors, a breathing apparatus, and an IV line—then stood back and collectively stared. I was there visiting an ailing relative, and I stared, too. 1

Here, in the ghastly white light of modern American medicine, writhed a real-life epidemiological specter: a 500-pound 22-year-old. The man, whom I'll call Carl, was propped up at a 45-degree angle, the better to be fed air through a tube, and lay there nude, save for a small patch of blood-spotted gauze stuck to his lower abdomen, where surgeons had just labored to save his life. His eyes darted about in abject fear. "Second time in three months," his mother blurted out to me as she stood watching in horror. "He had two stomach staplings, and they both came apart. Oh my God, my boy—." Her boy was suffocating in his own fat.

I was struck not just by the spectacle but by the truth of the mother's comment. This was a boy—one buried in years of bad health, relative poverty, a sedentary lifestyle, and a high-fat diet, to be sure, but a boy nonetheless. Yet how surprised should I have been? That obesity, particularly among the young and the poor, is spinning out of control is hardly a secret. It is, in fact, something that most Americans can agree upon. Along with depression, heart disease, and cancer, obesity is yet another chew in our daily rumination about health and fitness, morbidity and mortality. Still, even in dot-com America, where statistics fly like arrows, the numbers are astonishing. Consider:

- Today, one-fifth of all Americans are obese, meaning that they have a body mass index, or BMI, of more than 30. (BMI is a universally recognized cross-measure of weight for height and stature.) The epidemiological figures on chronic corpulence are so unequivocal that even the normally reticent dean of American obesity studies, the University of Colorado's James O. Hill, says that if obesity is left unchecked almost all Americans will be overweight within a few generations. "Becoming obese," he told the *Arizona Republic*, "is a normal response to the American environment."
- 5 Children are most at risk. At least 25 percent of all Americans now under age 19 are overweight or obese. In 1998, Dr. David Satcher, the new U.S. Surgeon General, was moved to declare childhood obesity to be epidemic. "Today," he told a group of federal bureaucrats and policymakers, "we see a nation of young people seriously at risk of starting out obese and dooming themselves to the difficult task of overcoming a tough illness."
- Even among the most careful researchers these days, *epidemic* is the term of choice when it comes to talk of fat, particularly fat children. As William Dietz, the director of nutrition at the Centers for Disease Control, said last year, "This is an epidemic in the U.S. the likes of which we have not had before in chronic disease." The cost to the general public health budget by 2020 will run into the hundreds of billions, making HIV look, economically, like a bad case of the flu.

Yet standing that day in the intensive care unit, among the beepers and buzzers and pumps, epidemic was the last thing on my mind. Instead I felt heartbreak, revulsion, fear, sadness—and then curiosity: Where did this boy come from? Who and what had made him? How is it that we Americans, perhaps the most health-conscious of any people in the history of the world, and certainly the richest, have come to preside over the deadly fattening of our youth?

The beginning of an answer came one day last fall, in the same week that the Spanish-language newspaper *La Opinion* ran a story headlined "*Diabetes epidemia en latinos,*" when I attended the opening of the newest Krispy Kreme doughnut store in Los Angeles. It was, as they say in marketing circles, a "resonant" event, replete with around-the-block lines, celebrity news anchors, and stern cops directing traffic. The store, located in the heart of the San Fernando Valley's burgeoning Latino population, pulsed with excitement. In one corner stood the new store's manager, a young Anglo fellow, accompanied by a Krispy Kreme publicity director. Why had Krispy Kreme decided to locate here? I asked.

"See," the manager said, brushing a crumb of choco-glaze from his fingers, "the idea is simple—accessible but not convenient. The idea is to make the store accessible—easy to get into and out of from the street—but just a tad away from the mainstream so as to make sure that the customers are presold and very intent before they get here," he said, betraying no doubts about the company's marketing formula. "We want them intent to get at least a dozen before they even think of coming in."

But why this slightly nonmainstream place? 10

"Because it's obvious . . . " He gestured to the stout Mayan donas queuing around the building. "We're looking for all the bigger families."

Bigger in size?

"Yeah." His eyes rolled, like little glazed crullers. "Bigger in size."

Of course, fast food and national restaurant chains like Krispy Kreme that serve it have long been the object of criticism by nutritionists and dietitians. Despite the attention, however, fast-food companies, most of them publicly owned and sprinkled into the stock portfolios of many striving Americans (including mine and perhaps yours), have grown more aggressive in their targeting of poor inner-city communities. One of every four hamburgers sold by the good folks at McDonald's, for example, is now purchased by inner-city consumers who, disproportionately, are young black men.

In fact, it was the poor, and their increasing need for cheap meals consumed 15
outside the home, that fueled the development of what may well be the most important fast-food innovation of the past 20 years, the sales gimmick known as "supersizing." At my local McDonald's located in a lower-middle-income area of Pasadena, California, the supersize bacchanal goes into high gear at about 5 P.M., when the various urban caballeros, drywalleros, and jardineros get off work and head for a quick bite. Mixed in is a sizable element of young black kids traveling between school and home, their economic status apparent by the fact that they've walked instead of driven. Customers are cheerfully encouraged to "supersize your meal!" by signs saying, "If we don't recommend a supersize, the supersize is free!" For an extra 79 cents, a kid ordering a cheeseburger, small fries, and a small Coke will get said cheeseburger plus a supersize Coke (42 fluid

ounces versus 16, with free refills) and a supersize order of french fries (more than double the weight of a regular order). Suffice it to say that consumption of said meals is fast and, in almost every instance I observed, very complete.

But what, metabolically speaking, has taken place? The total caloric content of the meat has been jacked up from 680 calories to more than 1,340 calories. According to the very generous U.S. dietary guidelines, 1,340 calories represent more than half of a teenager's recommended daily caloric consumption, and the added calories themselves are protein-poor but fat- and carbohydrate-rich. Completing this jumbo dietetic horror is the fact that the easy availability of such huge meals arrives in the same years in which physical activity among teenage boys and girls drops by about half.

Now consider the endocrine warfare that follows. The constant bombing of the pancreas by such a huge hit of sugars and fats can eventually wear out the organ's insulin-producing "islets," leading to diabetes and its inevitable dirge of woes: kidney, eye, and nerve damage; increased risk of heart disease; even stroke. The resulting sugar-induced hyperglycemia in many of the obese wreaks its own havoc in the form of glucose toxicity, further debilitating nerve endings and arterial walls. For the obese and soon to be obese, it is no overstatement to say that after supersized teen years, the pancreas may never be the same. Some 16 million Americans suffer from Type 2 diabetes, a third of them unaware of their condition. Today's giggly teen burp may well be tomorrow's aching neuropathic limb.

Diabetes, by the way, is just the beginning of what's possible. If childhood obesity truly is "an epidemic in the U.S. the likes of which we have not had before in chronic disease," then places like McDonald's and Winchell's Donut stores, with their endless racks of glazed and creamy goodies, are the San Francisco bathhouses of said epidemic, the places where the high-risk population indulges in high-risk behavior. Although open around the clock, the Winchell's near my house doesn't get rolling until 7 in the morning, the Spanish-language talk shows frothing in the background while an ambulance light whirls atop the Coke dispenser. Inside, Mami placates Miguelito with a giant apple fritter. Papi tells a joke and pours ounce upon ounce of sugar and cream into his 20-ounce coffee. Viewed through the lens of obesity, as I am inclined to do, the scene is not so feliz. The obesity rate for Mexican-American children is shocking. Between the ages of 5 and 11, the rate for girls is 27 percent; for boys, 23 percent. By fourth grade the rate for girls peaks at 32 percent, while boys top out at 43 percent. Not surprisingly, obesity-related disorders are everywhere on display at Winchell's right before my eyes—including fat kids who limp, which can be a symptom of Blount's disease (a deformity of the tibia) or a sign of slipped capital femoral epiphysis (an orthopedic abnormality brought about by weight-induced dislocation of the femur bone). Both conditions are progressive, often requiring surgery.

The chubby boy nodding in the corner, waiting for his Papi to finish his cafi, is likely suffering from some form of sleep apnea; a recent study of 41 children with severe obesity revealed that a third had the condition and that another third presented with clinically abnormal sleep patterns. Another recent study indicated that "obese children with obstructive sleep apnea demonstrate clinically significant decrements in learning and memory function." And the lovely but very chubby little girl tending to her schoolbooks? Chances are she will begin puberty before the age of 10, launching her into a lifetime of endocrine bizarreness that not only will be costly to treat but will be emotionally devastating as well. Research also suggests that weight gain can lead to the development of pseudotumor cerebri, a brain tumor most common in females. A recent review of 57 patients with the tumor revealed that 90 percent were obese. This little girl's chances of developing other neurological illnesses are profound as well. And she may already have gallstones: Obesity accounts for up to 33 percent of all gallstones observed in children. She is 10 times more likely than her nonobese peers to develop high blood pressure, and she is increasingly likely to contract Type 2 diabetes, obesity being that disease's number-one risk factor.

Of course, if she is really lucky, that little girl could just be having a choco- 20
sprinkles doughnut on her way to school.

What about poor rural whites? Studying children in an elementary school in a low-income town in eastern Kentucky, the anthropologist Deborah Crooks was astonished to find stunting and obesity not just present but prevalent. Among her subjects, 13 percent of girls exhibited notable stunting; 33 percent of all kids were significantly overweight; and 13 percent of the children were obese—21 percent of boys and 9 percent of girls. A sensitive, elegant writer, Crooks drew from her work three important conclusions: One, that poor kids in the United States often face the same evolutionary nutritional pressures as those in newly industrializing nations, where traditional diets are replaced by high-fat diets and where labor-saving technology reduces physical activity. Second, Crooks found that "height and weight are cumulative measures of growth . . . reflecting a sum total of environmental experience over time." Last, and perhaps most important, Crooks concluded that while stunting can be partially explained by individual household conditions—income, illness, education, and marital status—obesity "may be more of a community-related phenomenon." Here the economic infrastructure—safe playgrounds, access to high-quality, low-cost food, and transportation to play areas—was the key determinant of physical-activity levels.

Awareness of these national patterns of destruction, of course, is a key reason why Eli Lilly & Co., the $75 billion pharmaceutical company, is now building the largest factory dedicated to the production of a single drug in industry history. That drug is insulin. Lilly's sales of insulin products totaled $357 million in the third quarter of 1999, a 24 percent increase over the previous third quarter. Almost every leading pharmaceutical conglomerate has like-minded ventures under way, with special emphasis on pill-form treatments for non-insulin-dependent forms of the disease. Pharmaceutical companies that are not seeking to capture some portion of the burgeoning market are bordering on fiduciary mismanagement. Said James Kappel of Eli Lilly, "You've got to be in diabetes."

Wandering home from my outing, the wondrous smells of frying foods wafting in the air, I wondered why, given affluent America's outright fetishism about diet and health, those whose business it is to care—the media, the academy, public-health workers, and the government—do almost nothing. The answer, I suggest, is that in almost every public-health arena, the need to address obesity as a class issue—one that transcends the inevitable divisiveness of race and gender—has been blunted by bad logic, vested interests, academic cant, and ideological chauvinism.

Consider a story last year in the *New York Times* detailing the rise in delivery-room mortality among young African-American mothers. The increases were attributed to a number of factors—diabetes, hypertension, drug and alcohol abuse—but the primary factor of obesity, which can foster both diabetes and hypertension, was mentioned only in passing. Moreover, efforts to understand and publicize the socioeconomic factors of the deaths have been thwarted. When Dr. Janet Mitchell, a New York obstetrician charged with reviewing several recent maternal mortality studies, insisted that socioeconomics were the issue in understanding the "racial gap" in maternal mortality, she was unable to get government funding for the work, "We need to back away from the medical causes, she told the *Times,* clearly exasperated, "and begin to take a much more ethnographic, anthropological approach to this tragic outcome."

25 In another example, a 1995 University of Arizona study reported that young black girls, who are more inclined toward obesity than white girls, were also far less likely to hold "bad body images" about themselves. The slew of news articles and TV reports that followed were nothing short of jubilant, proclaiming the "good news." As one commentator I watched late one evening announced, "Here is one group of girls who couldn't care less about looking like Kate Moss!" Yet no one mentioned the long-term effects of unchecked weight gain. Apparently, when it comes to poor black girls the media would rather that they risk diabetes than try to look like models.

"That's the big conundrum, as they always say," Richard MacKenzie, a physician who treats overweight and obese girls in downtown L.A., told me recently. "No one wants to overemphasize the problems of being fat to these girls, for fear of creating body-image problems that might lead to anorexia and bulimia." Speaking anecdotally, he said that "the problem is that for every one affluent white anorexic you create by 'overemphasizing' obesity, you foster 10 obese poor girls by downplaying the severity of the issue." Judith Stem, a professor of nutrition and internal medicine at UC Davis, is more blunt. "The number of kids with eating disorders is positively dwarfed by the number with obesity. It sidesteps the whole class issue. We've got to stop that and get on with the real problem."

Moreover, such sidestepping denies poor minority girls a principal, if sometimes unpleasant, psychological incentive to lose weight: that of social stigma.

Only recently has the academy come to grapple with this. Writing in a recent issue of the *International Journal of Obesity,* the scholar Susan Averett looked at the hard numbers: 44 percent of African-American women weigh more than 120 percent of their recommended body weight yet are less likely than whites to perceive themselves as overweight.[1] Anglo women, poor and otherwise, registered higher anxiety about fatness and experienced far fewer cases of chronic obesity. "Social stigma may serve to control obesity among white women," Averett reluctantly concluded. "If so, physical and emotional effects of greater pressure to be thin must be weighed against reduced health risks associated with overweight and obesity." In other words, maybe a few more black Kate Mosses might not be such a bad thing.

While the so-called fat acceptance movement, a very vocal minority of super-obese female activists, has certainly played a role in the tendency to deny the need to promote healthy thinness, the real culprits have been those with true cultural power, those in the academy and the publishing industry who have the ability to shape public opinion. Behind much of their reluctance to face facts is the lingering influence of the 1978 best-seller, *Fat Is a Feminist Issue,* in which Susie Orbach presented a nuanced, passionate look at female compulsive eating and its roots in patriarchal culture. But although Orbach's observations were keen, her conclusions were often wishful, narcissistic, and sometimes just wrong. "Fat is a social disease, and fat is a feminist issue," Orbach wrote. "Fat is not about self-control or lack of will power . . . It is a response to the inequality of the sexes."[2]

Perhaps so, if one is a feminist, and if one is struggling with an eating disorder, and if one is, for the most part, affluent, well-educated, and politically aware. But obesity itself is preeminently an issue of class, not of ethnicity, and certainly not of gender. True, the disease may be refracted though its concentrations in various demographic subgroupings—in Native Americans, in Latinos, in African Americans, and even in some Pacific Island Americans—but in study after study, the key adjective is poor: poor African Americans, poor Latinos, poor whites, poor women, poor children, poor Latino children, etc. From the definitive *Handbook of Obesity:* "In heterogeneous and affluent societies like the United States, there is a strong inverse correlation of social class and obesity, particularly for females." From *Annals of Epidemiology:* "In white girls . . . both TV viewing

[1]Certainly culture plays a role in the behavior of any subpopulation. Among black women, for example, obesity rates persist despite increases in income. A recent study by the National Heart, Lung, and Blood Institute concludes that obesity in black girls may be "a reflection of a differential social development in our society, wherein a certain lag period may need to elapse between an era when food availability is a concern to an era of affluence with no such concern." Other observers might assert that black women find affirmation for being heavy from black men, or believe themselves to be "naturally" heavier. Such assertions do not change mortality statistics.

[2]At the edges of the culture, the inheritors of Susie Orbach's politics have created websites called FAT GIRL and Largesse: the Network for Size Esteem, which claim that "dieting kills" and instruct how to induce vomiting in diet centers as protest.

and obesity were strongly inversely associated with household income as well as with parental education."

Yet class seems to be the last thing on the minds of some of our better 30
social thinkers. Instead, the tendency of many in the academy is to fetishize or "post modernize" the problem. Cornell University professor Richard Klein, for example, proposed in his 1996 book, *Eat Fat,* "Try this for six weeks: Eat fat." (Klein's mother did and almost died from sleep apnea, causing Klein to reverse himself in his epilogue, advising readers: "Eat rice.") The identity politics of fat, incidentally, can cut the other way. To the French, the childhood diet has long been understood as a serious medical issue directly affecting the future of the nation. The concern grew directly from late-19th-century health issues in French cities and the countryside, where tuberculosis had winnowed the nation's birthrate below that of the other European powers. To deal with the problem, a new science known as puericulture emerged to educate young mothers about basic health and nutrition practices. Long before Americans and the British roused themselves from the torpor of Victorian chub, the French undertook research into proper dietary and weight controls for the entire birth-to-adolescence growth period. By the early 1900s, with birthrates (and birth weights) picking up, the puericulture movement turned its attention to childhood obesity. Feeding times were to be strictly maintained; random snacks were unhealthy for the child, regardless of how "natural" it felt for a mother to indulge her young. Kids were weighed once a week. All meals were to be supervised by an adult. As a result, portion control—perhaps the one thing that modern obesity experts can agree upon as a reasonable way to prevent the condition—very early became institutionalized in modern France.

The message that too much food is bad still resounds in French child rearing, and as a result France has a largely lean populace.

What about the so-called Obesity Establishment, that web of researchers, clinicians, academics, and government health officials charged with finding ways to prevent the disease? Although there are many committed individuals in this group, one wonders just how independently minded they are. Among the sponsors for the 1997 annual conference of the North American Association for the Study of Obesity, the premier medical think tank on the subject, were the following: the Coca-Cola Company, Hershey Foods, Kraft Foods, and, never to be left out, Slim Fast Foods. Another sponsor was Knoll Pharmaceuticals, maker of the new diet drug Meridia. Of course, in a society where until recently tobacco companies sponsored fitness pageants and Olympic games, sponsorship hardly denotes corruption in the most traditional sense. One would be hard-pressed to prove any kind of censorship, but such underwriting effectively defines the parameters of public discussion. Everybody winks or blinks at the proper moment, then goes on his or her way.

Once upon a time, however, the United States possessed visionary leadership in the realm of childhood fitness. Founded in 1956, the President's Council on Youth Fitness successfully laid down broad-based fitness goals for all youth and established a series of awards for those who excelled in the effort. The council spoke about obesity with a forthrightness that would be political suicide today, with such pointed slogans as "There's no such thing as stylishly stout" and "Hey kid, if you see yourself in this picture, you need help."

By the late 1980s and early 1990s, however, new trends converged to undercut the council's powers of moral and cultural suasion. The ascendancy of cultural relativism led to a growing reluctance to be blunt about fatness, and, aided and abetted by the fashion industry's focus on baggy, hip-hop-style clothes, it became possible to be "stylishly stout." Fatness, as celebrated on rap videos, was now equated with wealth and power, with identity and agency, not with clogging the heart or being unable to reach one's toes. But fat inner-city black kids and the suburban kids copying them are even more disabled by their obesity. The only people who benefit from kids being "fat" are the ones running and owning the clothing, media, food, and drug companies.

35 In upscale corporate America, meanwhile, being fat is taboo, a surefire career-killer. If you can't control your own contours, goes the logic, how can you control a budget or a staff? Look at the glossy business and money magazines with their cooing profiles of the latest genius entrepreneurs: to the man, and the occasional woman, no one, I mean no one, is fat.

Related to the coolification of homeboyish fat—perhaps forcing its new status—is the simple fact that it's hard for poor children to find opportunities to exercise. Despite our obsession with professional sports, many of today's disadvantaged youth have fewer opportunities than ever to simply shoot baskets or kick a soccer ball. Various measures to limit state spending and taxing, among them California's debilitating Proposition 13, have gutted school-based physical-education classes. Currently, only one state, Illinois, requires daily physical education for all grades K–12, and only 19 percent of high school students nationwide are active for 20 minutes a day, five days a week, in physical education. Add to this the fact that, among the poor, television, the workingman's babysitter, is now viewed at least 32 hours a week. Participation in sports has always required an investment, but with the children of the affluent tucked away either in private schools or green suburbias, buying basketballs for the poor is not on the public agenda.

Human nature and its lazy inclinations aside, what do America's affluent get out of keeping the poor so fat? The reasons, I'd suggest, are many. An unreconstructed Marxist might invoke simple class warfare, exploitation fought through stock ownership in giant fast-food firms. The affluent know that the stuff will kill them but need someone (else) to eat it so as to keep growing that retirement portfolio. A practitioner of vulgar social psychology might argue for "our" need for the "identifiable outsider." An economist would say that in a society as overly competitive as our own, the affluent have found a way to slow down the striving poor from inevitable nipping at their heels. A French semiotician might even say that with the poor the affluent have erected their own walking and talking "empire of signs." This last notion is perhaps not so far-fetched. For what do the fat, darker, exploited poor, with their unbridled primal appetites, have to offer us but a chance for we diet- and shape-conscious folk to live vicariously? Call it boundary envy. Or, rather, boundary-free envy. And yet, by living outside their boundaries, the poor live within ours; fat people do not threaten our way of life; their angers entombed in flesh, they are slowed, they are softened, they are fed.

Meanwhile, in the City of Fat Angels, we lounge through a slow-motion epidemic. Marm buys another apple fritter. Papi slams his second sugar and cream. Another young Carl supersizes and double supersizes, then supersizes again. Waistlines surge. Any minute now, the belt will run out of holes.

The Fat of the Land

BILL BRYSON

1 I HAVE BEEN thinking a lot about food lately. This is because I am not getting any. My wife, you see, recently put me on a diet. It is an interesting diet of her own devising that essentially allows me to eat anything I want so long as it contains no fat, cholesterol, sodium, or calories and isn't tasty. In order to keep me from starving altogether, she went to the grocery store and bought everything that had "bran" in its title. I am not sure, but I believe I had bran cutlets for dinner last night. I am very depressed.

Obesity is a serious problem in America (well, serious for fat people anyway). Half of all adult Americans are overweight and more than a third are defined as obese (i.e., big enough to make you think twice before getting in an elevator with them).

Now that hardly anyone smokes, it has taken over as the number one health fret in the country. About three hundred thousand Americans die every year from diseases related to obesity, and the nation spends $100 billion treating illnesses arising from overeating—diabetes, heart disease, high blood pressure, cancer, and so on. (I hadn't realized it, but being overweight can increase your chance of getting colon cancer—and this is a disease you really, really don't want to get—by as much as 50 percent. Ever since I read that, I keep imagining a proctologist examining me and saying: "*Wow!* Just how many cheeseburgers have you *had* in your life, Mr. Bryson?") Being overweight also substantially reduces your chances of surviving surgery, not to mention getting a decent date.

Above all, it means that people who are theoretically dear to you will call you "Mr. Blimpy" and ask you what you think you are doing every time you open a cupboard door and, entirely by accident, remove a large bag of Cheez Doodles.

5 The wonder to me is how anyone can be thin in this country. We went to an Applebee's Restaurant the other night where they were promoting something

called "Skillet Sensations." Here, verbatim, is the menu's description of the Chili Cheese Tater Skillet:

> We start this incredible combination with crispy, crunchy waffle fries. On top of those we generously ladle spicy chili, melted Monterey jack and cheddar cheeses, and pile high with tomatoes, green onions, and sour cream.

You see what I am up against? And this was one of the more modest offerings. The most depressing thing is that my wife and children can eat this stuff and not put on an ounce. When the waitress came, my wife said: "The children and I will have the De Luxe Supreme Goo Skillet Feast, with extra cheese and sour cream, and a side order of nachos with hot fudge sauce and biscuit gravy."

"And for Mr. Blimpy here?"

"Just bring him some dried bran and a glass of water."

10 When, the following morning over a breakfast of oat flakes and chaff, I expressed to my wife the opinion that this was, with all respect, the most stupid diet I had ever come across, she told me to find a better one, so I went to the library. There were at least 150 books on diet and nutrition—*Dr. Berger's Immune Power Diet, Straight Talk about Weight Control, The Rotation Diet*—but they were all a little earnest and bran-obsessed for my tastes. Then I saw one that was precisely of the type I was looking for. By Dale M. Atrens, Ph.D., it was called *Don't Diet.* Now here was a title I could work with.

Relaxing my customary aversion to consulting a book by anyone so immensely preposterous as to put "Ph.D." after his name (I don't put Ph.D. after my name on my books, after all—and not just because I don't have one), I took the book to that reading area that libraries put aside for people who are strange and have nowhere to go in the afternoons but nonetheless are not quite ready to be institutionalized, and devoted myself to an hour's reflective study.

The premise of the book, if I understood it correctly (and forgive me if I am a little sketchy on some details, but I was distracted by the man opposite me, who was having a quiet chat with a person from the next dimension), is that the human body has been programmed by eons of evolution to pack on adipose tissue for insulating warmth in periods of cold, padding for comfort, and energy reserves in times of crop failures.

The human body—mine in particular evidently—is extremely good at doing this. Tree shrews can't do it at all. They must spend every waking moment eating. "This may be why tree shrews have produced so little great art or music," Atrens quips. Ha! Ha! Ha! Then again, it may be because the tree shrew eats leaves, whereas I eat Ben and Jerry's double chocolate fudge ice cream.

The other interesting thing Atrens points out is that fat is exceedingly stubborn. Even when you starve yourself half to death, the body shows the greatest reluctance to relinquish its fat reserves.

15 Consider that each pound of fat represents 5,000 calories—about what the average person eats in total in two days. That means that if you starved yourself

for a week—ate nothing at all—you would lose no more than three and a half pounds of fat, and, let's face it, still wouldn't look a picture in your swimsuit.

Having tortured yourself in this way for seven days, naturally you would then slip into the pantry when no one was looking and eat everything in there but a bag of chickpeas, thereby gaining back all the loss, plus—and here's the crux—a little something extra, because now your body knows that you have been trying to starve it and are not to be trusted, so it had better lay in a little extra wobble in case you get any more foolish notions.

This is why dieting is so frustrating and hard. The more you try to get rid of your fat, the more ferociously your body holds on to it.

So I have come up with an ingenious alternative diet. I call it the Fool-Your-Body-Twenty-Hours-a-Day Diet. The idea is that for twenty hours in each twenty-four you ruthlessly starve yourself, but at four selected intervals during the day—for convenience we'll call them breakfast, lunch, dinner, and midnight snack—you feed your body something like an 18-ounce sirloin steak with a baked potato and extra sour cream, or a large bowl of double chocolate fudge ice cream, so that it doesn't *realize* that you are actually starving it. Brilliant, eh?

I don't know why this didn't occur to me years ago. I think it may be that all this bran has cleared my head. Or something.

Fat Like Me

LESLIE LAMBERT

FOR ONE heartbreaking, exhausting week, I lived as an obese woman—and endured, every day, the kind of openly contemptuous behavior most people never have to suffer. If you have ever laughed at an overweight person—or are overweight yourself—you must read this story. 1

One morning I gained one hundred fifty pounds, and my whole life changed. My husband looked at me differently, my kids were embarrassed, friends felt sorry for me, and strangers were shamelessly disgusted by my presence. The pleasures of shopping, family outings, and going to parties turned into wrenchingly painful experiences. In truth, I became depressed by just the thought of running even the most basic errands; a trip to the grocery store or the video shop was enough to put me in a bad mood. But mostly, I became angry. Angry because what I experienced in the week that I wore a "fat suit"—designed to make me look like a two-hundred-fifty-plus-pound woman—was that our society not only hates fat people, it feels entitled to participate in a prejudice that at many levels parallels racism and religious bigotry. And in a country that prides itself on being sensitive to the handicapped and the homeless, the obese continue to be the target of cultural abuse.

To many, obesity symbolizes an inability to control oneself or to maintain personal health. Fat people are often perceived as smelly, dirty, lazy failures (whose extra girth must also be expected to shield them from cruel insults and blatant disdain). The issue of personal space also plays a prominent role in this prejudice—many feel that fat people take up more than their justifiable territory on the bus, in movie theaters, in store aisles, in general. Judging from my recent experience as a counterfeit obese person, it seems we are more tolerant of ill-mannered, indecent individuals who are slim than we are of honorable, oversize citizens.

We are a society that worships slimness and fears the full figure. I am no different. After having given birth to three children, waved good-bye to thirty long ago and succumbed to the natural laws of gravity, I found myself holding on to twenty or so pounds that I've never looked upon in a friendly way. And anyone who knows me could reveal my own on-off-on-off dieting battles. But nothing could have prepared me for the shame and disrespect imposed upon the clinically obese (that is, those more than 20 percent over ideal weight for a given height).

When Goldie Hawn was weighted down with two hundred extra pounds in 5
last year's movie *Death Becomes Her,* I thought, I wonder what it would really be like to look so big? Then I asked myself, What would it be like to live like that? And so this experiment was born.

Each morning during the first week, I slipped into a custom-made "fat suit" designed by special-effects artist Richard Tautkus of New York City (he's responsible for costumes worn in The Ringling Bros. Circus, the upcoming Star Wars road show, and a number of hit movies and Broadway shows), and made my way into a world where I was alternately treated as invisible or regarded as a spectacle. Following is my diary:

FRIDAY

10 A.M.: I take a taxi from the *Ladies' Home Journal* offices in Manhattan to Richard Tautkus Studio, in Long Island City, for Richard and his assistants, Jim and Steven, to finish sculpting me into my new persona. I am nervous about this assignment, especially when I recall a recent newspaper series reporting a study of former fat people (all of whom had lost significant amounts of weight after intestinal bypass surgery) who said they'd rather be blind, deaf, or have a leg amputated than be fat again. Can it really be that bad?

The costumers can hardly believe the swelled-up me before them. The costume—made from air-conditioner filters—is surprisingly lightweight, but its bulk is already making me sweat. I'm led to a three-way, full-length mirror. I'm stunned. I look authentic. Too authentic!

I am uncomfortable seeing myself like this. "You're still pretty," comforts one of the guys jokingly, "—for a fat girl." I do not laugh.

12 P.M.: I take my first taxi ride in the fat suit. Did the driver sneer at me? I must 10
be imagining it. It took me a little longer than usual to maneuver myself into the cab. Was the driver impatient? I arrive at the photo studio and, with difficulty, get out of the car. Did I say something funny? The driver is openly laughing.

8 P.M.: I show my husband and kids the before-and-after pictures from the photo session. My husband reconsiders his willingness to go out to dinner with me in my disguise. "It makes me sad to think of you this fat," he says. "I'll be uncomfortable knowing that people will be staring at you and making fun of you." My kids chorus, "Don't pick me up at school looking like that."

We talk about fat discrimination. "I don't dislike fat people," says Elizabeth, my ten-year-old. "It's just that I wouldn't want anyone to say mean things about you." Nine-year-old Amanda says flatly, "You scare me." Alex, my seven-year-old son, laughs nervously and wants to try on the costume.

11 P.M.: I am trying to fall asleep in my own body. My husband is quietly snoring. I am hurt by his reaction to the fat me. While he's never made a disparaging comment about my body in the twelve years we've been married, I feel awful at having seen the look of repulsion on his face when he saw the photos.

MONDAY

7 A.M.: I suit up and take the commuter train to work. No one sits next to me. I feel incredibly self-conscious. People look long enough to let me know that they disapprove, then go back to reading their morning newspapers. Two women go as far as to whisper blatantly, glaring at me with a how-could-you-let-yourself-get-like-that attitude. I take up one and a half seats, and, yes, I feel embarrassed. Yet shame takes a backseat to the resentment I'm feeling. How dare these people judge me on the basis of my dress size?

8 A.M.: At the office, everyone is eager to hear about my experiences and to see 15
if my disguise has had an impact on the real me. One editor remarks that in my fat suit, my body movements seem more aggressive. A staff member asks me how I'll feel if while on assignment I bump into an old boyfriend. Another one says I seem depressed. Yes, I am depressed—and, suddenly, very hungry.

1 P.M.: I am lunching with two colleagues at a swank restaurant uptown. I am cranky, conscious of all the smirks and stares. In an effort to seem helpful, the waiter pulls my chair way out so that I can fit at the table. My embarrassment at having to shimmy into the chair with too-tight armrests is certainly noticed by the other patrons, who are sneaking looks whenever they can.

Okay, I'm fat, I'm thinking. But I'll bet some of you are pill-poppers, embezzlers, adulterers, and lousy parents. I wish you had to display symbols of those character flaws as openly as I have to reveal my above-average body size (which some medical experts are beginning to define as a genetically linked trait—not a personality weakness). We skip dessert and leave.

5:30 P.M.: Driving home from the train station, I stop at a red light next to a car with two teenage boys in it. I look over. The boy on the passenger side puffs out his cheeks at me and bursts out laughing.

6:30 P.M.: Pick up the kids at school and go to a take-out chicken shop to get dinner. My kids make me walk in first.

I order two roast chickens, potatoes, gravy, veggies, corn, and a half-dozen 20
brownies. Some kids in the restaurant refer to me as that Fat Lady; the adults with them muffle their amusement.

While the man at the cash register is ringing up my order, he asks me how many people I'm feeding. I reply indignantly, "Six people. Why?" He says that had he known, he could have suggested a less expensive family-pack meal. I am upset for assuming he was trying to ridicule me.

TUESDAY

10 A.M.: On my way to Bloomingdale's to go shopping, I stop for ice cream at Häagen-Dazs. I order a double scoop of chocolate-chocolate chip, and as I watch the youngster behind the counter evaluate my size, I fight the urge to say something defensive. Walking down the street eating the cone, I see one well-dressed man shake his head in disparagement and another laugh out loud as he passes me.

Walking into Bloomingdale's is difficult. First, I can barely fit in the revolving door, and when I get inside, I feel all eyes are on me. Interestingly, I am not ignored the way I thought I would be. Two perfumers practically attack me with their latest fragrance. One man behind the counter asks me if I want a makeover.

I proceed to the elevator. Have to squeeze in. A couple of women giggle. I ask the saleswoman for help in the sportswear section. She refers me nicely to the "big gals" department.

On the way home, I buy a dozen bagels at a bakery in Grand Central Ter- 25
minal. I eat one on the train. Why do people find it so repulsive to watch a large person eat? I do not give in to the frowning looks. I am hungry.

WEDNESDAY

10 A.M.: I'm having a consultation at a beauty salon near my home. I tell the hair-stylist, who's thin as a rail, that I want a different look. She gently explains that I need a fuller hairstyle to compensate for my ample figure. I am not offended. She has been honest, but not insulting. We talk about the difficulties of dieting. I have made a friend.

1 P.M.: I am meeting some friends for lunch at a restaurant in the suburbs. They can't wait to see my transformation and hear about my project. I am feeling depressed and do not want to go. I am getting tired of constantly being on the defensive. My friends jokingly argue over who gets to sit next to me, so that they can feel skinny. I am delighted when I see another large woman seated at the table next to us. I notice that she is eating a salad. I order one, too.

2:30 P.M.: I go grocery shopping. Everyone peers into my cart to see what the fat lady is buying. A couple of women are exasperated at not being able to get by me in the canned goods aisle. I apologize and turn sideways. I dread the candy aisle, but I promised my kids Skittles. I grab the bag of candy and look to see if anyone is watching. I discreetly put it in my cart. I feel like a criminal.

4 P.M.: I worry that I'm getting paranoid about others' reaction to me. I decide to talk to an overweight woman to see if she has the same feelings. Unfortunately, she does. "I am sick of being judged by what I put in my mouth," Denise Rubin says. Rubin, thirty-two, an attorney, is five feet two and weighs over two hundred pounds. "I'm tired of being regarded as less-than because of my more-than size. When are we going to understand that fat is an adjective, not an epithet?"

I listen sympathetically, but do not have an answer for her. 30

THURSDAY

9:30 A.M.: Elizabeth has told her fifth-grade class about my assignment, and the teacher has asked me to come, in my fat suit, to share my experience with the students. Elizabeth is no longer embarrassed to let her friends see me. During this week, we have all been transformed. We are anxious to tell my story to others; to make people understand the prejudice. The kids in this classroom—most of whom know me—laugh at first, and then fire questions faster than I can answer them: How did I feel? Were people mean to me? What's it like to be fat?

2 P.M.: I drive to the city to finish up some work at the office. I must admit, being behind the wheel at this weight has not been easy. I have had to adjust my seat to the farthest position so that I can fit comfortably, but, as a result, I can barely reach the pedals.

7:30 P.M.: I'm having dinner at a see-and-be-seen kind of place in the city with my costumer, Richard. We have made plans to meet in the lobby of a nearby hotel, so that I wouldn't have to walk into the chic restaurant all by myself. Richard is late, so I window-shop in the lobby. I am met with the looks of disdain that I have come to expect. Richard finally arrives at seven forty-five, and he kisses me hello. We walk arm-in-arm to dinner. I feel safe.

The nightmare begins. A sea of beautiful people are sitting at the bar. It is so crowded I can barely manage to take off my coat. Richard, a good-looking man, whispers from behind. He can't believe how blatantly I am being made fun of by the crowd at the bar. I wait in line to tell the hostess we have arrived, but she pretends not to see me. Richard steps in, gives her our name, and she shows us to our table.

We had asked for a table in front. We get seated in the back by the hostess. 35 The two thirtysomething women next to me can barely contain their horror as I clumsily try to pass through the space between our tables to slide onto the banquette seat. The water glasses shake as I unwittingly rock both tables. Richard and I order a drink, and I take a roll from the bread basket. The two women are glaring at me. I order a goat-cheese salad and pasta with cream sauce. They giggle. The rest of the meal proceeds in much the same manner. Richard and I look at the dessert menu, ignoring the two women.

I excuse myself to go to the ladies room. Once there, I change out of my fat suit and into my own clothes. I know that sounds crazy, but I'm so upset that I have to do it. I come back and slink into my place. The two women are stupefied. Richard is ready to take revenge. He tells me that as soon as I left, one of them asked him, "What are you doing with that fat pig?" He replied, "She's my girlfriend." "That's not possible," said one woman. "You must be a hustler." My blood is boiling. Richard tells them about my project. They are angry at me. *Angry* at me! They quickly pay the check and leave.

Richard and I leave after our coffee. I am put off by flirtatious looks from the same men at the bar who were previously so rude to me.

FRIDAY

4 P.M.: I take my kids to the mall to buy clothes for our upcoming trip down south. Today while we're shopping I get two "Wows," countless dirty looks, and one snort from various strangers. But I care less about what people are thinking. Perhaps it's because I know the project is coming to an end; perhaps I am resigned to society's disfavoring of me, the fat person. I still feel the sting of the everyday prejudice I experienced, but I feel less rebellious. I feel worn out.

7:30 P.M.: I'm out to dinner with my husband (sans fat suit). I am surprisingly sulky, not at all rejoicing in my instant weight loss. Instead, I feel ashamed of my culture and how much pain we cause people who are less than our concept of ideal. I'm thinking about ways I can help obese people feel more powerful; what I can do to deliver the message about maintaining positive self-esteem. Yet I am still using all my willpower to refrain from ordering dessert.

Chapter 5

Writing Arguments.

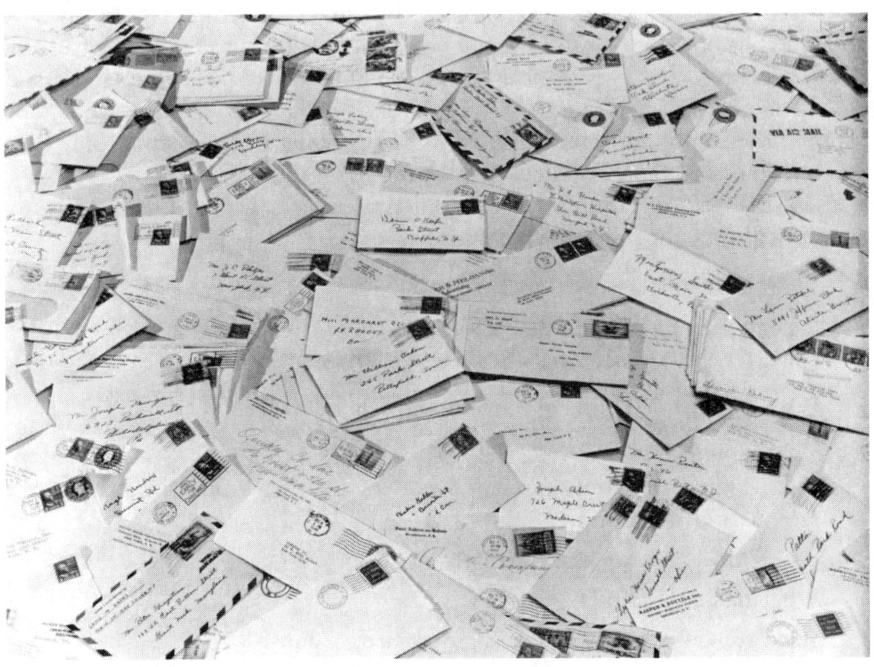

The Process of Writing an Argument

Since communities are so different from one another and each argument has its particular complexities, it is difficult to propose a general method for engaging all arguments. Much depends upon your ability to analyze and understand the features of the particular community you find yourself in. Still, arguments found in all communities do have some features in common, so a process may assist you in joining the conversation:

- Identify a controversial issue or claim you want to know more about.
- Identify a community that discusses or cares about this issue (or that should care).
- Understand the organization of the community and your place within that organization.
- Identify kairos, the right times and places for discussion to occur.
- Identify and record the conversation about your issue.
- Analyze and evaluate the various arguments being made about the issue.
- Find or create a place from which you can contribute to the conversation.

Remember, though, that this is a process rather than a method or procedure. It is intended to be flexible and may vary for different issues or communities. For instance, the steps may not always follow the same order. You may already have formed your opinion on an issue, but you should still try to find out what others have said. Or you may belong to a community that cares about the issue. Also, you may not need to go through every step. If you already have a good sense of the community and the kairos for a particular issue, you may only need to go through the final few steps of the process.

To use argumentation to resolve differences within communities, it is important to apply the following questions:

What is the issue?

What claims do people make about the issue?

What kind of claims are they?

What reasons do people give to support those claims?

What assumptions are implied by these reasons?

What additional reasons or chains of reasons support the point made in the reasons and assumptions?

Where do I agree or disagree with this argument?

What claims can I make?

What reasons would I give to support these claims?

What assumptions are implied by these reasons?

Analyzing an argument in this way helps you to evaluate and respond to the argument. If it is a convincing argument, then the process of analysis may give you good reasons to believe as you do or may cause you to change your opinion. If the argument is not convincing, then you are in a position to respond with a better argument or to help others see the weaknesses in the argument. When pursued in the proper manner, in a spirit of cooperation, such analysis may resolve conflicts within a community (not necessarily removing disagreements, but perhaps helping members to accept differences or to understand why others hold the opinions they do). Ethical persuasion presupposes an investigation of evidence, an examination of assumptions, a commitment to values, and, most of all, a commitment to the membership of the community, to taking responsibility for the effects of one's attempts at persuasion. It requires a realization that knowledge is created and sustained by the community, that it depends upon compromise and adherence, and that people may still disagree and remain faithful members of the community. It requires that you focus on ideas rather than on individuals and that you respect others. Questioning long-held assumptions can create tension and conflict in a community. Sometimes the community resolves this tension through force or violence, persecuting those who dare to question the "common sense" of the community. Responding through violence may solve the conflict, but no learning or self-awareness results. When a community responds to questioning by allowing for debate and discussion in a spirit of goodwill, there may still be tension, but negotiating this tension will lead to new levels of understanding and ultimately strengthen the community.

Once you have framed your ideas to your own satisfaction, it is time to go public, to make your ideas available to the community. Doing so means adapting your argument to the needs of that community, and here is where your argument gains its persuasive power. Adapting an argument to a community involves finding community-based reasons and organizing the argument for its audience.

Adapting to the Community

FINDING COMMUNITY-BASED REASONS

In the process of analyzing arguments, you may begin to think that any claim can be called into question. In addition, reasons and assumptions can themselves become claims in need of additional support, leading to a chain of reasoning with no apparent solid intellectual ground upon which you can build with any certainty. Where does the justifying come to an end? Couldn't a stubborn person keep asking for more and more support, disputing every statement in an argument, asking—as a young child does—"Why? Why? Why?" If one wants to be stubborn, yes; but such orneriness becomes ridiculous after a while. When arguments have a context, when they are a meaningful part of the life of a community, then at some point they can be grounded in what the community accepts as credible, authoritative, or true—the common sense or common knowledge of the community. This stock of knowledge differs from one community to another, and not all members of any community completely agree on that community's "common knowledge." This is why disagreements arise. But still there are statements and beliefs that most members of a community accept as true, and an argument will be persuasive only when the reasons and assumptions that justify the claim are grounded in this core of common belief. Reasons grounded in the common beliefs of the community are called "community-based reasons."

The danger in relying on community-based reasons and adapting your argument to the needs of the community is that you may compromise the integrity of your own views. In other words, you may end up telling people what they want to hear rather than what you really believe. Some people can accept being insincere or deceitful, and telling people what they want to hear may help them get what they want in the short run. But insincerity and deceit are usually discovered in time. If you want to make a long-term commitment and any real contribution to a community, you should be wary of such compromises. The trick is to find reasons that the community will find persuasive and that you can accept and believe in. These may not be the most compelling reasons for you, but they may be the most compelling for those you are addressing. And if you can still accept these reasons, you preserve your integrity.

I once had a student writing an essay about a controversy in the small town she came from. A town ordinance forbade the consumption and sale of alcohol in city parks. Some citizens wanted to change the ordinance to make the sale and consumption of alcohol legal by special permit. The intent of this proposed change was to make it possible for the town to attract concerts to the city parks, which many believed would help the town's economy. At the same time, influential religious groups in the town opposed the change because public drinking violated their religious beliefs or because they believed that such access to alcohol would destroy the morality of the town, making it an unhealthy place to raise a family. These groups argued that giving in on this drinking law would open the door to all other kinds of compromises in the name of economic development.

The issue had polarized the town. Supporters of the change saw members of the religious groups as being self-righteous and judgmental or as trying to protect their own economic interests. When my student wrote her discovery draft (her argument for herself), she sided with those who objected to the proposed change on religious and moral grounds. But she realized that because the town was so polarized, these reasons might not be convincing to the community as a whole or to the town council.

Being an emergency room nurse at the local hospital, which was in a neighboring city that did allow the sale of alcohol for park concerts, she knew that on concert nights the emergency room was overloaded with concert-goers who had had too much to drink or had run into trouble with those who had. Her own son had even had to wait for emergency medical care on a concert night. So in her draft she argued that allowing alcohol at concerts in her town—as well as the neighboring town—would overload the local medical system and ultimately cost the town much more in human and monetary terms than it would gain.

Even though this was not the most compelling reason for my student, it was a reason that she nonetheless believed in strongly and one that added a new dimension to the debate, an argument centered in the common values of the community. After all, who would deny the value of reliable medical care?

Here is another example of finding community-based reasons. A few years ago the State of Utah voted on a proposition to allow individual counties to decide whether to legalize gambling between individuals (on sporting events, horse racing, and "friendly" games of chance). At the time such gambling was illegal under state law, but a majority of citizens in several counties favored legalizing gambling between individuals because of the economic benefits they thought it would bring to their communities.

The religious groups in the state opposed the proposition. They believed gambling of any sort was immoral. But these groups realized that the immorality of gambling was not the best community-based reason because it would polarize the state along religious lines. So these groups argued instead that legalizing gambling would actually bring economic problems to the state. They used the examples of other states, such as Wyoming, that had relaxed their gambling laws and showed how the economic costs of doing so had outweighed any benefits. Even though the most compelling reason for these religious groups was that they considered gambling immoral, they could still accept the argument about economic harm. The argument about economic harm was a community-based reason because it relied on one of the values held by the proponents of gambling, showing how their proposal actually ran counter to that value.

The proposition was defeated by an overwhelming majority of voters, some of whom may have believed it was immoral, some of whom may have been persuaded by the argument about economic disadvantages. Some claimed that they voted against the proposition because they felt its proponents were self-serving in basing their argument on economic benefits. In other words, the proponents of the gambling proposition made the mistake of arguing for the reason that they found most convincing rather than finding community-based reasons. Rather than arguing for economic benefits, they might have been more successful had they argued for the importance of local government: The proposition did not actually legalize gambling, but only made it possible for individual counties to determine the issue locally. If they had argued that the issue was not gambling but rather decentralization of government, this value might have had wider appeal.

FOLLOWING THE CONVENTIONS

When you adapt your argument to the needs of an audience, you need to be careful to follow the conventions that guide the particular conversation you are joining. Each site of communication has its own types of discourse, its own rules governing what is and is not acceptable or understandable, and its own recognized experts and authorities. Generally, the more you conform to a community's conventions, the more credibility you will have with that community and the more persuasive you will be.

When you observe conversations, pay attention not only to what people say, but also to how they say it. Saying the right thing in the right way is an important part of kairos. Pay particular attention to those who are recognized as experts or authorities.

How do they organize their arguments?

What kind of language do they use?

What kind of evidence do they use?

How do they incorporate what others have said into their own arguments?

What kind of ethos do they construct?

How do they use emotional appeals and give their arguments presence?

Newcomers to a community often learn to become accepted by imitating more experienced and respected members of the community. Very young children imitate their parents. Teenagers imitate members of their peer group. Aspiring artists or athletes may imitate the style of a master or champion. The same is true of those who are joining the conversation of a community. You can become accepted by imitating others around you, by gaining a keen sense of kairos. At the same time, however, you risk losing some of your identity and integrity if you merely follow what others have done and tell others what they want to hear. There is a balance between following the conventions of a conversation and preserving your own voice. Maintaining this balance is part of the whole tension between the individual and the community that characterizes living in a community and makes arguing such an important part of that life.

Challenging the Community

Generally, the best way to persuade others is to identify with them in some way, to build upon common assumptions, beliefs, and values. Typically, you have to speak the language and follow the conventions of the community you want to address. Still, there are some who are successful as arguers by doing just the opposite. Refusing to follow the conventions of a community, particularly if done in a dramatic way, can get a conversation going, redirect a conversation, or draw attention to an issue that might go unnoticed otherwise.

Much of what we do, we do without thinking about it. Our experience becomes habitual and automatic. Think about some things you do every day—driving the car, taking a shower, getting dressed, eating breakfast. You have probably developed some routines that have become so mechanical that you don't even have to think about what you're doing; it's what you take for granted. A community develops similar kinds of routine and habitual ways of thinking and doing. A newcomer or stranger to the community will notice these things, but those who are members of the community will not. The philosopher Jean-Paul Sartre wrote that we are like fish in a fish bowl: We don't notice the water because it surrounds us. Those who challenge the community cause us to see the familiar in unfamiliar ways. They make the ordinary seem strange and new. They cause us to think about things that we would otherwise take for granted. By doing this, those who challenge the community play an important role in maintaining its vitality.

You can challenge the conventions of a community in many ways. One approach is through humor. Humor, by definition, is a way of seeing the world in a different way: It results from unexpected relationships among objects and ideas, and we laugh because we see something in a new way. Children think it's really funny when adults act like children because this behavior surprises them. Adults are amused when they see children playing like grownups. They see children and themselves in a new way. Perhaps they notice things about themselves that they had never noticed before. Stand-up comics, comedy writers, satirists, political cartoonists, and advertisers all use humor to draw our attention to what might otherwise go unnoticed. The comedian Jerry Seinfeld has built his entire career around fairly ordinary observations about ordinary things, but his somewhat twisted way of looking at things draws our attention to them. We say, "That's really true" or "I wish I had thought of that." Seinfeld says that his television show was about "nothing," but he discusses nothing in such a way that it becomes "something." Artists, philosophers, and writers may also challenge our ways of seeing, thinking, and perceiving the world. Andy Warhol was able to draw our attention to Campbell's soup cans by framing them as art, challenging thinking about what is really "art." Socrates challenged the conventional thinking of fifth century Athens. Abraham Lincoln credited Harriet Beecher Stowe with starting the Civil War because of the way *Uncle Tom's Cabin* caused a nation to reconsider its attitudes toward slavery. Political activists and protestors may be able to draw the attention of the community to an issue that would otherwise go unnoticed.

Although those who challenge the community can perform a valuable function, they do so at considerable personal risk. Not all members of the community will welcome the challenge and may threaten those who do things differently. Those who challenge the community also risk destroying the common values and beliefs that define the community itself.

Organizing Your Argument

When you adapt your argument to the community, you need to organize your argument in such a way that it meets the needs of your audience. You do this, first, by identifying the relationship you have to others who are participating in the conversation. Are you appealing to those who are undecided or uninformed (a middle-group)? Are you trying to build some common ground with those who disagree with you (an out-group)? Or are you trying to motivate those who basically feel the same way you do (an in-group)?

CLASSICAL ARGUMENT

If you are addressing community members who are uninformed or uncommitted, you will want to make sure that you address multiple perspectives on the issue (to avoid stacking the deck or manipulating your audience) and that you treat these other perspectives fairly (to maintain an ethos of goodwill). At the same time, you will want to answer the best reasons offered by those who disagree with you and provide strong support for your own beliefs. One approach that allows you to achieve these purposes is the classical argument.

Classical argument is the form taken by a lot of academic writing, and it is often used by philosophers as a way of exploring and evaluating their ideas. To begin, you might summarize the situation that leads you to make your claim, the "space" in the conversation that your argument is going to fill. You might begin by summarizing the issue being debated as well as the various positions others take on this issue. You can then clarify where your claim differs from these others—the points at which you disagree, whether your disagreement be with reasons or assumptions. In academic writing, this usually serves as the introduction of an essay. At the end of your introduction, you should state your claim. In academic writing, this is called the thesis of the essay. Your thesis may also include the reasons you will present to support your claim, possible objections to your thesis, and perhaps even your response to these objections.

Here is an example: "Although some activists are concerned about the effect that tax reform would have on the poor, introducing a flat rate tax is a good idea because such a tax would make the government more efficient and will have long-term benefits for the economy." This sample thesis consists of one claim (introducing a flat rate tax is a good idea) and two reasons (such a tax would make the government more efficient and would have long-term benefits for the economy). This thesis also states a possible reservation or objection (some activists are concerned about the effect that tax reform would have on the poor).

After the introduction, the body of a classical argument essay contains two sections. In the first of these, you present and support each of your reasons as best you can. You may also wish to identify and support the assumptions implied by your reasons. In the second section of the body, you respond to possible objections to your argument. A classical argument typically concludes with a review of the major points that have been made, a discussion of what this argument adds to the conversation, or a presentation of the action those who accept the argument should take. Here is an overview of the classical argument:

Introduction: background, context, review of the conversation.

Thesis: statement of claim and reasons.

Support of reasons and assumptions.

Answers to possible objections.

Conclusion: review of major points, the contribution of this argument, call to action.

For example, let's say that you are addressing the following issue: Should businesses be allowed to use popular music in advertising without paying a fee to the songwriter who holds the copyright on the music? Small business owners have argued that Congress should change copyright law to allow them to use popular songs in their advertising without paying the songwriter. They argue that popular songs allow them to reach a lot of customers, but as small businesses, they can't afford the daily fees for the rights to replay these songs. This puts them at a disadvantage when competing with larger companies with larger advertising budgets. They argue further that popular songs have paid the songwriter many times over, so there is no real harm to the artist. Songwriters argue that these songs are their intellectual property and that they have the same right to be compensated as authors of books and creators of software. They argue further that the popularity of the song has nothing at all to do with this basic right. If small business owners can't afford their songs, then they are free to use another song or hire someone to write a song for them.

Most of the public is either unaware of or uninterested in this issue. It doesn't affect most people directly, because they are neither songwriters nor small business owners. Whether you wanted to argue for or against the business owners' claim, you could use a classical argument. It might look something like this:

Introduction: Problems faced by small business owners and songwriters. History of appeals made to Congress. Review of the claims made for and against amending the law.

Thesis: Small business owners should not have to pay fees to use popular songs in advertising because these fees don't allow them to compete fairly with large corporations and because their use of the songs doesn't harm the artist, who has already profited from the song many times over.

Support of reasons: The first reason is based on a causal claim that permission fees lead to unfair competition. This causal claim has a related claim about language regarding the definition of "unfair competition." In this section you would need to provide a definition of unfair competition and show how these permission fees lead to a situation that meets this definition. Finally, you would need to show the harm of unfair competition (a causal claim related to values).

Answers to objections: You acknowledge the fact that not paying these fees does take some money away from songwriters, but you answer this objection by showing that in the case of popular songs often used in commercials, the songwriters have already profited many times over. You will need to give some examples of what qualifies as a "popular" song and show how the writers of these songs really won't lose much if small business owners are allowed to use them without charge.

Conclusion: Here you would need to explain why this issue matters to the audience, how higher advertising budgets lead to higher costs for consumers and how fair competition reduces prices and improves products. You would also explain what your audience should do to act on this issue.

In this example, I have explained one approach to this issue through the classical argument. The structure of the argument helps the writer identify burdens of proof that must be met to address the needs of the audience. Changing the audience changes the structure of the argument and the types of proof required.

DELAYED THESIS

When you are addressing those who are familiar with an issue but committed to a position that opposes yours, you may want to approach them more indirectly. If their opposition is somewhat conditional or qualified, then you might try a delayed thesis. An argument with a delayed thesis is like a classical argument in reverse because the thesis comes near the end. This approach allows you to address those who might not listen to your argument if they knew your position from the beginning but might be willing to accept some of what you say after hearing your reasoning.

A delayed thesis argument generally begins with a discussion of assumptions, values, or definitions that you hold in common with your audience. You would then show how these common assumptions provide support for a set of beliefs that will become the chain of reasons to support the claim. Like a classical argument, a delayed thesis essay is organized around reasons and assumptions, but the chain of reasoning leads the audience to the claim or thesis at the end.

The delayed thesis argument may also begin with objections to the claim. Then the writer answers these objections and leads the audience through the chain of reasons that support the claim. Such a pattern might work, for instance, when a moderate Republican advocate addresses moderate Democratic opponents on the subject of welfare reform. If the claim were presented at the beginning of the argument, such an audience's initial reaction might be so hostile that the subsequent reasoning would be ignored. But after considering the writer's reasoning, a Democratic audience might be willing to accept the Republican proposal when it is presented at the end.

A delayed thesis argument requires a fair amount of skill on the part of the writer because it doesn't follow a set form or pattern. In addition, the writer must maintain the interest and the assent of his or her audience throughout, without giving a sense that the audience is being manipulated or "trapped."

Let's return to my example about songwriters and small business owners. Let's say that you are a songwriter and are addressing a group of small business owners. Perhaps they don't know a lot about this issue and haven't formed a very strong opinion, but their immediate reaction would be to side with their fellow small business owners against the songwriters. Using the direct approach of the classical argument might set your audience against you from the beginning. Using the delayed thesis, however, you can begin from a position of goodwill and common ground. You could, for instance, begin by discussing the struggles of small business owners and the importance of fair competition to the growth of a business and the production of a quality product. You could then describe how you, as a songwriter, are also trying to run a business where the product is your music. You would then describe the importance to small business owners, like yourselves, of profiting from all their hard work. Then you could discuss how this proposal before Congress, although it claims to help small business owners, is really undermining the property rights of all business owners. If you use the delayed thesis, your audience may still not be persuaded, but you have a better chance of presenting your best reasons and building some common ground in the process. Perhaps you can at least move some closer to your position.

CONCILIATORY ARGUMENT

The conciliatory argument is closely related to the delayed thesis argument. It also begins by discussing common assumptions, values, or definitions, but it does not move on to any statement of the author's claim. The goal of this kind of argument is to move the audience from a position of unconditional opposition to a more moderate position, even one of conditional support. The writer tries to build a basis for further conversation, establishing some common ground with the audience in order to win a degree of consent.

This kind of argument is most effective when a writer is addressing his or her most extreme out-group. It might work, for instance, when an advocate for tolerance of homosexuality addresses fundamentalist Christians. The positions of the two are so far apart that the audience would probably not even accept a delayed thesis. But perhaps the writer could open the possibility for dialogue by emphasizing common ground (however remote from the actual issue) and arguing for an assumption, value, or belief that could lay the groundwork for future discussion. For example, he or she could argue for a common belief in the right to privacy and tolerance for difference without ever mentioning homosexuality, perhaps discussing the persecution endured in the past by religious minorities. This argument would not convince its audience to support gay rights, but it might move the audience toward a more moderate position in relation to the writer's position.

You, as a representative of songwriters, might find yourself talking to those lobbying Congress to allow business owners to use songs without paying permissions fees. You would make little progress by using a classical argument, since they are well acquainted with the issues and have already formed some strong beliefs with good reasons of their own to support their claims. Even the delayed thesis would probably not work, because they might see where the argument is heading from the beginning and would likely reject your claim outright. To address this kind of extreme out-group, you need a conciliatory argument. Perhaps you could remove the debate from the particulars of the legislation to discuss the beneficial effects of property law in general and copyright law in particular. This approach would strengthen the value upon which you would eventually build your argument. Perhaps you could discuss the commonalities between you as small business owners and the struggles you share. This approach would strengthen the connection between you and other small business owners and between intellectual property and other kinds of products.

MOTIVATIONAL ARGUMENT

The prime concern in addressing an in-group is to build motivation and inspire members to action. An in-group already agrees with the writer's position but may not be motivated to act or respond. There are many ways to build motivation, all generally involving an appeal to a common vision or common set of values. In addition, the emotional appeal is often central to a motivational argument. Most advertisements are motivational arguments, trying to move us to acquire things we already want or value. A lot of religious discourse, such as preaching, is also motivational: A preacher describes a religious or moral vision and encourages those who accept this vision to change their behavior. Some business consultants have made millions of dollars because of their ability to deliver motivational arguments.

Monroe's motivated sequence is one type of motivational argument. It begins with the description of a need or a problem. In the next section, the writer describes the negative effects or consequences of that need or problem, trying to make it real for the audience, to give it presence. The writer then presents a way to fill the need or solve the problem, followed by a description of a "vision" of this solution, how things would be better if the solution were put in place. The argument ends with a specific action that readers can take to contribute to the solution: making a phone call, writing a letter, contributing money, making an immediate change in behavior, making a commitment, signing a contract, and so on. The motivational argument usually includes the means to take the action. For instance, if the argument ends by asking you to write to your senator or representative, it will also include the names and addresses of those you should write to, and perhaps even a sample letter. If the argument ends by asking you to make an immediate change in your behavior, it might include a step-by-step guide for doing so. If you are to make a phone call, the argument will include the phone number and an example of what you should say.

Let's say, for this example, that you are a small business owner lobbying Congress to allow businesses to use popular songs without paying fees. You are addressing a group of your fellow business owners and are trying to give them good reasons for supporting this legislation and to motivate them to call their congressional representatives. In this case, your audience already shares a lot of the same values and beliefs that you do; they just need to get more involved. You might organize your appeal as follows:

Need: Describe how small business owners struggle with the unfair competition of larger businesses with larger advertising budgets.

Effects: Show how these budgets allow corporations to build their images using popular songs, which have a powerful effect on consumers. To keep up, small business owners have to spend a larger percentage of their budgets. Describe in vivid detail the economic problems this causes. Relate a couple of particular examples to give the argument presence.

Solution: Explain the legislation and how it would allow business owners to compete with corporations.

Vision: Return to the particular examples you gave before and show how life would have been different for these business owners under this legislation. You could even show some sample commercials that business owners could now afford.

Action: Provide the names and numbers of the congressional representatives involved and the specific actions each member of the audience needs to take to influence these representatives.

If you anticipate some opposition to your actions, the motivational sequence might also include some answers to these objections and some specific ways to meet this opposition.

ROGERIAN ARGUMENT

Rogerian argument is based on the theories of psychologist Carl Rogers. Rogers developed a theory of negotiation and conflict management that was nonconfrontational, nonjudgmental, and cooperative. This type of argument works well when you find yourself in the position of mediator, trying to bring two opposing groups together, or when you want to establish common ground between your in-group and an out-group.

Rogerian argument begins with a description of the context for the argument and a brief statement summarizing the various positions. All parties should agree that the mediator has stated their positions accurately. In the next section, the mediator tries to outline each position as clearly as possible, without passing judgment on any position or seeking to favor one side over the other. Again, this description should be one that all parties can accept as accurate. The third section attempts to describe assumptions, values, and definitions that the different parties share. The argument concludes with a presentation of claims that all the parties can accept based on what they share.

A Rogerian argument may not bring the differing parties into complete agreement, but it will at least show precisely where they disagree and what they have in common. A Rogerian argument may result in an agreement to disagree, but at least it will be an informed disagreement.

Rogerian argument is an excellent way to begin a dialogue among parties that might not get together otherwise. Its success depends upon the ability of the mediator to describe the various positions and what the differing parties have in common, in terms that everyone will agree to. This type of argument works with groups whose interests seem to be in serious conflict, such as the parties to a labor dispute or at a diplomatic summit. A careful Rogerian argument can help stalemated groups begin talking.

As the dispute between business owners and songwriters heats up, you might find yourself, as a concerned observer, in the role of mediating the dispute. Perhaps you see the merits of both sides and would like to help work out a solution acceptable to both parties. You might structure your argument in this way:

Introduction: You would rehearse the history of the dispute and state the claims and reasons made by both sides in such a way that both feel that they have been fairly represented.

Position #1: You outline the position of the business owners and explore in detail the reasons and assumptions they use to support their claim.

Position #2: You outline the position of the songwriters in response to the proposal made by the business owners and you outline the reasons for their objections and the assumptions implied by these reasons.

Common ground: You try to find values, beliefs, and assumptions that both parties share. For instance, you might point out that both parties are entrepreneurs, that both are trying to profit from their creativity and hard work in the face of fierce competition, and that both believe in the responsibility of the government to protect property rights. You try to explain how these groups could benefit from helping one another.

Negotiated solution: Here is the hard part. You try to find a solution that everyone can agree on. Perhaps you could argue that the problem is that both parties struggle with large corporations that dominate the market. Perhaps the business owners could withdraw their attack on the property rights of songwriters if songwriters developed a different scale for charging permissions fees. Perhaps songwriters could charge according to television and radio ratings so that larger corporations that could afford prime commercial time would pay a higher percentage of fees. Such an arrangement might benefit songwriters and small business owners, who could use the same songs for a lower fee during less expensive commercial time.

Rogerian argument doesn't always lead to solutions that everyone can agree on, but it does attempt to defuse highly emotional conflicts by getting the parties involved focusing on what they share rather than what divides them.

OPTION THREE

The term *option three* was coined by William Safire, a political columnist and language expert for the *New York Times.* He first identified this argument in political and corporate strategies for negotiation. The option three argument is related to Rogerian argument in form, but its goal is quite different: It is used

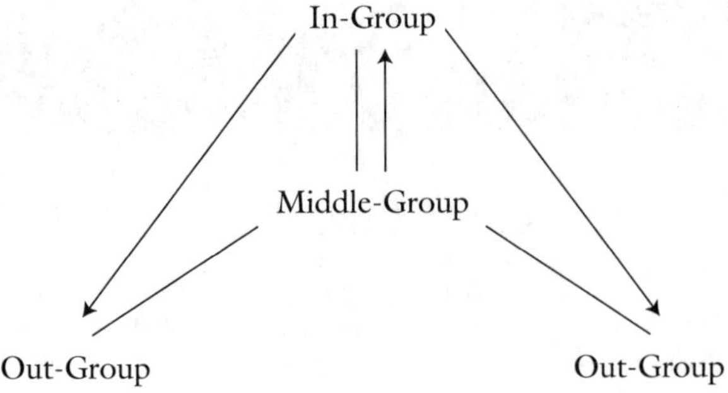

Diagram of Option Three

when a writer is trying to appeal to a moderate group that lies between two extreme out-groups. In this case, the writer is not a mediator trying to bring two extreme groups together. Instead, the writer rejects both groups and presents a more moderate third option. In a sense the writer creates an in-group of those who are leaning toward one or the other extremes or who are uncommitted. The writer achieves this aim by pushing two out-groups away and attracting a middle-group.

An option three argument follows a form similar to Rogerian argument with a few important differences. Like Rogerian argument, an option three argument begins by describing the controversy, its context, and the positions that are currently set forth. In the next section, the writer describes each extreme position in detail, showing its weaknesses and disadvantages. In the third section, the writer describes the beliefs, values, and definitions that he or she shares with the audience (a more moderate group, a potential in-group for the author). The writer then presents a third option that lies between the two extremes, a position that builds on what he or she and the audience (the middle-group) share.

The option three argument is often used in political campaigns when candidates try to identify with the political center, hoping to win votes from both parties. The option three is also used in the corporate world when a company, for instance, wants to show its stockholders that it is steering a middle course between two extremes.

Let's return to the example of songwriters and business owners. Let's say that you represent a citizens' group that thinks consumers suffer unfairly from copyright laws that offer too much protection and from business owners who too easily pass their costs on to the consumer. You might address a middle-group by explaining how songwriters and business owners are both extremists, acting in their own economic interests rather than trying to provide a quality product at a fair price. You would appeal to consumers to reject both of these groups and support your citizens' group that seeks to advance the rights of consumers against manipulative advertisers, pampered musicians, and greedy business owners.

■■ TYPES OF ARGUMENTS

	Classical Argument	*Delayed Thesis*	*Conciliatory Argument*
STRUCTURE (each number is a section)	1. Summarize situation (use question, quote, anecdote, history, social context, facts, or narration) and then make claim/thesis 2. Discuss reasons and assumptions with evidence 3. Respond to opposition 4. Conclusion: review main points, discuss how this adds to the community conversation, or call for action	1. Discuss assumptions, values, or definitions 2. Show how common assumptions provide support for chain of reasons 3. Give reasons 4. State claim/thesis in conclusion OR 1. Discuss objections to claim 2. Answer objections and proceed through claim of reasons 3. State claim/thesis in conclusion	1. Discuss common assumptions, values, or definitions 2. Show common assumptions as support for chain of reasons 3. Give reasons 4. State claim/thesis in conclusion
PURPOSE	To get readers interested in and support your argument (but show both sides)	To get audience to agree with writer by the end	To emphasize common ground and move audience from opposing to a more moderate position, or possible conditional support
AUDIENCE	Uninformed or uninterested in your argument (a middle-group to the argument)	Opposed to your argument (out-group)	Opposed to your argument (extreme out-group)
STRATEGY	Get readers interested in argument and then convince them of claim	Maintain readers' interest without making them feel "trapped"	Build consensus using common ground

Motivational Argument	*Rogerian Argument*	*Option Three (Safire)*
1. Describe need or problem 2. Describe negative effects or consequences of problem 3. Present argument or solution 4. Describe "vision" of solution (what the result looks like) 5. Call to specific action, showing means of action	1. Describe context of argument, summarize the various views 2. Outline each side clearly and fairly (show no judgment for either side) 3. Describe assumptions, values, definitions that the different parties share 4. Present claims that all parties can accept based on shared views	1. Describe context of argument, summarize the various views 2. Outline each side clearly and show weaknesses and disadvantages of each side 3. Describe beliefs, values, and definitions that writer shares with moderate group 4. Present third option that lies between two opposing sides (the moderate view)
To inspire and motivate readers to action through appeal to common vision or common set of values	To bring two opposing sides together, to mediate between two sides; to establish common ground To show the two sides where they differ in view and what they have in common To get them talking to each other	To get two opposing sides to agree to a third, moderate solution
Those who agree with you (the in-group); "preaching to the converted"	Two opposing groups	A moderate group between two extreme groups
Use emotional appeal	Nonconfrontational, non-judgmental, cooperative for conflict management	Reject both extreme views and present a more moderate third option

Used with permission from Katherine Ploeger.

The Principles in Action: Readings

ADAPTING TO THE COMMUNITY

The following section examines one of the most famous arguments of all time: "Letter from Birmingham Jail," by Martin Luther King, Jr. Although King's 1963 essay is familiar to many students, you may not realize the extent to which King is adapting his discourse to multiple audiences: the eight clergymen that make up his named audience; the community of Birmingham, Alabama; King's own supporters; and the national news audiences. King was trained as a preacher, and when he spoke to his predominantly black congregations, he used the idiom and conventions of the African-American folk pulpit. This style is evident in his political speeches, such as the powerful "I Have a Dream" speech delivered at the Lincoln Memorial during the March on Washington. "Letter from Birmingham Jail," on the other hand, has a different audience than do King's sermons or "I Have a Dream." His immediate audience is represented by the eight Alabama religious leaders who issued a public statement objecting to King's political activities in Birmingham. This statement was a powerful show of solidarity among leaders from various sects and denominations—Catholic, Protestant, and Jewish. To answer this statement, King had to draw upon the language, values, and beliefs of these religious leaders. In addition to these religious leaders, King was addressing the citizens of Birmingham and of Alabama through the local media as well as a national audience through network television news and major newspapers. Perhaps an even more important audience for King were the readers of *Christian Century,* where this letter was published—liberal, white Protestants, many of whom were financial supporters of King's work. King had to choose an approach that would meet the needs of all these communities as well as motivate and support those who suffered with him in Birmingham.

As you read the "Public Statement by Eight Alabama Clergymen," consider the following questions:

1. Before this public statement, these same religious leaders issued "An Appeal for Law and Order and Common Sense." What is implied by placing together the terms "law," "order," and "common sense"?
2. The clergymen claim, "When rights are consistently denied, a cause should be pressed in the courts and in negotiations among local leaders and not in the streets." What assumptions and values underlie this statement?
3. How do the names and titles at the end of this statement create ethos? How credible is this ethos?
4. What role does emotion play in this argument? What would be the effect of using more or less emotion?
5. How is this argument organized? What are the advantages and disadvantages of this organization?
6. In what ways do you think these clergymen are trying to adapt their argument to the needs of their community?

As you read "Letter from Birmingham Jail," consider the following questions:

1. What specific strategies does King use to address his multiple audiences? How does he adapt his argument to the needs of several communities?
2. How does King establish his credibility? What authorities does he cite to strengthen his ethos? Who does he compare himself to? How does he use the Bible, particularly the New Testament?
3. What emotional appeals does King use? How do these appeals give presence to his argument? What would be the effect of using more or less emotion?
4. How does King address the "white moderate"? What effect might these paragraphs (27 and 28) have had on his liberal white supporters?
5. How is King's essay organized? What are the advantages and disadvantages of this organization?

The third essay in this set, "Letter from Jail," is an excerpt from Keith D. Miller's book *Voice of Deliverance* (1998). In this excerpt, Miller explains the historical context for King's essay and the various audiences King is trying to address. Miller than analyzes King's speech within this context. Miller's book was written for both a scholarly audience and a general educated readership. As you read Miller's article, consider the following questions:

1. What is Miller's claim about King and his essay? What reasons does he use to support this claim? What assumptions are implied in these reasons?
2. How does Miller create his own credibility as an expert on King and his rhetoric?
3. How does Miller use emotion in his argument? What would be the effect of more or less emotion?
4. What is Miller's tone (his attitude toward his subject as evidenced in his language)?
5. How is Miller's argument organized? What are the advantages and disadvantages of this organization?
6. How well does Miller's evaluation of King's essay match your own? Where do you agree or disagree with Miller?

Public Statement by Eight Alabama Clergymen

April 12, 1963

WE THE undersigned clergymen are among those who, in January, issued 1
"An Appeal for Law and Order and Common Sense," in dealing with racial problems in Alabama. We expressed understanding that honest convictions in racial matters could properly be pursued in the courts, but urged that decisions of those courts should in the meantime be peacefully obeyed.

Since that time there had been some evidence of increased forbearance and a willingness to face facts. Responsible citizens have undertaken to work on various problems which cause racial friction and unrest. In Birmingham, recent public events had given indication that we all have opportunity for a new constructive and realistic approach to racial problems.

However, we are now confronted by a series of demonstrations by some of our Negro citizens, directed and led in part by outsiders. We recognize the natural impatience of people who feel that their hopes are slow in being realized. But we are convinced that these demonstrations are unwise and untimely.

We agree rather with certain local Negro leadership which has called for honest and open negotiation of racial issues in our area. And we believe this kind of facing of issues can best be accomplished by citizens of our own metropolitan area, white and Negro, meeting with their knowledge and experience of the local situation. All of us need to face that responsibility and find proper channels for its accomplishment.

Just as we formerly pointed out that "hatred and violence have no sanction 5
in our religious and political traditions," we also point out that such actions as incite to hatred and violence, however technically peaceful those actions may be, have not contributed to the resolution of our local problems. We do not believe that these days of new hope are days when extreme measures are justified in Birmingham.

We commend the community as a whole, and the local news media and law enforcement officials in particular, on the calm manner in which these demonstrations have been handled. We urge the public to continue to show restraint should the demonstrations continue, and the law enforcement officials to remain calm and continue to protect our city from violence.

We further strongly urge our own Negro community to withdraw support from these demonstrations, and to unite locally in working peacefully for a better Birmingham. When rights are consistently denied, a cause should be pressed in the courts and in negotiations among local leaders, and not in the streets. We appeal to both our white and Negro citizenry to observe the principles of law and order and common sense.

Signed by:

C.C.J. Carpenter, D.D., LL.D.,
Bishop of Alabama

Joseph A. Durick, D.D.,
Auxiliary Bishop, Diocese of Mobile, Birmingham
Rabbi Milton L. Grafman,
Temple Emanu-El, Birmingham, Alabama
Bishop Paul Hardin,
Bishop of the Alabama-West Florida Conference of the Methodist Church
Bishop Nolan B. Harmon,
Bishop of the North Alabama Conference of the Methodist Church
George M. Murray, D.D., LL.D.,
Bishop Coadjutor, Episcopal Diocese of Alabama
Edward V. Ramage,
Moderator, Synod of the Alabama Presbyterian Church in the United States
Earl Stallings,
Pastor, First Baptist Church, Birmingham, Alabama

Letter from Birmingham Jail

MARTIN LUTHER KING, JR.

MY DEAR fellow clergymen,

While confined here in the Birmingham city jail, I came across your recent statement calling our present activities "unwise and untimely." Seldom, if ever, do I pause to answer criticism of my work and ideas. If I sought to answer all of the criticisms that cross my desk, my secretaries would be engaged in little else in the course of the day, and I would have no time for constructive work. But since I feel that you are men of genuine good will and your criticisms are sincerely set forth, I would like to answer your statement in what I hope will be patient and reasonable terms. 1

I think I should give the reason for my being in Birmingham, since you have been influenced by the argument of "outsiders coming in." I have the honor of serving as president of the Southern Christian Leadership Conference, an organization operating in every southern state, with headquarters in Atlanta, Georgia. We have some eighty-five affiliate organizations all across the South—one being the Alabama Christian Movement for Human Rights. Whenever necessary and possible we share staff, educational and financial resources with our affiliates. Several months ago our local affiliate here in Birmingham invited us to be on call to engage in a nonviolent direct-action program if such were deemed necessary. We readily consented and when the hour came we lived up to our promises. So I am here, along with several members of my staff, because we were invited here. I am here because I have basic organizational ties here.

Beyond this, I am in Birmingham because injustice is here. Just as the eighth-century prophets left their little villages and carried their "thus saith the Lord" far beyond the boundaries of their hometowns; and just as the Apostle Paul left his little village of Tarsus and carried the gospel of Jesus Christ to practically every hamlet and city of the Graeco-Roman world, I too am compelled to carry the gospel of freedom beyond my particular hometown. Like Paul, I must constantly respond to the Macedonian call for aid.

Moreover, I am cognizant of the interrelatedness of all communities and states. I cannot sit idly by in Atlanta and not be concerned about what happens in Birmingham. Injustice anywhere is a threat to justice everywhere. We are caught in an inescapable network of mutuality, tied in a single garment of destiny. Whatever affects one directly affects all indirectly. Never again can we afford to live with the narrow, provincial "outside agitator" idea. Anyone who lives in the United States can never be considered an outsider anywhere in this country.

You deplore the demonstrations that are presently taking place in Birming- 5
ham. But I am sorry that your statement did not express a similar concern for the conditions that brought the demonstrations into being. I am sure that each of you would want to go beyond the superficial social analyst who looks merely at effects, and does not grapple with underlying causes. I would not hesitate to say that it is unfortunate that so-called demonstrations are taking place in Birmingham at this time, but I would say in more emphatic terms that it is even more unfortunate that the white power structure of this city left the Negro community with no other alternative.

In any nonviolent campaign there are four basic steps: (1) collection of the facts to determine whether injustices are alive, (2) negotiation, (3) self-purification, and (4) direct-action. We have gone through all of these steps in Birmingham. There can be no gainsaying of the fact that racial injustice engulfs this community.

Birmingham is probably the most thoroughly segregated city in the United States. Its ugly record of police brutality is known in every section of this country. Its unjust treatment of Negroes in the courts is a notorious reality. There have been more unsolved bombings of Negro homes and churches in Birmingham than any city in this nation. These are the hard, brutal and unbelievable facts. On the basis of these conditions Negro leaders sought to negotiate with the city fathers. But the political leaders consistently refused to engage in good faith negotiation.

Then came the opportunity last September to talk with some of the leaders of the economic community. In these negotiating sessions certain promises were made by the merchants—such as the promise to remove the humiliating racial signs from the stores. On the basis of these promises Rev. Shuttlesworth and the leaders of the Alabama Christian Movement for Human Rights agreed to call a moratorium on any type of demonstrations. As the weeks and months unfolded we realized that we were the victims of a broken promise. The signs remained. Like so many experiences of the past we were confronted with blasted hopes, and the dark shadow of a deep disappointment settled upon us. So we had no alternative except that of preparing for direct action, whereby we would present our very bodies as a means of laying our case before the conscience of the local and national community. We were not unmindful of the difficulties involved. So we decided to go through a process of self-purification. We started having workshops on nonviolence and repeatedly asked ourselves the questions, "Are you able to accept blows without retaliating?" "Are you able to endure the ordeals of jail?" We decided to set our direct-action program around the Easter season, realizing that with the exception of Christmas, this was the largest shopping period of the year. Knowing that a strong economic withdrawal program would be the by-product of direct action, we felt that this was the best time to bring pressure on the merchants for the needed changes. Then it occurred to us that the March election was ahead and so we speedily decided to postpone action until after election day. When we discovered that Mr. Connor was in the run-off, we decided again to postpone action so that the demonstrations could not be used to cloud the issues. At this time we agreed to begin our nonviolent witness the day after the run-off.

This reveals that we did not move irresponsibly into direct action. We too wanted to see Mr. Connor defeated; so we went through postponement after postponement to aid in this community need. After this we felt that direct action could be delayed no longer.

10 You may well ask, "Why direct action? Why sit-ins, marches, etc.? Isn't negotiation a better path?" You are exactly right in your call for negotiation. Indeed, this is the purpose of direct action. Nonviolent direct action seeks to create such a crisis and establish such creative tension that a community that has constantly refused to negotiate is forced to confront the issue. It seeks so to dramatize the issue that it can no longer be ignored. I just referred to the creation of tension as a part of the work of the nonviolent resister. This may sound rather shocking. But I must confess that I am not afraid of the word *tension*. I have earnestly worked and preached against violent tension, but there is a type of constructive nonviolent tension that is necessary for growth. Just as Socrates felt that it was necessary to create a tension in the mind so that individuals could rise from the bondage of myths and half-truths to the unfettered realm of creative analysis and objective appraisal, we must see the need of having nonviolent gadflies to create the kind of tension in society that will help men to rise from the dark depths of prejudice and racism to the majestic heights of understanding and brotherhood. So the purpose of the direct action is to create a situation so crisis-packed that it will inevitably open the door to negotiation. We, therefore, concur with you in your call for negotiation. Too long has our beloved Southland been bogged down in the tragic attempt to live in monologue rather than dialogue.

One of the basic points in your statement is that our acts are untimely. Some have asked, "Why didn't you give the new administration time to act?" The only answer that I can give to this inquiry is that the new administration must be prodded about as much as the outgoing one before it acts. We will be sadly mistaken if we feel that the election of Mr. Boutwell will bring the millennium to Birmingham. While Mr. Boutwell is much more articulate and gentle than Mr. Connor, they are both segregationists, dedicated to the task of maintaining the status quo. The hope I see in Mr. Boutwell is that he will be reasonable enough to see the futility of massive resistance to desegregation. But he will not see this without pressure from the devotees of civil rights. My friends, I must say to you that we have not made a single gain in civil rights without determined legal and nonviolent pressure. History is the long and tragic story of the fact that privileged groups seldom give up their privileges voluntarily. Individuals may see the moral light and voluntarily give up their unjust posture; but as Reinhold Niebuhr has reminded us, groups are more immoral than individuals.

We know through painful experience that freedom is never voluntarily given by the oppressor; it must be demanded by the oppressed. Frankly, I have never yet engaged in a direct-action movement that was "well-timed," according to the timetable of those who have not suffered unduly from the disease of segregation. For years now I have heard the word "Wait!" It rings in the ear of every Negro with a piercing familiarity. This "Wait" has almost always meant "Never." It has been a tranquilizing thalidomide, relieving the emotional stress for a moment, only to give birth to an ill-formed infant of frustration. We must come to see with the distinguished jurist of yesterday that "justice too long delayed is justice denied." We have waited for more than 340 years for our constitutional and God-given rights. The nations of Asia and Africa are moving with jet-like speed toward the goal of political independence, and we still creep at horse and buggy pace toward the gaining of a cup of coffee at a lunch counter. I guess it is easy for those who have never felt the stinging darts of segregation to say, "Wait." But when you have seen vicious mobs lynch your mothers and fathers at will and drown your sisters and brothers at whim; when you have seen hate-filled policemen curse, kick, brutalize and even kill your black brothers and sisters with impunity; when you see the vast majority of your twenty million Negro brothers smothering in an airtight cage of poverty in the midst of an affluent society; when you suddenly find your tongue twisted and your speech stammering as you seek to explain to your six-year-old daughter why she can't go to the public amusement park that has just been advertised on television, and see tears welling up in her little eyes when she is told that Funtown is closed to colored children, and see the depressing clouds of inferiority begin to form in her little mental sky, and see her begin to distort her little personality by unconsciously developing a bitterness toward white people; when you have to concoct an answer for a five-year-old son asking in agonizing pathos: "Daddy, why do white people treat colored people so mean?"; when you take a cross-country drive and find it necessary to sleep night after night in the uncomfortable corners of your automobile because no motel will accept you; when you are humiliated day in and day out by nagging signs reading "white" and "colored"; when your first name becomes "nigger" and your middle name becomes "boy" (however old you are) and your last name becomes "John," and when your wife and mother are never given the respected title "Mrs."; when you are harried by day and haunted by night by the fact that you are a Negro, living constantly at tiptoe stance never quite knowing what to expect next, and plagued with inner fears and outer resentments; when you are forever fighting a degenerating sense of "nobodiness"; then you will understand why we find it difficult to wait. There comes a time when the cup of endurance runs over, and men are no longer willing to be plunged into an abyss of injustice where they experience the blackness of corroding despair. I hope, sirs, you can understand our legitimate and unavoidable impatience.

You express a great deal of anxiety over our willingness to break laws. This is certainly a legitimate concern. Since we so diligently urge people to obey the Supreme Court's decision of 1954 outlawing segregation in the public schools, it is rather strange and paradoxical to find us consciously breaking laws. One may well ask, "How can you advocate breaking some laws and obeying others?" The answer is found in the fact that there are two types of laws: there are *just* and there are *unjust* laws. I would agree with Saint Augustine that "An unjust law is no law at all."

Now what is the difference between the two? How does one determine when a law is just or unjust? A just law is a man-made code that squares with the moral law or the law of God. An unjust law is a code that is out of harmony with the moral law. To put it in the terms of Saint Thomas Aquinas, an unjust law is a human law that is not rooted in eternal and natural law. Any law that uplifts human personality is just. Any law that degrades human personality is unjust. All segregation statutes are unjust because segregation distorts the soul and damages the personality. It gives the segregator a false sense of superiority, and the segregated a false sense of inferiority. To use the words of Martin Buber, the great Jewish philosopher, segregation substitutes an "I-it" relationship for the "I-thou" relationship, and ends up relegating persons to the status of things. So segregation is not only politically, economically and sociologically unsound, but it is morally wrong and sinful. Paul Tillich has said that sin is separation. Isn't segregation an existential expression of man's tragic separation, an expression of his awful estrangement, his terrible sinfulness? So I can urge men to disobey segregation ordinances because they are morally wrong.

Let us turn to a more concrete example of just and unjust laws. An unjust 15
law is a code that a majority inflicts on a minority that is not binding on itself. This is difference made legal. On the other hand a just law is a code that a majority compels a minority to follow that it is willing to follow itself. This is sameness made legal.

Let me give another explanation. An unjust law is a code inflicted upon a minority which that minority had no part in enacting or creating because they did not have the unhampered right to vote. Who can say that the legislature of Alabama which set up the segregation laws was democratically elected? Throughout the state of Alabama all types of conniving methods are used to prevent Negroes from becoming registered voters and there are some counties without a single Negro registered to vote despite the fact that the Negro constitutes a majority of the population. Can any law set up in such a state be considered democratically structured?

These are just a few examples of unjust and just laws. There are some instances when a law is just on its face and unjust in its application. For instance, I was arrested Friday on a charge of parading without a permit. Now there is nothing wrong with an ordinance which requires a permit for a parade, but when the ordinance is used to preserve segregation and to deny citizens the First Amendment privilege of peaceful assembly and peaceful protest, then it becomes unjust.

I hope you can see the distinction I am trying to point out. In no sense do I advocate evading or defying the law as the rabid segregationist would do. This would lead to anarchy. One who breaks an unjust law must do it *openly, lovingly* (not hatefully as the white mothers did in New Orleans when they were seen on television screaming, “nigger, nigger, nigger”), and with a willingness to accept the penalty. I submit that an individual who breaks a law that conscience tells him is unjust, and willingly accepts the penalty by staying in jail to arouse the conscience of the community over its injustice, is in reality expressing the very highest respect for law.

Of course, there is nothing new about this kind of civil disobedience. It was seen sublimely in the refusal of Shadrach, Meshach and Abednego to obey the laws of Nebuchadnezzar because a higher moral law was involved. It was practiced superbly by the early Christians who were willing to face hungry lions and the excruciating pain of chopping blocks, before submitting to certain unjust laws of the Roman Empire. To a degree academic freedom is a reality today because Socrates practiced civil disobedience.

We can never forget that everything Hitler did in Germany was “legal” and 20
everything the Hungarian freedom fighters did in Hungary was “illegal.” It was “illegal” to aid and comfort a Jew in Hitler’s Germany. But I am sure that if I had lived in Germany during that time I would have aided and comforted my Jewish brothers even though it was illegal. If I lived in a Communist country today where certain principles dear to the Christian faith are suppressed, I believe I would openly advocate disobeying these anti-religious laws. I must make two honest confessions to you, my Christian and Jewish brothers. First, I must confess that over the last few years I have been gravely disappointed with the white moderate. I have almost reached the regrettable conclusion that the Negro’s great stumbling block in the stride toward freedom is not the White Citizens Counciler or the Ku Klux Klanner, but the white moderate who is more devoted to “order” than to justice; who prefers a negative peace which is the absence of tension to a positive peace which is the presence of justice, who constantly says, “I agree with you in the goal you seek, but I can’t agree with your methods of direct action”; who paternalistically feels that he can set the timetable for another man’s freedom; who lives by the myth of time and who constantly advised the Negro to wait until a “more convenient season.” Shallow understanding from people of good will is more frustrating than absolute misunderstanding from

people of ill will. Lukewarm acceptance is much more bewildering than outright rejection.

I had hoped that the white moderate would understand that law and order exist for the purpose of establishing justice, and that when they fail to do this they become dangerously structured dams that block the flow of social progress. I had hoped that the white moderate would understand that the present tension of the South is merely a necessary phase of the transition from an obnoxious negative peace, where the Negro passively accepted his unjust plight, to a substance-filled positive peace, where all men will respect the dignity and worth of human personality. Actually, we who engage in nonviolent direct action are not the creators of tension. We merely bring to the surface the hidden tension that is already alive. We bring it out in the open where it can be seen and dealt with. Like a boil that can never be cured as long as it is covered up but must be opened with all its pus-flowing ugliness to the natural medicines of air and light, injustice must likewise be exposed, with all of the tension its exposing creates, to the light of human conscience and the air of national opinion before it can be cured.

In your statement you asserted that our actions, even though peaceful, must be condemned because they precipitate violence. But can this assertion be logically made? Isn't this like condemning the robbed man because his possession of money precipitated the evil act of robbery? Isn't this like condemning Socrates because his unswerving commitment to truth and his philosophical delvings precipitated the misguided popular mind to make him drink the hemlock? Isn't this like condemning Jesus because His unique God-consciousness and never-ceasing devotion to his will precipitated the evil act of crucifixion? We must come to see, as federal courts have consistently affirmed, that it is immoral to urge an individual to withdraw his efforts to gain his basic constitutional rights because the quest precipitates violence. Society must protect the robbed and punish the robber.

I had also hoped that the white moderate would reject the myth of time. I received a letter this morning from a white brother in Texas which said: "All Christians know that the colored people will receive equal rights eventually, but it is possible that you are in too great of a religious hurry. It has taken Christianity almost two thousand years to accomplish what it has. The teachings of Christ take time to come to earth." All that is said here grows out of a tragic misconception of time. It is the strangely irrational notion that there is something in the very flow of time that will inevitably cure all ills. Actually time is neutral. It can be used either destructively or constructively. I am coming to feel that the people of ill will have used time much more effectively than the people of good will. We will have to repent in this generation not merely for the vitriolic words and actions of the bad people, but for the appalling silence of the good people. We must come to see that human progress never rolls in on wheels of inevitability. It comes through the tireless efforts and persistent work of men willing to be co-workers with God, and without this hard work time itself becomes an ally of the forces of social stagnation. We must use time creatively, and forever realize that the time is always ripe to do right. Now is the time to make real the promise of democracy, and transform our pending national elegy into a creative psalm of brotherhood. Now is the time to lift our national policy from the quicksand of racial injustice to the solid rock of human dignity.

You spoke of our activity in Birmingham as extreme. At first I was rather disappointed that fellow clergymen would see my nonviolent efforts as those of the extremist. I started thinking about the fact that I stand in the middle of two opposing forces in the Negro community. One is a force of complacency made up of Negroes who, as a result of long years of oppression, have been so completely drained of self-respect and a sense of "somebodiness" that they have adjusted to segregation, and, of a few Negroes in the middle class who, because of a degree of academic and economic security, and because at points they profit by segregation, have unconsciously become insensitive to the problems of the masses. The other force is one of bitterness and hatred, and comes perilously close to advocating violence. It is expressed in the various black nationalist groups that are springing up over the nation, the largest and best known being Elijah Muhammad's Muslim movement. This movement is nourished by the contemporary frustration over the continued existence of racial discrimination. It is made up of people who have lost faith in America, who have absolutely repudiated Christianity, and who have concluded that the white man is an incurable "devil." I have tried to stand between these two forces, saying that we need not follow the "do-nothingism" of the complacent or the hatred and despair of the black nationalist. There is the more excellent way of love and nonviolent protest. I'm grateful to God that, through the Negro church, the dimension of nonviolence entered our struggle. If this philosophy had not emerged, I am convinced that by now many streets of the South would be flowing with floods of blood. And I am further convinced that if our white brothers dismiss as "rabble-rousers" and "outside agitators" those of us who are working through the channels of nonviolent direct action and refuse to support our nonviolent efforts, millions of Negroes, out of frustration and despair, will seek solace and security in black nationalist ideologies, a development that will lead inevitably to a frightening racial nightmare.

Oppressed people cannot remain oppressed forever. The urge for freedom 25
will eventually come. This is what happened to the American Negro. Something within has reminded him of his birthright of freedom; something without has reminded him that he can gain it. Consciously and unconsciously, he has been swept in by what the Germans called the *Zeitgeist,* and with his black brothers of Africa, and his brown and yellow brothers of Asia, South America and the Caribbean, he is moving with a sense of cosmic urgency toward the promised land of racial justice. Recognizing this vital urge that has engulfed the Negro community, one should readily understand public demonstrations. The Negro has many pent-up resentments and latent frustrations. He has to get them out. So let him march sometime; let him have his prayer pilgrimages to the city hall; understand why he must have sit-ins and freedom rides. If his repressed emotions do not come out in these nonviolent ways, they will come out in ominous ex-

pressions of violence. This is not a threat, it is a fact of history. So I have not said to my people "get rid of your discontent." But I have tried to say that this normal and healthy discontent can be channelized through the creative outlet of nonviolent direct action. Now this approach is being dismissed as extremist. I must admit that I was initially disappointed in being so categorized.

But as I continued to think about the matter I gradually gained a bit of satisfaction from being considered an extremist. Was not Jesus an extremist in love—"Love your enemies, bless them that curse you, pray for them that despitefully use you." Was not Amos an extremist for justice—"Let justice roll down like waters and righteousness like a mighty stream." Was not Paul an extremist for the gospel of Jesus Christ—"I bear in my body the marks of the Lord Jesus." Was not Martin Luther an extremist—"Here I stand; I can do none other so help me God." Was not John Bunyan an extremist—"I will stay in jail to the end of my days before I make a butchery of my conscience." Was not Abraham Lincoln an extremist—"This nation cannot survive half slave and half free." Was not Thomas Jefferson an extremist—"We hold these truths to be self-evident, that all men are created equal." So the question is not whether we will be extremist but what kind of extremist will we be. Will we be extremists for hate or will we be extremists for love? Will we be extremists for the preservation of injustice—or will we be extremists for the cause of justice? In that dramatic scene on Calvary's hill, three men were crucified. We must not forget that all three were crucified for the same crime—the crime of extremism. Two were extremists for immorality, and thusly fell below their environment. The other, Jesus Christ, was an extremist for love, truth and goodness, and thereby rose above his environment. So, after all, maybe the South, the nation and the world are in dire need of creative extremists.

I had hoped that the white moderate would see this. Maybe I was too optimistic. Maybe I expected too much. I guess I should have realized that few members of a race that has oppressed another race can understand or appreciate the deep groans and passionate yearnings of those that have been oppressed and still fewer have the vision to see that injustice must be rooted out by strong, persistent and determined action. I am thankful, however, that some of our white brothers have grasped the meaning of this social revolution and committed themselves to it. They are still all too small in quantity, but they are big in quality. Some like Ralph McGill, Lillian Smith, Harry Golden and James Dabbs have written about our struggle in eloquent, prophetic and understanding terms. Others have marched with us down nameless streets of the South. They have languished in filthy roach-infested jails, suffering the abuse and brutality of angry policemen who see them as "dirty nigger-lovers." They, unlike so many of their moderate brothers and sisters, have recognized the urgency of the moment and sensed the need for powerful "action" antidotes to combat the disease of segregation.

Let me rush on to mention my other disappointment. I have been so greatly disappointed with the white church and its leadership. Of course, there are some notable exceptions. I am not unmindful of the fact that each of you has taken some significant stands on this issue. I commend you, Rev. Stallings, for your Christian stance on this past Sunday, in welcoming Negroes to your worship service on a nonsegregated basis. I commend the Catholic leaders of this state for integrating Springhill College several years ago.

But despite these notable exceptions I must honestly reiterate that I have been disappointed with the church. I do not say that as one of the negative critics who can always find something wrong with the church. I say it as a minister of the gospel, who loves the church; who was nurtured in its bosom; who has been sustained by its spiritual blessings and who will remain true to it as long as the cord of life shall lengthen.

I had the strange feeling when I was suddenly catapulted into the leadership 30
of the bus protest in Montgomery several years ago that we would have the support of the white church. I felt that the white ministers, priests and rabbis of the South would be some of our strongest allies. Instead, some have been outright opponents, refusing to understand the freedom movement and misrepresenting its leaders; all too many others have been more cautious than courageous and have remained silent behind the anesthetizing security of the stained-glass windows.

In spite of my shattered dreams of the past, I came to Birmingham with the hope that the white religious leadership of this community would see the justice of our cause, and with deep moral concern, serve as the channel through which our just grievances would get to the power structure. I had hoped that each of you would understand. But again I have been disappointed. I have heard numerous religious leaders of the South call upon their worshippers to comply with a desegregation decision because it is the *law,* but I have longed to hear white ministers say, "Follow this decree because integration is morally *right* and the Negro is your brother." In the midst of blatant injustices inflicted upon the Negro, I have watched white churches stand on the sideline and merely mouth pious irrelevancies and sanctimonious trivialities. In the midst of a mighty struggle to rid our nation of racial and economic injustice, I have heard so many ministers say, "Those are social issues with which the gospel has no real concern," and I have watched so many churches commit themselves to a completely otherworldly religion which made a strange distinction between body and soul, the sacred and the secular.

So here we are moving toward the exit of the twentieth century with a religious community largely adjusted to the status quo, standing as a taillight behind other community agencies rather than a headlight leading men to higher levels of justice.

I have traveled the length and breadth of Alabama, Mississippi and all the other southern states. On sweltering summer days and crisp autumn mornings I have looked at her beautiful churches with their lofty spires pointing heavenward. I have beheld the impressive outlay of her massive religious education buildings. Over and over again I have found myself asking: "What kind of people worship here? Who is their God? Where were their voices when the lips of Governor Barnett dripped with words of interposition and nullification? Where were they when Governor Wallace gave the clarion call for defiance and hatred? Where were their voices of support when tired, bruised and weary Negro men and women decided to rise from the dark dungeons of complacency to the bright hills of creative protest?"

Yes, these questions are still in my mind. In deep disappointment, I have wept over the laxity of the church. But be assured that my tears have been tears of love. There can be no deep disappointment where there is not deep love. Yes, I love the church; I love her sacred walls. How could I do otherwise? I am in the rather unique position of being the son, the grandson and the great-grandson of preachers. Yes, I see the church as the body of Christ. But, oh! How we have blemished and scarred that body through social neglect and fear of being nonconformists.

35 There was a time when the church was very powerful. It was during that period when the early Christians rejoiced when they were deemed worthy to suffer for what they believed. In those days the church was not merely a thermometer that recorded the ideas and principles of popular opinion; it was a thermostat that transformed the mores of society. Wherever the early Christians entered a town the power structure got disturbed and immediately sought to convict them for being "disturbers of the peace" and "outside agitators." But they went on with the conviction that they were "a colony of heaven," and had to obey God rather than man. They were small in number but big in commitment. They were too God-intoxicated to be "astronomically intimidated." They brought an end to such ancient evils as infanticide and gladiatorial contest.

Things are different now. The contemporary church is often a weak, ineffectual voice with an uncertain sound. It is so often the arch-supporter of the status quo. Far from being disturbed by the presence of the church, the power structure of the average community is consoled by the church's silent and often vocal sanction of things as they are.

But the judgment of God is upon the church as never before. If the church of today does not recapture the sacrificial spirit of the early church, it will lose its authentic ring, forfeit the loyalty of millions, and be dismissed as an irrelevant social club with no meaning for the twentieth century. I am meeting young people every day whose disappointment with the church has risen to outright disgust.

Maybe again, I have been too optimistic. Is organized religion too inextricably bound to the status quo to save our nation and the world? Maybe I must turn my faith to the inner spiritual church, the church within the church, as the true *ecclesia* and the hope of the world. But again I am thankful to God that some noble souls from the ranks of organized religion have broken loose from the paralyzing chains of conformity and joined us as active partners in the struggle for freedom. They have left their secure congregations and walked the streets of Albany, Georgia, with us. They have gone through the highways of the South on tortuous rides for freedom. Yes, they have gone to jail with us.

Some have been kicked out of their churches, and lost support of their bishops and fellow ministers. But they have gone with the faith that right defeated is stronger than evil triumphant. These men have been the leaven in the lump of the race. Their witness has been the spiritual salt that has preserved the true meaning of the gospel in these troubled times. They have carved a tunnel of hope through the dark mountain of disappointment.

I hope the church as a whole will meet the challenge of this decisive hour. But even if the church does not come to the aid of justice, I have no despair about the future. I have no fear about the outcome of our struggle in Birmingham, even if our motives are presently misunderstood. We will reach the goal of freedom in Birmingham and all over the nation, because the goal of America is freedom. Abused and scorned though we may be, our destiny is tied up with the destiny of America. Before the Pilgrims landed at Plymouth we were here. Before the pen of Jefferson etched across the pages of history the majestic words of the Declaration of Independence, we were here. For more than two centuries our foreparents labored in this country without wages; they made cotton king; and they built the homes of their masters in the midst of brutal injustice and shameful humiliation—and yet out of a bottomless vitality they continued to thrive and develop. If the inexpressible cruelties of slavery could not stop us, the opposition we now face will surely fail. We will win our freedom because the sacred heritage of our nation and the eternal will of God are embodied in our echoing demands.

I must close now. But before closing I am impelled to mention one other 40
point in your statement that troubled me profoundly. You warmly commended the Birmingham police force for keeping "order" and "preventing violence." I don't believe you would have so warmly commended the police force if you had seen its angry violent dogs literally biting six unarmed, nonviolent Negroes. I don't believe you would so quickly commend the policemen if you would observe their ugly and inhuman treatment of Negroes here in the city jail; if you would watch them push and curse old Negro women and young Negro girls; if you would see them slap and kick old Negro men and young boys; if you will observe them, as they did on two occasions, refuse to give us food because we wanted to sing our grace together. I'm sorry that I can't join you in your praise for the police department.

It is true that they have been rather disciplined in their public handling of the demonstrators. In this sense they have been rather publicly "nonviolent." But for what purpose? To preserve the evil system of segregation. Over the last few years I have consistently preached that nonviolence demands that the means we use must be as pure as the ends we seek. So I have tried to make it clear that it is wrong to use immoral means to attain moral ends. But now I must affirm that it is just as wrong, or even more so, to use moral means to preserve immoral ends. Maybe Mr. Connor and his policemen have been rather publicly nonviolent, as Chief Pritchett was in Albany, Georgia, but they have used the moral means of nonviolence to maintain the immoral end of flagrant racial injustice.

T. S. Eliot has said that there is no greater treason than to do the right deed for the wrong reason.

I wish you had commended the Negro sit-inners and demonstrators of Birmingham for their sublime courage, their willingness to suffer and their amazing discipline in the midst of the most inhuman provocation. One day the South will recognize its real heroes. They will be the James Merediths, courageously and with a majestic sense of purpose facing jeering and hostile mobs and the agonizing loneliness that characterizes the life of the pioneer. They will be old, oppressed, battered Negro women, symbolized in a seventy-two-year-old woman of Montgomery, Alabama, who rose up with a sense of dignity and with her people decided not to ride the segregated buses, and responded to one who inquired about her tiredness with ungrammatical profundity: "My feet is tired, but my soul is rested." They will be the young high school and college students, young ministers of the gospel and a host of their elders courageously and nonviolently sitting-in at lunch counters and willingly going to jail for conscience's sake. One day the South will know that when these disinherited children of God sat down at lunch counters they were in reality standing up for the best in the American dream and the most sacred values in our Judeo-Christian heritage, and thusly, carrying our whole nation back to those great wells of democracy which were dug deep by the Founding Fathers in the formulation of the Constitution and the Declaration of Independence.

Never before have I written a letter this long (or should I say a book?). I'm afraid that it is much too long to take your precious time. I can assure you that it would have been much shorter if I had been writing from a comfortable desk, but what else is there to do when you are alone for days in the dull monotony of a narrow jail cell other than write long letters, think strange thoughts, and pray long prayers?

If I have said anything in this letter that is an overstatement of the truth and is indicative of an unreasonable impatience, I beg you to forgive me. If I have said anything in this letter that is an understatement of the truth and is indicative of my having a patience that makes me patient with anything less than brotherhood, I beg God to forgive me.

I hope this letter finds you strong in the faith. I also hope that circumstances 45
will soon make it possible for me to meet each of you, not as an integrationist or a civil rights leader, but as a fellow clergyman and a Christian brother. Let us all hope that the dark clouds of racial prejudice will soon pass away and the deep fog of misunderstanding will be lifted from our fear-drenched communities and in some not too distant tomorrow the radiant stars of love and brotherhood will shine over our great nation with all of their scintillating beauty.

Yours for the cause of Peace and Brotherhood,

Martin Luther King, Jr.

Letter from Jail

KEITH D. MILLER

IN THE SPRING of 1963 Cleo Kennedy, a soloist at St. Luke's Church in 1
Birmingham, began her a cappella rendition of "Swing Low, Sweet Chariot."[1] The slow, lullaby-like tempo of the most famous of all spirituals fit perfectly with the quiet joy of its lyrics. The resplendent expression of a calm expectation to reach heaven, "Swing Low" is a perfect song of religious contemplation. No one would ever tinker with it. But someone did. Without warning, organist Carlton Reese and his choir dove into Kennedy's solo and began belting "Rock Me, Lord," a pounding, extremely upbeat variation of "Swing Low." The pews began to quiver as Reese's whitehot solo proved beyond doubt that every jazz pianist should have played the organ instead. Sopranos leapt boldly into the few spaces the skittering organist left open. And the low, steady bass notes riveted the building to its foundation, which it threatened to desert.

The crowd shouted, clapped, and stomped, celebrating not only the heavenly music, but also their own earthly crusade to eliminate segregation from their city, a bastion of American apartheid.

King stepped up to the pulpit, into the excitement generated by sublime music and by a grassroots protest that had galvanized the attention of the world. He addressed the church in placid, measured tones, transforming his followers' zeal into calm as he prepared them to face the wrath of the city. He and they realized that Sheriff Bull Connor would continue to confront peaceful marchers with powerful fire hoses and angry police dogs. But he insisted that, though greeted with dogs and hatred, protestors should remain nonviolent and patiently accept jail sentences for themselves and their children.[2]

Nonviolence was finally winning the Battle of Birmingham. King and SCLC had already dispatched twenty-five hundred people to jail, for the first time meeting their objective of literally filling the jails.

The Birmingham movement gained the sympathy of millions of Americans, 5
who were horrified by police violence, especially when applied to innocent black children. But police brutality in Birmingham and elsewhere did not automatically signify that segregation was evil. The public needed to understand police barbarism as symptomatic and symbolic of an entire racist system. King and the movement had to convince America that Connor was no aberration, that every-

[1]Listen to Carawan, *Birmingham*.

[2]For King's oration, listen to *Birmingham*. King distinguishes the three types of love, as debreated by the Greek words *eros, philia,* and *agape*. This discussion has become his standard analysis of love, which he borrowed from Fosdick's *On Being Fit* (6–7) and in "Pilgrimage," "Loving Your Enemies," and elsewhere. He relied on it so often that "there were few who followed [King's] career who have not heard his favorite discourse on the meaning and significance of *eros, philia,* and *agape*" (David Lewis 44).

day segregation was just as horrific as Connor's police. By sacrificing themselves to the hoses and dogs, King's activists essentially claimed that Connor's violence represented the hidden, daily violence of racism.

Just as police brutality served as an apt symbol for the less dramatic, quotidian evil of segregation, so did jail. As they presented themselves for jail, African Americans in effect argued that jail symbolized racism.[3] They could stand jail because segregation already locked them in jail. If segregation was already a prison, then why not go behind bars?

Providing this equation explicitly in "Shattered Dreams," King equates Paul's suffering in prison with the experience of enslaved and segregated blacks. He argues that African Americans in "the prison of segregation" recapitulate Paul's experiences in prison.[4] King's "Letter from Birmingham Jail" implicitly offers the same comparison: life in jail matches life under segregation.

King could provide this equation because his conception of religious leadership came from the Old Testament prophets, the Apostle Paul, and the black church. Early in this letter he compares himself to the eighth-century Old Testament prophets and to Paul.[5] His readers realized that Paul was often incarcerated and wrote letters from jail. Like the prophets, Paul was simultaneously a preacher, a theologian, and a disturber of the peace. And Paul made no distinction between his sermons, his theology, and his letter-writing. Refusing to cultivate an elite, he preferred to evangelize anyone who would listen.

Long before King was born, black churches often insisted on vesting in a single person the duties of theologian, preacher, and activist. In many black communities, mastering all these roles has been almost a requirement for becoming an authoritative religious leader. Until the advent of black theology about the time of King's death, blacks rarely recognized theology as something distinct from sermons. Believing that the brightest and best-educated people should instruct whole congregations, African-American leaders have historically gained authority by combining the roles of expert and public speaker. The finest black theologians—Richard Allen, Henry Highland Garnet, Vernon Johns, C. L. Franklin, and others—delivered theology through their sermons, not by way of erudite theological prose. They also engaged in protest; indeed, their church "was born as a protest movement."[6] And, while its impulse to protest has sometimes remained dormant, the impulse has never died.

By contrast, in the first half of this century liberal white Protestants treated 10
sermons, theology, and social protest as discrete concerns. No one regarded Fosdick, Buttrick, and Hamilton as theologians. Nor were they activists of any note. Though Tillich often preached, his reputation rests on his theological volumes, which he clearly valued more than his sermons. Though Niebuhr ventured across the tidy demarcations of religious roles, he, like Tillich, regarded his

[3]I thank John Doebler for this observation.
[4]See King, Jr., *Strength* 83.
[5]For the Pauline qualities of "Letter," see Snow.
[6]Kelly Miller Smith 72.

theology—not his sermons—as the most important expression of his thought. In fact, the extremely prolific Niebuhr never published a collection of sermons and never used theology to organize a movement.[7] Like other white Protestants, King's professors regarded theology, homiletics, and social ethics as separate subjects to be taught in separate classes.

While many would rank King as the greatest American preacher of the century, one could easily wonder how he could become a stellar homilist and essayist while also directing a social revolution. He managed to become both the most accomplished preacher and the most successful reformer of the century partly because he did not begin the process of fusing the roles of preacher, theologian, and activist. Unlike white religious leaders, he preached by protesting, protested by preaching, and wrote theology by stepping into a jail cell. His successful theology consists of his sermons, speeches, civil rights essays, and political career—not his formal theological work. Had he accepted the white division of theology, homiletics, and politics, he never would have gone to jail to gain the authority to speak. By rejecting white models, he achieved the apotheosis of his own community's understanding of religious leadership, an understanding the nation came to cherish.

Nowhere is this black conception of theology more evident than in "Letter from Birmingham Jail." Along with the Sermon on the Porch, the essay is more completely inseparable from the civil rights movement than any other example of King's discourse. Indeed a better match between words and deeds is difficult to imagine. King perfectly tailored his letter to the particulars of Birmingham in 1963, including its recent mayoral election and an unsolved rash of bombings. The principles outlined in "Letter" mandated his trip to jail, and a stay in jail mandated the explanation supplied by "Letter." Getting arrested set the stage for "Letter," "Letter" set the stage for future arrests.

Yet, as King masterfully performed the simultaneous roles of preacher, theologian, and activist, he wrote an essay that, unlike his other discourse, actually reflects his study of Euro-American philosophy and theology. "Letter" also manifests the powerful and more familiar influences of the black folk pulpit, *Christian Century,* Fosdick, Wofford, and two other religious writers. All these influences converge in this extraordinary essay.

Although King's epistolary essay was inspired by Paul, his more immediate stimulant was *Christian Century.*[8] In 1959, six months after joining the edito-

[7]Unhappy with what his sermons might look like in print, Niebuhr revised a fairly small number of them into "sermonic essays," which were homilies shaped into miniature theological excursions.

[8]Ostensibly "Letter" is King's response to eight moderate clergy, who wrote not a letter but a statement for a local newspaper, directing their remarks *not* to King, but to "our own white and Negro citizenry" (Snow 321). For that reason, the clergy did not invent the context for "Letter." Together with the editor of *Christian Century,* King invented the context. The comment by the clergy gave King an ostensible context that has been widely mistaken for the real context.

rial staff of the journal, he informed its editor that he wanted to write “occasional articles and letters” that could reach “the Protestant leadership of our country.”[9] The editor agreed that his readership would appreciate “an occasional personal letter which you could write.”[10] Six months later the editor gave more explicit instructions, telling King and his other editors-at-large to write Christmas letters “in such a form that they can actually be sent to the people to whom they are addressed as well as appearing in the columns of the magazine.”[11] The recipients responded with a set of public letters printed in the Christmas issue of the journal. Like “Letter,” these letters ostensibly focused on their real-life addressees but actually on readers of *Christian Century.* Like “Letter,” some of them combined a cordial and respectful tone with forceful criticism of their addressees. Although King did not write a public letter on this occasion, he did so a few years later in Birmingham.

Ostensibly serving as King’s response to eight moderate clergy, “Letter” 15
first surfaced in *Christian Century, Liberation,* and *Christianity and Crisis*—three left-of-center journals—and in pamphlets disseminated by the Fellowship of Reconciliation (FOR) and another leftist, pacifist organization, the American Friends Service Committee.[12] Soon afterwards other readers encountered King’s epistle in *The Progressive, Ebony,* and other liberal periodicals. Publication in the *New York Post* and the *San Francisco Chronicle* further expanded King’s readership. (He claimed that “nearly a million copies . . . have been widely circulated in churches of most of the major denominations.”[13]) He also installed the instantly popular essay as the centerpiece for *Why We Can’t Wait,* his longer account of the Birmingham movement.

Given that King wrote “Letter” for *Christian Century* and other left-of-center outlets, one can say that its original and primary audience was not the ostensible audience of eight moderate clergy. Nor was it other moderate readers. Instead, King carefully crafted a letter that could actually be mailed to its addressees while engaging the readers of *Christian Century* and other liberal Protestants. The progressive ministers and laity who raved about King’s sermons at Cathedral of St. John, Riverside Church, the Chicago Sunday Evening Club, and elsewhere were the same people who subscribed to *Christian Century.* Because this journal had promulgated racial equality not merely for years, but for several decades prior to “Letter,” the vast majority of its subscribers wholeheartedly agreed with King’s attack on segregation long before he wrote his essay. Had the editors of the journal failed to sympathize with King, they would not have published “Pilgrimage” several years prior to “Letter.” Nor would they have welcomed him as an editor-at-large every year from 1958 until a year after the publication of “Letter.” Equally sympathetic were those who read “Letter”

[9]King, Jr. Letter to Harold Fey, 30 March 1959, KC BU.
[10]See Harold Fey, letter to King, Jr., 11 May 1959, KC BU.
[11]Harold Fey, letter to King, Jr., 23 November 1959, KC BU.
[12]American Friends Service Committee is an arm of the Quakers.
[13]King, Jr., “*Playboy*” 351.

in other liberal forums. Although the essay eventually reached large numbers of moderates, King's main purpose was to convert the converted and reinforce their earlier support. He carefully preached to the choir, targeting an audience of liberals by asking them to invoke the role of moderates. The essay was so well written that it reached a large, spillover audience of moderates as well.

All readers perused an essay composed under trying conditions. By every account, King entered Birmingham jail with nothing to read and with no notes or examples of his own writing. However, he remembered earlier speeches and sermons and insinuated several familiar passages into his essay, including material he had originally obtained from sources. Because he relied on his memory—not directly on texts—the borrowed passages in "Letter" do not resemble his models as closely as usual. Still, several of his sources can be clearly identified.

For his arguments about nonconformity, he recalled his own sermon "Transformed Nonconformist," including passages that came from Fosdick's *Hope of the World* and from a sermon by H. H. Crane:

> FOSDICK: We Christians were intended to be that [creative] minority. We were to be the salt of the earth, said Jesus. We were to be the light of the world. We were to be the leaven in the lump of the race. . . . That is joining the real church . . . *ecclesia* . . . a minority selected from the majority. . . . There was a time . . . when Christianity was very powerful. Little groups of men and women were scattered through the Roman Empire. . . . They were far less than two per cent and the heel of persecution was often on them, but they flamed with a conviction. . . .
>
> Do you remember what Paul called them. . . . "We are a colony of heaven," he said. . . . [Christianity] stopped ancient curses like infanticide. It put an end to the . . . gladitorial shows.[14]
>
> CRANE: Consider first the thermometer. Essentially, it . . . records or registers its environment. . . . Instead of being *conformed* to this world, [man] can *transform* it. . . . For when he is what his Maker obviously intended him to be, he is not a thermometer; he is a thermostat . . . there is a thermostatic type of religion . . . and its highest expression is called vita Christianity.[15]
>
> KING: There was a time when the church was very powerful. . . . In those days the church was not merely a thermometer that recorded the ideas and principles of popular opinion; it was a thermostat that transformed the mores of society. Whenever the early Christians entered a town, the people in power . . . immediately sought to convict the Christians for being "disturbers of the peace." . . . But the Christians pressed on in the conviction that they were a "colony of heaven." . . . Small in number, they were big in commitment. . . . By their effort and example they brought an end to such ancient evils as infanticide and gladitorial contests. Perhaps I must turn . . . to the inner spiritual church as the true *ekklesia* and hope of the world. These [ministers who support civil rights] have been the leaven in the lump of the race. Their witness has been the spiritual salt that has preserved the true meaning of the Gospel. . . . [16]

[14]Fosdick, *Hope* 5–6.
[15]Crane 30, 32, 38.
[16]King, Jr., "Letter," *Why* 91, 92.

King here eschewed the King James version of the Bible, which he normally used, and followed Fosdick in quoting from the 1922 Moffatt translation of Philippians 3:20 ("We are a colony of heaven").[17] Significantly, the King James translation of this verse—"For our conversation is in heaven"—fails to provide *any* Biblical support for nonconformity. Here King owes a debt not only to Fosdick's lines, but also to Fosdick's choice of a specific scripture *and* a specific translation of that scripture. This translation contrasts substantively not only with the King James edition, but with almost all other available English translations.

Turning to another familiar source, King marshalled his arguments for nonviolence and civil disobedience by refashioning ideas and language from two of Wofford's speeches. He reworded a passage from Wofford that he had used earlier in *Stride:*

> WOFFORD: [Civil disobedience] involves the highest possible respect for the law. If we secretly violated the law, or tried to evade it, or violently tried to overthrow it, that would be undermining the idea of law, Gandhi argued. But by openly and peacefully disobeying an unjust law and asking for the penalty, we are saying that we so respect the law that when we think it is so unjust that in conscience we cannot obey, then we belong in jail until that law is changed.[18]
>
> KING: In no sense do I advocate evading or defying the law. . . . One who breaks an unjust law must do so openly, lovingly, and with a willingness to accept the penalty. I submit that an individual who breaks a law that conscience tells him is unjust, and who willingly accepts the penalty of imprisonment in order to arouse the conscience of the community over its injustice, is in reality expressing the highest respect for the law.[19]

King also paraphrased Wofford's citation of Socrates, Augustine, and Aquinas as
proponents of civil disobedience and Wofford's call for nonviolent gadflies.[20] 20

For part of his analysis of segregation, King turned to George Kelsey, his professor at Morehouse, whose remarks on segregation proved useful on several occasions. In *Stride,* "A Challenge to Churches and Synagogues," and "Letter," King sometimes reiterated and sometimes adapted passages from Kelsey:

> KELSEY: segregation is itself utterly un-Christian. It is established on pride, fear, and falsehood. . . . It is unbrotherly, impersonal, a complete denial of the

[17]See Moffatt. Preceding Fosdick, who published *Hope* in 1933, Luccock quoted the "colony of heaven" translation in the late 1920s. See Chapter 4. Conceivably, Luccock, Fosdick, and King were drawing on some translation other than Moffatt's but that seems unlikely, inasmuch as Moffatt's translation appeared shortly before Luccock's book and inasmuch as the "colony of heaven" metaphor represents a decidedly unusual translation of the original passage. I thank Ernest Miller for the importance of the Luccock/Fosdick/King translation from Philippians.

[18]Wofford. "Non-violence and the Law" 65–66.

[19]King, Jr., "Letter," *Why* 83–84.

[20]Compare Wofford, "The Law" 2 and King, Jr., "Letter," *Why* 84; Wofford's "Nonviolence and the Law" 65, 68 and King, Jr., "Letter," *Why* 79, 82.

> "*I–Thou*" relationship, and a complete expression of the "*I–Thou*" relation. Two segregated souls never meet in God.[21]

Compare King's statement in "A Challenge to the Churches and Synagogues":

> [S]egregation is morally wrong and sinful. It is established on pride, hatred, and falsehood. It is unbrotherly and impersonal. Two segregated souls never meet in God. . . . To use the words of Martin Buber, segregation substitutes an "I–it" relationship for the "I–thou" relationship and ends up relegating persons to the status of things.[22]

King distilled this analysis in "Letter":

> Segregation, to use the terminology of . . . Martin Buber, substitutes an "I–it" relationship for an "I–thou" relationship and ends up relegating persons to the status of things.[23]

For his affirmation of interdependence, King borrowed another passage from Fosdick. Fosdick's "We are intermeshed in an inescapable mutuality" became King's "We are caught in an inescapable network of mutuality."[24]

The black church originally supplied King with ideas about nonconformity, nonviolence, segregation, interdependence, and other themes trumpeted in "Letter." Invoking sacred time, he compared himself to the prophets and Paul and talked about Jesus, Martin Luther, John Bunyan, Lincoln, and Jefferson as though they shared his cell block in Birmingham. Wielding his customary argument from authority, he also cited Socrates, Augustine, Aquinas, Tillich, Niebuhr, T. S. Eliot, and three Old Testament heroes.[25] He skillfully wove each of these references into the fabric of an astute analysis of segregation and civil disobedience in Birmingham.

While King drew on familiar sources for the content of "Letter," the intricate structure of his argument reflects his exposure to famous Euro-American philosophers, whose works offer many precedents of fine-spun philosophical persuasion. *Christian Century* and black and white sermons provide far fewer examples of the carefully layered appeals that structure "Letter."

King's essay can be seen as an exemplary, modern version of an oration from ancient Greece or Rome.[26] Basically "Letter" follows the steps of a typical classical speech: introduction, proposition, division, confirmation, refutation, and peroration. His tendency to move his argument forward through skillful digressions is a standard classical strategy. Offering a modest variation of classical form,

[21]Kelsey, "Christian Way" 44.

[22]King, Jr., "Challenge" 158–159.

[23]King, Jr., "Letter," *Why* 82. For correspondences between Kelsey's text and King's *Stride* and "Challenge," compare Kelsey, "Christian Way" 29, 40, 44, 47–48; King, Jr., *Stride* 104, 205–206, 210; and King, Jr., "Challenge" 158–159, 168.

[24]Compare Fosdick, *Riverside* 251–252 and King, Jr., "Letter," *Why* 77.

[25]The heroes were Shadrach, Meshach, and Abednego.

[26]Fulkerson makes this argument, which I summarize in this paragraph.

he packed the bulk of his argument into his refutation, effectively refuting both major and minor premises of the eight clergymen's implicit syllogisms.[27] He practiced "multipremise refutation" by expressing disappointment at being labelled an extremist, then folding that argument into a vigorous defense of certain forms of extremism.[28] His "tone of sadness and compulsion" and expert understatement (e.g., "I cannot join you in your praise of the Birmingham police department") also enjoy precedents in classical rhetoric.[29] By registering his humility, his understatements paradoxically buttress his claims instead of undermining them.

Layered philosophical argument is just as crucial to "Letter" as the black 25
conception of religious roles that made it possible in the first place. *Christian Century,* white sermons, and black folk religion also inform King's essay in powerful ways. "Letter" masterfully interlaces themes of Fosdick, Wofford, Crane, and Kelsey; invokes multiple authorities; reinvigorates the sacred time of the folk pulpit; and supplies rich Pauline allusions and other Biblical echoes. King carefully subsumed each of these appeals within a larger inductive argument consisting of box-within-a-box, multipremise refutation—an argument as lucid as it is intricate. His keen awareness of the readership of *Christian Century* enabled him to choose truisms from appropriate authorities (including Tillich, Niebuhr, and Martin Buber) that would fit suitably into his larger scheme.

King's study of philosophy and theology during his years at Crozer and Boston accounts for the classical argument that structures his essay. Classical rhetoric directly or indirectly influenced every masterpiece of Western philosophy and theology that King's professors assigned him to read. Though he often expressed the major themes of "Letter"—sometimes with remarkably similar wording—at no other time did he ever summon its rigorously ordered, predominantly inductive logic and controlled understatement.

The uniqueness of the essay results primarily from his decision to go to jail, which reflects Biblical and African-American precedents for combining the roles of preacher, theologian, and agitator. His isolation in Birmingham jail—an isolation he never again experienced—enabled him to translate into popular terms the kind of argument he learned in the academy.

CHALLENGING THE COMMUNITY

Despite the personal risk involved in challenging a community to which you are a member, writers do this all the time. Some writers identify their role as being a "gadfly" or "muckraker," someone who is willing to say what no one else wants to say. They believe that trying to find common ground would compro-

[27]See Fulkerson 129.

[28]Fulkerson 129.

[29]For "tone of sadness," see Fulkerson 126. For "I cannot . . . ," see King, Jr., "Letter," *Why* 936.

mise their values. And some writers—particularly those who use humor and satire—challenge the community because they think it is the most effective means of persuasion for the given moment.

Each of the following writers chooses to challenge the values of his or her community, but they all use different strategies. The first of these essays, "A Modest Proposal," by Jonathan Swift, is familiar to many students and is probably the most famous satirical work in English. Swift (1667–1745) was a clergyman, poet, and satirist, and either a personal friend or enemy of most of the writers in 18th-century England. He is best known for *Gulliver's Travels* (1726), a satirical novel later adapted as a children's story for Victorian readers. "A Modest Proposal," written in 1729, was Swift's response to the oppression of the impoverished Irish by their English rulers. The second essay, "We Do Abortions Here," describes Sallie Tisdale's experience as a nurse at an abortion clinic. Tisdale is the award-winning author of several nonfiction books, many of them written from her background in medicine. In some of her other writings, Tisdale identifies herself as a feminist (though not in this essay), and she holds a "pro-choice" position inasmuch as she believes that abortion is necessary and that women should have access to abortion, but she doesn't make this choice comfortable. In fact, Tisdale's essay is frequently used by anti-abortion groups as evidence of the horrors of an abortion clinic. "The Ones Who Walk Away from Omelas," by Ursula Le Guin, is a short story, not an essay, but it is still clearly an argument. Le Guin is the author of several science fiction and fantasy novels and short stories as well as critical essays on science fiction and fantasy. This speculative story arose from Le Guin's reading of "The Moral Philosopher and the Moral Life," an essay by psychologist and philosopher William James attacking the Utilitarian philosophy of John Stuart Mill and Jeremy Bentham ("the greatest good for the greatest number.") This story also has clear connections to the biblical ritual of the "scapegoat," where all the sins of the people were placed on the head of a goat, who was then led out into the desert to die. Le Guin's imaginary place, Omelas, is just "Salem, O." (Oregon) spelled backward. Le Guin said she got the idea from a street sign. The final selection in this set is "The Childswap Society," an essay by Sandra Feldman, president of the American Federation of Teachers, a national teacher's union. It was first published in the *New York Times,* January 4, 1998.

As you read these selections consider the following questions:

1. What is each author's claim? What reasons does each author give to support the claim? What assumptions are implied by these reasons? Are the claims, reasons, and assumptions explicit or implicit?
2. What impression do you form of the author? Is it necessary in some cases to distinguish the author from the speaker or narrator? How reliable is the speaker or narrator in each selection?
3. How does each author establish his or her credibility? In particular, how does each author establish the "moral authority" necessary to challenge the beliefs and values of the community?

4. What emotions do you feel as you read these essays? How does each author use emotional arguments? Which use humor? Which use horror? Do any use both?
5. Are there instances where the author restrains the use of emotion adopting an objective stance? What are the effects of such a detached, restrained presentation of highly emotional subject matter?
6. Children play an important role in each of these arguments. How does each author use children? In particular, what role do children play in emotional arguments? How would the arguments be different in each case if you substituted adults for children?
7. How does each author challenge the beliefs and values of the community? Do you find any of these arguments personally challenging?
8. Which authors use an indirect approach such as humor or satire? Which use a more direct approach? What are the advantages or disadvantages of one approach over another?

A Modest Proposal

For preventing the Children of Poor People in Ireland from Being a Burden to Their Parents or Country, and for Making Them Beneficial to the Public

JONATHAN SWIFT

IT IS A melancholy object to those who walk through this great town or travel in the country, when they see the streets, the roads, and cabin doors, crowded with beggars of the female sex, followed by three, four, or six children, all in rags and importuning every passenger for an alms. These mothers, instead of being able to work for their honest livelihood, are forced to employ all their time in strolling to beg sustenance for their helpless infants, who, as they grow up, either turn thieves for want of work, or leave their dear native country to fight for the Pretender in Spain, or sell themselves to the Barbados.[1] 1

I think it is agreed by all parties that this prodigious number of children in the arms, or on the backs, or at the heels of their mothers, and frequently of their fathers, is in the present deplorable state of the kingdom a very great additional grievance; and therefore whoever could find out a fair, cheap, and easy method of making these children sound, useful members of the commonwealth would deserve so well of the public as to have his statue set up for a preserver of the nation.

[1]The Pretender was James Stuart, the Catholic son of James II. Exiled in Spain, he sought to gain the throne his father had lost to the Protestant rulers William and Mary in 1688. Attempting to escape from destitution, many Irish people went to Barbados and other colonies as indentured servants.

But my intention is very far from being confined to provide only for the children of professed beggars; it is of a much greater extent, and shall take in the whole number of infants at a certain age who are born of parents in effect as little able to support them as those who demand our charity in the streets.

As to my own part, having turned my thoughts for many years upon this important subject, and maturely weighed the several schemes of other projectors, I have always found them grossly mistaken in their computation. It is true, a child just dropped from its dam may be supported by her milk for a solar year, with little other nourishment; at most not above the value of two shillings, which the mother may certainly get, or the value in scraps, by her lawful occupation of begging; and it is exactly at one year that I propose to provide for them in such a manner as instead of being a charge upon their parents or the parish, or wanting food and raiment for the rest of their lives, they shall on the contrary contribute to the feeding, and partly to the clothing, of many thousands.

There is likewise another great advantage in my scheme, that it will prevent 5
those voluntary abortions, and that horrid practice of women murdering their bastard children, alas, too frequent among us, sacrificing the poor innocent babes, I doubt, more to avoid the expense than the shame, which would move tears and pity in the most savage and inhuman breast.

The number of souls in this kingdom being usually reckoned one million and a half, of these I calculate there may be about two hundred thousand couples whose wives are breeders; from which number I subtract thirty thousand couples who are able to maintain their own children, although I apprehend there cannot be so many under the present distress of the kingdom; but this being granted, there will remain an hundred and seventy thousand breeders. I again subtract fifty thousand for those women who miscarry, or whose children die by accident or disease within the year. There only remain an hundred and twenty thousand children of poor parents annually born. The question therefore is, how this number shall be reared and provided for, which, as I have already said, under the present situation of affairs, is utterly impossible by all the methods hitherto proposed. For we can neither employ them in handicraft or agriculture; we neither build houses (I mean in the country) nor cultivate land. They can very seldom pick up a livelihood by stealing till they arrive at six years old, except where they are of towardly parts; although I confess they learn the rudiments much earlier, during which time they can however be looked upon only as probationers, as I have been informed by a principal gentleman in the county of Cavan, who protested to me that he never knew above one or two instances under the age of six, even in a part of the kingdom so renowned for the quickest proficiency in that art.

I am assured by our merchants that a boy or a girl before twelve years old is no salable commodity; and even when they come to this age they will not yield above three pounds, or three pounds and half a crown at most on the Exchange; which cannot turn to account either to the parents or the kingdom, the charge of nutriment and rags having been at least four times that value.

I shall now therefore humbly propose my own thoughts, which I hope will not be liable to the least objection.

I have been assured by a very knowing American of my acquaintance in London, that a young healthy child well nursed is at a year old a most delicious, nourishing, and wholesome food, whether stewed, roasted, baked, or boiled; and I make no doubt that it will equally serve in a fricassee or a ragout.

I do therefore humbly offer it to public consideration that of the hundred 10
and twenty thousand children, already computed, twenty thousand may be reserved for breed, whereof only one fourth part to be males, which is more than we allow to sheep, black cattle, or swine; and my reason is that these children are seldom the fruits of marriage, a circumstance not much regarded by our savages, therefore one male will be sufficient to serve four females. That the remaining hundred thousand may at a year old be offered in sale to the persons of quality and fortune through the kingdom, always advising the mother to let them suck plentifully in the last month, so as to render them plump and fat for a good table. A child will make two dishes at an entertainment for friends; and when the family dines alone, the fore or hind quarter will make a reasonable dish, and seasoned with a little pepper or salt will be very good boiled on the fourth day, especially in winter.

I have reckoned upon a medium that a child just born will weigh twelve pounds, and in a solar year if tolerably nursed increaseth to twenty-eight pounds.

I grant this food will be somewhat dear, and therefore very proper for landlords, who, as they have already devoured most of the parents, seem to have the best title to the children.

Infant's flesh will be in season throughout the year, but more plentiful in March, and a little before and after. For we are told by a grave author, an eminent French physician,[2] that fish being a prolific diet, there are more children born in Roman Catholic countries about nine months after Lent than at any other season; therefore, reckoning a year after Lent, the markets will be more glutted than usual, because the number of popish infants is at least three to one in this kingdom; and therefore it will have one other collateral advantage, by lessening the number of Papists among us.

I have already computed the charge of nursing a beggar's child (in which list I reckon all cottagers, laborers, and four-fifths of the farmers) to be about two shillings per annum, rags included; and I believe no gentleman would repine to give ten shillings for the carcass of a good fat child, which, as I have said, will make four dishes of excellent nutritive meat, when he hath only some particular friend or his own family to dine with him. Thus the squire will learn to be a good landlord, and grow popular among the tenants; the mother will have eight shillings net profit, and be fit for work till she produces another child.

[2]François Rabelais (1494?–1533) was the author of *Gargantua and Pantagruel,* a five-volume satire much admired by Swift.

15 Those who are more thrifty (as I must confess the times require) may flay the carcass; the skin of which artificially dressed will make admirable gloves for ladies, and summer boots for fine gentlemen.

As to our city of Dublin, shambles may be appointed for this purpose in the most convenient parts of it, and butchers we may be assured will not be wanting; although I rather recommend buying the children alive, and dressing them hot from the knife as we do roasting pigs.

A very worthy person, a true lover of his country, and whose virtues I highly esteem, was lately pleased in discoursing on this matter to offer a refinement upon my scheme. He said that many gentlemen of his kingdom, having of late destroyed their deer, he conceived that the want of venison might be well supplied by the bodies of young lads and maidens, not exceeding fourteen years of age nor under twelve, so great a number of both sexes in every country being now ready to starve for want of work and service; and these to be disposed of by their parents, if alive, or otherwise by their nearest relations. But with due deference to so excellent a friend and so deserving a patriot, I cannot be altogether in his sentiments; for as to the males, my American acquaintance assured me from frequent experience that their flesh was generally tough and lean, like that of our schoolboys, by continual exercise, and their taste disagreeable; and to fatten them would not answer the charge. Then as to the females, it would, I think with humble submission, be a loss to the public, because they soon would become breeders themselves; and besides, it is not improbable that some scrupulous people might be apt to censure such a practice (although indeed very unjustly) as a little bordering upon cruelty; which, I confess, hath always been with me the strongest objection against any project, how well soever intended.

But in order to justify my friend, he confessed that this expedient was put into his head by the famous Psalmanazar,[3] a native of the island of Formosa, who came from thence to London about twenty years ago, and in conversation told my friend that in his country when any young person happened to be put to death, the executioner sold the carcass to persons of quality as a prime dainty; and that in his time the body of a plump girl of fifteen, who was crucified for an attempt to poison the emperor, was sold to his Imperial Majesty's prime minister of state, and other great mandarins of the court, in joints from the gibbet, at four hundred crowns. Neither indeed can I deny that if the same use were made of several plump young girls in this town, who without one single groat to their fortunes cannot stir abroad without a chair, and appear at the playhouse and assemblies in foreign fineries which they never will pay for, the kingdom would not be the worse.

Some persons of a desponding spirit are in great concern about that vast number of poor people who are aged, diseased, or maimed, and I have been desired to employ my thoughts what course may be taken to ease the nation of so

[3]George Psalmanazar (1679?–1763) published an imaginary description of Formosa (Taiwan) and became well known in English society.

grievous an encumbrance. But I am not in the least pain upon that matter, because it is very well known that they are every day dying and rotting by cold and famine, and filth and vermin, as fast as can be reasonably expected. And as to the younger laborers, they are now in almost as hopeful a condition. They cannot get work, and consequently pine away for want of nourishment to a degree that if any time they are accidentally hired to common labor, they have not strength to perform it; and thus the country and themselves are happily delivered from the evils to come.

20 I have too long digressed, and therefore shall return to my subject. I think the advantages by the proposal which I have made are obvious and many, as well as of the highest importance.

For first, as I have already observed, it would greatly lessen the number of Papists, with whom we are yearly overrun, being the principal breeders of the nation as well as our most dangerous enemies; and who stay at home on purpose to deliver the kingdom to the Pretender, hoping to take their advantage by the absence of so many good Protestants, who have chosen rather to leave their country than to stay at home and pay tithes against their conscience to an Episcopal curate.

Secondly, the poorer tenants will have something valuable of their own, which by law may be made liable to distress, and help to pay their landlord's rent, their corn and cattle being already seized and money a thing unknown.

Thirdly, whereas the maintenance of an hundred thousand children, from two years old and upwards, cannot be computed at less than ten shillings a piece per annum, the nation's stock will be thereby increased fifty thousand pounds per annum, besides the profit of a new dish introduced to the tables of all gentlemen of fortune in the kingdom who have any refinement in taste. And the money will circulate among ourselves, the goods being entirely of our own growth and manufacture.

Fourthly, the constant breeders, besides the gain of eight shillings sterling per annum by the sale of their children, will be rid of the charge of maintaining them after the first year.

25 Fifthly, this food would likewise bring great custom to taverns, where the vintners will certainly be so prudent as to procure the best receipts for dressing it to perfection, and consequently have their houses frequented by all the fine gentlemen, who justly value themselves upon their knowledge in good eating; and a skillful cook, who understands how to oblige his guests, will contrive to make it as expensive as they please.

Sixthly, this would be a great inducement to marriage, which all wise nations have either encouraged by rewards or enforced by laws and penalties. It would increase the care and tenderness of mothers toward their children, when they were sure of a settlement for life to the poor babes, provided in some sort by the public, to their annual profit instead of expense. We should see an honest emulation among the married women, which of them could bring the fattest child to the market. Men would become as fond of their wives during the time of their pregnancy as they are now of their mares in foal, their cows in calf, or sows when they are ready to farrow; nor offer to beat or kick them (as is too frequent a practice) for fear of a miscarriage.

Many other advantages might be enumerated. For instance, the addition of some thousand carcasses in our exportation of barreled beef, the propagation of swine's flesh, and improvements in the art of making good bacon, so much wanted among us by the great destruction of pigs, too frequent at our tables, which are no way comparable in taste or magnificence to a well-grown, fat, yearling child, which roasted whole will make a considerable figure at a lord mayor's feast or any other public entertainment. But this and many others I omit, being studious of brevity.

Supposing that one thousand families in this city would be constant customers for infants' flesh, besides others who might have it at merry meetings, particularly weddings and christenings, I compute that Dublin would take off annually about twenty thousand carcasses, and the rest of the kingdom (where probably they will be sold somewhat cheaper) the remaining eighty thousand.

I can think of no one objection that will possibly be raised against this proposal, unless it should be urged that the number of people will be thereby much lessened in the kingdom. This I freely own, and it was indeed one principal design in offering it to the world. I desire the reader will observe, that I calculate my remedy for this one individual kingdom of Ireland and for no other that ever was, is, or I think ever can be upon earth. Therefore let no man talk to me of other expedients: of taxing our absentees five shillings a pound: of using neither clothes nor household furniture except what is of our own growth and manufacture: of utterly rejecting all materials and instruments that promote foreign luxury: of curing the expensiveness of pride, vanity, idleness, and gaming in our women: of introducing a vein of parsimony, prudence, and temperance: of learning to love our country, in the want of which we differ even from Laplanders and the inhabitants of Topinamboo: of quitting our animosities and factions, nor acting any longer like the Jews, who were murdering one another at the very moment their city was taken: of being a little cautious not to sell our country and conscience for nothing: of teaching landlords to have at least one degree of mercy toward their tenants: lastly, of putting a spirit of honesty, industry, and skill into our shopkeepers; who, if a resolution could now be taken to buy only our native goods, would immediately unite to cheat and exact upon us in the price, the measure, and the goodness, nor could even yet be brought to make one fair proposal of just dealing, though often and earnestly invited to it.

Therefore I repeat, let no man talk to me of these and the like expedients, 30
till he hath at least some glimpse of hope that there will ever be some hearty and sincere attempt to put them in practice.

But as to myself, having been wearied out for many years with offering vain, idle, visionary thoughts, and at length utterly despairing of success, I fortunately fell upon this proposal, which, as it is wholly new, so it hath something solid and real, of no expense and little trouble, full in our own power, and whereby we can incur no danger in disobliging England. For this kind of commodity will not bear exportation, the flesh being of too tender a consistence to admit a long continuance in salt, although perhaps I could name a country which would be glad to eat up our whole nation without it.

After all, I am not so violently bent upon my own opinion as to reject any offer proposed by wise men, which shall be found equally innocent, cheap, easy, and effectual. But before something of that kind shall be advanced in contradiction to my scheme, and offering a better, I desire the author or authors will be pleased maturely to consider two points. First, as things now stand, how they will be able to find food and raiment for an hundred thousand useless mouths and backs. And secondly, there being a round million of creatures in human figure throughout this kingdom, whose sole subsistence put into a common stock would leave them in debt two millions of pounds sterling, adding those who are beggars by profession to the bulk of farmers, cottagers, and laborers, with their wives and children who are beggars in effect; I desire those politicians who dislike my overture, and may perhaps be so bold as to attempt an answer, that they will first ask the parents of these mortals whether they would not at this day think it a great happiness to have been sold for food at a year old in the manner I prescribe, and thereby have avoided such a perpetual scene of misfortunes as they have since gone through by the oppression of landlords, the impossibility of paying rent without money or trade, the want of common sustenance, with neither house nor clothes to cover them from the inclemencies of the weather, and the most inevitable prospect of entailing the like or greater miseries upon their breed forever.

I profess, in the sincerity of my heart, that I have not the least personal interest in endeavoring to promote this necessary work, having no other motive than the public good of my country, by advancing our trade, providing for infants, relieving the poor, and giving some pleasure to the rich. I have no children by which I can propose to get a single penny; the youngest being nine years old, and my wife past childbearing.

We Do Abortions Here: A Nurse's Story

SALLIE TISDALE

WE DO abortions here; that is all we do. There are weary, grim moments 1
when I think I cannot bear another basin of bloody remains, utter another kind phrase of reassurance. So I leave the procedure room in the back and reach for a new chart. Soon I am talking to an eighteen-year-old woman pregnant for the fourth time. I push up her sleeve to check her blood pressure and find row upon row of needle marks, neat and parallel and discolored. She has been so

hungry for her drug for so long that she has taken to using the loose skin of her upper arms; her elbows are already a permanent ruin of bruises. She is surprised to find herself nearly four months pregnant. I suspect she is often surprised, in a mild way, by the blows she is dealt. I prepare myself for another basin, another brief and chafing loss.

"How can you stand it?" Even the clients ask. They see the machine, the strange instruments, the blood, the final stroke that wipes away the promise of pregnancy. Sometimes I see that too: I watch a woman's swollen abdomen sink to softness in a few stuttering moments and my own belly flip-flops with sorrow. But all it takes for me to catch my breath is another interview, one more story that sounds so much like the last one. There is a numbing sameness lurking in this job: the same questions, the same answers, even the same trembling tone in the voices. The worst is the sameness of human failure, of inadequacy in the face of each day's dull demands.

In describing this work, I find it difficult to explain how much I enjoy it most of the time. We laugh a lot here, as friends and professional peers. It's nice to be with women all day. I like the sudden, transient bonds I forge with some clients: moments when I am in my strength, remembering weakness, and a woman in weakness reaches out for my strength. What I offer is not power, but solidness, offered almost eagerly. Certain clients waken in me every tender urge I have—others make me wince and bite my tongue. Both challenge me to find a balance. It is a sweet brutality we practice here, a stark and loving dispassion.

I look at abortion as if I am standing on a cliff with a telescope, gazing at some great vista. I can sweep the horizon with both eyes, survey the scene in all its distance and size. Or I can put my eye to the lens and focus on the small details, suddenly so close. In abortion the absolute must always be tempered by the contextual, because both are real, both valid, both hard. How can we do this? How can we refuse? Each abortion is a measure of our failure to protect, to nourish our own. Each basin I empty is a promise—but a promise broken a long time ago.

5 I grew up on the great promise of birth control. Like many women my age, I took the pill as soon as I was sexually active. To risk pregnancy when it was so easy to avoid seemed stupid, and my contraceptive success, as it were, was part of the promise of social enlightenment. But birth control fails, far more frequently than our laboratory trials predict. Many of our clients take the pill; its failure to protect them is a shocking realization. We have clients who have been sterilized, whose husbands have had vasectomies; each one is a statistical misfit, fine print come to life. The anger and shame of these women I hold in one hand, and the basin in the other. The distance between the two, the length I pace and try to measure, is the size of an abortion.

The procedure is disarmingly simple. Women are surprised, as though the mystery of conception, a dark and hidden genesis, requires an elaborate finale. In the first trimester of pregnancy, it's a mere few minutes of vacuuming, a neat tidying up. I give a woman a small yellow Valium, and when it has begun to relax her, I lead her into the back, into bareness, the stirrups. The doctor reaches in her, opening the narrow tunnel to the uterus with a succession of slim, smooth bars of steel. He inserts a plastic tube and hooks it to a hose on the machine. The woman is framed against white paper that crackles as she moves, the light bright in her eyes. Then the machine rumbles low and loud in the small windowless room; the doctor moves the tube back and forth with an efficient rhythm, and the long tail of it fills with blood that spurts and stumbles along into a jar. He is usually finished in a few minutes. They are long minutes for the woman; her uterus frequently reacts to its abrupt emptying with a powerful, unceasing cramp, which cuts off the blood vessels and enfolds the irritated, bleeding tissue.

I am learning to recognize the shadows that cross the faces of the women I hold. While the doctor works between her spread legs, the paper drape hiding his intent expression, I stand beside the table. I hold the woman's hands in mine, resting them just below her ribs. I watch her eyes, finger her necklace, stroke her hair. I ask about her job, her family; in a haze she answers me; we chatter, faces close, eyes meeting and sliding apart.

I watch the shadows that creep up unnoticed and suddenly darken her face as she screws up her features and pushes a tear out each side to slide down her cheeks. I have learned to anticipate the quiver of chin, the rapid intake of breath and the surprising sobs that rise soon after the machine starts to drum. I know this is when the cramp deepens, and the tears are partly the tears that follow pain—the sharp, childish crying when one bumps one's head on a cabinet door. But a well of woe seems to open beneath many women when they hear that thumping sound. The anticipation of the moment has finally come to fruit; the moment has arrived when the loss is no longer an imagined one. It has come true.

I am struck by the sameness and I am struck every day by the variety here—how this commonplace dilemma can so display the differences of women. A 21-year-old woman, unemployed, uneducated, without family, in the fifth month of her fifth pregnancy. A 42-year-old mother of teenagers, shocked by her condition, refusing to tell her husband. A 23-year-old mother of two having her seventh abortion, and many women in their thirties having their first. Some are stoic, some hysterical, a few giggle uncontrollably, many cry.

I talk to a 16-year-old uneducated girl who was raped. She has gonorrhea. 10
She describes blinding headaches, attacks of breathlessness, nausea. "Sometimes I feel like two different people," she tells me with a calm smile, "and I talk to myself."

I pull out my plastic models. She listens patiently for a time, and then holds her hands wide in front of her stomach. "When's the baby going to go up into my stomach?" she asks.

I blink. "What do you mean?"

"Well," she says, still smiling, "when women get so big, isn't the baby in your stomach? Doesn't it hatch out of an egg there?"

My first question in an interview is always the same. As I walk down the hall with the woman, as we get settled in chairs and I glance through her files, I am trying to gauge her, to get a sense of the words, and the tone, I should use. With some I joke, with others I chat, sometimes I fall into a brisk, business-like patter. But I ask every woman, "Are you sure you want to have an abortion?" Most nod with grim knowing smiles. "Oh yes," they sigh. Some seek forgiveness, offer excuses. Occasionally a woman will flinch and say, "Please don't use that word."

Later I describe the procedure to come, using care with my language. I 15
don't say "pain" any more than I would say "baby." So many are afraid to ask how much it will hurt. "My sister told me—" I hear. "A friend of mine said—" and the dire expectations unravel. I prick the index finger of a woman for a drop of blood to test, and as the tiny lancet approaches the skin she averts her eyes, holding her trembling hand out to me and jumping at my touch.

It is when I am holding a plastic uterus in one hand, a suction tube in the other, moving them together in imitation of the scrubbing to come, that women ask the most secret question. I am speaking in a matter-of-fact voice about "the tissue" and "the contents" when the woman suddenly catches my eye and asks, "How big is the baby now?" These words suggest a quiet need for a definition of the boundaries being drawn. It isn't so odd, after all, that she feels relief when I describe the growing bud's bulbous shape, its miniature nature. Again I gauge, and sometimes lie a little, weaseling around its infantile features until its clinging power slackens.

But when I look in the basin, among the curdlike blood clots, I see an elfin thorax, attenuated, its pencilline ribs all in parallel rows with tiny knobs of spine rounding upwards. A translucent arm and hand swim beside.

A sleepy-eyed girl, just 14, watched me with a slight and goofy smile all through her abortion. "Does it have little feet and little fingers and all?" she'd asked earlier. When the suction was over she sat up woozily at the end of the table and murmured, "Can I see it?" I shook my head firmly.

"It's not allowed," I told her sternly, because I knew she didn't really want to see what was left. She accepted this statement of authority, and a shadow of confused relief crossed her plain, pale face.

Privately, even grudgingly, my colleagues might admit the power of abor- 20
tion to provoke emotion. But they seem to prefer the broad view and disdain the telescope. Abortion is a matter of choice, privacy, control. Its uncertainty lies in specific cases: retarded women and girls too young to give consent for surgery, women who are ill or hostile or psychotic. Such common dilemmas are met with both compassion and impatience: they slow things down. We are too busy to chew over ethics. One person might discuss certain concerns, behind closed doors, or describe a particularly disturbing dream. But generally there is to be no ambivalence.

Every day I take calls from women who are annoyed that we cannot see them, cannot do their abortion today, this morning, now. They argue the price, demand that we stay after hours to accommodate their job or class schedule. Abortion is so routine that one expects it to be like a manicure: quick, cheap, and painless.

Still, I've cultivated a certain disregard. It isn't negligence, but I don't always pay attention. I couldn't be here if I tried to judge each case on its merits; after all, we do over a hundred abortions a week. At some point each individual in this line of work draws a boundary and adheres to it. For one physician the boundary is a particular week of gestation; for another, it is a certain number of repeated abortions. But these boundaries can be fluid too: one physician overruled his own limit to abort a mature but severely malformed fetus. For me, the limit is allowing my clients to carry their own burden, shoulder the responsibility themselves. I shoulder the burden of trying not to judge them.

This city has several "crisis pregnancy centers" advertised in the Yellow Pages. They are small offices staffed by volunteers, and they offer free pregnancy testing, glossy photos of dead fetuses, and movies. I had a client recently whose mother is active in the anti-abortion movement. The young woman went to the local crisis center and was told that the doctor would make her touch her dismembered baby, that the pain would be the most horrible she could imagine, and that she might, after an abortion, never be able to have children. All lies. They called her at home and at work, over and over and over, but she had been wise enough to give a false name. She came to us a fugitive. We who do abortions are marked, by some, as impure. It's dirty work.

When a deliveryman comes to the sliding glass window by the reception desk and tilts a box toward me, I hesitate. I read the packing slip, assess the shape and weight of the box in light of its supposed contents. We request familiar faces. The doors are carefully locked; I have learned to half glance around at bags and boxes, looking for a telltale sign. I register with security when I arrive, and I am careful not to bang a door. We are all a little on edge here.

Concern about size and shape seem to be natural, and so is the relief that 25
follows. We make the powerful assumption that the fetus is different from us, and even when we admit the similarities, it is too simplistic to be seduced by form alone. But the form is enormously potent—humanoid, powerless, palm-sized, and pure, it evokes an almost fierce tenderness when viewed simply as what it appears to be. But appearance, and even potential, aren't enough. The fetus, in becoming itself, can ruin others; its utter dependence has a sinister side. When I am struck in the moment by the contents in the basin, I am careful to remember the context, to note the tearful teenager and the woman sighing with something more than relief. One kind of question, though, I find considerably trickier.

"Can you tell what it is?" I am asked, and this means gender. This question is asked by couples, not women alone. Always couples would abort a girl and keep a boy. I have been asked about twins, and even if I could tell what race the father was.

An 18-year-old woman with three daughters brought her husband to the interview. He glared first at me, then at his wife, as he sank lower and lower in the chair, picking his teeth with a toothpick. He interrupted a conversation with his wife to ask if I could tell whether the baby would be a boy or girl. I told him I could not.

"Good," he replied in a slow and strangely malevolent voice, "cause if it was a boy I'd wring her neck."

In a literal sense, abortion exists because we are able to ask such questions, able to assign a value to the fetus which can shift with changing circumstances. If the human bond to a child were as primitive and unflinchingly narrow as that of other animals, there would be no abortion. There would be no abortion because there would be nothing more important than caring for the young and perpetuating the species, no reason for sex but to make babies. I sense this sometimes, this wordless organic duty, when I do ultrasounds.

We do ultrasound, a sound-wave test that paints a faint, gray picture of the 30
fetus, whenever we're uncertain of gestation. Age is measured by the width of the skull and confirmed by the length of the femur or thighbone; we speak of a pregnancy as being a certain "femur length" in weeks. The usual concern is whether a pregnancy is within the legal limit for an abortion. Women this far along have bellies which swell out round and tight like trim muscles. When they lie flat, the mound rises softly above the hips, pressing the umbilicus upward.

It takes practice to read an ultrasound picture, which is grainy and etched as though in strokes of charcoal. But suddenly a rapid rhythmic motion appears—the beating heart. Nearby is a soft oval, scratched with lines—the skull. The leg is harder to find, and then suddenly the fetus moves, bobbing in the surf. The skull turns away, an arm slides across the screen, the torso rolls. I know the weight of a baby's head on my shoulder; the whisper of lips on ears, the delicate curve of a fragile spine in my hand. I know how heavy and correct a newborn cradled feels. The creature I watch in secret requires nothing from me but to be left alone, and that is precisely what won't be done.

These inadvertently made beings are caught in a twisting web of motive and desire. They are at least inconvenient, sometimes quite literally dangerous in the womb, but most often they fall somewhere in between—consequences never quite believed in come to roost. Their virtue rises and falls outside their own nature: they become only what we make them. A fetus created by accident is the most absolute kind of surprise. Whether the blame lies in a failed IUD, a slipped condom, or a false impression of safety, that fetus is a thing whose creation has been actively worked against. Its existence is an error. I think this is why so few women, even late in a pregnancy, will consider giving a baby up for adoption. To do so means making the fetus real—imagining it as something whole and outside oneself. The decision to terminate a pregnancy is sometimes so difficult and confounding that it creates an enormous demand for immediate action. The decision is a rejection: the pregnancy has become something to be rid of, a condition to be ended. It is a burden, a weight, a thing separate.

Women have abortions because they are too old, and too young, too poor, and too rich, too stupid, and too smart. I see women who berate themselves with violent emotions for their first and only abortion, and others who return three times, five times, hauling two or three children, who cannot remember to take a pill or where they put the diaphragm. We talk glibly about choice. But the choice for what? I see all the broken promises in lives lived like a series of impromptu obstacles. There are the sweet, light promises of love and intimacy, the glittering promise of education and progress, the warm promise of safe families, long years of innocence and community. And there is the promise of freedom: freedom from failure, from faithlessness. Freedom from biology. The early feminist defense of abortion asked many questions, but the one I remember is this: Is biology destiny? And the answer is yes, sometimes it is. Women who have the fewest choices of all exercise their right to abortion the most.

Oh, the ignorance. I take a woman to the back room and ask her to undress; a few minutes later I return and find her positioned discreetly behind a drape, still wearing underpants. "Do I have to take these off too?" she asks, a little shocked. Some swear they have not had sex, many do not know what a uterus is, how sperm and egg meet, how sex makes babies. Some late seekers do not believe themselves pregnant; they believe themselves *impregnable*. I was chastised when I began this job for referring to some clients as girls: it is a feminist heresy. They come so young, snapping gum, sockless and sneakered, and their shakily applied eyeliner smears when they cry. I call them girls with maternal benignity. I cannot imagine them as mothers.

The doctor seats himself between the woman's thighs and reaches into the 35
dilated opening of a five-month pregnant uterus. Quickly he grabs and crushes the fetus in several places, and the room is filled with a low clatter and snap of forceps, the click of the tanaculum, and a pulling, sucking sound. The paper crinkles as the drugged and sleepy woman shifts, the nurse's low, honey-brown voice explains each step in delicate words.

I have fetus dreams, we all do here: dreams of abortions one after the other; of buckets of blood splashed on the walls; trees full of crawling fetuses. I dreamed that two men grabbed me and began to drag me away. "Let's do an abortion," they said with a sickening leer, and I began to scream, plunged into a vision of sucking, scraping pain, and being spread and torn by impartial instruments that do only what they are bidden. I woke from this dream barely able to breathe and thought of kitchen tables and coat hangers, knitting needles striped with blood, and women all alone clutching a pillow in their teeth to keep the screams from piercing the apartment-house walls. Abortion is the narrowest edge between kindness and cruelty. Done as well as it can be, it is still violence—merciful violence, like putting a suffering animal to death.

Maggie, one of the nurses, received a call at midnight not long ago. It was a woman in her twentieth week of pregnancy; the necessarily gradual process of cervical dilation begun the day before had stimulated labor, as it sometimes does. Maggie and one of the doctors met the woman at the office in the night. Maggie helped her onto the table, and as she lay down the fetus was delivered into Maggie's hands. When Maggie told me about it the next day, she cupped her hands into a small bowl—"It was just like a little kitten," she said softly, wonderingly. "Everything was still attached."

At the end of the day I clean out the suction jars, pouring blood into the sink, splashing the sides with flecks of tissue. From the sink rises a rich and humid smell, hot, earthy, and moldering; it is the smell of something recently alive beginning to decay. I take care of the plastic tub on the floor, filled with pieces too big to be trusted to the trash. The law defines the contents of the bucket I hold protectively against my chest as "tissue." Some would say my complicity in filling that bucket gives me no right to call it anything else. I slip the tissue gently into a bag and place it in the freezer, to be burned at another time. Abortion requires of me an entirely new set of assumptions. It requires a willingness to live with conflict, fearlessness, and grief. As I close the freezer door, I imagine a world where this won't be necessary, and then return to the world where it is.

The Ones Who Walk Away from Omelas (Variations on a Theme by William James)

URSULA K. LE GUIN

WITH A CLAMOR of bells that set the swallows soaring, the Festival of Summer came to the city Omelas, bright-towered by the sea. The rigging of the boats in harbor sparkled with flags. In the streets between houses with red roofs and painted walls, between old moss-grown gardens and under avenues of trees, past great parks and public buildings, processions moved. Some were decorous: old people in long stiff robes of mauve and grey, grave master workmen, quiet, merry women carrying their babies, and chattering as they walked. In other streets the music beat faster, a shimmering of gong and tambourine, and the people went dancing, the procession was a dance. Children dodged in and out, their high calls rising like the swallows' crossing flights over the music and the singing. All the processions wound towards the north side of the city, where on the great water-meadow called the Green Fields boys and girls, naked in the bright air, with mud-stained feet and ankles and long, lithe arms, exercised their restive horses before the race. The horses wore no gear at all but a halter without bit. Their manes were braided with streamers of silver, gold, and green. They flared their nostrils and pranced and boasted to one another; they were vastly excited, the horse being the only animal who had adopted our ceremonies as his own. Far off to the north and west the mountains stood up half encircling Omelas on her bay. The air of morning was so clear that the snow still crowning the Eighteen Peaks burned with white-gold fire across the miles of sunlit air, under the dark blue of the sky. There was just enough wind to make the banners 1 that marked the racecourse snap and flutter now and then. In the silence of the broad green meadows one could hear the music winding through the city streets, farther and nearer and ever approaching, a cheerful faint sweetness of the air that from time to time trembled and gathered together and broke out into the great joyous clanging of the bells.

Joyous! How is one to tell about joy? How describe the citizens of Omelas?

They were not simple folk, you see, though they were happy. But we do not say the words of cheer much any more. All smiles have become archaic. Given a description such as this one tends to make certain assumptions. Given a description such as this one tends to look next for the King, mounted on a splendid stallion and surrounded by his noble knights, or perhaps in a golden litter borne by great-muscled slaves. But there was no king. They did not use swords, or keep slaves. They were not barbarians. I do not know the rules and laws of their society, but I suspect that they were singularly few. As they did without monarchy and slavery, so they also get on without the stock exchange, the advertisement, the secret police, and the bomb. Yet I repeat that these were not simple folk, not dulcet shepherds, noble savages, bland utopians. They were not less complex than us. The trouble is that we have a bad habit, encouraged by pedants and sophisticates, of considering happiness as something rather stupid. Only pain is intellectual, only evil interesting. This is the treason of the artist: a refusal to admit the banality of evil and the terrible boredom of pain. If you can't lick 'em, join 'em. If it hurts, repeat it. But to praise despair is to condemn delight, to embrace violence is to lose hold of everything else. We have almost lost hold; we can no longer describe a happy man, nor make any celebration of joy. How can I tell you about the people of Omelas? They were not naïve and happy children—though their children were, in fact, happy. They were mature, intelligent, passionate adults whose lives were not wretched. O miracle! but I wish I could describe it better. I wish I could convince you. Omelas sounds in my words like a city in a fairy tale, long ago and far away, once upon a time. Perhaps it would be best if you imagined it as your own fancy bids, assuming it will rise to the occasion, for certainly I cannot suit you all. For instance, how about technology? I think that there would be no cars or helicopters in and above the streets; this follows from the fact that the people of Omelas are happy people. Happiness is based on a just discrimination of what is necessary, what is neither necessary nor destructive, and what is destructive. In the middle category, however—that of the unnecessary but undestructive, that of comfort, luxury, exuberance, etc.—they could perfectly well have central heating, subway trains, washing machines, and all kinds of marvelous devices not yet invented here, floating light-sources, fuelless power, a cure for the common cold. Or they could have none of that: it doesn't matter. As you like it. I incline to think that people from towns up and down the coast have been coming in to Omelas during the last days before the Festival on very fast little trains and double-decked trams, and that the train station of Omelas is actually the handsomest building in town, though plainer than the magnificent Farmers' Market. But even granted trains, I fear that Omelas so far strikes some of you as goody-goody. Smiles, bells, parades, horses, bleh. If so, please add an orgy. If an orgy would help, don't hesitate. Let us not, however, have temples from which issue beautiful nude priests and priestesses already half in ecstasy and ready to copulate with any man or woman, lover or stranger, who desires union with the deep godhead of the blood, although that was my first idea. But really it would be better not to have any temples in Omelas—at least, not manned temples. Religion yes, clergy no. Surely the beautiful nudes can just wander about, offering themselves like divine soufflés to the hunger of the needy and the rapture of the flesh. Let them join the processions. Let tambourines be struck above the copulations, and the glory of desire be proclaimed upon the gongs, and (a not unimportant point) let the offspring of these delightful rituals be beloved and looked after by all. One thing I know there is none of in Omelas is guilt. But what else should there be? I thought at first there were no drugs, but that is puritanical. For those who like it, the faint insistent sweetness of *drooz* may perfume the ways of the city, *drooz* which first brings a great lightness and brilliance to the mind and limbs, and then after some hours a dreamy languor, and wonderful visions at last of the very arcana and inmost secrets of the Universe, as well as exciting the pleasure of sex beyond all belief; and it is not habit-forming. For more modest tastes I think there ought to be beer. What else, what else belongs in the joyous city? The sense of victory, surely, the celebration of courage. But as we did without clergy, let us do without soldiers. The joy built upon successful slaughter is not the right kind of joy; it will not do; it is fearful and it is trivial. A boundless and generous contentment, a magnanimous triumph felt not against some outer enemy but in communion with the finest and fairest in the souls of all men everywhere and the splendor of the world's summer: this is what swells the hearts of the people of Omelas, and the victory they celebrate is that of life. I really don't think many of them need to take *drooz*.

Most of the processions have reached the Green Fields by now. A marvelous smell of cooking, goes forth from the red and blue tents of the provisioners. The faces of small children are amiably sticky; in the benign grey beard of a man a couple of crumbs of rich pastry are entangled. The youths and girls have mounted their horses and are beginning to group around the starting line of the course. An old woman, small, fat, and laughing, is passing out flowers from a basket, and tall young men wear her flowers in their shining hair. A child of nine or ten sits at the edge of the crowd alone, playing on a wooden flute. People pause to listen, and they smile, but they do not speak to him, for he never ceases playing and never sees them, his dark eyes wholly rapt in the sweet, thin magic of the tune.

He finishes, and slowly lowers his hands holding the wooden flute. 5

As if that little private silence were the signal, all at once a trumpet sounds from the pavilion near the starting line: imperious, melancholy, piercing. The horses rear on their slender legs, and some of them neigh in answer. Soberfaced, the young riders stroke the horses' necks and soothe them, whispering, "Quiet, quiet, there my beauty, my hope. . . ." They begin to form in rank along the starting line. The crowds along the racecourse are like a field of grass and flowers in the wind. The Festival of Summer has begun.

Do you believe? Do you accept the festival, the city, the joy? No? Then let me describe one more thing.

In a basement under one of the beautiful public buildings of Omelas, or perhaps in the cellar of one of its spacious private homes, there is a room. It has one locked door, and no window. A little light seeps in dustily between cracks in the boards, secondhand from a cobwebbed window somewhere across the cellar. In one corner of the little room a couple of mops, with stiff, clotted, foul-smelling heads, stand near a rusty bucket. The floor is dirt, a little damp to the touch, as cellar dirt usually is. The room is about three paces long and two wide: a mere broom closet or disused tool room. In the room a child is sitting. It could be a boy or a girl. It looks about six, but actually is nearly ten. It is feeble-minded. Perhaps it was born defective, or perhaps it has become imbecile through fear, malnutrition, and neglect. It picks its nose and occasionally fumbles vaguely with its toes or genitals, as it sits hunched in the corner farthest from the bucket and the two mops. It is afraid of the mops. It finds them horrible. It shuts its eyes, but it knows the mops are still standing there; and the door is locked; and nobody will come. The door is always locked; and nobody ever comes, except that sometimes—the child has no understanding of time or interval—sometimes the door rattles terribly and opens, and a person, or several people, are there. One of them may come in and kick the child to make it stand up. The others never come close, but peer in at it with frightened, disgusted eyes. The food bowl and the water jug are hastily filled, the door is locked, the eyes disappear. The people at the door never say anything, but the child, who has not always lived in the tool room, and can remember sunlight and its mother's voice, sometimes speaks. "I will be good," it says. "Please let me out. I will be good!" They never answer. The child used to scream for help at night, and cry a good deal, but now it only makes a kind of whining, "eh-haa, eh-haa," and it speaks less and less often. It is so thin there are no calves to its legs; its belly protrudes; it lives on a half-bowl of corn meal and grease a day. It is naked. Its buttocks and thighs are a mass of festered sores, as it sits in its own excrement continually.

They all know it is there, all the people of Omelas. Some of them have come to see it, others are content merely to know it is there. They all know that it has to be there. Some of them understand why, and some do not, but they all understand that their happiness, the beauty of their city, the tenderness of their friendships, the health of their children, the wisdom of their scholars, the skill of their makers, even the abundance of their harvest and the kindly weathers of their skies, depends wholly on this child's abominable misery.

10 This is usually explained to children when they are between eight and twelve, whenever they seem capable of understanding; and most of those who come to see the child are young people, though often enough an adult comes, or comes back, to see the child. No mater how well the matter has been explained to them, these young spectators are always shocked and sickened at the

sight. They feel disgust, which they had thought themselves superior to. They feel anger, out-rage, impotence, despite all the explanations. They would like to do something for the child. But there is nothing they can do. If the child were brought up into the sunlight out of that vile place, if it were cleaned and fed and comforted, that would be a good thing, indeed; but if it were done, in that day and hour all the prosperity and beauty and delight of Omelas would wither and be destroyed. Those are the terms. To exchange all the goodness and grace of every life in Omelas for that single, small improvement: to throw away the happiness of thousands for the chance of the happiness of one: that would be to let guilt within the walls indeed.

The terms are strict and absolute; there may not even be a kind word spoken to the child.

Often the young people go home in tears, or in a tearless rage, when they have seen the child and faced this terrible paradox. They may brood over it for weeks or years. But as time goes on they begin to realize that even if the child could be released, it would not get much good of its freedom: a little vague pleasure of warmth and food, no doubt, but little more. It is too degraded and imbecile to know any real joy. It has been afraid too long even to be free of fear. Its habits are too uncouth for it to respond to humane treatment. Indeed, after so long it would probably be wretched without walls about it to protect it, and darkness for its eyes, and its own excrement to sit in. Their tears at the bitter injustice dry when they begin to perceive the terrible justice of reality, and to accept it. Yet it is their tears and anger, the trying of their generosity and the acceptance of their helplessness, which are perhaps the true source of the splendor of their lives. Theirs is no vapid, irresponsible happiness. They know that they, like the child, are not free. They know compassion. It is the existence of the child, and their knowledge of its existence, that makes possible the nobility of their architecture, and poignancy of their music, the profundity of their science. It is because of the child that they are so gentle with children. They know that if the wretched one were not there snivelling in the dark, the other one, the flute-player, could make no joyful music as the young riders line up in their beauty for the race in the sunlight of the first morning of summer.

Now do you believe in them? Are they not more credible? But there is one more thing to tell, and this is quite incredible.

At times one of the adolescent girls or boys who go to see the child does not go home to weep or rage, does not, in fact, go home at all. Sometimes also a man or woman much older falls silent for a day or two, and then leaves home. These people go out into the street, and walk down the street alone. They keep walking, and walk straight out of the city of Omelas, through the beautiful gates. They keep walking across the farmlands of Omelas. Each one goes alone, youth or girl, man or woman. Night falls; the traveler must pass down village streets, between the houses with yellow-lit windows, and on out into the darkness of the fields. Each alone, they go west or north, towards the mountains. They go on. They leave Omelas, they walk ahead into the darkness, and they do not come back. The place they go towards is a place even less imaginable to most of us than the city of happiness. I cannot describe it at all. It is possible that it does not exist. But they seem to know where they are going, the ones who walk away from Omelas.

The Childswap Society

SANDRA FELDMAN

1 MANY YEARS ago, when I was a teenager, I read a science fiction story that I've never been able to forget. It came back to me with special force this holiday season because I was thinking about this country's national shame—a child poverty rate of 25 percent—and about our lack of urgency in dealing with the problems this poverty creates.

The story described a society with a national child lottery which was held every four years. Every child's name was put into it—there were no exceptions—and children were randomly redistributed to new parents, who raised them for the next four years.

Babies were not part of this lottery. Parents got to keep their newborn children until the next lottery, but then they became part of the national childswap. The cycle was broken every third swap and kids were sent back to their original parents until the next lottery. So by the time you were considered an adult, at age 26, the most time you could have spent with your birth parents was 10 years. The other 16 were simply a matter of chance.

THE LUCK OF THE DRAW

Maybe one of your new parents would be the head of a gigantic multinational company and the most powerful person in the country or the president of a famous university. Or you might find yourself the child of a family living in a public housing project or migrant labor camp.

5 The whole idea sounded horrible to me, but people in the childswap society took the lottery for granted. They didn't try to hide their children or send them away to other countries; childswapping was simply part of their culture. And one thing the lottery did was to make the whole society very conscientious about how things were arranged for kids. After all, you never knew where your own child would end up after the next lottery, so in a very real sense everyone's child was—or could be—yours. As a result, children growing up under this system got everything they needed to thrive, both physically and intellectually, and the society itself was harmonious.

What if someone wrote a story about what American society in the late twentieth century takes for granted in the arrangements for its children? We might not want to admit it, but don't we take for granted that some kids are going to have much better lives than others? Of course. We take for granted that some will get the best medical treatment and others will be able to get little or none. We take for granted that some kids will go to beautiful, well-cared-for schools with top-notch curriculums, excellent libraries, and computers for every child and others will go to schools where there are not enough desks and textbooks to go around—wretched places where even the toilets don't work.

We take for granted that teachers in wealthy suburban schools will be better paid and better trained than those in poor inner-city or rural schools. We take for granted, in so many ways, that the children whom the lottery of birth has made the most needy will get the least. "After all," we say to ourselves, "it's up to each family to look after its own. If some parents can't give their children what they need to thrive, that's *their* problem."

WHAT WOULD HAPPEN?

Obviously I'm not suggesting that the United States adopt a childswap system. The idea makes me cringe, and, anyway, it's just a fable. But I like to imagine what would happen if we did.

We'd start with political figures and their children and grandchildren, with governors and mayors and other leaders. What do you suppose would happen when they saw that their children would have the same chance as the sons and daughters of poor people—no more and no less? What would happen to our schools and health-care system—and our shameful national indifference to children who are not ours?

I bet we'd quickly find a way to set things straight and make sure *all* chil- 10
dren had an equal chance to thrive.

TAKING YOUR TURN

Newsweek magazine runs a weekly feature called "My Turn," a column that allows ordinary people the chance to tell their story to a national audience. According to *Newsweek,* some "My Turn" essayists "try to persuade readers to take action or agree with a point of view"; others "simply share experiences, feelings or reflections. The personal experience or observation draws readers into the essay and helps them make a connection with the writer and the ideas." The experiences of "My Turn" essayists usually aren't profound, and the writers are rarely well known or influential. But they show the ability to use their direct experience to address a national readership and to offer thoughtful, fresh insights. The following essays are a sampling of "My Turn" columns from *Newsweek.* As a class, you could just as easily make your own collection. As you read these essays, consider the following questions:

1. What is the claim or main idea of each essay? Are some more expressly argumentative than others? What reasons and assumptions support the author's claim?
2. Since readers know very little about each author, how does each author establish credibility and a sense of self? What role does personal experience play in establishing credibility?
3. How does each author use emotion? How does the author make the emotion real for the reader?
4. Which essays do you personally relate to? Why?

SUVs: Fuel-Wasting Garbage Trucks?

TITO MORALES[1]

I SUPPOSE we should be gloating a bit right now, those of us who don't drive sport utility vehicles. What with the rising cost of gasoline putting the squeeze on folks who tool about town in the reputedly bigger-is-better tanks, the current gas crunch is merely a case of "what goes around, comes around," right? But whenever I think about how truly wasteful those behemoths are, I feel despondent, not smug, because I know that their gross fuel inefficiency affects us all. 1

I admit it. I have never liked SUVs, and I'm as tired of their overblown proportions as anyone else. I'm frustrated when I have to strain to see through or around them while I'm driving in traffic. And I'm fed up with having to squeeze into my parked car because an SUV driver has wedged his or her vehicle too close to mine. I'm pretty sure I could learn to cope with these minor inconveniences, if there wasn't the much broader issue of how SUVs hurt our environment.

Many of us are old enough to remember the gasoline shortage of the '70s, when car owners waited to refuel on the day of the week that corresponded with their odd- or even-numbered license plates. We vividly remember when there were so many cars lined up at the pumps that they overflowed out of the service-station driveways. We can recall when terms such as "Earth Day," and "recycling" came into our collective consciousness. And while a subject such as ozone depletion may have initially seemed too remote to concern us, all we've needed to do lately is look at changing weather patterns to realize that hey, our actions *do* affect our environment.

Why, then, do our automakers mass-produce vehicles that burn through precious fossil fuel and spew pollution? Why have so many consumers been so quick to embrace SUVs? I know one family of four—two adults and two

[1]Morales lives in Pacific Palisades, California.

teenagers—who each drive their own SUV. The front of their house resembles a truck stop more than a residential driveway. Any day I'm half-expecting them to install a gas pump next to the mailbox.

We've all heard SUV owners' arguments for these testaments to excess: how 5
they're ideal for off-road driving and convenient for carpooling and hauling. In my neighborhood, though, the tires of the SUVs are always showroom-clean and there's rarely ever more than one passenger and a Labrador retriever inside (and never a boat or horse trailer attached to them). And it may be true that SUVs provide a measure of safety for their occupants, but what about the other drivers on the road? Not long ago a friend of mine was involved in a collision with an SUV. While damage to the light truck was minimal, the injuries to my friend and her car were greatly exacerbated by the disparity in vehicle sizes.

Reports of the SUV's poor emissions records have been trumpeted by environmental groups for years. Some of the vehicles, we read, actually spew as much pollution as two average-size cars. "It's basically a garbage truck that dumps its pollution into the sky," said the director of the Sierra Club's Global Warming and Energy Program when Ford unveiled its nine-passenger, 12-mile-per-gallon Excursion back in February of 1999. You read right—12. The Model T probably did better than that.

Last month Ford took an important first step when it admitted publicly that its approach to SUVs and the environment has not always been a responsible one. Admission or no, Ford and the rest of the auto industry continue to reap tremendous profits from our insatiable appetite for these steroid-pumped vehicles, and they don't appear likely to dramatically alter their latest recipe for success.

If there's one positive thing that can be said about the current gas dilemma, it's that maybe a few potential SUV buyers will come to their senses when they realize how much it will cost to keep these giants fueled. But I sometimes wonder whether these trend-followers are too self-involved to possess any sense in the first place. I find it extremely insulting, for example, to see how many of these gas guzzlers are now sporting environmental-protection-theme license plates. I don't know if those drivers are trying to alleviate their guilt by directing a nominal portion of their annual DMV fees toward environmental causes. The truth is they may as well be using the images of Yosemite, the Everglades and Cape Cod for target practice.

Yes, I suppose we should be feeling somewhat smug, we non-SUVers.

But we're not. Maybe we're bigger than that.

What Does Online Shopping Cost Us?

PATRICK VALA-HAYNES[1]

IT'S NOT about the money. It's never been about the money. As a young 1
couple with degrees in humanities and history, my wife, Robbie, and I didn't buy a bicycle shop 20 years ago near the Oregon Coast Range because we had dreams of great riches. We simply hoped that being self-employed would allow us to pursue our many interests—gardening, horses, theater—and maybe support a family. Robbie chose another career a few years after our daughter and son were born, but I've yet to find a good reason to change my profession.

Four days before Christmas last year, a gentleman walked into my shop near closing time. He wore a fine wool suit and a silk tie.

"How are you tonight?" I asked.

"Good, good," he huffed, his eyes wandering around the store.

"Can I help you find something?" 5

"Yes, yes. I'm looking for a—I'm not sure what you call it—one of those!" He pointed at a bicycle touring trailer and seemed relieved to have found it. "I've been searching for one all week."

"Really? Where have you looked?" I was curious as to why he hadn't bothered to check our store first, since we have the only bicycle shop in town. I wheeled the trailer to the counter.

"All over the Internet," he said. "I've been doing all my Christmas shopping that way. This is the first store I've set foot in all season." He seemed proud.

I offered to give him the name of some Web sites where he could buy the device, but he admitted that it was too late, he'd never get it before Christmas. I told him that I knew the going price of the item on the Net, and had he purchased the trailer online he could have saved $7.50 on his $185 purchase. "Of course, the assembly would have taken you about an hour," I added.

"Longer than that. I don't own a single wrench." He spun around on his feet and held up one hand as though he was hoping to sight land. "You know, I've never been in this store before tonight."

As I collapsed the item, what struck me was the man's genuine sense of unease that he was wasting valuable minutes of his day in a brick-and-mortar store, conversing with a merchant. He could have been at his keyboard, spending money by making even more purchases, more quickly. He tossed his Visa card on the counter, and tapped his thumb against his palm as we waited for the electronic transaction to be completed.

"Must be a lot of people shopping right now, for this to take so long," he 10
said impatiently. He signed the slip and I handed him his receipt. When I offered to carry his purchase to his car, he froze as though in shock. I'd wondered if I'd accidentally hit his OFF switch.

[1]Vala-Haynes lives in Carlton, Oregon.

"Really?" he asked.

"No problem," I said. "I might even thank you and tell you to have a good evening," I teased.

He laughed, and we stepped outside into the clear night. The street lights glowed pale yellow on Third Street. A few cars crept by. I loaded the trailer and waved as the man pulled away.

As I closed up my shop I pictured a world where people had no reason to extend the common courtesies of "thank you" and "you're welcome," in which all their transactions were electronic. Such a world wasn't hard to imagine. I've owned my business for 20 years, and, like most merchants, I've worried about the impact of Internet and mail-order shopping on my livelihood. Though I have noticed some effect, moments like the one I experienced a few days before Christmas steel my resolve to survive, and point up the need all communities have for businesses such as mine. Yes, shop owners provide a needed service, but just as important, we provide a forum where people from different circles of society rub elbows with each other.

In the early '70s, an obscure writer from Texas, W.D. Norwood Jr., wrote 15
that progress was a myth. Culture is a seesaw, he contended. Something goes up, something comes down. There is no gain without loss. As Americans communicate faster and faster, exchanging more and more money and words in an electronic world, we have to begin to question the value of all this speed. If we believe that commerce is only about the exchange of money for products in as short a time as possible, then we as a culture have suffered a terrible loss of perspective. The seesaw is tipping.

I think my customer had a pleasant time in my shop. For just one moment, his heart calmed and he laughed. And he found something he wanted. I hope he'll come back. I can't promise I'll always have what he wants, but if I don't, I'll help him find it elsewhere. He won't have wasted his time.

Good retail business is a dialogue, not the punching of a few keys and the exchange of an address and a credit-card number. Those little moments of contact that we brick-and-mortar shops can offer are part of our social contract. Maybe we are meant to slow the world down.

The Full-Time Stress of Part-Time Professors

MICHELE SCARFF[1]

YOU KNOW that common student nightmare—the one where you know 1
you have a class, but you don't know where and you don't know what class it is? And you haven't done the homework—you don't even know what the homework is? As a student taking more than the maximum-allowed number of credits, I never had this nightmare. Later, I worked full time and went to school full time, and still I never had this nightmare. Then I became an adjunct professor. And that's when I experienced the horror of waking up in the middle of the night sweating.

Last fall I taught four freshman-composition courses at two colleges: one state, one private. At these schools, a full-time professor usually teaches five courses in a whole year. From August to December, I made $7,000 teaching a load almost equal to a full-time professor's, for which he or she would usually earn a minimum of $45,000. If I divided my pay by the number of hours I worked, it would be well below the minimum wage. And I was not alone, not by far.

Retiring professors are rarely replaced by full-time professors anymore. Why should administrators worry about tenure and sabbaticals when they can hire part-time or temporary adjuncts for a fraction of the cost? Unfortunately, these savings don't usually benefit the student.

In each of my four courses, students wrote five essays, plus a research paper, during the semester, and they were required to rewrite at least two of them. If I wasn't prepping for a class or driving to a class or teaching a class or meeting with students, I was reading papers, rereading papers and marking papers. I wrote comments, and I deliberated for some time before assigning grades. I needed to reassure myself that the grade was deserved, that I wasn't misgrading because I was burnt out.

Then there was the question of plagiarism. I allowed students to write their 5
research essays on any subject of their choice. I wanted students to be enthusiastic, but giving them so much freedom meant I lost control over the sources. When I read paragraph after paragraph without errors I wanted to believe that students had improved so much between writing their last essay and their research paper but, and I say it with great sadness, many were not able to resist temptation. Does anybody know how many search engines there are? Do you have any idea how much work it is to try to find the original source?

My students were also required to keep journals, which I collected in the middle and at the end of the semester. It surprised and distressed me to read how unhappy most first-year students were. They were lonely. They missed their hometowns, their parents (to their surprise), their friends, their girlfriends or

[1]Scarff studies at SUNY, New Paltz, New York.

boyfriends. Often I worried about what I read and felt guilty that I didn't have enough time to talk with each student about what they wrote. Because of time constraints our meetings were reserved for talking about their essays. Personal problems were a luxury I could hardly afford. I did as much as I could, but some of those students needed more. Much more.

Adjuncts are so busy juggling jobs that they're underavailable to students who, at private institutions, can pay as much as $30,000 for tuition, room and board. Students need teachers who are accessible, teachers who have permanent offices and time to spend in them. I gave my students my e-mail address and I got back to them as soon as I could, but I never felt that was enough. I've heard stories of an expensive New York City university where students meet their advisers in the stairwells because the advisers don't have offices. I don't want to put adjuncts out of work, but if I were a student looking for a college, I'd ask about full-time-to-adjunct-faculty ratios. Full-time professors aren't necessarily better teachers than adjuncts, but they have more time—they're there to stay.

While earning my M.F.A., I worked at a small liberal-arts college as an assistant to the associate dean who hired the adjuncts, so I saw them from the other side. Adjuncts try to do their job well because, in my experience, most of them are over-achievers who care a great deal about their students and what they teach. They also know they're being taken advantage of, and that if they speak up too loudly, they're easy to replace.

I say "they" because I'm not an adjunct anymore. I've gone back to school. I am a student, yet again. This time, I'm getting certified to teach grades seven to 12, to get one job at one school with benefits and vacation and my own desk. Then I can get on with teaching, which is what I wanted to do in the first place. It won't be worry-free, but there'll be no more sweating in the middle of the night.

When Living Is a Fate Worse Than Death

CHRISTINE MITCHELL[1]

THE BABY died last winter. It was pretty terrible. Little Charlotte (not her real name) lay on a high white bed, surrounded by nurses and doctors pushing drugs into her veins, tubes into her trachea and needles into her heart, trying as hard as they could to take over for her failing body and brain. She was being coded, as they say in the ICU. It had happened several times before, but this time it would fail. Her parents, who were working, weren't there. 1

Charlotte was born with too few brain cells to do much more than breathe and pull away from pain. Most of her malformed brain was wrapped in a sac that

[1]Mitchell lives in Massachusetts.

grew outside her skull and had to be surgically removed to prevent immediate death.

Her parents were a young, unmarried couple from Haiti. They loved Charlotte and wanted her to live. The nurses and doctors thought she should be allowed to die peacefully. They recommended that a Do Not Resuscitate order be placed in Charlotte's chart. The new parents disagreed. Surely, they thought, medical care in the United Sates could save their baby. They bought their daughter a doll.

For 16 months Charlotte bounced back and forth—between hospital, home, the ER and pediatric nursing homes. Wherever she was, every time her body tried to die, nurses and doctors staved off death. Each time, Charlotte got weaker.

Charlotte's medical team at the hospital asked to talk with the Ethics Advi- 5
sory Committee and, as the hospital's ethicist, I got involved. Is it right to keep doing painful things just to keep Charlotte alive a little longer, her doctors and nurses asked us. To whom are we most obligated: the patient or the family? The committee advised that in this case the parents' rights superseded the caregivers' beliefs about what was right. Painful procedures should be avoided, the panel believed, but the care that Charlotte's parents wanted for her should be provided unless there was a medical consensus that it would not prolong her life. Such a consensus was elusive. There's almost always another procedure that can be tried to eke out a little more time until the patient dies despite everything—as Charlotte did.

A week after Charlotte's death, I met with the doctors, nurses and therapists who had done everything they could for her and yet felt terrible about having done too much. We talked for almost two hours about how Charlotte had died.

"It was horrible," said a doctor. "We tried to resuscitate her for over an hour. It's the worst thing I've ever done. I actually felt sick." A nurse talked about the holes that were drilled in Charlotte's bones to insert lines they couldn't get in anywhere else.

Why didn't Charlotte's parents spare Charlotte—and us—the awfulness of her death? Because they were too young? Too hopeful? Because they were distrustful of white nurses and doctors who they thought might really be saying that their black baby wasn't worth saving? Or because they believed that a "good" death is one in which everything possible has been tried?

Why didn't the hospital staff, including the ethics committee, save Charlotte from that kind of death? Maybe we feared that her parents would take us to court, like the mother in Virginia who got a judge to order the hospital to provide life-saving treatment for her anencephalic baby, who was born without most of her brain. Maybe we were afraid of seeing ourselves in the news—as the staff of a Pennsylvania hospital did when they withdrew life support, against the parents' wishes, from a comatose 3-year-old with fatal brain cancer. Maybe we were thinking about what was best for the parents, not just the child. Maybe we were wrong.

The nurse sitting next to me at the meeting had driven two hours from the 10
nursing home where she used to care for Charlotte. She had attended the wake.

She said the parents had sobbed; that Dad said he felt terrible because he wasn't there when his little girl died, that Mom still couldn't believe that she was dead.

It could have been different. They could have been there holding her. That's the way it happens most of the time in ICUs today. Family and staff make the decision together, machines are removed and death comes gently.

As a hospital ethicist, a large part of my job is helping staff and families distinguish between sustaining life and prolonging death. Sometimes I join the staff, as I did that night, in second-guessing decisions and drawing distinctions between the dignified death of a child held by parents who accept their child's dying, and the death that occurs amid technologically desperate measures and professional strangers.

Sooner or later, every person will die. I wish, and the hospital staff I work with wishes, almost beyond telling, that people could know what they are asking when they ask that "everything" be done.

Pay Your Own Way! (Then Thank Mom)

AUDREY ROCK-RICHARDSON[1]

IS IT ME, or are students these days lazy? I'm not talking about tweens who 1
don't want to do their homework or make their bed. I'm referring to people in legal adulthood who are in the process of making hugely consequential life decisions. And collectively, their attitude is that they simply cannot pay for college.

Don't get me wrong. I realize that there are people out there who pay their own tuition. I know that some cannot put themselves through school because of disabilities or extenuating circumstances. But I have to say: the notion that parents must finance their children's education is ridiculous.

During college I consistently endured comments from peers with scholarships and loans, peers who had new Jeeps and expensive apartments, all who would say to me, eyes bulging, "You mean your parents didn't help you at *all*?"

I resented my fellow students for asking this, first because they made it sound like my parents were demons, and second because they were insinuating that I wasn't capable of paying my own way. "How did you pay tuition?" they'd ask. My response was simple: "I worked." They would look at me blankly, as though I had told them I'd gone to the moon.

As an undergrad (University of Utah, 1998), I put myself through two solid 5
years of full-tuition college by working as a day-care provider for $4.75 an hour. I then married and finished out seven more quarters by working as an interpreter for the deaf and a tutor in a private school.

[1]Rock-Richardson lives in Stansbury Park, Utah.

I didn't work during high school or save for years. I simply got a job the summer following graduation and worked 40 hours a week. I didn't eat out every weekend, shop a lot or own a car. I sacrificed. I was striving for something bigger and longer-lasting than the next kegger.

Looking at the numbers now, I'm not sure how I managed to cover all the costs of my education. But I did. And I bought every single textbook and pencil myself, too.

I remember sitting in a classroom one afternoon during my senior year, listening to everyone introduce themselves. Many students mentioned their part-time jobs. There were several members of a sorority in the class. When it came to the first girl, she told us her name and that she was a sophomore. "Oh," she added, "I major in communications." After an awkward silence, the teacher asked, "Do you work?"

"Oh, no," she said emphatically, "I go to school full time." (As if those of us who were employed weren't really serious about our classes.)

The girl went on to explain that her parents were paying tuition and for her 10
to live in a sorority house (complete with a cook, I later found out). She was taking roughly 13 credit hours. And she was too busy to work.

I, on the other hand, was taking 18, count'em, 18 credit hours so I could graduate within four years. I worked 25 hours a week so my husband and I could pay tuition without future loan debt. And here's the kicker: I pulled straight A's.

I caught a glimpse of that same girl's report card at the end of the quarter, and she pulled C's and a few B's, which didn't surprise me. Having to juggle tasks forces you to prioritize, a skill she hadn't learned.

I'm weary of hearing kids talk about getting financial help from their parents as though they're entitled to it. I am equally tired of hearing stressed-out parents groaning, "How are we going to pay for his/her college?" Why do they feel obligated?

I do not feel responsible for my daughter's education. She'll find a way to put herself through if she wants to go badly enough. And (I'm risking sounding like my mom here), she'll thank me later. I can say this because I honestly, wholeheartedly thank my parents for giving me that experience.

I'm not saying that it's fun. It's not. I spent the first two years of school 15
cleaning up after 4-year-olds for the aforementioned $4.75 an hour and taking a public bus to campus. My husband and I spent the second two struggling to pay out our tuition. We lived in a cinder-block apartment with little privacy and no dishwasher.

Lest I sound like a hypocrite, yes, I would have taken free college money had the opportunity presented itself. However, because my parents put themselves through school they expected me to do the same. And, frankly, I'm proud of myself. I feel a sense of accomplishment that I believe I couldn't have gained from 50 college degrees all paid for by someone else.

Getting through school on our own paid off in every way. My husband runs his own business, a demanding but profitable job. I write part time and work as a mother full time. I believe the fact that we are happy and financially stable is a direct result of our learning how to manage time and money in college.

So, kids, give your parents a break. Contrary to popular belief, you can pay tuition by yourself. And you might just thank your mother for it, too.

Grieving for a Pet? I Won't Roll My Eyes.

JUDY PUTNAM[1]

IT WAS THE kind of news story that, until a few months ago, would have 1
made me roll my eyes in exasperation. Grief counselors would be available for the families of the 60 cats and dogs that had died in an early-morning kennel fire.

So very sad, but grief counseling? Come on. I could never understand why stories of animal tragedies can sometimes seem to provoke more public reaction than reports of abused or neglected children. For the pets lost in the fire, our community mobilized—even holding a memorial service in their honor.

I now understand the need to grieve. The news of the kennel deaths came two months after we lost our own family pet, Ernie, a big, loopy, black Labrador. He died after hours of surgery to try to correct a case of bloat, where his stomach twisted and swelled painfully, cutting off circulation to much of his body.

Like the deaths of the dogs and cats lost in the fire, Ernie's death at the age of 11 was unexpected. He was lean and tall and frequently ran in a field near our home, where he was off the leash and free to romp. People often mistook him for a young dog. I thought he would live for years.

I am not a diehard dog person, and Ernie and I had, at times, a tense rela- 5
tionship. I need to be honest about the dog: he was loud, messy and generally a pain in the neck. He also had the world's worst sense of timing. Start to drift off to sleep for a well-earned nap? He'd bark. Have company? He would supply some after-dinner gas for their enjoyment. Late for work? He'd burst away to freedom while being marched from the house to the dreaded tether.

He was difficult. But he forced us out to exercise, even during the worst weather. He loved my son so thoroughly it would bring tears to your eyes. And he sat by me, his head resting on the couch pillows, his big, brown eyes full of sympathy, as I cried my way through four miscarriages.

After 11 years with a hardheaded dog worming his way into my hardhearted existence, I miss him every day. My heart sinks a little each time I come home and automatically scan the yard for Ernie, ready to grab him before he com-

[1] Putnam lives in East Lansing, Michigan.

mences a loud and joyful welcome. Instead, I can take my time. My house is cleaner, too. It's cold comfort.

Despite my complaints about him, I always, secretly, liked the fact that we never truly owned Ernie. He never bent to our will. It was quite the opposite.

We first got him for hunting purposes. My husband, an avid sportsman, joked that Ernie would wait for him to clear a path through the brush. And although Labs are natural-born swimmers, Ernie hated the water.

He didn't like hunting or swimming, but we discovered, after moving to a 10
college town, that he loved keggers. I'd find him at yard parties near campus, surrounded by beer-drinking, adoring students who'd put a red bandanna around his neck.

Ernie was an escape artist. Although he never jumped fences, he could open doors and latches like a canine Houdini. He'd find other ways to get away, snapping cables, digging under fences, slipping his collar. He frequently took himself on walks, flouting the city ordinance requiring dogs to be on a leash.

We picked him up at gas stations, by the Christian Science reading room and at a restaurant with a patio bar. Once, when he slipped his collar and left his identification behind, he lived with a lovely family for three days before we tracked him down.

The police brought him home twice in a squad car. We had to bail him out of the dog pound five or six times, enduring lectures and fines. Often he'd end his romps by returning on his own. I would find him in the backyard in the middle of the night, hours after his escape from our house, surrounded by shoes, gardening tools and other objects from the neighbors' yards. The biggest mystery was a fake-fur hat with a Bloomingdale's label. I never found its true owner.

I was ready to help Ernie through his old age, his love earning our understanding and patience. But it was not to be. He died in his prime. As always, his sense of timing was off. I realize now that I took him for granted. When I dug through stacks of photos, I found only a few of Ernie. My favorite: Ernie as a
pup on a park bench, with a tongue that was somehow wider than the mouth 15
from which it was hanging.

I've gone through the stages of grief. There's guilt: if only I had taken him to the vet when he first got sick, in the morning before work, instead of racing him there, desperately ill, at lunchtime. There's the blues: I find myself depressed or cranky some days. There's a tremendous need to talk about my dog with friends or family. Yes, I understand the need for counseling. As many people told me, we lost a member of the family. Indeed we did. I won't roll my eyes.

What Do I Get the Boy Who Has Everything?

DONNA CORNACHIO[1]

1 MY SON IS turning 7 this month. The age of reason, according to conventional wisdom. But in my house, it's more the age of materialism, for my son covets money and goods and whatever toy he's encountered on his most recent play date.

Andrew, my oldest child, is obsessed with money and the things it buys. He becomes giddy at the sight of crisp dollar bills, the sound of silver jingling in a coat pocket.

Our children get an allowance each Sunday and, of the three, he is the first to demand it and the first to spend it. Their take is $3 each, with the stipulation that the first dollar goes into the collection plate at church, the second is to be saved in their piggy banks and the third dollar can be spent as they wish. No sooner does Andrew get his dollar to spend than he is champing at the bit to indulge his fantasy: baseball cards, a die-cast plane, a new ball.

Over time Andrew has learned the advantage of saving for something big rather than frittering his allowance on a cheap toy that rarely lasts the car ride home. A first grader, he now has a firm grasp on numbers and a beginning appreciation for value: $10 is worth more than $5 and takes longer to save, but you can buy something a little better as a result. Which is not to say that Andrew always lives within his means. Many's the time my husband and I have overheard Andrew negotiating with his sisters for a hefty loan on their allowance for some plaything he desires: "You'll love it, you'll really love it," he earnestly assures them.

5 There's a fine line, I've discovered, between giving your children whatever they desire and spoiling them rotten. As a child growing up, my siblings and I were given gifts at Christmas, on our birthdays and, very occasionally, when we were sick (I still remember a royal blue Fisher-Price phonograph my father bought me after a nasty late-summer bout of chicken pox). There were seven of us children, and though we were certainly comfortable, my parents did not buy us presents on a mere whim.

I also remember the summer I was 10, when my rather spoiled best friend got a pogo stick for no other reason than that she wanted a pogo stick. I loved bouncing on that pogo stick of hers more, I think, than my friend did. So much so that she suggested I ask my parents to buy me one. "I can't," I said. "I have to wait until my birthday." Come September, and my birthday, I got my pogo stick. While my friend had long since tired of hers, I spent hours practicing until I could navigate our driveway at top speed.

My children, on the other hand, seem to get gifts almost daily. Not from

[1]Cornachio lives in Hastings-on-Hudson, New York.

their father and me but from their grandmothers, 15 aunts and uncles, 18 cousins and family friends. When one child has a birthday, the other two get a token gift. ("They're so little," I'm told by a doting relation. "They don't understand why one's getting a present and they're not.") It certainly keeps the peace but I think it mars an important lesson: sometimes you get and sometimes you just have to wait.

Andrew has already chosen his birthday present from us this year: an aircraft carrier complete with electronic sounds and eight planes and four helicopters. It cost $49.95—an amount I told Andrew it would take him nearly a year to save. I thought that might make a connection for him between the dollars in his piggy bank and the credit-card number I recite over the telephone. But he was too busy flipping through the catalog for what he "really, really" wanted for Christmas.

I don't begrudge him his desire but I wonder how I can really celebrate his birthday. What gift can I give him that he will cherish as I have the pogo stick and the phonograph?

Recently I came across an obituary of Pepi Deutsch, a Holocaust survivor 10
who died not long ago at the age of 101. During the '40s Pepi and her teenage daughter Clara managed to stay together through a Hungarian ghetto, deportation, Auschwitz-Birkenau and three detention camps. They suffered bone-breaking labor, the brutalities of the German soldiers and near starvation—surviving at one point on a daily ration of three slices of bread and a soup of potato peels.

In January 1945 Pepi also found a way to celebrate her daughter's 17th birthday in the labor camp: she hoarded her three slices of bread, coated them with marmalade and created a birthday cake.

Andrew is too young to appreciate this parable of sacrifice. But as I make his party plans, I can't get Pepi's story out of my mind. When Andrew blows out the candles on his Carvel ice-cream cake, I know I'll be thinking of that other cake. And someday, when he's a bit older, I'll tell him about Pepi and the things that no money can ever buy.

Why Teachers Are Not "Those Who Can't"

EMILY MOORE[1]

NATURALLY, I began teaching for the money. And the prestige. Who 1
wouldn't want to stand around at cocktail parties listening to some puffed-up acquaintance on a six-month consulting stint drone "Yeah, I mean teaching is great and all. But what will you do next?"

Shortly after completing my student teaching last fall, I applied for a summer job outside the field of education. The interviewer lit a cigarette and reviewed my résumé. "Phillips Academy. Very good. Princeton! Good schools you've got. Magna cum laude. Thesis prize. Teaching experience: English. Teaching?" She looked up from the paper. "But you have such a good degree! Why waste it teaching?"

I would like to say that nobody has asked me this before. That up until this point, I've had no need to defend my ambition. The truth, of course, is bleaker. So bleak that I am always ready with a response.

"Who would you rather have teaching your children?"

The interviewer sat back and took a long drag. "Well, I never thought of it 5
like that," she conceded.

We live in an age when people seem to lament the state of public education in the same breath that they dismiss teachers as "those who can't." I cannot count the number of times a well-meaning acquaintance has assured me that I am qualified to do other things besides teach. That, by implication, I don't have to teach.

In fact, I want to spend my life teaching. I love teaching. And ritzy degrees aside, I don't think I will ever feel qualified to do it as well as I'd like.

I feel extraordinarily blessed to have been called to a profession which I am always learning. It is grueling, exciting, gratifying work. As a student teacher in New Jersey last fall, I looked out at my high-school students and saw a field of possibilities. I looked at their clunky boots and spiked hair and adored them.

Naturally, there were downsides. On bad days, I felt I was preaching to a swarm of gnats. Yet as wretched as my students could be, it's been far more distressing to be told by adults that I have wasted my degree.

There are notable exceptions. Fellow teachers have been nothing but kind, 10
witty and encouraging. Without a fiercely funny, intelligent mentor teacher who believed in what she was doing, I never would have survived my student teaching. Many parents with children in the public-school system are deeply invested in recruiting and retaining gifted teachers. Yet there are people both inside and outside this public-school culture who continue to wrestle with assumptions

[1]Moore, who recently received her New Jersey State Certification in Secondary English, lives in New York.

about who is and isn't teaching, often arriving at troublesome conclusions: that teachers are poorly educated, ill suited for high-powered jobs, unwilling or unable to have more glamorous careers.

Though it is decidedly unglamorous—I spent all three months of my student teaching exhausted and encrusted with chalk—teaching is deeply rewarding. In my classroom, there was nothing more exciting to me than witnessing a student write first a good sentence and then a good essay. Yet as victorious as I felt when a student nailed down a provocative thesis, employed a stellar verb or gracefully wove textual evidence into his or her paper, I was even more gratified to hear that I had touched a student personally. "She was the only teacher who didn't question my blue hair and understood the meaning of my having it," one student wrote in an evaluation. "I think you will be a great teacher someday," one of my more challenging students told me as I passed back his essay, "because you always make me feel like I'm doing good." I look forward to the day when teachers are as rewarded outside the classroom—with both higher salaries and greater respect—as they are within.

Students, not teachers, may be the greatest beneficiaries of increased respect for educators. If insinuations that teachers are unqualified for other careers upset educators, these notions alienate students. I remember one afternoon proctoring in-school suspension. Eager to chat after a morning of enforced silence, a tall, gangly boy asked: "You a student teacher?"

"Yes."

"Where from?" he inquired, his words reverberating off the dusty linoleum.

"Princeton," I responded. 15

"Princeton University?" he asked, flashing a broad smile. "Damn! What are you doing here? I mean, you could have been like a doctor or a lawyer or something!"

"I'm here because I want to be here," I said, smiling at his sudden animation. "Don't you think you deserve good teachers?"

"You *know* I deserve only the best," a sullen boy in the far corner cracked, raising his head up off the desk. As humorous as I found the moment, I could not help wincing at his irony.

Practicing the Principles: Activities

VARIATIONS ON A BRIEF ARGUMENT

Select a brief argument, either one from this chapter or one you have written—even an outline will do—and try organizing this argument according to the needs of different audiences. See how varying the audience and purpose affects the structure. Try to use three or four of the structures outlined in this chapter.

WRITING A LETTER TO THE EDITOR

Bring to class several recent issues of your campus newspaper or a local paper and analyze letters to the editor. As you read these letters, consider the following questions:

1. To what extent do the authors of these letters try to find community-based reasons to support their views?
2. What persuasive strategies do they use?
3. How do they organize their arguments to meet the needs of their audience?

After you have analyzed these letters, try composing a letter on an issue of current interest to your campus or local community. Instead of just explaining why you believe your claim, try to find compelling reasons for others to believe your claim, reasons that you can accept but that are centered in the values, beliefs, and attitudes of the community. Then send your letter to the editor of the newspaper.

As you compose your letter, consider the following tips[1]:

- State your position in the first or second paragraph of the letter.
- Although letters to the editor are traditionally addressed to the editor of the paper, your audience is the readership.
- Be specific. Support your arguments with facts, quotations, and examples.
- Address local issues. Don't try to solve all of the world's problems in one letter.
- Don't just repeat your opinion over and over. Be economical in your use of words.
- Focus on issues, not individuals. Don't resort or respond to name-calling.
- Be willing to admit the validity of other viewpoints. Don't present every issue as two-sided.
- Avoid stating the obvious.

[1]These suggestions are adapted from Ashley Baker, opinion editor for the *Daily Universe,* Brigham Young University's campus newspaper.

- Have someone read your letter before you send it in.
- Conclude your letter by restating your opinion and what action should be taken.

WRITING A MEMBER OF CONGRESS

Research issues currently being debated in Congress, or identify an issue you care about that you would like Congress to consider. Find the name, address, phone number, and e-mail address of the congressional representative for the district your college is in or for your hometown district. You can find this information online at <www.house.gov> or <www.senate.gov>. Then write a persuasive letter to this individual. You can even submit your letter to a congressional representative online at <www.house.gov/writerep>.

Remember that senators and representatives are very busy and can't keep up on every piece of legislation. On a few issues of considerable public interest, they may receive a lot of mail from their constituents, but on most legislation, they receive very little. Even a few letters may influence how they vote. Don't be afraid to write or encourage others to write, but don't just send form letters. Obvious letter-writing campaigns are usually not as effective as genuine mail from constituents. You should also remember that because they are busy, your representative probably won't read your letter. It may be read by an aide and summarized as part of a report, or it may just be recorded as mail for or against a particular issue. Your letter may also be forwarded to a government employee. Because constituent mail receives very brief attention, you should make sure that you focus your letter on an identifiable issue and make your point clearly and quickly.

As you write your letter, consider the following guidelines:

- Stick to one or two typewritten pages. Try to make your argument concise and direct. Use language that your representative and his or her staff will understand.
- Use your own stationery or letterhead and your own words. Don't just send in a form letter.
- Focus on one issue and get right to your point. Clearly outline your reasons in support of your claim. Remember that you can write in support of legislation as well as in opposition.
- If you are addressing a particular piece of legislation, make sure to give the name and number of the bill of resolution. You can find these in committee reports, in the *Congressional Record,* and online at the House and Senate websites.
- State explicitly where you agree or disagree with the legislation. Suggest some practical alternatives, if appropriate.

- Sign your letter and include your name, address, phone number, and e-mail address. If you have a particular connection to the issue, make sure that you explain this.
- Get a sense of the kairos of legislation. If the bill is in its early stages, you might have some input as to what goes into it. If the bill is in committee, you might be able to influence the hearings about the legislation. When the bill comes up for a vote, you might help your representative decide how to vote. For a bill in committee, you should probably address the chair of the committee or subcommittee. For legislation you want to propose or for a bill coming up for a vote, you should probably address your representative. Find information about committees and the legislative agenda online at the House and Senate websites.
- Use the following addresses and style:

  The Honorable ___________
  United States House of Representatives
  Washington, DC 20515
  Dear Representative ___________

  The Honorable ___________
  United States Senate
  Washington, DC 20510
  Dear Senator ___________

YOUR TURN

Write a letter for *Newsweek* magazine that could be published in the "My Turn" column. As a class, gather additional samples of "My Turn" essays and examine these to identify the features of successful essays. Then write an essay from your own experience. *Newsweek* provides the following information for writers who want to submit "My Turn" essays. (For more information see www.newsweek.com.):

> "My Turn" submissions should be sent to:
>
> My Turn Editor, *Newsweek*
> 251 W. 57th St.
> New York, NY 10019-1894
> e-mail: letters@newsweek.com
> fax: 212-445-4120 (attn: My Turn Editor)
>
> The essay should be (*a*) an original piece, (*b*) 850–900 words, (*c*) personal in tone, and (*d*) about any topic, but not framed as a response to a *Newsweek* story or another "My Turn" essay. Submissions must not have been published elsewhere. Please allow two months for your submission to be considered; if your story is time sensitive, it may not be appropriate. Please include your full name, phone number, and address with your entry. The competition is very

stiff—we receive over 600 entries per month—and we can only print one a week. We are fully aware of the time and effort involved in preparing an essay, and each manuscript is given careful consideration.

POST AND RIPOSTE

The Atlantic Unbound has a forum called "Post and Riposte" where you can debate current issues. In small groups, formulate an opinion on a contemporary social issue and enter your argument on "Post and Riposte," <www.theatlantic.com/pr/index.htm>.

FINDING A CONTEXT FOR ARGUMENTS: *HARPER'S MAGAZINE*

Sallie Tisdale's essay on abortion clinics first appeared in *Harper's* in October 1987. Examining this issue of *Harper's* may help you understand something about the communities of readers that Tisdale is challenging. Find out what other articles were published in the same issue. Skim the six months or so before and after the October issue to get a feel for what kind of articles *Harper's* regularly published at the time of Tisdale's essay. Analyze the ads that appear in a few issues. Whom do you think these ads target? What assumptions do the ads and articles make about the audience? How well do the intended audiences for the ads fit the possible audiences for the articles? From what you can infer about the intended readership of *Harper's,* how well does Tisdale's essay fit?

TELLING A FABLE

One way some writers have challenged the community is through stories. In the New Testament, Jesus challenged the conventional thinking of the Jews through his parables. In his book *Animal Farm,* George Orwell criticized contemporary political leaders by portraying them as barnyard animals. And although you may not realize it, Aesop's *Fables* has been used throughout history to challenge prevailing political and social beliefs.

Try your hand at challenging the conventions of a community you belong to by writing a fable. Take a common situation in your community, something people routinely do without giving it much thought. Substitute animals for humans or even machines for humans in this situation, paying particular attention to which animals or machines you use to characterize which humans. Share these as a class and consider how changing the perspective causes you to view ordinary events in unfamiliar ways.

As an alternative, try changing the gender, race, or nationality of those in the situation to point out unstated assumptions about how we view these differences.

Applying the Principles: Analytical Project

HUMOR, SATIRE, AND IRONY

Each of the following selections uses humor, satire, or irony to make a serious point. As a class, use what you have learned in this chapter to analyze and evaluate these selections as arguments. The first of these is a cartoon from Garry B. Trudeau, famous for his controversial political cartoon, "Doonesbury." This cartoon was first syndicated in 1985. The second selection is "In Defense of *##@&$%#," by Anna Quindlen. Quindlen is the author of several nonfiction books, collections of essays, novels, and books for children. She is also a frequent contributor to *Newsweek's* "The Last Word," where this column was published September 25, 2000. "How I'm Doing," by David Owen was first published July 3, 2000, in the "Shouts & Murmurs" section of *The New Yorker.* Owen is a *New Yorker* staff writer. "Day Trading Made Easy," by Andy Borowitz, was also published in "Shouts & Murmurs" (May 8, 2000). Borowitz is a frequent contributor to *The New Yorker* and other magazines, and he has also written *The Trillionaire Next Door: A Greedy Investor's Guide to Day Trading and Rationalizations to Live By.* Borowitz is also a successful film and television producer. George F. Will's "The Perils of Brushing" first appeared in *Newsweek's* "The Last Word" on May 10, 1999. Will is a syndicated conservative political columnist. The final selection, "A Liberating Curriculum," was written by Roberta F. Borkat, until her recent death a professor of English and comparative literature at San Diego State University.

Doonesbury

GARRY B. TRUDEAU

In Defense of *$##@&$%#

ANNA QUINDLEN

As the train hurtles through the dark of the subway tunnels, three teenagers consider aloud the events of their school day. In the fashion of adolescent boys, they seem to occupy more space than the simple size of their bodies would suggest. They stand around a center pole only a few feet from two women who appear old enough to be their grandmothers. And this is what they say: 1

Actually, verbatim quotes won't work here. There was a guy who banged into one of them in gym, and an early-morning problem with the trains that caused one of them to be late, and there were girls, naturally. And in the recounting, all of this was peppered with a single word, the word that during the teenage years of the women sitting opposite, and in my teenage years, too, was considered the ultimate swear word. There, you've got it, right? These boys were using it as a verb, an adverb, even a participle. And each time one of them would use the word, I thought I saw a scarcely visible *frisson* in the shoulders of one of the women, as though someone had hit her with a low-voltage cattle prod.

But this will not be a rant about the decline of standards, or a sad lament that the dirtying up of movies and television has resulted in potty-mouthed American children. Rather, it raises an interesting question, particularly for someone in the literary line of work: what does it mean when a word doesn't mean what it meant anymore?

What does it mean that stories about swearing at the highest levels of American public life have been in the news during this election season, and have raised far less of a stink than stories about soft money and subliminal commercial messages? George W. Bush called a reporter what was once considered a dirty word in front of an open microphone, and seemed far from contrite afterward. Hillary Rodham Clinton was quoted as ripping a campaign aide with a double-barreled obscenity a quarter century ago, but the accusation quickly evaporated.

Writing about all this has sometimes been a comical exercise in shifting standards. In a variation on the game Hangman, *Newsweek* said Bush had referred to the reporter as a "major-league a-----e." Taxing the reader's imagination even more, the *New York Times* used "expletive deleted." But *The New Yorker* went the whole way, printing the word itself. "So long as we're not using or quoting such a word mindlessly," says David Remnick, the magazine's editor, "it seems patronizing to me to invent euphemisms or insert dashes. The readers are grown-ups. They've heard these things before." 5

This seems a reasonable response to an event in which the word's the thing, especially since those watching television could, to quote Bush's father, read his lips. But publications are still feeling their way toward community standards in a nation that is swearing more and caring about it less. Or is what we're doing swearing at all? The boys on the subway were clearly not trying to offend, or using the word as the euphemism for sexual intercourse for which it once stood. You could make the argument that they were insensitive to the sensibilities of their elders; and unimaginative in their range of vocabulary. But their language was by way of being a verbal tic, as unself-conscious and, absent an audience, as inoffensive as the word "like," which also acts as a space holder in the conversation of many adolescents.

Slang, particularly teenage slang, has a rich history of taking words and morphing them into something they never were before, stripping them of previous meaning. It's vivid, powerful and perishable. The very fact that the Republican presidential candidate used the term "major league" means that "major league" is so not happening. Today things are "mad," which means very: mad cool, mad fun, mad stupid. Oh, and they're "ill," too, which means the ultimate, the best, as in "that's an ill bike." A "son" is an inferior, a weakling; a "herb" is a jerk.

And an expletive deleted is nothing much. In his study "Cursing in America"—yes, I'm not making this up—psychologist Timothy Jay says that curses count for 8 percent of leisure conversation among college students, but a full 13 percent among their elders. And what counts as cursing changes from era to era, even place to place. That's why producers were fined for allowing the word "damn" in the curtain line of *Gone With the Wind*. That's why Americans blithely took their kids to a movie called "Austin Powers: The Spy Who Shagged Me," while the British were slightly breathless at the marquee use of a verb that, in their country, is a vulgar term for sexual congress.

Defenders of swearing say that sometimes it's the only way to express strong emotion. Opponents say it's a reflection of a culture poised between Sodom and Gomorrah. But they're both wrong. The words that were once considered so objectionable have now lost both their edge and their sense. They've been cleansed by use, and by overuse. According to a poll done by the Shorenstein Center at Harvard's Kennedy School of Government, only 18 percent of those aware of Bush's vulgarity said it affected their opinion of him. Seven percent said it made him rise in their estimation.

It's easier to put our moment where our mouths are by looking at the case 10
of Mrs. Clinton. The pejorative she was accused of once delivering consisted of an expletive adjective, the word "Jew" and an expletive noun. Reporters who had heard the account of the outburst in the past said that the participants had conveniently added the religious angle only after Mrs. Clinton ran for the Senate in a state with many Jewish voters; Jewish leaders sprang to the First Lady's defense and said her past actions made it impossible to believe she was a bigot. But no one seemed particularly ruffled by those other two obscenities. So today the words that still have the power to shock and offend us are not the words that reflect bodily functions or bedroom. They are the words that express prejudice and hatred. Isn't that ill?

How I'm Doing

DAVID OWEN

IN THE HOPE of establishing a more equitable framework by which the public can evaluate my effectiveness as a father, husband, friend, and worker, I am pleased to announce that the methodology heretofore used in measuring my performance is being revised. Beginning tomorrow, my reputation and compensation will no longer be based on year-long, cumulative assessments of my attainments but will instead be derived from periodic samplings of defined duration, or "sweeps." 1

From now on, ratings of my success as a parent will be based solely on perceptions of my conduct during the two weeks beginning March 7th (a.k.a. "spring vacation"), the two weeks beginning August 1st (a.k.a. "summer vacation"), the seven days ending December 25th, and my birthday. No longer will my ranking be affected by unsolicited anecdotal reports from minors concerning my alleged "cheapness," "strictness," and "loser" qualities, or by the contents of viewing diaries maintained by my dependents. Page views, click-throughs, and People Meter data concerning me will also be disregarded, except during the aforementioned periods. The opinions of my children will no longer be counted in evaluations of my sense of humor.

Public appraisals of my behavior at parties will henceforth not be drawn from overnight ratings provided by my wife; instead, my annual ranking will be based on a random sampling of my level of intoxication during the week following January 2nd. My official weight for the year will be my median weight during the four weeks beginning July 1st. All measures of my geniality, thoughtfulness, romantic disposition, and willingness to compromise will henceforth be calculated just three times per year: on September 15th (my wife's birthday), August 26th (our anniversary), and February 14th. My high-school grades, S.A.T. scores, college grades, and income history will no longer be available for inclusion in any of my ratings, and in fact they will be expunged from my personal database. Evaluations of my success as a stock-market investor will no longer include the performance of my portfolio during the month of October.

Beginning in 2001, my annual compensation will cease to consist of my total income over the twelve months of the fiscal year; instead, my yearly pay will be adjusted to equal not less than thirteen times my nominal gross earnings during the four weeks beginning February 1st, when the holiday season is over, my children are back in school, and my local golf course has not yet reopened for the spring. My critics may object that my output during February is not representative of my output during the rest of the year, especially when I am at the beach. However, I believe (and my auditors concur) that the work I do during periods of cold, miserable weather provides the best available indication of my actual abilities as a worker and therefore constitutes the only fair and objective basis for calculating my true contribution to the economy. Conversely, my federal income-tax liability will henceforth be based on an annualized computation of my total earnings between Memorial Day and Labor Day.

5 These changes are being made as a part of my ongoing effort to insure that public data concerning me and my personality are the very best available. This new protocol may be further modified by me at any time without advance notice, and, in any case, is not legally binding. In addition, all assessments of my performance are subject to later revision, as improved information becomes available. Specifically, my lifetime ratings in all categories may be posthumously adjusted, within thirty days of my death, to reflect the content of newspaper obituaries regarding me, should any such be published, and the things that people say about me at my funeral.

Day Trading Made Easy

ANDY BOROWITZ

1 The stock-market turmoil of the last few weeks has caused many to point the finger of blame at a convenient target: me. I'm used to it. Ever since I became a full-time day trader, I have been called everything from "a cyber-speculator" to "an embarrassment to your father and me." Contrary to what its critics may think, however, day trading is a science, like chemistry or astrology, with its own rigorously tested set of principles. You wouldn't perform open-heart surgery without first going to two years of medical school; similarly, you shouldn't risk your life savings on the Internet without spending the thirty minutes it takes to learn these rules. The rules of stock selection apply equally to all industries: automotive companies, like Ford and General Motors, or chip makers, like Intel and Frito-Lay.

Remember, day trading is not the same thing as gambling. You're not betting on stocks. You're betting on yourself—and yourself is betting on stocks.

1. *The "Name Game."* Often, when novice investors do "research" on a stock, they breeze right past the name of the stock and delve into obscure and mind-numbing data like profits, cash flow, earnings projections, etc. They are making a common "beginner's mistake," because, nine times out of ten, the most important information about a stock is contained in the name of the stock itself. The old adage "You can't judge a book by its cover" does not apply to stocks, and for a very simple reason: stocks do not have covers.

Let's start with some simple examples. Amazon.com, America Online, and Amgen have been three of the stock market's biggest success stories. What do these stocks have in common? They all begin with the letters "Am." Using history as my guide, I recommend the following stocks for every day trader's portfolio:

- Amalgamated Toxic Spilling
- American Lint Supply
- Amorouschimps.com

To take another example, Microsoft, Cisco Systems, Sun Microsystems, and Advanced Micro Devices have all zoomed in price over the last few years, and little wonder: they all have the words "micro" or "systems" in their names. Be on the lookout for new stock offerings that contain either of these words: these stocks will always go up, big time.

What is a "system"? What is a "microsystem"? You're asking the wrong guy. 5
It's safe to say that they both have something to do with technology. And I'll go out on a limb and say that a "microsystem" is probably smaller than a "system." But just how small is a microsystem? So small that it could be lost in shipping, or fall down a grate? You got me. Which leads me to another ironclad rule of stock selection:

2. *Never own a stock long enough to know what the company does.* I'm sure some of you will bristle at this notion. You'll say it is the duty of every investor, before buying a stock, to know the company inside out. Well, it *is* someone's job to know what business a company is in—*the CEO's, not the day trader's!* Nothing irritates me more than the idea that we are supposed to spend all the livelong day trying to figure out what a company's profits are, etc., while some CEO calls it quits at five and hits the links with his Martini-swilling pals.

As investors, we demonstrate our faith in a company by tirelessly buying, selling, and buying it again twenty or thirty times in a given day. So we should demand accountability of these slacker CEOs and deliver the following message, loud and clear: Hey, Mr. CEO—figure out what your company does so we don't have to.

3. *The "Dartboard Portfolio."* Every so often, the *Wall Street Journal* runs a feature in which a panel of so-called experts is asked to put together theoretical stock portfolios. The results of these portfolios are then compared with a "dartboard portfolio": a portfolio assembled by throwing darts at a newspaper's stock listings. Surprisingly, the dartboard portfolio sometimes yields better results than those designed by the "pros." What does this tell us? *A dartboard is an excellent way to choose stocks.*

In your home office, hang up a dartboard covered with a newspaper's stock page. Tape a line across the floor six feet from the dartboard, and remain behind the line as you hurl the darts. Remember, stepping over the line is cheating, and it may affect your investment results. To resist the temptation to cheat, I remain seated at my desk, throwing darts with my left hand while operating the mouse with my right. This maximizes both throws and trades per minute.

All of these day-trading rules are important, but there is one final rule that 10
is more important than the rest. Simply put: When you are day trading, if something sounds too good to be true, go for it.

The Perils of Brushing

GEORGE F. WILL

1 ALL OF US have seen lots of them, those words of warning or instruction that appear on products we buy. "Do not eat this sled." "For best results do not apply this floor wax to your teeth." "This antifreeze is not intended for pouring on breakfast cereal." We hardly notice them, let alone consider what they say about the times in which we live. The sled, wax and antifreeze warnings are apocryphal. But you could not know that. After all, *The American Enterprise* magazine offers these from real life:

On a bag of Fritos: "You could be a winner! No purchase necessary. Details inside." On a bread pudding: "Product will be hot after heating." On a bar of Dial soap: "Use like regular soap." On a hotel shower cap: "Fits one head." On a package of Nytol sleeping aid: "May cause drowsiness." On a string of Christmas lights: "For indoor or outdoor use only." On the packaging of a Rowenta iron. "Do not iron clothes on body."

The warning about a product's being hot after heating may be a response to the famous case wherein a woman successfully sued McDonald's because she was burned when she spilled—she was a passenger in a stationary car at the time, with the cup between her legs—the hot McDonald's coffee she had just bought. (If the coffee had been cool, a complaint about that could have been packaged as a lawsuit.) But try to picture in your mind the event involving two or more heads that the manufacturer of the shower cap was worried about.

Give up? Well, then, answer this: If there are people who press their pants while in their pants, are they the sort of people whose behavior will be changed by a warning on the packaging the iron comes in? If there are people who have done that once, are there any who have done it twice? If not, does that demonstrate that even the dimmest among us has a learning curve that actually curves?

5 Such questions are stirred by the great toothbrush litigation just getting underway in Chicago. What Charles Dickens did with *Jarndyce v. Jarndyce* in *Bleak House* as an index of cultural conditions, perhaps some modern novelist will do with *Trimarco v. Colgate Palmolive et al.*

The et al.'s include some other manufacturers of toothbrushes, and the American Dental Association. All are to be hauled before the bar of justice by Mark Trimarco, speaking for himself and—this is a class-action suit—"all others similarly situated." The others are suffering from what Trimarco's complaint calls "a disease known as 'toothbrush abrasion'." Abrasion a disease? The plaintiff's materials also call it "an injury." And "a distinct clinical entity caused by toothbrushes of the following bristle types: firm, medium and soft, both natural and synthetic."

The complaint says people suffering from this self-inflicted injury are consumers who were not "informed or warned about the danger of toothbrush abrasion." And: "It was the duty of the defendant manufacturers to furnish a product, i.e., toothbrush, which was in reasonably safe condition when put to a use in a manner that was reasonably foreseeable considering the nature and intended function of the product."

But the toothbrushes "were unsafe and unreasonably dangerous for their intended use in that the packaging contained no warning as to the risks of toothbrush abrasion or instructions on how to brush to avoid toothbrush abrasion." The American Dental Association is a defendant because it gave its seal of approval to the toothbrushes.

The complaint charges negligence because the manufacturers knew or should have known about the disease/injury/clinical entity since "at least 1949" but continued to manufacture toothbrushes that were "likely" to cause abrasion. *Likely?* If the result is "likely," you would think that the class of plaintiffs would be a majority of all who brush their teeth.

If toothbrushes are, as charged, "unreasonably dangerous" because of the 10
absence of warnings and instructions, try to imagine the words which, if printed on toothbrush packages, would immunize manufacturers against such a complaint. "Warning: In brushing, too much is too much." "Instructions: Hold brush in hand. Insert the end with the bristles into your mouth. Move brush up and down. Stop before you wear out your teeth." Or perhaps: "Look, this toothbrush is not normally a dangerous implement, but neither is it intended for ninnies who can't figure out how to brush their teeth without doing them irreparable harm."

This suit is just part of a great American growth industry—litigation that expresses the belief that everyone has an entitlement to compensation for any unpleasantness; litigation that displaces responsibility from individuals to corporations with money. This industry was, of course, up and running before the tobacco litigation, but that taught lawyers just how lucrative it could be to blame individuals' foolishness on, say, Joe Camel.

Now many cities are suing gun manufacturers for the "costs"—the numbers are guesses—of shootings. In a new wrinkle in tort law—a move that would make a trial lawyer blush, if that were possible—individuals who have been shot are suing groups of manufacturers without claiming to have been injured by a product made by any of the targeted manufacturers.

If you—your teeth *are* suddenly feeling a bit abraded, are they not?—want to climb aboard the latest gravy train pulling out of the station, log on to www.toothbrushlawsuit.com. You will be greeted warmly: "Welcome to the Toothbrush Lawsuit Web Site." Illinois residents can dial 1-877-SORE GUMS. From the Web site you will learn that the disease is "progressive." That means not that Al Gore likes it, but that it gets worse if you keep making it worse. You also will learn that toothbrush abrasion "is most prevalent in those with good oral hygiene, i.e., people who brush their teeth." And "there are studies that show that people who do not brush their teeth, never develop" symptoms of toothbrush abrasion. Consider yourself warned.

A Liberating Curriculum

ROBERTA F. BORKAT

1 A BLESSED change has come over me. Events of recent months have revealed to me that I have been laboring as a university professor for more than 20 years under a misguided theory of teaching. I humbly regret that during all those years I have caused distress and inconvenience to thousands of students while providing some amusement to my more practical colleagues. Enlightenment came to me in a sublime moment of clarity while I was being verbally attacked by a student whose paper I had just proved to have been plagiarized from *The Norton Anthology of English Literature*. Suddenly, I understood the true purpose of my profession, and I devised a plan to embody that revelation. Every moment since then has been filled with delight about the advantages to students, professors and universities from my Plan to Increase Student Happiness.

The plan is simplicity itself: at the end of the second week of the semester, all students enrolled in each course will receive a final grade of A. Then their minds will be relieved of anxiety, and they will be free to do whatever they want for the rest of the term.

The benefits are immediately evident. Students will be assured of high grade-point averages and an absence of obstacles in their march toward graduation. Professors will be relieved of useless burdens and will have time to pursue their real interests. Universities will have achieved the long-desired goal of molding individual professors into interchangeable parts of a smoothly operating machine. Even the environment will be improved because education will no longer consume vast quantities of paper for books, compositions and examinations.

Although this scheme will instantly solve countless problems that have plagued education, a few people may raise trivial objections and even urge universities not to adopt it. Some of my colleagues may protest that we have an obligation to uphold the integrity of our profession. Poor fools, I understand their delusion, for I formerly shared it. To them, I say: "Hey, lighten up! Why make life difficult?"

5 Those who believe that we have a duty to increase the knowledge of our students may also object. I, too, used to think that knowledge was important and that we should encourage hard work and perseverance. Now I realize that the concept of rewards for merit is elitist and, therefore, wrong in a society that aims for equality in all things. We are a democracy. What could be more democratic than to give exactly the same grade to every single student?

One or two forlorn colleagues may even protest that we have a responsibility to significant works of the past because the writings of such authors as Chaucer, Shakespeare, Milton and Swift are intrinsically valuable. I can empathize with these misguided souls, for I once labored under the illusion that I was giving my students a precious gift by introducing them to works by great poets, playwrights and satirists. Now I recognize the error of my ways. The writings of such authors may have seemed meaningful to our ancestors, who had nothing better to do, but we are living in a time of wonderful improvements. The writers of bygone eras have been made irrelevant, replaced by MTV and *People* magazine. After all, their bodies are dead. Why shouldn't their ideas be dead, too?

JOYOUS SMILES

If any colleagues persist in protesting that we should try to convey knowledge to students and preserve our cultural heritage, I offer this suggestion: honestly consider what students really want. As one young man graciously explained to me, he had no desire to take my course but had enrolled in it merely to fulfill a requirement that he resented. His job schedule made it impossible for him to attend at least 30 percent of my class sessions, and he wouldn't have time to do much of the reading. Nevertheless, he wanted a good grade. Another student consulted me after the first exam, upset because she had not studied and had earned only 14 points out of a possible 100. I told her that, if she studied hard and attended class more regularly, she could do well enough on the remaining tests to pass the course. This encouragement did not satisfy her. What she wanted was an assurance that she would receive at least a B. Under my plan both students would be guaranteed an A. Why not? They have good looks and self-esteem. What more could anyone ever need in life?

I do not ask for thanks from the many people who will benefit. I'm grateful to my colleagues who for decades have tried to help me realize that seriousness about teaching is not the path to professorial prestige, rapid promotion and frequent sabbaticals. Alas, I was stubborn. Not until I heard the illuminating explanation of the student who had plagiarized from the anthology's introduction to Jonathan Swift did I fully grasp the wisdom that others had been generously offering to me for years—learning is just too hard. Now, with a light heart, I await the plan's adoption. In my mind's eye, I can see the happy faces of university administrators and professors, released at last from the irksome chore of dealing with students. I can imagine the joyous smiles of thousands of students, all with straight-A averages and plenty of free time.

My only regret is that I wasted so much time. For nearly 30 years, I threw away numerous hours annually on trivia: writing, grading and explaining examinations; grading hundred of papers a semester; holding private conferences with students; reading countless books; buying extra materials to give students a feeling for the music, art and clothing of past centuries; endlessly worrying about how to improve my teaching. At last I see the folly of grubbing away in meaningless efforts. I wish that I had faced facts earlier and had not lost years because of old-fashioned notions. But such are the penalties for those who do not understand the true purpose of education.

STUDENT VOICES

You don't have to be published in *Newsweek* or *The New Yorker* to have something to say. The following essays were all written for Professor Martha F. Bowden's first-year writing class at Kennesaw State University in Georgia. As a class, use what you have learned in the first section of this book to analyze and evaluate these essays as arguments.

Rachel Rosshirt

Our Actors Need Help: Entertainment Is in Danger

Since May of 2000, the Screen Actor's Guild (SAG) and the American Federation of Television and Radio Artists (AFTRA) have been on strike against commercial advertisers. Advertisers want to cut out the "pay-per-play" system, which pays the actors a fee each time their commercial is aired ("Striking Actors"). The situation does not harm so much the famous rich actors as it does the new actors starting out in commercials. The exclusion of the "pay-per-play" system would cause struggling actors not to make enough money to even pay their bills. SAG and AFTRA want the advertisers not only to keep the "pay-per-play" system, but to apply it to commercials aired on cable television as well. As of now, commercial actors are getting paid a flat fee for commercials aired on cable TV. SAG is fighting for the "pay-per-play" system because over 80 percent of their members make an annual income of less than $5,000 ("Striking Actors").

Actors deserve more from advertisers. How would companies be able to advertise their products without actors? Actors are the heart of entertainment and advertising. We need to support our actors because without them there would not be movies to watch on dates or with friends, or television shows to entertain us at night or with family. Life would be pretty boring without television and movies. Support from fans, friends, and family is key to the unions' success.

There are far more actors than television and film industries can hire, but whose right is it to say that actors cannot try to live out their dream of acting just because there are already too many actors? Many new actors start out by doing commercials; this is a great way to be seen by millions of television and film viewers, as well as casting directors. Commercial work needs to pay actors so that they can actually make a living. It's a job that should pay the bills, just like working in a factory, a law firm, or a major corporation. Many people working in these types of jobs make a decent living. Why should the actors' union strike be any different than a factory union strike? There are a lot of rich, famous actors out there, but they are not fighting for themselves, they are fighting for the struggling actors because many of the rich actors started out in commercials.

So far the strike has had pretty good success. In the first half of June the number of commercial permits issued in Los Angeles has dropped 67 percent from the 1999 levels. SAG's president, William Daniels, says, "It's the most effective strike we've ever had" (qtd. in "Striking Actors"). SAG and AFTRA have also gained the support of other unions, including those of professional athletes. Athlete members of these unions have even canceled commercial shoots at the last minute to respect the picket line. Some companies have even signed an "'interim agreement'--which stipulates that the company will honor the unions' proposed contract terms" ("Striking Actors").

Not only would the omission of the "pay-per-play" system harm the new adult actors, but it would also really hurt the child actors. There are many child actors, especially in commercials. It is one thing to "rip off" an adult, but to "rip off" a child is unethical. Think about it. Why are there are so many commercials with children in them? Because children sell! If advertisers start to pay actors a flat fee for the airing of commercials, then they can easily air the commercial 7,000 times or more, causing the actor to become overexposed. Overexposure can cause people to lose interest in that actor (Petersen). Loss of interest in a child actor can really hurt that child's career before it even takes off. Commercials are a gateway into the world of acting, especially for child actors (Petersen). If children are taken advantage of in the commercial industry, many parents could easily stop their children from joining the industry. Many child actors want to be actors. When parents get in the way, the child's dream is killed. If the industry treats children in an appealing way, parents will be more likely to allow their children to step into the acting world and live out their dream.

The common opinion states that the "pay-per-play" system benefits the actor but hurts the advertiser. Not so. The "pay-per-play" system does not hurt the advertiser, but discarding it produces more money for them. At the same time, though, the actors are in a sense giving away their talent without the system. Actors sell their talent when they are in commercials, movies, or television shows. Advertisers may realize this, but they choose to ignore it. Actors deserve more. Acting is a love and a passion for many actors, and taking away the income causes actors to turn to other jobs to make a living. When actors must go elsewhere for money, they lose time for acting work. If the advertisers do not give in to the unions, eventually the entertainment industry will slowly fade away because the gateway into the acting world will no longer serve the purpose it does today. Actors will no longer be able to get as much exposure in commercials because the unions will always stand in the way. The only way to keep the entertainment industry alive is for the unions and the advertisers to come to an agreement that works for all.

Works Cited

Petersen, Paul. "Union Kids Strike the Commercial World." A Minor Consideration. 1 May 2000. 25 Oct. 2000 <http://www.minorcon.org/strike.html>.

"Striking Actors Won't Be Turned Out." Union Trends and Data. 11 Jul. 2000. Labor Research Association. 23 Oct. 2000 <http://laborresearch.org/strikes/actors.htm>.

Kayla Crawford

Quit Blaming Teachers for Low Academic Achievement

When my mother was thirty-six years old, she decided to go back to school to become a teacher. At the time, she had a six-year-old daughter, an unsupportive husband, and a full-time job as an accountant. Despite all of these situations against her, she managed to graduate with honors from Kennesaw State College in four years with a bachelor's degree in elementary education. All of her life she had wanted to be a teacher. Now, seven years later, she is a first grade teacher at McGarity Elementary School in Paulding County. She loves her job. But just a few weeks ago, she told me that she does not want to teach anymore.

The reason that she no longer wants to teach is Governor Barnes's education reform bill. According to the bill, teachers are held accountable for their students' shortcomings on standardized tests and other academic measures. The number of students in elementary classrooms will be dramatically reduced (to no more than nineteen per teacher) and new programs targeted at "at-risk" students (those who are below level) will be implemented to improve classroom achievement (Governor's). To someone who is distanced from the education field (those who have no school-aged children or those who are uninvolved in their child's education), the reforms seem to be a step in the right direction to improve Georgia's academic achievement. But to an educator, these reforms are pointing fingers in the wrong direction: at the teachers instead of at the parents.

Another one of the controversial proposals in the governor's education reforms is to increase academic achievement by "weeding out" the bad teachers and making room for the good (Governor's). While this proposal sounds good, a child's academic achievement is not entirely up to the teachers. The effect that parents have on their young child's education is much stronger than that of the teacher. No matter how phenomenal the teacher, if the parents do not prepare their child for what will be learned and reinforce what was learned, school is a waste of the child's time. But the governor's proposals do not attempt to ensure that parents prepare for school and reinforce what is being taught. Instead, Governor Barnes's answer is to punish teachers based on the academic progress of their students. If these teachers were really "held accountable" (as Governor Barnes says) for their students' academic progress, the state would be firing teachers at an alarming rate. And this would only solve half the problem!

Many parents have their children involved in after-school activities: football, cheerleading, dance, etc. Sometimes these activities do not end until eight or nine o'clock at night. When the child gets home and still has to do homework, take a bath, and other nighttime rituals, the child may not get into bed until ten or eleven o'clock. This time is much too late for a young child to be awake on a school night! Often homework is neglected in order to allow the child to sleep. This situation demands the question: which is more important to a child's future, education or recreation activities?

The governor also has big plans for those children who come from a home environment that is not conducive to successful child rearing (so-called "at risk" children) and consequently are not prepared for school. He proposes to implement new programs designed to bring these children up to the normal standards for their grade level (Governor's). Again, these new programs will work in theory, but when a teacher attempts to recommend a student for these programs, there are tests to be administered (many that require parental consent) and forms to be filled out and submitted. This process can take up to six months to complete. By then, the child is too far behind in academics, and it is almost pointless to place him or her in the program. There are more flaws in this plan than just this aforementioned one: as I mentioned above, many of these tests require parental consent, something that many parents are unwilling to give for various reasons. Without that all-important signature, the child is forced to struggle in his or her regular classroom, not really learning anything. In addition, if a child does struggle in class and consequentially fails all of his or her subjects, parental consent is required to retain a child in the current grade instead of promoting him or her to the next. If the parent denies the consent, then the child is legally required to be "placed" in the next grade, where he or she will undoubtedly fail and the process will repeat itself (Crawford).

State School Superintendent Linda Schrenko says in a press release that "Instead of real education reform, the [state] House and Senate passed a bill that only gives false hopes of education reform" (qtd. in HB1187). It seems that if Governor Barnes really were interested in increasing Georgia's academic achievement, he would do more than just point fingers at the teachers. If a child fails to improve, maybe the parents should be held accountable before even examining the teacher. Education starts with the parents when the child is a toddler (or perhaps even earlier). If children do not receive stimulation from their parents in these first few years, they are like brick walls in the classroom: they will not absorb anything and the material will bounce off them. My mother constantly receives praise from her students' parents who say that she is a wonderful teacher. My mother also is doing something that she loves. If she does indeed decide to quit teaching to pursue another career, the state would lose a great contribution to the education system.

Works Cited

Crawford, Ginger. Personal Interview. 24 Oct. 2000.

Governor's Education Reform Study 2000- Legislation. 23 October 2000 <http://www.gagovernor.org/governor/edreform_2000/legislation.html>.

HB 1187 Georgia Department of Education. 23 October 2000 <http://www.doe.k12.ga.us/communication/releases/hb1187summary.html>.

Jeff Jones

The Law of the New Economy

During the 1920s, the government established Prohibition to augment social order at the price of a nation's right to drink. In the 1960s, the government was forced to create legislation granting equal rights to minorities, thereby increasing individual freedoms. In the

United States, there have been many times of tension between social order and individual freedoms. It is a central issue that affects all governments and the people they govern. There must be a balance established between the laws that are necessary to maintain order and the protection of the rights of the people. However, there are certain freedoms that must not be compromised in order to maintain a democratic and free society. The government should not regulate the Internet because that infringes on the freedom of speech, stifles creativity, and prevents growth of the New Economy.

One of the great things in this country is the right guaranteed to all citizens to freely express themselves and communicate without undue restraint. The First Amendment of the Constitution was created to prevent the government from taking away the most vital elements of a democratic society. The government cannot regulate the Internet because that would infringe upon these essential freedoms. This fact has been proven with the Supreme Court's overturning of the Communications Decency Act in 1998. The law violated the freedom of speech by dictating what materials cannot be publicly posted on the World Wide Web and was inherently unconstitutional. To ensure the continued freedom of our society, it is necessary to prevent government censorship and regulation of the Internet. On the Late Show with David Letterman, Al Gore said, "Remember America: I gave you the Internet, and I can take it away." (qtd. in Thyfault 74) It was intended as a joke but doubles as a reminder of how nothing should be taken for granted.

Government regulation of the World Wide Web would destroy creativity and freedom of expression. These elements must be protected and are essential to the function of a democracy. Without any creativity or personal expression, we would all be identical. Communist countries have tried to force conformity and revoke individual freedoms with terrible failure. All people have an instinctive need to be different and to be creative as human beings. Art is an area of little or no government censorship because it is widely accepted as a way for people to express themselves. The Internet is only a new medium of communication that is no different from art or the press. It allows individuals to convey their personal thoughts and ideas digitally. Any actions taken by the government to restrain this new medium would not only demolish creativity, but it would also be an unconstitutional infringement of the people's right to express themselves freely.

Necessity may be the mother of invention, but it is most certainly not the means by which innovation occurs. Technology has advanced greatly because of the freedom and creativity the Internet offers. The Web allows all people access to information and gives them an outlet for expression of their own ideas. The Internet has sped innovation and the development of technology around the world in a very short time. It has increased the efficiency of business, allowed people in different countries to talk in real-time, and created a new platform of thought without physical limits. The potential of the Web is virtually limitless and has only begun to be explored. A New Economy has been formed of companies that take advantage of this frontier, such as Intel, Cisco, and Microsoft. They realize the ability of the Web to make money and create a worldwide marketplace. Government interference with these businesses would result in lost productivity, lost innovation, and lost potential. The taxes, laws, and bureaucracy that government uses to control would cause complete and utter annihilation of the New Economy's potential. Robert Holleyman, president and CEO of the Business Software Alliance, agrees with this fact when he says, "It's in the best interest of the economy to maintain only the lightest touch regarding regulating this industry." (qtd. in Bacheldor 55)

The government must not regulate the Internet so that the free and economically healthy world we live in today may continue to strive. There is nothing to gain and everything to lose by restraining the potential of the World Wide Web. It has allowed us to perform tasks that were not even imaginable one hundred years ago. Who knows what the future may hold? The economy of the nineties has been one of the most prosperous in history because of great technological advances. The Internet is a vital tool that will ensure future innovation for generations to come as long as it is preserved. However, the Web is useless without the right to use it freely. The freedoms that we so commonly take for granted such as the freedom of expression and the freedom of speech are fragile and should be protected at all cost. Without them, the government can become an unchecked totalitarian force of destruction to both technology and freedom.

Works Cited

Bacheldor, Beth. "Undue Influence?" Information Week 9 Oct. 2000: 54-68.

Thyfault, Mary E. "Presidential Focus." Information Week 9 Oct. 2000: 74.

Erin Beavers

The Case for Graduated Driver Licensing

Amongst teenage drivers motor vehicle accidents are the leading cause of death. In fact, on the basis of miles driven teenagers are involved in three times as many fatal accidents as are all drivers, and though young people make up only 6.7 percent of the total driving population in the country, they are involved in 14 percent of all fatal accidents ("Saving," appendix C). Based on these figures it is obvious that something needs to be done to improve teenage driving; however, the course of action that should be taken is fiercely debated. Though there are many suggestions, the two most popular solutions at this time are putting driver's education back in the public school curriculum and raising the legal driving age from the present age of sixteen to the age of seventeen, or possibly even eighteen. In order to choose a solution, the reasons for poor teen driving need to be examined. According to the National Highway Transportation Safety Administration in its online publication Saving Teenage Lives, the three main factors are inexperience, risk-taking behavior and immaturity, and greater risk exposure (referring to the high likelihood of teens driving at night or with other teens in the car). Thus, the proper solution would be one in which all of these areas are considered. While the suggestion to put driver's education back in schools may solve the problem of inexperience, it does not address the issues of immaturity and greater risk exposure. Similarly, raising the legal driving age may be the solution to the problem of immaturity, but the problems of experience and greater risk exposure remain. I believe, however, that there is a solution that takes into account each of these factors and that is the use of graduated driver licensing.

Graduated driver licensing is a system in which "new drivers typically go through a three-stage process that involves their gradual introduction to full driving privileges . . . after the young driver demonstrates responsible driving behavior, restrictions are systematically lifted until the driver 'graduates' to full driving privileges" (Natl. Highway, sec. I). Graduated licensing has in fact already proven to be successful in states and countries that have adopted the program. Five years after the state of California began implementing the program fatal accidents among young drivers were reduced by 5.3 percent, and in Ontario, Canada, the crash rate of teenage drivers dropped 27 percent during the first two years of the program (Natl. Highway, sec. IV). In my opinion, the reason graduated driver licensing works is that it is a solution that encompasses the three main factors of poor teen driving: inexperience, risk-taking behavior/immaturity, and greater risk exposure.

To eliminate the problem of inexperience, the graduated licensing program requires the use of three levels of licensing, the first of which prevents inexperienced drivers from obtaining a license. The first license is a learner's permit. The core components of this permit are that the driver must be supervised by a parent or guardian twenty-one years of age or older, the driver must complete basic driver's education training, and the driver must have the permit for at least six months before moving on to the next stage (Natl. Highway, sec. II). States may choose to expand upon these core components by requiring a certain number of hours behind the wheel or extending the length of time the permit must be held before moving on. By setting up prerequisites to obtaining a license, drivers are forced to gain valuable driving experience.

The second stage of licensing, the intermediate or provisional license, combats the problem of greater risk exposure. To receive an intermediate license, a driver must complete the learner's permit stage and pass an on-road driving test, and the intermediate license must be kept for at least twelve months before the driver moves on to the next stage. While in possession of the provisional license, the driver is under established restrictions such as restricted nighttime driving hours unless supervised by parents and limits on the number of other teenage passengers allowed in the vehicle (Natl. Highway, sec. II). The use of conditional licensing and limiting driver privileges keeps young drivers from being at a greater risk of accidents caused by their own error by allowing new drivers to learn in controlled and low-risk environments.

In the third and final stage of licensing, drivers are given a license with all restrictions removed except for applicable laws such as alcohol restrictions. This stage addresses the problem of immaturity because before a driver can receive the full license, he or she must have passed all requirements for the two previous licenses and have had a minimum of a year and half of driving experience. Most plans, though, recommend having a minimum of two years of experience, one year of stage one and one year of stage two. Thus, a person who gets a learner's permit at the age of fifteen must be seventeen years of age before receiving a full license. This stage also tackles the problem of risk-taking behavior because, should the driver be involved in serious accidents in which he or she is at fault or be convicted of driving under the influence of alcohol before the age of twenty-one, the driver's license status will be demoted to that of a stage two provisional license (Natl. Highway, sec. II). Preventing drivers from gaining a restriction-free license until they have completed a minimum of a year and a half of training and downgrading the status of the license if the driver behaves irresponsibly encourages drivers to behave maturely and responsibly.

Some opponents of this solution argue that it forces parents or guardians to "chauffeur" their children or that the three-step program discriminates against teens by limiting their mobility. I would argue that preventing fatalities caused by young drivers is far more important than these few inconveniences. Though graduated licensing does require supervised driving time, it is not an unreasonable or extensive amount of time. As for the issue of limited mobility, a study of over fifty thousand students in seven states conducted by the Insurance Institute for Highway Safety reported that the social life and work patterns of sixteen-year-olds were generally unaffected by the age requirement necessary to receive a full license (Natl. Highway, sec. III). The issue of dangerous teenage driving is one that affects almost every member of the community, not just parents. Anyone who is on the road is at risk and should be aware of the problem and the available solutions. Based on the effectiveness and practicality of the graduated licensing system, I believe it to be the clear choice for a course of action. Some states have already adopted some form of graduated licensing, but many of these programs are not strict enough or are simply not enforced, and most states have not adopted any form of graduated licensing program at all. However, there is a way to let the government know that you want things to change. Every governor of every state has appointed a Governor's Highway Safety Representative to oversee highway safety programs in that state, and you can write or call your representative to voice your opinion. The teen driving situation must be taken seriously and needs to be resolved because it is literally a matter of life and death, not just for teens but also for everyone on the road.

Work Cited

Natl. Highway Transportation Safety Administration. Saving Teenage Lives. 23 Oct. 2000 <http://nhtsa.gov/people/injury/newdriver/SaveTeens/toc.html>.

Chapter 6

Writing Researched Arguments

What Research Contributes to an Argument

Once you have found an issue you care about, you should find what others have said about the issue. You need to do research. Research is the systematic gathering, recording, and evaluating of information. Doing research will help you become educated about a subject so that you can form your own opinion and so that you can find the best reasons to persuade others. Research also adds to your credibility as a writer because you are able to merge your voice with the voices of recognized experts in a subject. Research also strengthens your credibility because it allows you to see all sides of an issue—to understand an issue in all of its complexity—and to make a balanced presentation of the issue, communicating to your audience that you are fair-minded and have goodwill.

Another important reason to do research is to find your place in a larger conversation about ideas. Arguments occur within a context and are part of a conversation. Research is how you get caught up on that conversation. In a small community, keeping up on a conversation is fairly simple. Such a conversation usually takes place in real time and a real place and involves just a few participants. You may have a group of friends, for example, who form a small community for you. When you and your friends meet at some regular hangout, this occasion becomes the right time and place for a conversation. It is a moment of *kairos.* There may be more than one conversation occurring at the same time, but generally you can follow the thread of what others are saying. If other friends come in late, you can fill them in on what you've all been talking about because you have "recorded" the conversation in your head and can summarize it for them. In the same manner, if you attend a lecture or a meeting, you can fairly easily keep notes or minutes of what was said for your later reference or for someone who was not able to attend.

More formal conversations or virtual conversations can be more complex, however, and often require sophisticated means to gather and record information. In fact, some conversations are so large or have been going on for so long that no one person has recorded the conversation in his or her memory. Some very formal kinds of conversations are, nonetheless, recorded in great detail. For instance, the Supreme Court is a place for debating and deciding U.S. constitutional issues. The Court deals with a number of complex cases each year and has been doing so for more than 200 years, much longer than anyone on the present court has been alive. Imagine the problems that would ensue if the Court did not keep written records of its proceedings and decisions: The present justices would have to rely solely on what they had heard others say about past decisions.

Although you probably won't ever argue before the Supreme Court, when you argue about community issues, you will engage in conversations that have been going on for some time—often since before you were born. For instance, an essay about music piracy on the Internet might take you back to the original arguments about the first copyright laws. An argument about racial profiling may require that you review several years of research, legislation, and court decisions on civil rights, racial equality, and police practice. Writing, reading, and research have made it possible for people to follow the development of complex conversations such as these. But to use research to strengthen your argument, you need to know something about the kinds of sources that are available and about how to locate, record, and evaluate these sources.

Types of Research and Sources

PRIMARY SOURCES

Primary sources are those that you gather, describe, analyze, and report first-hand. Primary sources are interviews, surveys, questionnaires, observations, experiments, historical documents, eyewitness testimonies, literary texts, works of art. A scientist does primary research by observing nature or trying to reproduce natural conditions in a controlled environment through an experiment. For instance, a geologist would examine rock bodies and gather samples, a chemist would conduct experiments, a doctor might conduct clinical trials with patients, and a zoologist might examine the behavior of animals in the wild. A social scientist does primary research by conducting interviews, administering surveys and questionnaires, gathering statistical data, and observing human behavior. For instance, an anthropologist might live among a native tribe in New Guinea, a political scientist might use voting statistics to understand how people make decisions, an economist might gather data to understand consumer behavior, and a psychologist might conduct interviews or observe people in a controlled environment. Scholars in the humanities and historians use texts and artifacts as primary sources. For instance, a historian might use the diary and letters of someone from the past to reconstruct that person's life; an art historian would examine paintings, sketches, and notes of an artist; a literary critic might look at various drafts of a novel; and a musician might analyze early recordings of a particular performance.

Although, as a student, you may not have many opportunities to do sophisticated experiments or surveys, you should try to incorporate primary research into your writing as much as you can. Perhaps you can interview someone who is an expert on the issue you are studying or who has some personal experience relevant to your subject. You might be able to do some simple observations to strengthen your research. For instance, if you are doing a paper on water quality issues, you could schedule a visit to the local water treatment plant. Or if you are researching the judicial system, you could spend a few hours visiting a courtroom or prison. You may also be able to locate in your library or online some raw statistical data (such as census records, opinion polls, or consumer research) or some historical documents. Government documents often provide easy access to legislative reports, government reports and statistics, and court documents.

SECONDARY SOURCES IN PRINT AND ONLINE

Secondary sources are those that have been gathered, recorded, analyzed, and evaluated by someone else. These sources will provide you with the bulk of the information for your research. You should take advantage of the hard work of other researchers and build on what they have done to advance the conversation. Secondary sources include academic journals, popular magazines, trade magazines, newspapers, books, and most government documents and websites. Each of these sources has its own rules and conventions, its own way of carrying on the conversation.

Academic Journals Academic journals, for instance, are publications written and edited by scholars and researchers for other scholars. Academic journals provide a forum for scholars to report their own primary research. Editors of these journals usually assume an informed and engaged readership. These journals are usually published every three or four months, although some may be published only twice a year. Academic journals are typically bound in card stock (a kind of heavy paper) and are printed on plain paper with few advertisements or photographs. Because of limited distribution, academic journals can be expensive to produce, so publishers try to save money by eliminating frills. Because of the increasing costs of producing academic journals (particularly in the sciences), online journals are becoming more common. Academic journals meet the needs of very specialized academic communities and include titles such as *Protein Science, Harvard Law Review, Journal of Abnormal Psychology, Journal of Public Policy,* and *Shakespeare Quarterly.*

Academic journals are often associated with a formal scholarly organization. For instance, *PMLA* is a journal published by the Modern Language Association, an association of scholars devoted to the academic study of language, literature, and writing. It is the official site of conversation for members of this community. *The Quarterly Journal of Speech* is an official publication for the National Communication Association, and *The Journal of the American Medical Association* is sponsored by the national society for the medical profession. Although not every journal is affiliated with a particular scholarly organization, most are associated with a community of scholars, organized by their common interest in a particular field.

Although they may be difficult for nonspecialists to read, academic journals are generally recognized as sources of the highest quality and reliability. To be published in an academic journal, an essay must pass rigorous review by experts in the subject area who serve on the journal's board of editors. These reviewers will usually try to ensure that the essay makes an original contribution to knowledge in that field. This careful review process does not mean that everything published in an academic journal is true, accurate, or reliable, but it does mean that each essay has been carefully evaluated by a team of experts. This peer review also means that essays submitted to academic journals take a long time to be published. Often, the information published may be a few years out of date when it appears in print.

Popular Magazines Popular magazines are usually published more frequently than academic journals. Many appear at least once a month, and some are published weekly. Nearly all are published on slick paper, with high-quality, glossy photographs and professional page layout and design. Many popular magazines try to attract a large, national audience. Others focus on specific interest groups.

Popular magazines include titles such as *People, Seventeen, Sports Illustrated, Parenting, Newsweek, Time, Cosmopolitan, Woman's Day, Esquire,* and *Business Week.* Although they don't involve the same careful review found in an academic journal, articles published in popular magazines may be a valuable resource for your research. Often a popular magazine will discuss topics not found in scholarly journals, and popular magazines are usually more current. The articles may involve primary research based on the writer's firsthand experience, interviews, or observations. They may also report secondary research in a way that is understandable to a general readership. Your teacher may allow (or even require) you to supplement your research in scholarly sources with information found in popular magazines.

Trade Journals As popular magazines become more specialized, it is difficult to distinguish them from trade magazines. Trade magazines (or journals) often have a format similar to popular magazines, but they are geared toward particular trades, professions, or interest groups. They are usually published once a month, often on slick paper and with many advertisements and photographs. The advertising is typically aimed at the magazine's specialized readership. However, some trade magazines will look like academic journals, newspapers, or newsletters if the readership is somewhat limited. Trade magazines include titles such as *PC World* (for the computer software industry), *Waste Age* (for the sanitation industry), and *Photography* (for professional photographers as well as hobbyists). Although the submissions aren't reviewed in the way that academic journals are, articles in trade magazines are usually written by experts. Trade journals are a particularly good source for technical or specialized information.

Newspapers Newspapers are excellent sources for the most recent information on a subject, but not all newspapers are equal. Some newspapers are recognized as reliable sources for national and world news. These include the *New York Times, Washington Post,* and *Wall Street Journal.* These newspapers papers typically provide in-depth analysis and careful reporting. Newspapers such as these often provide information for other newspapers. *USA Today* is a popular national newspaper, and it is a good source for quick headlines, but it doesn't have the same quality and depth of reporting as the other national newspapers. Important regional newspapers provide the same kind of careful analysis and reporting but not on the same scale. These include papers such as the *Los Angeles Times, Arizona Republic, Chicago Sun-Times, Denver Post, Houston Chronicle,* or *Miami Herald.* These papers usually provide valuable information on the states and communities they serve. You should also rely on good local papers for coverage of local or campus issues. Your campus may have a newspaper as well, but campus papers vary considerably in quality. You should use more than one newspaper as a source. A national newspaper, such as the *New York Times,* will provide a different perspective on an issue than will a local paper. It can be useful to get both perspectives. Examining newspapers published in other countries will provide you with a fresh perspective on the world, and on the United States.

Books Books represent a range of quality from the carefully reviewed and edited publications of academic presses to the publications of vanity presses that will publish just about anything for any writer who will pay the cost of printing. Books provide a valuable resource for getting caught up on a conversation because if they are well written, they will review, analyze, and evaluate much of the previously published secondary research. But because books take even longer to edit and publish than academic journals, they are not a good source for the very latest information. Although you may examine several books through your research, try to limit the number of books you include. Two or three books will usually be enough. Skim through books, carefully examining their tables of contents, looking for just the right book. Searching for just the right book will also help you to focus your topic. For instance, instead of looking for every book ever written about the civil rights movement, you might choose one that focuses on a particular moment or individual.

Look for books that are published by reputable presses. Many universities publish books on scholarly topics. These books are usually reviewed by experts who try to ensure that the book makes an original contribution to research. Large national presses also use a careful editing process, but usually not peer review. Beware of material that is self-published, whether by an individual or an organization. As with all sources, you should compare what one author says against what others have said and draw your own conclusions.

Government Documents Government documents include the records and publications of local, county, and state governments, as well as publications of the U.S. government, some foreign governments, and international organizations such as the United Nations or the World Health Organization. Government documents include the proceedings of the U.S. Congress, as well as the reports of specific committees and subcommittees. Government documents usually resemble academic journals, printed on plain paper and bound in card stock. Government documents include a variety of sources. Some may just be transcripts, with no attempt to analyze or evaluate the source material. These transcripts can provide valuable information for primary research. The government also produces technical reports and books that are carefully edited and reviewed as well as brochures, pamphlets, and booklets directed to a popular audience.

Websites Websites can provide almost any kind of information, but websites generally are less carefully written, edited, and reviewed than print sources. The strength of the Internet is that it can conveniently provide up-to-the-minute information. The weakness is that anyone can publish anything. But more and more, you can find reputable information online. You just need to be extremely cautious in how you use Internet sources.

Secondary sources are all virtual places where people communicate with one another. Writers are separated from one another by time and space, but they "speak" to us and to each other from the shelves of the library. Of course, you can't ask a book questions the way you might ask friends questions to help you catch up on a conversation. But a book or academic journal can reveal a lot about the conversation of which it is a part and the communities that participate in that conversation.

VISUAL IMAGES AS SOURCES

As multimedia text becomes more common, visual elements of a text become more significant. Printed texts are using more visual elements. Even academic journals sometimes use black-and-white photographs or charts, graphs, and figures. Popular and trade magazines are highly visual. Electronic publication makes the use of visual information relatively inexpensive. Visual materials come in many forms and can be primary or secondary materials. In your research, you may wish to consult maps, diagrams, photographs, drawings, graphs, or charts. You may want to photograph or scan your own images to be used in your argument (particularly if you have gathered the information through your own observations). Be cautious, however, in how you use visual information. A picture reveals a lot, but it can also conceal. You never know for sure what is outside the frame of the camera, and photographers have a range of techniques for manipulating an image to achieve desired effects. Powerful computer graphic applications, such as Adobe Photoshop, can give anyone with a computer the ability to change images. As with all other sources, you need to evaluate the information conveyed by a visual image against the information you have gathered from other sources. Just as you shouldn't believe everything you read, you shouldn't believe everything you see.

Whenever you use a visual element in your essay, you should also make sure the visual element forms an integral part of your argument instead of mere decoration. Label each image properly and identify its source. If it is an image that you created, then identify yourself as the source. Be careful about downloading or copying images from the Internet or scanning images out of books. Some may be copyrighted, in which case you would need to gain the permission of the copyright holder as well as acknowledge the source.

What Research Looks Like in Arguments

When you record academic conversations that occur in classrooms or lecture halls, you take notes, jotting down ideas in your own words, summarizing or outlining extended lecture material, and perhaps quoting meaningful phrases. The principles used in note-taking also apply to research. You can take notes in many ways. Some people use note cards or half sheets of paper. Others may photocopy the source and then annotate it. And some may take notes on a laptop or even use a handheld scanner. How you take notes is up to you. Find a system that works for you, a system that allows you to record and retrieve information accurately and efficiently.

NOTE-TAKING AND DOCUMENTATION

Generally, you should keep two kinds of notes: bibliographic notes and content notes. The bibliographic note should provide publication information about the source you are using. For a book this would generally include the author's name, the title of the book, the place of publication, the publisher, and the year of publication. For a journal or magazine, this would generally include the author's name, the article title, the name of the journal, the volume, the year, and the inclusive page numbers. When you write your final paper, a "Works Cited" or "References" page at the end of the essay includes this information for each source you quoted, summarized, or paraphrased in your essay.

Academic communities have developed different formats for documenting sources. Two of the most common are the MLA and the APA styles, (named for the Modern Language Association and the American Psychological Association, two organizations within the academic community). You should find out from your instructor the style that is appropriate for your particular academic discipline. (Most college writing handbooks contain detailed information about documentation style.) Each documentation style has a particular form for reporting bibliographic information. Here are the basic forms for a book and for an academic journal in MLA style:

Book

Kessler, Ronald. The Bureau: The Secret History of the FBI. New York: St. Martin's, 2002.

Journal

Duffy, Edward. "Sentences in Harry Potter, Students in Future Writing Classes." Rhetoric Review 21 (2002): 170-87.

Here are the forms for a book and a journal in APA style:

Book

Halberstam, D. (2002) *Firehouse*. New York: Hyperion.

Journal

Klemperer, P. (2002) What really matters in auction design. *The Journal of Economic Perspectives, 16*(1), 169-189.

Whatever documentation style you use, I recommend that you memorize at least these basic forms for books and scholarly journals, and that you record the information for your bibliographic note in the proper form. Doing this will save you time when writing your paper. Since the bibliographic note is the record of the location of a conversation, you may also want to include whatever else you learned about the particular book, journal, magazine, or document—the context for the conversation—such as what you can discover about its readership or intended audience, its editorial policy, and any organizations affiliated with it. You will also want to include the call number and location of sources in the library.

The second type of note you need to take is a content note. This note contains information that you have learned from your source. It is difficult to copy everything by hand, and photocopying or scanning every page you might need is expensive and really only postpones the process of note-taking. I recommend taking notes in the form of summary, paraphrase, and occasional quotation. Use summary and paraphrase for most of the notes you take; use direct quotations sparingly. If you merely photocopy your sources or take all your notes as direct quotations, you will still have to summarize and paraphrase this material to include it in your essay. By taking most of your notes in the form of summary and paraphrase, you will save time in writing your essay and understand your research material better. Make sure that you include the information you will need to document this source in your essay: at least the author's name and the page number. You may also want to include a short title (if you are using more than one work by the same writer) or the year of publication (if you are using APA style).

Along with what you actually borrow from a source, you may want to include in your content notes any ideas you have about what you borrowed, perhaps your evaluation or response. I write my own ideas on the note within square brackets [like these] so that I can distinguish what I have borrowed from what is my own. (It is a typical practice to use square brackets in quoted material to indicate a comment from the writer who is quoting the passage.) If you think this might be confusing for you, use a separate card (or page break) and attribute the note to yourself. Keeping your own ideas separate from your summary or paraphrase of other ideas is important for avoiding plagiarism.

AVOIDING PLAGIARISM

Following proper guidelines for documenting source material is not just a matter of academic courtesy, and these guidelines don't just exist to help other scholars follow the trail of your research, although this is important. Being careful about documentation is essential for avoiding plagiarism, a serious crime in the academic community. Here are some examples of plagiarism:

- Copying another student's paper and handing it in as your own (even if the other student agrees to the copying). You should also not allow someone to copy your work.

- Handing in a paper written by someone else, hiring someone to write a paper for you, or copying a paper off the Internet. Many instructors will object to your handing in work that you completed in the past or that you are also using for another class. Make sure that you get both instructors' permission before using the same paper for two classes.
- Quoting the exact words of another author without proper acknowledgment, whether a sentence or a whole page.
- Using your own words to present the ideas of another author without proper acknowledgment. Even though the author may not be quoted, you should still credit the author as the source of the ideas you have borrowed. You must document anything you summarize or paraphrase from someone else.

Plagiarism is a serious offense and can get you in a lot of trouble—even when done unintentionally. You have a responsibility as a member of an academic community to learn how to avoid plagiarism. If you plagiarize, you may end up failing the assignment or the course, or even being suspended or expelled from college.

Documenting borrowed information allows your readers to locate your own writing within the context of a conversation and community and to identify your role as a contributor to that conversation. Your readers will be able to identify the conversations that you respond to and observe those conversations for themselves, understanding how you have extended or responded to other authors. Proper documentation also gives proper credit to other authors for their work. There are three ways of recording and reporting what someone else has contributed to the conversation: quotation, summary, and paraphrase. The ethics of academic writing require that you properly document any information that you quote, summarize, or paraphrase from an outside source.

QUOTATION

Quotation, the word-for-word transcription of what someone else said or wrote, may seem like the simplest method of recording a source's ideas, but it requires painstaking attention to detail. You have to record everything exactly as it is found in your source. This can take a lot of time if you copy by hand. It is a bit quicker if you have a laptop computer or a handheld scanner, or if you can find an electronic version of the original. Using the computer, you can simply cut and paste material to include in your own writing. Be very careful, though, to put quotation marks around anything you quote or to set off each longer quotation as an indented block. Again, failure to do so constitutes plagiarism and distorts your contribution to the conversation, leading readers to believe that you play a more important role than you actually do.

The MLA and APA styles call for "in-text" or "parenthetical" documentation. In this type of documentation, identifying information about the source is included in parentheses following the quoted material. MLA style includes the author's last name (if it has not been mentioned in the text) and the page number. APA style includes the author's last name, the year of publication, and the page number.

The following passages quote from the article "Employment-Based Health Insurance and Job Mobility," written by Brigitte C. Madrian, a University of Chicago economist. The first is in MLA style:

> Employers should note that "individuals with larger families are less likely to leave their jobs if they have health insurance than if they do not" (Madrian 52).

The documentation is in the parentheses following the quotation. It includes the author's last name and the page number of the source with no punctuation. Notice that the period comes after the parenthetical documentation. This is because the parenthetical material is actually part of the sentence (so it comes before the period) but not part of the quotation (so it comes after the last set of quotation marks).

Here is an example of APA style:

> Employers should note that "individuals with larger families are less likely to leave their jobs if they have health insurance than if they do not" (Madrian, 1994, p. 52).

Again, the documentation is in the parentheses following the quotation. In APA style the author's last name, the year of publication, and the page number of the source are included, separated by commas. Notice that in APA style, the abbreviation "p." is used for "page" ("pp." for "pages"); MLA style doesn't use this abbreviation.

You should generally give some kind of context or background for anything you quote, bringing your reader up to date on the conversation from which you are quoting. You may want to mention the author's full name, along with a bit about his or her background and a summary of the context from which you are quoting. When you introduce a quotation with the author's name, this information does not need to be repeated in the parentheses. Here is an example. The first is in MLA style:

> Brigitte Madrian, a University of Chicago economist, in her study of the effects of health insurance on job mobility found that "individuals with larger families are

> less likely to leave their jobs if they have health insurance than if they do not" (52).

Since the name of the author is given as part of the introduction to the quoted material, only the page number is included in the parentheses. Here is the same quotation following the APA format:

> In her study of the effects of health insurance on job mobility, Brigitte Madrian (1994) found that "individuals with larger families are less likely to leave their jobs if they have health insurance than if they do not" (p. 52).

In APA style, it is typical for the year of publication to follow the author's last name, and the page number to follow the actual quotation.

The previous two examples included the quoted material as part of a sentence that introduces that material. It is also possible for the quotation to follow a sentence, with a comma or colon introducing it. The following example uses MLA style:

> In a 1994 study, Brigitte Madrian, a University of Chicago economist, examined the effects of health insurance on job mobility: "Individuals with larger families are less likely to leave their jobs if they have health insurance than if they do not" (52).

It is even possible to interrupt quoted material with information about the context. This kind of interruption is set apart with commas. The following example uses APA style:

> "The majority of privately insured Americans obtain their health insurance through their own or a family member's employer," according to a recent study of the effects of health insurance on job mobility (Madrian, 1994). "The rationale for employers to provide health insurance is straightforward. By pooling the risks of individuals, employers can reduce adverse selection and lower administrative expenses" (p. 27).

SUMMARY

Summary is another common method of recording and reporting information. In a summary, you extract the main ideas from a larger piece of writing and report them in a much briefer form. You should use your own words, although it is acceptable in writing a summary to use some keywords and phrases from the original or to quote a memorable phrase. You may summarize a complete article or any part of it. As with quoted material, you must indicate where the summarized material came from using the appropriate style of documentation. Here is a summary of Brigitte Madrian's article on health insurance documented according to APA style:

> A recent study of the effects of health insurance on job mobility (Madrian, 1994, pp. 27-54) examined whether workers were "locked" into their jobs when their employers provided health insurance because prior medical conditions would not be insured if they left their jobs and had to obtain new coverage. For the years examined, this study found that in companies that provided health insurance the number of workers who willingly chose to change jobs decreased by 25 percent per year.

Note that in APA style you don't have to provide page number references following a summary, but it is recommended.

Here is the same summary in MLA format (with page number references):

> A recent study of the effects of health insurance on job mobility examined whether workers were "locked" into their jobs when their employers provided health insurance because prior medical conditions would not be insured if they left their jobs and had to obtain new coverage (Madrian 27-54). For the years examined, this study found that in companies that provided health insurance the number of workers who willingly chose to change jobs decreased by 25 percent per year.

Note that when you summarize, paraphrase, or quote from a Web page, you include the author's name (or a short title, if there is no author) but no page numbers.

When you write a summary, you should begin by previewing the essay: reading the first couple of paragraphs, the last few paragraphs, and the subheadings. Write down what you think the main ideas are in the essay, phrasing these ideas in your own words. Then read the article carefully and see how accurately you anticipated the writer's main ideas. Now try to summarize the main ideas of the writer. (The length of your summary depends on how much detail you need.)

PARAPHRASE

Paraphrase is the third method of recording and reporting information from sources. In a paraphrase, you rewrite a passage in your own words, preserving as much of the meaning of the original as you can. Think of paraphrase as an exercise in translation. You translate from the "language" of one community to the "language" of another. You may, for example, paraphrase a highly technical passage into language more familiar to nonspecialists or paraphrase highly formal language into more informal language. One method of paraphrasing is to read a passage carefully, cover it up, and then try to rewrite it in your own words. After you are finished, compare your paraphrase with the original. Cover the original again, revising your paraphrase to make sure that you have included the meaning of the original passage without using the actual language of the original. This may be difficult at first, but it will become easier as you become more skilled at rephrasing what others have said.

If this method does not work for you, then try the following two-step process. Substitute synonyms (words with similar meanings) for each keyword of the original passage. Be sure that you look up in a dictionary any words that are unfamiliar to you. Choose the words you substitute carefully so that they fit together in terms of their connotations, level of formality, and familiarity. Don't just open a thesaurus and pick any word from the list. For some particularly technical or precise words in the original, you may need to substitute an entire phrase to capture the right meaning. In fact, unlike a summary, a paraphrase is often longer than the original. After substituting keywords, revise the sentence and phrasal structure so that your paraphrase does not closely resemble the original.

As an example I will paraphrase the following passage from *The Communist Manifesto* by Karl Marx and Friedrich Engels:

> The bourgeoisie, wherever it has got the upper hand, has put an end to all feudal, patriarchal, idyllic relations. It has pitilessly torn asunder the motley feudal ties that bound man to his "natural superiors," and has left remaining no other nexus between man and man than naked self-interest, than callous "cash payment."

I will assume that I am using this passage in an essay addressed to a group that is not very familiar with the technical terminology of Marxist politics and economics, as well as other terms used in the passage, so that I need to paraphrase (or "translate") the passage to make the meaning more understandable. First, let's look up some of the unfamiliar terms. The following definitions come from *Webster's Tenth New Collegiate Dictionary:*

> *bourgeoisie:* the middle class or the social order dominated by the middle class
>
> *feudal:* relating to feudalism, the system of political organization prevailing in Europe from the 9th to about the 15th centuries, having as its basis the relation of lord to vassal with all land held in fee and as chief characteristics homage, the service of tenants under arms and in courts, wardship, and forfeiture
>
> *patriarchal:* relating to patriarchy, a social organization marked by the supremacy of the father in the clan or family, the legal dependence of wives and children, and the reckoning of descent and inheritance in the male line
>
> *idyllic:* pleasing or picturesque in natural simplicity
>
> *torn asunder:* torn into parts
>
> *motley:* composed of diverse often incongruous elements
>
> *nexus:* a connection or link
>
> *callous:* feeling no emotion, feeling no sympathy for others

When writing a paraphrase you cannot simply substitute dictionary definitions such as these for the words of the original. You must always consider whether or not the author is using these words according to the meaning expressed in the dictionary. And you must still put the paraphrase in your own words. Still, the dictionary can help you with unfamiliar or technical terms. Here is my first attempt at substituting my words for those of Marx and Engels:

> The middle class, wherever it has gained control, has eliminated any associations between lord and subject, father and family, or other natural ties. It has mercilessly broken apart the odd mix of agreements between the lord and his subjects that tied individuals to those who ruled over them by nature and has left behind no other connection between one individual and another than merely looking out for oneself, than emotion-free "monetary transaction."

In order to find some of these words, I consulted the dictionary. I also used a thesaurus to help me remember synonyms for words, but I was careful not to use any words from the thesaurus that I did not already know or that I did not look up in a dictionary to check for precise meaning.

Still, this paraphrase is not complete. It is only half of a paraphrase, relying too heavily on the structure and language of the original. Here is my attempt to recast the entire paragraph in my own words, using my own voice:

> In The Communist Manifesto Karl Marx and Friedrich Engels argue that whenever the middle class has gained control, it has done away with natural associations between individuals, such as those between lord and subject or father and family (60). They contend that the middle class mercilessly dissolved the odd mix of agreements found in the Middle Ages that tied individuals to those who ruled over them by nature. It has eliminated every connection between one individual and another except for looking out for oneself in a cold-hearted monetary transaction.

Evaluate this paraphrase. Does it capture the meaning without relying too heavily on the language of the original passage? Is it more understandable than the original? What kind of community would this kind of paraphrase be appropriate for? Could you revise this paraphrase and make it even less formal? (Notice that my paraphrase is longer than the original.)

In the sample above, I introduced the paraphrased passage by noting its source and included in-text documentation just as I might in a research paper. It is extremely important to introduce summarized and paraphrased material. Readers know when quoted material begins because you indicate this with quotation marks; but because a summary or paraphrase is in your own words, readers have no way of knowing when the borrowed passage begins unless you introduce it in some way. You can introduce summarized or paraphrased material by using the author's name or phrases such as "According to one author," "Studies show," "Research indicates," and "Some claim." Your parenthetical documentation will indicate where a borrowed passage ends.

DECIDING WHEN TO QUOTE, SUMMARIZE, OR PARAPHRASE

How do writers decide whether to quote, summarize, or paraphrase? Generally, beginning academic writers quote far too much, producing a paper that is more like a scrap-book of what others have said rather than a contribution to the academic conversation. You may want to quote in the following situations:

- When it is important to capture not only a writer's meaning but also the writer's language.
- When the writer writes with unusual authority and you want to include that sense of authority in your own writing.

- When you want to analyze a writer's exact words.
- When you want to distance yourself from what a writer has said so that it is clear to your audience that this is the writer's view and not yours.
- When the writer's words are famous or particularly memorable.

In nearly every other case, it is best to summarize or paraphrase. Use summary when you need only the main idea from an essay or long passage. Paraphrase passages when you want to include as much meaning as you can but when the language itself is not particularly significant.

The Process of Writing from Sources

A college or research library can seem an overwhelming and forbidding place for newcomers. Most college libraries are equipped with information desks and reference librarians, but if they are to assist you, you need to know what questions to ask. It helps to understand the process of library research. Students who don't know the process may simply wander about the library hoping their eye will catch a title somewhat related to their topic. If they pull down every book in the library, they will eventually find *something* related to their topic, but this is a very inefficient approach, akin to finding out what happened at a city council meeting by calling everyone in the phone book. Other students may at least ask a librarian, for example, "Does this library have any information on endangered species?" or look up "endangered species" in the catalog. This is slightly better than wandering around the library, but not much, because the library may have hundreds of books, articles, and documents related in some way to endangered species. Beginning with an Internet search is not much better than browsing the shelves of the library, and in most cases is much worse. If you used an Internet search engine to try to find material on "endangered species," you would track down every document among the billions of pages on the Internet with the words *endangered* and *species.* Such a search would probably generate tens of thousands of pages, but you would have no idea how to sort through them all. A more sensible approach is to learn how information is organized in a library.

Library research has five basic stages, as shown in Figure 6.1:

1. Finding background material on your topic.
2. Narrowing your topic and forming an issue question.
3. Finding research sources to use in your paper.
4. Evaluatory sources.
5. Taking notes and documentary sources.

Students are frequently tempted to skip the first two stages and try to go directly to the third, looking for books and articles or online information to include in their final paper. But following the first two stages is more efficient and will save

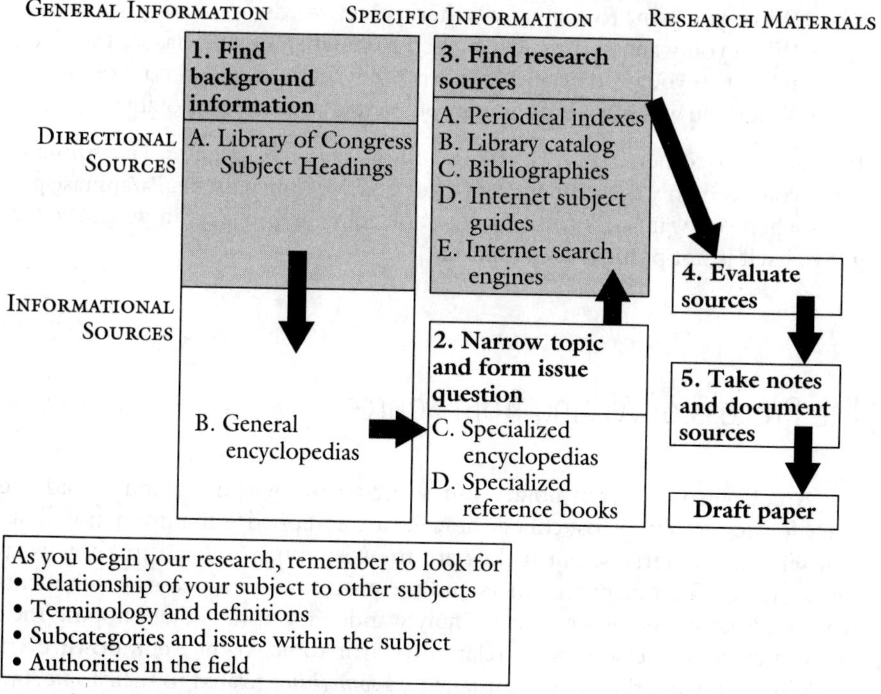

Figure 6.1 Research strategy model.
Source: Adapted from James E. Ford, "A General Research Model for Research Paper Introduction," *Literary Research Newsletter* 6 (1981), pp. 6–16.

you time in the long run. The strategy outlined in this diagram applies not only to your college writing courses but also to any kind of research project you undertake.

Library research begins with a topic or issue you wish to investigate. You may only have a vague notion of what you want to write about, perhaps something on biomedical ethics, water pollution, consumer product safety, or funding for the arts. You may have a more specific issue or controversy in mind. You may even have already formed an opinion on the issue and may be looking for evidence to support what you want to say. Even if you have a specific issue question in mind, however, it is probably best to begin by examining that issue within a broader context. Once you can see how your issue fits within the context of other conversations, you will be able to narrow your discussion of the issue and write about it more intelligently. First, get caught up on the general conversation; then, focus on your particular issue. Begin with a topic area for your research rather than a specific question to answer or thesis to prove.

The best way to conduct library research that will catch you up on the conversation is to begin with general sources and move on to more specific sources.

There are two kinds of library source material: informational and directional. Informational sources are part of the conversation I described earlier. They contain actual information related to your topic. General information sources, such as encyclopedias, dictionaries, and other reference works, summarize what others have said; they review the major issues related to a topic, nothing its major authors and contributors, and so are a quick way of catching up on the conversation. Particular scholarly communities and disciplines may also have their own encyclopedias, dictionaries, and reference works, containing more specific information. Journals, books, government documents, newspapers, magazines, and Internet pages are even more specific informational sources.

Directional sources help you locate informational sources and find out where academic conversations are taking place. Indexes, bibliographies, and catalogs are directional sources. As with informational sources, some directional sources are more specific than others, and some are related to particular scholarly disciplines.

STAGE ONE: FINDING BACKGROUND MATERIAL

Identifying Keywords and Subject Headings Where you begin library research depends on your level of familiarity with your issue and the sites of conversation related to it. An experienced member of a scholarly community working in his or her field of expertise can bypass the preliminary steps of library research. A less-experienced member of the community or a newcomer, however, will want to follow each step carefully. Begin by generating a list of possible terms associated with your subject. You can do this by consulting one of the most general of directional sources: the *Library of Congress Subject Headings* (LCSH) guide. The large red volumes of this guide are usually found near the reference desk, card catalog, or computer terminals in your library. Ask a librarian to help you find them. The LCSH lists the terms used by the Library of Congress to catalog library materials. Most library catalogs use these terms for subject searches. With this guide you can find some words used to describe your topic. If you have been following a conversation in a journal or magazine, you may already have some terms in mind. Jot down both general terms and more narrow terms. These will be important when you use other directional sources. Figure 6.2 shows a sample entry from the LCSH.

Words printed in bold in the LCSH are subject headings used in indexes organized according to the Library of Congress system. Catalogs at many colleges, for example, use these terms. Following most subject headings is a list of narrower, broader, and related terms that are also used to describe the topic. These terms are useful for keyword searches and for searching databases that do not use the Library of Congress terms or online indexes that allow for both Library of Congress subject searches and keyword searches on any term. The two-letter codes identify these keywords related to Library of Congress terms. UF stands for "Used For." Library of Congress terms are "used for"—or substitute for—

Cries *(May Subd Geog)*
[GT3450]
UF Street cries
Street songs
BT Cities and towns
Manners and customs
Sounds
Street music and musicians
NT Battle-cries
Peddlers and peddling

Crile family *(Not Subd Geog)*

Crime *(May Subd Geog)*
[HV6001-HV7220.5]
Here are entered works on the occurrence of crime. Works on the discipline that studies the causes, detection and prevention of crime, and the treatment or punishment of criminals, are entered under Criminology. Works on the criminal justice system are entered under Criminal justice, Administration of.
UF City crime
Crime and criminals
Crimes
Delinquency
Urban crime
BT Social problems
RT Criminal justice, Administration of
Criminal law
Criminals
Criminology
SA *headings beginning with the word* Criminal
NT Alcoholism and crime
Computer crimes
Crimes of passion
Crimes without victims
Drug abuse and crime
Education and crime
Employee crimes
Fear of crime
Hate crimes
Hypnotism and crime
Illegitimacy and crime
Impostors and imposture
Indians of North America—Crime
Juvenile delinquency
Mentally handicapped and crime
Narcotics and crime
Organized crime
Parapsychology and crime
Physically handicapped and crime
Reading disability and crime
Recidivism
Rural crimes
Sex crimes
Suburban crimes
Swindlers and swindling
Unemployment and crime
Violent crimes
War and crime
— Analysis
USE Crime analysis
— Authorship
USE Crime writing
— Classification
UF Classification of crimes
— Cross-cultural studies
— Fiction
UF Crime stories
— Forecasting
USE Crime forecasting
— Law and legislation
USE Criminal law
— Prevention
USE Crime prevention
— Religious aspects
[BL65.C7]
— — Buddhism, [Christianity, etc.]
— Sex differences
— Statistical methods
USE Criminal statistics
— Statistics
USE Criminal statistics
— Study and teaching
USE Criminology

Crime, Employee
USE Employee crimes

Crime analysis *(May Subd Geog)*
[HV7936.C88]
Here are entered works on the examination of data concerning criminal activity to assist in the planning, decision making, and administration of police and law enforcement work.
UF Crime—Analysis
BT Police administration

Crime and age
[HV6163]
UF Age and crime
BT Age
NT Aged—Crimes against
Youth—Crimes against

Crime and alcoholism
USE Alcoholism and crime

Crime and criminals
USE Crime
Criminals

Crime and criminals in mass media
USE Crime in mass media

Crime and criminals in the Bible

1130

Figure 6.2 Excerpt from Library of Congress Subject Headings.
Abbreviations Key: BT = broader term RT = related term UF = used for
NT = narrower term SA = see also USE = use instead

terms with this designation. In other words, a UF term won't show up in the Library of Congress subject search (although it may show up in another keyword search). BT stands for "broader term" and identifies a larger classification or more comprehensive topic than the term in bold. NT stands for "narrower term" and identifies a subtopic. RT stands for "related term" and is a cross-reference to similar subjects. SA stands for "see also" and refers to other main headings in the LCSH. Terms following dashes are subdivisions of the main term; those in boldface are also valid LCSH terms when entered after the main term and two hyphens ("crime—fiction," for example). USE identifies a term that you should use instead of the term listed if you want to conduct a Library of Congress subject search. *May Subd Geog* after the main term means that a topic may be divided further by geographical area, usually by nation. For instance, the subject "crime" may be further divided into "Crime—United States" or "Crime—England." Notice that most subject headings are followed by a Library of Congress call number (one or two letters followed by a series of numbers and letters). These call numbers indicate where materials on this topic will be shelved in libraries following the Library of Congress system.

The LCSH is useful because it can suggest topics that you may not have thought of. It can also help you focus your topic and even find specific material on your topic. It gives a broad overview of the possibilities for research and provides a list of terms you can use for subject and keyword searches. These keywords are particularly useful if you have access to an online catalog or index.

Using Encyclopedias The most general information sources are encyclopedias, such as the *Encyclopedia Britannica,* the *Encyclopedia Americana,* and *Collier's Encyclopedia.* Many libraries have online general encyclopedias, such as *Grolier's, Encarta,* or *Compton's.* Online encyclopedias offer more possibilities for keyword searching and often allow you to print or download the articles you need. They can also be updated quickly. They do not allow for the serendipitous discoveries that often result from browsing through a print encyclopedia, but you can benefit from using both kinds. Using the terms you generated, you can search encyclopedias for information on your topic. If you find too much information, use a narrower term; if you find too little, use a broader term.

An encyclopedia article provides one author's summary of the scholarly conversation related to a topic. Encyclopedia articles are usually written by experienced members of an academic community. Remember, though, that they are one person's view of the conversation; although they are generally reliable, some experts may disagree with the information as presented.

As you read, begin to record information about the scholarly conversation on your topic. Summarize the information you find. Write down the names of important contributors to the conversation and any informational sources (books, articles, and so forth) cited in the encyclopedia article. Look up unfamiliar terms in a dictionary. Remember to include full bibliographical information for material you record. Different scholarly communities use different styles, but you should generally record the author, title, place and date of publication, and page numbers.

Other general informational sources include almanacs and fact lists. *Facts on File,* for example, provides a yearly overview of significant news stories, and *Statistical Abstracts of the United States* gives all kinds of information (statistics, graphs, charts, tables) related to life in the United States.

Using Specialized Encyclopedias After your survey of general directional and informational sources, the next step is to locate more specific ones. Specialized encyclopedias and indexes are often located together in the reference section of the library according to subject area or academic discipline. Examples of specialized informational sources include the *International Encyclopedia of Social Sciences,* the *Dictionary of American History,* the *Encylopedia of World Art,* and the *McGraw-Hill Encyclopedia of Science and Technology.* A reference librarian can help you locate the specific sources you are looking for. (By now you should have some specific questions to ask.) The reference librarian usually has access to Balay's *Guide to Reference Books,* a directional source that lists reference works by subject area. (Check to see whether your library has the works listed.) If your library has an online catalog, you can do a keyword search with the general topic and a word such as *encyclopedia, bibliography, dictionary,* or index. For instance, if your topic is related to endangered species, you could do a keyword search on "endangered species and bibliography." Instead of finding every book or article with any information on endangered species, you would find only bibliographies specific to your topic. Such specialized bibliographies can help you find specific articles and books on your topic rather quickly.

STAGE TWO: NARROWING YOUR SEARCH

Once you have read several sources for background information, you should attempt to *intelligently* narrow your topic. General and specialized encyclopedias should have alerted you to subcategories of your topic on which you could focus your research. Understanding your topic from a variety of perspectives should help you select one aspect of the topic to research in greater detail. If the encyclopedias raised questions about that aspect of the topic, you can be confident that experts are also asking similar questions, and you can go forward assuming that there will probably be adequate research material to support your paper. Be sure to select an area that is of interest to you.

Identifying a Controversial Issue In writing argumentatively, you will focus on an issue that is controversial, an issue about which people disagree. A controversial issue will always have at least two opposing points of view, but often there will be more. You may want to begin with an issue that you already care about or want to know more about. Or you may want to listen in on the conversation for a while to see what issues arise.

As you define the issue you are going to analyze, resist the temptation to think of all controversies as two-sided: right/wrong, us/them, for/against, pro/con. Such dualistic thinking is popular in the United States, with its two main political factions: Republican/Democrat, conservative/liberal, anti-abortion/pro-choice, pro-business/pro-labor, and so on. Such binary thinking glosses over important distinctions and silences of those who do not feel comfortable in either camp. As you analyze controversial issues, try to identify as many views as you can. Identifying a diversity of viewpoints will provide you with the most complete understanding of the issue and help you prepare an effective response. Remember that diversity is a strength. To articulate your own opinions and justify them with the best reasons, you need to hear a number of different viewpoints. After all, the opinion you ultimately embrace as your own may be one that you haven't encountered yet. You may change your mind about your beliefs once you hear what others have to say. And even if you don't change your mind, listening to others will help you understand why you believe the way you do and will give you good reasons for explaining your beliefs to others.

Forming an Issue Question You can benefit greatly at this point by using prewriting techniques to focus your topic. For example, you might brainstorm or freewrite about all of the background information you have accumulated; you can then look over this material and decide which ideas look most interesting or most promising. You might also want to try clustering your ideas to develop a sense of what information you need to be looking for in your research.

Your background research and narrowing of your topic should result in an issue question, a specific question that you want to answer in your research. This should be a question that is "at issue" for the community you are addressing. In other words, it should be a question that people care about and disagree about. Here are some examples of issue questions:

> Should Congress provide compensation to property owners who lose equity in their property because of the Endangered Species Act?
>
> Should the National Endowment for the Arts fund individual artists, or should all NEA grants be disbursed through state humanities councils?
>
> Do live television broadcasts of trials encroach on the defendant's right to a fair trial?

You phrase these issues as questions to answer so that you can be open to what other people have to say rather than merely look for evidence to support what you already believe. You might want to brainstorm about the format of your issue question—try several different phrasings to see which one creates a sufficiently narrow area that will still allow room for developing important and interesting ideas in a paper. Once you have formed a specific issue question, you are ready to read books and articles related to your topic to find answers to your questions.

STAGE THREE: FINDING SOURCES

You have used background information to learn more about the conversation regarding your topic and to help narrow your topic to a workable focus. You are now ready to begin locating research material (as opposed to background material). With the subject terms you have defined from the LCSH guide and from your background reading, you can look for particular sources that respond to the issue question that you have formulated for your paper.

Finding Print Sources Once you have generated a list of key terms and subject headings and done some background reading on your topic, you are ready to look for print sources on your subject. To find books, you use your library's catalog. Some libraries still use a card catalog, but most now use electronic catalogs, which allow many possibilities for searches. You can look up the name of a recognized expert in the field; try your list of key terms as keyword, subject, or title searches; and even search by call number. To narrow your search, try combining your terms. If you find that your keywords generate too many sources, then consider narrowing your topic.

The library catalog will usually lead you to books. To find articles in periodicals (journals and magazines), you need to look in the periodical indexes. These may be bound volumes in the reference area or may be contained on CD-ROM disks, but more likely they will be found online with the catalog. Periodical indexes are usually organized by broad subject area: general knowledge, humanities and arts, social sciences, general sciences, technology and engineering, law, medicine, and so on. Search for the terms and subject headings on your list in these periodical indexes, but be aware that some periodical indexes require you to use terms from their own list of subject descriptors.

SUBJECT AREA INDEXES Below are some commonly used subject area indexes. Many of these are now available online, and some databases (such as *InfoTrac*, *Newsbank*, and *Lexis/Nexis*) are available only online. Libraries use these to keep track of scholarly conversations in journals.

Commonly Used Subject Area Indexes

CURRENT EVENTS AND POPULAR MEDIA

Reader's Guide to Periodical Literature
Social Sciences Index
Biography Index
Business Periodicals Index
General Science Index
New York Times Index
Wall Street Journal Index
Public Affairs Information Service (PAIS)
InfoTrac

Newsbank
Lexis/Nexis

EDUCATION

Education Index
Current Index to Journals in Education
Educational Resource Information Center (ERIC)

HISTORY AND HUMANITIES

America: History and Life
Annual Bibliography of English Language and Literature
Historical Abstracts
Humanities Index
MLA International Bibliography

NURSING AND MEDICINE

Cumulative Index to Nursing and Allied Health Literature
Index Medicus

PHILOSOPHY AND RELIGION

Philosopher's Index
Religion Index One: Periodicals

PSYCHOLOGY AND SOCIOLOGY

Psychological Abstracts
Social Sciences Index

GENERAL SCIENCE AND TECHNOLOGY

Applied Science and Technology Index
Biological and Agricultural Index
General Science Index

GOVERNMENT DOCUMENTS

Congressional Abstracts
Catalog of U.S. Government Publications

Once you have located specific print sources related to your topic, you can use the call number to locate additional books in the same subject area. Some catalogs will allow you to browse by catalog number, but you can also just browse the shelves.

LIBRARY REFERENCE SYSTEMS Knowing the Library of Congress or Dewey Decimal number for your subject area will help in your search for information. Each system uses a general number or letter for the major topic classifications, and each of these classifications then has additional numbers or letters for specific subdivisions. For instance, in the Library of Congress system, "P" is used for the general classification "language and literature," while "PS" is used for the subdivision "American literature" and "PR" for the subdivision "English literature." Following is an overview of these reference systems.

Dewey Decimal Classification System

000–099 General Works	500–599 Pure Science
100–199 Philosophy and Related Disciplines	600–699 Technology and Applied Science
200–299 Religion	700–799 The Arts
300–399 Social Sciences	800–899 Literature and Rhetoric
400–499 Language	900–999 General Geography and History

Library of Congress Classification System

A	General Works
B	Philosophy, Psychology, and Religion
C	Auxiliary Sciences of History (such as biography)
D	General and Old World History (except America)
E–F	American History
G	Geography, Anthropology, Recreation
H	Social Sciences (such as statistics, economics, sociology)
J	Political Science
K	Law
L	Education
M	Music
N	Fine Arts
P	Language and Literature
Q	Science
R	Medicine
S	Agriculture (including plant and animal culture and fisheries)
T	Technology
U	Military Science
V	Naval Science
Z	Library Science (including books and information resources)

Finding Electronic Sources

INTERNET SUBJECT GUIDES Part of the fun during the early years of the Internet was the freewheeling, disorganized nature of the sites. You could "surf" from one to another and turn up all kinds of surprises. Not too many years ago, you could keep up on all of the new sites that appeared during a day. However, as the Internet has grown exponentially, its disorganized nature has become more of a problem than an adventure. Keyword searches can turn up tens of thousands of documents. Surfing from page to page can still lead to some inter-

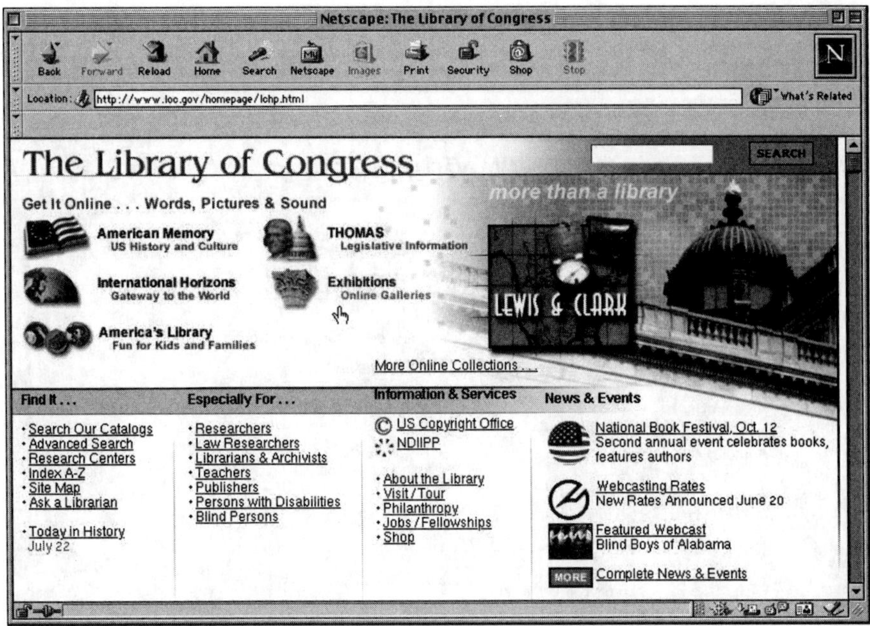

Figure 6.3 Library of Congress home page.

esting discoveries, but it can also take a lot of time and often just leads you in circles.

For the past few years, reference librarians have been trying to make some sense of the Internet. The pages they have constructed provide some great places to find the most useful sources quickly. These pages can save a lot of time because subject-area experts have done much of the sorting, sifting, and evaluating of sites for you. Remember to bookmark these pages and any other useful sites you discover so that you can find them again quickly.

One of the best places to start an Internet search is the Library of Congress home page (Figure 6.3) at <http://www.loc.gov>. The Library of Congress provides links to all online government resources as well as access to some of its own collections, such as selections from its Division of Prints and Photographs and its archives of motion picture and television footage. The Library of Congress website also provides easy access to an extensive array of additional online resources outside of its own collections. An excellent starting point is the "Ask a Librarian" page, which you can link to from the library's home page or go to directly at <http://www.loc.gov/rr/askalib/>. This page offers a chat service as well as links to the "Virtual Reference Shelf," an extensive selection of Web resources compiled by the Library of Congress. If you to to <http://lcweb.loc.gov/rr/news/extgovd.html#broad>, you'll find a link to "Official Federal Government Web Sites." Clicking on the link brings you to a list of the executive branch websites, with links to the legislative and judicial sites as well. By going to the executive branch, for example, you can find online material from the

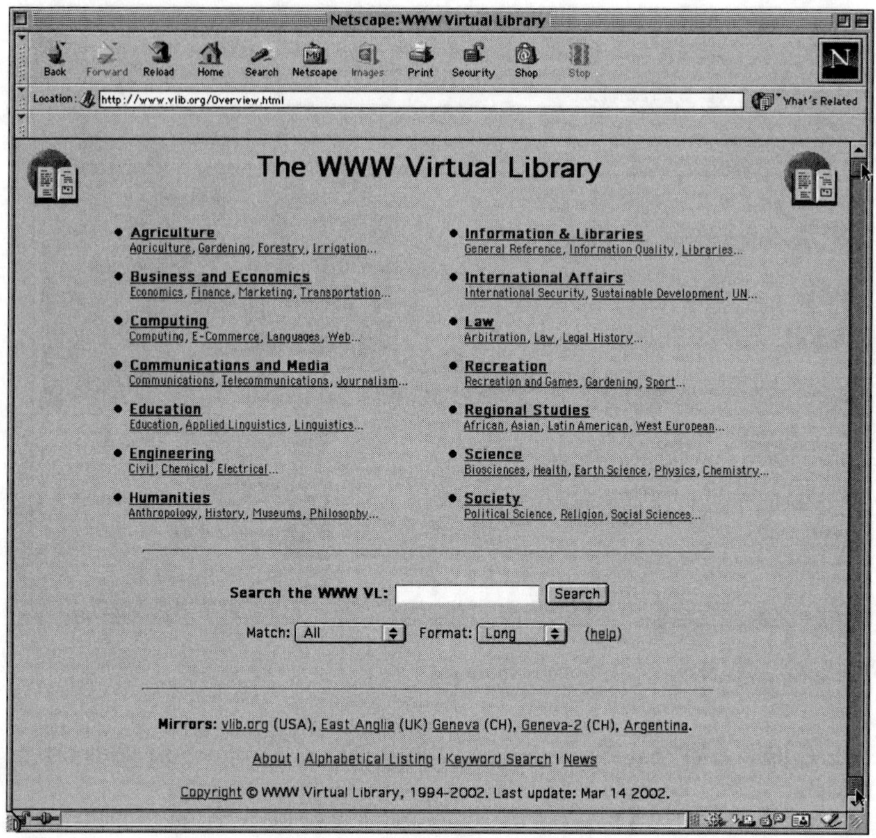

Figure 6.4 The Virtual Library home page.

White House; from each of the executive agencies, such as the Department of Agriculture or the Department of Defense; from independent agencies, such as NASA or the Peace Corps; from boards, commissions, and committees; and from quasi-official agencies, such as the Smithsonian Institution. The legislative branch includes information about both houses of Congress as well as numerous committees and subcommittees. At the judicial branch, you can find information about the Supreme Court and the federal court system, including transcripts and recent Supreme Court decisions.

Another valuable Internet guide is the *Virtual Library* (Figure 6.4) at <http://www.vlib.org>. This site is the oldest subject guide on the Internet, started by Tim Berners-Lee, the creator of the World Wide Web and html, the markup language used to create Web pages. Virtual librarians try to identify the most important sites for their subject specialty. Since the *Virtual Library* relies on volunteer subject-matter experts to locate and evaluate sites, it doesn't have the full coverage of some other catalogs, but the subjects included in the *Virtual Library* are covered very well.

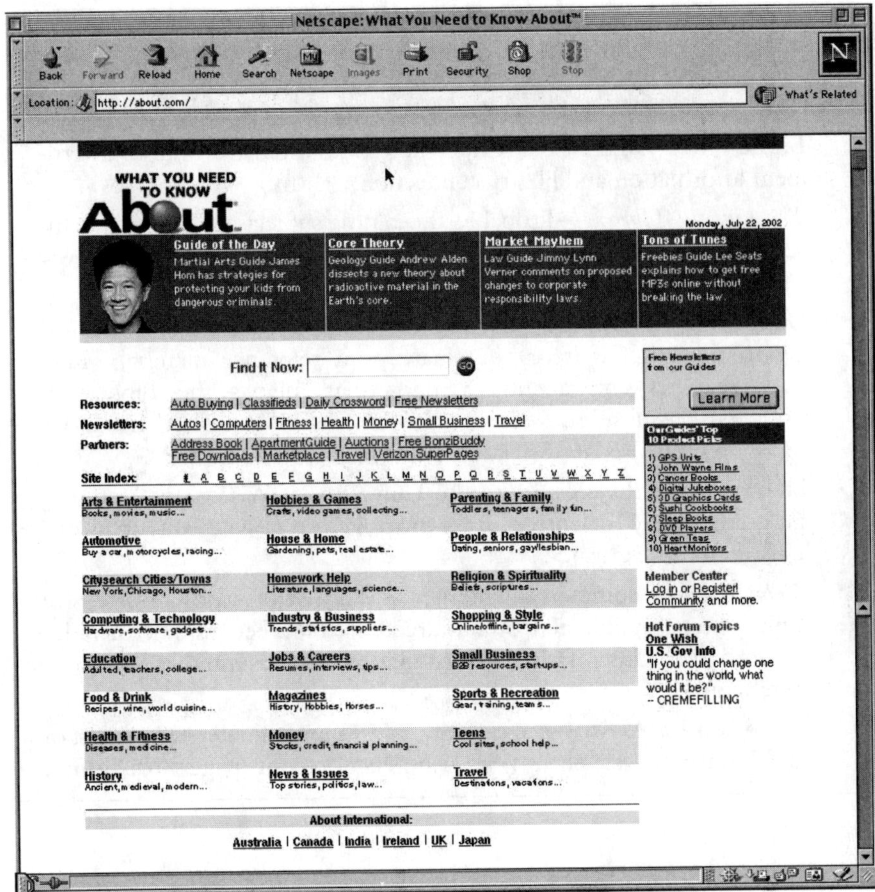

Figure 6.5 About.com home page.

Librarians at Iowa State University have created what they call the *CyberStacks,* a collection of important websites for research classified according to the Library of Congress system at <HTTP://WWW.PUBLIC.IASTATE.EDU/~CYBERSTACKS/homepage.html> (case sensitive). These librarians have tried to apply the principles of selecting library reference materials to selecting Internet sources. Before they include a site, they consider the "authority of the source," "accuracy of the information," "clarity of the presentation," "recency/timeliness," "favorable reviews," and "community needs." CyberStacks allows keyword searches of its sites.

Not all Internet subject guides are run by academic librarians. One of the best on the Internet is *About.com,* <http://www.about.com>, a commercial Internet portal that includes an extensive subject index maintained by an army of volunteers (Figure 6.5). The *About.com* "guides" don't just identify, evaluate, and organize sites; they also write brief articles about their subject area.

■■ INTERNET SUBJECT GUIDES

Library of Congress—Provides access to extensive online government information and library connections: <http://www.loc.gov>.

The Virtual Library—Probably the oldest subject guide on the Internet. Includes a subject guide and keyword searches: <http://www.vlib.org>.

CyberStacks—Created by librarians at Iowa State University according to the criteria used to evaluate print reference materials. Keyword searches and a subject index that follows the Library of Congress classification system: <HTTP://WWW.PUBLIC.IASTATE.EDU/~CYBERSTACKS/homepage.html> (case sensitive).

Internet Scout Project—From the University of Wisconsin–Madison, an academically oriented site: <http://scout.cs.wisc.edu/archives/lcshsearch/index.html>.

About.com—A commercial Internet portal that provides an extensive subject index maintained by hundreds of volunteer guides. Includes keyword searching of the subject guide and the Internet: <http://about.com>.

URLs for a Rainy Day—An extensive but somewhat unsystematic list of useful research sites: <http://www.purefiction.com/pages/res2.htm>.

About.com is a particularly useful guide for general culture and social issues. In addition to its subject guide, *About.com* allows for keyword searches of its subject database and of the Internet.

URLs for a Rainy Day, at <http://www.purefiction.com/pages/res2.htm>, lacks the systematic approach of these other subject guides. It is mostly a long list of useful sites. The sites listed here are suggested by experienced Internet users and collected by the site administrator. Despite its somewhat haphazard organization, *URLs for a Rainy Day* provides a good introduction to what resources are available to the Internet researcher.

INTERNET SEARCH ENGINES Despite the wealth of information found through Internet topical guides, you may still wonder whether you might be missing some important bit of information or some useful document. An Internet search engine will help you be sure that you have left no stone unturned. Internet search engines are computer applications that search documents on the Internet by keyword or phrase. They are useful for making connections that you otherwise may not have thought of, but you can also turn up far more information

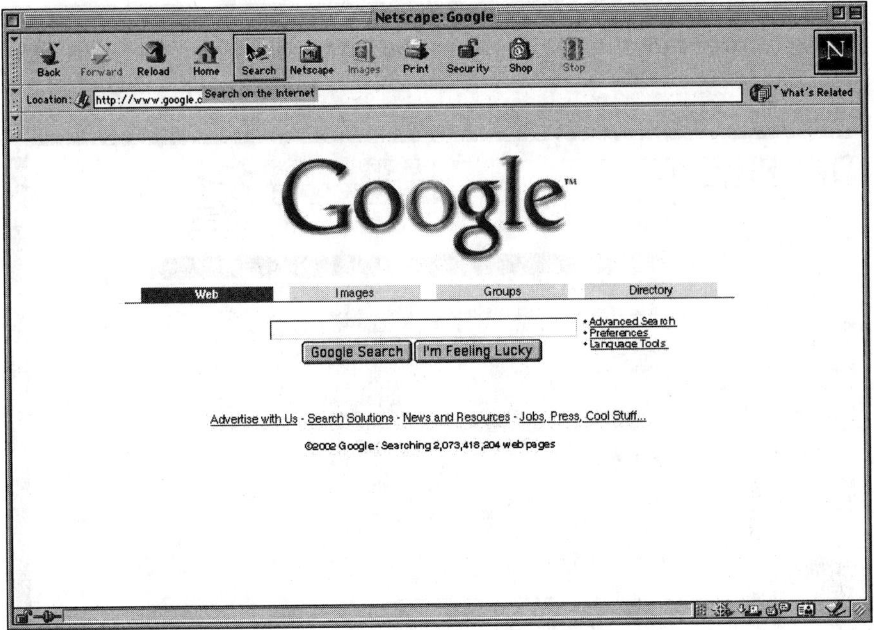

Figure 6.6 Google home page.

than you could ever sort through. First I'll talk about some of the more popular search engines, and then I'll describe an "all-in-one" approach.

The browsers Netscape Navigator and Microsoft Internet Explorer both direct users to some of the more popular Internet search engines such as *Yahoo!*, *Excite*, *Northern Light*, *Lycos*, *AltaVista*, *Google* (Figure 6.6), and *HotBot*. A lot of people have their favorite search engine, and some frequent Internet surfers can be quite fierce in defending the virtues of one search engine over another. Most of these search engines have some common features. They can all search for particular keywords and phrases, and most also have subject area indexes.

You need to be careful about what terms you use for keywords with these search engines. If you choose a broad term, you could turn up literally hundreds of thousands of sites. Return to the list of terms you generated and add to it any other useful terms you have found to describe your topic. Try to pick the most precise terms when using an Internet search engine.

You can expand the capability of the search engine and narrow your search by using advanced search features. Be aware that each search engine uses a slightly different protocol for advanced searches. You can usually find out how to do advanced searches by selecting a link labeled "advanced search" (or something less obvious like "more options") near the search window or looking for a "tips" or "help" link at the bottom of the main search page.

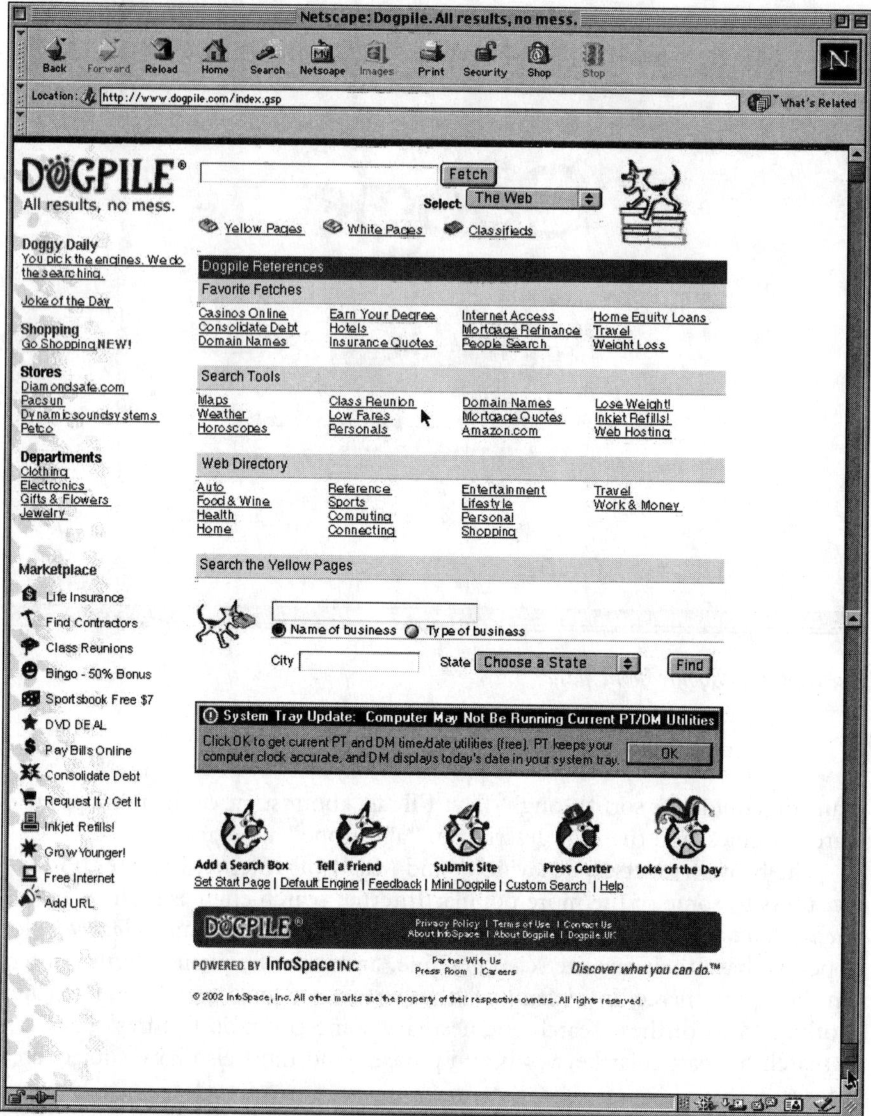

Figure 6.7 Dogpile home page.

If your search doesn't turn up any results, you will need to broaden your search. If you turn up several hundred documents, you will need to narrow your search by combining terms or using more precise terms.

You can save some time by using "all-in-one" or "meta-" search engines. These will usually allow you to search a number of smaller search engines at once. *All-in-one* and *Dogpile* (Figure 6.7) are good examples of meta-search engines.

■■ INTERNET SEARCH ENGINES

Different search engines have different special features. You may find the ones listed below particularly helpful for researching with the Internet. For more details about various search engines, go to <http://searchenginewatch.com/links>.

Alta Vista—(<http://www.altavista.com>) Searches the Web or directory sections; displays date page was created, modified, or located; automatically searches for phrases (no need to use " "); can search for related topics; Advanced Search can search for pages in various languages; can sort results by date; can limit search to a specific domain (e.g., .com or .edu), host name (e.g., <http://www.mhhe.com>), or word in a URL; can find images by word in file name (e.g., beaches or hats).

Excite—(<http://www.excite.com>) Searches Web pages or within directory sections; can search for photos, audio, or video pages. Advanced Search can search in a specific language and can search in a particular domain (e.g., .com or .edu) or country.

Google—(<http://www.google.com>) Searches Web pages or within directory sections; uses popularity as a link to rank results, ensuring relevancy; automatically searches for phrases (no need to use " "); shows cached pages (useful for pages that are temporarily inaccessible or that have disappeared); can find similar pages. Advanced Search can limit a search by language, domain, or website.

HotBot—(<http://hotbot.lycos.com>) Searches for related topics; can sort results by date; displays date page was created, modified, or located. Advanced Search can search for all pages in a particular website; can limit search by date; can search for pages that include images, audio, video, Java, Acrobat, and other elements.

Lycos—(<http://www.lycos.com>) Searches Web pages or sections of directory. Advanced Search can search by language or by links; can search in specific types of documents (e.g., books, music, news), including FTP files.

Northern Light—(<http://www.northernlight.com>) Contains "special collection" (mostly print) documents that are searchable for free but cost to view; search results display date pages were created or modified. Power Search can sort results by date or relevance, can search for words in page titles or URLs, can limit search to specific domains, can search for documents in particular languages and in particular countries.

Yahoo!—(<http://www.yahoo.com>) Searches Web pages or within directory sections; can search for Usenet documents. Advanced Search can sort results by date.

continued

■■ INTERNET SEARCH ENGINES (Continued)

Metasearch Engines Metasearch engines have different ways to let you search with multiple search engines. The list below indicates that variety. For more on metasearch engines, see <http://www.searchenginewatch.com/links/Metacrawlers>.

All-in-One—(<http://www.allonesearch.com>) Contains query boxes for more than 500 search engines, including dozens of specialized ones.

AskJeeves—(<http://www.ask.com>) Answers questions asked in natural language or lets you search in directory sections; results come from its own database and from several search engines.

Dogpile—(<http://www.dogpile.com>) Searches with any combination of over a dozen major and specialized search engines. Offers searches for images, audio, streatming media, Usenet, FTP, news wires, business news, stock quotes, weather, Yellow Pages, White Pages, and maps.

Finding Visual Sources Visual sources are becoming an increasingly important part of research, but graphics, especially photographs, are not always easy to find. There are not as many systematic indexes for visual materials as there are for print materials. To find photos and images, you should begin with your own school or hometown library. Your library may have a photo archive, digital library, or historical map and document collection that can provide valuable resources for your argument. The Library of Congress is beginning to assemble a digital library from its Division of Prints and Photographs, at <http://lcweb.loc.gov/rr/print/catalog.html>. The digital library is only a sampling of the library's collection, but it still has some interesting and valuable selections.

You can also find useful information online, but be careful not to do a keyword search using just the keywords "photographs" or "images" in an Internet search engine or you are likely to get something quite different from what you are looking for. However, the results of using the keywords "photo archives" are excellent, yielding links to numerous online museum, library, and historical society collections. Additionally, most of the major search engines will locate photographs and images for you, and offer the option on their main search pages. (Some even search specifically for video.)

Look for buttons labeled "images" or "photos," and type in keywords as you would for text documents. About.com also maintains a list of sites where you can search for and order stock photography, royalty-free photography, and public domain images. Look under "Web design" and then under "clip art" at

FINDING VISUAL IMAGES ONLINE

Library of Congress, Division of Prints and Photographs <http://www.lcweb.loc.gov/rr/print/catalog.html>.

Google <http://www.google.com>

HotBot <http://www.hotbot.lycos.com>

Alta Vista <http://www.altavista.com>

Excite <http://www.excite.com>

About.com <http://www.about.com>

<webdesign.about.com/compute/webdesign/cs/photos/index.htm>. One of the best of these sites is Corbis.com, which includes an archive of 17 million images, nearly 1 million in digital format. Corbis provides permission to use these photographs for a reasonable fee.

STAGE FOUR: EVALUATING SOURCES

Using library catalogs, appropriate subject indexes, and Internet guides should provide you with enough entries for a working bibliography of books, articles, and other documents related to your topic. A working bibliography is a list of sources you intend to examine because they look like they might answer the issue question you formulated in Stage Two of the research process. But not all sources you locate will be equally reliable. Sources address different audiences for different purposes. In some sources, the information is carefully screened by knowledgeable members of the community. Other sources allow anyone to say pretty much what he or she wants.

Librarians' Criteria Librarians use the following five criteria to evaluate source material:

- Accuracy. Is the information free from errors? Is there someone who checks the information? How well does the information correspond with information found in other sources?
- Authority. Who is the author? What are the author's credentials? Who is the publisher? What kind of editorial standards does the publisher use? Do the author and publisher have a reputation for rigorous scholarship?
- Objectivity. Does the source provide a balanced presentation? Is the source written or published by someone who has a direct personal or financial stake in the issue? Is the source free from bias? Is there any advertising in the source?

- Currency. How recent is the source? Does the author attempt to draw on the most current research? Does the author contribute primary research?
- Coverage. What topics are covered in the source? What is the scope and depth of research? Does the author show an awareness of the major secondary sources on this subject? What does this source provide that is not found elsewhere?

By applying these criteria to your research sources, you can discover which are most valuable. For example, academic journals and books are generally refereed. This means that before an article is published, it is evaluated and approved by knowledgeable members of that academic discipline. These referees or reviewers check to make sure that the information contained in the article is accurate, objective, and current. Because of this review process, academic journals typically have more authority than some other periodicals. Although trade journals, popular magazines, newspapers, and websites lack the authority of academic journals and books, they may provide more current information or broader coverage.

Check Online Sources Carefully Electronic sources present a credibility problem. Online sources are generally less reliable than print sources. (It is important to distinguish here between Web pages and print sources that are delivered on the Internet.) The Internet is full of truth, lies, hoaxes, and spoofs. For instance, *Clones-Я-Us* is sponsored by "Dream Technologies International," "the first and largest reproductive cloning provider," at <http://www.d-b.net/dti>. Is it truth or a hoax? *The Annals of Improbable Research,* <http://www.improb.com>, is an online journal that spoofs real scientific research. (Its acronym is AIR.) The editors claim, "About a third of what we publish is genuine research, about a third is concocted, and about a third of our readers cannot tell the difference." In the same humorous vein, *The Onion,* <http://www.theonion.com>, appears to be a normal online newsmagazine, but when you start reading the stories, you realize that things are not quite right. The Internet is full of sites that try to imitate legitimate sites. For instance, *martinlutherking.org* sounds like it should be a site devoted to Martin Luther King, Jr., but it is really run by Stormfront, a white supremacist group that uses the site to spread its racist views and misinformation about King.[1] Also, <http://www.gatt.org> presents itself as the official site of the World Trade Organization, <http://www.wto.org>, but it is really a protest site. And *gwbush.com* is attacking George W. Bush, whose official site is *georgewbush.com.* The site at <http://www.snopes2.com> is devoted to tracking misinformation spread through the Internet.

If you are careful, you can find reliable information online. Use the five criteria listed above and consider the credibility of the source. Typically, you

[1]Lee Hubbard discusses this site in "Dissing the King," published in *Salon,* a popular online magazine at <http://www.salon.com/news/feature/2000/01/24/mlk>. To find this essay, do a keyword search on "stormfront."

will want to favor websites that are part of a well-established organization, such as a university, government agency, or private foundation. These will have more authority than an individual's personal page. You will also want to rely on your background reading and look for the names of people who are considered experts. Always check what you find online against what you have found through more traditional sources. Look for online sources that are aware of the important issues, prior research, and important figures within your area of research. Be aware that you can't judge an online source by its appearance. A fancy design with a lot of sophisticated features does not necessarily mean that the information contained in the site is reliable. In fact, you should be suspicious of sites that appear to be all show and no substance. Using the Internet subject guides listed earlier in the chapter should help, because these are regularly reviewed by subject-area experts, but be careful to evaluate the information for yourself.

STAGE FIVE: ACKNOWLEDGING SOURCES

After evaluating the sources in your working bibliography, you should have an idea of which sources you will use in research. As you identify the sources you will actually quote, summarize, or paraphrase in your essay, the working bibliography will eventually become the "Works Cited" or "References" page of your essay. You can save a lot of time writing the paper and compiling this final page if you always put the sources for your working bibliography in proper bibliographic form for the documentation style you are using. Putting source information in proper form will become second nature to you if you memorize the most common forms: a book with one author, a journal, and an online document.

Now you are ready to start taking content notes—summaries, paraphrases, and quotations of the information you will use in your essay. (Review the first part of this chapter for information on quotation, summary, and paraphrase.) At first, you may be tempted to take your notes as quotations, but you should take most of your notes as either summary or paraphrase. Use quotations sparingly. They are difficult to record accurately, and most of the sources in your essay should be summarized or paraphrased anyway. If you do record a quotation, make sure that you use quotation marks to separate the quoted material from any paraphrased or summarized material. When you are summarizing or paraphrasing, make sure you clearly distinguish the paraphrase or summary from any of your own comments on the source material. I always put my own comments in square brackets so that I will remember that the ideas are my own. For any of your notes, you should be sure to include enough bibliographical information to relate the note to its source, usually the author's name, an abbreviated title, and the exact page numbers. Remember that you need a citation in the body of your essay for any information you summarize, paraphrase, or quote from an outside source. Failure to do so constitutes plagiarism. For quotations, you should indicate which part of the quotations came from which page. I do this by inserting a line in the quotation to show the page break. For summary and paraphrase, you should include all of the page numbers included in the note. Taking notes in this fashion may seem like more work than just photocopying your sources and underlining them with a highlighter, but if you take notes carefully, you will have a much better understanding of the material, and you will save yourself a lot of time in writing the essay.

DOCUMENTATION STYLES

The following sections provide samples of how to document various kinds of sources, first according to the style recommended by the Modern Language Association (MLA), followed by a sample student paper, and then according to the style recommended by the American Psychological Association (APA), again followed by a sample student paper.

In general, papers written for language and literature courses will be expected to conform to MLA style; those written for courses in the social sciences will be expected to conform to APA style. Other styles may be expected in the humanities and the biological/physical sciences. Check with your instructor to determine which style to use.

Sample Entries for a Works Cited Page: MLA Style For a more detailed discussion of MLA style, see the latest edition of the *MLA Handbook for Writers of Research Papers* or the *MLA Style Manual* (fifth edition, 1999), or go to <http://www.mla.org>.

BOOKS

Single Author

McDonough, Jimmy. Shakey: Neil Young's Biography. London: Random House UK. 2002.

Two or Three Authors

Hecht, Michael L., Mary Jane Collier, and Sidney A. Ribeau. African-American Communication: Ethnic Identity and Cultural Interpretation. Newbury Park: Sage, 1993.

Only the name of the first author is reversed.

Four or More Authors

You may cite the first author, last name first, followed by *et al.* for the remaining authors. (This Latin phrase means "and others.") You may also cite all names in the order they appear on the original work.

Editors

Solomon, William, and Robert McChesney, eds. Ruthless Criticism: New Perspectives in U.S. Communication History. Minneapolis: U of Minnesota P, 1993.

Author with an Editor

Crafts, Hannah. The Bondswoman's Narrative. Ed. Henry Louis Gates, Jr. New York: Time Warner Trade. 2002.

Translation

Dinesen, Isak. On Modern Marriage and Other Observations. Trans. Anne Born. New York: St. Martin's, 1986.

Corporate Author

Humane Farming Association. Bovine Growth Hormones. San Rafael: Humane Farming Assn., 1994.

Unknown Author

The Times Atlas of the World. 9th ed. New York: Times, 1992.

Two or More Works by the Same Author

Conway, Jill Ker. The Road from Coorain. New York: Random, 1990.

---. True North. New York: Knopf, 1994.

List works alphabetically by title.

Edition Other Than the First

Murray, Donald M. The Craft of Revision. 2nd ed. Fort Worth: Harcourt, 1995.

Multivolume Work

Smith. Adam. The Glasgow Edition of the Works and Correspondence of Adam Smith. Ed. A. S. Skinner. 6 vols. Oxford: Oxford UP. 1983.

One Volume from a Multivolume Work

Smith, Adam. Essays on Philosophical Subjects. Ed.

W. P. D. Wightman. Vol. 3 of The Glasgow Edition of the Works and Correspondence of Adam Smith. A. S. Skinner, gen. ed. 6 vols. Oxford: Oxford UP, 1983.

Encyclopedia or Dictionary Entry

"Value." Merriam-Webster's Collegiate Dictionary. 10th ed. 1993.

Dolling. W. R. "Bugs." The Encyclopedia of Insects. New York: Facts on File, 1986. 54-60.

Work in an Anthology

Callen, Michael. "AIDS: The Linguistic Battlefield." The State of the Language. Ed. Leonard Michaels and Christopher Ricks. Berkeley: U of California P, 1990. 171-84.

Foreword, Introduction, Preface, or Afterword

French, Marilyn. Introduction. The House of Mirth. By Edith Wharton. New York: Berkley, 1981. v-xxxv.

PERIODICALS

Article in a Monthly Magazine

Loftus, Elizabeth. "Eyewitnesses: Essential but Unreliable." Psychology Today Feb. 1984: 22-27.

Article in a Weekly Magazine

Shaheen, Jack. "The Media's Image of Arabs." Newsweek 29 Feb. 1988: 10.

Article in a Journal Paginated by Volume

Madrian, Brigitte C. "Employment-Based Health Insurance and Job Mobility: Is There Evidence of Job-Lock?" Quarterly Journal of Economics 109 (1994): 27-54.

Article in a Journal Paginated by Issue

Fotsch, Paul M. "Rap Music Resisting Resistance." Popular Culture Review 5.1 (1994): 57-74.

Article in a Daily Newspaper

Ivins, Molly. "Ban the Things. Ban Them All." Fort Worth Star-Telegram 11 Mar. 1993: 17A.

Unsigned Article in a Magazine or Newspaper

"Say It Ain't So, O. J." USA Today 14 June 1994: 1A.

Editorial in a Newspaper

"Wilderness Bill Offers No Protection." Editorial. Deseret News 8 July 1995: A17.

Letter to the Editor

Owens, Wayne. Letter. Deseret News 8 July 1995: A14.

ELECTRONIC SOURCES Citation forms for online sources are still being standardized by many scholarly organizations, so you will want to check the MLA's website (<http://www.mla.org>) for possible updates. Notice that each online entry needs to include the URL and the date that you accessed the site. (There is no period between the date and URL. URLS that are longer than one line are only broken after a forward slash, and all URLS are placed within angle brackets.)

CD-ROM Issued in a Single Edition

The Oxford English Dictionary. 1st ed. CD-ROM. Oxford: Oxford UP, 1987.

"Australia." Compton's Interactive Encyclopedia. CD-ROM. Compton's, 1994.

Online Scholarly Project

Perseus Project. Ed. Gregory Crane. 5 July 2002 <http://www.perseus.tufts.edu/>.

Professional Site

CNN Home Page. CNN. 1 July 2002 <http://www.cnn.com>.

Personal Site

Blakesley, David. Home page. 3 July 2002 <http://icdweb.cc.purdue.edu/~blakesle>.

Book

Drexler, Eric. Unbounding the Future. New York: William Morrow, 1991. 13 Aug. 1998 <http://www.web.net/~robbins/index.html>.

Poem

Frost, Robert. "Storm Fear." A Boy's Will. New York, 1913. Bartleby Library. Dec. 1995. Columbia U. 27 July 1998 <http://www.columbia.edu/acis/bartleby/frost/17.html>.

Article in a Library or Commercial Database

Koehn, Nancy F. "Henry Heinz and Brand Creation in the Late Nineteenth Century: Making Markets for Processed Food." Business History Review 73.3 (1999): 349+. InfoTrac OneFile. InfoTrac. San Francisco Public Lib., 3 May 2002 <http://www.infotrac.galegroup.com/>.

Article in a Journal

Lieberthal, Kenneth. "Hong Kong Between the U.S. and China." The Journal of the International Institute 5.1 (1997): 41 pars. 15 Mar. 1998 <http://www.umich.edu/~iinet/journal/vol5nol/hk4.html>.

Article in a Magazine

Doherty, Brendan. "Barefoot in the Park." Weekly Wire. 10 Aug. 1998. 15 Aug. 1998 <http://www.weeklywire.com/ww/current/alibi_featl.html>.

Newspaper Article

Claiborne, William. "From Casinos to Conglomerates." Washington Post 14 Aug. 1998: 37 pars. 15 Aug. 1998 <http://www.washingtonpost.com/wp-srv/frompost/aug98/indians14.htm>.

E-Mail Communication

Thulin, Craig. E-mail to the author. 15 May 1995.

Posting to a Discussion List

Dean, Thomas K. "Bowling and Community." Online posting. 20 Aug. 1996. H-Local: H-Net Discussion List for Local History. 3 May 1998 <http://www.h-net.msu.edu/logs/log9608/h-local>.

LEGAL REFERENCES If you are using a number of legal sources in your essay, consult the most recent edition of *A Uniform System of Citation* published by the Harvard Law Review Association.

15 US Code. Sec. 78j(b). 1964.

US Const. Art. 1, sec. 1.

Estes v. Texas. 381 USC 755. U.S. Supr. Ct. 1965.

OTHER SOURCES

Government Publication

United States. Cong. Committee on Agriculture. Subcommittee on Wheat, Soybeans, and Feed Grains. Formulation of the 1990 Farm Bill. 101st Cong., 1st sess. 8 vols. Washington: GPO, 1990.

Pamphlet

Shop Recycled!: A Consumer's Guide to Recycled Plastics. Washington: American Plastics Council, 1994.

Published Dissertation

Schmitz, Robert M. Hugh Blair. Diss. Columbia U, 1936. New York: King's Crown, 1936.

Unpublished Dissertation

Thulin, Craig D. "Posttranslational Processing and Human Profilaggrin." Diss. U of Washington, 1995.

Abstract of a Dissertation

Gaisford, John W. "Priorities in Health Care: A Resource Allocation Method and Empirical Investigation." Diss. U of Oregon, 1993. DAI 53 (1993): 2023A.

Published Proceedings of a Conference

Gretel, Richard, ed. Water Quality in Boston Harbor. Conf. on Water Quality and Pollution, 1968, Boston. Washington: GPO, 1970.

Work of Art

Hatcher, Brower. Seer. Brigham Young University Museum of Art, Provo.

Musical Composition

Gershwin, George. Rhapsody in Blue.

Beethoven, Ludwig van. Symphony no. 7 in A, op. 92.

Personal Letter

Thulin, Craig. Letter to the author. 15 May 1995.

Lecture or Public Address

Hallen, Cynthia. "Creating an Emily Dickinson Lexicon." Brigham Young University College of Humanities, Provo. 11 Nov. 1993.

Personal Interview

Rifberg, Klaus. Personal interview. 12 Dec. 1995.

Published Interview

Brooks, Gwendolyn. Interview. Literature and Belief 12 (1992): 1-12.

Radio or Television Interview

Welch, John W. Interview. Booktalk. KSL Radio. KSL, Salt Lake City. 5 June 1994.

Film or Videotape

Tom Jones. Dir. Tony Richardson. Screenplay by John Osborne. Perf. Albert Finney, Susannah York, Hugh Griffith, Edith Evans, and Joan Greenwood. United Artists, 1963.

Revising Prose. Narr. Richard Lanham. Videocassette. Macmillan, 1990.

Radio or Television Program

Sixty Minutes. KCBS, Los Angeles. 31 Aug. 1997.

"Amelia Earhart." The American Experience. Narr. Kathy Bates. Writ./Dir. Nancy Porter. PBS. WEDU, Tampa. 3 Nov. 1995.

Live Performance of a Play

The Comedy of Errors. By William Shakespeare. Dir. Marion Bentley. Perf. Richard Tullis, Harold Vance, Jan Nichols, and Phyllis Cundick. Brigham Young University Theatre, Provo. 10 Oct. 1995.

Sound Recording

McLachlan, Sarah. "Building a Mystery." Mirrorball. LP. BMG/Arista, 1999.

If the recording is not a CD, the medium precedes the manufacturer's name: *Audio-cassette. Reprise, 1992.* Other personnel (conductor, orchestra) may be listed if pertinent.

Cartoon

Yates, Bill. "The Small Society." Cartoon. Deseret News 8 July 1995: A14.

Map or Chart

Madrid. Map. New York: Baedeker's-Prentice-Hall, 1995.

Computer Software

Myst. Computer software. Novato: Brøderbund, 1992. Windows 3.1, 486, CD-ROM.

Provide identifying information in the upper-left corner of the first page. If your instructor asks for an outline, use a separate title page (see the sample paper in APA style on page 387).

Center the title.

Double-space throughout. Set top, bottom, and side margins at one inch. Indent paragraphs one-half inch, or five spaces.

In the upper right-hand corner of each page, include your name beside the page number. Most word processors have a running head feature that can be set up to do this automatically.

When you quote, paraphrase, or summarize without mentioning the author's name in your text, include the last name of the author (or authors) and the page number(s) in parentheses. For a cite at the end of a sentence, the period follows the close parenthesis.

Bryson 1

Will Bryson

Dr. Gideon Burton

English 312

27 November 2001

Free Press vs. Fair Trial:

The Right of a Defendant to Keep Pre-Trial Activities Private

The Constitution of the United States, along with the Bill of Rights, provides the framework to establish the human rights protected by the U.S. government for its citizens. Yet for all its genius and brilliance, the Constitution is not without flaws. What is to be done when two sections of the Constitution seemingly contradict each other? This question keeps the American judicial system busy in attempting to interpret the law fairly and accurately.

One major issue that has occupied the courts is the conflict between the right of the accused to a fair trial and the right of the mass media to report on the trial. Although the media has the right to report on criminal trial proceedings, given the media's current power it seems reasonable that a defendant should have the right to initiate a motion to have pre-trial hearings closed to the press and public, because doing so is the best way to ensure that the defendant's constitutional right to an impartial jury is protected.

The Sixth Amendment to the U.S. Constitution states, "In all criminal prosecutions, the accused shall enjoy the right to a speedy and public trial by an impartial jury." Some argue that these guarantees do not include a "fair trial" because those exact words are not explicitly mentioned in the Constitution (Donahue and Stoner 52). Even though a "fair trial" is not specified, however, the term is used more generally as a summary of the guarantees of the Sixth Amendment, guarantees included for the purpose of ensuring that the accused receives as fair a trial as possible. One

Bryson 2

way the legal system helps ensure a fair trial is through pre-trial activities. Pre-trial hearings help determine whether there is just cause to criminally try one who stands accused. In these hearings, evidence against the defendant is presented and its legality is tested. If there is sufficient evidence and probable cause, the defendant is brought to trial.

Pre-trial activities occur prior to jury selection. Therefore, if pre-trial hearings are highly publicized, the ability of the court to assemble an impartial jury is endangered. Evidence obtained illegally or deemed inadmissible can become known and could bias potential jurors. Paul C. Reardon and Clifton Daniel, in their 1968 report of the American Bar Association Advisory Committee of Fair Trial and Free Press, suggest that if a defendant feels his or her Sixth Amendment rights may be violated by heavy media coverage during pre-trial hearings, he or she should be given the option of requesting that these hearings be held in the judge's chambers or in closed court (16). The judge would then rule to grant or deny this motion, depending on his or her judgment of the circumstances. If deemed appropriate, the proceedings would be held in private, and a record would be kept to be made available to the press after jury selection is completed or after the case is disposed of without a trial.

It could be argued that closing pre-trial proceedings to the public and press would constitute a dangerous breach of the First Amendment guarantee of freedom of the press. Indeed, the Supreme Court has held that the news-gathering abilities of the press must be protected in order for the rights of a free press to be guaranteed (Branzburg 681). However, the Court has also found that the Sixth Amendment right to a fair trial must be protected at almost all costs, including that of other constitutional rights. In Nebraska Press Association v. Stuart, Supreme Court Justice William Brennan said, "The right to a fair trial is essential to the

When you mention the author's name, you need only include the page number(s) parenthetically.

The name of a court case is underlined in the essay but not in parenthetical citations or on the "Works Cited" list. Underlining is preferred to italics, which may not be as clearly distinguishable.

Underline for emphasis, but do so sparingly. If you add your own emphasis to a quotation, include the phrase "emphasis added" parenthetically at the end of the quotation.

preservation and enjoyment of all other rights, providing a necessary means of safeguarding personal liberties against government oppression" (586. emphasis added). According to the Sixth Amendment, the ability to face an impartial jury is essential to the right of a fair trial, and thus must be given consideration over the right of the press to have immediate access to pre-trial proceedings (586).

Perhaps one might think that keeping any information that comes from court proceedings private would violate the rights of a free press guaranteed in the First Amendment. However, if a transcript is recorded and later released to the press, then the media would still have access to the information. The argument then becomes one of the right of the press to instant information. In our contemporary world, our belief is that the faster the better, especially with such technological advances as the Internet and facsimiles to help speed news along the information superhighway.

However, when examined closely, the Constitution gives no provision to the press for immediate access to information. In Estes v. Texas, the Supreme Court found that the right to broadcast a court proceeding is not guaranteed to the press, especially when such broadcasting may interfere with the rights of the defendant. In writing the opinion of the court, Justice Clark noted that live coverage of a trial could have a negative impact on jurors, witnesses, judges (especially elected judges), and the defendant (535). Indeed, waiting to publish pre-trial information could lead to more press accuracy and reliability.

For example, in June of 1994 Nicole Brown Simpson and Ronald Goldman were murdered in Los Angeles. Immediately the media began publishing lists of evidence that would implicate Ms. Simpson's ex-husband, O. J. Simpson. Among the evidence mentioned in USA Today were a murder weapon and a bloody ski mask ("Say" 1A). Upon further investigation, no weapon or mask was found. Had USA Today waited to

For sources with anonymous authors, use the first word or two of the title in the "Works Cited" list.

Bryson 4

report on evidence until after a pre-trial hearing transcript was released, the news would have been more accurate and might have led to less prejudice in the minds of the public as to Simpson's guilt. This is not the first time this has happened.

In a similar case, Sheppard v. Maxwell, Dr. Sam Sheppard had been accused of the murder of his wife. The media was in a frenzy over the trial, and Dr. Sheppard was convicted in the local newspaper even before he was arraigned. The Cleveland Press ran front page editorials with such headlines as "Why Isn't Sam Sheppard in Jail?" and "Quit Stalling; Bring Him In" (Kane 10). Media coverage of the event was constant, and every bit of potential evidence was printed by the Press. In addition, names and addresses of all prospective jurors were printed, and free copies of the Press were delivered to their homes (11). Sam Sheppard was convicted of murder and spent ten years in jail before being released on a writ of habeas corpus. His case was reviewed by the U.S. Supreme Court, which found that his Sixth Amendment rights had been violated, and Sheppard was granted a new trial, in which he was acquitted. Had the pre-trial proceedings in the original action been held in the judge's chambers or in a closed courtroom, and information withheld until the selection of the jurors was complete, perhaps the first trial would have resulted in a more just decision. This could have saved ten years of Sam Sheppard's life and weeks of the court's time.

When citing additional material from a source just cited, you need only include the page number parenthetically.

Another case in which a defendant's Sixth Amendment rights were highlighted is Gannett Co. v. DePasquale. In this case, a trial judge closed off a preliminary hearing dealing with suppression of evidence. The Supreme Court upheld the right of the judge to do so. The Court found that a trial judge could bar access to pre-trial hearings if a "reasonable probability of prejudice" would occur from allowing the public to attend (Gannett 392-3). One could argue that this reasonable probability standard was later overturned by

Show where a summary begins by referring to the source. Show where it ends by providing parenthetical documentation.

Use ellipsis points (three spaced periods) enclosed in brackets to show where part of a quotation has been omitted. If the omission comes at the end of a sentence, use ellipsis points enclosed in brackets and followed by a period.

the Supreme Court in Richmond Newspapers v. Virginia. However, in this case the court only altered its previous decision, abandoning the "reasonable probability" standard in favor of a "substantial probability of prejudice" standard. Under this new standard, it has been held that a criminal hearing should be closed "only if specific findings are made demonstrating that [. . .] there is a substantial probability that the defendant's right to a fair trial will be prejudiced by publicity that closure would prevent [. . .]." (Press Enterprise 14). Thus, the ruling remains that "the defendant's right to a fair trial outweigh[s] the interests of the press and public" (Gannett 376). It may also be argued that the Court has upheld the right of the public to attend criminal trials and that the right to a public trial is not the exclusive right of the defendant. However, the Court has found in and since DePasquale that the right to an open courtroom is not an absolute right, and that pre-trial proceedings may be closed in "the interest of the fair administration of justice" (Richmond 563). Pre-trial hearings are separate from the actual trial, and neither the Constitution nor any Court ruling guarantees the right of the public to attend pre-trial activities. As long as the trial is accessible to the public, and transcripts of pre-trial proceedings are eventually made available, it is prudent to close pre-trial activities when the circumstances are deemed appropriate by the presiding judge.

Another example of a case in which the judge found it best to close pre-trial hearings is Federated Publications v. Swedberg. In this case, the judge found that the inclusion of the press would endanger the right of the defendant to a fair trial and excluded the press from the courtroom. The press appealed the decision to the Supreme Court of Washington State, which upheld the judge's decision. In giving the opinion of the court, Justice Rosellini said,

Bryson 6

> While this court has found a right of the public to attend a pre-trial hearing [. . .] that right is qualified by the court's right and duty to see that the defendant has a fair trial. The court may order closure, if the objectors fail to demonstrate the availability of some practical alternative. (634)

The U. S. Supreme Court supported this decision by refusing to grant certiorari, and even though this case is law only in the State of Washington, it sets a precedent which provides a judge the option to order closure to protect the Sixth Amendment rights of those who stand accused.

Returning to the O. J. Simpson murder trial, it is clear that this case could have benefited from closed pre-trial proceedings. The media coverage of the case was unparalleled in history. When Mr. Simpson was arrested for the crime, his picture was on the front page of nearly every newspaper in the country, and the coverage did not stop there. All the preliminary hearings and pre-trial motions were broadcast live on national television. Newsweek printed a list of thirty-four pieces of evidence that defense attorneys wished to suppress because they were illegally obtained (Turque et al. 23). All this publicity occurred before jury selection ever began. Even if Mr. Simpson had been convicted of the murders, he would have had grounds for appeal based on the argument that an impartial jury was practically impossible to find due to the media circus that surrounded his case. Perhaps, if the pre-trial proceedings had been closed, even more outrageous rumors and stories about evidence would have surfaced. Unethical journalists might have gone to unknown lengths to get a scoop. However, such practices would probably have been limited to sensational tabloids, and stories in such publications would have had less effect on potential jurors than a list of possibly illegal evidence published

Quotations of more than four typed lines are set off from the text and indented one inch from the left margin.

The parenthetical citation *follows* the final period in a block quotation. It is not followed by a period.

Bryson 7

in such a respected news magazine as Newsweek. Surely, if the pre-trial hearings and motions to suppress evidence had been held behind closed doors, the interest of justice would have been better served.

It could be argued that despite heavy media coverage, impartial jurors have been found in many cases, including the Mike Tyson and William Kennedy Smith rape trials, the Manuel Noriega drug case, and the trial of Los Angeles police officers in connection with the beating of Rodney King, among others (Litt 380). However, the jury selection process tends to produce uneducated jurors, resulting in easily persuaded juries and other problems. Mark Twain, in a criticism of the judicial process, told a story of jury selection in which anyone who had read or heard about the trial was automatically disqualified for jury duty. The jury ended up consisting of "two desperadoes, two low beer-house politicians, three barkeepers, two [illiterate] ranchmen and three dull, stupid, human donkeys. It actually came out afterwards that one of these latter thought that incest and arson were the same thing" (qtd. in Gillmour 485). Although the jurors selected for modern trials may not be ignorant to this extent, the problems addressed by Twain still exist. In the O. J. Simpson trial, over half of the jurors were not high school graduates, and Judge Lance Ito had problems keeping jurors; five were dismissed and only four alternates ultimately remained. Experts worried that the jury pool would run out and a mistrial would result (O. J. Simpson). In any case, if the jury had returned a guilty verdict, the problems experienced with jury members would probably have provided grounds for an appeal of the verdict. If the press were to be controlled until a jury was selected, perhaps there would be fewer problems finding and maintaining an impartial jury.

Of course, one could also argue that unless the press has access to pre-trial activities, secrecy and cover-ups could occur

Use brackets to indicate any brief explanatory comments you add to a quotation.

With an in-text quotation, the period follows the parenthetical citation.

Bryson 8

that might endanger the very rights a closed pre-trial is designed to protect. However, it should be remembered that the merits of a motion to close pre-trial activities would be left to the discretion of the judge, and a record of all proceedings would be kept for release to the press after jury selection. Many trials that have been surrounded in controversy over the question of the right to a fair trial could have been much less so had pre-trial activities occurred in private.

The conflict between the rights of a free press and the right to a fair trial is not a new one. The problem has been the subject of debate and court cases from the time the Constitution was written. A solution may be impossible to find. However, by limiting access to pre-trial hearings in appropriate situations, the interest of justice can be better served than it is under the present system of mass media hype which has led to "trial by newspaper" rather than "trial by jury" in so many instances.

Full bibliographic information for each source cited is included on a separate "Works Cited" page, which is double-spaced throughout. Entries are listed alphabetically by authors' last names (or the first main word in titles, for entries with no author). The first line of each entry is flush with the left margin; subsequent lines for the entry indent one-half inch. See pages 364–371 for MLA guidelines regarding the information required for specific types of sources.

Bryson 9

Works Cited

Branzburg v. Hayes. 404 USC 665. U.S. Supr. Ct. 1972.

Donahue, Hugh Carter, and Kevin R. Stoner. "Publication Delayed Is Justice Denied." Editor and Publisher 22 Dec. 1990: 52.

Esetes v. Texas. 381 USC 532. U.S. Supr. Ct. 1965.

Federated Publications v. Swedberg. 7 Media Law Reporter 1965. WA St. Supr. Ct. 1981.

Gannett Co. v. DePasquale. 443 USC 368. U.S. Supr. Ct. 1979.

Gillmour, Donald M., and Jerome A. Barron. Mass Communication Law: Cases and Comment. St. Paul: West. 1984.

Kane, Peter E. Murder, Courts, and the Press: Issues in Free Press/Fair Trial. Carbondale: Southern Illinois UP. 1982.

Litt, Marc O. "'Citizen Soldiers' and Anonymous Justice: Reconciling the Sixth Amendment Right of the Accused, the First Amendment Right of the Media and the Privacy Right of Jurors." Columbia Journal of Law and Social Problems 25.3 (1992): 371-421.

Nebraska Press Association v. Stuart. 427 USC 539. U.S. supr. Ct 1976.

O. J. Simpson on Trial. Cable News Network. 13 Apr. 1995.

Press-Enterprise v. Superior Court. 478 USC 1. U.S. Supr. Ct. 1986.

Reardon. Paul C., and Clifton Daniel. Fair Trial and Free Press. Washington: American Institute for Public Policy Research, 1968.

Richmond Newspapers, Inc. v. Virginia. 448 USC 555. U.S. Supr. Ct. 1980.

"Say It Ain't So, O. J." USA Today 14 June 1994: 1A.

Sheppard v. Maxwell. 384 USC 333. U.S. Supr. Ct. 1966.

Turque, Bill, Mark Miller, Andrew Murr, Jim Crogan, and Tim Pryor. "Body of Evidence." Newsweek 11 July 1994: 20-24.

Sample Entries for a References Page: APA Style For a more detailed discussion of APA style, see the most recent edition of the *Publication Manual of the American Psychological Association* (fifth edition, 2001), or go to <http://www.apastyle.org>. Note that the student format recommended by the APA differs somewhat from that required for papers being submitted for publication.

BOOKS

Single Author

Hewlett, S. A. (2002). *Creating a life: Professional women and the quest for children.* New York: Talk Miramax Books.

Note the initials are used for the author's first and second names and that the date follows, before the title.

Two or More Authors

Hecht, M. L., Collier, M. J., & Ribeau, S. A. (1993). *African-American communication: Ethnic identity and cultural interpretation.* Newbury Park, CA: Sage.

In titles and subtitles, only initial words and proper nouns are capitalized.

Editors

Solomon, W., & McChesney, R. (Eds.). (1993). *Ruthless criticism: New perspectives in U.S. communication history.* Minneapolis: University of Minnesota Press.

Corporate Author

Humane Farming Association. (1993). *Bovine growth hormones.* San Rafael, CA: Author.

An Article or Chapter in an Edited Book

Callen, Michael. (1990). AIDS: The linguistic battlefield. In L. Michaels & C. Ricks (Eds.), *The state of the language* (pp. 171-184). Berkeley: University of California Press.

Unknown Author

The Times atlas of the world (9th ed.). (1992). New York: Times Books.

Two or More Works by the Same Author

Conway, J. K. (1990). *The road from Coorain.* New York: Random House.

Conway, J. K. (1994). *True north.* New York: A. A. Knopf.

List works by date of publication, earlier date first. For two or more works by the same author in the same year, add lowercase letters following the year, beginning with *a:* (1990a), (1990b), and so on; works by the same author in the same year are listed alphabetically by title.

Edition Other Than the First

Williams, J. M. (2000). *Style: Ten lessons in clarity and grace* (6th ed.). New York: Longman.

Translation

Dinesen, I. (1985). *On modern marriage and other observations* (Anne Born, Trans.). New York: St. Martin's. (Original work published in 1981)

Encyclopedia Entry

Dolling, W. R. (1986). Bugs. In *The encyclopedia of insects* (Vol. 2, pp. 54-60). New York: Facts on File.

PERIODICALS

Article in a Magazine

Platt, C. (2001, May). The future will be fast but not free. *Wired, 9.05,* 120-27.

Gordimer, N. (1995, October 5). Adam's rib. *The New York Review of Books, XLII,* 28-29.

Include volume number, where available.

Article in a Journal Paginated by Volume

Madrian, B. C. (1994). Employment-based health insurance and job mobility: Is there evidence of job-lock? *Quarterly Journal of Economics, 109,* 27-54.

Article in a Journal Paginated by Issue

Fotsch, P. M. (1994). Rap music resisting resistance. *Popular Culture Review, 5*(1), 57-74.

Article in a Daily Newspaper

Ivins, M. (1993, March 11). Ban the things. Ban them all. *Fort Worth Star-Telegram*, p. 17A.

Unsigned Article in a Magazine or Newspaper

Say it ain't so, O. J. (1994, June 14). *USA Today*, p. 1A.

Letter to the Editor

Owens, W. (1995, July 8). Wilderness bill offers no protection [Letter to the editor]. *Deseret News*, p. A14.

ELECTRONIC SOURCES The current edition of the APA's *Publication Manual* (fifth edition, 2001) provides substantial guidance for writers citing online sources. The guidelines are also published on the organization's website, which includes additional updates (<http://www.apastyle.org/elecref.html>).

Article from a CD-ROM Database

Schmitz, S., & Christopher, J. C. (1997). Trouble in smurftown: Youth gangs and moral vision on Guam. *Child Welfare, 76*(3), 411-28. Retrieved from SilverPlatter database (Social Welfare Abstracts, CD-ROM, Item 35247).

Article from an Online Database

Morris, H.J. (2001, Sept. 3) Happiness explained. *U.S. News & World Report, 46*. Retrieved July 2, 2002, from InfoTrac OneFile database on the World Wide Web: http://www.infotrac.galegroup.com

Document on a Website

Electronic Reference Formats Recommended by the American Psychological Association. (2001, January 10). Washington, DC: American Psychological Association. Retrieved May 11, 2001, from the World Wide Web: http://www.apa.org/journals/webref.html

Article in an Online Journal

Lieberthal, K. (1997). Hong Kong between the U.S. and China. *The Journal of the International Institute, 5*(1). Retrieved January 12, 2001, from the World Wide Web: http://www.umich.edu/~iinet/journal/vol15no1/hk4.html

Article in an Online Magazine

Robbins, M. (2001, May 11). *Salon.* Retrieved May 11, 2001, from the World Wide Web: http://www.salon.com/mwt/feature/2001/05/11/test_revolt/index.html

Newspaper Article Online

Claiborne, W. (1998, August 14). From casinos to conglomerates. *Washington Post,* p. A1. Retrieved August 14, 1998, from the World Wide Web: http://www.washingtonpost.com/wpsrv.frompost/aug98/indians14.htm

Citation from a Discussion List or Mailing List Archive

MacDonald, A. (2001, April 30). A-bomb what if (message 1). *Google Groups, soc.history.what-if.* Retrieved May 11, 2001, from the World Wide Web: http://groups.google.com/groups?hl=en&lr=&safe=off&ic=1&th=8192a92c36f1e541,14

E-Mail Messages and Discussion or Mailing List Postings

E-mails and discussion-group exchanges, like print correspondence and telephone conversations, are not retrievable and are cited as personal communication in the text but are not included in the reference list.

Mark Wilhelm of Rice University and Mercury Technology Services said, "The short answer to the question of mercury pollution in rivers, especially the Amazon, is that you cannot get it out" (personal communication, April 5, 2000).

OTHER SOURCES

Government Publication

U.S. Congress. House Committee on Agriculture, Subcommittee on Wheat, Soybeans, and Feed Grains. (1990, August). *Formulation of the 1990 farm bill* (101st Cong., 1st sess.). Washington, DC: U.S. Government Printing Office.

Pamphlet

American Plastics Council. (1994). *Shop recycled!: A consumer's guide to recycled plastics* [Brochure]. Washington, DC: Author.

Unpublished Dissertation

Thulin, C. D. (1995). *Posttranslational processing and human profilaggrin.* Unpublished doctoral dissertation, University of Washington, Seattle.

Lectures, Speeches, and Addresses

Bizzell, P. (1985, March). *Separation and resistance in academic discourse.* Paper presented at the annual meeting of the Conference on College Composition and Communication, Minneapolis, MN.

Unpublished Paper

Jones, R. L. (1989). *Treating long-term depression.* Unpublished manuscript.

ERIC Microfilm Document

Hansen, K. (1987). *Relationships between expert and novice performance in disciplinary writing and reading.* (Report No. 2). East Lansing, MI: National Center for Research on Teacher Learning. (ERIC Document Reproduction Service No. ED 283 220)

Computer Software

Myst [Computer software]. (1992). Novato, CA: Brøderbund.

Videotape

National Geographic Society (Producer). (1987). *In the shadow of Vesuvius* [Videotape]. Washington, DC: National Geographic Society.

Television Broadcast

Porter, N. (1993). Amelia Earhart (N. Porter, Director). In J. Crichton (Producer). *The American experience.* Boston: WGBH.

For individual episodes of a series, list by writer's name; otherwise, list by the series producer's name: Crichton, J. (Producer). If pertinent, cite complete date of broadcast; otherwise, cite year of production.

Children Testifying in Sexual Abuse Trials:
Right to Emotional Safety vs. Right to Confrontation

Jessica Miskin
English 315
May 16, 2000

Provide identifying information on a separate title page. The running head (in the upper-right corner) includes a short title along with the page number. Most word processors include a feature for setting up such headers.

APA journals require an abstract, or brief summary of the main ideas of the paper, on a separate page following the title page. It should be accurate, self-contained, and specific. Some instructors may not require an abstract.

Abstract

As the incidence of child sexual abuse increases, so do concerns about having child victims testify in court against the alleged perpetrators of their abuse. The Sixth Amendment guarantees that the accused shall have the right to face the accuser; but when the accuser is a child, the trauma of facing the perpetrator may seriously impair the child's ability to give complete and credible testimony and may further hinder the child's recovery from the abuse. Because of these stresses, courts should seriously consider allowing children to use alternate methods of testimony, such as videotaped interviews and interviews using closed-circuit television or one-way screens. Although most courts have been reluctant to allow these methods, and although in some cases their use has been disallowed on appeal, the Supreme Court held in *Maryland vs. Craig* that "the Confrontation Clause does not prohibit the use of a procedure that, despite the absence of face-to-face confrontation, ensures the reliability of the evidence" (cited in Goodman, et al., 1991. p. 15). Therefore, when all the issues are weighed, society's responsibility to protect children from harm should have priority over protecting the accused's rights to confront the accuser.

Children Testifying 3

Children Testifying in Sexual Abuse Trials:
Right to Emotional Safety vs. Right to Confrontation

Child sexual abuse has existed at least since Biblical times, but in recent years reports of such abuse have grown dramatically, with the number of reported cases increasing by 593% from 1983 to 1993 (S. Norton, personal communication, January 15, 1993). It is impossible to know whether this is because the number of incidents is actually increasing or because people are just more willing than before to talk about the abuse. Experts in the field of social work vote both ways. But whatever the reason, caseworkers are swamped. Not that long ago in Utah County, workers only had fifteen cases each. In 1993 the number was up to twenty-five per worker (B. Peterson, personal communication, February 5, 1993), and the number of workers doubled from six to twelve (D. Crowley, personal communication, February 12, 1993).

The increased number of reported cases also led to an increased number of trials, and hence an increased number of children who must testify. In the past, children had no options but to testify in person. The Sixth Amendment mandates that the accused has the right to face the accuser, and in sexual abuse cases the accuser is the child. However, there has been on-going controversy about such children testifying in court. The court systems have historically been adult-oriented and were not prepared for the large number of children who have entered them. Adjustments have been made, but it has been suggested that further adjustments are necessary to accommodate these young witnesses.

While quite a few children are capable of testifying live without serious trauma, some children will experience great emotional harm if they aren't protected (Goodman, Levine, Melton, & Ogdens, 1991). The court may not arrive at the truth because of this harm. If children fear testifying, they may refuse to do so

Leave margins of at least one inch at top, side, and bottom.

Center title at top of first text page. Indent paragraphs five spaces, or half an inch.

Personal communication citations include the full date of the interview, letter, or e-mail. These are not included on the "References" list.

For the first parenthetical citation for a source by up to five authors, include the last name of each author. Use an ampersand (&) before the last author's name. (If you name the authors in your text, however, spell out *and*.) For a source by six or more authors, include only the first author's last name followed by "et al."

altogether, or they may withhold information. Neither trauma to the children nor incomplete evidence is in the best interest of the state. For this reason, court systems should seriously consider using alternate methods of testimony.

In this paper I will explain the stresses of live testimony on children: the benefits and detriments of live testimony; alternate methods for child testimony; and the legal system's reaction to these alternate methods. I believe that despite the controversy surrounding alternate methods of testimony, we must find ways to protect from unnecessary trauma these young accusers who are forced to enter our court systems.

Stress Associated With Testifying

Vulnerability

Whenever someone testifies in court, that person is bound to feel some anxiety. Goodman et al. (1991) note that this is true for adults, not just children: "As court dates approach, fear of testifying is one of adult rape victims' strongest fears" (p. 20). However, children are likely to feel more distress than adults for several reasons. First, children are at a very vulnerable period of life. They are still developing emotionally and mentally. Stress from court proceedings can interrupt this development, causing periods of stagnation and regression, occurrences which will affect them for the rest of their lives (Goodman et al., 1991).

In subsequent references to a source by three or more authors, include only the first author's last name, followed by "et al." Page numbers are included only for quotations, not for summaries.

Confusion About Proceedings

A second reason for increased distress in children is that they have less understanding of court proceedings than adults do. Goodman et al. (1991) state that by the latter part of elementary school, children have a fairly good understanding of legal processes. However, children who are still in preschool or lower grades have little, if any, understanding of the court system. Many people fear what they do not understand, and children are not exempt from this. Because they do not completely understand what is going to happen, they have higher levels of distress than adults do when testifying (Goodman et al., 1991).

Effects of Testifying Live

Beneficial Effects

High levels of stress do not have to create serious trauma to the child, however. If handled with a good deal of support, it can actually be a beneficial experience for children to testify, note Goodman et al. (1991). Appelbaum (1989) states that this is because it allows them "to participate in a process designed to redress the wrongs done to them" (p. 14). D. Crowley, (personal communication, February 12, 1993) says that testifying can be helpful in the child's healing process. In order to heal, one must talk about what has happened and deal with the emotions and the pain. While talking about one's experiences in front of strangers may not be helpful in every case, participating in the process of righting a wrong against oneself can be therapeutic.

Detrimental Effects

Increased Distress. However, in addition to possible benefits, there are potential detriments. Some children will be adversely affected by testifying live. Goodman et al. (1991) have found that children who participate in court proceedings experience more stress than children who do not have to testify. Some of the main reasons for this stress are having to testify more than once, facing the defendant, answering embarrassing questions, being harassed during cross-examination, and speaking in front of so many adults (Appelbaum, 1989; Goodman et al., 1991). Research indicates that testifying in front of the defendant is the most traumatic part of the court process (Appelbaum, 1989: Goodman et al., 1991; Naylor, 1989): "Indeed, research shows that the most frequent fear expressed by children awaiting testimony is a fear of facing the defendant" (Goodman et al., 1991, p. 21). When Goodman asked parents and children how some of the stress of testifying could have been alleviated, the most frequent response was "the use of

A first-level head is centered. A second-level head is flush left and italicized.

When you refer to the author in your text, indicate the date of the source's publication immediately following his or her last name. If you include a direct quotation, the page number(s) should follow it in parentheses.

A third-level head is indented and italicized.

If a citation is to more than one source, separate them with semicolons.

closed circuit television or videotaped testimony" (Goodman et al., 1991, p. 21).

The end punctuation follows the parenthetical cite, not the quotation. For direct quotations, page numbers follow the date (preceded by "p." or "pp.").

Obstructed Justice. Increased distress in child witnesses is not the only harmful effect of having the defendant in the courtroom or having to testify numerous times. The whole purpose of our legal system—arriving at the truth—can be obstructed. Goodman et al. (1991) note that some children will refuse to testify or may leave out important information if they are forced to testify with the defendant in the room; consequently, criminals sometimes go free due to lack of clear evidence. If alternate methods of testimony were used, this problem could be minimized. According to Goodman et al. (1991), "It is true that protective measures may be necessary in many cases to ensure that a child victim will be able to tell 'the whole truth and nothing but the truth'" (p. 18).

Alternate Methods of Testifying

Explanation

Certain innovations have been developed in the past several years to try to protect children from the harms of giving live testimony and to ensure that justice is served. Some of these are the use of videotaped interviews and interviews using closed-circuit television or one-way screens.

Videotaped interviews used as evidence are usually ones made by a social worker or psychologist. In recent decades social workers started taping their interviews with children reporting abuse in order to minimize the number of times the children would have to give statements, thereby decreasing confusion and trauma. In addition to social workers, children used to have to be interviewed by police, the prosecuting attorney, and the defense attorney. Now all those other people can just look at the tape. Pre-taped interviews were not admissible as evidence, however, until the mid-1980s, when a judge in a Dade County, Florida, child

sexual abuse case allowed such tapes to be used, along with a mixture of live testimony and closed-circuit television testimony (B. Peterson, personal communication, February 5, 1993).

Closed-circuit television testimony is broadcast to the courtroom from another room in the court house, often the judge's chambers. The child, the attorneys, and the judge leave the courtroom while the defendant, jury, and spectators remain. (In some countries it is the defendant who leaves [Naylor, 1989, p. 400.]) The accuser and the defendant can still see each other via television, but the child is spared the physical presence of the accused. Since that is considered by researchers to be the most traumatic aspect of testifying, closed-circuit television testimony is an effective method for protecting the child from trauma.

When a citation occurs within a parenthetical statement, it is enclosed in brackets. Brackets are also used to indicate explanatory comments within a quotation.

Another method that has been used to decrease the trauma associated with the presence of the defendant is a one-way screen or mirror (Naylor, 1989, p. 401), which is set up in the courtroom between the witness stand and the defendant. Neither the accused nor the accuser leaves the room. The child's view of the defendant is blocked, but the defendant can still see the child (Appelbaum, 1989, p. 13). This is to allow the child to concentrate more fully on testifying and to worry less about the defendant; while the defendant more or less retains the right to confront his or her accuser—and the jury can watch the defendant's reactions to the child and the child's testimony. In addition to decreasing the child's trauma associated with testifying, this method can also contribute to the search for truth because the child is more willing and able to testify completely.

History

In *Coy vs. Ohio* the defense appealed the decision of the presiding judge to allow the use of a one-way screen so that the accused could see the accuser, but not vice versa. The appeal went

Use italics (or underlining) for court cases.

Children Testifying 8

through several higher courts until it finally reached the U.S. Supreme Court. The Court overturned the judge's decision, declaring that the screen violated the accused's Sixth Amendment rights. The Justices qualified their decision with the statement that it may be too early in the history of child sexual abuse trials to be certain that rights are violated (Appelbaum, 1989).

Indeed, that statement turned out to be confirmed. In a more recent case, *Maryland vs. Craig* (cited in Goodman et al., 1991), the Supreme Court reached a similar decision, but clarified the use of protective measures. In *Craig*, the presiding judge ordered that the children testify outside of the courtroom, via closed-circuit television, in keeping with a state law allowing such a procedure. The defendant, a day-care operator, appealed her conviction on the basis that her Sixth Amendment right to face her accusers had been violated. The Court reversed her conviction, but it did not entirely rule out the usefulness of such protective measures, stating:

> Where necessary to protect a child witness from trauma that would be caused by testifying in the physical presence of the defendant . . . the Confrontation Clause does not prohibit the use of a procedure that, despite the absence of face-to-face confrontation, ensures the reliability of the evidence. (Goodman et al., 1991, p. 15)

Quotations of forty words or more are set off in a free-standing block of text indented five spaces, without quotation marks. The parenthetical citation for a block quotation *follows* the final period. No punctuation follows the close parenthesis.

In order to use these protective measures, the court must show the necessity of using them for each case. If it is shown, however, that the child will suffer great trauma from testifying in the same room as the defendant, that child's protection supersedes the defendant's right to confrontation (Goodman et al., 1991).

Controversy

Obstructed Truth. In the case of *Coy vs. Ohio*, one of the arguments against using the protective measures was that doing so could prevent finding the truth. Justice Scalia said, "It is always more difficult to tell a lie about a person 'to his face' than 'behind his back'" (cited in Appelbaum, 1989, p. 13). It was thought at the time of *Coy* that justice would be obstructed if the child did not have to see the accused face-to-face. The truth would be more elusive. *Maryland vs. Craig* addressed this idea two years later when the Supreme Court overturned that concept. Many experts believe that using protective measures can actually improve the quality of testimony given by a child. Children will generally feel more free to speak about what happened to them because they will have less fear (Bruck, Ceci, Hembrooke, 1998; Goodman et al., 1991; Koszuth, 1991).

Violated Rights. It is also argued that the defendant's Sixth Amendment rights are violated by using protective measures. One basic right is the right to face the accuser. If the child gives testimony from another room or by way of a pre-taped interview, then the defendant can't face the accuser (Appelbaum, 1989). Once again, this idea was addressed by *Craig*. The right of the child to be protected against trauma supersedes the right of the defendant to face-to-face confrontation. Thus, if the court can show sufficient evidence that serious harm will come to the child, protective measures can justifiably be used (Goodman et al., 1991).

In the face of the new definitions that *Maryland vs. Craig* established, definitions that are now two years old, one would think that people would understand the importance of protecting the interests of the child. Even today, however, judges are afraid to test these measures. Some states allow the use of one-way screens, video-taped evidence, and/or closed-circuit television. Many, however, still consider these measures unconstitutional (Naylor, 1989; D. Crowley, personal communication, February 12, 1993).

Juries' Views on Alternate Methods of Testifying

Decreased Credibility

Aside from being seen as unconstitutional in most states, alternate methods of testimony are also viewed as less credible. There is nothing so convincing as giving live testimony, even when faced with the threat of the accused in such close proximity (D. Crowley, personal communication, February 12, 1993). Justice Scalia's comment about lying seems to be a commonly held opinion. If children need to be out of the room to testify, it is because they aren't telling the truth. If they were telling the truth, they would be able to testify in front of the defendant easily, without feeling guilt or tripping up. If the jury can see them face-to-face, they are much more convinced of the truth of their testimonies (D. Crowley, personal communication, February 12, 1993).

This is only true if the child testifies confidently, however. Often, due to the pressure of being in the same room as the defendant, a child will give quiet, faltering testimony. Such children may thus be viewed as less credible because they are less confident. Research has indicated, though, that confidence and truthfulness are not related (Naylor, 1989). And so victimized children are in a double bind.

Declaration of Defendant's Guilt

However, juries can be led to believe the defendant is guilty through the use of alternate methods of testimony. If a child testifies out of the room or her pre-taped interview is used as testimony, the jury realizes that this is because the child is afraid of the defendant. If the child is so afraid that she can't testify live, the jury may assume that the defendant must be guilty. Their impartiality to "just the facts, ma'am" is already tainted (Naylor, 1989).

APA papers often end with a "Discussion" of the author's conclusions. Your instructor may not require such a section.

Discussion

While it is evident that constitutionality and credibility issues must still be resolved, it should also be evident that child-protective measures in the courtroom are vital to the emotional safety of children who must testify. While the measures still have limitations, they also have an impact on the lives of the children who testify, an impact that can be beneficial or detrimental, depending on whether and how the courts decide to use them. It is interesting to me that people seem unwilling to test the system. Crowley (personal communication, February 12, 1993) states that these methods are not used at all in Utah; in Texas they are unconstitutional (Naylor, 1989). This is surprising because the *Maryland vs. Craig* decision allowed their use. I realize that evidence must be shown that indicates that the trauma to the child will be severe enough to warrant these protective measures. I understand that proving this could take a long time, but children are worth the time.

I also realize that, although these measures address two of the largest sources of stress for child witnesses (facing the defendant and testifying numerous times), they don't address all sources of stress. There will still be the stress of answering embarrassing questions in front of many adults, being cross-examined, and reliving their horrible experiences of abuse. But if we can alleviate some of the stress, we should. Perhaps we can't make the court system perfect, but we could at least make it bearable for children and protect them from as much harm as we can.

Protecting our children from harm is the most important issue. We understand that people are innocent until proven guilty. We know that the prosecution has the burden of proof. It's horrible when an innocent person is convicted. But it's just as horrible when a perpetrator goes free. Children should not be treated as though they are on trial, yet sometimes they are. We should give them every chance to speak. If the only way for them to speak is through closed-circuit television or pretaped interviews, they should be allowed these avenues of speech. Their rights to emotional safety are more important than the defendant's right to face-to-face confrontation.

The children are the ones who have been harmed already. In our zeal to protect those who are "innocent until proven guilty," let's not forget to protect those who are truly innocent—our children.

Full bibliographic information for each source cited is included on a separate page titled "References," which is double-spaced throughout. Entries are listed alphabetically by authors' last names (or the first main word in titles, if no author is named). For papers that are not going to be typeset for publication, the first line of each entry is flush with the left margin; subsequent lines for the entry indent one-half inch, or five spaces. See pages 381–386 for APA guidelines regarding the information required and the format for specific types of sources.

Children Testifying 12

References

Appelbaum, P. S. (1989). Protecting child witnesses in sexual abuse cases. *Hospital and Community Psychiatry. 40.* 13-14.

Bruck, M., Ceci, S., Hembrooke, H. (1998, Feb.). Reliability and credibility of young children's reports: From research to policy and practice. *The American Pschologist, 53*(2), 136-52

Corder, B. F., & Whiteside, R. (1988). A survey of jurors' perception of issues related to child sexual abuse. *American Journal of Forensic Psychology. 6,* 37-43.

Goodman, G. S., Levine, M., Melton, G. B., & Ogdens, D. W. (1991). Child witnesses and the confrontation clause. *Law and Human Behavior, 15.* 13-29.

Koszuth, A. M. (1991). Sexually abused child syndrome. *Law and Psychology Review. 15,* 13-29.

Naylor, B. (1989). Dealing with child sexual assault: Recent developments. *British Journal of Criminology, 29.* 395-407.

The Principles in Action: Readings

THE DIHYDROGEN MONOXIDE CONTROVERSY

Over the past few years, a lively debate has occurred on the Internet regarding dihydrogen monoxide, a potentially toxic chemical used in many everyday situations. Although this controversy is not well known, how it is resolved may dramatically affect the lives of every American. The following selections are Web pages constructed by various groups attacking or defending the use of dihydrogen monoxide. As you read these Web pages, consider the following questions:

1. How accurate are these sources? Is the information free from errors? Is there someone who checks the information? How well does the information correspond with information found in other sources?
2. Who is the author for each source? What are the author's credentials? Who is the publisher? What kind of editorial standards does the publisher use? Do the author and publisher have a reputation for rigorous scholarship?
3. Does each source provide a balanced presentation? Is the source written or published by someone who has a direct personal or financial stake in the issue? Is the source free from bias? Is there any advertising in the source?
4. How recent is the source? Does the author attempt to draw on the most current research? Does the author contribute primary research?
5. What topics are covered in the source? What is the scope and depth of research? Does the author show an awareness of the major secondary sources on this subject? What does this source provide that is not found elsewhere?
6. What information is found in your library on dihydrogen monoxide?
7. What is dihydrogen monoxide? Based on your reading of these essays, what are its potential harms and benefits? Do you think it should be banned?

Coalition to Ban Dihydrogen Monoxide Home Page

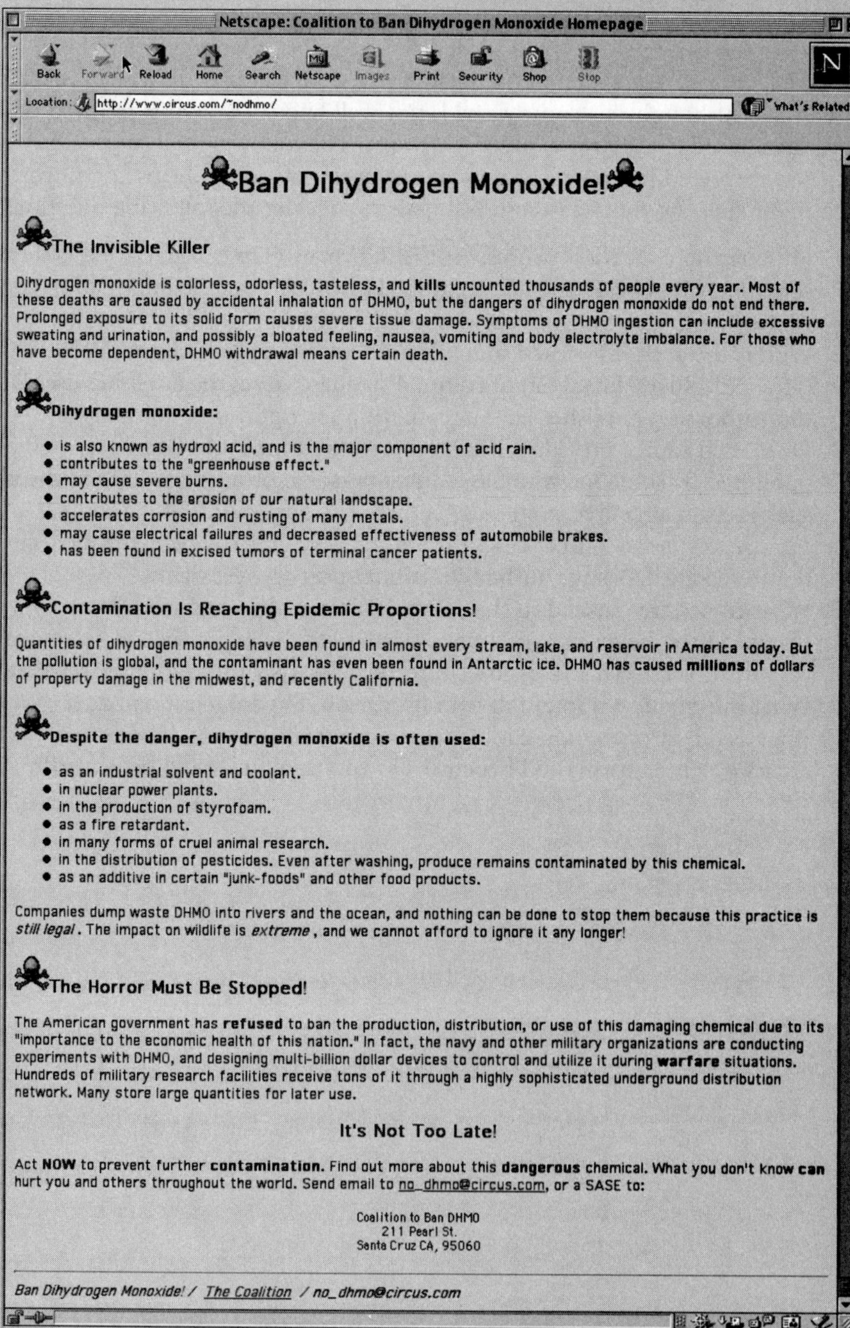

Netscape: Coalition to Ban Dihydrogen Monoxide Homepage

Back Forward Reload Home Search Netscape Images Print Security Shop Stop

Location: http://www.circus.com/~nodhmo/

What's Related

Ban Dihydrogen Monoxide!

The Invisible Killer

Dihydrogen monoxide is colorless, odorless, tasteless, and **kills** uncounted thousands of people every year. Most of these deaths are caused by accidental inhalation of DHMO, but the dangers of dihydrogen monoxide do not end there. Prolonged exposure to its solid form causes severe tissue damage. Symptoms of DHMO ingestion can include excessive sweating and urination, and possibly a bloated feeling, nausea, vomiting and body electrolyte imbalance. For those who have become dependent, DHMO withdrawal means certain death.

Dihydrogen monoxide:

- is also known as hydroxl acid, and is the major component of acid rain.
- contributes to the "greenhouse effect."
- may cause severe burns.
- contributes to the erosion of our natural landscape.
- accelerates corrosion and rusting of many metals.
- may cause electrical failures and decreased effectiveness of automobile brakes.
- has been found in excised tumors of terminal cancer patients.

Contamination Is Reaching Epidemic Proportions!

Quantities of dihydrogen monoxide have been found in almost every stream, lake, and reservoir in America today. But the pollution is global, and the contaminant has even been found in Antarctic ice. DHMO has caused **millions** of dollars of property damage in the midwest, and recently California.

Despite the danger, dihydrogen monoxide is often used:

- as an industrial solvent and coolant.
- in nuclear power plants.
- in the production of styrofoam.
- as a fire retardant.
- in many forms of cruel animal research.
- in the distribution of pesticides. Even after washing, produce remains contaminated by this chemical.
- as an additive in certain "junk-foods" and other food products.

Companies dump waste DHMO into rivers and the ocean, and nothing can be done to stop them because this practice is *still legal*. The impact on wildlife is *extreme*, and we cannot afford to ignore it any longer!

The Horror Must Be Stopped!

The American government has **refused** to ban the production, distribution, or use of this damaging chemical due to its "importance to the economic health of this nation." In fact, the navy and other military organizations are conducting experiments with DHMO, and designing multi-billion dollar devices to control and utilize it during **warfare** situations. Hundreds of military research facilities receive tons of it through a highly sophisticated underground distribution network. Many store large quantities for later use.

It's Not Too Late!

Act **NOW** to prevent further **contamination.** Find out more about this **dangerous** chemical. What you don't know **can** hurt you and others throughout the world. Send email to no_dhmo@circus.com, or a SASE to:

Coalition to Ban DHMO
211 Pearl St.
Santa Cruz CA, 95060

Ban Dihydrogen Monoxide! / The Coalition / no_dhmo@circus.com

Facts About Dihydrogen Monoxide

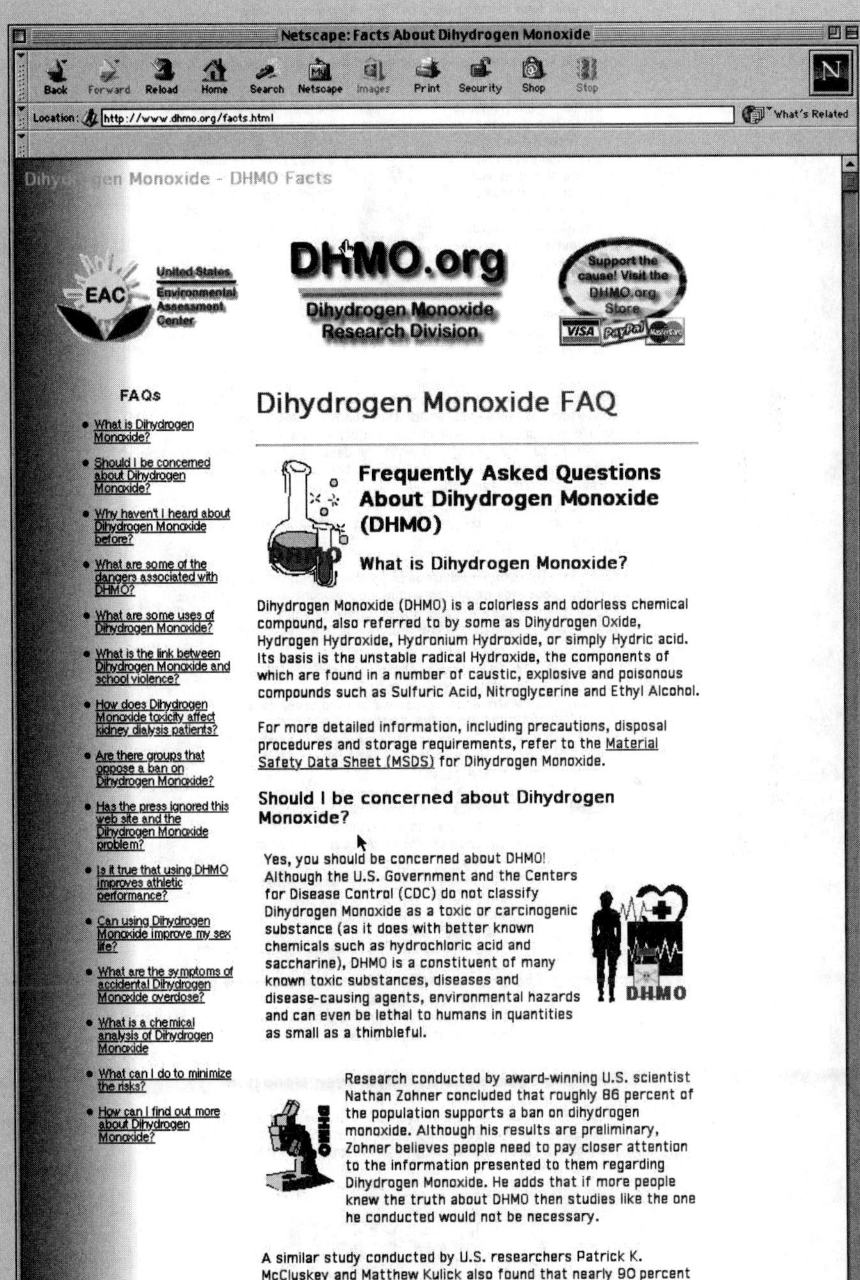

Netscape: Facts About Dihydrogen Monoxide

Back Forward Reload Home Search Netscape Images Print Security Shop Stop

Location: http://www.dhmo.org/facts.html What's Related

Dihydrogen Monoxide - DHMO Facts

United States Environmental Assessment Center

DHMO.org

Dihydrogen Monoxide Research Division

Support the cause! Visit the DHMO.org Store

FAQs

- What is Dihydrogen Monoxide?
- Should I be concerned about Dihydrogen Monoxide?
- Why haven't I heard about Dihydrogen Monoxide before?
- What are some of the dangers associated with DHMO?
- What are some uses of Dihydrogen Monoxide?
- What is the link between Dihydrogen Monoxide and school violence?
- How does Dihydrogen Monoxide toxicity affect kidney dialysis patients?
- Are there groups that oppose a ban on Dihydrogen Monoxide?
- Has the press ignored this web site and the Dihydrogen Monoxide problem?
- Is it true that using DHMO improves athletic performance?
- Can using Dihydrogen Monoxide improve my sex life?
- What are the symptoms of accidental Dihydrogen Monoxide overdose?
- What is a chemical analysis of Dihydrogen Monoxide
- What can I do to minimize the risks?
- How can I find out more about Dihydrogen Monoxide?

Dihydrogen Monoxide FAQ

Frequently Asked Questions About Dihydrogen Monoxide (DHMO)

What is Dihydrogen Monoxide?

Dihydrogen Monoxide (DHMO) is a colorless and odorless chemical compound, also referred to by some as Dihydrogen Oxide, Hydrogen Hydroxide, Hydronium Hydroxide, or simply Hydric acid. Its basis is the unstable radical Hydroxide, the components of which are found in a number of caustic, explosive and poisonous compounds such as Sulfuric Acid, Nitroglycerine and Ethyl Alcohol.

For more detailed information, including precautions, disposal procedures and storage requirements, refer to the Material Safety Data Sheet (MSDS) for Dihydrogen Monoxide.

Should I be concerned about Dihydrogen Monoxide?

Yes, you should be concerned about DHMO! Although the U.S. Government and the Centers for Disease Control (CDC) do not classify Dihydrogen Monoxide as a toxic or carcinogenic substance (as it does with better known chemicals such as hydrochloric acid and saccharine), DHMO is a constituent of many known toxic substances, diseases and disease-causing agents, environmental hazards and can even be lethal to humans in quantities as small as a thimbleful.

Research conducted by award-winning U.S. scientist Nathan Zohner concluded that roughly 86 percent of the population supports a ban on dihydrogen monoxide. Although his results are preliminary, Zohner believes people need to pay closer attention to the information presented to them regarding Dihydrogen Monoxide. He adds that if more people knew the truth about DHMO then studies like the one he conducted would not be necessary.

A similar study conducted by U.S. researchers Patrick K. McCluskey and Matthew Kulick also found that nearly 90 percent of the citizens participating in their study were willing to sign a petition to support an outright ban on the use of Dihydrogen Monoxide in the United States.

Why haven't I heard about Dihydrogen Monoxide before?

Good question. Historically, the dangers of DHMO, for the most part, have been considered minor and manageable. While the more significant dangers of Dihydrogen Monoxide are currently addressed by a number of agencies including FDA, FEMA and CDC, public awareness of the real and daily dangers of Dihydrogen Monoxide is lower than some think it should be.

Critics of government often cite the fact that many politicians and others in public office do not consider Dihydrogen Monoxide to be a "politically beneficial" cause to get behind, and so the public suffers from a lack of reliable information on just what DHMO is and why they should be concerned.

Part of the blame lies with the public and society at large. Many do not take the time to understand Dihydrogen Monoxide, and what it means to their lives and the lives of their families.

Unfortunately, the dangers of DHMO have increased as world population has increased, a fact that the raw numbers and careful research both bear out. Now more than ever, it is important to be aware of just what the dangers of Dihydrogen Monoxide are and how we can all reduce the risks faced by ourselves and our families.

What are some of the dangers associated with DHMO?

Each year, Dihydrogen Monoxide is a known causative component in many thousands of deaths and is a major contributor to millions upon millions of dollars in damage to property and the environment. Some of the known perils of Dihydrogen Monoxide are:

- Death due to accidental inhalation of DHMO, even in small quantities.
- Prolonged exposure to solid DHMO causes severe tissue damage.
- Excessive ingestion produces a number of unpleasant though not typically life-threatening side-effects.
- DHMO is a major component of acid rain.
- Gaseous DHMO can cause severe burns.
- Contributes to soil erosion.
- Leads to corrosion and oxidation of many metals.
- Contamination of electrical systems often causes short-circuits.
- Exposure decreases effectiveness of automobile brakes.
- Found in biopsies of pre-cancerous tumors and lesions.
- Often associated with killer cyclones in the U.S. Midwest and elsewhere.
- Thermal variations in DHMO are a suspected contributor to the El Nino weather effect.

What are some uses of Dihydrogen Monoxide?

Despite the known dangers of DHMO, it continues to be used daily by industry, government, and even in private homes across the U.S. and worldwide. Some of the well-known uses of Dihydrogen Monoxide are:

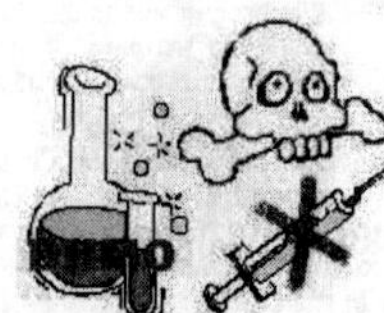

- as an industrial solvent and coolant,
- in nuclear power plants,
- by the U.S. Navy in the propulsion systems of some older vessels,
- by elite athletes to improve performance,
- in the production of Styrofoam,
- in biological and chemical weapons manufacture,
- as a spray-on fire suppressant and retardant,
- in abortion clinics,
- as a major ingredient in many home-brewed bombs,
- as a byproduct of hydrocarbon combustion in furnaces and air conditioning compressor operation,
- in cult rituals,
- by the Church of Scientology on their members and their members' families,
- by both the KKK and the NAACP during rallies and marches,
- by pedophiles and pornographers (for uses we'd rather not say here),
- by the clientele at a number of homosexual bath houses in New York City and San Francisco,
- historically, in Hitler's death camps in Nazi Germany, and in prisons in Turkey, Serbia, Croatia, Libya, Iraq and Iran,
- in World War II prison camps in Japan, and in prisons in China, for various forms of torture,
- by the Serbian military as authorized by Slobodan Milosevic in their recent ethnic cleansing campaign,
- in animal research laboratories, and
- in pesticide production and distribution.

What you may find surprising are some of the products and places where DHMO is used, but which for one reason or another, are not normally made part of public presentations on the dangers to the lives of our family members and friends. Among these startling uses are:

- as an additive to food products, including jarred baby food and baby formula, and even in many soups, carbonated beverages and supposedly "all-natural" fruit juices

- in cough medicines and other liquid pharmaceuticals,
- in spray-on oven cleaners,
- in shampoos, shaving creams, deodorants and numerous other bathroom products,
- in bathtub bubble products marketed to children,
- as a preservative in grocery store fresh produce sections,
- in the production of beer by all the major beer distributors,
- in the coffee available at major coffee houses in the US and abroad,
- in Formula One race cars, although its use is regulated by the Formula One Racing Commission, and
- as a target of ongoing NASA planetary and stellar research.

One of the most surprising facts recently revealed about Dihydrogen Monoxide contamination is in its use as a food and produce "decontaminant." Studies have shown that even after careful washing, food and produce that has been contaminated by DHMO remains tainted by DHMO.

What is the link between Dihydrogen Monoxide and school violence?

A recent stunning revelation is that in every single instance of violence in our country's schools, including infamous shootings in high schools in Denver and Arkansas, Dihydrogen Monoxide was involved. In fact, DHMO is often very available to students of all ages within the assumed safe confines of school buildings. None of the school administrators with which we spoke could say for certain how much of the substance is in use within their very hallways.

How does Dihydrogen Monoxide toxicity affect kidney dialysis patients?

Unfortunately, DHMO overdose is not unheard of in patients undergoing dialysis treatments for kidney failure. Dihydrogen Monoxide overdose in these patients can result in congestive heart failure, pulmonary edema and hypertension. In spite on the danger of accidental overdose and the inherent toxicity of DHMO in large quantities for this group, there is a portion of the dialysis treated population that continues to use DHMO on a regular basis.

Are there groups that oppose a ban on Dihydrogen Monoxide?

In spite of overwhelming evidence, there is one group in California that opposes a ban on Dihydrogen Monoxide. The Friends of Hydrogen Hydroxide is a group that believes that the dangers of DHMO have been exaggerated. Members claim that Dihydrogen Monoxide, or the less emotionally charged and more chemically accurate term they advocate for it, "Hydrogen Hydroxide," is beneficial, environmentally safe, benign and naturally occurring. They argue that efforts to ban DHMO are misguided.

Friends of Hydrogen Hydroxide is supported by the Scorched Earth Party, a radical and loosely-organized California-based group. Sources close to the Scorched Earth Party deny any outside funding from government, industry or pro-industry PACs.

Has the press ignored this web site and the Dihydrogen Monoxide problem?

For the most part, the press has not reported on the dangers of Dihydrogen Monoxide as much as some would like. Although many private individuals have put up web sites in a major grassroots effort to spread the word, major publications have not.

A notable exception is U.S. News & World Report which included a link the **DHMO.org** in a story on "Weird Science" in their October 11, 1999 issue. Unfortunately, the article ignores the dangers of Dihydrogen Monoxide, instead making light of various research projects by calling them "scientific satire."

The researchers at **DHMO.org** were disappointed that no mention of the risks of DHMO was made, but are thankful for the exposure on a national level in this very distinguished publication.

Is it true that using DHMO improves athletic performance?

Absolutely! With the numerous allegations of amateur and professional athletes using anabolic steroids and/or blood doping to enhance performance, virtually no attention has been paid to the performance enhancing properties of Dihydrogen Monoxide. It is perhaps the sporting world's dirtiest of dirty little secrets that athletes regularly ingest large quantities of DHMO in an effort to gain a competitive edge over an opponent.

One technique commonly used by endurance athletes in sports such as distance running and cycling is to take a large amount of DHMO immediately prior to a race. This is known within racing circles to dramatically improve performance.

Sports-medicine physicians warn that ingesting too much Dihydrogen Monoxide can lead to complications and unwanted side-effects, but do acknowledge the link to improved performance. DHMO is not currently considered a banned substance, so post-race urine tests do not detect elevated or abnormal levels of DHMO.

Can using Dihydrogen Monoxide improve my sex life?

This is a popular myth, but one which is also actually supported by a number of scientific facts. Dihydrogen Monoxide plays an instrumental role in the centers of the brain associated with increased libido and orgasm. So, much as with endurance athletes, moderate intake of DHMO prior to engaging in sexual activity may enhance performance, although the same caveats apply.

What are the symptoms of accidental Dihydrogen Monoxide overdose?

You may not always recognize that you have been a victim of accidental DHMO overdose, so here are some signs and symptoms to look for. If you suspect Dihydrogen Monoxide overdose, or if you exhibit any of these symptoms, you should consult with your physician or medical practitioner. The data presented here is provided for informational purposes only, and should in no way be construed as medical advice of any sort.

Watch for these symptoms:

- Excessive sweating
- Excessive urination
- Bloated feeling
- Nausea
- Vomiting
- Electrolyte imbalance
- Hyponatremia (serum hypotonicity)
- Dangerously imbalanced levels of ECF and ICF in the blood
- Degeneration of sodium homeostasis

A recently noted medical phenomenon involves small amounts of DHMO leaking or oozing from the corners of the eyes as a direct result of causes such as foreign particulate irritation, allergic reactions including anaphylactic shock, and sometimes severe chemical depression.

What is a chemical analysis of Dihydrogen Monoxide

Recently, German analytical chemist Christoph von Bueltzingsloewen at the Universitaet Regensburg identified what may be key reasons why the dangers of DHMO are ever present. According to von Bueltzingsloewen, the chemical separation of dihydrogenoxide from the hazardous oxygendihydride is extremely difficult. The two similar compounds curiously occur in nearly equimolar distribution wherever they are found. It is not clear how the two contribute directly to the dangers inherent in Dihydrogen Monoxide, although von Bueltzingsloewen believes that a synergetic mechanism, catalyzed by traces of hydrogenhydroxide, plays a major role.

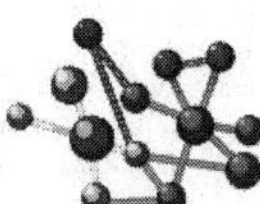

What can I do to minimize the risks?

Fortunately, there is much you can do to minimize your dangers due to Dihydrogen Monoxide exposure. **First,** use common sense. Whenever you are dealing with any product or food that you feel may be contaminated with DHMO, evaluate the relative danger to you and your family, and act accordingly. Keep in mind that in many instances, low-levels of Dihydrogen Monoxide contamination are not dangerous, and in fact, are virtually unavoidable. Remember, the responsibility for your safety and the safety of your family lies with you.

Second, exercise caution when there is the potential for accidental inhalation or ingestion of DHMO. If you feel uncomfortable, remove yourself from a dangerous situation. Better safe than sorry.

Third, don't panic. Although the dangers of Dihydrogen Monoxide are very real, by exercising caution and common sense, you can rest assured knowing that you are doing everything possible to keep you and your family safe.

How can I find out more about Dihydrogen Monoxide?

We would be happy to tell you more about DHMO! Send us email, and we'll gladly attempt to keep you up-to-date on current developments in the study of Dihydrogen Monoxide, its uses and misuses.

There are a number of sites on the world wide web that contain more information on DHMO and related topics. It should be noted that we do not endorse these sites, nor do we control their content or political bias.

Links to related information

DHMO web sites

- **Coalition to Ban Dihydrogen Monoxide (Headquarters)**
- **Coalition to Ban Dihydrogen Monoxide (Netreach)**
- **Friends of Hydrogen Hydroxide (DHMO supporters)**
- **Material Safety Data Sheet**

Environmental & Safety Information

- **SafetyBiz.com - Safety Engineer Jay Preston, expert in safety services and accident prevention**
- **Clean Air Engineering - promoting environmental responsibility and economic prosperity**

Back to DMRD main page

URL: http://www.dhmo.org/facts.html

Contact: <director@dhmo.org>

Material Safety Data Sheet for Dihydrogen Monoxide

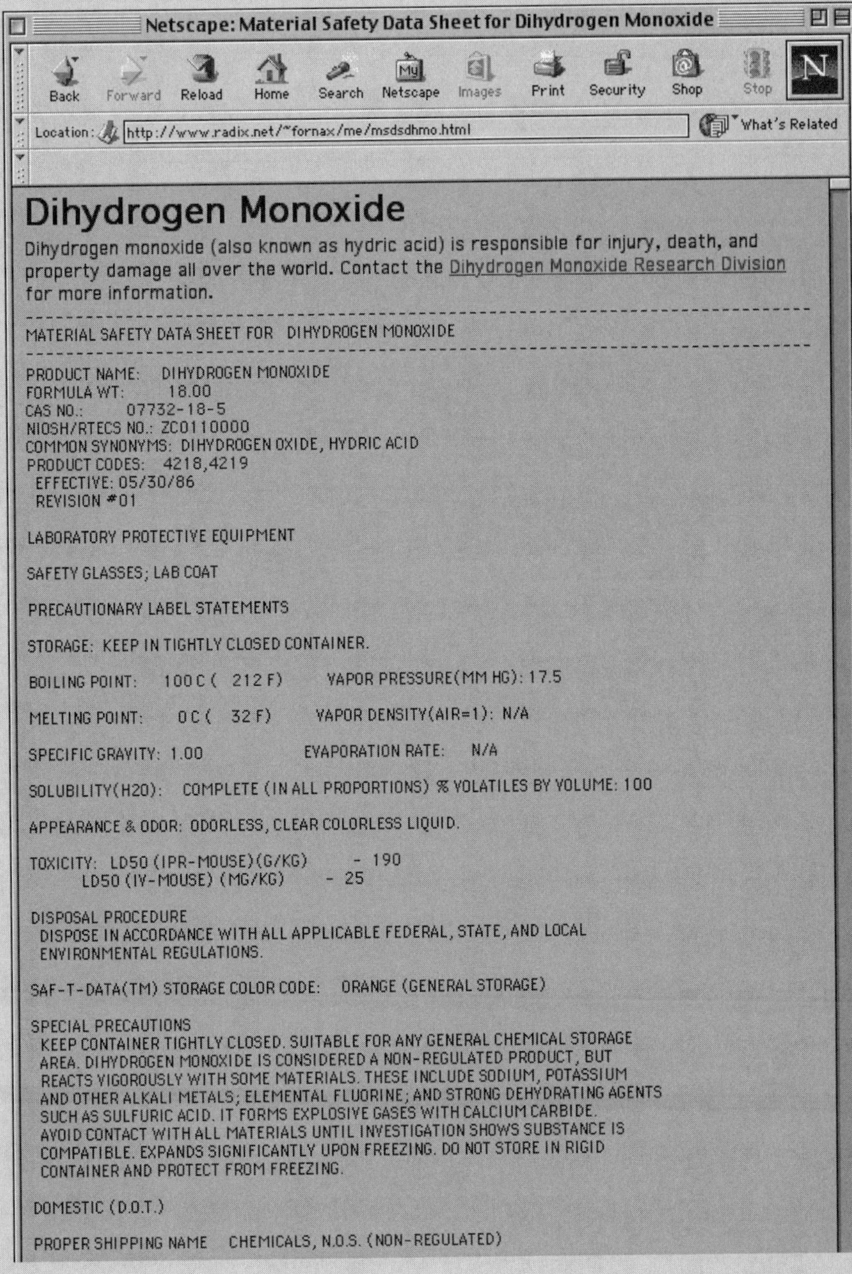

Netscape: Material Safety Data Sheet for Dihydrogen Monoxide

Back Forward Reload Home Search Netscape Images Print Security Shop Stop

Location: http://www.radix.net/~fornax/me/msdsdhmo.html What's Related

Dihydrogen Monoxide

Dihydrogen monoxide (also known as hydric acid) is responsible for injury, death, and property damage all over the world. Contact the Dihydrogen Monoxide Research Division for more information.

MATERIAL SAFETY DATA SHEET FOR DIHYDROGEN MONOXIDE

PRODUCT NAME: DIHYDROGEN MONOXIDE
FORMULA WT: 18.00
CAS NO.: 07732-18-5
NIOSH/RTECS NO.: ZC0110000
COMMON SYNONYMS: DIHYDROGEN OXIDE, HYDRIC ACID
PRODUCT CODES: 4218,4219
EFFECTIVE: 05/30/86
REVISION #01

LABORATORY PROTECTIVE EQUIPMENT

SAFETY GLASSES; LAB COAT

PRECAUTIONARY LABEL STATEMENTS

STORAGE: KEEP IN TIGHTLY CLOSED CONTAINER.

BOILING POINT: 100 C (212 F) VAPOR PRESSURE(MM HG): 17.5

MELTING POINT: 0 C (32 F) VAPOR DENSITY(AIR=1): N/A

SPECIFIC GRAVITY: 1.00 EVAPORATION RATE: N/A

SOLUBILITY(H2O): COMPLETE (IN ALL PROPORTIONS) % VOLATILES BY VOLUME: 100

APPEARANCE & ODOR: ODORLESS, CLEAR COLORLESS LIQUID.

TOXICITY: LD50 (IPR-MOUSE)(G/KG) - 190
LD50 (IV-MOUSE) (MG/KG) - 25

DISPOSAL PROCEDURE
DISPOSE IN ACCORDANCE WITH ALL APPLICABLE FEDERAL, STATE, AND LOCAL ENVIRONMENTAL REGULATIONS.

SAF-T-DATA(TM) STORAGE COLOR CODE: ORANGE (GENERAL STORAGE)

SPECIAL PRECAUTIONS
KEEP CONTAINER TIGHTLY CLOSED. SUITABLE FOR ANY GENERAL CHEMICAL STORAGE AREA. DIHYDROGEN MONOXIDE IS CONSIDERED A NON-REGULATED PRODUCT, BUT REACTS VIGOROUSLY WITH SOME MATERIALS. THESE INCLUDE SODIUM, POTASSIUM AND OTHER ALKALI METALS; ELEMENTAL FLUORINE; AND STRONG DEHYDRATING AGENTS SUCH AS SULFURIC ACID. IT FORMS EXPLOSIVE GASES WITH CALCIUM CARBIDE. AVOID CONTACT WITH ALL MATERIALS UNTIL INVESTIGATION SHOWS SUBSTANCE IS COMPATIBLE. EXPANDS SIGNIFICANTLY UPON FREEZING. DO NOT STORE IN RIGID CONTAINER AND PROTECT FROM FREEZING.

DOMESTIC (D.O.T.)

PROPER SHIPPING NAME CHEMICALS, N.O.S. (NON-REGULATED)

INTERNATIONAL (I.M.O.)

PROPER SHIPPING NAME CHEMICALS, N.O.S. (NON-REGULATED)

Back to Eric's Homepage.

Eric Schulman,
fornax@radix.net

Hydrogen Hydroxide: Now More Than Ever!

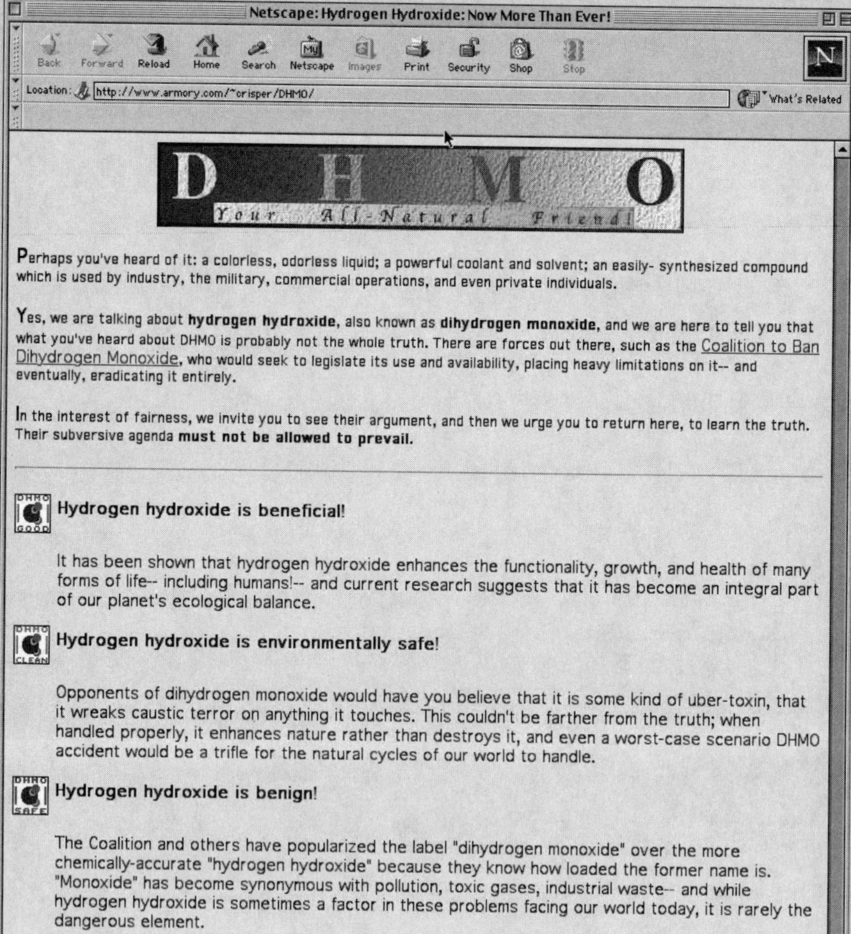

Perhaps you've heard of it: a colorless, odorless liquid; a powerful coolant and solvent; an easily- synthesized compound which is used by industry, the military, commercial operations, and even private individuals.

Yes, we are talking about **hydrogen hydroxide**, also known as **dihydrogen monoxide**, and we are here to tell you that what you've heard about DHMO is probably not the whole truth. There are forces out there, such as the Coalition to Ban Dihydrogen Monoxide, who would seek to legislate its use and availability, placing heavy limitations on it-- and eventually, eradicating it entirely.

In the interest of fairness, we invite you to see their argument, and then we urge you to return here, to learn the truth. Their subversive agenda **must not be allowed to prevail.**

DHMO GOOD

Hydrogen hydroxide is beneficial!

It has been shown that hydrogen hydroxide enhances the functionality, growth, and health of many forms of life-- including humans!-- and current research suggests that it has become an integral part of our planet's ecological balance.

DHMO CLEAN

Hydrogen hydroxide is environmentally safe!

Opponents of dihydrogen monoxide would have you believe that it is some kind of uber-toxin, that it wreaks caustic terror on anything it touches. This couldn't be farther from the truth; when handled properly, it enhances nature rather than destroys it, and even a worst-case scenario DHMO accident would be a trifle for the natural cycles of our world to handle.

DHMO SAFE

Hydrogen hydroxide is benign!

The Coalition and others have popularized the label "dihydrogen monoxide" over the more chemically-accurate "hydrogen hydroxide" because they know how loaded the former name is. "Monoxide" has become synonymous with pollution, toxic gases, industrial waste-- and while hydrogen hydroxide is sometimes a factor in these problems facing our world today, it is rarely the dangerous element.

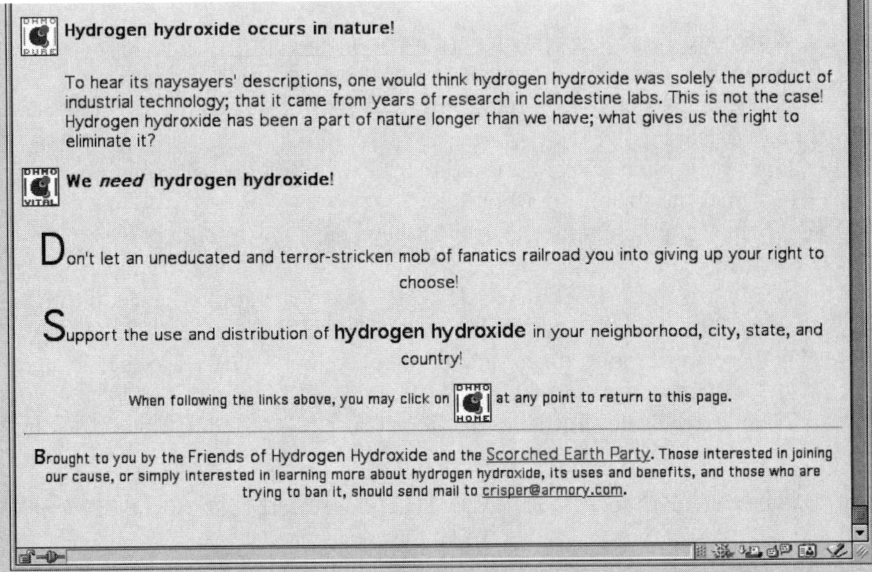

Hydrogen hydroxide occurs in nature!
To hear its naysayers' descriptions, one would think hydrogen hydroxide was solely the product of industrial technology; that it came from years of research in clandestine labs. This is not the case! Hydrogen hydroxide has been a part of nature longer than we have; what gives us the right to eliminate it?
We need hydrogen hydroxide!
Don't let an uneducated and terror-stricken mob of fanatics railroad you into giving up your right to choose!
Support the use and distribution of hydrogen hydroxide in your neighborhood, city, state, and country!
When following the links above, you may click on at any point to return to this page.
Brought to you by the Friends of Hydrogen Hydroxide and the Scorched Earth Party. Those interested in joining our cause, or simply interested in learning more about hydrogen hydroxide, its uses and benefits, and those who are trying to ban it, should send mail to crisper@armory.com.

Practicing the Principles: Activities

KNOW YOUR LIBRARY

Now that you have learned something about how academic conversations are recorded and organized in libraries, you need to check out your own library and get involved in some research. Keep in mind that the library is not only a depository of the records of conversations within academic communities, but it is also a community itself, so you'll need to know how to find your way around. You may even want to take a tour with other members of your class. You should be able to answer the following questions about your library:

- Where are the information desks located?
- What are the names of some librarians who can help you with your research?
- Where are the reference materials located? Is there a general reference area, or are reference areas spread throughout the library?
- Where is the library catalog located? Is it an online or card catalog?
- Where are computer terminals located? Are Internet connections available? Are computers available for word processing?
- Where are the books shelved?
- Where is the circulation desk? What do you have to do to obtain borrowing privileges?

- Where are current magazines and periodicals kept?
- Where are past issues of magazines or bound periodicals kept?
- Where are reserve materials kept? How can you get access to reserve materials?
- Does your library have an interlibrary loan office? If so, how do you obtain materials from other libraries?
- Where are the copy machines? Do they take coins or cards?
- Are there study areas? Can you arrange for group study rooms?
- Where are audiovisual materials kept? Does your library have a photo archive, film archive, video archive, or sound archive?
- Is there a rare-book room or special collections? Where are they located? Do students have access?
- What are the rules for using the library?

ANALYZING AN ACADEMIC JOURNAL

As a class, learn what you can about academic journals by each examining a different journal and reporting what you have learned to the class. Recent issues of academic journals are usually found in a "current periodicals" or "unbound serials" section of the library. Locate this part of the library and examine some journals that represent a field of study you are interested in. Learn what you can about the community that is represented by the journal and the conversations that are recorded there.

Examine the outside cover, the inside cover, and title pages. Usually, an academic journal will have some sort of editorial statement, defining the kinds of articles it publishes and the required format for submitting essays for publication. It usually lists the name and address of the editor, the place of publication, and an editorial board. The editorial board is generally made up of established members of the scholarly community associated with the journal. Members of this board review articles that are submitted to the journal and give the editor advice on which should be published and how they should be revised. A journal may also identify its association with a professional organization.

You can learn a lot about the community a journal represents by examining the contents of the journal. Find out what kind of writing is included. Are there essays, reviews, reader comments, calls for papers, announcements, or advertisements? Read a few of the essays. How are they organized? How do authors introduce and conclude the essays? What kind of documentation style is used? What counts as evidence? What issues are important? What questions are they trying to answer? What kind of claims do authors make? Scan some of the past issues of the journal. (Usually the library binds past issues of journals and shelves them either among the library books or in a separate "bound periodicals" section of the library.) By reviewing past issues, you can see how the conversation has evolved. Pay particular attention to the first issue. It will usually contain a statement about why the journal came into existence and what community it is designed to serve.

To understand how journals and magazines represent different types of communities, you may also want to examine journals that are directed toward a profession or trade and compare these journals with academic journals. As you briefly review the conversations in trade journals, how do they differ from academic journals? How do these academic and trade journals differ from some of the popular magazines you are familiar with?

ANALYZING A BOOK

You may think that you've looked at hundreds of books, but how many have you really analyzed? As a class, learn what you can about books and book publishing by each examining a book from a different press and reporting what you have learned to the class.

Examine a book from the outside to the inside. Check the cover and title page for as much information as you can find about the book and its author. Find out which company or press published the book and whether it is part of a series. Look up any information you can find about the book's publisher. Does the publisher have some statement of editorial policy and some sense of the community served? Is it an academic press or a trade press? What kinds of books does this press typically publish?

Look for biographical information about the author, often found at the end of the book or on the dust jacket. Read any forewords, prefaces, or acknowledgments, in which the author speaks to the reader about the book, often offering valuable information about how the book came into being. Read the table of contents and the opening section. Scan the remaining sections to discover what context the author provides for his or her writing. Survey the bibliography or list of works cited to get a sense of the conversation of which this book is a part. Finally, locate and read published reviews of the book to find out how other members relate the book to the larger conversation of the intellectual community. Your library may have the *Book Review Index* or *Book Review Digest* to help you find reviews of books. For reviews of recent books check a newspaper index, such as the *New York Times Index* or the *Washington Post Index*. The *New York Times Book Review* is also a very good place to find reviews of recent books. You can locate reviews online through newspapers or at <amazon.com> or <barnesandnoble.com>.

Applying the Principles On Your Own: Analytical Projects

NAPSTER

At the beginning of a new century, the controversy over Napster and the online sharing of digital music files has captured the attention of many college students and the music industry. The outcome of this controversy has multiple implications for the future of the Internet as well as the entertainment industry. Even normally law-abiding young people find themselves defending Shawn Fanning, the originator of the Napster file-sharing application, as a Robin Hood figure, taking on the big business of music to give power to the people. When Republican Senator Orrin Hatch (R-Utah) held Senate Judiciary Committee meetings in the summer of 2000 at politically and socially conservative Brigham Young University, in Provo, Utah, he no doubt expected a sympathetic audience. What he encountered was a group of students squarely in support of Fanning. After Fanning responded to the senator's questions, he received a standing ovation. (BYU has since filtered Napster from all campus Internet connections, primarily because it was taking up a huge amount of bandwidth.) This controversy clearly involves more than a simple disagreement about copyright law.

Although Napster lost its court case, the issues surrounding the case won't be going away soon—and in fact grow more complicated as new music-sharing companies—and technologies—develop. The following collection of essays presents various aspects of the Napster controversy as a starting point for further research. The first selection, "The Noisy War over Napster," is by Steven Levy, a correspondent for *Newsweek*. "It's Our Property," published in the same issue of *Newsweek*, was written by Lars Ulrich, drummer for Metallica, one of the plaintiffs in the Napster case. The third selection, "The Infoanarchist," was written by Adam Cohen and Chris Taylor, correspondents for *Time*. In this essay, Cohen and Taylor examine Freenet, a next-generation file-swapping application. "If It Feels Good . . . " was written by Vanessa Hua, a staff writer for the *San Francisco Chronicle*. This essay was accompanied in the same issue of the *Chronicle* by "Napster Use Can Be Research," a column by Dan Fost, regular author of the "Media Bytes" column on technology. "You Say You Want a Revolution" was written by Gina Arnold for the *East Bay Express*, a free weekly alternative newspaper distributed in the Berkeley area. The final selection is a research paper written by Keely Cosby for his first-year English class at Kennesaw State University in Georgia: "Should the Fate of Napster be Determined by the Interpretation of Law?"

For additional background reading on the music file-swapping controversy, you should also consult Charles C. Mann's lengthy article on Napster, "The Heavenly Jukebox," published as the cover story in the September 2000 issue of *The Atlantic Monthly*. This essay is also available online with additional interviews and Internet resources at <http://www.theatlantic.com>/issues/2000/

09>. Applying what you have learned in this chapter, you and your classmates can use these essays as background reading for a research project related to Napster. Consider the following activities:

1. Using library and Internet sources, gather additional information about Napster and Internet music sharing, bringing the controversy up to date.
2. Create a timeline for the Napster controversy and identify the various rhetorical moments in the life cycle of this debate.
3. Learn all you can about other Internet music file-swapping programs, such as Aimster, Freenet, Gnutella, Macster, and Mactella, and compare these to Napster.
4. As a group, synthesize what you learned and try to create a solution to the problem that addresses the needs of all the parties involved.
5. Write a proposal to your college administration recommending a campus policy on Napster and other Internet music file-swapping programs.

The Noisy War over Napster

STEVEN LEVY

1 MEET THE Napster Generation. Rachel is 14, an eighth grader in Potomac, Md., who loves lacrosse, basketball and guitar. Listens to 'NSync. Like millions of her peers with a computer and a clue, she's been using a program called Napster to download free music from the Internet, "because teenagers don't have that much money," she says. She doesn't think it's wrong to use Napster. "People don't think it's anything bad," she says. "Or think about it at all."

Smitha, a high-school student in Falls Church, Va., credits Napster, which gives her almost unlimited musical choices with a mouse-click, for expanding her musical horizons and "definitely" changing her buying habits. "I haven't purchased a CD in quite some time," she says.

Nor has Alejandro, a student at Stuyvesant High School in New York City, who downloads music while he sleeps. "Napster's the best thing ever created," he says. "I don't have to spend any money." Daniel, a Stanford comp-sci major, agrees: "I think almost all college students use it right now." The ethics issues of Napster don't bug him. "The main thing," he says, "is convenience."

Steve Bass does feel guilty about using the software. But then, he's 50, way past the age of senior citizenship in the Napster Generation. A Pasadena, Calif., writer and musician, he gets jazz tunes from Napster. "Morally, I've gotta stop," he says. "I've got a real conflict."

5 But conflict is what Napster, a deceptively simple computer program that's turned the Internet upside down, is all about. Conflicts between listeners and

record labels, labels and dot-coms, even artists against their audiences. According to one's point of view, Napster is a terrific way to acquire digital files that play tunes or a satanic jukebox that enables piracy on a scale not seen since Jean Lafitte cruised the seas. And sure enough, the popularity of Napster, the fastest-growing program in the highly incendiary history of the Internet, is tied to getting something for nothing. Napster allows you to search for almost any song you can think of, finds the song on a fellow enthusiast's hard drive and then permits you to get the song for yourself, *right now*. For the unbeatable cost of free, *nada*, gratis, *bupkes*, zero.

That's right. When you use Napster you simply download the program into your computer, make up a weird name for yourself and look for whatever song you want. Obscure Dylan tunes. "These Boots Are Made for Walkin.'" "American Pie," by Madonna *or* Don McLean. Within seconds you'll probably see a number of other users who have the song in the MP3 digital format. One click of the mouse and your computer hooks up with the one you choose, sucking up the bits that will allow you to play back the song on your computer, on a Walkman-like MP3 player or even on a CD that you might "burn" yourself. Fee to you: nothing. Royalties to artist, record company, songwriter: nothing. Guilt: optional.

The record companies are apoplectic. "The people who are on the board of directors and in the upper-level management of Napster all belong in prison," says Howie Klein, the president of Reprise Records. The Napster people, however, are not in prison: they're Silicon Valley heroes who have gotten $15 million in venture-capital funds. The downside is that they have no business model and are targets of several lawsuits charging them with copyright infringement and racketeering, including one by chest-baring heavy-metal rockers Metallica.

But that hardly matters. The fight over Napster has taken on a larger dimension, involving the future of music publishing, copyright law, 21st-century ethics and the relationship of artists to their audience. Pamela Samuelson, codirector of the Berkeley Center for Law and Technology, fears a "civil war" between artists, technology companies and desperate "copyright holders who want to control it all." For a few years now, the emergence of friction-free Internet pathways has raised a raft of questions about the future of entertainment and media, with no shortage of Chicken Little cyberpundits predicting an intellectual-property apocalypse—for music and everything else. But it took Napster to actually bring down the sky. And though there's hope that things will ultimately work out, right now no one is quite sure how to pick up the pieces.

Sitting at the center of all this controversy is Napster's creator: a slouchy, bullet-headed 19-year-old college dropout who suddenly finds himself the hottest star in the world's hottest industry. One evening last week Shawn Fanning steps out on the roof of his company's building in San Mateo—a drab, five-floor structure with a drive-through ATM and a red Union Bank sign on the façade—and squints at the sun while being interviewed by *Newsweek* and photographed by *Rolling Stone*. At that very moment, a 30-minute MTV special on

Napster is being shown to all of America, but he decides not to watch. "The media attention doesn't seem real," he says. As the photographer shoots, college-age Napster employees toss bean bags at him. It's just another night in Silicon Valley.

10 Only a year ago, Fanning was an obscure freshman at Northeastern University in Boston. After surviving a difficult childhood—his family was on welfare during his early years, and at one point he and his siblings were briefly shipped out to a foster home—he was a determined kid, according to his uncle John Fanning. The uncle had suffered a similarly rocky beginning and took an interest in his nephew, letting him work at his computer-game company near Cape Cod and purchasing a PC for him. According to Uncle John, Shawn applied to only two schools because he didn't have the $40 application fee—he was too proud to ask his uncle for the money—and one, Carnegie Mellon, turned him down.

Before finishing his freshman year, Shawn was bored and "partied out" at Northeastern, and spent much of his time on IRC, an Internet chat system. One IRC friend, Sean Parker, 20, lived in Virginia; another, Jordan Ritter, 23, was also in Boston. Fanning had noticed that his college roommates were into trading digital tunes on the MP3 format with each other but had difficulty finding files they wanted. He suggested the trio create a way for people to search for files and talk to each other, "to build communities around different types of music." File-sharing was almost an afterthought.

While writing the program—dubbed after his childhood nickname, from hairier days—Fanning spent "all waking moments on software." At first, he says, "we were just thinking of this as a cool project"—but they needed money for equipment and high-speed connections. Parker and Fanning's uncle convinced him it should be a business. The program went up in September 1999, and people instantly took to it, quickly creating a critical mass of tunes. As the audience grew—"we were doubling in users every five to six weeks," says John Fanning—the company found an angel investor, an interim CEO and a new home in Silicon Valley.

Fanning's program came at a pivotal moment. Ever since the VCR, the march of technology has created controversy over the way people make copies of artistic works. Film and TV studios hated the device, and tried to litigate it out of existence—an effort that ended with a Supreme Court ruling that consumers were allowed to copy television shows for personal use. (Now, of course, those same studios make the bulk of their profits from the device they tried to kill.) The use of the audiocassette was viewed with similar panic. But piracy from those media was limited by the difficulty of making multiple copies. The Internet changed that—it allows fast, unlimited file distribution, especially with high-speed connections. Still, anyone who tried to use the Net to sell illegal digital copies of songs or films was clearly breaking the law.

But because Napster simply allowed users to share their personal files with each other, Fanning and this new company claimed they were kosher. It's the digital equivalent of the piano player in the brothel: *hey, we don't know what goes on upstairs.* But that excuse went only so far, especially as the record companies began to notice that the Napster Generation had commenced swapping files *en masse.* Whereas most start-ups get changed by the arrival of the suits, Napster had to face the arrival of the lawsuits.

First came a filing from the Recording Industry Association of America 15
(RIAA) for copyright infringement. Then the heavy-metal Metallica crew found their music downloaded on Napster and were furious—they had their lawyer file another suit. For good measure they sued some of the *universities* whose students used Napster, including Yale and the University of Southern California. Further, the band took the drastic step of collecting the handles of 300,000 users who had allegedly downloaded Metallica songs, demanding they be removed from the system. Drummer Lars Ulrich personally delivered the names. Another suit was filed, by rapper Dr. Dre. (All are currently pending.)

Meanwhile, Napster's popularity kept increasing. At one point the program became so widespread that some colleges banned it—users were gobbling up more than half the computer resources of some schools, just swapping tunes on Napster. Log on at a given moment, and you could find about a million songs available for instant downloading.

And now Fanning is sort of a rock star himself, albeit of the Silicon Valley variety. Instead of a villa in the south of France, he lives with Parker in a dorm-like apartment a couple of blocks from the office. Two other Napster employees sleep on the floor every night. Fanning spends what little time he has outside work lifting weights at 24 Hour Fitness, every night between 11 and 2. He doesn't go out much. "San Francisco would be OK if I had a fake ID," he says. Fanning and his partners did make a trip to Berkeley last week to see the Smashing Pumpkins and ran into lead singer Billy Corgan backstage. They talked for an hour. "He was a huge supporter—he totally understands how it evolves," Fanning gushed to a friend.

Indeed, how Napster evolves is the big question for Fanning and partners. That's why the recent $15 million investment by the big-shot Silicon Valley venture-capitalist firm Hummer Winblad was so important. Other firms, nervous about the lawsuits, had demurred, a startling occurrence in an atmosphere where a few million bucks of VC money can be obtained by some nerd's vigorous sneeze. Hummer Winblad installed one of its VC's Hank Barry—a former copyright lawyer—as the new CEO. "We're trying to build a bridge to everybody involved in Napster," he says. "From music educators and users to record companies." Especially the latter. Barry's already been active in trying to reach a truce with the music industry, calling RIAA president Hilary Rosen and even Metallica. "He asked for a dialogue," says Ulrich. "It's a weird situation, though, cause we're in the middle of putting him out of business."

Many observers think that Napster's outlaw rep has permanently tainted the company. Some of the preliminary rulings have gone against it, more than 120 universities have banned it for legal reasons (including those sued by Metallica, which dropped them from the suit) and more bad news have come with a recent survey. Napster supporters had insisted that its users might actually buy more CDs after risk-free sampling of downloaded tunes. But a recent study, using the definitive Sound-Scan music-sales-measurement system, concluded that while overall CD sales have been significantly up, purchases have tanked at stores near college campuses—Napster country.

20 The "civil war" Samuelson referred to may have already begun. Not only the business people are taking sides, but the artists themselves. Napsterites like Limp Bizkit's frontman Fred Durst, whose free summer tour will be funded by the start-up, are excoriated by industry types. "Is [Durst] saying only kids with computers should get [his music] for free!" jokes Val Azzoli, co-CEO of the Atlantic Group. "He should give his music away for free at every retail store in America! The schmuck!"

While so far only Metallica and Dr. Dre have taken the step of moving against their fans, their lawyer Howard King says that at least five other artists have contacted him. Meanwhile, Ron Stone, manager of artists like Tracy Chapman and Bonnie Raitt, insists that the entire Napster movement is little better than thuggery. "Basically they're saying our art is worthless, it's free for the taking," he says. "Music used to be a collectible, now it's a disposable." With a few other artists and managers, he's starting an ad-hoc committee called Artists Against Piracy. Somehow it doesn't have the ring of Save the Rain Forest.

But even if the music industry succeeds in killing Napster, it is faced with a series of imitators, some of whom are even scarier from an industry point of view. In a way, Napster is a fat target for attackers: it uses a centralized database, which allows the company some control over its users. (And keeps a list of transfers handy for potential litigants.) But with some newer systems, the searching is done in a distributed manner that can't be shut down or modulated. One of these systems is Gnutella (pronounced New-tella). Unlike Napster, Gnutella could be used to exchange not just music files but any files, including movies, text and photos—a copyright holder's nightmare.

Amazingly, the program was written by Justin Frankel, a well-known programmer at Nullsoft, a company owned by America Online—which is in the process of purchasing Time Warner, the world's biggest collection of music labels. Within hours after Gnutella was posted on the Nullsoft site, AOL executives had it withdrawn. But the code circulated through the Net and now hundreds of programmers are supporting an active Gnutella community. If Napster is shut down, says Gene Kan, one of these pro bono developers, "the postapocalyptic pirates are going to be using Gnutella."

Even more radical is Freenet, created by 23-year-old Ian Clarke, an Irish computer scientist living in London. His program is not only decentralized but has safeguards to protect the privacy and identity of users. The actual files to be downloaded will be encrypted and then randomly distributed among the community of Freenetters, who won't even know what information is stored on their own disks. (Could be songs, could be kiddie porn.) File transfers will be untraceable. Clarke's motives are political—his dream is to liberate intellectual property. "My opinion is that people who rely on copyright probably need to change their business model," he says.

Most observers, however, are more sanguine about the eventual outcome of 25
the Napster Wars. Even the most virulent opponents of the software can recognize the popularity of Shawn Fanning's creation. "Despite all their scary characteristics, people love this stuff," says Samuelson. And just about everybody agrees that eventually the labels should muzzle the lawyers and view the Web experiments as potential partners. "How many industries try to kill off their biggest distribution channel on the Internet?" asks Gnutella developer Kan.

In fact, a number of Napster spinoffs intend to work within the system, getting licensing deals from record companies. One of these is Scour.com, whose key investor is superagent Mike Ovitz, who first heard of the company, founded by UCLA students, by reading the college paper. Ovitz notes that as a talent representative, his interest is in helping artists make the most of the new technologies. He thinks that eventually money will flow to those artists from models other than direct payments. "I'm looking at radio, sponsored shows, advertising-driven models, subscriptions," he says.

Rob Glaser, CEO of streaming-audio leader Real.com, thinks that when the record companies come to their senses and figure out ways to work with the Internet (expect some efforts by the year-end), the worst problems will fade. "All the illegal activity ends when prohibition ends," he says. "When there's a legal way for people to get what they want, mass bootlegging will recede."

The expectation is that music will become cheaper, and there will be more of it around, and it will be easier to find. But before that happens, the wars have to quiet down. The lawsuits have to be dropped. And the file-swappers have to come to grips with the fact that free isn't forever.

Meanwhile, the Napster Generation keeps searching for tunes, keeps downloading them and doesn't bother with concepts like intellectual property. "I sympathize [with bands, labels and music publishers] in the capitalist sense, but the technology isn't stoppable," says Rizwan Kassim, a 19-year-old sophomore at UCLA. Kassim's own experience is instructive. As one of the alleged violators identified by Metallica, his account was shut down by Napster. But Kassim simply began a new one under another name, and kept on downloading. He also stopped listening to the band, in any format, deleting all his Metallica tracks from CDs he burned using Napster.

In a final flourish, he took the one legit Metallica CD he owned and auc- 30
tioned it on eBay. "I think I got a couple dollars for it," he says.

At least *someone* is paying for music in the Age of Napster.

It's Our Property

LARS ULRICH

1 MY BAND WAS RECORDING A SONG CALLED "I Disappear" for the "Mission: Impossible 2" soundtrack when we heard that six different versions of the song—works in progress—had been made available on Napster. We don't know how the music got out, but somewhere in the chain of things it was leaked. But when we found out that people were trading these songs on this thing called Napster, which we hadn't even heard of, we felt a line had been crossed.

The whole notion of music and art and intellectual property is changing. People have been downloading copyrighted music for a couple years now for free, so they think they have the right to do it. But it isn't a right, it's a privilege. And you only have that privilege because the record industry let this stuff get totally out of control.

This is an argument about intellectual property. Right now we are talking about music. But it could apply to almost anything, from motion pictures to literature to fine art. In a year or two, when the technology advances and you start seeing illegal copies of big-budget mainstream Hollywood movies like "Gladiator" showing up on the Internet, Hollywood will certainly jump into this fight. But it goes beyond that. I mean, where does it end? Should journalists work for free? Should lawyers? Engineers? Plumbers?

The naysayers, the critics of Metallica, keep asking, "Who does Napster hurt?" Well, they're not really hurting us—yet—but I do know who they are hurting already: owners of small independent record stores. We heard from a guy in Syracuse, N.Y. The guy said that since Napster went up a few months ago, his business dropped like 80 percent and he had to shut it down. He said kids were coming into his store, checking out the bins for cool new records and then going home and downloading them instead of buying them.

5 We've also been hearing about a so-called fan backlash that has occurred as a result of our lawsuit, but I don't think it's any different from other so-called backlashes against us over the past 18 years. There has been a perception since the beginning that we've been a people's band, so to speak. That we are for the fans. I've always had a problem with that. We have always been friendly and connected to our fans, but being connected is very different than doing everything we do because of our fans. The truth is, what we do, we do for ourselves. We don't do it for anybody else. You really have to have that attitude, otherwise it will pollute or distort your creative purity. I've been preaching that same sermon for over 15 years. There is a selfishness in this band, but that leads to more artistic purity. I think people who are our true fans understand that and find that refreshing. You have to isolate yourself from putting the fan in the driver's seat, because we are not a product. We aren't toothpaste.

The bottom line is, Who cares about what people think of us? I don't care. We're doing this because we think it's the right thing to do, period. Other people have different opinions on this subject, people like rapper Chuck D, whom I respect greatly but with whom I totally disagree. We are bewildered by the lack of support from the record industry since we filed the lawsuit. Where are the record companies on this? Individually, virtually no one in the industry has really gone public in support of us. There is clearly a state of chaos in the industry, which has found itself mired in an anarchistic, mob-rules environment. But it's the industry's own fault. Basically the record industry let the boat leave the dock while they weren't watching. I am not pro-record company at all, but people are fantasizing if they think that unsigned bands can take their music to the public in any major way without record-industry backing. No acts from the Internet have ever broken into the wide mainstream. It's a fact.

I've been surprised that more artists haven't come out in support of what we are doing against Napster. Many artists are more concerned with their public images and with the perception of what they do and what they are. We just don't have those issues. We have always done what we want to do, what we believe in. The good thing about all of this is that the public debate is really opening up. At first some people just thought we were the bad guys in this debate, but as soon as I am allowed to explain my position I think most reasonable people understand where I'm coming from.

The Infoanarchist

ADAM COHEN and CHRIS TAYLOR

IAN CLARKE boots up a computer in a house he shares with two flatmates in a gritty London neighborhood, across the street from Brixton Prison. With a few quick keystrokes, he downloads a free copy of Britney Spears' new single, "Oops! . . . I Did It Again." As Britney's sugary lament fills his dorm-style bedroom, bouncing off the unmade bed and the laundry bag on the door, Clarke insists he feels no pangs of conscience. "Copyright is a crutch," he says. "It's inherent in nature that information wants to be free." 1

Ho-hum. Just another Gen Y geek pirating music on the Net. Napster—the file-sharing system that lets people download free music—and its close kin Gnutella seem so 10 minutes ago. The recording industry has Napster on the run, with a federal lawsuit pending to shut it down for copyright violations. And now MP3.com, another music-sharing service, has settled with two record companies (including Warner Music Group, a unit of this magazine's parent, Time Warner) on terms favorable to the industry.

But Clarke wasn't using Napster or MP3.com. He downloaded "Oops!" on Freenet, a next-generation Napster-like program of his own creation that ratchets file sharing up to the next level. What sets Freenet apart is that information on it travels from PC to PC anonymously. There's no way to tell who posts a document and no way to tell who downloads it.

The implications are profound. Dissidents in totalitarian states could use Freenet to post samizdat that once had to be cautiously hand-circulated. Whistle-blowers could safely bring smoking-gun documents to light. But Freenet could also be put to less high-minded use. Critics say it will be a boon to drug dealers, terrorists and child pornographers. And it poses a new threat to intellectual-property rights. With Napster, at least there's a company to sue and a way to trace individuals who have downloaded CDs. If Freenet catches on, it may be impossible to find anyone to punish.

5 Clarke, a lanky, earnest 23-year-old, became fascinated with computers after seeing the 1983 hacker-fantasy flick *War Games* as a child in Navan, Ireland. A computer-science major at the University of Edinburgh, Clarke developed Freenet as a student project over the summer of 1998. His key innovation was the element of anonymity. PCs hooked up to Freenet (the software can be downloaded from freenet.sourceforge.net) become "nodes," meaning they are host to data files deposited on them for varying amounts of time. There's no central server, as with Napster. And there's no need for users to sign on or identify themselves.

Clarke is a true anarchist about information. He believes no one should control it. Not governments, not corporations. "An attempt to control information should be just as disturbing as an attempt to control the air we breathe," he says. He dismisses critics' concerns. Musicians will always find ways to make money, Clarke insists, by sales of T-shirts and other ancillary items, perhaps, or even voluntary payments from their fans. As for terrorism and child pornography, he doesn't believe humanity should be denied free speech because "a few people might use it for something unsavory." Ultimately, Clarke says, Freenet makes debates of this kind moot. "If you had to convince everyone freedom of information is a good thing, it would never happen," he says. "The point is, I made it happen."

Or, more precisely, he's still trying to make it happen. Clark has a day job, working for a company that consults for online auctions. (He makes no money from Freenet, and since he doesn't claim to own it, he can't sell it.) He spends much of his free time—along with volunteer code writers from as far away as Stockholm and Houston—working out Freenet's kinks. It's in a creaky early version right now, so hard to use that only some 35,000 people have hooked up. High on Clarke's to-do list: create a search engine so users won't need to consult informal lists like "Steve's Key Index" that volunteers have assembled.

As for actual content, the pickings are still slim, but it's not hard to see Freenet's vast potential. Clarke scrolls down an index looking for items of interest and calls out what he finds. The Communist Manifesto. The U.S. Constitution.

A document purporting to be a British Intelligence report on Libyan spying activities in Britain. A lot of files have names suggesting they're pornographic; a few seem to be child porn. There are files that appear to contain secret "OT" documents of the Church of Scientology. If they're real, they illustrate Freenet's power: the Scientologists have obtained court orders in the past to yank such documents off the Net. Another file purports to be secret coding from Microsoft, also a vigilant defender of its copyrights. Clarke says he's never been contacted by Microsoft or any of the other entities whose content has been posted, and he doesn't expect to be. After all, he doesn't control what gets posted on Freenet. "There's nothing I can do, and they probably know that," he says.

Does this mean content providers will be steamrollered by Freenet? Not necessarily. Many media experts say people who create music and other copyrighted material will eventually find a way to charge for it. "Generating content is a valuable service," says Eric Scheirer, a media and Internet analyst at Forrester Research." And as long as it is, there will always be ways to monetize it." What's more, anonymous systems like Freenet are inherently vulnerable. "The record companies could flood Freenet with a million copies of static," Scheirer suggests, "and title them The New Britney Spears Song."

It turns out the brave new world of free-flowing information can be a bit dis- 10
concerting, even to infoanarchists. Clarke stops at a file named "Ian Clarke's Credit Card Numbers." He isn't worried, he says confidently. He's sure it's a joke, that it doesn't really contain his card numbers. Well, almost sure. He opens the file and checks. "I was right," he says with a trace of relief in his voice. "It was just a joke."

HOW TO BRING MP3S TO THE MASSES

A few weeks ago, the idea that the recording industry would embrace Michael Robertson as one of its own was about as ridiculous as, well, as the notion that the leaders of North and South Korea would shake hands. Robertson, founder and CEO of MP3.com, was trying to turn the music business on to the MP3 revolution, but all the suits saw was a maverick who went around claiming that they were dinosaurs who didn't get it. And when he launched the My.MP3.com service that allowed users to copy their CDs into his online folders and listen to them from anywhere they chose, those dinosaurs won a copyright-infringement court case that threatened to take the upstart dot-com for every penny it had.

But by the time that decision came down, the rise and rise of Napster had made My.MP3.com look like a littering violation in the middle of a full-scale riot. And Robertson, because he disavows the Napster free-for-all and sees a future in which record companies get paid for online distribution, has suddenly become a man the music industry can do business with. The settlement deal MP3.com cut with Warner and BMG two weeks ago—whereby Robertson will pay $100 million in damages and get a license to run My.MP3.com in return—is only the beginning of a beautiful friendship. If Robertson's vision is accurate, he and the record companies will streamline the $40 billion music business into a new digital-delivery system.

What he's banking on is that the majority of music fans will be prepared to pay a minimal monthly fee—around the price of a single CD—to have online access to thousands of albums. This music channel—along with the CDs already in their collections—will be available anywhere there's an Internet connection. Robertson believes the mainstream will choose this limited-pay model over legally dubious networks like Napster and Freenet. Thus far the rise of MP3s "has been painted as a college-kids-gone-crazy phenomenon," he says. "In fact, it cuts across all walks of life."

That includes classical-music aficionados, currently the fourth largest group on MP3.com, who made a willing audience for the site's first such monthly-fee channel. "They're the techno-elite," says Robertson. "Also, these people have disposable income." For $9.99 a month, there are thousands of fully downloadable tracks. It's all-you-can-eat Pavarotti, Itzhak Perlman and London Symphony. A second channel for children featuring fairy tales and nursery rhymes as well as songs is set for launch in July.

Suddenly it seems the once radical Robertson is offering a third way between 15
the rigid order of the old world and the chaos of Napster, a chance to make money out of wide but shallow channels of online music and still make a buck or two selling CDs in stores. That should be music to the dinosaurs' ears.

If It Feels Good . . .

VANESSA HUA

THOU SHALT not steal digital music. 1

Well, unless it's just one song from a costly album you wouldn't buy. Or if you're checking out a tune you will purchase later. Or if you're downloading a song you already own on tape or CD.

Or if everyone else is doing it.

So goes the thinking of Napster users who popularized the embattled online song-swapping program. Even though the recording industry may have prevailed over the Redwood City startup, the labels face an even more fundamental problem: unrepentant music fans.

"It's retribution for paying $20 per CD for years," said John Wang, 27, a Napster user and Los Angeles manufacturing engineer, criticizing what he deemed an inflated, antiquated pricing structure.

Wang, like many others, vowed to use other music-sharing alternatives in search of copyrighted songs blocked on Napster.

Are 67 million Napster users thieves? Put another way: Why is the definition 5
of "stealing" held by record companies and music fans so radically different?

Indeed, the Napster dilemma—to download or not to—reveals that matters of ethical standards are not always clear.

"Ethical norms are anchored in the culture," said James Post, a Boston University business ethics professor. "What Napster teaches us is that you can't have an ethical norm if the people refuse to accept it."

Otherwise law-abiding people who would never steal a compact disc from a 10
store say they are justified in downloading copyrighted music.

For many, song swapping has already become a socially acceptable practice. And it's not just cash-strapped teenagers and college students. Napster users around the globe range from tech-savvy Yuppies to homemakers.

"Until someone makes it clear that it's illegal, people are going to take chances," said David Barlin, 28, a marketing and product manager at an Internet startup in San Francisco and Napster user. Barlin said he would be willing to pay a monthly subscription fee for the service's convenience and vast selection.

Some users contend that pricing models should reflect the Internet age. They say Napster's technology creates cost-saving distribution efficiencies for record labels, allowing for freebies and other perks to customers.

"Personally, I've supported the industry enough that it's fair for me to grab some songs off the Internet," said Jeff Lee, 27, an El Sobrante native now living in Los Angeles.

"It doesn't feel like I'm ripping them off. It's more like a free add-on serv- 15
ice," said Lee, who likes to download hard-to-find 1980s bands and trance music. "It whets your appetite toward more music."

Randy Antin, 26, an online editor in San Francisco, views his usage of Napster as neither stealing nor sharing, but as "sampling."

"It is the same as hearing them played on the radio, listening to songs on a listening station at a record store or having a friend put a song on a mix tape," Antin said. "Napster allows users to choose what they want to listen to instead of a DJ or record company choosing for them."

As for the plight of artists, Napster users argue the service is helping, not harming musicians.

Two-thirds of college students who use Napster say they download songs so they can preview music before purchasing the CD, according to a recent study by market researchers Greenfield Online and YouthStream Media Networks.

"By getting their music out into the population, (artists) are already being 20
compensated with all the free advertising they could ever want," said Dwayne Saint Arnauld, 20, a Seattle office manager.

But musicians remain divided. Artists such as Metallica and Dr. Dre have sued to stop the enormous amount of downloading, which deprives them of hard-earned money and wrongly promotes the idea that artists should not be paid. Others such as the Dave Matthews Band and some indie groups say they appreciate the wider exposure.

Many users said they have a right to online music because they have been purchasing the same songs in various vinyl, cassette and CD formats over the years. Forcing them to buy the same song over and over is unfair, they say.

"Technology allows me to play what I have in my huge tape, CD and record collection," said Jennifer Sheekey, 39, of Mill Valley. "I don't have a tape player in the car. So now I can download, burn onto a CD and listen in my car."

Napster officials have said they believe their users are legally sharing songs, under the provisions of federal law that allow noncommerical copies for personal use and a limited amount of sharing.

But part of the murkiness in the stealing-sharing debate comes from differ- 25
ent interpretations of copyright law. Making copies for personal use is legally acceptable. Under review is Napster's ability to create infinite digital copies—a prospect neither anticipated nor spelled out in the legislation.

Furthermore, stealing a CD from a store and downloading songs online for free are not analogous, some legal experts say.

"When you take someone's personal property, they no longer have it. With intellectual property, (copyright holders) still have full use and enjoyment of it," said Robin Gross, an attorney at the Electronic Frontier Foundation in San Francisco.

The recording industry "is trying to color the language and mischaracterize that it's some kind of tangible product."

That distinction is important in matters of copyright law, whose protections are intended to increase the incentive for artists to produce while at the same time foster public good. The copyright holder receives a time-limited monopoly to protect work and ensure compensation. In return, the public has a right to access those works.

"The move to cut off the public's access—by say, digitally locking up music 30
and other work—is troubling," Gross said.

"It will have a chilling effect on the freedom of expression in cyberspace, for these technologies to be curtailed so early in their development because they threaten the interests of the five major labels," she said. "It's a murky area of law. What's sharing and what's stealing is anyone's guess."

Indeed, the same users the record industry calls cyber-shoplifters are the ones it wants to retain and attract as customers.

Record labels must work with, rather than attempt to squash, this powerful technology because it is exactly what users want, industry watchers say.

"Right now, sharing is easier than a legal purchase," said Rick Joyce, a media industry analyst at Accenture, a consulting firm in New York. "It has all the things that consumers are looking for in new content technology: wide availability, convenient to use, a credible standard and its playable on a device people have."

Legal digital music could become a $3.2 billion industry by the year 2005, 35
according to Accenture's projections.

"In my personal view, some variation on these 'illegal' practices will become the norm for delivery of digital information, with reasonable royalty payments built in," said Eric Easton, a University of Baltimore School of Law professor who specializes in Internet issues.

"These companies are only in court to ensure that they have some control over the paradigm shift."

Napster Use Can Be Research

DAN FOST

IF A REPORTER is covering a story about shoplifting, is it all right for that 1
reporter to pilfer a pair of shoes from Nordstrom?

Of course not. Why, then, is it so common for reporters covering the Napster case to download copyrighted music, an act the recording industry contends is illegal?

Reporters I spoke to offered a range of different explanations this week. At the very least, all of them use Napster so that they can understand what the case is about.

"How are you supposed to write about a program without using it?" asked Janelle Brown of Salon.com.

But some reporters also have more personal uses for Napster, an Internet 5
service that allows people to share digital files of songs. Some of those songs were put online by the artists themselves, which is fine, but many others were copied from compact discs onto people's home computers. The recording industry and artists such as Metallica and Dr. Dre contend file-sharing is tantamount to theft.

Brown, for one, contends that it isn't theft at all. "Using Napster right now is not illegal," she said. "Napster is going through the court system. It's unclear if it's going to be declared an illegal service."

Shoplifting, she said, is a bad analogy.

Something legal can still be unethical, according to Dave Enright, who staffs an advice hot line for journalists at the Loyola University Center of Ethics in Chicago.

Enright said reporters need to be careful of appearing to favor one side 10
through their actions. "So maybe it hasn't quite become a criminal act yet," Enright said. "But what is the appearance?"

Enright said one speaker at Loyola recently drew a standing ovation for saying any downloading of copyrighted material is inherently unethical.

Where the debate becomes clouded, however, is in the widespread use of Napster's service. Or, in the words of Matt Richtel, a reporter at the *New York Times,* "Can 65 million Napster users be wrong?"

Brad King, a reporter for *Wired News,* is a frequent downloader, at work and at home. "There hasn't been any indication that what Napster users are doing violates copyright law," King said. "The actual issue of what is copyright infringement will be decided at a jury trial."

King has downloaded Schoolhouse Rock, the Foo Fighters, Fat Boy Slim, Hansen, Led Zeppelin, Pink Floyd and Styx, among others. "I download Bon Jovi for my Bon Jovi Fridays," he said.

He's more fearful of getting grief for his abysmal musical taste—Hansen? Styx?—than of repercussions from the Recording Industry Association of America, which is suing Napster.

15 "I do give balanced coverage," he said. RIAA President Hilary Rosen still returns his calls, which he offered as proof of his fairness.

He recalled his first face-to-face meeting with Rosen last year, when he was standing on the first floor of San Francisco's Hotel W holding a bag with a Napster sticker on it. A woman approached and said, "You have got to be Brad King because no one else would have that sticker," he recalled. "I said, 'You must be Hilary, because nobody else would be that upset about it.'"

Brown, at Salon, has used Napster for her own purposes as well. "There's a real place for a system like Napster," said Brown, who can put her opinions in her columns. "I think it's a great service and a great system, and I think peer-to-peer file-sharing is the future."

Brown and other reporters almost invariably defended their use of Napster by noting they ultimately buy much of the music they initially download for free, although it's worth noting the industry doesn't accept that argument.

John Borland, who covers the controversy for Cnet's News.com, also uses Napster. "I don't think there are any issues about crossing ethical lines," he said. "It's like covering the car industry in Detroit and driving a car. Otherwise, you have no hope of understanding the legal and technical issues.

20 "A reporter can never be objective," Borland said. "That's a human impossibility, in my opinion. A good reporter is always balanced, and we've done a good job of that."

Richtel, of the *Times,* questioned that analogy. "To me, it's a question of whether you take the car for a test drive, or whether you borrow it for a summer vacation and let GM pay for the gas," he said.

There are plenty of other analogies—King, of *Wired News,* suggests it's like being a sportswriter and rooting for a team, or being a registered Democrat (or Republican) and covering politics.

Carl Hall, a science reporter at the *Chronicle,* wrote stories in which he bought Viagra online without a prescription to prove that companies were selling it illegally. "It's not a crime to buy it. It's a crime to sell it—to practice medicine without a license," he said.

Hall explained in his story exactly what he had done. (He still has the Viagra, but said, "I'm afraid to try it.")

But Hall, as a writer, said he has a problem with creative people taking copy- 25
righted material without paying for it. "By stealing the stuff, you're debasing the idea that this is something of value you can get money for," he said. And, after all, aren't writers creative people who get paid for their work?

The *Times'* Richtel has never used Napster to download copyrighted files. "It has become somewhat harder in light of the recent court decisions to justify more rampant downloading on the part of reporters," he said. "The courts have effectively deemed this direct copyright infringement."

That said, Richtel added he has always been fair to Napster in his coverage.

My colleague Benny Evangelista first got onto the Napster story with a tip from his son, Andrew, now 18. Evangelista said using Napster is important as a research tool: "Until you actually try it, you can't get a feel for how seductive it can be," he said.

Evangelista said he can't decide which side is right. "There is a compelling argument that this is a copyright violation," he said. "But was it right for the record industry to overcharge people for CDs all those years? That's why people say this is justified—it's righting a wrong."

Brad Stone of *Newsweek* used Napster to understand the service and found 30
it personally useful.

"I downloaded practically the entire soundtrack to 'O Brother Where Art Thou' after I saw the movie, then went out and bought the CD," he said. "Ditto with a few David Gray and Dido tunes—I ended up buying the CD in each case. I also recently downloaded Derek and the Dominoes' 'Bell Bottom Blues' to make sure (Eric) Clapton sings: 'I don't want to fade away, give me one more day.' Then I used the quote in my story to apply to Napster."

I should note that I have never used Napster, although when I was in college I did make tapes from friends' record albums (I'm that old), and I wear a Swiss Army watch bought on the streets of New York for $20.

You Say You Want a Revolution?

GINA ARNOLD

1 ALBERT LIN is the American recording industry's worst nightmare. In high school, he was a straight-A student, Eagle Scout, and captain of the diving team. As a first-year student at the university, the worst that can be said about him is that he drinks a lot of beer ("but," as he says, "I always recycle"). Lin is an engineering major and is taking 22 units this fall, but this fall is Year One of Napster, and as a consequence, he has been magically transformed into a scofflaw.

Napster has turned Lin into what Lars Ulrich of the rock band Metallica has characterized as "a common looter." He is a music pirate, in possible violation of US copyright infringement as well as the Fair Use statute and a few other federal regulations as well, but Lin doesn't feel the least bit guilty. "It's a capitalist society," he says. "I'm just bending the rules a little."

Actually, he admits, he hasn't thought about the morality much—although it *has* come to his attention, vaguely, that file-sharing is under fire. He certainly doesn't think of it as stealing. He thinks of it as sharing—especially since many of his downloads come from friends who send him MP3 files.

Lin lives in off-campus housing with four friends. All five of them have become devoted to file-sharing. While they are studying, he admits, more often than not they are simultaneously downloading music, for free, from Napster and other file-sharing services like Scour, Freenet, and Gnutella. Albert will set up some songs he wants to download on the school's computer, then skip to another screen and study engineering while the music is downloading.

5 "I don't think I would have used Napster in high school—if it had existed, I mean," he says. "It's a little bit weirder and harder to do than buying a CD was. And also, when you're in high school you don't stay in the house so much studying. In high school, I wanted to own the real thing."

Now, he says, things have changed. Like so many college students, his musical horizons are expanding rapidly. Growing up, Lin loved Top 40 radio station KFRC, and later he liked whatever rap songs were big on radio. But in the past year, he's heard more music than ever before—music picked by his friends, not by Live 105. I ask him for a list of what he's just downloaded. "Guster," he says. "Some Dave Matthews Band bootlegs. Some old songs I used to like when I was in 6th grade, like one called 'Paper Boy.'"

He likes to mix up the songs and use his CD burner to make mixed CDs. Whenever a whole CD that he wants is released, he borrows a copy from a friend—"there's always *someone* around who just *has* to have the real thing," he says. He's planning on doing this for the upcoming new Dave Matthews Band record, although DMB has long been his favorite band. "It'd be nice to own it," he shrugs, "but it's nicer to save $13."

I ask Lin, how much has he saved on CDs this year?

"Three hundred dollars."

What percentage of his friends do it? 10

"One hundred."

What's he going to do with all the money he's saved? "Buy beer. No, one of those MP3 players. No seriously, we're saving up for a foosball table."

The way Albert Lin talks about file-sharing, you'd think he'd been Napping for years. In fact, it's only been four months, and it's already an indispensable part of his and many other people's lives. That's why the phrase "the genie is out of the bottle" is used so frequently in reference to this remarkable phenomenon (which is also called "peer to peer" technology). To take Napster away from its many devoted users now would be like taking away the telephone. We want it. We need it. We use it. And we love it. Because far from being merely a new kind of audio experience—like DAT, CDs, and 8-track tapes—Napster is also a *social* experience. By adding the powerful concepts of "sharing" and "freedom" to the already attractive medium of popular music, it transforms the way one thinks and feels about what one's listening to.

For those of you who have not yet joined the revolution, here is a brief précis. The code that runs Napster was written less than two years ago by an eighteen-year-old college student named Shawn Fanning who wanted to share his music files with his friends. Presently, Fanning's uncle convinced him to set up a company and seek venture capital to develop his unique search engine. Napster, as the company was called, had no trouble getting funding, and by last spring it had begun, solely through word of mouth, to expand exponentially. It is estimated that Napster is currently running on ten percent of all American computers, while the peer-to-peer technology that Fanning set in motion is being considered for uses in numerous other fields.

What Napster does is provide an index of all the MP3 files—that is, songs— 15
that its users have in their collective files. Once you log on to Napster, you can type in the name of a song or an artist. Napster searches its database for another Napster user with that song in his or her system, then hooks the two computers up directly, and you download the song—for free. It's the electronic equivalent of borrowing a friend's CD to tape, only you don't personally know the person from whom you're borrowing it.

Another difference is that your friends only have a finite collection of music. Since Napster is currently boasting 38 million members, almost anything you want is available at any time—from the number-one chart topper of the week to the most obscure song you can think of by Blind Lemon Jefferson, from Iranian pop to the new U2. You name it, it's probably there. And if it's not there now, try again in an hour.

Essentially, Napster is a search engine. It is not involved directly in the recording or "ripping" (that is, turning a conventional CD or recording into digital data) of music; it merely provides an index for its users to consult. Searching the Internet is not currently against the law, nor is swapping MP3 files, but there are those who would like it to be, and they have very powerful lawyers. They are the members of the Recording Industry Association of America, aka the RIAA, and, at the moment, their argument—as set forth at a hearing for a preliminary injunction against Napster—is that Napster, by providing recorded music for free, is infringing on copyrights and impeding the ability of the industry and the artists it represents to make a living.

At the first *RIAA vs. Napster* hearing this summer, RIAA lawyer Russell Frackmann (representing five major labels and the publishers of most copyrighted music) argued that Napster was impeding their ability to collect revenues.

"They are taking advantage of [our] musicians, artists, retailers, and distributors—our clients," said Frackmann, "because, thanks to them, we are getting no return on our investment. Napster is piggybacking on our investment—the cost of recording, advertising, and marketing—and the longer it goes on, the harder it will be to do anything about it."

20 Some bands, like Metallica, agree that downloaded music cuts into the royalties they receive, both for CD sales and for publishing rights. In May, Metallica demanded that Napster bar the 334,000 people who had downloaded the band's music from accessing Napster's server. (Lists containing the names of the violators reportedly filled 60,000 pages.) Metallica, joined by rap star Dr. Dre, also sued Napster, claiming in a statement that those who download its music "have the moral fiber of common looters."

Metallica's rhetoric may be overheated, but the band is far from the only organization worried about its future as Napster's numbers continue to grow. According to court papers filed in conjunction with this suit, Napster's clientele went from 20,000 to 38 million in just six months. Fourteen thousand songs are downloaded every minute; 10,000 files a second. Court documents have estimated that three billion transactions will go down in the next six months, of which ninety percent will be of copyrighted material.

As you can imagine, these numbers have struck fear into the hearts of the record companies, which say they have lost $300 million in revenue in the past two months alone—and, to a lesser extent, artists everywhere. For if music can be had for free via the Internet, who on earth would ever buy it?

Apparently, a lot of folks. In fact most surveys are showing that CD sales are increasing nationwide. There is an exception to the trend, however: music stores near college campuses. That is why Metallica and Dr. Dre's lawyer, Howard E. King, sent a letter to many universities, including the University of California, asking them to block students' access to Napster through university servers. (UC refused, arguing that Napster's technology "could be used for legitimate purposes.")

Surely, if any place on earth is threatened by file-sharing, it's the three-block stretch of Telegraph Avenue between Bancroft Way and Haste Street, a 200-yard swatch housing three giant CD emporia: Rasputin, Amoeba, and Tower Records. Between the three of them, approximately 60,000 square feet are devoted to CDs. About 750,000 units are housed in the three buildings, and these three aren't even the only places to buy records around Berkeley. There are also Borders, HEAR, and speciality stores like Mod Lang and Down Home. In fact, if you walk into Amoeba on a rainy Saturday afternoon and see the sheer numbers of people trolling through the CD racks, it's hard to give any credence at all to the idea that record sales near college campuses are being affected by Napster.

They aren't, says store manager Alan Lewites. Not at all. "People like our 25
store, and they like buying stuff. The amount of money spent on entertainment in this neighborhood is really phenomenal," Lewites says. "People come to Telegraph Avenue specifically to buy records. It's a destination point for that, so I don't think we're in any danger."

At Rasputin Music, floor manager Dennis Bishop says that sales have, "if anything, gone up." Jim Sugarman, manager of Tower Records on Durant Avenue, agrees. Sales of CD singles are slightly down, Sugarman says, but he adds that since Tower now sells those in MP3 format online, it's not really a significant figure.

"What we see a lot of here is exposure to music through Napster—people coming in to buy the new Wheatus LP because they got it off their computer," he says. "There's a lot of new ears out there."

It seems kind of incredible that Napster could be processing the amount of transactions it apparently is, and that record sales could still be soaring. But what it reveals is just how acquisitive we are. Americans really like to *own* stuff—and MP3 files are, for better or worse, invisible. Free music is a great thing, but it has nothing on the cosmic process of purchasing. As long as kids can afford CDs—and, as Rasputin's Bishop points out, the economy is good—they're happy to buy them.

Berkeley resident Steve Tupper, whose distribution company Subterranean Records opened almost twenty years ago, agrees. Subterranean is still going strong, and Tupper says he isn't worried about file-sharing one bit.

"The majority of the sales we do are vinyl," he says. "And vinyl is an object. 30
You can hold it and look at it and turn it over . . . you can't do that with a file. Some customers really like to feel what they're buying. As a matter of fact, the latest thing in record collecting is extra-heavyweight vinyl, 220 grams per disc instead of 180." In which case, one of the major labels' big mistakes has been in cheapening production. "They don't have an appreciation of most people's attachment to physical objects," Tupper says. "To them, record sales are just a big money transfer." (One place where he has seen a drop in sales, however, is at record swaps such as those hosted by UC Berkeley's radio station KALX and Foothill College's KFJC. People do their swapping online now, he says.)

In drafting its arguments against Napster, Tupper points out, the RIAA is discounting certain key aspects of record-buying psychology. "What it comes down to is how involved you are in the music personally. Mainstream record consumers tend to have tiny record collections, whereas people who are collectors own thousands and thousands of LPs." Neither of these two groups, Tupper says, are a threat to the record companies' profit margins—in the case of first group, because they'll buy the few. CDs they *must* have, even if they download them as well. In the second case, it's because collectors are fixated on rarities.

Paul Bradshaw, owner of Mod Lang Records on Berkeley's University Avenue, agrees with Tupper, although he thinks there's a big difference between the mindset of a Limp Bizkit fan and a Smiths one. "If you're a Smiths collector," he says, "you need all the 7-inch singles and all the 12-inches with the thematic picture sleeves." A Limp Bizkit fan, he claims, "would be quite happy to burn twenty copies of the new record for his friends."

Mod Lang, he says, isn't threatened by file-sharing because it's a specialty store that deals in what he calls "information." Walk into Mod Lang on any given afternoon, and the cozy room will resound with the music of PJ Harvey or Mike Levy, or an obscure EP by Belle and Sebastian. A list of new releases will be prominently displayed near the checkout counter, and the racks are separated into arcane divisions: "Krautrock," for example, and "Japanese Psychedelia," and movie soundtracks from the '50s. It's almost like a clubhouse.

"I think of us as being more like an antiquarian bookstore than an ordinary record shop," says Bradshaw. "You come in here and chat to the clerk about the Mott the Hoople song you downloaded . . . and he can steer you in the right direction to more things like that. People come in here to just look and gaze and flip through the records, just like people go to bookstores to browse."

As for file-sharing, "I think any store that has a vision or a niche isn't going to be in trouble," he says. "My worry is just that, as time progresses the next generation of teenagers won't even *think* of going to record stores to hang out and shop. Right now, people still go shopping, but in ten years, file-sharing will become the norm." He entertains a grim vision of America one decade down the road as "a dysfunctional nation of teenage shut-ins."

Bradshaw's words reminded me of something I hadn't thought about for years. When I was a teenager, you can't imagine the high place record stores held in my psyche. I was too young to go to nightclubs, and I couldn't drive, so one of the ways I used to pass the time was to walk downtown to the local used record store and just walk up and down the aisles touching all the records. Much of my knowledge of obscure '70s rock groups comes from this time, when I used to memorize the song order on records I'd never even heard. Later on, when my parents lived in San Francisco, I used to go to Tower on Columbus at night and just hang out there, waiting in my naïve way for a rock star to walk in the door. (This never happened, though I always thought one day it would.) Berkeley, too, was even then a wealth of cool record stores: Rather Ripped, Odyssey, and Leopold's were the biggies, and I logged time in all of them. For me, record shopping was a pleasant way to pass the painful years before I could take a more active part in rock music—and more than that, it helped me to see that there was a world outside the shopping mall, where people who were interested in the same things as I was could meet and greet.

But Bradshaw may be right: all things must pass, and despite its current signs of health, perhaps the business of selling records may be on its way to obsolescence. The first time I used Napster was only in July of this year. It was just after the first court hearing, at a time when the word "Napster" seemed to be on everybody's lips. At the trial, RIAA lawyer Russell Frackmann talked about a kid in Hackensack, NJ, downloading something from another user who lived in Guam, as if the fact that the two were total strangers meant that the concept of "sharing" wasn't valid.

But Frackmann—and the Recording Industry Association of America—underestimates just how meaningful the word "share" is in the term "file-sharing." Since that first day, I've loaded down my hard drive with all kinds of MP3s: things like the Afghan Whigs doing "Straight Outta Compton" and Screamin' Jay Hawkins' version of "Old Man River," and there is not a single time that the upload arrow has appeared against one of them (meaning that a user somewhere in the world is "borrowing" my recording) when I haven't thought, Yippee!

That's what I mean when I say that Napster is a social revolution, not a technological one. I never cease to be profoundly gratified when people upload my MP3s. I *want* them to have them, in Guam and in Hackensack, because it makes me feel like a mini-DJ, like I'm doing a cultural exchange, like I'm influencing my peers, like there are potential friends out there who have the same taste in music that I do. It makes me feel like I am spreading that taste around in a much more practical way than I can by writing record reviews. And like all the best music, Napster makes its users feel less alone.

40 Napster has a function with which you can cruise through other users' MP3-file collections, just as if you were in their homes, flipping through their records. At my house, we like to speculate on what kind of person has tracks by the Backstreet Boys and Captain Beefheart. We wonder if it would be worth listening to some obscure band that that person has also collected. And sometimes we come upon someone whose collection mirrors our own, and that is always very heartening, because you can download the one thing they have that you don't and know that you'll like it.

The record industry has always been slow to appreciate the worth of technological advances to its economics, however, because it seldom looks at the way such changes affect consumers' hearts, rather than their pocketbooks. It took them a long time to catch on to the way cassette decks, especially when installed in cars, could be used to their advantage. And it never liked punk rock, despite its massive potential audience. Artist development is one of the record industry's weakest sciences, so the fact that Napster is the greatest promotional tool ever invented has not seemed to occur to the industry. Given the choice, it would rather have a consumer buy the last Limp Bizkit record than check out whoever might be the *new* Limp Bizkit, and start a buzz on *that* band instead.

Meanwhile, in its own defense, Napster's argument in court has been that it has many "non-infringing" uses, and in my case this is certainly true. I download songs by bands that I've heard of but not actually heard. I download tracks when I haven't gotten the advance copy of a new record fast enough for review. I download Spanish-language songs for my Spanish class (a use which ought to be covered by the Fair Use Doctrine, which protects professors from the consequences of photocopying material for classroom use). I download live tracks, which aren't copyrighted, and numbers that I already have on CD. (This practice, called space-shifting, is what the MYMP3.com program facilitates and is another use that's under dispute in court.)

As for downloading material without the artist's permission—that's a problem. I *do* like to think that if I called up some of the artists I download—Paul Westerberg, say, or Wayne Coyne—and asked, they'd give me permission. And others, like Shakira, should be grateful that I gave them a chance.

But it's true that artists differ greatly in their opinions on the subject. Metallica is of course the most extreme, but they're not alone. They Might Be Giants, for example, is a Brooklyn-based act with several hit singles ("Ana Ng," "Don't Let's Start"). They wrote the theme song for *Austin Powers: The Spy Who Shagged Me* and do the music for the TV sitcom *Malcolm in the Middle*. They are currently the number-one most legimately downloaded band in the world, and they make money online via their own site (Theymightbegiants.com).

45 Nevertheless, singer/guitarist John Flansburgh is one of the most vocal opponents of Napster. "One of the big draws of putting a free song on your Web site," says Flansburgh, "is that when someone downloads it, you get that name. We have tens of thousands of e-mail addresses of people who we know like us. That is a very efficient and affordable marketing tool. [But] if they all just get the music off Napster, not only are we iced out of making that connection, but we have our product given away with Napster and their creepy banner ads associated with us. We don't even let radio stations sponsoring our shows put up ad banners behind us. If we did, our fans would think we were creepy. Why should Napster get a check from gross banner ads while giving away our hard work?"

That said, he doesn't think his band has lost much revenue via Napster. "Our fans are very, very MP3-savvy, and very sensitive to our real-life struggle. They know that trading staff that is sold in stores and online directly affects us, and they pretty much keep it to the bootleg stuff online," he says. "There is a surprising amount of self-regulation. I'm honestly impressed with their integrity and respect for us."

Nevertheless, "What strikes me continually about the tremendous amount of discussion there has been about this issue is that twenty to thirty percent of the argument *for* Napster can be undone by the statement, 'stealing is wrong.' This is about seventeen-year-olds, people who don't work for a living and don't know the value of things. People are always saying, 'Information has to be set free', but, you know, a lot of things worth having aren't free. Music is one of the few things [about which] you really *can* say who made it. Can't we set other people's stuff free first, like—I don't know—lawyers' documents or something?

"Then there's this 'two wrongs make a right' argument," he continues. "That's the one where people say, 'Well, record companies have ripped off artists for years, so it's okay that Napster does.' But as bad as major labels are, it's better than being ripped off by a Web site. Record companies rip off artists, but they *do* pay the bills. It's a grossly unfair system, but there's a lot of grossly unfair systems in America—like buying houses and using lawyers."

There is, he adds, a solution to the copyright problem: Track the songs and pay the artists.

And herein lies the problem. The record industry would like you to think 50
that it cares about the intellectual property of its artists: that the problem with downloading, in its mind, is that the artists aren't getting paid. This is a crock of shit, except insofar as the intellectual property of songwriters is exactly what the record industry has thus far been exploiting. (In fact, the number of artists who have been forced to give up all royalties in order to get signed defies belief.) What really concerns the record industry is what is called the "bricks and mortar" aspect of the business: distribution and retail. This is what MP3 trading and even legitimate sales threaten, and this is what it is fighting to preserve.

Distribution is the dull end of the record industry—it's the trucks that schlepp the CDs from the warehouse to the store. It is dull, but it is profitable, because it is where the markup occurs. How much does it cost to press CDs in bulk? About one dollar a copy. How much are you paying for it in the store? The difference between those two figures is why distribution and retail are the best parts of the music business to be in. Bill Flanagan's novel *A & R* offers a wonderful summing-up of the industry's philosophy in the following quote by a character who heads a fictional record company:

"Nobody knows what's going to happen with the record business in the next ten years. I don't know if people will be punching up music online or over the telephone or through the radiator. I don't know how much longer we few old shops are going to get all the money just because we own all the trucks and pressing plants.

"But I can tell you this. We've had a great run. A hundred years of keeping 95 percent of the money and all the rights! Who'd have believed it? How can we complain?"

All of which shows how the industry has failed to understand, partly through ignorance and partly through greed, the public's needs and wants, willfully mistaking its deep love of music for rank stupidity—and author Bill Flanagan is in a position to know. "Working the music business today," he adds, "is a lot like working in the horse-and-carriage industry in 1905. All your life you've thought people will always go places by horse and you'll always be in business. And then all of a sudden there's this hint that maybe they won't."

Obviously, the music industry's greatest fear is that the digitalization of mu- 55
sic distribution will send down its costs—thus cutting the fat off the profit per

CD. After all, it takes a lot of money to make a superstar like Madonna. And as RIAA head Hillary Rosen pointed out recently, fifteen percent of the artists in the music industry pay for one hundred percent of the music produced by the industry. The Michael Jacksons of the world—even with their huge-budget videos and lifestyles and concomitant huge CD sales—pay for the Wilcos, the Tom Waitses, and so on.

That's why the place where any profit loss will be felt most strongly would be A&R. Flanagan thinks that, in the next few years, the A&R departments of the world "are going to mean less and less. I think Napster is an interim technology, like streetcars or the 8-track tape, that's going to go away, but eventually digital downloading is going to liberate musicians entirely, because listeners at home won't be prejudiced by whether music they hear is made by million-dollar labels or in a bedroom. They'll just decide what they like."

Given that prospect, it's no wonder the music business is reacting with fear and trepidation. EMI inaugurated a digital downloading system of its own—where consumers can, if they so desire, download MP3 files of CDs for the exact same price they would pay in the store (only with more restrictions on their use). Emusic.com has instituted a subscription service ($9.99 a month to download anything on their files), and other record companies will be following suit with various downloading methods and payment schemes and methods for compensating artists.

You can now legally download MP3 files from sites like Amazon.com, CD-Now, and even Towerrecords.com—as well as on dedicated MP3 sites like Liquid Audio, Emusic.com, Epitonic, and MP3.com. These are sometimes linked to the Web sites of magazines like *Rolling Stone,* and some provide free MP3s, licensed for promotional purposes, although most cost from $1 to $15. (The music has all been legally licensed from its owner.) You can also buy MP3s from label sites, like Sony's and Universal's, although not for any cheaper than you can get the CD in the store. Finally, you can usually get MP3s from the Web sites of your more forward-thinking bands, who've discovered that the Internet is the perfect publicity tool.

As for Napster, despite its enormous fan base, it still doesn't have a working business model or a way to make a profit—and it is still in the midst of two big court battles: the one against the RIAA and the one against Metallica and Dr. Dre. Things are beginning to look up for the embattled company, however. In July, when it faced Judge Marilyn Patel in a pre-injunction hearing, the court was definitely not in its pocket. In October, during the appeal hearing, it most definitely was.

At that time, Napster's CEO Hank Berry said the company was attempting 60
to strike a deal with its opponents. And last week it actually did, when Bertelsmann—the German media giant that oversees BMG, RCA, and Arista Records—signed a deal promising to help finance Napster's development of a membership-based service that would compensate artists, labels, and publishers for their work. The idea is that Napster users would be charged a monthly rate,

like users of AOL, for "all you can eat" music. But unless Napster can strike similar deals with the other four plaintiffs in the case—Warner Music, Sony, EMI, and Universal—the whole idea may backfire. And it might backfire anyway, if the court case currently pending goes against Napster in the court of appeals.

Besides, the whole point of Napster is the sheer volume of what's available on it. If its index is restricted to paying members, and if users offering rarities don't log on, I and many others will have no interest in it. We'll turn to services like Freenet and Gnutella that don't have corporate backing.

That would be more in the spirit of file-sharing, and less in the spirit of selling out to The Man—which, sad to say, is what Napster may well become, from the looks of things. After all, the history of rock has been one long line of cool new sounds and inventions being co-opted and exploited. So why should Napster turn out any differently? At least it's given us a great year 2000, and for that, respect is due.

[student essay]

Should the Fate of Napster Be Determined by the Interpretation of a Law?

Keely Cosby

Many musicians and record companies are concerned for their future and believe "they will lose billions in sales because fans are getting their music for free" ("Napster"). They think people will eventually stop buying CDs if Napster is allowed to continue to operate. A study by Forrester Research predicted that "within five years the music industry will lose $3.1 billion to piracy and the newfound independence of musicians" (Cohen 70). This prediction makes many musicians fear that they will no longer be able to profit from their music. Lars Ulrich, the drummer for Metallica, has been reported as saying that "what is at stake is nothing less than the future of his business" (qtd. in "Napster"). Some musicians feel they are being taken advantage of and believe they should be paid every time a song is digitally reproduced. They believe that their copyrights are being infringed and that Napster and other file-sharing software providers may force the music industry to drop the prices of CDs.

Napster is a program that allows computer users to swap music files with one another directly, without using a centralized file server. Every day "millions get music off the Internet from [Shawn] Fanning's creation, Napster" ("Napster"). On Napster, music is shared among its users. This type of sharing is not illegal because, as Napster's lawyer David Boies states, "noncommercial consumer copying is recognized as fair use under common-law theories and doctrines, and under the Supreme Court's criteria" (qtd. in Heilemann 255).

Many artists support Napster and are not afraid to speak out. Fred Durst of the band Limp Bizkit says that

Napster is "an amazing way to market and promote music" to a mass audience and is "a great way for fans to sample an album before buying it" (qtd. in Goodman). Along with many new musicians, I strongly agree with Durst. I personally have used Napster for just this purpose and then purchased a CD. Most average individuals probably do not have the equipment to produce their own CDs. Therefore the downloaded music never leaves their hard drive. Limp Bizkit showed their support of the company by joining with Napster to launch a free United States concert tour. Singer Courtney Love asked, "Why aren't record companies embracing this great opportunity? Why aren't they trying to talk to kids . . . to learn what they like?" (qtd. in Greenfeld 66). If the music industry had accepted file sharing, maybe it could have had a part in this technology. Many bands believe that by opposing Napster they will alienate their fans and that will lead to their ultimate downfall. By demonstrating their acceptance of Napster, many musicians are gaining more attention and respect from their fans. As David Boies states, "the Audio Home Recording Act directly says that noncommercial copying by consumers is lawful" (qtd. in Heilemann 255). The Recording Industry Association of America (RIAA) is afraid of losing money, and I believe this is why it wants to end Napster. Boies says that the RIAA has documents that indicate it wants "to shut Napster down and then take over the technology" (qtd. in Heilemann 256).

Napster should be allowed to support Internet users' desire to share music with one another. I agree with Boies' statement that "We never would have passed copyright laws in this country unless we believed they helped consumers by generating creative activity" (qtd. in Heilemann 257). If the music industry and musicians are still allowed to have too much control over the copyrights, the prices of CDs will continue to rise.

People are tired of paying ridiculous amounts of money for music. As Boies notes, "We know there needs to be a fair return to do that, but we don't want an excessive return, because the ultimate beneficiary is designed to be the consumer" (qtd. in Heilemann 257). The public has not benefited from these copyright laws for years, and this is why file-sharing programs like Napster have become such a success. Consumers have been taken advantage of by the high prices the members of RIAA have been able to charge because of their monopoly. Even if the courts decide to shut down Napster permanently, the problem will still exist because users will access other websites, such as Aimster, Gnutella, Macster, and Mactella. Before the industry starts zoning in on Napster, it needs to acknowledge all of the file-sharing programs that are available. In order to eliminate the sharing of music, not only will it have to defeat Napster, but it will eventually have to stop all of them. The truth is that using Napster, as David Boies puts it, "'is no different than using a photocopier or a VCR'" (qtd. in "Napster"). Is this really about copyright infringement, or is it about having ultimate control and making more money?

Works Cited

Cohen, Adam. "A Crisis of Content." Time 2 Oct. 2000: 68-73.

Goodman, Dean. "Jamming With Napster." ABC News Online 25 Apr. 2000. 24 Oct. 2000 <http://abcnews.go.com/sections/tech/DailyNews/napster000425.html>.

Greenfeld, Karl Taro. "Meet the Napster." Time 2 Oct. 2000: 60-68.

Heilemann, John. "David Boies: The Wired Interview." Wired Monthly Oct. 2000: 253-259.

"Napster." Sixty Minutes II. Narr. Charlie Rose. Prod. Phil Shimkin and Russ Torres. CBS. WGCL-TV, Atlanta. 10 Oct. 2000.

PART TWO

Types of Claims

Chapter 7
Arguing Claims about Existence

Our Differences about Experience

Our most immediate means of knowing the world around us is through our experience. Our senses constantly provide our brains with information about our environment, and we also experience our own thoughts and emotions inspired by that information. Sometimes, however, our experience of the world can mislead us. Perhaps we don't have enough sensory data to form correct conclusions. Perhaps we don't reflect sufficiently on the data we have received and so form false notions about our experience. Most people on occasion hear things that do not exist or see optical illusions. Seeing should not always mean believing. Yet, to interpret experience, most of us rely primarily on data from our physical senses or on reports of experience in print or pictures.

We usually consume this material uncritically because we lack the time or inclination to question every bit of reported data that comes to us. The scholarly community, however, attempts to scrutinize experience a bit more carefully. In fact, much of the writing you will do during your university career will involve writing about questions of existence and causality. Although it would be foolish to discount our experience of the world entirely, it is healthy occasionally to reflect on experience critically: What am I experiencing? What is causing this event? How can I understand it?

FACT AND OPINION

Because our human bodies are similar, we all share some of the same experiences. We all shiver when it gets cold enough or sweat when it gets hot. We all sleep and eat. We know what it's like to be tired. When a community comes to a general agreement about experience, that agreement is called a "fact," something that is accepted as true about the world of experience. But because each person is also unique, we each experience the world around us somewhat differently. We have different bodies. We have each had a different upbringing. We may speak different languages or varieties of the same language. We each have at least a somewhat different perspective of the world. Often, these differences are slight, but different perspectives of the world—separate ways of experiencing reality—can lead to disagreements within a community. When there is disagreement about the world of experience, then the various divergent interpretations are called "opinions" rather than facts. Opinions are less certain and less accepted in a community than facts are. Being less accepted, however, does not make an opinion less true; it is simply under dispute. Some of today's opinions may well be tomorrow's facts. And because our experience of the world is imperfect, what we accept as facts today may not be accepted in the future. New data and analysis can change our perception of what is real and true.

PAST, PRESENT, AND FUTURE

We often disagree about things that happened in the past. To know what happened in the past, we must rely either on our own memories or on someone else's report of past experience. And in addition to the fact that we all experience reality somewhat differently, we all have selective (and somewhat imperfect) memories. For example, my wife and I recall our first date differently. She remembers things that I don't, such as what she wore and where we went. I tend to remember what we ate. Occasionally, we disagree about particular details of other experiences: what we wore, where we went, what we did, who said what. I tend to remember events as much more dramatic than they probably were.

People can also disagree about present experiences. Someone asks, "Is it cold in here or is it just me?" and a debate ensues about whether or not it's cold enough to close the windows. A thermometer can provide a quantifiable reading of the temperature, but knowing that it is 78 degrees generally won't change the fact that someone's hands are cold.

In addition, people disagree about what will happen in the future. Where I grew up, farmers were always talking about the weather: Will it rain today? Do you expect a heavy winter? Their attempts to predict the weather could lead to some lively debates. Investors disagree about what will happen in the future in financial markets. Civil engineers disagree about the effect that a future earthquake might have on buildings, roads, and bridges. Environmental biologists and developers disagree about the effect that a new subdivision will have on the habitat of a threatened species.

Questions about Existence

Journalists are taught to ask six questions about experience: who? what? when? where? why? how? These questions are designed to help record experience in a complete and detailed way. They are also among the most basic questions we all ask about experience. The first four ask about the existence and nature of an experience. The final two address causality, the relationship between causes and effects. This chapter focuses on questions of existence. The next chapter discusses questions of causality.

The most basic of all questions about existence is whether something exists at all: Did it happen? Is it happening now? Will it happen again? Did it used to exist? Does it exist now? Will it ever exist? Here are some examples of specific questions about existence:

Do paranormal phenomena exist?

Are UFOs real?

Does ESP exist?

Has someone been in my room?

Does she have cancer?

Did the accused kill the victim?

An answer to any of these questions would be a statement affirming or denying a state of existence. This kind of statement is a claim about existence. When members of a community disagree about the state of existence there will be opposing claims:

Yes, UFOs are real. No, UFOs are not real.

Yes, the accused did kill the victim. No, the accused did not.

Someone has been in my room. No one has been in your room.

Some questions about existence relate to the nature of reality—not whether an event or object exists, but rather how we can describe this event or object: What kind? What size? How much? How many? How long? Here are some examples of questions that involve issues of reality:

Is that car green?

How large is the national debt?

Is Japan a world power?

Does Israel treat Palestinians fairly?

How serious a problem is nuclear proliferation?

How harmful is alcohol for humans?

Questions about existence can relate to questions about symbols and language. For instance, arguing about whether Japan is a world power may depend on how different parties define "world power." Then the argument becomes one about language as well as existence. But if all concerned agree on the definition of "world power," then the argument is simply about the nature of our experience of Japan: Does Japan fit the definition of "world power" on which we all agree?

Some questions about existence are so complex that the community as a whole may never come to complete agreement about them (for example, questions of the existence, power, and nature of a supreme being). But even if we cannot come to complete agreement about such complex issues of existence, we may be able to understand more clearly why we disagree, and we may then be better able to accept one another despite our differences.

ARGUING ABOUT THE NATURE OF REALITY

Because questions about existence and the nature of reality are so closely related, I have chosen to treat them together. We come to know that something exists in the same ways we come to know the nature of that object: through direct physical experience, introspection (inner experience), memory, and reports of the experiences of others.

As I mentioned before, although these ways of understanding experience serve us well most of the time, each can occasionally lead us to form false or incomplete impressions of reality. Francis Bacon, a contemporary of Shakespeare and a proponent of the scientific method, explained some of the problems of understanding experience in his *Novum Organum*, written in 1620. In that work, Bacon describes four "idols" or "false notions" that humans form about experience.

Bacon calls the first of these the *idols of the tribe*. The idols of the tribe are false notions that form because of our fallible human nature. Because we are all part of the human "tribe," we all suffer from limitations in how we perceive the world. Bacon states that the "human understanding is like a false mirror, which, receiving rays irregularly, distorts and discolors the nature of things by mingling its own nature with it." In addition to suffering from the weaknesses that beset all humans, we each have our own particular weaknesses that lead to false notions. Bacon calls these individual limitations the *idols of the cave.* Bacon points out that we have all had differing levels of education, experience, perception, and interaction with others. In addition, we all have different cognitive abilities and preferences that will lead us to form differing views of the world. The *idols of the marketplace* result from our interaction with others. As we seek to describe our experience of the world through the imperfect medium of language, we struggle to find just the right words to explain what we think and feel. In addition, those who listen to us struggle to make sense of our language in their own way. Some false notions are bound to result from these exchanges. For example, if you have been to another country, you might have some difficulty describing everything you saw and heard and experienced there. Your friends and family will no doubt form some inaccurate notions about the country because you haven't communicated your meaning precisely and because they haven't understood you exactly. As I have said before, the miracle of language is that we can communicate with others at all. The *idols of the theater* make up the fourth group of Bacon's idols. These idols are the false views that are formed through the influence of human philosophies. "In my judgment," writes Bacon, "all the received systems [of philosophy] are but so many stage-plays, representing worlds of their own creation after an unreal and scenic fashion."

In summary, Bacon argues that humans are bound to draw some false conclusions from their experience of the world. Humans are not perfect, our experience of the world is not complete, and how we perceive the world is influenced, to a certain degree, by our language and by the notions we have already formed. In addition, the moment of direct experience—the present—is constantly becoming the past.

Whenever present experience becomes past experience, we have to rely on our memories. Generally, our memories serve us quite well—particularly given that we do very little to train our memories. But, as attorneys are quick to point out in television courtroom dramas, memory is always imperfect. The problem is due partly to our imperfect perception of experience, as described by Bacon, and to the disorganized and chaotic state of memory itself. Problems also stem from the fact that we often remember what we want to remember—the way we want it to be remembered. In other words, our memories reconstruct reality, no matter how careful we are to remember the "truth."

EXPERIENCE AS EVIDENCE IN SCHOLARLY WRITING

Scholars tend to have a healthy distrust of direct experience, personal introspection, and memory. They try to discount their own perceptions and postpone judgment on a subject until they have gathered sufficient objective data on which to base their findings. But scholars also realize that personal observation and reflection are valuable sources of information about the world. One way for scientists to gather data is to go out into the field and experience an event firsthand. Usually, they observe with some purpose in mind, organizing their observations by looking for answers to a particular question; sometimes, however, scientists observe with no particular question or purpose other than to see what turns up. Scientists pay attention not only to *what* they are observing but also to *how* they are observing. Familiar with the limitations of sensory experience and memory, scientists improve their powers of observation and reflection by keeping *field notes* or a *log book,* carefully recording what they observe. Keeping a journal or log allows us to compare a report of an experience written shortly after it happened with our memory of the experience written shortly after it happened with our memory of the experience months or years later. Keeping a record can also sharpen our perceptions of the world around us and help us choose more careful language to report our observations. A log is usually organized by date and time.

Scientists may also use various instruments to gather more data than they can through their senses and then record these data in log books along with their own observations. Personal *journals* can provide opportunities for reflection as well as observation. Henry David Thoreau kept a detailed journal of his experiences with nature and used his journal to compose *Walden,* his 1854 treatise on the relationship between humans and the natural world. Prolific inventor Thomas Edison wrote hundreds of pages a day in his journal to keep track of all of his discoveries and ideas.

An *ethnography* is a particular kind of field report, a systematic record of one's experience of another community. It usually combines an ethnographer's personal observation and reflection with hard data and reports of experience from members of the community. Similar to an ethnography, a *case study* is the systematic observation of a particular event or object. Psychologists, sociologists, and journalists rely heavily on case studies. These kinds of studies suggest possibilities for generalizing, but there is a danger of hasty generalization or overgeneralization: Is the example studied typical? Are there countering examples? How accurate are the observations? Case studies usually are more reliable when there are multiple observers of multiple cases and if cases are used along with other kinds of evidence. At their best, cases and examples can be quite persuasive because they offer vivid portrayals of particular experience, giving an argument presence and making it seem more real and human.

REPORTED EXPERIENCE

Reported experience offers some of the immediacy and authenticity of direct experience. Primary sources or eyewitnesses can provide numerous specific details along with the credibility of personal testimony. But scholars approach the reported experience of others with a degree of skepticism, asking questions such as the following to determine a report's reliability:

1. Is the source reliable, fair, responsible, and capable? Does the source have a personal interest or obvious bias?
2. Is this a primary source or a "report of a report"? Is the source "a friend of a friend"?

3. How far removed was the source from the event? To what extent is the source relying on memory?
4. Are the statements in the report consistent with one another and with other reports and evidence?
5. Are the statements verifiable?
6. Is all relevant evidence included?
7. Is the language detailed, specific, and clear?

As Bacon points out, humans have a tendency to select details from experience to fit our own biases and conceptions of reality. We often see what we want to see.

This tendency to report experience selectively is evident in the following conflicting eyewitness accounts of the Battle of Lexington at the start of the American Revolution. Tension between the British army and the colonists had been building for some time when shots were fired at Lexington, Massachusetts, on April 19, 1775. Known as "the shot heard round the world," this incident was the first armed conflict of the revolution. The first account is by Thomas Fessenden, a colonist:

> *Lexington, April 23, 1775*
>
> I, Thomas Fessenden, of lawful age, testify and declare, that being in a pasture near the meeting-house at said Lexington, on Wednesday, last, at about half an hour before sunrise, . . . I saw three officers on horseback advance to the front of said Regulars, when one of them being within six rods of the said Militia, cried out, "Disperse, you rebels, immediately"; on which he brandished his sword over his head three times; meanwhile the second officer, who was about two rods behind him, fired a pistol pointed at said Militia, and the Regulars kept huzzaing till he had finished brandishing his sword, and when he had thus finished brandishing his sword, he pointed it down towards said Militia, and immediately the said Regulars fired a volley at the Militia and then I ran off, as fast as I could, while they continued firing till I got out of their reach. I further testify, that as soon as ever the officer cried "Disperse, you rebels," the said Company of Militia dispersed every way as fast as they could, and while they were dispersing the Regulars kept firing at them incessantly, and further saith not.
>
> THOMAS FESSENDEN

Here is an account of the same event from the diary of a John Barker, a British officer:

> 19th. At 2 o'clock we began our march by wading through a very long ford up to our Middles: after going a few miles we took 3 or 4 People who were going off to give intelligence; about 5 miles on this side of a Town called Lexington, which lay in our road, we heard there were some hundreds of People collected together intending to oppose us and stop our going on; at 5 o'clock we arrived there, and saw a number of People, I believe between 2 and 300, formed in a Common in the middle of the Town; we still continued advancing, keeping prepared against an attack tho' without intending to attack them; but, on our coming near them they fired one or two shots, upon which our Men without any orders, rushed in upon them, fired and put 'em to flight; several of them were killed, we cou'd not tell how many, because they were got behind Walls

> and into the Woods; We had a Man of the 10th light Infantry wounded, nobody else hurt. We then formed on the Common, but with some difficulty, the Men were so wild they cou'd hear no orders; we waited a considerable time there, and at length proceed on our way to Concord . . .

Who fired the first shots? Were the British ordered to fire by their officers, or did they fire on their own? Did the colonists disperse after the order of the British officers? Did the soldiers fire on the colonists after they began to disperse? Because of the differing eyewitness accounts, historians are still uncertain about what exactly transpired at Lexington. These two witnesses, for example, were probably not lying. The first was giving sworn testimony before a magistrate; the second was writing in his personal diary. The fact is that each saw and remembered a different sequence of events because his experience was filtered through his own individual perspective, position, and biases.

In addition to the selectivity of memory, direct experience of an event is limited by the observer's physical position in time and space or limited powers of observation: Some people have keener senses or longer attention spans than others. And, of course, the possibility exists that someone may knowingly give a false account. Sometimes what we take to be "facts" can be difficult to establish as true or false.

The difficulty of determining the truth of reported experience is greatest when the source of that report is lost or when the report has been passed from person to person. This is why scholars favor primary sources and are wary of claims where no source is disclosed: "Scientists say . . . ," "They say . . . ," "We know. . . . " You should also be suspicious when the source is "a friend of a friend" or when someone claims, "I read it in the paper," but can't produce the exact article. You may have played a party game in which one person whispers a message to someone else who whispers it to another until the message has been passed from person to person around the room. Usually, the message has become quite distorted by the time it reaches the final person. When a message contains complex, detailed, or ambiguous information, the distortion over time can be even greater.

Written testimony or an eyewitness report is one way of reporting experience. Another common form of reported experience is an interview. An interview has the advantage of face-to-face contact, allowing the interviewer to observe the body language of the source. But the quality of an interview depends not only on the quality of the source; the quality of the questions being asked is also important. Open-ended questions—such as the journalist's who? what? when? where? why? and how?—invite detailed responses. Questions answered "yes" or "no" invite commitment and confirmation from the source. Many interviewers like to ask questions in a particular sequence in order to determine the quality of the source and put him or her at ease. They begin with easy factual questions concerning background information, personal history, definitions, and key concepts, for example. They then ask application questions that require a more elaborate response, inquiring about processes, causes and effects, comparisons and analogies, relationships among ideas, interpretation and predictions.

They progress finally to questions that require judgment and commitment, asking about the source's views of right and wrong or good and bad, and about his or her recommendations, reactions, and evaluation. These final questions reveal the values of the person being interviewed.

When evaluating a published interview, it is important to know how it was conducted. Who did the interviewing? What questions were asked? In what order? How were the responses recorded? It is also important to know how the interview is reported. Is it a verbatim question-and-answer report of the interview or an edited transcript or summary? What was left out of the reporting?

Another form of reported experience common in scholarly writing and journalism is the survey or questionnaire. Surveys and questionnaires are a way of gathering a number of people's reports of their experience. The usefulness of surveys and questionnaires lies in their ability to sample a large amount of reported experience. Surveys also add the dimension of community. But it is important to remember that questionnaires record perceptions and reports, not actual experience. Surveys and questionnaires have the same limitations as other types of reported experience: Their quality depends on respondents answering honestly and reporting their experiences accurately. Surveyors must also avoid questions that skew the results with loaded questions or emotion-laden words that may prejudice respondents:

Should cold-blooded killers be executed?

Do you favor tax-and-spend liberalism or Republican fiscal responsibility?

Are you pro-life or in favor of killing babies?

Would you hire someone who was convicted of a felony?

Questions that are too vague or too rigid leave people unsure how to respond:

Are you happy?

Do you believe in angels?

Is your favorite sport baseball or hockey?

Are you in favor of health care reform?

Questions that use absolute terms leave no middle ground for respondents: Do you always eat out or never eat out? To allow greater flexibility, many surveyors use a *Likert scale,* a scale that allows for a range of answers (strongly disagree, disagree, unsure, agree, strongly agree), or allow respondents to rank their response on a numerical scale: How often do you eat out? Never, seldom, sometimes, often, always.

When evaluating data from a survey or questionnaire, it is important to ask how the survey was conducted:

1. Did the surveyors explain the purpose of the survey?
2. Did they give clear, concise directions?
3. Is the survey free of personal bias and slanted terms?
4. Does it include words the respondents will understand?

5. Is there a clear range of choices?
6. Did the researchers adhere to acknowledged ethical standards for human subject research, such as not conducting research on vulnerable populations (for example, the mentally disabled), informing participants of the nature of the research, securing informed consent, and making the results and report of the research available to the participants?
7. Were respondents selected to reflect an accurate sample of the population?

Many news programs today conduct telephone polls by asking people to call in and register their opinions according to the number they choose to dial, or they invite audience members to log on to their websites and register responses online. Similarly, many newspapers and magazines conduct opinion polls online through their websites. Even the Gallup organization, the long-standing leader of public opinion polling, now conducts polls and reports results at <http://www.gallup.com>. Since people who call in or go to a website have chosen to participate in the polls, they are probably more interested in the issue under question than a randomly selected group would be. Most of the news and entertainment organizations are careful to point out that their polls are not "scientific," yet they still report the outcomes as if the data could be meaningfully interpreted.

Does the means of contacting respondents affect their responses? When Franklin Roosevelt was running for president against Herbert Hoover in 1932, the Gallop organization surveyed people by phone about their presidential preference. This data predicted a Hoover victory; yet Roosevelt won overwhelmingly because he had strong support among the many people during the Depression who were too poor to own a telephone. To make a comparison to our own time, how accurate would a survey be that was conducted solely through the Internet?

MAKING INFERENCES ABOUT EXPERIENCE

Some phenomena are difficult, or even impossible, for humans to experience directly without the aid of instruments that extend the physical senses. For example, scientists know of the existence of microorganisms and faraway galaxies only through the aid of instruments that extends the power of sight. Weather satellites provide a perspective on the planet that no one but an astronaut could otherwise enjoy. Cameras allow us to observe phenomena that are too fast or too slow for the unaided human eye to follow. Instruments such as these can give us more data about experience than we would have through our physical senses alone, but even the most finely tuned scientific instruments cannot provide a complete picture of experience. Experience is too complex. And the data that these instruments provide must still be interpreted by humans.

Sometimes, even with the most sensitive instruments, humans cannot experience a phenomenon directly. For experience of the past or the future, we must rely upon "signs" or "evidence" that something occurred or existed or that something is likely to occur. *Jurassic Park* aside, no one has direct experience of dinosaurs, yet scientists don't doubt that such creatures existed because they left clear evidence: fossilized bones, teeth, eggs (some with fossilized embryos), footprints, skin impressions, DNA strands. The evidence is adequate (for the community of scientists) to eliminate any doubt about the existence of dinosaurs. But scientists still disagree about the nature of dinosaurs. Were they warm-blooded or cold-blooded? Are they more closely related to birds or lizards? Did they travel alone or in herds?

Even some phenomena in the present are too large or too small or too far away for humans to experience them directly—even with sensitive instruments. In such cases, we must "infer" their existence from what evidence is available. Most scientists believe, for example, that black holes exist, but this belief is based on inferences and mathematical models rather than direct observation of black holes.

Reports, reports of reports, and inferences all involve claims about existence. These are what people commonly call "facts" although it should be clear by now that there is a fair amount of interpretation in any report of experience. Take the hole in the ozone, for example. The layer of ozone around the earth is so large and remote that humans cannot experience it directly. Scientists must rely on instruments to gather data about the ozone, and then they make inferences based on these data. Is there actually a hole in the ozone? Does it exist? If it does exist, what is the nature of this ozone hole? Is it growing? Does it threaten the planet? Different experts will have different answers to these questions of "fact," of existence.

Evaluating Claims about Existence

Claims about existence can take many forms: eyewitness testimony, reports of reports, surveys, ethnographies, observation, inferences from data. Each kind of report about experience must be evaluated on its own terms, but you can use some general principles to analyze and evaluate claims about existence. Richard Fulkerson lists these four: sufficiency of grounds, typicality, accuracy, and reliability. He sums these principles up with the acronym STAR:

> *Sufficiency of grounds:* Is there *enough* evidence to warrant the claim drawn?
>
> *Typicality:* Are the data representative of the group of data being argued about?
>
> *Accuracy:* Is the information used as data true?
>
> *Relevance:* Is the claim asserted relevant to the information about the sample?[1]

[1]Richard Fulkerson, *Teaching the Argument in Writing* (Urbana, IL: NCTE, 1996), p. 44.

A good claim about experience requires sufficient evidence to support it. Of course, what is "sufficient" will depend somewhat on the situation. An audience that is receptive to the claim to begin with will probably require less evidence to believe in the claim than an audience that is suspicious. As a general rule, one example is not enough. Finding at least three sources to verify your claim is usually adequate for most purposes. But multiplying examples won't be convincing unless the evidence is also typical and accurate. The data you choose to support your argument should be representative of the data. In other words, you shouldn't pick one or two eccentric opinions just because they support your opinion, ignoring the bulk of the data. If hundreds of scientific studies support a position, it would be misleading to select as representative of the group, the one or two studies that draw different conclusions. Your data need to be accurate, as well. Pay close attention to how the information was gathered as well as to what the information states. Data gathered carefully, using precise measurements and accepted methods, will usually be more accurate and reliable than data gathered in a careless and haphazard manner. Your evidence should also be relevant to the claim you are making. Your readers should be able to make a clear connection between your evidence and your claim, following an assumption such as the following: "This evidence should reasonably verify this event."

The Principles in Action: Readings

THE RELIABILITY OF EYEWITNESS TESTIMONY

The following two essays discuss the reliability and unreliability of eyewitness testimony. The first is by a psychologist, Elizabeth F. Loftus, who speculates about whether it is possible for eyewitnesses to provide completely objective reports. The second is by Barry Winston, a practicing defense attorney. Winston talks about the consequences of believing too much in the objectivity of legal testimony. As you read these essays, consider the following questions:

1. What makes some witnesses more reliable or believable than others?
2. How often do you have to rely on accounts given by others? Do you tend to believe these accounts? What makes you believe some people more than others?
3. What happens when two people who experienced the same event disagree with one another? Is one of them necessarily lying or mistaken?
4. What should be the role of eyewitness testimony in legal cases?

Eyewitnesses: Essential but Unreliable

ELIZABETH F. LOFTUS

THE LADIES and gentlemen of William Bernard Jackson's jury decided that 1
he was guilty of rape. They made a serious mistake, and before it was discovered, Jackson had spent five years in prison. There he suffered numerous indignities and occasional attacks until the police discovered that another man, who looked very much like Jackson, had committed the rapes.

If you had been on the jury, you would probably have voted for conviction too. Two women had positively identified Jackson as the man who had raped them in September and October of 1977. The October victim was asked on the witness stand, "Is there any doubt in your mind as to whether this man you have identified here is the man who had the sexual activity with you on October 3, 1977?" She answered "No doubt." "Could you be mistaken?" the prosecutor asked. "No, I am not mistaken," the victim stated confidently. Jackson and other defense witnesses testified that he was home when the rapes occurred. But the jury didn't believe him or them.

This is just one of the many documented cases of mistaken eyewitness testimony that have had tragic consequences. In 1981, Steve Titus of Seattle was convicted of raping a 17-year-old woman on a secluded road; the following year he was proven to be innocent. Titus was luckier than Jackson; he never went to prison. However, Aaron Lee Owens of Oakland, California, was not as fortunate. He spent nine years in a prison for a double murder that he didn't commit. In these cases, and many others, eyewitnesses testified against the defendants, and jurors believed them.

One reason most of us, as jurors, place so much faith in eyewitness testimony is that we are unaware of how many factors influence its accuracy. To name just a few: what questions witnesses are asked by police and how the questions are phrased; the difficulty people have in distinguishing among people of other races; whether witnesses have seen photos of suspects before viewing the lineup from which they pick out the person they say committed the crime; the size, composition and type (live or photo) of the lineup itself.

I know of seven studies that assess what ordinary citizens believe about eye 5
witness memory. One common misconception is that police officers make better witnesses than the rest of us. As part of a larger study, my colleagues and I asked 541 registered voters in Dade County, Florida, "Do you think that the memory of law enforcement agents is better than the memory of the average citizen?" Half said yes, 38 percent said no and the rest had no opinion. When A. Daniel Yarmey of the University of Guelph asked judges, lawyers, and policemen a similar question, 63 percent of the legal officials and half the police agreed that "The policeman will be superior to the civilian" in identifying robbers.

This faith in police testimony is not supported by research. Several years ago, psychologists A. H. Tinkner and E. Christopher Poulton showed a film depicting a street scene to 24 police officers and 156 civilians. The subjects were asked to watch for particular people in the film and to report instances of crimes, such as petty theft. The researchers found that the officers reported more alleged thefts than the civilians but that when it came to detecting actual crimes, the civilians did just as well.

More recently, British researcher Peter B. Ainsworth showed a 20-minute videotape to police officers and civilians. The tape depicted a number of staged criminal offenses, suspicious circumstances and traffic offenses at an urban street corner. No significant differences were found between the police and civilians in the total number of incidents reported. Apparently neither their initial training nor subsequent experience increases the ability of the police to be accurate witnesses.

Studies by others and myself have uncovered other common misconceptions about eyewitness testimony. They include:

- *Witnesses remember the details of a violent crime better than those of a nonviolent one.* Research shows just the opposite: The added stress that violence creates clouds our perceptions.
- *Witnesses are as likely to underestimate the duration of a crime as to overestimate it.* In fact, witnesses almost invariably think a crime took longer than it did. The more violent and stressful the crime, the more witnesses overestimate its duration.
- *The more confident a witness seems, the more accurate the testimony is likely to be.* Research suggests that there may be little or no relationship between confidence and accuracy, especially when viewing conditions are poor.

The unreliability of confidence as a guide to accuracy has been demonstrated outside of the courtroom too; one example is provided by accounts of an aircraft accident that killed nine people several years ago. According to *Flying* magazine, several people had seen the airplane just before impact, and one of them was certain that "it was heading right toward the ground, straight down." This witness was profoundly wrong, as shown by several photographs taken of the crash site that made it clear that the airplane hit flat and at a low enough angle to skid for almost 1,000 feet.

Despite the inaccuracies of eyewitness testimony, we can't afford to exclude 10
it legally or ignore it as jurors. Sometimes, as in cases of rape, it is the only evidence available, and it is often correct. The question remains, what can we do to give jurors a better understanding of the uses and pitfalls of such testimony? Judges sometimes give the jury a list of instructions on the pitfalls of eyewitness testimony. But this method has not proved satisfactory, probably because, as studies show, jurors either do not listen or do not understand the instructions.

Another solution, when judges permit, is to call a psychologist as an expert witness to explain how the human memory works and describe the experimental findings that apply to the case at hand. How this can affect a case is shown by a murder trial in California two years ago. On April 1, 1981, two young men were walking along Polk Street in San Francisco at about 5:30 in the evening. A car stopped near them and the driver, a man in his 40s, motioned one of the men to get in, which he did. The car drove off. Up to this point, nothing appeared unusual. The area was known as a place where prostitutes hang out; in fact, the young man who got in the car was there hustling for "tricks." Three days later, he was found strangled in a wooded area some 75 miles south of San Francisco.

Five weeks later, the victim's friend was shown a six-person lineup and picked out a 47-year-old I'll call D. The quick selection of D's photograph, along with the strong emotional reaction that accompanied it (the friend became ill when he saw the photo), convinced the police that they had their man. D was tried for murder.

At his trial, the defense lawyer introduced expert testimony by a psychologist on the factors that made accurate perception and memory difficult. For example, in the late afternoon of April 1, the witness had been using marijuana, a substance likely to blur his initial perceptions and his memory of them. Furthermore, just before viewing the lineup, the witness had seen a photograph of D on a desk in the police station, an incident that could have influenced his selection. During the five weeks between April 1 and the time he saw the photographs, the witness had talked about and been questioned repeatedly about the crime, circumstances that often contaminate memory.

In the end, the jury was unable to reach a verdict. It is difficult to assess the impact of any one bit of testimony on a particular verdict. We can only speculate that the psychologist's testimony may have made the jury more cautious about accepting the eyewitness testimony. This idea is supported by recent studies showing that such expert testimony generally increases the deliberation time jurors devote to eyewitness aspects of a case.

15 Expert testimony on eyewitness reliability is controversial. It has its advocates and enemies in both the legal and psychological professions. For example, several judicial arguments are used routinely to exclude the testimony. One is that it "invades the province of the jury," meaning that it is the jury's job, not an expert's, to decide whether a particular witness was in a position to see, hear and remember what is being claimed in court. Another reason judges sometimes exclude such testimony is that the question of eyewitness reliability is "not beyond the knowledge and experience of a juror" and thus is not a proper subject matter for expert testimony.

In virtually all the cases in which a judge has prohibited the jury from hearing expert testimony, the higher courts have upheld the decision, and in some cases have driven home the point with negative comments about the use of psychologists. In a recent case in California, *People v. Plasencia,* Nick Plasencia, Jr., was found guilty of robbery and other crimes in Los Angeles County. He had tried to introduce the testimony of a psychologist on eyewitness reliability, but the judge refused to admit it, saying that "the subject matter about which (the expert) sought to testify was too conjectural and too speculative to support any opinion he would offer." The appellate court upheld Plasencia's conviction and made known its strong feelings about the psychological testimony:

> Since our society has not reached the point where all human conduct is videotaped for later replay, resolution of disputes in our court system depends almost entirely on the testimony of witnesses who recount their observations of a myriad of events.
>
> These events include matters in both the criminal and civil areas of the law. The accuracy of a witness's testimony of course depends on factors which are as variable and complex as human nature itself. . . . The cornerstone of our system remains our belief in the wisdom and integrity of the jury system and the ability of 12 jurors to determine the accuracy of witnesses' testimony. The system has served us well. . . .
>
> It takes no expert to tell us that for various reasons, people can be mistaken about identity, or even the exact details of an observed event. Yet to present these commonly accepted and known facts in the form of an expert opinion, which opinion does nothing more than generally question the validity of one form of traditionally accepted evidence, would exaggerate the significance of that testimony and give a "scientific aura" to a very unscientific matter.
>
> The fact remains, in spite of the universally recognized fallibility of human beings, persons do, on many occasions, correctly identify individuals. Evidence that under contrived test conditions, or even in real-life situations, certain persons totally unconnected with this case have been mistaken in their identification of individuals is no more relevant than evidence that in other cases, witnesses totally unconnected with this event have lied.
>
> It seems beyond question that the identifications in this case were correct. We find no abuse of discretion in the trial court's rejecting the proffered testimony.

Quite the opposite view was expressed by the Arizona Supreme Court in *State v. Chapple*. At the original trial, defendant Dolan Chapple had been convicted of three counts of murder and two drug-trafficking charges, chiefly on the testimony of two witnesses who identified him at the trial. Earlier they had selected him from photographs shown them by the police more than a year after the crime.

Chapple's lawyer tried to introduce expert psychological testimony on the accuracy of such identification. The judge refused to permit it on the grounds that the testimony would pertain only to matters "within the common experience" of jurors. The high court disagreed, maintaining that expert testimony would have provided scientific data on such pertinent matters as the accuracy of delayed identification, the effect of stress on perception and the relationship between witness confidence and accuracy. "We cannot assume," the court added, "that the average juror would be aware of the variables concerning identification and memory" about which the expert would have testified. Chapple's conviction was reversed, and he has been granted a new trial.

Like lawyers and judges, psychologists disagree on whether expert testimony is a good solution to the eyewitness problem. Two of the most outspoken critics are Michael McCloskey and Howard Egeth of The Johns Hopkins University. These experimental psychologists offer four reasons why they believe that expert testimony on eyewitness reliability is a poor idea. They say that there is no evidence that such testimony is needed; that the data base on which the expert must rely is not sufficiently well-developed; and that conflicting public testimony between experts would tarnish the profession's image. Given this sorry state of affairs, they argue, psychologists may do more harm than good by intruding into judicial proceedings.

20 Obviously, many psychologists disagree with this assessment and believe that both the law and psychology gain from mutual interaction. In the area of eyewitness testimony, information supplied by psychologists to lawyers has stimulated responses that have suggested a number of important ideas for future research.

For example, psychologists need to learn more about the ideas that the rest of us have about the operation of human perception and memory. When these ideas are wrong, psychologists need to devise ways to educate us so that the judgments we make as jurors will be more fully informed and more fair. Only through this give-and-take, and occasional biting controversy, will progress be made. It is too late to help William Jackson, or Steve Titus, or Aaron Lee Owens, but it is not yet too late for the rest of us.

Stranger Than True: Why I Defend Guilty Clients

BARRY WINSTON

1 LET ME TELL you a story. A true story. The court records are all there if anyone wants to check. It's three years ago. I'm sitting in my office, staring out the window, when I get a call from a lawyer I hardly know. Tax lawyer. Some kid is in trouble and would I be interested in helping him out? He's charged with manslaughter, a felony, and driving under the influence. I tell him sure, have the kid call me.

So the kid calls and makes an appointment to see me. He's a nice kid, fresh out of college, and he's come down here to spend some time with his older sister, who's in med school. One day she tells him they're invited to a cookout with some friends of hers. She's going directly from class and he's going to take her car and meet her there. It's way out in the country, but he gets there before she does, introduces himself around, and pops a beer. She shows up after a while and he pops another beer. Then he eats a hamburger and drinks a third beer. At some point his sister says, "Well, it's about time to go," and they head for the car.

And, the kid tells me, sitting there in my office, the next thing he remembers, he's waking up in a hospital room, hurting like hell, bandages and casts all over him, and somebody is telling him he's charged with manslaughter and DUI because he wrecked his sister's car, killed her in the process, and blew fourteen on the Breathalyzer. I ask him what the hell he means by "the next thing he remembers," and he looks me straight in the eye and says he can't remember anything from the time they leave the cookout until he wakes up in the hospital. He tells me the doctors say he has post-retrograde amnesia. I say of course I believe him, but I'm worried about finding a judge who'll believe him.

I agree to represent him and send somebody for a copy of the wreck report. It says there are four witnesses: a couple in a car going the other way who passed the kid and his sister just before their car ran off the road, the guy whose front yard they landed in, and the trooper who investigated. I call the guy whose yard they ended up in. He isn't home. I leave word. Then I call the couple. The wife agrees to come in the next day with her husband. While I'm talking to her, the first guy calls. I call him back, introduce myself, tell him I'm representing the kid and need to talk to him about the accident. He hems and haws, and I figure he's one of those people who think it's against the law to talk to defense lawyers. I say the D.A. will tell him it's O.K. to talk to me, but he doesn't have to. I give him the name and number of the D.A. and he says he'll call me back.

Then I go out and hunt up the trooper. He tells me the whole story. The 5
kid and his sister are coming into town on Smith Level Road, after it turns from fifty-five to forty-five. The Thornes—the couple—are heading out of town. They say this sports car passes them, going the other way, right after that bad turn just south of the new subdivision. They say it's going like a striped-ass ape, at least sixty-five or seventy. Mrs. Thorne turns around to look and Mr. Thorne watches in the rear-view mirror. They both see the same thing: Halfway into the curve, the car runs off the road on the right, whips back onto the road, spins, runs off on the left, and disappears. They turn around in the first driveway they come to and start back, both terrified of what they're going to find. By this time, Trooper Johnson says, the guy whose front yard the car has ended up in has pulled the kid and his sister out of the wreck and started CPR on the girl. Turns out he's an emergency medical technician. Holloway, that's his name. Johnson tells me that Holloway says he's sitting in his front room, watching television, when he hears a hell of a crash in his yard. He runs outside and finds the car flipped over, and so he pulls the kid out from the driver's side, the girl from the other side. She dies in his arms.

And that, says Trooper Johnson, is that. The kid's blood/alcohol content was fourteen, he was going way too fast, and the girl is dead. He had to charge him. It's a shame, he seems a nice kid, it was his own sister and all, but what the hell can he do, right?

The next day the Thornes come in, and they confirm everything Johnson said. By now things are looking not so hot for my client, and I'm thinking it's about time to have a little chat with the D.A. But Holloway still hasn't called me back, so I call him. Not home. Leave word. No call. I wait a couple of days and call again. Finally I get him on the phone. He's very agitated, and won't talk to me except to say that he doesn't have to talk to me.

I know I better look for a deal, so I go to the D.A. He's very sympathetic. But. There's only so far you can get on sympathy. A young woman is dead, promising career cut short, all because somebody has too much to drink and drives. The kid has to pay. Not, the D.A. says, with jail time. But he's got to plead guilty to two misdemeanors: death by vehicle and driving under the influence. That means probation, a big fine. Several thousand dollars. Still, it's hard for me to criticize the D.A. After all, he's probably going to have the MADD mothers all over him because of reducing the felony to a misdemeanor.

On the day of the trial, I get to court a few minutes early. There are the Thornes and Trooper Johnson, and someone I assume is Holloway. Sure enough, when this guy sees me, he comes over and introduces himself and starts right in: "I just want you to know how serious all this drinking and driving really is," he says. "If those young people hadn't been drinking and driving that night, that poor young girl would be alive today." Now, I'm trying to hold my temper when I spot the D.A. I bolt across the room, grab him by the arm, and say, "We gotta talk. Why the hell have you got all those people here? That jerk Holloway. Surely to God you're not going to call him as a witness. This is a guilty plea! My client's parents are sitting out there. You don't need to put them through a dog-and-pony show."

10 The D.A. looks at me and says, "Man, I'm sorry, but in a case like this, I gotta put on witnesses. Weird Wally is on the bench. If I try to go without witnesses, he might throw me out."

The D.A. calls his first witness. Trooper Johnson identifies himself, tells about being called to the scene of the accident, and describes what he found when he got there and what everybody told him. After he finishes, the judge looks at me. "No questions," I say. Then the D.A. calls Holloway. He describes the noise, running out of the house, the upside-down car in his yard, pulling my client out of the window on the left side of the car and then going around to the other side for the girl. When he gets to this part, he really hits his stride. He describes, in minute detail, the injuries he saw and what he did to try and save her life. And then he tells, breath by breath, how she died in his arms.

The D.A. says, "No further questions, your Honor." The judge looks at me. I shake my head, and he says to Holloway. "You may step down."

One of those awful silences hangs there, and nothing happens for a minute. Holloway doesn't move. Then he looks at me, and at the D.A., and then at the judge. He says, "Can I say something else, your Honor?"

All my bells are ringing at once, and my gut is screaming at me, Object! Object! I'm trying to decide in three quarters of a second whether it'll be worse to listen to a lecture on the evils of drink from this jerk Holloway or piss off the judge by objecting. But all I say is, "No objections, your Honor." The judge smiles at me, then at Holloway, and says, "Very well, Mr. Holloway. What did you wish to say?"

15 It all comes in a rush. "Well, you see, your Honor," Holloway says, "it was just like I told Trooper Johnson. It all happened so fast. I heard the noise, and I came running out, and it was night, and I was excited, and the next morning, when I had a chance to think about it, I figured out what had happened, but by then I'd already told Trooper Johnson and I didn't know what to do, but you

see, the car, it was upside down, and I did pull that boy out of the left-hand window, but don't you see, the car was upside down, and if you turned it over on its wheels like it's supposed to be, the left-hand side is really on the right-hand side, and your Honor, that boy wasn't driving that car at all. It was the girl that was driving, and when I had a chance to think about it the next morning, I realized that I'd told Trooper Johnson wrong, and I was scared and I didn't know what to do, and that's why"—and now he's looking right at me—"why I wouldn't talk to you."

Naturally, the defendant is allowed to withdraw his guilty plea. The charges are dismissed, and the kid and his parents and I go into one of the back rooms in the courthouse and sit there looking at one another for a while. Finally, we recover enough to mumble some Oh my Gods and Thank yous and You're welcomes. And that's why I can stand to represent somebody when I know he's guilty.

THE MEDIA AND REPORTED EXPERIENCE

"What Is News?" by Neil Postman and Steve Powers, focuses on the power of mass media, such as television, to shape our perceptions of reality and to create experience. The word *media* is the plural form of *medium,* which comes from a Latin word meaning "middle." A medium is "in the middle" of the receiver of a message and direct experience. In other words, a medium provides a selection and representation of experience, not experience itself. For instance, television provides images and sounds that you could not experience in any other way. During a typical news program, you can see footage from combat zones, crime scenes, and sporting events. You get satellite views of the weather and stock reports. All these images are accompanied by "expert" testimony to explain what you are seeing and experiencing. But what happens when viewers forget that television is *mediated* experience? As you read the following essays, consider these questions:

1. How would you answer the question posed by Neil Postman: "What is news?"
2. How often do you watch television, listen to radio, or read a newspaper? How is each of these media different from the others? What kind of information do you get from each?
3. How much confidence do you have in the media? Do you generally believe what you see on television, hear on the radio, or read in the newspaper?
4. What effect do you think the media have on public opinion?
5. Have the media ever covered a subject or event that you know quite well? If so, how closely did this coverage match your own experience?

What Is News?

NEIL POSTMAN and STEVE POWERS

ALL THIS TALK about news—what is it? We turn to this question because unless a television viewer has considered it, he or she is in danger of too easily accepting someone else's definition—for example, a definition supplied by the news director of a television station; or, even worse, a definition imposed by important advertisers. The question, in any case, is not a simple one, and it is even possible that many journalists and advertisers have not thought deeply about it. 1

A simplistic definition of news can be drawn by paraphrasing Justice Oliver Wendell Holmes's famous definition of the law. The law, Holmes said, is what the courts say it is. Nothing more. Nothing less. In similar fashion, we might say that the news is what news directors and journalists say it is. In other words, when you turn on your television set to watch a network or local news show, whatever is on is, by definition, the news. But if we were to take that approach, on what basis would we say that we haven't been told enough? Or that a story that should have been covered wasn't? Or that too many stories of a certain type were included? Or that a reporter gave a flagrantly biased account?

If objections of this kind are raised by viewers, then they must have some conception of the news that the news show has not fulfilled. Most people, in fact, do have such a conception, although they are not always fully conscious of what it is. When people are asked "What is the news?," the most frequent answer given is that the news is "what happened that day." This is a rather silly answer since even those who give it can easily be made to see that an uncountable number of things happen during the course of a day, including what you had for breakfast, that could hardly be classified as news by any definition. In modifying their answer, most will add that the news is "important and interesting things that happened that day." This helps a little but leaves open the question of what is "important and interesting" and how that is decided. Embedded somewhere in one's understanding of the phrase "important and interesting events" is one's definition of "the news."

Of course, some people will say that the question of what is important and interesting is not in the least problematic. What the President says or does is important; wars are important, rebellions, employment figures, elections, appointments to the Supreme Court. Really? We doubt that even the President believes everything he says is important. (Let us take, for example, President Bush's remark that he doesn't like broccoli.) There are, as we write, more than forty wars and rebellions going on somewhere in the world. Not even *The New York Times,* which claims to be the "newspaper of public record," reports on all of them, or even most. Are elections important? Maybe. But we doubt you'd be interested in the election in Iowa's Third Congressional District—unless you happen to live there. Some readers will remember the famous comedy routine of the 2,000-Year-Old Man who was discovered in the imaginations of Carl Reiner and Mel Brooks. Upon being asked what he believed to be the greatest invention of humankind during his life span, the 2,000-Year-Old Man replied unhesitatingly, "Saran Wrap." Now, there is a great deal to be said for Saran Wrap. We suspect that in the long run it may prove more useful to the well-being of most of us than a number of inventions that are daily given widespread publicity in the news media. Yet it is fair to say that no one except its manufacturer knows the date of Saran Wrap's invention, or even cares much to know. Saran Wrap is not news. The color of Liz Taylor's wrap is. Or so some people believe.

On the day Marilyn Monroe committed suicide, so did many other people, 5
some of whose reasons may have been as engrossing as, and perhaps more significant than, Miss Monroe's. But we shall never know about these people or their reasons; the journalists at CBS or NBC or *The New York Times* simply took no notice of them. Several people, we are sure, also committed suicide on the very day in 1991 when the New York Giants won the Super Bowl. We shall never learn about these people either, however instructive or interesting their stories may have been.

What we are driving at is this: "Importance" is a judgment people make. Of course, there are some events—the assassination of a president, an earthquake, etc.—that have near-universal interest and consequences. But most news does not inhere in the event. An event *becomes* news. And it becomes news because it is selected for notice out of the buzzing, booming confusion around us. This may seem a fairly obvious point but keep in mind that many people believe that the news is always "out there," waiting to be gathered or collected. In fact, the news is more often *made* rather than gathered. And it is made on the basis of what the journalist thinks important or what the journalist thinks the audience thinks is important or interesting. It can get pretty complicated. Is a story about a killing in Northern Ireland more important than one about a killing in Morocco? The journalist might not think so, but the audience might. Which story will become the news? And once selected, what point of view and details are to be included? After all, once a journalist has chosen an event to be news, he or she must also choose what is worth seeing, what is worth neglecting, and what is worth remembering or forgetting. This is simply another way of saying that every news story is a reflection of the reporter who tells the story. The reporter's previous assumptions about what is "out there" edit what he or she thinks is there. For example, many journalists believe that what is called "the intifada" is news-worthy. Let us suppose that a fourteen-year-old Palestinian boy hurls a Molotov cocktail at two eighteen-year-old Israeli soldiers. The explosion knocks one of the soldiers down and damages his left eye. The other soldier, terrified, fires a shot at the Palestinian that kills him instantly. The injured soldier eventually loses the sight of his eye. What details should be included in reporting this event? Is the age of the Palestinian relevant? Are the ages of the Israeli soldiers relevant? Is the injury to the soldier relevant? Was the act of the Palestinian provoked by the mere presence of Israeli soldiers? Was the act therefore justified? Is the shooting justified? Is the state of mind of the shooter relevant?

The answers to all of these questions, as well as to other questions about the event, depend entirely on the point of view of the journalist. You might think this is an exaggeration, that reporters, irrespective of their assumptions, can at least get the facts straight. But what are "facts"? In A. J. Liebling's book *The Press,* he gives a classic example of the problematic nature of "facts." On the same day, some years ago, both the *Wall Street Journal* and the now-defunct *World Telegram and Sun* featured a story about the streets of Moscow. Here is what the *Wall Street Journal* reporter wrote:

> The streets of central Moscow are, as the guidebooks say, clean and neat; so is the famed subway. They are so because of an army of women with brooms, pans, and carts who thus earn their 35 rubles a month in lieu of "relief"; in all Moscow we never saw a mechanical street-sweeper.

Here is what the *World Telegram and Sun* reporter wrote:

> Four years ago [in Moscow] women by the hundreds swept big city streets. Now you rarely see more than a dozen. The streets are kept clean with giant brushing and sprinkling machines.

Well, which is it? Can a dozen women look like an army? Are there giant machines cleaning the streets of Moscow or are there not? How can two trained journalists see events so differently? Well, one of them worked for the *Wall Street Journal,* and when these stories were written, it was the policy of the *Journal* to highlight the contrast between the primitive Russian economy and the sophisticated American economy. (It still is.) Does this mean the reporter for the *Journal* was lying? We doubt it. Each of our senses is a remarkably astute censor. We see what we expect to see; often, we focus on what we are paid to see. And those who pay us to see usually expect us to accept their notions not only of what is important but of what are important details.

That fact poses some difficult problems for those of us trying to make sense of the news we are given. One of these problems is indicated by a proposal, made years ago, by the great French writer Albert Camus. Camus wished to establish "a control newspaper." The newspaper would come out one hour after all the others and would contain estimates of the percentage of truth in each of their stories. In Camus's words: "We'd have complete dossiers on the interests, policies, and idiosyncrasies of the owners. Then we'd have a dossier on every journalist in the world. The interests, prejudices, and quirks of the owner would equal Z. The prejudices, quirks, and private interests of the journalist Y. Z times Y would give you X, the probable amount of truth in the story" (quoted in *The Press* by A. J. Liebling, p. 22n).

Camus was either a reckless mathematician or else he simply neglected to say 10
why and how multiplying Z and Y would tell us what we need to know. (Why not add or divide them?) Nor did he discuss the problem of how to estimate the

reliability of those doing the estimating. In any case, Camus died before he had a chance to publish such a newspaper, leaving each one of us to be our own "control center." Nonetheless, we can't help thinking how Camus's idea might be applied to television. Imagine how informative it would be if there were a five-minute television program that went on immediately after each television news show. The host might say something like this: "To begin with, this station is owned by Gary Farnsworth, who is also the president of Bontel Limited, the principal stockholder of which is the Sultan of Bahrain. Bontel Limited owns three Japanese electronic companies, two oil companies, the entire country of Upper Volta, and the western part of Romania. The anchorman on the television show earns $800,000 a year; his portfolio includes holdings in a major computer firm. He has a bachelor's degree in journalism from the University of Arkansas but was a C+ student, has never taken a course in political science, and speaks no language other than English. Last year, he read only two books—a biography of Cary Grant and a book of popular psychology called *Why Am I So Wonderful?* The reporter who covered the story on Yugoslavia speaks Serbo-Croatian, has a degree in international relations, and has had a Neiman Fellowship at Harvard University."

We think this kind of information would be helpful to a viewer although not for the same reason Camus did. Such information would not give an estimate of the "truth probability" of stories but it would suggest possible patterns of influence reflected in the news. After all, what is important to a person whose boss owns several oil companies might not be important to a person who doesn't even have a boss, who is unemployed. Similarly, what a reporter who does not know the language of the people he or she reports on can see and understand will probably be different from the perceptions of another reporter who knows the language well.

What we are saying is that to answer the question "What is news?" a viewer must know something about the political beliefs and economic situation of those who provide the news. The viewer is then in a position to know why certain events are considered important by those in charge of television news and may compare those judgments with his or her own.

But here's another problem. As we have implied, even oil magnates and poorly prepared journalists do not consult, exclusively, their own interests in selecting the "truths" they will tell. Since they want people to watch their shows, they also try to determine what audiences think is important and interesting. There is, in fact, a point of view that argues against journalists imposing their own sense of significance on an audience. In this view, television news should consist only of those events that would interest the audience. The journalists must keep their own opinions to themselves. The response to this is that many viewers depend on journalists to advise them of what is important. Besides, even if journalists were mere followers of public interest, not all members of the audience agree on what they wish to know. For example, we do not happen to think that Liz Taylor's adventures in marriage were or are of any importance whatsoever to anyone but her and Michael Wilding, Nicky Hilton, Mike Todd, Eddie Fisher, Richard Burton, John Warner, Larry Fortensky, and, of course, Debbie Reynolds and Sybil Burton. Obviously, most people don't agree, which is why an announcement of her intention to marry again is featured on every television news show. What's our point? A viewer must not only know what he or she thinks is significant but what others believe is significant as well.

It is a matter to be seriously considered. You may conclude, for example, that other people do not have a profound conception of what is significant. You may even be contemptuous of the taste or interests of others. On the other hand, you may fully share the sense of significance held by a majority of people. It is not our purpose here to instruct you or anyone else in what is to be regarded as a significant event. We are saying that in considering the question "What is news?" a viewer must always take into account his or her relationship to a larger audience. Television is a mass medium, which means that a television news show is not intended for you alone. It is public communication, and the viewer needs to have some knowledge and opinions about "the public." It is a common complaint of individuals that television news rarely includes stories about some special interest. We know a man, for example, who emigrated from Switzerland thirty years ago. He is an American citizen but retains a lively interest in his native land. "Why," he asked us, "are there never any stories about Switzerland?" "Because," we had to reply, "no one but you and a few others have any interest in Switzerland." "That's too bad," he replied. "Switzerland is an interesting country." We agree. But most Americans have not been in Switzerland, probably believe not much happens in Switzerland, do not have many relatives in Switzerland, and would much rather know about what some English lord has to say about the world's economy than what a Swiss banker thinks. Maybe they are right, maybe not. Judging the public mind is always risky.

And this leads to another difficulty in answering the question "What is 15
news?" Some might agree with us that Liz Taylor's adventures in marriage do not constitute significant events but that they ought to be included in a news show precisely for that reason. Her experiences, they may say, are amusing or diverting, certainly engrossing. In other words, the purpose of news should be to give people pleasure, at least to the extent that it takes their minds off their own troubles. We have heard people say that getting through the day is difficult enough, filled with tension, anxiety, and often disappointment. When they turn on the news, they want relief, not aggravation. It is also said that whether entertaining or not, stories about the lives of celebrities should be included because they are instructive; they reveal a great deal about our society—its mores, values, ideals. Mark Twain once remarked that news is history in its first and best form. The American poet Ezra Pound added an interesting idea to that. He defined literature as news that *stays* news. Among other things, Pound meant that the stuff of literature originates not in stories about the World Bank or an armistice agreement but in those simple, repeatable tales that reflect the pain, confusion, or exaltations that are constant in human experience, and touch us at

the deepest levels. For example, consider the death of Michael Landon. Who was Michael Landon to you, or you to Michael Landon that you should have been told so much about him when he died? Here is a possible answer: Michael Landon was rich, decent, handsome, young, and successful. Suddenly, very nearly without warning, he was struck down at the height of his powers and fame. Why? What are we to make of it? Why him? It is like some Old Testament parable; these questions were raised five thousand years ago and we still raise them today. It is the kind of story that *stays* news, and that is why it must be given prominence. Or so some people believe.

What about the kind of news that doesn't stay news, that is neither the stuff of history nor literature—the fires, rapes, and murders that are daily featured on local television news? Who has decided that they are important, and why? One cynical answer is that they are there because viewers take comfort in the realization that *they* have escaped disaster. At least for that day. It doesn't matter who in particular was murdered; the viewer wasn't. We tune in to find out how lucky we are, and go to sleep with the pleasure of knowing that we have survived. A somewhat different answer goes this way: it is the task of the news story to provide a daily accounting of the progress of society. This can be done in many ways, some of them abstract (for example, a report on the state of unemployment), some of them concrete (for example, reports on particularly gruesome murders). These reports, especially those of a concrete nature, are the daily facts from which the audience is expected to draw appropriate conclusions about the question "What kind of society am I a member of?" Studies conducted by Professor George Gerbner and his associates at the University of Pennsylvania have shown that people who are heavy television viewers, including viewers of television news shows, believe their communities are much more dangerous than do light television viewers. Television news, in other words, tends to frighten people. The question is, "Ought they to be frightened?," which is to ask, "Is the news an accurate portrayal of where we are as a society?" Which leads to another question, "Is it possible for daily news to give such a picture?" Many journalists believe it is possible. Some are skeptical. The early-twentieth-century journalist Lincoln Steffens proved that he could create a "crime wave" anytime he wanted by simply writing about all the crimes that normally occur in a large city during the course of a month. He could also end the crime wave by not writing about them. If crime waves can be "manufactured" by journalists, then how accurate are news shows in depicting the condition of a society? Besides, murders, rapes, and fires (even unemployment figures) are not the only way to assess the progress (or regress) of a society. Why are there so few television stories about symphonies that have been composed, novels written, scientific problems solved, and a thousand other creative acts that occur during the course of a month? Were television news to be filled with these events, we would not be frightened. We would, in fact, be inspired, optimistic, cheerful.

One answer is as follows: These events make poor television news because there is so little to show about them. In the judgment of most editors, people *watch* television. And what they are interested in watching are exciting, intriguing, even exotic pictures. Suppose a scientist has developed a new theory about how to measure with more exactitude the speed with which heavenly objects are moving away from the earth. It is difficult to televise a theory, especially if it involves complex mathematics. You can show the scientist talking about his theory but that would not make for good television and too much of it would drive viewers to other stations. In any case, the news show could only give the scientist twenty seconds of air time because time is an important commodity. Newspapers and magazines sell space, which is not without its limitations for a commercial enterprise. But space can be expanded. Television sells time, and time cannot be expanded. This means that whatever else is neglected, commercials cannot be. Which leads to another possible answer to the question "What is news?" News, we might say, may be history in its first and best form, or the stuff of literature, or a record of the condition of a society, or the expression of the passions of a public, or the prejudices of journalists. It may be all of these things, but in its worst form it can also be mainly a "filler," a "come-on" to keep the viewer's attention until the commercials come. Certain producers have learned that by pandering to the audience, by eschewing solid news and replacing it with leering sensationalism, they can subvert the news by presenting a "television commercial show" that is interrupted by news.

All of which leads us to reiterate, first, that there are no simple answers to the question "What is news?" and, second, that it is not our purpose to tell you what you ought to believe about the question. The purpose of this chapter is to arouse your interest in thinking *about* the question. Your answers are to be found by knowing what you feel is significant and how your sense of the significant conforms with or departs from that of others, including broadcasters, their bosses, and their audiences. Answers are to be found in your ideas about the purposes of public communication, and in your judgment of the kind of society you live in and wish to live in. We cannot provide answers to these questions. But you also need to know something about the problems, limitations, traditions, motivations, and, yes, even the delusions of the television news industry. That's where we can help you to know how to watch a television news show.

CONTROVERSIAL CLAIMS ABOUT EXISTENCE

The following essays analyze claims about existence that are controversial, even among scientists. In the first essay, "The HIV Disbeliever," David France analyzes Christine Maggiore's surprising claim that there is no connection between HIV and AIDS. She claims, instead, that AIDS symptoms are caused by the toxic drugs that are used to treat HIV. Although most scientists disagree quite strongly with Maggiore, she does find some scientific basis for her views in the work of Berkeley virologist Peter Duesberg. The second essay is an excerpt from Curtis Peebles' book *Watch the Skies! A Chronicle of the Flying Saucer Myth*

(1994). In this selection, Peebles analyzes the claims made by various authors about the reality of alien abductions. As you read these essays, consider the following questions:

1. What claim about existence are found in each of these essays?
2. What evidence supports these claims? Is the evidence sufficient, typical, accurate, and reliable?
3. Which people sound most credible? How is credibility affected by what the article reveals about the person's personal experience, education, or technical expertise?
4. How do those making controversial claims about existence account for counterevidence?
5. How well do these claims fit with your own experience and knowledge about these subjects? To what extent do you accept or reject a scientific world view?
6. What other controversial claims about existence are you familiar with?

The HIV Disbeliever

DAVID FRANCE

ONE SWELTERING California afternoon a few weeks ago, Christine Maggiore was sitting in her cramped office, still jet-lagged from the long flight home from South Africa, where she'd attended the International AIDS Conference. She hadn't yet found time to answer the "hundreds and hundreds, perhaps literally thousands" of e-mail messages she'd received from people she'd met there who were looking for AIDS literature or doctor referrals, or simply wanting to pat her on the back. "All your work and dedication is appreciated!!!" a typical message declared. She doesn't know when she'll find time to catch up—her whole life is behind schedule because of her AIDS work. "My fiancé and I have been trying to find time to get married for years!" she says. 1

But Maggiore, who heads Alive & Well AIDS Alternatives in Burbank, Calif., is not your typical AIDS activist. In South Africa some scientists spit nasty epithets at her. Protesters marching outside the meeting hall threatened to plug her and her galvanized followers with bullets. Why? Because Maggiore takes the strange contrarian stance that HIV, which has been blamed in the deaths of 18.8 million people worldwide, doesn't cause AIDS at all. She exhorts people to stop taking their medications and stop worrying about spreading their virus.

But Maggiore's influence here and abroad is swelling. The singer Nina Hagen wrote a song for her, and Esai Morales, the actor, is a big funder. The platinum-selling alternative rock band Foo Fighters promotes Maggiore's ideas on its Web site. And in South Africa Maggiore met privately with South African President Thabo Mbeki, who endorses many of her beliefs. Mbeki's call for more research into whether HIV causes AIDS dominated headlines from the important biennial meeting. In response, 5,000 flabbergasted scientists signed a declaration calling the laboratory evidence "clear-cut, exhaustive, and unambiguous."

Such consensus doesn't impress Maggiore, a bright and compelling former garment executive with no scientific training or college degree. Through emotional newspaper columns, e-mail postings and lectures in such disparate places as the University of Miami School of Medicine and the Rev. Al Sharpton's National Action Network in Harlem, she continues to try to pick apart the scientific literature, a strategy that especially appeals to people with a beef against the establishment. "We're not saying that anybody is 100 percent correct or incorrect on this issue," Foo Fighters bassist Nate Mendel told *Newsweek*. "Simply, there's information out there that is being blocked out."

5 Maggiore is convinced that HIV doesn't cause AIDS. No medical journal has ever proved to her it is dangerous. She calls standard HIV antibody tests so oversensitive that they can show positive "if you've had a flu shot or if you've ever been pregnant" (the Centers for Disease Control and Prevention disagree), and she cobbles together reams of footnotes, anecdotes and package inserts to prove it.

Then how does she explain all the deaths that have marked the pandemic? Here's where her argument takes a conspiratorial turn. In Africa, despite what health authorities say, people are simply not dying more than before, she asserts. And she thinks the 420,000 Americans who have died of AIDS are victims of the prescription drugs they hoped would save them. Or perhaps they died from recreational drugs. Or maybe they succumbed to "a profound fear of AIDS" itself. "We're not saying people haven't died of what is called 'AIDS'," Maggiore explained one afternoon in the sunny Burbank home she shares with her fiancé, a 31-year-old video editor named Robin Scovill, and her son. "We're just asking what is at the core of this incredible human tragedy. And by looking at other avenues, might we better resolve this?"

There is no way to know how many patients she has persuaded to abandon their medications or condoms, but Maggiore's detractors can barely contain their anger. "Many people will die because they will go untreated," says Dr. Luc Montagnier, the codiscoverer of HIV. White House AIDS-policy director Sandra Thurman says bluntly, "Christine is putting lives in jeopardy."

Disbelievers—"flat earth" types who fervently doubt the conclusions of science—have been around since the Enlightenment. But they are staging a resurgence today, partly in reaction to the unparalleled role science plays in society. Disbelievers fear Big Science the way millennialists feared Y2K. Fragments of contrarian evidence are enough to shake their faith in everything from water fluoridation to global-warming statistics, childhood vaccine programs to the artificial sweetener aspartame, the Holocaust to evolution. Huge parcels of the

World Wide Web are devoted to such exposés. "We're at a moment for a lot of things where skepticism becomes a dogma," says Michael Shermer, author of a book about the antiscience backlash, "Why People Believe Weird Things."

But what's in it for them? "The basis of denial is a need to escape something that is terribly uncomfortable," says Boston College psychology professor Joseph Tecce, who has studied Holocaust deniers and AIDS dissenters. "If something is horrific, I might want to pretend it doesn't exist."

Christine Maggiore's horrific event came on Feb. 24, 1992, when, she says, 10 a routine blood test came back positive for HIV. She was 36 years old, single and a partner in a successful clothing wholesaler. A former boyfriend also tested positive. "I was mortified," she says. "According to the conventional wisdom, I had just foolishly and irrevocably ruined my entire life."

Maggiore was not immediately a disbeliever. Initially, the oldest child of a Los Angeles advertising executive sought the advice of doctors and planned to start treatment. But some scientific principles of the disease never added up to her. For one thing, she felt fine—and still does. How could she have a killer virus? "There was this empirical data from my own body," she says, "I was ridiculously healthy."

Ultimately she discovered the work of Berkeley virologist Peter Duesberg, whose belief that AIDS is caused by lifestyle choices like promiscuity and drug use rather than infectious agents have long been dismissed by his peers. One spring evening in 1994, as she was sitting on a panel discussing AIDS prevention, it finally struck Maggiore that she no longer believed in the epidemic. "Being a practical person, it didn't seem to me after investigating this that there were good reasons for me to live my life as if I were dying," she says.

Now, nothing can dissuade her. Take the 1999 CDC report detailing the wild successes of protease inhibitors, the new class of AIDS drugs introduced in 1996. The study correlates a huge drop-off in classic AIDS-related infections with data on how many of the new drugs were prescribed. "Prescriptions don't mean people are actually taking the drugs," she objected. "Do you know how many people flush their drugs down the toilet?" (In fact, she says, the wholesale return to health is a direct result of that protest, in bathrooms across America.)

Today, Maggiore is the most prominent foe of what she calls "the HIV equals AIDS equals death paradigm," having sold or given away 28,500 copies of her self-published booklet since 1995, in addition to the copies in French, German, Italian, Spanish, Portuguese and Japanese. She founded Alive & Well, which has spun off chapters around the globe and is affiliated with dozens of like-minded groups representing perhaps tens of thousands of followers.

Their message has resonated among a number of gay men who, exhausted 15 by 20 years of medical vigilance and daily toxic drug regimens, are increasingly receptive to Maggiore's exhortation to "live in wellness . . . without fear of AIDS." And they have reinvigorated long-simmering AIDS conspiracy theories. According to a 1995 survey of 1,000 African-American churchgoers, one third believed HIV was concocted by the government for racial genocide. When she spoke before a crowded room in Harlem in 1998, spellbound members of the audience likened her to the abolitionists, interrupting her with cries of "John Brown lives!"

"If you told me five years ago I would be promoting the notion that HIV does not cause AIDS, I would have said you were nuts. I believed adamantly that HIV was a killer and these drugs were saving lives," says Michael Bellefountaine, 34, a friend of Maggiore's who decided against taking anti-HIV medication years ago. Now he attributes his survival to being drug-free. Last month he attended a protest in San Francisco and chanted. "HIV is a lie! It's toxic pills that made them die!"

AIDS educators already hold Maggiore and her acolytes responsible for an upswing in new infections. San Francisco authorities just announced that new HIV cases in 1999 were nearly twice as high as in 1997. "People are focusing on the wrong thing. They're focusing on conspiracies rather than protecting themselves, rather than getting tested and seeking out appropriate care and treatment," says Stephen Thomas, who directs the University of Pittsburgh's Center for Minority Health.

HIV renegades sometimes seem as if their main goal is mayhem, not constructive discourse. For instance, the San Francisco chapter of ACT UP, once a major force lobbying for more money for AIDS research, is now run by dissenters who stage protests against other AIDS leaders—regularly bathing them in cat-box litter or spit. On Aug. 9 police charged two ACT UP members with assault and battery for allegedly striking city health-department director Mitchell H. Katz and covering him with Silly String during a public meeting. Similar antics now prevail among a half-dozen ACT UP branches. "They're crazy," says Larry Kramer, who founded ACT UP in 1987. "They're undoing all we've fought for."

Picking over a black-bean wrap at her kitchen counter recently, Maggiore described herself simply as a person who asks questions others are overlooking. The fact that she provokes hostility only emboldens her. She sees only intolerance and recalcitrance among her detractors—they "smack of parental authority and religious authority," she said. Her brother Steven, 41, calls her a modern-day Copernicus.

But she soon made it clear that her disregard for HIV is not just an intel- 20
lectual gambit when her talkative 3-year-old son, Charlie, wandered into the kitchen after a midday nap. She talked about how she conceived him naturally and gave birth without drugs routinely given to prevent transmission. She continues to breast-feed him today, according to the family's pediatrician. Her family supports her in this, even though HIV can be transmitted through breast milk and judges have charged mothers in similar cases with child endangerment.

Maggiore and Scovill, Charlie's father, say they've never been curious to test the child for HIV (Scovill does not know his own status). Their pediatrician is not as sanguine. "I would not be opposed to testing his blood," admits Dr. Paul Fleiss, who says the boy has been very healthy. "But she is."

"He's a perfectly healthy little boy," says Scovill, bending to offer his son a macaroon. Charlie was skeptical. "They're really good," the father insisted patiently. "And for some reason they decrease viral load!" With that, both parents had a good laugh at the silly AIDS goblin. Such is the power of belief.

Abductions and Abductionists

CURTIS PEEBLES

THIS BOOK is a chronicle of the flying saucer myth—the system of beliefs that has developed around the idea that alien spacecraft are being seen in Earth's skies. These beliefs did not suddenly spring into existence fully formed. Rather, a set of conflicting ideas originated, the myth was defined, then the beliefs evolved over nearly half a century. Moreover, the flying saucer myth is not a single, monolithic set of doctrines. As soon as the flying saucer myth was defined, schisms began to develop among "believers"—those people who accepted the idea that flying saucers were extraordinary objects. Not all believers held the same beliefs, and these schisms soon led to open warfare. This interaction between believers has been a major influence on the myth's history. 1

The flying saucer myth not only concerns disk-shaped spaceships and the aliens who supposedly pilot them. Because it also involves how the believers view the role and nature of government, and how the government relates to the people, the U.S. government has had to deal with the flying saucer myth. Presidents have denied their existence; they were a twenty-two-year headache for the Air Force, and were investigated by Congress and the CIA. This interaction both fed the flying saucer myth and brought about the very things the government sought to avoid.

A similar interaction has taken place between the flying saucer myth and the larger society. The flying saucer myth is a mirror to the events of postwar America—the paranoia of the 1950s, the social turmoil of the 1960s, the "me generation" of the 1970s, and the nihilism of the 1980s and the early 1990s. As the flying saucer myth entered popular culture, images and ideas were created which, in turn, shaped the flying saucer myth itself. . . .

CLOSE ENCOUNTERS OF THE THIRD KIND

Although many films had used flying saucer themes, *Close Encounters of the Third Kind* was the only one to fully understand the flying saucer myth. The story is one of ordinary people trying to cope with mythic experiences. Roy Neary (Richard Dreyfuss) is a power company lineman who sees a UFO. He finds himself the victim of subliminal messages which cause him to undertake obsessive, bizarre actions which cause his family to leave. Neary finally realizes he is to go to Devil's Tower, Wyoming. He embarks on an arduous cross-country journey. Overcoming obstacles, he is rewarded with a meeting with the aliens. As the multicolored mothership lifts off with Neary aboard, he rises above his own mundane, earthly existence.

In earlier films, the flying saucers were sources of danger. In *Close Encoun-* 5
ters of the Third Kind, the meeting with the aliens was not to be feared, but to be anticipated. It was this "sense of wonder" that was so lacking in such films as *The Thing* or *Earth vs. the Flying Saucer.*

Close Encounters of the Third Kind defined the shape of the aliens. In the film, "they" were short, with large heads, slanted dark eyes, and light gray skins. Their noses were small and their ears were only small holes. The aliens' bodies were elongated and very thin. The fingers were also long. Their overall appearance was that of a fetus. By the early 1980s, this "shape" would come to dominate abduction descriptions.

THE GROWTH OF ABDUCTION REPORTS

Certain UFOlogists began to specialize in abduction cases. The first such "abductionist" was Dr. R. Leo Sprinkle, a psychologist at the University of Wyoming. Sprinkle was frequently quoted by the tabloids and was on the *National Enquirer's* Blue Ribbon Panel. Sprinkle's role was critical in shaping both the development of the abduction myth and its acceptance. His "hypnotic sessions with UFO abductees" began in 1967 and 1968 with three cases. It was not until 1974 that Sprinkle had another abduction case (reflecting the post-Condon Report decline in interest). In 1975 there were two cases. There were three cases each in 1976 and 1977 (after *The UFO Incident*). In 1978 (after *Close Encounters of the Third Kind*), Sprinkle worked with ten subjects, while in 1979 there were eighteen abductees. In 1980 he held the first of his annual conferences for UFO abductees and investigators.

This increase in abduction reports was not limited to Sprinkle. UFOlogist David Webb noted that a 1976 search of UFO literature (covering nearly thirty years) showed only 50 abduction-type cases. Yet, over the next two years, about 100 *more* cases were reported, bringing the total to some 150. By the end of the 1970s, the total number of cases exceeded 200. . . .

BUDD HOPKINS

With the 1980s, a new abductionist appeared—an artist named Budd Hopkins. Long interested in UFOs, the rise in abduction reports attracted Hopkin's attention in 1976. He met "Steven Kilburn had a vague memory of being afraid of a stretch of road, but no UFO sighting. To this point, people claiming to have been abducted said they had seen a UFO and/or occupant. This was followed by a period of "missing time." The "abduction" itself was "remembered" under hypnosis. Kilburn had no such memory. When he was hypnotized, however, Kilburn said he was grabbed by a "big wrench" and was taken aboard a UFO.

To Hopkins, this implied a person could be an "abductee" *without* any overt 10
memory. Hopkins began asking people if they had "uneasiness," recurring dreams, or "any event" which might indicate an abduction. It was no longer necessary for a person to have "missing time." *Anyone* could now be an abductee and not realize it. Hopkins believed there might be tens of thousands of abductees—what he called "an invisible multitude."

Hopkins published his conclusions in his 1981 book *Missing Time*. He believed "a very long-term, in-depth study is being made of a relatively large sample of humans." The "human specimens" were first abducted as young children. "Monitoring devices" would be implanted in the abductee's nose. This was described as a tiny ball on a long rod. The ball was left in the nasal cavity. The young abductees were then released with no memories of the (alleged) events. Years later, Hopkins believed, once the abductees reached puberty, they would be abducted a second time.

The aliens in Hopkins's abduction cases all followed the shape of those in *The UFO Incident* and *Close Encounters of the Third Kind*—large heads, thin bodies, slanted eyes, and gray skin. The book had several drawings of what became known as "the Grays." *Missing Time* completed the process of defining the shape of the aliens.

Hopkins also speculated on the aliens' motivation. He noted several abductees had scars from childhood. He believed tissue samples were being taken. Hopkins suggested the aliens needed a specific genetic structure. Hopkins also suggested the aliens were taking sperm and ova samples. These, he continued, might be for experiments in producing human/alien hybrids.

This expanded the abduction myth; it was now much more "intrusive." In the Pascagoula case, Hickson claimed he was passively "scanned." Now, tissue samples were being taken which left scars. The alleged abductees also showed emotional scars from their supposed experiences—long-lasting anxiety and fear. The "monitoring devices" were a further intrusion. The taking of sperm and ova was, symbolically, the most intrusive of all. Humans were depicted as helpless before the aliens' overwhelming power, reduced to a lab rat.

Hopkins further developed these themes in his 1987 book *Intruders*. In 15
September 1983, he received a letter from "Kathie Davis." She had read *Missing Time* and wrote him to describe a dream she had had in early 1978 of two small beings in her bedroom. From Davis's accounts and twelve other abductees, Hopkins came to believe the aliens had an unmistakable interest "in the process of human reproduction" going back to the Villas-Boas case.

Hopkins described the process as follows—female abductees were identified as donors during their childhood abductions. The implants allowed the aliens to "track" them. When they reached puberty, they would be reabducted. Ova would be removed, its genetic structure altered with alien characteristics, then replanted back in the human. The female abductees would carry the "baby" several months, then again be abducted. The human/alien child would be removed and brought to term.

Males were not immune to such breeding abductions, according to Hopkins. “Ed Duvall” recalled under hypnosis a sexual encounter with a hybrid alien. In this and other cases, a “suction device” was placed over the penis to remove the sperm. None of these breeding abductions could, according to Hopkins, be described as an erotic experience. “It was very perfunctory,” Duvall said, “a detached, clinical procedure.”

Once the hybrid children were born, the humans who had “donated” sperm or ova were (yet again) abducted and “shown” their “offspring.” The aliens even encouraged the humans to hold the “babies” in a kind of bonding exercise, according to Hopkins. Four women either dreamed or remembered under hypnosis being shown a tiny baby—gray in color and oddly shaped. Kathie Davis claimed to have seen two of her *nine* hybrid children and been allowed to name them. Nor did this cycle of abductions end here. Hopkins claimed the children of abductees were themselves targets for abductions.

Some of Hopkins’s abductees gave their impressions of why the aliens were doing these things. “Lucille Forman” had the impression of an alien society “millions of years old, of outstanding technology and intellect but not much individuality or warmth . . . the society was dying . . . children were being born and living to a certain age, perhaps preadolescence, and then dying.” The aliens were desperately trying to survive, through both taking new genetic material and exploiting human emotions.

Hopkins painted a progressively darker picture of the “relationship” be- 20
tween humans and aliens. “The UFO phenomenon,” Hopkins wrote, “seems able to exert nearly complete control over the behavior of the abductees.” He continued that the “implants” had “a controlling function as receivers” and that the abductees can “be made to act as surrogates for their abductors.” It is a basic tenet of the abduction myth that these alleged events were truly *alien* experiences—that they are not based on science fiction nor psychological aberrations. Hopkins said, “None of these recollections in any way suggests traditional sci-fi gods and devils . . . the aliens are described neither as all-powerful, lordly presences, nor as satanic monsters, but instead as complex, controlling, physically frail beings.”

Dr. David Jacobs (a pro-UFO historian) said in a 1986 MUFON[1] paper, “Contactee stories were deeply rooted in a science fiction model of alien behavior [while] abductee stories have a profoundly alien quality to them that are strikingly devoid of cultural programmatic content.”

Thomas E. Bullard said that Betty and Barney Hill had no cultural sources from which they could have derived their story, that they were “entirely unpredisposed.”

[1]MUFON (Mutual UFO Network) is an international scientific organization that studies UFOs.—Ed.

ENTIRELY UNPREDISPOSED?

Consider the following story—a group of men are in a rural area, at night, when they are abducted. They are rendered unconscious, loaded aboard strange flying machines, and taken to a distant place. They are then programmed with false memories to hide the time they were missing. One of them is converted into a puppet of his abductors. They are then released with no overt memories of what happened. But, years later, two of the group begin having strange, surreal dreams about what was done to them.

This story has many elements of abduction stories—loss of control, loss of memory (i.e., one's soul), and loss of humanity. It is not an abduction story. It has nothing to do with UFOs. It is the plot of the 1962 film *The Manchurian Candidate.*

Despite Hopkin's and Jacob's claims, the abductee myth has numerous sim- 25
ilarities with science fiction. Martin Kottmeyer has noted a number of these. In the film *Killers from Space* an abductee has a strange scar and missing memory. In *Invaders from Mars,* the Martians use implants to control humans. This includes not only adults, but their children as well. In the "Cold Hands, Warm Heart" episode of *The Outer Limits,* an astronaut (William Shatner) orbiting Venus loses contact with Earth for eight minutes. After returning to Earth, he has dreams that he landed on Venus and saw a Venusian approaching the ship. His body also starts changing into a Venusian.

"Dying planets" such as "Lucille Forman" described are a standard feature of science fiction—in H. G. Wells's masterpiece *War of the Worlds,* the Martians attacked because Mars was dying and Earth seemed their only hope for survival. Similar "dying planet" themes appeared in the films *This Island Earth, The 27th Day, Killers from Space,* and *Earth vs. the Flying Saucers. The Invaders* were "alien beings from a dying planet."

Crossbreeding between humans and aliens was a common science fiction film plot. They include *Devil Girl from Mars, I Married a Monster from Outer Space, The Mysterians, Village of the Damned, Mars Needs Women,* and the *Alien* film series.

The shape of aliens in abduction stories is well within the traditions of science fiction. The "bug-eyed monsters" of 1930s and 1940s pulp magazines often had large, bald heads. This was the shape of the projected image of the Wizard in the *Wizard of Oz.* The aliens in the film *Invasion of the Saucer Men* were "bald, bulgy-brained, googly-eyed, no-nosed," fitting the stereotyped image of UFO aliens. Kottmeyer noted that this "prompts worries that abductees are not only plagiarists, but have bad taste as well." In the 1960s, television series such as *The Twilight Zone* and *The Outer Limits* often featured dome-headed aliens. The original pilot for *Star Trek,* "The Cage" (telecast as the two-part episode "The Menagerie"), had short, large-headed, gray-skinned, bald, physically weak aliens with the power to control human minds.

The reasoning behind this particular shape was best expressed by an *Outer Limits* episode called "The Sixth Finger." The story involves the forced forward evolution of a human (David McCallum). As he evolves, his brain grows, his hair recedes, he becomes telepathic, and can control humans. The idea is that apes have small brains, are hairy, and strong. Modern man, in contrast, has a larger brain, has limited body hair, and is weaker. It therefore seems "right" that a future man would have a huge brain, no hair, and be physically frail.

All these similarities between science fiction concepts and the abduction 30
myth caused Kottmeyer to write, "It seems more sensible to flip Hopkins' allegation around. He says nothing about the aliens of UFO abductions resembling 'sci-fi.' I ask, is there anything about UFO aliens that does not resemble science fiction?"

A final note—Hopkins describes a half human/half alien being lacking the ability to feel emotions. It is just such a being which is the most famous character in all of science fiction—Mr. Spock of *Star Trek.* How "logical."

QUESTIONS ABOUT HYPNOSIS

Hopkin's abductees had no overt memories until they were hypnotized. The question becomes whether the abduction story is only a product of being hypnotized. A controlled test of hypnotic abduction accounts was conducted in 1977 by Dr. Alvin H. Lawson, a UFOlogist and English professor at California State University, Long Beach. He and others were dissatisfied with the hypnotic regression of abductees. They decided to ask a group of people with no significant UFO knowledge to imagine an abduction under hypnosis. The hypnotic sessions were conducted by Dr. William C. McCall, an M.D. with decades of clinical hypnosis experience. Lawson and the others had expected the imaginary abductees would need prompting. The result was quite different—Lawson wrote later:

> What startled us at first was the [subject's] ease and eagerness of narrative invention. Quite often, after introducing the situation—such as, "describe the interior"—Dr. McCall would sit back and the [subject] would talk freely with no more prompting than an occasional, "what's happening, now?"

Lawson compared four imaginary abduction accounts with features of four "real" abduction stories. The chart was an exact match. He concluded:

> It is clear from the imaginary narratives that a great many apparent patterns may originate in the mind and so be available to a witness—whether imaginary or "real." If a person who is totally uninformed about UFOs suddenly finds himself in the abduction sequence, it seems safe to assume that the individual's own sensibility will be able to provide under hypnotic regression, pattern details of his encounter which he may or may not have actually experienced in a "real" sense.

The implication of the Lawson study was not that there was a massive number of covert abductions. Rather, it shows that nearly anyone can, under hypnosis, provide an abduction story. Not surprisingly, abductionists and UFO groups have criticized and ignored the Lawson test.

35 The typical questioning during an abduction hypnotic session goes far beyond "what's happening, now." While researching the book *Mute Evidence,* Daniel Kagan was hypnotized by Dr. Sprinkle. During the session, Dr. Sprinkle said, "Imagine yourself in a spacecraft." There were no UFO images in the recurring dream Kagan was describing. Kagan was so shocked by the attempt to insert a UFO that he came out of the trance. Kagan concluded:

> Sprinkle had just demonstrated how much he had probably been responsible for the UFO imagery reported by so many of his hypnotic subjects. It meant that none of Sprinkle's case histories could be taken seriously, because his role as hypnotist could have been the single most powerful factor in introducing UFO images into the subjects' memories.

Another factor is that many of the stories originate with dreams. The dreams are real, but are they dreams of real events? One indication that they are, in fact, only dreams is the wildly irrational and contradictory nature of the stories. This includes one case in which an "abductee" reported hearing a voice from inside a UFO cry out, "I am Jimmy Hoffa!" Other psychological factors include the abductee's own mental state (even "normal" people can have hallucinations) and such organic brain disorders as temporal lobe epilepsy. Finally, there are the effects of personal experiences: under hypnosis, one abductee gave an extremely outlandish description of the aliens; when the hypnotist asked, "Are you sure?" the abductee responded, "No . . . that was something I saw in the Sunday comic section." Clearly, hypnosis is not the foolproof truth-finding technique the abductionists make it out to be.

In retrospect, it seems clear that the flying saucer myth was always an attempt to find a relationship with the aliens. Earlier myths were about contacts/interactions/struggles between humans and humanlike supernatural beings. Even the conservative Keyhoe had "Operation Lure." The contactees had their own "relationship," rooted in the worldview of the 1950s. When this faded, it was replaced, in the 1960s and 1970s, by the abduction myth, yet another attempt to find a relationship with mythological beings.

This human/alien relationship exactly mirrors society's changing attitudes toward authority, science, and sex. During the contactee era of the 1950s, the grandfatherly "Ike" was president. By the mid-1980s, authority was seen as absolutely evil. Science in the 1950s was seen as utopian. By the 1980s, this had changed into the belief science was antihuman. In 1978, Jose Inacio Alvaro described his alien sexual encounter as being pleasurable. By the 1980s, with the specter of AIDS haunting the bedroom, Hopkins was depicting it as a joyless, technological rape.

The function of mythology is to allow a society to relate to the larger world. This has not changed.

Practicing the Principles: Activities

KEEPING A RECORD OF YOUR EXPERIENCES

For one day try to keep a fairly complete record of your experiences. Record your experiences chronologically, but make sure that your record is more than just a chronology of events and when they happened. Try to describe in detail what you saw, heard, felt, and thought. Bring your record to class and discuss how keeping a record influenced your perceptions and memories of that day.

OBSERVING CAMPUS LIFE

Find an interesting spot on campus, and observe and record everything that takes place there for one hour. Keep track of the people who come by and what they do and say, but also pay attention to the plants, any animals or insects, the weather, the landscape, any buildings or machinery. Try to record as many details as you can. As an added dimension to this exploration, you might want to observe as a small group the same spot on campus for the same amount of time. Position yourselves so that you have different perspectives of the same general area, and then compare your observations. Discuss any differences you find.

THANKS FOR THE MEMORIES

If you have some photographs from your past, bring them to class. In a small group, share your photographs and take turns writing about the events portrayed in them. You can write about what you remember about the event depicted in the photograph. The other members of your group should write about what they can *infer* from the photograph and from what they know of you. Compare your accounts and discuss any differences. As an added dimension to this exploration, talk to friends and family who would also have memories of the same event. Compare their accounts of the photographed event with your own.

BECOMING AN EYEWITNESS

Try an experiment in being an eyewitness. Invite some actors to your class to stage a dramatic event (or use some members of the class who have a flair for the dramatic). This can be a short scene from a play or a "re-enactment" of a real event. (If you can't get actors, then show a short video clip.) Have half of the class watch the event while the other half takes a short break. Allow some of those who witness the event to take notes on what is happening. Ask the remainder of the witnesses to rely on their memories. After staging the event once, invite the rest of the class back in to ask questions about what happened. Then restage the event to compare the eyewitness testimonies with what actually happened. As a class, discuss any differences you discover in the testimonies of various participants.

READING THE NEWSPAPER

Bring to class three or four different newspapers: a large national daily, such as the *New York Times, Wall Street Journal,* or *Washington Post,* a regional or local paper, and a metropolitan daily from another town if you have access to one. Analyze these as a class and decide what counts as news for each newspaper and what perspective each paper provides on similar subjects. One obvious example will be differences in the coverage of sports: What is newsworthy about the Utah Jazz basketball team, for example, will certainly differ in Salt Lake City, Phoenix, Chicago, and New York City newspapers. But you will find that coverage of politics, crime, social events, and so forth differs as well. As an additional dimension to this activity, select a local event and write a brief news story that might be published in these different papers. Consider the differences in audience for a large national daily, a regional paper, and a local paper. Try to discover an aspect of the story that would interest each audience.

THE TRUTH IS OUT THERE

Accounts of the existence of UFOs, Bigfoot, ghosts, and the Loch Ness Monster all rely heavily on eyewitness reports. As a class, see how many accounts you can discover about one of these subjects. Consider a variety of sources: tabloid newspapers, scientific reports, government documents, Web pages—anything that might include such an account. Share these accounts in small groups, and evaluate them according to the following questions:

1. Is the source reliable, fair, responsible, and capable? Does the source have a personal interest or obvious bias?
2. Is this a firsthand account or a "report of a report"?
3. How far removed was the source from the event? To what extent is the source relying on memory?
4. Are the statements in the report consistent with one another and with other reports and evidence?
5. Are the statements verifiable?
6. Is all relevant evidence included?
7. Is the language detailed, specific, and clear?

SURVEYING INTERNET USE ON CAMPUS

Experts disagree about the extent to which families have access to computers and to the Internet in their homes. As a class, devise an informal survey that will measure how students at your college use computers and the Internet in their homes. (Remember to follow any college guidelines on using human subjects in research.) As you prepare this survey, consider whether college students may have had disproportionate access to computer technology. Try to measure computer and Internet access by race, income level, and geography. If you have time, try administering your survey off campus as well. Write an argument about computer access based on your data.

EXPLORING THE NET

What do people really miss if they don't have access to the Internet? As a class, do a quick survey of subject directories for the major search engines. (Perhaps each class member could choose a group of topics to focus on.) List what you consider useful and educational and what you consider frivolous. This list may say as much about you as it does about the Internet.) In particular, look for how government agencies and businesses use the Internet for important functions. After you share your lists with each other, try to come up with a class list of what kinds of important information would be available only through the Internet or would be much easier to find through the Internet.

Applying the Principles On Your Own

THE DIGITAL DIVIDE

The authors of the following essays are all trying to establish the existence and the size of a "digital divide," the difference between those who have access to computers and the Internet and those who don't. In addition to trying to discover whether such a gap exists, these authors also discuss the possible implications of such a technological gap.

The Digital Divide

CHRIS O'MALLEY

1 WILEY MIDDLETON is exactly the sort of fellow whom small towns love to welcome home. A 45-year-old graphics designer who honed his craft in bigger cities, Middleton moved back to his native Leadville, Colo., 18 months ago, eager to trade urban pressures for the serenity of this historic mining town of 3,421. But Leadville's telephone system is quaint too, and won't let his computer modem send the digital images that are his livelihood. This regularly forces Middleton to drive two hours to Denver to deliver electronic designs for brochures and ads. "I can't compete," he laments, again facing the prospect of leaving Leadville for the city. "The phone line is too small."

Or too narrow, to be more precise. The aging patchwork of thin wires and microwave towers that brings phone service to millions of Americans in remote spots like mountainous Leadville can barely transmit at speeds of 28.8 kilobits per second or less—assuming they can dial up a local Internet service at all. Meanwhile, much of the country has moved up to 56K modems or adopted one of the new broadband telephone and cable-company services that bring the Net to homes and businesses up to 100 times as fast. And the gap between online haves and have-nots appears to be widening.

"There is a growing digital divide," says Philip Burgess, president of the Center for the New West, an advocacy group whose board includes Solomon Trujillo, CEO of regional phone giant US West, and Utah Governor Michael Leavitt. The gulf, Burgess warns, could have "dire implications" for the social and economic fabric of many communities, particularly those in sparsely populated Western states.

Many of the start-up businesses that are driving employment and wealth in the new economy are built around the Internet and won't locate where it can't be speedily accessed. Even established businesses require high-speed Net connections to communicate effectively with customers, suppliers and employees. Professionals consider the bandwidth available in a locality when they decide where to work, live and buy vacation homes. The same calculation is made by affluent retirees who track investments online. At the same time, kids who aren't skilled on the Net face a growing disadvantage in college and the job market.

5 Not all the barriers to Internet access are geographic. The online population is still largely well educated, pale skinned and upper-middle income—a point the Rev. Jesse Jackson reinforced in recent speeches to Silicon Valley leaders. Whites are twice as likely as blacks to own a computer and three times as likely to be plugged into the Internet.

Dead zones in cyberspace can be found in states like Georgia, Mississippi and Maine, but the digital divide is particularly acute in Western states. Consider that in New Jersey the average distance between a customer and the phone company's nearest switching facility is about 2.6 miles. In Wyoming the distance is twice as far, and the cost to the phone company of reaching a customer is twice as high, according to figures from Sprint. Parts of the rural West have as few as half a dozen households per square mile (compared with thousands in urban and suburban areas); thus phone companies have less incentive to invest in stringing new lines there. "It does not make sense to build out into the rural market today," says Erik Olbeter, a telecommunications expert at the Economic Strategy Institute, a Washington-based think tank.

For decades Washington mandated subsidies that were aimed at putting a phone in every home, and some say that promise should extend to Internet service. "We're going to have to make a commitment to provide some level of [higher speed] Internet service to rural Americans," says Federal Communications Commission chairman William Kennard. Does that mean cable and computer companies could be required to chip into a universal service fund? "You bet," says Kennard.

That kind of equal-access talk incites the ire of many high-tech capitalists. "To tell me I've got to serve someone at a certain speed regardless of the cost because he chooses to live in the far reaches of Montana is not fair," says Garry Betty, president and CEO of Earthlink, a nationwide Internet-service provider. "Let them pay for it themselves."

Easier said than done, even if you've got the money. Total TV Network, a publisher of Bible-study materials and videos in Plano, Texas, considered moving to Durango, Colo., drawn by the pleasantly paced life-style and natural beauty. But the company was unable to get a couple of broadband T1 lines to approach what it had back home, so it ditched Durango. It's an all too familiar rejection for thousands of smaller cities and towns. In the past year, because Durango lacked sufficient bandwidth, it has had to turn away two firms seeking to open calling centers. Each might have hired 30 or 40 people.

Regional phone companies like US West complain that the FCC has been 10
slow to let them compete with long-distance giants such as AT&T, MCI and Sprint. The long-distance companies, in turn, accuse regional carriers of blocking access to their networks.

Despite the feuding, competition has come to some areas even well outside larger cities. But many of the service providers are cherry picking only the most lucrative business and professional customers, not smaller outfits or homes. For example, small-town ski meccas such as Aspen and Vail, while not far from blighted Leadville, enjoy fast and ready Internet access.

The problems are more than just economic. Not all the technological wizardry that permits high-speed Internet access in urban centers can work its magic in rural areas. So-called digital subscriber lines and 56K modems can't deliver higher speeds when your house is many miles from the nearest phone-switching office, and cable TV companies often leave the more remote spots to the satellite-dish sellers.

Satellite and other types of high-speed wireless technologies would seem to offer hope for spanning great distances and reaching the thinly wired. Indeed, the cost of downloading Web pages via a rooftop satellite dish is falling. Hughes'

DirecPC dish now sells for as little as $299, with monthly service starting at about $30. But this one-way technology won't serve the needs of many businesses and professionals like graphics designer Middleton.

Last month Motorola and Cisco Systems said they would jointly ante up $1 billion over four years to create wireless, high-speed Internet networks. AT&T and others are experimenting with cellular-like services that compress data and bring high-speed Web access into homes. That could help some rural areas. But while wireless towers can easily cover vast stretches of the plains, it's a far costlier matter to erect enough towers to throw signals around the Rocky Mountains. Moreover, many of the companies that are talking up wireless have densely packed urban businesses and mobile professionals in their sights, not rural customers.

15 A presidential panel this month recommended that federal funding for information-technology research be increased $1.3 billion over the next five years, in part to support an increasingly wired country. But a growing number of small towns have decided to take matters into their own hands. Some are forming cooperatives to string their own wire. Others are pulling strings. In Lusk, Wyo., a cajoling and farsighted mayor was able to get fiber-optic cable laid into his town of 1,600 and give its two schools access to a T1 line (and Lusk a starring role in Microsoft's ads on TV). Town leaders see it as a matter of survival. "We want our kids to come back here," says Twila Barnette, who manages the county Chamber of Commerce. "But we have to be able to offer them opportunities using this new technology."

A Nation of Net Have-Nots? No

THOMAS A. STEWART

1 INFORMATION technology has created more wealth faster than anything ever. The market value of Yahoo!, just three years public, has grown from $34 million to $27 billion—more than the entire U.S. steel industry is worth. An Internet bubble, some might say—and might be right—but surely Microsoft's no bubble, and it's worth more than General Motors, Ford, and DaimlerChrysler combined.

Technology has also created great opportunity. Each day 20 new U.S. technology and telecom companies are born. Some 1.2 million of the best jobs on the planet are held by Americans in the software and computer services industries. Other benefits are harder to quantify but no less real: the chance to buy any book in print, no matter how far you live from a decent bookstore; to fix a memo without retyping the whole damn thing; to leave phone messages when no one's home or call when you're stuck in traffic; to send mail around the world in seconds, not weeks; to see *Casablanca* every time you must.

Now the Internet—like telephones and televisions—is transforming society and markets. This has sparked debate about people who might be left behind. In studies called "Falling Through the Net," the Commerce Department presented 1994 and 1997 data that described a nation divided between information haves (white, prosperous, educated) and have-nots. For example, half the households with incomes of $75,000 or more had online service in 1997, vs. just 14% of those earning $25,000 to $35,000. There is a "digital divide" and a "digital apartheid," and—catchy phrases aside—a legitimate concern that it is wrong, even dangerous, if the wealth, work, and worthwhile things created by technology benefit only a few and leave the rest eating digital dust.

Rich people do get wired first, but that by itself is neither surprising nor worrisome. The rich owned horses while the poor walked, drove cars while others rode trams, watched color TV while others listened to AM radio.

5 Some technologies (Learjets, yachts) never spread beyond a few wealthy people, and no one cares.

The relevant questions are these:

How fast is the Internet spreading? Very. When this year's kindergartners were born, only the weird were wired. By December 1998, 61 million adult Americans were using the Internet, 50% more than did so 12 months earlier.

How deeply is it penetrating society? Also very. The Net shows signs of becoming as all-American as phones, TVs, and cars. The personal computer is less than 17 years old, yet 48% of U.S. households have at least one; 68% of American children live in a house with a PC. The number of schools with Internet connections zoomed from 65% in 1996 to 85% in 1998.

And the technology have-nots? The news—and it is news—is that their number is shrinking with stunning speed. The online gender gap is almost entirely gone. The age gap is narrowing; nearly a third of the membership of the American Association of Retired People owns a PC, and the number of wired fogies will steadily grow as death takes the oldest, who retired before the PC was born. The wage and race gaps are closing too. About 54% of Net veterans (online more than a year) earn more than $50,000 a year, according to a survey last November by the Pew Research Center; but 57% of newbies, online less than a year, earn under $50,000. Moore's Law is the poor's friend: As long as the cost of a given amount of processing power falls 50% every 18 months, fewer and fewer people will be unable to afford to compute.

10 One gap still yawns, that between the U.S. and the rest of the world. No other people have taken up the toys and tools of the Information Age as Americans have. The U.S. is also far and away the most wired big country. No. 3 in population, the U.S. has more phone lines and PCs than China, India, Indonesia, Brazil, Russia, Japan, Pakistan, Bangladesh, and Nigeria—the others in the big ten—combined. By global standards, nearly every American is an information Croesus.

Where will it stop? That's the 56 kilobits per second question. To achieve universal telephone service took an act of Congress—the Communications Act of 1934. No such help was needed with radios or television. At the start of the Clinton Administration, many thought the government should spend billions for a national information infrastructure; the private sector didn't wait. Later Newt Gingrich proposed that governments buy PCs for students; now they cost about the same as TV sets. The Net's hell-bent growth will plateau, but where? It could be as low as 67% (the percentage of households with cable TV); it could be as high as 95% (the percentage with telephones). Today, according to Forrester Research, 38% of households have Net access.

Someday people without Net access may be isolated or disadvantaged in a big way. The Kennedy-Nixon debates in 1960 mark a point at which anyone without TV was less than fully able to participate in the nation's life. The Net's not there yet. About the only things you can't do other than online are apply to MIT and listen to Steve Forbes announce his presidential rerun. If the advantages of being wired significantly outstrip the growth of the Netizenry, governments may need to help the last have-nots across the digital divide.

Why is this a management issue? Three reasons. First, for the CEO of Rip Van Winkle Enterprises: You have no choice. A plumber who is not online is on his way down the drain. In 1992 a friend told me that she found e-mail so compelling that she was starting to lose contact with friends without it. If you do not understand that, you are already losing suppliers, customers, and job candidates.

Second: Stop thinking of electronic commerce as a niche market. Sure, the money's small—today. E*Trade is a pimple on Merrill Lynch's nose—today. But just months after Merrill's executives derided Internet brokerage, they embraced it. If 61 million is a niche market, the Hall of Mirrors is a powder room.

Third: The medium is the message. The online population is demographi- 15
cally "normal," but that doesn't mean it's like mass markets of yore. Though human nature doesn't change, different media bring out different aspects of it. Television, Marshall McLuhan said, is a "cool" medium; that is, unintense. The Web is "kewl." It is intense. It is different. A while back (April) one of my colleagues wrote: "The Internet is not about creating ways to link people and ideas. It's all about marketing." *Fortune* is never wrong, so that was correct at the time. But times have changed.

Up on the Web (www.cluetrain.com) is a polite, in-your-face document called The Cluetrain Manifesto. The work of four longtime Web denizens, it's the subject of talk even in establishment places like the Conference Board. Some excerpts:

> Markets are getting smarter—and getting smarter faster than most companies. . . . People in networked markets have figured out that they get far better information and support from one another than from vendors. . . . The networked market knows more than companies do about their own products. And whether the news is good or bad, they tell everyone.

> Corporations do not speak in the same voice as these new networked conversations. . . . In just a few more years, the current homogenized "voice" of business—the sound of mission statements and brochures—will seem as contrived and artificial as the language of the 18th-century French court . . . Companies that speak in the language of the pitch, the dog-and-pony show, are no longer speaking to anyone.
>
> Can we talk?

Falling for the Gap

ADAM CLAYTON POWELL III

1 THE NEW YORK Jets have just won the Super Bowl. It must be true: There's a story on the front page of the *New York Times,* and there are color pictures in *Sports Illustrated*. And indeed it is true. Or, rather, it was true, a few decades ago. Only a truly inexperienced sports writer would suggest that the New York Jets are the current champions of the NFL.

Did you hear that the Dow Jones industrial average has topped 1,000? That, too, is old news, as even the most junior financial writer must know.

How about this one: There is a broad and widening gap on the Internet between white and minority Americans. This familiar claim, often asserted as a fact by policy makers and digerati alike, is also based on old information. Reinforced by White House press releases and presidential candidates' speeches, the idea is so ubiquitous that even the usually well-informed have come to believe that white Americans are online and minorities are not.

Not so. It may have been true in 1996 or 1997, when the Internet was only a few years old as a popular medium and personal computers cost thousands of dollars. But today, with dirt-cheap Internet access and computers approaching the costs of television sets, assertions of a "digital divide" or "racial ravine" are as correct as identifying Joe Namath as football's current MVP or pinning last week's Dow at 1,000.

5 Misled by stereotypes, misinformed about survey techniques, and misdirected by interest groups, the media have treated the "digital divide" as a crisis requiring government intervention. As a result, billions of dollars might be spent to address needs that no longer exist.

To understand how this happened, start with stereotypes. East Coast journalists typically equate "minority" with "African American," portraying the country as divided between black and white. This view omits the fastest growing minority group, Hispanic Americans, who in just a few years will be the largest minority group in the country.

Confusing "minority" with "African American" also leads journalists and analysts to forget that it is not among whites but among Asian Americans that Internet and computer use are approaching levels of penetration comparable to those of the telephone, television, and indoor plumbing. So even using the old survey data, it was always inaccurate to claim that minority Americans were not online in large numbers.

But the issue of dated information is crucial, especially because a year or two in "Internet time" is the equivalent of a decade for older media. The findings of the most frequently cited "digital divide" study, released last summer by the U.S. Department of Commerce, were presented and widely reported as new information. The study was actually an analysis of surveys in 1998 and earlier. When it was released, more-current information was already available from market research firms, but only a handful of news organizations reported the newer data.

The Commerce Department study made page one headlines with its conclusion that the United States faced a "racial ravine" dividing online white Americans from information-poor minorities. "For many groups, the digital divide has widened as the information 'haves' outpace the 'have nots' in gaining access to electronic resources," it said. "Between 1997 and 1998, the divide between those at the highest and lowest education levels increased 25 percent, and the divide between those at the highest and lowest income levels grew 29 percent."

That sounds impressive, but if you look more closely you may spot a crucial 10
methodological flaw. Among reporters for the major daily newspapers, only John Schwartz of the *Washington Post* noted the problem. "Last year's study did not collect information about out-of-home access," wrote Schwartz. "It is not possible, therefore, to say whether the digital divide is growing based on access from all places." In other words, the Commerce Department's claim of a "widened" gap was not supported by the data it cited, because the surveys asked different questions from year to year.

"We never stated that we have any information about widening with regard to anywhere access," says Larry Irving, who directed the government study before he resigned as assistant secretary of commerce. "But certainly we can prove the in-home access gap is widening."

Yet according to every survey taken in the last few years, Americans get their online access at work and at school in far larger numbers than at home. According to "The Internet News Audience Goes Ordinary," a 1999 report from the Pew Research Center for the People and the Press, 62 percent of employed Americans go online through their jobs, and 75 percent of students go online from their schools. The Commerce Department study reported only on use of personally owned computers, thus excluding the millions of users (including this writer) who are online every day but do not own a computer. This is like assuming you don't need a driver's license unless you buy a car.

Regardless of whether the questions in the federal survey were correctly phrased, they were asked in 1998. Surveys conducted this year have found not only that minorities are not falling behind but that they are catching up.

"If you missed Christmas [1998], you missed a big surge," says Ekaterina Walsh, author of "The Digital Melting Pot," a report based on 1999 data collected by Forrester Research of Cambridge, Massachusetts. "Quite a lot of people got cheap PCs. We were surprised ourselves, because we were projecting lower numbers for online penetration and commerce [than the study found]. Even a month made a big difference." Walsh adds that the federal report may undercount or ignore WebTV, which in 1998 was one of the lowest-priced devices enabling consumers to go online.

"I think we did miss a certain amount of information with regard to lower- 15
priced PCs since December," concedes Irving, the former Commerce Department official. But he stands firm on the question of whether the department's study was misleading because it tracked only computer use at home. "No one has been tracking out-of-home access, as far as we know," he says.

Larry Irving, meet Bob Mancuso. Mancuso, marketing manager for Nielsen Media Research in New York, says his firm produces a regular report on out-of-home Internet access and use. Forrester Research also provides tracking data on out-of-home use.

The *Orlando Sentinel* was one of the few newspapers that noted the problem with focusing exclusively on Internet use at home. The *Sentinel* also reported inconsistencies among the 1994, 1997, and 1998 federal surveys, noting that the earlier surveys did not even ask specifically about computer ownership; they asked whether respondents owned a modem. *Sentinel* reporter Maria Padilla also quoted comments from Walsh and other researchers challenging the government's conclusions. "Race has nothing to do with whether you adopt technology or not," Walsh told Padilla.

Donna Hoffman, an associate professor of management at Vanderbilt University who studies Internet access and popularized the term *digital divide,* says racial differences do indeed disappear when you measure access and use, rather than modem or computer ownership. "We do not find gaps in usage, given access," Hoffman says. But she defends the federal study because, however shaky its conclusions, it could have an impact on the policy debate, encouraging government spending on computers for poor people (a policy that Irving also favors). "Getting PCs into the homes of all Americans is critical," she argues.

Hoffman concedes that the research by Nielsen and Forrester, using 1999 data, was more current than her studies and the federal government's, which were based on data from 1998 or earlier. But she says older data are still useful. "We track events over time the better to understand the evolution in access and usage," she says. "We have learned an enormous amount about technology usage by carefully studying these events over time. The fact is that the data show a digital divide for those time points. The data also allow us to understand the likely impact of policy initiatives."

There is no shortage of those initiatives. Within hours of the federal report's 20
release, President Clinton, Vice President Gore, the National Association for the Advancement of Colored People, and the National Urban League all announced programs to buy computers for minority Americans.

But the recent data from Forrester and Nielsen suggest that such programs may be misdirected. According to Forrester, Hispanic Americans were slightly ahead of white Americans in computer use earlier this year, and African Americans were closing the black-white gap at a rate that could lead to parity within the next 12 months. In terms of Internet use, the truly disadvantaged may well be Native Americans, who were not covered by the federal report. Data from the Black College Communication Association and other sources also indicate disparities between educational institutions, including lower Internet access at predominantly minority colleges and universities. This, too, was lost in the focus on home computer ownership.

"Questions of colored folk and cyberspace are often plagued by overstatements of the bad news, understatements of the good news, and misplaced concern about the importance of computers," says Omar Wasow, an MSNBC commentator and founder of BlackPlanet.com and other black-oriented Web sites.

"For example, a few years ago people were concerned that women were dramatically underrepresented on the Internet. Yet because women were signing up at America Online and other access providers at an incredible clip, in a few short years women have practically achieved parity in their online access. . . . The critical statistic is not what are the current rates of usage but rather [what are] the current rates of adoption."

Wasow cites the history of another electronic medium. "We forget that once upon a time televisions were a rare and expensive device that only a few households were lucky enough to possess, and now every home has nearly a TV per person," he says. "Over time, most advanced technologies that are available only to an elite few become widely dispersed among the broader population."

In other words, there is no debate about the television-rich vs. the television-poor in America. Every American who wants one has a television set. And now that some personal computers cost less than TVs and Internet access is cheaper than cable (or even free), the data do indeed show that every American who wants one is getting a PC.

But the media echo chamber has drowned out updated information with old 25
studies and stereotypes. Even informed technology observers have mistaken last summer's federal report for current information. In the cover story for the August issue of *Yahoo! Internet Life* magazine, Farai Chideya of ABC News wrote that "the average Web user is different from the average American: more likely to be white or Asian . . . and less likely to be Latino, black or a blue collar worker." Her source? That Commerce Department report, based on interviews in 1998.

"Although middle-class blacks and other minorities are getting online in substantial numbers, there remains an enormous disparity between whites' computer use and blacks'," wrote the usually perceptive Internet observer Jon Katz in a late-summer column on the Freedom Forum Web site. His source? The new edition of the widely respected book *Technology and the Future,* edited by Albert Teich, the director of science and policy programs at the American Association for the Advancement of Science. And what was the book's source? The Commerce Department study. So Mayor Giuliani, where's the ticker-tape parade for Joe Namath?

Racial Digital Divide

LOGAN HILL

RECORD numbers of students are going online, according to UCLA's annual survey of college freshmen released this past January. But this new battery of Internet statistics—the latest in a field updated as rapidly as software—confirms that a digital divide persists between the races. Of the freshmen surveyed at private universities, 90.2 percent reported using the Internet for schoolwork, but just 77.6 percent of students at traditionally black public colleges said the same. The study reveals that this problem is linked to the lack of computer access at public high schools, which 92.2 percent of the respondents from black public colleges attended, compared with less than two-thirds of the students surveyed at private universities. 1

Unfortunately, the press garbled these results. First, the *New York Times*'s William Honan exaggerated the racial divide, reporting that the UCLA researchers found a "great disparity in computer mastery between students entering elite private colleges, 80.1 percent of whom say they use computers regularly, and those attending traditionally black public institutions, 41.1 percent of whom say that." These statistics actually refer to the percentage of students who use e-mail, not computers. The gap in scholastic Internet usage is significant (12.6 percentage points) but not inexplicably huge, while the e-mail discrepancy indicates that minority students, who are less likely to own PCs, are also less likely to have their own e-mail accounts or free time for nonessential computing at overburdened public terminals.

Honan's relatively benign conflation of these statistics soon mutated into a different and more troubling story. On January 25, *Slate* columnist Scott Shuger, dubbed a "cool cat" by William F. Buckley Jr. and recently wedged between Maureen Dowd and Matt Drudge as one of *Newsweek*'s "20 Stars of the New News," sent out his site's widely read "Today's Papers" e-mail brief. Shuger summarized the *Times*'s coverage but appended the following advice: "Before too much redistributive social policy gets made around such results, it might be good to add a question to the survey: 'Do you have a luxury sound system or a car less than two years old, or a luxury sound system in that car?'" Having stumbled upon such stereos—and students—at Freaknik, a spring break party for black college students in Atlanta, Shuger concluded that "computer/Internet paucity may be a function of [black students'] own interests and choices rather than that of affordability."

The *Times* granted Shuger three paragraphs of blustering self-defense (and just two words of quoted criticism) the following week, excusing him as a groggy nocturnal Web reporter. But logic like Shuger's is far from innocuous. In its report "The Myth of an Emerging Information Underclass," the Cato Institute opined that "the fact that people do not log on does not necessarily imply that they cannot afford to do so. They may simply have other priorities." Last year, a combination of such cyberculture-of-poverty arguments and hysteria over a "Gore Tax" led Congress to slash the VP's Internet access program from $2.5 billion to nearly half that.

Advocates like B. Keith Fulton, director of technology programs and policy 5
for the National Urban League, have little patience for such speculation. In predominantly white classrooms, Fulton points out, students are three times more likely to have Internet access than students in mostly minority classrooms. He says, "People like [Shuger] are not held accountable. They aren't out there working on studies, so they make a stereotyped comment and it gets attention. But we can train 1,400 people in an LA computer center, they can earn $31 million in salaries, and nobody talks about that." Fulton and the organizers of more than 250 community technology centers across the country (see www.ctcnet.org for more information) help provide computers, training and resources to minorities through schools, libraries and public centers.

The racial digital divide is real and cannot simply be attributed to income, as corroborated by a series of federal studies. With historically inferior technology access, minorities have been discouraged from computer education, recreation and professions. Currently, African-Americans and Latinos compose 22 percent of the Silicon Valley area's population, but only 4 percent of employees at its major firms are African-American, and just 8 percent are Latinos—and many work in service or support positions.

These stark numbers result from a systemic denial of training as well as access, which is bad news for techno-optimists who foresee democracy flourishing as every television set becomes an Internet node. Even as the Internet becomes more accessible, a skills gap will persist unless public schools are able to offer equitable teaching and other resources. Studies by the National Science Foundation and Vanderbilt University have found that even minority students who are able to surf do not receive the same levels of practical computer training that would allow them to share in the economic benefits of the high-tech boom.

Smaller class size and higher teacher pay might well do more to improve heavily minority schools than a blueberry iMac, but teachers can't even begin to impart technological knowledge until they have computers and support. Linda Sax, director of the UCLA survey, says that although "nearly everyone's misinterpreted something" about the study, it nonetheless offers some reason for hope in this regard: "Our survey shows that minority students are using the computers at school. That's excellent. That's working." But, she adds, African-American students own fewer computers, and "there won't be equity [in access] until every student has their own computer." Ramon Harris, who directs the Executive Leadership Foundation's Transfer Technology Project, a program that works to enhance computer course programs at traditionally black colleges, has the same goal in mind. He says, "Universal computing access is necessary and should be subsidized like a utility. Like water. Like light. It's that simple."

Crossing the Digital Divide

JENNIFER LACH

ASK FELIPE KORZENNY, cofounder of Cheskin Research in Belmont, California, what the future holds for the Hispanic digital marketplace and he's got one word: alliances. The recently announced partnership between computer maker Gateway and Web portal Quepasa.com supports his theory, he says. Gateway bought a 7.6 percent stake in Quepasa, which entitles it to be the exclusive provider of computer products on the Latino portal. The two companies will also engage in joint marketing and promotional programs targeted to Hispanics. Marketing to Hispanics isn't completely new to Gateway. Last fall, the computer maker launched toll-free phone lines for Spanish-speaking clients, tech support in Spanish, and other customer-friendly services. 1

Gateway, Korzenny contends, is on to something—and Cheskin's new study, "The Digital World of the U.S. Hispanic," proves it. While household computer penetration has increased 43 percent in the general U.S. population during the past two years, it's risen 68 percent among U.S. Hispanics. "In focus groups, Hispanic consumers tell us that they are adopting the technology because they don't want to be left behind, particularly for their kids' sake," says Korzenny. Roughly 58 percent of Hispanic households in the Cheskin study do not own computers, and of that group, 54 percent plan to buy one in the near future. What's holding back the rest? Price is cited most often—46 percent of Latino households without computers say they are too expensive—but other factors run close behind. Roughly 40 percent believe they don't need computers, and 29 percent say they are not familiar with them. High-tech companies, Korzenny contends, are partly to blame since few have bothered to educate Hispanics about the convenience of computers.

In some ways, wired Hispanics today differ significantly from Hispanics who aren't online. They tend to be better educated (14.4 years of schooling versus 9.5 years among nonusers), younger (34 versus 40), and much more likely to own a credit card (75 percent versus 39 percent). Latino Web users also consume fewer hours of Spanish-language media a week than non-users (13 versus 24). Overall, the study finds that Hispanic Web surfers lean more toward English than Spanish—and that preference carries over to the places they frequent online. Roughly 58 percent of Latinos online say they use Yahoo!; while only 11 percent mention Quepasa. And Quepasa ranked the highest of any Hispanic-targeted site, including Star Media, Yupi, and El Sitio.

Despite the results, Korzenny still believes there's room for Latino sites online, as long as they understand the needs of their target audience. "Hispanic sites must address the information needs of those who are coming on to the Internet for the first time," he says. "These consumers need orientation on what they can do online."

The study also finds that online Hispanics carry out many of the same 5
activities that the general population does. Three out of four use the Internet for information gathering; 31 percent for sending e-mail. Roughly 25 percent buy products online, with books, music, and airline tickets at the top of their shopping list.

Chapter 8
Arguing Claims about Causality

Types of Causes

Causality refers to a relationship between events in which an earlier event somehow causes or influences a later event or in which a later event somehow explains an earlier one. It is a statement about existence to say "The king died and then the queen died." The later event in this sequence merely follows the earlier one in time. But it is a statement about causality to say "The king died and so the queen died." This statement asserts that the death of the king (the earlier event) caused or influenced the death of the queen (the later event). Like questions about existence, questions about causality can focus on the past, present, or future: Why did this happen? Why is it happening now? Why will this happen again?

Unlike questions about existence, which are about whether an event or phenomenon occurred or about the nature of an event or phenomenon, questions about causality are about the relationship between two or more events or phenomena and between causes and effects. Did one cause the other? Did the second result from the first? Are they in some way connected? Here are sample questions about causality:

What causes sudden infant death syndrome?

How does work affect the family?

What are the causes of poverty?

How can famine in Africa be reduced?

What are the causes of terrorism?

How would school vouchers affect the country's educational system?

Complex decisions may involve questions of existence and causality. In a murder case the jury may need to consider how a killing occurred (causality), whether the killing was premeditated (existence), what motivated the killing (causality), and whether the accused killed the victim (existence). Understanding the differences between these two kinds of questions about experience can help us to solve a lot of misunderstandings and negotiate some of the disagreements about experience that inevitably arise in a community.

A number of relationships are included under the term *causality:*

- A *sufficient cause* describes a relationship in which, under normal conditions, one event or phenomenon (the sufficient cause) is always followed by a second: Something dropped from a height falls to the ground. Water that reaches 100 degrees celsius begins to boil.
- A *necessary cause* is an event or phenomenon that must exist for a second to occur but that is not sufficient in itself to cause the second. Heat, fuel, and oxygen are all necessary for a fire to burn, but no one of these can cause a fire by itself. A combination of necessary causes can become a sufficient cause. The right combination of heat, fuel, and oxygen will cause a fire to start all by itself.
- A *constraint* is a necessary element that, when removed, allows an event to occur. For instance, the relatively moderate communist government of Yugoslavia maintained peace amid ethnic tension for years. When the communists lost power, the constraint on ethnic violence was removed, and war erupted in Bosnia, Macedonia, and Kosovo. The government didn't cause the ethnic unrest or violence. Instead, the communist government constrained the forces that resulted in violence when that constraint was removed.
- A *contributing cause* is something that may enable or influence a second event or phenomenon but that is not necessary or sufficient to cause the

second. Snow on a road may enable an automobile accident, but snow does not cause the accident by itself. Nor is it a necessary condition for auto accidents; accidents occur without the presence of snow.

- A *correlation* is a relationship between two events or phenomena that occur together without it being clear whether one caused the other or whether both resulted from a third cause. For instance, philosophy majors have a higher rate of acceptance into law school than students with other undergraduate majors. The two phenomena are correlated. But does studying philosophy better prepare students for law school, or are students who choose to study philosophy naturally attuned to what law schools look for? Another correlation is between nearsightedness (the ability to see near objects better than distant objects) and reading ability. But does nearsightedness encourage reading (a preference for close tasks), or does excessive reading lead to nearsightedness? (Just notice how many English teachers wear glasses.)
- An *agent* is an individual who takes purposeful action to bring about a change: a person walking across a room to turn off a television, eating, throwing a baseball, playing the piano; a dog begging for food; a cat brushing up against a person's leg. All of these examples describe purposeful motion, motion with an intention to change some event or phenomenon.
- An *instrument* or *agency* is the means by which an agent can cause something to happen. The National Rifle Association makes this distinction in its famous line "Guns don't kill people. People kill people." People are the necessary agents for firing guns to kill others. A gun is the instrument or agency.
- A *logical cause* justifies or explains a situation. The "reason" in an argument that justifies a claim is a logical cause: You can't have any candy because you haven't eaten your dinner (the assumption is that you can only have candy after dinner).
- A *purpose* motivates action. It is a cause that follows what it causes, with the later event or phenomenon serving as the purpose of the earlier one: If you go to the refrigerator to get something to eat, you could think of yourself as an agent causing the motion that takes you to the refrigerator, but you could also think of your purpose or intention as a cause (getting something to satisfy your hunger).

The following terms signal a statement about causality:

X has the effect of

X facilitates

X leads to

X influences

X is a factor in

X is linked to

Because of X
X deters
As a result of X
X increases the likelihood that
X determines
X contributes to
X causes

Constructing Cause-and-Effect Diagrams

One way to sort through the many different types of causes is to use a cause-and-effect diagram. The cause-and-effect diagram, developed in Japan by Kaoru Ishikawa, is a simple way of representing causality visually, allowing you to explore the complexity of causal relationships and correlations. There are two kinds of cause-and-effect diagrams. The first is called a *dispersion analysis.* To construct a dispersion analysis diagram, you begin with an event, usually presented in Ishikawa's model as a "problem." Then you draw a line that represents the chronology leading up to the event or problem. Next you draw lines leading into this main line and label these as different causes. (Because of its appearance, a dispersion analysis is sometimes called a "fish" diagram. The ribs of the "fish skeleton" represent the possible causes for the event.) Figure 8.1 shows a simple model of a cause-and-effect diagram using dispersion analysis.

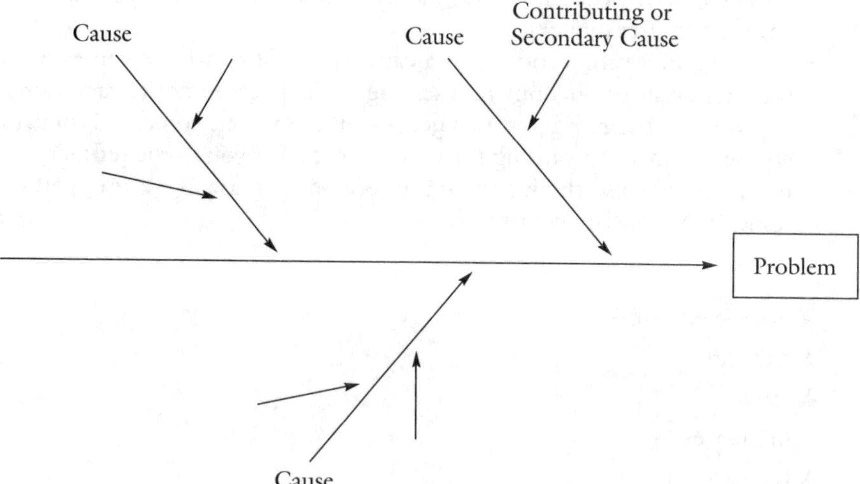

Figure 8.1 A simple cause-and-effect diagram.

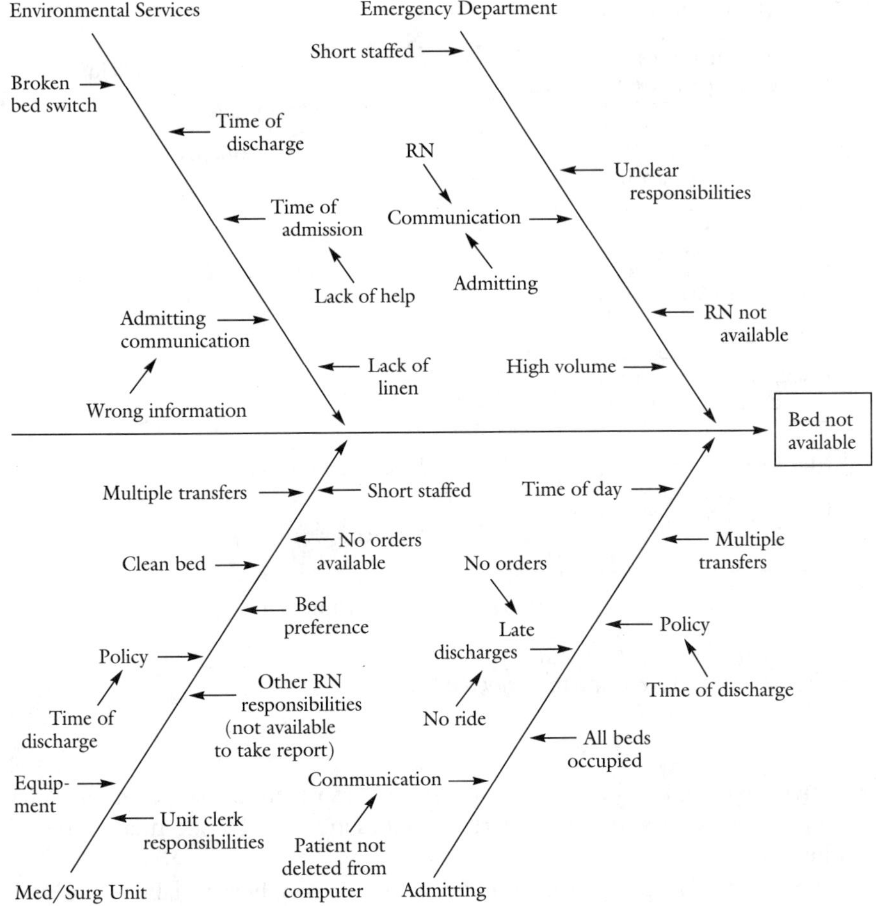

Figure 8.2 Cause-and-effect diagram for hospital emergency admission.

Let's assume you are trying to solve the following problem. A major hospital is continually running short of beds. Personnel face acute difficulties in moving patients from the emergency room to beds for recovery, and nothing hospital managers do has helped the problem. To understand the problem better, you might construct a dispersion analysis diagram identifying the four departments that cause the shortage: environmental services, emergency, the medical/surgery unit, and admitting. You would then identify several secondary or contributing causes. The dispersion diagram might look like Figure 8.2.

The second type of cause-and-effect diagram is a *process classification*. This diagram is a flowchart that represents the sequence of actions leading up to a particular event. Various causes that might influence the flow of the sequence are represented by lines extending from the boxes in the flowchart. To illustrate this diagram, let's say that you are trying to understand the problems affecting a

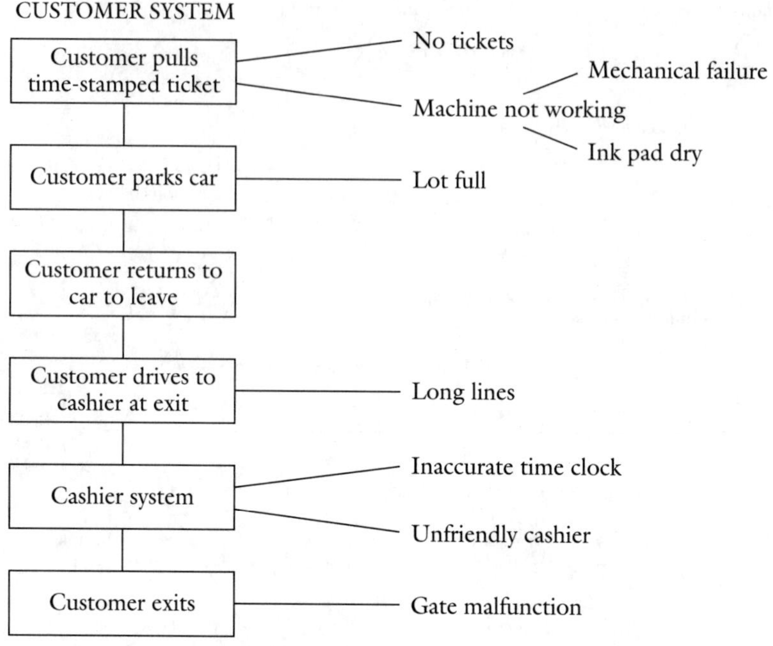

Figure 8.3 Process classification diagram.

parking garage. Figure 8.3 shows how you could represent the stages in the parking system in the form of a flowchart, as well as indicate the potential causes of malfunction.

When identifying causes on these diagrams, it may help to label what kind of cause each is: sufficient cause, necessary cause, constraint, contributing cause, or purpose. You also need to remember that developing cause-and-effect diagrams works best as part of a group brainstorming activity. Draw the diagrams quickly, with everyone suggesting causes, no matter how far-fetched, and then revise the diagram to describe more accurately the relationships among causes.

Explaining Causality

Arguing about causality is always a tricky affair. Causes are rarely self-evident. The fact that one event or phenomenon follows another does not mean that the first caused the second. Such an assumption is a *post hoc* fallacy (see Chapter 4), from the Latin *post hoc, ergo propter hoc* ("after this, therefore because of this"). Many superstitions arise from this fallacy. A black cat crosses your path on your way to school, and later that day you fail your chemistry test. Did the black cat bring you bad luck, or are there other possible causes? Experience is so complex and chaotic that the numbers of factors involved in a single event are usually multiple and changing. Rarely is causality as neat as one pool ball striking another and causing it to move.

Although knowledge of causal relationships is rarely absolute, some causal arguments are more believable or persuasive than others. Causal statements are based on probability and are more or less convincing depending on the reasons used to support them. Causal statements are usually most convincing when the cause and the effect are close to one another in time and space, when the event or phenomenon can be observed repeatedly, when the cause can be isolated by experiment, when there is a clear explanation of how one event or phenomenon leads to another, or when one can reason by analogy from a similar situation where the causes are known. Simpler explanations are usually more convincing than more complicated explanations (though complicated ones may in fact be true); such explanations are "models" or "theories" of the mechanism for the causal relationship.

To summarize, here are the most common ways to argue for a causal relationship:

1. Provide a model or theory to explain the mechanism for causation.
2. Use inductive methods, such as scientific experiments or statistical research, to show a probable link.
3. Use an analogous situation, a precedent or similar case, in which the causes are known.

PROVIDING A MODEL OR THEORY TO EXPLAIN CAUSALITY

A model or a theory is a detailed explanation of how something works. For instance, a car's engine is a complex series of causes and effects designed to be controlled by a human agent (the driver). The engineer's design for the engine is the model or theory describing how this complex system works. The theory of evolution describes an extremely complex system of causes and effects to explain changes in life forms over time. Whenever you plan something or act with purpose, you are using a model or theory to predict the possible outcomes of your actions. With many human actions, however, the model for action is so internalized as to be automatic. For example, I don't have to plan how to get from the couch to the cupboard to find something to eat, but my two-year-old daughter develops all kinds of plans for getting to the cupboard. Her actions are based on models and theories.

Sometimes there can be more than one theory to explain the causes of the same event. For instance, in a court trial, lawyers may disagree about what brought about the defendant's actions. The prosecution might argue that the defendant was an agent who acted intentionally and should therefore be considered guilty. The defense might argue that the defendant is legally insane and that the defendant's mental state caused the criminal behavior. This kind of debate requires some kind of model or theory about the human mind and the relationship between the mind and behavior. It also requires theories about action, intention, and guilt. The debate, in this case, might focus on the validity of the theories or else on the applicability of the theories to the defendant.

The debate surrounding the theory of organic evolution provides another example of a disagreement about models and theories. Life on earth is constantly changing, and it had to originate somewhere. Evolutionary biologists try to develop models that will explain the creation of the earth according to the standards of scientific proof. Some Christian theologians try to explain the origin of the earth by referring to the Bible as an authoritative text, using models that meet the standards of religious or spiritual truth. These models come into conflict because scientists and theologians do not agree on a common set of criteria for evaluating truth.

What happens when scientists themselves disagree about the models or theories used to explain causality? Generally, scientists favor a theory that explains phenomena in the most comprehensive way. For two theories that both explain equally well, scientists tend to favor the simpler one. Logicians call this preference for the simplest and most comprehensive explanation *Occam's razor* (named after a famous logician).

USING INDUCTIVE METHODS

A *laboratory experiment* re-creates direct experience in a controlled environment. Its validity relies on the similarity between the controlled environment and the event or phenomenon being re-created and on the ability of the scientists conducting the experiment to observe and record data. Experiments often use instruments to provide data not accessible to the unaided physical senses, data that must be interpreted by the scientists. Accurate observation and interpretation require precise language as well. The strength of an experiment lies in its ability to repeat conditions that will verify observations. Similar conditions should lead to similar results and conclusions.

USING AN ANALOGY, PRECEDENT, OR SIMILAR CASE

A third way to argue for a causal relationship to identify a precedent or similar case in which the causes are known and then make an analogy between that case and another where the causes are less certain. Arguing by analogy is difficult because analogies depend on similarities and any analogy contains some dissimilarities. Because there are always differences between two similar cases, the strength of an analogy depends upon the similarities being more important—not necessarily more numerous—than those differences. If the audience does not accept the assumption that the two cases are similar, the writer must support the analogy. One way to do so is to point out a number of specific similarities, based on the assumption that the two cases will be similar in other ways as well. Another way to support an analogy is to show that the two cases are similar in essential ways, even though they may be different in a number of other ways. The writer then has the burden of showing why these similarities are essential.

The danger in using an analogy is making a *false comparison*. A false comparison is a logical fallacy in which an analogy is made between two cases that are really more different than similar or that are different in essential ways. To test the similarities between two cases, try the following. First of all, list the features of each of the cases you are comparing. Then identify the features that they share. Finally, determine whether the two cases are more similar or different in terms of the features they share. For instance, many writers compared the war in Bosnia to the Vietnam War. The first step in testing this comparison is to list the features of the two wars. In what ways can a modern war be described? Here are some possibilities: level of U.S. involvement, level of United Nations involvement, types of weapons and tactics used, risk to U.S. security, risks to European security, number of civilian casualties, ideological differences, involvement of other countries. The next step is to compare the two wars according to the features listed. Is the level of U.S. involvement in Bosnia and Vietnam similar or different? Are the weapons and tactics similar or different? Is the risk to U.S. security similar or different? After asking about similarity or difference for each of the features, you can evaluate the similarities and differences to determine whether the war in Bosnia and the war in Vietnam are more similar than different or are similar in essential ways. If the audience accepts the similarities between the two wars, one could then argue that the results of U.S. involvement in Bosnia would be similar to the results of U.S. involvement in Vietnam.

The Principles in Action: Readings

The first two essays that follow describe the causes and effects of an American obsession, the lawn, and a primarily American tragedy, rampage killings. "The Lawn: A History of an American Obsession" is the conclusion of Virginia Jenkin's book-length study of the social history of Americans' obsession with lawns. She describes how Americans became enamored of green carpets of grass in the first place and then outlines the environmental effects of this obsession. Ford Fessenden's front page *New York Times* article, "Young Rampage Killers," presents an analysis of data profiling 102 killers and the circumstances surrounding 100 rampage killings that took place between 1949 and 1999. In the third essay, "Manure, Minerals, and Methane," Michael W. Fox examines the environmental and social consequences of factory farming, or agribusiness. Finally, in the fourth essay, "In and Out of Elevators in Japan," Terry Caesar examines aspects of Japanese culture by identifying the relationship between Japanese peoples' behavior inside and out of elevators. As you read these essays, consider the following questions:

1. What are the causes of our obsession with lawns? What are the effects of this obsession?
2. How do these authors explain causality? To what extent do they rely on a theory or mechanism f causation, use inductive reasoning or experimentation, or argue from precedent or analogy?
3. What is Virginia Jenkins's attitude toward lawns? Michael Fox's toward factor farms? And Terry Caesar's toward the Japanese?
4. How do these authors portray their expertise on the their topic?

After reading these essays, try constructing a cause-and-effect diagram for each one to understand the complex relationships of causes and effects.

From The Lawn: A History of an American Obsession

VIRGINIA JENKINS

FRONT LAWNS are the product of two elements: the ability and the desire to grow and tend lawn grasses. The desire for lawns developed as homeowners were exposed to a new landscape aesthetic in upper-class suburbs and on golf courses and as they were taught to care for their lawns through educational programs and cleanup campaigns, spearheaded by prominent citizens in communities across the nation. The ability to grow lawn grasses took a little longer. It became possible to grow lawn and pasture grasses in the northeastern section of the United States long before it became fashionable to have a lawn. In hotter and drier climates, the ability to grow lawns (and lawns themselves) had to wait for the agricultural revolution of the twentieth century. The American lawn industry began with the first lawn mower patent in 1869 and grew to be a multibillion-dollar industry with national and international companies serving homeowners from coast to coast. The industry nurtured the aesthetic that called for a smooth, green lawn in front of American homes. Advertising and popular magazines, the increasingly popular game of golf, labor-saving inventions, new grasses, and shifts in living and working patterns, combined with tremendous personal mobility, all contributed to a domestic landscape in the United States that is similar from coast to coast. Americans have used close-cut grass to beautify everything from graveyards to factories, from highways to the White House. 1

Lawns represent time, money, and labor. Both the idea of the lawn and lawn equipment were sold to the American public by appealing to a sense of status. In the early twentieth century, advertisements promised the homeowner the same grass seed or equipment used by men with large estates. After World War II, homeowners were assured by television stars and professional golfers that they too could have a good lawn, presumably like those in Hollywood and on the televised golf courses. More recently, the little "please stay off the grass" signs, placed on lawns after professional sprayings, offer a certain cachet to the homeowner who can afford to spend several hundred dollars a year for the service.

Lawns are so deeply rooted in American culture that they have become icons used to sell a whole range of products unconnected with the lawn. Seven Up used the image of a young woman sitting on a riding mower drinking a bottled soda to sell its product. An advertisement for Absorbine Junior, a muscle liniment, featured a cartoon character with a lawn mower and the caption "Oh! My aching back!" Fence manufacturers sold fences to protect lawns from neighbors' dogs and children. A manufacturer of cast-iron sewage pipes warned that accidents or problems with inferior pipes could wreck a lawn.

In addition to advertising, lawns and lawn mowing can be found throughout American popular culture. One hundred and fifty-five communities in thirty-six states have "lawn" as part of (or all of) their name. Lawn mowers are a stock item in the Sunday comic pages of the newspaper. In the spring and summer months of 1982, a performance artist named Bill Harding drove a grass-covered Buick through Kansas City. Several years later, he grew grass on his clothes and shoes and wore them in Chicago's Grant Park to make a statement about the environment. According to Harding, "Grass suits are a great communication tool." Stephen King's movie *The Lawnmower Man,* Richard Brautigan's story "Revenge of the Lawn," and popular songs such as the country hit "The Green, Green Grass of Home" and "Green Grass" by Gary Lewis and the Playboys are all deeply rooted in American popular culture.

Horticulture writers and advertisers portray the front lawn as an extension 5
of the home. Lawns symbolize domestic values and good domestic management. The image of the lawn as a green velvety carpet evokes the front parlor, which is used only for guests—like the front door and the front parlor, the front yard is formal space. It has been compared to "the plastic-wrapped living room sofa and the ever-virgin Encyclopaedia Britannica," the expensive yet seldom used symbols of a proper middle-class home. Those home furnishings, inside and out, indicate good housekeeping and good citizenship.

In our transient society, people are judged by the care taken of their lawns—a neatly kept front lawn indicates that the family's life is in order. In many American homes, family members use the side or back door nearest the garage or the driveway, and the front door is used by guests. Children and dogs are supposed to keep off the grass. Peer pressure is brought to bear on those who do not keep their lawns up to the standard of the neighborhood. Often, neighbors are willing to approach the homeowner with a badly kept yard to remind him to mow it, to complain about the number of dandelions, to offer to loan the necessary equipment, or even to pitch in and do the work if the homeowner is incapacitated. If all else fails, the homeowner may be reported to the local authorities, who will take responsibility for mowing the lawn. Municipal regulations about lawns may be justified by suspicions that long grass harbors vermin and insects, but the underlying reasons are moral and aesthetic.

American front lawns are a symbol of man's control of, or superiority over, his environment. Americans have moved from regional landscapes based on local vegetation and climate to a national landscape based on an aesthetic that considers grassy front yards necessary to domestic happiness. The philosopher Yi-Fu Tuan suggests that the garden, and by extension the lawn, is a pet. Man manages to dominate nature in order to create the lawn and thus makes a pet out of it, lavishing it with care and attention. Lawns must be maintained thoughtfully and systematically and, to be perfect, require constant attention. Otherwise they will revert to nature. Man's attempt to control nature has also been called "the Western way—in which the individual lives in alienation from his environment, competing with it, exploiting it, resisting it, or ignoring it." Lawns, however, often represent man's failure to achieve the perfect green velvety carpet. Despite the chemical and biological warfare that has raged for the past century, crabgrass and dandelions continue to flourish in most neighborhoods. Many homeowners have not learned the aesthetic lessons, have not been totally socialized. Good front lawns never have been completely the norm.

During the seventies and eighties, as developers built townhouse communities and condominiums became popular, fewer homeowners were responsible for maintaining their own lawns. People still wanted green velvety carpets surrounding their homes but paid others to take care of their lawns for them. Professional lawn companies catering to the estates of the wealthy widened their services to include the one-third-acre lawns of the suburban middle class.

The Environmental Protection Agency estimates that about 70 million pounds of chemicals are applied to lawns each year, and that number is growing by 5 to 8 percent annually. By the late eighties, the average lawn owner was using a higher concentration of chemicals than farmers use. Some homeowners began to question their effect on the environment. Several national organizations now monitor the use of pesticides, including the Bio-Integral Resource Center, Berkeley, California; the National Coalition Against the Misuse of Pesticides, Washington, D.C.; and the Rachel Carson Council, Chevy Chase, Maryland. Lawn companies are finding themselves under increasing attack for the overuse of pesticides and the herbicide 2,4-D, now a suspected carcinogen. Like the lawn mower companies in the sixties, they are attempting to police themselves before sweeping legislation is enacted to regulate them.

Lawn grass requires an inch of water a week, and a 25-by-40-foot lawn 10
needs about ten thousand gallons per summer. Scientists continue to search for drought-resistant grasses. The Washington Suburban Sanitary Commission, supplier of water to the Washington, D.C., area, is concerned about lawn watering, noting that the movement to reduce outdoor water use began in the Southwest, "where manicured lawns were even more impractical than they are

here." The commission advocates water-saving landscaping to conserve water and to protect the Chesapeake Bay from garden chemical runoff. In addition, the paradigm of the front lawn is being reexamined by those who are concerned about the future of the environment. If lawns are not natural, then the possibility of other options or choices arises. Some homeowners are replacing their front lawns with ground covers, cactus gardens, meadows, prairies, vegetables, or flower beds.

The ideals of democracy and equality continue to be expressed in suburban tract housing developments, in the belief that every family can and should own its own house with a yard, that a man's home is his castle or manor sited in a park. Americans, however, rarely stay in one house for more than five years, and the American dream home surrounded by grass and trees is perhaps more symbolic than real. The single-family house, while still a dominant democratic ideal, may become a relic of the past as energy and construction costs rise. Developers continue to construct residential communities around golf courses in popular retirement areas, but the open suburban landscape of the fifties and sixties is beginning to give way to fenced gardens and decks. Many households now live in condominiums or townhouse developments where the open space is taken care of by the management. The house-in-the-park aesthetic survives in planned communities such as Reston, Virginia, and Columbia, Maryland, where buildings are clustered to preserve parklike open space that is cared for by the corporation.

Privacy is becoming the new status symbol in a society that is increasingly crowded. As homeowners perceive a breakdown in the social order and must live closer to their neighbors, they are turning inward. In urban areas, fences go up around front lawns to keep the homeless from defecating on them. New walled suburban developments have gates and guard houses. As more households are supported by two working adults or only a single adult, there is less time for lawn care. Men, the traditional lawn caretakers, are now expected to spend more time in child care and domestic chores. In fact, spending time on the lawn may even be perceived as vaguely decadent.

Will the advocates of an alternative domestic landscape at the turn of the next century be as effective as those at the turn of this last century? The trend toward smaller homes and smaller cars came to a halt during the eighties as homes and cars started getting bigger again. Despite signs of movement away from manicured front lawns, there were 45 million lawns covering some 30 million acres of the United States in 1991. Homeowners may be able to keep their front lawns by relying on the work of scientists across the country who have developed drought- and disease-resistant grasses that require less chemical treatment. A new landscape aesthetic is a cultural creation, and it remains to be seen whether the environmental movement in this country can enlist as potent a group of supporters and teachers for the twenty-first century as the lawn industry, the Garden Club of America, the U.S. Golf Association, and the U.S. Department of Agriculture did during the twentieth century.

Young Rampage Killers

FORD FESSENDEN

1 THEY ARE NOT drunk or high on drugs. They are not racists or Satanists, or addicted to violent video games, movies or music.

Most are white men, but a surprising number are women, Asians and blacks. Many have college degrees, but most are unemployed. Many are military veterans.

They give lots of warning and even tell people explicitly what they plan to do. They carry semiautomatic weapons they have obtained easily and, in most cases, legally.

They do not try to get away. In the end, half turn their guns on themselves or are shot dead by others. They not only want to kill, they also want to die.

5 That is the profile of the 102 killers in 100 rampage attacks examined by the *New York Times* in a computer-assisted study looking back more than 50 years and including the shootings in 1999 at Columbine High School in Littleton, Colo., and one by a World War II veteran on a residential street in Camden, N.J., in 1949. Four hundred twenty-five people were killed and 510 people were injured in the attacks. The database, which primarily focused on cases in the last decade, is believed to be the largest ever compiled on this phenomenon in the United States.

Though the attacks are rare when compared with other American murders, they have provoked an intense national discussion about crime, education and American culture. The *Times* found, however, that the debate may have largely overlooked a critical issue: At least half of the killers showed signs of serious mental health problems.

The debate was most intense last year, which began with echoes of gunfire in a Salt Lake City television station in January and ended with seven Honolulu office workers dead in November. In between there was a berserk rampage by an Atlanta day trader that left 12 dead and 13 injured. A self-styled fascist attacked a Los Angeles day care center. Seven people died as a hymn ended in a Fort Worth church.

Probably the most shocking were the shootings by two students at Columbine High School who burst into suburban classrooms and killed 13 and wounded 23. The teenage killers were much like the adults the *Times* studied, but with important distinctions that may bring a better understanding to the problem. As the anniversary of that crime, April 20, approaches, the questions about crime and culture will inevitably reverberate again.

The *Times* set out to examine as many of these killings as possible in an effort to learn what factors they and the people who carried them out shared. For while many possible causes have been cited, including violent video games, a decline in moral values and the easy availability of guns, there has been little serious study of this explosive violence.

10 The *Times* included only rampage homicides—multiple-victim killings that were not primarily domestic or connected to a robbery or gang. Serial killers were not included, nor were those whose primary motives were political.

These are among the findings:

- While the killings have caused many people to point to the violent aspects of the culture, a closer look shows little evidence that video games, movies or television encouraged many of the attacks. In only 6 of the 100 cases did the killers have a known interest in violent video games. Seven other killers showed an interest in violent movies.
- In a decade that had a sharp decrease in almost all kinds of homicides, the incidence of these rampage killings appears to have increased, according to a separate computer analysis by the *Times* of nearly 25 years of homicide data from the Federal Bureau of Investigation. Still, these killings remain extremely rare, much less than 1 percent of all homicides.
- Society has turned to law enforcement to resolve the rampage killings that have become almost a staple of the nightly news. There has been an increasing call for greater security in schools and in the workplace. But a closer look shows that these cases may have more to do with society's lack of knowledge of mental health issues, rather than a lack of security. In case after case, family members, teachers and mental health professionals missed or dismissed signs of deterioration.

Whether they happen in a school, in a mall, in a crowded train or in a workplace, these crimes have been characterized in a language of incomprehension—"senseless," "random," "sudden," "crazy."

By contrast, murder in the heat of domestic passion or a tavern argument, in the desperation of armed robbery or in the cold calculation of gang competition, seems to make "sense."

But in reviewing court records and interviewing the police, victims and sometimes the killers themselves, the *Times* found that these killings, too, have their own logic, and are anything but random or sudden.

15 The rage that boiled over into homicide was clearly building in many. Of the 100 cases reviewed by the *Times,* 63 involved people who made threats of violence before the event, including 54 who threatened specific violence to specific people.

Richard Farley, for example, who was fired in 1987 for harassing a female co-worker, told acquaintances he was going to kill the people who had come between him and her before storming into his former workplace, killing seven. James Calvin Brady told psychiatrists he wanted to kill people, just days before he went on a rampage in an Atlanta shopping mall in 1990.

"These are not impulsive acts," said J. Reid Meloy, a forensic psychologist at the University of California at San Diego. "They are not acts of affective violence, where they drink a lot and go kill someone. There's a planning and purpose, and an emotional detachment that's very long-term."

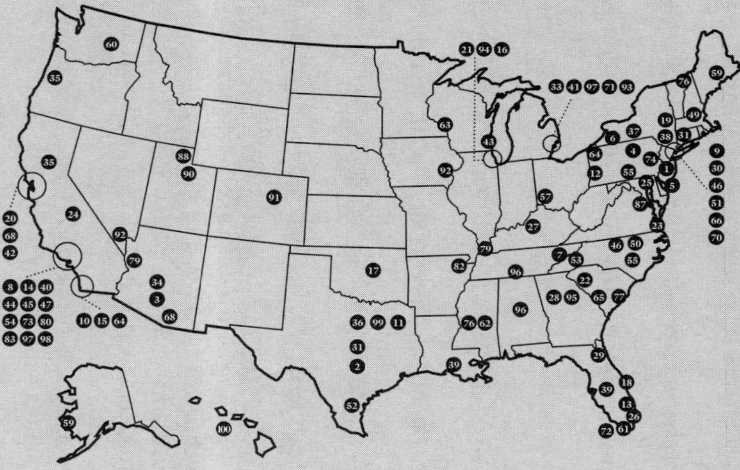

	YEAR KILLER	AGE	KILLED	INJURED*
1	'49 Howard B. Unruh	28	13	3
2	'66 Charles J. Whaitman	25	16	31
3	'66 Robert B. Smith	18	5	2
4	'67 Lwo Hald	40	6	6
5	'72 Edwin J. Grace	33	6	6
6	'74 Anthony Barbaro	17	3	9
7	'76 Robert D. Patty	43	3	2
8	'76 Charles E. Allaway	37	7	2
9	'77 Frederick W. Cowan	33	36	4
10	'79 Branda Spencer	16	2	9
11	'80 Alvin Lee King III	46	5	10
12	'80 Victor Belmanta	23	4	1
13	'82 Carl Brown	51	8	3
14	'84 Tyrone Mitchell	28	1	12
15	'84 James O. Huberty	41	21	19
16	'85 Sylvia Seegrist	25	3	7
17	'86 Patrick H. Sherrill	44	14	6
18	'87 William Cruse	59	6	12
19	'87 Robert L. Beebe	55	3	2
20	'88 Richard W. Farley	39	7	5
21	'88 Laurie Dann	30	1	6
22	'88 James W. Wilson	19	2	9
23	'88 Nicholas Elliott	15	1	1
24	'89 Patrick E. Purdy	24	5	31
25	'89 Emmanuel Tsegaye	33	3	31
26	'89 Joseph Besaraba Jr.	44	2	11
27	'89 Joseph T. Wesbecker	47	8	2
28	'90 James C. Brady	31	1	4
29	'90 James E. Pough	42	10	4
30	'91 Joseph M. Harris	35	4	0
31	'91 George Hannard	35	23	23
32	'91 Gng Lu	28	5	1
33	'91 Thomas Mclivane	31	4	4
34	'92 Pete C. Rogovich	27	4	0
35	'92 Eric Houston	20	4	10
36	'92 George Lott	45	2	3
37	'92 John T. Miller	50	4	0
38	'92 Wayne Lo	18	2	4
39	'93 Paul Calden	33	3	2
40	'93 Mark R. Hillbun	45	1	2
41	'93 Larry Jasion	45	3	0
42	'93 Gian Luigl Ferri	55	8	6
43	'93 Dion Terres	25	2	1
44	'93 Sergio Nelson	19	2	0
45	'93 Alan Winterbourne	33	4	4
46	'93 Colin Ferguson	35	6	19
47	'94 Tuan Nguyen	29	3	2
48	'94 Ladislav Antalik	38	2	2
49	'94 John C. Salvi	22	2	5
50	'95 Wendell Willamson	26	2	2
51	'95 Christopher Green	29	4	1
52	95 James Simpson	28	5	0
53	'95 James F. Davis	41	3	4
54	'95 Willie Woods	42	4	0
55	'95 William J Kreutzer J.	26	1	18
56	'95 Jaime Rouse	17	2	1
57	'95 Gerald Cemons	53	3	0
58	'95 Michael Vernon	22	5	3
59	'96 Mark Bechard	37	2	2
60	'96 Barry Loukaitis	14	3	1
61	'96 Cliftion McCree	41	5	1
62	'96 Kenneth Tornes	42	5	2
63	'96 Dan Copemen	40	2	2
64	''96 Frederick M. Davidson	36	3	0
65	'96 David M. Hill	36	3	0
66	'96 Jillian Robbins	19	1	1
67	'96 Gerald M. Atkins	29	1	3
68	'96 Jody T. Gordon	24	1	2
69	'97 Evan Ramsey	16	2	2
70	'97 All Hassan Abu Kamal	69	1	6
71	'97 Allen Griffin J.	21	3	2
72	'97 Jeffrey Wallace	36	1	3
73	'97 Daniel S. Marsden	38	2	4
74	'97 Drue Cade	69	1	2
75	'97 Katsuyuki Nishi	53	2	3
76	'97 Carl Drega	67	4	4
77	'97 Arthur H. Wise	43	4	3
78	'97 Luke T. Woodham	16	3	7
79	'97 Michael Carneal	14	3	5
80	'97 Arturo Reyes Torres	41	4	2
81	'98 Mathew Beck	35	4	0
82	'98 Mitchell Johnson	13	5	10
	Andrew Golden	11	5	10
83	'98 David Rothman	51	2	0
84	'98 Andrew Wurst	14	1	3
85	'98 Kipland Kinkel	15	4	22
86	'98 Gracie Verduzco	35	1	4
87	'98 Russell Weston Jr.	41	2	1
88	'99 Lisa Duy	24	1	1
89	'99 Shon Miller	22	4	4
90	'99 Sergel S. Babarin	70	2	5
91	'99 Eric Harris	18	13	23
	Dylan Klebold	17	13	23
92	'99 Zane Floyd	23	4	1
93	'99 Joseph Brooks Jr.	28	2	4
94	'99 Benjamin N. Smith	21	2	9
95	'99 Mark Barton	44	12	13
96	'99 Alan E. Miller	34	3	0
97	'99 Buford O. Furrow Jr.	37	1	5
98	'99 Dung Trinh	43	3	0
99	'99 Larry G. Ashbrook	47	7	7
100	'99 Byran K. Uyesugl	40	7	0

Yet there was often a precipitating event in addition to histories of failure and mental illness—a spark that set off the tinder, and gave the crime the appearance of being at the same time deliberate and impulsive.

"You can see someone who is morbidly depressed for a long time, and they have a suicide plan in place, but the timing is determined by impulse," said Kay Redfield Jamison, a professor of psychiatry at Johns Hopkins School of Medicine and author of *Night Falls Fast: Understanding Suicide* (Knopf, 1999).

By far the most common precipitator was the loss of a job, which was men- 20
tioned as a potential precipitator in 47 cases. A romantic issue—a divorce or breakup—was present in 22 cases.

"Some men see the loss of a job, or the loss of a mate, as irrevocable and catastrophic, something they can't get back or attain again," said David Buss, author of *The Dangerous Passion: Why Jealousy Is as Necessary as Love and Sex* (Free Press, 2000) and a professor of psychology at the University of Texas at Austin. "They set out on a course to inflict the maximum cost on their rivals, even sometimes killing the woman."

An analysis of the database found several recurring elements in rampage killings, including some that surprised the experts.

Perhaps the aspect that most set these crimes apart, aside from their spectacular nature, was this: Regular criminals try to get away with their crimes. More than a third of regular homicides went unsolved in 1997. But among the 102 killers in the *Times* database, not one got away. Eighty-nine never even left the scene of the crime.

In 1995, for example, after he killed three people at the Ohio trucking company where he had worked, Gerald Lee Clemons walked to the parking lot and leaned against his car calmly until the police arrived.

In 1997, Michael Carneal, a 14-year-old, killed three and wounded five at a 25
school in Louisville, Ky. Then he laid down his gun and said, "I'm sorry."

More tellingly, 33 of the offenders killed themselves after their crimes. Nine tried or wanted to commit suicide, and four killed themselves later. Nine were killed by the police or others, perhaps committing what some refer to as "suicide by cop."

"The number of people knowingly getting killed is striking," Prof. Alfred Blumstein of the Heinz School of Public Policy and Management at Carnegie Mellon University said after examining the review. Professor Blumstein is the director of the National Consortium on Violence Research.

Dr. Jamison said: "The link between suicide and homicide is a very real one, and it hasn't been studied nearly enough. It has always struck me about Columbine, people forget they committed suicide. And that's understandable—it was the least important thing from the public point of view."

Anthony Barbaro, a 17-year-old Regents scholar in upstate Olean, N.Y., offered a glimpse into this suicidal impulse in the note he left before he hanged himself with a knotted bedsheet in the county jail. He was awaiting trial after firing random shots out the window from the third floor of his high school, killing two passers-by and a school custodian, and wounding nine others.

"I guess I just wanted to kill the person I hate most—myself," he wrote. "I 30
just didn't have the courage. I wanted to die, but I couldn't do it, so I had to get someone to do it for me. It didn't work out."

One of the most remarkable insights to emerge from the survey is how much these killers differ from the typical American murderer.

Half of all murderers in this country are black. Eighty percent went to high school, and no further. Most of them killed someone they knew, or while committing another crime, like a robbery.

The rampage killers, on the other hand, were white, by far, though 18 of the 102 were black, and 7 Asian. The racial profile of the rampage killers is close to that of the entire population.

The rampage killers were overwhelmingly male—but not entirely. Six were 35
female, and they exhibited many of the same disturbed, aggressive characteristics of the males. Here again, however, was a distinction from regular murderers, who are about twice as likely as rampage killers to be women.

The rampage killers were far more likely to have a military background, and to kill strangers. There are intriguing age differences as well. The rampage killers were older than regular murderers, with more in their 40's and 50's and fewer in their 20's, compared with the typical killer.

Of the rampage killers who were over 25, a third had college degrees. Another third had some college education. Only nine had less than a high school diploma.

And there seemed to be no urban bias for these crimes, as there is for other violent crimes; 31 were in suburban areas, 25 were in small towns or rural areas. Forty two of those surveyed committed their crimes in urban areas.

That profile—a group that is largely suicidal, and shows few of the demographic patterns of poverty and race associated with regular crime—suggests that mental illness plays a huge role, psychiatrists say.

"Mental illness does not vary in different races, but socioeconomics do," said Dr. Lothar Adler, director of a psychiatric hospital in Muhlhausen, Germany, and author of *Amok,* a book on multiple murder.

The *Times* found much evidence of mental illness in its subjects. More than 40
half had histories of serious mental health problems—either a hospitalization, a prescription for psychiatric drugs, a suicide attempt or evidence of psychosis.

Of the 24 who had been prescribed psychiatric drugs, 14 had stopped taking them when they committed their crimes. Mr. Clemons, for instance, ran out of drugs a week before his crime, according to relatives.

Recent studies have shown that the mentally ill are no more violent than other people, except when they are off their medications, or have been abusing drugs or alcohol.

Indications of mental illness were far more common among the 100 cases than was evidence supporting popular explanations that emerged in the days after some of these spectacular events. Violent video games or television were mentioned in only a handful of cases. Three killers showed an interest in the occult. Racist ideas were apparent in the backgrounds of 16.

But 48 killers had some kind of formal diagnosis, often schizophrenia. Some of the diagnoses came after examinations by psychiatrists in trial preparations—which did not usually help in their defense, as only eight avoided conviction on grounds of insanity. Twenty-five killers received diagnoses before their crimes, which illustrates another recurring issue: They do not just suddenly snap. Many have long histories not only of mental illness but of failure and dislocation.

45 In spite of their education levels, for instance, a striking number—more than half—were unemployed.

"The high education level is one thing I hadn't anticipated, and the link to unemployment is another thing I didn't realize," Professor Blumstein said. "One of the things that education does is raise expectations, and raised ones are more readily frustrated."

For people without the emotional resources to accommodate it, frustration "can lead to rage, can lead to suicide," Professor Blumstein said.

These crimes are not new. Public rampage killings first entered the national consciousness with Charles Whitman, who stood on the University of Texas's tower in 1966, firing his rifle at students, killing 14 people.

Nor are they peculiarly American. The best scientific thinking, in a field that is admittedly understudied, now holds that multiple, public murder occurs at a fairly constant level across time and cultures. What some people call "running amok," a term first used in Malaysia to describe frenzied, indiscriminate killing, has been observed in many cultures, with weapons as varied as grenades and tanks in addition to high-powered handguns.

50 "Even though homicide rates and suicide rates are very different from country to country," said Peter M. Marzuk, a professor in the department of psychiatry at the Weil Medical College of Cornell University, "the rates of murder-suicide are really the same throughout the world."

Yet there is a strong impression that they have become more common. In an effort to confirm the trend, the *Times* analyzed F.B.I. reports of all homicides since 1976. Each year there were 15,000 to 22,000 homicides, but very few involved three or more victims.

That universe shrank even more, to just a few dozen, when the *Times* weeded out those involving robbery or gang violence, and those in which the primary victim was a family member.

What is left is the closest thing there is to a census of rampage killings—about one tenth of one percent of all killings.

And it shows that in the 1990's, they increased.

55 Their number remained fairly consistent from 1976 to 1989, averaging about 23 a year, only once going above 30. But between 1990 and 1997, the last year for which data was available, the number averaged over 34, dipping below 30 only once, in 1994.

"In the early 90's, for some reason, it increased, and seems to have a different level since," said Steven Messner, a criminologist at the State University of New York at Albany, who reviewed the numbers at the request of the *Times.*

There are many possible explanations. But the shift coincides, roughly at least, with a trend of increasing availability of more lethal weapons. In the late 1980's, the production of semiautomatic pistols in the United States overtook the production of revolvers, and with their larger ammunition magazines and faster reloading, semiautomatics have added to the potential for mayhem.

The effect may be apparent in the number of deaths per murderous incident, which suddenly increased in 1993 and has remained high since, according to the analysis of F.B.I. data by The *Times.*

"You have drastically increased the ability to inflict death and injury," said Tom Diaz, author of *Making a Killing: The Business of Guns in America* (New Press, 1999) and a senior policy analyst at the Violence Policy Center. "That means you can shoot more rounds faster and easier, what they call spray and pray."

In the *Times* study, wielders of semiautomatics inflicted more injuries. The 60
ratio of maimed to killed victims was 50 percent higher than for those who used other weapons. Yet, the increased availability of high-powered weapons may not explain everything. Some kinds of multiple murder have declined or remained static. Killings of three or more people to cover up another felony, like robbery, have not increased, for example. Neither have multiple killings of relatives. The number of incidents in which three or more died and the principal victim was a family member has remained fairly steady, around 30 cases a year.

"It used to be the most common type of this violence was in the family," said James Alan Fox, author of *Overkill: Mass Murder and Serial Killing Exposed* (Dell, 1996) and one of the nation's foremost experts on mass murder. "Now it's no longer true. It's in the workplace and in the schools."

Experts believe the crimes may be feeding on each other, particularly in an era of saturation coverage by cable television. Fourteen of the killers expressed knowledge about their predecessors.

For example, Ladislav Antalik, a Czech immigrant who killed two former co-workers and then himself after being fired from his job in Research Triangle Park, N.C., in 1994, had a newspaper article in his car describing a previous massacre.

The Columbine killers talked of doing it bigger and better than it had been done before. William Kreutzer, known as Crazy Kreutzer, as he set out to mow down a company of soldiers at Fort Bragg with an assault rifle and a semi-automatic pistol, told a friend he knew what the record number of multiple killings was.

But beyond the question of whether one event triggered the next, experts 65
say the recent increases in these crimes strongly suggest a social contagion.

"Why do you get a lot of people doing the same thing?" said Joseph Westermeyer, a psychiatrist at the University of Minnesota who has studied epidemics of explosive murder in other cultures. "I think there is this copycat element."

Dr. Adler, in his book, documented two cases of soldiers running amok with a tank in Germany in the 1980's after a widely publicized tank attack there. Army security was increased, and "tank amok never happened in Germany again," Dr. Adler said.

An angry, depressed, unstable, perhaps mentally ill person picks up a gun because it has become a known alternative. "Something that was inconceivable to many people suddenly becomes conceivable," Dr. Messner said.

"The transmission mechanism seems to be nothing more or less than that it's an idea that's in the air," said Philip Cook, a professor of public policy at Duke University, who has studied social contagions. "So you have these kind of catastrophic consequences from what seems a minor change in the environment."

How Youngest Killers Differ: Peer Support

FORD FESSENDEN

WHEN 16-YEAR-OLD Evan Ramsey strode into the lobby of his high school 1
in Bethel, Alaska, in 1997 and shot a popular basketball player in the stomach, there were already spectators gathered on the mezzanine above—students that he had told to be there to witness his "evil day."

Some may not have known exactly what was to transpire, but at least two students at Bethel Regional High had been intimately involved in the planning of Mr. Ramsey's crime, in which two people died. One student showed Mr. Ramsey how to load the shotgun the day before. The other carried a camera to record the event, but forgot to use it.

Such goading, sometimes even collaboration, is not uncommon among the school-age killers who were part of the *New York Times's* study of 100 rampage killings in the United States in the last 50 years. It is one of the principal factors that set them apart from adult killers.

For the most part, the adults were loners, who planned their crimes surreptitiously, even though they almost always broadcast their intentions. Some of the teenagers, on the other hand, sought, and often obtained, reinforcement from their peers and boasted of their plans.

In the most extreme cases, including the shootings at Columbine High 5
School, teenagers actually killed together. All of the adults killed alone.

In two other cases involving teenagers, including Mr. Ramsey's, collaborators were prosecuted, and in at least two more, the police have said they believed schoolmates or friends played a role.

As the country approaches the anniversary of the killings at Columbine, which crystallized public horror over rampage killings, this distinction is crucial to understanding, and even preventing, school shootings, many experts say.

A continuing study by the Secret Service's National Threat Assessment Center of 40 cases of school violence over the last 20 years has reached some of the same conclusions. The study, done in conjunction with the Department of

Education, found that teenage killers often communicated their plans or shared their feelings with other students, in sharp contrast to the pattern of adults.

In most ways, rampage killings involving young offenders are no different from those involving adults, the *Times* found in compiling its database. Young killers are as likely to strike in small towns as in big cities. Both groups are mostly white, but with some blacks and Asian-Americans. Both favor semiautomatic weapons.

But in other compelling ways, the teenage killers differ. While serious men- 10
tal health problems are common among them, fewer commit suicide after their crimes, the *Times* found. The younger killers are less emotionally detached and more susceptible to peer influence, experts said.

Overall, school violence is declining. The number of homicides and assaults at schools is down. But a series of mass killings at schools in the last four years has seemed to present the country with an ugly new face of school crime—the sudden, explosive rampage killing.

Although these shootings seem new, the *Times* study shows that teenage rampage killers were around far before the recent trend. Anthony Barbaro, an honor student, killed three and wounded nine at his high school in Olean, N.Y., in 1974. Sixteen-year-old Brenda Spencer, using a rifle given to her for her birthday, killed two and wounded nine at an elementary school near her house in San Diego in 1979. "I don't like Mondays," she told reporters. "This livens up the day."

Serious mental problems were reported in the histories of 10 of the 19 teenagers in the *Times* study. Two had been in psychiatric hospitals. Six showed evidence of psychotic delusions. Five had seen a mental health professional, and four had prescriptions for psychiatric drugs.

"I think it's quite possible that you're seeing incipient mental disorder," said J. Reid Meloy, a forensic psychologist at the University of California at San Diego who has just completed a study on juvenile rampage killers. "But a lot if times it will be minimized or not identified as readily as adults."

Dr. Anthony Hempel, chief forensic psychiatrist at the Vernon campus of 15
North Texas State Hospital and Dr. Meloy's co-author, said the fact that many of the adolescents were able to work with others was a strong argument that they were less likely to be mentally ill, or at least that their illness was in the early stages.

"When people pair up to commit one of these, the odds of a major mental illness go way down," Dr. Hempel said. "Very few people who don't have a mental illness can get together and plan something with someone with a major mental illness."

Some experts say that for many adolescents the plan to kill is a way of thinking about getting even, so the point is to discuss it. "Kids talk to kids about this stuff because fantasy is a process," said Frank C. Sacco, director of a mental health clinic in Springfield, Mass., who is researching school violence.

The companionship may even make the crimes possible. "Pairing then allows them to do these acts where acting alone doesn't," Dr. Meloy said. "It gives them courage or stamina."

But the fact that peers know in advance may make it easier to head off potential crimes. And immaturity may also point the way to hope for prevention.

"What we found is they're not as tightly wrapped emotionally when they do 20
mass murder," Dr. Meloy said. "Given their emotional ability they should be more accessible to interventions and treatment."

Manure, Minerals, and Methane: How Factory Farms Threaten the Environment

MICHAEL W. FOX

MANURE AS HAZARDOUS WASTE

ENABLING AMERICAN farmers to feed far more animals than the regional 1
land resources can sustain is detrimental to the land in many ways, not the least of which is the tremendous amount of animal waste produced by factory farms. This waste is not going back to the land from which the animal feed originated, to be used as fertilizer; instead, animal manure has become a costly environmental management hazard and is a cardinal indicator of bad farming practices and defunct agricultural policy.

All agricultural practices receiving federal government support are presumably subject to critical and objective environmental impact assessments under the National Environmental Policy Act (NEPA). However, the U.S. government does not exercise its authority as empowered by this act. In many states, federal subsidies and price supports of various agricultural commodities and practices have had well-documented adverse environmental impacts. Enforcement of the NEPA would provide the incentive for farmers and ranchers to adopt less harmful practices, but there is neither the will nor interest in government and agribusiness to do so.

There are many bioregions in the United States that are subject to environmentally destructive and costly agricultural and livestock enterprises. The Chesapeake Bay ecosystem, for example, is being destroyed along with the livelihood and culture of the people who live and work there. Agrichemical runoff from fields and the animal wastes from highly concentrated livestock industries are the primary cause. Fecal bacteria from livestock contaminate the bay, and ultimately the seafood that can then cause food poisoning.

Opponents of factory farming were outraged by the provision in the 1996 federal Farm Bill to provide $20 million annually of taxpayers' money to help factory livestock operators handle animal manure more safely using containment lagoons. Several manure spills from poorly maintained hog factory and large dairy feedlot lagoons caused serious pollution problems in 1995, and this legislated remedy, on the surface, looked reasonable. However, critics see this provision as a subsidy to encourage and underwrite the proliferation of large confinement operations for livestock production.

Some of the worst manure spills were from hog factories in North Carolina, 5
where North Carolina State University botanist Jo Ann Burkholder, Ph.D., identified a lethal phytoplankton that proliferated in streams polluted by hog manure. This microscopic organism called Pfiesteria piscidia produces a powerful toxin that was responsible for massive fish kills in polluted waters. This toxin can make people extremely ill, resulting in weight loss, abdominal cramps, festering sores, and memory loss. Phosphates in livestock manure stimulate this phytoplankton to bloom, an example of the inherent dangers of animal (and human) waste in aquatic ecosystems.

When farmers switch to indoor confinement systems and remove their animals from the land, they break the nutrient manure cycle. Now farmers have to pay for more chemical fertilizers to replace the livestock manure that once was recycled as fertilizer. Consider the waste of shipping corn from Iowa to feedlots in Texas: The manure from the feedlots does not go back to enrich the depleted soils in Iowa; instead, specialized, intensive livestock and poultry producers have a tremendous amount of unusable animal manure. If it is not managed correctly, it becomes a hazardous waste.

In areas where manure is put back into the soil, heavy metals, feed-additive chemicals, and pesticides residues, along with fecal bacteria, parasites, and residues of medications in the animals' feed, contaminate the land. These wastes from factory animal farms seep into the soil and groundwater and poison our lakes, rivers and coastal waters, and consequently the water we drink. Some 40 percent of the nitrogen and 35 percent of the phosphates contaminating the nation's rivers, lakes, and streams come from livestock wastes and feed fertilizers. For humans, nitrates in the drinking water can cause cancer. No one has yet determined the cost to clean animal wastes and agricultural chemical contaminants from our water supplies. However, the Environmental Protection Agency (EPA) estimates that it will cost $2 billion to simply survey contaminated wells.

In many regions, excessive waste from factory farms is too much for the land to sustain. This is especially true where there are large concentrations of intensively raised animals without a corresponding large area of farmland on which to spread the manure. In the United States, livestock and poultry excrete about 158 million tons of manure (dry weight basis) per year. If we put this much manure in boxcars, the train would stretch around the world four and a half times.

In Europe, scientists are finding that manure gases contribute to acid rain, which is killing their forests. In U.S. poultry and hog confinement operations, dust and slurry vapors are an occupational safety hazard. They do not do much for the chickens' and pigs' health and well-being either, or for the well-being of downwind neighbors, whose property values plummet because of the stench. The smell alone often forces local residents to sell their homes because they lack the resources and government support to sue and stop these factory farms.

I grew up in the north of England where we had a saying, "Where there's muck, there's money." Now animal muck has become an environmental and public health hazard that contains enough excess nitrates to kill fish, pollute the environment, and pose serious human health problems. We also have to reckon with phosphates, various feed additives, and drugs in the animal manure, some of which may actually accumulate in crops from soils soaked year after year with slurry or contaminated manure. Fecal bacteria and other fecal organisms can survive in the soil for some time, get into surface waters, and ultimately into our drinking water. Witness the April 1993 Lake Michigan mess, when Cryptosporidia from livestock waste mismanagement caused more than 1,000 people to get sick and everyone in Milwaukee had to boil their water for several days.

Much of this contaminated animal waste returns to the land to fertilize crops to feed these animals, who are in turn eaten. In other cases, it is fed back to the animals; some farmers even feed the rendered remains of "farm" animals to their cattle, along with dried poultry manure. To the agricultural economist and animal production scientist, that might seem an efficient and innovative improvement on nature. However, health and environmental risks far outweigh any cost savings. A recent outbreak of botulism in Australian feedlot cattle who were fed poultry manure is evidence of the risks of mishandling animal waste. Chemical residues and drugs in poultry manure can make cattle sick. Sheep on pastures sprayed with pig slurry can develop copper poisoning. It is no surprise that the United Kingdom's Royal Agricultural Society concludes that animal manure from conventional factory farms that use drugs is too hazardous for use as a fertilizer.

Integrating livestock production systems with organic crop and forage production systems will lessen the likelihood of problem diseases. A major tenet of sustainable agriculture is that well-managed manure is a valuable resource, not a hazardous waste.

TRACE MINERALS, HEAVY METALS, AND IMPOVERISHED SOILS

Concerns about trace minerals may seem of little importance to consumers and farmers, but they point to a much larger and very serious problem: trace-nutrient deficiency diseases, about which we know very little. What we do know is that vital nutrients like selenium and zinc are essential for the immune system's ability to fight infections and for neutralizing harmful free radicals in cells that can cause cancer and other diseases. Our resistance to disease may be considerably impaired by the use of chemical fertilizers—simple phosphates, potash, and nitrogen—along with other farming practices like monocropping (when farmers grow the same single crops on the same land year after year). These farming practices can result in the break of the molecular connections of the ecological food chain. The proper nutrients, especially trace minerals, needed to maintain the health of crops and all who eat these troubled harvests are not being returned to the soil. Instead of restoring the soil and testing it repeatedly, more business is made for the chemical and pharmaceutical industries, since farmers must now add essential trace minerals to animals' feed and consumers are advised to take trace mineral supplements as well.

Livestock producers use selenium, arsenic, and so-called heavy metals like copper and zinc extensively as feed additives. These chemicals should not be considered relatively safe nutrients, like an amino acid or complex carbohydrate. They can be toxic to animals when improperly mixed, and toxic to other animals when they become concentrated in manure and fertilized forage.

15 Chemicals such as selenium build up in the soil as well as in surface and groundwater, in aquatic life, and subsequently in birds and land animals. These chemicals even appear in certain plants that livestock consume, and in crops that humans consume from fields fertilized with animal manure that contains these trace minerals. Just as the government regulates veterinary pharmaceuticals and nonveterinary drugs such as antibiotics and other feed additives, it must also strictly regulate trace-mineral feed additives.

When the background level of a trace mineral is already high, the possibility of livestock being overdosed and poisoned when feed manufacturers and growers add a trace nutrient to animals' feed is very real. Sickness, impaired immunity and growth rate, lowered fertility, and decreased egg or milk production are some of the consequences. The toxicity of selenium and other additives may be increased further when used with other additives or medications. This can promote widespread disaster. However, the feed additive industry claims to be "self-regulated" and the government maintains that regulating it is expensive and unfeasible. It is incumbent upon the Food and Drug Administration (FDA) and responsible farmers to treat selenium and other trace-element additives with the same degree of concern as antibiotics and growth hormones.

CATTLE METHANE AND GLOBAL WARMING

Some scientists are concerned that giving cattle more forage to make them leaner will increase the amount of methane gas the animals produce. Each cow emits 200–400 quarts of methane gas daily. The world's cows contribute nearly 50 million metric tons of methane to the atmosphere every year. Methane is one of the gases associated with the trapping of infrared rays in the lower atmosphere, which leads to global warming. Animal nutritionist Donald Johnson has suggested feeding antibiotics to cattle to kill some of the methane-producing bacteria in their rumen, or first stomach. But even if this helps to reduce methane output by 30 percent and helps animals use their feed more efficiently, is administering more antibiotics the best solution?

Other scientists have proposed feeding livestock less forage and more grains. But that's not the answer either, because the very practice of expanding grain production results in two greenhouse gases, methane and nitrous oxide, which are respectively absorbed less and released more from chemically fertilized and heavily cultivated land. Natural range land actually absorbs atmospheric carbon dioxide and the methane gas released by cattle and other ruminant animals. This helps offset the contribution of livestock to global warming.

The fact remains that cattle do produce significant quantities of methane, as do the liquid manure lagoons adjacent to confinement livestock factories. One possible solution is to cover these lagoons to capture the gas and generate energy. A few U.S. dairy farmers are experimenting with methane-fired electric generators to provide electricity for their farms.

In 1992 the Center for Rural Affairs published a study on global warming 20
and climate change title "Mares' Tails and Mackerel Scales." According to the study, U.S. agriculture can reduce its greenhouse gas emissions by 28 percent through measures that will be good for farmers as well as the environment. The report details strategies for reducing emissions from each major source. It concludes that the top priorities are to reduce nitrogen fertilizer use, plant grass on highly erodible land, and reduce methane emissions from anaerobic lagoons where livestock waste decomposes without oxygen.

U.S. farms currently produce emissions of three major greenhouse gases that have the combined equivalent of about 643.6 million tons of carbon dioxide. Most startling is the finding that about one-fifth of all greenhouse gas emissions from major sources studied is from livestock waste that decomposes anaerobically in lagoons. Although only a small minority of farmers handle their animal waste this way, the percentage is growing as large-scale confinement facilities increase.

ENVIRONMENTAL COSTS OF FACTORY FARMS

The Federal Clean Water Act regulates pollution of surface waters in the United States, and considers concentrated animal feeding operations a source of pollution. Operators of livestock factory farms must obtain and install an expensive manure handling system. New or expanding facilities must also provide an Environmental Impact Statement. However, although most states have assumed responsibility for the Clean Water Act, there are serious concerns over lack of enforcement.

In 1993 several large factory farms and feedlots were operating or under construction in states that, at the time, still did not require permits. For example, National Farms, which was the nation's largest hog farm until it was sold to Premium Standard Farms, had built a 16,000-sow operation in Texas. In Oklahoma, Seaboard Corporation plans to construct a 4 million-head hog packing plant near Guymon. Circle Four, a conglomerate of Smithfield Foods, Murphy Farms, Carroll Foods, and Prestige Farms, has built a 2 million-pig factory farm in Utah.

While battles over new hog-raising facilities rage across the United States, one of the nation's leading pork-producing firms, North Carolina-based Carroll Foods, will build new hog factories in eastern Mexico's state of Veracruz, taking advantage of virtually nonexistent environmental regulations and cheap labor. The company says it will raise 600,000 hogs per year at 12 locations.

These factory farms are causing serious pollution and bacterial contamina- 25
tion of lakes, river basins, and drinking water. They have also caused several fish kills. Neighboring farmers and residents are filing lawsuits forcing the EPA to begin imposing costly livestock pollution controls since state authorities have refused to implement federal standards on their own.

One very good solution to these problems is to simply reduce the livestock population to an environmentally and ecologically balanced number and distribution. A decrease in consumer demand for animal products is the key to this solution working. What we buy at the grocery store and put into our mouths has a tremendous impact on the environment and the animal kingdom it sustains.

In and Out of Elevators in Japan

TERRY CAESAR

EVERY MORNING in the apartment building where I live I take the elevator 1
six floors down. One morning a woman appeared with her bicycle as I was waiting for the elevator. Though we live along the same corridor, I had scarcely seen her before, and we have never spoken. Japanese public behavior in residential space is customarily limited to either reserved nods of recognition or restrained "good mornings" and "good afternoons." Everything changes at the elevator, as I was especially surprised to see this particular morning.

Suppressing my annoyance (a bicycle takes half the space in the small elevator), I gestured for the woman to enter when the elevator arrived and the door opened. She acknowledged my courtesy, and positioned herself inside. There was just room enough to accommodate me in front of her. As the elevator descended, suddenly I felt a hand touch my collar, and smooth it down over my tie! "*Arigato gosaimas*" (thank you very much), I managed, when we reached the bottom floor and I could turn to face the woman. She smiled faintly and bowed in turn.

I was stunned for hours afterwards. Japanese never touch. It's not even customary among themselves when they meet to shake hands. So how to explain why this woman would so casually reach over and adjust my collar? In public! And yet, not exactly. The space of an elevator is small enough, and, perhaps more important, brief and ephemeral enough, to admit a private character. Therefore, an individual can relax, and accord another a degree of warmth inadmissible once the elevator doors open once more. My moment of contact, I concluded, could have only happened in an elevator, and then perhaps only in Japan. Suddenly the mundane seemed luminous with an entirely different meaning to transit space.

1.

Japanese courtesy is a staple of every handbook on the country designed for foreign consumption. In a typical recent one, *The Inscrutable Japanese,* organized around a chapter-by-chapter series of pointed questions, the following explanation is given in response to the question, "Why do Japanese yield to each other?": "Behind this custom lies the desire to be part of a group. Japanese value group harmony, and they don't like to stand out" (Hiroshi, 91). That is, Japanese are so courteous because their feeling for each other is already constituted—by their culture, by their very language—as collective in nature and consequence. What foreigners see as "courtesy" is in this sense merely an expression of the felt implication of their lives, each in one another. No wonder that they like to describe themselves, according to Ian Buruma, as "'wet and *yasashii.*' They stick together in mutual dependency like 'wet,' glutinous rice, so dear to the Japanese palate . . . They express themselves by 'warm, human emotions,' instead of 'dry, hard rational thought'" (Buruma, 219).

5 But this stereotype (as Buruma terms it) only operates according to very strict rules for public behavior. *The Inscrutable Japanese* strives to explain, for example, the cultural imperative against direct confrontation that results (to the consternation of foreigners) in Japanese saying "maybe" so often, or the ethical significance of learning *kata* (proper form) that comprehends (to the misunderstanding of foreigners) why Japanese appear so rigid in exchanging business cards. Nonetheless, the presumption of such a handbook is that unless you are Japanese it is finally very difficult not to see Japanese public behavior as severely "marked" in virtually every manifestation, and therefore as finally too ceremonial and cold—or, ironically, rather the opposite of the stereotype that the Japanese have of themselves.

Behavior at or near elevators would at first seem to follow from this presumption. Upon entrance, there is always some hesitation about who goes first among a group of people. Everyone is usually so pleased to yield to everyone else that there is often a real danger that no one will actually get into the elevator before it leaves. Once inside, the person nearest the floor buttons is quick either to press a button for everyone else's floor, or at least to demonstrate willingness to do so. Consideration of others is often so extreme that a person exiting will not only excuse himself or herself—*sumimasen* ("excuse me") being once more the most operative word in Japanese public life—but press the "close" button so that less time will be lost to those remaining in the elevator.

Yet if life outside the elevator dictates the social script by which people conduct themselves at entrance and exit points, behavior inside the elevator is another matter. Transit space is of course fluid by its very nature—too short in duration to fit very securely into the continuum between public and private behavior. In Japan, people are prepared to speak to each other more freely in elevators, rather in the manner of Westerners, and much in contrast to their behavior in the halls or on the street. In these more open, commodious public realms, quick nods of mutual recognition—visual or verbal—suffice. In the more restricted space of the elevator, however, questions are often ventured, opinions expressed, or even greetings exchanged that have a more expansive character.

Even a foreigner should not expect to be surprised to be spoken to in an elevator by someone who would normally refrain from speaking to him outside it. I do not think the mere fact of physical proximity explains this. Of course it does to a degree; people who find themselves close to each other are inclined to speak to each other, or at least find it less comfortable to avoid doing so. However, in any particular country they are neither inclined to speak to each other in the same way, nor for the same reasons. Transit space reveals cultural specificity like few other kinds, because such space consists in peculiar negotiations among the resources of both public and private social interaction.

Japanese behavior inside elevators is so distinctive because it is determined by the opportunity momentarily afforded for its felt relaxation from the burdens of role-governed behavior outside. The relaxation is culturally weighted by two specific factors. Although the second is more decisive than the first, as I will argue, granting each of these factors is crucial to understanding why such a mundane occasion as behavior in elevators becomes so fascinating and elusive, as well as instructive and important for the study of transit space generally.

2.

It is impossible to talk to another person very long on an elevator, which 10
functions exclusively to get its occupants to a fixed destination, because the floors of a building occur in such quick succession. Hence, elevator time lacks duration. This does not mean, however, that it lacks opportunity; indeed, one of the things that the study of transit space in general demonstrates is that its temporal coordinates, no matter how ephemeral, will be made nonetheless to perform social work. Depending upon the society, as well as the person, the limitations on conversation in an elevator can be either a great pity or a great relief.

To Japanese, they are both. The very brevity of the conversational horizon can yield an intensity that one can see invested in a wide range of other cultural phenomena, ranging from haiku to sumo or fireworks. The Japanese word for the latter, *hanabi,* or literally "flower fire," suggests a link between their fleeting beauty and its most celebrated cultural manifestation: the cherry blossom. We should not be surprised that the occasion of an elevator enables the operation of a venerable cultural code, in which precisely because something does not last long is the reason to invest it with significance and value.

For Peter Singer, this special feeling for brevity can be erected into a metaphysical principle: "[a Japanese] is satisfied with short moments of fulfillment rapidly shattered as cherry blossoms are, and even his fighting spirit was often said not to be well sustained. Able to show great bravery, bordering sometimes on madness, he does not like to endure long hardship and adversity. Unlike the Russian, he prefers suicide to silent despair" (Singer, 30). Such discourse is of course rather wildly unfashionable in sociology today. It posits a national essence, rather than proposing to examine a cultural construction. Furthermore, Singer assumes a condition of changelessness, and disdains the modifications of social development, much less the claims of history.

Behavior in elevators constitutes, I would only argue, one means to try to articulate something about national identity, as well as an especially distinctive way of studying how national identity, in turn, illustrates behavior in elevators. Japanese are attracted to attenuated temporal coordinates—in this case once established inside the elevator—for precisely the reasons others might despair of them. Suddenly, smiles can be ventured. Courtesy can allow or even risk disclosures of additional emotion. Suddenly, smiles can be ventured. Courtesy can allow or even risk disclosures of additional emotion. Suddenly, there need not be so much fear of being self-conscious. Talk will not last very long. Indeed, it may barely be possible to get started. Behavior inside an elevator therefore assumes the character of something exquisitely ephemeral, poignantly revealing, even surprisingly candid.

In effect, the space inside the elevator is so circumscribed by the public realm in Japan that it becomes private. Just so, it seems to me that we cannot ask in abstract terms whether this space is public or private, even if the most obvious initial factor remains the nature of the building in which the elevator operates. (Hence, the larger or more commercial the building, the more open its elevators to being governed strictly by public codes.) The distinction between public and private space is often difficult to stabilize in actual social practice because transit space is transit space precisely because it is unstable; roles are not clearly delineated, and so the easiest available role is often the suspension of any particular one—until the elevator door opens (or the train door), and social life can resume, scripted as before.

15 In Japan, nonetheless, I would maintain that elevator space is subject to much less individual negotiation or even suspension The space is private, if not entirely unproblematically. The primary reason is simple: virtually all other space is far less unproblematically public, including all other forms of transportation, ranging from trains and buses even to private automobiles, which must be open to more public monitoring—speed limits, toll fees, parking restrictions, maintenance checks—than vehicles in any nation on earth. (Foreigners new to Japan are surprised to see so many people relaxing or sleeping in cars, as if to reclaim their lost private dimension.) The easiest way to understand the common behavior whereby the person leaving the elevator first presses the "close" button is as a concession to the privacy of the remaining occupant or occupants. Just so, this same privacy is what prompts the person entering the elevator to apologize for doing so.

Once inside, what Erving Goffman venerably terms a "participation unit" is immediately formed (Goffman, 21). Of course the same unit is incipiently constituted everywhere in the world, any time an elevator door closes. But it does not always function—when it does—according to rules at variance with those outside the elevator door. Not only is the brief duration of the circumstance inescapably manifest as an opportunity for social interaction rather than as an inconsequence. In addition, the peculiar kind of participation possible inside an elevator in Japan is purchased against a formidable array of prohibitions, inhibitions, and sanctions concerning human relationships outside it. Each of these has a highly public character, which, in effect, robs the slightest contact between individuals of its potentially casual, accidental, or, in a word, mundane quality.

The inside of the elevator restores this quality, if only for a few instants. Speaking of the fact that relationships must both begin and end, Goffman writes elsewhere concerning a peculiar kind of farewell in which (because of death or geography) participants are about to be inaccessible to each other: "In these latter cases, a farewell can occur that marks the simultaneous termination of a moment or two of being in touch and the relationship that made being in touch in that way possible" (Goffman, 90). Precisely. The nature of human participation inside an elevator in Japan is that the contact is so fraught with farewell from the very moment of initiation that it terminates without having become a relationship at all. Such relationships are very rare in Japan. Or rather, the space for them is. Therefore this space exists to be cherished, even if it begs to persist almost beneath notice.

3.

It is undoubtedly the case that every society on earth has a considerable political investment in its transit spaces. Some monitor them more than others. However, the space of an elevator—now that the attendant who operates it (and by extension enforces orderly behavior) has fast become almost everywhere in the world an extremely rare figure—is not easily subject to surveillance. In Japan, at least, this particular space tends merely to be left to itself. It may be because people are taught to respect others, and, on the whole, they do. (For a recent popular explanation of the historical background, see Reid.) Even so, no less than any other people, Japanese are not without principles contrary to the society in which they find themselves.

How to make these principles manifest? For men, after-work bars—the world of the infamous "water trade"—can be seen as too prolonged, too systematic occasions. (For an incisive portrait of such establishments, see Morley.) People need mundane moments as well as significant ones in order to act out their own purely subjective or occasionally individual needs. Indeed, for these purposes mundane occasions are arguably the more precious, because they can be entirely free or careless of any sort of rationalization.

How to find such occasions? Perhaps they are best understood as given 20
rather than found. Transit space generally exemplifies them, and moments inside elevators in particular, at least in Japan. Of course this particular space abides as endangered, just as it does anywhere else in the world, and for the same reason: video cameras. These cameras are ubiquitous in modern society: in department stores, fast-food restaurants, offices, and of course elevators. They attest, if not to the relentless public definition of space, at least to the public claim that everywhere exists to be made (for whatever purpose) on space of any kind. One thing the study of elevator space in Japan reveals is that this claim is never made without resistance, even in a society whose formidable traditions of law, precept, cultural memory, and ethical wisdom would seem to rule out individual dissonance.

Instead, in a sense, the dissonance is made possible through one of these traditions: an exquisite sensitivity to the inside. Patrick Smith is the latest of a number of commentators on Japan who have called attention to the duality of outside and inside, the enclosed and the exposed, which, he states, is "the first thing to confront the arriving visitor. The standard term for oneself is *gaijin,* outside person. It is one's first notice that life in Japan will consist in a series of acceptances and rejections. Nothing is excepted" (Smith, 40). So, he continues, Japanese life can be comprehended as a series of variations on this duality, including everything from families, sports clubs, and companies to walls and paper screens. The reason elevator space in Japan is private is because it is seized by Japanese as a chance to create yet another inside.

Insides are not exclusively private; there would be little urgency to create them if they were not exposed to outsides. But insides always have a private coloration—won as it were over against the greater force of outsides, which are always public. (Compare in this respect the present furor over the existence of the ubiquitous "handy phones," so beloved of teenagers; these phones represent to Japanese a scandalous eruption of personal opportunity or whim into public life, and so the public service campaign against the use of these phones on trains or at meetings emphasizes their rudeness.) The nice thing about the emotional coloration of the inside of elevators is that we can see how private behavior can suddenly and momentarily reveal itself without shedding its public guise.

Private energies, in other words, need not be wholly effaced, for they need not be disruptive if expressed. Of course, once more, it helps immensely if the occasion is staged on a very small scale and is very brief. A final example: The other night I worked late in my office, and then took an elevator down, as usual, when I left. A woman got on at the third floor with a small cart. She inclined her head, upon entrance, and excused herself, faintly. Nothing surprising here. But her smile was, along with the fact that she stood to one side, facing me, rather than in front, with her back to me. One of those intricate little dances of civility ensued when the elevator stopped on the first floor. The woman gestured for me to precede her out. I, in turn, gestured for her. She was pleased to accept, and each of us was delighted to act out our respective acceptance with a degree of fervor unlikely to transpire away from the elevator.

Did we have to act this way? No. The social participation made possible by the inside of an elevator can remain inert, or wholly governed by the rules outside it. As it was, what further chances exist for extending the ephemeral moment of sociality that obtained between the woman and me? None. Or, to put it another way, further chances that could exist would cease to be charged with the peculiar intimacy that the most mundane occasions suddenly possess in Japan. They possess this intimacy because the social disposition of public space normally forbids it. But then the study of the mundane, I think, reveals that public space is never limited to what it forbids. Otherwise, none of us would have anything to bring to our relationships there, and social life may as well consist of empty action, going up and down like an elevator, with no inside and nobody to occupy it.

WORKS CITED

Buruma, Jan. *Behind the Mask: On Sexual Demons, Sacred Mothers, Gangsters, and Other Japanese Cultural Heroes.* New York: Meridian, 1984.

Goffman, Erving. *Relations in Public. Microstudies of the Public Order.* New York: Harper Books, 1971.

Hiroshi, Kagawa. *The Inscrutable Japanese.* Tokyo: Kodansha International, 1997.

Morley, John. *Pictures from the Water Trade. Adventures of a Westerner in Japan.* Boston: Atlantic Monthly Press, 1985.

Reid, T. R. *Confucius Lives Next Door.* New York: Random House, 1999.

Singer, Peter. *Mirror, Sword and Jewel. The Geometry of Japanese Life.* Tokyo: Kodansha International, 1971.

Smith, Patrick. *Japan: A Reinterpretation.* New York: Vintage, 1998.

Practicing the Principles: Activities

INVENTING A BETTER MOUSETRAP

As a class, choose a particular process or procedure that seems inefficient to you: registering for courses, applying for scholarships or grants, buying sports or concert tickets, clearing parking tickets, whatever. Develop a cause-and-effect diagram to understand the stages of the process and the possible causes for inefficiency. Then see if you can devise a more efficient process.

UNDERSTANDING AMERICAN OBSESSIONS

Over the years, Americans have demonstrated their tendency to follow fads and cultivate obsessions: hula hoops, pet rocks, Cabbage Patch Kids, Beanie Babies, to name only few. We have continuing love affairs with cars, lawns, television, sports, celebrities, fast food, and gadgets of all kinds. By the standards in other countries, Americans are also obsessive about personal hygiene. We have a whole array of personal-care products to help keep us squeaky clean and odor-free. As a class, brainstorm about some of the things Americans are obsessed with; then select a couple of these obsessions for analysis. Using cause-and-effect diagrams, outline some of the possible causes for these obsessions. Finally, on your own or as an in-class essay, turn your diagram into an essay analyzing an American obsession.

UNDERSTANDING SOCIAL ILLS

Poverty is one of the many social ills that our communities struggle to eliminate. You can probably think of others: physical and emotional abuse, drug addiction, violent crime, pollution, overcrowding, bigotry, and many more. As a class, select a social ill that you would like to understand better. Using diagrams, brainstorm about some possible causes and effects of this problem. From your diagrams generate a set of questions that you still need to answer, and do research to come up with further information. With other members of your class, write a collaborative essay about the possible causes and effects of the social ill you have researched. If possible come to a negotiated solution for alleviating the problem. Consider presenting your findings on a class website.

Applying the Principles On Your Own

MALE BODY IMAGE

The two essays that follow examine different aspects of maleness in today's society. The scholarly study "Evolving Ideals of Male Body Image as Seen through Action Toys" (Harrison Pope, Jr. et al) was first published in the *International Journal of Eating Disorders* in 1999. Richard Lacayo's essay, "Are You Man Enough?" focuses on the male hormone testerone. The essay first appeared in the April 24, 2000, issue of *Time*.

Evolving Ideals of Male Body Image as Seen Through Action Toys

HARRISON G. POPE, JR., ROBERTO OLIVARDIA, AMANDA GRUBER, and JOHN BOROWIECKI

INTRODUCTION

A GROWING body of literature has described disorders of body image among men. For example, such disturbances are frequently documented in men with eating disorders. In one study, college men with eating disorders reported a degree of body dissatisfaction closely approaching that of women with eating disorders, and strikingly greater than comparison men (Olivardia, Pope, Mangweth, & Hudson, 1995). Other studies of men with eating disorders have produced similar findings (Andersen, 1990; Schneider & Agras, 1987). Even in studies of male students without eating disorders, the prevalence of body dissatisfaction is often striking (Mintz & Betz, 1986; Drewnowski & Yee, 1987; Dwyer, Feldman, Seltzer, & Mayer, 1969). Body image disturbances may be particularly prominent in American culture. In a recent crosscultural comparison, groups of American college men reported significantly greater dissatisfaction with their bodies than comparable groups in Austria (Mangweth et al., 1997). 1

Another form of body image disturbance, also frequently affecting men, is body dysmorphic disorder (Phillips, 1991, 1997; Hollander, Cohen, & Simeon, 1993). Individuals with this disorder may develop obsessional preoccupations that their facial features are ugly, that their hairlines are receding, or that their penis size is too small—to name several of the more common presentations. Recently, we have described another form of body dysmorphic disorder found in both sexes, but probably more prevalent in men, which we have called "muscle dysmorphia" (Pope, Gruber, Choi, Olivardia, & Phillips, 1997). Individuals with muscle dysmorphia report an obsessional preoccupation with their muscularity, to the point where their social and occupational functioning may be severely impaired. For example, they may abandon important social and family relationships, or even relinquish professional careers, in order to spend more time at the gym (Pope et al., 1997). Many report that they refuse to be seen in public without their shirts on because they fear that they will look too small (Pope, Katz, & Hudson, 1993). Often they use anabolic steroids or other performance-enhancing drugs, continuing to take these agents even in the face of serious side effects because of persistent anxiety about their muscularity (Pope et al., 1993; Pope & Katz, 1994).

In many ways, muscle dysmorphia appears to be part of the "obsessive-compulsive spectrum" of disorders (Hollander, 1993; Phillips, McElroy, Hudson, & Pope, 1995). It is characterized by obsessional preoccupations and impulsive behaviors similar to those of classical obsessive-compulsive disorder. If this hypothesis is correct, it is natural to ask why modern American men with muscle dysmorphia would have developed this particular outlet for their obsessions, as opposed to a more traditional symptom pattern such as hand-washing or checking rituals.

One possible explanation for this phenomenon is that in our culture, the ideal male body is growing steadily more muscular. With the advent of anabolic steroids in the last 30 to 40 years, it has become possible for men to become much more muscular than is possible by natural means. Bodybuilders who won the Mr. America title in the presteroid era could not hope to compete against steroid-using bodybuilders today (Kouri, Pope, Katz, & Oliva, 1995). The public is exposed daily, in magazines, motion pictures, and other media, to increasingly—and often unnaturally—muscular male images. Some individuals, responding to these cultural messages, may become predisposed to develop muscle dysmorphia.

In an attempt to provide some quantitative data bearing on this hypothesis, 5
we examined the physiques of American action toys over the last 30 years.

METHODS

Action toys are small plastic figures, typically ranging from 3¾ in. to 12 in. in height, used by children in play, and frequently collected by adult hobbyists. Among the best known examples are the GI Joe figures, Star Wars and Star Trek characters, Superman, Spiderman, and Batman. Contemporary versions of these figures are readily available at toy stores and vintage figures may be purchased through a vast and well-organized collectors' market. Extensive reference works, such as the 480-page *Encyclopedia of GI Joe* (Santelmo, 1997), document the evolution of these figures over the years. We chose to study these toys because, unlike cartoon characters or movie stars, they can be readily physically measured, allowing accurate comparisons between figures of different eras.

We consulted with various action toy experts to ascertain toys which had been produced in various iterations by the same manufacturer over a period of 20 years or more. To obtain an objective index of the popularity of specific toys, we consulted the 1st through 15th annual sales surveys by *Playthings* magazine, published in the December issue of each year from 1983 to 1997 (*Playthings* magazine), to confirm that the toy had been among the 10 best-selling toy product lines in several years spanning the last two decades. We also required that the toy represent an actual male human being (such as a soldier or Luke Skywalker), rather than a nonhuman creature (such as Mr. Potato Head or the Teen-Age Mutant Ninja Turtles). Two toy product lines met all of these criteria: the GI Joe series manufactured by the Hasbro Toy Company since 1964 and the Star Wars figures manufactured by the Kenner Toy Company (a subsidiary of Hasbro) since 1978. We then purchased representative examples of these figures from different time periods. We also visited a branch of a large toy store chain and purchased additional examples of toys identified by store officials and by the most recent *Playthings* surveys as the most popular contemporary male action figures. Some of these latter figures, such as Batman and the Mighty Morphin Power Rangers, might not be considered completely "human," in that they possess powers beyond those of a real human being. Others, such as the X-Men, are mutants of human beings. However, they all possess essentially human bodies.

We then measured the waist, chest, and bicep circumference of all the figures and scaled these measurements using classical allometry (Norton, Olds, Olive, & Dank, 1996) to a common height of 1.78 m (70 in.).

RESULTS

GI JOE

The action toy with the longest continuous history is GI Joe. The Hasbro Toy Company first introduced GI Joe as an 11½-in. posable figure in 1964 (Santelmo, 1997). This figure continued without a change in body style as the GI Joe Adventurer in 1970 to 1973. It developed a new body style from 1973 to 1976 as the GI Joe Adventurer with kung-fu grip and lifelike body. In the late 1970s, production of the 11½-in. figures was discontinued, being replaced by a series of 3¾-in. figures that was introduced in 1982. These smaller figures continued through 11 series over the next 10 years, eventually attaining a height of 4½ in. and culminating in the GI Joe Extreme. This was a 5-in. figure (5.8 in. with knees and waist straightened) that was introduced in 1995 and is still available on the shelves of toy stores today. Meanwhile, the 11½-in. figures were reintroduced in 1991 and continue to be manufactured to the present.

We purchased three representative 11½-in. figures: a 1973 Adventurer with 10
the original body in use since 1964, a 1975 Adventurer with the newer lifelike body, and a 1994 Hall of Fame figure. [The dimensions] of these three figures . . . are shown in Table 1. Not only have the figures grown more muscular, but they have developed increasingly sharp muscular definition through the years. For example, the earliest figure has no visible abdominal muscles; his 1975 counterpart shows some abdominal definition; and the 1994 figure displays the sharply rippled abdominals of an advanced bodybuilder. The modern figure also displays distinct serratus muscles along his ribs—a feature readily seen in bodybuilders but less often visible in ordinary men.

We also purchased several of the smaller figures for comparison—a 1982 Grunt, a 1982 Cobra soldier (GI Joe's arch enemy), and a current GI Joe Extreme. . . . The contemporary GI Joe Extreme dwarfs his earlier counterparts with dramatically greater musculature and has an expression of rage which contrasts sharply with the bland faces of his predecessors. Although the body dimensions of the earlier small action figures cannot be accurately estimated because of their layer of clothing, the GI Joe Extreme is more easily measured (see Table 1). If extrapolated to 70 in. in height, the GI Joe Extreme would sport larger biceps than any bodybuilder in history.

Table 1 Measurements of Representative Action Toys Extrapolated to a Height of 70 In.

Toy, Date	Actual Measurements (in.)[a]				Extrapolated to Height of 70 In.[a]		
	Height	Waist	Chest	Biceps	Waist[b]	Chest[b]	Biceps[b]
GI Joe Land Adventurer, 1973 (with original body in use since 1964)	11.5	5.2	7.3	2.1	31.7	44.4	12.2
GI Joe Land Adventurer, 1975 (with new body introduced in 1974)	11.5	5.2	7.3	2.5	31.7	44.4	15.2
GI Joe Hall of Fame Soldier, 1994 (with body introduced in 1991)	11.5	4.8	7.1	2.7	29.2	43.2	16.4
GI Joe Extreme, 1998	5.8	3.0[c]	4.5[c]	2.2	36.5[c]	54.8[c]	26.8
The Gold Ranger, 1998	5.5	2.7[c]	3.6[c]	1.4[c]	34.4[c]	45.8[c]	17.8[c]
Ahmed Johnson, 1998	6.0	3.0	4.1	2.0	35.0	47.8	23.3
Iron Man, 1998	6.5	2.6	4.7	2.1	28.0	50.6	22.6
Batman, 1998	6.0	2.6	4.9	2.3	30.3	57.2	26.8
Wolverine, 1998	7.0	3.3	6.2	3.2	33.0	62.0	32.0

[a]Measurements estimated to the nearest 0.1 in.

[b]For comparison, the mean waist, chest, and biceps circumferences of 50 Australian soccer players, scaled to a slightly shorter height of 170.2 cm (67 in.), were found to be 29.6 in., 36.3 in., and 11.8 in., respectively (19).

[c]These numbers are reduced by about 5% from actual measurements to compensate for the thickness of the figure's clothes and equipment.

LUKE SKYWALKER AND HAN SOLO

A similar impression emerges upon examining the original (1978) versus the contemporary 3¾-in. figures of *Star Wars* characters Luke Skywalker and Han Solo (manufactured by the Kenner Toy Company). Luke and Han have both acquired the physiques of bodybuilders over the last 20 years, with particularly impressive gains in the shoulder and chest areas. Again, the clothing on these small plastic figures precludes accurate body measurements, so that they are not included in Table 1. . . .

DISCUSSION

We hypothesized that action toys would illustrate evolving ideals of male body image in the United States. Accordingly, we purchased and measured the most popular male human action figures which have been manufactured over the last 30 years. On both visual inspection and anthropomorphic measurement, it appears that action figures today are consistently much more muscular than their predecessors. Many modern figures display the physiques of advanced bodybuilders and some display levels of muscularity far exceeding the outer limits of actual human attainment.

These findings, however, must be interpreted cautiously for several reasons. First, we found only two lines of male human action toys which fully met our criterion of long-term documented popularity. Thus, it might be argued that these particular toy lines happened to favor our hypothesis by chance alone. However, on the basis of our discussions with action figure experts, we believe that the examples analyzed here are representative of the overall trend of body image in male action toys over the last several decades. The other leading contemporary toys . . . support the impression that this trend toward a bodybuilder physique is consistent. The only notable exception to this trend is the Mattel Company's Ken, the boyfriend of Barbie. However, although the Barbie toy line overall has frequently ranked among the top 10 toy lines, Ken is but a small part of this market. Among boys in particular, Ken almost certainly ranks well below the popularity of the other male action figure discussed above (*Playthings* magazine).

Second, it is uncertain whether action toys accurately mirror trends in other 15
media. It is our impression that comic strip characters, male models in magazines, and male motion picture actors have all shown a parallel trend toward increasing leanness and muscularity over the last several decades. However, more systematic studies will be required to confirm these observations.

Third, it is not clear to what extent these trends in toys, or parallel trends in other media, may be a cause or effect of an evolving cultural emphasis on male muscularity. Certainly, it would be premature to conclude that American men are prompted to develop disorders of body image purely as a result of boyhood exposure to muscular ideals of male physique. On the other hand, the impact of toys should not be underestimated. Male action toys as a whole accounted for $949 million in manufacturers' shipments in 1994 alone, with action figures accounting for $687 million of this total (*Playthings* magazine, 1995).

It should also be noted that similar theories have been advanced for many years regarding cultural ideals of thinness in women (Pope & Hudson, 1984; Cash & Pruzinsky, 1990). For example, one study found that both *Playboy* centerfold models and Miss America pageant contestants grew steadily thinner over the period of 1959 to 1978 (Garner, Garfinkel, Schwartz, & Thompson, 1980). A recent update suggests that this trend has continued at least through 1988 (Wiseman, Gray, Mosimann, & Ahrens, 1992). Similarly, in the area of toys, the literature has documented the inappropriate thinness of modern female dolls (Norton et al., 1996; Pederson & Markee, 1991; Rintala & Mustajoki, 1992; Brownell & Napolitano, 1995). Indeed, one report has found that Mattel Company's Barbie, if extrapolated to a height of 67 in., would have a waist circumference of 16 in. (Norton et al., 1996)—a figure approaching the impossibility of our male superheroes' biceps.

In any event, these striking findings suggest that further attempts should be made to assess the relationship between cultural messages and body image disorders in both men and women.

REFERENCES

Action figures duke it out. (1995). Playthings magazine, 93, 26–28.

Andersen, A.E. (Ed). (1990) Males with eating disorders. New York: Brunner Mazel.

Brownell, K.D., & Napolitano, M.A. (1995). Distorting reality for children: Body size proportions of Barbie and Ken dolls. International Journal of Eating Disorders, 18, 295–298.

Cash, T.F., & Pruzinsky, T. (Eds). (1990). Body images: Developments, deviance, and change. New York: Guilford.

Drewnowski, A., & Yee, D.K. (1987). Men and body image: Are males satisfied with their body weight? Psychosomatic Medicine, 49, 626–634.

Dwyer, J.T., Feldman, J.J., Seltzer, C.C., & Mayer, J. (1969). Body image in adolescents: Attitudes toward weight and perception of appearance. American Journal of Clinical Nutrition, 20, 1045–1056.

Garner, D.M., Garfinkel, P.E., Schwartz, D., & Thompson, M. (1980). Cultural expectations of thinness in women. Psychological Reports, 47, 483–491.

Hollander, E. (1993). Introduction. In E. Hollander, (Ed.), Obsessive-compulsive related disorders. Washington, DC: American Psychiatric Press.

Hollander, E., Cohen, L.J., & Simeon, D. (1993). Body dysmorphic disorder. Psychiatric Annals, 23, 359–364.

Kouri, E., Pope, H.G., Katz, D.L., & Oliva, P. (1995) Fat-free mass index in users and non-users of anabolic-androgenic steroids. Clinical Journal of Sport Medicine, 5, 223–228.

Mangweth, B., Pope, H.G., Jr., Hudson, J.I., Olivardia, R., Kinzl, J., & Biebl, W. (1997). Eating disorders in Austrian men: An intra-cultural and cross-cultural comparison study. Psychotherapy and Psychosomatics, 66, 214–221.

Mintz, L.B., & Betz, N.E. (1986). Sex differences in the nature, realism, and correlates of body image. Sex Roles, 15, 185–195.

Norton, K.I., Olds, T.S., Olive, S., & Dank, S. (1996). Ken and Barbie at life size. Sex Roles, 34, 287–294.

Olivardia, R., Pope, H.G., Jr., Mangweth, B., & Hudson, J.I. (1995). Eating disorders in college men. American Journal of Psychiatry, 152, 1279–1285.

Pedersen, E.L., & Markee, N.L. (1991). Fashion dolls: Representations of ideals of beauty. Perceptual and Motor Skills, 73, 93–94.

Phillips, K.A. (1991). Body dysmorphic disorder: The distress of imagined ugliness. American Journal of Psychiatry, 148, 1138–1149.

Phillips, K.A. (1997). The broken mirror. New York: Oxford University Press.

Phillips, K.A., McElroy, S.L., Hudson, J.I., & Pope, H.G., Jr. (1995). Body dysmorphic disorder: An obsessive-compulsive spectrum disorder, a form of affective spectrum disorder, or both? Journal of Clinical Psychiatry, 56 (Suppl. 4), 41–51.

Playthings. (1983–1997). New York: Geyer-McAllister Publications, Inc.

Pope, H.G., Jr., Gruber, A.J., Choi, P.Y., Olivardia, R., & Phillips, K.A. (1997). Muscle dysmorphia: An under-recognized form of body dysmorphic disorder. Psychosomatics, 38, 548–557.

Pope, H.G., Jr., & Hudson, J.I. (1984). New hope for binge eaters: Advances in the understanding and treatment of bulimia. New York: Harper and Row.

Pope, H.G., Jr., & Katz, D.L. (1994). Psychiatric and medical effects of anabolic-androgenic steroids: A controlled study of 160 athletes. Archives of General Psychiatry, 51, 375–382.

Pope, H.G., Jr., Katz, D.L., & Hudson, J.I. (1993). Anorexia nervosa and "reverse anorexia" among 108 male bodybuilders. Comprehensive Psychiatry, 34, 406–409.

Rintala, M., & Mustajoki, P. (1992). Could mannequins menstruate? British Medical Journal, 305, 1575–1576.

Santelmo, V. (1997). The complete encyclopedia to GI Joe (2nd ed.). Iola, WI: Krause Publications.

Schneider, J.A., & Agras, W.S. (1987). Bulimia in males: A matched comparison with females. International Journal of Eating Disorders, 6, 235–242.

Wiseman, C.V., Gray, J.J., Mosimann, J.E., & Ahrens A.H. (1992). Cultural expectations of thinness: An update. International Journal of Eating Disorders, 11, 85–90.

Are You Man Enough?

RICHARD LACAYO

WHATEVER ELSE YOU MAY THINK about testosterone, you can tell it's a hot topic. Every time you mention that you happen to be writing about it, the first thing people ask is "Can you get me some?" (Everybody, even the women.) Maybe that's not so surprising. If there is such a thing as a bodily substance more fabled than blood, it's testosterone, the hormone that we understand and misunderstand as the essence of manhood. Testosterone has been offered as the symbolic (and sometimes literal) explanation for all the glories and infamies of men, for why they start street fights and civil wars, for why they channel surf, explore, prevail, sleep around, drive too fast, plunder, bellow, joust, plot corporate takeovers and paint their bare torsos blue during the Final Four. Hey, what's not to like? 1

Until now, it was easy to talk about testosterone but hard to do much about it. About 4 million men in the U.S. whose bodies don't produce enough take a doctor-prescribed synthetic version, mostly by self-injection, every one to three weeks. But the shots cannot begin to mimic the body's own minute-by-minute micromanagement of testosterone levels. So they can produce a roller coaster of emotional and physical effects, from a burst of energy, snappishness and libido in the first days to fatigue and depression later. The main alternative, a testosterone patch, works best when applied daily to the scrotum, an inconvenient spot, to put it mildly. Some doctors recommend that you warm that little spot with a blow dryer, which may or may not be fun.

All of that will change this summer when an easy to apply testosterone ointment, AndroGel, becomes generally available for the first time by prescription. The company that developed it, Illinois-based Unimed Pharmaceuticals, promises that because AndroGel is administered once or more a day, it will produce a more even plateau of testosterone, avoiding the ups and downs of the shots. Though the body's own production of this hormone trails off gradually in men after the age of 30 or so, not many men now seek testosterone-replacement therapy (not that they necessarily need to) or even get their T levels tested. But replace the needles and patches with a gel, something you just rub into the skin like coconut oil during spring break at Daytona Beach, and suddenly the whole idea seems plausible.

Testosterone, after all, can boost muscle mass and sexual drive. (It can also cause liver damage and accelerate prostate cancer, but more on that later.) That makes it central to two of this culture's rising preoccupations: perfecting the male body and sustaining the male libido, even when the rest of the male has gone into retirement. So will testosterone become the next estrogen, a hormone that causes men to bang down their doctor's doors, demanding to be turned into Mr. T? Do not underestimate the appeal of any substance promising to restore the voluptuous powers of youth to the scuffed and dented flesh of middle age. If you happen to be a man, the very idea is bound to appeal to your inner hood ornament, to that image of yourself as all wind-sheared edges and sunlit chrome. And besides, there's the name: testosterone! Who can say no to something that sounds like an Italian dessert named after a Greek god?

5 But testosterone is at issue in larger debates about behavioral differences between men and women and which differences are biologically determined. A few Sundays ago, the *New York Times Magazine* ran a long piece by Andrew Sullivan, 36, the former editor of the *New Republic* in which he reported his own experience with testosterone therapy. In two years he has gained 20 lbs. of muscle. And in the days right after his once-every-two-weeks shot, he reports feeling lustier, more energetic, more confident and more quarrelsome—more potent, in all senses of the word.

Looking over the scientific research on testosterone, Sullivan speculated on the extent to which such traits as aggression, competitiveness and risk taking, things we still think of as male behavior, are linked to the fact that men's bodies produce far more testosterone than women's bodies. His answer—a lot—was offered more as an intuition than a conclusion, but it produced a spate of fang baring among some higher primates in the media and scientific world, since it implies that gender differences owe more to biology than many people would like to believe. Three researchers wrote the *Times* to complain that Sullivan had overstated their thinking. In the online magazine *Slate,* columnist Judith Shulevitz attacked Sullivan for favoring nature over environment in a debate in which nobody knows yet which is which. In the days that followed, Sullivan fired back at Shulevitz in *Slate,* she attacked again, and other writers joined in. If testosterone use becomes a true cultural phenomenon, expect the conversations about its role in gender differences to become even more, well, aggressive.

So just what does testosterone actually do for you? And to you? And how does it figure among the physical and environmental pressures that account for head-banging aggression, or even just the trading pit on Wall Street? One reason testosterone enjoys a near mythical status is that myth is what takes over when conclusive data are scarce. Though testosterone was first isolated in 1935, hormone-replacement therapy is one of the few areas of medicine where research on men lags behind that on women.

What we do know is that testosterone is an androgen, as the family of male sex hormones are called, and these hormones, in turn, are made up of the fat known as steroids. Both men and women produce testosterone in their bodies, men in the testes and adrenal glands, women in the adrenal glands and ovaries. But men produce much more—the average healthy male has 260 to 1,000 nanograms of testosterone per deciliter of blood plasma. For women the range is 15 to 70. But because men differ on how effectively their bodies process the substance—for instance, some have more receptors around their body that absorb it—a man on the low end of the normal range can still have all the testosterone he needs for normal sex drive and other benefits. In healthy men, levels also vary during the day, peaking around 8 a.m., which is why men commonly awaken in a state of sexual arousal, and dropping as much as half before bedtime.

Testosterone is the substance that literally turns boys into boys in the womb. In the first weeks after conception, all embryos are technically sexless. Around the sixth week of gestation, the presence of the Y chromosome in males triggers a complex set of signals that cause a surge in testosterone. Among other things, that sets in motion the formation of the penis and testes. In adolescence, boys undergo another eruption that deepens their voices, causes hair to form on their bodies and allows their muscles to enlarge. Testosterone in the blood of teenage boys can jump to as high as 2,000 nanograms, which helps explain teenage boys.

10 One possible danger of easy-to-use testosterone is that it might become a temptation to younger males looking to bulk up at the gym. Not many of them would be able to demonstrate the diminished T counts that would allow them to get it legally from their doctors, but the potential for a black market in AndroGel is not hard to imagine among teens and guys in their 20s—and older—who hear stories about a new substance stronger than the supplements available over the counter and easier to use than anabolic steroids that are injected. For teens in particular, the dangers of testosterone overload are not just acne and breast development but a shutting down of bone growth—though they may be at an age that makes them almost deaf to the risks. For older men, studies indicate that high levels of T do not necessarily cause prostate cancer but do fuel the growth of tumors once they occur, which is why chemical castration is one means of treating the disease in the advanced stages.

Gay men may have been one of the first populations to talk up testosterone replacement, which is often part of the treatment regimen for HIV-positive men like Sullivan, author of the *New York Times Magazine* piece. They produced a buzz about increased sex drive and better results at the gym, things that happen to be of interest to a lot of straight men too, especially middle-age baby boomers looking to put themselves back in the driver's seat as far as their sex drive is concerned. "These men already come in asking for [testosterone]," says Dr. Louann Brizendine, co-director of the program in sexual health at the University of California, San Francisco. "This generation came out of the sexual revolution. They really identify themselves as sexual beings. And they don't want to give that up."

At 66, Gene Teasley, who operates a family business that makes banners in Dallas, is a decade older than the baby boomers, but he gets the idea. About nine years ago, he went to his doctor complaining of less interest in sex. Since then, he has been getting testosterone shots once every two weeks. "I've enjoyed the results not just in the sexual way but also in a broader way of feeling healthier. I have more of a desire to work out, be outdoors and do more athletic things," he says. "Everybody wants to feel like they felt in their 20s and 30s."

Some researchers are taking seriously the still controversial notion of "male menopause," a constellation of physical changes, including fatigue, depression and drooping libido, that they believe can be traced to the decline of hormones, including testosterone, in men over 50. Others are not so sure. "One thing we have to recognize is that the decline in testosterone is also intertwined with changes, such as decrease in blood flow, and psychological and social changes too," says Dr. Kenneth Goldberg, medical director of the Men's Health Center in Dallas. "Simply expecting to take men who are androgen deficient and expecting testosterone to fix it all—it just can't be."

Yet even the passage of time doesn't guarantee that a particular man's testosterone will decline to a level that much affects how he feels, at least not by middle age. Middle-age men who preserve the body weight they had in their 20s may have no falloff at all, while overweight adult men of any age tend to have lower testosterone levels. This means that a couple of the *goombahs* on *The Sopranos* are probably deficient, though maybe I should let you be the one to tell them that.

Once you get past the proven links between testosterone, libido and muscle 15
mass, the benefits of having higher levels of testosterone become harder to prove, though no less interesting to hear about. Just how much of a role does this play in producing behaviors such as aggression, competitiveness and belligerence? Men who take testosterone by injection routinely report that in the first days after the shot, when their T counts are especially high, they feel increased confidence, well-being and feistiness—what you might call swagger. They also describe feeling snappish and fidgety.

Jim—not his real name—is a family therapist who was 40 when he started taking the shots because of fatigue and a so-so interest in sex, which had led him to get his T levels tested. The first day or two after the shot, he says, he's on pins and needles. "My fiancé knows to steer clear. I tend to be short-tempered, more critical, and I go around the house looking for problems. I live out in the country, so right after I get the shot I get out the weed whacker and the chain saw, and I just go crazy."

Gee. Even putting aside for a moment the much increased danger of prostate cancer, do we really want men to turn later life into a hormonal keg party? The thought could be mildly exasperating to women, who might be forgiven for greeting the news with the same feelings china shop-keepers have for bulls. But this is the point at which the discussion of testosterone veers into the metaphysical.

Outside the bedroom and the gym, just what does testosterone do for you? Studies in animals have repeatedly shown that testosterone and aggression go hand in hand. Castrate species after species, and you get a pussycat. Boost the testosterone with injections and the castrated animal acts more like a tiger. In one study of men, when the testosterone levels were suppressed (in this case by researchers using medications) libido and dominant behaviors dropped. But when a mere 20% of the testosterone was added back, libido and domination climbed to the levels where they had started. Which suggests that men do not need much of the stuff to go on doing whatever it is they have already learned to do.

Other studies have shown that men with naturally higher testosterone levels are more aggressive and take-charge than men with slightly lower levels. When two sports teams meet, both teams will show an increase in testosterone during the game. "In the face of competition, levels of testosterone will rise," says Alan Booth, a sociologist at Penn State University. "This prepares the competitor and may help increase the chances for a win. It could be that the rise in testosterone has physical benefits, such as visual acuity and increased strength. But only the winning team continues to show high testosterone after the game."

For this exercise, you don't even have to picture the Packers vs. the Vikings. 20
The T boost also happens during nonphysical competitions, like chess games and trivia contests. Whatever the game, in evolutionary terms this makes sense. Among the primates from whom we are descended, the victorious male in any encounter may have needed to maintain high testosterone levels in the expectation that his position in the pecking order would be challenged by the next guy coming up.

But here it gets complicated. Does higher testosterone produce more aggressive behavior? Or does the more aggressive male—whose aggression was learned, say, at home or in school or in the neighborhood or on the team or in the culture at large—call for a release of testosterone from within himself for assistance? And if testosterone really does determine male behaviors like aggression, then what are we to make of the fact that although testosterone levels are pretty equal in prepubescent children, boys and girls already demonstrate different behaviors?

What we know for certain is this: aggressive behavior and testosterone appear in the same place. And aggressive behavior seems to require some testosterone in your system. But researchers have yet to show conclusively that adding a little more in males who already have a normal range of the stuff does much to make them more aggressive or confrontational. In one study, Dr. Christina Wang of UCLA found that men with low testosterone were actually more likely to be angry, irritable and aggressive than men who had normal to high-normal levels of testosterone. When their testosterone was increased during hormone-replacement therapy, their anger diminished and their sense of well-being increased. "Testosterone is probably a vastly overrated hormone," says Robert Sapolsky, a Stanford University biologist and author of *The Trouble with Testosterone*.

All the same, there are social implications connected to the one area in which we know for a fact that testosterone matters—sex drive. Married men tend to have lower testosterone. It's evolution's way of encouraging the wandering mate to stay home. (In newly divorced men, T levels rise again, as the men prepare to re-enter the competition for a mate.) If aging men start to routinely boost their testosterone levels, and their sexual appetite, to earlier levels, will they further upset the foundations of that ever endangered social arrangement called the family? "What happens when men have higher levels than normal?" asks James M. Dabbs, a psychology professor at Georgia State University. "They are just unmanageable."

Dabbs, the author of *Heroes, Rogues and Lovers,* a book about the importance of the male hormone, is another researcher who believes that T counts for a lot in any number of male moods and behaviors. "It contributes to a boldness and a sense of focus," he insists. It's possible for the scientific community to come to such disparate conclusions on the stuff, not just because the research is slim but because the complexities of human behavior are deep. If we're verging on a moment when testosterone will be treated as one more renewable resource, we may soon all get to focus more clearly on just what it does. But if men, in a culture where the meaning of manhood is up for grabs, look to testosterone for answers to the largest questions about themselves, they are likely to be disappointed. One thing we can be sure of is that the essence of manhood will always be something more complicated than any mere substance in the blood.

COMPUTERS AND YOUTH CULTURE

The three essays that follow examine different aspects of the influence computers have on today's younger generations. Ian Zack's "Universities Find Sharp Rise in Computer-Aided Cheating," focuses on plagiarism, a problem many educators claim has only worsened since Zack's essay first appeared in the *New York Times* in 1998. "The Secret Life of Teens" examines the often-studied (and debated) topic of the relationship between the violent media (especially the Internet and video games) and youth violence. This essay, by John Leland, first appeared in *Newsweek* in 1999. In her 1998 *Arlington Star Telegram* article, "Study Says Net Use, Depression May be Linked," Amy Harmon reports on a Carnegie Mellon University research study of 169 Internet users (study participants) in the Pittsburgh area.

Universities Find Sharp Rise in Computer-Aided Cheating

IAN ZACK

IN A TROUBLING reminder of technology's darker side, Virginia Tech, the state's largest university, has acknowledged that computer-aided cheating by students is growing rapidly. 1

"We've had a lot more cases," said Leon Geyer, who oversees the student-run honor system at Virginia Polytechnic Institute and State University, which has 25,000 students. "In the olden days, you had to copy from the book. Now, you just copy and paste."

Officials at the university say that the number of cheating complaints has grown to 280 last year from 80 in 1995–96 and includes reports of plagiarizing information from the Internet, sharing answers or other information by electronic mail or diskette, and stealing information from a fellow student's computer screen or electronic mail system.

Virginia Tech is not the only university experiencing growth in such incidents or worrying about how to detect and prevent them. The personal computer, while enhancing teaching, has made cheating as simple as pointing and clicking a mouse or exchanging a floppy disk with the answers to a take-home test.

5 Stealing or copying someone's work has become so effortless, some say, that students may be inured to the ethical or legal consequences, much like drivers exceeding the speed limit.

"Let's say everyone in the class has a networked computer," said Chris Duckenfield, vice provost for computing and information technology at Clemson University. "They can exchange information electronically. They can pull down information electronically. Who's going to watch over every student's shoulder to see what they're doing?"

Last October, Boston University was so concerned about computer cheating that it filed a Federal lawsuit to stop eight companies from selling term papers over the Internet in Massachusetts. The university's action came a quarter century after the institution successfully sued term-paper mills hawking typewritten papers out of Volkswagen buses in Cambridge. The state now bans the sale of printed term papers.

At the University of California at Berkeley, a computer science professor, Alex Aiken, created software to identify plagiarism in his programming courses. He placed the software, called Moss, for Measure of Software Similarity, on the Internet (at www.cs.berkeley.edu/~aiken/moss.html), and it is now used by more than 500 professors at universities worldwide.

Professor Aiken attributes the rise to the anonymity of electronic communication, the vast resources of the Internet and the ever-multiplying speed of computers. "The fact that you can do it more quickly makes it easier to yield to an impulse," he said.

10 This is apparently what happened to the president of the student union at Oxford University in England, who was expelled after the university determined she had cheated on a final examination by downloading an essay she had written earlier.

At Virginia Tech last spring, dozens of students in a computer-programming course—roughly 10 percent of a class of 600—were accused of electronically sharing information on a year-end assignment. And recently, two graduating seniors downloaded another student's work to turn in as their own computer programming assignment. A piece of software similar to Professor Aiken's found them out.

"It does seem to be an increasing problem because it is so much easier," said Amanda Rich, a 21-year-old Virginia Tech senior from Clinton, Ill., who is chief justice of the university's honor system court, where accused cheaters are tried.

Ms. Rich said some incidents were obvious cases of wrongdoing, while others appear to be ignorance by students who do not understand the rules of scholarly research.

Whatever the reasons, professors and administrators at Virginia Tech do not quite know how to respond. "I don't know if this is the beginning of an ugly, awful trend or just a blip," said John Carroll, a computer science professor. "It's a new world out there."

15 But professors are not waiting around for a new set of computer commandments to take hold. Some routinely search the Internet when information in a term paper appears suspicious. Tom Rocklin, a University of Iowa professor who has written an electronic paper called "Downloadable Term Papers: What's a Prof to Do?" says that some teachers unwittingly encourage students to cheat by giving broad general-knowledge assignments or scheduling too many large projects at the end of a semester.

"If you tie assignments really tightly to what you're doing in class, it becomes more difficult to cheat," Professor Rocklin said. He also suggested that teachers require outlines and rough drafts for term papers, so they can see a student's work in progress.

Professor Geyer, the faculty adviser for Virginia Tech's honor system, said that while computer cheating was easy to do, once suspected it was also "easy to detect—and students haven't figured out the latter."

At Virginia Tech, students found guilty of computer-aided cheating have received punishments ranging from zeros and double-weighted zeros on tests—which can mean a failing grade in a course—to community service. Under the university's honor system, students rarely are expelled for a first offense.

But Professor Geyer said, "I know some graduating seniors who had to go to summer school."

The Secret Life of Teens

JOHN LELAND

1 "HI, KIDS, do you like violence? Wanna see me stick nine-inch nails through each one of my eyelids? Wanna copy me and do exactly like I did?" The bleached-blond pixie could be a refugee from the set of *Friends,* all smirk and glimmer. He is Marshall Mathers, better known as Eminem, whose debut rap album has been near the top of the charts for the last two months. In the secret lives of American teenagers, Eminem is large. "By the way," he raps, "when you see my dad, tell him I slit his throat in this dream I had."

Since they first emerged as a demographic entity earlier this century, adolescents of every era have carved out their own secret worlds, inventing private codes of style and behavior designed to communicate only within the in group and to exclude or offend adults. It is a central rite of American passage. But lately this developmental process has come under great strain. "In the past, the toughest decision [teens] had was whether to have sex, or whether to use drugs," says Sheri Parks, who studies families and the media at the University of Maryland. "Those are still there, but on top are piled all these other issues, which are very difficult for parents or children to decipher." New technologies and the entertainment industry, combined with changes in family structure, have more deeply isolated grown-ups from teenagers. The results are what Hill Walker, codirector of the Institute on Violence and Destructive Behavior in Oregon, calls "almost a virtual reality without adults."

With as many as 11 million teenagers now online, more and more of adolescent life is taking place in a landscape that is inaccessible to many parents. "That is apparent in the geography of households," says Marlene Mayhew, a clinical psychologist who runs an online mental-health newsletter. With the computer often in the teen's bedroom, Mayhew says, the power structure in the family is turned upside down. "Kids are unsupervised, looking at whatever they please." A parent who might eventually notice a stockpile of *Guns & Ammo* or pornographic magazines has fewer clues to a child's online activities. "We're missing the opportunity for an adult reality check, adult perspective on the stimulation [teens] are getting exposed to. Kids have less access to parents, more access to potentially damaging information."

The pop-culture industry, marketing tribal styles through MTV and the Internet, makes it harder than ever for adults to read their kids, even parents raised on rock and roll. Parents in the '50s could "read" the ripe sexuality of Elvis—they just might not have approved. But what to make of the much more densely encrypted messages and camp nihilism of Eminem or Marilyn Manson, who dare outsiders to take offense? How to distinguish a kid drawn to gangsta rapper DMX for the rhymes from one drawn to the crimes? Making the process harder, teens have long been adept at lying, dissembling and otherwise conniving to hide their secret lives. Robyn Sykes, a senior at Jordan High School in Long Beach, Calif., reports that the skills are still sharp. "Some girls," she says, "leave the house wearing one thing, and then change into tight, short skirts when they're here."

Mike L., 13, from suburban New York, is one of the unsupervised millions 5
online. A couple years ago his father spied on him through a window, catching him in a chat room where people swapped pirated software. But now Mike has his own laptop and can do what he wants. Like many kids, he mostly sends e-mail and hangs around chat rooms, where he encounters both adults and other teens. "You go in, and someone offers what they've got stored in their computer," he says. "And maybe one of the things is *The Anarchist Cookbook*," a notorious handbook that includes instructions for building bombs. Though he doesn't have it, he says, "one of my friends gets called down to the guidance counselor every day because somebody told a teacher that he knows how to make bombs. He's not the kind of guy who would do it. But he found out how on the Internet." Andrew Tyler, 13, from Haddonfield, N.J., used his Internet

freedom another way: two weeks ago, while his mother tended the family garden, Tyler placed bids on $3.2 million worth of merchandise via the online auction house eBay, including the winning bid on a $400,000 bedroom set. "I thought [eBay] was just a site," he told *Newsweek.* "It turned out to be a lot more than that."

The vast majority of adolescents' online activity ranges from edifying to harmless. Though hard numbers on Internet use are notoriously suspect, Malcolm Parks, an Internet researcher at the University of Washington in Seattle, says that most teens use the computer to send e-mail or instant messages, visit chat rooms or fan Web sites, do homework or download songs. For the most part, he says, "I worry more about poor quality of information online, and students' lack of skills for evaluating information, than I worry about frequently discussed evils like pornography."

At Neutral Ground in Manhattan on a recent afternoon, other skills are in play. The drafty, fourth-floor gaming room, undetectable from the street, is a teen oasis, dotted with interconnected computers. By a quarter to four, it is packed with adolescent boys. Robert, one of eight boys glued to the screens, suddenly curses and bangs on the table. "Die, you stupid whore," he shouts. Then, "I'm gonna go kill Sebastian now." Sebastian, three terminals down, calls back: "You take this game way too seriously."

They are playing Half-Life, known in video game parlance as a multiplayer "first-person shooter" game, or FPS. As Robert pushes a key, a red shell fires from an on-screen shotgun; arms fly off, blood spatters on the walls. "If my parents came down here now," says Mike, pausing from the carnage, "they'd probably drag me out." The best-known FPS is Doom, the game reportedly favored by the Littleton shooters, but to the kids at Neutral Ground, Doom is already passé. A new game, Kingpin, promises even hairier carnal gratifications. "Includes multiplayer gang bang death match for up to 16 thugs!" coos the ad copy. "Target specific body parts and actually see the damage done, including exit wounds."

The video game business last year topped $6.3 billion, much of it dedicated for play on the home computer. The more violent games are marked for sales to mature buyers only, but like R-rated movies, they are easily accessible to kids. "The people usually tell you you're not old enough," says Eddie, 14, a regular at Neutral Ground, "but they don't stop you from buying it." Eddie says most FPS games "make me dizzy," but he enjoys one called Diablo, which is not just another shoot-'em-up orgy. "It's more like slice 'em up." His parents don't like the games but rarely engage him on it. His mother, he says, "thinks it's too violent, so she doesn't watch."

Most teenagers seem to process the mayhem as mindless pyrotechnics. But 10
not all kids react the same way, warns Dan Anderson, a University of Massachusetts psychologist who has studied the effects of TV on children. "It's always been the case that the kids who have been vulnerable to violent messages on tel-

evision have been a small minority. But a small minority can cause serious havoc. If you're predisposed to violence and aggression, you can find like-minded people who will validate your experience. You can become part of an isolated group that family and friends don't know about, and that group can exchange information on getting or making weapons." Brad Bushman, an Iowa State University psychologist, argues that violent computer games are more harmful than movies, "because the person becomes the aggressor. They're the one that does the killing."

In Santa Monica last week Collin Williams and his friends, a multiracial group of eighth graders, describe a numbing effect. Sure, they shrugged, a tragedy like the one in Littleton could happen in their school. Though they don't spend much time on computers, says Williams, 14, "we see so much violence on TV and in the movies that it just seems like it's everywhere. We don't go to school thinking we're going to be killed. But maybe it's because we're so used to it."

The challenges for parents may be new, but they are not insurmountable. Many psychologists recommend changing the way the computer is used. Put it in a family room, where adults and teens have more opportunities to discuss what's coming into the house. Every Web browser records what sites users visit; parents can monitor their kids' activities with just elementary computer savvy. Filters, such as Net Nanny, restrict which sites users can visit, but smart kids can get around them, often by using a friend's computer. Idit Harel, founder of the kid-friendly site MaMaMedia, highly recommends playing videogames along with your kids. Even in violent games, she says, "there is learning, visualization; there is analysis of hints." Likewise, parents can either set limits on their kids' pop-cultural diets or just talk to the teens about what they're consuming. Say: "I don't understand this kid Eminem. What's he about?"

Even with such interaction, the secret lives of teenagers are likely to remain secret. They are as unbounded as the Internet and as plebeian as the Backstreet Boys, a daunting world for any parent to enter. But this remains the job of parenting. Today's teens command an electronic landscape more stimulating, vibrant and mysterious than any before. They are the masters of the new domain. But they still need adult guidance on their travels.

Study Says Net Use, Depression May Be Linked

AMY HARMON

IN THE FIRST concentrated study of the social and psychological effects of Internet use at home, researchers at Carnegie Mellon University have found that people who spend even a few hours a week online experience more depression and loneliness than those who use the computer network less frequently. 1

The participants who were lonelier and more depressed at the start of the two-year study, as determined by a standard questionnaire, were not more likely to use the Internet. Instead, Internet use itself appeared to lessen psychological well-being, the researchers said.

The results of the $1.5 million project are contrary to the expectations of the social scientists who designed it and many of the organizations that financed it. The backers include technology companies such as Intel Corp., Hewlett Packard, AT&T Research and Apple Computer, as well as the National Science Foundation.

"We were shocked by the findings, because they are counterintuitive to what we know about how socially the Internet is being used," said Robert Kraut, a social psychology professor at Carnegie Mellon's Human Computer Interaction Institute. "We are not talking here about the extremes. These were normal adults and their families, and on average, for those who used the Internet most, things got worse."

The Internet has been praised as superior to television and other "passive" media because it allows users to choose the kind of information they want to receive, and, often, to respond actively through e-mail exchanges, chat rooms or electronic bulletin board postings. 5

Research on the effects of watching television indicates that it tends to reduce social involvement. But the new study, "HomeNet," suggests that the interactive medium may be no more socially healthful than older mass media. It also raises troubling questions about the nature of "virtual" communication and the disembodied relationships that are often formed in the vacuum of cyberspace.

Study participants used inherently social features such as e-mail and Internet chat rooms more than they used passive information gathering such as reading or watching videos. But they reported a decline in interaction with relatives and a reduction in their circles of friends that directly corresponded to how much time they spent online.

At the beginning and end of the two-year study, the subjects were asked to agree or disagree with statements such as "I felt everything I did was an effort" and "I enjoyed life" and "I can find companionship when I want it." They were also asked to estimate how many minutes each day they spent with each member of their family and to quantify their social circle. Many of those questions are standard in psychological health assessments.

For the duration of the study, the subjects' use of the Internet was recorded. Depression and loneliness were measured independently, and each subject was rated on a subjective scale. In measuring depression, the responses were plotted on a scale of 0 to 3, with 0 being the least depressed and 3 being the most depressed. Loneliness was plotted on a scale of 1 to 5.

By the end of the study, the researchers found that one hour a week on the 10
Internet led to an average increase of .03, or 1 percent, on the depression scale, a loss of 2.7 members of the subject's social circle, which averaged 66 people, and an increase of .02, or four-tenths of 1 percent, on the loneliness scale.

The subjects exhibited wide variations in all three measured effects. The net effects are not large, but they are statistically significant in demonstrating deterioration of social and psychological life, Kraut said.

Based on the data, the researchers hypothesize that relationships maintained over long distances without face-to-face contact ultimately do not provide the kind of support and reciprocity that typically contribute to psychological security and happiness, such as being available to baby-sit in a pinch for a friend, or to grab a cup of coffee and talk.

"Our hypothesis is there are more cases where you're building shallow relationships, leading to an overall decline in feeling of connection to other people," Kraut said. . . .

Because the study participants were not randomly selected, it is unclear how the findings apply to the general population. It is also conceivable that some unmeasured factor caused simultaneous increases in use of the Internet and decline in normal levels of social involvement. Moreover, the effect of Internet use varied depending on an individual's life patterns and type of use. Researchers said that people who were isolated because of their geography or work shifts might have benefited socially from Internet use.

Even so, several social scientists familiar with the study vouched for its cred- 15
ibility and predicted that the findings will touch off a national debate over how public policy regarding the Internet should evolve and how the technology might be shaped to yield more beneficial effects.

"They did an extremely careful scientific study, and it's not a result that's easily ignored," said Tora Bikson, a senior scientist at Rand, the research institution. Based partly on previous studies that focused on how local communities such as Santa Monica, Calif., used computer networks to enhance civic participation, Rand has recommended that the federal government provide e-mail access to all Americans.

"It's not clear what the underlying psychological explanation is," Bikson said of the study. "Is it because people give up day-to-day contact and then find themselves depressed? Or are they exposed to the broader world of Internet and then wonder, 'What am I doing here in Pittsburgh?' Maybe your comparison standard changes. I'd like to see this replicated on a larger scale. Then I'd really worry."

Chapter 9

Arguing Claims about Language

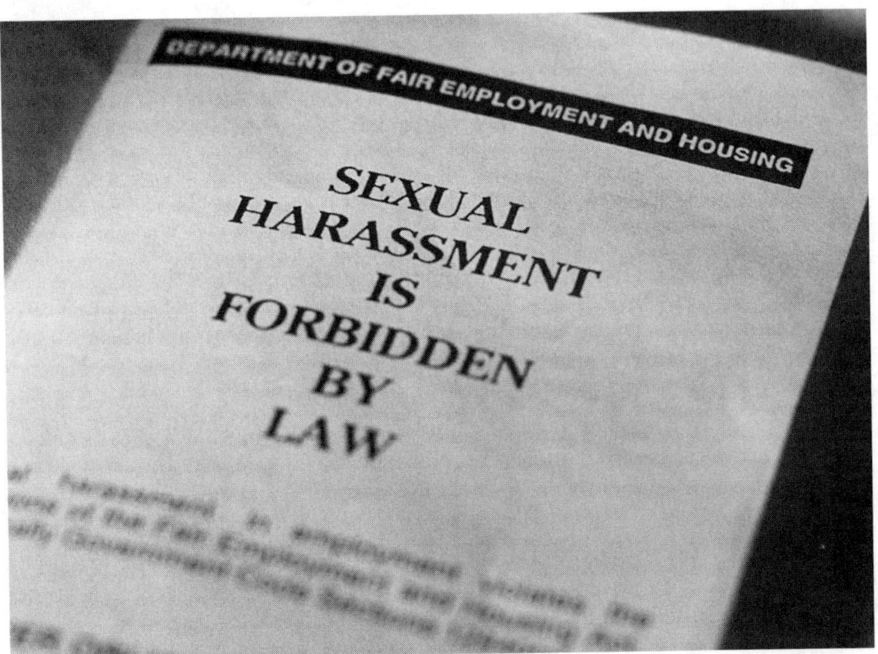

Our Differences about Language

The 17th-century English philosopher Francis Bacon listed language as one of the barriers to exact thinking. Paradoxically, it is also language that makes it possible for us to communicate our ideas at all. Language allows us to understand one another, but it is also through language that we misunderstand. The 20th-century philosopher Kenneth Burke argued that language is like a screen or a filter on a camera: It lets some meanings in and excludes others. Many disagreements in a community are about language. What do words mean? How should we interpret language? What language is appropriate or proper for a particular occasion? In addition to differences about language itself, there are also differences or disagreements caused by language, by the inability to communicate ideas in terms that others will understand. Sometimes disagreements are not really disagreements at all; they only seem so because people misunderstand each other. We often misunderstand each other because we assume that the meanings of words are obvious or that everyone is working with the same definitions and the same meanings. The process of arguing about language can help us to use language more precisely and to focus our attention on our real disagreements rather than on seeming disagreements that are actually misunderstandings.

Arguing about What Words Mean

DENOTATION AND CONNOTATION

Many arguments depend on determining the precise meanings of key terms, and many disagreements arise when those using key terms have not defined them for one another. For instance, the question "Is there more racism on college campuses today?" is about experience, but answering the question depends on how one defines *racism*. "Is pornography immoral?" is a question relating to values, but answering it requires not only a definition of *pornography* but also a definition of what is moral and immoral. Some may argue that abortion should be banned because it is murder. Is it really murder? It depends on one's definition. Some environmental activists argue that the clear-cutting of timber should be banned because it is ecological rape. Can the definition of rape be extended, even in a figurative sense, to the cutting of timber? Here are examples of other questions about defining key terms:

What is terrorism?

What is democracy or freedom?

What is courage?

What is justice?

What is sexual harassment?

What is a liberal?

What is a conservative?

These are terms that are used all the time in debates about political issues, but their definitions can be somewhat difficult to pin down.

One way to settle a dispute about definitions is to appeal to an authority, such as a dictionary or an expert, that is acknowledged by everyone involved in the dispute. When my friends and I play Scrabble, we agree before the game even starts on a dictionary that will be used to settle any disputes about whether a word is legitimate or not. As a student, you should become familiar with dictionaries that are considered authoritative, such as *Webster's Third International Dictionary, Black's Law Dictionary,* the *Random House Unabridged Dictionary,* and the *Oxford English Dictionary.* The *Oxford English Dictionary,* known as the OED, is particularly valuable because it not only gives the current meaning of a word, but also traces the changes in a word's meaning since its earliest appearances in print.

A dictionary, no matter how authoritative, has its limitations. It can describe how a community uses a word in very general terms, but it may not describe the shades of meaning the word has within different contexts. A dictionary provides the "denotative" definition of a word, what the word literally means, but dictionaries seldom provide "connotative" meanings, the associations a word carries with it. For instance, the following words all have roughly the same denotative meaning as the word *dead: deceased, departed, passed away, passed on, extinct, inanimate, late, lifeless, croaked, belly up, six feet under, pushing daisies, food for worms.* These words do not have the same connotation, however, and would not all be appropriate for the same contexts.

A word that has a particularly emotional connotation is often used in an argument to harm or injure. It is loaded language, language used as a weapon. Hate speech, the use of derogatory and demeaning terms to express anger or to attack others, provides a good example. In the academic community, as well as many others, this type of violence through language is not acceptable.

EUPHEMISMS AND DOUBLESPEAK

A word that is chosen for its positive connotations is called a *euphemism,* from the Greek for "good meaning." When you use *departed* or *passed on* for *dead,* you are using a euphemism, selecting a word for its positive connotations.

Sometimes euphemisms can be deceptive or misleading, giving an idea a more positive connotation than a straightforward statement will allow. Politicians have used the term *revenue enhancement* to hide the fact that they are imposing a *tax.* Military leaders have used the phrase "engaging the enemy on all sides" to hide the fact that their troops have become surrounded; and the phrase "collateral damage to soft targets" was used during the Persian Gulf War to hide the fact that U.S. bombs and missiles had harmed civilians. Governments refer to rebel groups they support as *freedom fighters* and rebel groups that they oppose as *terrorists,* even when both groups often use the same methods.

The use of language to obscure meaning in this way is called doublespeak, a term derived from George Orwell's novel *1984,* in which the government attempts to convince people that "war is peace" and "ignorance is knowledge," completely changing the denotative as well as connotative meanings of words.

Defining Troublesome Terms

Simply looking a word up in a dictionary may not be enough when complex questions and concepts are concerned. For instance, most dictionaries define *life* as an organism's ability to carry out metabolic functions, grow, respond to stimuli, and reproduce. This definition is generally useful, but how helpful is it in determining when human life begins or ends? A human cell does all of the above, but is it alive in the same sense that a human being is? At what stage does a fertilized egg change from a human cell to a human being? Life support can keep the human cells alive, but is the body on life support still a human life? And how helpful is this definition in determining whether something like a virus is really "alive"? In such cases you may need to formulate your own definition of the term for the purposes of argument. Here are some techniques for defining troublesome terms.

SYNONYMS AND PARAPHRASES

If a word requires a simple definition, then you can define it by choosing synonyms, words that mean approximately the same thing. You should seek out synonyms that are more familiar to your audience than the word you are trying to define. When you recast an entire passage in terms that are more familiar to the audience, then you have written a paraphrase.

CRITERIA AND MATCH

This is really a type of classification. You define the criteria that determine the members of a class, and then you examine a particular event or object to determine whether it fits those criteria. Criteria-and-match definitions take the following form:

If something possesses features A, B, and C, then it is a Y.

X possesses features A, B, and C.

Therefore, X is a Y.

In determining the criteria, you need to determine which criteria are necessary and which are optional. For instance, the chromosomal structure of a horse is a necessary criterion for determining whether an animal is a horse or not, but the color brown is optional: Some horses are brown and some are not.

Here is an example of defining and matching criteria using the argument that abortion is murder. To respond to this argument, you first determine the criteria for defining murder. The dictionary defines murder as the unlawful killing of a human being with malicious forethought. Using the criteria based on this definition, the act must

Kill a human being.

Be unlawful.

Be malicious.

Be done with forethought.

Do you accept these criteria? Are there others you would add? Are they all necessary, or are some optional? Certainly, the killing of a human being is necessary. But does murder only apply to human beings? Is it not possible to murder animals? If the killing is sanctioned by law is it, therefore, not murder? The systematic killing of Jews by the Nazis during World War II and the shooting of defectors by East German border guards were sanctioned by particular laws, yet the individuals who committed these acts were tried as murderers. Must the act be premeditated and malicious? The American legal system recognizes different degrees of murder, some of which do not require premeditation but are still considered murder. Establishing the criteria for what counts as murder and what doesn't is not as simple as it may first seem.

Let's say that you and your audience agree on these four criteria. You must now decide whether abortion matches these criteria for murder. Does an abortion kill a human being? It terminates a pregnancy and stops the growth of a fetus, but some dispute the stage at which a fetus can be considered a human being. Is a fertilized egg a human being? What happens when twinning occurs after the egg is fertilized? Did one human being turn into two? Is the differentiated zygote a human being? Some abortions are sanctioned by law. Does that mean they cannot be defined as murders? Or can these acts be judged by some higher law just as acts of the Nazis and East German border guards were? Is a doctor who performs an abortion performing a malicious act? Is the abortion always done with forethought, or could it be accidental or unintentional? If it is unintentional, is it still murder?

Of course, there are no easy answers to these questions: That is why there are disputes about definitions. But determining criteria and matching these to topics of debate can help to clarify complex issues.

FORMAL DEFINITIONS

A formal definition is similar to criteria-and-match definition, but there is an extra step. In a formal definition, after placing an object in a group, you go on to distinguish it from all other members of that group. It is usually stated in the following format: "An X is a Y that has features A, B, and C" (Y is the group, and A, B, C are the features that distinguish X from all other members of the group). Some formal definitions can be fairly simple: "Brigham Young University is a comprehensive four-year university sponsored by the Church of Jesus Christ of Latter-Day Saints (LDS), also known as the Mormon Church." Other colleges are sponsored by the LDS church, but they are not comprehensive four-year universities. There are other comprehensive four-year universities that are not sponsored by the LDS church. This definition places Brigham Young University in a class (comprehensive four-year university) and then distinguishes it from all other members of that class (sponsored by the LDS church).

ETYMOLOGY AND WORD HISTORY

Sometimes, when defining a word, it helps to know the etymology (origin) or history of the word. For instance, the word *obscene* comes from Greek and it refers to the story elements of a Greek tragedy that were shown "off stage," the literal meaning of the Greek word. In a Greek tragedy, no actual violence was shown on stage, only its results: The action of a character murdering her children or gouging out his own eyes took place off stage; the violence was often reported by a messenger, and then the character might appear covered in blood, but direct violence was "obscene." The meaning of *obscene* has changed in the last 2,000 years. Today it can indicate things that are repulsive, but it usually applies to something that is crude and sexually explicit.

The change in this word indicates a change in culture, a change in what we now consider repulsive or inappropriate. The fact that violence is no longer considered obscene in the same way that sex is may indicate our society has come to accept violence. At any rate, the etymology of this word provides an interesting perspective on its meaning, a perspective that could easily be incorporated into an argument about sex and violence.

OPERATIONAL DEFINITIONS AND PROTOTYPES

An operational definition is a precise or technical definition of a term developed for a specific purpose. It is much like a prototype but tends to be more scientific and verifiable. An operational definition often quantifies something or describes it in precise terms. For instance, a sociologist studying the effects of television violence on young children needs a definition of "violence." The dictionary definition—"the use of force to harm or abuse"—is not adequate because it cannot help *measure* violence. For the purposes of the study, the sociologist might define violence as certain types of violent acts: punching, slapping, or kicking a stuffed toy, for instance. This operational definition would allow the researcher to measure the effects of watching violent programs by counting the number of violent acts a child commits afterward.

EXAMPLES, COMPARISONS, AND ANALOGIES

An example or analogy is an attempt to use the familiar to explain the unfamiliar. These may be literal or figurative, real or imagined. Instructors often use examples to explain difficult concepts, as I have used examples throughout this book. When you are addressing a complex audience, made up of individuals with different experiences and background knowledge, it may be necessary to use multiple examples or comparisons in order to find something that is familiar to each individual.

NEGATION

One way to understand something is to describe what it is *not*. Theologians often use this approach in trying to describe the attributes of God. Scientists may use this approach to limit the possibilities for classifying or describing an unknown event. Be careful, though, not to mistake negation for definition. Negation limits the possibilities for what something may mean, but it doesn't reveal that meaning.

Arguing about How Language Should Be Used

Some disputes in a community may arise over the meaning of words. Other disputes may revolve around deciding what language is appropriate for the community. One recent such dispute in the United States is about the official language of the American community: The "English Only" movement has attempted to establish English as the only appropriate language for official, public use in the United States. Even so, English is made up of a number of varieties and dialects, some of which are considered more valuable or appropriate depending on the community.

Claims about how language should be used are closely related to claims about experience and claims about value and will usually be supported by reasons that are statements about experience or about values. For instance, an argument might state that using language in a particular way leads to harmful or beneficial effects. This argument about language includes an argument about experience (causality) and an argument about values (harmful and beneficial). Another argument might state that using language in a particular way violates some principle of correctness or morality. This argument also includes an argument about values (principles of correctness and morality).

Arguments about language use are not just about individual words; they are about metaphors as well. The metaphors that govern the way we think and act reveal themselves in the words we use. When we use them unconsciously they can do our thinking for us.

ARGUMENTS AS WAR

In their book *Metaphors We Live By,* George Lakoff and Mark Johnson describe how metaphors permeate our language and how our metaphors about arguing can often do our thinking for us. We talk about arguing as "war" without even realizing what we are doing:

Your claims are *indefensible.*

He *attacked every weak point* in my argument.

His criticisms were *right on target.*

I *demolished* his argument.

I've never *won* an argument with him.

You disagree? OK, *shoot!*

If you use that *strategy,* he'll *wipe you out.*

He *shot down* all of my arguments.

The violence of war is embedded in the way we talk about arguing and causes us to think that there must always be a winner and a loser. The war metaphor makes us think of arguing *against* others instead of arguing *with* others toward a common goal. What might be another metaphor for arguing? Lakoff and Johnson suggest that we should consider argument as a "dance" where each of the participants is a "performer." The object of the dance is to perfect the form and please others. Instead of "attacking" someone's "position," we could join with them in creating something new and mutually satisfying.

GENDER BIAS IN LANGUAGE

Other scholars have noted how unstated assumptions about gender permeate our language. Their findings have led to arguments about how we should use language to avoid gender bias. Linguist Alleen Pace Nilsen studied dictionary entries to see what they might suggest about sex bias in language. Reading through a dictionary, she made note cards growing to fill two shoe boxes. After completing her study and organizing her notes, Nilsen came to three conclusions about gender bias in language: Our language tends to portray women as "sexy" and men as "successful"; to portray women as "passive" and men as "active"; and to associate women with generally negative connotations and men with more positive connotations. Nilsen provides several examples of each of these relationships in order to establish a claim about experience: Gender bias can be found in our language. (Of course, this claim about experience relies on a claim about language, a definition of gender bias.)

Many communities, including most academic communities, have agreed that to the extent that sex bias does exist in language, it should be avoided. This claim leads to more arguments about the use of language. If there is gender bias in language, how should we avoid it? The National Council of Teachers of English (NCTE) has established some recommendations for how to avoid gender bias in language. First NCTE argues that because the generic *man* has come to refer primarily to men, it should be replaced with more gender-neutral terms: *humanity* instead of *mankind; human achievements* instead of *man's achievements; the best person for the job* instead of *the best man for the job; cave dwellers* instead of *cavemen;* and so on. Second, the council recommends using gender-neutral job titles instead of masculine and feminine forms: *chair, chairperson, coordinator, moderator,* or *head* instead of *chairman; business executive* or *manager* instead of *businessman; congressional representative* instead of *congressman; police officer* instead of *policeman; sales representative* or *sales clerk* instead of *salesman; firefighter* instead of *fireman; letter carrier* instead of *mailman;* and so on. The third recommendation has caused some of the most heated debate: the use of generic *he* and *his.* Traditionally, when referring to an indefinite pronoun (such as *one, anyone, someone, everyone*) or to a generalized singular noun, speakers and writers have used the pronoun *he.* "Everyone is entitled to *his* opinion" or "Every student should turn in *his* assignment on time." The NCTE recommends avoiding this generic *he* by recasting the sentence with a plural subject, by substituting *he or she* for *he* and *his or her* for *his,* or even by using the plural *their* with a singular subject. (This last suggestion has set off a heated debate among grammarians, but I'll bet that many of you use this construction without even thinking about it. Which would you say: "Has everyone got his passport?" or "Has everyone got their passport?")

Although discussions of gender bias in language and suggestions for avoiding bias often set off passionate discussion, many communities have adopted these guidelines. Government agencies, many corporations and businesses, and most universities expect writers at all levels to strive to eliminate gender and cultural bias from their work.

The Principles in Action: Readings

TWO VIEWS OF LANGUAGE AND ADVERTISING

Advertising is a particularly pervasive form of language use. Each day you probably encounter numerous messages advertising consumer products: billboards, television and radio commercials, magazine and newspaper ads, bumper stickers, T-shirts, even college classroom bulletin boards. With such a blur of messages, it is difficult to think critically about the arguments these messages contain. The following essays consider the persuasive potential of advertising. As you read them, consider the following questions:

1. How many different advertisements do you think you encounter every day? What kind of influence do you think advertising has?
2. What kind of persuasive strategies do you see in ads you encounter? What kind of claims, reasons, and assumptions do these ads contain? Are any of these strategies unfair or illegitimate?
3. To what extent do you accept the assumptions in ads?
4. Is advertising good or bad? Or is it both good and bad?

The Bribed Soul

LESLIE SAVAN

TELEVISION-WATCHING Americans—that is, just about *all* Americans—see approximately 100 TV commercials a day. In that same 24 hours they also see a host of print ads, billboard signs, and other corporate messages slapped onto every available surface, from the fuselages of NASA rockets right down to the bottom of golf holes and the inside doors of restroom stalls. Studies estimate that, counting all the logos, labels, and announcements, some 16,000 ads flicker across an individual's consciousness daily. 1

Advertising now infects just about every organ of society, and wherever advertising gains a foothold it tends to slowly take over, like a vampire or a virus. When television broadcasting began about 50 years ago, the idea of a network that would air nothing but commercials was never seriously considered, not even when single-sponsor shows were produced straight out of the sponsor's ad agency. But today, by the grace of cable, we have several such channels, including MTV, stylistically the most advanced programming on the air, and FYI, a proposed new channel that would run only ads—infomercials, home-shopping shows, regular-length commercials, and, for a real treat, programs of "classic" ads. Similarly, product placement in the movies started small, with the occasional Tab showing up in a star's hand, but now it's grown big enough to eat the whole thing. In its 1993 futuristic thriller *Demolition Man,* Warner Bros. not only scattered the usual corporate logos throughout the sets but it also rewrote the script so that the only fast-food chain to survive the "franchise wars" of the 20th century was Taco Bell—which, in return, promoted the movie in all its outlets.

Even older, far statelier cultural institutions have had their original values hollowed out and replaced by ad values, leaving behind the merest fossil of their founders' purpose. Modernist masters enjoy art museum blockbusters only when they can be prominently underwritten by an oil company or a telecommunication giant; new magazines are conceived not on the basis of their editorial content but on their ability to identify potential advertisers and groom their copy to fit marketing needs. In the process, the function of sponsored institutions is almost comically betrayed. The exotic bug exhibit at the Smithsonian Museum's new O. Orkin Insect Zoo, for example, opens with the red diamond logo of Orkin Pest Control and displays various little beasties, ever so subtly planting the suggestion that if they were to escape their glass cages you'd know who to call. Though the Smithsonian would never be so crass as to actually recommend Orkin's services, it is crass enough to never once mention in its exhibits the dangers of pesticides.

As for all those television-watching Americans, hit on by those 16,000 paid (and tax-deductible) messages a day, they're even more vulnerable than their institutions. Most admakers understand that in order to sell to you they have to know your desires and dreams better than you may know them yourself, and they've tried to reduce that understanding to a science. Market research, in which psychologists, polling organizations, trends analysts, focus group leaders, "mall-intercept" interviewers, and the whole panoply of mass communications try to figure out what will make you buy, has become a $2.5 billion annual business growing at a healthy clip of about 4.2 percent a year (after adjustment for inflation). Yet even this sophisticated program for the study of the individual consumer is only a starter kit for the technological advances that will sweep through the advertising-industrial complex in the 1990s. Today, the most we can do when another TV commercial comes on—and we are repeatedly told that this is our great freedom—is to switch channels. But soon technology will take even that tiny tantrum of resistance and make it "interactive," providing advertisers with information on the exact moment we became bored—vital data that can be crunched, analyzed, and processed into the next set of ads, the better to zap-proof *them*.

5 Impressive as such research may be, the real masterwork of advertising is the way it used the techniques of art to seduce the human soul. Virtually all of modern experience now has a sponsor, or at least a sponsored accessory, and there is no human emotion or concern—love, lust, war, childhood innocence, social rebellion, spiritual enlightenment, even disgust with advertising—that cannot be reworked into a sales pitch. The transcendent look in a bride's eyes the moment before she kisses her groom turns into a promo for Du Pont. The teeth-gnashing humiliation of an office rival becomes an inducement to switch to AT&T.

In short, we're living the sponsored life. From Huggies to Maalox, the necessities and little luxuries of an American's passage through this world are provided and promoted by one advertiser or another. The sponsored life is born when commercial culture sells our own experiences back to us. It grows as those experiences are then reconstituted inside us, mixing the most intimate processes of individual thought with commercial values, rhythms, and expectations. It has often been said by television's critics that TV doesn't deliver products to viewers but that viewers themselves are the *real* product, one that TV delivers to its advertisers. True, but the symbiotic relationship between advertising and audience goes deeper than that. The viewer who lives the sponsored life—and that is most of us to one degree or the other—is slowly re-created in the ad's image.

Inside each "consumer," advertising's all-you-can-eat, all-the-time, all-dessert buffet produces a build-up of mass-produced stimuli, all hissing and sputtering to get out. Sometimes they burst out as sponsored speech, as when we talk in the cadences of sitcom one-liners, imitate Letterman, laugh uproariously at lines like "I've fallen and I can't get up," or mouth the words of familiar commercials, like the entranced high school student I meet in a communication class who moved his lips with the voiceover of a Toyota spot. Sometimes they slip out as sponsored dress, as when white suburban kids don the baggy pants and backward baseball caps they see on MTV rappers. Sometimes they simply come out as sponsored equations, as when we attribute "purity" and "honesty" to clear products like Crystal Pepsi or Ban's clear deodorant.

To lead the sponsored life you don't really have to do anything. You don't need to have a corporate sponsor as the museums or the movies do. You don't even have to buy anything—though it helps, and you will. You just have to live in America and share with the nation, or at least with your mall-intercept cohorts, certain paid-for expectations and values, rhythms and reflexes.

Those expectations and how they unfold through advertising is the subject of this book. It's based on eight years of columns and articles I wrote about ads and other pop culture phenomena for *The Village Voice*. Despite advertising's enormous role in our lives, most of the media feel that, like hot dogs and military budgets, advertising goes down most easily when it's unexamined. They react this way, of course, because they're sponsored. Conveyors of commercial culture are free to question nearly all of modern life except their own life-support system. This conflict of interest means that unlike "official" cultural products—films, TV shows, books, paintings, and so on—advertising finds few regular critics in the mainstream press.

10 When the Center for the Study of Commercialism, a well-respected, Washington, D.C.–based nonprofit group, called a press conference in 1992 to announce the results of a study that showed the press repeatedly censoring itself under direct or anticipated advertiser pressure, not a single TV or radio reporter attended, and only a few papers even mentioned it. If journalism looks at ads at all, it usually settles for soft-shoe analysis, pieces that ask, essentially, "Does this ad work?" Most newspapers are pleased to do celebrity profiles of ad directors or agencies that have a few hits on their hands (possibly the agency will direct more ad dollars the paper's way, but more importantly over the long run, such stories prove that the publication offers a "positive environment" for advertisers). Ads are usually examined only when they make "news," through scandal, product failure, or superstar megadeals, like Madonna's or Michael Jackson's with Pepsi.

At the *Voice,* however, I could criticize ads in a fuller social and political context because, first of all, the paper is an alternative exception and does try to maintain a separation between advertising and editorial. And, as much to the point, I wasn't tearing into ads run by the futon shops, restaurants, and other local retailers that make up the bulk of *Voice* advertising.

That has allowed me to do the basic spadework of ad criticism—looking at the false claims ads occasionally make or the corporate misdeeds lurking behind the PR spin. But the real subject of my column, "Op Ad," has always been more *how* it works—how commercial values infiltrate our beliefs and desires, how we become more and more sponsored.

The chief expectation of the sponsored life is that there will and always should be regular blips of excitement and resolution, the frequency of which is determined by money. We begin to pulse to the beat, the one-two beat, that moves most ads: problem/solution, old/new, Brand X/hero brand, desire/gratification. In order to dance to the rhythm, we adjust other expectations a little here, a little there: Our notions of what's desirable behavior, our lust for novelty, even our visions of the perfect love affair or thrilling adventure adapt to the mass consensus coaxed out by marketing. Cultural forms that don't fit these patterns tend to fade away, and eventually *everything* in commercial culture—not just the 30-second spot but the drama, news segment, stage performance, novel, magazine layout—comes to share the same insipid insistence on canned excitement and neat resolution.

What's all the excitement about? Anything and nothing. You know you've entered the commercial zone when the excitement building in you is idly incommensurate with the content dangled before you: Does a sip of Diet Coke really warrant an expensive production number celebrating the rebel prowess of "ministers who surf," "insurance agents who speed," and "people who live their life as an exclamation not an explanation"?!? Of course not. Yet through the sympathetic magic of materialism we learn how to respond to excitement: It's less important that we purchase any particular product than that we come to expect resolution *in the form of* something buyable.

The way ads have of jacking up false excitement in the name of ultimately 15
unsatisfying purchases has given Western societies a bad case of commercial blue balls. You're hit on, say, by yet another guy on TV hawking fabric whitener, but—wait a minute—he "can't be a man" because he packs a different brand of smokes. And maybe you moan, "I can't get no, no no no. . . . "

Anyway, that's how the Rolling Stones put it in that seminal semiotic text "(I Can't Get No) Satisfaction" back in 1965. Commercials are the tinny jingles in our heads that remind us of all we've abandoned in exchange for our materially comfortable lives—real extended families, real human empathy, real rebel prowess. The result of stale promises endlessly repeated is massive frustration.

But Mick Jagger is younger than that now: Long after "Satisfaction" had dropped off the charts, the Rolling Stones became the first major band to tour for a corporate sponsor, Jovan perfumes, in 1981. By then Jagger had become a symbol of the most popular postmodern response to advertising's dominant role in our culture: the ironic reflex.

Irony has become a hallmark of the sponsored life because it provides a certain distance from the frustration inherent in commercial correctness. For some time now the people raised on television, the baby boomers and the "Generation Xers" that followed, have mentally adjusted the set, as it were, in order to convince themselves that watching is cool. They may be doing exactly what their parents do—but they do it *differently.* They take in TV with a Lettermanesque wink, and they like it when it winks back. In many cases (as Mark Crispin Miller has described so well in *Boxed In*), the winkers have enthusiastically embraced the artifice, even the manipulativeness, of advertising as an essential paradox of modern life, a paradox that is at the crux of their own identity.

The winkers believe that by rolling their collective eyes when they watch TV they can control *it,* rather than letting it control them. But unfortunately, as a defense against the power of advertising, irony is a leaky condom—in fact, it's the same old condom that advertising brings over every night. A lot of ads have learned that to break through to the all-important boomer and Xer markets they have to be as cool, hip, and ironic as the target audience likes to think of itself as being. That requires at least the pose of opposition to commercial values. The cool commercials—I'm thinking of Nike spots, some Reeboks, most 501s, certainly all MTV promos—flatter us by saying we're too cool to fall for commercial values, and therefore cool enough to want their product.

20 If irony is weak armor, how do we ward off the effect of billions of words and images from our sponsors? No perfect wolfsbane exists, but I can suggest some tactics to keep in mind.

When watching, watch out. Literally. Watch as an outsider, from as far a distance as you can muster (farther even than irony)—*especially* when watching ads that flatter you for being an outsider, as more and more are doing.

Big lie, little lie. All advertising tells lies, but there are little lies and there are big lies. Little lie: This beer tastes great. Big lie: This beer makes *you* great. Not all ads tell little lies—they're more likely to be legally actionable (while big lies by definition aren't). And many products do live up to their modest material claims: This car runs. But all ads *must* tell big lies: This car will attract babes and make others slobber in envy. Don't be shocked that ads lie—that's their job. But do try to distinguish between the two kinds of lies.

Read the box. Look not just at whether an ad's claims are false or exaggerated, but try to figure out what portion of an ad is about the culture as opposed to the product. Read the contents as you would a cereal box's: Instead of how much sugar to wheat, consider how much style to information. Not that a high ratio of sugar to wheat is necessarily more malevolent than the other way around. But it's a sure sign that they're fattening you up for the shill.

Assume no relationship between a brand and its image. Marlboro was originally sold as a woman's cigarette, and its image was elegant, if not downright prissy. It wasn't until 1955 that the Marlboro Man was invented to ride herd on all that. The arbitrary relationship between a product and its ads becomes even clearer when you realize how much advertising is created to overcome "brand parity"—a plague more troubling to marketers than bodily odors. Brand parity means that there's little or no difference between competing brands and that the best a brand can do is hire a more appealing image. When advertising works at all, it's because the public more or less believes that something serious is going on between a product and its image, as if the latter reveals intrinsic qualities of the former. Peel image off item, and you too can have more of the freedom that ads are always promising. Likewise . . .

25 **We don't buy products, we buy the world that presents them.** Over the long run, whether you actually buy a particular product is less important than that you buy the world that makes the product seem desirable. Not so long ago

a BMW or Mercedes was required if you seriously bought the worldview that their ads conveyed. Still, buying an attitude doesn't automatically translate into product purchase. If your income precluded a BMW, you might have bought instead a Ralph Lauren polo shirt or even a Dove bar (which is how yuppie snack foods positioned themselves—as achievable class). Sure, GE wants you to buy its bulbs, but even more it wants you to buy the paternalistic, everything's-under-control world that GE seems to rule. Buying *that* will result, GE is betting, not only in more appliance sales but also in more credibility when spokesmen insist that defrauding the Pentagon is not *really* what GE's all about. That is to say . . .

The promotional is the political. Each world that commercials use to sell things comes packed with biases: Entire classes, races, and genders may be excluded for the coddling of the sponsored one. Lee Jeans's world (circa 1989) is a place where young people are hip, sexual, and wear jeans, while old people are square, nonsexual, and wear uniforms. The class and age politics here is more powerful than the Young Republicans'. There is politics in all advertising (and, more obviously, advertising in all politics). It makes sense that these two professions call what they do "campaigns."

Advertising shepherds herds of individuals. When Monty Python's mistaken messiah in *The Life of Brian* exhorts the crowd of devotees to "Don't follow me! Don't follow anyone! Think for yourselves! . . . You are all individuals!" they reply in unison, "We are all individuals!" That is advertising in a nutshell.

Advertising's most basic paradox is to say: Join us and become unique. Advertisers learned long ago that individuality sells, like sex or patriotism. The urge toward individualism is a constant in America, with icons ranging from Thomas Jefferson's yeoman farmer to the kooky girl bouncing to the jingle "I like the Sprite in you!" Commercial nonconformity always operates in the service of . . . conformity. Our system of laws and our one-man-one-vote politics may be based on individualism, but successful marketing depends on the exact opposite: By identifying (through research) the ways we are alike, it hopes to convince the largest number of people that they need the exact same product. Furthermore, in modern pop culture, we construct our individuality by the unique combination of mass-produced goods and services we buy. I sip Evian, you slug Bud Light; I drive a Geo, you gun a Ford pickup; I kick sidewalk in cowboy boots, you bop in Reeboks. Individuality is a good angle for all advertising, but it's crucial for TV commercials. There you are sitting at home, not doing anything for hours on end, but then the very box you're staring at tells you that you are different, that you are vibrantly alive, that your quest for freedom—freedom of speech, freedom of movement, freedom to do whatever you damn well choose—will not be impeded! And you can do all that, says the box, without leaving your couch.

It's the real ad. The one question I'm most often asked is, Does advertising shape who we are and what we want, or does it merely reflect back to us our own emotions and desires? As with most nature-or-nurture questions, the answer is both. The real ad in any campaign is controlled neither by admakers nor adwatchers; it exists somewhere between the TV set and the viewer, like a huge hairball, collecting bits of material and meaning from both. The real ad isn't even activated until viewers hand it their frustrations from work, the mood of their love life, their idiosyncratic misinterpretations, and most of all, I think, their everyday politics. On which class rung do they see themselves teetering? Do they ever so subtly flinch when a different race comes on TV? In this way, we all co-produce the ads we see. Agency people are often aghast that anyone would find offensive meanings in their ads because "that's not what we intended." Intention has little to do with it. Whatever they meant, once an ad hits the air it becomes public property. That, I think, is where criticism should aim—at the fluctuating, multimeaning thing that floats over the country, reflecting us as we reflect it.

Follow the flattery. I use the word *flattery* a lot. When trying to under- 30
stand what an ad's really up to, following the flattery is as useful as following the money. You'll find the ad's target market by asking who in any 30-second drama is being praised for qualities they probably don't possess. When a black teenager plays basketball with a white baby boomer for Canada Dry, it's not black youth that's being pandered to. It's white boomers—the flattery being that they're cool enough to be accepted by blacks. Ads don't even have to put people on stage to toady up to them. Ads can flatter by style alone, as do all the spots that turn on hyperquick cuts or obscure meanings, telling us—uh, *some* of us—that we're special enough to get it.

We participate in our own seduction. Once properly flattered, all that's left is to close the sale—and only we can do that. Not only do we coproduce ads, but we're our own best voiceover—that little inner voice that ultimately decides to buy or not. The best ads tell us we're cool *coolly*—in the other meaning of the word. McLuhan[1] used to say that a cool medium, like television, involves us more by not giving us everything; the very spaces between TV's flickering dots are filled in by our central nervous system. He refers to "the involvement of the viewer with the completion or 'closing' of the TV image." This is seduction: We're stirred to a state so that not only do we close the image but, given the right image at the right time, we open our wallet. All television is erotically engaged in this way, but commercials are TV's G-spot. The smart ads always hold back a little to get us to lean forward a little. Some ads have become caricatures of this tease, withholding the product's name until the last second to keep you wondering who could possibly be sponsoring such intrigue. The seduction may continue right to the cash register, where one last image is completed: you and product together at last. It'd be nice to say that now that you've consumed, you've climaxed, and everyone can relax. But sponsorship is a lifetime proposition that must be renewed every day.

[1]Canadian philosopher Marshall McLuhan, whose focus was often on changes brought about by the mass media.

The Language of Advertising

CHARLES A. O'NEILL

1 TOWARD THE end of her concert in a downtown park in Manchester, New Hampshire—not far, as the wind blows, from the long-suffering nuclear power plant at Seabrook—Bonnie Raitt, the rock star, looked out over her audience and noticed the Marlboro and Dunkin' Donut signs in the distance. "If you think Marlboro country and donuts are where the flavor is, I've got news: it's not." She proceeded to tell the sympathetic, energized late-evening crowd that "where it is" was somewhere between a thing called love and a nonprofit group she supported, International Physicians for the Prevention of Nuclear War.

Ms. Raitt said nothing to indicate that she really had anything against Dunkin' Donuts—or, for that matter, cigarettes. And if she had anything against Miller beer, one of the sponsors of the event, she didn't say. Ms. Raitt's mid-concert comments were, after all, not meant to start a debate. But she was, in her own way, commenting on one aspect of something we in America have long accepted as part of our culture; something pervasive, often taken for granted but often criticized: advertising.

If Marlboro is not truly "where the flavor is," it's not for lack of effort. Perhaps they have not convinced Ms. Raitt, but the architects of "Marlboro country" know how to reach into millions of smokers' heads and touch the desired motivational lever: the one labelled "buy!" The "real truth" doesn't matter, for advertising is not about truth, virtue, love or positive social values; it is about making money. When the writers of Marlboro's ads sat down in front of their word processors, they set in motion a sequence of events that changed the buying habits of millions of people. The final test of any advertising program (whether for donuts, cigarettes, nonprofit groups, detergents, cereals, life insurance, or pantyhose) is simply the degree to which it creates that impulse, the impulse to buy.

What creates the impulse? The strategy may call for billboards in a city in New Hampshire, full-page ads in Rolling Stone, 30-second spots on the "CBS Evening News," T-shirts imprinted with a corporate logo, music videos—or, for that matter, Ms. Raitt at the microphone. Whatever the strategy, advertisements derive their power from a purposeful, directed combination of images. Images can take several forms: words—spoken or written—or visuals; or, most powerfully, a combination of the two. The precise formula is determined by the creative concept and the medium chosen. The combination is the language of advertising.

5 Everyone who grows up in the Western world soon learns that advertising language is different from other languages. Most children would be unable to explain how such lines as "With Nice 'n Easy, it's color so natural, the closer he gets the better you look!" (the famous ad for Clairol's Nice 'n Easy hair coloring

product) or Marlboro's "come to where the flavor is" differs from ordinary language, but they would be able to tell you, "It sounds like an ad." Whether printed on a page, blended with music on the radio or smoothly whispered on the sound track of a television commercial, advertising language is "different."

Over the years, the texture of advertising language has frequently changed. Styles and creative concepts come and go. But there are at least four distinct general characteristics of the language of advertising that make it different from other languages; characteristics that, taken together, lend advertising its persuasive power:

1. The language of advertising is edited and purposeful.
2. The language of advertising is rich and arresting; it is specifically intended to attract and hold our attention.
3. The language of advertising involves us; in effect, *we* complete the message.
4. The language of advertising holds no secrets from us; it is a simple language.

EDITED AND PURPOSEFUL

One easy way to develop a feeling for the basic difference between advertising language and other languages is to transcribe a television talk show. An examination of such a transcript will show the conversation skipping from one topic to another, even though the guest and the host may attempt to stick to a specific subject. The conversation also is rife with repetition. After all, informal, conversational language transactions are not ordinarily intended to meet specific objectives. Advertising language cannot afford to be so desultory. It *does* have a specific purpose—to sell us something.

In *Future Shock,* Alvin Toffler draws a distinction between normal "coded" messages and "engineered" messages. As an example of an uncoded message, Toffler writes about a random, unstructured experience:

> A man walks along a street and notices a leaf whipped along a sidewalk by the wind. He perceives this event through his sensory apparatus. He hears a rustling sound. He sees movement and greenness. He feels the wind. From these sensory perceptions he somehow forms a mental image. We can refer to these sensory signals as a message. But the message is not, in any ordinary sense of [the] term, man-made. It is not designed by anyone to communicate anything, and the man's understanding of it does not depend directly on a social code—a set of agreed-upon signs and definitions.[1]

The talk show conversation, however, is coded; the guests' ability to exchange information with their host, and our ability to understand it, depend, as Toffler puts it, upon social conventions.

Beyond coded and uncoded messages there is another kind—the engi- 10
neered message—a variation of the coded message. The language of advertising is a language of finely engineered, ruthlessly purposeful messages. By Toffler's calculation,[2] the average adult American is assaulted by at least 560 advertising messages a day. Not one of these messages would reach us, to attract and hold

our attention, if it were completely unstructured. Advertising messages have a clear purpose; they are intended to trigger a specific response.

RICH AND ARRESTING

Advertisements—no matter how carefully "engineered" and packed with information—cannot succeed unless they capture our attention in the first place. Of the hundreds of advertising messages in store for us each day, very few (Toffler estimates seventy-six) will actually obtain our conscious attention.[3] The rest are screened out. The people who design and write ads know about this screening process; they anticipate and accept it as a basic premise of their business. They expend a great deal of energy to guarantee that their ads will make it past the defenses and distractions that surround us. The classic, all-time favorite device used to penetrate the barrier is sex. The desire to be attractive to the opposite sex is an ages-old instinct, and few drives are more powerful. Whether it takes this approach or another, every successful advertisement contains a "hook." The hook can take the form of strong visuals (photos or illustrations with emotional value) or a disarming, unexpected—even incongruous—set of words:

"Reeboks let U B U."	(Reebok)
"My chickens eat better than you do."	(Perdue Chickens)
"Introducing the ultimate concept in air freight. Men that fly."	(Emery Air Freight)
"Look deep into our ryes."	(Wigler's bakery products)
"Me. 4 U."	(The State of Maine)
"If gas pains persist, try Volkswagen."	(Volkswagen)

Even if the text contains no incongruity and does not rely on a pun for its impact, every effective ad needs a creative strategy based on some striking concept or idea. In fact, the concept and execution are often so good that many successful ads entertain while they sell.

For example, consider the campaigns created by Ally and Gargano for Federal Express. A campaign was developed to position Federal Express as the company that would deliver packages, not just "overnight," but "by 10:30 A.M." the next day. The plight of the junior executive in "Presentation," one ad in the campaign, is stretched for dramatic purposes, but it is, nonetheless, all too real: The young executive, who is presumably trying to climb his way up the corporate ladder, is shown calling another parcel delivery service and all but begging for assurance that he will have his slides in hand by 10:30 the next morning. "No slides, no presentation," he pleads. Only a viewer with a heart of stone can watch without feeling sympathetic, as the next morning our junior executive struggles to make his presentation *sans* slides. He is so lost without them that he is reduced to using his hands to perform imitations of birds and animals in shadows on the movie screen. What does the junior executive *viewer* think when he or she sees the ad?

1. Federal Express guarantees to deliver packages "absolutely, positively overnight."
2. Federal Express packages arrive early in the day.
3. What happened to that fellow in the commercial will absolutely not happen to me, now that I know what package delivery service to call.

A sound creative strategy supporting a truly innovative service idea sold Federal Express. But the quality of execution and imagination doesn't really matter. An ad for Merit Ultra Lights (August 1990) made use of one slang word in its headline: "Yo!" Soft drink and fast food companies often take another approach. "Slice of life" ads (so-called because they purport to provide glimpses of people in "real life" situations), replete with beautiful babies frolicking at family picnics or Fourth of July parades, seduce us into thinking that if we drink the right beverage or eat the right hamburger, we'll fulfill our deep yearning for a world where old folks and young folks live together in perfect suburban bliss. Lifestyle—and the natural affiliation of a particular lifestyle with a product—has also been used effectively as an advertising strategy for other types of merchandise. This TV spot for Levi's Corduroys was produced by Foote, Cone & Belding (1985):

	Music up. (Open on quick shot of saxophone player. Cut to man at sink drying his face with a towel. Reflection seen in mirror.)
Male Singer:	Gotta be there at eight. Gotta luminate. (Cut to two women at a table in a 24-hour diner. A man tries to coax them.)
Male Singer:	Got to be lookin' much better than great. (Cut to man and woman walking down the street.)
Male Singer:	Grab a flash of color, add a little more style . . . (Cut to shot of two different women at a table. Man does a quick turn landing on a chair. He laughs. The women get up to leave.)
Male Singer:	. . . Looks like Levi's Corduroy night. (Cut to shot of large neon sign "Levi's Cords Tonight.")
Male Singer with Group Singers:	Levi's Corduroy night. (Cut back to last man on chair. He shrugs.)
Male Singer:	Lookin' good . . . (Quick cut to neon sign. Camera pulls back.
Male Singer with Group Singers:	It's a Levi's Corduroy night. (Cut to two women at phone booth. One is talking on phone, other waits impatiently.)
Male Singer:	Looks like it's gonna be another Levi's Corduroy night/ Levi's . . . (Cut back to first man at the mirror. He taps the mirror and walks away.)
Group Singers:	Corduroy night.
Super:	Levi's batwing. Quality never goes out of style. Music fade out.

Of course, the printed word cannot begin to capture the pace or ambiance of this ad; nonetheless, it is clear that this effort doesn't appeal to everyone, and that's just the point. It *will* appeal to the young people identified by Levi's marketing research as the prime target market for the product. The ad encourages the viewer to make a connection: "I'm a flexible, luminous, streetwise kind of guy, just like the man in the mirror. Levi's Corduroys are O.K. Better buy some soon."

15 The prominence of ads containing puns or cleverly constructed headlines would seem to suggest that ads emerge, like Botticelli's Venus from the sea, flawless and full grown. Usually they do not. The idea that becomes the platform for an effective creative strategy is most often developed only after exhaustive research. The product is examined for its potential, and the prospective buyers are examined for their habits, characteristics and preferences.

"Who will be interested in our product? How old are they? Where do they live? How much money do they earn? What problem will our product solve?" Answers to these questions provide the foundation on which the creative strategy is built.

The creative people in the advertising business are well aware that consumers do not watch television or read magazines in order to see ads. Ads have to earn the right to be seen, read, and heard.

INVOLVING

We have seen that the language of advertising is carefully engineered; we have seen that it uses various devices to get our attention. Frank Perdue has us looking at a photo of his chickens at a dinner table. Sneaker companies have us watching athletes at work, Marlboro has us looking at a cowboy on an outdoor billboard. Now that they have our attention, advertisers present information intended to show us that the product they are offering for sale fills a need and, in filling this need, differs from the competition. The process is called "product positioning." Once our attention has been captured, it is the copywriter's responsibility to express such product differences and to exploit and intensify them.

What happens when product differences do not exist? Then the writer must glamorize the superficial differences (for example, difference of color, packaging, or other qualities without direct bearing on the product's basic function) or else *create* differences. As long as the ad is trying to get our attention, the "action" is mostly in the ad itself, in the words and visual images. But as we read an ad or watch it on television, we become more deeply involved. The action starts to take place in *us.* Our imagination is set in motion, and our individual fears and aspirations, our little quirks and insecurities, superimpose themselves on that tightly engineered, attractively packaged message.

20 Consider, for example, the running battle among the low-calorie soft drinks. The cola wars have spawned many "look-alike" advertisements, because the product features and consumer benefits are generic, applying to all products in the category. Substitute one product name for another, and the messages are

often identical, right down to the way the cans are photographed in the closing sequence. This strategy relies upon mass saturation and exposure for impact. In contrast, consider the way sneaker companies have attempted to create a "sense" of product differentiation where few significant differences exist. Reebok said their sneakers were different—meriting their high price tag—because "Reeboks Let U B U" (presumably, other brands of footwear failed to deliver this benefit). To further underscore the difference between their brands and those of competitors, some sneaker companies in 1990 offered such "significant" innovations as inflatable air bladders, possibly in order to bring the wearer to a new state of walking ecstasy heretofore unavailable to mortals . . . but more likely in an effort to differentiate the product in a crowded, competitive field. Interestingly, competitors "rebelled," against Reebok's "innovation" (thus making themselves appear to be different). As reported in the *Boston Globe* (August 13, 1990), a print ad for Keds is to show a Reebok shoe, adjacent to its $65 price tag, with the headline, "U Gotta B Kidding." Not to be outdone, Puma ran ads depicting a sneaker they described as "too much," replete with bells, a whistle, electric sockets, wings and an air pump! (Guess whose sneaker, in contrast, is depicted as offering "just enough?") Sneakers are shoes, but they are also, in effect, "life-style indicators," or symbols: If I think of myself as somewhat rebellious, with a clear sense of independent spirit, I'll go with the Reeboks, since, after all, they'll Let me B Me; if I'm the practical sort—unswayed by technical hype—perhaps I'll go with the "practical" Keds or Pumas.

Symbols have become important elements in the language of advertising in other ways, too; not so much because they carry meanings of their own but because we bring a meaning to them: we charge them with significance. Symbols are efficient, compact vehicles for the communication of an advertising message; they are pervasive and powerful.

One noteworthy example of symbolism at work is provided by the campaign begun in 1978 by Somerset Importers for Johnnie Walker Red Scotch. Sales of Johnnie Walker Red had been trailing sales of Johnnie Walker Black, and Somerset Importers needed to position Red as a fine product in its own right. The Smith/Greenland Agency produced ads which made heavy use of the color red. One ad, often printed as a two-page spread, is dominated by a close-up photo of red autumn leaves. At lower right, the copy reads, "When their work is done, even the leaves turn to Red." Another ad—also suitably dominated by a photograph in the appropriate color—reads: "When it's time to quiet down at the end of the day, even a fire turns to Red." *Red.* Warm. Experienced. Seductive. A perfect symbol to use in a liquor advertisement; all the more for the fact that it offers great possibilities for graphic design and copywriting: more fuel for the advertiser's creative art.

From time to time, many people believe, a more disturbing form of symbolism is also used—the "hidden message" symbol. Take a close, hard look at liquor ads and occasionally you will see, reflected in the photograph of a glass of spirits, peculiar, demonlike shapes. Are these shapes merely the product of one consumer's imagination or an accident of photography? Were they deliberately superimposed onto the product photograph by the careful application of ink and airbrush?

The art of advertising contains many such ambiguities. Some are charged, like this one, with multiple shades of meaning. The demons may be taken to represent the problems and cares which one can presumably chase away through consumption of the advertised product. Or they can, just as easily, be taken as representations of the playful spirits which will be unleashed once the product has been consumed. The advertising creative director did not create the need to relax, or to get away from the stresses of daily life; he or she merely took advantage of these common human needs in developing a promotion strategy for the product.

Another human desire advertising writers did not invent (although they lib- 25
erally exploit it) is the desire to associate with successful people. All of us tend to admire or in some way identify ourselves with famous or successful people. We are therefore already primed for the common advertising device of the testimonial or personality ad. Once we have seen a famous person in an advertisement, we associate the product with the person. "I like Mr. X. If Mr. X likes (endorses) this product, I would like it too." The logic is faulty, but we fall for it just the same. That is how Joe DiMaggio sold Mr. Coffee. The people who write testimonial ads did not create our trust in famous personalities. They merely recognize our inclinations and exploit them.

The language of advertising is different from other languages because we participate in it; in fact, we—not the words we read on the magazine page or the pictures flashing before us on the television screen—charge the ads with most of their power.

A SIMPLE LANGUAGE

Clip a typical story from the publication you read most frequently. Calculate the number of words in an average sentence. Count the number of words of three or more syllables in a typical 100-word passage, omitting words that are capitalized, combinations of two simple words, or verb forms made into three-syllable words by the addition of *-ed* or *-es*. Add the two figures (the average number of words per sentence and the number of three-syllable words per 100 words), then multiply the result by .4. According to Robert Gunning, if the resulting number is seven, there is a good chance that you are reading *True Confessions*.[4] He developed this formula, the "Fog Index," to determine the comparative ease with which any given piece of written communication can be read. Here is the complete text of a typical cigarette advertisement.

> I demand two things from my cigarette. I want a cigarette with low tar and nicotine. But, I also want taste. That's why I smoke Winston Lights. I get a lighter cigarette, but I still get a real taste. And real pleasure. Only one cigarette gives me that: Winston Lights.

The average sentence in this ad runs seven words. *Cigarette* and *nicotine* are three-syllable words, with *cigarette* appearing four times; *nicotine,* once. Considering *that's* as two words, the ad is exactly fifty words long, so the average number of three-syllable words per 100 is ten.

7	words per sentence
+10	three-syllable words/100
17	
× .4	
6.8	Fog Index

According to Gunning's scale, this particular ad is written at about the seventh grade level, comparable to most of the ads found in mass circulation magazines.[5] It's about as sophisticated as *True Confessions;* harder to read than a comic book, but easier than *Ladies Home Journal.*

Of course, the Fog Index cannot evaluate the visual aspect of an ad. The 30
headline, "I demand two things from my cigarette," works with the picture (that of an attractive woman) to arouse consumer interest. The text reinforces the image. It is unlikely that many consumers actually take the trouble to read the entire text, but it is not necessary for them to do so in order for the ad to work.

Since three-syllable words are harder to read than one- or two-syllable words, and since simple ideas are more easily transferred from one human to another than complex ideas, advertising copy tends to use even simpler language all the time. Toffler speculates:

> If the [English] language had the same number of words in Shakespeare's time as it does today, at least 200,000 words—perhaps several times that many—have dropped out and been replaced in the intervening four centuries. The high turnover rate reflects changes in things, processes, and qualities in the environment from the world of consumer products and technology.[6]

It is no accident that the first terms Toffler uses to illustrate his point ("fastback," "wash-and-wear," and "flashcube") were invented not by engineers, or journalists, but by advertising copywriters.

Advertising language is simple language; in the engineering process, difficult words or images (which could be used in other forms of communication to lend color or fine shades of meaning) are edited out and replaced by simple words or images not open to misinterpretation.

WHO IS RESPONSIBLE?

Some critics view the entire advertising business as a cranky, unwelcomed child of the free enterprise system, a noisy, whining, brash kid who must somehow be kept in line, but can't just yet be thrown out of the house. Because advertising mirrors the fears, quirks, and aspirations of the society that creates it (and is, in turn, sold by it), it is wide open to parody and ridicule.

Perhaps the strongest, most authoritative critic of advertising language in recent years is journalist Edwin Newman. In his book *Strictly Speaking,* he poses the question, "Will America be the death of English?" Newman's "mature, well thought out judgement" is that it will. As evidence, he cites a number of examples of fuzzy thinking and careless use of the language, not just by advertisers, but by many people in public life, including politicians and journalists:

> The federal government has adopted the comic strip character Snoopy as a symbol and showed us Snoopy on top of his doghouse, flat on his back, with a balloon coming out of his mouth, containing the words, "I believe in conserving energy," while below there was this exhortation: savEnergy.
>
> savEnergy. An entire letter e at the end was savd. In addition, an entire space was savd. Perhaps the government should say onlYou can prevent forest fires . . . Spelling has been assaulted by Duz, E-Z Off, Fantastik, Kool, Kleen . . . and by products that make you briter, so that you will not be left hi and dri at a parti, but made welkom. . . . Under this pressure, adjectives become adverbs; nouns become adjectives; prepositions disappear; compounds abound.[7]

In this passage, Newman presents three of the charges most often levied against advertising:

1. Advertising debases English.
2. Advertising downgrades the intelligence of the public.
3. Advertising warps our vision of reality, implanting in us groundless fears and insecurities. (He cites, as examples of these groundless fears, "tattletale grey," "denture breath," "morning mouth," "unsightly bulge," "ring around the collar.")

Other charges have been made from time to time. They include: 35

1. Advertising sells daydreams; distracting, purposeless visions of lifestyles beyond the reach of most of the people who are most exposed to advertising.
2. Advertising feeds on human weaknesses and exaggerates the importance of material things, encouraging "impure" emotions and vanities.
3. Advertising encourages bad, even unhealthy habits like smoking.
4. Advertising perpetuates racial and sexual stereotypes.

What can be said in advertising's defense? Advertising is only a reflection of society; slaying the messenger (and just one of the messengers, at that) would not alter the fact—if it is a fact—that "America will be the death of English." A case can be made for the concept that advertising language is an acceptable stimulus for the natural evolution of language. (At the very least, advertising may stimulate debate about what current trends in language are "good" and "bad.") Another point: Is "proper English" the language most Americans actually speak and write, or is it the language we are told we should speak and write, the language of *The Elements of Style* and *The Oxford English Dictionary*?

What about the charge that advertising debases the intelligence of the public? Those who support this particular criticism would do well to ask themselves another question: Exactly how intelligent is the public? How many people know the difference between adverbs and adjectives? How many people *want* to know? The fact is that advertisements are effective, not because agencies say they are effective, but because they sell products.

Advertising attempts to convince us to buy products; we are not forced to buy something because it is heavily advertised. Who, for example, is to be blamed for the success, in the mid-70s, of a nonsensical, nonfunctional product—"Pet Rocks"? The people who designed the packaging, those who created the idea of selling ordinary rocks as pets, or those who bought the product?

Perhaps much of the fault lies with the public, for accepting advertising so readily. S. I. Hayakawa finds "the uncritical response to the incantations of advertising . . . a serious symptom of a widespread evaluational disorder." He does not find it "beyond the bounds of possibility" that today's suckers for national advertising will be tomorrow's suckers for the master political propagandist who will, "by playing up the 'Jewish menace,' in the same way as national advertisers play up the 'pink toothbrush menace,' in the same way as national glory and prosperity, sell fascism in America."[8]

Fascism in America is fortunately a far cry from Pet Rocks, but the point is 40
well taken. In the end, advertising simply attempts to change behavior. It is a neutral tool, just as a gun is a neutral tool, but advertising at least has not been known to cause accidental deaths. Like any form of communication, it can be used for positive social purposes, neutral commercial purposes, or for the most pernicious kind of paranoid propaganda. Accepting, for the purpose of this discussion, that propaganda is, at heart, an extension of politics and therefore is materially different from commercial advertising as practiced in the United States of America, circa 1990, *do* advertisements sell distracting, purposeless visions? Occasionally. But perhaps such visions are necessary components of the process through which our society changes and improves.

And recognize this: advertising is a mirror. It is not perfect; sometimes it distorts. When we view ourselves in it, we're not always pleased with what we see. Perhaps all things considered, that's the way it should be.

NOTES

1. Alvin Toffler, *Future Shock* (New York: Random House, 1970), p. 146.
2. Ibid., p. 149.
3. Ibid.
4. Curtis D. MacDougall, *Interpretive Reporting* (New York: Macmillan, 1968), p. 94.
5. Ibid., p. 95.
6. Toffler, *Future Shock,* p. 151.
7. Edwin Newman, *Strictly Speaking* (Indianapolis: Bobbs-Merrill, 1974), p. 13.
8. S. I. Hayakawa, *Language in Action* (New York: Harcourt, Brace, 1941), p. 235.

DEFINING A TROUBLESOME TERM: WHAT IS LOVE?

In the following chapter from his book *Love: Emotion, Myth, and Metaphor*, philosopher Robert Solomon tries to understand a troublesome term, *love*. He does so by examining several metaphors for love. These embedded metaphors affect how we think about love without our realizing it. Thomas Sowell also focuses on love, but in "Love and Other Four-Letter Words," he argues that love, as a concept, has fallen out of fashion and has been replaced by sex. He also addresses the social standing of the concepts/words "duty," "work," and "save." As you read these essays, consider the following questions:

1. How do metaphors about love affect how we express love?
2. What are some of the advantages and disadvantages of one metaphor over others?
3. Can you devise any additional metaphors for love? Is it possible to define "love" without using metaphors?
4. Can you think of any other concepts that helped society to function but have disappeared (or are noticeably rare)? What, if any, concepts have taken their place?

Models and Metaphors: "The Game of Love"

ROBERT SOLOMON

WE LOOK AT love, as we look at life, through a series of metaphors, each with its own language, its own implications, connotations and biases. 1

For example, if someone says that love is a game, we already know much of what is to follow: relationships will tend to be short-lived. Sincerity will be a strategy for winning and so will flattery and perhaps lying. ("All's fair. . . . ") The person "played with" is taken seriously only as an opponent, a challenge, valued in particular for his or her tactics and retorts, but quickly dispensable as soon as someone has "won" or "lost." "Playing hard to get" is an optional strategy, and being "easy" is not immoral or foolish so much as playing badly, or not at all.

On the other hand, if someone sees love as "God's gift to humanity," we should expect utter solemnity, mixed with a sense of gratitude, seriousness and self-righteousness that is wholly lacking in the "love is a game" metaphor. Relationships here will tend to be long-lasting, if not "forever," fraught with duties and obligations dictated by a "gift" which, in the usual interpretations, has both divine and secular strings attached.

The "game" metaphor is, perhaps, too frivolous to take seriously. The "gift of God" metaphor, on the other hand, is much too serious to dismiss frivolously.

We will discuss it, and the damage it has done, at length in several later chapters. In this chapter what I would like to do is display the variety and richness of the metaphors through which we tend to talk about, and experience, love. Not surprisingly, these love metaphors reflect our interests elsewhere in life—business, health, communications, art, politics and law as well as fun and games and religion. But these are not mere "figures of speech"; they are the self-imposed structures that determine the way we experience love itself. (For this reason, we should express some pretty strong reservations about some of them.)

TIT FOR TAT: LOVE AS A FAIR EXCHANGE

5 One of the most common love metaphors, now particularly popular in social psychology, is the *economic* metaphor. The idea is that love is an exchange, a sexual partnership, a trade-off of interests and concerns and, particularly, of *approval.* "I make you feel good about yourself and in return you make me feel good about myself." Of course exchange rates vary—some people need more than others—and there is a law of diminishing returns; that is, the same person's approval tends to become less and less valuable as it becomes more familiar. (This law of diminishing returns, which we experience as the gradual fading of romantic love, has been explored by the psychologist Eliot Arenson of the University of California at Santa Cruz. His theory has been aptly named by his students "Arenson's Law of Marital Infidelity.") In some relationships the balance of payments may indeed seem extremely one-sided but the assumption is, in the words of the Harvard sociologist Homans, that both parties must believe they are getting something out of it or they simply wouldn't stay around.

Now this economic model has much to offer, not least the fact that it gives a fairly precise account of the concrete motivation for love, which is left out of more pious accounts that insist that love is simply good in itself and needs no motives. But the problem is that it too easily degenerates into a most unflattering model of mutual buying and selling, which in turn raises the specter that love may indeed be, as some cynics have been saying ever since Marx (Karl) and Engels, a form of covert prostitution, though not necessarily—or even usually—for money. "I will sleep with you and think well of you or at least give you the benefit of the doubt if only you'll tell me good things about myself and pretend to approve of me."

It may be true that we do often evaluate our relationships in this way, in terms of mutual advantage and our own sense of fairness. The question, "What am I getting out of this, anyway?" always makes sense, even if certain traditional views of love and commitment try to pretend that such selfishness is the very antithesis of love. But the traditional views have a point to make too, which is, simply, that such tit-for-tat thinking inevitably undermines a relationship based on love, *not* because love is essentially "selfless" but because the bargain table is not the place to understand mutual affection. Love is not the exchange of affection, any more than sex is merely the exchange of pleasure. What is left out of these accounts is the "we" of love, which is quite different from mere "I and thou."

This is not to say that fairness cannot be an issue in love, nor is it true that "all's fair" in love. But while the economic exchange model explains rather clearly some of the motives for love, it tends to ignore the *experience* of love almost altogether, which is that such comparisons and evaluations seem at the time beside the point and come to mind only when love is already breaking down. It is the suspicion, not the fact, that "I'm putting more into this than you are" that signals the end of many relationships, despite the fact that, as business goes, they may have been "a good arrangement."

THE JOB OF LOVING: THE WORK MODEL

A very different model is the *work* model of love. The Protestant ethic is very much at home in romance. (Rollo May calls love the Calvinist's proof of emotional salvation.) And so we find many people who talk about "working out a relationship," "working at it," "working for it" and so on. The fun may once have been there, of course, but now the real *job* begins, tacking together and patching up, like fixing up an old house and refusing to move out until the roof caves in. This is, needless to say, a particularly self-righteous model, if for no other reason than that it begins on the defensive and requires considerable motivation just to move on. Personal desires, the other person's as well as one's own, may be placed behind "the relationship," which is conceived of as the primary *project.* Love, according to the work model, gets evaluated above all on its industriousness, its seriousness, its success in the face of the most difficult obstacles. Devotees of the work model not infrequently choose the most inept or inappropriate partners, rather like buying a run-down shack—for the challenge. They will look with disdain at people who are merely happy together (something like buying a house from a tract builder). They will look with admiration and awe at a couple who have survived a dozen years of fights and emotional disfigurements because "they made it work."

A MADNESS MOST DISCRETE: THE (MELO) DRAMATIC MODEL

In contrast to the work model, we can turn with a sense of recreation to the *dramatic* model of love, love as theater, love as melodrama. This differs from the game model in that one's roles are taken *very* seriously, and the notions of winners and losers, strategy and tactics are replaced by notions of performance, catharsis, tragedy and theatricality. Roles are all important—keeping within roles, developing them, enriching them. The dramatic model also tends to play to an audience, real (whenever possible) or imagined (when necessary). Fights and reconciliations alike will often be performed in public, and an evening at home alone may often seem pointless. Some dramatic lovers are prima donnas, referring every line or part back to themselves, but one can be just as theatrical by being visibly selfless, or martyred, or mad. Lunt and Fontanne or Bogart and Bacall might well be models, and lovers will strain without amusement to perfect for the appropriate occasion someone else's drawl, insult, posture or sigh.

Unfortunately the dramatic model too easily tends to confuse interpersonal problems with theatrical flaws, to praise and abuse itself in those mincing terms that are, appropriately, the vocabulary of the theater critic. (Clive Barnes as Cupid?) The worst that one could say of such love, therefore, is that it's "boring" or "predictable."

"RELATIONSHIPS": BANALITY AS METAPHOR

10 Blandness can be just as significant as profundity and excitement, and a metaphor may be intentionally noncommittal as well as precise. Thus we find the word "thing" substituted as a grammatical stand-in for virtually everything from sexual organs (a young virgin gingerly refers to her first lover's "thing") to jobs, hang-ups and hobbies (as in "doing your own thing"). Where love is concerned, the most banal of our metaphors, so pervasive and so banal that it hardly seems like a metaphor, is the word "relating," or "relationship" itself. There's not much to say about it, except to ponder in amazement the fact that we have not yet, in this age of "heavy relationships," come up with anything better. There is a sense, of course, in which any two people (or two things) stand in any number of relationships to one another (being taller than, heavier than, smarter than, more than fifteen feet away from . . . etc.). The word "relations" was once, only a few years ago, a polite and slightly clinical word for sex (still used, as most stilted archaisms tend to be, in law). People "relate" to each other as they "relate a story," perhaps on the idea that what couples do most together is to tell each other the events of the day, a less than exciting conception of love, to be sure. But metaphors can be chosen for their vacuousness just as for their imaginative imagery, and the fact that this metaphor dominates our thinking so much (albeit in the guise of a *meaningful* relationship) points once again to the poverty of not only our vocabulary but our thinking and feeling as well. Anyone who's still looking for a "meaningful relationship" in the 1980s may have a lot to learn about love, or not really care about it at all.

LOVE AND ELECTRONICS: THE COMMUNICATION METAPHOR

A powerful metaphor with disastrous consequences that was popular a few years ago was a "communication" metaphor, often used in conjunction with a "relating" metaphor, for obvious reasons. Both were involved with the then hip language of media and information theory: "getting through" to each other and "we just can't communicate any more" gave "relationships" the unfortunate appearance of shipwrecked survivors trying to keep in touch over a slightly damaged short-wave radio. The information processing jargon ("input," "feedback," "tuning in" and "turning off") was typically loaded with electronic gadget imagery, and good relationships appropriately were described in terms of their "good vibrations." But, like all metaphors, this one revealed much more than it distorted, namely, an image of isolated transmitters looking for someone to get their messages. It was precisely this milieu that gave birth to Rollo May's *Love and Will,* and his concern that we had rendered love between us impossible. Love was thought to be mainly a matter of self-expression, largely but not exclusively verbal expression. Talk became enormously important to love; problems were talked over, talked through and talked out. The essential moment was the "heavy conversation" and, appropriately, talk about love often took the place of love itself. Confession and "openness" (telling all) became the linchpins of love, even when the messages were largely hostility and resentment. Psychotherapist George Bach wrote a number of successful books, including *The Intimate Enemy* (with Peter Wyden), which made quite clear the fact that it was expression of feelings, not the feelings themselves, that made for a successful relationship. On the communication model, sex too was described as a mode of communication, but more often sex was not so much communicating as the desire to be communicated with. Sex became, in McLuhanesque jargon, a "cool" medium. And, like most modern media, the model put its emphasis on the medium itself (encounter groups, etc.) but there was precious little stress on the *content* of the programming. Not surprisingly, love became an obscure ideal, like television advertisements full of promise of something fabulous yet to come, hinted at but never spoken of as such. In fact the ultimate message was the idea of the medium itself.

THE ONTOLOGY OF LONELINESS: LOVE AND ALONENESS

In our extremely individualistic society we have come to see isolation and loneliness as akin to "the human condition," instead of as by-products of a certain kind of social arrangement, which puts mobility and the formation of new interpersonal bonds at a premium. This individualistic metaphor, which I call "the ontology of loneliness," is stated succinctly, for example, by Rollo May: "Every person, experiencing as he [sic] does his own solitariness and aloneness, longs for union with another" (*Love and Will,* p. 144). Similarly, Erich Fromm preoccupies himself with "our need to escape the prison of our aloneness," and the radical feminist Shulamith Firestone complains about the same need "to escape from the isolation of our own solitude." Love, then, is a refuge from an otherwise intolerable existence. Our "natural" state is aloneness; our escape from this state, hopefully, is love. "Love," writes the poet Rilke, "is two solitudes reaching out to greet each other."

This is a viewpoint that has been argued by many philosophers under the name of "solipsism" ("the only sure thing is one's own existence") and has been developed by the vulgar philosopher Ayn Rand into an argument for selfishness: "Each of us is born into the world alone, and therefore each of us is justified in pursuing our own selfish interests." But the premise is false and the inference is insidious. Not even Macduff (who was not, strictly speaking, "of woman born") came into the world by himself. And not only in infancy but in adulthood we find ourselves essentially linked to other people, to a language that we call our own, to a culture and, at least legally, to a country as well. We do not have to find or "reach out" to others; they are, in a sense, already *in us.* Alone in the woods of British Columbia, I find myself still thinking of friends, describing what I see as if they were there—and in their language. The idea of the isolated self is an American invention—reinforced perhaps by the artificially isolated circumstances of the psychiatrist's office and our fantasies about gunfighters and mountain men, but this is not true of most of us. And this means that love is not a refuge or an escape either. Our conception of ourselves is always a social self (even if it is an antisocial or rebellious self).

Our language of love often reflects this idea of natural isolation, for example in the "communication" metaphor in which isolated selves try desperately to "get through" to one another. But this is an unnecessarily tragic picture of life and love, and its result is to make love itself seem like something of a cure for a disease, rather than a positive experience which already *presupposes* a rather full social life. Indeed, it is revealing that, quite the contrary of social isolation, romantic love is usually experienced only *within* a rather extensive social nexus. "Sure, I have lots of friends and I like my colleagues at work but, still, I'm lonely and I want to fall in love." But that has nothing to do with loneliness. It rather reflects the tremendous importance we accord to romantic love in our lives, not as a cure for aloneness, but as a positive experience in its own right, which we have, curiously, turned into a need.

"MADE FOR EACH OTHER": THE METAPHYSICAL MODEL

15 Standing opposed to the "ontology of loneliness" is an ancient view which takes our *unity,* not our mutual isolation, as the "natural" state of humanity. The classic statement of this view, brilliant in its poetic simplicity, is Aristophanes' speech in the *Symposium,* in which he describes our "natural" state as double creatures, cleft in two by Zeus for our hubris, struggling to be reunited through love. Our own image of two people "being made for each other" is also an example of the metaphysical model, together with the idea that marriages are "made in heaven" and the idea that someone else can be your "better half." The metaphysical model is based not on the idea that love is a refuge from isolated individualism but, quite the opposite, on the idea that love is the realization of bonds that are already formed, even before one meets one's "other half."

The ontology of loneliness treats individuals as atoms, bouncing around the universe alone looking for other atoms, occasionally forming more or less stable molecules. But if we were to pursue the same chemical metaphor into the metaphysical model, it would more nearly resemble what physicists today call "field theory." A magnetic field, for instance, retains all of its electromagnetic properties whether or not there is any material there to make them manifest. So too, an individual is already a network of human relationships and expectations, and these exist whether or not one finds another individual whose radiated forces and properties are complementary. The old expression about love being a matter of "chemical attraction" (from Goethe to Gilbert and Sullivan[1]) is, scientifically, a century out of date; "attraction" is no longer a question of one atom affecting another but the product of two electromagnetic fields, each of which exists prior to and independently of any particular atoms within its range. So too we radiate charm, sexiness, inhibition, intelligence and even repulsiveness, and find a lover who fits in. The problem with this viewpoint, however, is that it leaves no room for the *development* of relationships but rather makes it seem as if, if the love is there at all, it has to be there, and be there in full, from the very beginning.

LOVE AND DISEASE: THE MEDICAL METAPHOR

"Love's a malady without a cure," wrote Dryden, and today, our favorite metaphor, from social criticism to social relationships, has become the disease metaphor, images of health and decay, the medicalization of all things human, from the stock market to sex and love. Not surprisingly, a large proportion of our books about love and sex are written by psychiatrists and other doctors. (They used to be written by priests and theologians.) Our society is described in terms of "narcissism" (a clinical term), as an "age of anxiety," and as "decadent" (the negative side of the biological process). For Rollo May and Erich Fromm, lack of love is the dominant disease of our times. For others, *Love and Addiction* author Stanton Peele, for instance, love is itself a kind of disease, an "addiction," waiting to be cured. Some feminists have seized on the disease metaphor (a disease invented by and carried by men): Ti-Grace Atkinson (in *Amazon Odyssey*) calls love "a pathological condition," and Erica Jong (in *Fear of Flying*) calls it "the search for self-annihilation." But whether love is the disease or love is the cure, what is obvious is that this model turns us all into *patients,* and one might well ask—the professional interests of the A.M.A. aside—whether that is the arena within which we want to talk about love.

THE ART IN LOVING: THE AESTHETIC MODEL

Perhaps the oldest view of love, the pivot of Plato's *Symposium,* is an *aesthetic* model: love as the admiration and the contemplation of *beauty.* The emphasis here is on neither relating nor communicating (in fact, unrequited love and even voyeurism are perfectly in order). On this model, it is not particularly expected that the lover will actually *do* much of anything except, perhaps, to get within view of the beloved at every possible opportunity, as one might stand before the fireplace and admire one's favorite painting over the mantel. It is this model that has dominated many of our theories about love, though not, luckily, our actual practices. It is this model that best fits the moaning troubadours in twelfth-century France, composing poetry about the inaccessible beauty of the maiden

[1] Hey diddle diddle with your middle-
class kisses.
It's a chemical reaction, that's all. (Gilbert and Sullivan)

up there on the tower balcony, visible but untouchable. It is this model that feminists rightly complain about when they accuse men of "putting them up on a pedestal," a charge that too often confuses the idealization that accompanies it with the impersonal distancing that goes along with the pedestal. The objection is not to the fact that it is a pedestal so much as the fact that it is usually a very *tall* pedestal, so that any real contact is pretty much out of the question and the fear of falling is considerable. Or else it is a very *small* pedestal, "and like any small place," writes Gloria Steinem, "a prison."

LOVE AND COMMITMENT: THE CONTRACT MODEL

An old view of love, which dominated much of the eighteenth and nineteenth centuries, was a *contract* model, a specific instance of a more general "social contract" theory that was then believed by most people to be the (implicit) basis of society itself. Contracts in love were exemplified, of course, by the quite explicit and wholly legal contract of marriage, but even then, and especially now, the idea of implicit contracts was taken for granted too. (*Cosmopolitan* magazine last year reran one of its most popular pieces, about "secret" contracts in love, two hundred years too late to be in vogue.) What is crucial to this metaphor, however, is the fact that *emotion* plays very little part in it. One accepts an obligation to obey the terms of the contract (implicit or explicit) whether or not (though hopefully whether) one wants to. The current term for this ever popular emasculation of emotion is *commitment.* In fact there seems to be an almost general agreement among most of the people I talk to that "commitment" is what constitutes love. (The contrast is almost always sexual promiscuity or purely "casual" affairs.) But commitment is precisely what love is *not* (though of course one can and often does make commitments on the basis of the fact that he or she loves someone). A commitment is an obligation sustained *whether or not one has the emotion that originally motivated it.* And the sense of obligation isn't "love."

FREUDIAN FALLACIES: THE BIOLOGICAL METAPHOR

The idea that science itself can be but a metaphor strikes us as odd, but 20
much of what we believe about love, it seems, is based on wholly unliteral biological metaphors. For example, we believe that love is "natural," even an "instinct," and this is supported by a hundred fascinating but ultimately irrelevant arguments about "the facts of life": the fact that some spiders eat their mates, that some birds mate for life, that some sea gulls are lesbians, that some fish can't mate unless the male is clearly superior, that chimpanzees like to gang bang and gorillas have weenies the size of a breakfast sausage, that bats tend to do it upside down and porcupines do it "carefully." But romantic love is by no means "natural"; it is not an instinct but a very particular and peculiar attitude toward sex and pair-bonding that has been carefully cultivated by a small number of modern aristocratic and middle-class societies. Even sex, which would seem to

be "natural" if anything is, is no more mere biology than taking the holy wafer at high mass is just eating. It too is defined by our metaphors and the symbolic significance we give to it. It is not a "need," though we have certainly made it into one. Sex is not an instinct, except in that utterly minimal sense that bears virtually no resemblance at all to the extremely sophisticated and emotion-filled set of rituals that we call—with some good reason—"making love." And where sex and love come together is not in the realm of nature either, but in the realm of expression, specific to a culture which specifies its meaning.

There is one particular version of the biological metaphor, however, which has enjoyed such spectacular scientific airplay, ever since Freud at least, that we tend to take it as the literal truth instead of, again, as a metaphor. It is the idea that love begins in—or just out of—the womb, and that our prototype of love—if not our one "true" love—is our own mother.

This would suggest indeed that love is, if not an instinct, common to all human beings. But the argument turns on a number of obvious fallacies, starting from the premise that, because of the extraordinarily slow development of human infants, all of us, from our very birth (and perhaps before), need love. But . . .

1. This isn't romantic love, in any case, and romantic love is in no way reducible to mere dependency. In fact, despite its "baby" imagery, romantic love presupposes just what infancy lacks: a sense of selfhood and a high degree of mobility and independence. Moreover, the view expresses an obvious male bias and leaves the romantic desires of women something of a mystery (for Freud in particular).
2. To need love is not to need *to* love. Some people need desperately to be loved but have no inclination whatever to love in return.
3. Babies need care and comfort, not necessarily love. In fact regular tender care is far more desirable than adoring but erratic attention. Romantic love, of course, thrives on the latter, gets too easily bored with the first.
4. In few societies is the care of a particular mother expected by either the infant or society, and the idea that one has special affection for one person exclusively is an anthropologically peculiar notion which in fact is disintegrating in our society too. In most societies, increasingly in our own, an infant is cared for by any number of different people, male as well as female, and the idea of a single utterly dominant dependency figure—which so obsessed Freud—is a peculiarity of the Victorian Viennese middle-class ethic, not a universal human characteristic.
5. It is most implausible that any adult emotion is simply reducible to an infantile need. To identify a radical politician's moral indignation with infantile rage would be offensive as well as simply wrong; to think of sexual jealousy as merely an adult extension of a child's possessiveness is not only to misunderstand jealousy but to misunderstand children as well. And even in those relatively few cases in which the so-called "Oedipal complex" reigns supreme, it is a mistake to reduce all subsequent affections to a mere repetition of family dynamics. Some psychologists, Gordon Allport for

example, have come to refer to this rejection of Freudian reductionism as "the autonomy of motives." No matter how revealing the origins of one's affections, it is their development and differences that define them. We think it noteworthy when a man dates a woman who resembles his mother, not when he does not. The Oedipal complex is desperately looking for an occasional instance as if to confirm it.

We sometimes plague ourselves with the idea that we are "hung up" on Oedipal images. In high school I worried about the fact that the girls I "dated" bore a sometimes striking resemblance to my mother. (They were usually short, bright, creative and Caucasian.) I had read enough Freud for this to worry me. Many years later a psychotherapist convinced me, or I "discovered," that, indeed, I was looking for a woman who was more like my father, which confused me considerably, needless to say, but worried me too. But this limited number of alternatives, always clouded by the threat of "neurosis," turns out to be nonsense, or worse—it is the Freudian doctrine of original sin, a new source of unnecessary guilt and just as much a myth as the original Original Sin. In fact our models and prototypes of love include not only our parents but brothers, sisters, teachers in junior high school, first dates, first loves, graduating-class heroes and heroines, hundreds of movie stars and magazine pictures as well as a dozen considerations and pressures that have nothing to do with prototypes at all. Indeed, even Freud insists that it is not a person's *actual* parent who forms the romantic prototype but rather a phantom, constructed from memory, which may bear little resemblance to any actual person. But if this is so, perhaps one's imagined mother is in fact a variation on one's first girl friend, or a revised version of Myrna Loy. Why do we take the most complex and at times exquisite emotion in most of our lives, and try to reduce it to the first and the simplest?

Or, if the Oedipal theory is right, why didn't Romulus, raised by a she-wolf, rape his dog, instead of the Sabine women? Mere motherhood is not everything, even in ancient mythology.

"THE FLAME IN MY HEART": THE EMOTION METAPHOR

Love is an emotion. But the way we talk about emotions is itself so pervaded
by metaphors that one begins to wonder whether there is anything there to ac- 25
tually talk about. We talk about ourselves as if we were Mr. Coffee machines, bubbling over, occasionally overflowing, getting too hot to handle, and bursting from too much pressure. We subscribe in metaphor if not in medicine to the medieval theory that the seat of the emotions is in the heart, and in love it is the heart that pounds, beats, breaks and is bound and occasionally butchered. We describe love in terms of heat, fire, flame—all of which are expressive and poetic but, it is sometimes hard to remember, metaphors all the same. But is love really that sense that one is going to burst? The warm flush that pours through one's body when *he* or *she* walks into the room: is that love? And if so, why do we set so much store by it? It is for this reason, no doubt, that the age-old wisdom about love has made it out to be more than a mere emotion—a gift from God,

a visitation from the gods, the wound of Cupid's arrow, the cure for a disease or a disease itself, the economics of interpersonal relations or even "the answer" to all life's problems. But then again, maybe we underestimate our emotions.

What is love? It seems to be almost everything except, perhaps, "never having to say you're sorry." Love is a series of metaphors, which we glorify selectively, picking one out and calling it "true" love, which itself is another metaphor.

Not all metaphors are created equal. Some are profound, some are banal, some increase our self-confidence, others make us feel slimy, defensive or sick. There is no "true" love, for there is no singly true metaphor, but this does not mean that one should not choose carefully. For choosing one's metaphor is, in fact, choosing one's love life as well.

Love and Other Four-Letter Words

THOMAS SOWELL

LOVE IS a four-letter word, but you don't hear it nearly as often as you hear 1
some other four-letter words. It may be a sign of our times that everyone seems to be talking openly about sex, but we seem to be embarrassed to talk about love.

Sex alone will not even reproduce the human race, because babies cannot survive the first week of life without incredible amounts of care. That care comes from love. If the parents are too wretched to give the infant the attention he needs, then a general love of babies must lead others to set up some backup system, so that the child does not die of neglect.

The shallow people who have turned our schools into propaganda centers for the counterculture try hard to take love out of human relations. Between men and women, for example, there is just sex, if you believe the clever anointed.

But why should we believe them? Why have there been such painful laments—in letters, literature, poetry and song—for so many centuries about the breakup of love affairs? Because there are no other members of the opposite sex available? Not at all.

Sex is almost always available, if only commercially. But love is a lot harder 5
to find. Some people do not even try after their loved one is gone. Some give up on life itself.

In short, what millions of people have done for hundreds of years gives the lie to the self-important cynics who want to reduce everything to an animal level.

Actually, many animals behave in ways which suggest that love is important to them, not only among their own species, but also with human beings. Stories of dogs who have rescued or defended their owners, even at the cost of their lives, go back for centuries.

Why is love so out of fashion with the intelligentsia and others who are striving to be "with it"?

Love is one of those bonds which enable people to function and societies to flourish—without being directed from above. Love is one of the many ways we influence each other and work out our interrelated lives without the help of the anointed. Like morality, loyalty, honesty, respect and other immaterial things, love is one of the intangibles without which the tangibles won't work.

Intellectuals are not comfortable with that. They want to be able to reduce 10
everything to something material, predictable and—above all—controllable. Many want to be in charge of our lives, not have us work things out among ourselves, whether through emotional ties or the interactions of the marketplace.

Another four-letter word that has fallen out of favor is "duty." It has not been banned. It has just been buried under tons of discussions of "rights." The two words used to be linked, but not anymore.

In the real world, however, rights and duties are as closely tied as ever. If A has a right to something, then B has a duty to see that he gets it. Otherwise A has no such right.

When it is a right to freedom of speech, then it is the duty of judges to stop the government from shutting him up—or to let him sue if it does. The big problem comes when it is no longer a question of rights to be left alone but rights to things that other people have to produce. When it is a right to "decent housing," for example, that means other people have a duty to produce that housing and supply it to you—whether or not you are willing to pay what it costs.

Only because the inherent link between rights and duties is broken verbally are advocates for all sorts of sweeping new rights able to sidestep the question as to why someone else must provide individuals with what they are unwilling to provide for themselves.

The claim is often made or implied that people may be willing to provide 15
for themselves but are simply unable to do so. But, when push comes to shove, many of the intelligentsia will admit that it doesn't matter to them why someone doesn't have something that he needs. He has a "right" to it. It also doesn't matter how someone caught AIDS. He has no duty to avoid it, but others have a duty to pay for it.

What is involved is not just some words but a whole vision of life. If one has the vision of the anointed who want to control other people's lives, then all those things which enable us to function independently of them and of government programs are suspect.

Four-letter words like *love, duty, work* and *save* are hallmarks of people with a very different vision, who make their own way through life without being part of some grandiose scheme of the anointed or of government bureaucracies that administer such schemes. No wonder those words are not nearly as popular as other four-letter words.

Practicing the Principles: Activities

KNOW YOUR RIGHTS

Prepare for this activity by brainstorming as a class the rights that you are guaranteed under the Constitution, relying just on your memory. Then carefully read a copy of the Bill of Rights and the Constitution to discover where these rights are spelled out. Are there any rights that you thought you had that are not stated explicitly in the document (such as a "right to privacy")? Are any rights stated that you were not aware of? Select one or more amendments to the Bill of Rights, such as the first, second, fourth, or fifth; then work through the language of the amendment, defining each word or phrase. To assist you, find in your library a Webster's dictionary from the early 19th century, a Johnson's dictionary from the 18th century, or the *Oxford English Dictionary.* Compare the historical definitions of these terms with definitions found in unabridged dictionaries or law dictionaries. For example, how has the meaning of the term *militia* (in the second Amendment) evolved over the years? As a class, try to come to some agreement about the meanings of some of the troublesome terms in the Constitution. After you have formulated your definitions, consider inviting some guest speakers to your class to discuss how the language of the Constitution is interpreted in legal decisions today.

DEFINING YOUR COLLEGE

Try writing a formal definition of your college or university, something that will place it within a class of colleges and then distinguish it from every other member of that class—a statement of what is unique about your college. Try to formulate your definition in one sentence in such a way that the definition excludes every other possible member of the group. To extend this activity, write an essay about your college that uses this definition as a thesis statement.

FINDING GENDER BIAS

As a class, try to reproduce some of Alleen Pace Nilsen's research on gender bias in language. Assign each member of the class a section of the dictionary (a few pages should do) to review quickly for words or phrases that reflect on gender. Write down the words you find on note cards, and discuss how many of them fit Nilsen's conclusions about gender bias in language. Once you have found some examples in the dictionary, try to find examples of gender bias or cultural bias in the popular media (or try to find obvious attempts to avoid gender bias or cultural bias). As an extension of this activity, write a research paper that focuses on whether gender and cultural bias exist and the possible effects of such bias. (Review Chapters 7 and 8 on questions of existence and causality).

CAVEAT EMPTOR: LET THE BUYER BEWARE

Charles O'Neill argues that the language of advertising "holds no secrets from us." Leslie Savan claims that "all ads *must* tell big lies." O'Neill admits that "the language of advertising involves us." Savan laments that "we participate in our own seduction." Which of these claims are true? Bring in examples of ads from various media that exemplify the claims made by these two authors. As a class, discuss how you can reconcile these seemingly contradictory positions.

Applying the Principles On Your Own

MASCULINITY

John Cloud's essay, "Never Too Buff," first appeared in the April 24, 2000, issue of *Time*. It addresses the dangerous trend of increased use of supplements and steroids among men to increase their sense of self-worth. Similarly, in her 1999 *Maclean's* essay, "The Lure of the Body Image," Susan McCelland explores today's idealized male body image and men's pursuit of it, including the development of eating disorders. Going beyond definitions of masculinity tied to body image, Gail Sheehy's essay "Men in Crisis," first published in *Ladies Home Journal* in 1998, also focuses on the psychological and emotional aspects of defining *masculinity*.

Never Too Buff

JOHN CLOUD

POP QUIZ. Who are more likely to be dissatisfied with the appearance of their chests, men or women? Who is more likely to be concerned about acne, your teenage son or his sister? And who is more likely to binge eat, your nephew or your niece? 1

If you chose the women and girls in your life, you are right only for the last question and even then, not by the margin you might expect. About 40% of Americans who go on compulsive-eating sprees are men. Thirty-eight percent of men want bigger pecs, while only 34% of women want bigger breasts. And more boys have fretted about zits than girls, going all the way back to a 1972 study.

A groundbreaking new book declares that these numbers, along with hundreds of other statistics and interviews the authors have compiled, mean something awful has happened to American men over the past few decades. They have become obsessed with their bodies. Authors Harrison Pope and Katharine Phillips, professors of psychiatry at Harvard and Brown, respectively, and Roberto Olivardia, a clinical psychologist at McLean Hospital in Belmont, Mass., have a catchy name to describe this obsession—a term that will soon be doing many reps on chat shows: the Adonis Complex.

The name, which refers to the gorgeous half man, half god of mythology, may be a little too ready for Oprah, but the theory behind it will start a wonderful debate. Based on original research involving more than 1,000 men over the past 15 years, the book argues that many men desperately want to look like Adonis because they constantly see the "ideal," steroid-boosted bodies of actors and models and because their muscles are all they have over women today. In an age when women fly combat missions, the authors ask, "What can a modern boy or man do to distinguish himself as being 'masculine'?"

5 For years, of course, some men—ice skaters, bodybuilders, George Hamilton—have fretted over aspects of their appearance. But the numbers suggest that body image concerns have gone mainstream: nearly half of men don't like their overall appearance, in contrast to just 1 in 6 in 1972. True, men typically are fatter now, but another study found that 46% of men of normal weight think about their appearance "all the time" or "frequently." And some men—probably hundreds of thousands, if you extrapolate from small surveys—say they have passed up job and even romantic opportunities because they refuse to disrupt workouts or dine on restaurant food. In other words, an increasing number of men would rather look brawny for their girlfriends than have sex with them.

Consider what they're spending. Last year American men forked over \$2 billion for gym memberships—and another \$2 billion for home exercise equipment. *Men's Health* ("Rock-hard abs in six weeks!" it screams every other issue) had 250,000 subscribers in 1990; now it has 1.6 million. In 1996 alone, men underwent some 700,000 cosmetic procedures.

At least those profits are legal. Anabolic steroids—the common name for synthetic testosterone—have led to the most dramatic changes in the male form in modern history, and more and more average men want those changes for themselves. Since steroids became widely available on the black market in the 1960s, perhaps 3 million American men have swallowed or injected them—mostly in the past 15 years. A 1993 survey found that 1 Georgia high school boy in every 15 admitted having used steroids without a prescription. And the Drug Enforcement Administration reports that the percentage of all high school students who have used steroids has increased 50% in the past four years, from 1.8% to 2.8%. The abuse of steroids has so alarmed the National Institute on Drug Abuse that on Friday it launched a campaign in gyms, malls, bookstores, clubs and on the Internet to warn teenagers about the dangers. Meanwhile, teenagers in even larger numbers are buying legal but lightly regulated food supplements, some with dangerous side effects, that purport to make you bigger or leaner or stronger.

As they infiltrated the bodybuilding world in the '70s and Hollywood a decade later, steroids created bodies for mass consumption that the world had literally never seen before. Pope likes to chart the changes by looking at Mr. America winners, which he called up on the Internet in his office last week. "Look at this guy," Pope exclaims when he clicks on the 1943 winner, Jules Bacon. "He couldn't even win a county bodybuilding contest today." Indeed, there are 16-year-olds working out at your gym who are as big as Bacon. Does that necessarily mean that today's bodybuilders—including those 16-year-olds—are 'roided? Pope is careful. "The possibility exists that rare or exceptional people, those with an unusual genetic makeup or a hormonal imbalance," could achieve the muscularity and leanness of today's big bodybuilders, he says.

But it's not likely. And Pope isn't lobbing dumbbells from an ivory tower: the professor lifts weights six days a week, from 11 a.m. to 1 p.m. (He can even mark historical occasions by his workouts: "I remember when the Challenger went down; I was doing a set of squats.") "We are being assaulted by images virtually impossible to attain without the use of drugs," says Pope. "So what happens when you change a million-year-old equilibrium of nature?"

10 A historical loop forms: steroids beget pro wrestlers—Hulk Hogan, for one, has admitted taking steroids—who inspire boys to be just like them. Steroids have changed even boys' toys. Feminists have long derided Barbie for her tiny waist and big bosom. The authors of "The Adonis Complex" see a similar problem for boys in the growth of G.I. Joe. The grunt of 1982 looks scrawny compared with G.I. Joe Extreme, introduced in the mid-'90s. The latter would have a 55-in. chest and 27-in. biceps if he were real, which simply can't be replicated in nature. Pope also points out a stunning little feature of the three-year-old video game Duke Nukem: Total Meltdown, developed by GT Interactive Software. When Duke gets tired, he can find a bottle of steroids to get him going. "Steroids give Duke a super adrenaline rush," the game manual notes.

To bolster their argument, the Adonis authors developed a computerized test that allows subjects to "add" muscle to a typical male body. They estimate their own size and then pick the size they would like to be and the size they think women want. Pope and his colleagues gave the test to college students and found that on average, the men wanted 28 lbs. more muscle—and thought women wanted them to have 30 lbs. more. In fact, the women who took the test picked an ideal man only slightly more muscular than average. Which goes a long way toward explaining why Leonardo DiCaprio can be a megastar in a nation that also idealizes "Stone Cold" Steve Austin.

But when younger boys took Pope's test, they revealed an even deeper sense of inadequacy about their bodies. More than half of boys ages 11 to 17 chose as their physical ideal an image possible to attain only by using steroids. So they do. Boys are a big part of the clientele at Muscle Mania (not its real name), a weightlifting store that *Time* visited last week at a strip mall in a Boston suburb. A couple of teenagers came in to ask about tribulus, one of the many over-the-counter drugs and bodybuilding supplements the store sells, all legally. "Friend of mine," one boy begins, fooling no one, "just came off a cycle of juice, and he heard that tribulus can help you produce testosterone naturally." Patrick, 28, who runs the store and who stopped using steroids four years ago because of chest pain, tells the kid, "The s---- shuts off your nuts," meaning steroids can reduce sperm production, shrink the testicles and cause impotence. Tribulus, Patrick says, can help restart natural testosterone production. The teen hands over $12 for 100 Tribulus Fuel pills. (Every day, Muscle Mania does $4,000 in sales of such products, with protein supplements and so-called fat burners leading the pack.)

Patrick says many of his teen customers, because they're short on cash, won't pay for a gym membership "until they've saved up for a cycle [of steroids]. They don't see the point without them." The saddest customers, he says, are the little boys, 12 and 13, brought in by young fathers. "The dad will say, 'How do we put some weight on this kid?' with the boy just staring at the floor.

"Dad is going to turn him into Hulk Hogan, even if it's against his will."

What would motivate someone to take steroids? Pope, Phillips and Olivar- 15
dia say the Adonis Complex works in different ways for different men. "Michael," 32, one of their research subjects, told *Time* he had always been a short kid who got picked on. He started working out at about 14, and he bought muscle magazines for advice. The pictures taunted him: he sweated, but he wasn't getting as big as the men in the pictures. Other men in his gym also made him feel bad. When he found out they were on steroids, he did two cycles himself, even though he knew they could be dangerous.

But not all men with body-image problems take steroids. Jim Davis, 29, a human services manager, told *Time* he never took them, even when training for bodybuilding competitions. But Davis says he developed a form of obsessive-compulsive disorder around his workouts. He lifted weights six days a week for at least six years. He worked out even when injured. He adhered to a rigid regimen for every session, and if he changed it, he felt anxious all day. He began to be worried about clothes, and eventually could wear only three shirts, ones that made him look big. He still felt small. "I would sit in class at college with a coat on," he says. You may have heard this condition called bigorexia—thinking your muscles are puny when they aren't. Pope and his colleagues call it muscle dysmorphia and estimate that hundreds of thousands of men suffer from it.

Even though most boys and men never approach the compulsion of Davis or Michael (both eventually conquered it), they undoubtedly face more pressure now than in the past to conform to an impossible ideal. Rippled male bodies are used today to advertise everything that shapely female bodies advertise: not just fitness products but also dessert liqueurs, microwave ovens and luxury hotels. The authors of "The Adonis Complex" want guys to rebel against those images, or at least see them for what they are: a goal unattainable without drug use. Feminists raised these issues for women years ago, and more recent books such as *The Beauty Myth* were part of a backlash against the hourglass ideal. Now, says Phillips, "I actually think it may be harder for men than women to talk about these problems because it's not considered masculine to worry about such things." But maybe there is a masculine alternative: Next time WWF comes on, guys, throw the TV out the window. And order a large pizza.

The Lure of the Body Image

SUSAN MCCELLAND

THE YEAR Ralph Heighton of Pictou, N.S., turned 30, he decided to lose some weight. At five-foot-nine, pushing 210 lb., Heighton says when he stood in front of the mirror, he knew something wasn't working. He joined the YMCA in the nearby town of New Glasgow, started taking nightly walks and altered his diet, cutting out the late-night pizzas and pitas with spiced beef, onions and sauce. Now, at 34, Heighton fluctuates around the 185 lb. mark, and has converted one of the three bedrooms in his new two-story home into a gym, complete with weights and a tattered heavy bag bound by duct tape. Heighton, a wildlife technician with Nova Scotia's department of fisheries, says he has achieved his goal of feeling better. Though still single, he says bashfully that he thinks he has never looked as good—which was one of his key reasons for getting in shape. "The magazines sort of force this body image on you of what it means to be a physically fit person," says Heighton. "Whether we want to admit it or not, this image is what we want to look like." 1

The idealized male body image nowadays is beefy and muscled, as epitomized in the Calvin Klein underwear advertisements showcasing the bulging pecs and rippling abdomen of Antonio Sabato Jr. And like Heighton, hundreds of thousands of men in Canada are flocking to gyms and health clubs in the quest to look buffed and toned. There are signs, however, that some men are taking the image to extremes. Statistics on steroid use show an alarming number of male teenagers across the country are using the substance illegally simply to put on muscle. Men are increasingly being diagnosed with eating disorders. And plastic surgeons report a general increase in men seeking their services to improve their appearance. "This is an early warning," said New York City author Michelangelo Signorile, whose book *Life Outside* chronicles the history of body image among homosexual men. "This 'cult of masculinity' isn't just in gay culture as so many like to believe. It envelops the entire culture. It is an obsessive devotion to an ideal."

Although worshipping the body is hardly new, the emphasis on the beefcake look has evolved gradually in North America over the past 100 years. Both Signorile and Brian Pronger, a philosopher in the faculty of physical education at the University of Toronto, say that many men, straight and gay, adopted a more masculine appearance after the Oscar Wilde trials in the 1890s associated effeminate behaviour with homosexuality in the popular mind. Pronger and Signorile also say that women's suffrage and, later, the modern feminist movement caused men to covet a larger appearance as a means of defending men's status. "As women take up more space in traditionally masculine places," says Pronger, "some men feel compelled to take up more in order to maintain their position."

It takes a lot of sweating and spending to achieve a hard-body look. According to a 1995 report published by the Canadian Fitness and Lifestyle Research Institute, men spend more than twice as much as women in all categories related to fitness, including clothing, exercise equipment, membership fees and instruction. Brad Whitehead, who works for one of the largest distributors of creatine, a controversial supplement that increases the energy capacity in muscles, says sales have increased 130 per cent since 1997.

5 Calvin Klein and other underwear merchants are not alone in using men with buffed bodies to sell products. Other advertisers include Coca-Cola, Nike and Marlboro, which has introduced a builder version of its original "Marlboro Man." As well, magazine stands now offer dozens of titles devoted to health, fitness and muscle, tantalizing readers with snappy headlines like "Great abs in eight weeks." Their pages are adorned with ads featuring big, bulky men selling muscle-building supplements.

One of the sad consequences of the push towards a hyper-masculine image is that it can rarely be obtained without the use of potentially harmful drugs. A 1993 study conducted for the Canadian Centre for Ethics in Sport concluded that four per cent of males aged 11 to 18—as many as 83,000 young Canadians—used anabolic steroids in 1992 and 1993. In the study, which involved 16,169 high-school and elementary students, one in five reported that they knew someone who was taking anabolic steroids. Among the reasons given for their use, nearly half said it was to change their physical appearance. That contrasted starkly with previously held notions that steroids were used mostly to increase athletic performance, says Paul Melia, the centre's director of education. "The reality is for most of these young men, even if they do get on a regimen of weight training, they are not going to look like these picture boys," said Melia. "And sustaining that look is a full-time job."

In a downtown Toronto gym, Mike, a 32-year-old former bodybuilder and weight lifter and a longtime user of anabolic steroids, says as many as four out of five of the 18-to-25-year-old men using the facility are on the illegal drugs. When he started using steroids 16 years ago, Mike says, he was part of an elite group of men who took them for competitive reasons. "Today it is for the body image," he says. "And these kids stack—they add steroid upon steroid, thinking they are going to get a certain look. They take this stuff, go out to night clubs, get drunk and mix everything together. It's all for image."

Mike says one result of working out seriously can be that, no matter how big their muscles get, men start thinking they are still not big enough. It is a phenomenon disturbingly similar to cases of eating disorders among women who believe they are too big, no matter how thin they get. Maintaining a hard body takes not only a regimen of heavy workouts, but also a dedication to eating right and at times dieting to avoid gaining fat, says Mike. And psychologists across the country say one result of those self-imposed pressures is an increased incidence of eating disorders among men. According to Dr. Howard Steiger, a clinical psychologist and director of the eating disorder program at Douglas Hospital in Montreal, surveys have shown that five to 10 per cent of eating disorder sufferers are men. He says most people with eating disorders have unstable self-esteem. He also says there are increasing sociocultural pressures on men to connect their self-esteem to body image. While there are no new national figures, specialists in many centres say that bulimia nervosa, characterized by binge eating and vomiting, is on the rise in men. "What you find," says Steiger, "are people who diet too much, who condition too much, and what you are doing is setting up this pressure of hunger—a constant state of undernutrition that eventually leads to bulimic-type eating patterns."

In addition to steroid use and erratic eating behaviour, John Semple, secretary treasurer of the Canadian Society of Plastic Surgeons, says he believes men are increasingly having plastic surgery to alter their body image. Dr. Bill Papanastasiou, a plastic surgeon in Montreal, estimates that only 10 per cent of his patients were male when he opened his practice 13 years ago. Today it is as high as 15 to 20 per cent In Halifax, plastic surgeon Dr. Kenneth Wilson says one of the most common surgeries he does for men is liposuction. For Nathan Estep, a 27-year-old from Detroit who spent $1,800 in Pontiac, Mich., in 1997 to have liposuction done on his waistline, the surgery has transformed his life. Since he was 10, Estep was a constant dieter, at times bulimic, and for many years tried to control his weight using diet drugs including Dexedrine, ephedrine and laxatives. Today, Estep says he can walk proudly, with his shirt off and with no hint of any fat from his childhood returning. "I was a fat kid—I had fat in the wrong places," he says. "The first thing I did after the liposuction was go to the beach, take my shirt off and eat a pint of Haagen-Dazs. I feel like a new man."

According to Pronger, who has been studying the philosophy of physical 10
fitness for five years, a person with a hard, fit body considers it a signal of discipline and a capacity for hard work "When you see somebody who is overweight," he says, "often the response is how did they let themselves get like that." The mistaken presumption, he adds, is that the person doesn't have the discipline to be a productive citizen. One of the solutions, says Pronger, is to teach children to look at body images in the same critical way they are told to consider art and literature—to be able to recognize what has merit. "If we were doing the same with physical education, people could learn to have a different reaction to these extreme body images," he says. "They would say, 'Hey, I don't want to be part of this pressure to fall in love with a highly commercialized image.'"

Men In Crisis

GAIL SHEEHY

1 HEADLINES and books trumpet the notion that manhood is on trial—or that it is dead altogether. The forties, which ought to be the peak decade in the lives of most men, are often filled with anxiety, dread and isolation. No less an icon than Clint Eastwood calls himself the "last cowboy." Robert Kincaid, the protagonist of *The Bridges of Madison County*—whom Eastwood played in the film of the same name—describes himself as obsolete: Computers and robots, he says, have replaced men of courage. Meanwhile, women's magazines instruct their readers in how to satisfy their own rising expectations: "Seize the Night!" they urge. "Your Sexual Peak Is Now!"

"Men in their forties feel quite threatened and attacked," says John Munder Ross, Ph.D., a pioneer in men's studies who teaches psychoanalysis and human development at the New York medical schools of Columbia, Cornell and New York University, and the author of *The Male Paradox* (Simon & Schuster, 1992). "On the work front and at home, they feel expendable. Women begin to look for positive changes in their forties, when their years of total parenthood are winding down. They become more invested in their careers, and often initiate separation from their mates. Men are much more dependent, and they have greater separation anxiety than they like to acknowledge."

CHANGES IN THE LANDSCAPE

It is commonly believed that men are hardwired to act aggressively and suppress emotion, and in fact it is true that in studies of temperament, one of the most striking gender differences is a man's ability to remain cool under physical attack. Yet there is also a basic need for intimacy that becomes more persistent as a man grows older.

What confuses this natural process for men today is the erosion of traditional male roles and privileges. For tens of thousands of years, men were warriors and hunters, dominant over women and indispensable as breadwinners. Their brawn was admired and feared. But in the past few decades—an evolutionary eyeblink—men have been asked to cool their aggressiveness, share their emotional secrets and be more polite about their sexual predation.

5 To make matters worse, millions of men at all social levels who expected to be secure by midlife are seeing their jobs disappear or their marriages disintegrate. The participation of adult males in the workforce is down from 87 percent in 1948 to just over 75 percent now.

Furthermore, American men in every age group under sixty-five have watched their income (in constant dollars) remain flat, decline or show only modest gains over the past two decades, while women's has steadily climbed. And the more economically independent women become, the less likely they are to remain in a miserable marriage.

Given these role-shattering changes, the historical model of masculinity is blurred at best. As in any era of profound change, there is a predictable backlash.

SOMETIMES A CIGAR IS MORE THAN A CIGAR

The scene is The Big Smoke, in San Francisco, at the Embarcadero Center. A thousand men are here to smoke big cigars, sip booze, get a little buzz and show off. Big steak-and-potatoes men with slaphappy smiles strut around the display booths. At the center of the swirl is the short, thick figure of Marvin Shanken, the prescient editor of *Cigar Aficionado*. When he launched his magazine in 1992, the antismoking wave was at its peak and the cigar market had dropped like a stone. But Shanken understood that men were famished for ways to express their maleness. He saw cigar smoking as a way for men to reassert a male preserve and adopt a status symbol that is considerably cheaper than a luxury car. During the next four years, the sales of premium cigars more than doubled, and circulation and ad sales for Shanken's magazine followed suit.

Of course, the cigar-smoking trend does not seriously address the confusion over a code of manliness appropriate to today. It is an elite version of a larger movement among men who feel displaced, disappointed and "dissed." Men need action-oriented ways and places they can get together with other men; many of those opportunities have been lost as a result of laws—justified and long overdue—against sexual discrimination.

"THE BIG IMPOSSIBLE"

10 Men's problem with defining their masculinity is an eternal one. In aboriginal North America, for example, among the nonviolent Fox tribe of the Iowa area, real manhood was described as "the Big Impossible." It was an elevated status that only an extraordinary few could achieve.

A man is *made* a man. Manhood is not something he's born with but something he earns. Anthropologist David D. Gilmore, in a cross-cultural study, finds that on every continent, among everyone from simple hunters to sophisticated urbanites, boys must pass a critical threshold, through harsh testing, before they can gain the right to be called men. There is no single line that, once passed, confers manhood, as menstruation marks womanhood for girls.

Even young men in their late twenties admit they are confused about what constitutes the code of manliness today. As one beefy blond Gen-Xer of twenty-eight raised in the American West says, with noticeable envy, "With my parents, there was a relationship of clear dominance and submission. My dad acted with godlike certainty. I mean, he assumed prerogative. My mother assumed it was her role to show deference." He summed up the dilemma: "There are no rules for how to be a man today."

When men today struggle to live up to the traditional mold of masculinity, they are trying to accomplish the big impossible. For some time now, women have been defying all the stereotypes with which they grew up, and they are measurably happier in midlife than any previous generation has been. It is time that men recognize that their old roles and rules are virtually impossible to live up to in the contemporary world. Trying to do so only limits their otherwise exhilarating possibilities for custom-designing a happier middle life.

HONOR AMONG MEN

"What men need is men's approval," notes playwright David Mamet. Traditionally, men have demonstrated their masculinity through displays of honor in the fields of sports, politics, business and war—all fields that until very recently excluded women. No matter how the roles of men have changed, one cultural truth remains: Men care most about what other men think of them. Their greatest fear is of being dominated or humiliated by a stronger man, particularly in front of other men. How then do they continue to demonstrate their manliness in middle life, even as their physical strength wanes and as the need arises to listen to and accommodate others in order to fulfill leadership roles?

15 Through sports, for one thing. The average American man watches twenty-eight hours of TV a week, much of it sports. Basketball, baseball, football and soccer are more than games. They constitute a culture—arguably, the dominant male culture today.

In a fascinating book called *The Stronger Women Get, the More Men Love Football* (Harcourt Brace & Co., 1994), Mariah Burton Nelson, a former professional female basketball player, points out that "manly sports comprise a world where men are in charge and women are irrelevant at best. . . . Sports offer a . . . world where men, as owners, coaches and umpires, still rule."

Sports also permit shared passion between men. It is most often the over-forty guys in the stands at games who shriek and groan and weep, uncovering raw emotions they would contain in front of other men in almost any other setting.

More important, true athletic heroes are champions at emotional control. If they weren't able to psych themselves up, control their anxieties, channel their anger and blot out the jeers of the crowd, they would never have the concentration necessary to kick that crucial field goal or come back from losing the first set. As Nelson writes, "When they fight, the fighting is deliberate masculine theater, not a momentary loss of control. The decision to [lose one's temper] involves rational considerations: not losing face, trying to win games, fulfilling expectations of fans and teammates and appearing on the evening news."

CURRENT MODELS OF MANHOOD

Men are finding ways to bolster themselves in this time of confusion, sometimes shifting back and forth among the following expressions of manliness, depending on mood or circumstances.

20 One of the strongest trends of the nineties is the reversion to the prefeminist, pre–Alan Alda form, **Resurgent Angry Macho Man (RAMM).** The

RAMM movement encourages a man to return to his primitive nature as the wild man with fire in his belly and a strong arm to put women back in their place. The prototype is the American cowboy. The tough loner who shoots from the hip, doesn't need love, doesn't stick around with women and doesn't react to loss was a cultural ideal through the 1950s. John Wayne, who has held up as a symbol of manhood for several generations, remains an inspiration to men of the RAMM type. As described by Garry Wills in his book *John Wayne's America* (Simon & Schuster, 1997), Wayne is the very embodiment of the country's receded frontier, "untrammeled, unspoiled, free to roam."

The opposite philosophy is represented by the **Sensitive New Age Guy (SNAG),** initially a man who discovered his nurturing side unexpectedly (or by default, as in the film *Kramer vs. Kramer*). In the extreme version, he switched roles and assumed the prerogatives of Mr. Mom. He expected his kids and wife to idealize his contribution, his hours would remain discretionary, and he wouldn't be responsible for mortgage payments. Or, having fought for custody after divorce, he was determined to prove he could outdo Mom. The results among men who actually try to perform this role without work outside the home are mixed. They can usually develop the necessary empathy and patience to care for the kids, but forgoing career ambitions and male posturing may eventually make them feel emasculated. And they often find themselves left behind by women, who desert them to seek wider horizons themselves.

However, many successful men in midlife have disclosed to me that they yearn to enjoy a period as Mr. Mom. This is an important cultural change, still small, but growing. It could be a very healthy way for a man in transition to exercise his nurturing side and feel useful while he is figuring out a new direction.

The currently popular Hollywood model of the SNAG is a successful but egocentric Yuppie who almost loses what is most important but is saved in the end by growing out of his macho posturing. The zany putty-face Jim Carrey scored a big hit with *Liar Liar,* which features a driven lawyer whose five-year-old son magically transforms a narcissistic no-show into a sensitive hands-on father.

Another expression of manliness is the **Dominant Male Model (DOM).** These men are the world-beaters, the wunderkinder, the high achievers who have to be on top to be happy. In contemporary terms, they were the hotshot bond traders of the greedy eighties so memorably labeled by Tom Wolfe as Masters of the Universe. In the nineties they are personified by the rogue elephants of the information and entertainment worlds: Bill Gates, Rupert Murdoch, Donald Trump.

Yet a fourth philosophy is the **Messenger of God** model (**MOG**), pro- 25
pounded by a new wave of evangelism, which calls upon men to band together in spiritually inspired mass movements that bear a great resemblance to twelve-step programs. Men are recruited to these movements by powerful autocratic figures: Louis Farrakhan, for example, the militantly anti-Semitic Muslim who presided over the Million Man March, or Bill McCartney, the messianic former

football coach who created the Promise Keepers. Both of these movements tap into a longing for ideals, discipline, spiritual guidance and a resurgence of male authority. They appeal particularly to boomers and Gen-Xers, with their use of rock music, an athletic "uniform," martial speeches, the pointed exclusion of women and permission for heterosexual men to show love for one another. Adherents recite vows to become better fathers, husbands and community leaders and dedicate themselves to restoring Scriptural values.

A true grassroots movement is the **Partner and Leader** model (**PAL**). Men are finding ways to bond in small groups that form spontaneously—through a school or church connection, among men cruelly downsized at a workplace or shut out of their children's lives as noncustodial fathers. In these smaller groups, men are encouraged to act as partners as well as leaders, rather than being led by any higher authority. They are not bonding for the historical purpose of attacking or defending turf, but as chosen brothers who can offer each other support and solace or aid in unlearning the socialization that keeps them locked up with inscrutable feelings and secret failings.

These groups are not usually religious, but there are reverberations among men in the Christian communities, who are being called by their churches to find new meaning in service and community leadership. Wives are welcomed as full partners. The new manhood ideal here is servant-leader. Christian counseling is blended with psychotherapy. The call is to spiritual transformation, stressing the movement from success to significance.

REINVENTING MANHOOD

In truth, no man is just one of these types. Men's lives today call upon a full range of capacities—from brute force to gentle empathy—and it is no longer necessary or useful to lock oneself into the old stereotypes. With military confrontations increasingly being replaced by trade wars, men have a greater chance to develop new "manly arts."

To speak of the end of manhood is both brute and destructive. What is needed is a new definition of manliness, one that celebrates the strengths of the post-patriarchal male in midlife and uses his individual gifts. Such ideals are indispensable to the healthy functioning of any culture, to give men a purpose in life regardless of their age, and urgently necessary to bind men psychologically into the family and the community.

DEFINING POVERTY AND RACE

The three essays that follow take on the challenge of defining two of our society's most complex terms, *poverty,* and what is possibly the most complex, *race.* Louis Uchitelle's "Devising New Math to Define Poverty," first published in the *New York Times* in 1999, focuses on families in Indianapolis, Indiana, to analyze the U.S. Census Bureau's formulas for determining poverty levels. Originally published in the *New York Times Magazine* in June 1999, Jeffrey Goldberg's "The Color of Suspicion" explores racial profiling from a variety of perspectives, and Richard Dyer traces representations of whiteness in Western culture in "The Matter of Whiteness," an excerpt from his 1997 book *White*.

Devising New Math to Define Poverty

LOUIS UCHITELLE

1 THE CENSUS Bureau has begun to revise its definition of what constitutes poverty in the United States, experimenting with a formula that would drop millions more families below the poverty line.

The bureau's new approach would in effect raise the income threshold for living above poverty to $19,500 for a family of four, from the $16,600 now considered sufficient. Suddenly, 46 million Americans, or 17 percent of the population, would be recognized as officially below the line, not the 12.7 percent announced last month, the lowest level in nearly a decade.

A strong economy has undoubtedly lifted many families, but not nearly as many as the official statistics suggest.

"It is certainly our opinion, and the opinion of every researcher we have talked to, that something should be done to update the poverty measure," said Edward Welniak, chief of the Census Bureau's Income Statistics Branch.

5 Fixing a poverty line has always been a subjective endeavor. The current formula was created for President Lyndon B. Johnson to keep score in his "war on poverty" and has remained unchanged since 1965 except for adjustments for inflation. It is based on a minimal food budget that no longer represents American eating habits or spending. The Census Bureau's new Experimental Poverty Measures are an effort to determine what poor people must spend on food, clothing, housing and life's little extras.

"There is no scientific way to set a new poverty line," said Rebecca M. Blank, dean of the School of Public Policy at the University of Michigan. "What there is here are a set of judgment calls, now being made, about what is needed to lift people to a socially acceptable standard of living."

Sociologists and economists who study what people must earn to escape poverty in the United States place the line even higher than the Census Bureau's experimental measures, which were published in July and are now the focus of a growing debate. They put the threshold for a family of four somewhere between $21,000 and $28,000. That is partly because the bureau's criteria, based largely on a study by the National Academy of Sciences, do not allow extra cash for emergencies—to fix a car, say, or repair a leaky roof, or to buy health insurance.

Ordinary Americans, in opinion polls, draw the poverty line above $20,000, saying it takes at least that much, if not more, to "get along in their community," to "live decently" or to avoid hardship.

But a higher threshold means government spending would rise to pay for benefits tied to the poverty level, like food stamps and Head Start. That would require an incursion into the budget surplus that neither Republicans nor Democrats seek.

Not surprising, the White House, which would have to authorize a change 10
in the poverty formula, is proceeding cautiously. "We have at least a couple of years more work to do," an Administration official said, passing the decision for redefining poverty to the next administration. . . .

The new thinking has several facets. It redefines income to include for the first time noncash income like food stamps and rent subsidies. It puts child care and other work-related expenses in a separate category because they vary so much from family to family. And it tries to determine what a low-income family must spend in the 1990's not only to survive, but to preserve a reasonable amount of self-respect.

A telephone is considered essential. So is housing in good repair. Clothing is no longer just to keep warm or covered; looking decent is a critical status symbol. That is why Isaac Pinner, 16 and in ninth grade, and his sister, Lea, 12 and in seventh grade, insist they are not poor. Sitting in the living room of their rundown rented home with their mother, Julie Pinner, 35, a receptionist and clerk, they resent her decision to talk to a reporter about poverty. "I get what I want," Lea said, and Isaac agreed. "Why talk to us?" he asked.

Judging by their clothes, they do not seem poor, although their mother's income of $15,500, including a rent subsidy, while higher than the official poverty line for a single mother of two, puts the Pinners right at the dividing line in the Census Bureau's experimental measures.

"They think I am richer than I am," said Ms. Pinner, who noted that the gas was turned off recently when she could not pay the bill. She also lacks money to fix her car.

"But," Ms. Pinner said of her children, "he wears the latest Nike brand 15
shoes and she the latest Levi's. I like them to look nice, and here in the ghetto there are standards of dress. If they don't dress up to the standards, other kids tend to pick on them. I am not the only poor person who dresses her kids."

Most proposed definitions of poverty include a car—an old one—which is deemed necessary not only for work but for the odd outing, or the supermarket. "Not having a car is a big dividing line between the poor and the not so poor," said Christopher Jencks, a sociologist at Harvard's Kennedy School of Government.

More often than not, poor Indianapolis families own used cars, but they are often at risk. Austin Johnson, for example, says he cannot afford car insurance. Neither can Nevada Owens, who is also short of money to fix a flat tire. She drives her 1985 Delta Oldsmobile with a spare doughnut tire permanently on a rear wheel. The car was a gift from her church, but the cost of gasoline for this guzzler eats up 7 percent of her $17,300 in annual income.

Her income, from welfare, food stamps, rent and tuition subsidies and a $3,000 gift from her mother, puts Ms. Owens, a single mother, and her three children just above the official poverty line. But at 21, studying to be a licensed practical nurse, she needs the car. The course work requires her to travel from her school to two different hospitals, about 25 miles a day.

Then there is the Saturday outing in Ms. Owens's old car, which she drives to her grandfather's home in a rural area outside the city—the one family luxury. "We have a cookout," she said, "and the kids play on the swings and my mother comes over—she lives two doors away. We have a good time."

In a 1993 study of impoverished single mothers, published as the book *Making Ends Meet,* Kathryn Edin, a sociologist at the University of Pennsylvania, reported that the mothers found themselves forced to spend more than their acknowledged incomes. They got the difference from family members, absent boyfriends, off-the-books jobs and church charity. 20

"No one avoided the unnecessary expenditures," Ms. Edin said recently, "such as the occasional trip to the Dairy Queen, or a pair of stylish new sneakers for the son who might otherwise sell drugs to get them, or the cable subscription for the kids home alone and you are afraid they will be out on the street if they are not watching TV."

The Color of Suspicion

JEFFREY GOLDBERG

SGT. LEWIS of the Maryland State Police is a bull-necked, megaphone-voiced, highly caffeinated drug warrior who, on this shiny May morning outside of Annapolis, is conceding defeat. The drug war is over, the good guys have lost and he has been cast as a racist. "This is the end, buddy," he says. "I can read the writing on the wall." Lewis is driving his unmarked Crown Victoria down the fast lane of Route 50, looking for bad guys. The back of his neck is burnt by the sun, and he wears his hair flat and short under his regulation Stetson. 1

"They're going to let the N.A.A.C.P. tell us how to do traffic stops," he says. "That's what's happening. There may be a few troopers who make stops solely based on race, but this—they're going to let these people tell us how to run our department. I say, to hell with it all. I don't care if the drugs go through. I don't."

He does, of course. Mike Lewis was born to seize crack. He grew up in Salisbury, on the Eastern Shore—Jimmy Buffett country—and he watched his

friends become stoners and acid freaks. Not his scene. He buzz-cut his hair away 5
and joined the state troopers when he was 19. He's a star, the hard-charger who made one of the nation's largest seizures of crack cocaine out on Route 13. He's a national expert on hidden compartments. He can tell if a man's lying, he says, by watching the pulsing of the carotid artery in his neck. He can smell crack cocaine inside a closed automobile. He's a human drug dog, a walking polygraph machine. "I have the unique ability to distinguish between a law-abiding person and an up-to-no-good person," he says. "Black or white." All these skills, though, he's ready to chuck. The lawsuits accusing the Maryland State Police of harassing black drivers, the public excoriation—and most of all, the Governor of New Jersey saying that her state police profiled drivers based on race, and were wrong to do so—have twisted him up inside. "Three of my men have put in for transfers," he says. "My wife wants me to get out. I'm depressed."

What depresses Mike Lewis is that he believes he is in possession of a truth polite society is too cowardly to accept. He says that when someone tells this particular truth, his head is handed to him. "The superintendent of the New Jersey State Police told the truth and he got fired for it," Lewis says.

This is what Carl Williams said, fueling a national debate about racial profiling in law enforcement: "Today, with this drug problem, the drug problem is cocaine or marijuana. It is most likely a minority group that's involved with that." Gov. Christine Todd Whitman fired Williams, and the news ricocheted through police departments everywhere, especially those, like the Maryland State Police, already accused of racial profiling—the stopping and searching of blacks because they are black.

The way cops perceive blacks—and how those perceptions shape and misshape crime fighting—is now the most charged racial issue in America. . . .

Neither side understands the other. The innocent black man, jacked-up and humiliated during a stop-and-frisk or a pretext car stop, asks: Whatever happened to the Fourth Amendment? It is no wonder, blacks say, that the police are so wildly mistrusted.

And then there's the cop, who says: Why shouldn't I look at race when I'm looking for crime? It is no state secret that blacks commit a disproportionate amount of crime, so "racial profiling" is simply good police work.

Mike Lewis wishes that all this talk of racial profiling would simply stop.

As we drive, Lewis watches a van come up on his right and pass him. A 10
young black man is at the wheel, his left leg hanging out the window. The blood races up Lewis's face: "Look at that! That's a violation! You can't drive like that! But I'm not going to stop him. No, sir. If I do, he's just going to call me a racist."

Then Lewis notices that the van is a state government vehicle. "This is ridiculous," he says. Lewis hits his lights. The driver stops. Lewis issues him a warning and sends him on his way. The driver says nothing.

"He didn't call me a racist," Lewis says, pulling into traffic, "but I know what he was thinking." Lewis does not think of himself as a racist. "I know how to treat people," he says. "I've never had a complaint based on a race-based stop. I've got that supercharged knowledge of the Constitution that allows me to do this right."

In the old days, when he was patrolling the Eastern Shore, it was white people he arrested. "Ninety-five percent of my drug arrests were dirt-ball-type whites—marijuana, heroin, possession-weight. Then I moved to the highway, I start taking off two, three kilograms of coke, instead of two or three grams. Black guys. Suddenly I'm not the greatest trooper in the world. I'm a racist. I'm locking up blacks, but I can't help it."

His eyes gleam: "Ask me how many white people I've ever arrested for cocaine smuggling—ask me!"

I ask. 15

"None! Zero! I debrief hundreds of black smugglers, and I ask them, 'Why don't you hire white guys to deliver your drugs?' They just laugh at me. 'We ain't gonna trust our drugs with white boys.' That's what they say."

Mike Lewis's dream: "I dream at night about arresting white people for cocaine. I do. I try to think of innovative ways to arrest white males. But the reality is different." . . .

WHY A COP PROFILES

This is what a cop might tell you in a moment of reckless candor: in crime fighting, race matters. When asked, most cops will declare themselves color blind. But watch them on the job for several months, and get them talking about the way policing is really done, and the truth will emerge, the truth being that cops, white and black, profile. Here's why, they say. African-Americans commit a disproportionate percentage of the types of crimes that draw the attention of the police. Blacks make up 12 percent of the population, but accounted for 58 percent of all carjackers between 1992 and 1996. (Whites accounted for 19 percent.) Victim surveys—and most victims of black criminals are black—indicate that blacks commit almost 50 percent of all robberies. Blacks and Hispanics are widely believed to be the blue-collar backbone of the country's heroin- and cocaine-distribution networks. Black males between the ages of 14 and 24 make up 1.1 percent of the country's population, yet commit more than 28 percent of its homicides. Reason, not racism, cops say, directs their attention.

Cops, white and black, know one other thing: they're not the only ones who profile. Civilians profile all the time—when they buy a house, or pick a school district, or walk down the street. Even civil rights leaders profile. "There is nothing more painful for me at this stage in my life," Jesse Jackson said several years ago, "than to walk down the street and hear footsteps and start thinking about robbery—and then look around and see somebody white and feel relieved." Jackson now says his quotation was "taken out of context." The context, he said, is that violence is the inevitable by-product of poor education and health care. But no amount of "context" matters when you fear that you are about to be mugged.

At a closed-door summit in Washington between police chiefs and black community leaders recently, the black chief of police of Charleston, S.C., Reuben Greenberg, argued that the problem facing black America is not racial profiling, but precisely the sort of black-on-black crime Jackson was talking about. "I told them that the greatest problem in the black community is the tolerance for high levels of criminality," he recalled. "Fifty percent of homicide victims are African-Americans. I asked what this meant about the value of life in this community." 20

The police chief in Los Angeles, Bernard Parks, who is black, argues that racial profiling is rooted in statistical reality, not racism. "It's not the fault of the police when they stop minority males or put them in jail," Parks told me. "It's the fault of the minority males for committing the crime. In my mind it is not a great revelation that if officers are looking for criminal activity, they're going to look at the kind of people who are listed on crime reports." . . .

PROFILING IN BLACK AND WHITE

"Some blacks, I just get the sense off them that they're wild," Mark Robinson says. "I mean, you can tell. I have what you might call a profile. I pull up alongside a car with black males in it. Something doesn't match—maybe the style of the car with the guys in it. I start talking to them, you know, 'nice car,' that kind of thing, and if it doesn't seem right, I say, 'All right, let's pull it over to the side,' and we go from there."

He is quiet and self-critical, and the words sat in his mouth a while before he let them out. "I'm guilty of it, I guess."

Guilty of what?

"Racial profiling." 25

His partner, Gene Jones, says: "Mark is good at finding stolen cars on the street. Real good."

We are driving late one sticky Saturday night through the beat-down neighborhood of Logan, in the northern reaches of Philadelphia. The nighttime commerce is lively, lookouts holding down their corners, sellers ready to serve the addict traffic. It's a smorgasbord for the two plainclothes officers, but their attention is soon focused on a single cluster of people, four presumptive buyers who are hurrying inside a spot the officers know is hot with drugs.

The officers pull to the curb, slide out and duck behind a corner, watching the scene unfold. The suspects are wearing backward baseball caps and low-slung pants; the woman with them is dressed like a stripper.

"Is this racial profiling?" Jones asks. A cynical half-smile shows on his face.

The four buyers are white. Jones and Robinson are black, veterans of the street who know that white people in a black neighborhood will be stopped. Automatically: Faster than a Rastafarian in Scarsdale. 30

"No reason for them to be around here at this time of night, nope," Jones says.

Is it possible that they're visiting college friends? I ask.

Jones and Robinson, whose intuition is informed by experience, don't know quite what to make of my suggestion.

"It could be," Jones says, indulgently. "But, uhhhh, no way."

Are you going to stop them? 35

"I don't know what for yet, but I'm going to stop them." . . .

"DRIVING WHILE BLACK," AND OTHER EXAGGERATIONS

Here's the heart of the matter, as Chief Greenberg of Charleston sees it: "You got white cops who are so dumb that they can't make a distinction between a middle-class black and an under-class black, between someone breaking the law and someone just walking down the street. Black cops too. The middle class says: 'Wait a minute. I've done everything right, I pushed all the right buttons, went to all the right schools, and they're jacking me up anyway.' That's how this starts."

So is racism or stupidity the root cause of racial profiling?

Governor Whitman, it seems, would rather vote for stupidity.

"You don't have to be racist to engage in racial profiling," she says. We are 40
sitting in her office in the State House in Trenton. She still seems a bit astonished that her state has become the Mississippi of racial profiling.

Whitman, though burned by the behavior of her state troopers, is offering them a generous dispensation, given her definition of racial profiling. "Profiling means a police officer using cumulative knowledge and training to identify certain indicators of possible criminal activity," she told me. "Race may be one of those factors, but it cannot stand alone."

"Racial profiling," she continues, "is when race is the only factor. There's no other probable cause."

Her narrow, even myopic, definition suggests that only stone racists practice racial profiling. But the mere sight of black skin alone is not enough to spin most cops into a frenzy. "Police chiefs use that word 'solely' all the time, and it's such a red herring," says Randall Kennedy, Harvard Law professor and author of the book *Race, Crime, and the Law*. "Even Mark Fuhrman doesn't act solely on the basis of race."

The real question about racial profiling is this: Is it ever permissible for a law-enforcement officer to use race as one of even 5, or 10, or 20 indicators of possible criminality?

In other words, can the color of a man's skin help make him a criminal 45
suspect?

Yes, Whitman says. She suggests she doesn't have a problem with the use of race as one of several proxies for potential criminality. "I look at Barry McCaffrey's Web site," she says, referring to the Clinton Administration's drug czar, "and it says certain ethnic groups are more likely to engage in drug smuggling."

It is true. . . . The Office of National Drug Control Policy's Web site helpfully lists which racial groups sell which drugs in different cities. In Denver,

McCaffrey's Web site says, it is "minorities, Mexican nationals" who sell heroin. In Trenton, "crack dealers are predominantly African-American males, powdered cocaine dealers are predominantly Latino."

The link between racial minorities and drug-selling is exactly what Whitman's former police superintendent, Carl Williams, was talking about. So was Williams wrong?

"His comments indicated a lack of sensitivity to the seriousness of the problem."

But was he wrong on the merits? 50

"If he said, 'You should never use this solely; race could be a partial indicator, taken in concert with other factors' "—she pauses, sees the road down which she's heading, and puts it in reverse—"but you can't be that broad-brushed."

"Racial profiling" is a street term, not a textbook concept. No one teaches racial profiling. "Profiling," of course, is taught. It first came to the public's notice by way of the Federal Bureau of Investigation's behavioral-science unit, which developed the most famous criminal profile of all, one that did, in fact, have a racial component—the profile of serial killers as predominantly white, male loners.

It is the Drug Enforcement Administration, however, that is at the center of the racial-profiling controversy, accused of encouraging state law-enforcement officials to build profiles of drug couriers. The D.E.A., through its 15-year-old "Operation Pipeline," finances state training programs to interdict drugs on the highway. Civil rights leaders blame the department for the burst of race-based stops, but the D.E.A. says it discourages use of race as an indicator. "It's a fear of ours, that people will use race," says Greg Williams, the D.E.A.'s operations chief.

Cops use race because it's easy, says John Crew, the A.C.L.U.'s point man on racial profiling. "The D.E.A. says the best profile for drug interdiction is no profile," he says. "They say it's a mistake to look for a certain race of drivers. That's their public line. But privately, they say, 'God knows what these people from these state and local agencies do in the field.' "

The A.C.L.U. sees an epidemic of race-based profiling. Anecdotes are plen- 55
tiful, but hard numbers are scarce. Many police officials see the "racial profiling" crisis as hype. "Not to say that it doesn't happen, but it's clearly not as serious or widespread as the publicity suggests," says Chief Charles Ramsey of Washington. "I get so tired of hearing that 'Driving While Black' stuff. It's just used to the point where it has no meaning. I drive while black—I'm black. I sleep while black too. It's victimology. Black people commit traffic violations. What are we supposed to say? People get a free pass because they're black?"

The Matter of Whiteness

RICHARD DYER

1 RACIAL[1] IMAGERY is central to the organisation of the modern world. At what cost regions and countries export their goods, whose voices are listened to at international gatherings, who bombs and who is bombed, who gets what jobs, housing, access to health care and education, what cultural activities are subsidised and sold, in what terms they are validated—these are all largely inextricable from racial imagery. The myriad minute decisions that constitute the practices of the world are at every point informed by judgements about people's capacities and worth, judgements based on what they look like, where they come from, how they speak, even what they eat, that is, racial judgements. Race is not the only factor governing these things and people of goodwill everywhere struggle to overcome the prejudices and barriers of race, but it is never not a factor, never not in play. And since race in itself—insofar as it is anything in itself—refers to some intrinsically insignificant geographical/physical differences between people, it is the imagery of race that is in play.

There has been an enormous amount of analysis of racial imagery in the past decades, ranging from studies of images of, say, blacks or American Indians in the media to the deconstruction of the fetish of the racial Other in the texts of colonialism and post-colonialism. Yet until recently a notable absence from such work has been the study of images of white people. Indeed, to say that one is interested in race has come to mean that one is interested in any racial imagery other than that of white people. Yet race is not only attributable to people who are not white, nor is imagery of non-white people the only racial imagery.

[I write] about the racial imagery of white people—not the images of other races in white cultural production, but the latter's imagery of white people themselves. This is not done merely to fill a gap in the analytic literature, but because there is something at stake in looking at, or continuing to ignore, white racial imagery. As long as race is something only applied to non-white peoples, as long as white people are not racially seen and named, they/we function as a human norm. Other people are raced, we are just people.

There is no more powerful position than that of being "just" human. The claim to power is the claim to speak for the commonality of humanity. Raced people can't do that—they can only speak for their race.[2] But non-raced people can, for they do not represent the interests of a race. The point of seeing the racing of whites is to dislodge them/us from the position of power, with all the inequities, oppression, privileges and sufferings in its train, dislodging them/us by undercutting the authority with which they/we speak and act in and on the world.

5 The sense of whites as non-raced is most evident in the absence of reference to whiteness in the habitual speech and writing of white people in the West. We (whites) will speak of, say, the blackness or Chineseness of friends, neighbours,

colleagues, customers or clients, and it may be in the most genuinely friendly and accepting manner, but we don't mention the whiteness of the white people we know. An old-style white comedian will often start a joke: "There's this bloke walking down the street and he meets this black geezer," never thinking to race the bloke as well as the geezer. Synopses in listings of films on TV, where wordage is tight, none the less squander words with things like: "Comedy in which a cop and his black sidekick investigate a robbery," "Skinhead Johnny and his Asian lover Omar set up a laundrette," "Feature film from a promising Native American director" and so on. Since all white people in the West do this all the time, it would be invidious to quote actual examples, and so I shall confine myself to one from my own writing. In an article on lesbian and gay stereotypes,[3] I discuss the fact that there can be variations on a type such as the queen or dyke. In the illustrations which accompany this point, I compare a "fashion queen" from the film *Irene* with a "black queen" from *Car Wash*—the former, white image is not raced, whereas all the variation of the latter is reduced to his race. Moreover, this is the only non-white image referred to in the article, which does not however point out that all the other images discussed are white. In this, as in the other white examples in this paragraph, the fashion queen is, racially speaking, taken as being just human.

This assumption that white people are just people, which is not far off saying that whites are people whereas other colours are something else, is endemic to white culture. Some of the sharpest criticism of it has been aimed at those who would think themselves the least racist or white supremacist. bell hooks, for instance, has noted how amazed and angry white liberals become when attention is drawn to their whiteness, when they are seen by non-white people as white.

> Often their rage erupts because they believe that all ways of looking that highlight difference subvert the liberal belief in a universal subjectivity (we are all just people) that they think will make racism disappear. They have a deep emotional investment in the myth of "sameness," even as their actions reflect the primacy of whiteness as a sign informing who they are and how they think.[4]

Similarly, Hazel Carby discusses the use of black texts in white classrooms, under the sign of multiculturalism, in a way that winds up focusing "on the complexity of response in the (white) reader/student's construction of self in relation to a (black) perceived 'other.'" We should, she argues, recognise that "everyone in this social order has been constructed in our political imagination as a racialized subject" and thus that we should consider whiteness as well as blackness, in order "to make visible what is rendered invisible when viewed as the normative state of existence: the (white) point in space from which we tend to identify difference."[5]

The invisibility of whiteness as a racial position in white (which is to say dominant) discourse is of a piece with its ubiquity. When I said above that [I am not] merely seeking to fill a gap in the analysis of racial imagery, I reproduced the idea that there is no discussion of white people. In fact for most of the time white people speak about nothing but white people, it's just that we couch it in terms of "people" in general. Research—into books, museums, the press, advertising, films, television, software—repeatedly shows that in Western representation whites are overwhelmingly and disproportionately predominant, have the central and elaborated roles, and above all are placed as the norm, the ordinary, the standard.[6] Whites are everywhere in representation. Yet precisely because of this and their placing as norm they seem not to be represented to themselves *as* whites but as people who are variously gendered, classed, sexualised and abled. At the level of racial representation, in other words, whites are not of a certain race, they're just the human race.

We are often told that we are living now in a world of multiple identities, of hybridity, of decentredness and fragmentation. The old illusory unified identities of class, gender, race, sexuality are breaking up; someone may be black *and* gay *and* middle class *and* female; we may be bi-, poly- or non-sexual, of mixed race, indeterminate gender and heaven knows what class. Yet we have not yet reached a situation in which white people and white cultural agendas are no longer in the ascendant. The media, politics, education are still in the hands of white people, still speak for whites while claiming—and sometimes sincerely aiming—to speak for humanity. Against the flowering of a myriad postmodern voices, we must also see the countervailing tendency towards a homogenisation of world culture, in the continued dominance of US news dissemination, popular TV programmes and Hollywood movies. Postmodern multiculturalism may have genuinely opened up a space for the voices of the other, challenging the authority of the white West,[7] but it may also simultaneously function as a side-show for white people who look on with delight at all the differences that surround them.[8] We may be on our way to genuine hybridity, multiplicity without (white) hegemony, and it may be where we want to get to—but we aren't there yet, and we won't get there until we see whiteness, see its power, its particularity and limitedness, put it in its place and end its rule. This is why studying whiteness matters.

It is studying whiteness *qua* whiteness. Attention is sometimes paid to 10
"white ethnicity,"[9] but this always means an identity based on cultural origins such as British, Italian or Polish, or Catholic or Jewish, or Polish-American, Irish-American, Catholic-American and so on. These however are variations on white ethnicity (though . . . some are more securely white than others), and the examination of them tends to lead away from a consideration of whiteness itself. John Ibson, in a discussion of research on white US ethnicity, concludes that being, say, Polish, Catholic or Irish may not be as important to white Americans as some might wish.[10] But being white is.

NOTES

1. I use the terms race and racial . . . in the most common though problematic sense, referring to supposedly visibly differentiable, supportedly discrete social groupings.

2. In their discussion of the extraordinarily successful TV sitcom about a middle-class, African-American family, *The Cosby Show,* Sut Jhally and Justin Lewis note the way that viewers repeatedly recognise the characters' blackness but also that "you just think of them as people"; in other words that they don't only speak for their race. Jhally and Lewis argue that this is achieved by the way the family conforms to "the everyday, generic world of white television," an essentially middle-class world. The family is "ordinary" *despite* being black; because it is upwardly mobile, it can be accepted as "ordinary," in a way that marginalises most actual African-Americans. If the realities of African-American experience were included, then the characters would not be perceived as people." Sut Jhally and Justin Lewis, *Enlightened Racism The Cosby Show, Audiences and the Myth of the American Dream* (Boulder: Westview Press, 1992).

3. Richard Dyer, "Seen to Be Believed: Problems in the Representation of Gay People as Typical," in *The Matter of Images: Essays on Representation* (London: Routledge, 1993), pp. 19–51.

4. bell hooks, "Representations of Whiteness in the Black Imagination," in *Black Looks: Race and Representation* (Boston: South End Press, 1992), p. 167.

5. Hazel V. Carby, "The Multicultural Wars," in *Black Popular Culture,* ed. Gina Dent (Seattle: Bay Press, 1992), p. 193.

6. . . . The research findings are generally cast the other way round, in terms of non-white under-representation, textual marginalisation and positioning as deviant or a problem. Recent research in the US does suggest that African-Americans (but not other racially marginalised groups) have become more represented in the media, even in excess of their proportion of the population. However, this number still falls off if one focuses on central characters.

7. See, for example, Craig Owens, "The Discourse of Others: Feminists and Postmodernism," in *The Anti-Aesthetic: Essays on Postmodern Culture,* ed. Hal Foster (Port Townsend, Wash.: Bay Press, 1983), pp. 57–82.

8. *The Crying Game* (GB, 1992) seems to me to be an example of this. It explores with fascination and generosity, the hybrid and fluid nature of identity: gender, race, national belonging, sexuality. Yet all of this revolves around a bemused but ultimately unchallenged straight white man—it reinscribes the position of those at the intersection of heterosexuality, maleness and whiteness as that of the one group which does not need to be hybrid and fluid.

9. See, for example, Richard D. Alba, *Ethnic Identity: The Transformation of White America* (New Haven, Conn.: Yale University Press, 1990).

10. John Ibson, "Virgin Land or Virgin Mary? Studying the Ethnicity of White Americans," *American Quarterly* 33 (1981): 284–308.

Chapter 10
Arguing Claims about Values

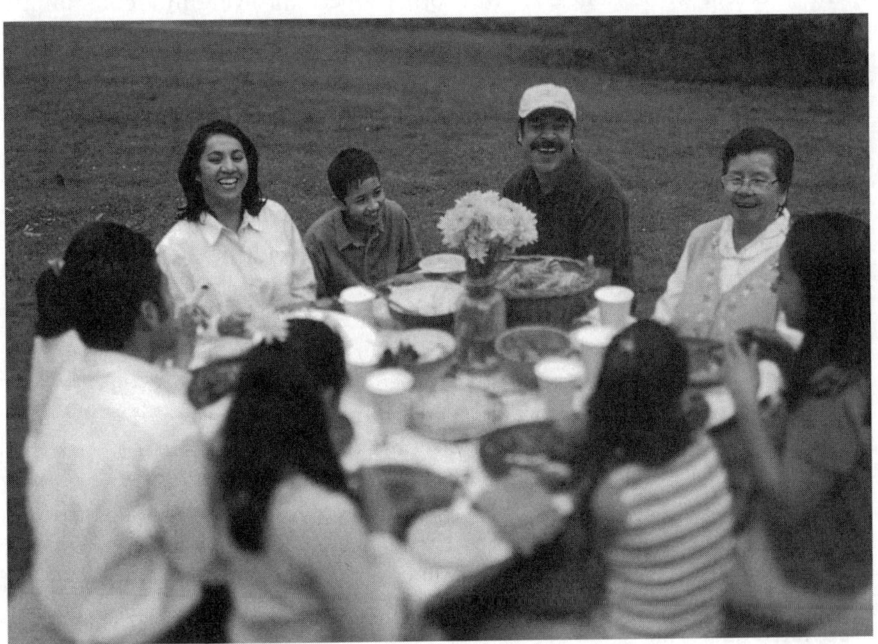

Our Disagreements about Values

Personal tastes are often informal and private. As the saying goes, "There is no accounting for taste." Some people like Chinese food; some don't. Some like one kind of music; some prefer another. It is difficult to argue about personal tastes. It is difficult to argue that someone else should like Chinese food just because you do or that Chinese food is somehow better than other kinds of food just because you think it is. One who disagrees can always respond, "You like what you like, and I'll like what I like."

To be meaningful, arguments about values must be based in the common values of a community, those things that we value collectively. It is one thing to say that you like or don't like Shakespeare. It is quite another to say that Shakespeare is the greatest English writer and then support that claim with community-based reasons. The first is a statement about personal taste; the second is a statement about community values. The fact that you personally like or don't like Shakespeare does nothing to change how the community values Shakespeare as a writer.

If you find yourself at odds with the values of the community, then you can seek to change them through arguing. Or if you encounter members of the community who disagree with the community's values, you can seek to persuade them to accept those values. As with other aspects of living in a community, there is a tension here between what individuals desire or value and what the community as a whole desires and values. Because individuals are so different from one another and individual desires are so various, disputes about values are frequent in communities. In fact, nearly all disputes in communities are in some way related to values, to what we desire.

Values are often expressed as abstract ideas or principles about what is "good" or "bad," "desirable" or "undesirable," "advantageous" or "disadvantageous," "moral" or "immoral," "good" or "evil," "righteous" or "wicked," "beautiful" or "ugly." These abstract terms carry the force of judgment. The philosopher Richard Weaver calls them "ultimate terms," terms that express the ultimate values of a society, around which other values are clustered. Something "good" is something we accept and desire. Something "bad" is something we reject. (See Chapter 3 for a more detailed discussion of ultimate terms.)

But these abstractions have little meaning outside the context of a particular community. In other words, the key to understanding the values of a community is understanding how that community defines "good" and "bad," "beautiful" and "ugly." What do members of the community accept and reject, and why? That is to say, what do they value?

Here are some abstract terms commonly used to describe things people in the United States value:

adventure
ambition
autonomy
collective responsibility
comfort
competition
cooperation
courage
creativity
equality of condition
equality of opportunity
excellence
flexibility
freedom of speech
generosity
harmony
honesty
justice
novelty
order
patriotism
peace
rationality
security
spontaneity
tolerance
tradition
wisdom

How do you define these terms? What examples would you give of each? For you, are these values good, bad, or mixed?

Think about the things you desire. Are there abstract terms to describe what you value? If you desire a college education, for example, ask yourself why. Will a college education bring you something else you desire: financial security, prestige, respect? Is education itself a value for you? If you desire a happy family life, then how would you describe that value? Consider the things you think your community values. How do your personal values compare with the community's values?

As you examine your personal values, you may notice some conflicts. For instance, you may value both adventure and security, even though the two don't always go together. You may value the freedom to do what you want but also the order that comes when everyone follows the same rules. You may value reliability and spontaneity, saving money and spending money, tradition and novelty, and so on. It is often the case in arguments about values that the dispute is not over accepting one value and rejecting another; rather the dispute is an attempt to find a balance among conflicting values.

Arguments about values take two basic forms. The first, the argument about what a community should value, takes the form "X is good (or bad)." "Good" or "bad" in such claims can be replaced by any of the "ultimate terms" used by a community: "right" or "wrong," "moral" or "immoral," "beautiful" or "ugly," and so on. Here are some sample claims:

Anyone who is involved in an abortion is evil.

Giving tax breaks to the wealthy is unfair.

Pornography is immoral.

Plagiarism is wrong.

The right to freedom of speech is inviolable.

It is unethical for politicians to mislead the public.

The second type of value argument is the argument about evaluating. In this argument the focus is not on what constitutes "goodness" or "badness" but rather on whether a particular object or event fits the criteria for determining what is "good" or "bad." This argument takes the form "X is a good (or bad) X," again with any of the ultimate terms possibly substituting for "good" or "bad." Comparative and superlative forms of the terms (*better, best, worse, worst*) can also be used to show the relation among the objects being evaluated. For instance, to say that an object is "best" in its class is to say that it is closest to the ideal of what is valuable or desirable for that class. To say that one object is "better than" another is to say that the better object is closer to the ideal than the other. Here are some sample claims:

William Faulkner is the greatest American writer.

Star Trek: The Next Generation is better than the original *Star Trek* series.

That car is worth more than $6,000.

This place serves the worst Mexican food I've ever had.

Arguing about What We Value

APPEAL TO AUTHORITY AND PRINCIPLES

How does a community negotiate the various personal tastes and preferences of its individual members in order to come up with a common set of values? One way is appeal to an acknowledged authority, such as an expert, judge, critic, or arbitrator. For instance, ethical questions related to the law are usually resolved by a judge, with the Supreme Court being the highest authority on legal questions in the United States. Aesthetic questions (questions about what is beautiful) may be decided by a critic, such as a movie or book reviewer or art critic. The authority may be a written statement of what the community believes and values: the Constitution, the Declaration of Independence, religious texts like the Bible or the Koran. Sometimes, the role of the expert is to interpret these foundational writings. The Supreme Court interprets the Constitution in deciding issues of legal "right" or "wrong." Religious leaders interpret sacred texts in deciding religious values. Art critics may examine what artists have written about their own work or what philosophers have said about what is valuable in art.

Once specific principles are laid down by authoritative members of the community or authoritative texts, the principles themselves may take on a certain authority. Principles are values that have been codified. The Ten Commandments are part of the legacy of Moses, an authoritative text for Jews and Christians, but many of the principles set forth in the Ten Commandments—"Thou shalt not kill," "Thou shalt not steal," and so forth—have taken on an authority of their own. The so-called Golden Rule—"Do unto others as you would have others do unto you"—is based on the teachings of Jesus in the New Testament, but it has also taken on an authority of its own in American culture. The Declaration of Independence, the Constitution, and the Bill of Rights provide good examples of authoritative texts for the community defined by the United States.

APPEAL TO CONSEQUENCES

Another way a community determines its values is by considering the consequences for the community of pursuing one or another value. What is in the best interest of the community as a whole? Most people value both airline safety and saving money, for example, but what are the consequences of pursuing one value over the other? How much would it cost to make flying absolutely riskfree? Probably so much that no one could afford to fly—if it could be done at all. But what about cutting costs at the expense of safety? If the risk of flying became so great that no one was willing to fly, then the lower costs wouldn't matter. Most people value the efforts of the government to eliminate crime, but what would be the consequences of trying to capture and prosecute every criminal? Is there a point at which the costs outweigh the benefits? To eliminate crime entirely might require turning the country into a police state and forgoing many of our civil rights. Many of our values have what economists call a "point of diminishing returns," a point after which the consequences of pursuing what we desire out-weigh any benefits we gain.

PRINCIPLES VERSUS CONSEQUENCES

Neither authority and principles nor consequences are without problems for determining values. For instance, when authorities or principles conflict with one another, how does a community decide among these conflicting opinions? One way is to appeal to a higher authority. Another is to consider consequences along with principles, to consider the effects of following one principle rather than another. However, if a community only considers consequences, always making decisions based on what is popular or expedient at the moment, then its decisions will be arbitrary, and there will be no justice or integrity. Usually, a community combines these two approaches, deferring to principles or authorities while also considering the consequences for the community.

Consider ethical issues, for example. Ethical issues involve claims about values: "X is right (or wrong)." Because individuals in a community do not all share the same values or the same beliefs about what constitutes ethical behavior, there are bound to be disputes. One way to resolve such disputes is by appealing to authority or principle. When Gandhi and Martin Luther King argued that there are higher laws which supersede the unjust laws passed by particular governments, they were basing their arguments on principle. When the philosopher Immanuel Kant argued that no one should use another as a means to an end and that one should always act as if every action could become universal law, he was outlining a set of principles to govern human behavior. It would be difficult, however, to follow Kant's principle without ever considering consequences or weighing costs against benefits. For instance, when someone serves you lunch or helps you at a store, you are using that person as a means to an end. On the other hand, that person is also using you, the customer, as a means to an end. The interaction is mutually beneficial: You get served, while the person helping you gets paid. At the same time, following Kant's principles can have beneficial effects. There are other times when using a person as a means to an end, such as extorting money from someone or becoming emotionally dependent on someone, has adverse consequences. Considering only consequences without being guided by principles at all would destroy the fabric of a community. Selfishness would guide every decision. Those who were most powerful would get their way.

Evaluation

As explained earlier, evaluation involves applying values to particular objects or events in order to judge their worth. In such arguments the values themselves may not be under dispute. The focus of the argument may rather be on the application of these values. The form of evaluation ("X is a good X") is similar to the form of the criteria-and-match definition outlined in the previous chapter. First, you develop the criteria for deciding what constitutes a "good X." Then you apply these criteria to a particular object or event to see how well it matches these criteria. The criteria are based on the values of the community, the "ultimate terms" used to characterize "good" and "bad" (and so on). Here are the steps to follow when conducting an evaluation.

First, determine the group to which the object belongs. You can't agree that "X is a good X" if it is not an "X" at all. For instance, you can't say that a horror movie is a bad romantic comedy. It's not a romantic comedy at all. Choose the group carefully. If you make it too large, then the grouping becomes meaningless. One problem with the awards for a year's "best movie," for example, is that movies are so different from one another that grouping them together as "movies" becomes almost meaningless for purposes of evaluation. Similarly, imagine trying to select the "best computer program." On the other hand, if the category is too small, then it can become a category of one, in which case evaluation becomes completely meaningless. Imagine giving an award for the "best full-length animated feature by a Disney studio for the year 1998."

Second, determine what the community values in the members of this group. What does the community value in a sports car or sport utility vehicle? One way to determine the values of a community is to find a model or standard system of measurement by which all others of the group can be judged. For instance, one can make claims about the relative values of two objects by comparing their cost. Money is a symbol Americans use to mark the value of things. If one object from a group costs more than another, you can examine the features of each object to determine what makes one more expensive. These features will give you a clue about what the community values. For instance, by examining

THE FIVE STEPS OF EVALUATING

1. Determine the group to which the object belongs.
2. Determine what the community values in the members of this group.
3. Determine criteria based on these values.
4. Weigh the criteria against each other.
5. Match the object against the criteria.

the features that make a home more valuable, you can determine what the community values in a home. By comparing two pieces of property, you can determine what the community values in land. Does the community value a coal mine more than a red rock desert? Which costs more?

Third, determine criteria based on these values. What does an object have to have to meet the values of the community? Which criteria are absolutely necessary and which are recommended or beneficial?

Fourth, weigh the criteria against one another. The word *critic* comes from a Greek word meaning "to weigh." A critic or evaluator must weigh the criteria against one another to decide which are essential or most important and which are optional or less important.

Evaluating Claims about Values

In their basic form, arguments about values are very similar to arguments about language. *Value* is typically a troublesome term that can be defined in different ways depending on one's perspective. A value is really a definition that carries with it the force of judgment—acceptance or rejection based on whether the value meets the criteria that the community considers important. Because a claim about value involves definitions, the first step in evaluating a values claim is to evaluate the quality of the definitions upon which the claim is based. Ask yourself the following question: "What is the effect of defining a value in this way?" For example, what would be the consequences of defining *honesty* more broadly or more narrowly? If honesty is something we as a community value, what happens when you make a definition more or less inclusive? You can ask the same questions of values that you ask of definitions generally:

1. Is the value term sufficiently inclusive?
2. Is the value term sufficiently exclusive?
3. Is the language clear?
4. Does the definition of the value emphasize detail, excluding unnecessary detail?
5. What would be the implications of this definition of the value if it were used in a different context?
6. Who gains and who loses by defining the value in this particular way?

The next step in evaluating a value claim is to consider the value in light of other values, to consider the importance of the value within your own or your community's hierarchy of values. What would you gain or lose by emphasizing this particular value? Does this value correspond to or violate principles that you hold absolute? If not, then how do you judge this value relative to other values? As the term *value* suggests, there isn't really one right answer to these questions

THE PROCESS OF EVALUATING VALUE CLAIMS

Step 1—Define the value.

Step 2—Decide how important the value is to you and to your community.

Step 3—Determine whether the claim really fits the definition.

that can be objectively verified or accepted by all. A value requires you to make a decision about what is really important to you and to your community.

If you accept the value implicit in the claim, then the final step is to determine whether the claim really does match the value. For example, if someone argues that a particular action violates the First Amendment to the Constitution, you first have to decide whether the First Amendment is important to you. If it isn't, then the argument doesn't matter. If it is important, then you need to determine whether the action really *does* violate the First Amendment.

Evaluating a claim about evaluation works the same way. Let's say that you are evaluating the claim that a particular car is the best in its class because of its low cost and high performance. First of all, you would need to clarify the terms, defining exactly what is meant by "low cost" and "high performance." Second, you need to decide whether the values implicit in this claim are important to you. Do you value low cost and high performance, or do you look for something else in a car? If you do value these attributes, then you need to complete the third step: determining whether the car really does match the criteria set forth in the definitions of "low cost" and "high performance."

The process of evaluating claims about values seems fairly simple, but it can be difficult because of the complex nature of defining values and deciding what is really important to us. But despite the difficulty in defining values, learning to evaluate claims about values is important because most arguments that really matter usually have some kind of implicit claim about values.

The Principles in Action: Readings

VALUE SYSTEMS

The following two essays consider where we derive our values. In the first, Robert L. Simon considers the problems he sees with values derived from "moral relativism," the idea that it isn't possible to take an absolute stand on questions of morality. As a professor of philosophy at Hamilton College, Simon takes a particular interest in the unwillingness of students to take a stand. In the second essay, Richard Rieke and Malcolm Sillars identify six basic value systems that help to clarify why Americans value what they do. As you read these essays, consider the following questions:

1. For each author, what is the source of our values? To what extent are values derived from principles or consequences (or some combination or these)? What role does authority play in determining values?
2. How would each author address the problem of competing values? How would each decide which values are more important than others?
3. What are the consequences of a relative approach to values? What are the consequences of an absolute approach? Is it possible to take a relative position in some situations and an absolute position in others?
4. How would you describe your value system? To what extent does your value system correspond to the six described by Rieke and Sillars? How would you modify or add to their models?
5. How well would these author's views work in deciding moral issues facing your community?

Get Students Past "Absolutophobia"

ROBERT L. SIMON

A STUDENT of mine made this comment: "Of course, I dislike the Nazis, but who is to say they are morally wrong?" Other students in my classes on moral and political philosophy have made similar remarks about apartheid, slavery, and ethnic cleansing. They say it as though it were self-evident; no one, they say, has the right even to criticize the moral views of another group or culture. 1

In an increasingly multicultural society, it is not surprising that many students believe that criticizing the codes of conduct of other groups and cultures is either unwise or prohibited. They equate such criticism with intolerance and the coercive imposition of a powerful culture's norms on the less powerful.

Does a decent respect for other cultures and practices really require us to refrain from condemning even the worst crimes in human history? Does it make moral judgment impossible?

I maintain that it does not. The growing moral paralysis of some of our best students arises because they have become entangled in abstract premises that, however fashionable they may be, are grounded in confusion and misunderstanding.

To begin with, note that students—and others—who feel that a respect for other cultures requires them not to criticize practices different from their own already are making moral judgments, even if they do not recognize their own 5 presuppositions. They believe, for example, that we ought to respect other cultures, that we ought to be tolerant of practices different from our own, and that we ought to welcome diversity rather than fear it. In fact, not only are they making moral judgments, they are making precisely the ones that should lead to condemnation of the Nazis.

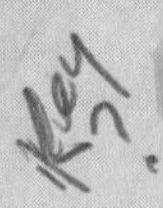

How, then, can we explain this unwillingness to condemn great evils? Although there probably is no simple explanation, several assumptions by students play a role.

The first is that making a moral judgment is, in effect, drawing a line in the sand. Those who make moral judgments are felt to be "absolutists," and, of course, we all know there are no absolutes. The idea seems to be that those who assert absolutes are dogmatic and intolerant, and that they advance simple, inflexible general principles that allow no exceptions.

Students, therefore, believe that making moral judgments means that they are closed to further discussion—that they would be taking an inflexible stand that they must maintain, come what may. Perhaps the inflexibility and closed-mindedness of much of what passes for political debate in our society reinforces this image.

But, although there may be some absolutists among us, and perhaps even some "absolutes," there is nothing about moral judgment that requires inflexibility, intolerance, fanaticism, unwillingness to argue and debate, or an inability to recognize that many issues exist on which reasonable people of good will may disagree. In fact, as I've noted, the claim that we ought to be tolerant and willing to consider the viewpoints and arguments of others is itself a moral judgment, one that many of our skeptical students make, however unwilling they may be to acknowledge it.

An antidote to this reluctance to make moral judgments is to replace "ab- 10
solutophobia" with an appreciation of the richness, diversity, and openness that make up moral discourse and moral judgment. Discussion of moral issues need not consist of two fanatics asserting conflicting principles they regard as self-evident; it can involve dialogue, the consideration of the points raised by others, and an admission of fallibility on all sides.

The second assumption that students should examine is that we are so inextricably embedded in our own individual perspectives—or those of our social or ethnic group, race, or gender—that the kind of impartiality or detachment from our own viewpoint that moral judgment requires is impossible. One of my students summed up this view on a recent exam paper, arguing that the social constructions of race, gender, and class make impartial assessment of a moral issue impossible.

What this student failed to consider is that if our race, gender, or class memberships really make impartial assessment of evidence impossible, how can we ever be confident that the evidence shows that race, gender, and class actually distort our thinking? Similarly, if we are all so biased, how can we claim that we ought to be tolerant, argue that we ought to respect diversity, or, indeed, defend any social or political goal at all?

Accordingly, although we certainly do need to be aware of biases that may taint our evaluations, asserting that such biases are so pervasive and inescapable that they make objectivity impossible undercuts the very possibility of having reasons for our opinions at all—including reasons for thinking that we are all biased.

Perhaps more important, the students who dismiss the possibility of moral inquiry ignore the role of critical dialogue in detecting and correcting personal or social prejudices. Surely one benefit of moral dialogue with others is that it can expose our own biases and open them to critical examination.

Crude forms of relativism, then, are open to strong logical objection. What, 15
then, makes these views, which are so vulnerable to reasoned criticism, so pervasive? What gives them so strong a hold on so many students?

Part of the answer probably lies in students' interpretations (or misinterpretations) of multiculturalism and postmodernism. As understood by the relativist student, these views suggest that any criticism of another culture's practices is a kind of cultural imperialism. Second, the postmodern rejection of many of the ideals of the Enlightenment is taken to imply that, because we all speak from some particular perspective, truly objective moral knowledge is impossible to attain.

Sophisticated multiculturalists surely do not want to assert that all views are equally justified, for on many issues they claim that multicultural approaches are more justified than traditional ones. Similarly, sophisticated postmodernists surely want to claim that their own critique of many ideals of the Enlightenment is itself well-founded. So if multicultural and postmodernist approaches are to avoid intellectual incoherence, they cannot support the crude relativism that we are hearing from our students.

A more cynical explanation for such relativism rests less on current intellectual trends that on old-fashioned intellectual laziness. Crude relativism is an easy and undemanding position to hold. Rather than think through a problem to a reasoned conclusion, students can throw up their hands and ask, "Well, who's to say, anyway?" This conveniently allows them to ignore the moral issues that arise on their own campuses, such as excessive consumption of alcohol or improper conduct in personal relationships.

What can faculty members do to combat such views, without appearing dogmatic or authoritarian? We can begin by pointing out the hidden contradictions in the relativism espoused by students. That is, students simply cannot have it both ways, claiming that justifiable moral judgments cannot be made and yet that colleges should encourage the values of tolerance and respect for diversity.

Second, faculty members can point out that students themselves not only 20
expect moral standards to be applied to them, but can offer explicit and coherent arguments for why they should be. Few students will be satisfied by "Who's to say one grade is more deserved than any other?" when that is a professor's explanation for giving them a failing grade on an important examination.

Third, we can demand that students not avoid difficult issues by asking "Who's to say?" but instead require them to state what constitutes a justifiable response to the issue at hand. The "Who's to say?" response should be clearly exposed for what it is—an excuse for refusing to engage in sustained inquiry.

Most important, we can require students to engage in the kinds of reasoning that can appropriately be applied to moral issues. Students can be asked if specific social practices can be defended for all those affected by them, and, if not, whether they can be regarded as fair to anyone. For example, can the support provided for men's and women's athletics on their own campuses be regarded as reasonable from the perspective of both male and female athletes?

Or we might ask students if their own views on different issues are totally consistent. Surely a student who believes both that the affluent have no moral obligations to the disadvantaged and that a 16-year-old girl who is pregnant as the result of rape has an obligation to carry her fetus to term needs to explain how these two views can be compatible.

Although different forms of ethical argument may or may not yield one final moral truth, it is unlikely that people who actually engage in moral reasoning and discussion will be able to conclude that all moral claims are equally reasonable, let alone that the views of the Nazis are as defensible as those of their opponents.

It is possible to reach relativist students, I believe, precisely because, deep 25
down, they are not true moral relativists or skeptics. Rather, they actually hold to a disguised morality that emphasizes tolerance and respect for diversity.

However, by denying themselves the moral authority to condemn such great evils of human history as the Holocaust, slavery, and racial oppression, these students lose the basis for morally condemning wrongdoing anywhere, and so must ultimately abandon the very values that led them to advocate tolerance and respect for diversity in the first place.

Isn't it our responsibility as teachers to show, by directly confronting the confusions underlying absolutophobia, that students need not be inflexible dogmatists to have a moral ground on which to stand? If we allow the legitimate desire to avoid moral fanaticism to drive us to the point where even condemnation of the Holocaust is seen as a kind of unwarranted intellectual arrogance, then the truly arrogant and the truly fanatical need not fear moral censure no matter what evil they choose to inflict on us all.

American Value Systems

RICHARD D. RIEKE and MALCOLM O. SILLARS

BY CAREFUL analysis individual values can be discovered in the arguments of ourselves and others. There is a difficulty, however, in attempting to define a whole system of values for a person or a group. And as difficult as that is, each of us, as a participant in argumentation, should have some concept of the broad systems that most frequently bring together certain values. For this purpose, it is useful for you to have an idea of some of the most commonly acknowledged value systems. 1

You must approach this study with a great deal of care, however, because even though the six basic value systems we are about to define provide a fair view of the standard American value systems, they do not provide convenient pigeonholes into which individuals can be placed. They represent broad social categories. Some individuals (even groups) will be found outside these systems. Many individuals and groups will cross over value systems, picking and choosing from several. Note how certain words appear as value terms in more than one value system. The purpose of this survey is to provide a beginning understanding of standard American values, not a complete catalog.[1]

THE PURITAN-PIONEER-PEASANT VALUE SYSTEM

This value system has been identified frequently as the *puritan morality* or the *Protestant ethic*. It also has been miscast frequently because of the excessive emphasis placed, by some of its adherents, on restrictions of personal acts such as smoking and consuming alcohol.[2] Consequently, over the years, this value system has come to stand for a narrow-minded attempt to interfere in other people's business, particularly if those people are having fun. However, large numbers of people who do not share such beliefs follow this value system.

We have taken the liberty of expanding beyond the strong and perhaps too obvious religious implications of the terms *puritan* and *Protestant*. This value system is what most Americans refer to when they speak of the "pioneer spirit," which was not necessarily religious. It also extends, we are convinced, to a strain of values brought to this country by Southern and Eastern European Catholics, Greek Orthodox, and Jews who could hardly be held responsible for John Calvin's theology or even the term *Protestant ethic*. Thus, we have the added word *peasant*, which may not be particularly accurate. Despite the great friction that existed between these foreign-speaking immigrants from other religions and their native Protestant counterparts, they had a great deal in common as do their ideological descendants today. On many occasions after describing the puritan morality we have heard a Jewish student say, "That's the way my father thinks," or had a student of Italian or Polish descent say, "My grandmother talks that way all the time."

The Puritan-Pioneer-Peasant value system is rooted in the idea that persons 5
have an obligation to themselves and those around them, and in some cases to their God, to work hard at whatever they do. In this system, people are limited in their abilities and must be prepared to fail. The great benefit is in the striving against an unknowable and frequently hostile universe. They have an obligation to others, must be selfless, and must not waste. Some believe this is the only way to gain happiness and success. Others see it as a means to salvation. In all cases it takes on a moral orientation. Obviously, one might work hard for a summer in order to buy a new car and not be labeled a "puritan." Frequently, in this value system, the instrumental values of selflessness, thrift, and hard work become terminal values where the work has value beyond the other benefits it can bring one. People who come from this value system often have difficulty with retirement, because their meaning in life, indeed their pleasure, came from work.

Likewise, because work, selflessness, and thrift are positive value terms in this value system, laziness, selfishness, and waste are negative value terms. One can see how some adherents to this value system object to smoking, drinking, dancing, or cardplaying. These activities are frivolous; they take one's mind off more serious matters and waste time.

Some of the words that are associated with the Puritan-Pioneer-Peasant value system are:

Positive: *activity, work, thrift, morality, dedication, selflessness, virtue, righteousness, duty, dependability, temperance, sobriety, savings, dignity*

Negative: *waste, immorality, dereliction, dissipation, infidelity, theft, vandalism, hunger, poverty, disgrace, vanity*

THE ENLIGHTENMENT VALUE SYSTEM

America became a nation in the period of the Enlightenment. It happened when a new intellectual era based on the scientific finding of men like Sir Isaac Newton and the philosophical systems of men like John Locke were dominant. The founders of our nation were particularly influenced by such men. The Declaration of Independence is the epitome of an Enlightenment document. In many ways America is an Enlightenment nation, and if Enlightenment is not the predominant value system, it is surely first among equals.

The Enlightenment position stems from the belief that we live in an ordered world in which all activity is governed by laws similar to the laws of physics. These "natural laws" may or may not come from God, depending on the particular orientation of the person examining them; but unlike many adherents to the Puritan value system just discussed, Enlightenment persons theorized that people could discover these laws by themselves. Thus, they may worship God for God's greatness, even acknowledge that God created the universe and natural laws, but they find out about the universe because they have the power of reason. The laws of nature are harmonious, and one can use reason to discover them all. They can also be used to provide for a better life.

Because humans are basically good and capable of finding answers, restraints 10
on them must be limited. Occasionally, people do foolish things and must be restrained by society. However, a person should never be restrained in matters of the mind. Reason must be free. Thus, government is an agreement among individuals to assist the society to protect rights. That government is a democracy. Certain rights are inalienable, and they may not be abridged; "among these are life, liberty and the pursuit of happiness." Arguments for academic freedom, against wiretaps, and for scientific inquiry come from this value system.

Some of the words that are associated with the Enlightenment value system are:

Positive: *freedom, science, nature, rationality, democracy, fact, liberty, individualism, knowledge, intelligence, reason, natural rights, natural laws, progress*

Negative: *ignorance, inattention, thoughtlessness, error, indecision, irrationality, dictatorship, fascism, bookburning, falsehood, regression*

THE PROGRESSIVE VALUE SYSTEM

Progress was a natural handmaiden of the Enlightenment. If these laws were available and if humans had the tool, reason, to discover them and use them to advantage, then progress would result. Things would continually get better. But although progress is probably a historical spin-off of the Enlightenment, it has become so important on its own that it deserves at times to be seen quite separate from the Enlightenment.

Richard Weaver, in 1953, found that "one would not go far wrong in naming progress" the "god term" of that age. It is, he said, the "expression about which all other expressions are ranked as subordinate . . . Its force imparts to the others their lesser degrees of force, and fixes the scale by which degrees of comparison are understood."[3]

Today, the unmediated use of the progressive value system is questioned, but progress is still a fundamental value in America. Most arguments against progress are usually arguments about the definition of progress. They are about what "true progress is."

Some of the key words of the Progressive value system are: 15

Positive: *practicality, efficiency, change, improvement, science, future, modern, progress, evolution*

Negative: *old-fashioned,*[4] *regressive, impossible, backward*

THE TRANSCENDENTAL VALUE SYSTEM

Another historical spin-off of the Enlightenment system was the development of the transcendental movement of the early nineteenth century. It took from the Enlightenment all its optimism about people, freedom, and democracy, but rejected the emphasis on reason. It argued idealistically that there was a faculty higher than reason; let us call it, as many transcendentalists did, intuition.

Thus, for the transcendentalist, there is a way of knowing that is better than reason, a way which *transcends* reason. Consequently, what might seem like the obvious solution to problems is not necessarily so. One must look, on important matters at least, to the intuition, to the feelings. Like the Enlightenment thinker, the transcendentalist believes in a unified universe governed by natural laws. Thus, all persons, by following their intuition, will discover these laws, and universal harmony will take place. And, of course, little or no government will be necessary. The original American transcendentalists of the early nineteenth century drew their inspiration from Platonism, German idealism, and Oriental mysticism. The idea was also fairly well limited to the intellectuals. By and large, transcendentalism has been the view of a rather small group of people throughout our history, but at times it has been very important. It has always been somewhat more influential among younger people. James Truslow Adams once wrote that everyone should read Ralph Waldo Emerson at sixteen because his writings were a marvel for the buoyantly optimistic person of that age but that his transcendental writings did not have the same luster at twenty-one.[5] In the late 1960s and early 1970s, Henry David Thoreau's *Walden* was the popular reading of campus rebels. The emphasis of anti-establishment youth on Oriental mysticism, like Zen, should not be ignored either. The rejection of contemporary society and mores symbolized by what others considered "outlandish dress" and "hippie behavior" with its emphasis on emotional response and "do your own thing" indicated the adoption of a transcendental value system. Communal living is reminiscent of the transcendental "Brook Farm" experiments that were attempted in the early nineteenth century and described by Nathaniel Hawthorne in his novel *The Blithedale Romance.*

In all of these movements the emphasis on humanitarian values, the centrality of love for others, and the preference for quiet contemplation over activity has been important. Transcendentalism, however, rejects the common idea of progress. Inner light and knowledge of one's self is more important than material well-being. There is also some tendency to reject physical well-being because it takes one away from intuitive truth.

It should be noted that not everyone who argues for change is a transcendentalist. The transcendental white campus agitators of the late 1960s discovered that, despite all their concern for replacing racism and war with love and peace, their black counterparts were highly pragmatic and rationalistic about objectives and means. Black agitators and demonstrators were never "doing their thing" in the intuitive way of many whites.

It should also be noted that while a full adherence to transcendentalism has been limited to small groups, particularly among intellectuals and youth, many of the ideas are not limited to such persons. One can surely find strains of what we have labeled, for convenience, transcendentalism in the mysticism of some very devout older Roman Catholics, for instance. And perhaps many Americans become transcendental on particular issues, about the value to be derived from hiking in the mountains, for example.

Here are some of the terms that are characteristic of the Transcendental value system: 20

Positive: *humanitarian, individualism, respect, intuition, truth, equality, sympathetic, affection, feeling, love, sensitivity, emotion, personal kindness, compassion, brotherhood, friendship, mysticism*

Negative: *science,*[6] *reason, mechanical, hate, war, anger, insensitive, coldness, unemotional*

THE PERSONAL SUCCESS VALUE SYSTEM

The least social of the major American value systems is the one that moves people toward personal achievement and success. It can be related as a part of the Enlightenment value system, but it is more than that because it involves a highly pragmatic concern for the material happiness of the individual. To call it selfish would be to load the terms against it, although there would be some who accept this value system who would say, "Yes, I'm selfish." "The Lord helps those who help themselves" has always been an acceptable adage by some of the most devout in our nation.

You might note that the Gallup poll . . . is very heavily weighted toward personal values. Even "good family life" rated as the top value can be seen as an item of personal success. This survey includes only a few social values like "helping needy people" and "helping better America," and even those are phrased in personal terms. That is, the respondents were asked "how important you feel each of these is to you." The personal orientation of the survey may represent a bias of the Gallup poll, but we suspect it reflects much of American society. We are personal success–oriented in an individual way which would not be found in some other cultures (e.g., in the Japanese culture).

Here are some of the terms that tend to be characteristic of the Personal Success value system:

Positive: *career, family, friends, recreation, economic security, identity, health, individualism, affection, respect, enjoyment, dignity, consideration, fair play, personal*

Negative: *dullness, routine, hunger, poverty, disgrace, coercion, disease*

THE COLLECTIVIST VALUE SYSTEM

Although there are few actual members of various socialist and communist groups in the United States, one cannot ignore the strong attachment among some people for collective action. This is, in part, a product of the influx of social theories from Europe in the nineteenth century. It is also a natural outgrowth of a perceived need to control the excesses of freedom in a mass society. Its legitimacy is not limited to current history, however. There has always been a value placed on cooperative action. The same people today who would condemn welfare payments to unwed mothers would undoubtedly praise their ancestors for barnraising and taking care of the widow in a frontier community. Much rhetoric about our "pioneer ancestors" has to do with their cooperative action. And anticollectivist presidents and evangelists talk about "the team." At the same time many fervent advocates of collective action in the society argue vehemently for their freedom and independence. Certainly the civil rights movement constituted a collective action for freedom. Remember the link in Martin Luther King, Jr.'s speech between "freedom" and "brotherhood"?

But whether the Collectivist value system is used to defend socialist propos- 25
als or promote "law and order" there is no doubt that collectivism is a strong value system in this nation. Like transcendentalism, however, it is probably a value system that, at least in this day, cannot work alone.

Here are some of the terms that tend to characterize the Collectivist value system:

Positive: *cooperation, joint action, unity, brotherhood, together, social good, order, humanitarian aid and comfort, equality*

Negative: *disorganization, selfishness, personal greed, inequality*

Clearly, these six do not constitute a complete catalog of all American value systems. Combinations and reorderings produce different systems. Two values deserve special attention because they are common in these systems and sometimes operate alone: *nature* and *patriotism.* Since the beginning of our nation the idea has prevailed that the natural is good and there for our use and preservation. Also, since John Winthrop first proclaimed that the New England Puritans would build "a city on the hill" for all the world to see and emulate, the idea has endured that America is a fundamentally great nation, perhaps God-chosen, to lead the world to a better life. This idea may be somewhat tarnished in some quarters today, but there is no doubt that it will revive as it has in the past. Linked to other value systems we have discussed, it will once more be a theme that will draw the adherence of others to arguments.

NOTES

1. The following material draws from a wide variety of sources. The following is an illustrative cross section of sources from a variety of disciplines: Virgil I. Baker and Ralph T. Eubanks, *Speech in Personal and Public Affairs* (New York: David McKay, 1965), pp. 95–102; Clyde Kluckhohn, "An Anthropologist Looks at the United States," in *Mirror for Man* (New York: McGraw-Hill, 1949), pp. 228–261; Stow Persons, *American Minds* (New York: Holt, Rinehart and Winston, 1958); Jurgen Ruesch, "Communication and American Values; A Psychological Approach," in *Communication: The Social Matrix of Psychiatry,* eds. Jurgen Ruesch and Gregory Bateson (New York: W. W. Norton, 1951), pp. 94–134; Edward D. Steele and W. Charles Redding, "The American Value System: Premises for Persuasion," *Western Speech,* 26 (Spring 1962), pp. 83–91; Richard Weaver, "Ultimate Terms in Contemporary Rhetoric," in *The Ethics of Rhetoric* (Chicago: Henry Regnery, 1953),

pp. 211–232; Robin M. Williams, Jr., *American Society,* 3rd ed. (New York: Alfred A. Knopf, 1970), pp. 438–504.

2. It is ironic that the original American Puritans did not have clear injunctions against such activity.

3. Weaver, p. 212.

4. Note that "old-fashioned" is frequently positive when we speak of morality and charm but not when we speak of our taste in music.

5. James Truslow Adams, "Emerson Re-read," in *The Transcendental Revolt,* ed. George F. Whicher (Boston: D.C. Heath, 1949), pp. 31–39.

6. It is interesting to note, however, that one of the major organizations in the United States with transcendental origins, the Christian Science Church, combines transcendentalism with science.

ETHICAL DECISIONS IN BUSINESS, LAW, AND MEDICINE

In the first two essays, Albert Z. Carr and Monroe H. Freedman address issues related to honesty and professional ethics in the practice of business and law. Carr asks whether it is acceptable to lie when conducting business as long as that lying is a form of bluffing. He argues that a different set of ethical values applies to business than, for example, to religion. Freedman focuses on the frequent dilemma faced by the criminal defense lawyer between betraying the confidence of the client/lawyer relationship and knowingly giving false information to the court. Freedman's views were so controversial when he first presented them to the American Bar Association that some of his colleagues tried to have him suspended or disbarred. In the third essay, Raymond S. Duff and A. G. M. Campbell address ethical issues faced by doctors and nurses in special care nurseries. In particular, they describe the circumstances under which medical professionals together with families would decide to withhold care from a severely ill infant.

As you read these three essays, consider the following questions:

1. What claim is each author making about values? What does each author value (either stated or implied)?
2. What reasons or assumptions does each author use to support these claims?
3. To what extent does each author rely on authorities and principles or consequences to support a claim?
4. How do the authors' values in each essay correspond with your personal values or the values of the different communities you belong to?
5. What argument would you use either to support or oppose the claims made in these essays?

Is Business Bluffing Ethical?

ALBERT Z. CARR

A RESPECTED businessman with whom I discussed the theme of this article 1
remarked with some heat, "You mean to say you're going to encourage men to bluff? Why, bluffing is nothing more than a form of lying! You're advising them to lie!"

I agreed that the basis of private morality is a respect for truth and that the closer a businessman comes to the truth, the more he deserves respect. At the same time, I suggested that most bluffing in business might be regarded simply as game strategy—much like bluffing in poker, which does not reflect on the morality of the bluffer.

I quoted Henry Taylor, the British statesman who pointed out that "falsehood ceases to be falsehood when it is understood on all sides that the truth is not expected to be spoken"—an exact description of bluffing in poker, diplomacy, and business. I cited the analogy of the criminal court, where the criminal is not expected to tell the truth when he pleads "not guilty." Everyone from the judge down takes it for granted that the job of the defendant's attorney is to get his client off, not to reveal the truth; and this is considered ethical practice. I mentioned Representative Omar Burleson, the Democrat from Texas, who was quoted as saying, in regard to the ethics of Congress, "Ethics is a barrel of worms"—a pungent summing up of the problem of deciding who is ethical in politics.

I reminded my friend that millions of businessmen feel constrained every day to say *yes* to their bosses when they secretly believe *no* and that this is generally accepted as permissible strategy when the alternative might be the loss of a job. The essential point, I said, is that the ethics of business are game ethics, different from the ethics of religion.

We can learn a good deal about the nature of business by comparing it with 5
poker. While both have a large element of chance, in the long run the winner is the man who plays with steady skill. In both games ultimate victory requires intimate knowledge of the rules, insight into the psychology of the other players, a bold front, a considerable amount of self-discipline, and the ability to respond swiftly and effectively to opportunities provided by chance.

No one expects poker to be played on the ethical principles preached in churches. In poker it is right and proper to bluff a friend out of the rewards of being dealt a good hand. A player feels no more than a slight twinge of sympathy, if that, when—with nothing better than a single ace in his hand—he strips a heavy loser, who holds a pair, of the rest of his chips. It was up to the other fellow to protect himself. In the words of an excellent poker player, former President Harry Truman, "If you can't stand the heat, stay out of the kitchen." If one shows mercy to a loser in poker, it is a personal gesture, divorced from the rules of the game.

Poker has its special ethics, and here I am not referring to rules against cheating. The man who keeps an ace up his sleeve or who marks the cards is more than unethical; he is a crook, and can be punished as such—kicked out of the game or, in the Old West, shot.

In contrast to the cheat, the unethical poker player is one who, while abiding by the letter of the rules, finds ways to put the other players at an unfair disadvantage. Perhaps he unnerves them with loud talk. Or he tries to get them drunk. Or he plays in cahoots with someone else at the table. Ethical poker players frown on such tactics.

Poker's own brand of ethics is different from the ethical ideals of civilized human relationships. The game calls for distrust of the other fellow. It ignores the claim of friendship. Cunning deception and concealment of one's strength and intentions, not kindness and openheartedness, are vital in poker. No one thinks any the worse of poker on that account. And no one should think any worse of the game of business because its standards of right and wrong differ from the prevailing traditions of morality in our society. That most businessmen are not indifferent to ethics in their private lives, everyone will agree. My point is that in their office lives they cease to be private citizens; they become game players who must be guided by a somewhat different set of ethical standards.

The point was forcefully made to me by a Midwestern executive who has 10
given a good deal of thought to the question: "So long as a businessman complies with the laws of the land and avoids telling malicious lies, he's ethical. If the law as written gives a man a wide-open chance to make a killing, he'd be a fool not to take advantage of it. If he doesn't, somebody else will. There's no obligation on him to stop and consider who is going to get hurt. If the law says he can do it, that's all the justification he needs. There's nothing unethical about that. It's just plain business sense."

The illusion that business can afford to be guided by ethics as conceived in private life is often fostered by speeches and articles containing such phrases as, "It pays to be ethical," or "Sound ethics is good business." Actually this is not an ethical position at all; it is a self-serving calculation in disguise. The speaker is really saying that in the long run a company can make more money if it does not antagonize competitors, suppliers, employees, and customers by squeezing them too hard. He is saying that oversharp policies reduce ultimate gains. That is true, but it has nothing to do with ethics. The underlying attitude is much like that in the familiar story of the shopkeeper who finds an extra $20 bill in the cash register, debates with himself the ethical problem—should he tell his partner?—and finally decides to share the money because the gesture will give him an edge over the s.o.b. the next time they quarrel.

I think it is fair to sum up the prevailing attitude of businessmen on ethics as follows:

We live in what is probably the most competitive of the world's civilized societies. Our customs encourage a high degree of aggression in the individual's striving for success. Business is our main area of competition, and it has been ritualized into a game of strategy. The basic rules of the game have been set by the government, which attempts to detect and punish business frauds. But as long as a company does not transgress the rules of the game set by law, it has the legal right to shape its strategy without reference to anything but its profits. If it takes a long-term view of its profits, it will preserve amicable relations, so far as possible, with those with whom it deals. A wise businessman will not seek advantage to the point where he generates dangerous hostility among employees, competitors, customers, government, or the public at large. But decisions in this area are, in the final test, decisions of strategy, not of ethics.

If a man plans to take a seat in the business game, he owes it to himself to master the principles by which the game is played, including its special ethical outlook. He can then hardly fail to recognize that an occasional bluff may well be justified in terms of the game's ethics and warranted in terms of economic necessity. Once he clears his mind on this point, he is in a good position to match his strategy against that of the other players. He can then determine objectively whether a bluff in a given situation has a good chance of succeeding and can decide when and how to bluff, without a feeling of ethical transgression.

To be a winner, a man must play to win. This does not mean that he must 15
be ruthless, cruel, harsh, or treacherous. On the contrary, the better his reputation for integrity, honesty, and decency, the better his chances of victory will be in the long run. But from time to time every businessman, like every poker player, is offered a choice between certain loss or bluffing within the legal rules of the games. If he is not resigned to losing, if he wants to rise in his company and industry, then in such a crisis he will bluff—and bluff hard.

Every now and then one meets a successful businessman who has conveniently forgotten the small or large deceptions that he practiced on his way to fortune. "God gave me my money," old John D. Rockefeller once piously told a Sunday school class. It would be a rare tycoon in our time who would risk the horse laugh with which such a remark would be greeted.

In the last third of the twentieth century even children are aware that if a man has become prosperous in business, he has sometimes departed from the strict truth in order to overcome obstacles or has practiced the more subtle deceptions of the half-truth or the misleading omission. Whatever the form of the bluff, it is an integral part of the game, and the executive who does not master its techniques is not likely to accumulate much money or power.

Professional Responsibility of the Criminal Defense Lawyer: The Three Hardest Questions

MONROE H. FREEDMAN

IN ALMOST any area of legal counseling and advocacy, the lawyer may be 1
faced with the dilemma of either betraying the confidential communications of his client or participating to some extent in the purposeful deception of the court. This problem is nowhere more acute than in the practice of criminal law, particularly in the representation of the indigent accused. The purpose of this article is to analyze and attempt to resolve three of the most difficult issues in this general area:

1. Is it proper to cross-examine for the purpose of discrediting the reliability or credibility of an adverse witness whom you know to be telling the truth?
2. Is it proper to put a witness on the stand when you know he will commit perjury?
3. Is it proper to give your client legal advice when you have reason to believe that the knowledge you give him will tempt him to commit perjury?

These questions present serious difficulties with respect to a lawyer's ethical responsibilities. Moreover, if one admits the possibility of an affirmative answer, it is difficult even to discuss them without appearing to some to be unethical.[1] It is not surprising, therefore, that reasonable, rational discussion of these has been uncommon and that the problems have for so long remained unresolved. In this regard it should be recognized that the Canons of Ethics, which were promulgated in 1908 "as a general guide," are both inadequate and self-contradictory.

I. THE ADVERSARY SYSTEM AND THE NECESSITY FOR CONFIDENTIALITY

At the outset, we should dispose of some common question-begging responses. The attorney is indeed an officer of the court, and he does participate in a search for truth. These two propositions, however, merely serve to state the problem in different words: As an officer of the court, participating in a search

[1] The substance of this paper was recently presented to a Criminal Trial Institute attended by forty-five members of the District of Columbia Bar. As a consequence, several judges (none of whom had either heard the lecture or read it) complained to the Committee on Admissions and Grievances of the District Court for the District of Columbia, urging the author's disbarment or suspension. Only after four months of proceedings, including a hearing, two meetings, and a *de novo* review by eleven federal district court judges, did the Committee announce its decision to "proceed no further in the matter." Professor Freedman has expanded and updated his analysis in his latest book, *Understanding Lawyers' Ethics* (Matthew Bender/Irwin, 1990).

for truth, what is the attorney's special responsibility, and how does that responsibility affect his resolution of the questions posed above?

The attorney functions in an adversary system based upon the presupposition that the most effective means of determining truth is to present to a judge and jury a clash between proponents of conflicting views. It is essential to the effective functioning of this system that each adversary have, in the words of Canon 15, "entire devotion to the interest of the client, warm zeal in the maintenance and defense of his rights and the exertion of his utmost learning and ability." It is also essential to maintain the fullest uninhibited communication between the client and his attorney, so that the attorney can most effectively counsel his client and advocate the latter's cause. This policy is safeguarded by the requirement that the lawyer must, in the words of Canon 37, "preserve his client's confidences." Canon 15 does, of course, qualify these obligations by stating that "the office of attorney does not permit, much less does it demand of him for any client, violations of law or any manner of fraud or chicane." In addition, Canon 22 requires candor toward the court.

The problem presented by these salutary generalities of the Canons in the 5
context of particular litigation is illustrated by the personal experience of Samuel Williston, which was related in his autobiography. Because of his examination of a client's correspondence file, Williston learned of a fact extremely damaging to his client's case. When the judge announced his decision, it was apparent that a critical factor in the favorable judgment for Williston's client was the judge's ignorance of this fact. Williston remained silent and did not thereafter inform the judge of what he knew. He was convinced . . . that it was his duty to remain silent.

In an opinion by the American Bar Association Committee on Professional Ethics and Grievances, an eminent panel headed by Henry Drinker held that a lawyer should remain silent when his client lies to the judge by saying that he has no prior record, despite the attorney's knowledge to the contrary. The majority of the panel distinguished the situation in which the attorney has learned of the client's prior record from a source other than the client himself. William B. Jones, a distinguished trial lawyer and now a judge in the United States District Court for the District of Columbia, wrote a separate opinion in which he asserted that in neither event should the lawyer expose his client's lie. If these two cases do not constitute "fraud or chicane" or lack of candor within the meaning of the Canons (and I agree with the authorities cited that they do not), it is clear that the meaning of the Canons is ambiguous.

The adversary system has further ramifications in a criminal case. The defendant is presumed to be innocent. The burden is on the prosecution to prove beyond a reasonable doubt that the defendant is guilty. The plea of not guilty does not necessarily mean "not guilty in fact," for the defendant may mean "not legally guilty." Even the accused who knows that he committed the crime is entitled to put the government to its proof. Indeed, the accused who knows that he is guilty has an absolute constitutional right to remain silent. The moralist might quite reasonably understand this to mean that, under these circumstances, the defendant and his lawyer are privileged to "lie" to the court in pleading not guilty. In my judgment, the moralist is right. However, our adversary system and related notions of the proper administration of criminal justice sanction the lie.

Some derive solace from the sophistry of calling the lie a "legal fiction," but this is hardly an adequate answer to the moralist. Moreover, this answer has no particular appeal for the practicing attorney, who knows that the plea of not guilty commits him to the most effective advocacy of which he is capable. Criminal defense lawyers do not win their cases by arguing reasonable doubt. Effective trial advocacy requires that the attorney's every word, action, and attitude be consistent with the conclusion that his client is innocent. As every trial lawyer knows, the jury is certain that the defense attorney knows whether his client is guilty. The jury is therefore alert to, and will be enormously affected by, any indication by the attorney that he believes the defendant to be guilty. Thus, the plea of not guilty commits the advocate to a trial, including a closing argument, in which he must argue that "not guilty" means "not guilty in fact."[2]

There is, of course, a simple way to evade the dilemma raised by the not guilty plea. Some attorneys rationalize the problem by insisting that a lawyer never knows for sure whether his client is guilty. The client who insists upon his guilt may in fact be protecting his wife, or may know that he pulled the trigger and the victim was killed, but not that his gun was loaded with blanks and that the fatal shot was fired from across the street. For anyone who finds this reasoning satisfactory, there is, of course, no need to think further about the issue.

It is also argued that a defense attorney can remain selectively ignorant. He 10
can insist in his first interview with his client that, if his client is guilty, he simply does not want to know. It is inconceivable, however, that an attorney could give adequate counsel under such circumstances. How is the client to know, for example, precisely which relevant circumstances his lawyer does not want to be told? The lawyer might ask whether his client has a prior record. The client, assuming that this is the kind of knowledge that might present ethical problems for his lawyer, might respond that he has no record. The lawyer would then put the defendant on the stand and, on cross-examination, be appalled to learn that his client has two prior convictions for offenses identical to that for which he is being tried.

Of course, an attorney can guard against this specific problem by telling his client that he must know about the client's past record. However, a lawyer can

[2] "The failure to argue the case before the jury, while ordinarily only a trial tactic not subject to review, manifestly enters the field of incompetency when the reason assigned is the attorney's conscience. It is as improper as though the attorney had told the jury that his client had uttered a falsehood in making the statement. The right to an attorney embraces effective representation throughout all stages of the trial, and where the representation is of such low caliber as to amount to no representation, the guarantee of due process has been violated," Johns v. Smyth, 176 E. Supp. 949, 953 E.D. Va. (1959); Schwartz, *Cases on Professional Responsibility and the Administration of Criminal Justice* 79 (1962).

never anticipate all of the innumerable and potentially critical factors that his client, once cautioned, may decide not to reveal. In one instance, for example, the defendant assumed that his lawyer would prefer to be ignorant of the fact that the client had been having sexual relations with the chief defense witness. The client was innocent of the robbery with which he was charged, but was found guilty by the jury—probably because he was guilty of fornication, a far less serious offense for which he had not even been charged.

The problem is compounded by the practice of plea bargaining. It is considered improper for a defendant to plead guilty to a lesser offense unless he is in fact guilty. Nevertheless, it is common knowledge that plea bargaining frequently results in improper guilty pleas by innocent people. For example, a defendant falsely accused of robbery may plead guilty to simple assault, rather than risk a robbery conviction and a substantial prison term. If an attorney is to be scrupulous in bargaining pleas, however, he must know in advance that his client is guilty, since the guilty plea is improper if the defendant is innocent. Of course, if the attempt to bargain for a lesser offense should fail, the lawyer would know the truth and thereafter be unable to rationalize that he was uncertain of his client's guilt.

If one recognizes that professional responsibility requires that an advocate have full knowledge of every pertinent fact, it follows that he must seek the truth from his client, not shun it.[3] This means that he will have to dig and pry and cajole, and, even then, he will not be successful unless he can convince the client that full and confidential disclosure to his lawyer will never result in prejudice to the client by any word or action of the lawyer. This is, perhaps, particularly true in the case of the indigent defendant, who meets his lawyer for the first time in the cell block or the rotunda. He did not choose the lawyer, nor does he know him. The lawyer has been sent by the judge and is part of the system that is attempting to punish the defendant. It is no easy task to persuade this client that he can talk freely without fear of prejudice. However, the inclination to mislead one's lawyer is not restricted to the indigent or even to the criminal defendant. Randolph Paul has observed a similar phenomenon among the wealthier class in a far more congenial atmosphere:

> The tax advisor will sometimes have to dynamite the facts of his case out of the unwilling witnesses on his own side—witnesses who are nervous, witnesses who are confused about their own interest, witnesses who try to be too smart for their own good, and witnesses who subconsciously do not want to understand what has happened despite the fact that they must if they are to testify coherently.

Paul goes on to explain that the truth can be obtained only by persuading the client that it would be a violation of a sacred obligation for the lawyer ever to reveal a client's confidence. Beyond any question, once a lawyer has persuaded

[3] "Counsel cannot properly perform their duties without knowing the truth." Opinion 23, Committee on Professional Ethics and Grievances of the American Bar Association (1930).

his client of the obligation of confidentiality, he must respect that obligation scrupulously.

II. THE SPECIFIC QUESTIONS

The first of the difficult problems posed above will now be considered: Is it proper to cross-examine for the purpose of discrediting the reliability or the credibility of a witness whom you know to be telling the truth? Assume the following situation. Your client has been falsely accused of a robbery committed at 16th and P Streets at 11:00 P.M. He tells you at first that at no time on the evening of the crime was he within six blocks of that location. However, you are able to persuade him that he must tell you the truth and that doing so will in no way prejudice him. He then reveals to you that he was at 15th and P Streets at 10:55 that evening, but that he was walking east, away from the scene of the crime, and that, by 11:00 P.M., he was six blocks away. At the trial, there are two prosecution witnesses. The first mistakenly, but with some degree of persuasion identifies your client as the criminal. At that point, the prosecution's case depends on this single witness, who might or might not be believed. Since your client has a prior record, you do not want to put him on the stand, but you feel that there is at least a chance for acquittal. The second prosecution witness is an elderly woman who is somewhat nervous and who wears glasses. She testifies truthfully and accurately that she saw your client at 15th and P Streets at 10:55 P.M. She has corroborated the erroneous testimony of the first witness and made conviction virtually certain. However, if you destroy her reliability through cross-examination designed to show that she is easily confused and has poor eyesight, you may not only eliminate the corroboration, but also cast doubt in the jury's mind on the prosecution's entire case. On the other hand, if you should refuse to cross-examine her because she is telling the truth, your client may well feel betrayed, since you knew of the witnesses' veracity only because your client confided in you, under your assurance that his truthfulness would not prejudice him.

15 The client would be right. Viewed strictly, the attorney's failure to cross-examine would not be violative of the client's confidence because it would not constitute a disclosure. However, the same policy that supports the obligation of confidentiality precludes the attorney from prejudicing his client's interest in any other way because of knowledge gained in his professional capacity. When a lawyer fails to cross-examine only because his client, placing confidence in the lawyer, has been candid with him, the basis of such confidence and candor collapses. Our legal system cannot tolerate such a result.

> The purposes and necessities of the relation between a client and his attorney require, in many cases, on the part of the client, the fullest and freest disclosures to the attorney of the client's objects, motives and acts . . . To permit the attorney to reveal to others what is so disclosed, would be not only a gross violation of a sacred trust upon his part, but it would utterly destroy and prevent the usefulness and benefits to be derived from professional assistance.

The client's confidences must "upon all occasions be inviolable," to avoid the "greater mischiefs" that would probably result if a client could not feel free "to repose [confidence] in the attorney to whom he resorts for legal advice and assistance." Destroy that confidence, and "a man would not venture to consult any skillful person, or would only dare to tell his counsellor half his case."

Therefore, one must conclude that the attorney is obligated to attack, if he can, the reliability or credibility of an opposing witness whom he knows to be truthful. The contrary result would inevitably impair the "perfect freedom of consultation by client with attorney," which is "essential to the administration of justice."

The second question is generally considered to be the hardest of all: Is it proper to put a witness on the stand when you know he will commit perjury? Assume, for example, that the witness in question is the accused himself, and that he has admitted to you, in response to your assurances of confidentiality, that he is guilty. However, he insists upon taking the stand to protect his innocence. There is a clear consensus among prosecutors and defense attorneys that the likelihood of conviction is increased enormously when the defendant does not take the stand. Consequently, the attorney who prevents his client from testifying only because the client has confided his guilt to him is violating that confidence by acting upon the information in a way that will seriously prejudice his client's interests.

Perhaps the most common method for avoiding the ethical problem just posed is for the lawyer to withdraw from the case, at least if there is sufficient time before trial for the client to retain another attorney.[4] The client will then go to the nearest law office, realizing that the obligation of confidentiality is not what it has been represented to be, and withhold incriminating information or the fact of his guilt from his new attorney. On ethical grounds, the practice of withdrawing from a case under such circumstances is indefensible, since the identical perjured testimony will ultimately be presented. More important, perhaps, is the practical consideration that the new attorney will be ignorant of the perjury and therefore will be in no position to attempt to discourage the client from presenting it. Only the original attorney, who knows the truth, has that opportunity, but he loses it in the very act of evading the ethical problem.

The problem is all the more difficult when the client is indigent. He cannot retain other counsel, and in many jurisdictions, including the District of Columbia, it is impossible for appointed counsel to withdraw from a case except for extraordinary reasons. Thus, appointed counsel, unless he lies to the judge, can successfully withdraw only by revealing to the judge that the attorney has received knowledge of his client's guilt. Such a revelation in itself would seem to be a sufficiently serious violation of the obligation of confidentiality to merit

[4] Unless the lawyer has told the client at the outset that he will withdraw if he learns that the client is guilty, "it is plain enough as a matter of good morals and professional ethics" that the lawyer should not withdraw on this ground.

severe condemnation. In fact, however, the situation is far worse, since it is entirely possible that the same judge who permits the attorney to withdraw will subsequently hear the case and sentence the defendant. When he does so, of course, he will have had personal knowledge of the defendant's guilt before the trial began.[5] Moreover, this will be knowledge of which the newly appointed counsel for the defendant will probably be ignorant.

The difficulty is further aggravated when the client informs the lawyer for the first time during trial that he intends to take the stand and commit perjury. The perjury in question may not necessarily be a protestation of innocence by a guilty man. Referring to the earlier hypothetical of the defendant wrongly accused of a robbery at 16th and P, the only perjury may be his denial of the truthful, but highly damaging, testimony of the corroborating witness who placed him one block away from the intersection five minutes prior to the crime. Of course, if he tells the truth and thus verifies the corroborating witness, the jury will be far more inclined to accept the inaccurate testimony of the principal witness, who specifically identified him as the criminal.[6]

If a lawyer has discovered his client's intent to perjure himself, one possible solution to this problem is for the lawyer to approach the bench, explain his ethical difficulty to the judge, and ask to be relieved, thereby causing a mistrial. This request is certain to be denied, if only because it would empower the defendant to cause a series of mistrials in the same fashion. At this point, some feel that the lawyer has avoided the ethical problem and can put the defendant on the stand. However, one objection to this solution, apart from the violation of confidentiality, is that the lawyer's ethical problem has not been solved, but has only been transferred to the judge. Moreover, the client in such a case might well have grounds for appeal on the basis of deprivation of due process and denial of the right to counsel, since he will have been tried before, and sentenced by, a judge who has been informed of the client's guilt by his own attorney.

A solution even less satisfactory than informing the judge of the defendant's guilt would be to let the client take the stand without the attorney's participation and to omit reference to the client's testimony in closing argument. The latter solution, of course, would be as damaging as to fail entirely to argue the case to the jury, and failing to argue the case is "as improper as though the

[5] The judge may infer that the situation is worse than it is in fact. In the case related in note 8, the attorney's actual difficulty was that he did not want to permit a plea of guilty by a client who was maintaining his innocence. However, as is commonly done, he told the judge only that he had to withdraw because of "an ethical problem." The judge reasonably inferred that the defendant had admitted his guilt and wanted to offer a perjured alibi.

[6] One lawyer, who considers it clearly unethical for the attorney to present the alibi in this hypothetical case, found no ethical difficulty himself in the following case. His client was prosecuted for robbery. The prosecution witness testified that the robbery had taken place at 10:15, and identified the defendant as the criminal. However, the defendant had a convincing alibi for 10:00 to 10:30. The attorney presented the alibi, and the client was acquitted. The alibi was truthful, but the attorney knew that the prosecution witness had been confused about the time, and that his client had in fact committed the crime at 10:45.

attorney had told the jury that his client had uttered a falsehood in making the statement."

Therefore, the obligation of confidentiality, in the context of our adversary system, apparently allows the attorney no alternative to putting a perjurious witness on the stand without explicit or implicit disclosure of the attorney's knowledge to either the judge or the jury. Canon 37 does not proscribe this conclusion; the canon recognizes only two exceptions to the obligation of confidentiality. The first relates to the lawyer who is accused by his client and may disclose the truth to defend himself. The other exemption relates to the "announced intention of a client to commit a crime." On the basis of the ethical and practical considerations discussed above, the Canon's exception to the obligation of confidentiality cannot logically be understood to include the crime of perjury committed during the specific case in which the lawyer is serving. Moreover, even when the intention is to commit a crime in the future, Canon 37 does not require disclosure, but only permits it. Furthermore, Canon 15, which does proscribe "violation of law" by the attorney for his client, does not apply to the lawyer who unwillingly puts a perjurious client on the stand after having made every effort to dissuade him from committing perjury. Such an act by the attorney cannot properly be found to be subornation—corrupt inducement—of perjury. Canon 29 requires counsel to inform the prosecuting authorities of perjury committed in a case in which he has been involved, but this can only refer to perjury by opposing witnesses. For an attorney to disclose his client's perjury "would involve a direct violation of Canon 37." Despite Canon 29, therefore, the attorney should not reveal his client's perjury "to the court or to the authorities."

Of course, before the client testifies perjuriously, the lawyer has a duty to attempt to dissuade him on grounds of both law and morality. In addition, the client should be impressed with the fact that his untruthful alibi is tactically dangerous. There is always a strong possibility that the prosecutor will expose the perjury on cross-examination. However, for the reasons already given, the final decision must necessarily be the client's. The lawyer's best course thereafter would be to avoid any further professional relationship with a client whom he knew to have perjured himself.

The third question is whether it is proper to give your client legal advice 25
when you have reason to believe that the knowledge you give him will tempt him to commit perjury. This may indeed be the most difficult problem of all, because giving such advice creates the appearance that the attorney is encouraging and condoning perjury.

If the lawyer is not certain what the facts are when he gives the advice, the problem is substantially minimized, if not eliminated. It is not the lawyer's function to prejudge his client as a perjurer. He cannot presume that the client will make unlawful use of his advice. Apart from this, there is a natural predisposition in most people to recollect facts, entirely honestly, in a way most favorable to their own interest. As Randolph Paul has observed, some witnesses are nervous, some are confused about their own interests, some try to be too smart for their own good, and some subconsciously do not want to understand what has happened to them. Before he begins to remember essential facts, the client is entitled to know what his own interests are.

The above argument does not apply merely to factual questions such as whether a particular event occurred at 10:15 or at 10:45.[7] One of the most critical problems in a criminal case, as in many others, is intention. A German writer, considering the question of intention as a test of legal consequences, suggests the following situations. A young man and a young woman decide to get married. Each has a thousand dollars. They decide to begin a business with these funds, and the young lady gives her money to the young man for this purpose. Was the intention to form a joint venture or a partnership? Did they intend that the young man be an agent or a trustee? Was the transaction a gift or a loan? If the couple should subsequently visit a tax attorney and discover that it is in their interest that the transaction be viewed as a gift, it is submitted that they could, with complete honesty, so remember it. On the other hand, should their engagement be broken and the young woman consult an attorney for the purpose of recovering her money, she could with equal honesty remember that her intention was to make a loan.

Assume that your client, on trial for his life in a first-degree murder case, has killed another man with a penknife but insists that the killing was in self-defense. You ask him, "Do you customarily carry the penknife in your pocket, do you carry it frequently or infrequently, or did you take it with you only on this occasion?" He replies, "Why do you ask me a question like that?" It is entirely appropriate to inform him that his carrying the knife only on this occasion, or infrequently, supports an inference of premeditation, while if he carried the knife constantly, or frequently, the inference of premeditation would be negated. Thus, your client's life may depend upon his recollection as to whether he carried the knife frequently or infrequently. Despite the possibility that the client or a third party might infer that the lawyer was prompting the client to lie, the lawyer must apprise the defendant of the significance of his answer. There is no conceivable ethical requirement that the lawyer trap his client into a hasty and ill-considered answer before telling him the significance of the question.

A similar problem is created if the client has given the lawyer incriminating information before being fully aware of its significance. For example, assume that a man consults a tax lawyer and says, "I am fifty years old. Nobody in my immediate family has lived past fifty. Therefore, I would like to put my affairs in order. Specifically, I understand that I can avoid substantial estate taxes by setting up a trust. Can I do it?" The lawyer informs the client that he can successfully avoid the estate taxes only if he lives at least three years after establishing the trust or, should he die within three years, if the trust is found not to have been created in contemplation of death. The client then might ask who decides whether

[7] Even this kind of "objective fact" is subject to honest error. See note 6.

the trust is in contemplation of death. After learning that the determination is made by the court, the client might inquire about the factors on which such a decision would be based.

At this point, the lawyer can do one of two things. He can refuse to answer the question, or he can inform the client that the court will consider the wording of the trust instrument and will hear evidence about any conversations which he may have or any letters he may write expressing motives other than avoidance of estate taxes. It is likely that virtually every tax attorney in the country would answer the client's question, and that no one would consider the answer unethical. However, the lawyer might well appear to have prompted his client to deceive the Internal Revenue Service and the courts, and this appearance would remain regardless of the lawyer's explicit disclaimer to the client of any intent so to prompt him. Nevertheless, it should not be unethical for the lawyer to give the advice.

In a criminal case, a lawyer may be representing a client who protests his innocence, and whom the lawyer believes to be innocent. Assume, for example, that the charge is assault with intent to kill, that the prosecution has erroneous but credible eyewitness testimony against the defendant, and that the defendant's truthful alibi witness is impeachable on the basis of several felony convictions. The prosecutor, perhaps having doubts about the case, offers to permit the defendant to plead guilty to simple assault. If the defendant should go to trial and be convicted, he might well be sent to jail for fifteen years, on a plea of simple assault, the maximum penalty would be one year, and sentence might well be suspended.

The common practice of conveying the prosecutor's offer to the defendant should not be considered unethical, even if the defense lawyer is convinced of his client's innocence. Yet the lawyer is clearly in the position of prompting his client to lie, since the defendant cannot make the plea without saying to the judge that he is pleading guilty because he is guilty. Furthermore, if the client does decide to plead guilty, it would be improper for the lawyer to inform the court that his client is innocent, thereby compelling the defendant to stand trial and take the substantial risk of fifteen years' imprisonment.[8]

[8] In a recent case, the defendant was accused of unauthorized use of an automobile, for which the maximum penalty is five years. He told his court-appointed attorney that he had borrowed the car from a man known to him only as "Junior," that he had not known the car was stolen, and that he had an alibi for the time of the theft. The defendant had three prior convictions for larceny, and the alibi was weak. The prosecutor offered to accept a guilty plea to two misdemeanors (taking property without right and petty larceny) carrying a combined maximum sentence of eighteen months. The defendant was willing to plead guilty to the lesser offenses, but the attorney felt that, because of his client's alibi, he could not permit him to do so. The lawyer therefore informed the judge that he had an ethical problem and asked to be relieved. The attorney who was appointed in his place permitted the client to plead guilty to the two lesser offenses, and the defendant was sentenced to nine months. The alternative would have been five or six months in jail while the defendant waited for his jury trial, and a very substantial risk of conviction and a much heavier sentence. Neither the client nor justice would have been well served by compelling the defendant to go to trial against his will under these circumstances.

Essentially no different from the problem discussed above, but apparently more difficult, is the so-called *Anatomy of a Murder* situation. The lawyer, who has received from his client an incriminating story of murder in the first degree, says, "If the facts are as you have stated them so far, you have no defense, and you will probably be electrocuted. On the other hand, if you acted in a blind rage, there is a possibility of saving your life. Think it over, and we will talk about it tomorrow." As in the tax case, and as in the case of the plea of guilty to a lesser offense, the lawyer has given his client a legal opinion that might induce the client to lie. This is information which the lawyer himself would have, without advice, were he in the client's position. It is submitted that the client is entitled to have this information about the law and to make his own decision as to whether to act upon it. To decide otherwise would not only penalize the less well-educated defendant, but would also prejudice the client because of his initial truthfulness in telling his story in confidence to the attorney.

III. CONCLUSION

The lawyer is an officer of the court, participating in a search for truth. Yet no lawyer would consider that he had acted unethically in pleading the statute of frauds or the statute of limitations as a bar to a just claim. Similarly, no lawyer would consider it unethical to prevent the introduction of evidence such as a murder weapon seized in violation of the fourth amendment or a truthful but involuntary confession, or to defend a guilty man on grounds of denial of a speedy trail. Such actions are permissible because there are policy considerations that at times justify frustrating the search for truth and the prosecution of a just claim. Similarly, there are policies that justify an affirmative answer to the three questions that have been posed in this article. These policies include the maintenance of an adversary system, the presumption of innocence, the prosecution's burden to prove guilt beyond a reasonable doubt, the right to counsel, and the obligation of confidentiality between lawyer and client.

Moral and Ethical Dilemmas in the Special-Care Nursery

RAYMOND S. DUFF and A. G. M. CAMPBELL

ABSTRACT. Of 299 consecutive deaths occurring in a special-care nursery, 43 (14 percent) were related to withholding treatment. In this group were 15 with multiple anomalies, eight with trisomy, eight with cardiopulmonary disease, seven with meningomyelocele, three with other central-nervous system disorders, and two with short-bowel syndrome. After careful consideration of each of these 43 infants, parents and physicians in a group decision concluded that prognosis for meaningful life was extremely poor or hopeless, and therefore rejected further treatment. The awesome finality of these decisions, combined with a potential for error in prognosis, made the choice agonizing for families and health professionals. Nevertheless, the issue has to be faced, for not to decide is an arbitrary and potentially devastating decision of default.

—N. ENGL. J. MED. 289: 890–894, 1973

DISCUSSION. That decisions are made not to treat severely defective infants 1
may be no surprise to those familiar with special-care facilities. All laymen and professionals familiar with our nursery appeared to set some limits upon their application of treatment to extend life or to investigate a pathologic process. For example, an experienced nurse said about one child, "We lost him several weeks ago. Isn't it time to quit?" In another case, a house officer said to a physician investigating an aspect of a child's disease, "For this child, don't you think it's time to turn off your curiosity so you can turn on your kindness?" Like many others, these children eventually acquired the "right to die."

Arguments among staff members and families for and against such decisions were based on varied notions of the rights and interests of defective infants, their families, professionals, and society. They were also related to varying ideas about prognosis. Regarding the infants, some contended that individuals should have a right to die in some circumstances such as anencephaly, hydranencephaly, and some severely deforming and incapacitating conditions. Such very defective individuals were considered to have little or no hope of achieving meaningful "humanhood."[1] For example, they have little or no capacity to love or be loved. They are often cared for in facilities that have been characterized as "hardly more than dying bins,"[2] an assessment with which, in our experience, knowledgeable parents (those who visited chronic-care facilities for placement of their children)

[1] J. Fletcher, Indicators of humanhood: A tentative profile of man, *The Hastings Center Report,* 2, no. 5 (Hastings-on-Hudson, N.Y., Institute of Society, Ethics and the Life Sciences, November 1972), pp. 1–4.

[2] H. E. Freeman, O. G. Brim, Jr., G. Williams, *New dimensions of dying. The dying patient,* edited by O. G. Brim, Jr. (New York: Russell Sage Foundation, 1970), pp. xii–xxvi.

agreed. With institutionalized well children, social participation may be essentially nonexistent, and maternal deprivation severe; this is known to have an adverse, usually disastrous, effect upon the child.[3] The situation for the defective child is probably worse, for he is restricted socially both by his need for care and by his defects. To escape "wrongful life,"[4] a fate rated as worse than death, seemed right. In this regard, Lasagna[5] notes, "We may, as a society, scorn the civilizations that slaughtered their infants, but our present treatment of the retarded is in some ways more cruel."

Others considered allowing a child to die wrong for several reasons. The person most involved, the infant, had no voice in the decision. Prognosis was not always exact, and a few children with extensive care might live for months, and occasionally years. Some might survive and function satisfactorily. To a few persons, withholding treatment and accepting death was condemned as criminal.

Families had strong but mixed feelings about management decisions. Living with the handicapped is clearly a family affair, and families of deformed infants thought there were limits to what they could bear or should be expected to bear. Most of them wanted maximal efforts to sustain life and to rehabilitate the handicapped; in such cases, they were supported fully. However, some families, especially those having children with severe defects, feared that they and their other children would become socially enslaved, economically deprived, and permanently stigmatized, all perhaps for a lost cause. Such a state of "chronic sorrow" until death has been described by Olshansky.[6] In some cases, families considered the death of the child right both for the child and for the family. They asked if that choice could be theirs or their doctor's.

As Feifel has reported,[7] physicians on the whole are reluctant to deal with 5
the issues. Some, particularly specialists based in the medical center, gave specific reasons for this disinclination. There was a feeling that to "give up" was disloyal to the cause of the profession. Since major research, teaching and patient-care efforts were being made, professionals were expected to discover, transmit and apply knowledge and skills; patients and families were supposed to co-operate fully even if they were not always grateful. Some physicians recognized that the wishes of families went against their own, but they were resolute. They commonly agreed that if they were the parents of very defective children, withholding treatment would be most desirable for them. However, they argued that aggressive management was indicated for others. Some believed that allowing death as a management option was euthanasia and must be stopped for fear of

[3] R. A. Spitz, Hospitalism: An inquiry into the genesis of psychiatric conditions in early childhood, *Psychoanal. Study Child, I:* 53–74, 1945.

[4] H. T. Engelhardt, Euthanasia and children: The injury of continued existence. *J. Pediatr., 83:* 170–171, 1973.

[5] L. Lasagna, *Life, death, and the doctor* (New York: Alfred A. Knopf, 1968).

[6] S. Olshansky, Chronic sorrow: A response to having a mentally defective child, *Soc. Casework, 43:* 190–193, 1962.

[7] H. Feifel, Perception of death, *Ann. N. Y. Acad. Sci. 164:* 669–677, 1969.

setting a "poor ethical example" or for fear of personal prosecution or damage to their clinical departments or to the medical center as a whole. Alexander's report on Nazi Germany[8] was cited in some cases as providing justification for pressing the effort to combat disease. Some persons were concerned about the loss through death of "teaching material." They feared the training of professionals for the care of defective children in the future and the advancing of the state of the art would be compromised. Some parents who became aware of this concern thought their children should not become experimental subjects. . . .

Is it possible that some physicians and some families may join in a conspiracy to deny the right of a defective child to live or to die? Either could occur. Prolongation of the dying process by resident physicians having a vested interest in their careers has been described by Sudnow.[9] On the other hand, from the fatigue of working long and hard some physicians may give up too soon, assuming that their cause is lost. Families, similarly, may have mixed motives. They may demand death to obtain relief from the high costs and the tensions inherent in suffering, but their sense of guilt in this thought may produce the opposite demand, perhaps in violation of the sick person's rights. Thus, the challenge of deciding what course to take can be most tormenting for the family and the physician. Unquestionably, not facing the issue would appear to be the easier course, at least temporarily; no doubt many patients, families, and physicians decline to join in an effort to solve the problems. They can readily assume that what is being done is right and sufficient and ask no questions. But pretending there is no decision to be made is an arbitrary and potentially devastating decision of default. Since families and patients must live with the problems one way or another in any case, the physician's failure to face the issues may constitute a victimizing abandonment of patients and their families in times of greatest need. As Lasagna[10] pointed out, "There is no place for the physician to hide."

Can families in the shock resulting from the birth of a defective child understand what faces them? Can they give truly "informed consent" for treatment or withholding treatment? Some of our colleagues answer no to both questions. In our opinion, if families regardless of background are heard sympathetically and at length and are given information and answers to their questions in words they understand, the problems of their children as well as the expected benefits and limits of any proposed care can be understood clearly in practically all instances. Parents *are* able to understand the implications of such things as chronic dyspnea, oxygen dependency, incontinence, paralysis, contractures, sexual handicaps and mental retardation.

Another problem concerns who decides for a child. It may be acceptable for a person to reject treatment and bring about his own death. But it is quite a dif-

[8] L. Alexander, Medical science under dictatorship. *N. Engl. J. Med. 241:* 39–47, 1949.
[9] D. Sudnow, *Passing on* (Englewood Cliffs, N.J.: Prentice-Hall, 1967).
[10] Lasagna, *Life, death, and the doctor.*

ferent situation when others are doing this for him. We do not know how often families and their physicians will make just decisions for severely handicapped children. Clearly, this issue is central in evaluation of the process of decision making that we have described. But we also ask, if these parties cannot make such decisions justly, who can?

We recognize great variability and often much uncertainty in prognoses and in family capacities to deal with defective newborn infants. We also acknowledge that there are limits of support that society can or will give to assist handicapped persons and their families. Severely deforming conditions that are associated with little or no hope of a functional existence pose painful dilemmas for the laymen and professionals who must decide how to cope with severe handicaps. We believe the burdens of decision making must be borne by families and their professional advisers because they are most familiar with the respective situations. Since families primarily must live with and are most affected by the decisions, it therefore appears that society and the health professions should provide only general guidelines for decision making. Moreover, since variations between situations are so great, and the situations themselves so complex, it follows that much latitude in decision making should be expected and tolerated. Otherwise, the rules of society or the policies most convenient for medical technologists may become cruel masters of human beings instead of their servants. Regarding any "allocation of death"[11] policy we readily acknowledge that the extreme excesses of Hegelian "rational utility" under dictatorships must be avoided. Perhaps it is less recognized that the uncontrolled application of medical technology may be detrimental to individuals and families. In this regard, our views are similar to those of Waitzkin and Stoekle.[12] Physicians may hold excessive power over decision making by limiting or controlling the information made available to patients or families. It seems appropriate that the profession be held accountable for presenting fully all management options and their expected consequences. Also, the public should be aware that professionals often face conflicts of interest that may result in decisions against individual preferences. 10

What are the legal implications of actions like those described in this paper? Some persons may argue that the law has been broken, and others would contend otherwise. Perhaps more than anything else, the public and professional silence on a major social taboo and some common practices has been broken further. That seems appropriate, for out of the ensuing dialogue perhaps better choices for patients and families can be made. If working out these dilemmas in ways such as those we suggest is in violation of the law, we believe the law should be changed.

[11] B. Manning, *Legal and policy issues in the allocation of death. The dying patient,* edited by O. G. Brim, Jr. (New York: Russell Sage Foundation, 1970), pp. 253–274.

[12] H. Waitzkin and J. D. Stoeckle. The communication of information about illness, *Adv. Psychosom. Med., 8:* 180–215, 1972.

EVALUATING THE QUALITY OF CONSUMER GOODS

The magazine *Consumer Reports* is published by the Consumer's Union, a nonprofit, nonpartisan organization dedicated to educating consumers, testing products and services, and reporting its findings about a whole host of products. Many readers refer to *Consumer Reports* before buying a car, a stereo, a camera, or some other major purchase. The articles in *Consumer Reports* provide excellent examples of evaluation. Each article describes the product being evaluated, makes recommendations, and rates each brand according to a set of common criteria. The following selections from *Consumer Reports* evaluate common products: bottled water, chocolate, ice cream, and toilet paper. Each essay includes a chart that provides a detailed evaluation of different brands of each product according to common criteria. The authors try to develop standard measures for each criterion, and they include brief descriptions of features or qualities that may interest consumers but that are not covered by the standard criteria. There is also an assessment of overall quality. For example, in addition to rating the overall quality of each brand of toilet paper, the authors also evaluate each brand according to the following criteria: sheets per roll, cost per 100 sheets, strength, disintegration, softness, and absorption.

As you read each essay, consider the following questions:

1. What group do the objects being compared to all belong to? Do these different items really have enough in common to be considered in one category?
2. What do members of your community value in each of the products being compared? What do you personally value in each product?
3. To what extent do the criteria used by *Consumer Reports* match what most people would value in the product? How inclusive are the criteria? How well do these criteria provide a standard measure for comparison? Would you add or delete any criteria?
4. Which criteria are more important than others? Which are necessary and which are optional? How would you determine the overall quality of a product?
5. How does *Consumer Reports* determine whether the objects being evaluated match the criteria? How accurate are these measurements? (You may want to do some firsthand consumer research of your own to answer this question.)

It's Only Water, Right?

CONSUMER REPORTS

EVERY MINUTE of every day, Americans shell out more than $10,000 for 1
something many don't even have to buy: water. The figures are no Y2K blip, either. Sales of bottled water have been rising steadily for years. In 1976, Americans drank 1.5 gallons of bottled water per person; in 1999, they drank 15.5 gallons.

You might think that all bottled waters taste pretty much alike and that none could harbor the kind of contaminants occasionally found in tap water. They don't, and they can. In fact, a four-year study of 103 bottled waters released last year by the Natural Resources Defense Council, an environmental group, revealed concerns. Among them: Several waters had levels of chlorine by-products or arsenic that were above the threshold set by California, though within limits set by the U.S. Food and Drug Administration (FDA).

For our report, we bought multiple samples of 39 bottled waters—still (noncarbonated), carbonated, and mineral. We focused mainly on taste but also had a lab analyze the waters for harmful substances that can occur naturally or stem from treatment procedures or bottling. In a nutshell, we found:

- The major differences in taste were due to the type of plastic in the water's bottle. In most cases, waters in clear PET plastic (usually bottles of 1.5 liters or smaller) tasted better than those in cloudy, softer HDPE plastic (usually 1-gallon bottles).
- None of the waters we tested harbored contaminants above current standards. That said, some occasionally had a bit more than we'd like to see of one or more substances that shouldn't be prevalent in drinking water.
- Although the top-rated water costs 29 cents per 8-fluid-ounce glass, some waters that cost half as much tasted very good. . . .

THE TERMS, THE SOURCES

Technically, there are more choices in bottled water than just with fizz or 5
without:

Spring water comes from an underground formation and must flow naturally to the earth's surface. Water is collected at the spring or through a hole that taps the source, and the source must be stated on the label. Spring water is typically protected from microorganisms sometimes found in surface water. Carbon dioxide can be added to make it "sparkling."

Purified drinking water has been processed by reverse osmosis, distillation, or similar procedures that remove minerals and contaminants. The source need not be named and is often tap water.

Naturally sparkling water is naturally carbonated and often comes from a spring. Bubbles lost during treatment or collection may be replaced with the same amount of carbon dioxide the water held originally.

Soda water and seltzer are not considered bottled water. The FDA regulates them as soft drinks, under rules less strict than those for bottled water, and some products may have added sugar, flavors, or salts. They're often carbonated municipal water, sometimes with extra filtration.

Mineral water contains at least 250 parts per million of dissolved solids— 10
usually calcium, magnesium, sodium, potassium, silica, and bicarbonates. Minerals must occur naturally. Mineral water is typically spring water and can be sparkling or still.

Despite formal definitions, labels can be confusing. *Aquafina Purified Drinking Water,* one of America's top-selling bottled waters, sounds like an Italian import, and its label favors the deep blues and snow-capped mountains many brands use to telegraph the idea of faraway glacial springs. In fact, *Aquafina* is produced by the Pepsi Cola Company. Its name? From "the marketing folks," says Pepsi spokesman Larry Jabbonsky. The water originates from 16 sources—mainly municipal water supplies. Sources include venues no more exotic than Cheraw, S.C.; Detroit; Fresno, Calif.; and Munster, Ind. *Aquafina* is "not in the high end of water," Jabbonsky concedes.

Pepsi is now being challenged by—who else?—Coca-Cola. Coke's water, *Dasani,* is purified from municipal sources, "enhanced with a mix of minerals for a crisp taste," a Coke spokesman told us. (*Aquafina* and *Dasani* fell in the middle of our Ratings.)

Something else the label may not reveal is that a single brand of spring water can come from many sources. *Dannon Natural Spring Water,* another recent entry into the national market, taps four springs, in Florida, Pennsylvania, Utah, and Quebec. Different sources can mean different tastes.

THE TASTE OF TASTELESS

Good drinking water should taste like nothing. However, nothing can still taste a little like *something,* and water should taste clean, fresh, lively, and a little crisp.

Waters bottled in PET plastic generally tasted better than those bottled in 15
HDPE. That was true even within the same brand. *Arrowhead Mountain Spring Water,* for example, was very good when bottled in PET, which imparted a hint of sweet, fruity plastic flavor (imagine the scent when you blow up a beachball). But *Arrowhead* was only fair when bottled in HDPE, which made it taste a bit like melted plastic (imagine the smell when you get a plastic container too close to a flame). For waters that come in both kinds of bottle, the Ratings list two scores (and two prices—water is apt to cost more in PET). The only water bottled in PVC plastic, Winn-Dixie's *Prestige Premium 100% Spring Water,* rated good overall.

Why did different plastics impart different tastes? There's no one answer. Some plastics more easily allow nearby odors and tastes into water. Small amounts of chemicals in the plastic itself could leach into the water. Even the process used in making the plastic could affect taste. . . .

Still Waters

Only *Volvic Natural Spring Water* was excellent. A French import, *Volvic* comes from an area rich in volcanic rock, a company spokesman said. Several other waters were very good and cost much less.

Carbonated Waters

All are bottled in PET, and differences among the seven brands we tasted were subtle. The best—*Vintage Old Original Seltzer Water* and *Canada Dry Original Seltzer*—were very good. Both were less bitter than others.

Mineral Waters

Each of the five we tried has a different taste. Which you choose will depend on whether you like mineral water more or less fizzy or mineral-y. For that reason, we didn't rate these waters.

TROUBLED WATER? 20

The nation's thirst for bottled water, we suspect, has grown at least in part because its confidence in tap water has been shaken. Concerns were fueled in 1993, when cryptosporidium, a parasite from animal waste, entered Milwaukee's water supply. It killed more than 50 people, sent 4,400 to hospitals, and sickened hundreds of thousands.

The U.S. Environmental Protection Agency (EPA) has standards for some 80 contaminants in public drinking water and maintains that the U.S. enjoys some of the safest water in the world. You can check for yourself: Since 1999, Federal law has required local water utilities to send "consumer confidence reports" to their customers each year. The reports detail ongoing laboratory testing, name system trouble spots, and outline measures being taken to fix problems. If you haven't received one, contact your local water department, call the Safe Drinking Water Hotline at 800 426-4791, or visit *www.epa.gov/safewater/dwinfo.htm.*

The bottled-water industry falls under the jurisdiction of the FDA, which has borrowed from the EPA's standards for tap water. The International Bottled Water Association, the industry's trade group, has its own model code, with some standards stricter than the FDA's. Member companies, which produce 85 percent of the bottled water sold in the U.S., must also allow annual surprise inspections at processing plants by an independent nonprofit group.

Bottlers often imply their product is purer than tap water. Some play up "protected sources," often underground springs whose output the company tests regularly. Others say their waters have undergone ozonation (it disinfects but leaves no chlorine aftertaste) or "one-micron absolute" filtration (water is strained through pores small enough to catch cryptosporidium).

We tested all the bottled waters for trihalomethanes (THMs), a potentially harmful by-product of the chlorine treatment to which tap water is subjected. We confined tests for other contaminants to waters in which they would most likely be found. Without comprehensive nationwide tests, no one can say how much cleaner bottled water might be than tap water. We do know that none of the waters in our analyses—bottled or tap—harbored contaminants at levels above current standards. However, several samples of bottled water were above the EPA's *proposed* standard for arsenic, a couple of samples had a fairly high level of bacteria that can indicate spotty sanitation, and eight of ten polycarbonate jugs leached a potentially problematic plastic component into water.

RECOMMENDATIONS

It's important to drink enough water—eight glasses per day; more in hot 25
weather or if you're especially active. Drinking too little water can cause fatigue, weakness, dizziness, and headaches. Over the long term, drinking too little water has been linked to constipation, kidney stones, and even some cancers. Yet despite the rise in consumption of bottled water, one American in ten doesn't typically drink water at all, according to a recent survey for the bottled-water industry and Rockefeller University.

Where should that water come from? You can take it from the tap, of course, and incidents of contamination by harmful chemicals or parasites in public drinking water are very rare. Taste is another matter. Some of the tap waters we sampled tasted almost swampy. (Bad taste doesn't necessarily mean water is unhealthful, however.)

Some carafe filters and faucet-mounted filters improve tap water's taste—for far less money than a bottle or two of water per day. . . .

If you prefer bottled water, you have plenty of choices in a wide price range. One overall finding to keep in mind: Water in PET plastic bottles generally tasted better than water in HDPE plastic, though water in HDPE is usually cheaper. Note also that taste differences are most obvious when water is at room temperature. When the water is ice-cold, differences will be less noticeable.

Volvic Natural Spring Water, 29 cents per 8-fluid-ounce glass, was excellent, with no off-tastes. Next best was *Dannon Natural Spring Water,* 14 cents. Very good when bottled in PET (but not in HDPE) were *Arrowhead Mountain Spring Water, American Fare Natural Spring Water* (Kmart), and *Albertson's A+ Natural Spring Water,* all 12 cents.

The best carbonated water, *Vintage Old Original Seltzer Water,* was also the 30
cheapest, at 11 cents a glass.

Mineral waters have very individual tastes. *Vittel* and *Calistoga* were less expensive than the others, at 23 cents per serving.

Overall Ratings Within types, in order of flavor score

PRODUCT	SOURCE	COST PER GLASS	PLASTIC	FLAVOR SCORE (0–100: P F G VG E)	COMMENTS
STILL WATER					
Volvic Natural Spring Water	S	29¢	PET		Very clean, no off-flavors.
Dannon Natural Spring Water	M	14	PET		Relatively clean; hint of sweet, fruity plastic flavor.
Arrowhead Mountain Spring Water	M	12	PET		Hint of sweet, fruity plastic flavor.
		7	HDPE		Pronounced melted-plastic flavor, hint of wet-dust flavor.
American Fare Natural Spring Water (Kmart)	M	12	PET		Hint of sweet plastic flavor.
American Fare Spring Water (Kmart)		4	HDPE		Pronounced melted-plastic flavor.
Albertson's A+ Natural Spring Water	M	12	PET		Hint of sweet plastic flavor.
		5	HDPE		Hint of melted-plastic flavor; hint of wet-dust flavor in some samples.
Prestige Premium 100% Spring Water (Winn-Dixie)	M	8	PVC		Hint of plastic flavor.
Prestige Natural Spring Water (Winn-Dixie)		12	PET		Hint of sweet plastic flavor.
Crystal Geyser Natural Alpine Spring Water	M	12	PET		Hint of sweet plastic flavor.
Zephyrhills Natural Spring Water	S	6	HDPE		Hints of plastic and mineral flavors.
		14	PET		Hint of sweet plastic flavor.
Evian Natural Spring Water	S	28	PET		No plastic flavor; hint of mineral flavor.
Sparkletts Crystal-Fresh Drinking Water[1]	—	12	PET		Hint of sweet plastic flavor.
		7	HDPE		Pronounced melted-plastic flavor.
Dasani Purified Water	—	23	PET		Hint of sweet, fruity plastic flavor.
Pure American Spring Water	M	12	PET		Hint of sweet, fruity plastic flavor.
		5	HDPE		Pronounced melted-plastic flavor.
Poland Spring Natural Spring Water	S	7	HDPE		Hind of melted-plastic flavor.
		15	PET		Hint of sweet plastic flavor.
Kroger Natural Spring Water	M	11	PET		Hint of plastic flavor.
		6	HDPE		Hind of melted-plastic flavor.
Deer Park Spring Water	M	13	PET		Hint of sweet plastic flavor.
		6	HDPE		Pronounced melted-plastic flavor; hint of wet-dust flavor in some samples.
Aquafina Purified Drinking Water	—	19	PET		Hint of sweet, fruity plastic flavor.
Maya Canadian Natural Spring Water	M	19	PET		Hints of sweet, fruity plastic and mineral flavors.
Ozarka Natural Spring Water	M	14	PET		Hint of sweet plastic flavor.
		6	HDPE		Pronounced melted-plastic flavor.
Aberfoyle Springs Imported Natural Spring Water	M	11	PET		Hints of sweet plastic and mineral flavors.
Great Bear Natural Spring Water	M	6	HDPE		Hint of melted-plastic flavor.
Calistoga Mountain Spring Water	M	14	PET		Pronounced sweet, fruity plastic flavor.
Safeway Drinking Water	M	6	HDPE		Hint of melted-plastic flavor.
Crystal Springs Mountain Spring Water[2]	M	13	PET		Hint of melted-plastic flavor.
		7	HDPE		Pronounced melted-plastic flavor.
Pathmark Natural Spring Water	M	5	HDPE		Hints of melted-plastic and wet-dust flavors.
		12	PET		Pronounced plastic flavor.
Great Value Spring Water (Wal-Mart)	M	4	HDPE		Hints of melted-plastic and mineral flavors.
Walgreens Drinking Water	M	5	HDPE		Pronounced melted-plastic flavor.
America's Choice Natural Spring Water (A&P stores)[3]	M	5	HDPE		Pronounced melted-plastic flavor; hint of wet-dust flavor.
CARBONATED WATER					
Vintage Old Original Seltzer Water	—	11	PET		Strong effervescence; hint of bitterness and occasional hint of fruity flavor; cleaner-tasting than most.
Canada Dry Original Seltzer[4]	—	23	PET		Strong effervescence; hint of bitterness and occasional hint of fruity flavor.
Albertson's A+ Original Seltzer	—	16	PET		Occasional hint of fruity flavor.
Safeway Select Seltzer Water	—	18	PET		Strong effervescence; occasional hint of fruity flavor.
Schweppes Original Seltzer Water	—	26	PET		Strong effervescence; occasional hint of fruity flavor.
Kroger Golden Crown Sparkling Seltzer Water	—	19	PET		Occasional hint of fruity flavor.
Poland Spring Sparkling Spring Water	—	22	PET		Hint of mineral flavor, and occasional hint of fruity flavor.

[1] Also sold as Alhambra Crystal-Fresh Drinking Water.
[2] Also sold as Crystal Springs Spring Water.
[3] As of 2000, mfr. says, water will also be bottled in PET.
[4] Also sold as Canada Dry Original Sparkling Water.

Figure 10.1

Mmmm Chocolate

CONSUMER REPORTS

1 TO THE connoisseur, chocolate can be as subtle, as varied, and as rewarding as fine wine or exotic coffee.

Milk chocolate, the favorite type in the U.S., is sweeter, with a mellower, less chocolaty flavor than dark chocolate. In Europe, dark chocolate dominates. Whether sweet, semisweet, bittersweet, or extra-bittersweet, dark chocolate is complex and somewhat bitter; it's a sophisticated treat favored by those who crave a more intense chocolate hit. (The difference between, say, sweet and bittersweet is determined by the amount of chocolate liquor—the substance produced when cacao beans are roasted and ground and that makes chocolate taste like chocolate.) Some dark chocolates have a pronounced nutty or woody character, others have a distinct fruity note, too. And dark chocolate should feel smooth and silky as it melts in the mouth.

Milk chocolate bars vary the most in flavor. Some have more chocolate than milk flavor; others, more milk than chocolate. They tend to have a thicker, creamier melted texture in the mouth than dark chocolate.

For many, it's enough that chocolate just tastes good. That's what treats are for, after all. But the medical verdict on chocolate is also more favorable than you might expect.

- You don't have to feel guilty about an occasional indulgence. A 1½-ounce serving of a typical chocolate bar contains around 200 calories and 12 to 15 grams of fat. That's a fair percentage of a single day's intake of fat and calories. But unless people eat chocolate every day, chocolate bars don't contribute much to the overall calorie and fat intake.
- A majority of the fat in cocoa butter (which contributes the fat in a chocolate bar) is saturated fat. But about half that fat is stearic acid, a saturated fat believed to have a neutral effect on cholesterol.
- You can tell doubting teen-agers that chocolate doesn't beget acne.
- There's even some preliminary research indicating that chocolate may help people live longer. In a recent study of 7,841 male college graduates, the ones who ate a moderate amount of chocolate lived almost a year longer than those who abstained. The reason may lie with phenols, antioxidants that can help prevent fatlike substances from forming in the blood and clogging arteries. This study is very tentative, however.

THE QUEST FOR QUALITY

5 For this report we tested 37 chocolate bars: plain dark chocolate, plain milk chocolate, and milk chocolate with extras like nuts, toffee crisps or nougat bits. They ranged from the classic *Hershey's* milk chocolate bar that costs less than a dollar to the superpremium *Teuscher* dark chocolate bar that costs nearly $8. We

also included three "dietetic" bars, sweetened with maltitol or fructose and promoted to diabetics.

Our trained panelists diligently nibbled and tasted several bars from each brand, describing how close each came to meeting our criteria for high-quality chocolate. (We may have given low marks to some of your favorite brands, and we recognize that "good" chocolate is very much a matter of personal preference.)

Here's what we looked for and what we found:

Dark Chocolate

A high-quality bar should be quite firm and deliver a sharp snap when you bite it. It should have a sharp melt—that is, begin to melt rather slowly, then quickly take on a thin and smooth texture, with no grittiness. The chocolate hit—the intensity of the flavor—should be fairly high and quite complex. It can consist of nutty and fruity flavors, which are typical of the cacao bean that's refined to form chocolate, as well as a touch of vanilla. The sweetness can vary, although a dark chocolate bar should never be intensely sweet. It should also have a distinct bitter note and a hint of sourness.

The nine bars we tested show that good-tasting dark chocolate doesn't have to be expensive. Most were judged very good. The *Teuscher* was excellent. So was the $2.25-a-bar *Godiva*. But we also gave high marks to *Dove*—at only 50 cents a bar.

Milk Chocolate

Milk chocolate is usually softer than dark to begin with. It turns thick and 10
creamy when it melts in your mouth. The more milk in the bar, the thicker and creamier it tends to be when it melts. Milkier milk chocolate will have a relatively low chocolate hit. The milk flavor can be cooked, caramelized, or even slightly sour; it depends on how the milk is processed. Although the underlying nutty and fruity components of the chocolate will be less obvious, you still should be able to detect a distinct chocolate flavor.

The fairly pricey *Godiva* and *Teuscher* bars led the pack, followed by the *Dove* bar. *Godiva* and *Dove* had the strongest chocolate flavor. And *Hershey's*? The bar most Americans consider synonymous with chocolate landed near the bottom. It lacked the smooth melt-in-the-mouth texture of the better milk chocolate bars. It was a little gritty rather than smooth. We rated the *Hershey's* merely good.

The only bars faring worse were two "dietetic" bars. Among their several shortcomings: a stale, distinctly dry-milk flavor and not much of a chocolate hit at all. The other dietetic bar, *Guylian No Sugar Added,* was considerably better—one of the higher-rated milk chocolate bars, in fact.

Milk Chocolate with Extras

Pair high-quality chocolate with high-quality extras, and the result is a very flavorful candy bar. Nuts and cereal crisps should taste fresh. Toffee should have a buttery, caramelized flavor.

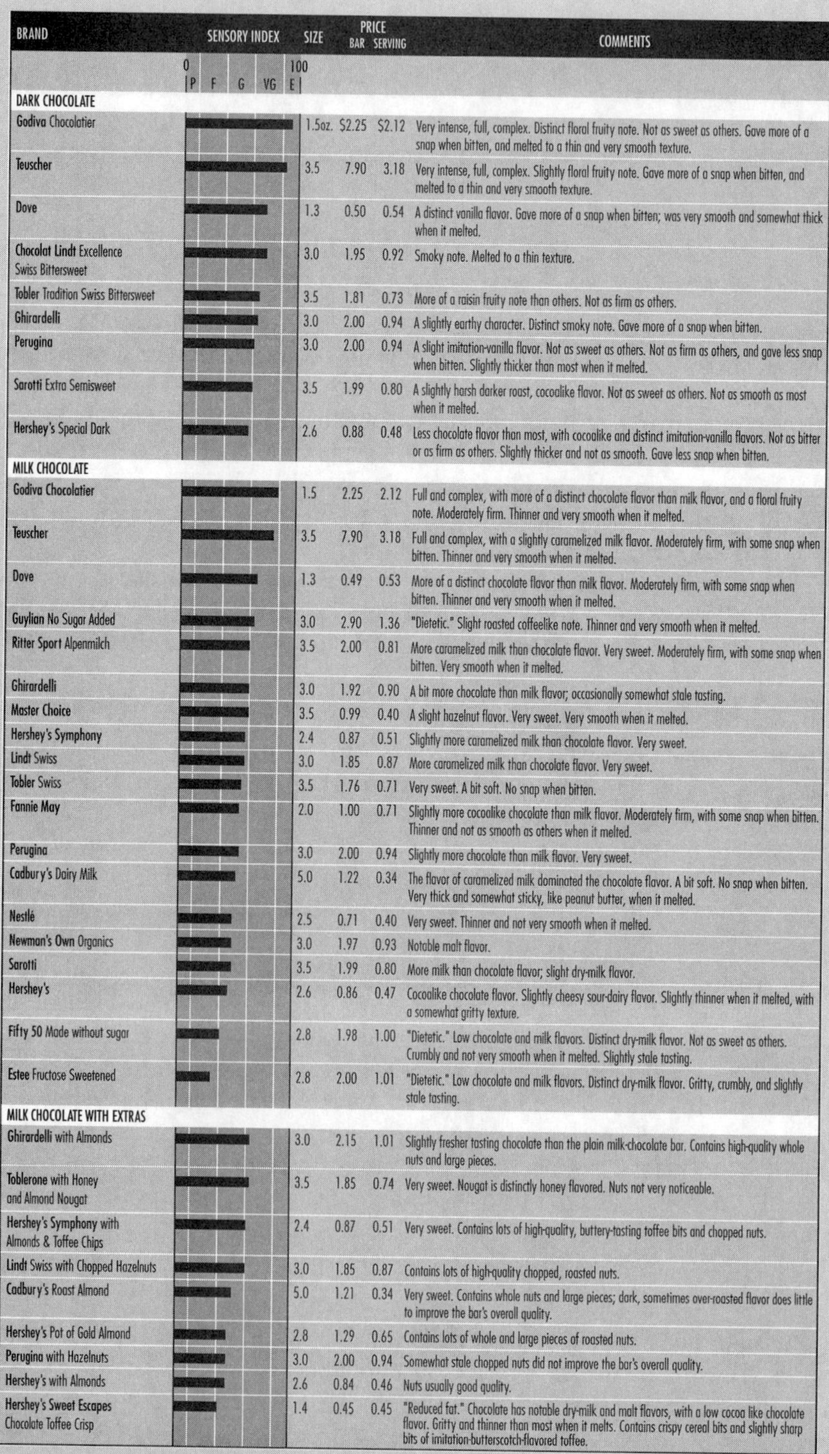

BRAND	SENSORY INDEX (0–100: P, F, G, VG, E)	SIZE	PRICE BAR	PRICE SERVING	COMMENTS
DARK CHOCOLATE					
Godiva Chocolatier		1.5oz.	$2.25	$2.12	Very intense, full, complex. Distinct floral fruity note. Not as sweet as others. Gave more of a snap when bitten, and melted to a thin and very smooth texture.
Teuscher		3.5	7.90	3.18	Very intense, full, complex. Slightly floral fruity note. Gave more of a snap when bitten, and melted to a thin and very smooth texture.
Dove		1.3	0.50	0.54	A distinct vanilla flavor. Gave more of a snap when bitten; was very smooth and somewhat thick when it melted.
Chocolat Lindt Excellence Swiss Bittersweet		3.0	1.95	0.92	Smoky note. Melted to a thin texture.
Tobler Tradition Swiss Bittersweet		3.5	1.81	0.73	More of a raisin fruity note than others. Not as firm as others.
Ghirardelli		3.0	2.00	0.94	A slightly earthy character. Distinct smoky note. Gave more of a snap when bitten.
Perugina		3.0	2.00	0.94	A slight imitation-vanilla flavor. Not as sweet as others. Not as firm as others, and gave less snap when bitten. Slightly thicker than most when it melted.
Sarotti Extra Semisweet		3.5	1.99	0.80	A slightly harsh darker roast, cocoalike flavor. Not as sweet as others. Not as smooth as most when it melted.
Hershey's Special Dark		2.6	0.88	0.48	Less chocolate flavor than most, with cocoalike and distinct imitation-vanilla flavors. Not as bitter or as firm as others. Slightly thicker and not as smooth. Gave less snap when bitten.
MILK CHOCOLATE					
Godiva Chocolatier		1.5	2.25	2.12	Full and complex, with more of a distinct chocolate flavor than milk flavor, and a floral fruity note. Moderately firm. Thinner and very smooth when it melted.
Teuscher		3.5	7.90	3.18	Full and complex, with a slightly caramelized milk flavor. Moderately firm, with some snap when bitten. Thinner and very smooth when it melted.
Dove		1.3	0.49	0.53	More of a distinct chocolate flavor than milk flavor. Moderately firm, with some snap when bitten. Thinner and very smooth when it melted.
Guylian No Sugar Added		3.0	2.90	1.36	"Dietetic." Slight roasted coffeelike note. Thinner and very smooth when it melted.
Ritter Sport Alpenmilch		3.5	2.00	0.81	More caramelized milk than chocolate flavor. Very sweet. Moderately firm, with some snap when bitten. Very smooth when it melted.
Ghirardelli		3.0	1.92	0.90	A bit more chocolate than milk flavor; occasionally somewhat stale tasting.
Master Choice		3.5	0.99	0.40	A slight hazelnut flavor. Very sweet. Very smooth when it melted.
Hershey's Symphony		2.4	0.87	0.51	Slightly more caramelized milk than chocolate flavor. Very sweet.
Lindt Swiss		3.0	1.85	0.87	More caramelized milk than chocolate flavor. Very sweet.
Tobler Swiss		3.5	1.76	0.71	Very sweet. A bit soft. No snap when bitten.
Fannie May		2.0	1.00	0.71	Slightly more cocoalike chocolate than milk flavor. Moderately firm, with some snap when bitten. Thinner and not as smooth as others when it melted.
Perugina		3.0	2.00	0.94	Slightly more chocolate than milk flavor. Very sweet.
Cadbury's Dairy Milk		5.0	1.22	0.34	The flavor of caramelized milk dominated the chocolate flavor. A bit soft. No snap when bitten. Very thick and somewhat sticky, like peanut butter, when it melted.
Nestlé		2.5	0.71	0.40	Very sweet. Thinner and not very smooth when it melted.
Newman's Own Organics		3.0	1.97	0.93	Notable malt flavor.
Sarotti		3.5	1.99	0.80	More milk than chocolate flavor; slight dry-milk flavor.
Hershey's		2.6	0.86	0.47	Cocoalike chocolate flavor. Slightly cheesy sour-dairy flavor. Slightly thinner when it melted, with a somewhat gritty texture.
Fifty 50 Made without sugar		2.8	1.98	1.00	"Dietetic." Low chocolate and milk flavors. Distinct dry-milk flavor. Not as sweet as others. Crumbly and not very smooth when it melted. Slightly stale tasting.
Estee Fructose Sweetened		2.8	2.00	1.01	"Dietetic." Low chocolate and milk flavors. Distinct dry-milk flavor. Gritty, crumbly, and slightly stale tasting.
MILK CHOCOLATE WITH EXTRAS					
Ghirardelli with Almonds		3.0	2.15	1.01	Slightly fresher tasting chocolate than the plain milk-chocolate bar. Contains high-quality whole nuts and large pieces.
Toblerone with Honey and Almond Nougat		3.5	1.85	0.74	Very sweet. Nougat is distinctly honey flavored. Nuts not very noticeable.
Hershey's Symphony with Almonds & Toffee Chips		2.4	0.87	0.51	Very sweet. Contains lots of high-quality, buttery-tasting toffee bits and chopped nuts.
Lindt Swiss with Chopped Hazelnuts		3.0	1.85	0.87	Contains lots of high-quality chopped, roasted nuts.
Cadbury's Roast Almond		5.0	1.21	0.34	Very sweet. Contains whole nuts and large pieces; dark, sometimes over-roasted flavor does little to improve the bar's overall quality.
Hershey's Pot of Gold Almond		2.8	1.29	0.65	Contains lots of whole and large pieces of roasted nuts.
Perugina with Hazelnuts		3.0	2.00	0.94	Somewhat stale chopped nuts did not improve the bar's overall quality.
Hershey's with Almonds		2.6	0.84	0.46	Nuts usually good quality.
Hershey's Sweet Escapes Chocolate Toffee Crisp		1.4	0.45	0.45	"Reduced fat." Chocolate has notable dry-milk and malt flavors, with a low cocoa like chocolate flavor. Gritty and thinner than most when it melts. Contains crispy cereal bits and slightly sharp bits of imitation-butterscotch-flavored toffee.

Figure 10.2

The best of the batch: *Ghirardelli* with almonds, *Toblerone* with honey and almond nougat. *Hershey's Symphony* with almonds and toffee chips, and *Lindt* with chopped hazelnuts. The *Hershey's* is the bargain, at less than $1 a bar.

RECOMMENDATIONS

Of the chocolate we tested, *Godiva* and *Teuscher* were by far the best. You 15
won't find either one at the corner candy store, but you can order them by mail. Call 800 554-0924 for information about *Teuscher;* 800 946-3482 for *Godiva.*

High quality doesn't have to mean high price, though. The *Dove* milk and dark chocolate bars were among the best—and, at about 50 cents a bar, among the lowest priced.

Cream of the Crop

CONSUMER REPORTS

IF YOU'VE come back to full-fat ice cream after trying to stem your crav- 1
ings with reduced-fat products, you're not alone. The real thing is now the fastest-growing segment of all frozen dairy treats—while sales of light and lower-fat ice cream and wanna-bes like frozen yogurt have declined.

To help you find the products that are worth the calorie and fat hit, our trained panelists tasted 18 vanilla, 17 chocolate, and 6 coffee ice creams. We focused on "premium" and "super-premium" products—unofficial categories used to describe products that, according to the International Ice Cream Association, generally contain from 40 to 80 percent more milk fat than the minimum government standard for ice cream. We included several of the new "homemade style" products, which promise a creamy taste similar to that of hand-cranked ice cream. And because limiting fat in the diet *is* still important, we added a "light" ice cream in each flavor to see how it would compare.

All the ice creams we tested were at least good. But only *Häagen-Dazs* was consistently excellent. Also notable: *Breyers Vanilla* and a new arrival that was too late for our main test, *Godiva Belgian Dark Chocolate.*

PREMIUM TASTE?

The quality of an ice cream depends on what it's made of and how it's made. To make ice cream, a manufacturer pasteurizes and homogenizes milk, cream, sweeteners, and other ingredients such as gums and emulsifiers; cools the mixture; adds flavors and colors; and whips air into it as it freezes.

Too much air and too many gums can result in a light, airy ice cream; 5
too little air makes for an extremely dense and heavy product. An ice cream's

texture can also be affected by how it's handled between the plant and the store. Sharp variations in temperature, for example, can turn a smooth ice cream into an icy one.

As for flavor, here's what our panelists looked for in each category, and what they found.

Vanilla

A high-quality vanilla ice cream should be mild but not bland, sweet but not overpoweringly so. The dairy should be balanced with a vanilla-bean, quality vanilla-extract, or other real vanilla flavor. There might be a slight alcohol note from the extract. There may also be a slight egg flavor. The ice cream should be creamy smooth with little or no iciness, and it should melt in your mouth to almost the thickness of heavy cream, but with no obvious gums or thickeners.

Breyers Vanilla and *Häagen-Dazs Vanilla* were both excellent—and quite different from each other. *Häagen-Dazs* was more creamy smooth with a very full dairy flavor and very distinct vanilla-extract flavor; *Breyers* had a fresh, clean dairy flavor with a somewhat milder, high-quality, real vanilla flavor, which more than offset its slightly icy texture.

Breyers Light actually tasted better than most full-fat vanillas (though it had just 20 calories per serving less than regular *Breyers*). *ShopRite Premium Vanilla Bean,* the best of the store brands, was a good value.

As for the "homemade" vanillas, they were nothing special. In fact, *Breyers* 10
Homemade—which, unlike its regular brandmate, contains gums—had a generic vanilla flavor and was rather light and airy.

Chocolate

A high-quality chocolate ice cream should have more chocolate than dairy flavor. The chocolate should have a touch of bitterness and astringency, but be mellow rather than harsh. The texture should be like that of an excellent vanilla ice cream, but a slight chalkiness—a natural component of cocoa and chocolate—is acceptable.

Häagen-Dazs, with its creamy smooth texture and mellow chocolate and full dairy flavors, was far superior to most other chocolate ice creams. The only contender was an expensive superpremium ice cream new to the market: *Godiva Belgian Dark Chocolate.* Although it contains gums, it did not have an excessively gummy texture.

Among the runners-up, several premium store brands made a strong showing. Only *Dreyer's/Edy's Grand* tasted slightly better than store-brand chocolates from Winn Dixie, A&P-owned stores, Publix, and chains that carry *Sensational Premium.* These products topped the quality of even the superpremium *Starbuck's Doubleshot Chocolate,* which costs about four times as much and averages nearly twice the calories.

The "homemade" chocolate ice creams from *Breyers* and *Dreyer's/Edy's Grand* were both inferior to the regular offerings of those brands. *Breyers Home-*

made Double Chocolate Fudge included fudge sauce and mediocre-tasting chocolate chunks.

Coffee

A high-quality coffee ice cream should have more brewed-coffee than dairy 15
flavor, with a sweetness and texture about the same as in a high-quality vanilla. Again, *Häagen-Dazs* was best. *Breyers* also had a very good overall score and was about one-third the price of the top-rated ice cream in this category.

Think carefully before downing a few scoops of coffee ice cream before bedtime. The caffeine in the coffee ice creams we tested varied from less than 10 milligrams per half-cup for *Breyers* and *Dreyer's/Edy's Grand* to as much as 45 milligrams per half-cup of *Starbuck's Coffee Italian Roast.* Eating a big bowl of some of these ice creams could give you as big a hit as you'd get from an eight-ounce cup of brewed coffee, which can contain about 137 milligrams of caffeine.

THE PRICE YOU PAY

Ice cream contains protein, calcium, vitamin A, and other vitamins and minerals. But there's no getting around it: With every spoonful of the full-fat products you also get a hefty dose of fat and calories. A standard half-cup serving (but who are they kidding?) of most of the tested ice creams ranged from 140 to 170 calories, with 8 to 10 grams of fat. The same serving of a superpremium such as *Häagen-Dazs* or *Ben & Jerry's* has about 100 more calories and twice the amount of fat.

Part of the reason is that super-premiums are denser—less air and more ice cream. You get more ice cream per half-cup serving than you get with premiums or regular ice creams. Finish off a pint of *Häagen-Dazs Chocolate* in one sitting, which some people have been known to do, and you will have consumed 72 grams of fat—more than the government's daily recommended limit of 65 grams of fat for people who eat about 2,000 calories in a day—and 1,080 calories.

One bit of good news: Ice cream may cost a bit less this season. Last summer, a domestic butterfat shortage hiked consumer prices on high-fat dairy products, ice cream included. This year, however, there's a glut, and butterfat prices have plunged. Ice cream prices should follow suit.

RECOMMENDATIONS

Häagen-Dazs was the only brand to have a consistently high-quality flavor 20
and smooth and creamy texture in all three flavors tested. *Breyers,* at a fraction of the cost, fat, and calories of the superpremiums, weighed in with an excellent vanilla ice cream which we've rated A CR Best Buy. *Breyers* coffee ice cream, another CR Best Buy, is also a very good tasting, less fattening alternative to *Häagen-Dazs.*

Breyers Light Vanilla is a very good choice for people who watch their fat intake. It was tastier than most other regular vanilla ice creams but had only about half the fat and somewhat fewer calories per serving.

PRODUCT	FLAVOR AND TEXTURE SCORE (0–100: P F G VG E)	CONTAINER SIZE	HALF-CUP SERVING COST	CALORIES	FAT	COMMENTS
VANILLA ICE CREAM						
Breyers A CR Best Buy[†]		1/2 gal.	23¢	150	9g	Big fresh dairy, notable cream, and distinct real vanilla flavors. Slightly icy, a slightly thinner melt than most, no gumminess.
Häagen-Dazs		pt.	73	270	18	Big full dairy with a notable cream flavor, very distinct vanilla flavor with a strong alcohol note, hint of egg. Very dense, creamy smooth, with no gumminess.
Ben & Jerry's		pint	73	250	16	Full dairy with a notable cream flavor, very distinct real vanilla flavor with a distinct alcohol note, hint of egg. Very dense, little gumminess.
ShopRite Premium **A CR Best Buy**[†]		1/2 gal.	18	160	8	Big fresh dairy and distinct real vanilla flavors. Noticeably icy with a thinner melt than most and no gumminess.
Breyers Light		1/2 gal.	24	130	4	Distinct vanilla flavor, very sweet. Slightly thinner melt than most and little gumminess.
Sensational Premium		1/2 gal.	21	150	8	Distinct real vanilla flavor. Little gumminess. (Sold at Stop & Shop, Giant, Bi-Lo, Edwards, and Tops.)
Blue Bell Homemade		1/2 gal.	23	180	9	Distinct vanilla and slight custardlike flavors, very sweet. Slightly thin melt and little gumminess.
Newman's Own		qt.	48	170	10	Overpowering vanilla flavor with a harsh alcohol note.
Dreyer's/Edy's Homemade		1/2 gal.	23	140	7	Slightly cooked-milk flavor with a caramellike note, imitation vanilla flavor, very sweet.
America's Choice Premium (A&P-owned stores)		1/2 gal.	19	150	9	Slightly low vanilla flavor. Somewhat light and airy.
Breyers Homemade		1/2 gal.	23	150	8	Slightly cooked-milk flavor, very sweet. Somewhat light and airy.
Dreyer's/Edy's Grand		1/2 gal.	21	140	8	Very sweet. Somewhat light and airy.
Prestige Premium (Winn Dixie)		1/2 gal.	23	160	9	Very sweet.
Turkey Hill Premium		1/2 gal.	17	140	8	Low dairy flavor. Light and airy, noticeably thick, gummy melt.
Publix Premium		1/2 gal.	20	160	9	Low dairy, poor-quality vanilla flavor, very sweet. Light and airy, noticeably thick, gummy melt.
Albertsons		1/2 gal.	23	150	8	Low dairy and vanilla flavors, slight chemical note. Somewhat light and airy, noticeably thick, gummy melt.
Safeway Select Premium		1/2 gal.	28	160	10	Low dairy and vanilla flavors. Somewhat light and airy, noticeably thick, gummy melt.
Texas Gold Premium (Kroger)		1/2 gal.	28	170	10	Low dairy and imitation vanilla flavors, very sweet. Somewhat light and airy, thick, gummy melt.

CHOCOLATE ICE CREAM						
Häagen-Dazs		pt.	73	270	18	Big full dairy with a notable cream flavor, very distinct chocolate flavor with a smoky note, a bit less sweet than most. Very dense, creamy smooth, with no gumminess.
Dreyer's/Edy's Grand		1/2 gal.	23	150	8	Very distinct chocolate flavor with a smoky note.
Prestige Premium (Winn Dixie)		1/2 gal.	23	170	10	Very distinct chocolate flavor, a bit less sweet than most.
America's Choice Premium (A&P-owned stores)		1/2 gal.	19	140	8	Slightly thin melt.
Publix Premium		1/2 gal.	19	160	9	A bit less sweet than most.
Sensational Premium		1/2 gal.	21	150	9	Slightly icy, with a slightly thin melt and little gumminess. (Sold at Stop & Shop, Giant, Bi-Lo, Edwards, and Tops.)
Breyers		1/2 gal.	22	160	9	Slightly thin melt and no gumminess.
Starbuck's Doubleshot Chocolate		pt.	82	290	17	Very distinct chocolate flavor with a smoky note. Very sweet with a very slight saltiness. Streak of chocolate syrup has a hazelnut flavor.
Blue Bell Dutch Chocolate		1/2 gal.	23	170	9	Very distinct chocolate flavor. Slightly icy, with a slightly thin melt and little gumminess.
Newman's Own		qt.	48	190	10	Very distinct chocolate flavor.
Dreyer's/Edy's Homemade Double Chocolate Chunk		1/2 gal.	24	190	10	Very distinct chocolate flavor, very sweet. Somewhat gummy. Has high-quality chocolate chunks that taste better than the ice cream.
ShopRite Premium		1/2 gal.	18	160	8	Slightly icy, with a slightly thin melt and no gumminess.
Albertsons Chocolate Chunky Chocolate		1/2 gal.	22	170	9	Less chocolate flavor than most. Slightly thin melt. Has chocolate chunks that taste better than the ice cream.
Turkey Hill Premium Dutch Chocolate		1/2 gal.	17	150	8	Very distinct chocolate flavor. Somewhat gummy.
Safeway Select Premium Dutch Chocolate		1/2 gal.	28	150	8	A bit less sweet than most. Somewhat gummy.
Dreyer's/Edy's Grand Light Chocolate		1/2 gal.	24	110	3	Somewhat gummy. Has streaks of chocolate syrup.
Breyers Homemade Double Chocolate Fudge		1/2 gal.	23	180	9	Very sweet. Somewhat gummy. Has mediocre-tasting slightly soft chocolate chunks and syrup.
COFFEE ICE CREAM						
Häagen-Dazs		pt.	73	270	18	23 mg. caffeine. Full dairy with notable cream and high-quality coffee flavors, a hint of egg. Very dense, creamy smooth, with no gumminess.
Breyers A CR Best Buy[†]		1/2 gal.	22	150	9	8.8 mg. caffeine. Big, high-quality dairy flavor; coffee flavor is milder than most. Slightly icy, with a thin clean melt and no gumminess.
Dreyer's/Edy's Grand		qt.	37	140	8	9.8 mg. caffeine. Milder coffee flavor than most. Very slight gumminess.
Starbuck's Coffee Italian Roast		qt.	50	230	12	33-45 mg. caffeine. Intense harsh coffee flavor with slight smoky note.
Turkey Hill		1/2 gal.	20	140	8	16 mg. caffeine. Poor-quality, candylike coffee flavor.
Starbuck's Coffee Lowfat Latte		qt.	50	170	3	35mg. caffeine. Intense harsh coffee flavor, very sweet.

Flavor and texture score is based on blind taste tests by trained panelists. One product goes by two brand names—Dreyer's in the West and Edy's in the rest of the country. In a half-cup serving (4 fluid oz.), cost is calculated from the national or regional average price of the most common container size. Calories and fat come from manufacturers' label information. About two-thirds of the fat is saturated. Caffeine per half-cup serving, listed only for the coffee ice creams, is based on analyses in our laboratories. For the Starbuck's Coffee Italian Roast, which differed greatly from sample to sample in its caffeine content, we list a range. Comments are based on the judgments of our trained panel.

Flavor and texture notes: Most of the ice creams were quite sweet, moderately dense, and had no noticeable iciness. Melted, they had a texture like heavy cream and a very slight to slight gumminess. Most vanilla ice creams had distinct dairy and vanilla flavors with a slight cream flavor. The chocolates generally had a distinct chocolate flavor with a maltlike note, and a moderate dairy with a slight cream flavor. Most coffees had a distinct coffee flavor and a moderate dairy with a slight cream flavor.

† A CR Best Buy means a Consumer Reports Best Buy

Figure 10.3

You can save money by purchasing a store-brand ice cream. The best were *ShopRite Premium Vanilla* (another CR Best Buy), *Sensational Premium Vanilla* and *Chocolate* (Stop & Shop and other stores), *Prestige Premium Chocolate* (Winn Dixie), *America's Choice Premium Chocolate* (A&P-owned stores), and *Publix Premium Chocolate.*

Roll Models

CONSUMER REPORTS

Consider what you're asking of your toilet paper: It should be soft (never scratchy) and absorbent, should quickly disintegrate in water (to avoid clogging your plumbing) and yet be strong enough to hold together when used. It should be made in a way that's easy on the environment. And this perfect roll should be priced reasonably, or you'll push your cart farther along the supermarket aisle. 1

For this report, we put 30 toilet papers through tests for the attributes mentioned above. We tested the rolls you see advertised ad nauseam. Those include Procter & Gamble's best-seller *Charmin* (at 83, the actor who plays Mr. Whipple is back to say that the new *Charmin* is stronger and more absorbent), *Quilted Northern* (which claims to leave less lint—in sensitive areas or on glasses, presumably—than *Charmin*), and *Kleenex Cottonelle* (whose "thick cushy ripples leave you feeling clean and fresh"). We tested *Scott,* whose 1,000-sheet rolls are among the least costly per 100 sheets. We tested *Purely Cotton,* an expensive product made entirely of recycled cotton fibers.

We also tested "green" products—*Green Forest, Marcal, Publix Green,* and *Seventh Generation*—made with recycled paper. . . . And we tested store brands from Costco, Wal-Mart, and several supermarket chains that are sold in packages of as many as 24 rolls.

We discovered decided differences in strength, disintegration, softness, and absorption among the toilet papers. Moreover, we found big differences in their price—from 6 cents per 100 sheets to 25 cents.

PRICE POINTS

Not surprisingly, those 24-roll packages are among the best bargains, selling for 8 to 10 cents per 100 sheets. Still, there are so many variables in toilet paper that it's hard to compare cost in any meaningful way. The number of sheets per roll varies almost sixfold (from 170 to 1,000), and some brands are sold in double-size and triple-size rolls (they have, respectively, two times and three times as many sheets, not more plies). 5

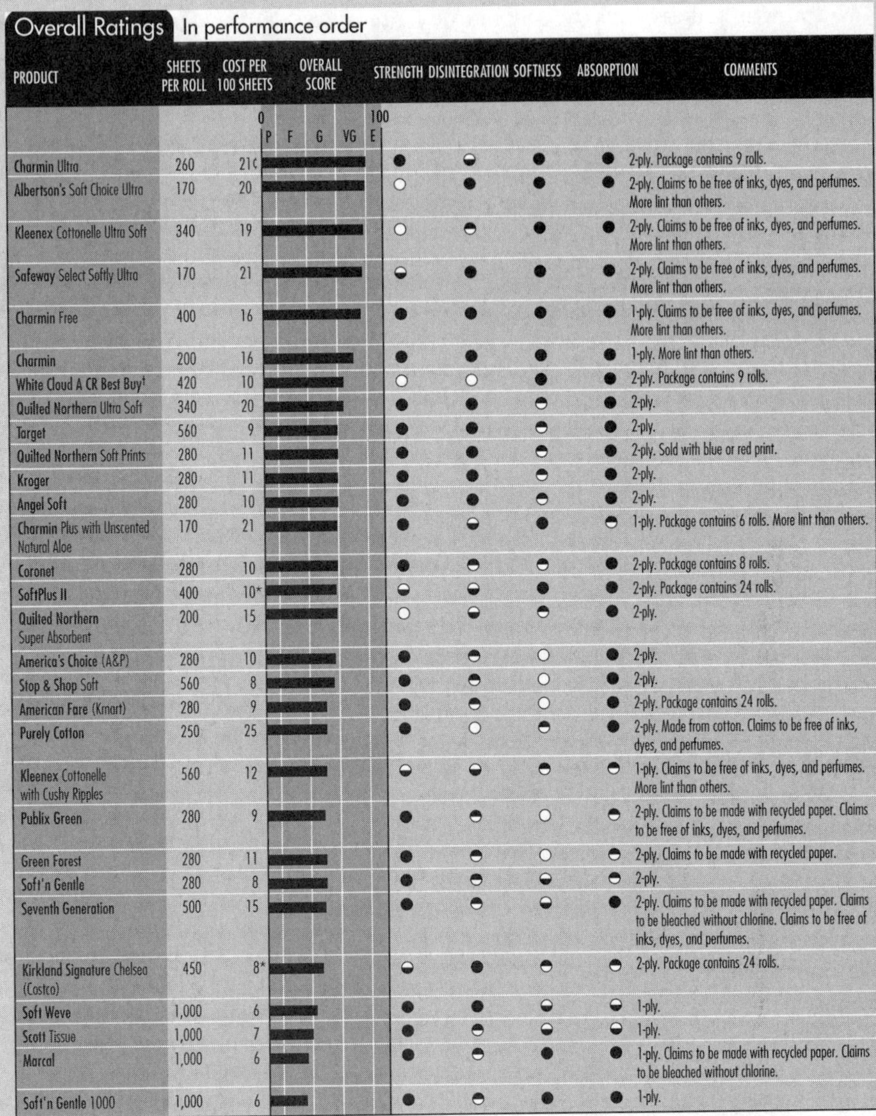

Overall Ratings In performance order

PRODUCT	SHEETS PER ROLL	COST PER 100 SHEETS	OVERALL SCORE (0–100: P F G VG E)	STRENGTH	DISINTEGRATION	SOFTNESS	ABSORPTION	COMMENTS
Charmin Ultra	260	21¢		●	◒	●	●	2-ply. Package contains 9 rolls.
Albertson's Soft Choice Ultra	170	20		○	●	●	●	2-ply. Claims to be free of inks, dyes, and perfumes. More lint than others.
Kleenex Cottonelle Ultra Soft	340	19		○	◓	●	●	2-ply. Claims to be free of inks, dyes, and perfumes. More lint than others.
Safeway Select Softly Ultra	170	21		◒	●	●	●	2-ply. Claims to be free of inks, dyes, and perfumes. More lint than others.
Charmin Free	400	16		●	●	●	●	1-ply. Claims to be free of inks, dyes, and perfumes. More lint than others.
Charmin	200	16		●	●	●	●	1-ply. More lint than others.
White Cloud A CR Best Buy†	420	10		○	○	●	●	2-ply. Package contains 9 rolls.
Quilted Northern Ultra Soft	340	20		●	●	◓	●	2-ply.
Target	560	9		●	●	◓	●	2-ply.
Quilted Northern Soft Prints	280	11		●	●	◓	●	2-ply. Sold with blue or red print.
Kroger	280	11		●	●	◓	●	2-ply.
Angel Soft	280	10		●	●	◓	●	2-ply.
Charmin Plus with Unscented Natural Aloe	170	21		●	◒	●	◓	1-ply. Package contains 6 rolls. More lint than others.
Coronet	280	10		●	◓	◓	●	2-ply. Package contains 8 rolls.
SoftPlus II	400	10*		◒	◒	●	●	2-ply. Package contains 24 rolls.
Quilted Northern Super Absorbent	200	15		○	◒	◓	●	2-ply.
America's Choice (A&P)	280	10		●	◓	○	●	2-ply.
Stop & Shop Soft	560	8		●	◓	○	●	2-ply.
American Fare (Kmart)	280	9		●	◓	○	●	2-ply. Package contains 24 rolls.
Purely Cotton	250	25		●	○	◓	●	2-ply. Made from cotton. Claims to be free of inks, dyes, and perfumes.
Kleenex Cottonelle with Cushy Ripples	560	12		◒	◒	◓	◓	1-ply. Claims to be free of inks, dyes, and perfumes. More lint than others.
Publix Green	280	9		●	◓	○	◓	2-ply. Claims to be made with recycled paper. Claims to be free of inks, dyes, and perfumes.
Green Forest	280	11		●	◓	○	◓	2-ply. Claims to be made with recycled paper.
Soft'n Gentle	280	8		●	◓	◒	◓	2-ply.
Seventh Generation	500	15		●	◓	◒	●	2-ply. Claims to be made with recycled paper. Claims to be bleached without chlorine. Claims to be free of inks, dyes, and perfumes.
Kirkland Signature Chelsea (Costco)	450	8*		◒	●	◓	◓	2-ply. Package contains 24 rolls.
Soft Weve	1,000	6		●	●	◒	◒	1-ply.
Scott Tissue	1,000	7		●	◓	◒	◒	1-ply.
Marcal	1,000	6		●	◓	●	●	1-ply. Claims to be made with recycled paper. Claims to be bleached without chlorine.
Soft'n Gentle 1000	1,000	6		●	◓	●	●	1-ply.

The overall score is based on strength, disintegration, softness, and absorption. We tested strength by weighing how much lead shot a dampened sheet of paper could hold before it broke. Disintegration, important mainly to owners of low-flow toilets or septic tanks, reflects the time it took a sheet of paper to break up in a swirling beaker of water. Papers with the highest scores disintegrated fastest. A trained panel judged softness by feeling the products with their hands. Absorption reflects the time it took a sheet of paper to soak up a single drop of water. Sheets per roll is for the size tested; other sizes are available for some brands. Cost per 100 sheets is the estimated average, based on a national survey. An asterisk denotes the approximate price.

Most products: Fit in the typical wall dispenser. Have sheets that measure 4 1/2 inches wide by between 4 and 4 1/2 inches long. Come in plain white; a few may be available in colors or colored prints. Are scent-free. Are sold in 4-roll packages.

† A CR Best Buy means a Consumer Reports Best Buy

Figure 10.4

You won't always save by buying the larger sizes; regular *Charmin* costs 16 cents per 100 sheets in the 200-sheet size but 18 cents in the 300-sheet size. (We found that whatever its roll size, regular *Charmin* performed essentially the same.)

The 200-sheet roll of the new regular *Charmin* is the successor to a 280-sheet roll of the old regular *Charmin;* double-size and triple-size rolls have also shrunk. That fact didn't escape the notice of some of our readers, who complained to us about the apparent price increase. Procter & Gamble no doubt expected that kind of suspicion; when we contacted them to ask for basic information about their toilet papers, they wrote us that "this is not an example of . . . 'down counting.' . . . The new *Charmin* contains 22% more fibers and is 35% thicker [than old *Charmin*]." We didn't count fibers, but we did determine that new *Charmin* is thicker, and it scored higher overall than old *Charmin*.

Some toilet-paper sheets are plain and thin, some thick and textured. Some have one ply, others two. Some sheets measure 4 × 4½ inches, others 4½ × 4½—a difference of about 12 percent. We've even seen one brand that comes in 3 × 4½-inch sheets (for elves, no doubt). But would you use a lot less of a thick paper than you would of a thin paper? And would that make up for any difference in price?

To find out, we performed a limited test in some men's and women's bathrooms at our Yonkers, N.Y., testing center. It turned out that people did use less of thicker papers—sometimes enough less to make up for the price difference.

IN THE LABORATORY, NOT THE LAVATORY

We used lab instruments to measure most attributes, but we asked trained 10
panelists to judge softness. Specifics about each roll are in the Ratings.

Strength

Everything else matters little if the toilet paper falls apart when you use it. We poured lead shot onto a sheet of dampened paper held horizontally and weighed the amount that made it break. The result? Well, it turns out that Mr. Whipple has a point: Three varieties of *Charmin* (*Ultra, Free,* and regular) were the strongest products by far. A large number of papers, in a wide range of prices, proved to be much weaker.

More plies didn't always indicate greater strength; two of the top-scoring *Charmins* are one-ply papers.

Disintegration

Strength is great, but only up to a point. If you have a toilet that's apt to clog or a low-flow toilet (one that uses about 1.6 gallons of water per flush), it's especially important that your toilet paper break up quickly. Otherwise, your home's drainpipes could clog. Quick disintegration is also advantageous if you have a septic system, in which the remnants of toilet paper should sink to the bottom, not float. We tested disintegration by measuring the time it took a single sheet to break up in a beaker of water being stirred.

For the most part, there were no surprises: The papers that did best in our strength test took longest to break up; those that did worst broke up fastest. Among those that were reasonably strong yet broke up reasonably fast were *Albertson's Soft Choice Ultra, Kleenex Cottonelle Ultra Soft,* and *White Cloud.* They would make good choices, especially for anyone whose toilets or pipes tend to clog. Regular *Charmin, Charmin Free,* and *Kirkland Signature* were among the products that would be poor choices for those people.

Softness

15 Our trained panelists judged the components of softness: pliability, cushioning, smoothness, thickness, and the absence of scratchiness. The panelists also checked how likely sheets were to tear in use and how well the plies of two-ply rolls stayed together.

The result? Right again, Mr. Whipple. The four *Charmins* we tested proved among the softest. Other brands with top scores in softness included the *Albertson's* supermarket brand, *Kleenex Cottonelle Ultra Soft, Safeway Select Softly Ultra, White Cloud,* and *SoftPlus II.*

Most of the products with a low score for softness were 1,000-sheet rolls, which were quite thin, felt kind of like tissue paper, and were somewhat scratchy. Despite its name, 1,000-sheet *SoftWeve,* for instance, scored only fair in softness. Furthermore, *Purely Cotton* may be made of cotton, but it was not as cottony soft as some of the purely paper competition.

That said, unless your skin is especially sensitive, none of the toilet papers should be objectionable.

Absorption

We measured the time it took each paper to soak up a drop of water. Most of the papers did fine, absorbing the drop in less than five seconds. But the *Marcal* and *Soft'n Gentle* 1,000-sheet rolls took more than 20 times longer—about two minutes to absorb one drop.

20 We did one more test, to see if there was anything to *Quilted Northern's* claim of having less lint than *Charmin.* The claim proved true for *Charmin* regular, *Free,* and *Plus* and for a few other brands, all of which left noticeable lint on a piece of black felt. If you use toilet paper to clean your glasses, consider yourself warned.

RECOMMENDATIONS

- If you want a strong, soft, absorbent paper, consider one of the three *Charmin* varieties that got excellent scores for all three of those attributes: *Charmin Ultra,* 21 cents per 100 sheets; *Charmin Free,* 16 cents; and regular *Charmin,* 16 cents. Keep in mind, however, that all three took a long time to disintegrate, which could be a problem if your pipes tend to clog or if you have a septic system or a low-flow toilet.

- Several brands disintegrated quickly and had a very good overall score. They include *White Cloud* (sold in Wal-Mart stores), A CR Best Buy at 10 cents per 100 sheets; *Kleenex Cottonelle Ultra Soft,* 19 cents; and *Albertson's Soft Choice Ultra,* 20 cents (available mainly in the West).
- If you want to buy a toilet paper made from recycled ingredients, you'll have to accept less strength and softness. The best bets are *Publix Green,* 9 cents per 100 sheets (sold in Publix supermarkets in the South), and *Green Forest,* 11 cents. *Marcal* scored poor in every test but disintegration.

Practicing the Principles: Activities

THE RAW AND THE COOKED

In his book *The Raw and the Cooked,* cultural anthropologist Claude Lévi-Strauss discusses how attitudes toward what is "raw" and what is "cooked" vary from one culture to another. Invariably, "raw" is seen as "bad" and "cooked" as "good," but different communities disagree about what is raw and what is cooked. Freewrite for five minutes to generate a list of foods that are all right to eat raw and food that must be cooked. As a class, compare your lists and compile a list that everyone agrees on. If there are any differences of opinion, then work these out. For example, some people believe that carrots and cauliflower cannot be eaten cooked, only raw. For some, a rare steak is raw; for others, it is "cooked." For some hot dogs eaten right out of the package are "raw"; for others, they are "cooked." Some people eat raw cookie dough; others want it cooked. As a class, try to figure out the point at which raw becomes "cooked" for each of the kinds of food you listed. Are there degrees of being cooked? How do you decide what is raw and what is cooked?

Now freewrite for about five minutes about what is "good" or "bad" in music: rap, big band, Broadway musical, Barney the Dinosaur, country, disco, heavy metal, classical, Muzak, Doctor Demento, whatever—the more outrageous, the better. If you complete this list at home, you might consider bringing a few selections to class to illustrate what you consider bad and good in music. As a class, try to compile a list that you all agree on. What criteria do you use to decide what is bad and what is good?

Finally, freewrite for about five minutes to generate a list of things or actions that are always bad or always good (always right or always wrong, always moral or always immoral). As a class, compare your lists to compile a list of what you as a class consider always good and always bad. Work out any differences of opinion. For instance, most people agree that lying, stealing, and killing are bad, but are there cases in which these may be justified or desirable? Are there some people that might consider these actions (or other actions on your "bad" list) to be good? Are there some that might consider actions on your good list to be bad? What criteria do you use to decide what is good and what is bad?

COMPARISON SHOPPING

Select a group of consumer products or services with which you are familiar or that you would like to know more about: fast food, cellular phones, computers, sports shoes, stereos, long-distance phone service, movie theaters, restaurants, bookstores, music stores, anything at all. In small groups, decide on criteria for evaluating these products, and develop a chart like the one reproduced in the *Consumer Reports* article. Use numerical values or the famous *CR* circles to indicate "excellent," "very good," "good," "fair," and "poor." If you have spreadsheet or graphing software available, then try to present your findings in a table. Consider publishing your results, along with the findings of other groups in your class, on a class website. Perhaps you could even make your findings available to other students as a consumer guide to your local community.

BLAND, BEAUTIFUL, AND BOY CRAZY

In an article for *TV Guide,* Mary Pipher (author of *Reviving Ophelia*) criticizes television's portrayal of women. She quotes an American Psychological Association study which found that the women represented on television "tend to be young, beautiful, passive, and dependent." The same study also found that "older, competent, less attractive, and minority women are underrepresented, almost invisible." Pipher is particularly concerned that young women will take the world of television to be a reflection of the real world rather than a distortion. She recommends that television networks make the following changes in order to provide more realistic and responsible images of women:

- Girls of all ethnic backgrounds, degrees of attractiveness, and socioeconomic levels would be featured. Being different wouldn't be mocked or punished.
- Girls would be the active subjects of their own lives, not the objects of others' attention. Their main characteristics would be their talents, intelligence, and character, not their appearance.
- Plots would show girls in diverse roles—not just as prom queens, rape victims, or call girls—with diverse interests. They wouldn't all be mall rats.
- Girls would be shown with people of all ages, and adults wouldn't always be portrayed as adolescents themselves. Other characters would relate to girls as interesting people worthy of respect.

- Interactions between teens would encourage kind and decent behavior. Mean-spiritedness, smugness, harassment, and superficiality wouldn't be regarded as clever. Girls would like each other.

As a class, discuss Pipher's argument. Do you see a problem with the way women are portrayed on television? Are there problems with how men are portrayed as well? Are there problems with how minority racial and cultural groups are portrayed? What might you do to improve the representation of characters on television?

Using Pipher's criteria (and any others that you have developed as a class), review the current television season's offerings. You might consider assigning each class member (or pairs of class members) to review a show for a couple of weeks and then report on their findings to the class. After viewing the shows and analyzing them, then visit the websites for each of the networks and learn as much as you can about the shows. If possible, send your report to the networks.

Applying the Principles On Your Own

THE INTERNET AND THE RIGHT TO PRIVACY

As the Internet continues to expand at a rapid rate, more and more information is available at the click of a mouse. But some harbor growing concerns that too much information is available—especially information that these detractors consider private. The first essay, "The Eroded Self," was written by Jeffrey Rosen for the *New York Times Magazine*. Rosen is a professor at the George Washington University Law School and the legal affairs editor for *The New Republic*. In this essay, he describes how new technology has blurred the distinction between public and private. In the second essay, Tom Cattapan, a media associate for Starcom Worldwide, describes the potential problems of "cookies," small pieces of text placed on a computer's hard drive when an individual visits a website. Cattapan argues that cookies provide e-business marketers with information about consumers without them being aware that a company is gathering such information. Cattapan suggests some ways that Internet companies can continue to gather valuable market information without violating Internet users' privacy.

The Eroded Self

JEFFREY ROSEN

IN CYBERSPACE, there is no real wall between public and private. And the 1
version of you being constructed out there—from bits and pieces of stray data—is probably not who you think you are.

Monica Lewinsky is a rather unlikely spokeswoman for the virtues of reticence. But in addition to selling designer handbags, she has emerged after her internship as an advocate of privacy in cyberspace. "People need to realize that your e-mails can be read and made public, and that you need to be cautious," she warned recently on "Larry King Live." Lewinsky was unsettled by Kenneth Starr's decision to subpoena Washington bookstores for receipts of her purchases; in her underappreciated biography, *Monica's Story,* she points to the bookstore subpoenas as one of the most invasive moments in the Starr investigation. But she was also distraught when the prosecutors subpoenaed her home computer. From the recesses of her hard drive, they retrieved e-mail messages that she had tried unsuccessfully to delete; along with the love letters she had drafted—but never sent—to the president. "It was such a violation," Lewinsky complained to her biographer, Andrew Morton.

Many Americans are beginning to understand just how she felt. As reading, writing, health care, shopping, sex and gossip increasingly take place in cyberspace, it is suddenly dawning on us that the most intimate details of our daily lives are being monitored, searched, recorded and stored as meticulously as Monica Lewinsky's were. For most citizens, however, the greatest threat to privacy comes not from special prosecutors but from employers and from all-seeing Web sites and advertising networks that track every online move we make.

Consider the case of DoubleClick Inc. For the past few years, DoubleClick, the Internet's largest advertising-placement company, has been compiling anonymous data on our browsing habits by placing "cookie" files on millions of our hard drives. Cookies are electronic footprints that allow Web sites and advertising networks to monitor our online movements with granular precision. Some Web sites can monitor the search terms you enter and the articles you skim. After DoubleClick sends you a cookie, you will find yourself receiving targeted ads when you visit the Web sites of its 2,500 clients. So, for example, if you were to visit Alta Vista's auto section, DoubleClick might send you cheerful ads from G.M. or Ford, thoughtfully ensuring that you don't see them more than two or three times.

As long as users were confident that their virtual identities weren't being 5
linked to their actual identities, many were happy to accept cookies without thinking about them. Then last November, DoubleClick bought Abacus Direct, a database of names, addresses and information about the off-line buying habits of 90 million households, collected from the largest direct mail catalogs and

retailers in the nation. In January, using Abacus's detailed records, DoubleClick began to compile profiles linking individuals' actual names and addresses with their online and off-line purchases. Suddenly, shopping that had once seemed anonymous was being archived in personally identifiable dossiers.

Under pressure from privacy advocates and from dot-com investors, DoubleClick announced last month that it would postpone its profiling scheme until the federal government and the e-commerce industry agree on privacy standards. Still, the DoubleClick controversy points to the inherent threat to privacy in a new economy that is based, in unprecedented ways, on the recording and exchange of intimate personal information.

There are many fearful consequences to the loss of privacy, but none perhaps more disquieting than this: privacy protects us from being misdefined and judged out of context. This protection is especially important in a world of short attention spans, a world where information can easily be confused with knowledge. When intimate personal information circulates among a small group of people who know you well, its significance can be weighed against other aspects of your personality and character. (Monica Lewinsky didn't mind that her friends knew she had given the president a copy of Nicholson Baker's "Vox" because her friends knew that she was much more than a person who would read a book about phone sex.) But when your browsing habits or e-mail messages are exposed to strangers, you may be reduced, in their eyes, to nothing more than the most salacious book you once read or the most vulgar joke you once told. And even if your Internet browsing isn't in any way embarrassing, you run the risk of being stereotyped as the kind of person who would read a particular book or listen to a particular song. Your public identity may be distorted by fragments of information that have little to do with how you define yourself. In a world where citizens are bombarded with information, people form impressions quickly, based on sound bites, and these brief impressions tend to oversimplify and misrepresent our complicated and often contradictory characters.

The sociologist Georg Simmel observed nearly 100 years ago that people are often more comfortable confiding in strangers than in friends, colleagues or neighbors. Confessions to strangers are cost-free because strangers move on; you never expect to see them again, so you are not inhibited by embarrassment or shame. In many ways the Internet is a technological manifestation of the phenomenon of the stranger. There's no reason to fear the disclosure of intimate information to faceless Web sites as long as those Web sites have no motive or ability to collate the data into a personally identifiable profile that could be disclosed to anyone you actually know. By contrast, the prospect that your real identity might be linked to permanent databases of your online—and off-line—behavior is chilling, because the databases could be bought, subpoenaed or traded by employers, insurance companies, ex-spouses and others who have the ability to affect your life in profound ways.

The retreat of DoubleClick may seem like a victory for privacy, but it is only an early battle in a much larger war—one in which many expect privacy to be vanquished. "You already have zero privacy—get over it," Scott McNealy, the C.E.O. of Sun Microsystems, memorably remarked last year in response to a question at a news conference introducing a new interactive technology called Jini. Sun's rosy Web site promises to usher in the "networked home" of the future, in which the company's "gateway" software will operate "like a congenial party host inside the home to help consumer appliances communicate intelligently with each other and with outside networks." In this chatty new world of electronic networking, your refrigerator and coffee maker can talk to your television, and all can be monitored from your office computer. The incessant information exchanged by these gossiping appliances might, of course, generate detailed records of the most intimate aspects of your daily life. Your liquor cabinet might tell Pinkdot.com, the online grocer, that you are low on whiskey, prompting your television to start blaring ads for Alcoholics Anonymous. But this may not be what Sun Microsystems has in mind when it boasts about the pleasures of the "connected family."

New evidence seems to emerge every day to support McNealy's grim ver- 10
dict about the triumph of online surveillance technology over privacy. A former colleague of mine who runs a Web site for political junkies recently sent me the "data trail" statistics that he receives each week. They disclose not only the Internet addresses of individual browsers who visit his site, clearly identifying their universities or corporate employers, but also the Web sites each user visited previously and the articles he or she downloaded there. And it is increasingly common to find programs in the workplace that report back to a central server all the Internet addresses that employees visit. After the respected dean of the Harvard Divinity School was forced to step down in 1998 for downloading pornography on his home computer, a former Harvard computer technician wrote an article for *Salon,* the online magazine, criticizing his former colleagues for snitching on the dean. "In the server room of one of my part-time jobs," the techie confessed, "I noticed that a program called Gatekeeper displayed all the Internet usage in the office as it happened. I sat and watched people send e-mail, buy and sell stocks on e-trade and download pictures of Celine Dion. If I had wanted I could have traced this usage back to the individual user."

A survey of nearly a thousand large companies conducted last year by the American Management Association found that 45 percent monitored the e-mail, computer files or phone calls of their workers, up from 35 percent two years earlier. Some companies use Orwellian computer software with names like Assentor or Investigator, available for as little as $99, that can monitor and record every keystroke on the computer with videolike precision. These virtual snoops can also be programmed to screen all incoming and outgoing e-mail for forbidden words and phrases—involving racism, body parts or the name of your boss—and can forward suspicious messages to a supervisor for review. E-mail can be resurrected from computer hard drives even after it has ostensibly been deleted. And companies are increasingly monitoring jokes and e-mail sent from home as well as work over company servers.

The most common justification for Internet and e-mail monitoring in the workplace is fear of liability under sexual harassment law, which requires companies to protect workers from speech that might be construed to create a "hostile or offensive working environment." Because employers can't be sure in advance what sort of e-mail or Web browsing a particular employee might find offensive, they have an incentive to monitor far more Internet activity than the law actually forbids.

Changes in the delivery of books, music and television are extending the technologies of surveillance beyond the office, blurring the boundaries between work and home. Last summer, for example, Amazon.com was criticized for a feature that uses ZIP codes and domain names to identify the most popular books purchased online by employees at prominent corporations. (The top choice at Charles Schwab: *Memoirs of a Geisha.*) And anonymous browsing continues to be under assault. The Sprint wireless Web phone that I bought in March promptly revealed my new telephone number to Amazon's preprogrammed Web site when I dialed in the hope of discreetly looking for ordering information about my new book.

The same technologies that are making it possible to download digitally stored books, CDs and movies directly onto our hard drives will soon make it possible for publishers and entertainment companies to record and monitor our browsing habits with unsettling specificity. "Snitchware" programs can track not only which books you read but also how many times you read them, charging different royalties based on whether you copy from the book or forward part of it to a friend. Television, too, is being redesigned to create precise records of our viewing habits. A new electronic device known as a personal video recorder makes it possible to store up to 30 hours of television programs; it also enables viewers to skip commercials and to create their own lineups. One of the current models, TiVo, establishes viewer profiles that it then uses to make viewing suggestions and to record future shows. And in a world where media conglomerates like AOL–Time Warner can monitor your activities in cyberspace and then use your browsing habits to determine the content that is beamed to you through television, books, movies and magazines, the integrated media box of the future may have surveillance capabilities that make DoubleClick's database look benign.

As if that weren't bad enough, Globally Unique Identifiers, or GUIDs, are 15
making it possible to link every document you create, message you e-mail and chat with your real-world identity. GUIDs are a kind of serial number that can be linked with your name and e-mail address when you register online for a product or service. Last November, RealJukebox, one of the most popular Internet music players, with 30 million registered users, became a focus of media attention when privacy advocates noted that the player could relay information to its parent company, RealNetworks, about the music each user downloaded, and that this could be matched with a unique ID number that pinpointed the user's identity. At a conference about privacy in cyberspace held at the Stanford

Law School in February, a lawyer for RealNetwork, Bob Kimball, insisted that the company had never, in fact, matched the GUIDs with the data about music preferences. Nevertheless, hours after the media outcry began, RealNetworks disabled the GUIDs to avoid a DoubleClick-like public relations debacle. But some currently available software products, like Microsoft's Word 97 and Powerpoint 97, embed unique identifiers into every document. Soon, all documents created electronically may have invisible markings that can be traced back to the author or recipient.

There is nothing new about the fear that technologies of surveillance and communication are altering the nature of privacy. A hundred years ago, in the most famous essay on privacy ever written, Louis D. Brandeis and Samuel Warren worried that new media technologies—in particular the invention of instant photographs and the tabloid press—were invading "the sacred precincts of private and domestic life." What outraged Brandeis and Warren was a mild society item in Boston's Saturday *Evening Gazette* that described a lavish breakfast party that Warren himself had put on for his daughter's wedding. Although the information wasn't inherently salacious, Brandeis and Warren were appalled that a domestic ceremony would be described in a gossip column and discussed by strangers.

At the beginning of the 21st century, the Internet has vastly expanded the aspects of private life that can be monitored and recorded. As a result, cyberspace has increased the danger that personal information originally disclosed to friends and colleagues may be exposed to, and misinterpreted by, a less-understanding audience. Gossip that in Brandeis and Warren's day might have taken place in a drawing room is now recorded in a chat room and can be retrieved years later anywhere on earth.

Several months ago, for example, the *Washington Post* described the case of James Rutt, a man who worried that his Internet past might be misconstrued if taken out of context. Rutt had spent years unburdening himself in a chat group. Although he had been happy to speak candidly in the sympathetic confines of a space characterized as "a virtual corner bar," once he was appointed to a new position as C.E.O. of Network Solutions Inc., he feared that his musings about sex, politics and his own weight problem might embarrass him, or worse. Fortunately for Rutt, the chat group offered a special software feature called Scribble that allowed him to erase a decade of his own postings. But as intimate information about our lives is increasingly recorded, archived and not easily deleted, there is a growing danger that a part of our identities will come to be mistaken for who we are.

In certain circles today it's not uncommon for prospective romantic partners, before going out on dates, to perform background checks on each other; scouring the Internet for as much personal information as possible. And these searches can be a deal-breaker: a friend of mine, after being set up on a blind date, ran an Internet search and discovered that her prospective partner had been described in an article for an online magazine as one of the 10 worst dates of all time; the article included intimate details about his sexual equipment and performance that she was unable to banish from her mind during their first—and only—dinner. These are the sorts of details, of course, that friends often exchange in informal gossip networks. The difference now is that the most intimate personal information is often recorded indelibly and can be retrieved with chilling efficiency by strangers around the globe.

In a famous essay on reputation published in 1890, E. L. Godkin, the edi- 20
tor of *The Nation,* elaborated on the distinction between oral and written gossip. As long as gossip was oral, and circulated among acquaintances rather than strangers, Godkin wrote, its objects were often spared the mortification of knowing they were being gossiped about. Oral gossip is a flexible way of enforcing communal norms while still respecting privacy. When neighbors gossip about one another's intimate activities, those who behave badly will soon feel the indirect effects of social disapproval. The wrongdoers can then correct their misbehavior without feeling that their public faces have been assaulted. And because all of the relevant parties know one another well based on close personal observation, individual transgressions can be weighed against the broader picture of an individual's personality.

Cyberspace, however, has blurred the distinction between oral and written gossip by recording and publishing the kind of private information that used to be exchanged around the water cooler. Unlike oral gossip, Internet gossip is hard to answer, because its potential audience is anonymous and unbounded. A Web site called *Disgruntled Housewife,* for example, offers an appalling feature designed to promote "girly solidarity through bile-spewing," in which women from around the country write in to describe the most intimate secrets of former lovers they dislike. (The men are identified by their hometowns and sometimes by their full names, a few letters of which are fatuously omitted.) Furthermore, when gossip is archived, it can come back to haunt you. If, in a moment of youthful enthusiasm, I posted intemperate comments to an Internet newsgroup, those comments could be retrieved years later simply by typing my name or Internet protocol address into a popular search engine.

For more and more citizens the most important way of exchanging gossip is e-mail. But instead of giving private e-mail the same legal protections as private letters, courts are increasingly treating e-mail as if it were no more private than a postcard. In an entirely circular legal test, the Supreme Court has held that constitutional protections against unreasonable searches depend on whether citizens have subjective expectations of privacy that society is prepared to accept as reasonable. This means that as technologies of surveillance and data collection have become ever more intrusive, expectations of privacy have naturally diminished, with a corresponding reduction in constitutional protections. More recently, courts have held that merely by adopting a written policy that warns employees that their e-mail may be monitored, employers will lower expectations of privacy in a way that gives them virtually unlimited discretion to monitor whatever they please.

Even when employers promise to respect the privacy of e-mail, courts are upholding their right to break their promises without warning. A few years ago in a case in Pennsylvania, the Pillsbury Company repeatedly promised its employees that all e-mail would remain confidential and that no employee would be fired based on intercepted e-mail. Michael Smyth, a Pillsbury employee, received an e-mail message from his supervisor over the company's computer network, which he read at home. Relying on the company's promise about the privacy of e-mail, he sent a heated reply to the supervisor, supposedly saying at one point that he felt like killing "the backstabbing bastards" on the sales force, and referring to a holiday party as the "Jim Jones Kool-Aid affair."

Despite the company's promises, it proceeded to retrieve from its computers dozens of e-mail messages that Smyth had sent and received, and then fired him for transmitting "inappropriate and unprofessional comments." Smyth sued, arguing that the company had invaded his right to privacy by firing him. But the court blithely dismissed his claim on the grounds that Pillsbury owned the computer system and therefore could intercept e-mail sent from home or work without invading its workers' legitimate expectations of privacy.

This can't be right. I'm at home as I type these words, but the computer on 25
which I'm typing is owned by the law school I teach at, as is the network that supplies my e-mail access. I would be appalled if anyone suggested that the provision of these research tools gave my law school the right to monitor all the e-mail I send and receive. In 1877, the Supreme Court held that postal inspectors need a search warrant to open first-class mail, regardless of whether it is sent from the office or from home. And searches of e-mail can be even more invasive than searches of written letters. Georg Simmel wrote about the ways in which written letters are peculiarly subject to misinterpretation. Because letters lack the contextual accompaniments—"sound of voice, tone, gesture, facial expression"—that, in spoken conversation, are a source of clarification, Simmel argued, letters can be more easily misinterpreted than speech. With e-mail, the possibilities for misinterpretation are even more acute. E-mail combines the intimacy of the telephone with the infinite retrievability of a letter. And because e-mail messages are often dashed off quickly, they may, when taken out of context, provide an inaccurate window onto someone's emotions.

In 1997, for example, Judge Thomas Penfield Jackson chose Lawrence Lessig of Harvard Law School to advise him in overseeing the antitrust dispute between the government and Microsoft. When Microsoft challenged Lessig's appointment as a "special master," Netscape officials turned over to the Justice Department an e-mail message that Lessig had written to an acquaintance at Netscape in which he joked that he had "sold my soul" by downloading Microsoft's Internet Explorer. The Justice Department, in turn, gave Lessig's e-mail to Microsoft, which claimed he was biased and demanded his resignation.

In fact, Lessig's e-mail had been quoted out of context. As the full text of the e-mail makes clear, Lessig had downloaded Microsoft's Internet Explorer to enter a contest to win a PowerBook. After installing the Explorer, he discovered that his Netscape bookmarks had been erased. In a moment of frustration, he fired off the e-mail to the Netscape acquaintance, whom he had met at a cyberspace conference, describing what had happened and quoting a Jill Sobule song that had been playing on his car stereo: "Sold my soul, and nothing happened." And although a court ultimately required Lessig to step down as special master for technical reasons having nothing to do with his misinterpreted e-mail, he discovered that strangers were left with the erroneous impression that the e-mail "proved" that he was biased, and that this forced him to resign. The experience taught Lessig that in a world where most electronic footsteps are recorded and all records can be instantly retrieved, it is very easy for sentiments to be taken out of their original context by people who want to do someone ill.

"The thing I felt most about the Microsoft case was not the actual invasion (as I said, I didn't really consider it an invasion)," Lessig wrote in an e-mail message to me after the ordeal. "What I hated most was that the issue was just not important enough for people to understand enough to understand the truth. It deserved one second of the nation's attention, but to understand the issue would have required at least a minute's consideration. But I didn't get, and didn't deserve, a minute's consideration. Thus, for most, the truth was lost." Lessig felt ill treated, in short, not because he wasn't able to explain himself, but because in a world of short attention spans, he was never given the chance. In what might be seen as poetic justice, Microsoft itself was embarrassed in the antitrust trial that followed when e-mail from top executives, from Bill Gates on down, was turned over to the government and introduced in court.

Unchastened by my friend Lessig's experience, I behave as if my online life isn't virtually transparent, even though I understand on some level that it is. Not long ago, I visited my law school's computer center to find out how many of my online activities were in fact being monitored. "If I happen to be in the server room, I can watch you send e-mail, and I'll know who you're sending it to," said the discreet head of the center. Beyond that, I was pleased to learn, the law school has decided not to install the programs that many companies use to monitor the browsing, reading and writing of their employees in real time, or to make regular copies of hard drives, including the cache files that record all the Internet documents a user has downloaded. But if I, like the former dean of Harvard Divinity School, asked school technicians to repair my home computer, the school would be able to reconstruct my personal and professional online activities with telescopic precision.

30 Perhaps the only sane response to the new technologies of surveillance in cyberspace is unapologetic paranoia. If so, my candidate for the perfectly rational man is K., one of my former students. K. wears green Army fatigues and black boots and spends much of his day shredding and covering his electronic tracks. "In my home office, I have five computers with AtGuard personal firewalls," he explained to me not long ago. "With AtGuard you can monitor how many backdoors you have open to the Internet, so if someone is spying on you with a hacking program like BackOrifice or NetBus, you can kill that connection." Whenever a Web site tries to send K. a cookie, AtGuard fires back a cookie that

says, "Keep your cookies off my hard drive." Aware that files and e-mail can be resurrected from his hard drive even after they are deleted, K. also uses a suite of security tools called Kremlin. Every time K. turns off his computer, Kremlin does a "secure total wipe" of his 20 gigabyte hard drive, scribbling electronic graffiti, in the form of zeroes and ones, over all the free space so that any lurking, partly deleted files will be rendered illegible. This takes more than an hour. K. also uses Kremlin to encrypt his personal documents in a secure folder on his hard drive, and he carefully chose a nonsense password, garbled with upper- and lowercase letters and numbers, so that it can't easily be cracked by a "brute force attack program" that might hypothetically bombard his computer with millions of random words generated from an electronic dictionary. Impressed by his vigilance, I asked K. what, precisely, he was trying to hide. "It's more an ideological act than anything else," he said. "I know that I can be surveilled at all times, so I feel like I have a responsibility to resist."

Not everyone agrees that there is reason to resist the brave new world of virtual exposure. This is, after all, an exhibitionistic culture in which people cheerfully enact the most intimate moments of their daily lives on Web cams and on Fox TV. It is a culture in which 2,000 confessional souls have chosen to post their most private thoughts on a site called Diarist.net, which boasts, "We've got everything you need to know all about the people who tell all." Defenders of transparency argue that there's no reason to worry about privacy if you have nothing to hide and that more information, rather than less, is the best way to protect us against being judged out of context. We might think differently about a Charles Schwab employee who ordered the eminently respectable *Memoirs of a Geisha* from Amazon.com, for example, if we knew that she also listened to the Doors and subscribed to *Popular Mechanics.*

But the defenders of transparency are confusing secrecy with privacy, and secrecy is only a small dimension of privacy. Even if we saw an Amazon.com profile of everything the Charles Schwab employee had read and downloaded this week, we wouldn't come close to knowing who she really is. (Instead, we would misjudge her in all sorts of new ways.) In a surreal world where complete logs of every citizen's reading habits were available on the Internet, the limits of other citizens' attention spans would guarantee that no one could focus long enough to read someone else's browsing logs from beginning to end. Instead, overwhelmed by information, citizens would change the channel or click to a more interesting Web site.

Even the most sophisticated surveillance technologies can't begin to absorb, analyze and understand the sheer volume of information. The F.B.I. recently asked Congress for $75 million to finance a series of surveillance systems, including a new project called Digital Storm, which will allow it to vastly expand its recordings of foreign and domestic telephone and cell-phone calls, after receiving judicial authorization.

But because it can't possibly hire enough agents to listen to the recordings from beginning to end, the F.B.I. plans to use "data mining" technology to search for suspicious key words. This greatly increases the risk that information will be taken out of context: as "60 Minutes" reported, an analyst at the Canadian Security Agency identified a mother as a potential terrorist after she told a friend on the phone that her son had "bombed" in his school play. Filtered or unfiltered, information taken out of context is no substitute for the genuine knowledge that can emerge only slowly over time.

Moreover, defenders of transparency have adopted a unified vision of human 35
personality, which views social masks as a way of misrepresenting the true self. But as the sociologist Erving Goffman argued in the 1960's, this view of personality is simplistic and misleading. Instead of behaving in a way that is consistent with a single character, people reveal different parts of themselves in different contexts. I may—and do—wear different social masks when interacting with my students, my editors, my colleagues and my dry cleaner. Far from being inauthentic, each of these masks helps me try to behave in a manner that is appropriate to the different roles demanded by these different social settings. If these masks were to be violently torn away, what would be exposed is not my true self but the spectacle of a wounded and defenseless man.

Goffman also maintained that individuals, like actors in a theater, need backstage areas where they can let down their public masks, tell dirty jokes, collect themselves and relieve the tensions that are an inevitable part of public performance. But in the new economy of information exchange, white-collar workers are increasingly forced to work under constant surveillance like the dehumanized hero of *The Truman Show,* a character who has been placed on an elaborate stage set without his knowledge or consent and whose every move, as he interacts with the actors who have been hired to play his friends and family, is broadcast by hidden video cameras.

The inhibiting effects on creativity and efficiency are palpable. Surveys of the health consequences of monitoring in the workplace suggest that electronically monitored workers experience higher levels of depression, tension and anxiety and lower levels of productivity than those who are not monitored. Unsure about when, precisely, electronic monitoring may take place, employees will necessarily be far more guarded and less spontaneous, and the increased formality of conversation and e-mail can make communication less efficient. Moreover, spying on people without their knowledge is an indignity. It fails to treat its objects as fully deserving of respect, and treats them instead like animals in a zoo, deceiving them about the nature of their own surroundings.

In *The Unbearable Lightness of Being,* Milan Kundera describes how the police destroyed an important figure of the Prague Spring by recording his conversations with a friend and then broadcasting them as a radio serial. Reflecting on his novel in an essay on privacy, Kundera writes, "Instantly Prochazka was discredited: because in private, a person says all sorts of things, slurs friends, uses coarse language, acts silly, tells dirty jokes, repeats himself, makes a companion laugh by shocking him with outrageous talk, floats heretical ideas he'd never admit in public and so forth." Freedom is impossible in a society that refuses to respect the fact that "we act different in private than in public," Kundera argues, a reality that he calls "the very ground of the life of the individual." By requiring citizens to live in glass houses without curtains, totalitarian societies deny their status as individuals, and "this transformation of a man from subject to object is experienced as shame."

A liberal state should respect the distinction between public and private speech because it recognizes that the ability to expose in some contexts aspects of our identity that we conceal in other contexts is indispensable to freedom, friendship and love. Friendship and romantic love can't be achieved without intimacy, and intimacy, in turn, depends upon the selective and voluntary disclosure of personal information that we don't share with everyone else. Also, as Kundera recognized, privacy is necessary for the development of human individuality. Any writer will understand the importance of reflective solitude in refining arguments and making unexpected connections. (In an odd but widely shared experience, many of us seem to have our best ideas when we are in the shower.) Indeed, studies of creativity show that it's during periods of daydreaming and seclusion that the most creative thought takes place, as individuals allow ideas and impressions to run freely through their minds without fear that their untested thoughts will be exposed and taken out of context.

40 It is surprising how recently changes in law and technology have been permitted to undermine sanctuaries of privacy that Americans have long taken for granted. Even more surprising has been our relatively tepid response to the new technologies of exposure. There is no reason to surrender to technological determinism; no reason to accept the smug conclusion of Silicon Valley that in the war between privacy and technology, privacy is doomed. On the contrary, a range of technological, legal and political responses might help us rebuild in cyberspace some of the privacy and anonymity that we demand in real space.

The most effective responses may be forms of self-help that allow citizens to cover their electronic tracks, along the lines of the Kremlin technology that my student K. uses to scour his hard drive or the Scribble technology that James Rutt used to erase his own chat. The fact that e-mail, for example, is hard to delete and easy to retrieve is partly a consequence of current technology, and technology can change. Companies with names like Disappearing Inc. and ZipLip have introduced a form of self-deleting e-mail that uses encryption technology to make messages nearly impossible to read soon after they are received. When I send you a message, Disappearing Inc. scrambles the e-mail with an encrypted key and then gives you the same key to unscramble it. I can specify how long I want the key to exist, and after the key is destroyed, the message can't be read without a herculean code-breaking effort.

At the moment, the most advanced technology of anonymity and pseudonymity in cyberspace is offered by companies like Zero-Knowledge Systems, which is based in Montreal. For a modest fee, you can disaggregate your identity with a software package called Freedom, which initially gives you five digital pseudonyms, or "nyms," that you can assign to different activities, from discussing politics to surfing the Web. (Why any of us needs five pseudonyms isn't entirely clear, but the enthusiasm of the privacy idealists is sweet in its way.) On the Freedom system, no one, not even ZeroKnowledge itself, can trace your pseudonyms back to your actual identity.

"You can trust us because we're not asking you to trust us," says Austin Hill, Zero-Knowledge's 26-year-old president. Hill has a messianic air about his role in vindicating what he considers to be the universal human rights of privacy, free speech and the possibility of redemption in a world where youthful errors can follow you for the rest of your life. "Twenty years from now, I'm going to be able to talk to my grandkids and say I played an instrumental role in making the world a better place," he says. "As the Blues Brothers say, everyone here feels that we're on a mission from God."

Freedom makes traceability difficult by encrypting e-mail and Web-browsing requests and sending them through at least three intermediary routers on the way to their final destinations: each message is wrapped like an onion in three layers of cryptography, and each router can peel off only one layer of the onion to learn the next stop in the path of the message. Because no single router knows both the source of the message and its destination, the identity of the sender and the recipient is difficult to link. Zero-Knowledge assigns pseudonyms using the same technology, and so the company itself can't link the pseudonyms to individual users; if it is subpoenaed it can only turn over a list of its customers, who can hope for anonymity in numbers.

But should people be forced to resort to esoteric encryption technology 45
with names like ZipLip and Zero-Knowledge every time they want to send e-mail or browse the Web? Until anonymous browsers become widespread enough to be socially acceptable, their Austin Powers–like aura may deter all but the most secretive users who have something serious to hide. Moreover, every technological advance for privacy will eventually provoke a technological response. For this reason, some privacy advocates, like Marc Rotenberg, the director of the Electronic Privacy Information Center, argue that anonymity on the Internet should be a legal right, rather than something achieved with a commercial product.

Americans increasingly seem to agree that Congress should save us from the worst excesses of online profiling. In a *Business Week*/Harris poll conducted last month, 57 percent of the respondents said that the government should pass laws regulating how personal information can be collected and used on the Internet. The European Union, for example, has adopted the principle that information gathered for one purpose can't be sold or disclosed for another purpose without the consent of the individual concerned. But efforts to pass comprehensive privacy legislation in the United States have long been thwarted by a political reality: the beneficiaries of privacy—all of us, in the abstract—are anonymous and diffuse, while the corporate opponents of privacy are well organized and well heeled.

In the hope that the political tide may be turning, Senator Robert Torricelli has introduced a bill that would forbid a Web site to collect or sell personal data unless users checked a box allowing it to do so. This "opt in" proposal has been vigorously and successfully resisted by the e-commerce lobby, which insists that it would cripple the use of online profiling and cause advertising revenues to plummet.

The e-commerce lobby prefers a more modest Senate proposal that would require Web sites to display a clearly marked box allowing users to "opt out" of data collection and resale. But it's not clear that "opt out" proposals would provide meaningful protection for privacy. Many users, when confronted with boilerplate privacy policies, tend to click past them as quickly as teenage boys click past the age certification screens on X-rated Web sites.

Moreover, many people seem happy to waive their privacy rights in exchange for free stuff. There is now a cottage industry of companies that offer their users product discounts, giveaways or even cash in exchange for permission to track, record and profile every move they make, and to bombard them with targeted ads on the basis of their proclivities.

This is about as rational as allowing a camera into your bedroom in exchange 50
for a free toaster. But as Monica Lewinsky discovered, it's easy to forget why privacy is important until information you care about is taken out of context, and by that point, it's usually too late. "One of the things that I was a little bit disappointed about," Lewinsky told Larry King, "was that people didn't seem to pay too much attention about their privacy issues." In the latest indignity for Lewinsky, some of her previously undisclosed e-mail messages to Betty Currie may have surfaced a few weeks ago, when the White House announced that it had discovered backup computer tapes. In cyberspace, as in cheap horror movies, your ghosts can rise up to haunt you just when you think the danger has passed.

There is no single solution to the erosion of privacy in cyberspace: no single law that can be proposed or single technology that can be invented to stop the profilers and surveillants in their tracks. The battle for privacy must be fought on many fronts—legal, political and technological—and each new assault must be vigilantly resisted as it occurs. But the history of political responses to new technologies of surveillance provides some grounds for hope. Although Americans are seldom roused to defend privacy in the abstract, the most illiberal and intrusive technologies of surveillance have, in fact, provoked political outrage that has forced the data collectors to retreat. In 1967, after the federal government proposed to create a national data center that would store personal information from the I.R.S., the census and labor bureaus and the Social Security administration, Vance Packard wrote an influential article for this magazine that helped to kill the plan.

We are trained in this country to think of all concealment as a form of hypocrisy. But we are beginning to learn about how much may be lost in a culture of transparency—the capacity for creativity and eccentricity, for the development of self and soul, for understanding, friendship and even love. Perhaps someday we will look back with nostalgia on a society that still believed opacity was possible and was shocked to discover what happened when it was not. There is nothing inevitable about the erosion of privacy in cyberspace, however, just as there is nothing inevitable about its reconstruction. We have the ability to rebuild some of the private spaces we have lost. What we need now is the will.

Destroying E-Commerce's "Cookie Monster" Image

TOM CATTAPAN

"Without responsible actions, this medium can go away as quickly as it came."
JERRY YANG, FOUNDER OF YAHOO!

WHEN YOU think about it, it's all about who you can trust with your cookies. Growing up we learn who we can tell our secrets to and who we cannot tell. If you guess wrong, suddenly everyone knows who you have a crush on, or that you're actually a Cubs fan. But if that person keeps your secret, you're well on your way to building a new friendship. 1

For e-commerce to succeed, online marketers must successfully build trust with millions of consumers. According to a Louis Harris & Associates study of 1,009 participants, 61 percent of non-Internet users say that privacy concerns keep them from going online. William Daley, U.S. Secretary of Commerce, has said "more than 80 percent of Americans are concerned about threats to their privacy online." And this past January, DoubleClick, one of the fast growing Internet advertising companies, was sued by a woman who believes her privacy rights were violated. Privacy, more than bandwidth or any other Internet issue, is e-commerce's greatest hurdle.

One of the major concerns about Internet privacy involves the use of Internet cookies to track consumers on the Web. Use and knowledge of these cookies are growing among businesses and Internet users. Cookies can provide a wealth of information to marketers and has unfortunately created a load of anxiety for consumers. The hope is to teach consumers the benefits of using Internet cookies and self-regulating businesses to use the information they gather ethically, fairly, and with the permission of the consumer. How this can be done is the focus of this article. But first, what exactly is an Internet cookie?

A COOKIE'S INGREDIENTS

Cookies are unique, small pieces of text that are created by a Web site and sent to a computer's hard drive. When the same visitor returns to the Web site, it grabs the cookie from the computer and recalls the information provided previously. Without cookies, Internet administrators do not know who is a new visitor, what visitors come back, how often they come back, where they went, and what they came to see. This lack of information makes it difficult to improve sites and make them more profitable. So sites place cookies to identify users as repeaters or new visitors and to research what visitors want from them.

"COOKIE MONSTERS" ARE NOT SCIENCE FICTION

5 Cookies are created as anonymous tracking numbers. Marc Rotenberg, director of Electronic Privacy Information Center (EPIC), is quoted in *Internetweek* saying, "If the user is not actually ID-ed (tagged), there's no real privacy issue." The problem occurs when marketers match their customer databases with the databases they get from the cookies.

This is just what DoubleClick has started to do. This past November, they paid Abacus Direct Corp. $1.7 billion for its list of catalog purchasers' names and addresses. They then linked these names with their cookies so they not only knew where these people are online, but where they live, who they are, and what their phone number is. This sent a woman from Marion County, California, crying foul. She says she doesn't want her personal information sold without her consent, but DoubleClick argues that they have given consumers notice and that they give consumers the option to opt-out of giving personal information.

However, some privacy advocates say that Web site privacy policies are not clear enough or adhered to by the creators. This is when consumers start to see Internet marketers as monsters selfishly gathering cookies.

Even with these positive steps online marketers have made in regards to consumer privacy, there are still some legitimate concerns that consumers have regarding cookie usage. Many companies are using cookies to simply keep better track of their consumers so that they can better assist them. However, others may sell this information to other marketers, which many consumers consider an invasion of privacy.

CAUGHT WITH THEIR HAND IN THE COOKIE JAR

In 1998, GeoCities was caught by the Federal Trade Commission for releasing personal details about its customers, which was in violation with its own privacy policy. The company gave "optional" information supplied by its users to a third party. Brace Zanca, the vice president of communications for GeoCities, said that the incident was a mistake and that it was rectified quickly. The site now has a revised privacy policy and has a link to the FTC's site.

10 America Online released sensitive information about one of its customers in 1998. In doing so, AOL is considered to have violated the Electronic Communications Privacy Act, which prohibits most disclosures of personal information by Internet services. This is not the only time online services have been accused of giving away personal information. Can AOL and other giants keep apologizing?

THE BIGGEST COOKIE OF THEM ALL

Intel caused controversy by placing a unique identifying number on its Pentium III processors. Such a number could be used to track a user's presence on the Internet. Privacy activists called for a boycott of the Pentium III and the state of Arizona was going to outlaw the sale of the chips in that state. Intel, in reaction, gave a solution within a matter of hours. A software utility would allow consumers to leave the number off permanently. However, some privacy advocates still fear the ID number.

"It's still there," according to Jason Catlett, president of Junkbusters Corporation. He said in an *Electronic News* article, "We're still considering whether it is sufficiently dangerous to leave it in at all." The fear is that somehow it will get turned back on, and all of a user's movements can be tracked on the Internet by anyone who knows how to read the ID number Intel planted.

ARE WE BECOMING "COOKIE MONSTERS"?

The Louis Harris & Associates survey found that 82 percent of net users believe that "consumers have lost all control over how personal information about them is collected and used by companies." This remains the same from a similar survey done in 1995. Consumers feel they are losing control, but they do not know what to do to stop it or what the benefits of sharing information are.

Although only 28 percent of respondents knew what an online cookie referred to, once given an explanation, 85 percent of all respondents believe that "telling users in advance how the cookie tagging will be used and what benefits it could offer" is "very" or "somewhat important." As consumers learn more and more about the capabilities of cookies, it is important that they know the benefits and the concerns they create.

WHERE THE COOKIE CRUMBS CAN LEAD

Cookies can be more than just a treat for marketers; it can help both consumers and marketers communicate more effectively. By using Internet cookies we can: 15

1. Target ads that are relevant to specific consumers needs and interests.

Not only will marketers get a higher ROI with more targeted ads, consumers will no longer be bothered by hundreds of unnecessary, bothersome ads. Instead they will receive messages that are relevant to them. Surfing the net and only viewing relevant ads could be the future of Internet banner ads and possibly interactive television.

Infoseek, the second ranked search engine behind Yahoo!, has worked with Aptex Inc. to develop InfoMatch, a program that uses cookies to find people with a lilting for the advertised product or history of clicking on similar ads. Infoseek's targeted InfoMatch banner ads have led to a 10 percent click-through rate. Untargeted click-through rates have dropped to 0.5 percent. "Personalization techniques" are what experts insist will be essential for Internet commerce to blossom. By using cookies, ads will be better targeted and will lead to higher response rates and more advertisers going to companies like Infoseek.

2. Prevent repetitive banner ads.

Cookies also come from the ad banners that appear within a Web page. For 20
example, if you are visiting Yahoo! and a banner ad for Amazon.com shows up, a cookie may be placed by the bookstore. These cookies were placed by Internet Marketing companies like Focalink Inc., DoubleClick, Inc., and the Interse Corp. These companies can use cookies to make sure an Internet user does not have to see the same ads over and over. The effectiveness of a banner ad drops significantly after the first viewing and close to zero after the sixth. Cookies let sites count how many times visitors have seen their banner ad and how many times, if any, they have clicked it.

3. Better understand the habits of consumer behavior.

This data can also work on more than just an individual basis. Information technology departments are working with marketers to understand consumer behavior. By compiling data on hundreds of thousands of consumers, advanced data miners, such as NCR Inc. and Sift Inc., can anticipate and react to high volume traffic. Jeff Wilkins, president of Sift Inc., said in an *Internetweek* article, "What the Internet allows for direct marketers is to go through data in a much finer granularity than we could before." This will enable marketers to better meet the needs of all consumers.

WHERE THE COOKIE CRUMBS END

Although cookies can be very helpful in tracking people's use of a site, Internet cookies are not made by the Keebler Elves. Many consumers have myths about what cookies can do. Cookies cannot:

Read cookies from other sites.

Steal information from a hard drive.

Plant viruses that would destroy the hard drive.

Track movements from one site to another site.

Take credit card numbers without permission.

Lastly, cookies cannot track to find out names, addresses, and other personal information unless consumers have provided such information voluntarily.

In other words, cookies do not track people, as much as they track the 25
cookie crumbs the site has previously laid. Some consumers fear giving voluntary information because they are concerned marketers will use their information improperly and become "cookie monsters."

UNCLE SAM WANTS TO KILL THE "COOKIE MONSTER"

When computer users were asked their views regarding "how personal information can be collected and used on the Internet," 58 percent of them said "yes" to government regulation. This has prompted representatives and senators into action. The United States Congress is working on 250 bills on Internet related issues, and 80 of those are to protect consumer privacy.

Some of the bills currently pending government action include the Consumer Internet Privacy Protection Act (H.R. 313), which would regulate use of subscribers' personally identifiable information by interactive computer services. Vice President Gore's Privacy Working Group has been working with the Interactive Service Association (ISA), which allows online services to sell subscriber names as long as they notify before enrollment. Sites must also provide easy opt-out methods for subscribers. Their proposal only allows "names, addresses, and broad usage patterns" to be exchanged. "No list may include data on individual session activities." This would narrow the amount of information marketers could receive, but would keep the door open for cookies if consumers agree to let them be used.

The FTC did a survey in 1998 of 1,400 Web sites that are "likely to be of interest to consumers" to find out how many had privacy statements. It found that 92 percent of sites collect some kind of personal information. Only 14 percent of them (also noted by fellow contributor Fred Newell) provide any type of notice as to what they will do with the information. The FTC did not pose any questions as to what the sites did with any cookies they collected. In March of 1999, President Clinton appointed Peter Swire, Ohio State University law professor and prolific author on privacy, to coordinate the administration's position on Internet Privacy.

CHILDREN ARE NOT AFRAID OF THIS MONSTER

There is a growing concern that children will give information voluntarily to Web sites. Over 11 million 2-to-17-year-olds were estimated to be online in 1998. With 97 percent of net parents agreeing that sites "should not ask children for their names and addresses to buy products or to register for a site," most online marketers are avoiding targeting kids on the Internet.

However, with $24 billion spent on advertising for ages 4 to 12 in 1997, In- 30
ternet advertisers are taking the plunge. Already the Children's Television Workshop Web site has a few ads, and Nickelodeon's Web site has links to Web pages like GapKids. As a response to this outcry, the government started to send warnings to marketers. Last October, these warnings turned into laws.

Starting on April 21, 2000, the FTC's new privacy rules to protect kids will have taken effect. These roles require that Web sites get parental permission before collecting information from kids. The rules give a "sliding scale" of acceptable ways to gather information. If the information is going to be given to a third party, or displayed in a public setting, then there must be written consent that has been sent to the [site] either via the post office or a fax. If sent electronically, the parent must give a pin, credit card or digital signature. However, if the information is for internal use only, the consent can be sent via e-mail but the site must be able to insure that it really is the parent giving consent.

If this is the future of government regulation, it's not just marketers who are going to be getting a headache. Every household will have to send letters and e-mails to let sites know it is permissible for the child to visit their site. This is a sign that the trust between consumers and marketers doesn't look too healthy.

"People will stop shopping if their data is abused," said Daley, the Secretary of Commerce. He later added, "I want self-regulation to work, but if it doesn't, we'll have to consider other options." Some other countries are already considering those options.

THEY SAY "KUCHEN," WE SAY "COOKIE"

Privacy policies vary by different nations. With e-commrce being a global venture, an international privacy alliance may be necessary. The European Union has already formed their set of rules in the "European Union Data Directive" which went into implementation in October of 1998. The EU is threatening to take U.S. businesses to court if they do not adhere to their policies.

In the book, *Civilizing Cyberspace,* the director of Privacy International, Si- 35
mon Davies, said, "The U.S. stands alone as an example of what a superpower should not do in privacy." The EU has adopted strict privacy policies to avoid marketers from obtaining too much information from consumers. In the U.S. some consumers are taking matters into their own hands.

FOR THOSE ON A COOKIE-FREE DIET

Consumers are not waiting for the government or self-regulation. Some are searching out ways of deleting cookies so they can keep their anonymity. There are a number of ad blockers or cookie-busters available for downloading. Some are available at www.download.com. Ad blockers include Zero-Knowledge systems, Freedom 1.0 Atgaurd, Adwipe, and Junkguard. Going through the Web site www.anonymizer.com will not stop cookies, but it will allow you to surf the Internet while withholding your IP address and other information about yourself. Another example is Cookie Pal, which asks each time a cookie appears whether or not you want to accept it. These blockers range from free to $20.

Jason Catlett, who distributes Junkguard, estimated in a 1998 *Star Tribune* article that less than 1 percent of all online users use software that blocks cookies. Usually, this is because consumers have never heard about them or don't want to download the software. Those who don't want to see banner ads are most likely not going to click on them; therefore, consumers who use ad blockers may be doing marketers a favor by cutting themselves out of circulation. This is similar to consumers on direct marketers' "don't call" or "don't mail" lists.

There are disadvantages and limitations to what cookies can do for marketers. Marketing directly to consumers by addressing them by name and reciting their past purchase history can come off as being a bit eerie. Amazon.com greets repeat consumers on their home page by giving their name and a list of recommended books based on their previous selections. However, one book purchase doesn't necessarily indicate a consumer is interested in that topic. But one book will show up as part of a purchase history and effect a cookie profile on Amazon.com. Cookies may not always be the solution to marketers, but they can be a treat.

COOKIES AS TREATS

With so much debate over whether or not cookies are ethical, should online marketers abandon them? If cookie use came to an end, advertisers would have a difficult time targeting their ads. One of the major complaints among Internet users is that ads are junk that they are not interested in seeing.

Consumers also must remember that the ads are paying for the Web site. 40
Bob Colvin, who runs Interactive Media Partners, says the Internet is "now a mass medium. Who's going to pay for it? It's not subscription fees, or the government. It's got to be the advertising." The Internet's growth is a result of online ads subsidizing its content. This leads to another philosophical question asked by Beth Snyder of *Advertising Age*. "Because consumers are getting Web sites for free, are they obligated to view them?" Cookie busters are blocking the ads that pay the cost of producing and updating sites for users to view.

The solution is creating banner ads that are "clickable," ads that consumers will be interested in seeing. If cookies became more sophisticated, they would be able to better target consumers and provide more relevant ads while eliminating the junk.

Cookies are one of the best ways to find out consumer wants and needs. However, marketers need to place cookies with the consumer's consent.

HOW CONSUMERS LIKE THEIR COOKIES

Consumers want: (1) easy to use software tools that would allow them to chose what personal information they will give; and (2) to be able have input regarding how sites could be made acceptable. Consumers would like some choice over how much and what kind of information they give to online stores.

A July of 1999 Harris Interactive Poll found that 68 percent of Internet users said that they would provide personal information in order to receive tailored banner ads, if notice and opt-out were provided. A similar 1997 Louis Harris & Associates study showed that 78 percent of computer users who buy products on the Internet would be "very" or "somewhat interested" in a software tool that would check the [site's] privacy policy and inform the user if it meets their privacy preferences. Consumers want cookies as treats, not as a forced commodity.

CREATING A BRAND YOU CAN TRUST WITH YOUR COOKIES

Even though the majority of computer users would like to see government 45
regulation, 70 percent of computer users favor voluntary policies over legislative rules for consumer privacy protection. The Online Privacy Alliance was formed in June of 1998 by 50 companies to form a self-regulatory policy for Internet companies. Since then, they have decided to use a seal system to promote Web sites with fair privacy policies. One of the most established seal programs is TRUSTe, founded in 1997 by the Electronic Frontier Foundation. Seals are only given to sites that promote TRUSTe's three goals for e-commerce and abide by their policies. TRUSTe's goals are to:

Give online consumers control over their personal information.

Provide Web publishers with standardized, cost effective solutions to satisfy businesses and address consumer's anxiety over sharing information.

Provide governmental regulators with evidence that the industry can self-regulate.

The TRUSTe's logo is a link to the site's own privacy policy. These policies must be in compliance with TRUSTe's established policies, which are:

Implementing a policy that factors in the goals of the site as well as consumers['] anxiety over sharing information.

Posting notice and disclosure of collection and practices of personal data.

Giving users a choice over how their personal data will be used and shared.

Putting data security and quality measures in place to safeguard, update, and correct personal information.

These policies comply with the fair information practices of the FTC, the U.S. Department of Commerce, and associations and organizations involved with privacy concerns. An estimated 80 percent of Web traffic is on pages that are members of this alliance. With that much of the Web market, e-commerce appears to be on its way to self-regulation.

Two-thirds of online consumers say they would increase their purchases on the Internet if sites contained seals of approvals that would be given by a "reputable business rating service." Although this survey did not specifically spell out TRUSTe, it does bring hope that such organizations can lead to better communication between online marketers and consumers.

MAY I DUNK MY OREO? PERMISSION MARKETING

Communication between consumers and marketers can make marketing on the Web a very exciting phenomenon. By asking consumers if marketers can obtain specific information from them, consumers can decide what is in their best interest, and marketers can have smaller, more useful lists of relevant consumers. One of the most difficult aspects of direct marketing has been finding a profitable list. If consumers have openly asked for information, marketers are going to have higher ROI over standard lists.

50 TRUSTe and the FTC are suggesting this same idea of asking for voluntary information. Permission marketing asks potential consumers if a site can use cookies so that marketers can better meet their needs later in the future. Permission marketing can make marketing on the Internet personal and relevant. It gives consumers power. It is what will make interactive advertising work or fall apart. It all depends on trust.

BUILDING A TWO-WAY PRIVATE BRIDGE LEADING TO A MINT OF COOKIES

Imagine a bridge built out of trust. The bridge connects online consumers and marketers. The more trust that's built, the faster the information flows on the bridge. If the information superhighway is going to become a fast, resourceful medium, advertisers are going to have to give financial support to pave it. Just as television and radio need advertising dollars, so does the Internet.

What makes the Internet different is its ability to specifically target individuals through one-to-one marketing. Messages can be sent individually, catered to each person's needs and wants. This means less waste for marketers and no more annoying "junk" ads for consumers. This relationship, just like any relationship, is built on trust and communication. Any break in communication can lead to distrust, which may cause the bridge to shake. And if the bridge shakes enough, it may crumble. Just like a cookie.

BIBLIOGRAPHY

Alster, Norm, Amy Bores, Heather Green, and Catherine Yang (2000), "Privacy: Outrage on the Web." *Business Week* (February 14) 38–40.

Barrett, Neil (1997), *Advertising on the Internet.: How to Get Your Message Across on the World Wide Web*, London: Kogan. 67–69.

Beaven, Colin (1997), "They're Watching You." *Esquire* (August) 104.

Brady, Regina, Edward Forrest, and Richard Mizerski, (1997) *Cybermarketing: Your Interactive Consultant*, Chicago: NTC. 296–298.

Bridis, Ted (1998), "What Price the Internet: Ads or No Ads?" *Star Tribune* (August 27) 1998.

Buckler, Grant (1998), "Web Sites Often Put the Bite on Net Cookies," *Computer Dealer News* (October 19) 20.

Croot, Andrea (1998), "Who's Watching the Web? With Concern over Online Privacy Growing, the AAF Has Joined an Industry Group Committed to Developing Effective Self-Regulatory Policies." *American Advertising* (Fall) 11–16.

Furger, Roberta (1998), "Look Out—You Are Being Followed." *PC World* (October) 33.

Godin, Seth (1998), "The Power of Permission." *The DMA Insider* (Fall) 20–23.

Gross, Neil, and Ira Sager (1999), "Caution Signs Along the Road: Business, Consumers, and Techies are Grappling With the Net's Perils." *Business Week* (June 22) 166–68.

Harris, Louis, and Associates (1997), "Internet Privacy Survey." *Privacy & American Business* (July, August) 1–11.

Hesseldahl, Ark (1999), "Inlet Bows to Privacy Protests on Pentium IIL." *Electronic News* (February 1) 43.

Kent, Andrew (1997), "It's Hot!" *Australian Accountant* (March) 73.

Kenworthy, Karen (1998), "Cookie Crumbs." *Windows Magazine* (September) 205.

Kuchinskas, Susan (1998), "In Web Sites We Trust?: As E-Commerce Grows, So Does Concern About Privacy." *Adweek* (February 15) 48, 50.

Lewis, Anne. "Victory for Privacy." *FamilyPC.* (March 2000) 93.

Mand, Adrienne (1998), "It's None of Your Business." *Adweek* (October 1998) 54–56.

McAllester, Matthew (1998), "Identity Crisis." *Newsday* (September 30), C3–C4.

McCullagh, Declan, and James Glave (1999), "Clinton Tabs Privacy Point Man." *Wired News* (March 3).

Miller, Steven (1996), *Civilizing Cyberspace*, New York: ACM. 272–73, 312–13.

Mosquera, Mary (1999), "Tech Bills on Target in Congress." *CMPnet* (February 17).

Moozakis, Chuck (1998), "New Company Sifts through Internet Data." *Internetweek* (March 30) 39.

Opel, Darren, D. (1999), "Privacy and the Internet." *Healthcare Executive* (January/ February) 53.

Petersen, Andrea (1999), "Price of Internet Banner Ads Slips as Web Sites Proliferate." *Wall Street Journal* (February 24) B8.

Shachtman, Noah (1998), "Get Personal: Business Sites Are Trying to Match Products and Services More Closely to Customers Needs. Is it Working?" *Internetweek* (November 2) 36.

Sprenger, Polly (1998), "Sun on Privacy: 'Get Over It.'" *Wired News* (January 26).

Sullivan, Eamonn (1996) "Are Web-Based Cookies a Treat or a Recipe for Trouble?" *PC Week* (June 24) 75.

Weissman, Rachel X. (1998), "The Kids Are All Right—They're Just a Little Converged." *American Demographics* (December) 30–32.

Zimmerman, Jan, and Michael Mathiesen (1998), *Marketing on the Internet Gulf Breeze,* Maximum Press, ix.

Web sites mentioned include:

www.TRUSTe.org

www.download.com

www.anonomizer.com.

ETHICAL ISSUES RELATED TO CLONING

Recent advances in biomedical technology raise many ethical issues. As scientists refine the processes of cloning and engineering genes, the question of whether human genes should be cloned or engineered is an obvious concern. But cloning involves many other potential problems as well. The following essays examine some of these ethical issues. "The Last Taboo" is an editorial written for *New Scientist,* a British science magazine. In this essay, the editorial writers wonder whether refined techniques in genetic engineering might eventually reverse the public's opposition to engineering human genes. The second essay, "Of Mice, Jellyfish, and Us," is an editorial for *Commonweal,* a magazine that discusses controversial social issues primarily for an educated American Catholic audience. In this essay, the authors argue that although scientists involved in genetic engineering face serious ethical questions, they resist doing anything to answer them. In "Could a Clone Ever Run for President?" *Time* magazine writer Michael Lemonick takes a sideways look at the cloning debate, setting science aside for the moment to wonder what the possibility of cloning humans might mean for a presidential election in 2044. The final two essays in this section examine whether people could or should use genetic engineering to preserve their favorite pets. "Clone of Silence" was written for the *New York Times Magazine* by Margaret Talbot, senior fellow at the New America Foundation, an organization devoted to bringing new ideas and new voices to the forefront of American public discourse. Talbot examines efforts to clone animals to replace family pets and preserve endangered species. She asks whether the commonplace cloning of animals might be the first step toward genetically reproduced humans. In "Clone-a-Friend," first published in *New Scientist,* Oliver Morton offers his reflections on the cloning of pets and what this procedure might mean for the cloning of humans.

The Last Taboo

NEW SCIENTIST

FIRST IT WAS transgenic lab mice. Then came the pigs with humanised or- 1
gans and Dolly the sheep. Now there is talk of creating artificial life forms from scratch. So relentless has the march of biomedicine become that even the experts are locked in a perpetual game of catch-up.

The latest development offers no respite for the footsore. Indeed, even hardened observers could be forgiven for blinking at the news that scientists have invented [an] artificial chromosome that can be inserted into the cells of mammals and passed from one generation to the next.

At first glance the invention might look like no more than a neat trick for genetically engineering laboratory mice or farm animals. But there are good grounds for thinking it represents far more than this. The research to date is based on mice. But if human versions of these—or similar—chromosomes were inserted into human embryos, they and their children and their children's children would all inherit them. The chromosomes, and any genes they carry, would enter our gene pool.

That sounds pretty scary. Should we be alarmed? As ever, there are no easy answers. So far, genetic experiments on humans have been limited to altering genes in small numbers of cells—in the lungs, say—of patients with serious illnesses. Such changes are often temporary and can never be passed on. People have talked about introducing genetic changes that could be inherited. But so far, that is all it's been: talk.

One obvious reason for this is that many ethicists, scientists and govern- 5
ments fear genetic engineering would put us on a slippery slope to a nightmare world of superhumans and designer babies. But there's another reason why it's been all talk and no action—the techniques for manipulating embryos have so far been too haphazard to use on humans. Artificial chromosomes could change that. If they fulfill their promise, they could revolutionise scientists' ability to genetically engineer embryos. They may never make the outcome totally predictable, but they could make it safe enough to ease the worst fears about genetic accidents.

And that could change perceptions. It's easy to say genetic engineering should simply never be carried out on humans when the technology is so primitive nobody would dream of using it. But when more reliable techniques exist, dogmatic opposition becomes harder to maintain. More people begin to think the unthinkable and imagine scenarios in which human genetic engineering might be justified.

Should anything be done? The kneejerk response would be to impose a blanket ban on research using artificial chromosomes in human tissues. This would be a bad move for several reasons.

First, Europe already has what amounts to a ban on genetically engineering human embryos, while the US Food and Drug Administration has said it will not approve such experiments without a major public debate. Secondly, a ban would prevent researchers from using the chromosomes in conventional gene therapy, or worse still, drive research underground.

And finally, there is a growing feeling among some scientists that engineering human embryos might actually be our best hope of dealing with some inherited diseases. This is partly because gene therapy is proving harder than anyone imagined, and partly because the initial horror of human genetic engineering is beginning to fade.

It may be naive to think the public is out of step with this trend. In polls, a 10
sizable minority consistently say they would accept human genetic engineering for the treatment of serious illnesses. If artificial chromosomes really can be made safe, their invention could nudge more people this way. As for designer babies, nobody is going to approve of them in the abstract. But if you ask would-be parents if they'd like to give their children a head-start at school or on the athletics track, don't be too surprised to find that the opposition is less than absolute.

For all these reasons, it would be a mistake to expect the taboo on human genetic engineering to last forever. Some day someone will want to try it. The invention of artificial chromosomes doesn't make that desirable—only people can make that judgment. But it does add to the forces that are now beginning to make it seem inevitable.

As for taboos, they are simply a bad excuse for not thinking.

Of Mice, Jellyfish, and Us

COMMONWEAL

1

ONE OF THE great challenges of the twenty-first century will be our response to the combined power of new reproductive technologies and manipulation of the human gene. Two recent news stories illustrate the heart of the problem: scientists recognize they now face serious ethical problems but continue to do more or less nothing about them.

A *New York Times* story (December 23, 1999) reports a successful experiment in which jellyfish genes were mixed with the sperm cells of the rhesus monkey. The sperm, subsequently injected into monkey eggs, bypassed the natural fertilization process, allowing the jellyfish gene to enter the monkey egg. This process produced monkey embryos carrying the jellyfish gene. How do scientists know their experiment worked? One-third of the embryos glowed when a fluorescent light was shone on them; in another experiment, eleven of fifty-seven mice born through the same technique had green-glowing tails. This is scientific progress?

Some scientists think so. These seemingly modest developments in reproductive technology may eventually pave the way for sophisticated programs of genetic engineering, ultimately with human genes. Technical difficulties remain to actually inserting a human gene, for example, into a mouse egg, or the even more humanly compatible pig egg. We are promised, however, that these techniques will help in the development of spare human organs. And someday inserting a modified gene into a human egg could reduce susceptibility to diseases such as AIDS or Alzheimer's. Who can doubt that when it can be done, it will be done? Progress and profits beckon.

Of course, all of this lies in the future. But not wholly, for these reproductive techniques work their way into human medicine in the form of infertility treatments. The direct insertion of a single sperm into an egg is already possible and some ten to twenty thousand efforts a year are made on human eggs. But as the jellyfish experiments showed, direct insertion of sperm into an egg provides none of the protective functions of natural fertilization that separate the sperm's outer protein coat (and extraneous matter such as viruses) from its genetic material. Who knows what children born of such techniques may have floating around as extraneous genetic or viral material? Not jellyfish genes, we hope. 5

Consider the second story. Remember Dolly the clone, that singular sheep and media sensation of 1997?

She has been surpassed. A prize Japanese bull has been cloned from skin cells scraped from its own ear (*New York Times,* January 5, 2000). Four calves were produced with far greater efficiency and less expense than the cumbersome technique that produced Dolly. But they haven't gotten the attention she did—where are the baby pictures? For experiments creating cloned calves and jellyfish-enhanced monkeys have become everyday science and ho-hum media events. Yet in these stories and others like them, one thing has not changed, the invocation of ethical dilemmas.

Funny thing though, they are the same ethical dilemmas we've heard about for twenty-five years, and their invocation does not bring reflection or resolution. Ethical hand-wringing might better describe what scientists say in stories announcing their successful experiments. More fascinating than jellyfish genes in monkey tails, then, is ethical agnosticism in the face of scientific advance.

The most obvious ethical dilemmas are presented in moving from animal to human genetic experimentation. What risks will it pose? Who can know before the actual experiments take place? In the face of uncertainty, who can give informed consent? Gene replacement therapy promises to cure our ills. But children given modified genes at conception may be born and raised, perhaps reaching adulthood, before the full effects of any alteration or treatment can be known. Even now, one physician who does direct insertion of a human sperm into an egg acknowledges that extraneous material may enter the egg—although no infants born as a result of this technique have yet shown a tendency to unusual diseases or conditions. Does that mean nothing is amiss?

Another physician, who describes himself as "an ethical religious man," says he will include the new information in counseling patients, but "they can decide whether they want to go forward or not." Presumably this meets his ethical obligation. The same physician also claims that he would not recommend to his patients every advance in technology, "just because there is a market for it." But are there "treatments" before physicians and their scientific colleagues work to develop them through animal experiments? And are there markets before physicians themselves offer treatments?

Down the road, cloning human organs in monkeys or pigs will present the same round of ethical hand-wringing. Yes, it presents risks. Once the technical barriers are breached, how can the risks to humans be fully known without actually transplanting cloned organs? Fully consenting to the risks, sick and dying people will acquiesce in the hope of renewed health and life. Who will stop them? Perhaps, at first, health insurance companies will say "no"; predictably, they will be beaten back by "compassionate" legislation. Institutional review boards in hospitals and research institutes seem ready to approve potentially effective treatments (especially for fatal conditions), leaving the risk questions to the future. And then, of course, millions [or] even billions of dollars are being invested in these projects. Who will really say no to the market?

Is this any way to approach ethical decision making in matters of novel and 10
risky experiments that will affect not just individuals, but the whole human community and the animal and plant world that sustains us?

What is all of this doing to creation? For if natural selection is part of the marvelously adaptive nature of all life on earth, who are scientists to decide that some genes should be enhanced or modified, while others are disabled? If the process of selection and adaptation takes eons, how can we foresee the consequences of even the simplest alteration in our genetic make-up, or that of the jellyfish and rhesus monkey?

We are all original sinners, but do we know nothing about hubris or heedlessness? If we learn nothing from the story of Adam and Eve, can we learn something from the development of the atomic bomb or the overuse of antibiotic medicines? Do we know nothing about the power of nature to strike back? Have we not learned that ethical questions are real questions? They require real reflection and real answers. Yes, there is medical progress to be made in genetic research, but real progress also requires us to say: Stop and think.

Could a Clone Ever Run for President?

MICHAEL D. LEMONICK

SURE, WHY NOT? Scientists used to think it would be difficult to clone an 1
animal as complex as a mammal, but Dolly the sheep neatly demolished that theory. If you can clone a sheep, a human isn't much tougher. Whether it is ethical to do so is another matter, and in fact human cloning has been outlawed in a number of countries and states. But illegal or not, someone's going to do it—and having been conceived by a convicted felon is no bar to public office.

The U.S. Constitution, moreover, doesn't have a clone clause. As long as you are a citizen and 35 or older, you're eligible. The age requirement means it can't happen for a while—2036 at the earliest (presuming that someone hasn't already secretly created the first human clone). But 2036 is not that far away. While some may insist that a clone should not be eligible for citizenship, the argument won't fly. If you are human and born in the U.S., you're a citizen. A clone will be born in the conventional way, with a mother, a belly button and a full complement of human DNA.

The obstacle to President Clone will come if cloning carries serious side effects. Dolly the sheep, it turns out, has prematurely aged cells, probably attributable to the fact that she is the biological extension of an animal that was already an adult. Human clones could have the same problem—plus cloning-related mental or behavioral defects that might not be apparent in a sheep.

If these difficulties can be overcome, political campaigns could get pretty interesting. Biologists today are talking of using cloning to bring the woolly mammoth and other extinct animals back to life. Maybe Democrats and Republicans would want to try something similar. After all, candidates are always trying to link themselves to great leaders of the past. Why not cut out the middlemen? Given the pace of scientific progress, plus sufficiently audacious party leaders, the presidential debates of 2044 could feature some pretty impressive lineups. Imagine Abraham Lincoln taking on F.D.R. Or J.F.K. going up against Thomas Jefferson. Or Millard Fillmore vs. Warren Harding.

On second thought . . . 5

Clone of Silence

MARGARET TALBOT

PERHAPS I should start by saying that I have never had a dog I would 1
have wished to replicate. There was Nappy, the poodle-shaped blur of my toddler years. Sweet little Woof, never the brightest bulb in the canine kingdom. Lawrence, the Labrador, who barked at suitcases on wheels. My sister's Irish setter, who gathered up the ripest of our unwashed laundry and slept in it. I won't bore you with the rest of my dog-owning history, except to add that I liked all my dogs, toilet-drinkers though they were, mourned their passing—and trooped cheerfully off to the animal shelter when the time came for a new one.

I am not, in other words, the target customer for Genetic Savings and Clone, a company that offers to store the DNA of your aging dog or cat so that one just like it may someday be cloned for you, at a cost, initially, of about \$200,000 each. The company is itself an offshoot of the Missyplicity Project, founded in 1998 when an anonymous couple gave \$2.3 million to Texas A&M University so that biologists there might devote their considerable time and expertise to the remaking of the couple's pet dog, Missy. Researchers hope to meet that goal by the end of this year.

In the purity of its self-indulgence and the frivolousness of its purpose, the Missyplicity project is unique. Why invest millions in pet cloning when the world is full of sick children and stray dogs? But in another sense, it is an entirely representative case—a riveting reminder of the way in which the idea of cloning has been normalized, even cute-ified, in remarkably short order.

Remember how it was just three years ago? In February 1997, when scientists in Edinburgh unveiled Dolly, a cloned sheep, the whole idea of cloning mammals—and the path it seemed to open to the cloning of humans—struck countless observers as a hideous portent of science out of control. Writing of cloning's potential for commodifying human life and further depersonalizing reproduction, the moral philosopher Leon Kass warned, "Shallow are the souls that have forgotten how to shudder."

Who shudders now? Last month, when PPL Therapeutics, a biotech com- 5
pany, revealed that it had produced five cloned pigs, the story didn't even make the front page of many newspapers. When the Discovery Channel sponsored the thawing of a woolly mammoth—which scientists hoped to clone—Larry Agenbroad, a paleontologist involved with the project, crowed: "When people say; 'Why clone a woolly mammoth?' I say, 'Why not?'" His swagger was so convincing that the skeptical biologist who protested that "life isn't something you start and stop like a record. It has to go on in continuum" sounded like a querulous Luddite—even to millions who had applauded the didactic ending of *Jurassic Park*.

"There are theological objections to this work, but the objectors have to back off," Michael Archer, a scientist working on the cloning of the extinct Tasmanian tiger, has said. "This is the way science, and life, is going."

Not all cloning projects are alike, and cloned pigs, it must be said, may someday save the lives of people in need of transplants. And yet, every news account that wallows in porcine cuteness ("the baby pigs playfully wrestled and nibbled on one another's ears at the news conference") or matter-of-factly reports their beneficial effect on stock price, makes the whole Frankensteinian business seem that much more banal. Every breakthrough in animal cloning makes human cloning not just more technically plausible, but more emotionally plausible. In February, the European Patent Office admitted that it had—by mistake—issued a patent that could include human cloning.

It's true that many technological innovations that once seemed disturbingly unnatural—in vitro fertilization, for one—have been folded more or less smoothly into the fabric of modern life. But human cloning is different. It would be a quantum leap toward the manufacture of children as consumer goods. And it would introduce a new kind of intergenerational tyranny: who can doubt that a child endowed with—specifically chosen to have—a previously used genotype would grow up fettered by parents' Procrustean expectations of how those genes should perform? "It is pertinent to ask," wrote Ian Wilmut and Keith Campbell, the scientists who brought us Dolly, "whether curiosity, vanity, the wish for personal power or an undoubtedly misguided desire for immortality really are good enough reasons for bringing a child into the world."

In its own small or maybe not so small way, the Missyplicity Project is the cloning frontier's worst moral offender. That's because it represents the first example of cloning for sentimental reasons, the first attempt to re-create a specific animal, and so feeds the illusion that those we love can be replaced by genetic copies. It doesn't matter that Missyplicity's backers admit a clone can duplicate only a creature's genetic material, not its identity. The fantasy they are playing to is of resurrection. The Texas A&M scientists say they have already been inundated with requests from people whose pet "is dying or got hit by a car or . . . is just getting old." And for three years, Ian Wilmut has been taking calls from grieving parents and others begging him to clone their loved ones back to life. Cloyingly, incrementally, Missyplicity and its ilk make the manufacture of replacement-model humans seem that much more imaginable. And that, I think, is still worth a shudder.

Clone-a-Friend

OLIVER MORTON

1 LAST SUMMER, Tigger—our neighbour's cat—learned how to hurl himself from the roof of the adjacent library through the open window of our first-floor kitchen. After the initial surprise, we quickly adjusted to life with an occasional cat. I never much liked cats before, but I have become rather smitten with Tigger.

If the neighbours moved house, which they regularly threaten to do, we would lose a dear friend. Which is why I have become fascinated with the idea of cloning pets. A team at Texas A&M University in College Station is trying to clone Missy, the dog of a Silicon Valley billionaire known only as Mr E (*New Scientist,* 19 December 1998, p 28). He is apparently so besotted with Missy that he is investing millions of dollars in a genetically identical replacement. Once this pioneering experiment is complete, other pet owners will be able to do the same for considerably less money, the scientists claim. They believe this may be the most immediately profitable form of cloning, and I think they may be right.

So, in a more technologically advanced world, were Tigger's owners ever to move, we could simply FedEx a cheque and a few cells—perhaps just a whisker—to a clone-a-cat laboratory and in a few months receive a sweet little Tiggoid kitten in return. Would this cat be as enchanting? Who knows? But finding out would be fun in a way most nature/nurture conflicts aren't. People could bring up the "same" pet under the same conditions again and again, or they could raise it in different environments. As my wife Nancy points out, cloning would remove the need for those newfangled pet passports. People would just have different copies of their pets in different countries. (Before anyone writes in to complain, she doesn't mean it.)

However, simply cloning Tigger would not be good enough, because Nancy is allergic to him and his visits have to be rationed. So ideally I'd like to snip out the allergen-encoding genes from Tigger's genome. This may turn out to be impractical—allergen production is probably too closely tied up with Tigger's cat-ness for the two to be disentangled—but as an idea, it's a winner.

5 Since humans have more in common with cats than cauliflowers, you might expect that the unease people feel about agricultural biotechnology would be nothing compared with the revulsion such Frankentiggers would engender. But I suspect the reverse is true. One of the problems with cloning and genetic modification is that the technology is associated with mass production and conformity, with identikit herds and monoculture cereals. Cloning and tweaking a pet would be all about individualisation. It would prize personality above everything. And there would be less of a sense of the unnatural. Pets, after all, are not natural—they have been bred and trained to be part of the human world. If you had to draw a distinction between "us" and "nature," pets would be with us.

Biotechnology forces us to rethink our attitudes to the natural and the artificial. In the context of the countryside, people might find this difficult, even without the health worries associated with GM food. But in the context of the cat on their mat, it may be not so hard at all. Especially if the cat is as unnaturally charming as Tigger.

Chapter 11

Arguing Claims about Actions

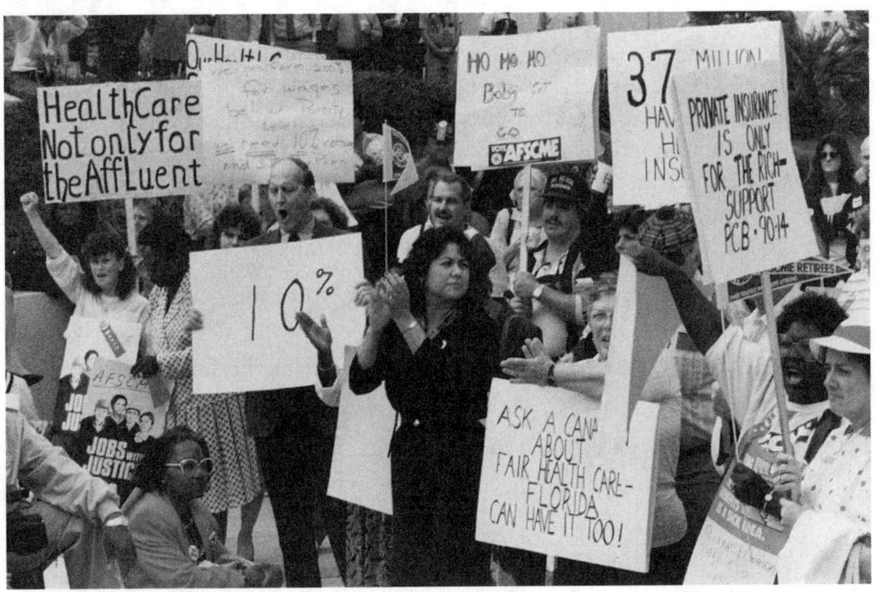

Kaizen and Our Disagreements about Actions

One of the most important issues that people disagree about, and one of the most complex to negotiate, is how one should act. Questions about actions may refer to the past: How should we have acted in the past? Most legal systems and studies of human history turn on this question. Questions about actions may also refer to the present and the future: How should we be acting right now? Should we be doing what we are doing? How should we act in the future? Most political debates turn on these questions. But people also face questions about actions on a smaller scale each day. And within our individual communities, the decisions we make about actions can have far-reaching consequences.

In the United States, we often don't start arguing about what we should do until the problem has become so large that we can't ignore it any longer. Once a problem reaches a certain size, then the media get involved, our political leaders get involved, people start discussing it in a variety of forums. As a result of this process, we have come to see arguing as a way of responding to problems, threats, and crises rather than as an ongoing aspect of the life of the community. Japanese culture has a different way of addressing problems. The Japanese regard discussion and negotiation as an ongoing part of a process called *kaizen* (ky'zen) or "improvement." *Kaizen* focuses on a general process for discussion rather than on finding particular solutions for particular problems. *Kaizen* teaches that focusing on results (solutions to problems and crises) means that communities have to invent a new process for each solution. Focusing on the process itself means that developing solutions will become a routine part of the life of a community. The models for decision making I present here are based on the Japanese idea of *kaizen*, models that provide the ongoing improvement of a community through dialogue and discussion—that is, through arguing.

Arguing about actions is a complex activity because it involves each of the subjects described in earlier chapters: arguing about existence, arguing about causality, arguing about language, and arguing about values. Disagreements about actions are often phrased as "should" questions:

Should the United States intercede more forcefully in the Arab-Israeli conflict?

Should the U.S. government have acted earlier in the fight against AIDS?

Should Congress pass legislation to regulate gun ownership more strictly?

Should society legally sanction homosexual marriages?

Should the U.S. legalize the use of peyote in Native American religious ceremonies?

Should the federal government regulate Internet content?

When members of a community have conflicting answers to questions such as these, then they may become the issues for debate.

The reasons offered to justify actions are usually one of the types of claims already discussed. For instance, one could argue that abortion should be banned because it is murder (a claim about language), because it is physically and psychologically harmful to the mother (a claim about causality), or because it violates the Judeo-Christian system of ethics (a claim about values). One could argue, on the other hand, that banning abortions would create a black market for abortions (a claim about causality) and would violate a woman's right to privacy (a claim about values). Claims about actions almost always involve claims about existence because the question of whether we *should* do something is related to the question of whether we *can* do it. Because the reasons used to justify actions take the form of claims themselves, they may require further reasons, leading to a chain of reasons and claims. For example, if you argue that abortion should be banned because it is murder, then you may need to defend the claim implicit in the reason (abortion is murder) with a further reason. Refer to Chapter 4 for a discussion of chains of reasons.

Problems and Solutions

An argument about actions often takes the form of an argument about problems and solutions. Some members of a community feel that there is something wrong with the current state of the community (a "mess"), isolate problems that have led to the "mess," and propose actions to address these problems (solutions). The first step in an argument about problems and solutions is to analyze the problem. The following questions are useful for doing so:

What is the "mess" (the situation that we find dissatisfying)?

What are the problems (the causes of the "mess")?

What happens if we don't do anything about the problems?

How desirable or undesirable are these effects?

The next step is to analyze possible solutions:

What actions may possibly solve the problems?

What would be the effects of these changes?

How desirable or undesirable would these changes be?

Once this analysis is complete, the next stage is to identify how the action or actions will be carried out:

Who should take the action?

What means should they use?

Where and when should the action take place?

What purpose or motives are behind these actions? Who wants to make these changes and why?

Every action must have an agent, some person or group of people who will carry it out, although not every claim about action will reveal the proposed agent explicitly. (In some instances, such as advertising, the person who is supposed to do the action is the reader.) Every solution requires an agent because action is purposeful. It is driven by human intention and motives. If I trip and fall down a flight of stairs, I may be moving, but I am not acting, unless I caused myself to trip. When I decide to go to the refrigerator for a snack, I am acting. My movement is purposeful and intentional. But the beating of my heart and the functioning of my digestive tract involve only motion; they are not actions because they are not purposeful.

Every action is also accomplished through some means. Like the agent, the means is frequently not stated in the claim, but it is useful to ask not only who will perform the action but also how it will be carried out.

Every action also has kairos, a time and place proper for the action. Often, the occasion is "here and now" or "as soon as possible." Sometimes the time and place must be determined precisely for the action to succeed. Determining the life cycle of the particular situation provides a guide to the proper time and place for action.

The final question about action relates to causality, to purpose or motive as cause. This question leads us to discover whether there are other purposes, besides solving the particular problem under consideration, that will be served by the action. What interests do particular parties in the community have in the proposed action or actions?

Individual and Collective Action

The agent performing the action can be either an individual or a group. For instance, questions about actions may involve personal decisions: Should I buy a car? Should I major in English? Should I get married? Should I go skiing this weekend? Or they may involve deciding actions for a group: Should the English Department get a new computer lab? Should my friends and I go fishing this weekend? Should our family take a trip to Disneyland? Should the city put a new stop sign at the intersection near our house? Should the state of Utah spend money on a light rail transport system? Should the federal government regulate children's television programming?

A MODEL FOR INDIVIDUAL DECISION MAKING

The process of making a decision about individual action can take two forms. First, you might be facing a problem that has no clear solution. In this case, you have to brainstorm about possible solutions before you can decide among them. In the second case, you may not be trying to solve a problem as much as choose among possible actions: Should I do X or Y? As an example of the first model for decision making, let's say you face a problem with one of your assignments: You've put off working on a paper. It's due in a couple of days, and you are just now realizing that it may require more time than you originally thought. This situation leaves you feeling dissatisfied: You are in a "mess." You begin by defining the problem, its causes, and effects.

The problem is that you think you won't be able to do a good job on your assignment and complete it by the due date. This is a claim about existence, about what things may be like in the future. You may start by examining whether what you think is really the case. What evidence do you have that you will not be able to complete the essay on time? Your performance on past assignments? Your estimate of how much time will be required for each part of the task of writing? Is the problem really a problem?

You decide, based on past experience, that the problem really exists. The next step is to define what caused this problem. What brought this situation about? You go over your activities for the semester and realize that you had the assignment in plenty of time, but you put off working on it until the last minute. Perhaps you recognize that you have done this sort of thing before on assignments. You just had other things on your mind. You resolve to do better in the future, but what about the present?

What are the effects of the problem? What will happen if you don't turn this paper in or don't do very well on it? If the harmful effects are not great, you may want to turn in what you can finish in two days and hope for the best. You read through the syllabus and realize that you have to turn in the paper to get credit for the course and that it counts for a large portion of your final grade. Using the syllabus as evidence to predict your instructor's action, you reason that this problem will have a negative, or undesirable, effect on your grade. You can take your analysis of effects further: What will be the effect of not doing well in this class or not getting credit for it? Is it required for graduation? How badly will this affect your overall grade point average? And what effect might this have on your prospects for graduate study or employment?

Once you have defined the problem and its effects, you need to use brainstorming and research to determine solutions that will solve this problem. What are your possibilities? You could choose not to write the paper at all, a decision to let the problem stand. You could choose to do what you can in two days and hope for the best. You could try to adapt a paper that someone else has written. You could talk to the instructor and see whether you could arrange to turn in the paper a couple of days late.

Next you look at these solutions in terms of their causes and effects. First, what is the motivation behind each of these proposals? The decision to let the problem stand might be motivated by your conclusion that none of the other solutions will make much of a difference. It could also be motivated by laziness or irresponsibility. What about the decision to do what you can and hope for the best? This might be motivated by a desire to make the best of a poor situation and to learn from your mistakes, as well as a fear of discussing this problem with the instructor. What would motivate the decision to use someone else's paper? Certainly not a desire to learn what you could from working on the paper. Perhaps it is the desire to do well in the class no matter what it takes, without any regard for what is right. The decision to talk to the instructor might be motivated by a desire to admit your mistakes and to try to do your best on the assignment, taking the time to learn what you can in the process.

What are the effects of these proposed solutions? We've already examined the effects of letting the problem stand. If you do what you can in two days, you might not produce a very good paper, but you would probably get credit for the assignment and pass the course. This solution would require a lot of work, possibly pulling a couple of all-nighters, and it might have a negative effect on your work for other classes. Using someone else's paper would save you a lot of work, and you might even do well on the assignment if it were a good paper to begin with and if you could adapt it successfully. But if you were to be caught, you could fail the class or even be kicked out of school. In addition, you wouldn't learn what the assignment was intended to teach, which is one reason you came to school in the first place. Moreover, you might not be able to live with yourself knowing that you cheated. If you decide to talk to the instructor, you might get more time to work on the paper without penalty, which would allow you the advantage of completing the assignment without the disadvantage of it affecting your work for other classes. Of course, your instructor might not give you any more time and would also know in advance how little time you had to spend on the paper.

What would you decide to do? After going through this process, I think I would call the instructor right away, plead my case, and try to make some arrangement to turn the paper in a little late. If this didn't work, I would do what I could in the time I had and hope for the best. Borrowing a paper from someone else would violate my sense of right and wrong and could have very undesirable effects.

Of course, when I decide to include the teacher in my decision-making process, then my decision is no longer an individual decision; it becomes a group decision. The teacher and I must use language to negotiate a consensus about collective action.

You follow a similar process when you are presented with actions to choose among. Let's say that you apply to graduate school and are accepted at three different places. In this case, you are not really searching for a solution to a problem; you are trying to decide among competing possibilities. First, examine some questions of existence: Is it really possible for you to take each of these actions? Must you really choose among them? Does choosing one exclude choosing the others? You decide, in this case, that you can really only go to one graduate school.

Now you consider each of these actions in terms of its causes and effects. What is motivating your decision to go to each school? What will happen if you choose one school over the others? What will happen if you decide not to go to any of them at all?

FORMULATING AN ARGUMENT ABOUT PROBLEMS AND SOLUTIONS

1. *Analyze the problem.* Define the problem, its causes and effects.
2. *Analyze possible solutions.* Consider possible solutions and weigh their advantages and disadvantages.
3. *Identify how the solution will be implemented.* Determine who should take action, what they should do, what means they should use, where and when they should act, and what purpose should guide them.

Once you have identified the possible causes and effects, you then consider the values attached to these causes and effects: What are the advantages and disadvantages of each choice? Which values are most important to you?

You make so many decisions about actions each day that you don't always have the time or the inclination to examine each decision in such detail. This kind of analysis is an action in itself that has positive and negative effects. You can't spend all day deciding what you will eat for breakfast. Sometimes you have to act on the knowledge you have and hope for the best.

A MODEL FOR COLLECTIVE DECISION MAKING

Few decisions are truly individual. When you start considering who else might be affected by your decisions and try to involve them in the decision-making process, then what at first was an individual decision quickly becomes a group decision. But collective decision making is tricky: The further you move away from what you control as an individual, the more difficult it is to have a full voice in the decisions that are made. When I was single, I could make many decisions on my own, but I still had to work things out with a boss or a roommate and occasionally my parents or siblings. When I got married, I started participating in a lot more group decisions. My wife and I had to work out how we were going to decide our collective actions: Who would decide what? What kind of input would others have? Who would carry out what kind of actions? Now that we have children, decision making becomes even more complicated.

What my example shows is the effect on decision making of membership in a community—in this case the community defined by my individual family. As you become more involved in any community, you will find that you participate in more group decisions and that you have more responsibility to consider others when contemplating your own actions. As a student passing through the English Department at Brigham Young University, I did not have a lot of say in what took place there: what classes were offered, who was hired and assigned to teach those classes, what books were ordered, how the money was spent. I was part of the English Department community, but I was not nearly as involved in that community as I am now as a faculty member. Because of my greater involvement in the English Department community, I find that my actions have greater impact within the community and that more of my actions are group actions. I serve on committees to decide who gets into our graduate program and who gets to teach our composition courses. As a teacher, my actions in the classroom have much more effect than my actions as a student did.

Collective decisions are complex and involve related claims about existence, causality, language, values, and actions. Here are some examples:

Only people who can pass a literacy test should be allowed to vote.

Health care reform should be administered by the states rather than the federal government.

Season ticket holders should be allowed to vote on a salary cap for major league baseball.

Unless there is an immediate threat to American interests, the president should seek congressional approval before sending American troops into combat situations.

The federal government should subsidize the charitable work of churches.

To have an effect on group decision making, it is important to understand how the community considering the action is organized. The "journalistic questions" are helpful for identifying the organization of a community: who? what? when? where? why? and how?

Who makes decisions?

What kind of decisions can they make?

When do they typically make decisions?

Where do they make decisions?

Why do they make decisions? (What is the mission or purpose of the community?)

How do they make decisions?

You can ask the same questions about how decisions are implemented and enforced.

When groups make decisions, they can follow much the same process described for making individual decisions: defining the nature of a problem, identifying solutions, and examining positive and negative causes and effects. Group decision making involves the additional task of resolving differences and disagreements about existence, causality, language, and values.

Arguments about collective action are at the very heart of community life. Addressing such actions is really the purpose of this book: How can we use language to participate more fully in the collective decisions and actions of the communities we belong to? By participating regularly in constructive arguments about collective action, we can achieve kaizen, the continual improvement of our community.

Evaluating Claims about Actions

Because claims about actions include one or more of the other types of claims, evaluating claims about actions may seem complex. But evaluating action claims doesn't require any skills different from those discussed in previous chapters. Evaluating these kinds of claims can be a little more complicated because you have to evaluate different types of claims in connection with one another. As discussed earlier in this chapter, the reasons given to support a claim about actions could be a claim about existence, about causality, about language, or about values. A claim about actions might be supported by more than one of these different types of claims. Or the assumptions implied in these reasons may be one of the other types of claims. For example, you could argue that the government should take a particular action because the advantages of acting outweigh the disadvantages. Although this is a claim about actions, the reasons given include a claim about causality, that these advantages really will happen. This argument would also include an implicit claim about existence (as arguments about causality typically do) and an implicit claim about values (that the "advantageous" results really are valuable).

Since claims about actions may involve one or more of the other types of claims, the first step in evaluating claims about actions is to identify the structure of the argument and the types of claims involved. (Chapter 4 explains how to identify the claims, reasons, and assumptions in an argument, how to outline chains of reasons and assumptions, and how to classify the different types of claims.) Once you have identified the types of claims involved, you can then evaluate these claims according to the methods described in previous chapters. For claims about existence, you would use Richard Fulkerson's STAR system: sufficiency of grounds, typicality, accuracy, and reliability. Here are the questions you need to ask when evaluating claims about existence:

> *Sufficiency of grounds:* Is there *enough* evidence to warrant the claim drawn?
>
> *Typicality:* Are the data representative of the group of data being argued about?
>
> *Accuracy:* Is the information used as data true?
>
> *Relevance:* Is the claim asserted relevant to the information about the sample?

Because claims about causality involve claims about existence, you need to use the STAR system to evaluate these as well, but you should also ask questions such as the following:

1. Has the author given an adequate explanation or model for how one event could reasonably cause the second?
2. Has the author accounted for all possible causes? Is the author careful not to mistake correlation for cause?
3. Are there repeated observations or experiments that document the relationship? Do these observations or experiments follow one of the five methods of causal reasoning?
4. If the causal argument is based on an analogy, comparison, or precedent, do the two situations being compared have enough important features in common to make the analogy?

Claims about language and claims about values are similar because both involve definitions (a value is a "troublesome term" with a judgment attached). As you

THE PROCESS OF EVALUATING CLAIMS ABOUT ACTIONS

1. Identify the claims, reasons, and assumptions in the argument.
2. Classify the claims implicit in the reasons and assumptions as claims about existence, causality, language, or values.
3. Evaluate each of these types of claims according to the principles discussed in earlier chapters. For example, use the STAR system to evaluate claims about existence.

consider these kinds of claims, ask yourself the following question: "What is the effect of defining a term in this way?" What happens when you make a definition more or less inclusive? Here are some particular questions you can use to evaluate definitions and values:

1. Is the definition or value sufficiently inclusive?
2. Is the definition or value sufficiently exclusive?
3. Is the language clear?
4. Does the definition or value emphasize detail, excluding unnecessary detail?
5. What would be the implications of this definition or value if it were used in a different context?
6. Who gains and who loses by defining the term in this particular way?

Because claims about values require you to make a judgment, you also need to consider the value in light of other values, to consider the importance of the value within your own or your community's hierarchy of values. What would you gain or lose by emphasizing this particular value? Does this value correspond with or violate principles that you hold absolute? If not, then how do you judge this value relative to other values? If the value *is* important, then you need to determine whether the claim really does match the value.

The Principles in Action: Readings

RESPONDING TO CONTROVERSIAL SOCIAL ISSUES

In each of the following essays, the author addresses one of those controversial social issues that seem never to be resolved: gun violence, capital punishment, gambling. In the first, Molly Ivins, syndicated political columnist for the *Fort Worth Star-Telegram,* argues that the way to solve gun violence is to prevent ordinary citizens from owning any guns. The second essay is written by Coretta Scott King, civil rights activist and founder of the Martin Luther King Center for Nonviolent Social Change. In "The Death Penalty is a Step Back," King argues that responding to murder by executing the murderer only perpetuates the cycle of violence in our society. In the third essay, Russell Baker, a Pulitzer Prize–winning journalist for the *New York Times,* argues that America should address the social ills of gambling by making it illegal. As you read each of these essays, consider the following questions:

1. What problems does each author identify? According to each author, what are the causes and effects of these problems? How significant are these problems?
2. What solutions does each author propose? What are the advantages and disadvantages of these solutions? How would these solutions be implemented?
3. Are the decisions required to achieve these solutions individual or collective? If they are collective, then who would be involved in making the decisions?
4. What reasons does each author provide to support his or her claims about actions? What assumptions are implied in these reasons?
5. To what extent do you accept the arguments presented by each of these writers? If you disagree, what is the crux of your disagreement?
6. If you were going to respond to each of these writers, what common assumptions or beliefs could you build on? How would you mediate between these authors and those who hold opposing viewpoints?

Ban the Things. Ban Them All.

MOLLY IVINS

GUNS. Everywhere guns.

Let me start this discussion by pointing out that I am not anti-gun. I'm 1
pro-knife. Consider the merits of the knife.

In the first place, you have to catch up with someone to stab him. A general substitution of knives for guns would promote physical fitness. We'd turn into a whole nation of great runners. Plus, knives don't ricochet. And people are seldom killed while cleaning their knives.

As a civil libertarian, I of course support the Second Amendment. And I believe it means exactly what it says: "A well-regulated militia being necessary to the security of a free state, the right of the people to keep and bear arms shall not be infringed." Fourteen-year-old boys are not part of a well-regulated militia. Members of wacky religious cults are not part of a well-regulated militia. Permitting unregulated citizens to have guns is destroying the security of this free state.

I am intrigued by the arguments of those who claim to follow the judicial 5
doctrine of original intent. How do they know it was the dearest wish of Thomas Jefferson's heart that teenage drug dealers should cruise the cities of this nation perforating their fellow citizens with assault rifles? Channeling?

There is more hooey spread about the Second Amendment. It says quite clearly that guns are for those who form part of a well-regulated militia, i.e., the armed forces including the National Guard. The reasons for keeping them away from everyone else get clearer by the day.

The comparison most often used is that of the automobile, another lethal object that is regularly used to wreak great carnage. Obviously, this society is full of people who haven't got enough common sense to use an automobile properly. But we haven't outlawed cars yet.

We do, however, license them and their owners, restrict their use to presumably sane and sober adults and keep track of who sells them to whom. At a minimum, we should do the same with guns.

In truth, there is no rational argument for guns in this society. This is no longer a frontier nation in which people hunt their own food. It is a crowded, overwhelmingly urban country in which letting people have access to guns is a continuing disaster. Those who want guns—whether for target shooting, hunting or potting rattlesnakes (get a hoe)—should be subject to the same restrictions placed on gun owners in England—a nation in which liberty has survived nicely without an armed populace.

The argument that "guns don't kill people" is patent nonsense. Anyone who 10
has ever worked in a cop shop knows how many family arguments end in murder because there was a gun in the house. Did the gun kill someone? No. But if there had been no gun, no one would have died. At least not without a good footrace first. Guns do kill. Unlike cars, that is all they do.

Michael Crichton makes an interesting argument about technology in his thriller *Jurassic Park.* He points out that power without discipline is making this society into a wreckage. By the time someone who studies the martial arts becomes a master—literally able to kill with bare hands—that person has also undergone years of training and discipline. But any fool can pick up a gun and kill with it.

"A well-regulated militia" surely implies both long training and long discipline. That is the least, the very least, that should be required of those who are permitted to have guns, because a gun is literally the power to kill. For years, I used to enjoy taunting my gun-nut friends about their psycho-sexual hangups—always in a spirit of good cheer, you understand. But letting the noisy minority in the National Rifle Association force us to allow this carnage to continue is just plain insane.

I do think gun nuts have a power hangup. I don't know what is missing in their psyches that they need to feel they have the power to kill. But no sane society would allow this to continue.

Ban the damn things. Ban them all.

You want protection? Get a dog. 15

The Death Penalty Is a Step Back

CORETTA SCOTT KING

1 When Steven Judy was executed in Indiana [in 1981] America took another step backwards towards legitimizing murder as a way of dealing with evil in our society.

Although Judy was convicted of four of the most horrible and brutal murders imaginable, and his case is probably the worst in recent memory for opponents of the death penalty, we still have to face the real issue squarely: Can we expect a decent society if the state is allowed to kill its own people?

In recent years, an increase of violence in America, both individual and political, has prompted a backlash of public opinion on capital punishment. But however much we abhor violence, legally sanctioned executions are no deterrent and are, in fact, immoral and unconstitutional.

Although I have suffered the loss of two family members by assassination, I remain firmly and unequivocally opposed to the death penalty for those convicted of capital offenses.

5 An evil deed is not redeemed by an evil deed of retaliation. Justice is never advanced in the taking of a human life.

Morality is never upheld by legalized murder. Morality apart, there are a number of practical reasons which form a powerful argument against capital punishment.

First, capital punishment makes irrevocable any possible miscarriage of justice. Time and again we have witnessed the specter of mistakenly convicted people being put to death in the name of American criminal justice. To those who say that, after all, this doesn't occur too often, I can only reply that if it happens just once, that is too often. And it has occurred many times.

Second, the death penalty reflects an unwarranted assumption that the wrongdoer is beyond rehabilitation. Perhaps some individuals cannot be rehabilitated; but who shall make that determination? Is any amount of academic training sufficient to entitle one person to judge another incapable of rehabilitation?

Third, the death penalty is inequitable. Approximately half of the 711 persons now on death row are black. From 1930 through 1968, 53.5 percent of those executed were black Americans, all too many of whom were represented by court-appointed attorneys and convicted after hasty trials.

10 The argument that this may be an accurate reflection of guilt, and homicide trends, instead of a racist application of laws lacks credibility in light of a recent Florida survey which showed that persons convicted of killing whites were four times more likely to receive a death sentence than those convicted of killing blacks.

Proponents of capital punishment often cite a "deterrent effect" as the main benefit of the death penalty. Not only is there no hard evidence that murdering murderers will deter other potential killers, but even the "logic" of this argument defies comprehension.

Numerous studies show that the majority of homicides committed in this country are the acts of victim's relatives, friends and acquaintances in the "heat of passion."

What this strongly suggests is that rational consideration of future consequences are seldom a part of the killer's attitude at the time he commits a crime.

The only way to break the chain of violent reaction is to practice nonviolence as individuals and collectively through our laws and institutions.

Taking the Saps

RUSSELL BAKER

THERE ARE many explanations for why America is highballing down the 1
low road to Doomsday. One of my favorites is government-sponsored gambling. Any people who let their own government sucker them into throwing their money away on games with prohibitively high odds haven't the wit needed to save great nations from doom.

Here is this human mass that thinks of itself as "the great American people," and what does it amount to? A bunch of saps who sat meekly by while their own once-honorable and respectable government—a government whose flag we saluted every morning before tackling arithmetic—while this once decent government took over the gambling racket from the mob.

The states are chiefly to blame for this, of course, but the Feds quietly acquiesce. When gangsters ran things, muscling in on their rackets could leave you bullet-riddled. Unfortunately the gangsters couldn't do that when government started muscling in. All the gangsters had for enforcing discipline was the machine gun; government had the atom bomb.

It debases a nation to let its governors take over the rackets. It is a no-class thing for a government to do.

You hear the argument that, if millions are determined to gamble anyhow, 5
it's better for government to take their money than for mobsters to do it. Government, the argument goes, will put the money to good use; the mob will use it to set up love nests and indulge depraved tastes.

Everything about this argument is specious, starting with the idea that government will use the money to improve the public condition. Any government that exploits the weakness of its citizens to enrich itself cheapens its own character and thus damages the public interest.

As for the perverse uses to which the mob might put the money, let us not be too quick with denunciations. The mob's record is not so bad.

It has pumped a great deal of its gambling profits into creating Las Vegas, an American entertainment landmark in a class with Disney World, Camden Yards, and Cape Cod. Without Las Vegas, Hollywood would have no place to set half of its movies, and motion picture box-office receipts might suffer gravely, with who knows what consequences for one of the nation's few industries not yet transported to Asia or Latin America.

Let no one suppose that despising government sponsoring of vice marks me as either unduly moral or foolishly sentimental about human nature. I am certain that millions will always enjoy gambling and will continue enjoying it without government assistance.

This appetite should be satisfied, however, by criminals, not by government. 10
Human character is improved when each citizen must settle for himself the moral question of whether the pleasure of vice justifies breaking the law to enjoy it.

As everybody has probably known since pre-biblical times, pleasure's delights are intensified when the pleasure cannot be realized without taking risks. The truth of this antique wisdom was illustrated during the recent "sexual revolution" when the birth-control pill eliminated virtually all the risks of casual sex. As a result sex often declined into just another humdrum social ritual, which might require a delightfully forbidden drug to give it a little zest.

America was a healthier land when its gamblers had to break the law to get rid of their money. As a police reporter long ago in Baltimore, a great horse-player's town, I was struck by the high spirits of American betting men hauled in by the vice squad after a raid on some gambling den.

Being arrested seemed to make their day. They clumped together in the police station waving like celebrities and exchanging jokes while waiting to be bailed out, bantering with the uniformed cops who respected bettors and despised vice squads, and otherwise basking in the rare experience of being under arrest.

It was usually professional gamblers who got caught. What a contrast that robust gambler's America was to the dreary bureaucracies we now find in state-run betting offices and in the sadness of candy-store lines where incurable dreamers queue to buy lottery tickets.

Let us return to an America that worked: Re-criminalize gambling. 15

SOLVING COMPLEX PROBLEMS

The authors of each of the following essays propose specific solutions to complex problems. The first essay, "Distinguishing between Felons and Truants," first appeared in the *Los Angeles Times.* The author, Gil Garcetti, was district attorney for Los Angeles County at the time this essay was published. In this essay, Garcetti proposes some specific steps for separating violent juvenile criminals from youth who can be rehabilitated. The second essay, "Deadly

Dosing," was written for *Vegetarian Times* by Dave Plank. In this essay, Plank calls upon his readers to contact their government representatives to initiate a ban on using antibiotics in livestock. In "A Global Disaster," written for *The Economist,* the author outlines the steps that governments need to take to address the growing worldwide spread of AIDS. As you read these essays, consider the following questions:

1. What problems does each author identify? According to each author, what are the causes and effects of these problems? How significant are these problems?
2. What solutions does each author propose? What are the advantages and disadvantages of these solutions? How would these solutions be implemented?
3. Are the decisions required to achieve these solutions individual or collective? If they are collective, then who would be involved in making the decisions?
4. What reasons does each author provide to support his or her claims about actions? What assumptions are implied in these reasons?
5. To what extent do you accept the arguments presented by each of these writers? If you disagree, what is the crux of your disagreement?
6. If you were going to respond to each of these writers, what common assumptions or beliefs could you build on? How would you mediate between these authors and those who hold opposing viewpoints?

Distinguishing between Felons and Truants

GIL GARCETTI

THE JUVENILE justice system is failing to protect us from the surge in violent crimes committed by young people. 1

The patchwork of laws put on the books over the past thirty years isn't working. One problem is that the system was designed to help troubled youths who committed minor offenses, but 75 percent of the current cases in juvenile court are felonies. We need to act immediately to replace it with a coherent program that protects society from violent juvenile criminals, efficiently rehabilitates youths who can be saved—and also knows how to tell the difference.

CORE PRINCIPLES

Here are some principles that could form the core of a revision:

Remove many violent offenders from the juvenile system. Violent youths who are seventeen years old should be sent directly to adult court. In 1993, about 50 percent of the juveniles referred to the Probation Department for possible criminal offenses were seventeen years old. So were many juveniles charged with the most serious crimes.

5 Prosecutors should have discretion to transfer even much younger juveniles accused of the most serious crimes to adult courts. State legislators have proposed lowering the age at which a youth can be tried as an adult from sixteen to fourteen, but the numbers matter less than letting prosecutors use their own judgment. For instance, a fifteen-year-old is in juvenile court, accused of a double murder. If the murders had occurred nine days later, on his sixteenth birthday, he could have been tried as an adult and, if convicted, sentenced to life without the possibility of parole. Convicted juvenile offenders must be freed by age twenty-five.

Limit juvenile confidentiality. Society needs to identify juveniles who commit serious crimes and know what happens to them in court. Improvements have been made over the years, but there are still instances where agencies charged with providing services to children are not aware of criminal proceedings involving a child. School officials, for instance, concerned about violating confidentiality laws, have often not told teachers about students who had been convicted of crimes.

Deliver real rehabilitation. Juvenile justice has to efficiently deliver rehabilitative services to juveniles who commit minor offenses. The first step is coordination among all the agencies that assist young people at risk. We need to identify and help the growing number of children who have never had structure or hope in their lives. Government can also offer parents help with parenting skills and intervention before the family structure falls apart.

The present juvenile system puts truants and murderers through the same procedures, including the appointment of attorneys at public expense and long judicial hearings. We need laws that allow better choices between punishment and guidance, and that use resources more wisely.

ACCOUNTABILITY

Make juveniles—and their parents—accountable. Punishment that fits the crime must be meted out fairly and with certainty. Currently, juvenile burglars are often sent straight home on probation while adults who commit the same offense get a mandatory prison sentence; this sort of thing makes juvenile offenders believe they can get away with almost anything.

10 Parents must be held responsible for keeping their children in school. We can enforce violations of the Education Code and at the same time assist parents with "stay in school" programs. Parents must also pay for the damage their children cause, including the cost of graffiti cleanups. Current law provides for restitution of up to $10,000 to victims of juvenile crime. New laws should simplify this recovery and reinforce parental responsibility, while also offering parenting assistance.

Intervene early to prevent violence later. This is the most important step we can take to stop juvenile crime. Legislators need to change the laws that prohibit and punish as well as provide programs and funding to give children the skills and motivation to stay in school and away from gangs, drugs and crime.

Keep juveniles away from guns. We must substantially stiffen laws and penalties for juveniles in possession of guns and for adults who make guns available to juveniles. No loopholes, no exceptions.

A new juvenile justice system would quickly reduce the level of fear we all feel. Over the long term, it would reduce the number of juvenile and adult violent criminals. We need to put reformers to work right away and give them a time limit, no more than 180 days, to produce a framework for a new juvenile justice system. I offer one of my senior prosecutors to this effort.

The reformers should be nonpartisan; this is not about olitics. It is about making California a safe, desirable place to live.

Deadly Dosing

DAVE PLANK

PUMPING livestock full of antibiotics has become so commonplace that we almost take it for granted. Now, thanks to emerging research, scientists from powerful institutions like the National Academy of Sciences (NAS), the World Health Organization (WHO) and even the Food and Drug Administration (FDA) are worried that drug-resistant strains of bacteria produced as a result of this practice may become the next millennium's most daunting human public-health challenge. 1

Over the past few decades, ranchers have been aggressively using antibiotics to ward off diseases and fatten up cattle, sheep, swine and poultry by allowing them to metabolize more feed and grow at an accelerated rate. According to the U.S. Department of Agriculture, 60 to 80 percent of all American livestock animals are given the drugs. And scientists believe that this rampant overuse of antibiotics is causing the DNA of infectious pathogens like salmonella, E. coli and campylobacter to change and make the diseases resistant to the drugs that traditionally wiped them out. Once resistant, the deadly bacteria can easily survive in the animals and be transmitted to humans as contaminated meat, explains Kansas State University's James Coffman, D.V.M., chairman of the NAS panel that produced a report called "The Use of Drugs in Food Animals." "That threat," warns Coffman, "is real, and is documented."

Coffman says that animals are routinely kept on low doses of antibiotics, such as penicillin, tetracycline and streptomycin, to neutralize the repercussions of filthy living conditions. Modern, high-density feed lots crowd tens or even hundreds of thousands of animals into pens with only a few square feet of living area for each. Waste is supposed to be carried away by drainage systems operating beneath the animals, but the systems don't always work. The end result is a cramped, dirty, stressed-out animal that often needs drugs to stay healthy or even alive. However, should a disease get passed into the food supply, the antibiotics prescribed to combat it in humans are often useless, as the bacteria that cause the disease are already resistant to the "cure."

Even the FDA, which regulates agricultural antibiotic use, is wary of the practice. In a recent press release, the FDA stated that it "believes the current use of subtherapeutic [small doses to stop disease] drugs by livestock producers is safe, but favors more research into the area of antibiotic resistance among livestock-borne pathogens." While the number of deaths due to antibiotic resistance is low, it is growing annually, according to the Centers for Disease Control in Atlanta. And with tens of thousands of cases of food-borne illnesses reported every year, the situation is primed to get worse. "We've seen an explosion in the numbers of organisms that don't respond to therapies with drugs that have worked for years. We need to start paying closer attention to what we give out [antibiotics] for," says Julius Franke, M.D., an expert in infectious diseases at the University of Colorado.

5 Halting the widespread use of antibiotics won't be easy. The Center for Science in the Public Interest, a consumer advocacy group based in Washington, D.C., estimates that a ban would raise the cost of beef, poultry, pork and dairy products by $1.2 billion to $2.5 billion per year. Such an increase would stem from the greater expense of raising animals without antibiotics—in other words, in cleaner, more humane conditions. Still, the group is urging the FDA to ban subtherapeutic use of these drugs, calling it a "significant hazard to public health." Agricultural and medical experts at the WHO concur, saying there is indeed cause for concern, as well as for government monitoring. It recommends raising livestock in lower-density quarters and doing more research into the development of nonantibiotic drugs.

Unfortunately, the government has no plans to tighten up regulation, and experts fear that antibiotic resistance will have to reach epidemic proportions before the government takes action. At this point, pressuring your congressperson through letters and phone calls is the most viable option.

A Global Disaster

THE ECONOMIST

PIETERMARITZBURG, Harare, Kampala 1

The AIDS virus has infected 47 million people, and shows no signs of slowing. It cannot be cured. Can it be curbed?

In rich countries AIDS is no longer a death sentence. Expensive drugs keep HIV-positive patients alive and healthy, perhaps indefinitely. Loud public-awareness campaigns keep the number of infected Americans, Japanese and West Europeans to relatively low levels. The sense of crisis is past.

In developing countries, by contrast, the disease is spreading like nerve gas in a gentle breeze. The poor cannot afford to spend $10,000 a year on wonder-pills. Millions of Africans are dying. In the longer term, even greater numbers of Asians are at risk. For many poor countries, there is no greater or more immediate threat to public health and economic growth. Yet few political leaders treat it as a priority.

Since HIV was first identified in the 1970s, over 47 million people have been 5
infected, of whom 14 million have died. Last year saw the biggest annual death toll yet: 2.5 million. The disease now ranks fourth among the world's big killers, after respiratory infections, diarrhoeal disorders and tuberculosis. It now claims many more lives each year than malaria, a growing menace, and is still nowhere near its peak. If India, China and other Asian countries do not take it seriously, the number of infections could reach "a new order of magnitude," says Peter Piot, head of the UN's AIDS programme.

The human immuno-deficiency virus (HIV), which causes acquired immune deficiency syndrome (AIDS), is thought to have crossed from chimpanzees to humans in the late 1940s or early 1950s in Congo. It took several years for the virus to break out of Congo's dense and sparsely populated jungles but, once it did, it marched with rebel armies through the continent's numerous war zones, rode with truckers from one rest-stop brothel to the next, and eventually flew, perhaps with an air steward, to America, where it was discovered in the early 1980s. As American homosexuals and drug injectors started to wake up to the dangers of bath-houses and needle-sharing, AIDS was already devastating Africa.

So far, the worst-hit areas are east and southern Africa. In Botswana, Namibia, Swaziland and Zimbabwe, between a fifth and a quarter of people aged 15–49 are afflicted with HIV or AIDS. In Botswana, children born early in the next decade will have a life expectancy of 40; without AIDS, it would have been nearer 70. Of the 25 monitoring sites in Zimbabwe where pregnant women are tested for HIV, only two in 1997 showed prevalence below 10%. At the remaining 23 sites, 20–50% of women were infected. About a third of these women will pass the virus on to their babies.

The region's giant, South Africa, was largely protected by its isolation from the rest of the world during the apartheid years. Now it is host to one in ten of the world's new infections—more than any other country. In the country's most populous province, KwaZulu-Natal, perhaps a third of sexually active adults are HIV-positive. Asia is the next disaster-in-waiting. Already, 7 million. Asians are infected. India's 930 million people look increasingly vulnerable. The Indian countryside, which most people imagined relatively AIDS-free, turns out not to be. A recent study in Tamil Nadu found over 2% of rural people to be HIV-positive: 500,000 people in one of India's smallest states. Since 10% had other sexually transmitted diseases (STDs), the avenue for further infections is clearly open. A survey of female STD patients in Poona, in Maharashtra, found that over 90% had never had sex with anyone but their husband; and yet 13.6% had HIV. China is not far behind.

No one knows what AIDS will do to poor countries' economies, for nowhere has the epidemic run its course. An optimistic assessment, by Alan Whiteside of the University of Natal, suggests that the effect of AIDS on measurable GDP will be slight. Even at high prevalence, Mr Whiteside thinks it will slow growth by no more than 0.6% a year. This is because so many people in poor countries do not contribute much to the formal economy. To put it even more crudely, where there is a huge over-supply of unskilled labour, the dead can easily be replaced. Some people argue that those who survive the epidemic will benefit from a tighter job market. After the Black Death killed a third of the population of medieval Europe, labour scarcity forced landowners to pay their workers better.

Other researchers are more pessimistic. AIDS takes longer to kill than did 10
the plague, so the cost of caring for the sick will be more crippling. Modern governments, unlike medieval ones, tax the healthy to help look after the ailing, so the burden will fall on everyone. And AIDS, because it is sexually transmitted, tends to hit the most energetic and productive members of society. A recent study in Namibia estimated that AIDS cost the country almost 8% of GNP in 1996. Another analysis predicts that Kenya's GDP will be 14.5% smaller in 2005 than it would have been without AIDS, and that income per person will be 10% lower.

THE COST OF THE DISEASE

In general, the more advanced the economy, the worse it will be affected by a large number of AIDS deaths. South Africa, with its advanced industries, already suffers a shortage of skilled manpower, and cannot afford to lose more. In better-off developing countries, people have more savings to fall back on when they need to pay medical bills. Where people have health and life insurance, those industries will be hit by bigger claims. Insurers protect themselves by charging more or refusing policies to HIV-positive customers. In Zimbabwe, life-insurance premiums quadrupled in two years because of AIDS. Higher premiums force more people to seek treatment in public hospitals: in South Africa, HIV and AIDS could account for between 35% and 84% of public-health expenditure by 2005, according to one projection.

Little research has been done into the effects of AIDS on private business, but the anecdotal evidence is scary. In some countries, firms have had to limit the number of days employees may take off to attend funerals. Zambia is suffering power shortages because so many engineers have died. Farmers in Zimbabwe are finding it hard to irrigate their fields because the brass fittings on their water pipes are stolen for coffin handles. In South Africa, where employers above a certain size are obliged to offer generous benefits and paid sick leave, companies will find many of their staff, as they sicken, becoming more expensive and less productive. Yet few firms are trying to raise awareness of AIDS among their workers, or considering how they will cope.

In the public sector, where pensions and health benefits are often more generous, AIDS could break budgets and hobble the provision of services. In South Africa, an estimated 15% of civil servants are HIV-positive, but government departments have made little effort to plan for the coming surge in sickness. Education, too, will suffer. In Botswana, 2–5% of teachers die each year from AIDS. Many more take extended sick leave.

At a macro level, the impact of AIDS is felt gradually. But at a household level, the blow is sudden and catastrophic. When a breadwinner develops AIDS, his (or her) family is impoverished twice over: his income vanishes, and his relations must devote time and money to nursing him. Daughters are often forced to drop out of school to help. Worse, HIV tends not to strike just one member of a family. Husbands give it to wives, mothers to babies. This correspondent's driver in Kampala lost his mother, his father, two brothers and their wives to AIDS. His story is not rare.

OBSTACLES TO PREVENTION

The best hope for halting the epidemic is a cheap vaccine. Efforts are under 15
way, but a vaccine for a virus that mutates as rapidly as HIV will be hugely difficult and expensive to invent. For poor countries, the only practical course is to concentrate on prevention. But this, too, will be hard, for a plethora of reasons.

- Sex is fun. Many feel that condoms make it less so. Zimbabweans ask: "Would you eat a sweet with its wrapper on?" And discussion of it often taboo. In Kenya, Christian and Islamic groups have publicly burned anti-AIDS leaflets and condoms, as a protest against what they see as the encouragement of promiscuity. A study in Thailand found that infected women were only a fifth as likely to have discussed sex openly with their partners as were uninfected women.
- Myths abound. Some young African women believe that without regular infusions of sperm, they will not grow up to be beautiful. Ugandan men

use this myth to seduce schoolgirls. In much of southern Africa, HIV-infected men believe that they can rid themselves of the virus by passing it on to a virgin.

- Poverty. Those who cannot afford television find other ways of passing the evening. People cannot afford antibiotics, so the untreated sores from STDs provide easy openings for HIV.
- Migrant labour. Since wages are much higher in South Africa than in the surrounding region, outsiders flock in to find work. Migrant miners (including South Africans forced to live far from their homes) spend most of the year in single-sex dormitories surrounded by prostitutes. Living with a one-in-40 chance of being killed by a rockfall, they are inured to risk. When they go home, they often infect their wives.
- War. Refugees, whether from genocide in Rwanda or state persecution in Myanmar, spread HIV as they flee. Soldiers, with their regular pay and disdain for risk, are more likely than civilians to contract HIV from prostitutes. When they go to war, they infect others. In Africa the problem is dire. In Congo, where no fewer than seven armies are embroiled, the government has accused Ugandan troops (which are helping the Congolese rebels) of deliberately spreading AIDS. Unlikely, but with estimated HIV prevalence in the seven armies ranging from 50% for the Angolans to an incredible 80% for the Zimbabweans, the effect is much the same.
- Sexism. In most poor countries, it is hard for a woman to ask her partner to use a condom. Wives who insist risk being beaten up. Rape is common, especially where wars rage. Forced sex is a particularly effective means of HIV transmission, because of the extra blood.
- Drinking. Asia and Africa make many excellent beers. They are also home to a lot of people for whom alcohol is the quickest escape from the stresses of acute poverty. Drunken lovers are less likely to remember to use condoms.

HOW TO FIGHT THE VIRUS

Pessimists look at that list and despair. But three success stories show that the hurdles to prevention are not impossibly high.

First, Thailand. One secret of Thailand's success has been timely, accurate information-gathering. HIV was first detected in Thailand in the mid-1980s, among male homosexuals. The health ministry immediately began to monitor other high-risk groups, particularly the country's many heroin addicts and prostitutes. In the first half of 1988, HIV prevalence among drug injectors tested at one Bangkok hospital leapt from 1% to 30%. Shortly afterwards, infections soared among prostitutes.

The response was swift. A survey of Thai sexual behaviour was conducted. The results, which showed men indulging in a phenomenal amount of unprotected commercial sex, were publicised. Thais were warned that a major epidemic would strike if their habits did not change. A "100% condom use" campaign persuaded prostitutes to insist on protection 90% of the time with non-regular customers.

By the mid-1990s, the government was spending $80 million a year on AIDS education and palliative care. In 1990–93, the proportion of adult men reporting non-marital sex was halved, from 28% to 15%; for women, it fell from 1.7% to 0.4%. Brothel visits slumped. Only 10% of men reported seeing a prostitute in 1993, down from 22% in 1990. Among army conscripts in northern Thailand, a group both highly sexed and well-monitored, the proportion admitting to paying for sex fell from 57% in 1991 to 24% in 1995. The proportion claiming to have used condoms at their last commercial entanglement rose from 61% in 1991 to 93% in 1995.

People lie about sex, so reported good behaviour does not necessarily mean actual good behaviour. But tumbling infections suggest that not everyone was fibbing. The number of sexually transmitted diseases reported from government clinics fell from over 400,000 in 1986 to under 50,000 in 1995. Among northern conscripts, HIV prevalence fell by half between 1993 and 1995, from over 7% to under 3.5%.

Most striking was the government's success in persuading people that they were at risk long before they started to see acquaintances die from AIDS. There was no attempt to play down the spread of HIV to avoid scaring off tourists, as happened in Kenya. Thais were repeatedly warned of the dangers, told how to avoid them, and left to make their own choices. Most decided that a long life was preferable to a fast one.

Second, Uganda. Thailand shows what is possible in a well-educated, fairly prosperous country. Uganda shows that there is hope even for countries that are poor and barely literate. President Yoweri Museveni recognised the threat shortly after becoming president in 1986, and deluged the country with anti-AIDS warnings.

30 The key to Uganda's success is twofold. First, Mr Museveni made every government department take the problem seriously, and implement its own plan to fight the virus. Accurate surveys of sexual behaviour were done for only $20,000–30,000 each. Second, he recognised that his government could do only a limited amount, so he gave free rein to scores of non-governmental organisations (NGOs), usually foreign-financed, to do whatever it took to educate people about risky sex.

The Straight Talk Foundation, for example, goes beyond simple warnings about AIDS and deals with the confusing complexities of sex. Its staff run role-playing exercises in Uganda's schools to teach adolescents how to deal with romantic situations. Its newsletter, distributed free, covers everything from nocturnal emissions to what to do if raped. Visiting AIDS workers from South Africa and Zimbabwe asked the foundation's director, Catharine Watson, how she won government permission to hand out such explicit material, and were astonished to hear that she had not felt the need to ask.

The climate of free debate has led Ugandans to delay their sexual activity, to have fewer partners, and to use more condoms. Between 1991 and 1996, HIV prevalence among women in urban ante-natal clinics fell by half, from roughly 30% to 15%.

Third, Senegal. If Uganda shows how a poor country can reverse the track of an epidemic, Senegal shows how to stop it from taking off in the first place. This West African country was fortunate to be several thousand miles from HIV's origin. In the mid-1980s, when other parts of Africa were already blighted, Senegal was still relatively AIDS-free. In concert with non-governmental organisations and the press and broadcasters, the government set up a national AIDS-control programme to keep it that way. In Senegal's brothels, which had been regulated since the early 1970s, condom use was firmly encouraged. The country's blood supply was screened early and effectively. Vigorous education resulted in 95% of Senegalese adults knowing how to avoid the virus. Condom sales soared from 800,000 in 1988 to 7 million in 1997. Senegalese levels of infection have remained stable and low for a decade—at around 1.2% among pregnant women.

Contrast these three with South Africa. On December 1st, World AIDS Day, President Nelson Mandela told the people of KwaZulu-Natal that HIV would devastate their communities if not checked. The speech was remarkable not for its quality—Mr Mandela is always able to move audiences—but for its rarity. Unlike Mr Museveni, South Africa's leader seldom uses his authority to encourage safer sex. It is a tragic omission. Whereas the potholed streets of Kampala are lined with signs promoting fidelity and condoms, this correspondent has, in eight months in South Africa, seen only two anti-AIDS posters, both in the UN's AIDS office in Pretoria.

HOW TO DITHER AND DIE

South Africa has resources and skills on a scale that Uganda can only marvel at. It even has an excellent AIDS prevention plan, accepted by the new cabinet in 1994. But the plan was never implemented. The government likes to consult every conceivable "stakeholder," so new plans are eternally drafted and redrafted. Local authorities cannot act without orders from the central government. NGOs, many of them dependent on the powers-that-be for their finance, waste months making sure that enough of their senior management posts are filled with blacks to satisfy the ruling African National Congress. And they have minimal freedom to experiment.

"There's an idea that if you disagree with the government, you are betraying the liberation struggle," says Mary Crewe, head of the Greater Johannesburg AIDS project. As a result, soldiers in the South African army are so ignorant that they snip the tips off their free condoms, and HIV has spread through South Africa as fast, according to Dr Neil McKerrow of Grey's Hospital in Pietermaritzburg, as if no preventive measures at all had been taken.

Such bungling is not unique to South Africa. Most governments have been slow to recognise the threat from AIDS. From Bulawayo to Beijing, apathy and embarrassment have hamstrung preventive efforts.

In anarchic countries, such as Congo and Angola, there have been almost no preventive efforts. Many people believe that the cause—a bid to restrain one of the most basic human instincts—is hopeless. As a Zimbabwean novelist, Chenjerai Hove, puts it with disturbing fatalism: "Since our women dress to kill, we are all going to die." But if the sexual drive is basic, so is the desire to live. If governments in poor countries wake up to the need to persuade their citizens that unprotected sex is Russian roulette, Mr Hove could be proved wrong.

This article is indebted to a number of UN AIDS reports, including AIDS epidemic update (December 1998), AIDS in Africa (November 1998), and "A measure of success in Uganda" (May 1998).

ADDRESSING INCIVILITY

The authors of the following essays each consider actions themselves as a problem. In the first essay, "No, Please, After You," David Taylor describes his attempts to personally address the growing problem of incivility in large cities such as Los Angeles. This essay was originally published in *Forbes.* The second essay, "Campus Climate Control," was written by college student Katie Roiphe for the *New York Times.* In this essay, Roiphe tries to find a way to address the growing incivility on college campuses without severely limiting the personal freedom that distinguishes the college experience. As you read these two essays, consider the following questions:

1. How does each author characterize incivility in our society? What examples does each author provide? Can you think of counterexamples?
2. According to each author, what are the causes and effects of incivility? From your experience, how significant are these problems?
3. What solutions does each author propose? What are the advantages and disadvantages of these solutions? How would these solutions be implemented?
4. How would you individually address the problem of incivility? How could a group collectively address this problem? Who would be involved in a collective decision?
5. What reasons does each author provide to support his or her claims about actions? What assumptions are implied in these reasons?
6. To what extent do you accept the arguments presented by each of these writers? If you disagree, what is the crux of your disagreement?

7. If you were going to respond to each of these writers, what common assumptions or beliefs could you build on? How would you mediate between these authors and those who hold opposing viewpoints?

No, Please, After You

DAVID TAYLOR

1 IF PRESSED, I would call myself a reasonably civil man, but there I was, neck veins distended, eyes bulging, anger heating my blood to lava as I shouted futilely through the windshield at the oblivious, car phone–talking, lane-jumping dimwit who had just cut me off in order to gain a car length's advantage in the morning traffic crawl. My daughter looked at me with teenage clarity—I had lost my mind. At that moment, I had an out-of-body experience and saw myself from a distance, and it was an ugly sight. I realized that my grip on simple manners and common "seevility" was weakening. And I realized that I was not alone. I was doing unto others what they were doing to me.

Somewhere in the jumbled closet of my memory, there is a half-remembered article on a psychological experiment conducted at Yale in the 1960s by J. B. Calhoun. The experimenters created a lab rat population in an environment with restrictive boundaries and allowed normal rat society to establish itself. Then they began adding to the population without expanding the boundaries. When population density reached a certain point, rat society went to hell. The animals stopped breeding. Formerly mild-mannered family members turned on each other. Rat considerateness, rat manners, went out the window, and they weren't even using cell phones. Rats attacked each other at the slightest provocation. They had descended into a societal phenomenon the experimenters called "the behavioral sink."

According to the U.S. Census Bureau, the present population of the country is some 266 million. A hundred years ago it was only 63 million.

I live in Los Angeles, a city that has increased its population from 2.9 million people to 3.6 million in the last 16 years. Maybe population density is the root cause of our present slide. But I also blame the car for the dramatic rise in rudeness.

5 Walking is nearly unheard of here unless one is wearing sweat clothes and carrying a stopwatch and an air of grim and healthy purpose. We drive everywhere, often alone, sealed into our cars, distanced from life, viewing it through the windshield as if watching a television show. This isolation has eroded our consideration for others, and our facility for calm interaction is degrading toward nil. We are becoming so self-centered, we are in danger of spiraling back into our own navels.

People park to block one lane of a two-lane street while they dash in to pick up their dry cleaning—"I'll only be a second"—unconcerned for the ten people stacked up behind. I have seen spandex-clad women, glowing from an hour of aerobics with their personal trainers, park in the handicap spots at grocery stores to save steps while they run in to buy arugula and Swedish water, their four-wheel-drive vehicles legitimized by disability placards bought from their plastic surgeons.

"Please" and "thank you" are grudgingly delivered, and "excuse me" is a phrase heard no more often than Urdu. The customer is almost always wrong. If, as they say, the future of America is bred here, better buckle up, we're in for a bumpy ride.

I wanted to do my bit to break the cycle, to push back against this tide, but how could one person have an effect? I don't own a gun, and, though I have lived here 20 years, gunfire still seems an extreme reaction to rudeness. Swearing is petty and can get your nose broken. Irony was out; it is not understood.

The only option appeared to be Gandhian resistance, satyagraha, the technique for redressing wrongs by inviting, rather than inflicting, suffering; for resisting an adversary without rancor and fighting him without violence. I would meet rudeness with politeness, inconsiderateness with considerateness, anger with a smile. I would change the world one person at a time. Eventually someone would step back and hold a door. Someone would offer a seat, allow another's car to make a turn. Someone would defer his need for someone else's. We would enter a new golden age. Once again L.A. would lead, this time toward paradise!

Crusades can be dangerous. I discovered that the results of civility were not 10
always what I anticipated. Once I found myself in a race toward a restaurant door with a white-haired man 15 years my senior. I was hoping to hold it open for him. He mistook my intent for competition and accelerated to be the first one through. I put on a burst of speed and managed to edge him out. I held the door. "Please, after you." He looked at me with profound suspicion. "Right," he snorted, and disappeared inside.

I found that if I held the door for a woman carrying a baby, six people stampeded in after her. Slow down at an intersection to let another car clear, and the person behind leans on the horn. Stand when someone enters the room, and your seat is gone when you turn around. Offer a hand, lose an arm.

My smile became a rictus. My "excuse me's" and "after you's" came through clenched teeth. I fought to suppress the urge to smack the unenlightened. How did Gandhi do it year after year? Didn't he ever want to pick up the spinning wheel and just beat the marmalade out of those arrogant, beef-eating, stiff-upper-lip, lime-sucking . . .

The trick was to keep the goal in sight and a shoulder to the wheel. I would chant the mantras—"please," "thank you," no, no, after you."

Then one day, I returned a dropped wallet in the public library. The owner gave me a grudging "thanks," and waited politely until he thought I wasn't looking to check that I hadn't stolen the money. A woman walled off by bumper-to-bumper traffic at a gas station exit smiled and waved when I slowed to let her out. A couple of blocks later, I saw her offer the same favor to another car. A young man held the door for me as I staggered out of Sears carrying a case of motor oil and waved away my astonished thanks. I redoubled my efforts.

Soon I was deferring to everyone about everything, a situation that caused 15
confusion in my house where I am known to have firm opinions on all matters, including those that are none of my business. What did I want for dinner? Anything was fine with me. What movie did I want to see? Whatever anybody else wanted. May I use the car? Of course. Take it.

Weeks went by. I held doors till my arm grew tired. To avoid offending, I took no stances, offered no judgments. My friends found me increasingly dull. Family meals were silent. No one wanted to risk another welter of my sweet agreeableness. Politeness had become tyranny.

My wife and I were on our way to a meeting that was important to her. We were already late. I held the door as we entered the building; she went ahead. I was still there holding it for others when she came back to find me. She nailed me with a look that I have seen before.

She was silent on the way home, one of those brooding silences that men know will cost them. It distracted me, and when the car in the next lane cut me off, it caught me by surprise. Without thinking, I learned on the horn and shouted futilely behind the windshield. My wife raised an ironic eyebrow and smiled. I had an urge to apologize, but I stifled it, and at that moment, a great weight was lifted from me.

I still defer when common sense dictates. I aim to be polite in the common understanding of the word. But if that white-haired gentleman barges through as I hold open a restaurant door, I am going to hip-check him into the salad bar.

Campus Climate Control

KATIE ROIPHE

I REMEMBER the butter pats that covered the soaring ceiling of my fresh- 1
man dining hall. They were the first sign that I had entered a world utterly devoid of adults. I remember my best friend passing out from inhaling nitrous oxide. I remember someone I know falling drunkenly off a fire escape and ending up in the hospital. I remember groups of us breaking into the pool at night and swimming naked. This was not 1967. This was 1990.

By the time I arrived at college, the idea of adult authority had been chipped away and broken down by a previous generation—by Watergate and Vietnam and drugs. And though we would have died rather than admit it, without it some of us were feeling lost. We had the absolute, shimmering freedom that had been dreamed up for us during the 60's. We had the liberating knowledge that no one cared what we did.

But it wasn't making us as happy as it was supposed to. I remember moments of exultation walking through the pink campus at dawn, but I also remember moments of pure terror.

During a particularly wild period of my senior year, a professor looked up from my essay on Robert Lowell's falling out-of-love poetry, glanced at the violet circles under my eyes and said, "You really need to get some sleep." I stood there in my ripped jeans. I felt suddenly reassured. The adult world, where people wake up in the morning, pay their bills and take out the trash, was still intact.

It therefore does not surprise me that students now want universities to act 5
in loco parentis again, and that slightly perplexed babyboom administrators are trying to find ways to accommodate them. Some of the practical ideas being floated around campuses seem absurd. Alcohol-free adult-supervised student centers? Students will mock them. But they may serve a function by their mere existence.

Parents of teen-agers are always embarrassing to adolescents, and institutions acting in loco parentis will also be embarrassing. The alcohol-free, adult-supervised student centers (or trips to the theater with professors, or more resident advisers) are simply signs of an adult presence. They offer tangible monuments to an authority that you can avoid or rebel against, but that nonetheless exists. You can find it on a campus map.

I remember the stories my mother told of climbing into her dorm room, wedging open the window, when she got back after curfew. Part of the thrill of rules, the perverse allure, is that they can be broken. Even when students are deliberately ignoring them, the fact of their existence is comforting. Rules give order to our chaos; they give us some sort of structure for our wildness so that it doesn't feel so scary.

At the heart of the controversy over whether colleges should act in loco parentis is the question of whether college students are adults or children, and of course they are neither. They are childish and sophisticated, naive and knowing, innocent and wild, and in their strange netherworld, they need some sort of shadow adult, some not-quite-parent to be there as a point of reference.

That said, some new rules being considered on campuses seem extreme—like the rule at Lehigh that there can be no campus parties without a chaperone. Surely there must be a way of establishing a benign and diffuse adult presence without students having to drink and dance and flirt and pick people up around actual adults.

Many students . . . seem to like the superficial wholesomeness of the 50's. 10
But what about the attitudes that informed it, like the sexism that tainted any college girl who enjoyed sex?

There must be a way to create some sort of structure without romanticizing or fetishizing the 50's. There must be a way of bringing back an adult presence on college campuses without treating students like children, a way of correcting the excesses of the sexual revolution without throwing away all of its benefits.

Americans are always drawn to extreme ideologies, to extremes of freedom or repression, of promiscuity or virginity, of wildness or innocence, but maybe there is a middle ground, somewhere closer to where people want to live their actual lives: a university without butter pats on the ceiling or 10 o'clock curfews.

Practicing the Principles: Activities

CREATING KAIZEN

By this point in the term, you should have analyzed how issues on your campus are debated and decided. You should also have a pretty good idea of how arguing functions within the communities you belong to. Remember that the principle of kaizen stresses that discussion and arguing should be a continual part of improving the life of the community. Select a community that you belong to that could be improved through kaizen. Analyze how issues are debated and decided within this community, and recommend some processes that better apply the principles of kaizen.

ADOPTING A CAUSE

Most communities have meaningful issues that few people really know or care about. As a class, try to find an important issue that would normally concern only a few people: planning and zoning decisions, local environmental issues, school funding, mental health care, local jail conditions, business planning and development. Adopt one of these issues as a class project and find out as much as you can about the issue. Attend the meetings where this issue is discussed. Meet with those who are directly involved in the issue. Try to raise public awareness of this issue through informational fliers or brochures, educational meetings, and letters to the editor. Try to provide a service for people or organizations that don't have the resources or ability to promote their own cause. As a class, try to come to a negotiated solution to the problem raised by the issue you have adopted, and present your solution to local decision makers.

A MOCK PARLIAMENT

Organizing the class as a mock parliament allows you to debate about actions that should be taken in the future. The activity usually requires two or three class periods. Begin by brainstorming about issues you would like to consider. I recommend that you focus on local issues, particularly campus issues, or issues that you have all researched and are familiar with. You will have more to say about familiar issues, and they will probably mean more to you. Divide yourselves into "parties" (usually about four or five). Prepare resolutions ahead of time that address the issues you've agreed to discuss. Circulate these to the rest of the class, and allow class members to take them home to draft arguments for and against the resolutions.

Once all the parties have had time to prepare, vote to choose a class member to be the chair of the parliament and approve some rules. I recommend using a simplified form of Roberts' Rules of Order. The U.S. House of Representatives and Senate use rules very similar to these:

- Speakers must be recognized by the chair before they are allowed to speak. They ask for permission to speak by rising and saying, "Mr. (or Madame) Chair." The chair then says, "The chair recognizes . . . " Speakers are then allowed to speak or make a motion.
- Each motion or resolution must be seconded. If there is no second, then the motion fails to carry. Once a motion has been moved and seconded, the chair should call for debate on the motion.
- Each speaker is allowed five minutes to speak, but he or she can yield any unused time to another speaker.
- The chair should alternate recognizing speakers for and against a motion or resolution.
- Speakers may propose amendments to resolutions. When a motion to amend has been made and seconded, the chair should call for debate on the proposed amendment. The body should vote on the amendment before voting on the resolution itself.
- When everyone who desires to speak has had a chance, the chair should call for the question (vote) on the resolution. If someone objects to calling for the question, the chair should call for the previous question (hold a vote on whether to vote), ensuring that everyone gets a chance to speak. The vote is carried out by saying "yea" or "nay," although the chair can entertain a motion for a hand count. The vote on the call for the previous question is always a hand count and needs a ⅔ vote to carry.
- Once the group has voted on a resolution (with any amendments), the chair should entertain additional resolutions.

These rules are just suggestions, and you may want to modify these as a class. I recommend that you write your rules down and elect a class member to be parliamentarian to make sure that the group follows the rules. Remember that the point of this activity is to give yourselves practice in arguing, so make sure that everyone has a chance to participate.

The mock parliament may sound complicated at first, but you will catch on quickly. Try to make this fun so that class members will not feel intimidated. Ask your instructor to provide some prizes for the chair and for the best speakers from each party (as well as treats for the class).

A MOOT COURT

A moot court, or mock trial, is a good way to argue about actions that occurred in the past. Try to keep procedure to a minimum. As with the mock parliament, this activity takes two or three class periods. To begin, you should brainstorm about issues you want to discuss. Once you have agreed on some issues, select a prosecution and defense team (of two or three people each) and a judge. Divide the rest of the class into witnesses for the prosecution and defense. Each side prepares its case, dividing the research among the witnesses. Each team prepares its arguments, and witnesses prepare to represent different viewpoints or historical sources. Once you have finished your research and preparation, begin by having each team make a brief opening statement. The prosecution then presents its case in detail and calls witnesses. The defense has a chance to cross-examine each witnesses. The defense then makes its case and calls witnesses. The prosecution cross-examines, and each team makes closing statements. The prosecution speaks first in opening and closing statements. After the entire case has been presented, everyone becomes a member of the jury and votes on the case by secret ballot. (You should vote on what you have generally been persuaded to believe, not on which side you were assigned to represent.)

MODEL UNITED NATIONS

Many colleges and universities have a Model United Nations program. Sometimes this is offered as a separate class in political science or international relations. Some students participate in national conferences and competitions to learn more about global issues and to explore careers in diplomacy. For information about the American Model United Nations association, contact its website at www.amun.org. At this site you will find information about researching global issues, writing UN resolutions, and simulating UN debates. If you have an AMUN chapter on your campus, invite someone to come to your class to speak about global issues. Or contact the American Model United Nations (mail@amun.org) for information about people at your college who could speak about the United Nations. If you don't have time to simulate a complete council or committee, then consider writing a resolution as a class. The AMUN handbook provides some guidelines for writing resolutions at <www.amun.org/amun_handbook.html>.

MEET THE PRESS

Another format for arguing about actions is that used in many presidential debates. This activity can be accomplished in one or two class periods and is simpler than the mock parliament or mock trial. To begin, brainstorm as a class about some current controversial issues facing your community. Agree on the issues you want to focus on in the debate, and write questions that address these issues. For each question, every class member should prepare arguments both for and against the issue being raised. Before you begin the debate, elect a class member to serve as moderator. The moderator will write everyone's name on a slip of paper and put the slips in a box. Before each question, the moderator draws two names from the box. The first person whose name is drawn will speak first. The second person will speak second and will take the opposing view of the first person. (If you have prepared properly, you should be able to discuss either side of an issue.) The debate format is as follows: the moderator draws two names and asks a question of the two speakers. The first speaker speaks for 60 seconds.

Applying the Principles on Your Own

GRADING: PROBLEMS AND SOLUTIONS

As college students and parents become increasingly conscious of grades, some have wondered whether letter grades are the best way to motivate student learning and to reward student achievement. The first essay, "A for Effort," was written by John Leo, a columnist for *U.S. News and World Report.* In this essay, Leo expresses his concerns about the problem of grade inflation. The second essay, "A Proposal to Abolish Grading," is taken from Paul Goodman's book *Compulsory Miseducation.* The third essay, "Making the Grade," was originally published for *Newsweek* by Kurt Wiesenfeld, a physics professor at Georgia Tech in Atlanta.

A for Effort

JOHN LEO

WHAT IS THE hardest mark to get at many American colleges? 1

Answer: C. Like the California condor, it is a seriously endangered species. It may need massive outside help to survive. Otherwise, it could easily go the way of marks like D, E and F, all believed to be extinct.

Harvard instructor William Cole put it this way in an article in the *Chronicle of Higher Education:* A generation or two ago, students who mentally dropped out of classes settled for "a gentleman's C." Now, he says, perfunctory students get "a gentleperson's B," and "a gentleperson's A−" is not out of the question, especially in the humanities. An English tutor told *Harvard Magazine,* "In our department, people rarely receive a grade lower than B−. Even B− is kind of beneath mediocre."

As college tuition has climbed, grade inflation has risen right along with it, perhaps muting complaints about what it all costs. At Harvard in 1992, 91 percent of undergraduate grades were B− or higher. Stanford is top-heavy with A's and B's too; only about 6 percent of all grades are C's. At Princeton, A's rose from 33 percent of all grades to 40 percent in four years.

Because of grade inflation, outstanding students and average students are of- 5
ten bunched at the top. "In some departments, A stands for average," Harvard senior Dianne Reeder said at a panel discussion on inflated grades last spring. "Since so many of us have A− averages, our grades are meaningless."

The avalanche of A's is producing a similar avalanche of students graduating with honors. *Harvard Magazine* cites an unidentified dean of admissions at a top-six law school saying his office ignores magna cum laude and cum laude honors from Harvard because so many applicants have them. In 1993, 83.6 percent of Harvard seniors graduated with honors.

Vanishing breed. This is a national problem. Outside of economics, science and engineering, collegians are getting such good marks these days that it seems average students are disappearing from the campus, all replaced by outstanding achievers. It's reminiscent of Garrison Keillor's fictional Lake Wobegon, where "all the children are above average."

What is going on here? Market forces surely play a role. Colleges are competing for a pool of students who expect and sometimes demand high marks. "Students complain in ways they didn't before," says Martin Meyerson, former president of the University of Pennsylvania. "Teachers find it easier to avoid the hassle and just give higher grades." And good marks sustain enrollments in academic departments, a sign of success for professors.

Many people think grade inflation started with the generous marks professors gave to mediocre students in the '60s to keep them out of the draft during the Vietnam War. Fallout from the '60s is involved; during the campus upheavals, radicals attacked grading as a display of institutional power over the young. And, in general, the post-'60s makeover of campuses has been crucial.

"Relativism is the key word today," says Cole. "There's a general conception 10
in the literary-academic world that holding things to high standards—like logic, argument, having an interesting thesis—is patriarchal, Eurocentric and conservative. If you say,'This paper is no good because you don't support your argument,' that's almost like being racist and sexist."

The current campus climate makes professors reluctant to challenge grade inflation. Harvard Prof. Harvey Mansfield said during the panel discussion on grading that "professors have lost faith in the value of reason and hence lost faith in the value of their status. Their inability to give grades that reflect the standards of their profession is a sign of a serious loss of morale." Boston University Prof. Edwin Delattre says, "If everything is subjective and arbitrary, and you try to apply standards, you run afoul of the prevailing ethos of the time."

Still, whatever the failings of the academy, inflated grades don't start there. The same virus has afflicted high schools for at least two decades. Since 1972, when the College Board began keeping tabs, the percentage of college-bound seniors reporting high marks in school has almost tripled. In 1972, 28.4 percent of those taking the test said they had A or B averages in high school. By 1993, it was 83 percent. This happened while SAT scores were falling from a mean combined score of 937 to the current 902.

For whatever reasons (and the feel-good self-esteem movement is surely one), marks have broken free of performance and become more and more unreal. They are designed to please, not to measure or to guide students about strengths and weaknesses.

Give A's and B's for average effort and the whole system becomes a game of "Let's Pretend." Parents are pleased and don't keep the pressure on. Students tend to relax and expect high rewards for low output. What happens when they join the real world where A and B rewards are rarely given for C and D work?

A Proposal to Abolish Grading

PAUL GOODMAN

LET HALF a dozen of the prestigious Universities—Chicago, Stanford, the Ivy League—abolish grading, and use testing only and entirely for pedagogic purposes as teachers see fit. 1

Anyone who knows the frantic temper of the present schools will understand the transvaluation of values that would be effected by this modest innovation. For most of the students, the competitive grade has come to be the essence. The naive teacher points to the beauty of the subject and the ingenuity of the research; the shrewd student asks if he is responsible for that on the final exam.

Let me at once dispose of an objection whose unanimity is quite fascinating. I think that the great majority of professors agree that grading hinders teaching and creates a bad spirit, going as far as cheating and plagiarizing. I have before me the collection of essays, *Examining in Harvard College,* and this is the consensus. It is uniformly asserted, however, that the grading is inevitable; for how else will the graduate schools, the foundations, the corporations *know* whom to accept, reward, hire? How will the talent scouts know whom to tap?

By testing the applicants, of course, according to the specific task requirements of the inducting institution, just as applicants for the Civil Service or for licenses in medicine, law, and architecture are tested. Why should Harvard professors do the testing *for* corporations and graduate schools?

The objection is ludicrous. Dean Whitla, of the Harvard Office of Tests, 5
points out that the scholastic-aptitude and achievement tests used for *admission* to Harvard are a super-excellent index for all-around Harvard performance, better than high-school grades or particular Harvard course-grades. Presumably, these college-entrance tests are tailored for what Harvard and similar institutions want. By the same logic, would not an employer do far better to apply his own job-aptitude test rather than to rely on the vagaries of Harvard section-men? Indeed, I doubt that many employers bother to look at such grades; they are more likely to be interested merely in the fact of a Harvard diploma, whatever that connotes to them. The grades have most of their weight with the graduate schools—here, as elsewhere, the system runs mainly for its own sake.

It is really necessary to remind our academics of the ancient history of Examination. In the medieval university, the whole point of the grueling trial of the candidate was whether or not to accept him as a peer. His disputation and lecture for the Master's was just that, a masterpiece to enter the guild. It was not to make comparative evaluations. It was not to weed out and select for an extramural licensor or employer. It was certainly not to pit one young fellow against another in an ugly competition. My philosophic impression is that the medievals thought they knew what a good job of work was and that we are competitive because we do not know. But the more status is achieved by largely irrelevant competitive evaluation, the less will we ever know.

(Of course, our American examinations never did have this purely guild orientation, just as our faculties have rarely had absolute autonomy; the examining was to satisfy Overseers, Elders, distant Regents—and they as paternal superiors have always doted on giving grades, rather than accepting peers. But I submit that this set-up itself makes it impossible for the student to *become* a master, to *have* grown up, and to commence on his own. He will always be making A or B for some overseer. And in the present atmosphere, he will always be climbing on his friend's neck.)

Perhaps the chief objectors to abolishing grading would be the students and their parents. The parents should be simply disregarded; their anxiety has done enough damage already. For the students, it seems to me that a primary duty of the university is to deprive them of their props, their dependence on extrinsic valuation and motivation, and to force them to confront the difficult enterprise itself and finally lose themselves in it.

A miserable effect of grading is to nullify the various uses of testing. Testing, for both student and teacher, is a means of structuring, and also of finding out what is blank or wrong and what has been assimilated and can be taken for granted. Review—including high-pressure review—is a means of bringing together the fragments, so that there are flashes of synoptic insight.

There are several good reasons for testing, and kinds of test. But if the aim 10
is to discover weakness, what is the point of down-grading and punishing it, and thereby inviting the student to conceal his weakness, by faking and bulling, if not cheating? The natural conclusion of synthesis is the insight itself, not a grade for

having had it. For the important purpose of placement, if one can establish in the student the belief that one is testing *not* to grade and make invidious comparisons but for his own advantage, the student should normally seek his own level, where he is challenged and yet capable, rather than trying to get by. If the student dares to accept himself as he is, a teacher's grade is a crude instrument compared with a student's self-awareness. But it is rare in our universities that students are encouraged to notice objectively their vast confusion. Unlike Socrates,[1] our teachers rely on power-drives rather than shame and ingenuous idealism.

Many students are lazy, so teachers try to goad or threaten them by grading. In the long run this must do more harm than good. Laziness is a character-defense. It may be a way of avoiding learning, in order to protect the conceit that one is already perfect (deeper, the despair that one *never* can be). It may be a way of avoiding just the risk of failing and being downgraded. Sometimes it is a way of politely saying, "I won't." But since it is the authoritarian grown-up demands that have created such attitudes in the first place, why repeat the trauma? There comes a time when we must treat people as adult, laziness and all. It is one thing courageously to fire a do-nothing out of your class; it is quite another thing to evaluate him with a lordly F.

Most important of all, it is often obvious that balking in doing the work, especially among bright young people who get to great universities, means exactly what it says: The work does not suit me, not this subject, or not at this time, or not in this school, or not in school altogether. The student might not be bookish; he might be school-tired; perhaps his development ought now to take another direction. Yet unfortunately, if such a student is intelligent and is not sure of himself, he *can* be bullied into passing, and this obscures everything. My hunch is that I am describing a common situation. What a grim waste of young life and teacherly effort! Such a student will retain nothing of what he has "passed" in. Sometimes he must get mononucleosis to tell his story and be believed.

And ironically, the converse is also probably commonly true. A student flunks and is mechanically weeded out, who is really ready and eager to learn in a scholastic setting, but he has not quite caught on. A good teacher can recognize the situation, but the computer wreaks its will.

[1] Socrates (469–399 BC), an important Greek philosopher, emphasized the importance of self-knowledge. The acquisition of such knowledge could be facilitated by dialogue between a teacher and a student, now called the Socratic method.

Making the Grade

KURT WIESENFELD

IT WAS A rookie error. After 10 years I should have known better, but I 1
went to my office the day after final grades were posted. There was a tentative knock on the door. "Professor Wiesenfeld? I took your Physics 2121 class? I flunked it? I wonder if there's anything I can do to improve my grade?" I thought: "Why are you asking me? Isn't it too late to worry about it? Do you dislike making declarative statements?"

After the student gave his tale of woe and left, the phone rang. "I got a D in your class. Is there any way you can change it to 'Incomplete'?" Then the e-mail assault began: "I'm shy about coming in to talk to you, but I'm not shy about asking for a better grade. Anyway, it's worth a try." The next day I had three phone messages from students asking *me* to call *them.* I didn't.

Time was, when you received a grade, that was it. You might groan and moan, but you accepted it as the outcome of your efforts or lack thereof (and, yes, sometimes a tough grader). In the last few years, however, some students have developed a disgruntled-consumer approach. If they don't like their grade, they go to the "return" counter to trade it in for something better.

What alarms me is their indifference toward grades as an indication of personal effort and performance. Many, when pressed about why they think they deserve a better grade, admit they don't deserve one but would like one anyway. Having been raised on gold stars for effort and smiley faces for self-esteem, they've learned that they can get by without hard work and real talent if they can talk the professor into giving them a break. This attitude is beyond cynicism. There's a weird innocence to the assumption that one expects (even deserves) a better grade simply by begging for it. With that outlook, I guess I shouldn't be as flabbergasted as I was that 12 students asked me to change their grades *after* final grades were posted.

That's 10 percent of my class who let three months of midterms, quizzes 5
and lab reports slide until long past remedy. My graduate student calls it hyperrational thinking: if effort and intelligence don't matter, why should deadlines? What matters is getting a better grade through an unearned bonus, the academic equivalent of a freebie T-shirt or toaster giveaway. Rewards are disconnected from the quality of one's work. An act and its consequences are unrelated, random events.

Their arguments for wheedling better grades often ignore academic performance. Perhaps they feel it's not relevant. "If my grade isn't raised to a D, I'll lose my scholarship." "If you don't give me a C, I'll flunk out." One sincerely over-wrought student pleaded, "If I don't pass, my life is over." This is tough stuff to deal with. Apparently, I'm responsible for someone's losing a scholarship, flunking out or deciding whether life has meaning. Perhaps these students see me as a commodities broker with something they want—a grade. Though intrinsically worthless, grades, if properly manipulated, can be traded for what has value: a degree, which means a job, which means money. The one thing college actually offers—a chance to learn—is considered irrelevant, even less than worthless, because of the long hours and hard work required.

In a society saturated with surface values, love of knowledge for its own sake does sound eccentric. The benefits of fame and wealth are more obvious. So is it right to blame students for reflecting the superficial values saturating our society?

Yes, of course it's right. These guys had better take themselves seriously now, because our country will be forced to take them seriously later, when the stakes are much higher. They must recognize that their attitude is not only self-destructive, but socially destructive The erosion of quality control—giving appropriate grades for actual accomplishments—is a major concern in my department. One colleague noted that a physics major could obtain a degree without ever answering a written exam question completely. How? By pulling in enough partial credit and extra credit. And by getting breaks on grades.

But what happens once she or he graduates and gets a job? That's when the misfortunes of eroding academic standards multiply. We lament that schoolchildren get "kicked upstairs" until they graduate from high school despite being illiterate and mathematically inept, but we seem unconcerned with college graduates whose less blatant deficiencies are far more harmful if their accreditation exceeds their qualifications.

Most of my students are science and engineering majors. If they're good at 10
getting partial credit but not at getting the answer right, then the new bridge breaks or the new drug doesn't work. One finds examples here in Atlanta. Last year a light tower in the Olympic Stadium collapsed, killing a worker. It collapsed because an engineer miscalculated how much weight it could hold. A new 12-story dormitory could develop dangerous cracks due to a foundation that's uneven by more than six inches. The error resulted from incorrect data being fed into a computer. I drive past that dorm daily on my way to work, wondering if a foundation crushed under kilotons of weight is repairable or if this structure will have to be demolished. Two 10,000-pound steel beams at the new natatorium collapsed in March, crashing into the student athletic complex. (Should we give partial credit since no one was hurt?) Those are real-world consequences of errors and lack of expertise.

But the lesson is lost on the grade-grousing 10 percent. Say that you won't (not can't, but won't) change the grade they deserve to what they want, and they're frequently bewildered or angry. They don't think it's fair that they're judged according to their performance, not their desires or "potential." They don't think it's fair that they should jeopardize their scholarships or be in danger of flunking out simply because they could not or did not do their work. But it's more than fair; it's necessary to help preserve a minimum standard of quality that our society needs to maintain safety and integrity. I don't know if the 13th-hour students will learn that lesson, but I've learned mine. From now on, after final grades are posted, I'll lie low until the next quarter starts.

CHANGING THE EDUCATIONAL ENVIRONMENT

The educational system is a constant site for reform. It seems like students never measure up to society's expectations, and a host of experts present a variety of solutions to solve the problems faced by schools. Each of these essays considers ways to improve education by reforming the educational environment in some way. In "Hold Your Horsepower," Lyla Fox examines the problems high school students face by buying their own cars. This essay was originally published in the "My Turn" column for *Newsweek*. In "The Great Campus Goof-Off Machine," Nate Stulman describes how attempts by universities to improve education by giving students easy access to computers or by requiring students to purchase computers may actually inhibit student learning. Stulman was a sophomore at Swarthmore College when he wrote this essay for the *New York Times*. In the third essay, Patricia King suggests that a single-sex educational environment may help female students learn better, particularly in math and science. Her essay was originally published in *Newsweek*.

Hold Your Horsepower

LYLA FOX

FOLKS IN THE small Michigan town where I grew up revere the work ethic. Our entire culture lauds those who are willing to work their tails off to get ahead. Though there's nothing wrong with hard work, I suggest that our youngsters may be starting too young—and for all the wrong reasons. 1

Increasingly I identify with Sisyphus trying to move that stone. There are more mornings than I would like to admit when many of my students sit with eyes glazed or heads slumped on their desks as I try to nurture a threatening-to-become-extinct interest in school. These are not lazy kids. Many are high-achieving 16- and 17-year-olds who find it tough to reconcile 7:30 A.M. classes with a job that winds down at 10:30 P.M. or later.

"What's wrong?" I asked a student who once diligently completed his homework assignments. He groggily grunted an answer. "I'm tired. I didn't get home until 11 P.M." Half the class nodded and joined in a discussion about how hard it is to try to balance schoolwork, sports and jobs. Since we end up working most of our adult life, my suggestion to the class was to forgo the job and partake of school—both intra- and extracurricular.

"Then how do I pay for my car?" the sleepy student, now more awake, asked. Click. The car. That's what all these bleary eyes and half-done papers are about. My students have a desperate need to drive their own vehicles proudly into the school parking lot. The car is the teenager's symbolic club membership. I know because I've seen the embarrassed looks on the faces of teens who must answer "No" to the frequently asked "Do you have a car?" National Merit finalists pale in importance beside the student who drives his friends around in a shiny new Ford Probe.

My own son (a senior at the University of Michigan) spent a good part of 5
his high-school years lamenting our "no car in high school" dictate. When he needed to drive, we made sure he could always borrow our car. Our Oldsmobile 88, however, didn't convey the instant high-school popularity of a sporty Nissan or Honda. Our son's only job was to do as well as he could in school. The other work, we told him, would come later. Today I see students working more than the legally permitted number of hours to pay for their cars. I also see once committed students becoming less dedicated to schoolwork. Their commitment is to their cars and the jobs that will help them make those monthly car payments.

Once cars and jobs enter the picture, it is virtually impossible to get students focused on school. "My parents are letting me get a car," one of my brightest students enthused a few months ago. "They say all I have to do is get a job to make the payments." *All.* I winced, saying nothing because parents' views are sacrosanct for me. I bit my cheeks to keep from saying how wrong I thought they were and how worried I was for her schoolwork. Predictably, during the next few months, her grades and attitude took a plunge.

I say attitude because when students go to work for a car, their positive attitude frequently disappears. Teachers and parents are on the receiving end of curved-lip responses to the suggestion that they should knuckle down and do some schoolwork. A job and car payments are often a disastrous combination.

These kids are selling their one and only chance at adolescence for a car. Adults in their world must help them see what their children's starry eyes cannot: that students will have the rest of their lives to own an automobile and pay expenses.

Some parents, I know, breathe a sigh of relief when their children can finally drive themselves to orthodontist appointments and basketball practice. This trade-off could mean teens' losing touch with family life. Having a car makes it easy for kids to cut loose and take part in activities far from home. Needing that ride from Mom and Dad helps to keep a family connection. Chauffering teens another year or two might be a bargain after all.

What a remarkable experience a school day might be if it were the center of 10
teens' lives, instead of that much-resented time that keeps them from their friends and their jobs. Although we may not have meant to, parents may have laid the groundwork for that resentment. By giving kids permission to work, par-

ents are not encouraging them to study. Parents have allowed students to miss classes because of exhaustion from the previous night's work. By providing a hefty down payment on a $12,000 car and stressing the importance of keeping up the payments, they're sending a signal that schoolwork is secondary.

The kids I'm writing about are wonderful. But they are stressed and angry that their day has too few hours for too much work. Sound familiar? It should. It is the same description adults use to identify what's wrong with their lives.

After reading this, my students may want to hang me in effigy. But perhaps some of them are secretly hoping that someone will stop their world and help them get off. They might also concede that it's time to get out of the car and get on mass transit. For students in large metropolitan areas, public transportation is the only way to get around.

Adults should take the reins and let teens off the hook. We must say "no" when we're implored to "Please let me get a job so I can have a car." Peer pressure makes it hard for kids to turn away from the temptation of that shiny four-wheeled popularity magnet. It's up to the grown-ups to let kids stay kids a little longer.

The subject of teens and cars comes up in my home as well as in my classroom. My 15-year-old daughter gave me some bone-chilling news yesterday. "The Springers got Suzi her own car!" she announced. "All she has to do is make the payments."

I smiled and went back to correcting the essays that would have been lovely 15
had their authors had some time to put into constructing them. The payment, I told myself after my daughter went grudgingly to begin her homework, may be greater than anyone in the Springer family could possibly imagine.

The Great Campus Goof-Off Machine

NATE STULMAN

CONVENTIONAL wisdom says that computers are a necessary tool for higher 1
education. Many colleges and universities these days require students to have personal computers, and some factor the cost of one into tuition. A number of colleges have put high-speed Internet connections in every dorm room. But there are good reasons to question the wisdom of this preoccupation with computers and the Internet.

Take a walk through the residence halls of any college in the country and you'll find students seated at their desks, eyes transfixed on their computer monitors. What are they doing with their top-of-the-line PC's and high-speed T-1 Internet connections?

They are playing Tomb Raider instead of going to chemistry class, tweaking the configurations of their machines instead of writing the paper due tomorrow, collecting mostly useless information from the World Wide Web instead of doing a math problem set—and a host of other activity that has little or nothing to do with traditional academic work.

I have friends who have spent whole weekends doing nothing but playing Quake or Warcraft or other interactive computer games. One friend sometimes spends entire evenings—six to eight hours—scouring the Web for images and modifying them just to have a new background on his computer desktop.

And many others I know have amassed overwhelming collections of music 5
on their computers. It's the searching and finding that they seem to enjoy: some of them have more music files on their computers than they could play in months.

Several people who live in my hall routinely stay awake all night chatting with dormmates on-line. Why walk 10 feet down the hall to have a conversation when you can chat on the computer—even if it takes three times as long?

You might expect that personal computers in dorm rooms would be used for nonacademic purposes, but the problem is not confined to residence halls. The other day I walked into the library's reference department, and five or six students were grouped around a computer—not conducting research, but playing Tetris. Every time I walk past the library's so-called research computers, it seems that at least half are being used to play games, chat or surf the Internet aimlessly.

Colleges and universities should be wary of placing such an emphasis on the use of computers and the Internet. The Web may be useful for finding simple facts, but serious research still means a trip to the library.

For most students, having a computer in the dorm is more of a distraction than a learning tool. Other than computer science or mathematics majors, few students need more than a word processing program and access to E-mail in their rooms.

It is true, of course, that students have always procrastinated and wasted 10
time. But when students spend four, five, even ten hours a day on computers and the Internet, a more troubling picture emerges—a picture all the more disturbing because colleges themselves have helped create the problem.

Science for Girls Only

PATRICIA A. KING

THE SUBJECT of the day is electrical circuits, and the sixth graders are tinkering intently with wires and batteries. But the real subjects of this experiment are the students themselves, a pioneer class of 35 who have enrolled since last September in the new Girl's Middle School in Mountain View, Calif., the heart of Silicon Valley. They're having a little trouble with defective batteries and miswiring, but they're not fazed. Earlier in the year they built suspension bridges out of Popsicle sticks and arch bridges out of Styrofoam, so they're not about to be bested by some stupid loose connection. They are intent on understanding how Christmas lights work—why some blow out singly and why some blow out a whole string at a time—and how to repair them. "Then," notes Aliya Lakha, 12, "we won't have to ask men to fix it." 1

Making girls electrically independent on Christmas Eve is only a microcosm of the school's mission. The teachers (including a Stanford-trained structural engineer) and the curriculum (where 40 percent of class time is devoted to science, technology and math) were both chosen to make the girls as comfortable in technical subjects as they are in writing and history, says founder Kathleen Bennett, a former teacher and technical writer for Apple. The math, science and tech courses emphasize hands-on learning and working in groups, both of which promote girls' interest and learning. (The program also includes language arts, Spanish, fine arts and performing arts.) The first class—chosen by an admissions committee from 80 applicants—is not all science whizzes; their career ambitions range from computer engineer to horse trainer to teacher to lawyer.

You'd think that Silicon Valley would be the last place where girls would need to be sold on science. Not so. Even here, says Bennett, girls "hit the wall of femininity," when the formerly feisty and intellectually daring become afraid to stand out. As a result, far fewer girls than boys enroll in high-level math and science classes, particularly physical science, found a 1992 report [titled] "How Schools Short-change Girls," by the American Association of University Women. The failure of those teachers to give girls as much attention and computer time as boys seemed to be part of the reason, as was peer pressure on girls to hide their brains and zip their lips. Although the gender gap has closed some, the AAUW concluded this year that "girls' failure to take more top math and science courses . . . threatens to make women bystanders in the burgeoning technology industry of the 21st century."

Not our girls, they said in the Valley. The warning that girls are getting the short end of the mouse has attracted to GMS an all-star advisory council that includes CEOs Carol Bartz of Autodesk and Trip Hawkins of 3DO. It has also attracted $2.5 million for start-up costs. Venture capitalist Dan Lynch was first in line with a $100,000 gift. His daughter, now 29, quit science when middle-school peer pressure kicked in, he says; he fears his 9-year-old (who for now is "interested in absolutely everything like squashing bugs and seeing what they bleed") will make the same mistake. "Girls are still afraid not to be cool," especially in front of boys, Lynch says. Other parents agree: nationwide enrollment in girls' schools has gone up 20 percent in the last eight years.

All-girl classes can be especially helpful in middle school, a transition period 5
when conflicting messages about femininity and achievement, and the need to fit in, often erode girls' self-image. But at the $10,000-per-year GMS, which will expand to eighth grade in 2000, girls get all the teachers' attention and all the leadership roles. Sixth grader Divya Dujari, 11, who wants to be the CEO of a computer company, raves about the help she gets from teachers and the chance to do cool projects. Kris Bobier says her daughter Audrey has been sold on GMS ever since the open house, when she built a tower of cards. But there was an even stronger draw. "We were losing her," says Bobier. "She was shutting down to school. She really is a free spirit. This school gives her room for that." As for Audrey, she's so delighted with her boy-free school that she's hoping to remain at a girls' school until college.

Critics argue that a single-sex environment gives girls a false idea of what they'll face in the real world. Also, studies of girls' schools have produced conflicting results, with some suggesting that it is small classes, innovative curricula and great teaching that really help. But even if no one has figured out a sure-fire way to hook girls on science and tech, GMS probably has a better shot than most. After all, if they can't do it in Silicon Valley, where can they?

Chapter 12

Arguing with Images

Although most of the arguments you have encountered in this book have been verbal arguments (arguments through language), many of the arguments you encounter each day are primarily visual. That is, they are arguments that rely heavily, sometimes exclusively, on images. As a visual representation of meaning, an image doesn't just convey an argument (as words convey the meaning of verbal arguments); an image *is* the argument. Visual arguments are therefore quite direct and immediate, and so tend to be much more economical than verbal arguments—hence the saying "A picture is worth a thousand words." A visual argument is especially effective if it meets the needs of its intended audience. For example, you may be familiar with how lawyers often use visual arguments in a courtroom. In addition to written arguments and oral arguments, lawyers often use charts, graphs, pictures, and objects to strengthen their case. This visual evidence is usually called an "exhibit," something that is "shown" to the judge and jury. It's a dramatic moment in a court when the prosecutors produce Exhibit A: the murder weapon. Or the visual arguments could include photographs of the crime scene, fingerprints, blood spatter diagrams, DNA charts, or even a bloody glove. In the murder trial of O. J. Simpson, considered by some to be the "trial of the 20th century," the prosecution tried to create a dramatic visual argument by asking Simpson to try on a bloody glove found at his Brentwood, California, home. This glove was an important piece of physical evidence in the prosecution's case, and they not only wanted to demonstrate that it was Simpson's, they also wanted to leave the image in the jury's mind of Simpson with the glove. But this strategy backfired when Simpson was unable to get the glove over his hand. Even though the prosecution later had Simpson try on another pair of the same gloves to show that the gloves must have shrunk from contact with the blood, it was too late. Despite all of the evidence the prosecution had prepared and presented, what remained in the juror's mind was a glove that didn't fit—a powerful visual argument. In his closing argument in the case, defense lawyer Johnnie Cochran reinforced this visual argument with his memorable phrase, "If it doesn't fit, you must acquit." Not all visual arguments we encounter are found in this kind of dramatic context. Most are everyday arguments, but these can still be quite powerful because they are immediate and memorable, and often influence our emotions.

We encounter many types of visual arguments, and below I'll delve into a few of them, but visual arguments appear in only four basic forms. A visual argument can be one still image: a magazine ad, news photograph, editorial cartoon, poster, T-shirt, bumper sticker, product logo. It can also be a pair of images, such as the "before and after" photographs used to sell fad diets. A series of more than two images presented together can tell a story or show a cause-and-effect relationship, as in presentation slides, comic strips, comic books, children's picture books, and "graphic novels" (a more serious kind of comic book such as Japanese mangas or Art Spiegelman's *Maus,* a story about the Holocaust). And when a sequence of images is passed before our eyes very quickly, the sequence provides the illusion of movement—the moving images found in movies, television, videos, CD-ROMS, and websites. This last form of visual argument almost always includes sound—whether spoken words, music, representational sounds (a doorbell ringing, squealing car tires), or symbolic sounds (whoosh, wham)—and is considered multimedia, as it employs multiple media to persuade us. Multimedia arguments are exceptionally powerful, as anyone knows whose heart has started to race during a horror movie with just a change in background music.

■■ TYPES OF IMAGES

Still images: magazine ads, news photographs, editorial cartoons, posters, bumper stickers, product logos

Sequential images: side-by-side comparisons, comic strips, comic books, children's picture books, graphic novels

Moving images: movies, television, television ads, videos, animation

Multimedia arguments: websites, CD-ROMs, multimedia presentation

The Variety of Visual Arguments

PRODUCT LOGOS

In Chapter 1, I discussed the importance of product logos as arguments, using Nike's "swoosh" logo as an example. This logo is so common and so closely identified with Nike and with the traditional values of sports that Nike doesn't even need to include its name or anything about its products. The Nike logo is instantly recognizable to most people, and some argue that it is one of the most easily recognized symbols in the world. Nike has taken one simple shape and associated with it a collection of values, beliefs, and attitudes, including competitiveness, endurance, fair play, sacrifice, and excellence.

Although other companies haven't had the remarkable success of Nike, product logos are still important visual arguments. Intel, the maker of Pentium computer chips, asks consumers to look for the "Intel inside" brand on computers to make sure they are getting a quality product. Car companies, such as Ford, Chevy, Chrysler, Nissan, or Volvo, have created memorable logos to identify the wide range of cars they produce. But no car company has been quite as successful as Mercedes-Benz at associating with its logo a whole set of attitudes, beliefs, and values. Particularly during the 1980s, the Mercedes-Benz logo meant wealth and status. The mere presence of the logo is an argument.

Because logos can be such effective visual arguments, companies work very hard to make sure no one else uses them. For instance, even though it is a non-profit organization and supporter of amateur sport, the International Olympic Committee (IOC) aggressively protects its logo, the five Olympic rings representing the five continents that participate in the Olympics. The IOC sells a lot of merchandise as part of the Olympics—pins, shirts, hats, athletic clothing, mugs, pens, paperweights—just about anything can become a valuable souvenir with the Olympic logo on it. Many colleges and universities also try to create memorable logos that identify the school and its values but also sell products.

ADVERTISEMENTS

There are ads everywhere, and most ads rely heavily on visual images: print ads, TV ads, movie trailers, product packaging, Internet banners, product websites, and music videos. An advertiser has to make a powerful, persuasive argument in a very short time or very brief space. A television ad may be as short as 15 seconds. A magazine or newspaper ad may cover only a few square inches. An Internet ad banner may run for only a few seconds in a narrow strip at the top of a Web page. And a movie trailer or music video must compete for a viewer's attention against all the other trailers and videos. But despite the challenge of presenting an argument in such a brief format, ads are persuasive because they rely so heavily on visual arguments, which, as I mention above, are immediate, memorable, and affect our emotions. In Chapter 3, I describe how advertisements work as emotional arguments. They appeal to humor, fear, vanity, pride, greed as well as other emotions and needs.

POLITICAL COMMUNICATION

Politicians use advertising in much the same way that businesses do. But the products they are selling are themselves and their ideas. As part of campaigning, politicians will run traditional print or television ads that show images of themselves doing things that promote American values: kissing babies, playing touch football with a group of soldiers, visiting a memorial to fallen police officers or firefighters, meeting with other important people, visiting an elementary school. Politicians want to present themselves as someone who can get things done. They will often show pictures that illustrate clean cities, clean parks and forests, safe schools, or a prosperous economy. These pictures might show a clean and busy downtown area (without any homeless people), families having a picnic, children eagerly learning in a classroom, or people in hard hats building a new stadium. Such visual arguments are meant to identify important community values with the candidate so that people will want to vote for him or her.

Of course, visual arguments can work in negative campaigns as well. They can be used to attack a candidate by showing images associated with negatives values: polluted rivers and lakes, vandalism and crime, schools plagued by drugs and violence, or people lined up at the unemployment office. When George Bush ran for the presidency in 1988, a Republican political action group ran a controversial ad attacking Bush's Democratic opponent, Michael Dukakis, governor of Massachusetts. This ad tried to show that Dukakis was "soft on crime" by showing a picture of Willie Horton, a convicted murderer who was released on a weekend pass under Dukakis' prison furlough program and committed a rape. The ad was controversial because many thought it played into the stereotypical and racist fears that some Americans have about black men and crime. But some argue that the ad was so effective that it cost Dukakis the election. You can see a copy of the ad at <www9.cnn.com/ALLPOLITICS/1996/candidates/ad.archive>.

In addition to paid advertisements, politicians can also gain credibility through the traditional media by how they present themselves. National politicians usually have "image consultants" who help them choose what to wear, what kinds of facial expressions or gestures to use, how to inflect their voice, and how to stand. A politician wants to look and act confident to gain the trust of the people. A candidate wants to look "presidential." This is usually easier for a incumbent president because he has the White House, the Oval Office, and the other trappings of the presidency to support his credibility. In the film *The American President,* the fictional president says, "The White House is the single greatest home-court advantage in the modern world." A whole range of visual arguments support the credibility of the presidency regardless of who holds the office. Flags, emblems, marine guards, historical documents and artifacts, portraits of past presidents: Visual elements such as these all combine to give a sitting president a real rhetorical advantage.

PROPAGANDA

Political communication that is particularly one-sided, distorted, or manipulative is called propaganda. Propaganda is especially common in countries where the government has exclusive access to the mass media and where freedom of speech and freedom of the press are limited. In democratic countries, the media usually provide a check on propaganda. But propaganda still exists in democratic countries, particularly during times of war or political uncertainly when the government may have more control than usual over the media.

Although all governments use propaganda techniques to an extent, the German Nazi party perfected the art of modern propaganda, particularly the use of the mass media of the time—books, newspapers, posters, pamphlets, radio, and film. The Nazi propaganda machine reflected the peculiar genius of Joseph Goebbels, German minister for public information, who gave the Nazi party rhetoric a unified vision. Under Goebbels, the Nazis attacked Jews, blacks, communists, gays, and anyone else different from their Aryan ideal. Particularly in posters, pamphlets, and films, the Nazis presented their visual ideal of racial purity as the norm and portrayed as monsters anyone who didn't fit this ideal. One vicious example of Nazi propaganda is a film called *The Eternal Jew (Der Ewige Jude*, 1940). In this film, the Jews of Poland (which was invaded by Germany in 1939) are shown in the worst possible light: as evil, vicious, filthy, murderous monsters bent on taking over the world. The film portrays Jews as rats who have spread throughout the world, making frequent cuts between poor Jews living in the Polish ghettos and rats living in the sewers. The film ends with footage from Hitler's speech before the German parliament in 1939 where he called for "the annihilation of the Jewish race in Europe." Like most propaganda, *The Eternal Jew* is transparent, and by today's standard almost laughable in its crude and obvious attempts to demonize Jews. But the hatred behind the film is real and equally obvious, and by playing upon the fears and prejudices of the people, *The Eternal Jew* was very influential at the time in gaining support for Hitler's plan to exterminate all Jews. It is still frequently used to teach students about the dangers of propaganda and the reality of the Holocaust.

NEWS

Although they are primarily a print medium, newspapers have always relied on visual arguments. The most overtly persuasive visual elements in newspapers are the editorial cartoons. An editorial cartoonist has the difficult job of conveying in one panel an opinion about current events. And a cartoonist usually has to do this every day. The saying among editorial cartoonists is that you are only as good as your last drawing. Often, a newspaper will have its own staff cartoonist, but many of the better cartoonists are also syndicated, appearing in newspapers throughout the country. For example, Steve Benson is the staff cartoonist for the *Arizona Republic,* but his cartoons can be found in syndication in many other newspapers.

Other obvious visual elements in a newspaper are the photographs. A news photographer tries to give a story presence by capturing some element of it in a single moment: horror, fear, grief, excitement, tension, relief, or humor of a newsworthy event. News photographs may not look like arguments because they present themselves as a reliable record of what actually happened. We sometimes treat a photograph as the ultimate eyewitness that puts the viewer at the scene of the event. We trust that reliable news sources have not altered or manipulated the photograph. However, it's important to remember that a photograph is still a selection of reality. Although it is based in reality, it only shows what the photographer has chosen to frame within her lens. And what the photographer chooses to photograph, or which photograph the editor chooses to run, represents an attitude toward the event, even though it looks objective. A news photograph shows truth, but truth from the perspective of the photographer. It can't show what lies outside the frame of the lens or what happened before or after the shot was taken.

In addition to editorial cartoons and photographs, many newspapers include other visual elements such as charts, graphs, maps, and diagrams. As you review newspapers, you will also notice that some use more visual elements than others. For example, *USA Today* includes a lot of photographs, charts, diagrams, and graphs and a lot of color. On the other hand, the *Wall Street Journal* includes only engraved images, not real photographs, and very little color. And when the *Wall Street Journal* includes a chart, it is typically full of data, not graphics.

Newsmagazines, such as *Time, Newsweek,* or *U.S. News and World Report* rely even more heavily on visual arguments than do newspapers. Like newspapers, they have editorial cartoons, news photographs, graphics, charts, diagrams, and graphs, but a newsmagazine usually has more of these than a typical newspaper. And the quality of photographs in a magazine is usually much higher. A newspaper publishes on inexpensive newsprint, but newsmagazine comes out on glossy paper that allows for high-quality color reproductions. The high quality of these images gives the photographs in news magazines an even greater sense of presence and reality.

The most important image for the newsmagazine is the image that appears on the front cover. The cover of a newsmagazine usually relates to the lead story in the magazine, the story that the editors believe is the most important. As a visual argument, the cover of the magazine tries to attract the attention of possible readers and makes a statement about what is newsworthy. Like any news photograph, the cover photograph also represents a selection of reality from the point of view of the photographer and the editors. It just occupies a much more prominent place than most other news photographs.

When television news first started, it was heavily influenced by radio, and in early television news broadcasts, the news anchors would read the news to viewers. Even this image-poor environment was a visual argument because it was a statement to those suspicious of this new medium that television news was as serious as any other kind of news. Now that television is a well-established medium, television news is all about images. Because it includes a sequence of images along with sound, television video creates more of a sense of reality than a still photograph. And because television news can cover breaking news better than a newspaper can, television news images have a greater sense of immediacy. Television news give a sense that the recorded event is really happening. Handheld cameras, particularly digital cameras, have made television news even more immediate as amateur eyewitness photographers often capture remarkable images before a news crew even reaches the scene. For example, on the morning of September 11, 2001, millions of stunned Americans watched news video showing terrorists slamming a 767 airliner into the south tower of the World Trade Center. Several amateur photographers captured photos and video footage of this event, as well as the attack on the north tower, from different perspectives. The ability of news media to show this event from these different perspectives emphasized the reality and horror of what had really happened.

Of course, just as a still photograph is a selection of reality, so also is video. Video footage still represents the perspective of the videographer, and video still goes through editing before it is shown on television. Like a still photograph, video footage is based in reality but is also one perspective on the event that can reveal something about the attitude of those reporting the event.

As viewers, we generally trust that news agencies have not altered or manipulated the images that they present as real. But good video footage is not always available. And since television news relies so heavily on images, news programs will occasionally create images to accompany the story. Sometimes these images are animations; sometimes they are "dramatic re-creations," where actors are used to show what probably happened. These kind of re-creations are a step removed from reality, so a news agency will usually announce in some way that it is a re-creation.

Because of its reliance on striking images, some argue that television news is really more about entertainment than news. (For a detailed discussion of this topic, read "What Is News?" by Neil Postman and Steve Powers, in Chapter 7.) Television news is heavy on fires, car accidents, murder scenes, combat footage, and natural disasters not because these are necessarily the most important events of the day but rather because these events produce memorable images. Because images can often determine what is newsworthy and because of the immediacy and striking reality of news video, those who get most of their news from television often consider the world a more dangerous place than those who get their news from newspapers or magazines.

INTERNET NEWS SOURCES

ABC News Online: <www.abcnews.com>

BBC News Online: <news.bbc.co.uk>

CBS News Online: <www.cbsnews.com>

CNN.com: <www.cnn.com>

MSNBC Cover: <www.msnbc.com>

New York Times on the Web: <www.nytimes.com>

PBS News Hour Online: <www.pbs.org/newshour>

Washington Post: <www.washingtonpost.com>

With the phenomenal growth of the Internet, television networks and newspapers have often joined to provide both breaking news and analysis around the clock. Like other websites, news sites are highly visual, allowing viewers access to still photographs, digitized video, as well as charts, graphs, and diagrams. Internet news sources also allow users access to databases of stories, photographs, and video, providing potentially greater depth of understanding on a topic. And news websites often include additional content or features not found on television news programs or in newspapers or magazines. Many Internet news sites look like newspapers. They have a banner at the top and headlines, and many even use three columns. Like newspapers, they usually run still photographs with captions. The headlines and images are usually links to more information about the story, and there is typically a frame on the top or the left side that allows the user to view the news by category: opinion, sports, national news, world news, and so on. The layout of the news website itself is a kind of visual argument. Why, for example, don't news sites use much flash animation or dramatic splash pages (like you find on a lot of entertainment sites)? Since the Internet itself is a relatively new medium, the newspaper layout of these sites announces that these are serious, reliable sources of information.

ENTERTAINMENT

While news sources at least make the attempt to present themselves as serious sources of information, most media sources are designed to entertain rather than inform, and images are increasingly important to entertainment. Popular magazines freely engage in altering and manipulating images. Unlike news video, television shows and movies rely on scripts, careful set design and decoration, controlled lighting, multiple cameras, and multiple takes to get the images just right. Even shows that are "taped before a live audience" involve multiple takes and considerable postproduction editing before the show is aired. Very little "live" television is actually live anymore. Even shows that present themselves as "reality television," shows like "Survivor," "The Fear Factor," "MTV's Real World," and "Temptation Island," use actors, not real people, in highly artificial situations, and the "reality" of these shows is carefully controlled to entertain. (If you really recorded the "reality" of most people's lives, it would not be very entertaining.)

Visual images in entertainment, whether magazines, television, or film, often make arguments about what we value rather than what is real. We are presented images of our ideals of beauty, femininity, masculinity, strength, courage, cowardice, goodness, or evil. As entertainment, television and movies in particular reveal our fears, hopes, and desires, what we wish the world was like (or fear it may become) rather than how it really is. In addition to these arguments about values, visual images in entertainment also make an argument about actions: You should buy the products of those who sponsor the entertainment. And some television shows are just long advertisements. Infomercials, for example, follow the format of a talk show or news program, but they really exist not to provide information per se but to sell a product or service.

Television and magazines obviously exist to promote products, but movies do as well. First, they promote other movies. Movie trailers (or "previews") shown before the feature presentation try to ensure a big opening weekend for future releases. Second, movies actually place products prominently in the film to promote them. In older movies, no brand names were shown, but now movies are full of brand names, paid promotions from the companies whose products are featured. This is called "product placement." Sales of Reese's Pieces jumped 65 percent after being featured in Steven Spielberg's *E.T.: The Extraterrestrial* (1982). Mars had passed on the offer to feature M&Ms. Budget Rent-A-Truck paid to have its product featured in *Home Alone* (1990). Recent James Bond movies have featured Visa credit cards, Avis car rentals, BMW cars and motorcycles, Smirnoff vodka, Heineken beer, Omega watches, Ericsson cell phones, and L'Oreal makeup. And could you argue that Tom Hanks's *Castaway* is the longest commercial for FedEx ever made? In addition to product placement, movies exist to sell a line of products associated with the film. These are called product tie-ins. Sometimes we might even wonder, do movies exist to sell McDonald's Happy Meals? Or do Happy Meal toys exist to promote movies? Finally, like television shows, movies promote a set of attitudes and values. In the famous western *High Noon* (1952), Gary Cooper plays a peaceful U.S. marshal who must face an old enemy on his own when his townspeople refuse to support him. Some claim that this film, which was produced at a time when the United States was struggling with its role in the Cold War against communism, argues in favor of the United States standing up against communism, even in the face of wavering support from its allies. But even if you don't accept this kind of allegorical interpretation of the film, it is clear that *High Noon* is reinforcing traditional American values of individuality and standing up for what's right even though it may not be popular.

ART

Although visual art is not as blatantly commercial as most entertainment, fine art often does make an argument. You could say that all art is an argument about the nature of art itself, particularly about what constitutes art. In particular, avant-garde art (experimental art) often responds to common beliefs about what is proper, appropriate, or correct in the subject matter, technique, or context of art. For instance, the Impressionist painters such as Monet and Renoir challenged the prevailing conventions of the French salon about what was the proper subject matter for art. Instead of mythological themes or heroic battles, they painted flowers, haystacks, or ponds in natural light rather than in the studio. In a similar manner, their Impressionistic technique challenged the academic and precise style of other artists, many of whom considered the Impressionists unskilled amateurs. Another painter that makes a visual argument about art is Georges Seurat, best known for his large painting *A Sunday Afternoon on the Island of La Grande Jatte*. Seurat's painting portrays Parisians enjoying a Sunday afternoon in a park, but it is also an argument about technique and visual theory. Seurat's technique was to paint in dots, and was called "pointillism" or "divisionism." His visual theory was that small dots of pure color would produce brighter colors than mixing paints on a palate and painting in strokes. This large painting took Seurat over two years to complete, one dot at a time. And his work anticipates the color theory used by television and computers, where points of colored light are combined by the eye to produce a mixture of colors.

Art can also argue about values. Some art reinforces the common beliefs of the community, but more often than not, artists use their medium to challenge what is commonly accepted. Artists may deliberately produce something that others consider obscene, profane, or disrespectful to challenge what the community considers appropriate. Some art responds to a particular political situation while also addressing community values more broadly. Delacroix's famous *Liberty Leads the People* reinforces the values of the French Revolution—liberty, fraternity, equality—and portrays in heroic style those of all ages who fought against the French aristocracy. Francisco de Goya presents another version of the French Revolution and the Napoleonic Wars in *The Disasters of War,* his series of etchings on the horrors of war. Goya makes another emotional visual argument in his painting *The Shootings of May Third 1808,* which depicts the execution of innocent civilians during the War of Spanish Independence (see Figure 12.1). Consider also what some consider art's most powerful statement against war: Pablo Picasso's *Guernica* (see chapter opener). This large mural was the centerpiece of the Spanish Pavilion of the 1937 World's Fair in Paris and depicts the horrible attack on Guernica, a small Basque village in northern Spain, which was

Figure 12.1 The Shootings of May 3, 1808

chosen for bombing and strafing practice by Hitler's air force, with the permission of Spain's fascist dictator Francisco Franco. The village was bombed with high-explosive and incendiary bombs for over three hours, leaving 1,600 civilians killed or wounded. After the fair, *Guernica* toured Europe and North America, where it helped to raise awareness of the growing fascist threat in Europe.

DESIGN

Visual design refers to the appearance of objects that are not necessarily works of art: cars, dishes, silverware, furniture, appliances, computers, toys, interiors of buildings, or clothing. The design of an object can make a lot of arguments about the object itself. For example, during the 1950s and 1960s, many cars were made to look like jets or rockets, with large fins on the back fenders. Although these designs look out of place today, these features argued that these cars were fast and powerful. They also had a "futuristic" look that many consumers found appealing. Some cars were designed to look streamlined, like a missile or a bullet, making a similar argument about speed. Even kitchen appliances from the time—toasters, blenders, hand mixers—were given a sleek, streamlined, futuristic space-age look. These ordinary objects argued that they should be purchased and used by people who are modern and sophisticated.

Currently popular sport utility vehicles are designed to look rugged and outdoorsy even though they will never go off-road. Luxury car companies produce safari-looking vehicles, even though they will only be driven around the city, because this is a look that sells. Some design features are tied to what economist Thorstein Veblen called conspicuous consumption—the purchase of luxurious items as a sign of status and wealth. Whatever products have become status symbols will soon set the style for the design of other objects, even when that design doesn't really match the function of the object itself. In the West, for example, some people wear cowboy hats and boots even though they've never been near a horse. (Real cowboys often wear baseball caps.) And teenagers from predominantly white suburbs can be seen wearing the hip-hop fashions, traditionally associated with the predominantly black inner city, because these fashions represent values and a kind of cool status that has a broad appeal among youth.

The Rhetorical Situation and Visual Arguments

Much of what you've already learned about verbal arguments can be applied to visual arguments. As with verbal arguments, for instance, visual arguments make more sense when they are analyzed within the context of a particular community. Understanding the context for a visual argument is even more important because visual arguments don't usually explain themselves. Taken away from its context, a visual argument can seem puzzling and open to a variety of interpretations. But within its context, a visual argument is often instantly recognizable to viewers.

Because visual arguments rely more heavily on images than words, they often have to be explained through language to those who are not participants in the immediate context, much as I described and then briefly explained the ad about Extreme Polo Sport. Begin with the rhetorical situation: Who produced this image? Where is it located? What is its context? Who are its intended viewers? What issue does it address? Then try to identify the kairos of the issue: What other arguments is the image responding to? What is the life cycle of the situation it is addressing? Where is the image located within that life cycle?

Images and Persuasion

Like verbal arguments, visual arguments relate to the three means of persuasion outlined in Chapter 1: ethos, pathos, and logos.

VISUAL ETHOS

Visual arguments can be used to create and maintain credibility. You gain credibility as an individual by how you present yourself, how you dress, groom, and behave. For example, when you dress up for a job interview, you are making a visual argument. You might call it "trying to make a good impression," but you are making the visual argument through your clothes and appearance that you are the right person for the job. For some jobs, this would mean wearing a suit; for other jobs, you would dress more casually. You establish credibility by dressing in the right way for the right occasion. You would expect servers at a restaurant to have a neat and clean appearance (after all, they are handling your food), but you might be suspicious of a mechanic who didn't look a little greasy.

In addition to appearance, individuals may also have visual evidence of their education, training, or certification. Doctors dress like doctors and they often have a diploma on their wall as well. Both the doctor's dress and the diploma are visual arguments that the doctor is competent and credentialed. Even the little letters that follow a person's name can be a visual argument of that person's competence or authority: MD, PhD, CPA, JD, MSW, DDS, RN. Other certifications and awards, particularly if displayed in a person's office, also contribute visually to that person's credibility and authority.

Sometimes visual credibility comes from the office or position a person holds rather than from the individual. This is one reason firefighters and police officers wear uniforms. And even a plainclothes police officer will have a badge, a visual symbol that this individual has authority to enforce the law. A judge's black robe and gavel are visual reminders that the judge has the authority of the state to rule on criminal guilt or legal disputes. And the formal dress of many religious leaders identifies them as authorized representatives of their church.

Credibility can come from identifying visually with an organization as well. This is one reason that corporations, universities, and nonprofit organizations usually have an official seal, motto, or logo that shows up on official publications, letterhead, and business cards. These brief visual arguments transfer some of the credibility of the organization to the individual.

The visual design of a document also helps to reinforce the credibility of the author. If what you write has a neat, professional appearance, people will take your argument more seriously than if your writing looks sloppy. For example, if you turn in an essay that is handwritten on cheap paper with a lot of surface errors, then it will be difficult for your readers to take your argument seriously, even if it is well written. On the other hand, if your argument is neat and correct and looks professional, then you will most likely have more credibility with your readers. The visual appearance of the essay itself is an argument supporting your ethos. You can also support your ethos through visual design by meeting the expectations of your audience and the design conventions of the genre you are writing. Your choice of typeface, paper or screen color, headings, layout, and illustrations should all be governed by the nature of the situation. A more formal situation might call for black type on white paper with few illustrations (mostly of a technical nature). A less formal situation might call for a colored background (or a mix of colors) with a distinctive typeface and splashy illustrations designed to catch the eye and hold the reader's attention. You can observe the visual conventions of the situation you are writing for by reading what others have written for similar situations and paying close attention to how they have used color, typeface, layout, and illustration. In academic writing, you will be required to follow the design conventions of a particular academic style guide (see page 372–398 in Chapter 6), such as MLA, APA, or *Chicago Manual of Style* (CMS). These style guides provide details with regard to where you put your name, title, page numbering, and how you document source materials. Following these details may seem tedious to you, but it is an important part of strengthening your credibility as an academic author.

VISUAL PATHOS

Because of their immediacy and vividness, visual arguments are particularly effective at evoking an emotional response in a reader/viewer. A visual argument gives a claim presence; it makes it real for readers. In evoking an emotional response, a picture really is worth a thousand words. A skilled writer can still evoke an emotional response through careful description, but a skilled photographer, artist, or cinematographer can give the subject an even more immediate and dramatic rendering.

One way to create visual pathos is through the choice of image. The human image in particular is an effective means of evoking emotion. For example, people may feel bad when they hear about thousands of children starving in a distant country such as Somalia, Iraq, or Afghanistan, but they will feel an even more powerful emotion if they are shown images of these starving children, particularly if the focus is on their faces. A visual image puts a human face on suffering. A photographer may capture excitement and joy by showing an action shot of a sporting event. One television sports program, "The Wide World of Sports," used to show "the thrill of victory" by showing a team running out onto a field after scoring the winning point and "the agony of defeat" by showing a downhill skier suffering a tremendous crash. These visual images, shown at the beginning of the sports coverage, made the visual argument that "whether you win or lose, it is exciting to watch sports," enticing the viewer to spend an afternoon watching sports broadcasts. Choosing scenes from nature is another way to evoke emotion. Environmentalists can make a visual argument by showing pictures of endangered animals in their natural habitat. Just think what showing visual images of whales has done worldwide for protecting these animals from hunting. Ansel Adam's black-and-white photographs of Yosemite, the remarkable photography in *Arizona Highways* magazine and *National Geographic,* and the efforts of early 20th-century landscape painters did much to portray the wilderness of the American West as something worth preserving.

Symbols are visual arguments that can often awaken an immediate response in those who recognize the symbol. For instance, the symbols of the United

States awaken feelings of patriotism in many people. The flag, the White House, the Capitol, the Washington Monument, the Lincoln Memorial, the Vietnam Veteran's Memorial, the bald eagle, the Liberty Bell, fireworks: All of these are visual reminders of the values identified with the United States. Other countries would have a different set of symbols to evoke feelings of patriotism. Every state also has symbols, usually presented on a seal or flag, that represent the values of the state. Many of these are instantly recognizable to those who live in the state, and they create a sense of community identity. Religious symbols are also visual arguments, promoting the beliefs and values of those who adhere to the religion. The cross for Christians, the Star of David for Jews, the crescent for Muslims, the yin-yang symbol for Taoists: These symbols identify these systems of belief, and there are many others. Some Christians use the fish as a symbol for Christ. The menorah is another important symbol for Jews. The five-pointed star represents for Muslims the five pillars of Islam and is often shown together with the crescent, particularly on many flags.

Finally, colors themselves may evoke certain emotions within members of a community. Some claim that blue is a peaceful and tranquil color. Blue will help people resolve conflicts and accept difficult decisions. Some say green is also a very soothing and relaxing color and that, for instance, after the Blackfriar's Bridge in London was painted green, suicides at the bridge decreased by 34 percent. Of course, many believe red is an angry color that leads to tension and irritability. If you do a little research, you will find many different psychological theories of color. Most agree that brighter, more intense colors lead to more powerful emotions. And many argue that emotional responses to color are somewhat determined by culture. For example, in the United States, most brides wear white (as a symbol of purity), and people wear black to funerals as a sign of mourning. A black wedding dress or white funeral attire would be unusual. But in some Asian cultures, black is a symbol of good luck, so brides wear black, and white is a symbol of death. There is no question that colors can evoke an emotional response in viewers, but you need to be careful to examine these responses within the context of a particular community.

VISUAL LOGOS

Visual arguments appeal to reason in two primary ways: evidence of existence or causality and visual representation of data. If you can observe an object or event firsthand, you have a pretty good visual argument (for yourself, at least) that the object really exists or that the event really happened. But how do you convince others? You can make a written report of the event, but a picture or physical evidence (such as a piece of the object) would be much more convincing. If you had an encounter with a UFO, you could describe your experience (which could then be compared with other reports for consistency), but a photograph of the UFO would be even better—especially if you are in the photograph, too. And imagine what a convincing argument you could make if you had a piece of the spaceship.

Many objects or events are not directly observable. Visual evidence plays an important role here, too. Historians or archeologists can't observe the ancient world directly, but they can uncover artifacts: bits of pottery, bones, teeth, tools, ruins, engravings, carvings, and so on. By collecting these artifacts or making visual records of them through drawings, photographs, or video, historians can present visual arguments to support their theories about past civilizations. Scientists also make visual records of natural phenomena that are not easily observed or measured with the eye. Telescopes, satellites, and space probes can take photographs or measurements of planets, stars, and galaxies that are too remote for scientists to see. Satellites can even tell us more about our own earth than scientists can observe from the earth's surface. You can make a weather forecast using the clouds as visual evidence, but you can make a much more accurate forecast using satellite imaging.

Visual evidence also plays an important role in arguing about causality. Causality relies on a change in an object or event, and visual evidence can help to identify and explain such changes. For example, military intelligence uses before-and-after satellite images of a target to measure the effectiveness of a bombing raid. Scientists will gather physical evidence, photographs, and measurements at the scene of a tornado to measure its strength and behavior. And detectives will gather a lot of physical evidence at a crime scene (fingerprints, photographs, blood samples, bits of cloth, weapons, etc.) to determine who committed the crime. Later, prosecutors may use this visual evidence to try to convict someone. Visual evidence, such as photographs, drawings, or images, are usually identified as "figures" in academic writing. Remember that if you use someone else's visual evidence, you need to identify the source in your caption for the figure.

Not all evidence is visual, but if the evidence can be represented quantitatively, it can usually also be represented visually through charts, graphs, diagrams, and maps. Pie charts are very effective at representing percentages. They might be used to show the amount of money in a budget allocated to different items. Or they could be used to show the racial makeup of a particular community, based on census data.

Line graphs are very good at showing causal relationships, particularly the changes in an object or event over time. A line graph can express mathematical functions, where one object or event changes in relation to another. For example, a line graph can be used to show a company's changing profitability over time or to record an athlete's training record. An economist could use a line graph to show demand for a product as a relationship of the price of the product. Bar graphs are good for making comparisons, particularly when several items are being compared. For example, a bar graph could provide a company with information about production and sales for a particular product over a series of years. Or it could be used to compare by voting district how many people voted in a recent election.

Diagrams can be used to represent causal relationships be explaining visually how something works. Diagrams can represent a process and often take the form of a set of instructions, demonstrating, for instance, how an object should be put together. Diagrams are useful in simplifying complex objects or events. For instance, a geologist might use a diagram to identify the different rock layers and faults in a mountain range or to show the internal structure of a volcano.

Maps are also a simplification of complex information that make a visual appeal to reason. Political maps simplify the relationships among different countries to identify countries by their names and boundaries. Although maps may look very objective, they don't always agree with one another. A map showing Taiwan as an independent country rather than a province of mainland China is a political statement as well as a geographic one. The names of countries can be disputed, too. Does your map show Cambodia or Kampuchea? It depends on which government was in power at the time. Most maps present themselves as accurate and reliable reports in information. As such, maps may be used as visual evidence to support a variety of arguments. A county surveyor's map, for example, may be used in a dispute between property owners about a boundary line. A geologist's resource map can be used as evidence by environmentalists in a dispute about water quality or water resources. When maps disagree with one another or when the accuracy of the map itself becomes suspect, then the map as visual argument becomes the focus of debate.

Strategies of Visual Argument

Visual arguments can be used to accomplish many different purposes, and some strategies of visual argument are used frequently. If you learn to recognize these strategies, you will be much more effective in analyzing and responding to these arguments.

METAPHOR

In literature classes, you have probably heard *metaphor* defined as a figurative comparison between two objects. Seeing one object in terms of another is the essence of metaphor, and visual metaphor involves representing such a comparison to the viewer. For instance, a little kid who is angry at his sister might draw a picture of his sister as a pig. Or he might draw a picture of a pig and label it "my sister." This is a visual metaphor. He has found an animal that represents how he feels about his sister, and he expresses this visually. Much propaganda uses visual metaphor that is not much more sophisticated than this. When the Nazis showed Jews as rats, they were using visual metaphor. In propaganda issued by the Allied forces during World War II, the Germans and Japanese were similarly dehumanized through visual metaphor. Enemy soldiers were shown as ravenous wolves or demons or monsters, making them much easier for people to hate. One famous Nazi poster shows Hitler as a white knight sitting on horseback. The Nazi propaganda machine was presenting him as a crusading knight, who had come to the salvation of the German people. In this way, a visual metaphor can make an argument about values by associating someone with something good or with something bad.

Another kind of metaphor is used to explain or illustrate an idea. When evolutionary biologists talk about the "primordial soup" from which life on earth developed, they aren't talking about a literal soup. They are using soup as a metaphor to explain the mixture of chemicals, heat, and forces that produced the right combination for life. In a similar fashion, some people try to use mechanical metaphors to explain the human body. The body can be illustrated as a complex machine, divided into different systems. It consumes "fuel" (food, water, air) and produces "waste." At the same time, the human body becomes a metaphor for understanding machines as well. Even robots that don't look much like humans may have "arms," "legs," or "eyes." In the information age, the human brain is often compared to a computer. Both the brain and a computer have memory. Both use electrical "switches" to transmit information. Both can adapt and learn. Both can do mathematical calculations or solve logical problems (although a computer can do these much more quickly). Both have a remarkable ability to recognize patterns and make quick decisions based on these patterns. Some people even talk about meeting with other people as "interfacing." In the 18th century, astronomers compared the solar system to a clock, a metaphor that emphasizes the precise movements of the planets. You may have seen a miniature model of the solar system that runs like a clock. This type of mechanical model of the solar system is called an orrery. The first one was invented in the 18th century by George Graham, and it was later named after Charles Boyle, Earl of Orrery. This mechanical model is a visual representation of the clock metaphor, and it illustrates the power of a visual metaphor. Once you see one of these little machines, it is difficult to think of the solar system as something other than a large clockwork mechanism.

ALLUSION

In literature, an allusion is a reference to something or someone outside of the literary work: another work of literature, a historical figure or event, a famous person, a proverb or famous saying. Allusion can be persuasive, particularly in building credibility when the allusion helps to identify the argument with something or someone admired by the community. For example, in his famous "Letter from Birmingham Jail," Martin Luther King, Jr., alludes frequently to the New Testament as well as to well-known secular and religious thinkers. These allusions help to strengthen King's credibility by showing that he is well-educated, but they also help King to identify himself with these figures, who would be admired by his readers. Allusions can also create a comparison that leads the community toward a conclusion. For example, after the destruction of the World Trade Center on September 11, 2001, many people immediately began comparing the terrorist attack to the surprise attack by the Japanese navy on Pearl Harbor, the event that led the United States into World War II. Although some people think that this allusion suits the situation well, it also carries with it an implied course of action, a military retaliation. On the other hand, those who express concerns about the increasing involvement of the United States in a war in Afghanistan might compare it to Vietnam, a comparison that also carries with it an implied course of action.

Allusions are found in visual arguments as well. Visual allusions are images from other works, or images that represent famous events or people or that illustrate famous stories, proverbs, or sayings. Over the past several years, moviemakers have been fascinated with visual allusions. For instance, in nearly every one of its animated films produced in the last decade, Disney includes a reference to one of its other animated films. Product tie-ins from *A Bug's Life* turn up in *Toy Story 2.* And a child is listening to the soundtrack from *The Lion King* in *Toy Story.* The crab from *The Little Mermaid* makes a brief appearance in *Aladdin,* and Scar, the evil brother from *The Lion King,* makes a cameo appearance in *Hercules.* In one scene from *Aladdin,* the genie (voiced by Robin Williams) asks, "Aladdin, you've just won the heart of the princess. What are you going to do now?" The understated answer is "I'm going to Disney World." This scene alludes to a famous television moment. After the San Francisco 49ers had just won the Super Bowl, a reporter asked quarterback Joe Montana, "What are you going to do now?" He replied, "I'm going to Disney World." Disney later reenacted this scene and turned it into a commercial. A lot of other films and television shows follow this same practice.

These visual allusions provide a point of interest for the audience. The filmmakers are "winking" at their audience, sharing a little inside joke. But in the case of Disney, where all of the allusions are to other Disney films and characters, the allusions also subtly promote Disney product tie-ins (toys, games, action figures) as well as Disney films on video. Subtle and clever allusions favor a video age, where children may watch the same Disney film dozens of times. These allusions remind young viewers that Disney isn't just one film—it's a whole line of films, videos, products, hotels, cruise ships, and theme parks.

Another example of visual allusion involves one of the most famous news photographs of all time, Joe Rosenthal's Pulitzer Prize–winning photograph of a group of marines raising the U.S. flag over Mt. Suribachi during the battle of Iwo Jima in World War II (see Figure 12.2). Following the war, this photograph provided the image for the U.S. Marine Corps war memorial near Arlington, Virginia. The image of this moment has been reproduced in many different contexts, usually to celebrate the values of determination, strength, patriotism, and sacrifice. An interesting parallel to the Iwo Jima photograph was captured by Thomas Franklin, photographer for *The Record* (Bergen County, New Jersey). This now-famous photograph shows three firefighters raising a flag over the rubble of one of the World Trade Center towers, and it bears such a striking resemblance to Rosenthal's photo that people immediately began to recognize the allusion and to place the photos side by side. (The photo is widely available online:

Figure 12.2 Flag Raising over Iwo Jima

do an image search using the photographer's name, "Thomas Franklin," as your search term.) But visual similarities aside, the reason that the comparison works so well is that Americans were eager to associate the values represented by the marines on Iwo Jima to the firefighters in New York. In related examples of visual allusion, a torn flag from the World Trade Center flew over Yankee Stadium during the 2001 World Series and aboard the U.S.S. Theodore Roosevelt as it left to support the war in Afghanistan. The flags in these examples are more than just flags; they become symbols of heroism and sacrifice through the power of allusion.

JUXTAPOSITION

One common strategy of visual argument involves juxtaposition, placing images side by side. This technique can be used to emphasize similarities or differences. In arguments about values, juxtaposition is used to identify a person or event with another person or event that assigns the first positive or negative value. After the photograph was taken of the firefighters raising the flag at the World Trade Center, it was circulated around the Internet along with the Iwo Jima photo. Placing these two photographs side by side emphasizes the comparison and invites the viewers to recognize the common values celebrated in the two photographs.

Mt. Rushmore, a famous American image, involves a similar kind of juxtaposition. The images of George Washington, Thomas Jefferson, Abraham Lincoln, and Theodore Roosevelt are placed next to each other in a heroic sculpture, inviting the viewer to see each of these presidents as ideal leaders and all of these presidents in relationship to one another. On the other hand, political cartoons showing Osama bin Laden along with Hitler and Stalin (the epitome of evil in the 20th century) invites viewers to see bin Laden in terms of these two dictators.

Juxtaposition can also be used to emphasize contrasts. This often happens in advertising where one brand is shown next to another in a magazine ad or television commercial so that potential buyers can clearly see the superiority of one over the other.

In arguments about causality, juxtaposition can be used to show the changes that have taken place, the "effects" of the "cause." The famous "before and after" photographs promoting weight loss programs attempt to illustrate the physical differences in a person who has followed the diet. The first picture is usually a very bad photo of a severely overweight person. Often, to emphasize the contrast, other things about the person are bad as well—pale skin, bad haircut, clothing that is out of fashion, poor lighting, no makeup. In the second picture, the person is shown after losing weight (often from a side shot, rather than a front shot). They may be wearing a swimsuit or holding a pair of their old pants. But they are usually also wearing better makeup and better clothes. They will also have a better tan and haircut, too. Of course, not all of these differences can be attributed to the diet, but the side-by-side comparison invites the viewer to see the striking differences, attribute these differences to the diet, and decide to go on the diet as well. One striking antismoking ad makes its point by placing an X-ray of a healthy set of lungs next to an X-ray of a smoker's lungs. This visual argument points out how harmful smoking can be and encourages people not to smoke. And side-by-side or before-and-after images are often used in news photography to show the effects of a natural disaster or military strike.

THE HUMAN FIGURE

Human figures are used in many of the visual arguments described in this chapter, and representing the human figure is a frequent element of visual arguments because humans respond well to other humans and because the human body is capable of expressing so much meaning.

The face is the primary focus of the human body. The human face is capable of more than 10,000 expressions, and scientists estimate that over 3,000 of these convey some kind of emotion. Many of these expressions vary from one culture to another, but anthropologist Paul Ekman says there are six universal expressions: joy, sorrow, surprise, fear, disgust, and anger. Ekman bases his research on early work by Charles Darwin, who tried to capture facial expressions of human emotion on film. An accurate facial expression as part of a visual argument can intensify the power of the image to convey emotion. These expressions can be captured in the moment, as a news photographer tries to do, or they can be rehearsed and staged by actors.

Just as the face is the primary focus of the human body, the eyes are the primary focus of the face. If someone's eyes are shifty and evasive, if the person avoids making eye contact, some people conclude that the person is lying or trying to hide something. But, in some cultures, direct and sustained eye contact can be seen as a sign of aggression. Children learn early in life how to make "sad puppy eyes" to try to get sympathy from their parents. Widened eyes usually express fear or surprise, while narrowed eyes may communicate anger or disagreement. Rapid blinking of the eyes may show excitement.

Other features of the face can also signal emotion. A heartfelt smile shows joy, contentment, or excitement, while a posed smile might conceal true contempt or deception. Pursing of the lips often shows disagreement or anger, while pouting can show uncertainty or sadness. A canine snarl might show disgust, while a grimace may show terror.

In addition to the face, other parts of the body can be used as visual cues in an argument. Gestures, posture, and body movement can communicate a lot. Americans almost universally use the "OK" gesture to signal that everything is all right. But a thumbs-up works as well. And two thumbs up is even more emphatic. During World War II, the "V" for victory sign became a quick visual argument to boost the morale of Allied troops. This sign eventually became identified with Winston Churchill, but it signified the determination of the British in particular to triumph over Nazi Germany. Richard Nixon later identified himself by his trademark double victory sign. And the meaning of some gestures is unmistakable. When the U.S.S. Pueblo was captured by North Korea in 1968, the crew members were forced to appear in a propaganda picture. The North Koreans were arguing that the crew members were "contrite and cooperative"; however, in this picture, the sailors on the first row all display what *Time* magazine called "the U.S. hand signal of obscene derisiveness and contempt"—the elevated middle finger.[1] The crew had told their captors that this gesture was "The Hawaiian good luck sign," but this visual argument sent a clear message to Americans of how the crew members really felt about their North Korean captors. The handshake is a very important part of American culture. A firm grip can show confidence and determination. A death grip might indicate that someone is overbearing and pushy. And a limp handshake might indicate that someone is tentative or weak.

People also communicate a lot by how they walk, stand, or sit. Someone sitting on the edge of her seat indicates that she is engaged and interested, while someone leaning back might show a lack of interest. Often, people cross their arms when they are going on the defense, while outstretched arms can indicate openness. Where someone sits in relation to another person or how close someone stands can communicate a lot, too. Sitting behind a desk creates a barrier between you and someone else, signaling a position of power and a formal relationship, while sitting next to someone can indicate a more equal relationship.

Although not strictly part of the human figure, clothing can also tell you a lot about a person: gender, social class, age, economic status, nationality,

[1] North Korean Propaganda Photograph of Room 13, *Time,* October 18, 1968.

ethnicity, status, role, group identity, emotional state, physical climate, period in history (as in a photograph), or attitude.

Appearance does matter for persuasiveness. Research indicates that people who are considered physically attractive are generally treated better at stores and restaurants, are often considered more successful, and even get lighter punishments when they commit a crime. Advertisers, in particular, know this, and they make good use of the human figure as a strategy for argument. They know that many people are more willing to trust and listen to someone who is considered physically attractive. Advertisers will do a lot of research to find out just the right kind of "look" that will appeal to a particular demographic group (age, region, ethnicity, etc.), and they will use makeup, clothing, modeling techniques, and even image manipulation to make that person look as appealing as possible. Even the models in the pictures don't look as good as the image that is created once the art people are through. An advertiser may take an already attractive woman, for example, and enhance her bust, lengthen her legs, narrow her waist, lighten her skin tone, and remove any physical blemishes to create an image that fits an ideal of physical beauty. Those skilled in visual argument can use color, figure, shape, texture, line, and image to argue just as effectively as others can with words.

Applying the Principles: Readings

IMAGES GO TO WAR

In the following essay, Steven Perry describes how Hitler uses metaphors to characterize Jews and to argue in favor of their extermination. Although these metaphors were an important part of Hitler's verbal rhetoric, they were important to the visual rhetoric of German propaganda, too. As a class, review the images stored on the websites listed below, and then after reading Perry's essay, consider the following questions:

1. How do the Nazis use images to build their credibility, appeal to reason, or appeal to the emotions?
2. What types of visual metaphors are typical in Nazi propaganda? Which metaphors are positive and which are negative?
3. How do the Nazis use allusion? What style of art dominates their positive images? To what other civilizations do they compare themselves?
4. How do the Nazis use juxtaposition? To what extent is juxtaposition used to invite value judgments or demonstrate causality?
5. How do the Nazis represent the human figure? What positive and negative portrayals of the human figure do they use?
6. In what ways are the strategies of Nazi propaganda still used by hate groups today?

■■ SOURCES OF NAZI PROPAGANDA

Poster art from World War II, National Archives and Records Administration:

<http://www.nara.gov/exhall/powers/powers.html>

Anti-Defamation League, Hate Symbols Database:

<http://www.adl.org>

United States Holocaust Memorial Museum, 1936 Nazi Olympics:

<http://www.ushmm.org/olympics>

German Propaganda Archive at Calvin College:

<http://www.calvin.edu/cas/gpa/index.htm>

Museum of Tolerance, Multimedia Learning Center, "The Nazis":

<http://motlc.wiesenthal.org/pages>

Infestations of the National Body: Hitler's Rhetorical Portrait of the Jews

STEVEN PERRY

The highest purpose of a folkish state is concern for the preservation of those original racial elements which bestow culture and create the beauty and dignity of a higher mankind. We, as Aryans, can conceive of the state only as the living organism of a nationality which not only assures the preservation of this nationality, but by the development of its spiritual and ideal abilities leads it to the highest freedom.

HITLER'S USE of natural, organic imagery to characterize the German nation is so frequent and has been touched upon so often by critics and commentators that its prevalence hardly needs to be proven anew here. What I propose to explore instead are Hitler's extensions of this organic metaphor to the characterization of the natural enemy of the nation—the Jew—in terms of metaphors of organic infestation. Such references abound in *Mein Kampf* and in Hitler's speeches; a useful sampling of these references occurs in Richard Koenigsberg's *Hitler's Ideology: A Study in Psychoanalytic Sociology.* Working from the texts of *Mein Kampf* and Norman Baynes' two-volume 1942 collection of Hitler's speeches, Koenigsberg cites 43 exemplary statements character- 1 izing the Jews and Bolsheviks (the latter being a subset of the former) as disease-causing agents of various types, 19 statements in which the Jew is referred to as a parasite, and 23 statements referring to the Jew as a poison in the national body. For example: "For hundreds of years Germany was good enough to receive these elements [Jews], although they possessed nothing except infectious political and physical diseases." And: "[The Jew] is and remains the typical parasite, a sponger who like a noxious bacillus keeps spreading as soon as a favorable medium invites him." Further: "National Socialism has sought to remove from the organism of our people those weaknesses which might have favoured the inflow of Bolshevist poisons."

I should note at this point that the metaphors I include here—viral-bacterial, parasitic, and poison—stretch the treatment of disease metaphors. . . . I include them together here under the rubric of "disease/infestation metaphors" because all three refer to an attack on the national body by an insidious and invisible exogenous force. Hence, all contain the element of horror and mystification, and can be accorded an equivalent value in terms of how they help metaphorically to explain the Jewish question and to cast it in a particular moral light. The point of my analysis, then, will be to describe how these metaphors function to provide such explanations and moral legitimations for National Socialism's militant anti-semitism.

The strategy of rhetorically renaming one's enemies in a conflict situation is a common one. It is done in order to depersonalize the enemy, to de-humanize him or her, and thus to ameliorate the prospect of extreme action against that enemy. The most visible examples of such renamings are those which occur in wartime, as for instance when we rechristened the Japanese during World War II with labels such as "Gook," "Nip," and various other terms of derogation. But raising the example of wartime renamings points us to the special problem encountered by Hitler in renaming the Jews. In wartime, that is, the identity of the enemies and the ostensible reasons for opposition to them are in a sense given. Usually, some momentous threat is perceived as having been voiced or carried out. This demarcation of "the enemy" is part of the stock of public knowledge, independent of the process of renaming the enemies so as to de-humanize them.

Hitler's rhetorical situation, however, was different. Though there was unquestionably a very real current of anti-semitism in central Europe at the time of National Socialism's rise, the Jews nonetheless were not popularly perceived as enemies of the German nation. Hitler had to shape and channel popular anti-semitism; particularly, he had to explain how it was that the heretofore *scorned* Jew was actually a dangerous and foreign threat to the very foundations of the German nation. The use of infestation metaphors provided Hitler with the answer. Such metaphors were suitably de-humanizing, and, even more important, they provided a figurative explanation of the Jewish threat: The Jew was like the disease-causing microbe, the internal parasite, or the secretly-administered poison, wreaking an invisible but ultimately fatal havoc on the national body. Hence, it was not as though the Jew had somehow suddenly metamorphosed from a worthless but harmless object of scorn into a full-blown national threat. Rather, the Jew had always posed such a threat, and the German masses had only needed a savior, a Hitler, to rise and show them the real workings of the insidious, invisible Jewish plague.

Similarly, an appreciation of the figurative logic of the infestation metaphor 5
allows one to dissolve a paradox which seems apparent when one tries to read Hitler's words in terms of a more rational logic: That is, if the Jews are so clearly and emphatically inferior to Aryans, then how can they pose such a grave threat to the Aryan order? The answer, of course, is that the Jew is to the Aryan as the parasite is to the host—a lesser, dependent being, but one ultimately capable of bringing about the destruction of the biologically superior host organism. In addition to helping to explain the character of the jewish threat, Hitler's infestation metaphors carry certain figurative entailments which function to convey a vision of the moral dynamics associated with this threat.

As noted earlier, the application of disease or infestation metaphors to human agents is quite different from their application to inanimate objects. In the latter case, the repugnance evoked by the disease metaphor is primarily aesthetic, for we do not feel any *danger* emanating from the *lepreuse* stone facade mentioned by Sontag; we are simply expressing a distaste for its appearance. When used in public discourse to characterize whole groups of people, however, such metaphoric labels function differently. Sontag notes: "The melodramatics of the disease metaphor in modern political discourse assumes a punitive notion: of the disease . . . as a sign of evil, something to be punished" (p. 79). This is because (as Sontag neglects to explain) disease metaphors in political contexts are associated with willful human agents. They retain the sense of horror and mystery which inheres in the metaphors' vehicles, and add to this the implication that a certain group of human agents share these attributes, or are willfully responsible for the inculcation of these horrors into the national body. It follows naturally that such agents would come to participate in an aura of mysterious but unmistakable *evil*. Thus, in a most basic sense, Hitler's application of infestation metaphors to the Jews coded them as intrinsically, biologically evil. It is worth noting that in *Mein Kampf*, the most fully-developed expression of the National Socialist world-view, Hitler repeatedly devotes lengthy passages solely to the underlining of the Jew's natural malevolence toward the Aryan race and its cultural goals.

Infestation metaphors further imply a fundamental impurity, a profanation of the natural order. Black and Sontag describe at length how the cancer metaphor functions to convey this meaning. Sontag notes: "Cancer is a metaphor for what is most ferociously energetic; and these energies constitute the ultimate insult to the natural order" (p. 67). Hitler does not often refer directly to cancer, but the sorts of infestation images which he does use (e.g., "incurable tumors," "malignant tumors," "inner decay," "deadly cancerous ulcers") have an equivalent value in that they all point to the consumption from within of the national body by a sinister and ultimately fatal force of exogenous origins. For example:

"They think that they must demonstrate . . . that they are ready for appeasement so as to stay the deadly cancerous ulcer through a policy of moderation." According to the logic of Hitler's figures, the Jews are the most fundamental anti-natural force, and extensions of this logic reverberate through *Mein Kampf*: The Jews are parasites upon Aryan culture; they are incapable of operating in accordance with the highest laws of nature; and they threaten ultimately to destroy the purity of the Aryan race (and thus to consume the national body, of which pure Aryan blood is the substance).

My commentary on the moral implications of the infestation metaphor thus far has focused upon the characterizations of the Jews themselves implied by these metaphors. In addition, the logic of these metaphors implies a vision of the moral ramifications for Germans of National Socialist anti-semitism, and a general characterization of the Nazi-Jewish conflict.

The logic of the infestation metaphor removes the moral ambiguities from the prospect of treating the Jews as enemies. In a general sense, as noted, these metaphors serve to de-humanize the Jews, which makes categorical opposition to them more psychologically feasible. More precisely, the infestation metaphor suggests that traditional moral categories of human social interaction are inoperative in dealing with Jews, for in putting a patient on the road to recovery, the doctors need not worry about whether the disease-causing agent is treated fairly, "humanely." This would be absurd. The only real priority is to provide a cure, and the means used to achieve this end are not in themselves very important. Any cure is acceptable which snuffs out the disease and stops short of killing the patient.

10 The infestation metaphor thus implies an end-over-means, moral *carte blanche* for the National Socialist saviors of Germany. Further, the metaphor provides a general characterization of the Nazi-Jewish struggle, by casting the stakes of the battle as the survival of the national body itself. Hitler is emphatic about this: "State after state will either fall a victim to the Jewish-Bolshevist plague or must take measures for self-protection." "[If] the development we are seeing today . . . continued unobstructed . . . the Jew would really devour the peoples on the Earth." "All great cultures of the past perished . . . from blood poisoning." The sense of urgency conveyed by this vision of the Jewish threat heightens the sense of moral *carte blanche* implicit in the metaphor. Pushed to its extreme, in fact, one may even say that the logic of the metaphor *necessitates* the elimination—by whatever means—of the Jewish agent of infestation.

My analysis of Hitler's rhetoric has been based entirely upon pre-1940 documents. As this analysis implies, we can find significant foreshadowings of the character of the Final Solution in Hitler's rhetorical treatment of the Jews from the beginning of his career onward. I do not mean to claim that Hitler's figurative treatment of Jews should be seen as an instrumental means of creating an atmosphere conducive to annihilation. This is too simplistic a view. Rather, I mean to suggest that exploring and appreciating the figurative logic of National Socialism helps us to understand the moral universe in which a Holocaust could occur. According to the terms of the metaphor as I have spelled them out, the Jews were evil, unnatural, and wantonly destructive, and their elimination was essential to the national body's survival. When we understand this aspect of the Nazi world-view, it becomes easier than before to understand the National Socialists' choice to systematically eliminate German Jewry.

FRAMING NEWS PHOTOGRAPHS

In her book *On Photography,* Susan Sontag argues that "photographs may be more memorable than moving images, because they are a neat slice of time, not a flow."[2] Sontag sees a photograph as a "privileged moment" that the viewer can return to again and again. Several photographs have become defining moments for the 20th century: Joe Rosenthal's photo of marines raising the U.S. flag over Iwo Jima Robert Capa's famous images of the D-Day invasion at Omaha Beach John F. Kennedy, Jr., saluting his father's casket Eddie Adam's picture of a street execution during the Vietnam War Nick Ut's photo of a naked Vietnamese girl fleeing a napalm attack John Filo's image of a distraught girl kneeling over a dead student at Kent State Alan Diaz's photograph of INS agents seizing Elian Gonzales the raising of the U.S. flag over the ruins of the World Trade Center. Each of these is one of Sontag's "privileged moments" that defined an entire event. But if a photograph is a slice of time, then what happened on either side of the photograph? What does the framing of the photograph leave out?

The following essay by Associated Press writer Terry Spencer describes how Alan Diaz planned to get his famous photograph of Elian Gonzalez. Following this essay are several famous photographs. As a class you may want to conduct some research on the context for these photographs. (Look for information about the photographs by searching for the photographer.) As you read the essays and report your research on these photographs, consider the following questions:

1. What memories do you have of any of these photographs? What have you learned or what do you remember about the events depicted in the photo? In what ways does the photograph characterize the event as a whole?
2. What emotions does each photograph evoke? What visual elements bring about this emotional response?
3. How many shots did each photographer take of the event in addition to the famous shot? What other images exist of the same event? What makes one image more famous or more powerful than another?
4. Although all of these photographs look spontaneous, how much preparation can a photographer do to capture just the right shot? How much of getting the shot is just being in the right place at the right time?

[2] Susan Sontag, *On Photography* (New York: Farrar, Straus, Giroux, 1977), p. 18.

5. What happened before and after each photograph was taken? What have historians or journalists said looking back on these photographs after many years?
6. In 1977, Susan Sontag argued that "the images that have virtually unlimited authority in a modern society are mainly photographic images."[3] Is the photograph still the authoritative image? What is the role of video and Internet images in a modern society? What memorial images from video and Internet have defined important events?

Months of Preparation Got Miami Photographer Winning Shot

TERRY SPENCER

1 ALAN DIAZ had been preparing for his Pulitzer Prize–winning photograph long before he heard the footsteps of federal agents running toward the house where Elian Gonzalez slept.

For months, the photojournalist had been talking to the Cuban boy's family and getting to know the house and its surroundings. Now, in the pre-dawn darkness last April 22, that preparation was about to pay off.

"It's going down," Diaz yelled as he grabbed his camera, which he'd placed beneath a towel to protect it from the early morning dew. He jumped the fence into the side yard of the Gonzalez family's Little Havana home, paused to set his shutter speed and strobe light and then ran through a door a family member had opened.

"Where's the boy?" he yelled in Spanish, as Elian's frantic relatives scurried around the living room. A man pushed Diaz toward the boy's bedroom, where he threw on the light. Elian wasn't there.

5 He pounded on the bedroom door across the hall, which Elian's aunt opened. Diaz could see 6-year-old Elian being held in the closet by Donato Dalrymple, who'd helped pull the boy from the Atlantic Ocean five months earlier.

Inside the room, Diaz took the photograph of a federal agent with an assault rifle confronting a screaming Elian and a stunned Dalrymple.

That photo won Diaz, 53, the Pulitzer for best spot news photograph of 2000. He will receive $7,500. It is the AP's 47th Pulitzer—19 for writing and 28 for photographs.

[3] Ibid., p. 153.

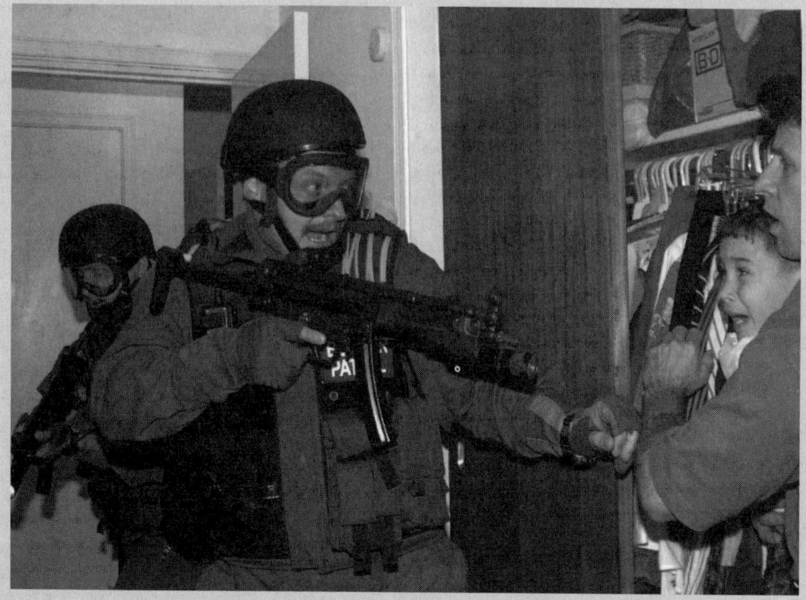

"It's awesome, I can't believe it," Diaz said Monday as he was mobbed by co-workers.

"It's a great picture, just a great picture, and we're very pleased for Alan that he won," AP President Louis Boccardi said.

"It's an amazing job by an amazing, talented photographer," said Vin Al- 10
abiso, an AP vice president and the executive photo editor.

Diaz, then a free-lance photographer, had been hired by the AP on Nov. 30, 1999, to take daily pictures of Elian. His mother and 13 other Cubans had tried to flee across the Florida Straits, but their boat sank.

Elian had been lashed to an innertube and was rescued when Dalrymple and his cousin found him while fishing two miles off Fort Lauderdale. Two adults who'd used another innertube washed ashore near Miami, but Elian's mother and the others died.

Diaz said Monday that Elian's great-uncle Lazaro Gonzalez was not enthusiastic when the photographer first arrived at the house. But Diaz, whose parents are from Cuba, struck up a conversation with Lazaro across the fence.

"We talked about everything—politics, coffee, sports, women—until he was comfortable with me," Diaz said.

Diaz, who spent at least 16 hours daily covering Elian, said that in the first 15
days he was often the only still photographer at the house. He would take pictures of the boy going to school and playing in the yard and the demonstrations that occasionally happened outside.

By April, the tension surrounding Elian was high. The Clinton administration was demanding that Elian be turned over so he could return to Cuba with his father, but the Miami relatives were balking. Four days before the raid, Diaz decided he would not leave the house until the case was resolved.

At 5:15 A.M. that Saturday, the streets surrounding the Gonzalez home were quiet as most of the family's supporters had gone home. Diaz had thought about taking a nap, but he couldn't sleep. For months he had thought about what he would do if agents raided the house—how he would try to get inside and where he would shoot from if he couldn't.

Since the photo, Diaz's life has changed dramatically. A free-lancer for 12 years, the AP hired him for a full-time position last June. He has won many awards and been sought after for interviews by other journalists.

"Everything turned around on me," the self-effacing Diaz said. "I don't mean that in a bad sense of the word, but now everybody wanted to hear from me.

"I'm not used to that." 20

D-Day, Omaha Beach, Normandy, France

ROBERT CAPA

John F. Kennedy, Jr., Saluting His Father's Casket

HARRY LEADER/CORBIS BETTMANN

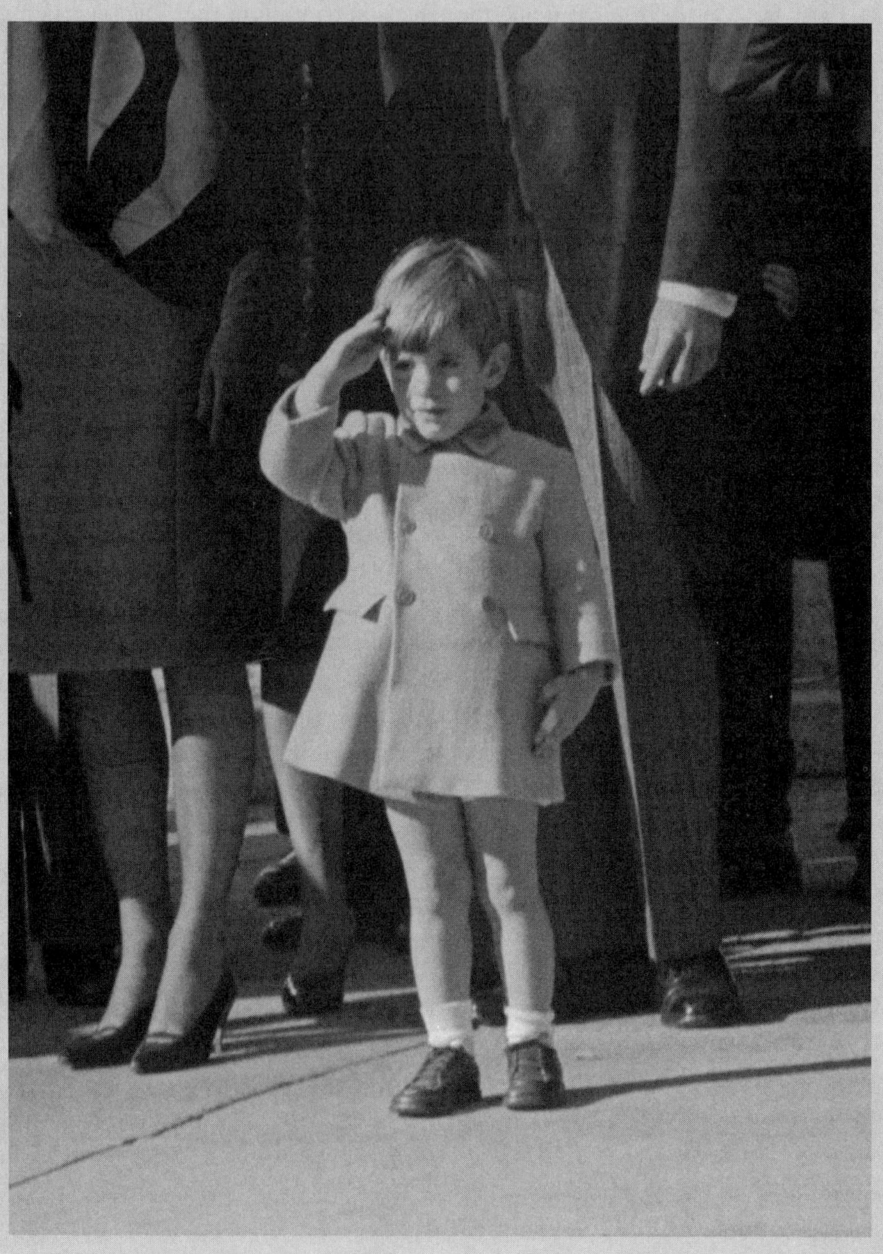

Vietnamese Brig. Gen. Nguyen Ngoc Loan Executing a Viet Cong Prisoner on a Saigon Street

EDDIE ADAMS

Vietnamese Girl Fleeing a Napalm Attack

NICK UT

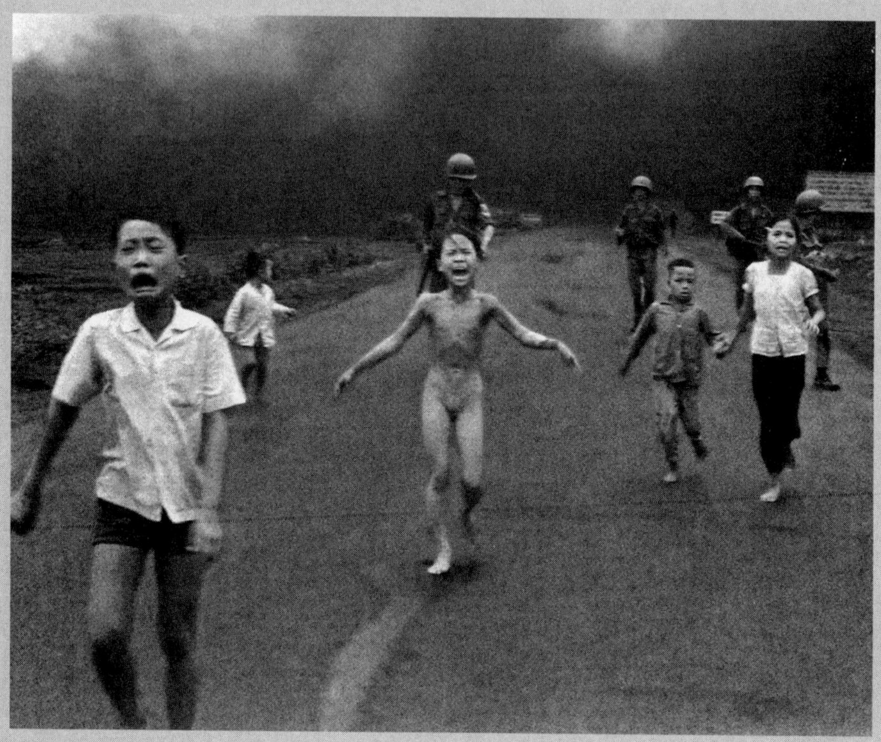

CAMPAIGN ADVERTISEMENTS

Political campaigns have always used visual arguments (posters, leaflets, buttons, cartoons), but the advent of television made the image even more important to what political theorist Murray Edelman has called "the political spectacle." In fact, some historians looking back at the 1960 presidential election claim that one reason John Kennedy won a narrow victory over Richard Nixon is that Kennedy looked much better than Nixon on television. Of course, the Internet has made visual argument even more important to campaigning because the Internet allows candidates to mix media and to exercise much more control over the content of the message they broadcast. Networks have certain restrictions. They are required to give candidates equal time, and they limit the amount of time a candidate can use to deliver his or her message. But the Internet has few restrictions, and websites have been set up by individual candidates, political parties, and political action groups. Despite the importance of the Internet to contemporary campaigning, the campaign advertisement is still an important factor in determining how Americans vote. The following essay, "What's the Spin?" explains what goes into the making of a political ad, particularly the nonverbal elements, what Esther Thorson calls the "structural features" of an ad. After reading this essay, review the following websites, which provide an archive of political advertisements from past campaigns along with analysis of political ads:

<http://www9.cnn.com/ALLPOLITICS/1996/candidates/ad.archive/>

<http://www.pbs.org/pov/ad/index.html>

As you read this essay and analyze these advertisements, consider the following questions:

1. What are the structural features of a political ad? Which of these elements involve visual argument?
2. How prevalent are visual arguments in the political ads you examined?
3. How do the ads use visual argument to build the credibility of the candidate?
4. What emotions do the ads evoke? What visual elements contribute to this emotional response?
5. In what ways do the ads appeal to reason? To what extent do the visual elements of the ad reinforce or run counter to the logical argument of the ad?
6. In what ways do the ads use visual metaphor, allusion, or juxtaposition? How does the ad use juxtaposition? Does the use of juxtaposition make a claim about values, causality, or both?
7. How are human figures used in the ads? In addition to what people in the ad say, how are people presented visually?

What's the Spin?

ESTHER THORSON

MOST POLITICAL consultants agree that television is the most persuasive advertising tool available. A large body of studies carried out in the last 15 years shows quite clearly that political commercials have major effects on people. In presidential elections television commercials consume most of the money spent by candidates in their attempts to get elected. This is also true of state-level elections. 1

Over 99% of US homes have a television, and in the average home, television sets are turned on more than four hours a day. Television advertising reaches more people than all other forms of advertising combined. In addition, the visual nature of television makes its messages more powerful than anything shy of a candidate's personal visit to a voter's living room.

Like any persuasive message developed by a professional communicator, every aspect of their few-seconds duration is carefully designed to influence. Aspects of ads beyond their verbal content are called structural features.

Most political ads broadcast on television (commonly called "spots") run for 30-seconds, though 15- and 60-second spots are sometimes used. All 30-second spots aim to provide information and tell stories about candidates, but the best spots blend visual, verbal and aural images into a cohesive whole. Visual images are used to highlight points, verbal cues (both oral and textual) are used to persuade, and music is used to impassion the viewer.

This guide describes ten of the structural features that political ads use most 5
commonly to craft powerful, cohesive messages. Regardless of what verbal content an ad uses, it will employ one or most of these persuasive tools.

CANDIDATE MYTHOLOGIES

When people think about a political office-holder like the president, vice president, governor, or senator, they often, unbeknownst to themselves, associate mythological features to that person. Common mythologies about the president represent him as:

a. War hero
b. Man of the people
c. Father
d. Savior
e. Friend

These "myths" are used to create emotion in viewers. If that face up on the screen asking for your vote is "your friend," you feel differently about him. If he's a "hero," he may make you feel proud or safe. If he's "your father," you may feel trustful of him.

Myths like these are generally not spoken, but represented in images. A candidate shown with people trying to touch him, shake his hand, or clapping for him, is being represented as a hero. Shown with his family, he's obviously a father, but he's also a father when shown kissing babies or supporting laws that aid children. Probably the most common spoken myth is "friend." "Friend of the people," "the working man's friend," are popular ad phrases. Clasping a voter around the shoulders or a warm hand-shake visually represents "friend."

BACKGROUND LOCATIONS

Where the candidate is when he is shown or where the opponent is shown in an attack ad is critically important to what is being communicated. John F. Kennedy was shown walking along the beach. Ross Perot was almost always in a paneled den or office. Bill Clinton was most frequently surrounded by people.

Each of the backgrounds is used to communicate a variety of things about the candidate.

PROPS

10 Props are objects shown in the scenes. The most common prop is the American flag. Desks are important props. Headlines in newspapers are props used to verify statistical and factual claims ("If the newspaper said it, it must be true.") A podium is a prop, or sometimes other people serve as props. A recent Senate candidate in Wisconsin used a cardboard standup of Elvis as a prop!

EMOTION-COMMUNICATING FACES

While any scene, any piece of music, any statement can induce emotion, the most common emotional device is the human face: the fear and anger in the face of teen druggie, the admiration and enthusiasm in crowd faces, babies' faces crying, fierce, uncaring expressions on the faces of opponents. All of these faces and their expressions are carefully planted in ads. A most common approach is to take the face of an opponent at its most unattractive and show that face as background for words written on the screen to indicate what awful things he has done. Faces are probably a candidate's most direct conduit to creating feelings in viewers.

APPEALS

Every ad is designed to appeal to something in the viewer him- or herself. Insurance ads appeal to fears of disasters. Cosmetics appeal to personal ego. Many high-ticket products appeal to greed. Candidates appeal to feelings of patriotism, fears of such things as war, crime, loss of jobs, poor education for children and so on. Attack ads usually appeal to fear—of a variety of sorts. "You can't trust this guy." "This guy will take health benefits away from your parents." "This guy will lead us into war." And so on. Every political ad has a central appeal and sometimes several more minor appeals. Appeals are often what political consultants search for and term "hot buttons." Hot buttons are appeals that work very effectively with a large percent of the population of voters.

MUSIC AND BACKGROUND SOUNDS

Almost all political ads use music. It is usually orchestral, stately, designed to sound inspiring to a broad spectrum of listeners. Volume of music is very important. A common approach is have a crescendo of sound at the end an ad. Background music is borrowed from horror movies when the ad attacks an opponent. Music is often fiercely patriotic-sounding.

Background noises are important and seldom consciously noticed by viewers. Sirens, traffic noise and drumbeats are commonly employed. A good way to pick up use of music and background sounds, of course, is to look away from the screen during the ad. You'll find a lot going on there that you'd otherwise be unlikely to notice.

FILM EDITING AND CAMERA USE

Slow-motion is commonly used to increase the salience of an image. Extreme close-ups increase our perceptions of importance. They are also used to emphasize emotion, evil and truthfulness. Often the camera comes in closer to the candidate as he begins his pledge to voters—whatever that pledge may be. Jump-cuts occur when scenes are edited together and the central figure moves suddenly from one location to another. Shooting from above the candidate when he's greeting a crowd provides an impression of warmth and bonding. Black and white pictures usually mean the topic is serious and most likely negative. 15

CLOTHING

What a candidate is wearing is carefully chosen to show the viewer something "important" about him. An expensive suit shows power, taste and authority. Shirt sleeves show hard work and empathy with ordinary people. Jacket over the shoulder shows ease, warmth and confidence. A loosened tie usually indicates the same characteristics.

DEPICTED ACTIONS

What the candidate is doing in a support ad and what the opponent is doing in an attack ad is important. Getting off a plane shows characteristics like international expertise and concern, familiarity and caring about the whole country or just plain old power. Interacting with the family shows caring. Holding hands with a spouse does the same. Signing papers shows ability to get important things done. Greeting ordinary people shows popularity and caring. Speaking from a podium emphasizes power and good ideas.

In the opponent, the activity is sometimes representing as "silly" or weak. A good example is the 1988 ad which featured Dukakis's helmeted head popping out of the top of an army tank. The opponent is sometimes shown with an incriminating "other." Candidates are usually doing things in color. Opponents are usually doing things in black and white.

SUPERS AND CODE WORDS

Supers are words printed in large letters on the screen. They appear over a background that is supposed to exemplify whatever is represented in the super. A super says, "Pay attention to this factoid or claim." It often communicates outrage at something the opponent has done: RAISED TAXES THREE TIMES IN THREE YEARS. It often emphasizes the appeal that is being taken in the whole ad: WRONG FOR YESTERDAY. WRONG FOR TOMORROW. Supers often try to make maximum use of code words. These are words that sound simple but carry vast stereotyped and sometimes unconscious meaning for viewers. Good examples of code words and phrases include:

- **Values.** Although it's never clear just what values are involved, the implication is that the candidate has them and the opponent doesn't.
- **Crime.** Many argue that this word involves racial aspects for many viewers.
- **Welfare.** Another word that is often code for race.
- **Yesterday.** Not just occurring in the past, but too old, no longer relevant.

This article is adapted from an essay by Esther Thorson, Graduate Dean of Journalism at the University of Missouri.

Practicing the Principles: Activities

TIME MAGAZINE COVERS

The cover of a magazine usually presents an image that reinforces the most important story in the magazine. This is particularly true in newsmagazines. *Time* magazine online, <www.time.com/time/magazine/archive>, includes an archive of *Time* covers for each weekly issue from the present to 1985. These covers provide an interesting visual summary of the historical events of the past 15 years. These archives also include summaries of the stories contained in *Time* for that issue. As a class, review these covers and analyze how the editors used the strategies of visual argument discussed in this chapter to make a statement about the cover story. To learn more about the story for a particularly interesting cover, divide up stories among class members and review the back issues of *Time* in your library. Each cover story was considered the most important story for the week that issue was published. As you look back over these issues, how significant is the story now?

THE 30-SECOND CANDIDATE

The PBS Democracy Project, <www.pbs.org/democracy>, is devoted to helping citizens become more engaged in the political process. One part of this project is a special called "The 30-Second Candidate." At the interactive site for this special, you can learn more about the growing importance of the 30-second television commercial for candidates running for offices throughout the nation. And you can also build your own campaign ad for a fictional candidate, <www.pbs.org/30secondcandidate>.

THE HUMAN FACE

In the BBC special "The Human Face," John Cleese analyzes how the human face relates to human interaction, our identity, our notions of beauty, fame, and success. In 2001, this special aired on the Learning Channel (part of the Discovery Channel network). The video for this special is available from BBC Online or the Discovery Channel store. But the Discovery Channel also has a website that includes information about the series, <http://tlc.discovery.com/convergence/humanface/humanface.html>. You can, for example, place the "beauty mask" over your own picture to see how well you measure up to the classical ideal of beauty. Or you can take the "face value" quiz to see what kinds of judgments you make about people based on their appearance. This site also includes links to other sites about the human face, including the original BBC online site for the special, <http://www.bbc.co.uk/science/humanbody/humanface>.

YOU ARE WHAT YOU WEAR

According to Hamlet, "The apparel doth oft proclaim the man" ("William Shakespeare," *Hamlet, Prince of Denmark,* I.iii). This line is often paraphrased as "The clothes make the man" (or woman). What does your clothing reveal about you? How do you "read" the clothing of other members of your class? What kind of arguments are you each making about yourselves and your world? As a class, collect some images from magazines, newspapers, advertisements, television news programs, and other sources. In these images, what are people saying by what they wear? Are some people presented as an "ideal" of fashion (as models or actors would be)? In what ways do ordinary people try to emulate the rich and famous through their clothing? What kinds of arguments do people make by rejecting fashion trends?

BECOMING AN AD CRITIC

Adcritic.com includes hundreds of examples of television ads, including several new ads each week. As a class, review these ads and analyze how the visual elements in this chapter are used in different kinds of ads. What seems to be the intended audience for each ad? How does the ad use visual elements to appeal to this audience?

IMAGES OF SEPTEMBER 11, 2001

The terrorist attack of September 11, 2001, left an indelible impression on those who witnessed it, either firsthand or through the media. September 11 News.com, <www.september11news.com/index.html>, includes an extensive archive of images related to the attack and its aftermath. As a class, use the principles you have learned in this class to analyze the visual arguments related to this event.

EDITORIAL CARTOONS

Editorial cartoonist Daryl Cagle keeps an extensive archive of editorials by professional cartoonists, <cagle.slate.msn.com>. And the archive is updated regularly to reflect the changing news. As a class, you could use this archive either to analyze cartoons about current events or to research visual arguments about a news event in the recent past (such as editorial cartoons on the September 11, 2001, attack on the World Trade Center, or on school shootings).

Glossary

ad populum A logical fallacy wherein a statement is assumed to be true because of the number of people who believe in it. (The Latin phrase means "to the people.") This fallacy depends on the assumption that just because an idea is popular or commonly held, it is true or right.

agency The means by which an agent brings about a change.

agent An individual who takes purposeful action to bring about a change.

analogy A comparison between two objects or events wherein a familiar idea is used to explain an unfamiliar one.

appeal to force A logical fallacy that takes the form of a threat, diverting attention from the real issue to the negative consequences of not accepting the argument. Extortion, blackmail, intimidation, and sexual harassment are all examples of the appeal to force.

appeal to ignorance A logical fallacy wherein the burden of proof is refused and a statement is claimed to be true because no one has ever proved it otherwise.

appeal to reward A logical fallacy that takes the form of a reward or bribe, diverting attention from the real issue to the positive consequences of accepting the argument. Buying votes, trading favors, and bribery are all examples of the appeal to reward.

arguing, argument A form of rational persuasion. The word *argument* comes from the Latin word for "silver" and literally refers to making an idea clear. An argument consists of three parts: claims, reasons, and assumptions.

assumptions The information necessary to move logically from the reasons to the claim in an argument. Assumptions "fill in the gaps" in arguments, answering the question, If I accept the reasons, what else do I have to believe to accept the claim? They are often left unstated. Stephen Toulmin refers to assumptions as "warrants."

begging the question A logical fallacy wherein a reason offered to support a conclusion or claim is really just a restatement of that conclusion or claim.

brainstorming A group activity to generate ideas. In brainstorming, a group generally focuses on a problem and determines a specified amount of time for discussing it. Members of the group all suggest ideas without any being evaluated or rejected until the brainstorming session has ended.

causality A relationship between events such that (1) an earlier event in some way causes or influences a later event or (2) a later event in some way explains an earlier one. A number of elements may be components in analyzing causality: sufficient cause, necessary cause, contributing cause, logical cause, constraint, correlation, agent, instrument or agency, and purpose.

claims Along with reasons and assumptions, one of the three parts of an argument. A claim is a statement under dispute that takes a stand on a controversial issue about which at least some people disagree. It is the focus of the argument. In academic writing, the claim is often the thesis. Claims may be made about existence, causality, language, values, or actions.

classical argument An argument that takes the following form: introduction, thesis, supporting reasons and assumptions, answers to possible objections, and conclusion.

clustering A type of mapping to discover ideas that involves writing down and circling a topic or issue in the center of a sheet of paper, jotting down and circling related words and ideas around this central topic, and then joining or "clustering" these ideas by drawing lines among those that are related.

communication The process of sharing or achieving a common understanding through language. The word *communication* comes from the same Latin root as the word *community* does.

community A group of people who have something in common. The word *community* comes from a Latin word meaning "common" or "shared." For instance, a community may be defined by shared interests, common ancestors, or shared language or geographic location.

community-based reasons Reasons that are grounded in the beliefs shared by a community.

complex question A logical fallacy wherein two different questions are phrased as if they were one, so that the same answer must be given for both. This is also called a "loaded question."

conciliatory argument An argument that focuses on common assumptions, values, or definitions but does not assert the specific claim. The goal of this kind of argument is to move a hostile audience from a position of unconditional opposition to a more moderate position, even one of conditional support for the unstated claim.

connotation The associations a word carries, what it suggests in addition to its literal meaning.

constraint A necessary element that, when removed, allows an event or phenomenon to occur.

contributing cause A cause that may enable or influence a second event or phenomenon but that is not necessary or sufficient to cause the second.

correlation A relationship between two events or phenomena occurring together that is not necessarily causal; both may actually be caused by something else. Mistaking correlation for cause results in the post hoc fallacy.

criteria and match A type of classification and definition wherein the criteria that determine the members of a class are first defined and then a particular event or object is examined to determine whether it fits those criteria.

delayed thesis An argument that is similar to classical argument except that the thesis is not stated until the conclusion.

denotation The dictionary definition of a word, what the word means literally.

dicto simpliciter A logical fallacy wherein statements that are true in simple cases are applied to more complex cases without qualification. This Latin phrase literally means "simple speech."

discourse community A community defined by a common language and body of knowledge.

doublespeak The use of language to obscure meaning.

ethos Along with pathos and logos, one of the three means of persuasion described by Aristotle. Related to the English word *ethics,* ethos refers to the trustworthiness or credibility of a speaker or writer, based on how others perceive his or her character. Ethos or credibility depends to a certain degree on an individual's standing or status in the community and to a degree on how he or she uses language.

etymology The history of a word.

euphemism A word chosen for its positive connotations. The Greek root for this word means "good meaning." Euphemisms are used as substitutes for more blunt language.

fact A statement or belief that is commonly accepted as true within a given community.

false analogy An analogy that is fallacious because the differences between the two things being compared are greater than their similarities.

false dilemma A logical fallacy wherein the audience is misleadingly presented with only two options, one of which is clearly more desirable than the other. This is also called the "either/or fallacy."

formal definition A definition wherein a term is placed in a group and then distinguished from other members of the group: *X is an A (group) that B (distinguishing characteristics).*

freewriting A method for discovering ideas by writing down everything that comes into one's mind, without stopping, for a set period of time.

guilt by association A logical fallacy wherein all members of a group are stereotyped based on how only some members of the group behave. This is another name for "stereotyping."

hasty generalization A logical fallacy wherein a conclusion is formed based on inadequate evidence. This is another name for "jumping to conclusions."

in-group In audience analysis, a group whose opinions on a controversial issue are most similar to the writer's or speaker's.

instrument See *agency.*

Internet A network of computers across the world that makes possible e-mail, discussion lists, bulletin boards, gopher space, and the World Wide Web.

kairos Greek term used to describe times and places of significance. A critical or opportune moment.

loaded question See *complex question.*

logical cause A justification or explanation. A "reason" that justifies the claim in an argument is a logical cause.

logos Along with ethos and pathos, one of the three persuasive appeals described by Aristotle. Logos involves an appeal to reason. It is rational persuasion, the structure of the argument.

mapping A visual representation for planning the relationships among ideas in an essay. A map may be a formal outline, a branching tree diagram, a series of pictures, or a set of circled words joined by lines ("cluster").

middle-group In audience analysis, a group that is uninformed or uncommitted or whose position on a controversial issue lies between the writer's or speaker's position and that of those who hold the opposite opinion.

Monroe's motivational sequence A motivational argument that begins with a description of a need or problem, followed by a description of the consequences of not meeting that need or solving that problem. The argument then offers a solution to the problem, followed by a "vision" of how the situation would be improved by the adoption of this solution. This sequence ends by suggesting specific actions the audience can take to achieve the solution.

motivational arguments An argument that aims to motivate those who already accept the claim. Monroe's motivated sequence is an example of a motivational argument.

necessary cause An event or phenomenon that must exist for a second to occur but that is not sufficient in itself to cause the second.

negation Defining something by describing what it is not.

non sequitur A reason or chain of reasons that cannot be connected logically to the claim. This Latin phrase literally means "does not follow" and refers to an argument in which the claim does not clearly follow from the reasons.

operational definition A precise or technical definition of a term developed for a specific purpose or task.

opinion A statement or belief about which at least some people disagree, and which is controversial or under dispute in a community.

option three An argument that appeals to a moderate position between two extreme positions.

out-group In audience analysis, a group whose opinions on a controversial issue are furthest opposed to the writer's or speaker's.

oversimplified cause A logical fallacy wherein a complex event or phenomenon is reduced to one simple cause.

paraphrase A method of recording and reporting information from sources. In a paraphrase the original passage is rewritten using different words and sentence structure but preserving as much of the meaning of the original as possible.

pathos Along with ethos and logos, one of the three persuasive appeals described by Aristotle. Pathos involves creating an emotional response in others by using emotionally charged language and description. Trying to generate a greater emotional response than is warranted by the situation is considered a fallacious appeal to the emotions.

personal attack A logical fallacy wherein an attack on a person's character is used to distract the audience from a serious evaluation of the argument.

persuasion Urging, influencing, or enticing through language in a manner that is not constraining or threatening. The word persuasion originally comes from a Latin word that means "sweet" and is related to the Greek word for "pleasure" or "sweetness." According to the ancient Greek philosopher Zeno, persuasion is represented by an open hand rather than a closed fist. Persuasion involves three appeals: ethos, pathos, and logos.

plagiarism Knowingly presenting the ideas or language of others as one's own. Plagiarism is considered a kind of academic fraud.

point of view The relationship that a writer establishes with his or her audience and subject. Use of "I" or "we" indicates a first-person point of view. Use of "you" is second-person. Use of "they," "he," "she," "it," or "one" establishes a third-person point of view.

poisoning the well A logical fallacy wherein an argument is presented in such an emotionally biased way that it is difficult for a critic to respond without seeming dishonest or immoral. This strategy is intended as a distraction from the real issue and may involve personal attacks or fallacious appeals to emotion.

post hoc, ergo propter hoc A logical fallacy wherein it is assumed that just because one event follows another, the first caused the second. This Latin phrase means "after this, therefore because of this."

purpose A cause that follows what it causes, with the later event or phenomenon serving as the reason for the earlier one.

quotation A word-for-word transcription of what someone else said or wrote.

rational Relating to the ability to think and reason, but also to the ability to offer reasons as justification.

reasons Statements offered to justify, explain, or increase adherence to a claim. The reasons answer the question, What do I need to believe in order to accept the claim the author is making? Along with claims and assumptions, one of the three parts of an argument.

red herring A logical fallacy wherein an attempt is made to draw attention away from the issue at hand by raising irrelevant issues.

Rogerian argument A type of negotiation based on the theories of psychologist Carl Rogers. In this kind of argument, the opposing views are described as objectively as possible and common values and goals are identified in order to bring opposing parties to a consensus.

stacking the deck A logical fallacy wherein any evidence or arguments that do not support the claim are ignored.

sufficient cause An event or phenomenon that, under normal conditions, can by itself cause a second.

summary A method of recording and reporting information from sources. In a summary the main ideas of a larger piece of writing are reported in a much briefer form and in the summarizer's own words.

synonyms Words with similar meanings.

troping A means of drawing attention to an argument by deviating intentionally from conventions, presenting ideas in a surprising or unexpected way.

virtual space The sites of communication created electronically through computer networks. The Internet's World Wide Web is the largest virtual site.

visual rhetoric The term that both names a sub-area of rhetorical study and acknowledges that visuals communicate meaning and influence behavior in ways that are significant and similar to verbal communication.

Credits

PHOTO/ART CREDITS

Page 3, © Michael Newman/PhotoEdit; **page 45,** Copyright © 1999 *San Diego Union-Tribune*–Copley News Service. Reprinted by permission of Steve Kelley.; **page 60,** Courtesy of San Diego State University; **page 67,** © David Young–Wolff/PhotoEdit; **page 109,** © Mark Richards/PhotoEdit; **page 111,** © Reuters NewMedia Inc./CORBIS; **page 118,** no credit; **page 119,** Courtesy of the American Red Cross; **page 120,** Courtesy of The Humane Farming Association; **page 124,** Courtesy of www.columbine-memorial.org; **page 129,** © AFP/CORBIS; **page 138,** Courtesy of DEVITO/VERDI; **page 139,** © Frank Pedrick/Index Stock; **page 221,** © Vivian Archive Holdings/Getty Images/The Image Bank; **page 303,** Doonesbury © 1985 G. B. Trudeau. Reprinted with permission of Universal Press Syndicate. All rights reserved.; **page 327,** © Adam Wollfitt/CORBIS; **page 353,** Courtesy of the Library of Congress; **page 354,** Courtesy of The WWW Virtual Library; **page 355,** Courtesy of About.com; **page 357, page 358,** Courtesy of Dogpile.com; Courtesy of Google Inc.; **page 445,** © ART MONTES DE OCA/Getty Images/FPG; **page 499,** © Mark Richards/PhotoEdit; **page 555,** © Michael Newman/PhotoEdit; **page 619,** © Brand X Pictures; **page 711,** © UPI/Corbis-Bettmann; **page 757,** © John Bigelow Taylor/Art Resource, NY; **page 767,** © Erich Lessing/Art Resource, NY; **page 776,** © CORBIS; **page 786,** Alan Diaz/AP Wide World; **page 787,** © Robert Capa/Magnum Photos; **page 788,** © Bettmann/CORBIS; **page 789,** Eddie Adams/AP Wide World; **page 790,** Nick Ut/AP Wide World

TEXT CREDITS

DEVON ADAMS, "Mourn for the Killers, Too," from *Newsweek,* August 23, 1999. Copyright © 1999 Newsweek, Inc. All rights reserved. Reprinted by permission.

JAMES AJEMIAN, "Is the SDSU Aztec Logo Offensive?" Letter to the Editor, from the *San Diego Union-Tribune,* October 4, 2000. Reprinted by permission of the author.

GINA ARNOLD, "You Say You Want a Revolution?" from *East Bay Express,* November 17, 2000. Reprinted by permission of the author.

REGINA AVILA, JUDI ACRE, and JAN TROPHY, "Columbine Timeline," compiled by Regina Avila, Judi Acre, and Jan Tropy, from *The Denver Post,* April 20, 1999. Copyright © 2000 *The Denver Post.* Reprinted by permission of *The Denver Post.* All rights reserved.

RUSSELL BAKER, "Taking the Saps," from *The New York Times,* June 15, 1996. Reprinted by permission of The New York Times Agency.

ROBERT D. BALLARD, Excerpt from "How We Found Titanic" from *National Geographic,* December 1985. As found in Zachary Seech, *Logic in Everyday Life,* p. 127, Wadsworth, 1987. Reprinted by permission of National Geographic.

ANDREA BALTAZAR, "Is the SDSU Aztec Logo Offensive?" Letter to the Editor, from the *San Diego Union-Tribune,* October 4, 2000.

JANET BINGHAM, "Gerda Weissmann Klein and Melissa Pillow: Holocaust Survivor Comforts Columbine Survivor" and "Crystal Woodman: Columbine Library Survivor," from *The Denver Post,* April 16, 2000. Copyright © 2000 *The Denver Post.* Reprinted by permission of *The Denver Post.* All rights reserved.

ROBERTA BORKAT, "A Liberating Curriculum," by Roberta F. Borkat, *Newsweek,* April, 12, 1993. Reprinted by permission.

ANDY BOROWITZ, "Day Trading Made Easy," from *The New Yorker,* May 8, 2000. Reprinted by permission of the author.

AMY BRUCKMAN, reprinted with permission from *Technology Review,* "Finding One's Own in Cyberspace," January 1996, published by the Association of Alumni and Alumnae of MIT. Copyright © 1998 Association of Alumni and Alumnae of MIT. Reproduced by permission of the publisher via Copyright Clearance Center, Inc.

BILL BRYSON, "The Risk Factor," "The Numbers Game," and "The Fat of the Land," from *I'm a Stranger Here Myself* by Bill Bryson. Copyright © 1999 by Bill Bryson. In Canada, all extracted from *Notes from a Big Country* by Bill Bryson. Copyright © 1998 by Bill Bryson. Reprinted by permission of Broadway Books, a division of Random House, Inc., and by Doubleday Canada, a division of Random House of Canada Limited.

STEPHEN BUDIANSKY, "The Numbers Racket: How Polls and Statistics Lie," from *US News and World Report,* July 11, 1988. Copyright © 1988 U.S. News & World Report, L.P. Reprinted with permission.

TERRY CAESAR, "In and Out of Elevators in Japan," from the *Journal of Mundane Behavior,* as found on www.mundanebehavior.org.

CHRISTOPHER CALDWELL, "Levittown to Littleton: How the Suburbs Have Changed," from *National Review,* May 31, 1999, p. 30. Copyright © 1999 by National Review, Inc., 215 Lexington Avenue, New York, NY 10016. Reprinted by permission.

ALBERT Z. CARR, reprinted by permission of *Harvard Business Review* from "Is Business Bluffing Ethical?" January/February 1968. Copyright © 1967 by the Harvard Buisness School Publishing Corporation. All rights reserved.

SYLVIA CARY, "The Big Bash," from *Men's Fitness,* October 1998. Copyright © October 1998 Weider Publications, Inc. Reprinted with permission.

TOM CATTAPAN, "Destroying E-Commerce's Cookie Monster Image," by Tom Cattapan, from *Direct Marketing,* April 2000. Reprinted by permission of the author and the publisher.

JOHN CLOUD, "Never Too Buff," from *Time,* April 24, 2000, p. 64. Copyright © 1999 Time Inc. Reprinted by permission.

JONATHAN COLVIN, "Me, My Clone, and I (or In Defense of Human Cloning)," from *The Humanist,* May/June 2000. Reprinted by permission of the author.

COMMONWEAL EDITORS, "Of Mice, Jellyfish & Us" by The Editors, *Commonweal,* January 28, 2000. Copyright © 2000 Commonweal Foundation. Reprinted with permission. For subscriptions, www.commonwealmagazine.org.

CONSUMER REPORTS, "Cream of the Crop" and "Mmmm Chocolate." Copyright © 1999 by Consumers Union of U.S., Inc., Yonkers, NY 10703-1057, a nonprofit organization. "It's Only Water, Right?" and "Roll Models." Copyright © 2000 by Consumers Union of U.S., Inc., Yonkers, NY 10703-1057, a nonprofit organization. All adapted with permission from the July 1999 and 2000 issues, respectively, of *Consumer Reports®* for educational purposes only. No commercial use or photocopying permitted. To learn more about Consumers Union, log onto www.ConsumerReports.org.

DONNA CORNACHIO, "What Do I Get the Boy Who Has Everything?" from *Newsweek,* April 10, 2000. Copyright © 2000 Newsweek, Inc. All rights reserved. Reprinted by permission.

GREG CRITSER, "Let Them Eat Fat," from *Harper's Magazine,* March 2000. Copyright © 2000 by *Harper's Magazine.* All rights reserved. Reproduced from the March issue by special permission.

GERARDO DERARDO, "Is the SDSU Aztec Logo Offensive?" Letter to the Editor, from the *San Diego Union-Tribune,* October 4, 2000.

DIHYDROGEN MONOXIDE RESEARCH DIVISION, "Dihydrogen Monoxide FAQ," as found on www.dhmo.org/facts.html. Reprinted by permission of the DHMO Organization.

RAYMOND S. DUFF and A. G. M. CAMPBELL, excerpted from "Moral and Ethical Dilemmas in the Special-Care Nursery," from *The New England Journal of Medicine,* 1973, vol. 289, pp. 893–894. Copyright © 1973 Massachusetts Medical Society. All rights reserved. Reprinted by permission.

RICHARD DYER, "The Matter of Whiteness," from *White,* by Richard Dyer. London: Routledge, 1997, pp. 1–4. Reprinted by permission of Taylor and Francis Books Ltd.

THE ECONOMIST, "A Global Disaster," from *The Economist,* January 2, 1999, p. 42. © 1999 The Economist Newspaper Ltd. All rights reserved. Reprinted with permission. Further reproduction prohibited. www.economist.com.

CAROLYN EDY, "Single Motherhood Is a Joy, Not a Disaster," from *Newsweek,* May 10, 1999. Copyright © 1999 Newsweek, Inc. All rights reserved. Reprinted by permission.

SANDRA FELDMAN, "The Childswap Society," from *The New York Times,* January 4, 1998. Reprinted with permission from the January 1998 "Where We Stand," a monthly column of the American Federation of Teachers.

FORD FESSENDEN, "Young Rampage Killers" and "How Youngest Killers Differ: Peer Support," *The New York Times,* April 9, 2000, front page. Copyright © 2000 New York Times. Reprinted by permission of The New York Times Agency.

JAMES E. FORD, adapted from "A General Research Model for Research Paper Introduction," *Literary Research Newsletter* 6, 1981. Reprinted by permission of the author.

DAN FOST, "Napster Use Can Be Research" from *San Francisco Chronicle,* March 8, 2001, B1. Copyright © 2001 San Francisco Chronicle. Reprinted by permission.

LYLA FOX, "Hold Your Horsepower," from *Newsweek,* March 25, 1996. Copyright © 1996 by Newsweek, Inc. All rights reserved. Reprinted by permission.

MICHAEL W. FOX, "Manure, Minerals, and Methane," from *The Animals' Agenda,* May/June 1998, Animal Rights Network, Inc., Westport. Reprinted with permission from *The Animals' Agenda,* P.O. Box 25881, Baltimore, MD 21224; 410-675-4566; www.animalsagenda.org.

DAVID FRANCE, "The HIV Disbeliever," from *Newsweek,* August 28, 2000. Copyright © 2000 Newsweek, Inc. All rights reserved. Reprinted by permission.

MONROE H. FREEDMAN, "Professional Responsibility of the Criminal Defense Lawyer: The Three Hardest Questions," reprinted from *Michigan Law Review,* June 1966, vol. 64, no. 8. Copyright © 1966 by The Michigan Law Review Association. Used with permission.

GIL GARCETTI, "Distinguishing between Felons and Truants," from *Los Angeles Times,* February 7, 1994. Reprinted by permission of the author.

JAMES GILLIGAN, "Reflections from a Life Behind Bars," by James Gilligan, from *Chronicle of Higher Education,* October 16, 1998, pp. B7–B9. Reprinted by permission of the author.

JEFFREY GOLDBERG, "The Color of Suspicion," from *The New York Times Magazine,* June 20, 1999, pp. 51–56. Reprinted by permission of The New York Times Agency.

ROBERT GOLDMAN and STEPHEN PAPSON, excerpt from "Suddenly the Swoosh Is Everywhere" from *Nike Culture (Cultural Icons),* Sage Publications, 1999. Copyright © 1998 Robert Goldman and Stephen Papson. Reprinted by permission of Sage Publishing.

PAUL GOODMAN, "A Proposal to Abolish Grading," excerpted from *Compulsory Miseducation and the Community of Schools,* by Paul Goodman. Copyright © 1962, 1964 by Paul Goodman. Used by permission of Random House, Inc.

CHUCK GREEN, "It's Time to Find Out What's Wrong with Our Hateful Society," from *The Denver Post,* April 21, 1999. Copyright © 1999 *The Denver Post.* Reprinted by permission of *The Denver Post.* All rights reserved.

AMY HARMON, "Study Says Net Use, Depression May Be Linked," first published as "Sad, Lonely World Discovered in Cyberspace" in *The New York Times,* August 30, 1998. Used by permission of The New York Times Agency.

CHARLTON HESTON, Address to Denver, Colorado, May 1, 1999, NRA meeting. Copyright © 1999 National Rifle Association. Authorized by permission of the National Rifle Association.

LOGAN HILL, "Racial Digital Divide." Reprinted with permission from the April 26, 1999 issue of *The Nation.*

VANESSA HUA, "If It Feels Good . . . ," from *San Francisco Chronicle,* March 8, 2001, B1. Copyright © 2001 San Francisco Chronicle. Reprinted by permission.

MOLLY IVINS, "Ban the Things, Ban Them All," from *Nothin' But Good Times Ahead,* by Molly Ivins. Copyright © 1993 by Molly Ivins. Used by permission of Random House, Inc.

CRAIG JACKSON, ERIC LECHNER, and LARS NORPCHEN, "Ban Dihydrogen Monoxide!" by the Coalition to Ban DHMO, as found on www.circus.com/~nodhmo/. Reprinted by permission of the authors.

SIMON JARA, "Is the SDSU Aztec Logo Offensive?" Letter to the Editor, from the *San Diego Union-Tribune,* October 4, 2000.

VIRGINIA JENKINS, From *The Lawn: A History of an American Obsession.* Copyright © 1994 Smithsonian Institution Press. Used by permission of the publisher.

DAN CURTIS JOHNSON, "DHMO: Your All-Natural Friend," Friends of Hydrogen Hydroxide, DHMO as found on www.armory.com/~crisper/DHMO/. Reprinted by permission of the author.

RALPH JOHNSON and J. ANTHONY BLAIR, *Exercises from Logical Self Defense,* excerpts from pp. 90–2, 112, 114, 143–5, 165–6, 190, 203. McGraw-Hill Higher Education, 1994. Reprinted with permission of The McGraw-Hill Companies.

DAVID P. KILEY, "Is the SDSU Aztec Logo Offensive?" Letter to the Editor, from the *San Diego Union-Tribune,* October 4, 2000. Reprinted by permission of the author.

CORETTA SCOTT KING, "The Death Penalty is a Step Back." Copyright © 1985 Coretta Scott King, copyright renewed 1991 Coretta Scott King. Reprinted by arrangement with the Estate of Martin Luther King, Jr., c/o Writers House as agent for the proprietor, New York, NY.

MARTIN LUTHER KING, JR., "Letter from a Birmingham Jail," Copyright © 1963 Dr. Martin Luther King, Jr., copyright renewed 1991 Coretta Scott King. Reprinted by arrangement with the Estate of Martin Luther King, Jr., c/o Writers House as agent for the proprietor, New York, NY.

PATRICIA A. KING, "Science for Girls Only," from *Newsweek,* June 21, 1999. Copyright © 1999 by Newsweek, Inc. All rights reserved. Reprinted by permission.

RICHARD LACAYO, "Are You Man Enough?" from *Time,* April 24, 2000, p. 60. Copyright © 1999 Time Inc. Reprinted by permission.

JENNIFER LACH, "Crossing the Digital Divide," from *American Demographics,* June 2000. Copyright © 2000 Primedia Business Magazines and Media. All rights reserved. Reprinted by permission.

LESLIE LAMBERT, "Fast Like Me," from *Ladies Home Journal,* May 1993. Copyright © June 1998 Meredith Corporation. All rights reserved. Used with the permission of Ladies' Home Journal.

URSULA K. LE GUIN, "The Ones Who Walk Away from Omelas (Variations on a Theme by William James)." Copyright © 1973, 2001 by Ursula K. Le Guin. First appeared in *The Wind's Twelve Quarters.* Permission granted by the author and the author's agents, the Virginia Kidd Agency, Inc.

JOHN LELAND, "The Secret Life of Teens," from *Newsweek,* May 10, 1999. Copyright © 1999 Newsweek, Inc. All rights reserved. Reprinted by permission.

MICHAEL LEMONICK, "Could a Clone Ever Run for President?" from *Time,* November 8, 1999, p. 96. Copyright © 1999 Time Inc. Reprinted by permission.

JOHN LEO, "'A' for Effort." *U.S. News & World Report,* Oct 18, 1993. Copyright © 1993 U.S. News & World Report, L.P. Reprinted with permission.

BARBARA LERNER, "The Killer Narcissists: The Missing Explanation," from *National Review,* May 17, 1999, p. 34. Copyright © 1999 by National Review, Inc. Reprinted by permission.

GRETCHEN LETTERMAN, "Tobacco's Tiniest Victims," from *St. Petersburg Times,* City Edition, Sunday, April 16, 1995, p. 6D. Copyright © 1995 St. Petersburg Times. Reprinted by permission.

STEVEN LEVY, "The Noisy War over Napster," from *Newsweek,* June 5, 2000. Copyright © 2000 Newsweek, Inc. All rights reserved. Reprinted by permission.

ELIZABETH F. LOFTUS, "Eyewitnesses: Essential but Unreliable." Reprinted with permission from *Psychology Today Magazine.* Copyright © 1984 Sussex Publishers, Inc.

SUSAN MCCELLAND, "The Lure of the Body Image," *MacLean's,* February 22, 1999, vol. 112, issue 8, p. 38. Reprinted by permission of MacLean's Magazine.

MARC B. LOGAN, "SDSU Alumni Want Aztec Mascot Kept," Letter to the Editor, from the *San Diego Union-Tribune,* October 22, 2000.

GEORGE LONGWORTH and MELISSA DRESCHER, "Is the SDSU Aztec Logo Offensive?" Letter to the Editor, from the *San Diego Union-Tribune,* October 4, 2000. Reprinted by permission of the authors.

WILLIAM LUTZ, "Beware of the Polls," from *Doublespeak,* by William Lutz, pp. 43–51. Copyright © 1989 by Blonde Bear, Inc. Reprinted by permission of HarperCollins Publishers, Inc.

JIM MALIK, "Aztec Heritage Runs Deep," Letter to the Editor, from the *San Diego Union-Tribune,* October 8, 2000. Reprinted by permission of the author.

MATERIAL SAFETY DATA SHEET FOR DIHYDROGEN MONOXIDE, adapted by Eric Schulman from J. T. Baker, MSDS#W0600.

BILL MILLER, "Logo Drop Nonsensical," Letter to the Editor, from the *San Diego Union-Tribune,* October 8, 2000.

KEITH D. MILLER, "Letter from Jail," from *Voice of Deliverance: The Language of Martin Luther King, and Its Sources,* University of Georgia Press, 1998. Copyright © 1992 by Keith D. Miller. Reprinted by permission of the University of Georgia Press.

CHRISTINE MITCHELL, "When Living Is a Fate Worse than Death," from *Newsweek,* August 28, 2000. Copyright © 2000 Newsweek, Inc. All rights reserved. Reprinted by permission.

EMILY MOORE, "Why Teachers Are Not 'Those Who Can't,'" from *Newsweek,* April 3, 2000. Copyright © 2000 Newsweek, Inc. All rights reserved. Reprinted by permission.

TITO MORALES, "SUV's: Fuel-Wasting Garbage Trucks?" from *Newsweek,* June 26, 2002. Copyright © 2000 Newsweek, Inc. All rights reserved. Reprinted by permission.

OLIVER MORTON, "Clone-a-Friend," by Oliver Morton, from *New Scientist,* April 15, 2000. Reprinted by permission.

NEW SCIENTIST, "The Last Taboo," from *New Scientist,* October 23, 1999. Reprinted by permission.

CHRIS O'MALLEY, "The Digital Divide," from *Time,* March 22, 1999, p. 86. Copyright © 1999 Time Inc. Reprinted by permission.

CHARLES A. O'NEILL, "The Language of Advertising." Reprinted by permission of the author.

NEWSWEEK, "Moving Beyond the Blame Game," Panel Discussion, from *Newsweek,* May 17, 1999. Copyright © 1999 Newsweek, Inc. All rights reserved. Reprinted by permission.

DAVID OWEN, "How I'm Doing," from *The New Yorker,* July 3, 2000. Copyright © 2000 by David Owen. Reprinted from *The New Yorker.* Used by permission of the author.

CURTIS PEEBLES, from *Watch the Skies: A Chronicle of the Flying Saucer Myth.* Copyright © 1994 Smithsonian Institution Press. Used by permission of the publisher.

STEVEN PERRY, "Infestations of the National Body," from *Central States Speech Journal,* vol. 34 (Winter 1983), pp. 231–235. Reprinted by permission of *Central States Speech Journal.*

DAVE PLANK, "Deadly Dosing," article by Dave Plank, from *Vegetarian Times,* February 1999. Copyright © 1999 Vegetarian Times. Reprinted by permission of Vegetarian Times.

HARRISON G. POPE, JR., "Evolving Ideals of Male Body Image as Seen through Action Toys," from *International Journal of Eating Disorders,* vol. 26, 1999. Copyright © 1999 by John Wiley & Sons, Inc. This material is used by permission of John Wiley & Sons, Inc.

NEIL POSTMAN and STEVE POWERS, "What Is News," from *How to Watch TV.* Copyright © 1992 by Neil Postman and Steve Powers. Used by permission of Viking Penguin, a division of Penguin Putnam Inc.

ADAM CLAYTON POWELL III, "Falling for the Gap." Reprinted with permission from the November 1999 issue of *Reason Magazine.* Copyright © 2002 by Reason Foundation, 3415 S. Sepulveda Blvd., Suite 400, Los Angeles, CA 90034. www.reason.com

J. B. PRIESTLEY, "Wrong Ism," from *Essays of Five Decades,* by J. B. Priestley. Copyright © 1968 by J. B. Priestley. Reprinted by permission of Sterling Lord Literistic, Inc.

JUDY PUTNAM, "Grieving for a Pet? I Won't Roll My Eyes," from *Newsweek,* April 24, 2000. Copyright © 2000 Newsweek, Inc. All rights reserved. Reprinted by permission.

ANNA QUINDLEN, "In Defense of *##@&$%#," from *Newsweek,* September 25, 2000. Copyright © 2000 by Anna Quindlen. First appeared in Newsweek. Reprinted by permission of International Creative Management, Inc.

RICHARD D. RIEKE and MALCOLM O. SILLARS, from *Argumentation and the Decision Making Process,* 2d ed., pp. 118–124 Copyright © 1984 by Scott, Foresman and Company. Reprinted by permission of Pearson Education, Inc.

RICK REILLY, "The Swooshification of the World," by Rick Reilly, *Sports Illustrated,* February 24, 1997. Copyright © 1997, Time Inc. All rights reserved. Reprinted courtesy of Sports Illustrated.

JUDITH A. REISMAN, "Cultivating Killers: Pop Culture Is Getting Away with Murder." This copyrighted article first appeared in *The New American* from June 7, 1999, and is reprinted with permission.

AUDREY ROCK-RICHARDSON, "Pay Your Own Way! (Then Thank Mom)," from *Newsweek,* September 11, 2000. Copyright © 2000 Newsweek, Inc. All rights reserved. Reprinted by permission.

KATIE ROIPHE, "Campus Climate Control," from *The New York Times,* March 5, 1999. Reprinted by permission of the author.

JEFFREY ROSEN and AUSTIN BUNN, "The Eroded Self." This article first appeared in *The New York Times Magazine* and is reprinted by permission of Jeffrey Rosen.

ROGER ROSENBLATT, "A Note for Rachel Scott," from *Time,* May 10, 1999. Copyright © 1999 Time Inc. Reprinted by permission.

LESLIE SAVAN, "The Bribed Soul," from *The Sponsored Life.* Copyright © 1994 by Leslie Savan. Reprinted by permission of Don Congdon Associates, Inc.

MICHELE SCARFF, "The Full-Time Stress of Part-Time Professors," from *Newsweek,* May 15, 2000. Copyright © 2000 Newsweek, Inc. All rights reserved. Reprinted by permission.

DARRELL SCOTT, Darrell Scott's speech to Congress after the Columbine Massacre, as found on http://cssa.org/articles/scott_may99.html

ZACHARY SEECH, from *Logic in Everyday Life,* 1988. Reprinted with permission of Wadsworth, an imprint of the Wadsworth Group, a division of Thomson Learning. Fax 800 730-2215.

GAIL SHEEHY, from *Understanding Men's Passages* by Gail Sheehy. Copyright © 1998 by G. Merritt Corporation. Endpapers and charts copyright © 1998 by Nigel Holmes. Used by permission of Random House, Inc.

LESLIE MARMON SILKO. Reprinted with the permission of Simon & Schuster Adult Publishing Group from *Yellow Woman and a Beauty of the Spirit* by Leslie Marmon Silko. Copyright © 1996 by Leslie Marmon Silko. Originally appeared in The Nation Magazine.

ROBERT L. SIMON, "Get Students Past 'Absolutophobia,'" *Education Digest,* October 1997, vol. 63, no. 2, p. 48(4). Reprinted by permission.

ANNA L. SKALAK, "Is the SDSU Aztec Logo Offensive?" Letter to the Editor, from the *San Diego Union-Tribune,* October 4, 2000. Used by permission of the author.

ROBERT C. SOLOMON, from "The Game of Love," in *Love, Emotion, Myth & Metaphor,* Amherst, NY: Prometheus Books. Copyright © 1990 by Robert C. Solomon. Reprinted by permission of the publisher.

MIKE SORAGHAN, "Tragedy Focuses Attention on Gun Bills," from *The Denver Post,* April 21, 1999. Copyright © 1999 The Denver Post. Reprinted by permission of The Denver Post. All rights reserved.

THOMAS SOWELL, "Love and Other Four-Letter Words," *Forbes,* January 1, 1996, vol. 157, no. 1, p. 64. Copyright © 2002 Forbes, Inc. Reprinted by permission of Forbes Magazine.

TERRY SPENCER, "Months of Preparation Got Miami Photographer Winning Shot," Associated Press. Copyright © 2001 The Associated Press. Reprinted with permission of The Associated Press.

THOMAS A. STEWART, "A Nation of Net Have-Nots? No," from *Fortune,* July 5, 1999, vol. 140, issue 1, p. 184. Reprinted by permission of Fortune.

TON STODGHILL II, "In Search of Brotherhood," *Essence,* November 1999. Reprinted with permission of Essence magazine.

NATE STULMAN, "The Great Campus Good-Off Machine," *The New York Times,* March 15, 1999, p. A25. Reprinted by permission of The New York Times Agency.

MARGARET TALBOT, "Clone of Silence," from *New York Times Magazine,* April 16, 2000. Reprinted by permission of The New York Times Agency.

CHRIS TAYLOR, "The Infoanarchist," from *Time,* June 26, 2000, p. 46. Copyright © 1999 Time Inc. Reprinted by permission.

DAVID TAYLOR, "No, Please, After You," from *Forbes FYI,* September 22, 1997, vol. 160, no. 6, p. S36. Copyright © 2002 Forbes Inc. Reprinted by permission of Forbes FYI Magazine.

TENTH GRADE WORLD HISTORY CLASS AT SAN DIEGO HIGH SCHOOL, "Is the SDSU Aztec Logo Offensive?" Letter to the Editor, from the *San Diego Union-Tribune,* October 4, 2000.

ESTHER THORSON, "What's the Spin?," adapted from an essay by Esther Thorson, Graduate Dean of Journalism at the University of Missouri. From PBS's *The Democracy Project,* 2000. Reprinted by permission of the author.

CHAN-LIN TIEN, "A View from Berkeley," from *New York Times,* March 31, 1996, Special Education Section, p. 30. Reprinted by permission of The New York Times Agency.

SALLIE TISDALE, "We Do Abortions Here: A Nurse's Story," by Sallie Tisdale, *Harper's Magazine.* Copyright © 1987 by *Harper's Magazine.* All rights reserved. Reproduced from the October issue by special permission.

LOUIS UCHITELLE, "Devising New Math to Define Poverty," from *The New York Times,* October 18, 1999, pp. A1, A4. Reprinted by permission of The New York Times Agency.

LARS ULRICH, "It's Our Property," from *Newsweek,* June 5, 2000. Reprinted by permission of the author.

PATRICK VALA-HAYNES, "What Does Online Shopping Cost Us?" from *Newsweek,* June 12, 2000. Copyright © 2000 Newsweek, Inc. All rights reserved. Reprinted by permission.

JERRY WALDRON, "Keeping the Faith," Letter to the Editor, from the *San Diego Union-Tribune,* October 8, 2000. Reprinted by permission of the author.

KURT WIESENFELD, "Making the Grade," from *Newsweek,* June 17, 1996. Copyright © 1996 by Newsweek, Inc. All rights reserved. Reprinted by permission.

GEORGE F. WILL, "The Perils of Brushing," from *Newsweek,* May 10, 1999. Copyright © 1999 George F. Will. Reprinted with permission. All rights reserved.

BARRY WINSTON, "Stranger than True: Why I Defend Guilty Clients," from *Harper's Magazine.* Copyright © 1986 by *Harper's Magazine.* Reproduced from the December issue by special permission.

BILL WODRASKA, "The Gentle Art of Hunkering," reprinted with permission from *Mother Earth News Magazine,* July/August 1986. Copyright © 1986 Sussex Publishers. Inc.

KENNETH WOODWARD, "The Making of a Martyr," from *Newsweek,* June 14, 1999. Copyright © 1999 Newsweek, Inc. All rights reserved. Reprinted by permission.

IAN ZACK, "Universities Find Sharp Rise in Computer-Aided Cheating," from *The New York Times,* September 23, 1998, p. A26. Reprinted by permission of The New York Times Agency.

Index